120°  140°  160°

Lena

Bering Sea

KAMCHATKA
PENINSULA

S I B E R I A

Sea of Okhotsk

Irkutsk

Lake Baikal

KURILES

Amur

HOKKAIDO
Sapporo

Harbin    Vladivostok

Ulan Bator

Sea of Japan

HONSHU    JAPAN    Tokyo

MONGOLIAN
PEOPLE'S
REPUBLIC

DEMOCRATIC
PEOPLE'S
REPUBLIC
OF KOREA

Shenyang
(Mukden)

P'yŏngyang

Kyoto
Osaka

G o b i

Beijing    Seoul

Dalian

REPUBLIC OF
KOREA

SHIKOKU

20°

Tianjin

Huang He

Taiyuan    Qingdao

Pusan

Kitakyushu

CHINA

Yellow Sea

CHEJU    KYUSHU

(Yellow River)    Nanjing

Xi'an

Shanghai

East China Sea

Yangtze    Wuhan

P  a  c  i  f  i  c

Chengdu

OKINAWA

Chongqing

RYŪKYŪ ISLANDS

O  c  e  a  n

Taipei

TAIWAN

Irrawaddy    Salween

Guangzhou
(Canton)
Hong Kong
(Brit.)

Mandalay

LUZON

Philippine Sea

Hanoi    HAINAN

BURMA    LAOS    South China
Sea

PHILIPPINES

Chiang Mai    Vientiane

Manila

SAMAR

Rangoon

Gulf of
Tonkin

MINDORO

0°

Mekong

Andaman Sea

THAILAND    VIETNAM

KAMPUCHEA
(CAMBODIA)

PALAWAN    Sula Sea

MINDANAO

Bangkok

Phnom Penh    Ho Chi Minh City
(Saigon)

Gulf of
Thailand

HALMAHERA

M  A  L  A  Y  S  I  A    SABAH
BRUNEI

Kuala Lumpur    SARAWAK

Sibu    Sulawesi Sea

MALAYA

SINGAPORE    KALIMANTAN    SULAWESI
(CELEBES)    Banda Sea    Arafura Sea

BORNEO

SUMATRA    Banjarmasin

I  N  D  O  N  E  S  I  A

Java Sea    Timor Sea

Jakarta    Surabaya    BALI    LOMBOK
Bandung    JAVA    SUMBA    FLORES    TIMOR    A  U  S  T  R  A  L  I  A

100°    120°    140°

# ENCYCLOPEDIA
## OF
# ASIAN
# HISTORY

# ENCYCLOPEDIA
## OF
# ASIAN
# HISTORY

Prepared under the auspices of
The Asia Society

Ainslie T. Embree

EDITOR IN CHIEF

Volume 2

Charles Scribner's Sons
New York

Collier Macmillan Publishers
London

Charles Scribner's Sons
Macmillan Publishing Company
866 Third Avenue, New York, N.Y. 10022

Collier Macmillan Canada, Inc.


Library of Congress Catalog Card Number: 87–9891

*Library of Congress Cataloging-in-Publication Data*

Encyclopedia of Asian History

Includes bibliographies and index
1. Asia—History—Dictionaries   I. Embree, Ainslie Thomas
DS31.E53   1988      950      87-9891
ISBN 0–684–18619–5 (set)
ISBN 0–684–18899–6 (v. 2)


Acknowledgments of permissions to reproduce photographs
are gratefully made in a special listing in volume 4.

Printed in the United States of America

printing number

2  3  4  5  6  7  8  9  10

# ENCYCLOPEDIA
## OF
# ASIAN
# HISTORY

# G

(CONTINUED)

GUANGDONG is a large and populous province on the southeast coast of China. It lies to the south of the Nanling mountain range, separating the West River valley of South China from the Yangtze River valley of central China. Most of Guangdong lies within the lower portion of the West River basin below neighboring Guangxi Province. However, it also takes in, to the east, the small Han River valley adjacent to Fujian Province and, to the west, the Leizhou Peninsula and Hainan Island bordering the Gulf of Tonkin.

Armies of the Qin dynasty in the late third century BCE conquered the region and made it a lasting part of the Chinese empire. Because of its remoteness, however, Han Chinese immigrants from the populated North did not settle in Guangdong in any significant numbers until the Tang period (618–907). Natives of Guangdong thus refer to themselves as "people of Tang" rather than, as elsewhere in China, "people of Han." A new wave of refugees arrived during the Southern Song period (1127–1279), when North China was overrun by Jurchen and Mongol invaders.

The population of Guangdong in 1982 was 59,299,000. Much of that population is concentrated in the Pearl River delta in central Guangdong, where the West River converges with its two principal tributaries, the North and East rivers, and fans out through an intricate system of channels and streams before emptying into the South China Sea. Canton (Guangzhou), situated along the northern edge of the delta, has been the provincial capital since the Qing dynasty (1644–1911) and, excluding British Hong Kong, is the most populous city of the region and the province. Portuguese Macao, opposite Hong Kong across the broad mouth of the Pearl River, is nearby.

The rest of the province is generally hilly and far less densely populated than the delta. Settlements lie in scattered pockets of arable lowlands along the coast or in interior river valleys. The principal regional centers are Shantou (Swatow), a coastal port at the mouth of the Han River in eastern Guangdong; Shaoguan, a way station on the ancient imperial highway (and now modern railroad) along the North River in northern Guangdong; and Zhanjiang, a new industrial city at the base of the Leizhou Peninsula in western Guangdong.

Ethnically, the population of Guangdong is composed overwhelmingly of Han Chinese; only a very small number of non-Han minorities inhabit the mountainous fringes of the province, such as the Yao along the border with Hunan and Guangxi and the Li on Hainan Island. Linguistically, the situation is much more complex. Most of the Han Chinese in the West River drainage basin, particularly the Pearl River delta, speak the Cantonese dialect of Chinese. Natives of eastern Guangdong and of Hainan Island, however, generally speak either the Hakka dialect or a variant of the Min dialect of southern Fujian Province; these dialects are mutually unintelligible.

The economy of Guangdong was and, to a large extent, still is based on the cultivation of irrigated rice. Because of the temperate climate, the long growing season, and an abundance of water, the land generally can yield two rice crops a year. Other agricultural products for which Guangdong is noted include silk, sugar, and a tremendous variety of tropical fruits. Commercial fishing is also important, particularly along the coast. Manufacturing has developed steadily and in all parts of the province since the Communist takeover. The Canton-Hankou railroad, completed in 1936, is the main transport link between Guangdong and the rest of the country to the north. Another, earlier railway, built in 1911, connects Canton with Hong Kong. With its long coastline and its extensive network of internal wa-

1

terways, however, shipping remains a vital form of transportation within the province.

Because of its coastal location and its proximity to Southeast Asia, Guangdong has had a long history of maritime commerce and foreign contact. Canton in particular was a center of the Arab trade in the Tang period and of the trade with the maritime nations of Europe in the Qing period. In addition, Guangdong is the ancestral home of many of the overseas Chinese presently living in Southeast Asia and in the Americas. Most Chinese in Thailand, for example, migrated from the Shantou area of eastern Guangdong, while those in the United States generally came from the Pearl River delta of central Guangdong. Their continuing remittances of funds from abroad to relatives in Guangdong have contributed significantly to the economic development of their home districts.

Edward J. M. Rhoads, *China's Republican Revolution: The Case of Kwangtung, 1895–1913* (1975). Theodore Shabad, *China's Changing Map: National and Regional Development, 1949–1971* (1972). Herold J. Wiens, *China's March Toward the Tropics* (1954).

EDWARD J. M. RHOADS

GUANGXI, mountainous province on the southern periphery of China adjoining Vietnam. Guangxi lies in the upper basin of the West River above Guangdong Province.

Administratively, Guangxi has been a part of China since the Qin dynasty in the late third century BCE. Because of its remoteness and its malarial climate, however, it was relatively undeveloped until the Ming (1368–1644) and Qing (1644–1911) periods, when land-hungry immigrants pushed their way into its river valleys from the neighboring provinces of Hunan and Guangdong. It was, historically, a poor and lawless province, which, for example, spawned the massive Taiping Rebellion of the mid-nineteenth century.

The population of Guangxi in 1982 was 36,421,000. The majority are Han Chinese, divided between Mandarin speakers in the north along the Hunan border and Cantonese speakers in the east adjacent to Guangdong. However, one-third of the inhabitants, mostly in the west, belong to the indigenous Zhuang nationality. An agriculturalist people, they share some cultural traits with the Tai of Southeast Asia but otherwise are barely distinguishable from the Han Chinese. The Zhuang are one of the most numerous of China's fifty-odd ethnic minorities. Other minority groups living in Guangxi include the Yao, Miao, and Dong.

Guangxi's economy is primarily agricultural, with wet-rice cultivation as the principal activity. Its main commercial link with the rest of China has traditionally been the West River down to Canton (Guangzhou), but the Hunan-Guangxi railroad, built in the 1930s, now offers a more direct route to the Yangtze Valley. Another railroad, completed in the early 1950s, connects Guangxi with Vietnam. The major cities of the province, all river ports and railroad towns, include Guilin, the provincial capital during the Ming and Qing periods and a scenic attraction famous for its bizarre limestone formations; Nanning, the capital since 1912; and Liuzhou, a new industrial center.

Diana Lary, *Region and Nation: The Kwangsi Clique in Chinese Politics, 1925–1937* (1974). Theodore Shabad, *China's Changing Map: National and Regional Development, 1949–1971* (rev. ed., 1972). Herold J. Wiens, *China's March Toward the Tropics* (1954).

EDWARD J. M. RHOADS

GUANGXI CLIQUE, a military faction based on the Guangxi provincial army that played a major role in the fortunes of the Republic of China. Generals Bai Chongxi, Li Zongren, and Huang Shaohong were its chief leaders. They gave vital military support during the Northern Expedition but rebelled in 1929 when Chiang Kai-shek pressured them to disband part of their armies. In 1932 they reconciled their differences with Chiang and increased their control of a rather backward and poor southern province.

During World War II the Guangxi clique again became a major factor in the Republic of China. Pushed out of the rich eastern part of China by the Japanese, Chiang Kai-shek was forced to rely more heavily on support from the Guangxi clique, most of whose resources were not destroyed or occupied by the Japanese. Both Bai Chongxi and Li Zongren were forward looking, but their support for Chiang Kai-shek was tempered with self-interest and the Republic of China eventually became more reliant on their political and military resources than was desirable. During these years when they were close to the center of power in the Republic of China, the Guangxi clique's leadership lost its cohesion. Bai Chongxi loyally followed Chiang Kai-shek to Taiwan in 1949, but Li Zongren broke with him and went to the United States before returning to China in 1966. Huang Shaohong remained in China after 1949.

[*See also* Bai Chongxi; Li Zongren; Chiang Kai-shek; China, Republic of; and Warlord Cliques.]

Diana Lary, *The Kwangsi Clique in Chinese Politics, 1927–1937* (1974).         DAVID D. BUCK

**GUANGZHOU.** See Canton.

**GUANZHONG,** also called Guannei or Guanxi; geographical region situated in the Wei River basin of China, around the modern city of Xi'an (ancient Chang'an) in Shaanxi Province. Guanzhong served as an important political, military, and cultural center from late Warring States times (403–221 BCE) down through the Tang dynasty (618–907). The literal meaning of the name, "within the passes," points to the region's strategic importance as a relatively impregnable military stronghold. Guanzhong was the location of capitals of the Western Zhou, Qin, Former Han, Sui, and Tang dynasties, among others. According to the Han historian Sima Qian, in Han times Guanzhong contained one-third of the total population of China and 60 percent of its wealth. As China's political and economic center moved east and southward, however, Guanzhong's fortunes declined. After the tenth century it settled into relative insignificance.    HOWARD J. WECHSLER

**GUILIN,** a former capital of Guangxi Province, China, now called Guangxi Zhuang Autonomous Region. Guilin's traditional importance came from its proximity to the canal and portage system linking the rivers flowing north to the Yangtze River with those running south to Guangzhou (Canton).

Modern Guilin, with a population of 413,000 (1981), is a major tourist attraction, famous for caves and for the limestone karst formations that rise in abrupt and fantastic shapes out of the broken plain and along the verdant Li River, which flows through the city.    LYMAN P. VAN SLYKE

**GUIYANG,** capital and most important city in the rather poor and relatively undeveloped southwestern Chinese province of Guizhou. Guiyang became more important during the Ming and Qing dynasties, when Chinese migration was encouraged at the expense of the original non-Chinese inhabitants of the region. The city thus became a strategic outpost of imperial political and military power. It also lies astride a principal transportation route connecting Yunnan and Guizhou provinces with the rest of China. Guiyang's population in 1983 was estimated at 1.3 million.    LYMAN P. VAN SLYKE

**GUIZHOU,** province in southwest China; capital, Guiyang. Located on the rugged Yungui (Yunnan-Guizhou) Plateau, Guizhou is 174,000 square kilometers in area. About one-fourth of Guizhou's population is non-Han, the largest minorities being the Miao and the Buyi; the Han are concentrated in the lowlands of central and northern Guizhou. The total population in 1982 was 28.5 million.

Part of the Tai state of Nanzhao (Dali) until the Mongol conquest in 1253, Guizhou became a province during the Ming dynasty (1368–1644). In the following centuries it was settled by Han Chinese immigrants from Guangdong, Hunan, and Sichuan. In the early eighteenth century the Manchu governor-general Ortai (1680–1745) brought the aboriginal tribes under direct Chinese control. Conflicts between the tribes and the Han Chinese resulted in several rebellions, most notably the Miao rebellion of the mid-nineteenth century.

The province remained isolated and economically backward into the twentieth century. During World War II, however, Guizhou became strategically important as the Japanese invasion drove the Chinese government into southwest China. Highways and railroad links to neighboring provinces were built. Mining and industry have been developed since the 1950s.    ROBERT ENTENMANN

**GUJARAT.** With the longest coastline (992 miles) of any state of India, Gujarat has long been famous as a home of trade. Rojdi, Lothal, and other ancient sites bear evidence from the second millennium BCE of trade and cultural relations with the ancient Indus Valley civilization. [*See also* Indus Valley Civilization.] Throughout the centuries, sailors have traveled from Gujarat's ports to East Africa, Southeast Asia, and Indonesia. Among Gujarat's principal castes are Hindu Vaishnavite Banias and Jain religious and trading communities. Since the eighth century Gujarat has also been home to the Parsi community of Zoroastrians, who have excelled in business and trade. [*See* Parsis.]

With 72,236 square miles and a population of 36,000 (1981), however, Gujarat holds a great diversity of topographic and human types. Its two large western peninsulas—the desert and salt plains of Kutch to the north and the semiarid Saurashtra to the south—as well as the northern part of the mainland, share in the Rajput influences of Rajasthan, the bordering state to the north. [See Rajput.] Their language, too, blends into Rajasthani. The southernmost area, a hilly forest area called the Dangs, is inhabited by tribals whose language blends into the Marathi of the border state to the south. Along the eastern fringes of the state are other tribal groups blending into those of Madhya Pradesh to the east. [See Adivasis.] The central and southern areas of the mainland are the sites of the cities of Ahmadabad, Baroda, Surat, Broach (Bharuch), and Cambay (Khambat)—historical centers of trade and rule with pan-Indian significance. They provide markets for the rich farmlands—well watered by the Tapti, Narmada, Mahi, and Sabarmati rivers—dominated in the north and central areas by farming communities of Patels and in the South by Anavil brahmans. [See Baroda and Surat.]

The area that is today Gujarat was consolidated as a state in 1960 on the basis of linguistic identity as suggested by Mohandas Gandhi beginning in the 1920s and carried out after independence by the States Reorganization Committee, following considerable discussion as well as protest in the streets. Historically the region takes its name from the Gurjaras, a people of indeterminate origin who dominated much of Northwest India from a base in central and southern Rajasthan during the period from 550 to 950 and again in the eleventh century. A centralization of power within the current borders of Gujarat, however, first took place under Jayasimha Siddharaja of the Chalukya dynasty, who established in Anhilwad Pattan the capital of an empire that lasted almost two centuries. [See Chalukya Dynasties.] During this time a Gujarati literary and linguistic consciousness also began to form in the region, led by Hemachandra, a Jain saddhu whose works also indicate the growing importance of Jainism in Gujarat. [See Jainism.]

In 1299 the Delhi sultanate conquered Gujarat, again indicating the tension between a growing internal sense of identity and the political power of external rulers. [See Delhi Sultanate.] A century later Muslim rulers declared a separate sultanate of Gujarat, consolidated by Ahmad Shah I and symbolized in his transfer of the capital to the new city of Ahmadabad, which he built in 1411 and named for himself. In 1572 the region fell again to outsiders, the centralizing Mughal empire under Akbar. Despite its somewhat peripheral location, the Mu-

ghals valued Gujarat's wealth in agriculture and handicrafts, and Surat became the chief port of their empire. But as that empire weakened in the eighteenth century, Gujarat became a battleground between the Mughals and various Maratha forces.

In 1818 Gujarat fell to the British, who registered their perception of the wealth and pivotal position of the central area by ruling five districts directly: Ahmadabad, Kaira (Kheda), Broach, Surat, and the Panch Mahals. The rest of the region, considered peripheral, was left to be ruled by native princes, varying from the large and powerful state of Baroda to many of the 220 tiny principalities that made up Saurashtra.

The formation of the present linguistic state in 1960 followed two earlier divisions after independence: (1) the 1948 establishment of Saurashtra and Kutch as two separate states, with the mainland merged into a bilingual Bombay State; and (2) the 1956 merger of all these areas into the greater Bombay State. [See Rann of Kutch.]

Noted primarily for its natural wealth and successful business classes, Gujarat has also spawned eminent political leaders including, in this century, Mohandas Gandhi, Sardar Patel, and Mohammad Ali Jinnah. Since 1960 Gujarat has been noted for its economic advancement in both industry and agriculture, its caste-based politics, and social mobility and violence, despite its Jain and Gandhian legacies of nonviolence.

[See also Indian Ocean; Princely States; Gandhi, Mohandas Karamchand; Patel, Sardar Vallabhbhai; and Jinnah, Mohammad Ali.]

M. S. Commissariat, A History of Gujarat, 2 vols. (1938, 1957). K. R. Dikshit, Geography of Gujarat (1970). A. K. Forbes, Ras-mala: Hindu Annals of Western India, with Particular Reference to Gujarat (1878; reprint, 1973). M. F. Lokhandwala, trans., Mirat-i-Ahmadi; A Persian History of Gujarat (1965). K. M. Munshi, Gujarat and Its Literature, from Early Times to 1852 (3d ed., 1967). Howard Spodek, Urban-Rural Integration in Regional Development: A Case Study of Saurashtra, India, 1800–1960 (1975).   HOWARD SPODEK

GU JIEGANG (1893–1980), historian and folklorist, known for his acclaimed critical studies of Chinese antiquity. Brought up in the classics, Gu developed an early interest in China's past. Under the influence of the young American-trained Hu Shi while enrolled at Beijing University, Gu began to use a new critical approach, known as "the doubting of antiquity," to reexamine Chinese history and the classics. The results of his work and his discussions with scholars were published in the seven-volume *Gushi bian* (*Critical Discussions of Ancient History;* 1926–1941), a monumental work that permanently altered the contours of Chinese historiography. Gu was also a pioneer in the Chinese folklore movement, avidly promoting the study of folk songs, legends, and other folklore disciplines.

[*See also* Hu Shi *and* May Fourth Movement.]

Chang-tai Hung, *Going to the People: Chinese Intellectuals and Folk Literature, 1918–1937* (1985). Laurence A. Schneider, *Ku Chieh-kang and China's New History: Nationalism and the Quest for Alternative Traditions* (1971).                                CHANG-TAI HUNG

GUNAWARDENA, DON PHILIP RUPASINGHE (d. 1972), Sri Lankan statesman. Upon entering the state council, Gunawardena cofounded the Trotskyist Lanka Sama Samaja Paksa (Ceylon Socialist Peace Party) in 1936. He worked to help S. W. R. D. Bandaranaike win the 1956 elections. As minister of lands and agriculture Gunawardena single-handedly created the Paddy Lands Act of 1958, which attempted to improve tenant security.

[*See also* Lanka Sama Samaja Party *and* Bandaranaike, Solomon West Ridgeway Dias.]

George Lerski, *Origins of Trotskyism in Ceylon: A Documentary History of the Lanka Sama Samaja Party, 1935–1942* (1968).                    PATRICK PEEBLES

GUOMINDANG (Kuomintang, KMT, or Nationalist Party), one of the major political forces in China in the first half of the twentieth century. Sun Yatsen dominated the party until his death in 1925, followed by Chiang Kai-shek in later years.

The Guomindang was the descendant of Sun Yatsen's earlier revolutionary organizations—the Xingzhonghui (Revive China Society) formed in 1894 and the Tongmenghui (Revolutionary Alliance) formed in 1905. Sun was a charismatic leader who brought together disparate groups under his rather vague philosophy of *sanmin zhuyi* ("three principles of the people"). His personality and skills as a fundraiser were crucial in holding together his movement.

*Early Organization.* The Guomindang itself was organized in the summer of 1912 to replace the old Tongmenghui. After the success of the 1911 (Xinhai) Revolution, Sun and his followers sought to broaden their political base in preparation for the impending parliamentary elections. On 25 August 1912 they inaugurated this new coalition. Although Sun was a dominant leader, Song Jiaoren, a brilliant political organizer, actually directed much of the electoral campaign. The KMT triumphed, capturing 45 percent of the membership of the two houses of parliament in the December 1912/January 1913 elections, far more than any other party.

The victory was short-lived. Yuan Shikai, president and military leader of the Republic of China, did not wish to share power with the KMT and on 20 March 1913 had Song assassinated. The so-called second revolution followed in the summer of 1913, a showdown between Yuan and the KMT. Yuan's guns won the day; the KMT's strength was shattered by September 1913 and Sun fled to Japan.

Discouraged by the failure of his parliamentary party, Sun reorganized the KMT in Tokyo into a centralized, disciplined, and secret group. All members had to take an oath of allegiance to the party and agree to obey Sun's leadership; all had to pledge to sacrifice their life and freedom for the revolutionary cause if called upon to do so; all had to affix a fingerprint to the oath statement. Many of Sun's followers rejected the new approach. Huang Xing, a key KMT leader, broke with Sun and left for America, although such figures as Chen Qimei, Liao Zhongkai, and Hu Hanmin remained loyal to Sun. [*See also* Huang Xing; Chen Qimei; *and* Hu Hanmin.]

On 1 September 1914 the new party, now renamed the Zhonghua Gemingdang (China Revolutionary Party), issued its manifesto. The platform revealed Sun's newfound pessimism concerning parliamentary democracy. While repeating the old Tongmenghui program of a three-stage process of political change (military rule, party tutelage, followed by constitutional rule), it set no time limit for the period of tutelage. The earlier platform had called for a nine-year span between the first and third stages.

Japan's Twenty-one Demands made on the Yuan Shikai government weakened the Gemingdang's campaign against its archrival. Not only did Yuan gain popular support for resisting the most onerous demands, but Sun continued to hope for Japanese assistance and refused to denounce Tokyo. His already divided movement further splintered. Only Yuan Shikai's ill-timed bid to become emperor in late 1915 followed by his sudden death in June 1916 saved the day for Sun, rallying his followers and allowing the party leader to return to Shanghai in the spring of 1916. [*See also* Twenty-one Demands *and* Yuan Shikai.]

With Yuan removed from the scene, Sun briefly revived his hopes for parliamentary government in China, and Gemingdang members participated in the restored parliament of August 1916. Yuan's death did not end military domination of the Beijing government, however; it merely ushered in a long period of unstable warlord rule. When militarist Zhang Xun briefly captured Beijing in July 1917 and tried to restore the Qing dynasty, Sun Yat-sen gathered one hundred KMT followers, all former parliament members, in Canton (Guangzhou). In September 1917 Sun's regime proclaimed itself the government of China, although Sun lacked an army and his position was unstable. In 1918 local warlords forced Sun to retreat to Shanghai, where he languished until November 1920, when he was invited back to Canton courtesy of the militarist Chen Jiongming.

The centralized and secretive Gemingdang had not been able to unite earlier KMT supporters behind Sun, particularly overseas groups, nor had the new party achieved great success. When the May Fourth Movement of 1919 spread throughout China, party leaders sought to maximize their base by reorganizing. In October 1919 the Zhonghua Gemingdang was reformed as the Zhongguo (China) Guomindang, a more open and democratic party. Sun's energies, however, were applied to the creation of a political regime in Canton, and the party itself was weak. The party's misfortune continued. In June 1922 Chen Jiongming broke with Sun and forcibly ejected the KMT elements from Canton.

Following this loss, the fortunes of Sun Yat-sen and the KMT appeared to be at their nadir. The party was a powerless entity; the first decade of republican rule—Sun's earlier dream—had brought chaos and weakness to China. From his exile in Shanghai's foreign concessions, however, Sun continued the struggle for a strong republican government. Sun was now convinced that the party must have its own military base and strong financial backing to succeed. At the same time, Sun drifted further from the parliamentary model and became increasingly disillusioned with the Western democracies that had so conspicuously failed to help the KMT. By contrast, party leaders looked with increasing favor on the new Bolshevik government in Russia. Anti-imperialist statements and acts by the Soviet regime found a receptive audience in China. Sun had met with Comintern representatives as early as November 1920 and held discussions with Maring (Hendricus Sneevliet) in December 1921. Moscow looked with some favor on the KMT as a progres-

sive, anti-imperialist party, particularly since the new Chinese Communist Party (CCP) formed in July 1921 remained minuscule.

***Alliance with Communists.*** Sun's interest in a Soviet tie naturally increased following his ouster from Canton. Shortly after arriving in Shanghai, he met with Comintern agent Adolph A. Joffe. Sun rejected suggestions for a two-party (KMT-CCP) alliance, but agreed to a reorganization of the KMT and participation by CCP members. In September a nine-member committee of representatives from both parties convened to draft the new organizational plan. In January 1923 Sun and Joffe issued their famous joint declaration in which both sides acknowledged that conditions in China were not ripe for the establishment of communism, but that China should strive to achieve national unification and complete independence. Sun Yat-sen's motivation in seeking the KMT-Comintern tie has been the subject of extensive historical debate, much of which has been fueled by political concerns. Unquestionably, Sun was partially motivated by his quest for aid, and had other countries been forthcoming, he might not have pursued the communist link so vigorously. Nonetheless, there is strong evidence that Sun was ideologically attracted to the Comintern connection. Joffe assisted Sun in reorganizing the KMT into a centralized, disciplined political party, modeled after Lenin's Bolshevik Party. Sun, who continued to serve as director (*zongli*) of the party, had attempted this earlier with the formation of the Gemingdang. Sun's doctrine of *sanmin zhuyi* (nationalism, democracy, and people's livelihood), always an amorphous ideology, had become increasingly radical and anti-imperialist.

Events continued to move rapidly. Just days after the Sun-Joffe statement in February 1923, Sun returned to Canton, where, despite the precarious military situation, he reestablished the KMT regime. Soviet aid, perhaps $1 million, arrived during that year. Equally important, in October 1921 Michael Borodin arrived in Canton as the permanent representative of the Comintern. For the next four years Borodin was to play a major role in KMT politics as an adviser and participant. He immediately assisted in the reorganization of the party structure, grafting on the Leninist form of "democratic centralism." Borodin pressed Sun to adopt more radical labor and peasant policies, with only partial success. Sun began to call for rent reductions for farmers and eight-hour working days for urban laborers. Borodin's hand was strengthened in late 1923 when the Western powers forcefully rejected Sun's demand for control of Canton's customs revenue. The Soviet tie was Sun's only hope for outside aid. [*See also* Comintern *and* Borodin, Michael.]

In January 1923 the reorganized KMT convened its first party congress. The assembly, which broke to observe three days of mourning for Lenin, incorporated many of the radical changes proposed by Borodin. "Ever since the 1911 Revolution . . . the exploitation and encroachment of our national rights by the militarists and imperialists are getting worse every day, making China more of a sub-colony," declared the congress's manifesto of 30 January 1924. The solution was to be a national revolution led by the KMT to implement the Three Principles of the People. "The success of the national revolution depends upon the participation of the peasants and laborers of the whole country," the statement continued. The party must engage in a "determined struggle against imperialism and militarism, against the classes opposed to the interests of the peasants and laborers. . . . Such is the meaning of the Three Principles." The manifesto thus demonstrated the KMT's new emphasis on social revolution, and its desire for mass mobilization of peasants and workers. In foreign policy it called for abolition of the unequal treaties.

The assembly contained almost 200 delegates, of whom 20 were also members of the CCP. The body claimed to represent almost 30,000 members. Sun Yat-sen was made party leader for life and given veto power over the decisions of party organs. Authority was otherwise entrusted to the Central Executive Committee (CEC), which was to meet between sessions of the party congress. Communist leader Li Dazhao was elected to the CEC; Mao Zedong was an alternate member.

Sun Yat-Sen turned his attention to creation of a KMT army, which he now considered essential. In June 1924 the government inaugurated the Whampoa Military Academy near Canton to train officers from the new army. Chiang Kai-shek, a Japanese-trained military specialist who had recently returned from Moscow, was appointed head of the academy. Liao Zhongkai, longtime KMT stalwart, and Zhou Enlai of the CCP were on its political staff. Soviet aid, arms, and advisers were crucial in the growth of the academy and the KMT army. General P. A. Pavlov and Vasilii K. Blykher (Galen) headed the military mission, which included numerous advisers and instructors by 1925. Sun was impatient to use the new force. In 1924 he attempted to launch a northern expedition prematurely. The effort failed, although Sun did attract additional military support.

*The Northern Expedition.* The reorganized KMT began to recognize the importance of mass mobili-

zation as part of the party's revolutionary strategy. It established bureaus for labor, peasants, and women in an effort to tap these social forces. Liao Zhongkai headed the labor division, which tried to rally workers and laborers to the KMT cause. The peasant bureau began organizing rural associations during the summer of 1924. Although KMT policies were relatively moderate, involving rent reduction rather than land confiscation, these party-led peasant groups frequently clashed with landlords and their agents. Although the mobilization campaigns were crucial in setting the stage for the Northern Expedition, they tended to benefit the CCP more than the KMT. The most successful organizers in the labor and peasant bureaus were young CCP members.

In November 1924 Sun Yat-sen left Canton for Beijing, where he was to open talks with northern leaders. While there his health suddenly deteriorated, and he died of cancer on 12 March 1925. From its beginning Sun had been the center of the KMT; his charisma, his fund-raising ability, and his flexibility created an appeal to a wide range of constituencies. Sun's removal from the scene not only created a crisis of leadership at the center but also unleashed the strains of the KMT-CCP tie. Factions within both parties were distrustful of the other.

Ironically, Sun's death and the leadership crisis occurred just as the political climate in China suddenly favored the revolutionaries. Workers in Shanghai had been striking Japanese-owned factories in the spring of 1925. On 30 May foreign-concession police fired on and killed several Shanghai students who were demonstrating in favor of the workers. The May Thirtieth Incident, as it came to be called, created a firestorm of protest throughout urban China—strikes, boycotts, and riots developed in most cities. On 23 June in Canton foreign police fired machine guns into a Chinese crowd, precipitating a successful and long-lived boycott of Hong Kong. [*See also* May Thirtieth Incident.]

This outburst of Chinese nationalism fueled the KMT-CCP movement. Students and young Chinese flocked to Canton to join the cause. Workers and labor organizations were able to recruit support throughout China. This explosive growth favored both the KMT and the CCP, but particularly the latter.

At the very moment when the hope of a successful Northern Expedition seemed more likely than ever, the unity of the movement came into grave doubt. On 20 August 1925, Liao Zhongkai, a strong supporter of the Communist alliance, was assassinated. Right-wing KMT elements were blamed, and Hu

Hanmin, a key contender for party leader, left China under a cloud. Two other KMT stalwarts, Lin Sen and Zou Lu, departed Canton for Beijing, where they gathered conservative leaders in November. Meeting in the western hills of the capital, they denounced the Canton KMT as Communist-dominated. This "Western Hills" faction later assembled in Shanghai and claimed to be the legitimate KMT, electing their own CEC and expelling the Communists and leftists. Prominent KMT theorist Dai Jitao also demanded expulsion of the Communists.

Within the Canton regime itself, the left-KMT and CCP leaders gained ascendancy. Wang Jingwei and Borodin consolidated the leftist position while Chiang Kai-shek, as commander of the first army corps of the party's military, increased his standing. Throughout the fall of 1925 the KMT finally secured its military domination of Guangdong Province. By January 1926 the leftist forces felt secure enough to call the Second National Party Congress to curb formally the dissident conservative elements. The new congress had 250 delegates, one-third of whom were members of the CCP, and claimed to represent 200,000 KMT members. The congress elected a new CEC, heavily dominated by the left.

The steady rise of the left was suddenly thwarted on 20 March 1926 by the *Zhongshan* gunboat incident, a power play by Chiang Kai-shek. He suddenly declared martial law and arrested several CCP leaders. Chiang, considered by many to be a leftist at that time, was actually quite disturbed by the political shift in Canton. Ambitious, he perhaps hoped to counter Wang Jingwei's rise. The KMT army still needed Soviet aid, however, so Chiang stopped well short of a solid break. Borodin and the Comintern likewise felt the need to compromise, having invested so heavily in the KMT. Borodin conceded to most of Chiang's demands and CCP activities within the KMT were restricted. Chiang increased his power within the party apparatus. His patron, the conservative Zhang Renjie, was elected chairman of the standing committee of the CEC, and Chiang and his sworn brother Chen Guofu took over the party's organization bureau. Although the Zhongshan Incident curbed the CCP's strength within the KMT, its total power continued to grow, particularly within the labor and peasant movements.

On 9 July 1926 Canton finally launched the long-discussed Northern Expedition led by Chiang Kai-shek, newly appointed commander in chief of KMT forces. Chiang pushed northward into Hunan and Hubei, achieving victory over warlord opponents whose troops often lacked the discipline and political motivation of the KMT army. The Northern Expedition also became a political crusade, firing up peasant and labor groups and creating sometimes violent attacks on foreign interests in China. [*See also* Northern Expedition.]

**Internal Struggles.** The success and turbulence of the Northern Expedition brought a climax to the struggle between left and right. On 1 January 1927 the civilian KMT government moved to Wuhan, where Borodin and the leftists reasserted control. Wang Jingwei (who had gone overseas after the Zhongshan Incident) returned as well. Chiang Kai-shek, meanwhile, captured Nanjing and Shanghai in March 1927. Possessing the wealthy industrial and banking center of China in Shanghai, Chiang could now afford a break with the Soviets. On 12 April 1927 Chiang, allied with underworld elements, launched a violent attack on labor and CCP groups in Shanghai. Six days later he created his own conservative KMT regime in Nanjing. Both Wuhan and Nanjing condemned the other and purged its leaders.

Wuhan's own leftist coalition proceeded to collapse. Stalin ordered the CCP to take strong independent action, which enraged Wang Jingwei and the KMT left. The Wuhan regime expelled Borodin and the CCP leaders and began a violent crackdown on the left. The Nanjing regime was plagued by disagreement among its leaders and military defeat during these weeks. In June 1927 Chiang successfully concluded an alliance with northern militarist Feng Yuxiang, who had been courted by both Wuhan and Nanjing.

**The Rise of Chiang Kai-shek.** The Northern Expedition thus seemed on the verge of self-destruction. Chiang retired in August and traveled to Japan, breaking the deadlock. The Western Hills faction attempted to unite the two groups through a new Nanjing regime established in September but much of the military remained loyal to Chiang. In January 1928 he was invited back to head a new KMT government as commander in chief and chairman of the CEC. The conservatives had triumphed. Allied with Feng and Yan Xishan, KMT forces captured Beijing in June 1928.

The success of the Northern Expedition might seem the culmination of the KMT's long struggle and indeed the symbols of victory were present. The KMT one-party regime and its flag dominated China and achieved international standing as its recognized government. Behind the facade of success, however, lurked grave weaknesses. Chiang's military victories were achieved by dint of alliances with such men as Feng Yuxiang, Yan Xishan, Zhang Xueliang, and the Guangxi clique. These powerful regional leaders resisted Chiang's authority, and civil war, sometimes quite costly, plagued the Nanjing government. The CCP continued to fight after the 1927 split. Following several defeats in urban areas, the party created a rural base with the Jiangxi Soviet. Chiang chased the Communists to the northwest in 1934 and 1935 but did not defeat them. Finally, Japan was alarmed at the rise of Chinese nationalism and seized control of the three northeastern provinces of Manchuria in September 1931 and pressed into North China. In sum, the KMT government was beset by serious internal and external problems.

Nor was the KMT itself united. Dissident elements and leaders continued to challenge Chiang's dictatorship. In March 1929 Chiang summoned the Third Party Congress to purge left-wing ideas and members. Later, however, the leading rightist Hu Hanmin challenged Chiang's authority and was arrested in the spring of 1931. Opponents of Chiang then created a separate KMT regime in Canton and both called simultaneous Fourth Party Congresses. Chiang resigned temporarily in late 1931, easing the crisis, but returned in January 1932, now allied with the old leftist Wang Jingwei. Although the mid-1930s brought somewhat greater stability to China, a renewed crisis developed in 1935 and 1936 as a result of Japanese pressure in North China.

Chiang Kai-shek controlled the Nanjing government. Although theoretically a period of one-party KMT tutelage, in fact the Nanjing era saw little independent party authority. As long as it had been out of power the KMT had been a center of power and politics. After the creation of the Nanjing government, the locus of power shifted to Chiang and the military. The party itself swelled in size (to more than 600,000 by 1929) but membership became *pro forma* for government employees and soldiers. The organization of the party was controlled by the Chen brothers and their CC clique. Few decisions were made within the party structure. The Central Political Council, headed by Chiang, was nominally a committee of the CEC and it controlled the government. In practice it mattered little which hat Chiang wore, as he made all of the decisions. The KMT was moribund, serving largely as a propaganda device for the regime.

During the mid-1930s Chiang tried to appease Japan and avoid war, a policy increasingly unpopular in urban China. Student demonstrations in De-cember 1935 demanded resistance and in December 1936 Chiang was forcibly detained in Xi'an by Zhang Xueliang. As a consequence Chiang halted the civil war against the Communists and opened negotiations. When the Sino-Japanese War erupted after 7 July 1937, the KMT and CCP formed a United Front against Japan, although the agreement had more form than substance in the later years of the war. [See also Xi'an Incident and United Front.]

The Nanjing government was devastated by the war and retreated inland to Chongqing. Wang Jingwei, still a potent KMT figure, decided that China's position was hopeless and defected to the Japanese in December 1938. He later established a puppet government under the KMT aegis in Nanjing. Its flag and its army's insignia were that of the old KMT government, a circumstance that undermined somewhat the KMT regime in Chongqing.

The actual role of the party in Chiang's government dwindled in the war as power tilted even further into the hands of the military. Chiang was honored by being named director-general (zongcai) of the KMT in March 1938 by an extraordinary congress. As part of the United Front strategy, the KMT regime broke the tradition of one-party tutelage and summoned a parliamentary-style body, the People's Political Council. While it did allow for CCP and minority-party representation, the government gave the council only advisory powers.

When World War II ended the KMT regime was weak and demoralized. Even the Sixth Party Congress of the KMT, held in May 1945, reflected the despair that characterized the Chongqing regime. Under American pressure it held a Political Consultative Conference in January 1946 with representation by the KMT, CCP, and minority parties. Agreements were reached but never successfully implemented; civil war resumed. After some early success, the KMT position rapidly eroded and finally collapsed in 1949.

Chiang Kai-shek and the KMT established a rump government on Taiwan that continues today, still essentially a KMT one-party regime. The KMT itself, as during the Nanjing years, serves as a propaganda organ for the government, not the locus of political power.

[See also China, Republic Period; China, Republic of; Taiwan; Sun Yat-sen; Chiang Kai-shek; Chen Guofu; and Wang Jingwei.]

Gerald E. Bunker, *The Peace Conspiracy: Wang Ching-wei and the China War, 1937–1941* (1972). Hsi-sheng Ch'i, *Nationalist China at War: Military Defeats and Po-

*litical Collapse, 1937–1945* (1982). Lloyd E. Eastman, *The Abortive Revolution: China under Nationalist Rule, 1927–1937* (1974) and *Seeds of Destruction: Nationalist China in War and Revolution, 1937–1949* (1984). James E. Sheridan, *China in Disintegration: The Republican Era in Chinese History, 1912–1949* (1975). Milton J. T. Shieh, *The Kuomintang: Selected Historical Documents, 1894–1965* (1970). Hung-mao Tien, *Government and Politics in Kuomintang China, 1927–1937* (1972). George T. Yu, *Party Politics in Republican China, The Kuomintang, 1912–1924* (1966).                    PARKS M. COBLE, JR.

**GUO MORUO** (1892–1978), Chinese literary figure whose chiefly bureaucratic career was founded on his standing as a creative artist. In Japan (1913–1921), Guo was inspired by Western romanticism. His Creation Society (founded 1921), journals, and self-celebratory, Whitmanesque poems added to the lively 1920s literary scene. Guo repudiated this for Marxism in 1924, notably in the confused but influential essay "Revolution and Literature" (1927). Prolific in many genres and in scholarship, Guo in his early poems, translations (especially from German), and autobiographies showed an erratic promise. Later writings, however, largely served the party line. Guo was the expositor of Mao Zedong's poems, president of the Academy of Science, and chairman of the All-China Federation of Literary and Art Circles.

Leo Ou-fan Lee, *The Romantic Generation of Modern Chinese Writers* (1973), pp. 177–200. David T. Roy, *Kuo Mo-jo: The Early Years* (1971).                    SHAN CHOU

**GUPTA EMPIRE.** Including most of northern India under direct rule, at its peak, the Gupta empire wielded power and influence over a much wider area. Although the empire was established as a petty state toward the end of the third century CE under its first king, Sri Gupta, it did not rise to prominence until the reign of its third king, Chandragupta I, in about 320 CE, a year that marks the beginning of the Gupta era. Through military conquest and a timely marriage to Kumaradevi, a Licchavi princess whose name and effigy appear on coins along with his own, Chandragupta I created the nucleus of an empire that included most of Bihar and the eastern half of Uttar Pradesh, with Pataliputra as capital.

Chandragupta's son and successor, Samudragupta (r. 335–375), is remembered in an epigraphic record engraved on an Ashokan pillar at Allahabad describing his military campaigns. Having exterminated nine kings of Aryavarta, Samudragupta brought the larger part of the northern heartland under his direct administration, and having subjugated five monarchical states from Assam to Himachal Pradesh and nine nonmonarchical ones from the Punjab, Rajasthan, and Madhya Pradesh, he created a ring of tributary states as a buffer zone. He defeated twelve kings who ruled the Deccan and lands as far south as Kanchi, but allowed them to rule over their kingdoms in amicable subservience. Several Kushan splinter states in the northwest acknowledged his power and sent gifts, and the rulers ·of Lanka had a friendly relationship with him. His coins give epigraphic testimony to his performance of the Ashvamedha sacrifice and to his excellence in music and the fine arts.

Samudragupta's son Chandragupta II Vikramaditya (reigned c. 375–415), an equally great king, destroyed the Saka power in western India and thereby obtained access to the benefits of trade with the Western world. He entered into matrimonial alliance with the Vakatakas of the Deccan and perhaps made successful campaigns in the northwest. His reign saw the consolidation of the empire. Chandragupta II was a great patron of arts and letters; Faxian, the Chinese Buddhist monk who visited India at that time, reported on the security and prosperity of the people.

The Gupta empire reached its zenith in the period of Kumaragupta I (reigned c. 415–455). Without any military campaigns he provided peace with splendor for almost four decades. But after these successive long reigns the empire began showing signs of weakness. While the Pushyamitras created a disturbance in the southwest, the Hunas threatened in the northwest. Kumaragupta's successor, Skandagupta (reigned c. 455–467), was on the front attempting to save the empire from these dangers when his father died. He kept the empire intact, but after him there were succession rifts and brief reigns; an exception was the reign of Budhagupta, who had a comparatively longer tenure (reigned c. 477–495). After Budhagupta there followed a period of further internal dissensions, disputed successions, truant feudatories, and Huna incursions. The empire not only contracted but became divided among the leading scions of the family. One of them, Bhanugupta, is known from the Eran inscription in Madhya Pradesh, dated 510 CE, to have fought a battle with the Hunas in which his general Góparaja was killed, and the wife of the general became a *sati*. [*See* Sati.]

The Huna harassment continued with mixed success, but Narasimhagupta, probably the Baladitya of Xuanzang's account, and Yashodharman, an

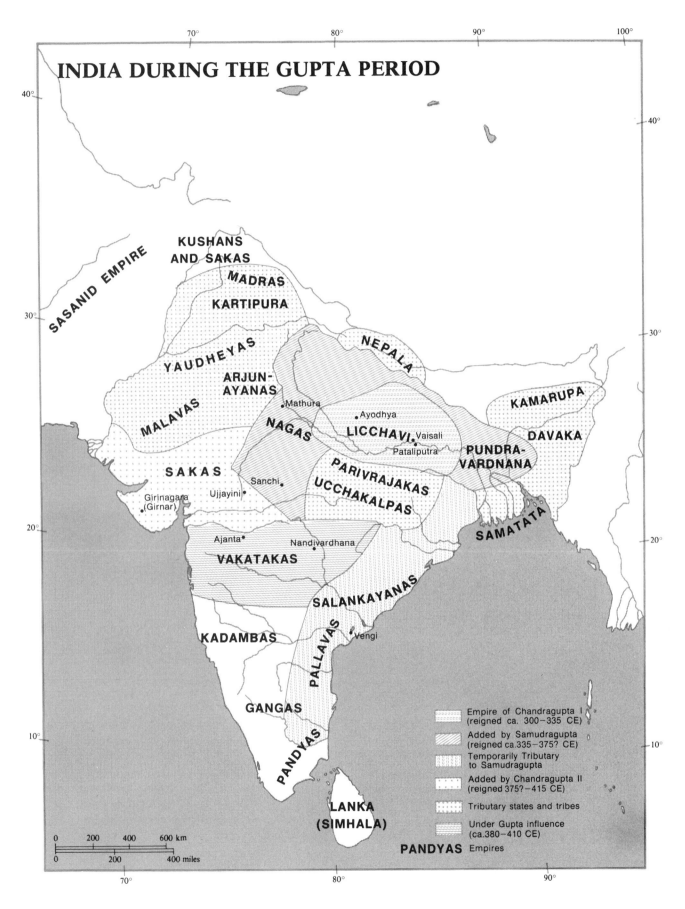

# INDIA DURING THE GUPTA PERIOD

SASANID EMPIRE

KUSHANS AND SAKAS

MADRAS

KARTIPURA

YAUDHEYAS

ARJUN-AYANAS

MALAVAS

NAGAS

Mathura

NEPALA

Ayodhya

LICCHAVI

Vaisali

Pataliputra

KAMARUPA

DAVAKA

PUNDRA-VARDNANA

SAKAS

Sanchi

Ujjayini

PARIVRAJAKAS

UCCHAKALPAS

SAMATATA

Girinagara
(Girnar)

Ajanta

Nandivardhana

VAKATAKAS

SALANKAYANAS

KADAMBAS

PALLAVAS

Vengi

GANGAS

PANDYAS

LANKA
(SIMHALA)

Empire of Chandragupta I
(reigned ca. 300–335 CE)

Added by Samudragupta
(reigned ca.335–375? CE)

Temporarily Tributary
to Samudragupta

Added by Chandragupta II
(reigned 375?–415 CE)

Tributary states and tribes

Under Gupta influence
(ca.380–410 CE)

**PANDYAS** Empires

0    200    400    600 km

0    200    400 miles

FIGURE 1. *Shakyamuni Buddha*. Although influenced by the earlier Kushan style, this Gupta-period bronze statue, dated to the first half of the sixth century, shows the development of the more geometric Gupta style. Height 68.6 cm.

eminent feudatory who had risen to independence, inflicted a crushing defeat on the Hunas and forced their confinement in the northwest. Nonetheless, these wars took their toll on the security and economy of the empire and hastened its disintegration by the middle of the sixth century CE, although nominal allegiances to the Guptas were recorded in Bengal and Orissa for another two decades.

By the standard of most early empires the government of the Guptas was remarkably mild. The general benevolence of the government is evident from the numerous inscriptions and from Faxian's account. By and large the system was decentralized; local bodies and institutions, social groups, and trade guilds appear to have enjoyed much autonomy. The legal system was liberal and the death penalty was not imposed, even for the most serious crimes. There was freedom of movement and trade routes were generally safe. The economy was in excellent condition for most of the Gupta era. Gupta gold coins, known as *dinars*, were based on Roman weight standards carried over from Kushan times. These coins are known for their artistic variety and quality and are perhaps the only series in the world bearing poetic compositions.

The Gupta age was productive in the fields of literature, science, and technology. Classical Sanskrit was at its height, and featured such poets as Kalidasa. The two national epics of India, the *Ramayana* and the *Mahabharata*, along with the major Puranas, attained their definitive forms in this period. Treatises on law, such as the *Yajnavalkya Smriti*, updated social norms. Authoritative books of the diverse religious systems, their philosophies, and their rituals, as well as standard works on aesthetics, ethics, erotica, dance, drama, and technical arts, were produced. Notable advances were made in mathematics and astronomy; two famous names in this area, Aryabhata and Varahamihira, belong to the Gupta period. The iron pillar of Mehrauli at Delhi stands as an example of the technological development of the age.

The period of the Gupta empire is generally considered the "golden" or "classical" age of Indian history. Although there are dissenting views, this period was probably the most outstanding in Indian history. The preceding centuries of interaction between the indigenous and foreign elements had already introduced ingredients and incentives for a new synthesis and idealism. The long period of peace and security, religious freedom and toleration, friendly interstate relations, decentralized administration, favorable foreign trade balance, and economic prosperity left hardly anything wanting for the effulgence of art and culture, and above all gave a sense of maturity and confidence so very necessary for all great ages of history.

[*See also* Pataliputra; Kalidasa; Ramayana; Mahabharata; Indo-Aryan Languages and Literatures; *and* Architecture: South Asian Architecture.]

A. S. Altekar, *The Coinage of the Gupta Empire* (1957). P. L. Gupta, *The Imperial Guptas*, 2 vols. (1975, 1979).

S. K. Maity, *The Imperial Guptas and Their Times* (1975). R. C. Majumdar, ed., *The Classical Age* (1954). Romila Thapar, *A History of India*, vol. 1 (1966).

A. K. NARAIN

GURJARA-PRATIHARA DYNASTY. Among several Gurjara families ruling in Rajasthan during the mid-sixth century, the Gurjara-Pratiharas were most powerful. Their descendants, rising to power under Nagabhata (reigned c. 730–756), are known as the Imperial Pratiharas, one of the great dynasties in North India. Ruling from Kanauj, the Pratihara monarchs of the ninth and tenth centuries were frequently involved in battles with the powerful Rashtrakuta and Pala dynasties; several times the Pratiharas temporarily annexed large portions of their territory. For example, inscriptions of the Pratihara king Mahendrapala (reigned c. 885–910) are known in Bihar and Bengal, indicating his hold over eastern India as well. The military strength of the Pratiharas served as a barrier to Muslim armies seeking conquest of North India at least until 1027, the last known date of a Pratihara king.

[*See also* Kanauj.]

R. C. Majumdar, "The Gurjara-Pratīhāras," *Journal of the Department of Letters* 10 (1923): 1–76. R. S. Tripathi, *History of Kanauj to the Moslem Conquest* (1964).

FREDERICK M. ASHER

GURKHAS, soldiers of the British and Indian armies recruited largely from the hill populations of Nepal. British officers leading the Kumaon campaign against the raja of Gorkha in 1815 were so impressed with the courage and stamina of the enemy troops that they began recruiting prisoners taken in battle. By the war's end, nearly three thousand "Goorkhas"—as the British came to refer to all the "martial" tribes of the Himalayan foothills—were organized into four battalions of the Bengal Native Infantry. A decade later the British resident at Kathmandu recommended the employment of Nepalese troops as mercenaries in the Indian army with the dual purpose of augmenting the strength of the Gurkha units and undermining the capacity of the Nepalese to wage further war against the Raj.

Despite the opposition of Nepal's rulers to their subjects serving the British, the ranks of the Gurkhas were expanded steadily during the nineteenth century. Gurkha soldiers played a major role in the consolidation of British rule over the subcontinent in campaigns against the Marathas, Sikhs, Afghans,

and Burmese, during the Mutiny of 1857, and in the opening of Tibet. Two hundred thousand Nepalese soldiers saw action with Allied forces during each of the world wars, and Gurkha units were instrumental in checking Japanese expansion into Northeast India on the Burma Front in 1944. Following the partition of India in 1947 the Gurkha regiments were divided between the British and Indian armies, each of which now recruits separately. England continues to maintain a force of seven thousand Gurkhas recruited directly from Nepal for service throughout the British commonwealth, especially Hong Kong, Brunei, Singapore, and Belize. India employs nearly seventy-five thousand Nepalese troops, the majority of whom are recruited from Nepalese communities in India.

[*See also* Gurungs.]

H. James and D. Sheil-Small, *The Gurkhas* (1965). J. B. R. Nicholson, *The Gurkha Rifles* (1974). W. B. Northey and C. J. Morris, *The Gurkhas* (1974).

RICHARD ENGLISH

GURUNGS, a Mongoloid people living mainly in the central Nepal hills between Gurkha and Parbat districts and known outside of Nepal mainly as Gurkha soldiers in the British, Indian, and Nepalese armies. They profess Tibetan Buddhism and speak Gurung, a Tibeto-Burman dialect. They are agriculturalists-cum-pastoralists, and those among them who live at higher altitudes raise sheep and weave woolen blankets. The Gurungs seem to have been organized under a system of chieftains before the Hindus overran them in the sixteenth century. As alcohol drinkers, they are assigned to a relatively low status by Hindu social organization.

[*See also* Gurkhas *and* Nepal: History of Nepal.]

Donald A. Messerschmidt, *The Gurungs of Nepal* (1976). Francis Tuker, *Gorkha: The Story of the Gorkhas of Nepal* (1957). PRAYAG RAJ SHARMA

GUWEN. The term *guwen* had two different meanings in China's late imperial period: "ancient script" and "ancient-style prose," both terms referring to pre-Han writings. When used in contradistinction to the term *jinwen*, "modern script," *guwen* referred to the ancient textual versions of the classical canon. As a literary genre, *guwen* was properly translated "ancient-style prose," a major innovation in literary expression that drew upon models of expository prose dating from before the Han dynasty (206 BCE–220 CE). The term "ancient-style prose" was adopted to distinguish it from the style known as "rhymed prose." Favored by writers during the Period of Disunion (265–589), "rhymed prose" grouped words into phrases of four or six characters and applied rules of tight parallel construction between phrases and sentences. *Guwen* contained no artificial rules and allowed the writer freely to adopt any rhythms or constructions, thus affording "maximum scope to individual expression, absorption of current vocabulary, and the development of new syntax."

Initially promoted by the late Tang (618–907) prose masters Han Yu and Liu Zongyuan, *guwen* was further developed during the Song dynasty by Ouyang Xiu (1007–1072), Su Shi (Su Dongpo; 1036–1101), and Zhu Xi (1130–1200). In the Qing period, the more conservative scholars from Tongcheng, Anhui Province, Fang Pao (1668–1749) and Yao Nai (1732–1815), promoted *guwen* because it facilitated didactic exposition of moral principles to promote moral education basic to sociopolitical reform. It was also the stylistic medium used by Song Neo-Confucian philosophers. The prestige of *guwen* was challenged by Ruan Yuan, who favored "rhymed prose" because it was untainted by association with the "eight-legged" (*ba gu*) style of exposition demanded of civil service examinations candidates.

[*See also* Chinese Literature; Confucianism; Jinwen; Neo-Confucianism; Ouyang Xiu; Su Dongpo; *and* Zhu Xi.]

James T. C. Liu, *Ou-yang Hsiu* (1967).

JUDITH A. WHITBECK

GU YANWU (1613–1682), anti-Manchu Chinese scholar, proponent of evidential scholarship (*kaozheng xue*). Descended from a respected lineage in Kunshan, Jiangsu Province, Gu Yanwu was adopted and raised by the widow of his natal father's first cousin. As a young man, Gu participated in Fushe activities and was involved in the resistance to the invading Manchus, but he never served in the Southern Ming court. As hopes for a loyalist restoration faded, and faced with a hostile creditor in Kunshan, Gu turned to a life of restless wandering, teaching, and scholarship—successfully resisting service in the Manchu court.

In the course of Gu's travels in north and central China he wrote on a vast range of contemporary concerns including institutional practices, ethical and historical questions, geographical conditions in

areas of military strategic importance, and controversial textual problems relating to the classical inheritance. His goal throughout was to pursue knowledge applicable to understanding and ordering the present. Gu's writings were enormously influential in the Qing period (1644–1911), when he became revered as the founder of evidential scholarship and a staunch critic of the late Ming intellectual tendency toward metaphysical speculation. Countering centralist tendencies during the imperial era, Gu recommended principles for local administration to increase the status and power of the district magistrate and to strengthen the clan system.

[*See also* Kaozheng Xue; Neo-Confucianism; *and* Qing Dynasty.]

R. Kent Guy, "The Development of the Evidential Research Movement: Ku Yen-wu [Gu Yanwu] and the *Ssuk'u ch'üan-shu*," *Tsing Hua Journal of Chinese Studies* (1986). David Kornbluth, "Ku Yen-wu and the Reform of Local Administration," *Select Papers from the Center for Far Eastern Studies,* no. 1 (1955–1957): 7–46. Willard J. Peterson, "The Life of Ku Yen-wu," *Harvard Journal of Asiatic Studies* 28 (1968): 114–156, 29 (1969): 201–247.

JUDITH A. WHITBECK

GU ZUYU (1631–1692), a native of Wuxi, China, carried on his father's historical and geographical research, which emphasized military strategy, an interest shared by the more famous contemporary scholar Gu Yanwu. Gu Zuyu was a Ming loyalist who lent support to the Three Feudatories Rebellion, abandoning the cause only when his superior surrendered to the Qing. Gu's *Essentials of Geography* gained wide acclaim in the early nineteenth century, largely through the sponsorship of Li Zhaoluo (1769–1841).

[*See also* Gu Yanwu *and* Three Feudatories Rebellion.]

Arthur Hummel, ed., *Eminent Chinese of the Ch'ing Period* (1943), pp. 419–420.

JUDITH A. WHITBECK

GWALIOR, city in India located about sixty-five miles south of Agra. Although the fort of Gwalior has existed since the ninth century, it became the capital of the most powerful Maratha princely state in India only in the 1770s. Ranoji Scindia (d. 1750), the founder of Gwalior state, started his political career reputedly as a slipper-bearer at the court of the *peshwa*, or prime minister, of the Marathas, but soon rose to high office. His youngest son, Mahadaji Scindia (d. 1794), became the greatest general of the *peshwa* and expanded Maratha power north through Central India toward Delhi. After an inconclusive war, Mahadaji Scindia, as a representative of the *peshwa*, concluded the Treaty of Salbai with the British in 1782. The Scindias and the British engaged in desultory battles until a treaty in 1818 adjusted boundaries and confirmed Scindia as a British client.

Maharaja Madho Rao (r. 1894–1925) was a modernizing administrator within his state, an ardent supporter of Maratha revivalism, and an active participant in the Chamber of Princes. In 1931 Gwalior had an area of 26,382 square miles (the sixth-largest state) and a population of 3,523,070 (the fifth most populous state). Gwalior was integrated into the Madhya Bharat union of princely states in 1946 and was incorporated into Madhya Pradesh state in 1956.

[*See also* Madhya Pradesh; Princely States; *and* Marathas.]

H. M. Bull and K. N. Haksar, *Madhav Rao Scindia of Gwalior, 1876–1925* (1926). Surendra Nath Roy, *A History of the Native States of India*, vol. 1, *Gwalior* (1888).

BARBARA N. RAMUSACK

# H

HACHIMAN, popular Japanese deity of uncertain origins, widely thought to be the special protector of warriors. Hachiman's cult, believed to have originated in the Usa district on the island of Kyushu, combines elements of Buddhism, Shinto, and shamanism. The Chinese characters with which his name is written literally mean "eight banners" and may be read as "Hachiman" or "Yahata." This unusual name may have derived from that of the region where he was first worshiped.

In the eighth century, the Hachiman cult spread from Kyushu to the imperial capital, Nara. There a shrine was dedicated to him on the grounds of Tōdaiji, the headquarters of state Buddhism. In Nara Hachiman was venerated as a special guardian of Buddhism, of the nation, and of the imperial family.

Following the transfer of the capital to Kyoto in 794, a new Hachiman shrine was established at Iwashimizu (on the outskirts of the city), where he was worshiped together with two female deities. His identification with the legendary emperor Ōjin (r. 270–310) and that of the god's female attendants with the emperor's mother, Empress Jingū, and consort, Nakatsuhime, sealed the cult's already close ties with the imperial family.

By 1185, when the Minamoto established their military headquarters at Kamakura, the worship of Hachiman had spread throughout northeastern Japan. The Minamoto, who had adopted Hachiman as their tutelary deity, founded a shrine in his honor at Tsurugaoka. Together with those at Usa and Iwashimizu, it remains a major center of the official cult to the deity. Hachiman's association with members of the Minamoto warrior clan led to the growth of his role as a war god and the overshadowing of his earlier ties with the imperial family. In this new guise Hachiman also achieved a wide popular following. Today, Hachiman shrines are found in cities, towns, and villages throughout Japan.

[See also Minamoto and Shinto.]

Jean Herbert, *Shinto: At the Fountainhead of Japan* (1967). Alicia Matsunaga, *The Buddhist Philosophy of Assimilation* (1969). CHRISTINE M. E. GUTH

HACIENDA. The Spanish system of landed estates (*haciendas*), owned by a Spanish *hacendado* and worked by tenant laborers, developed in the late eighteenth century in the Philippines. After they could no longer depend on profits from the Manila galleon trade to support them, Spaniards and mestizos began to take a more active interest in developing haciendas to grow export crops. Frequently, Philippine haciendas incorporated existing village networks, and since the early Spanish settlers were content to remain in Manila, Filipino chiefs or other members of the indigenous population were recruited to become the local agents or estate managers.

The Spanish clergy's early organizational efforts in the Luzon hinterland resulted in the Roman Catholic church's control over large haciendas, which were sold off to Philippine elite under the American colonial administration, in power during the early twentieth century. At this time contracts between sugar mill owners and *hacendados* expanded sugar cultivation. In Luzon the *hacendado* delivered his tenants' sugar production to the mills; in Negros, however, *hacendado* families owned the sugar mills and thus had total control over the production and processing of sugar. Conflict between Luzon *hacendados* and their tenants over the division of sugar profits resulted or contributed to the development of political and revolutionary movements in the 1930s.

[See also Philippines; Spain and the Philippines; Friars; and Manila Galleon.]

Nicholas P. Cushner, "Meysapan: The Formation and Social Effects of a Landed Estate in the Philippines," *Journal of Asian History*, 7.1 (1973): 30–53.

KENNETH R. HALL

**HADITH**, a technical term in Arabic used to designate those reports that claim to relate a saying or deed of the Prophet. Although of interest to the Muslim community from the beginning, it was not until the early ninth century that these prophetic traditions came to be viewed as an authoritative source for Muslim belief and practice, thanks largely to the efforts of al-Shafi'i and the traditionist movement. The study of these traditions, eventually gathered into written collections, became one of the most characteristic features of Muslim scholarship throughout the lands of Islam.

[*See also* Shafi'i *and* Shari'a.]

Alfred Guillaume, *The Traditions of Islam* (1924). J. Robson, "Hadith," in *The Encyclopaedia of Islam* (new ed., 1960–).           MERLIN SWARTZ

**HAFIZ** (1327–1391), literary name of Shams al-Din Muhammad Shirazi, by common consent the greatest and most popular poet of *ghazals* (lyrics) in the Persian language. As with many other poets of Iran, very little is known about his life. Efforts to glean references to his personal life from his poetry have always led to scholarly controversies that are often of little significance.

Hafiz's father, Baha al-Din, was a petty businessman from Isfahan who had settled in Shiraz, where Hafiz was born. The poet's mother was from Kazirun, a town to the southwest of Shiraz. The death of Baha al-Din left the family in dire poverty. Shams al-Din had to earn his living (reportedly as a baker's apprentice) at a young age, but he managed to receive a sound education in his hometown, which, despite repeated political turmoil, was still a major center of learning in the Islamic world. He mastered the Arabic language, studied religious sciences, and attained the status of *hafiz* (one who has learned the Qur'an by heart, hence his pen name, Hafiz). His poetry bears witness to his thorough knowledge of the early masters of Persian poetry.

Hafiz lived in troubled times, witnessing the fall of two dynasties. His first royal patron was Shaikh Abu Ishaq Inju, under whose liberal rule Hafiz seems to have enjoyed the comforts of life. But Abu Ishaq was defeated and killed in 1353 by the Muzaffarid Mubariz al-Din Muhammad, who decided to make Shiraz his capital. Muhammad was a ruthless religious zealot who had no use for Hafiz and his poetry, although his vizier seems to have patronized the poet. Muhammad's stern religious restrictions imposed on the wine-loving Shirazis gave him the sobriquet Muhtasib ("one who restricts") that Hafiz

has immortalized in more than one ode. But in 1358 he was deposed and blinded by his son, Shah Shoja, himself a poet of some merit. Hafiz could not but express his delight at the turn of events, but for reasons that are not entirely clear he lost the new monarch's favor and had to try his fortune at Isfahan and Yazd, other centers of Muzaffarid rule. Disappointed, he returned to Shiraz after a year or two, calling Yazd "Alexander's Prison." In 1387 Shiraz was captured by Timur, who reportedly had an encounter with the poet and, impressed with his wit, granted him royal favor.

Except for short sojourns in Isfahan and Yazd and a reported trip as far as Hormuz on the way to India, Hafiz spent all his life in his beloved Shiraz, which he has characterized as "Solomon's Dominion" (Mulk-i Sulayman). He is reported to have had a teaching job at a religious college in Shiraz, but his main source of income seems to have been the allowances and gifts he received from the court and the nobles whom he panegyrized. Particularly in his old age, however, he led a life of poverty. His poetry is rich in Sufi symbolism and imagery, but we have no report concerning his attachment to any particular Sufi order.

Hafiz died and was buried in Shiraz; his wife and son had predeceased him. His mausoleum (the Hafiziyya) in Shiraz is the best-known monument there and a site frequently visited by tourists. During the last ten years of the Pahlavi regime parts of the much-publicized annual art festival of Shiraz were held in the Hafiziyya.

[*See also* Shiraz; Inju Dynasty; Muzaffarid Dynasty; *and* Timur.]

A. J. Arberry, *Shiraz, the Persian City of Saints and Poets* (1960), pp. 139–168. E. G. Browne, *A Literary History of Persia* (1928), vol. 3, pp. 271–319. J. Rypka, *History of Iranian Literature* (1968), pp. 263–274. G. M. Wickens, "Hāfiz," in *The Encyclopaedia of Islam* (new ed., 1960–). John D. Yohannan, *Persian Poetry in England and America: A Two Hundred Year History* (1977).

MANOUCHEHR KASHEFF

**HAIBUTSU KISHAKU** ("abolish Buddhism and destroy Buddhist images"), a slogan describing a surge of anti-Buddhist sentiment and attacks on Buddhism that swept through Japan in the first few years of the Meiji period (1868–1912). The movement to eradicate Buddhism was unleashed by the Meiji government's policy of separating Shinto from Buddhism (*shinbutsu bunri*) and elevating Shinto to the status of a national faith. It was intensified by the resentment many Shinto priests and scholars of Kokugaku ("national learning") felt at the influence of Buddhism in social and intellectual life.

For more than a millennium, the characteristic pattern of Japanese religion had been one of accommodation between Buddhism and Shinto, with Buddhism the dominant partner. In the Edo (Tokugawa) period this traditional synthesis came under criticism from Shinto advocates who wanted to assert the primacy of Shinto and from Kokugaku scholars, like Motoori Norinaga and Hirata Atsutane, who praised Shinto as a pure and ancient native faith and attacked Buddhism as an alien superstition. There were purges of Buddhism in a number of domains during the Edo period. The most severe were those in domains where the daimyo or *han* government was influenced by Shinto or Kokugaku theorists, as in Mito, Okayama, Aizu, Tsuwano, Satsuma, and Chōshū. Some of the anti-Buddhist reformers from domains like Tsuwano were given positions in the Department of Rites (Jingikan) of the new Meiji government and used these positions to pursue their crusade against Buddhism.

In the third month of 1868 the Meiji government issued the first of several edicts for the separation of Shinto and Buddhism. Although the government's avowed policy was separation of the two faiths, not eradication of Buddhism, the policy was clearly intended to end the influence of Buddhism over Shinto, to undercut the economic and material strength of Buddhism, and to reduce the role of Buddhism in Japanese society. Extremists in many parts of the country seized on the edicts as an excuse to launch local attacks on Buddhism. There was little loss of life but much desecration of temples, burning of images, and humiliation of the clergy. That there was not a nationwide revulsion against Buddhism is indicated by the sporadic character of the outbursts and by the fact that in several parts of the country Buddhist laity rallied to the support of their clergy in pro-Buddhist demonstrations. Although the economic and social reduction of Buddhism continued for a decade, the worst of the *haibutsu kishaku* fever was over by 1874, and the various Buddhist institutions began to make a gradual recovery.

One effect of *haibutsu kishaku* was a drastic reduction in the scale of the Buddhist establishment in Japan. On the positive side, the challenge of eradication forced many Buddhists to face the spiritual challenges posed by the new conditions of the Meiji period. What survived of Buddhism had been strengthened by the ordeal and was better prepared to answer the needs of a country undergoing rapid change and modern development.

[*See also* Tokugawa Period *and* Meiji Restoration.]

Martin Collcutt, "Buddhism," in *Japan in Transition: From Tokugawa to Meiji*, edited by Marius B. Jansen and Gilbert Rozman (1985).          MARTIN COLLCUTT

**HAIDAR ALI KHAN** (1721–1782), the de facto ruler of Mysore, was known for his opposition to the British in India. The son of a soldier, he learned the art of warfare and diplomacy in the Anglo-French wars of 1751 to 1755 and supplanted his own master, Nanjaraj, in 1761. Haidar Ali enlarged the Mysore kingdom and endowed it with an efficient system of administration and a well-disciplined army; he fought constant wars with his neighbors, the Marathas and the *nizam*, who remained unreconciled to his rise as a power; and he inflicted severe blows on the English and damaged their reputation as an invincible power in India. In the First Mysore War (1767–1769), he appeared before the gates of Madras and dictated terms to the British. In the Second Mysore War (1780–1784), he caused them greater embarrassment by defeating their armies and by occupying large tracts of their territories. He died, however, before he could conclude the war.

[*See also* Mysore.]

B. Sheik Ali, *British Relations with Haidar Ali* (1963). N. K. Sinha, *Haidar Ali* (1959). M. Wilks, *History of Mysore* (1980).          B. SHEIK ALI

**HAIKAI**, a form of Japanese poetry that flourished in the sixteenth through eighteenth centuries, reaching its zenith with the work of Matsuo Bashō (1644–1694). *Haikai*—the word originally signified comic or unconventional poetry—evolved in the late fifteenth century as an informal alternative to linked verse *(renga)*. Both *haikai* and linked verse were usually produced as a poetic sequence by a small group. The most eminent poet present at a session began by composing the first stanza, in seventeen syllables. This is the *hokku*, or opening verse; in the late nineteenth century, it became an independent form of poetry, the *haiku*. The next most prominent poet at a session followed the *hokku* with a fourteen-syllable verse that was "linked" by theme, image, or subject; the third poet would link another seventeen-syllable stanza to the preceding one. Then, assuming that the group consisted of only these three people, the first poet would continue the sequence by contributing a fourteen-syllable link, the second poet followed with a seventeen-syllable link, and so on until a fixed number of stanzas (usually one hundred) was composed. Occasionally a virtuoso would compose a *haikai* sequence of one hundred or one thousand stanzas by himself. The novelist Ihara Saikaku (1642–1693) pushed such performances to the limit by composing 23,500 stanzas in the course of one day and night in 1684.

The principal difference between early *haikai* and linked verse is in the vocabulary used. Linked verse, a highly refined art by the mid-fifteenth century, required that participants use only a limited range of native Japanese words. The subject of each stanza was also confined to a few approved categories. *Haikai,* however, permitted colloquialisms and Chinese loanwords, as well as commonplace, vulgar, and even risqué subjects. Another difference lay in the intended effect of the poetry. Linked verse aimed for a smooth, subtle flow of themes and images, while *haikai* constantly sought out novel and sometimes shocking styles and subjects.

Early *haikai* was a diversion rather than a literary art. Its practitioners included eminent linked verse poets like Sōgi (d. 1502), who evidently composed *haikai* as a means of relaxation. One kind of *haikai* sequence from the early period takes the form of a riddle and proposed answers. A poet composes a riddle in fourteen or seventeen syllables, to which the other poets present must respond with a link solving the riddle. The preferred answer was a witty mélange of puns and double entendres. One riddle-verse, "Spring has come indeed / To the chessboard," elicited this response from Yamazaki Sōkan (fl. c. 1520), an early *haikai* poet: "For the warbler is / Settling into its nest / To keep a check on its mate."

Matsunaga Teitoku (1571–1653) brought respectability to *haikai,* transforming what had been a frivolous pastime into a relatively serious literary activity. The son of a professional poet of linked verse and himself a practitioner of that art, Teitoku was also trained in court poetry. His knowledge of these more refined genres enabled him to formulate analogous rules for composing *haikai* sequences. As the status of *haikai* rose, Teitoku attracted talented pupils who perpetuated his light, polished style. Teitoku is remembered for *hokku* such as this: "Why be so dejected? / Are apricot blossoms prey to / Some secret concern?" In the original Japanese, the apricot blossoms are given human emotions through a dexterous use of puns.

Teitoku's conservative tradition was challenged in the mid-seventeenth century by an iconoclastic group, the Danrin school. Founded by Nishiyama Sōin (1605–1682) and including the prolific Saikaku, the Danrin school stressed the importance of stating one's own feelings and perceptions in poetry, rather than concentrating on wordplay and intellectual games. Sōin's poetry is often a direct expression of emotion: "My thoughts go on and on, / Accumulating with the snow: / Silent, unspoken."

Teitoku's codification and the Danrin style of subjectivity are the bases for the poetry of Bashō, the greatest composer of *haikai.* An eclectic reader, Bashō was deeply influenced by the poetry of Saigyō (1118–1190) and Sōgi, as well as by Chinese literature and Zen Buddhism. [*See* Saigyō.] Some of his most famous *haikai* synthesize these interests. One of his most admired poems, "Upon a withered branch / Crows have come to rest: / Autumnal twilight," has been seen as the verbal equivalent of a Chinese ink painting, as a Zen scene pared to the minimum, and as a work embodying the mystery and depth of the *Shinkokinshū,* a poetry anthology. Other *hokku* by Bashō juxtapose the eternal and the transitory: "Ancient pond: / A frog jumps into / The sound of water," or again, "Wildflowers of summer: / All that remain of / Warriors' dreams." Bashō's mature work provides the reader with a glimpse of eternity through an unadorned portrayal of nature.

The transcendental "Bashō style" influenced all future *haikai.* It is reflected in the objective poetry of Yosa Buson (1716–1783): "In an ancient garden, / Warblers sing / Throughout the day." Buson also excels in conjuring up scenes from the past, as in this allusion to an episode from the *Tale of Genji (Genji monogatari)*: "Inside the wide sleeve of / A casual court robe / Creeps a firefly." Bashō's simple diction and attraction to nature also appear in the *haikai* of Kobayashi Issa (1763–1827). Although Issa does not rank with Bashō and Buson as one of the great *haikai* poets, he remains popular for straightforward verses on small animals and insects: "Oh, sparrow chick, / Better go now, better go— / Milord's horse is coming!" But Issa was an exception among increasingly uninspired *haikai* poets. In 1892 *haikai* came under attack by the poet Masaoka Shiki (1867–1902), who asserted that it had been reduced to a word game for elderly gentlemen. He advocated the objective portrayal of nature through the form of *haiku.* Shiki's manifesto marks the beginning of the "*haiku* revival" and the end of *haikai* as a literary genre.

[*See also* Matsuo Bashō.]

Harold G. Henderson, *An Introduction to Haiku* (1958). Donald Keene, *Japanese Literature: An Introduction for Western Readers* (1953) and *World within Walls* (1976). Earl Miner, *Japanese Linked Poetry* (1979). Makoto Ueda, *Matsuo Bashō* (1970; reprint, 1982).

AILEEN GATTEN

HAILEYBURY COLLEGE, the training school for East India Company civil servants from 1806 until 1855. Because the expansion of British power in India created the need for trained administrators rather than commercial agents, the company opened Haileybury in England along with Fort William College in Calcutta. Students at Haileybury studied three Indian languages, as well as law, political economy, history, and science. T. R. Malthus taught political economy at the college until 1834, and the famous Orientalist H. H. Wilson had official connections there. The college was officially closed after the India Act of 1858 established open and competitive exams for the Indian civil service.

Bernard S. Cohn, "Recruitment and Training of British Civil Servants in India 1600–1860," in *Asian Bureaucratic Systems Emergent from the British Imperial Tradition*, edited by Ralph Braibanti (1966).    LYNN ZASTOUPIL

HAINAN, island located about ten miles off the South China coast; excluding Taiwan, it is China's largest island possession. Hainan was first incorporated within the Chinese empire in the second century BCE during the early Han dynasty, and it has long been administratively a part of Guangdong Province. Because of its unhealthy tropical climate, however, Hainan remained for most of its history relatively sparsely populated and underdeveloped. Its population in 1982 was about 3,740,000. The majority of its inhabitants are Han Chinese who migrated originally from southern Fujian Province and who speak a variant of the Min dialect; they make their living farming the lowlands along the coast. The main urban center is the northern port of Haikou opposite the mainland. In the highlands of south-central Hainan live more than 300,000 Li, an indigenous agriculturalist people related to the Tai of Southeast Asia. Some of China's Miao population also reside on Hainan.

Edward H. Schafer, *Shore of Pearls* (1970). Theodore Shabad, *China's Changing Map: National and Regional Development, 1949–1971* (rev. ed., 1972).

EDWARD J. M. RHOADS

HAI SAN SOCIETY, Chinese secret society in Malaya. It was most prominent between 1860 and 1880 among the Hakka tin miners of Perak but was also active in Selangor, Penang, and Singapore. The Penang lodge was founded in 1820 and is said to be the oldest Hai San lodge in Malaya. The Perak Hai San, under Chung Keneg Kwee, were a part of the Penang branch and allied themselves with the Mentri of Larut in his struggle against the Ghi Hin and Raja Abdullah. A similar struggle between the Selangor Hai San, under the leadership of Yap Ah Loy (founder of Kuala Lumpur), and Ghi Hin rivals contributed to the disorders that brought about British intervention in the peninsular states in 1873. Hai San headmen held prominent positions in their respective areas as tin miners, merchants, and revenue farmers for many years after British intervention.

[*See also* Perak; Selangor; Ghi Hin; Yap Ah Loy; *and* Tin.]

Emily Sadka, *The Protected Malay States 1874–1895* (1968).    CARL A. TROCKI

HAJI, RAJA (r. 1777–1784), fourth Bugis *yang di pertuan muda* of Johor/Riau. Raja Haji controlled the state during the minority of Sultan Mahmud III. He is credited in the *Tufhat al-Nafis* (written by his grandson) with spreading the influence of Riau throughout the western part of the archipelago and with bringing Riau to a high point of economic prosperity. Fearing that he might unite the Malays against them, the Dutch attacked Riau in 1784. Breaking the siege, Raja Haji led an attack on Dutch Melaka. There, he was shot and killed, whereupon the Dutch sacked Riau and effectively destroyed the state.

[*See also* Bugis; Johor; Riau; *and* Mahmud Riayat Syah III.]

Raja Ali Haji, *Tufhat al-Nafis (The Precious Gift)*, edited and translated by Virginia Matheson and Barbara Watson Andaya (1981). Carl A. Trocki, *Prince of Pirates: The Temenggongs and the Development of Johor and Singapore 1784–1885* (1979).    CARL A. TROCKI

HAKKA, Han Chinese who originated in North China but migrated to the South. During the Southern Song dynasty (1126–1279), they were pushed southward by invading Central Asian tribes; by the nineteenth century they had reached as far south as Guangdong and Guangxi provinces. The inhabitants who had settled these provinces centuries earlier, who referred to themselves as "original people" (*bendi;* pronounced *punti* in Cantonese), called these newcomers "guest people" (*kejia;* Cantonese, *hakka*).

Because the Hakka maintained their own dialect and customs—they did not bind their women's feet, for example—they were not assimilated among the original settlers, whose tenants they became. Forced onto poor hillside soil, the impoverished Hakka often fought the original settlers over land. They became the first participants in the Taiping Rebellion (1851–1864). Seeking relief from their poverty, thousands of Hakka emigrated to Southeast Asia and North America.                P. RICHARD BOHR

HALEBID. *See* Hoysala Dynasty.

HALI, ALTAF HUSAIN (1837–1914). Poet, critic, and social reformer, Altaf Husain chose the pen name *Hali* ("contemporary"), which aptly expressed his deepest concerns. Born in Panipat, near Delhi, into a respected family, he ran away to Delhi at the age of seventeen and came under the influence of some of the best minds of the time, including the poet Mirza Asadullah Khan Ghalib. In 1871 Hali obtained an educational position in Lahore; together with Muhammad Husain Azad and a group of liberal British educators he was active in the Anjuman-e Panjab, a society dedicated to social and literary reform. During this period he wrote poetry on patriotic and naturalistic themes. He returned to Delhi in 1875, became an active supporter of Sir Sayyid Ahmad Khan's reformist programs, and wrote his famous hortatory long poem *Musaddas* in 1879.

Retiring to Panipat in 1887, he wrote his most influential poetry and prose, including his *Muqaddama* (introduction to his *divan*, 1894), *Yadgar-e Ghalib* (a literary biography of the poet, 1897), *Hayat-e javed* (a biography of Sayyid Ahmad Khan, 1901), and *Chup ki dad* (1905), a moving poem on the silent suffering and noble qualities of Indian women. Hali attempted a Western interpretation of the nature of poetry and pleaded for a literature that was socially responsible, realistic, and "natural."

[*See also* Ghalib, Mirza Asadullah Khan *and* Ahmad Khan, Sir Sayyid.]

Laurel Steele, "Hali and His *Muqaddamah*: The Creation of a Literary Attitude in Nineteenth Century India," *Annual of Urdu Studies* 1 (1981): 1–45.

                FRANCES W. PRITCHETT

HALIFAX, VISCOUNT. *See* Wood, Edward Frederick Lindley.

HALL, D. G. E. (1891–1979), English historian of Southeast Asia, professor of history at the University of Rangoon (1921–1934), and founding professor of the history of Southeast Asia at the University of London (1949–1959). Hall's scholarly writings fall into two main areas: those concerned with the activities of Europeans in Burma, including *Early English Intercourse with Burma, 1587–1743* (1928); and those predominantly concerned with the indigenous history of the region, such as *A History of South-East Asia* (first published in 1955). The latter was of crucial importance in establishing Southeast Asia as a major field of academic interest. As a historical introduction to the region, Hall's *History* has rarely been equaled and never surpassed.

C. D. Cowan, "D. G. E. Hall: A Biographical Sketch," *Southeast Asian History and Historiography: Essays Presented to D. G. E. Hall*, edited by C. D. Cowan and O. W. Wolters (1976). D. G. E. Hall, *A History of South-East Asia* (4th ed., 1981).                IAN BROWN

HAMADAN, or Hamadhan, a major city of the western Iranian Plateau, located on a strategic route connecting western Asia and the Mediterranean lands to the east. The population of Hamadan in 1975 was 155,846.

There are reasons to believe that Hamadan is the city referred to as *Amdana* in the Assyrian tablets of the twelfth century BCE. The Greek historian Herodotus mentions the city as being the creation of the first Median king (c. seventh century BCE), who called it *Agbatana*. The name reappears in later Greek and Roman sources as *Ecbatana*. *Hamadan* seems to be a compound of the Iranian words *hang* or *hag* ("assembly") and *mata* ("place").

Hamadan stands at the edge of a fertile and well-watered plain at the foot of the majestic Mount Alwand (or Alvand); it possesses a cool climate. The city has always been a major urban area, serving as the capital of the Medes and as the summer capital of the Achaemenid dynasty. In the Bible (Ezra 6:2) the city is mentioned as Akhmeta; the legendary tombs of Queen Esther and her uncle Mordechai there are the most revered Jewish shrines in Iran.

Hamadan remained important under the Seleucid, Parthian, and Sasanid dynasties. Conquered by Muslim forces early in the seventh century CE, the city sank to the level of a provincial town until the twelfth century, when it served as a Seljuk capital. It was sacked by the Mongols in 1221 and again in 1224, and later by Timur in 1389. Under the Safavids Hamadan prospered, only to take another plunge in the aftermath of the downfall of the dynasty. Thereafter it reverted from Persian to Turkish control and back again several times. In 1910 and 1912 a number of civil disturbances resulted in the entry of Russian troops directed to restore order. The city exchanged hands several times more during World War I until it was finally brought under firm Persian rule in the 1920s.

The city was until the present century one of the four premier cities of the Jibal Province and later of Iraq-i Ajami. Historically the city has shown a curious dearth in producing first-class cultural luminaries. It is true that the city was conquered and ruined many times, but this is a fate shared by many other cities on the Iranian Plateau and the Transoxiana. Another peculiarity is the apparent eclipse of Hamadan by smaller neighboring towns in the twentieth century. The population has remained stagnant. Although the city had the fourth- or fifth-largest population in nineteenth- and early twentieth-century Iran, in the past fifty years it has grown by less than 40 percent, while in the same period the growth of its ancient rival cities has been spectacular.

Hamadan has a mixed ethnic and religious population. Luri (a local dialect of Persian), a number of Turkic dialects, Kurdish, and certain "Median" dialects are spoken in Hamadan. Linguistically, the city may still have a "Persian" plurality, but the growing number of Kurdish speakers is steadily eroding that position. The ancient and once-large Jewish community has been diminished in numbers and importance by the past half-century of emigration.

Few relics of the city's long past have survived the onslaught of the ages. A set of Achaemenid rock inscriptions, a Parthian stone lion, a small number of Islamic mausoleums, and the modern tombs of Ibn Sina and Baba Tahir (the rustic poet and the favorite son of Hamadan) are all that remain standing. The strategic centrality of Hamadan has prompted the present Iranian government to set up one of the country's largest military air bases in the environs of this city.

G. Le Strange, *The Lands of the Eastern Caliphate* (1905)      MEHRDAD IZADY

## HAMAGUCHI OSACHI (1870–1931), Japanese politician, prime minister from 1929 to 1931. Hama-

guchi died in Tokyo from gunshot wounds inflicted by a fanatic nationalist.

Born in Tosa (now Kōchi Prefecture), Hamaguchi lived during a period that produced the beginnings of a parliamentary system and the emergence of contemporary Japan. Hamaguchi's political career reached its peak in the wake of Japan's first election on the basis of universal manhood suffrage. His assassination signaled an ominous turn in Japan's rising militarism in the 1930s and 1940s.

Upon graduation from Tokyo Imperial University, Hamaguchi entered the Ministry of Finance. He was elected to the House of Representatives in 1915. Within a little more than ten years, Hamaguchi became an established party politician with a reputation as a policymaker. Prior to becoming the president of Rikken Minseitō, which represented the merger of two major parties, he served as minister of finance and as minister of home affairs. Following the collapse of the cabinet of Tanaka Giichi as a result of the 1928 assassination of the Chinese warlord Zhang Zuolin, Hamaguchi became prime minister in 1929.

Hamaguchi's austere fiscal policy did not endear him to the military, which had grown wary of party politics in the 1910s and 1920s. In 1930 Hamaguchi further displeased the military by skillfully forcing approval of agreements reached at the London Naval Conference. This success ultimately cost him his life.      MICHIO UMEGAKI

## HAMENGKUBUWANA, name of all sultans of

Yogyakarta (Java) since Mangkubumi (Hamengkubuwana I, r. 1749–1792) assumed it in 1755. His son Hamengkubuwana II (r. 1792–1810, 1811–1812, 1826–1828) contributed to the fall of Yogyakarta to British forces in 1812 by his arbitrary rule, intrigues, and mishandling of relations with Britain. Among his successors the most noteworthy are Hamengkubuwana V (r. 1822–1826, 1828–1855), a noted patron of literature, and Hamengkubuwana IX, who assumed the throne in 1939 and introduced progressive reforms in Yogyakarta from 1945 onward. He played a leading role in the revolution (1945–1949) and in national affairs thereafter, eventually serving as vice president of Indonesia (1973–1978).

[*See also* Yogyakarta; Mangkubumi; *and* Indonesian Revolution.]

M. C. Ricklefs, *A History of Modern Indonesia c. 1300 to the Present* (1981). Selosoemardjan, *Social Changes in Jogjakarta* (1962).      M. C. RICKLEFS

**HAMI**, town in eastern Xinjiang (Chinese Turkestan), important since ancient times for its position on the trade route that linked China to Persia. Held intermittently by the Han dynasty from about 73 to 136, Hami was occupied briefly by the Sui, but brought firmly into China's orbit only by Tang Taizong, whose forces reached it in 630. Subsequently Hami was conquered by Turfan, then by the Uighurs, and ultimately by the Mongols, who called it Qomul; it was visited by John of Marignolli and mentioned by Marco Polo. Hami was of strategic importance to the Ming, whose court debated policy toward it but were unable to maintain influence there. Hami formed part of the Qing empire and of China subsequently.          ARTHUR N. WALDRON

**HAM NGHI** (c. 1871–1947), seventh Nguyen emperor (r. 1884–1888). Enthroned at the age of thirteen, he fled Hue with his regent, Ton That Thuyet, upon the arrival of French troops in July 1885. Hiding in Quang Tri and later in the Quang Binh-Ha Tinh area, he was the focus of loyalty for the scattered resistance groups who responded to the Can Vuong ("loyalty to the king") edict. Although able to escape capture for several years, Ham Nghi was betrayed by a Muong lieutenant and caught by the French in November 1888. He was deported to Algeria, where he spent the rest of his life.

[*See also* Can Vuong *and* Ton That Thuyet.]

Truong Buu Lam, *Patterns of Vietnamese Response to Foreign Intervention: 1858–1900* (1967). David Marr, *Vietnamese Anticolonialism, 1885–1925* (1971).

BRUCE M. LOCKHART

**HAN**, one of the Warring States of ancient China. Located on the North China Plain along the course of the Yellow River in present-day Shanxi and Henan provinces, Han was one of three states formed in the breakup of the state of Jin in 453 BCE. The Zhou dynasty recognized Han's independence formally in 403 BCE. Han was the smallest of the seven major contending states in the fourth and third centuries BCE; the philosopher Shen Buhai was its most famous minister. Han was conquered by Qin in 225 BCE.          EDWARD L. FARMER

**HANAFI**, one of the four orthodox schools of law in Sunni Islam, named after Abu Hanifa al-Nu'man ibn Thabit, who died in Baghdad in 767. Hanafi grew out of a tradition of legal thought that first took form in Kufa and from there established itself as the dominant legal orientation throughout much of southern Iraq during the late Umayyad and early Abbasid periods. The development of Hanafi law into a distinctive school of jurisprudence, however, was the work of Abu Hanifa's disciples, principally Abu Yusuf (d. 798) and Muhammad al-Shaibani (d. 805), whose writings laid the basis for a more or less coherent system of jurisprudence. While Hanafi doctrine from the beginning recognized the importance of the Qur'an as an essential source of law, Hanafis were at pains to insist on the indispensability of personal judgment or reason *(ijtihad/ra'y)* as a tool of juridical elaboration. The freedom and flexibility that they sought to secure for juridical doctrine were given concrete expression in such concepts as *istihsan* (juridical preference) and *qiyas* (analogical reason). Although these concepts are to be found in Maliki and Shafi'i law, it was the Hanafis who applied them most consistently and extensively. The Hanafi school, however, did not entirely escape the influence of the traditionist movement, as a consequence of which Hanafis, too, were compelled to concede a larger role to prophetic tradition *(hadith)* as a source of law.

While the Hanafi school had its origins in southern Iraq and reflected the legal consensus of that particular region, it rapidly established itself as the dominant school of law in the eastern provinces of the Abbasid empire, thanks in no small measure to the favor shown it by the court in Baghdad. From Iraq and Persia the Hanafi school found its way to Central Asia, Afghanistan, and India. With the penetration of Islam into China, especially from the thirteenth century, the Hanafi school became the dominant legal influence there as well. In each of these areas the Hanafi school remains the legal affiliation of the vast majority of Muslims.

[*See also* Hadith *and* Shari'a.]

Noel J. Coulson, *A History of Islamic Law* (1964). Joseph Schacht, *The Origins of Muhammadan Jurisprudence* (1950).          MERLIN SWARTZ

**HANBALI**, youngest of the four orthodox schools of law in Sunni Islam, named after Ahmad ibn Hanbal (d. 855), whose teaching, together with that of his immediate disciples, laid the basis for a system of law and theology decidedly traditionalist in orientation. While not rejecting reason altogether as a source of law, the Hanbali school sought vigorously to circumscribe its scope, emphasizing rather the Qur'an and the *sunna* as the primary sources of law.

Among the Sunni schools of law it was closest to that of the Shafi'is, differing from it mainly in the role assigned to reason. Founded in Baghdad, the Hanbali school came to play a significant role in the revival of Sunni Islam following the collapse of the Buyid dynasty in 1055. During the late eleventh and the twelfth centuries, a period that may be regarded as the golden age of Hanbalism, the school produced some of its most influential spokesmen, among them Ibn Aqil (d. 1120), Abd al-Qadir al-Jilani (d. 1166), and Ibn al-Jauzi (d. 1200).

Although Baghdad remained the stronghold of Hanbalism until the middle of the thirteenth century, its influence spread both eastward and westward from an early date. By the end of the eleventh century, the school was represented in a number of Persian cities as well as in Mesopotamia and Syria. Through the writings of Ibn Taimiyya (d. 1328) and the efforts of the Wahhabi movement in the eighteenth century, Hanbali influences made their way to India and Southeast Asia, where even today they continue to be felt.

[See also Hadith; Qur'an; Shafi'i; and Shari'a.]

Henri Laoust, "Hanābila," in The Encyclopaedia of Islam (new ed., 1960–).                    MERLIN SWARTZ

**HAN DYNASTY.** Established in the wake of the collapse of the authority of the Qin dynasty, the Han dynasty (206/202 BCE–220 CE) further consolidated China into a unified empire in which many Chinese political and social patterns were set. With the Tang dynasty (618–907), the Han period is considered an era in which Chinese culture achieved its greatest heights. The dynasty is divided into two periods separated by the Wang Mang interregnum. The Former, or Western, Han (206 BCE–9 CE) had its capital in Chang'an; the Latter, or Eastern, Han (23–220) was centered in Luoyang.

***Establishment of the Dynasty.*** Beginning in 209 BCE, numerous rebel groups joined to overthrow the despotic Qin government. Several years of civil war followed in which the rebel leaders each fought for the imperial title. Two major contenders finally emerged. One was Xiang Yu, the descendant of a formerly aristocratic family in the southern state of Chu; the other, Liu Bang, was of peasant background and had been a minor village official. The competition was not a struggle between the social classes, however, because both men had supporters from diverse backgrounds. Liu Bang's strategy was to establish alliances with leaders of armed groups by recognizing them as equals, which gave him an important edge over Xiang Yu, who organized other leaders as his subordinates. Xiang Yu was finally defeated in 202 BCE and committed suicide. Liu Bang (Gaozu; r. 206/202–195), who had taken the title king of Han in 206, now proclaimed himself emperor of the Han dynasty. [See also Liu Bang.]

The early years of the dynasty were characterized by power struggles among Liu Bang's old comrades. Several of these meritorious generals had been given large domains to govern as vassal states of the Han court and could not resist the temptation of the imperial throne. After the first generation, however, the internal disturbances were mainly created by succession disputes among children of the Liu imperial house. It was not until the reign of Emperor Jin (157–141) that stability in the Han court was secured.

Externally, however, the Han faced serious challenges from the newly rising nomadic empire of the Xiongnu. The Xiongnu had headed a confederation of various ethnic groups along the Eurasian steppe even before the Qin dynasty (221–207) was founded. By the end of the third century BCE, the confederation had been welded into a strong empire that stretched from Central Asia to eastern Siberia. Han China, just emerging from hardship under the despotic Qin and from decades of civil wars, lacked sufficient resources to fight the Xiongnu, whose cavalry surpassed the Chinese infantry. Thus, in its first century of rule the Han was vulnerable both internally and externally.

***The Reign of Emperor Wu.*** With a fresh memory of Qin authoritarianism, which had penetrated almost every aspect of life, the Han leaders did not actively adopt measures to reorganize China. The government structure inherited from the Qin was kept virtually intact. Nevertheless, codified law was simplified in practice. Tax rates were reduced, few public projects requiring large corvée labor were conducted, and large-scale foreign campaigns were not initiated. After a century of recovery China gradually gathered strength. Agricultural productivity was improved and commercial and manufacturing activities increased. Several urban centers rose in population and became extremely prosperous.

Emperor Wu (r. 141–87), who succeeded to the throne as a dynamic young prince, aided by other equally energetic leaders of his generation, began to take positive action to transform China into a splendid empire. The primary task was to release China from the constant threat imposed by the Xiongnu. Not only were large armies sent beyond China's border to penetrate into their territory, but expe-

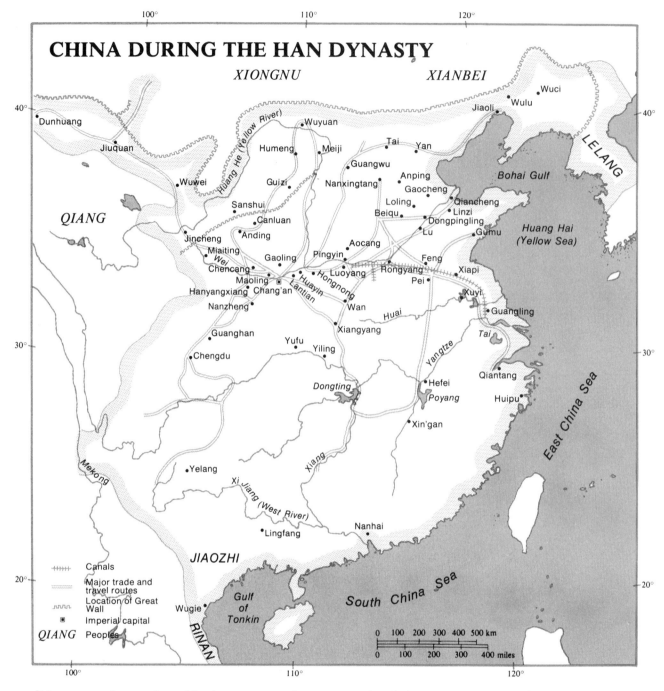

# CHINA DURING THE HAN DYNASTY

*XIONGNU*          *XIANBEI*

Wuci
Wulu
Jiaoli
Dunhuang
Wuyuan
Jiuquan
Tai     Yan
Humeng     Meiji
Guangwu     *LELANG*
Wuwei     Guizi     Anping
Nanxingtang     Gaocheng     *Bohai Gulf*
Sanshui     Loling     Qiancheng
*QIANG*     Beiqu     Linzi
Canluan     Dongpingling
Jincheng     Anding     Aocang     Lu     Gumu     *Huang Hai
(Yellow Sea)*
Miaiting     Gaoling     Pingyin     Feng
*Wei*     Luoyang     Rongyang     Xiapi
Chencang     Hongnong     Pei
Maoling     Huayin     Xuyi
Hanyangxiang     Chang'an     Lantian     *Guangling*
Nanzheng     Wan
Xiangyang     *Tai*
Guanghan     *Huai*
Yufu     Qiantang
Chengdu     Yiling     *Yangtze*     Huipu
Hefei
*Dongting*     Poyang     *East China Sea*
Xin'gan

*Xiang*

Yelang
*Xi Jiang
(West River)*

Lingfang     Nanhai

*JIAOZHI*

*Mekong*

*Huang He (Yellow River)*

| | |
|---|---|
| ++++++ | Canals |
| | Major trade and travel routes |
| nnnnn | Location of Great Wall |
| ▣ | Imperial capital |
| *QIANG* | Peoples |

*RINAN*     Wugie     *Gulf
of
Tonkin*

*South China Sea*

0  100 200 300 400 500 km
0  100  200  300  400 miles

---

ditions were also conducted in the western regions for the purpose of severing the Xiongnu from their potential allies in Central Asia. Chinese campaigns finally drove the Xiongnu out of the pasturelands near China. The emptied land between the Great Wall and the Gobi Desert was given to other nomads, who supposedly served as a buffer between China and the Xiongnu.

The Han operations in the west brought all of Central Asia into the orbit of the Han empire. In order to locate new routes to Central Asia, the Han explored the mountainous southwest, where a variety of native states were made tributary and finally were governed by Chinese after the Han administration was established. In the northeast, Chinese troops entered northern Korea to establish provinces there, presumably to flank the Xiongnu on their eastern border. [*See also* Xiongnu *and* Commanderies in Korea, Chinese.]

All of these operations, plus the extravagant life of the young emperor, emptied the imperial treasury, which had accumulated over the three previous generations. The Han court, therefore, was compelled to raise revenues by levying various kinds of taxes. The one that caused the most profound impact was imposed upon private business. Boats, carts, shops, and other facilities were made subject to property taxes. The government also gained additional income from the confiscation of the personal property of those who were found guilty of tax fraud. The worst blow to private businesses, however, was delivered when the government entered market competition by selling the commodities that had been collected either as tribute or taxes paid in kind. The result was that the private sector of the national economy withered drastically. During the early period of the Han dynasty, prosperity in the private portion of the economy had produced specialization of trade and manufacturing as well as rapid urbanization. After private business interests suffered this tremendous setback, Han China became dominated by an agrarian economy, a pattern that was to continue throughout Chinese history.

*Han Bureaucracy.* The Han government structure was inherited from the model of its Qin predecessor. In the central government, the chancellor headed the government, or outer court, while the personal secretaries of the emperor constituted an inner court that balanced the authority of the chancellor and the outer court. Military command was in the hands of the grand general, whose status was equal to that of the chancellor and who had the confidence of the emperor. The government treasury and the private imperial treasury were separated so that the emperor could not touch the public funds. A board of inspectors was empowered to supervise the conduct and performance of all government officials, even of the emperor himself.

At the provincial level, China was divided into more than one hundred provinces, which in turn were divided into counties. The court of a provincial governor was a miniature replica of the imperial court. The provincial governor, however, was constantly supervised by an imperial inspector who was in residence and who monitored the conduct and performance of officials in the province.

The situation could have functioned despotically if the Han dynasty had not developed a recommendation system to counterbalance that potentiality. In the Qin period, there had been a rudimentary recommendation system to select capable or wealthy people in local communities to serve as policemen, clerks, sheriffs, and other such officers. In the Han, an elaborate recommendation system was gradually developed in order to draw talent from all over the empire to serve in the government. Eventually the bureaucracy became a self-generating mechanism that was so powerful that the personal power of the emperor (or those who acted in his behalf) could not prevail absolutely.

In order to avoid nepotism at the local level, only those who were not natives could be appointed to the position of chief official of a particular region, such as provincial governor or county magistrate. Nevertheless, the staff of the local governments was drawn exclusively from native elites. The system therefore prevented the buildup of local power in any region that might lead to segmentation of the empire, while local interests were protected by the presence of native sons in the government.

*Ascent of Confucian Intellectuals.* Confucian scholars had suffered purges under the First Emperor of Qin, an ardent practitioner of Legalist theories. During the early reigns of the Han dynasty, Confucianism did not fare well either, for the ruling class embraced Daoism as a philosophy to justify their laissez-faire policies. Nevertheless, Confucian scholars had already found a path to government as experts on ritual and precedents and in other areas that were indispensable to a functioning bureaucracy.

Emperor Wu, who did not wish to continue the monopoly on government jobs held by a small group of aristocrats, appointed Confucian scholars to serve in high positions. Their number steadily increased because of the recommendation system. Meanwhile, in the Imperial Academy, Confucian classics were the exclusive curricula. Provincial schools were also established. After graduating from a local school, a talented student could continue his academic training at the Imperial Academy. Fellowships and assistantships were available so that the poorer students could also receive higher education. The graduates of the Imperial Academy became candidates for government service to be appointed to mid-ranking positions. Such an education system definitely helped to regenerate Confucian participation in the government.

Confucian influence in the court grew steadily after the reign of Emperor Wu, especially during the rule of emperors Yuan (r. 49–33) and Cheng (32–7), both of whom were educated by Confucian tutors. The enrollment of the Imperial Academy increased from a few hundred students in Emperor Wu's time to more than thirty thousand by the beginning of the first century CE. The criteria for advancing a candidate in the recommendation system were based on a Confucian standard of conduct

FIGURE 1. *Early Han Plate. Pan,* bronze core enveloped with gilded sheet silver and decorated with animal motifs. Diameter 50.8 cm.

rather than on the candidate's successful completion of a particular mission. The recommendation system was thus transformed into a mechanism that supported Confucian ideology, then regarded as the guiding principle for a Han bureaucrat to carry on governance. The end product of the confucianization of the bureaucracy was the long-lasting ideological influence of the system, which had acquired political support to sustain its status as an orthodoxy.

*Wang Mang's Interregnum.* The Western Han ended in 9 CE when the throne was usurped by Wang Mang (r. 9–23), a member of a family of imperial consorts, several of whom had become empresses. The Han imperial power was very often shared by matrimonial relatives, who would hold key positions. The accumulation of power within the Wang family over many generations was partly the result of their repeated marriages of daughters to the throne. Wang Mang initially served as a regent since the emperor was too young to hold court. Finally he simply took the throne for himself, as emperor of the Xin ("new") dynasty.

Wang Mang was a Confucian who was probably sincere in his attempt to implement several programs discussed in the classics. First he changed the titles of the government officials to those included in the *Rites of Zhou (Zhouli)* to symbolize the reinstalla-tion of an ancient Zhou institution. His major projects of reform were in the economic sphere. He proclaimed that all slaves were to be called imperial subjects and that all land was to be regarded as an "imperial field." It is not clear whether this meant that the slaves were emancipated as freemen or were simply being shifted to the status of imperial slaves nor whether this implied a nationalization of landholdings.

While there had been a government monopoly on salt and iron during the Western Han period, Wang Mang expanded the monopolized items to include wine and natural resources (such as woods and swamps) on government land. He also levied taxes on business profits to establish a public loan fund from which the poor could borrow without paying usurious interest rates. These measures ensured that excessive profit would not become the source of accumulated wealth for private citizens, thereby helping to create a more just society that would reduce the excessive differences between the rich and the poor.

Wang Mang's reforms, however, were probably too drastic and too hastily put into practice. He also weakened the empire economically by issuing too much money, which led to runaway inflation. In foreign affairs he brought on wars with irritated nomads on China's borders. The compounded effects of all of these problems finally brought down his regime. In 23 CE Wang Mang was killed by rebel forces and the Han dynasty was restored. [*See also* Wang Mang.]

*Han Restoration.* The rebels who ended Wang Mang's Xin regime consisted of hungry peasants who were the victims of inflation; landlords whose property and profits had been greatly reduced; Confucian intellectuals who regarded Wang Mang as a usurper of the legitimate imperial house; and royalists, many of whom were members of the deposed Liu house. The leader who succeeded in restoring the Han imperial sovereignty was Liu Xiu, a Confucian student, landlord, and member of the imperial family, although distantly related to the former ruling line. Many of his lieutenants were his Confucian schoolmates and landlords, while his soldiers were mainly reorganized from armed gangs of starving peasants.

Liu Xiu, also known as Emperor Guangwu (r. 23–57), restored the Han dynasty, which lasted until 220. The capital was moved from Chang'an eastward to Luoyang, and the dynasty was thus later known as the Eastern, or Latter, Han. The Chinese territory remained largely the same as it had been in the Western Han, and rebellious nomads in the north and west were again subjugated. The southernmost location of Chinese authority was in northern Vietnam. The western regions in Central Asia were once again brought under the control of Chinese commissioners. It is through the consolidation brought about during the four centuries of Han rule that the Chinese as a nation conceived of their homeland as the territory held during the Han period.

Within these bounds, the Chinese migrated to peripheral areas, especially the fertile land of the Yangtze River and the vast plains of Manchuria. Chinese migrants first settled in river valleys, where footholds were established. Gradually they moved upward along river systems and pushed farther inland, forcing the indigenous inhabitants out of the plains and the valleys into the marginal areas in the mountainous highlands. The Chinese population shifts to the South during the Eastern Han period were so numerous that demographic distribution was permanently changed and administrative units in the South were constantly added.

*Conflict Between State and Society.* The balance between the inner and the outer courts in the Western Han period had been tipped once under Emperor Wu's strong monarchy. Generally, however, there was mutual respect between the imperial power and the power of the elite, who were deeply rooted in the bureaucracy. The new government of the Eastern Han saw a shift to a much stronger monarchy because the imperial authority firmly belonged to the throne. The inner court was the decision-making body, while the power of the chancellor was drastically reduced. Furthermore, the inner court during the Eastern Han period was composed exclusively of eunuchs, while the Western Han imperial secretariat had often been a mixed body of bureaucrats and those who enjoyed imperial confidence, including the eunuchs. The Eastern Han inner court, therefore, lacked the participation of people who could serve as a link between the government and the palace.

In addition, the Eastern Han intellectuals, predominantly Confucians, expanded their numbers and their influence in the society because of increased educational opportunities, becoming a strong autonomous body. They regenerated their own power by taking selection of officials into their own hands. Some of them became extremely powerful community leaders, while a few families actually could be regarded as a new national aristocracy. The tension between these two mutually independent power groups—the socially elite intellectuals and those of the inner court—led to competition and confrontation between the state and the society.

In the latter half of the Eastern Han, the eunuchs and imperial relatives were engaged in a power struggle for imperial authority. They created a vicious cycle of revolving power groups, placing on the throne young emperors whom they could manipulate; if the ruler died early they installed an even younger heir from a collateral branch. Palace control changed hands frequently, with the adversaries trying to enlist the outer court as allies in the struggles. The later reigns of the Eastern Han witnessed mass persecution of ranking officials and finally a coup d'état. As a result of their failure to support

FIGURE 2. *Tomb Figure of a Male Attendant.* Gray earthenware with white slip and traces of polychromy. Height 54 cm.

particular inner-court factions, Confucian intellectuals suffered at least two massive purges (161–169 and 171–184), with hundreds jailed, exiled, or even massacred. Both the state and the society in the Han dynasty were severely damaged by such bloody conflicts.

*Fall of the Han.* The last reigns of the Han dynasty saw the final disintegration of the unified empire. The Han government structure was built upon a balance between the central government and the local provincial administrations. As long as the central government functioned effectively, the local units were held together through cultural unity and imperial sovereignty. Nevertheless, because of its great size China had been difficult to govern throughout the Han period. Regionalism was a natural tendency for such a vast empire because of the interaction and competition between rival districts or states. Once the weakened central government failed to perform routine administrative duties, widespread discontent provoked peasant uprisings and the empire began to disintegrate. The most serious uprising was that of the Yellow Turbans, an early Daoist sect, in 184. Numerous provinces in North China were affected. The provincial governors organized local armies and developed de facto independence. Along the Chinese borders there also were disturbances. Large armies were mobilized to fight the Yellow Turbans, then to defend the borders of the empire; these troops became private armies. [*See also* Yellow Turbans.]

In 189 a power struggle in the imperial court brought the army of a warlord to the capital. Chaos brought down the central government. The provinces then engaged in a long civil war in which China was eventually divided into three contending kingdoms. A puppet Han court survived for thirty years, but in 220 the last Han emperor was forced by Cao Pei to give up the throne, with Cao Pei declaring himself emperor of a new dynasty, the Wei.

[*See also* Three Kingdoms.]

Hans Bielenstein, "The Restoration of the Han Dynasty," *Bulletin of the Museum of Far Eastern Antiquities* 26 (1954): 1–209 and 31 (1959): 1–287. T'ung-tsu Ch'ü, *Han Social Structure* (1972). Rafe de Crespigny, trans., *The Last of the Han* (1969). Cho-yun Hsu, *Han Agriculture* (1980) and *Bibliographic Notes on Studies of Ancient China* (1982). Michael Loewe, *Crisis and Conflict in Han China, 104 B.C. to A.D. 9* (1974). Burton Watson, *Records of the Grand Historian of China: Translated from the Shih chi of Ssu-ma Ch'ien* (1961). Ying-shih Yu, *Trade and Expansion in Han China* (1967).

CHO-YUN HSU

**HAN FEIZI** (280?–233 BCE), the great architect of the Chinese Legalist school of philosophy. With Li Si (280?–208 BCE), the future prime minister of the Qin dynasty, he was a student of the prominent Confucian Xunzi (fl. 298–238 BCE). Unlike the often humble origins of early Chinese philosophers, Han Feizi was born a prince of the royal family of the state of Han. This linked him inexorably to the fortunes of Han in the political instabilities of his age. He was acutely aware of the growing threat of Qin and equally the need for reform within Han. Several times he memorialized the king, but to no avail. He suffered apparently from a speech impediment and was incapable of arguing his ideas before the king, a severe handicap in an age that prided itself upon the dialectician's arts. His recourse was to write, and that he did, leaving as his legacy the major text of Legalist thought.

The standard biography of Han Feizi in the *Shiji* enumerates the problems that Han Feizi tried to bring to the attention of the king: the need for reform in the laws and institutions of a state that no longer reflected the feudal order; the strengthening of the power and authority of the ruler to match the needs of an emerging bureaucracy; the strengthening of the army to face the aggression of Qin; and the need for new methods of selection of officials, particularly in the void left by the ending of hereditary officialdom. The formulation of Han Feizi's thought was in direct response to these conditions.

Han Feizi synthesized several different trends in Legalism and as a result created a unified system of thought, focused first and last upon the power and authority of the state and its ruler. From Shang Yang, or Lord Shang (d. 338 BCE), he took the idea of *fa,* law. From Shen Buhai (d. 337 BCE) he took *shu,* methods or techniques. From Shen Dao (350–275 BCE) he took the concept of *shi,* power. In his system of thought all three elements were essential to the art of governance.

These principles rested upon the assumption for Han Feizi that human nature was evil. Most consider this a teaching he received from his teacher Xunzi. There is no innate moral nature of goodness. Man is motivated only by what will benefit him personally and permit him to avoid suffering. Altruistic ideals are applicable only as schemes of corporate interest to avoid undesired results. The ruler then was justified in utilizing laws as well as methods and power to maintain order and authority.

The application of law and methods meant stringent legal codes without concern for special moral relations. All were equal under the law. It also meant techniques for the ruler to maintain his own power against the populace as well as his own ministers. One dominant principle employed was *xingming,* actualities and names. Names were the specific duties and functions assigned to particular positions; actualities, the individual and his particular position. These were to correspond. If they corresponded, then the one who held authority over the names also held control over the actualities. The position of the individual could only be to seek to conform to the name or the position he was given.

Laws and methods were still not necessarily totally adequate. Power was also needed, seen primarily in the exalted position given to the ruler. The ruler's authority was maintained by the sheer exalted nature of the position itself. Throughout the system a severe series of rewards and punishments enforced the principles. The ruler rewarded or punished in strict adherence to the duties performed correctly or incorrectly and to the letter of the law.

Han Feizi's own biography ended sadly. In 234 BCE Qin attacked Han. The king of Han sent Han Feizi to Qin as a special envoy. His own former classmate Li Si, who was now prime minister of Qin, suggested to the king of Qin that Han Feizi, as a member of the royal family of Han, would always harbor loyalties to Han. As a result, even though the king respected Han Feizi and his Legalist writings, he had Han Feizi imprisoned for investigation, and at the instigation of Li Si, Han Feizi committed suicide. Thus, the major teacher of Legalism met his death at the hands of those who most venerated the very teachings he espoused.

[*See also* Legalism; Li Si; Qin Dynasty; Shen Buhai, *and* Xunzi.]

Fung Yu-lan, *A History of Chinese Philosophy,* vol. 1, translated by Derk Bodde (1952). W. K. Liao, trans., *The Complete Works of Han Fei Tzu,* 2 vols. (1939–1959). Arthur Waley, *Three Ways of Thought in Ancient China* (1939). Burton Watson, *Han Fei Tzu: Basic Writings* (1964).                    RODNEY L. TAYLOR

**HANGZHOU,** capital of China's Zhejiang Province and historically a leading political, economic, and cultural center; its population in 1980 was estimated at 1.13 million.

Hangzhou's history extends back over two millennia. Located near the sea on the northwest bank of the Qiantang River, Hangzhou was originally part of the ancient kingdom of Wu, but did not become prominent until after the Sui dynasty (581–618) made it the southern terminus of the Grand Canal in the early seventh century. During the Tang dynasty (618–907), Hangzhou was greatly expanded by filling in an old harbor between two large hills. At the same time, the scenic West Lake was created on the western edge of the city. On the other side, sea walls were constructed to protect the city from damage caused by the unusually large tidal waves arriving annually about the time of the fall equinox. Two famous poet-governors of Hangzhou are still honored for their engineering feats: Bai Juyi (772–846) and Su Dongpo (1036–1101).

From 893–978, Hangzhou served as the capital of the Kingdom of Wuyue. After the Song capital of Kaifeng fell to Jurchen invaders in 1126, Hangzhou became the Southern Song capital. When the fleeing Gaozong emperor came upon Hangzhou, he declared it his "temporary residence" (*xingzai,* whence Marco Polo's name for the city, "Quinsai") in part because he shrewdly observed that the surrounding countryside, crisscrossed with irrigation canals and waterways, would provide an effective deterrent against the Jurchen cavalry. In peacetime, the city grew rapidly to become a flourishing metropolis of nearly one million people. Jacques Gernet has vividly described the life of this "richest and most populous city in the world" at the peak of its glory. (Polo still found Hangzhou's grandeur impressive even after the dynasty had fallen.)

Hangzhou has been known through time as an important trade and handicraft center, and especially as a city of silk weavers. As early as the seventh century it was called the "home of silk and satin." Although by Ming times Hangzhou had lost its once-important status as a seaport owing to heavy silting of navigational channels, some small-scale shipping continues today along with transport by rail and canal. The city was opened to foreign commerce in 1895 by the Treaty of Shimonoseki, and its modern economy still rests largely on silk production, greatly expanded since 1949. In addition, Hangzhou produces cotton textiles, some steel and chemicals, hemp, mulberries, the famous Longjing (Dragon Well) tea, and traditional crafts like sandalwood fans, bambooware, and silk parasols.

Nevertheless, it is for its wide reputation as one of China's major scenic tourist spots that modern Hangzhou stands out in the world today. As generations of Chinese have been fond of saying, "Above, there is Heaven; below, Hangzhou and Suzhou."

Jacques Gernet, *Daily Life in China on the Eve of the Mongol Invasion, 1250–1276* (1962).

ROLAND L. HIGGINS

HAN LINER (d. 1367), figurehead emperor of the so-called Song rebel regime (fl. 1355–1363), which figured prominently in the Chinese rebellions against the Mongol Yuan dynasty (1260–1368). The founding emperor of the succeeding Ming dynasty (1368–1644), Zhu Yuanzhang (d. 1398), originally served the Song as well. Han Liner's father, Han Shantong, was the hereditary head of a branch of the ramified White Lotus sect; he also pretended to be the legitimate heir of the historical Song dynasty (960–1279), which the Mongols had conquered. Han organized his followers in secret lodges throughout the regions of the lower Yangtze and Huai rivers; their ideology combined the Buddhist rebel tradition of the descent to earth of Maitreya and the Manichaean doctrine of the triumph of the Prince of Light (Mingwang) with Song restorationism.

In 1351 the White Lotus instigated a rebellion among the workers assembled to carry out the canal-dredging project of the Yuan chancellor Toghto. Now known popularly as Red Turbans or Incense Armies, the rebels overran the Huai area, triggering similar rebellions in the middle Yangtze. Toghto organized and led the Yuan counterattack, whose first objectives were the already established regional rebel regimes of Fang Guozhen and Zhang Shicheng. In 1355 Han Shantong was executed by Yuan authorities. Soon afterward, the dismissal of Toghto by the emperor Toghon Temur (r. 1333–1370) led to the rapid disintegration of Yuan power in South China.

In the same year Liu Futong, by now the de facto leader of the Red Turbans, brought Han Liner out of hiding and proclaimed him "Song" emperor at Bozhou. Affiliated rebel bands ranged widely through North China. In 1358 Liu Futong took Kaifeng, the capital of the historical Song. In the following year, however, the Red Turbans were driven south to Anfeng by the growing power of the Yuan loyalist warlord Chaghan Temur. The "Song" court then became a backwater as the real strength of the Red Turban movement passed into the hands of Zhu Yuanzhang at Nanjing. Zhu rescued Han Liner when the rebel leader Zhang Shicheng's forces captured Anfeng in 1363. Even this early, Zhu was trying to win Confucian support for his regime, despite the continued loyalty of many of his soldiers

to the millennial ideology symbolized by Han Liner. Han Liner survived until 1367, when he died in a boating accident allegedly ordered by Zhu. Zhu afterwards systematically eliminated the remnants of Red Turban ideology, although his choice of Ming ("brightness") as a dynastic name has been interpreted as an allusion to these beliefs.

[See also White Lotus Society; Red Turbans; Fang Guozhen; Zhang Shicheng; and Zhu Yuanzhang.]

John Dardess, "The Transformations of the Messianic Rebellion and the Founding of the Ming Dynasty," *Journal of Asian Studies* 29.3 (1970): 539–558.

EDWARD L. DREYER

HANOI (Dong Do, Thang Long), capital and largest city (1979 population, 2,570,000) of the Socialist Republic of Vietnam, located near the apex of the Hong (Red) River delta, at the juncture of the To Lich and Red rivers.

This site has been inhabited since Neolithic times and was the chief population and administrative center of the delta throughout the period of Chinese domination, during which it was known as Tong Binh. The names Dai La, La Thanh, and Dai La Thanh, sometimes associated with this location, refer more specifically to the various fortresses built there by the Chinese.

In 1010 Ly Thai To designated this site as his new capital and renamed it Thang Long ("ascending dragon"). Thang Long remained the Viet capital until 1802, except for the years 1397–1407, when Le (Ho) Qui Ly moved the court to Tay Do ("western capital"), the new city he had ordered built in Thanh Hoa Province. During this decade and the twenty-year Ming occupation that followed, Thang Long was known variously as Dong Do ("eastern capital") and Dong Quan ("eastern frontier post").

In 1430 Le Loi officially named the capital Dong Kinh ("eastern capital"; source of the Western-language toponym Tonkin), but the name Thang Long continued in use until the nineteenth century. The Nguyen emperors moved the capital to Hue in 1802, but the former capital retained much of its importance. In 1831 the Minh Mang emperor created the province of Ha Noi ("within the river") and gave the same name to the citadel constructed within the old capital. Hanoi later served as the headquarters of the Indochinese Union (1887–1945) and as capital of the Democratic Republic of Vietnam (1954–1976), after which it achieved its present status.

Little of Hanoi's precolonial architecture remains. Although the Ly, Tran, Later Le, Restored Le, and, to a lesser extent, the Nguyen rulers built extensively in the city, successive invasions and internal strife have brought about the destruction of most of their works. Most extant precolonial structures date from the mid-seventeenth century or later.

In the twentieth century Hanoi's principal importance has again been as an administrative and communications center. Most large-scale commercial and industrial activity within Vietnam has been based in other northern cities, such as Haiphong and Nam Dinh, or in the former southern capital of Saigon (Ho Chi Minh City).

[*See also* Dai La Thanh; Vietnam, Democratic Republic of; Indochinese Union; Tonkin; *and* Vietnam.]

Thomas Hodgkin, *Vietnam: The Revolutionary Path* (1981). "Hanoi: From the Origins to the 19th Century," *Vietnamese Studies* 48 (1977).    JAMES M. COYLE

## HAN SHANTONG. *See* Han Liner.

**HAN YU** (768–824), great literary figure and Confucian moralist of the mid- to late Tang dynasty of China and forerunner of the Neo-Confucian movement that began in the tenth century. Han Yu was from modern Henan Province, the youngest son of a county magistrate. Although his family was not wealthy, he was able to pass the *jinshi* examination in 792 at the relatively young age of twenty-five. Han's political career was a stormy one; he was twice exiled, in 804 and 819, to the region of Lingnan in southernmost China (modern Guangdong Province) for boldly criticizing the throne. His second exile was occasioned by his protest against emperor Xianzong's plan to parade into the palace a finger bone that was purported to be a relic of the Buddha. In his memorial, Han charged that Buddhism was a superstitious and un-Chinese faith, dangerous to public morals.

Han's attack on Buddhism was part of a wider contemporary movement of literary reform and ethical regeneration, known as *fugu,* or "restore antiquity," of which he was a leader. *Fugu* sought to defend China's cultural orthodoxy, especially Confucian morality, against the subversive influences of Buddhism and Daoism by affirming tradition and restoring the ideals of antiquity. Literature, too, was part of this reform. As opposed to the flowery and highly abstruse "parallel prose" style of the Southern Dynasties and the early Tang, Han advocated a more substantial and straightforward prose style on the model of the pre-Qin and Han periods, known as *guwen,* or "ancient prose." The *guwen* style, which Han created with the help of friends like Liu Zongyuan (733–819), served to revitalize Tang prose. Reaching the height of its popularity during the Song dynasty, it remained influential in Chinese literature down through late-Qing times. For his literary genius, Han is ranked as one of the "eight masters of the Tang and Song periods" *(Tang Song badajia).*

[*See also* Chinese Literature; Guwen; Neo-Confucianism; *and* Tang Dynasty.]

Stephen Owen, *The Poetry of Meng Chiao and Han Yü* (1975).    HOWARD J. WECHSLER

**HAOMA.** The Zoroastrian *haoma* was a plant, a drink made from the plant, and a divinity created by recurrent acts of worship using the drink. The identity of the plant is unknown. It may have been ephedra, which is used by Zoroastrians today, but recently it has been proposed that it was originally a mushroom, the *Amanita muscaria.* The core of the Zoroastrian liturgy consists of the preparation, consecration, and consumption of *haoma,* first by the priests, then by the congregation.

*Haoma* was an intoxicant that gave warriors courage and inspired priests and poets. It was also believed to be the elixir of immortality and was therefore regarded as a healer. *Haoma* is identical with the Vedic *soma* and was an important feature in the cult and mythology of the Indo-Iranians before the Iranians and Indians became two peoples.

[*See also* Zoroastrianism.]

Mary Boyce, *A History of Zoroastrianism* (1975), vol. 1. R. G. Wasson, *Soma: Divine Mushroom of Immortality* (1968).    LUCIANNE C. BULLIET

## HARAPPA. *See* Indus Valley Civilization.

**HARA TAKASHI** (1856–1921), Japanese politician; prime minister from 1918 to 1921. Hara was born into a very high-ranking samurai family of Nambu *han* (Iwate). The *han* opposed the new Meiji government's military forces in the final battles of the imperial restoration, and throughout his life Hara carried with him antipathetic feelings toward the Meiji government. Still, he owed much to the patronage of such prominent Meiji leaders as Inoue Kaoru and Itō Hirobumi.

Hara went to Tokyo (1871), entered a French Catholic seminary (1872), and was baptized David (1873). In 1876 he attended the Justice Ministry's law school but was expelled in 1879 for protesting school policies. He then worked for the *Yūbin hōchi shimbun*, an antigovernment paper in Tokyo, until 1882. These nonconformist acts that marked his early years did not prevent him from calculating the benefits accruable from government connections, for he soon became editor of the *Daitō nippō*, a progovernment newspaper in Osaka (1882). He then entered the Foreign Ministry (1882), came to Inoue Kaoru's attention (1884), and was posted to the Paris legation (1885–1889). Upon his return, he became by turns private secretary to Inoue (1889) and to Agriculture and Commerce Minister Mutsu Munemitsu (1890). The next few years saw him in the bureaucracy and the Foreign Ministry (1892); in the Foreign Ministry he rose to become vice-minister (1895) and minister to Korea (1896–1897).

Hara left government service to become president of the *Osaka mainichi shimbun* (1897–1900), a post he in turn left to help Itō Hirobumi form a new party, the Rikken Seiyūkai. In 1900 he became communications minister in Itō's fourth cabinet. He subsequently assumed the powerful home minister's position three times (1906–1908, 1911–1912, and 1913). He was elected to the House of Representatives from Iwate Prefecture in 1902 and was elected eight times in all until the fourteenth general election in 1920. He assumed the presidency of the Seiyūkai in 1914 and became prime minister on 29 September 1918. He was known as "the commoner prime minister" because he declined peer's rank.

Hara was a consummate politician who made full use of his journalistic experience, ties with Kansai financial circles, and Chōshū patronage. His overriding aim after the Seiyūkai's formation was to strengthen it. He did this by solidifying local support for the party through pork-barrel projects and by building power bases in the central bureaucracy and in the House of Peers. He also took pains to cultivate people as disparate as Itō Hirobumi, Katsura Tarō, Saionji Kimmochi, Yamamoto Gonnohyōe, and Yamagata Aritomo. His tenure as prime minister was cut short by an ultrarightist assassin's knife on 4 November 1921, but not before he had helped to establish the precedent that the head of the majority party in the House of Representatives could become prime minister.

[*See also* Seiyūkai.]

GEORGE K. AKITA

HARBIN, capital of Heilongjiang, the northernmost province of China. The city has become an important industrial and transportation center in northeast China with a 1982 population of 2,550,000. Located on the Sungari River (Chinese, Songhua) near the southern border of the province, Harbin was first developed in the 1890s when the Chinese Eastern Railway was built jointly by the Manchu Qing dynasty and the Russians to become a branch of the Trans-Siberian Railway system. The city also became a haven for large numbers of White Russians fleeing the 1917 Revolution.

In 1932, Harbin was captured by the Japanese forces invading Manchuria and remained in Japanese control until 1945. During this period, Harbin developed into an important food processing center of the northeast region. Since 1949 Harbin's industrial sector has expanded to include the production of heavy machinery, electrical equipment, precision tools, tractor bearings, cement, chemicals, paper manufacturing, and sugar refineries.

ANITA M. ANDREW

HARDWAR, one of the most sacred sites of Hindu pilgrimage in India, located 120 miles north of New Delhi on the Ganges River. Hardwar is thought to be the site of the ancient city Mayapuri, which the Chinese Buddhist pilgrim Xuanzang visited in the fifth century CE. Hardwar is a prominent venue in the mythic traditions of India but it has a particularly intimate association with the deity Vishnu (Hari), from whom the city derives its name, that is, "the gateway to Hari." Pilgrims believe that bathing in the Ganges at Hardwar on the first day of the Hindu solar year, especially once every twelve years on the occasion of the Khumba Mela, will absolve them of all their sins.

[*See also* Hinduism *and* Vaishnavism.]

S. M. Bhardwaj, *Hindu Places of Pilgrimage in India* (1973).          RICHARD ENGLISH

HARIHARALAYA, site of the capital of Angkor in the ninth century. It is a few miles southeast of Angkor proper, where later capitals clustered, and is marked by the Roluos group of monuments. *Hariharalaya* means "the abode of Harihara," the Hindu deity consisting of Vishnu and Shiva conjoined, whose cult was popular in the early Zhenla period of Cambodian history. There was probably a settlement at Roluos before Jayavarman II, founder of Angkor, made his capital there early in the century. His successors Jayavarman III and Indravarman I (who built the Bakong and Preak Koh monuments there) also ruled from Hariharalaya. Yasovarman I moved the capital during his reign to Angkor. Hariharalaya became the prototype of the Angkor style of monarchy, whereby kings sought to build a reservoir, an ancestor temple, and a temple mountain as signs of their authority.

[See also Angkor.]

Lawrence P. Briggs, *The Ancient Khmer Empire* (1951). G. Coedès, *The Indianized States of Southeast Asia*, translated by Susan B. Cowing (1968).    IAN W. MABBETT

**HARMAND, FRANÇOIS-JULES** (1845–1921), French explorer and diplomat in Indochina. After participating in Francis Garnier's 1873 Tonkin campaign, Harmand traveled extensively throughout Vietnam and Cambodia. In May 1883, while serving as consul to Siam, he was sent to Tonkin, where the French were vigorously fighting to expand their influence. Appointed general commissioner of Tonkin, he worked to establish a formal protectorate over the rest of Vietnam. Delivering an ultimatum to Hue, he was able to achieve this goal provisionally with the agreement of 25 August 1883, later superseded by the 1884 Patenotre Treaty. Because of continual conflict with French military commanders, he was replaced by Admiral Courbet.

[See also Garnier, Francis *and* Patenotre Treaty.]

BRUCE M. LOCKHART

**HARRIS, TOWNSEND** (1804–1878), first American consul in Japan. The Kanagawa Treaty (1854) made provision for an American consular representative in Japan, a post to which Townsend Harris, a merchant with experience in East Asia, was appointed in August 1855. He went to Japan via Siam, where in May 1856 he negotiated a commercial treaty similar to those concluded earlier with China. Arriving in Shimoda in August, he soon opened talks about practical questions concerning the American position in Japan, chiefly in regard to currency and rights of residence. A convention was signed on 17 June 1857 settling these points, opening Nagasaki to American ships, and making Americans in Japan subject to American law.

Harris also pressed the Japanese officials on larger issues: first, to grant him an audience with the shogun; second, to negotiate a commercial treaty, modeled on the one he had concluded with Siam. During the summer of 1857 Japanese official opinion slowly moved toward accepting the inevitability of relaxing trade restrictions. In October treaties were signed with the Netherlands and Russia. Against this background, Harris was at last given permission to go to Edo.

On 7 December he had an audience with the shogun, then began talks on trade, seeking to persuade the *bakufu* to permit freer trade than the Dutch and Russian treaties allowed. He was, he wrote in his journal, "engaged in teaching the elements of political economy to the Japanese." He was also threatening them, stating that it would be better to negotiate with an American envoy, acting alone, than to wait until Britain made demands at gunpoint. The argument proved effective. By the end of February 1858 a treaty had been drafted along the lines he wished, opening the following ports and cities to trade: Hakodate, Nagasaki, Kanagawa (Yokohama), Hyōgo (Kobe), Niigata, Edo, and Osaka.

Before this treaty could be signed, Japanese feudal opinion had to be brought to accept it. This proved difficult. Opposition came both from daimyo and from the imperial court. Failure to overcome it led to the resignation of Hotta Masayoshi, the senior official responsible for the negotiations. His successor, Ii Naosuke, faced crisis, partly owing to a Tokugawa succession dispute, partly to news that British warships were on their way to Japan. He acted firmly. First he settled the succession, putting his opponents under restraint. Then, on 29 July 1858, he signed the American treaty, ignoring the emperor's refusal to sanction it.

These events precipitated political turmoil, in which the treaty was a central issue. They therefore did not end Harris's diplomatic problems. Once the ports were opened in 1859 there began a series of attacks on foreigners, in one of which his own secretary, Henry Heusken, was killed (January 1861). Despite this, Harris worked to prevent a major clash. His influence on events was declining, however, as was his health. In April 1862, at his own request, he retired from his post and left Japan.

[See also Kanagawa Treaty *and* Shimoda.]

W. G. Beasley, ed., *Select Documents on Japanese Foreign Policy, 1853–1868* (1955). M. E. Cosenza, ed., *The Complete Journal of Townsend Harris, First American Consul General and Minister to Japan* (1930; rev. ed., 1959). Payson J. Treat, *Diplomatic Relations between the United States and Japan, 1853–1895* (1932; reprint, 1963).    W. G. BEASLEY

**HARRISON, FRANCIS BURTON** (1873–1957), American governor-general of the Philippines during the presidency of Woodrow Wilson

(1913–1921). As the first Democrat to become governor-general, Harrison faced the hostility of Republican appointees to the Philippine civil service when he asked senior American members to resign. The flight of Americans from the Manila government necessitated the appointment of underqualified Filipinos. This isolated Harrison from the American community and threw him upon Filipino politicians for support and counsel. On 29 August 1916, the Jones Bill, which granted Filipinos control of the upper branches of their government, was enacted into law. Harrison was instrumental in its passage, although the Wilson administration had reservations about the part of the bill that promised Filipinos independence if they proved their capacity for self-government.

For the next five years, Harrison interpreted the Jones Act liberally. By turning the government over to Filipino political leaders, he advanced Filipino desires for self-rule. Although his actions were not in keeping with the Jones Act, Harrison was not censured by President Wilson. By giving more than token power to the Filipinos, he won the gratitude of politically minded Filipinos but earned the enmity of most Americans in the islands and of high-placed Republicans in Washington. In 1919 Harrison returned home to plead for Philippine independence before a skeptical administration and Republican-dominated Congress. His tenure in office was marred in its last years by financial crises, cattle diseases, and wide-scale smallpox outbreaks. In mid-1921, Leonard Wood and former governor-general William Cameron Forbes conducted an investigation of the Philippines. Harrison left Manila on 5 March 1921.

[See also Philippines; Jones Act; Wood, Leonard; and Forbes, William Cameron.]

William Cameron Forbes, The Philippine Islands (1928). Francis Burton Harrison, The Corner-stone of Philippine Independence (1922) and Origins of the Philippine Republic, edited by Michael P. Onorato (1974). Peter W. Stanley, A Nation in the Making: The Philippines and the United States, 1899–1921 (1974).

MICHAEL PAUL ONORATO

HARSHA (r. 606–647), the last monarch of classical India to build an empire that extended from the Himalayas to the Vindhyas and from Bengal to Gujarat. Ascending the throne of the small kingdom of Sthanvishvara (modern Thaneswar in Haryana), Harsha rescued his sister, the queen of the slain Maukhari king of Kanyakubja, and campaigned for control of the Ganges Plain. He assumed Maukhari rule in 612 and shifted his capital to Kanyakubja (modern Kanauj). Harsha thereafter subjugated numerous rulers to the north but failed to overpower the southern overlord Chalukya Pulakeshin II, which would have created a pan-Indian empire.

Harsha is one of the few Indian kings to have a biography, written by his court poet Bana, and to have hosted a foreign visitor, the Chinese Buddhist pilgrim Xuanzang, who recorded his royal patron's achievements in a comprehensive account of India. Harsha is renowned for his just rule, for his authorship of Sanskrit plays, for his patronage of Buddhism and of Nalanda University, and for his liberality, distinguished by the quinquennial distribution of his entire treasury at the sacred confluence of the Ganges and Yamuna rivers.

[See also Maukhari Dynasty; Nalanda; and Kanyakubja.]

D. Devahuti, Harsha: A Political Study (1970).

SHIVA BAJPAI

HART, ROBERT (1835–1911), trusted adviser to the Qing government and a powerful Chinese employee who was a longtime inspector general of the Chinese Maritime Customs Service (1863–1908). Hart was a prime mover in China's modernization, symbolized the constructive side of the unequal treaty system, and represented Victorian Britain's informed empire in East Asia.

Born in Northern Ireland, Hart showed early promise of unusual ability. After graduating from Queen's College in Belfast at age eighteen, he joined the British consular service in China, arriving at Ningbo in 1854. He moved to the British consulate in Guangzhou (Canton) in 1858, joined the newly established customhouse there the following year, and replaced Horatio N. Lay as the inspector general of maritime customs in 1863. Hart thus modestly began a career that was to bring him great influence within China and worldwide recognition.

Working hard and supported by Chinese and foreign governments, Hart built up the Customs Service as a modern, administrative arm of the Qing central government that provided financial support to various reform efforts. His concern for the future of the Customs led to his refusal in 1885 to accept the prestigious post of British minister to China. Behind the scenes Hart also was a diplomat who settled the Sino-French War, changed Macao's status, got boundaries delimited with Burma and India, and mitigated the disasters of imperialism.

Hart's tact and capability, coupled with the fact that he was bilingual, endeared him to the court, which took him into confidence as a trusted adviser. In 1865 he submitted a memorandum to the Zongli Yamen (Foreign Office) entitled "Observations by an Outsider," in which he stressed the advantages of mining, railroads, steamships, the telegraph, and Western diplomatic practices. He became deeply involved in the creation of the Naval Yamen in 1885. He promoted the Society for the Diffusion of Christian and General Knowledge (SDK) among the Chinese, translated Western works on international law, started the publication of medical reports, and advocated the inclusion of science and mathematics in the traditional civil service examinations. He returned to England in 1908 and died on 20 September 1911. The Chinese government conferred on him its highest honors, his own country gave him the hereditary rank of baronet in 1893, and he was decorated by thirteen other countries as well.

[See also Maritime Customs Service and Qing Dynasty.]

John K. Fairbank, K. F. Bruner, and E. M. Matheson, eds., The I. G. in Peking: Letters of Robert Hart, Chinese Maritime Customs, 1868–1907, 2 vols. (1975). Robert Hart, These from the Land of Sinim (1901). Stanley F. Wright, Hart and the Chinese Customs (1950).

YEN-P'ING HAO

HARYANA, one of the states of India, with an area of approximately seventeen thousand square miles and a population of about fourteen million (in 1986). The popular explanation of the name is that it means "home of Hari," Hari being a name of the god Vishnu. Haryana came into existence as a separate political entity in 1966 when the former state of the Punjab was divided along linguistic grounds into the Hindi-speaking state of Haryana and the Punjabi-speaking state of the Punjab.

While a new political division, and with few important monuments, it has rich historical associations, since it is on the pathway of migrants and invaders moving from the northwest into the Indian heartland, as well as being contiguous with the Delhi area, which has been a central point for most rulers of northern India. The Aryan people settled in the region in the second millennium BCE, and the modern Kurukshetra is regarded as the site of the battle described in the Mahabharata, the great Sanskrit epic poem. Such identifications depend almost wholly upon literary allusions, but there is epigraphical evidence to suggest that Haryana was part of the Maurya empire in the third century BCE. It was successively part of the Kushan and Gupta empires, and then at the end of the sixth century CE it was controlled by Harsha, who began his career as ruler of Thaneswar. Later it came under under the rulers of Delhi, who were increasingly attacked by the Turco-Afghan rulers who had conquered the northern Punjab in the eleventh century. In 1192 Muhammad Ghuri defeated the Delhi rulers at Taraori in Haryana and the region became part of the Delhi sultanate. Another decisive battle took place in Haryana in 1526 when new invaders from the northwest, the Mughals, defeated the Delhi sultan and established their own great empire. After the decay of the Mughal empire the region was fought over by the Marathas and the Sikhs, but the eventual victors were the British, when the East India Company took over the area in 1803. In 1858, after the Mutiny of 1857, the region became part of the new province of the Punjab, and the region tended to be overshadowed by the shift of political and economic power to Lahore and the northern part of the state.

Even before independence, there was a strong demand that the region be formed into a separate state to recognize its cultural and linguistic differences from the Punjab, since the majority of the people were Hindus, in contrast to the Sikhs in the northern districts of the Punjab. With the very strong sentiment in the northern regions for a measure of autonomy for the Sikhs, the Haryanvis, as the people of the area are known, were anxious to have a state where they would be dominant. Thus the creation of the new state in 1966 was widely welcomed. Until 1986 the two states shared a common capital at Chandigarh, but in that year the central government awarded it to the Punjab, and Haryana had to create a new capital.

Haryana is one of the most productive agricultural regions in India, with most of its land being arable. Wheat is the principal crop, and its production doubled in the first ten years of statehood, owing to the government's encouragement of irrigation and the use of fertilizer. Sugarcane, cotton, and pulses are also important crops. Small-scale industries have grown rapidly, and Haryana has shared in the prosperity that characterizes the Punjab and the Delhi area.

[See also Chandigarh; Delhi; Delhi Sultanate; East India Company; Mughal Empire; and Kurukshetra.]

Government of Haryana, Statistical Abstract of Haryana (yearly). R. S. Sharma, Haryana Directory and Who's Who (1968).

AINSLIE T. EMBREE

FIGURE 1. *Jar and Stand.* Hasanlu, ninth century BCE. Unglazed earthenware. Height of jar 21.7 cm., height of stand 19.7 cm.

**HASANLU**, archaeological site near the southeast corner of Lake Urmia, regarded as the best example of an Iron Age settlement in Iran. Excavations by R. H. Dyson, Jr., in the 1960s revealed various occupational levels on the site's main mound, which dates from the early prehistoric period to the middle of the first millennium BCE. The most important phase of the Hasanlu settlement is indicated by a fort with defensive walls of mud brick, a columned hall, and storerooms dating from the ninth century BCE. Among the finds in the storerooms are weapons, ceramic utensils, and gold, silver, and bronze vessels that were ornamented with religious scenes depicting chariot-mounted deities and mortals. The site was an important cultural link between Mesopotamia and eastern Iran.

Sylvia A. Matheson, *Persia: An Archaeological Guide* (2d ed., 1976), pp. 91–95, 116–117, 291, with references. Edith Porada, *The Art of Ancient Iran* (1965), pp. 102–122.          A. SHAHPUR SHAHBAZI

**HASTINAPUR**, an ancient city in the Meerut district of Uttar Pradesh, India, was the capital of the Kaurava kings celebrated in the epic *Mahabharata.*

Archaeological excavations confirm its antiquity, dating it to the beginning of the first millennium BCE, and the tradition that it was finally swept away by a flood of the Ganges.

[*See also* Mahabharata.]

B. B. Lal, "Ancient India," *Bulletin of the Archaeological Survey of India* 10 (1954) and 11 (1955).

A. K. NARAIN

**HASTINGS, WARREN** (1732–1818), governor-general of India and governor of Bengal (1772–1785). Hastings was one of the most remarkable figures in India's history. A scholarly orphan, destined for Cambridge, he might have had a very different career. But on his uncle's death, his guardian arranged for him to be sent out to Calcutta. The youth thrived, making friends, learning languages (including Bengali and Persian), and faithfully serving his masters, insomuch that he "arose to become a ruler in Pharaoh's household." As such, he established peace and order, ending much oppression and corruption within higher levels of government. With patience and skill he made "friends" for the East India Company among both peoples and princes of India. Not wishing to expand directly company dominions but hoping to safeguard them by an adroit balancing of powers, he "persuaded" many princes to join a system of subsidiary alliance. By such means he gained recognition for the company as the leading power in India. In all these doings, even to the gold-decorated parchment Persian documents that he signed, his style was that of the Mughals.

Indeed, Hastings's Mughal titles—*jaladat jang* ("daring in war") and *umdat-ul-mulk* ("the support of the realm")—made Hastings seem all too Indian to many in London. He represented the taint of oriental despotism and all things corrupt. His conspicuous consumption, his Arabian horses and lavish palaces—even the gold-crusted uniform of his doorkeeper, which some said cost more than the coronation robes of George III—aroused envy. Indeed, the fact that he actually commanded more troops (90,000) than any other English commander made him seem even dangerous. Allegations of dark deeds served to make him to look like a sinister Machiavellian, a menace to his own country. His harsh treatment of Muhammad Reza Khan, Raja Chait Singh, Raja Nanda Kumar, the *begums* of Awadh, and others, while hardly strange in a Mughal emperor, shocked the public in Britain.

In 1786 twenty-two "articles of charge of high

crimes and misdemeanors" were brought against him by Edmund Burke and others. Hastings's impeachment trial before the House of Lords lasted until 1795. Acquitted, in the end he survived all his enemies. But controversy lingers. About no other British ruler of India has so much been written, embellished with so many colorful sidelights. His sponsorship of scholarship, of William Jones, of the Calcutta Madrasa, of the Asiatic Society of Bengal, and of similar cultural pursuits put him among the first "orientalists." His marriage to Baroness von Imhoff—his "Beloved Marion"—is a saga of romantic love. His duel with Philip Francis, his quarrels with councillors, and many other vivid tales are woven around this seemingly quiet and outwardly unassuming personality.

[See also East India Company and Governor-General of India.]

Keith Feiling, *Warren Hastings* (1954). T. B. Macaulay, "Warren Hastings," *Edinburgh Review* (1841). P. J. Marshall, *The Impeachment of Warren Hastings* (1965).

ROBERT E. FRYKENBERG

HATAMOTO ("liege vassal" or "bannerman"), direct retainers of Japan's Tokugawa shogunate (1600–1868), with incomes of at least 100 *koku* (a measure of value in terms of rice equivalance); *hatamoto* largely staffed the shogunate's civilian bureaucracy and military establishment.

The *hatamoto* were the descendents of warriors who supported Tokugawa Ieyasu's successful rise to national hegemony in the late sixteenth century. *Hatamoto* status was hereditary but could be revoked for criminal or immoral behavior. Theoretically, *hatamoto* status bestowed on its holder the privilege of direct shogunal audience. Five thousand in number at the beginning of the eighteenth century, their number had increased by an additional thousand by the end of that century.

*Hatamoto* income usually ranged from 100 *koku* to 10,000 *koku* (those with income in excess of 10,000 *koku* achieved daimyo status) and consisted of the family's stipend (*hondaka*) plus an office salary (*yakudaka*) attached to the bureaucratic position, if any, held by the *hatamoto* family. The income came through fief (*chigyō*), rice stipend (*kirimai*), "support rice" (*fuchi*), or some combination of these. Statistics of the Kansei period (1789–1800) reveal that approximately 2,260 *hatamoto* received their incomes mostly in the form of *chigyō*, while an additional 2,500 received their income in the form of *kirimai*. The former category obviously constituted the elite stratum of the Tokugawa *hatamoto*.

From their incomes the *hatamoto*, as members of the shogunate's standing army, were expected to support not only themselves and their families, but also a certain number of fighting men and their equipment. Regulations for 1649 (which remained in effect for the duration of the Tokugawa period) stipulated that a *hatamoto* with a 200-*koku* income support a total of 5 persons (1 lancer, 1 swordsman, and 3 servants), while a 10,000-*koku* bannerman was required to maintain a total of 238 fighting men (20 riflemen, 10 archers, 30 lancers, 16 swordsmen, and 10 cavalry), flag bearers (3), and servants (149).

Most *hatamoto* lived in Edo (modern Tokyo) on land provided by the shogunate, on which they built their residences as well as quarters for their stipendiaries; consequently, the fief-holding *hatamoto* seldom saw their fiefs, which they came to view as distant sources of income. Education consisted of attendance at schools designed to provide expertise in the martial arts, calligraphy, and the fine arts, such as the tea ceremony. Research has revealed that the *hatamoto* came to resemble urbanized, stipended bureaucrats more than the crude, rural samurai of Ieyasu's time.

As shogunal officials, the bannermen filled all but the top sixty offices (which were reserved for daimyo) of the shogunate's national and regional bureaucracies. High status accompanied those offices whose incumbents' names were officially recorded for posterity; included in this category were such important posts as chamberlain (*sobashū*), masters of court ceremony (*kōke*), inspectors-general (*ōmetsuke*), and finance commissioners (*kanjō bugyō*), as well as administrative positions at Nagasaki, Osaka, Kyoto, Hakodate, Nikko, Sado, and Sunpu.

Militarily, the *hatamoto* constituted the officer corps of the four principal units of the shogun's standing army: Great Guard (*ōban*), Bodyguard (*shoinban*), Inner Guard (*koshōban*), and New Guard (*shinban*), as well as several specialized units (such as Color Guard, Escort Guard, Coast Guard, etc.). Although the history of the *hatamoto* during the Tokugawa period was replete with such problems as increasing impoverishment, chronic unemployment among the lower echelons of society (which Edo tried to solve by creating "make-work" positions), boredom, and declining morale, the scholarly consensus is that they served the Tokugawa rulers competently and well.

[See also Tokugawa Period.]

Conrad Totman, *Politics in the Tokugawa Bakufu, 1600–1843* (1967). Kozo Yamamura, *A Study of Samurai Income and Entrepreneurship* (1974).

RONALD J. DiCENZO

**HATEM, GEORGE** (Ma Haide; b. 1910), medical adviser in modern China. A Lebanese-American born in North Carolina, Hatem went to Shanghai in 1934 after completing medical studies in Switzerland. Shaken by the turmoil and health conditions around him, he was persuaded by Agnes Smedley to visit Communist-led guerrilla units in northwest China. Hatem made the trip with Edgar Snow in 1936 and never returned. In Yan'an he married a Chinese actress, joined the Chinese Communist Party, and became the backbone of a new health care system in guerrilla-held areas during World War II. After the Communists came to power in 1949, Hatem helped to design health policies for the entire nation. He is noted in particular for leading a successful campaign to wipe out venereal disease in the 1950s. In recent years his chief focus has been on the eradication of leprosy. In 1986 he received the Lasker Award in recognition of his efforts to conquer these diseases in China.

STEPHEN R. MACKINNON

**HATOYAMA ICHIRŌ** (1883–1959), Japanese politician; prime minister from 1954 to 1956. Hatoyama was one of the more popular Liberal-Democratic (Conservative) Party politicians. His popularity stemmed not so much from his policies as from his challenge to his predecessor, Yoshida Shigeru, who had engineered Japan's survival during the Occupation period (1945–1952) and Japan's recovery of independence. For the majority of the Japanese who had grown weary of Yoshida's often arrogant political style, Hatoyama appeared especially appealing for his ability to survive two debilitating setbacks in his political career. The first setback came when the Hatoyama-led Japan Liberal Party won the election of 1946. Instead of allowing Hatoyama to form his government, the Occupation authorities issued an order purging him from public office for his alleged antiliberal measures as minister of education before the war. Then, in 1951, still waiting for an order lifting the purge, he suffered a stroke, temporarily ending his opportunity to lead the government.

Hatoyama Ichirō was born in Tokyo, the eldest son of Hatoyama Kazuo, himself an established party politician. After graduating from Tokyo Imperial University in 1907 and beginning a legal practice, Hatoyama launched his parliamentary career as a city assembly member for Tokyo City. First elected to the Diet in 1915, Hatoyama quickly established his reputation as a shrewd politician. His prewar career was full of major appointments both in the government and in his party, the Seiyūkai, the predecessor of the postwar Japan Liberal Party.

As premier, Hatoyama was strongly committed to lessening Japan's one-sided reliance on the United States. He hoped to revise the 1947 constitution, written under the pressure of the Occupation authorities; he intended to strengthen Japan's self-defense capability; and he also wished to broaden Japan's diplomatic contacts with East Asian neighbors. Hatoyama could achieve only one of his many goals, the reestablishment of diplomatic relations with the Soviet Union in 1956. His unprecedented popularity notwithstanding, Hatoyama's ability to realize policy goals was severely limited by instability within the Liberal-Democratic Party, which had come into existence by way of a merger only in 1955.

MICHIO UMEGAKI

**HATTA, MOHAMMAD** (1902–1980), vice-president of Indonesia (1945–1956).

A Minangkabau born in Bukittinggi and educated in Dutch primary and secondary schools in Padang and Batavia, Hatta gained his early political experience as treasurer of the Jong Sumatranen Bond in Padang and Batavia. In 1922 he proceeded to tertiary studies in Rotterdam, where he remained for ten years. He was involved in converting the Indische Vereeniging, the Indies students' society in the Netherlands, from a social club into the politically active Perhimpunan Indonesia (Indonesian Union). He became chairman in 1926 and contributed to the planning of a new nationalist party in the Indies, became involved with the League against Imperialism, was arrested in 1927, tried for subversive activities, and acquitted. He returned to Batavia in 1932.

In 1931 Hatta was instrumental in founding the Club Pendidikan Nasional Indonesia (National Education Club), arguing that educating nationalist cadres was more important than forming mass parties, such as the Indonesian Nationalist Party (PNI), that could be easily suppressed by the authorities. Arrested in 1935, Hatta was exiled first to Boven Digul and then to Banda Naira. He was brought back to Java just before the Japanese invasion and served during the occupation regime as vice-chairman of its mass organizations. In August 1945 he, together with Sukarno, signed Indonesia's Proclamation of Independence, and he became vice-president. In 1948, during a period of acute factional rivalry, Sukarno commissioned him to form a government, and as prime minister Hatta presided over negotiations with the Dutch and the transfer of sovereignty to the republic. Increasingly disturbed by political trends in the early fifties, he resigned as vice-president in December 1956.

A social democrat in political outlook, Hatta was a devout Muslim who believed in the possibility of a synthesis of Islam and socialism. He advocated the development of cooperatives as a solution to Indonesia's economic problems. As vice-president, Hatta was seen as balancing Sukarno in a two-in-one unity *(dwi-tunngal)*: Java-Sumatra, Javanism-Islam, passion-intellect, nation builder-administrator. After his resignation, Hatta remained a respected elder statesman until his death.

[*See also* Indonesia, Republic of; Sukarno; *and* Indonesian Revolution.]

Mohammad Hatta, *Portrait of a Patriot* (1972) and *Memoir* (1979). J. E. Ingleson, *The Road to Exile: The Indonesian Nationalist Movement 1927–1934* (1979). George McT. Kahin, *Nationalism and Revolution in Indonesia* (1952).     JOHN D. LEGGE

**HAWKINS, WILLIAM** (fl. 1595), English seaman, captain of the *Hector,* which sailed to Surat, India, in 1607. Hawkins is credited with having obtained permission from the Mughal emperor Jahangir (in 1609–1611) for the establishment of an English factory at Surat. [*See also* East India Company *and* Jahangir.]     USHA SANYAL

**HAW PEOPLE.** *See* Ho.

**HAYAM WURUK** (1334–1389), king of the Javanese kingdom of Majapahit (r. 1350–1389). His reign represents the apogee of Java's Singosari-Majapahit era. By virtue of the composition of the poem "Nagarakertagama" at his court in 1365, a great deal is known of fourteenth-century Javanese government, religion, and cultural life. Despite the dramatic events at its beginnings—for example, the Bubat bloodbath of 1351, in which the Sundanese king and his retinue perished—the reign was noted for a stability unusual in Javanese history. Some of it is attributable to the Majapahit chief minister Ga-

jah Mada (d. 1364). Yet in the final analysis Hayam Wuruk's own governmental talents must have come to the fore; his reign, apparently peaceful, outlived his chief minister by nearly a quarter of a century and contrasts with the troubles of his successors.

[*See also* Majapahit; Singosari; Nagarakertagama; *and* Gajah Mada.]

M. C. HOADLEY

**HAYASHI SHIHEI** (1738–1792), Japanese political and economic thinker of the mid-Edo (Tokugawa) period. Hayashi Shihei's father was a *bakufu* retainer who lost warrior status for some wrongdoing, and as a result Shihei and his siblings were adopted by an uncle. Through marital connections an older brother obtained a samurai post with a stipend of 150 *koku* (measures of rice) in Sendai domain in 1756. The next year Shihei went to live with this brother. He was a hanger-on his whole life: much of his scholarly activity was motivated by the ambition to win fame and employment. He traveled to Nagasaki three times and associated with scholars of Dutch learning *(rangaku)* in Edo from 1783 to 1791. His two major works, *Illustrated Accounts of Three Lands* (1786) and *Military Talks for a Maritime Nation* (1787–1791), were based for the most part on information obtained verbally from *bakufu* interpreters at Nagasaki.

His *Illustrated Accounts* introduced conditions in Korea, the Ryukyu Islands, and Ezo (Hokkaido) from a strategic standpoint. He warned against Russian encroachments on Japan's northern frontier and advocated Japanese colonization of Hokkaido. In *Military Talks*, he criticized Japanese works on strategy and tactics, which until then had heavily relied on Chinese military classics and had dealt only with domestic warfare between feudal lords. He argued that Japan, unlike landlocked China, was an island nation that should direct attention to maritime defense against foreign enemies. In 1791, the *bakufu* banned his works and sentenced him to house arrest for publicly airing views on national defense. His ambitions frustrated, he died the next year.

[*See also* Rangaku *and* Tokugawa Period.]

Donald Keene, *The Japanese Discovery of Europe* (1969).     BOB TADASHI WAKABAYASHI

**HAZARAJAT,** the central, mountainous geographic zone of Afghanistan, is the source of several river systems. The Hazaras generally have been the chief inhabitants of its wider valleys. The high-altitude summer pastures of Hazarajat have been the grazing lands of Pakhtun nomads since the 1880s. Hazarajat has never constituted one administrative unit; it is currently a part of four provinces.

[*See also* Hazaras.]

*Imperial Gazetteer of Afghanistan, Kabul Province,* 2 vols. (1910).                    ASHRAF GHANI

**HAZARAS** have inhabited the mountainous zone of Hazarajat in central Afghanistan for at least four hundred years. Their origin is uncertain, and although their name may refer to a division in the Mongol army, the Persian dialect they speak contains larger numbers of Turkish than of Mongolian words.

Between 1747 and 1919, Hazaras were subjected to continual Pakhtun expansion. The trend began in the 1750s with the loss of their lands in the Kandahar region to the Durranis and culminated in the full conquest of Hazarajat by Abd al-Rahman, who declared the Shi'ite Hazaras infidels fit for slavery. In 1919 Amanullah abolished slavery, and many Hazaras migrated to Kabul, the capital, during his reign. By 1978 Hazara merchants had emerged as a significant economic power in Kabul. Although presently Keshtmand, a Hazara, is prime minister, the Hazaras have not rallied to the Soviet-backed regime.

[*See also* Durranis; Hazarajat; *and* Pakhtun.]

H. Schurmann, *The Mongols of Afghanistan* (1961).

ASHRAF GHANI

**HEARN, LAFCADIO** (known to the Japanese as Koizumi Yakumo; 1850–1904), American journalist and writer. The son of an Anglo-Irish father and a Greek mother, Hearn was born in Greece and spent his youth in Ireland and England. In 1869 he was sent to Cincinnati, Ohio, where he worked as a newspaper reporter. After further jobs in New Orleans, New York, and the West Indies, he traveled to Japan in 1889. Hearn taught English at a school in Matsue, Shimane Prefecture, married the daughter of an old samurai family in 1891 and moved to Kumamoto, and was naturalized as a Japanese citizen in 1895. He taught English literature at the University of Tokyo from 1896 to 1903, when he was replaced by Natsume Sōseki. [*See* Natsume Sōseki.]

Although a minor author in his own right, Hearn is best known for his vignettes and sketches of life in Meiji Japan and his renditions of traditional Japanese stories: *Glimpses of Unfamiliar Japan* (1894), *Kokoro* (1896), *In Ghostly Japan* (1899), *Shadowings* (1900), *A Japanese Miscellany* (1901), *Kottō* (1902), and *Kwaidan* (1904). In retrospect he has been blamed for much of the exoticism in early Western attitudes toward Japan. His reputation in Japan is far higher, perhaps because he was one of the first Westerners to become naturalized. His criticism of brash Meiji modernism also finds a responsive chord. Much admired as a teacher of English literature, he is reputed to have instilled great loyalty in his students. His essays on Japanese life are primarily of interest for what they show of Western attitudes at the time and make an interesting comparison with the acerbic essays of B. H. Chamberlain, with whom Hearn carried on a long correspondence. Hearn's renditions of Japanese tales have been translated back into Japanese and are read as stories on their own merit, containing as they do an exoticism that comes from his own somewhat Western interpretations.

A. E. Kunst, *Lafcadio Hearn* (1969). Elizabeth Stevenson, *Lafcadio Hearn: A Biography* (1961; reprint, 1979). Beongcheon Yu, *An Ape of Gods* (1964).

RICHARD BOWRING

**HEBEI**, Chinese province, includes the northern plateau and uplands stretching to the north and west toward Inner Mongolia and a broad alluvial plain in the south known during the Qing dynasty (1644–1911) as Zhili. Hebei's population is reported as 53,560,000 (1982). Shijiazhuang, an important textile center and railway junction, became the provincial capital in 1958. Hebei is also the home of two provincial-level independent municipalities, Tianjin and Beijing.

The southern Hebei plain was brought under cultivation some two thousand years ago and became established as the center of Chinese agriculture and population until it was surpassed in the eighth century by the economic development of the Yangtze River valley. Agriculture is still a primary concern of this region. Wheat, cotton, oilseed, and fruit are among the most important crops. The exploitation of coal has been a key to Hebei's industrial development since 1949. Tangshan, in eastern Hebei, has become the center of the province's coal mining industry. Hebei is also important for its fishing, iron and steel, and textile industries. ANITA M. ANDREW

HEBER, REGINALD (1783–1826), bishop of Calcutta from 1822 to 1829. He traveled widely throughout his vast diocese, which included all the three provinces (Bengal, Madras, and Bombay) of British India, and his account of his travels, *Journey through India*, published in 1828, is one of the best early accounts of Indian life. One of the founders of Bishop's College, Calcutta, he helped to lay the foundation for the work of the Anglican Church in India. He was the author of many well-known hymns.                                    AINSLIE T. EMBREE

HEFEI, formerly Luzhou, capital and largest city of Anhui Province, China. Located in the center of Anhui north of Lake Chao, Hefei is linked by rail to the city of Huainan and by water to the Yangtze River. Until the founding of the People's Republic, Hefei was a small administrative center with a population of less than 40,000. Since the late 1950s, following the relocation of many light industries from Shanghai, the establishment of a small steel plant, and the development of engineering and aluminum industries, Hefei has grown to an estimated population of 810,000 (1982).          JOHN A. RAPP

HEIAN PERIOD. The Heian period of Japanese history, covering the four centuries from 794 to 1185 CE, from the move of the capital to Heian (Kyoto) to the establishment of warrior power in Kamakura, is named for the city that became during this time the political and cultural center of Japan. Historiographically, it may be meaningful to divide the period at the tenth century, when changes in economic organization and local government made for a state quite different from the previous one. Traditionally, however, the Heian period, taken as a whole, is viewed as an important epoch of Japanese history, the height of the nation's aristocratic era, when some of its finest literary works were produced and when one of the world's most exquisitely aesthetic cultures flourished. Japan came of age in the Heian period, assimilating the elements of Chinese society that the Japanese had been importing for several centuries. Chinese material culture remained fashionable during the Heian period, and the basic Chinese political ideals remained philosophically important, but in economics and politics, literature and art the Japanese created institutions and genres that bore little resemblance to Chinese prototypes.

*Moving the Capital.* In 784 Emperor Kammu (Kanmu) ordered the capital moved from Heijō (Nara) northwest to Nagaoka in Yamashiro Province, but this city was abandoned within a decade for the final move to Heian. The two moves of the capital were related to tense political rivalries at the imperial court. One imperial desire was to escape the baneful influence of the Buddhist clergy on the civil government. The dominance of the priest Dōkyō during the reign of Empress Shōtoku (764–770) was the most blatant example of priestly intrusion into secular matters.

There were other political problems at Nara. After Empress Shōtoku's death, Fujiwara Momokawa enthroned the aging Emperor Kōnin and paved the way for Emperor Kammu by removing Crown Prince Osabe, who died later in prison with his mother, Empress Inoue. Much of the nobility opposed the succession of Kammu, whose own mother was of low rank. Thus Shōtoku was succeeded by a descendant of Emperor Tenji (Kōnin), marking a shift away from Temmu's line. Temmu had seized the throne after the death of his elder brother Tenji in 672. The Temmu line remained powerful in the Yamato area around Nara, while the Tenji line was dominant in Yamashiro. Thus, several factors—a desire to escape Buddhist influence, fear of vengeful spirits, and the advantages of moving to an area of Tenji power—lay behind the move from Nara. Emperor Kammu may have also wished to impress the local population with the power of the throne.

Fujiwara Tanetsugu was in charge of construction of Nagaoka, and the project commenced in 784 with a huge complement of conscripted labor working night and day. When the palace was finished, Kammu moved to Nagaoka, though the city was far from completed. Although Tanetsugu enjoyed Kammu's favor, he had an enemy in Kammu's younger brother, Crown Prince Sawara, who hoped to become emperor. Tanetsugu favored Kammu's eldest son, Prince Ate. One evening while Tanetsugu was inspecting the construction of Nagaoka, he was attacked and killed. The investigation implicated Prince Sawara and members of the Ōtomo clan.

Sawara was exiled to Awaji, where he soon died. Prince Ate (Emperor Heizei) became crown prince. Besides removing Sawara, the courtiers close to Kammu also curtailed the power of the Ōtomo clan. Historians regard this incident as simply a plot to remove Prince Sawara from the line of succession.

The court rushed to complete the capital. But as the project neared completion, Kammu decided to move again, to Heian, further north in Yamashiro

Province. The motive was apparently fear of the vengeful spirit of Prince Sawara. Deaths of people close to Kammu, epidemics, and other untoward events were attributed to this spirit. Despite the financial sacrifice, the courtiers abandoned the cursed capital at Nagaoka.

*Heian Institutions.* Heian political and economic institutions were based upon the *ritsuryō* system, the penal *(ritsu)* and administrative *(ryō)* codes of the Tang dynasty of China. Japan had been in the process of adopting the Chinese institutional superstructure since the time of Prince Shōtoku in the seventh century, and by early in the Nara period the experiment was largely complete. The impressive imperial city of Nara represented the transcendent magnificence of the emperor, and a detailed administrative and penal code—the *ritsuryō* of the Taihō and Yōrō eras—described the political and economic workings of the state.

The *ritsuryō* system never functioned in Japan as envisioned, and in the Heian period many of its provisions were adapted or abandoned. But the nobility remained faithful to the *ritsuryō* ideals. In particular, the basic concept of a "public" peasantry and land system, that is, a system in which peasantry and land belong to the emperor, as opposed to a system in which they are controlled by "private" interests, never died, despite the extensive development of private estates *(shōen)* in Heian times. Even a courtier owning numerous *shōen* himself could lament this development as contrary to the spirit of the *ritsuryō* system. [*See also* Ritsuryō State.]

*Politics and Government.* There are several ways to divide the political history of the Heian period, but perhaps the most useful is a four-period scheme. The first period, roughly the century from 794 to the end of the ninth century, was characterized first by Emperor Kammu's efforts to reinvigorate the *ritsuryō* system through a change in the military system, the subjugation of the Ezo peoples, and reform of provincial governance. This attempt to revive the *ritsuryō* system, still focusing on the Chinese pattern, was furthered by measures instituted by other early Heian emperors: legal codifications; establishment of new, non-*ritsuryō* offices to improve governmental efficiency, such as the *kebiishi* (imperial militia) and the *kurōdo-dokoro* (secretariat); and so forth. These initiatives helped restore a degree of political stability.

But the creation of extracodal offices provided new avenues to power for nonimperial families among the nobility. Partially through control of such offices, the Fujiwara clan, already a leading courtier family at Nara, reached a position of competition with the royal house itself. Through a series of incidents planned or exploited by Fujiwara clansmen (the Jōwa Incident of 842, the Ōtemmon Incident of 866, and the Ako Incident of 866) the Fujiwara eliminated many rival families and drew close to the imperial family, serving as regent *(sesshō* or *kampaku).* From this base the Fujiwara later established a permanent regency acting in the name of the monarchy. [*See also* Fujiwara Lineage.]

In the second period, late ninth century to 967, the imperial house preserved both power and authority despite the rise of the Fujiwara. Emperors Uda and Daigo reigned without the "assistance" of a Fujiwara regent during the Engi and Tenryaku eras. For this reason, scholars have idealized the period as a high point of imperial rule. But the court faced a serious decline in revenue because of the breakdown of the complex land allotment system. To meet the crisis, the government abandoned certain *ritsuryō* principles. Henceforth, control of the provinces was entrusted to the local governors, requiring only that they meet the tax quota set for their province. Further, the central government abandoned the tax based upon persons, switching to a tax on the land itself.

Despite the promulgation of the *Engishiki,* the governmental regulations of the Engi era (901–923), as well as extensive compilation of court histories and a splendid cultural environment among the aristocracy during the period, *ritsuryō* institutions continued to break down as local landholders, frustrated by the land allotment system, sought more secure tenure over lands by establishing *shōen.* Court control of land and people continued to weaken.

In 967 Fujiwara no Saneyori reestablished the Fujiwara regency after a hiatus of almost twenty years. (Under Uda and Daigo, there had been no regent from 890 to 930; Tokiyori had held the post from 931 until his death in 949.) Once Saneyori succeeded as regent, the Fujiwara held the post for the rest of premodern Japanese history. After the leading non-Fujiwara courtier, Minamoto Takaaki, was exiled in 969, the Fujiwara dominated the Heian polity.

This initiated a third period, from 967 to 1068, the period of Fujiwara regency rule *(sekkan seiji),* when the northern branch of the Fujiwara clan established a permanent regency through which it ruled in the emperor's name. The basis of the regency lay in marriage politics: the Northern Fujiwara controlled the position of empress. Consequently, emperors were sons of Fujiwara mothers dominated by their maternal relatives, in whose households they normally lived, since uxorilocal marriage was the common practice. Fujiwara Michinaga (966–1027), for example, was father of four women who married emperors and grandfather of three emperors. This helped his son Yorimichi, a high-ranking courtier for three-quarters of a century, maintain Fujiwara supremacy until 1068, when the clan's marital ties to the imperial house were broken.

This third period is so celebrated in Japan that its highly refined aristocratic life is often considered representative of the entire Heian epoch. Lady Murasaki's *Tale of Genji,* perhaps the world's first novel, brilliantly depicts the aura of mid-Heian court life. Fujiwara dominance was so extensive that many consider "Heian" synonymous with "Fujiwara"; in art history, the Fujiwara epoch covers the last three centuries of Heian Japan. [*See also* Fujiwara Period.]

Emperor Go-Sanjō, the first sovereign in one hundred years not related to the Fujiwara regent's line, succeeded in 1068, initiating the fourth and final Heian period, one of rule by "cloistered emperors" *(insei),* when three powerful ex-emperors, Shirakawa, Toba, and Go-Toba, emerged as supreme political figures, filling the roles played by the emperors during the early Heian and the regents during the mid-Heian.

Lasting until the ultimate political ascendancy of the warrior class (the shoguns) in 1185, the *insei* period was an era of imperial revival, when the royal house organized itself like other noble houses in order to compete more effectively for power. Under the headship of ex-emperors, the imperial family developed a strong household system with a large number of clients and the largest block of *shōen* in the country.

In this period, however, the *ritsuryō* system all but disappeared, as powerful military cliques continued onslaughts on public land and the major Buddhist institutions fought among themselves for both economic and ecclesiastical rewards, terrorizing the court when their demands were not met. According to a popular Buddhist doctrine, in 1052 Japan had entered the dreaded "Latter Day of the Law" *(mappō),* that final phase of human decline, and the courtiers felt powerless to combat the disasters foretold for this era.

Thus, reliance upon the warrior class to maintain civil government became necessary even in the Heian period, as clearly demonstrated in the Hōgen (1155) and Heiji (1159) incidents. The subsequent rise of the warrior Taira family has led some scholars to argue for a final epoch of Heian times, the period of Taira rule, from 1160 to 1185. [*See also* Hōgen and Heiji Wars.]

*The Landholding System.* The Taika Reforms of 645 initiated a process of centralization culminating in the *ritsuryō* system, modeled on Chinese practices. The *ritsuryō* system provided for government (royal) control of all rice-paddy land and productive human labor, in contrast to the pre-Taika era, when individual *uji* (clans) controlled private lands *(tadokoro)* and the labor *(be)* on those lands. However, while adopted in principle, the *ritsuryō* system never functioned as envisioned. Primarily, this was because the Yamato *uji,* the imperial house, was too weak to force other *uji* to surrender control of their extensive resources. To secure cooperation, the Yamato *uji* appointed members of large *uji* to bureaucratic positions carrying stipends in land and labor. Thus, these new bureaucrats maintained much of their resources when they became nobles in the new imperial system. *Uji* leaders acquiesced because the system appeared to provide for at least the maintenance, if not the possibility for expansion, of their economic interests. [*See also* Taika Reforms.]

Under the *ritsuryō* system, all land belonged to the government. The government did not "own" it, but exercised administrative control over and taxation rights to the land. The Land Allotment Law *(handen shūjuhō)* allocated rice land on a fixed basis to males, females, and slaves. Households pooled their allotted lands, called *kubunden,* for the purpose of cultivation.

A census recording recipients of land allotments was compiled every six years. Land was redistributed in accordance with demographic changes—new household members received land, and land held by deceased members reverted to the state. Cultivators could work their lands for life, provided they paid the taxes the state levied upon them: a rice tax, probably 3 to 5 percent; a tax in kind (paid mostly in cloth); and corvée, amounting to as much as a hundred days for males aged twenty to fifty-nine. Military corvée was levied on the general population as well. It was necessary to accommodate the interests of powerful *uji* to ensure cooperation. Consequently, the *uji* nobility came to control large tracts of land and numerous cultivators. Independent cultivators were often reduced to marginal circumstances; they thus sought alternate solutions when available.

Land-hungry nobles and religious institutions had the capital to open new lands and the political power to guarantee their security, but they needed labor. A natural economic alliance between poor cultivators and nobles and religious institutions allowed for the development of *shōen* (private estates). Ironically, the government was unable to check this development because it faced a population increase without a concomitant rise in taxable paddy fields. Several measures were adopted in the early Nara period to entice cultivators to open new lands that the government would still control, but all failed. Finally, in 743, the government decided to allow permanent ownership to anyone who cultivated new rice lands.

This incentive proved successful, and nobles and institutions with capital lured cultivators away from their fields—either on a part-time basis or by providing the impetus for the peasant to abscond—and opened new lands on which the incentives for the cultivator were greater than on allotment lands. Thus began the acquisition of *shōen,* a trend counter to the *ritsuryō* system, but one supported by government officials, for whom it was profitable.

The decline of the *kubunden* system continued in the Heian period as it became even more difficult to administer; land was redistributed only twice in the ninth century. The system had become all but a dead letter, and both nobles' and cultivators' desire for lands to own or cultivate were accommodated by private means, leading to a further increase in the growth of *shōen.* Private lands expanded in the ninth century by reclamation, by purchase, by occupation of lands abandoned by its cultivators, and by commendation from cultivators. At the turn of the century, *shōen* regulation was attempted, but it succeeded mainly in checking private holdings only of the imperial family. Land acquisition by other noble families continued unabated.

By the end of the ninth century the problems of provincial government resulting from the unworkability of the *ritsuryō* provisions were of major concern to conscientious ministers and governors. Cultivators resisted *ritsuryō* levies by absconding, by falsifying census registers both to avoid losing lands and to escape corvée, and by colluding with powerful persons to privatize holdings and escape taxes. Such acts seriously reduced the resources of the central government, thereby exacerbating the worsening relationship between it and local authorities.

To combat the situation, the court adopted two major changes in provincial governance and taxation during the early tenth century. The *ritsuryō* system of taxing individuals was complex, and registers were easily falsified. People were difficult to count, but land under cultivation was easier to measure. As an aid to administration, the government created *myō,* taxation units based on paddy fields, upon which both rent and corvée could easily be levied. Next, the central government entrusted local administration entirely to governors, in return for payment of stipulated revenues calculated for each province.

Government fields were now generally referred to by the term "public lands" *(kōden).* Although allotment was no longer carried out, the registers of provincial land *(kokuzu)* were used as a record of the amount of *kōden,* that is, taxable land, in each province. These *kōden* had "owners," cultivators whose families had worked the land perhaps for many generations, but the government claimed ultimate administrative control and tax rights. Thus from the tenth century the amount of public taxable land in each province was set, and it was divided for exploitative purposes into units called *myō.*

Non-*kōden* lands, mostly *shōen,* increased tremendously during the eleventh and twelfth centuries, constituting more than half Japan's paddy fields by the end of the period. The growth of *shōen* reduced the amount of taxable *kōden,* thus forcing the nobility to seek further *shōen* revenues to replace lost public income.

There were several types of *shōen,* but in late Heian most were those commended by local owners to central nobles or temples. This commendation produced the typical *shōen,* with several levels of administrative and fiscal control, each characterized by rights, called *shiki,* to a share of the estate's income.

A *shōen* resembled a stockholding company: the lowest level cultivator and the highest-level protector enjoyed some interest. Normally, a cultivator, pressed by local government for taxes on traditional family holdings, commended his land as an estate to a noble. The commender adopted a title of *shōen* administrator *(shōkan, azukaridokoro),* while the capital proprietor was known as a *ryōke.* Proper documentation recognizing the *shōen* as tax-exempt and immune to entry by officials could be obtained by commendation to a more powerful noble or religious institution. [See also Shōen.]

By the twelfth century, *shōen* were seriously undermining state revenues. Under the system of proprietary control of provinces, nobles treated even public lands (referred to as *kōryō,* "public holdings") essentially as private possessions, managed by the governor. Although much land shifted from public to *shōen* status, considerable *kōryō* survived into Kamakura times, and, in fact, most warriors rose to power from public lands, for which they served hereditarily in an administrative capacity. Nonetheless, the *ritsuryō* ideal of national control of land and people was long dead by the end of Heian times.

*Cultural Life.* In the Heian period Japan turned from Chinese models toward more indigenous patterns. In the institutional area scholars see this process negatively, referring to the "decline" or "dissolution" of the *ritsuryō* system. But in the cultural sphere the assessment is positive, since the Japanese created a truly native, that is, non-Chinese, culture for the first time. In fact, it is its cultural achievements that most define the Heian period: the absorption of Buddhist ideas, the perfection of a writing system that allowed for a truly Japanese literary expression, and the emergence of a secular artistic tradition freeing Japanese artists from rigid Chinese traditions.

*Religion.* Despite the undue political influence of the Buddhist establishment during Nara times, Buddhism flourished in Heian times, but in new forms. Shortly after the move of the capital, two monks returned from China to establish new sects of Buddhism that were soon to dominate Heian religious culture.

Saichō (767–822), founder of Enryakuji on Mount Hiei, established the Tendai sect there upon his return. Saichō was determined to create a monastic order that would serve the country more positively than the older orders in Nara. Although the Enryakuji temple stood to the northeast, in this position protecting the capital against evil spirits, the priests of Saichō's temple later became more of a bane than a blessing to the city. [*See also* Saichō *and* Tendai.]

Kūkai (Kōbō Daishi, 744–835) returned from China to found his temple on Mount Kōya in Kii Province, where he introduced Tantric Buddhism to Japan in the form of the Shingon (True Word) sect. Because it emphasized rituals, incantations, and magical formulas and stressed visual representation of the Buddhist cosmology (mandalas), Shingon soon became popular at court. It was important not only as a religion providing personal comfort but also as one offering encouragement of the arts. Kūkai's own personality was also crucial in popularizing esoteric Shingon, which eclipsed Tendai as the most important religion in Heian times. [*See also* Kūkai *and* Shingon.]

The headquarters of these new sects were located outside the capital, in accord with Kammu's wish that the new capital be protected from the negative influence of priests. Only two temples were built in the original city, while others developed in the suburbs of the city. By late Heian times, however, the aristocracy had constructed many private temples in the city, and monks were as common a sight in Heian as they had been in Nara. In fact, they were in certain ways even more threatening to court interests.

During the Heian period the major temples of the capital region nurtured armed monks, mostly recruited from provincial estates, to aid in disputes within or among temples over ecclesiastical, political, or economic issues. These armed monks, termed *akusō* ("unruly monks") by the courtiers, were also effective in opposing government decisions on religion or economics. If the temple's demands were not met, the monks might carry the sacred palanquin housing the temple's protective Shinto deity to the gates of the palace as a threat. [*See also* Akusō.]

Although the *akusō* threatened the court and some priests were engaged in corrupt practices, the clergy never influenced the government as Nara priests had done. The court nobles remained devout, and pilgrimages to the Buddhist and Shinto establishments were a common part of the lives of the aristocracy.

There was also some popularization of Buddhism in the form of Amidism, centering on faith in Amida, Buddha of Boundless Light, who lived in the "Western Paradise." It was Amida's "original vow" that all who called on him through *nembutsu* (the recitation of Amida's name) would be reborn into his Western Paradise, the so-called Pure Land. Pure Land Buddhism was introduced by priests such as Ennin, returning from China, and it was popularized by Kōya, who preached to common folk in the streets, dancing and singing with a bell tied around his neck. The most influential Heian Pure Land priest was Genshin, whose *Essentials of Salvation (Ōjōyōshū)* depicted graphically the horrors of hells and the delights of the Pure Land.

Although it did not become a separate sect until the Kamakura period, Pure Land Buddhism was popular from mid-Heian times. Pure Land doctrine rested on the Mahayana concept of *mappō*, the "Latter Days of the Law," which held that after the death of the Buddha the Buddhist Law would develop through three stages: a prosperous period of five hundred years, a period of decline of one thousand years, and finally its destruction in the ten thousand years of *mappō*. Once *mappō* began (1052, according to the most popular Japanese reckoning), enlightenment through one's own powers, as preached in most Buddhist sects, was deemed impossible; one's only hope was the saving grace of Amida. [*See also* Amidism *and* Pure Land.]

Thus, court nobles and ladies chanted the *nembutsu* to attain rebirth in Amida's Western Paradise. Fujiwara no Michinaga, for example, records that during a five-day period he repeated the *nembutsu* ("All hail to Amida Buddha") 700,000 times! Like many courtiers, Michinaga also built an Amida Hall for the worship of this Buddha. Perhaps the greatest such private Amida temple was the Phoenix Hall of the Byōdōin, built by his son Yorimichi at Uji.

Buddhism thus flourished during the Heian period—at the old Nara temples, in the new Tendai and Shingon centers, and in the more popular Pure Land devotionalism. But the religious belief of the nobility was highly eclectic. Courtiers seemingly made little distinction between various Buddhist beliefs, native Shinto beliefs, and Chinese-derived concepts of yin and yang and the "five elements." Thus, for example, Fujiwara Michinaga visited Tendai and Shingon Shinto shrines, called on the services of exorcists, chanted the *nembutsu,* and reposed great faith in Miroku (the Buddha of the future).

*Literature.* The height of the Heian creative spirit was reached in the field of literature, especially poetry. The thirty-one-syllable *tanka* form became so popular among the aristocracy that failure to compose a proper *tanka* at the appropriate occasion exposed one to ridicule. A narrative style of prose literature also developed from the mid-Heian period, in two general forms: the *monogatari,* or tale, and the *nikki,* or diary.

In the early Heian period, however, concern with Chinese literary models continued under the strong patronage of Emperor Saga, paralleling the attempt to restore the *ritsuryō* system institutions. Anthologies of Chinese poetry were compiled under imperial authorization, and the Japanese poetry of the *Man'yōshū,* the classic anthology of the Nara period, was virtually ignored.

After 838, the year of the last official mission to the Tang court, the Japanese turned increasingly to more native modes of expression. The development of the *kana* syllabary lay behind the surge of creativity in both poetry and prose writing. Although *kana* developed gradually, tradition attributes its "invention" to Kōbō Daishi. Sanskrit may have inspired this phonetic writing system, and priests like Kōbō Daishi were clearly responsible for perfecting it. *Kana* also represented a refinement of *man'yōgana,* a writing system whereby Chinese

characters were borrowed for sound only, without regard to meaning. The refinement led to two forms of *kana: hiragana,* which were simplifications of entire Chinese characters, and *katakana,* created by using only one part of a character. These *kana,* numbering about fifty symbols, made writing far simpler than it had been using difficult Chinese characters, for by using these syllabaries one could theoretically write a "pure" Japanese sentence using no (Chinese) characters at all. But Japanese already contained many borrowed Chinese words, including all the abstract terms from Confucian and Buddhist philosophies. In practice then, the mixing of Chinese characters and the *kana* syllabary was common, indeed unavoidable, and persists to this day in standard written Japanese.

The evolution of *kana* affected Heian literature in another way. The Heian court noble typically devoted himself to the Chinese written language (perhaps because the knowledge of Chinese separated aristocrat from commoner) and kept diaries in classical Chinese, relying upon *kana* only for poetry. Thus it was primarily Heian court women who wrote the great works of the period's literature.

As direct interest in China waned, courtiers turned increasingly to the *tanka,* a thirty-one-syllable poem in lines of five, seven, five, seven, and seven syllables. The *tanka* focused on emotional imagery rather than narrative discourse to move the reader. Allusions were widely employed, as were devices such as pivot words (*kakekotoba*) and words evoking the seasons. Because *tanka* were so short, skill in adding nuances to earlier poems was valued more than originality.

Skill in poetic composition was important for the Heian courtier. There were informal and formal poetry competitions, some held at imperial command. Lovers exchanged poems, and there were even public occasions when officials communicated via poems. The inability to recognize an allusion to a famous poem or to compose a passable verse could condemn a court noble or lady to social disgrace.

Among the many anthologies of Japanese poetry compiled in Heian times, the *Kokin wakashu* (905) was the greatest. Ki no Tsurayuki's introduction superbly captures Japanese poetic sensibilities:

Japanese poetry has for its seed the human heart, and grows into countless leaves of words. In this life many things touch men: they seek then to express what they see or hear. Who among men does not compose poetry on hearing the song of the nightingale among the flowers, or the cries of the frog who lives in the water? Poetry it is which, without effort, moves heaven and earth, and stirs to pity the invisible demons and gods;

which makes sweet the ties between men and women; and which can comfort the hearts of fierce warriors.

(quoted in Earl Miner, *Japanese Poetic Diaries*,1969)

The development of *kana* also stimulated the birth of a native prose literature. The *monogatari* and *nikki,* the former being a true narrative tale (such as Lady Murasaki's *Tale of Genji*) and the latter a collection of personal impressions of daily events, shared at least one common feature: the inclusion of poems interspersed throughout the narrative. In fact, one type of *monogatari,* the *uta monogatari,* or poem tale, consisted of little more than brief introductory prose remarks linking a large number of verses. The Japanese found this form of expression quite moving, and the best example of this genre, the *Tales of Ise (Ise monogatari),* is regarded as a classic.

The *Tosa nikki (Tosa Diary)* by Ki no Tsurayuki, a man writing in a manner that would be recognized as that of a woman, is considered the first of the *nikki.* Later the genre was completely taken over by women; two of its most representative works are the *Kagerō nikki (Gossamer Years)* and the diary of Genji's author, Lady Murasaki. Unlike the *Tosa nikki,* which focuses on a specific journey, *Kagerō nikki* covers a long period of time by focusing on scattered instances, chronicling the author's despair as her husband, the regent Fujiwara Kaneie, visits her with decreasing frequency, leaving her and her son to fend for themselves. The *Pillow Book (Makura no sōshi)* of Sei Shōnagon (like Murasaki, a serving lady at court) is a collection of reminiscences, anecdotes, and frank personal opinions about people and events at court. The work is light and witty, what the Heian courtiers referred to as *okashi.* Sei Shōnagon wrote in a style that foreshadowed the genre known as *zuihitsu* ("running brush"), miscellany that demonstrate the Japanese preference for rambling collections of episodes relying upon polished short sequences for intense emotional appeal.

The *Tale of Genji* remains the classic work of Heian, indeed of Japanese, literature, a work immensely more sophisticated in language and structure than anything that preceded it. Diary entries reveal that *Genji* was circulated widely at court while Murasaki was writing it, between 1008 and 1020. Compared to other Heian works, *Genji* is a massive tale. Its fifty-four chapters deal with court life and focus on the hero Genji, the "shining prince." Genji is the epitome of courtly virtues: handsome, a brilliant poet, dancer, musician, and calligrapher, and practiced at courtly love. The *Tale of Genji* deals with relations between men and women in Heian Japan, seen usually from the viewpoint of either Genji or his male companions. Both the language and mood of *Genji* are elegant; the work is a masterpiece of psychological narrative.

Yet *Genji* resembles the *Pillow Book* in that it lacks the structural coherence modern theorists of the novel expect. The book divides somewhat naturally into two parts with the death of Genji. The moods of the two sections are quite different, the Genji section depicting the court at its zenith and the latter section tinged with uncertainty over the future. Some have even suggested that the difference is the result of multiple authorship.

If the *Pillow Book* represents the Heian aesthetic value of *okashi,* the bringing of amusement, then *Genji* is the epitome of *mono no aware,* a sensitivity to the sadness inherent in the things of this world—a preference for the beauty of the falling of blossoms over their budding, for example.

*Genji* has had enormous impact upon Japanese literary and cultural history. It is the towering work of Japanese fiction, often imitated—even its division into fifty-four chapters was a convention for later writers—but never surpassed. One of the world's largest novels (630,000 words in Arthur Waley's translation), *Genji* has over four hundred characters, most of whom are related in some way. In Japan today a potter might create a series of plates, each named for a character from *Genji,* while in Tokugawa times, courtesans might be named for *Genji* characters. [*See also* Genji Monogatari.]

**Art.** Art historians distinguish early and late Heian eras, dividing at the cessation of official relations with China in 838. The first century is known as the Jōgan, or Kōnin, era, while the last three centuries are called the Fujiwara age. Jōgan was an era of strong Chinese influence, and development was especially striking in the arts associated with Esoteric Buddhism: sculpture and the mandala.

Nara-period statues were of bronze, dry lacquer, or clay; in the Jōgan era the Japanese relied largely upon wood. Customarily, a statue was carved from one block of wood, left unpainted (except for lips) so as not to interfere with the natural aroma of the wood (sandalwood was especially favored). Consequently, most Jōgan statues were smaller than earlier ones. Declining imperial support for Buddhism reduced the need for massive statues like the Tōdaiji *daibutsu,* the function of which seems to have been as much nationalistic as religious. The smaller scale of such works meant that the concerted efforts of government-supported artisans were no longer necessary; the Jōgan epoch witnessed the emergence of individual craftsmen. The extant statues show a rigid stance, which together with the stylized "wave" patterned robe of the Buddha creates a severe, unearthly appearance. The most famous Jōgan sculptures are the depiction of Yakushi (the Healing Buddha) at the Jingoji in Kyoto and that of the historical Buddha at the Murōji, south of Nara.

The most numerous surviving examples of early-Heian painting are mandalas, aids in meditation, which in Japan were most often painted on hanging scrolls or sometimes on temple walls. They normally depict the cosmic Buddha, Dainichi (Sanskrit, Vairochana), surrounded by other figures from the Shingon pantheon.

The only other Jōgan paintings are the fierce representations of the colored (blue, red, or yellow) Fudō. Regarded as a manifestation of the cosmic Buddha, Fudō was pictured as a grotesque, muscular guardian who subdues enemies of the faith with rope and sword. A fine example is the Yellow Fudō of Onjōji.

As in literature, the art of the Fujiwara period showed great change. An important factor was the rise of Pure Land Buddhism. Statues of Amida Buddha became popular, the most noteworthy being that sculpted by the priest Jōchō in the Phoenix Hall of the Byōdōin. The serene, gentle countenance contrasts markedly with the more stiff and severe Jōgan images. Jōchō was perhaps the first craftsman to be considered a true artist. The Amida faith was not only influential in the field of sculpture. A popular theme in painting was the raigō, a representation of Amida coming to lead the believer to the Pure Land. Amida is normally shown riding on a wisp of clouds, surrounded by bodhisattvas praying or playing musical instruments. An excellent example of the raigō theme is the wall painting at Byōdōin.

Perhaps the most significant change in Fujiwara-era painting was the development of a secular art, known as Yamato-e, "Japanese pictures," to distinguish it from what were considered "Chinese pictures." In earlier periods, nonreligious art consisted of Chinese-style landscapes and portraits of great ecclesiastical figures like the Chinese priest Ganjin. But in the Fujiwara period there was an outburst of secular painting, landscapes and scenes of court life, painted on folding screens (byōbu) and paper doors. These we known only by description, however, since neither the paintings nor buildings that contained them survive.

Perhaps the finest surviving examples of Fujiwara painting are the emakimono, or narrative scrolls, which came into vogue in the eleventh and twelfth centuries. Some, such as the Ban Dainagon scroll, deal with famous historical incidents; some are more religious in nature, treating, for example, the history of a temple, as in the Shigisan scroll; and some even depict in graphic details the Buddhist hells. Best known are the four extant Genji scrolls, which depict in elegant color the world of Murasaki's novel. Characteristic of emakimono are a cutaway of the roof, allowing the viewer to look down into the rooms, and stylized figure drawing, wherein faces are indistinguishable because of the "straight lines for eyes and hooks for noses" technique. [See also Painting: Japanese Painting.]

Freed from the constraints of religion, painting developed in many directions. The Yamato-e style initiated the development of forms quite different from those of the Chinese. Subsequently, new Chinese artistic traditions were introduced and flourished (ink painting, for example), but by returning to the Yamato-e style the Japanese continued to produce new and distinctive forms.

John Whitney Hall, *Japan: From Prehistory to Modern Times* (1970). G. Cameron Hurst III, *Insei: Abdicated Sovereigns in the Politics of Late Heian Japan* (1976). George B. Sansom, *Japan: A Short Cultural History* (1932) and *A History of Japan to 1334* (1958).

G. CAMERON HURST III

**HEIJI WAR.** *See* Hōgen and Heiji Wars.

**HEIJŌ,** the city (later called Nara) where Japan's capital was located for most of the Nara period (710–784 CE). Modeled after Chang'an, the capital of Tang China, Heijō was the focal point of wide-ranging change, along Chinese lines, that was associated not only with the formation of bureaucratic institutions to support imperial rule but also with remarkable achievements in art and learning.

Gemmei Tennō apparently assumed that a new emperor (tennō) should have a new capital, and she therefore issued an edict in the second year of her reign (708) announcing the establishment of an office responsible for planning and building a new capital at Heijō. Early in 710, at the beginning of the Nara period, Heijō was officially designated Japan's capital. Several years passed before construction was completed, as is deduced from the appointment in 724 of an official who was charged with prodding builders to finish the work.

As with other capitals modeled after Chang'an, Heijō had straight parallel streets that divided the city into segments of equal size. The Imperial Palace and the buildings of the various ministries and bureaus were located in the north-central portion of the city, facing south. Much of the new construction resulted from moving such famous Buddhist temples as Asukadera, the Yakushiji, and the Daianji into the capital from Asuka. There were also government-managed markets.

The entire city, however, was only about one-fourth the size of Chang'an. Heijō had a population of around 200,000, whereas Chang'an's was close to 1.2 million. Also, Heijō was not surrounded by a wall, while Chang'an was encircled by a wall about thirty meters high.

[*See also* Nara Period.]

DELMER M. BROWN

**HEILONGJIANG**, China's northernmost province, forms part of the region known as Dongbei ("northeast") or Manchuria. Its capital is Harbin. Heilongjiang is China's fourth-largest province in total area; census figures report a population of 32,810,000 (1982). Traditionally, Heilongjiang occupied territory on the frontier of the Chinese empire. Its border with the Soviet Union has been disputed since the seventeenth century and in recent decades has been the site of numerous skirmishes between the two superpowers.

Since 1949, Heilongjiang has been an important agricultural region in China, producing wheat, corn, soybeans, sugar beets, sunflowers, and lumber. Oil has become the most important natural resource of the province largely owing to the discovery of vast reserves at Daqing in the early 1960s. In addition, gold is mined in the Manchurian uplands and along the Heilongjiang (Amur) River and coal is extracted from deposits throughout the province.

ANITA M. ANDREW

**HE LONG** (1896–1969), general; marshal of the Chinese People's Liberation Army; member, Chinese Communist Party (CCP) Politburo; vice-premier, State Council; chairman, Physical Culture and Sports Commission.

He Long is one of the most popular and romanticized military heroes in China's recent history. Born in a poor district of northwest Hunan, he became an outlaw in the Liang Shan (Robin Hood) tradition in his youth. In his twenties he joined the

Nationalist Army, but later defected, playing a key role in the Nanchang Uprising of 1 August 1927 that established the Communist Red Army. From 1928 to 1935 he commanded troops in the Hunan-Hubei base area. Following the Long March, he became the commander of the 120th Division of the Communist Eighth Route Army during the war with Japan.

After the founding of the People's Republic of China in 1949, He held a number of leading positions in the party and government, and was frequently sent abroad on diplomatic missions. He was attacked as a revisionist in the early phases of the Cultural Revolution but was later rehabilitated.

[*See also* Chinese People's Liberation Army; Eighth Route Army; *and* Great Proletarian Cultural Revolution.]

Donald W. Klein and Anne B. Clark, *Biographic Dictionary of Chinese Communism, 1921–1965* (1971). Edgar Snow, *Red Star over China* (1938).

PETER J. SEYBOLT

**HEMU** (d. 1556), a Hindu of the mercantile caste, appointed prime minister (1552–1554) by Muhammad Adil Shah Sur, for whom he won twenty-two victories. On Humayun's accidental death (January 1556), Hemu tried to prevent Akbar, heir to the throne, from taking possession of his father's kingdom. When Hemu declared himself an independent ruler and assumed the title of *vikramaditya*, Bairam Khan and Akbar marched with an army against him. At the historic Battle of Panipat an accidental arrow pierced his brain and he fell unconscious. At Bairam Khan's request, Akbar cut off Hemu's head with his sword. The head was sent to Kabul to be exposed, while the trunk was gibbeted at one of the gates of Delhi.

[*See also* Panipat, Battles of.]

V. A. Smith, *Akbar the Great Mogul* (1919), pp. 34–39. I. H. Qureshi, *Akbar, the Founder of the Mughal Empire* (1978), pp. 51–54.    KHALIQ AHMAD NIZAMI

**HENAN**, province in north-central China; its area is 167,000 square kilometers and its population in 1982 was 74,422,739. Henan is one of the smallest, most densely populated, and earliest settled of China's provinces. Northern Henan was the site of Neolithic and Bronze Age settlements and the homeland of the Shang state in the second millennium BCE. The city of Luoyang in northwestern Henan was the second capital of the Eastern Zhou dynasty (770–221) and capital of many later dynasties of the first millennium CE, when the plain of eastern Henan was the most heavily populated area of China. The commercial city of Kaifeng in north-central Henan was the capital of the Song dynasty (960–1127). After that time the province became less politically prominent, although it remained economically important in spite of the frequent flooding of the Yellow River and other natural disasters. Since 1949, water control projects have reduced flooding and made irrigated agriculture more extensive, with winter wheat, gaoliang (Chinese sorghum), corn, sweet potatoes, and cotton the most important crops. Since the 1950s, the region around Luoyang, Kaifeng, and the capital, Zhengzhou, has been turned into a modern industrial center. Zhengzhou, along with Xinxiang in the north and Nanyang in the southwest, is also an important commercial, communications, and transport center.

JOHN A. RAPP

**HENG SAMRIN** (b. 1934), Cambodian political figure. He has been president of the People's Republic of Kampuchea (PRK) since 1979 and secretary general of the Kampuchean People's Revolutionary Party since 1981. Heng Samrin was born in southeastern Cambodia and actively supported the Vietnamese civil war in the late 1950s. During the Cambodian communist uprising against the Khmer Republic (1970–1975) he rose to the rank of regimental commander. He was a brigade commander in the eastern zone of Democratic Kampuchea in 1976. The following year he took refuge in Vietnam to avoid purges of party members being carried out at the behest of Pol Pot, the party's secretary-general. After returning secretly to Cambodia, Heng Samrin assumed command of an uprising against Pol Pot in 1978, which was soon followed by a Vietnamese invasion. Heng Samrin was named president of the pro-Vietnamese PRK regime in January 1979.

[See also Kampuchea, People's Republic of; Kampuchea, Democratic; Khmer Republic; and Pol Pot.]

Michael Vickery, Cambodia 1975–1982 (1984).

DAVID P. CHANDLER

**HENRIQUEZ, HENRY** (1520–1600). Born of Jewish parents in Vilavicosa, Portugal, and later a student of law at Coimbra, Henriquez came to India

as a Jesuit in 1547. In fifty-three years of ministry at Punneikayal, Manaar, and Tuticorin, he was distinguished for his roles as parish priest, catechist, educator, organizer of Christian confraternities, and Tamil scholar. He is credited with writing and printing the first Catholic books in Tamil.

[See also Jesuits: Jesuits in India.]

J. Haupert, A South Indian Mission: The Madura Catholic Mission (1937).
PATRICK ROCHE

**HEPBURN, JAMES CURTIS** (1815–1911), pioneer Presbyterian missionary to Japan, teacher, translator, and inventor of the Hepburn system of romanization. Born in Pennsylvania, Hepburn was educated at Princeton College and at the University of Pennsylvania Medical School. After serving as a medical missionary in China from 1840 to 1846, he practiced medicine in New York until 1859, when he was sent to Japan. One of the first Presbyterian missionaries to settle in Kanagawa, Hepburn opened a medical dispensary and school. Teaching English and healing the sick, he quickly developed a reputation as a man of integrity and unusual linguistic ability. Concerned about the lack of teaching aids for those hoping to master the difficulties of the Japanese language, he compiled a dictionary (published in Shanghai in 1869), and developed a system of romanizing Japanese that still remains in use.

Later, Hepburn turned his medical work over to Japanese physicians and devoted himself to translating scripture and developing Meiji Gakuin, the Presbyterian college in Tokyo, which he served as president and as a professor of hygiene and physiology. A man of wide scientific interests, with a warm and open personality and a deep belief that Christianity required social involvement as well as spiritual outreach, Hepburn was one of the most effective, and well liked, of the foreign missionaries and teachers active in Meiji Japan.

F. G. NOTEHELFER

**HEPTHALITES.** See Huns.

**HERAT** (Harat), a city and province in western Afghanistan centered on the fertile river valley of the Hari Rud. Herat's location at the juncture of trade routes linking Iran with Central Asia and India assured its strategic importance, and its capture was often the object of invading armies. Old Herat is noted for its square layout and strong inner citadel, and until the twentieth century it was surrounded by a massive embankment topped by high walls.

Herat has existed since antiquity; some attribute its founding to Alexander the Great. In the fifth and sixth centuries CE it was an important Sasanid military base. In the seventh century it was conquered by the Arabs. One of the four great cities of medieval Khurasan (along with Nishapur, Balkh, and Merv), Herat was very prosperous; the city also produced many learned men, including the Sufi poet Khwaja Abd Allah Ansari (d. 1088).

Herat was destroyed by the Mongols in 1222 but was rebuilt in the fourteenth century under the Kart dynasty. It reached its greatest cultural and artistic florescence—particularly in miniature painting—in the fifteenth century under the Timurid ruler Husain Baiqara. Herat formed part of the Safavid empire for much of the sixteenth and seventeenth centuries, although possession was contested by the Uzbeks. During the eighteenth and nineteenth centuries the Persian Qajar dynasty unsuccessfully sought to regain possession of the city.

In the nineteenth century Herat also became the focus of international rivalry. The British, who wanted to maintain Afghanistan as a buffer between India and Russia, regarded Herat as the "key to India." They were determined to exclude both Russian and Persian influence. Persian occupation of Herat in 1856 precipitated the brief British-Persian War, won by the British. Herat has been part of the modern state of Afghanistan since 1863. Its population in the 1960s was around 100,000; since the Soviet invasion of 1979 this number has declined, perhaps drastically, and about half the city is reported to have been destroyed.

[See also Ansari; Khurasan; Kart Dynasty; Timurid Dynasty; Baiqara, Husain; and Painting: Iranian and Central Asian Painting.]

Ludwig Adamec, ed., Historical and Political Gazetteer of Afghanistan, vol. 3, Herat and Northwestern Afghanistan (1975). Wilhelm Barthold, An Historical Geography of Iran, translated by Svat Soucek (1984). Heinz Gaube, Iranian Cities (1979).    LAWRENCE POTTER

HESHEN (1750–1799), Manchu bannerman who became the notorious favorite and chief minister of the Qianlong emperor during the Qing dynasty (1644–1911) in China. Heshen became an imperial bodyguard in the Forbidden City at the age of twenty-two and within three years managed to catch the eye of the emperor. Whatever the reason for his infatuation with the handsome and clever young

man, the aging emperor showered him with titles, honors, special privileges (including permission to issue edicts), and the high office of grand councillor. Heshen's meteoric rise to power was so complete that he thoroughly dominated the government for the next twenty-three years.

Heshen greedily and blatantly abused his lofty position in order to enrich himself and his accomplices, especially through extortion and embezzlement of military funds. Fearing his influence with the increasingly senile emperor, few dared stand in his way. When the emperor finally died in 1799, Heshen was swiftly arrested and his wealth confiscated. As punishment, he was "permitted" to commit suicide. Heshen contributed greatly to the deterioration of Qing rule and the onset of dynastic decline. He not only spread corruption but also provoked large popular uprisings such as the White Lotus Rebellion (1796–1805).

[See also Grand Council; Qianlong Emperor; and Qing Dynasty.]

Harold L. Kahn, Monarchy in the Emperor's Eyes: Image and Reality in the Ch'ien-lung Reign (1971).

ROLAND L. HIGGINS

HIBIYA INCIDENT, major riot in Tokyo ensuing from a mass rally held in Hibiya Park on 5 September 1905 to protest the Treaty of Portsmouth, which settled the Russo-Japanese War. The public, ignorant of the actual war situation, judged the treaty disgraceful to their victorious nation. While the Katsura government ignored the popular indignation, some minor political party members, lawyers, and newspapermen organized the Kōwa Mondai Dōshi Rengōkai (Joint Council of Fellow Activists on the Peace Question). Against a government ban, they convened a protest meeting at the park and appealed to the emperor to reject the treaty, while also demanding that the army in Manchuria continue fighting.

After the rally, some two thousand protesters proceeded to march on the Imperial Palace grounds, where they clashed with police. Similar skirmishes followed in other parts of the city. The Imperial Guards and the First Army Division were mobilized to suppress the rioters. On 6 September martial law was declared throughout the city. Before the rioting finally subsided the next day, partly as a result of a heavy rain, more than 350 structures were demolished, including the home minister's official residence, the office of the progovernment newspaper Kokumin shimbun, nine police stations, thirteen

Christian churches, and fifty-three private homes. In addition, fifteen streetcars were burned. The recorded casualties exceeded one thousand, including seventeen dead.

Some historians have characterized the riot as the precursor of the so-called Taishō Democracy, viewing it as evidence of a growing mass political consciousness. Others have maintained that the protest was fundamentally a manifestation of nationalistic chauvinism, brought about by an indoctrinated, blind loyalty to the imperial state.

[*See also* Russo-Japanese War; Portsmouth, Treaty of; *and* Taishō Political Change.]

Shumpei Okamoto, "The Emperor and the Crowd: The Historical Significance of the Hibiya Riot," in *Conflict in Modern Japanese History: The Neglected Tradition,* edited by Tetsuo Najita and J. Victor Koschmann (1982), pp. 258–275.                    SHUMPEI OKAMOTO

**HIDEYOSHI'S INVASION OF KOREA.** The military invasion launched by Toyotomi Hideyoshi of Japan against Korea from 1592 to 1598, which also brought China into the conflict at a later stage, had a far-reaching impact on the course of East Asian history. The genesis of the invasion dates from the time when, as Hideyoshi's goal of achieving a national unification of Japan was nearing completion, he openly expressed his desire to launch a military expedition against Korea and China for the purpose of territorial conquest. Such a venture abroad would also give a convenient outlet to the excess energies of the Japanese warriors. Hideyoshi apparently hoped to win Korea's support for his military venture, but when his demand that his troops be allowed to pass through Korea on their way to invade China was refused, he ordered his forces of more than 158,000 men to attack Korea in April 1592.

The first contingent, commanded by Konishi Yukinaga, landed at Pusan on 23 May and quickly overran the fortress of Tongnae. [*See* Konishi Yukinaga.] Soon thereafter, other Japanese troops rushed to Korea. Korea was woefully ill prepared to meet the Japanese invasion. The diplomatic mission sent to Japan in 1590 returned with conflicting reports on the possible intent of Hideyoshi toward Korea. The peace Yi-dynasty Korea had enjoyed for two centuries, coupled with the pacifist sentiment of Neo-Confucian idealism, had left Korea totally unprepared for military crisis. Japan, on the other hand, showed military superiority on land in all aspects. The Korean defenders were especially helpless against the firearms the Japanese employed. Thus,

as the Japanese troops advanced along the three main routes toward Seoul, Korea could offer little effective resistance. In desperation, the Yi court pinned its hopes on General Sin Ip to halt the Japanese in a gallant but hopeless stand at T'an'gŭmdae, outside Ch'ungju. When the news of General Sin's defeat reached the capital the king and his court fled, to the taunts and jeers of an angry crowd. On 12 June, only twenty days after the initial landing, the Japanese occupied Seoul. After a brief pause, they pushed northward, Konishi seizing P'yŏngyang in July and Katō Kiyomasa leading his troops into Hamgyŏng Province. Driven to the border town of Ŭiju, the Korean court finally appealed to Ming China for military assistance.

As the initial shock of defeat began to wear off, Korea was able to put up more effective resistance. On sea, along the southern coast, Admiral Yi Sun-sin was achieving spectacular victories against the Japanese navy using his heavily armed "turtle" ships, thus interrupting Japanese supply and communication lines. [*See also* Yi Sun-sin.] On land, numerous militia units, known as the "righteous armies," were organized by the local gentry and Buddhist monks to fight the intruders. In the meantime, China, regarding the Japanese occupation of Korea as a threat to its own security, dispatched more than forty thousand troops, retaking P'yŏngyang in February 1593 and forcing the Japanese to retreat to the north of Seoul, where, at Pyŏkchegwan, the Japanese ambushed the Chinese. Not long thereafter, the regrouped Korean army, under the command of Kwŏn Yul, defeated the Japanese at the mountain fortress of Haengju, compelling the Japanese to withdraw to the south of Seoul. The military situation now reached a stalemate, forcing negotiations between China and Japan.

The negotiations followed circuitous routes amid trickery and misunderstanding until 1597. Hideyoshi's demands included the marriage of a Chinese princess to the Japanese emperor, the restoration of tally trade, and the cession of four southern provinces of Korea. Hideyoshi's negotiators misled him about the Chinese response to these demands, and he was astonished and enraged to find that the Chinese mission of "submission" was actually bearer of a document certifying him as king of Japan and a vassal of the Ming emperor. A second invasion was mounted in August 1597. In the temporary absence of Yi Sun-sin, who was in disfavor, the Japanese navy fared better. This time, however, the Japanese were met by more effective resistance from the allied armies of Korea and China, and the Japanese advance was stopped near Seoul at Chiksan.

There was now growing awareness among the Japanese commanders of the futility in further bloodshed. The sudden death of Hideyoshi in September 1598 provided a convenient excuse to withdraw all the Japanese troops from Korea.

The war was extremely costly for Korea in both human and material terms. Korea lost innumerable cultural and artistic treasures, and the war left bitter scars of fear and resentment in the minds of the Koreans toward Japan. Ming China also suffered greatly as the costly war weakened its control over the border region, allowing the Manchu tribe to gain strength. Japan, on the other hand, benefited in cultural terms. The Neo-Confucianism of Zhu Xi was transmitted to Japan, Japan acquired the technique of movable-type printing, and a large-scale relocation of Korean ceramic artists enabled Japan to enrich its ceramic industry with porcelain ware.

[*See also* Toyotomi Hideyoshi *and* Yi Dynasty.]

Ki-baik Lee, *A New History of Korea,* translated by Edward W. Wagner (1984). George Sansom, *A History of Japan, 1334–1615* (1961), chap. 22. Yi Sun-sin, *Nanjung ilgi: War Diary of Admiral Yi Sun-sin,* translated by Ha Tae-hung and edited by Sohn Pow-key (1977), and *Imjin Changch'o: Admiral Yi Sun-sin's Memorials to Court* (1981).                        YŎNG-HO CH'OE

**HIMACHAL PRADESH,** state in northwestern India bounded on the south by Haryana, on the west by the Punjab, on the east by the Tibetan Autonomous Region of China, and on the north by Kashmir, covering a total area of 21,490 square miles. The landscape of Himachal Pradesh is crowned by the snowy mountains from which it takes its name. Its capital, Simla, is 7,262 feet above sea level and is the largest town in what is India's least urbanized state. The population of Himachal Pradesh, approximately 3.6 million, is ethnically and linguistically diverse, and although it is predominantly Hindu, it includes Muslims, Sikhs, Buddhists, and Christians as well. Originally constituted in 1948 as an administrative unit comprising thirty hill states, Himachal Pradesh grew to include the former states of Bilaspur, Kulu, Simla, Lahul-Spiti, and Kangra before achieving full statehood on 26 June 1971.

[*See also* Simla.]

BRUCE MCCOY OWENS

**HIMALAYAS,** mountain system bounded by the Indus and Brahmaputra rivers forming the great northern watershed of the Indian subcontinent. The Himalayas (the name is Sanskrit and means "abode of snow") stretch nearly fifteen hundred miles from India's northeastern borders with China and Burma to the Hindu Kush of Pakistan's northwest frontier, forming an almost impenetrable barrier between the densely populated Ganges Plain and the arid steppeland of the Tibetan plateau.

Source of the holy Ganges and site of the fabled Mount Kailash, the Himalayas are held sacred by Hindu and Buddhist alike. "As the dew is dried up by the morning sun," the *Skanda Purana* proclaims, "so are the sins of mankind at the sight of the Himalayas." The world's tallest mountain system, with a dozen peaks exceeding twenty-five thousand feet, the Himalayas were formed by the collision of the Indian subcontinent with the central Asian mainland during the Eocene period, some forty-five million years ago. Frequent earthquakes throughout the region, such as the one that leveled over 60 percent of the Kathmandu Valley in 1933, testify to the persistent activity of geological forces that continue to push up the continental crust.

Geographers conventionally divide the Himalayas into three parallel zones. The malarial lowlands of the Tarai, lying at the base of the mountains, have been colonized by the surplus populations of neighboring regions for subsistence and commercial agriculture only within the last century. The rugged and populous Middle Hills, which have been intensively terraced for the cultivation of wet rice over the past three to four hundred years, have long been settled by Indo-Aryan populations migrating from northwestern India and Tibeto-Burman peoples from southwestern China. Society in this region reflects a distinctive *pahari* (hill) culture in contrast to the Tarai, where cultural continuities with the North Indian heartland are pronounced. The Great Himalayan Range constitutes the third zone. Vast tracts of snow, ice, and glacial moraine are interspersed with alpine meadows that extend into the Inner Himalayas of the Tibetan plateau. The populations of Tibetan origin inhabiting this region combine limited agriculture with transhumant pastoralism and trade across the high mountain passes. The crest of the range demarcates the border between Nepal and Chinese-occupied Tibet, and between Bhutan and the Indian states of Arunachal Pradesh, Sikkim, Uttar Pradesh, and Himachal Pradesh; in the northwest, it separates Ladakh from Kashmir.

This diversity of settlement, combined with the isolating tendencies of the natural environment, long obstructed the Buddhist, Hindu, and indigenous rulers from expanding the borders of their very localized and typically fragmented domains. It was not until the late 1700s that the Hindu rajas of Gorkha consolidated their rule over much of the central Himalayas. The Buddhist monastic principalities that controlled access to the high mountain passes along the Himalayan periphery remained independent of Hindu domination from the south, both because of their religious and political alliances with Tibet and because of their importance in the trans-Himalayan trade between India and Central Asia.

Under the governorship of Warren Hastings, the British East India Company initiated efforts to gain access to trans-Himalayan trade through intervention in a number of the region's political rivalries. In addition to the lure of gold and luxury fabrics exported from Tibet, Hastings saw great opportunity to open up markets in Tibet and China for company commodities such as broadcloth. By the middle of the nineteenth century, the British had annexed all the Himalayan territories exclusive of Bhutan and Nepal. The subsequent expansion of British commercial interests in the region, in the form of timber harvesting and the development of a plantation economy for such cash crops as tea, cinchona, indigo, and rubber, brought about the rapid integration of the region into the international economy.

In 1959 the Communist Chinese assumed direct control over Tibet, and from 1963 to 1965 Chinese troops pressed their government's claims to Himalayan regions in Ladakh and Arunachal Pradesh. These actions led to the Sino-Indian War of 1965. Although the settlement of this dispute resulted in a mutually recognized border, the area remains a ilitarily strategic and sensitive zone of geopolitical concern.

[See the articles on the various Himalayan states mentioned herein. See also Hastings, Warren; East India Company; McMahon Line; and Aksai Chin.]

G. Berreman, "Peoples and Cultures of the Himalayas," *Asian Survey* (1963). M. Fisher, L. Rose, and R. Huttenback, *Himalayan Battlegrounds* (1963). T. Hagen, *Nepal* (1961). J. Preble, *John Company at War* (1972).

RICHARD ENGLISH

HINDI. *See* Indo-Aryan Languages and Literatures.

HINDUISM. The term *Hinduism* has no single traditional equivalent in the indigenous languages of South Asia. It came to be used by Western scholars and administrators in the nineteenth century to designate what they took to be the broad ritual and ideological framework of the religion of the vast majority of people in the subcontinent. Today this term is a standard part of both scholarly and official usage, in English and in many South Asian vernaculars.

The category "Hindu," although it has more complex etymological and historical roots, is today fundamentally a matter of social identity rather than of specific doctrinal assent or sacramental induction. In South Asia, a Hindu is a person who is born into a social group (often a caste or community of worshipers) that has not explicitly converted to Islam, Christianity, Zoroastrianism, or Judaism. The complicated personal law of India allows for quite a liberal definition of who shall be considered Hindu, whereas the official census is more conservative. Yet, even by the most conservative measures, between 60 and 70 percent of the population of South Asia must be regarded as Hindu.

*Historical Formation.* From a modern perspective, Hinduism can be viewed as the product of the interaction of a variety of forces during a period of approximately seventeen centuries, from about 1000 BCE to the seventh century of the common era. These forces were ecological as well as literary, political as well as philosophical. Although important changes did occur after 700 CE, Hinduism had by then acquired its basic intellectual and social form.

In the course of the first millennium BCE, Indo-Aryan speakers with ethnic roots in West and Central Asia brought their nomadic life-style, martial culture, and sacrificial religion to substantial portions of the north and west of the South Asian subcontinent. This social and geographical expansion of Indo-Aryan culture had as its concomitant a number of changes in religious ideology. The religion of the Vedas (the sacred hymns that formed the foundation of Indic religion) evolved gradually from a cosmology centered on sacrifice to a complex system anchored in highly abstract philosophical reflections that were expressed in detailed ritual and legal codes, historicized in a rich epic and narrative tradition, dramatized through the public generosity of the elite, and socially reproduced in the cults of many diverse localities. Brahmans—the priestly and scholarly elite—played a pivotal role both in the intellectual aspects of this transformation and in its social enactment.

The major economic shift that formed the backdrop for these ideological changes was the shift from an economy based on interaction between the mobile pastoralists and the hunting and gathering populations of the heavily forested subcontinent, to a gradual integration of both populations into complex, stratified, and multi-ethnic agricultural communities. These communities were formed on a model of society to be found as far back as one of the hymns of the *Rig Veda* (c. 1800–1300 BCE). According to this hymn, the primeval man (Purusha) was dismembered in a cosmic sacrifice. His mouth became the *brahman* caste (priests and teachers), his arms the *kshatriya* caste (warriors and kings), his thighs the *vaishya* (traders and agriculturalists), and his feet the *shudra* (servants and laborers for the three other ranks). This hierarchical model is the founding charter of Hindu society. In later centuries a very detailed body of teachings and codes (the Dharmasutras and the Dharmashastras) was evolved to describe and define the duties *(dharma)* and mutual relations of these social ranks. Built upon a hierarchical model of occupational specialization and moral interdependence, these codes became the cultural basis of a complex agricultural civilization, which continued to extend its economic and cultural influence over previously nonagricultural peoples and regions. This process of expansion continues today.

These economic and ideological developments were paralleled by changes in political theory and practice, which also had a religious basis. Even in the Vedic period, the king was regarded as a special vehicle of divinity, who through his great sacrifices maintained the proper balance in the universe. Increasingly, kings came to be identified as the upholders of *dharma,* that is, guardians of the social order and protectors of their subjects. The waging of war—and thus the conquest of new territories—was always regarded as the proper expression of the dominion *(kshatra)* of the righteous king. It is clear that by the early centuries of the common era the settled portions of the subcontinent supported many small states (and some large ones) that encompassed localized agricultural communities linked together by trade, crafts, pilgrimage, and migration.

Accompanying and facilitating these various developments in thought and social life was a major shift in the practical ethos of Indic religion. This is the shift from *yajna,* or worship through sacrifice, to *puja,* or the worship of vivified icons. The mature Vedic sacrifice was a cosmogonic ritual performance directed to invisible gods invited to temporary sacrificial spaces. *Puja,* on the other hand, was a rite of adoration offered to iconicized deities who were permanently established in the small-scale prayer rooms of households or the large-scale public sancta

of wood and stone temples. The rise of *puja* is also associated with the growth of temples, the rise of Shiva and Vishnu (the great gods of contemporary Hinduism), and, in general, the evolution of the various forms of theistic ideology and practice that we now call Hinduism. The gradual replacement of *yajna* by *puja* was supported, in part, by shifts in the forms of royal generosity, away from the periodic redistributive contexts of sacrifice and toward the permanent endowment of temples and brahman settlements through gifts of land. In the context of expanding kingdoms, the extension of agriculture, and the absorption of a variety of local cults into the Brahmanic fold, these shifts in elite patterns of generosity were probably not arbitrary.

These major transformations in the social history of early Hinduism were not always smooth or consensual processes. Buddhism and Jainism, the two great early heterodoxies of South Asia, represented major challenges to the power of the brahmans and the social order of Brahmanical society in the period from 600 to 300 BCE. The new forms of thought and practice that have been characterized here as constituting Hinduism were in large part the orthodox response to these challenges. In subsequent periods there were other challenges to Hindu dominance in the subcontinent and attendant changes in Hindu philosophy and practice, but by the end of the seventh century the social and intellectual edifice of Hinduism was firmly established in South Asia.

*Worldview.* The intellectual essentials of Hinduism are summarized only at some risk, for Hindu thought, as with all living traditions, has evolved through temporal processes of conflict and debate, reform and revival, addition and subtraction. Moreover, Hinduism encompasses arcane doctrines and speculations, and simple maxims and assumptions. These many strands have been transmitted in a wide variety of written texts (both in Sanskrit, the language of learning and orthodox ritual, and in the vernaculars) as well as through oral traditions. Written and oral traditions, furthermore, have always engaged in lively intercourse.

Hindu thought has always been resolutely utilitarian: even the most abstruse Hindu philosophical speculations (such as those contained in the Upanishads) regard knowledge as an instrument for liberation *(moksha)* from the bonds of phenomenal existence *(samsara)*. The most widely shared and deeply felt ontological assumption behind this pragmatic and soteriological orientation is the doctrine of karma and the closely linked doctrine of rebirth. Hindus assume the existence of an essential and permanent self *(atman)* that through ignorance *(avidya),* is plunged into a series of births that constitute entanglement in the illusory web *(maya)* of phenomenal existence. The law of karma (which can be glossed as the moral law of acts and consequences) dictates that every action must inexorably have a moral consequence and that consequences that are unfulfilled in one birth *(janma)* must necessitate another birth. These closely related theories supply not only a deterministic view of the link between worldly action and transmigration but also a distinctively Hindu theodicy. Much Hindu speculation as well as the bulk of Hindu ritual technique is directed, either directly or indirectly, at breaking the bonds of karma, at escaping the snare of rebirth, and at restoring the original serenity of the undivided self by reuniting it with godhead.

But the special genius of Hindu thought is to have linked in importance the law of karma (and the subsequent quest for liberation from rebirth) to *dharma,* the performance of one's social duties. Particularly emphasized are the duties of caste. It is probably the case that the peculiar tenacity of Hindu ideology is owed to the interdependence of those two concepts: while the prescriptions of *dharma* anchor the long-term abstractions of the law of karma in a very concrete here and now, the social injunctions of *dharma* acquire the special appeal of being dependable routes to liberation. This link is at the heart of Hindu social thought, although it is framed and contextualized by a plethora of theories and teachings about other matters. In popular Hinduism, these high-level ideas (and the textual traditions that embody them) have become internalized as assumptions and are less dwelt upon than the particulars of life-cycle rites, inquiries to astrologers, petitions to favored deities, pilgrimages to holy places, and a widespread concern with the doings and sayings of ascetics and holy persons of every type. Yet these two aspects of Hinduism acquire their significance only by reference to each other, and in the context of social life.

*Social Life.* The life of the average Hindu is everywhere touched by Hinduism, and sometimes dominated by it. Time is regulated by a lunar calendar that is the basis for popular Hindu almanacs. These almanacs provide detailed guides for discriminating between auspicious and inauspicious times for initiating any serious action. Astrology (and astrologers) provide more refined skills for prognostication and planning. The year is punctuated by feasts and fasts, festivals and celebrations, many of which honor specific deities, publicize particular

cults, and revive the social memory of the epics and the Puranas. There is, thus, considerable regional variation in the rhythms of the Hindu calendar.

Daily domestic life, particularly for members of the three upper castes, is filled with ritual prescriptions and prohibitions that govern the details of personal purity, social contact, and professional interaction. The landscape of most of the subcontinent is dotted with holy rivers, rocks, and trees, which, when taken together with the many monasteries and temples, compose a spatial and living archive of Hindu history. Often these sacred places are tied to the temporal traditions of the epics and Puranas. Monasteries frequently provide nodes of leadership and organization for translocal followings *(sampradaya)* whose continuity is maintained through teacher-disciple *(guru-shishya)* relationships. Temples attract regular local worshipers and servants as well as occasional, and more distant, pilgrims. Human motion is an important part of Hinduism. On the one hand, householders periodically undertake journeys to local (and distant) places of pilgrimage. On the other hand, a variety of ascetics and professional "wanderers" provide constant contact between places of habitation and places of worship or meditation. The sacred geography of Hinduism, which lays out the location of these places and the various routes and networks that link them, has roots as far back as the epics and the Puranas.

Crucial among the prescriptions of *dharma* are those that fall under the rubric of *varnashramadharma* (duties of caste and life stage). These roles are especially important for the three upper castes, who are conceived of as "twice-born" *(dvija)* by virtue of a rite of initiation called the *upanayana.* The ideal stages of life for these three upper castes are (1) student, (2) householder, (3) hermit, and (4) ascetic. The rules for how to handle these stages have been refined historically both by law *(shastra)* and by custom *(achara)* to account for a variety of special considerations of time and place. The Hindu understanding of pure and impure substances (their nature, powers, and risks) is a critical part of these rules and is the basis for regulating the interactions between castes.

Thus, from an ideological point of view, conformity with caste etiquette is part of the endless pursuit of purity and of liberation. Liberation itself is considered the most inclusive and superior of the four ends of Hindu life, the other three of which are duty *(dharma),* wealth *(artha),* and sensual pleasure *(kama).* In traditional Indic society, these complex and multiple social aims were held together by the mutual alliance of rulers and brahmans, who, by their sharing of ritual and political prerogatives and their domination of religious discourse, maintained social control.

*Protest and Withdrawal.* Internal criticisms of Hindu orthodoxy and brahman control of society have a long history in the subcontinent. Buddhism and Jainism, both of which reflected urban, mercantile, and *kshatriya* opposition to the excesses of Brahmanic ritualism and Vedic orthodoxy, are the historical models for such protest. In the early medieval period, starting in South India, movements based on multicaste participation, intense devotionalism, and vernacular poetry and theology swept through many parts of the subcontinent. These devotional *(bhakti)* movements have since represented a permanent repository of alternatives to the hierarchical, ritualistic, and rationalistic orthodoxies of Hinduism.

The introduced religions—notably Islam, but to some extent Christianity as well—provided incentives for conversion, especially to groups that were disenfranchised from within the Hindu framework. Islamic ideology provided the impetus and the model for certain reformist movements within Hinduism, and also provided a partial model for the latest major break from Hinduism: the Sikh faith. [*See* Sikhism.] In the nineteenth century, partly in response to the social changes of the colonial period and partly in response to direct Western criticisms of Hinduism, a variety of urban-based reform movements swept the Hindu middle classes, the most important of these being the Arya Samaj in Punjab, the Brahmo Samaj in Bengal, and the Theosophical movement in Madras. [*See* Arya Samaj *and* Brahmo Samaj.] The nationalist movement of the late nineteenth and twentieth centuries drew a good part of its vocabulary and sentiment from these "neo-Hindu" movements. Historically, the social basis for most of these movements has been provided either by disenchanted elites, by disenfranchised followings, or by both. However, such movements have had great difficulty at the level of social life, for, since they were defined as deviant castes or sects, they were neutralized.

But the oldest and most profound criticism of the Hindu mainstream is to be found in the tradition of asceticism, of religious renunciation and social withdrawal. The renouncer has been the alter ego of the brahman priest from the earliest periods of Indian history, and in some ways the constant reminder to all Hindus of the objective of life, which is to escape all lives. All Hindu injunctions, however mundane,

reflect some of the appeal and prestige of the renunciatory model, which has been described as a counterculture in light of orthodox Hinduism. To some degree, every conscientious Hindu enacts in his life choices and aspirations the tug-of-war between the obligations of *dharma* and the enchantment of *sannyasa* (ascetic withdrawal). Yet, since ascetics and holy men *(sadhus)* remain, by and large, within the Hindu fold and thus are accessible to laymen, the tension between renunciation and involvement in worldly affairs remains vital and generative, and not divisive or sterile. In the ideal processual model of the stages of life, all Hindus bridge the gap between these poles as they make their way through the vicissitudes and puzzles of *samsara*.

[*See also* Shaivism; Vaishnavism; Bhakti; Indo-Aryan Languages and Literatures; *and* Dravidian Languages and Literatures.]

A. L. Basham, *The Wonder That Was India* (1954). W. Norman Brown, *Man in the Universe: Some Continuities in Indian Thought* (1966). J. D. M. Derrett, *Religion, Law and the State in India* (1968). L. Dumont, *Homo Hierarchicus: The Caste System and Its Implications* (1970). Thomas J. Hopkins, *The Hindu Religious Tradition* (1971). K. W. Morgan, ed., *The Religion of the Hindus* (1958). Max Weber, *The Religion of India* (1958).

ARJUN APPADURAI

# HINDUIZATION. *See* Indianization.

# HINDU KUSH,

known as Caucasus Indicus by the ancient Greeks, is a mountain chain extending through east-central Afghanistan, merging with the Pamirs and Karakorams to the east. Averaging 150 miles in width, this range of granitic and metamorphic rock stands at a general height of fifteen thousand feet, reaching its highest peak, Tirich Mir, in Pakistan. Although the Hindu Kush, literally "killer of the Hindus," was a barrier for trade and movement, it could be crossed at two major passes, the Shibar (10,696 feet) and Salang (13,370 feet).

MICHAEL BONINE

# HINDU LAW.

In the Indian tradition law does not exist as a separate subject but, together with religion and mores, is an integral part of a broader concept, *dharma;* even as *dharma,* Hindu law is therefore based on the eternal and inalterable Veda. The earliest Sanskrit sources that focus on legal precepts are the Dharmasutras—which are entirely or mostly in prose and are attributed to Gautama, Apastamba, Baudhayana, Vasishtha, and Vishnu—and the versified Dharmashastras, attributed to Manu, Yajnavalkya, Narada, Brihaspati, Katyayana, and others. All these texts together make up the *smriti*, a literature the authoritativeness of which is surpassed only by that of the Veda itself.

The dates of the *smritis* are highly uncertain. It is generally assumed that the prose texts, in *sutra* style, are older than the *shastras*, in *shloka* meter. All that can be reasonably ascertained is that the principal texts of the *smriti* literature mentioned above were composed between 500 BCE and 500 CE, although some minor *smritis* may be of a more recent date.

With regard to legal procedure (*vyavahara*), the *smritis* recognize the authority of a variety of law courts whose judgments are based on the uncodified customs of tribes, guilds, merchants, the army, and so forth. Judgments in the highest court, presided over by the king (raja) assisted by learned brahman assessors, are founded on the Dharmashastras. The texts distinguish two kinds of evidence: human evidence, which includes the testimony of witnesses, written documents, and prolonged, undisturbed possession; and divine evidence, which consists of oaths and ordeals.

Substantive law (*vivada*) is invariably divided into eighteen *vivadapadas* ("titles of law" or "heads of litigation"). The several lists show minor variations, but the one in the *Manusmriti* is as follows: (1) nonpayment of debts, (2) deposit and pledge, (3) sale by one not the owner, (4) concerns among partners, (5) recovery of gifts, (6) nonpayment of wages, (7) breach of regulations within associations, (8) rescission of sale and purchase, (9) disputes between the owner of a herd and his herdsmen, (10) disputes regarding boundaries of villages and properties, (11) assault, (12) insult, (13) theft, (14) robbery and violence, (15) adultery, (16) duties of husband and wife, (17) partition and inheritance, and (18) gambling and betting.

The composition of *smritis* came to a close in about the eighth century CE. A vast commentarial literature then developed, with two types of commentaries: explications of particular *smritis* with only occasional references to other *smritis*, and digests (*nibandhas*) that consolidate provisions from a variety of *smritis* on specific topics. Even though we therefore have, in the *nibandhas*, a number of texts devoted entirely to *vivada* or *vyavahara* or both, in most cases these represent only subdivisions of larger compositions, other sections of which deal with different, nonlegal aspects of *dharma*.

Commentators consider all rules contained in the *smritis* to be authoritative, and make it their task to bring seemingly inconsistent or contradictory rules into harmony. Since different commentators, however, take different rules as their points of departure, and severally interpret other rules so as to fit them into congruent schemes, each of them creates a construct unlike that of any other. Some of these texts, the composition of which continued into the eighteenth century, are among the best specimens of panditic learning and casuistry.

The British administration of Hindu law began in 1772, with an order by Governor-General Warren Hastings proclaiming that "in all suits regarding inheritance, marriage, caste and other religious usages or institutions, the law . . . of the Shaster with respect to the Gentoos shall invariably be adhered to." This order led to the composition of the *Code of Gentoo Laws* commissioned by Hastings (1776), to Sir William Jones's studying Sanskrit to translate the *Manusmriti* (1794), and, most importantly, to the translation of *Two Treatises on the Hindu Law of Inheritance* by Henry Thomas Colebrooke (1810). The acceptance of one of these treatises, Jimutavahana's *Dayabhaga* (a section of a *nibandha*), as the law for Bengal, and of the other, the chapter on inheritance in Vijnaneshvara's *Mitakshara* (a commentary on the *Yajnavalkyasmriti*), as the law for the rest of India, introduced the concept of different "schools of Hindu law" for separate parts of the subcontinent. The subsequent translations of other commentaries and their acceptance as the law texts for subschools of the *Mitakshara* led to further geographical disparity in Hindu law. [*See also* Hastings, Warren *and* Jones, Sir William.]

Innovations in Anglo-Hindu law include focusing on law as distinct from religion; reliance on precedents and interpretations of Sanskrit texts recorded in earlier judgments, rather than on the texts themselves; priority of valid custom over written texts; application of the principles of justice, equity, and good conscience when the provisions of the texts were felt to be unacceptable; and the introduction of a number of acts overruling sections of Hindu law.

The Constituent Assembly of independent India stated as one of its goals the elimination of separate family laws not only for Hindus living in different parts of the country, but also for Hindus as distinct from other Indian citizens. According to the constitution, "The State shall endeavour to secure for the citizens a uniform civil code throughout the territory of India" (article 44). Yet, after the failure of the Hindu Code Bill, which was to provide all Hindus with a uniform family law, the system developed during the British period was carried over unaltered into independent India. The most important developments since independence have been four acts passed by Parliament, which made major sections of Hindu law obsolete and substituted modern laws based on entirely different principles: in 1955, the Hindu Marriage Act, and in 1956, the Hindu Succession Act, the Hindu Minority and Guardianship Act, and the Hindu Adoptions and Maintenance Act. Those sections of Hindu family law that are not covered by these and other minor acts remain, however, administered by Hindu law as it developed after 1810.

[*See also* Law: Judicial and Legal Systems of India; Indo-Aryan Languages and Literatures; *and* Hinduism.]

J. D. M. Derrett, *Hindu Law Past and Present* (1957) and *Dharmaśastra and Juridical Literature* (1973). P. V. Kane, *History of Dharmaśastra*, 5 vols. in 7 (2d rev. ed., 1968–1975). Robert Lingat, *The Classical Law of India*, translated by J. D. M. Derrett (1973). *Sacred Books of the East*, vols. 2, 7, 14, 25, 33 (1859).    LUDO ROCHER

HINDU MAHASABHA, an Indian political party founded in 1913 as a central body bringing together several provincial-level "Hindu *sabhas*," especially those in the Punjab and Bengal. The predecessor bodies had been founded partially in reponse to the formation of the Muslim League in 1906 and partly in opposition to what appeared to some Hindus to be concessions to the Muslims in the two provinces. Thus the Hindu Mahasabha strongly opposed the Lucknow Pact of 1916 in which the Congress accepted separate electorates and agreed to an allocation of seats among the various communities.

The Hindu Mahasabha also supported the process of *shuddhi* (reconversion of Muslims and others to Hinduism). In elections the party was never strong, although some with Mahasabha sympathies were elected under such labels as "Congress Nationalist." In the 1930s and 1940s, the principal leader of the party was Vinayak Damodar Savarkar (1883–1966), who said, "A Hindu means a person who regards this land of Bharatvarsha from the Indus to the seas as his Fatherland as well as his Holyland"(Savarkar, *Hindutva*, 1942, p. 1); thus adherents of "foreign religions" had no place in India. A more moderate leader, Shyama Prasad Mookerjee (1901–1953), was included briefly in Jawaharlal Nehru's first ministry and later helped found the

Bharatiya Jana Sangh, to which many Hindu Mahasabha members went after 1951. Although it won a few seats in Parliament in the first three general elections, the party has had little importance since independence.

[*See also* Savarkar, Vinayak Damodar; Shuddhi; Jana Sangh; All-India Muslim League; *and* Indian National Congress.]

Craig Baxter, *The Jana Sangh, a Biography of an Indian Political Party* (1969). Indra Prakash, *A Review of the History and Work of the Hindu Mahasabha and the Hindu Sanghatan Movement* (1952).    CRAIG BAXTER

HINDU RENAISSANCE, term applied to a period of renewed creativity in India resulting from the nineteenth-century synthesis of Hindu and Western culture. The introduction of Western education into their country exposed Indians to Western culture and institutional forms and encouraged them to adapt these to their own society. New religious societies such as the Brahmo Samaj in Bengal and the Arya Samaj in western India demanded the reform of traditional Hindu religion. New journals, magazines, and newspapers appeared in English, and revitalized Indian vernaculars employed the Western literary genres of the short story and the essay to express Indian concerns. Local societies such as the Puna Sarvajanik Sabha (1870) and the Madras Mahajana Sabha (1884) and pan-Indian groups such as the All-India National Congress (1885) used Western-style organizations to address indigenous political concerns.

[*See also* Arya Samaj *and* Brahmo Samaj.]

Charles Heimsath, *Indian Nationalism and Hindu Social Reform* (1964). Amit Sen, *Notes on the Bengal Renaissance* (1964).    JUDITH E. WALSH

HINDU SHAHI DYNASTY, name given by Muslim chroniclers to Hindu powers controlling northwestern India and eastern Afghanistan during the tenth and eleventh centuries. Between 977 and 1001 they successfully attacked the Ghaznavids three times, once reputedly with unified Hindu support. By 1010, however, the Hindu Shahi Anandapala became a Ghaznavid vassal. After his death hostilities were renewed, resulting in the final defeat of the Hindu Shahis about 1019, which ultimately facilitated the Islamic conquest of India. [*See also* Ghaznavid Dynasty.]    CATHERINE B. ASHER

HINDUSTAN. Although its literal meaning, in Persian, is "the country of the Hindus," or, broadly speaking, India, *Hindustan* may also connote a more restricted, but variously conceived, region north of the Vindhya Escarpment or of the Narmada River, which flows slightly to its south. In its most limited sense, *Hindustan* was taken to mean northern India exclusive of its eastern portion, referred to as Purab, but the inclusiveness of Purab is itself vague, sometimes seen as extending as far west as Awadh and Varanasi (Banaras) and sometimes no farther than Bihar. In Muslim histories (e.g., by Abu'l Fazl) *Hindustan* indicated an even smaller region: eastern Punjab, the areas now including Haryana and Delhi, eastern Rajasthan, and the greater part of modern Uttar Pradesh. More inclusive views (e.g., Jean de Thévenot, 1665) held that Hindustan extended all the way from the Indus to the Ganges. For those accepting these western and eastern limits and also the inclusion of peninsular India, Hindustan was the equivalent of the Ptolemaic "India intra Gangem" ("India within the Ganges"). This is in opposition to "India extra Gangem" ("India beyond the Ganges"), roughly Southeast Asia. (Following Ptolemy, European maps until well into the eighteenth century portrayed the Ganges as running almost due north-south.) Some European maps of the sixteenth and later centuries bore titles that equated Hindustan with the Mughal empire, whose limits were in more or less constant flux, but which did extend for long periods both east of the Ganges and south of the Narmada. At present, *Hindustan* is used by persons in various Muslim countries to refer to the area of the Republic of India.

[*See also* India *and* Ganges River.]

"Hindustan," in *Imperial Gazetteer of India, New Edition* (1908–1909), vol. 13, pp. 140–141. Henry Yule and A. C. Burnell, *Hobson-Jobson* (1903), pp. 416–418.

JOSEPH E. SCHWARTZBERG

HIRADO, island off northwest Kyushu, Japan. From 1550 to 1640 Hirado was a major port in Japan's foreign trade, the domain of the Matsuura family of daimyo. In ancient times a port on the diplomatic and trading routes between Japan and the continent, Hirado was first visited by Portuguese traders in 1550, who called there annually until 1561; the Portuguese were later joined by the Spanish, from 1584, the Dutch, in 1609, and the English, in 1613. Hirado also had a large community of resident Chinese traders until 1635, when all Chinese trade was restricted to the port of Nagasaki.

After the cession of Nagasaki to the Portuguese in 1580, Hirado's importance as a port of trade declined until the early seventeenth century, when it once more flourished under the influence of English and Dutch trade. But the English factory failed in 1622, and in 1641 the Tokugawa *bakufu* ordered the Dutch operations transferred to the island of Deshima, in Nagasaki harbor. Thereafter, Hirado was significant only as the seat of the Matsuura daimyo, a fishing port, and a center of local trade.

[*See also* Deshima.]

C. R. Boxer, *The Christian Century in Japan, 1549–1650* (1951). Richard Cocks, *Diary Kept by the Head of the English Factory in Japan, Diary of Richard Cocks, 1615–1622*, 3 vols. (1978–1980). Iwao Seiichi, "Li Tan, Chief of the Chinese Residents at Hirado, Japan in the Last Days of the Ming Dynasty," *Memoirs of the Research Department of the Toyo Bunko* 17 (1958): 27–83. Kato Eiichi, "The Japan-Dutch Trade in the Formative Period of the Seclusion Policy, Particularly on the Raw Silk Trade by the Dutch Factory at Hirado, 1620–1640," *Acta Asiatica* 30 (1976): 84–104.    RONALD P. TOBY

HIROHITO. Born on 29 April 1901, Hirohito is the 124th sovereign of Japan since the mythological founding emperor of Japan, Jimmu, who is alleged to have reigned from 660 to 585 BCE. Having acceded to the "sun throne" in 1926, Hirohito (the Shōwa emperor, or Shōwa Tennō) has had the longest reign of any Japanese emperor whose birth and reign dates have been historically verified (those from the sixth century CE onward).

The eldest of four sons born to Taishō Tennō (1879–1926, r. 1912–1926), Hirohito was reared and educated in a manner befitting both a Japanese sovereign and a modern world-monarch. Formal education at the Peers School and private tutoring included Japanese and Chinese history as well as world history and French language, and the Chinese classics and poetry as well as economics, natural history, and military affairs. He was especially interested in biology, and later became an authority on marine organisms and certain forms of plant life, publishing books on both subjects. Those entrusted with his overall education were for the most part prominent naval and army officers, such as Admiral Tōgō Heihachirō (1847–1934). Although instilled with virtues appropriate to his constitutional position as commander in chief of the imperial armed forces in pre–World War II Japan, Hirohito was not a military person either by temperament or by physical bearing.

Hirohito was installed as crown prince in 1912, and his engagement to Princess Nagako, daughter of Imperial Prince Kuni Kunihiko, was made public in 1919. Although a controversy arose over alleged color blindness on Princess Nagako's maternal side, the marriage took place in 1924. The marriage signaled the end of the ancient system of court ladies and the establishment of monogamy in the palace.

In 1921, after completion of his formal education, Hirohito toured Britain and Western Europe, the first crown prince in Japan's history to go abroad. When he returned that year he was made regent for his father, who had suffered ill health almost from birth; Taishō Tennō died on 25 December 1926.

Hirohito's reign was designated Shōwa, "enlightened harmony." The first half of his rule was far from harmonious, however, both domestically and internationally. His enthronement in November 1928 took place in the midst of the Zhang Zuolin affair, which marked the point of no return for Japanese militarism in China. Assassinations, culminating in the 26 February 1936 coup attempt, which paralyzed Tokyo for over four days, ended the promising start of party government made in the late 1910s. War with China in 1937 and the Pacific War in 1941 led to Japan's defeat in 1945 and to the unprecedented occupation of Japan by foreign troops from 1945 to 1952.

During this tumultuous period Hirohito remained a moderate, insisting that the precepts of constitutional government set down by his grandfather, Mutsuhito, the Meiji emperor, be followed. Hirohito's opposition to the militarist coup of 26 February 1936 was instrumental in its suppression. In August 1945 he broke the deadlock among his ministers and accepted the Potsdam Declaration, thereby surrendering Japan to occupation by Allied forces. His radio broadcast announcing Japan's surrender to his subjects paved the way for their acceptance of the Occupation.

During the Occupation, Japan's constitution of 1889 underwent a drastic revision under which the emperor lost all political power. Sovereignty was vested in the people and the emperor was made "symbol of the State and of the unity of the people." Apparently with the endorsement of Hirohito, some members of the imperial family, and the palace bureaucracy in general, a massive public effort was made to "democratize" and popularize the emperor and imperial institution. Touring his war-torn country in a worn and baggy Western suit, Hirohito was no longer seen as the sacrosanct glory of Japan but as an all-too-human monarch symbolizing defeat and failure. Since then, the government, palace bureaucracy, and mass media have portrayed Hirohito and his family as somewhat idealized human beings; they are presented to the public as warm, close, "modern," and devoted to their people. Japan's efforts at a new and peaceful internationalism were symbolized by Hirohito's visit to Western Europe in 1971 and his visit to the United States in 1975; he is the first reigning emperor of Japan to have traveled abroad.

Hirohito has reigned over possibly the most momentous period in Japan's history, witnessing the rise of a potential parliamentary democracy in the 1920s, the bureaucratic fascism and militarism of the 1930s and the Occupation of the 1940s, and the establishment of a parliamentary democracy with the world's second-largest gross national product. A man of frugal habits, scientific interests, and disciplined attention to public duties throughout his reign, he perhaps symbolizes more than any other person or institution the trauma of Japan's emergence as a modern democratic state.

[See also Shōwa Period.]

Hane Mikiso, *Emperor Hirohito and His Chief Aide-de-Camp: The Honjo Diary, 1933–36* (1982). Leonard Mosley, *Hirohito, Emperor of Japan* (1966). David A. Titus, "The Making of the 'Symbol Emperor System' in Postwar Japan," *Modern Asian Studies* 14.4 (1980). Herschel Webb and David A. Titus, "Emperor," in *Encyclopedia of Japan*, vol. 2 (1983).        DAVID A. TITUS

HIROSHIMA, the name of both a city and prefecture in the Chūgoku region of southwestern Honshu, Japan. On 6 August 1945, near the end of World War II, with an aerial bombing by the United States the city became the site of the first explosion of an atomic device over a populated area. The city's Atomic Bomb Dome (the only building left unreconstructed after the bombing) and Peace Memorial Park today serve as grim monuments to the approximately 200,000 lives lost in the blast.

During the Tokugawa period (1600–1868) the city was the site of a castle town under the administration of the Asano daimyo. The fief that the Asano held had an assessed productivity of 426,000 *koku*, or approximately 2.2 million bushels of rice. The castle itself had been constructed by Mōri Terumoto in 1589, but after the Battle of Sekigahara in 1600 Tokugawa Ieyasu awarded control to Fukushima Masanori. Fukushima lost the castle to Asano Nagaakira when he attempted to implement an unauthorized expansion of its defenses. After the

Meiji Restoration (1868) the city became, during the Sino-Japanese War, the temporary command post of the Meiji emperor.

The modern city is part of the Hiroshima-Kure industrial district, the most important manufacturing district between Kobe and northern Kyushu. The region is a major center for shipbuilding and the production of steel, heavy machinery, and automobiles. Kure holds the distinction of having been, before World War II, the greatest fortified naval base and arsenal in East Asia. The region is located along the Sanyō railway line at the mouth of Hiroshima Bay, which is famous for its oyster beds. Hiroshima, with a population of 717,000 in 1975 (1981 est., 910,700), is the eleventh largest city in Japan.

Hiroshima Prefecture was created in 1877 by the amalgamation of three former prefectures: Hiroshima, Fukuyama, and Nakatsu. It supports a population of 2.52 million in an area of 8,448 square kilometers (3,258 square miles). The prefectural capital and largest city is Hiroshima City.

THOMAS R. SCHALOW

**HIZBU'LLAH AND SABILI'LLAH,** two Indonesian Islamic guerrilla organizations that fought the Dutch between 1945 and 1950. Both formed part of Masjumi, an Islamic party. Hizbu'llah ("Allah's forces"), founded in December 1944, was intended to become a PETA reserve corps in the war against the Allies and was open to youths between seventeen and twenty-five years of age. Its first chairman was Zainul Arifin and its first vice-chairman Moh Roemn. In August 1945 it had about five hundred trained members. Only after the declaration of Indonesian independence did the Hizbu'llah become one of Indonesia's largest irregular guerrilla organizations.

Sabili'llah (or Sabil Allah, "the way of God") was founded in November 1945 to serve as an instrument for the general mobilization of the Islamic population in the struggle against the Dutch. Founded alongside Hizbu'llah, it was intended for all who could not join Hizbu'llah (for instance, because they were too old). In practice, the distinction between the two was not as clear-cut as on paper.

[*See also* Masjumi *and* PETA.]

C. VAN DIJK

**HIZEN,** premodern Japanese province (modern Nagasaki Prefecture) located on the northwestern coast of Kyushu. Because of its proximity to the Asiatic mainland, Hizen was important early in Japan's history as the most important point of contact with Chinese culture. Buddhism, Confucianism, the Chinese script, and Chinese arts were but a few of the continental influences that entered the archipelago through Hizen.

In the sixteenth century, Hizen was under the control of the Ryūzōji house, one of the powerful Warring States (Sengoku) daimyo families of Kyushu, and it was also a center of Catholic missionary activity and Western trade.

During the Tokugawa period (1600–1868), Hizen was divided among several daimyo houses, the largest being the *tozama* daimyo house of Nabeshima at Saga, assessed at 357,000 *koku* (measures of rice). Hizen also saw the start of the Shimabara Rebellion of 1637–1638, in which Christian peasants rose to protest excessive taxation by local daimyo. The shogunate viewed the rebellion as a Christian, and hence foreign, threat and, after crushing it, issued the Seclusion Edicts, which banned Christian proselytization and practice, expelled all missionaries and foreigners, and closed the country to foreign contact with the exceptions of the Dutch and the Chinese. [*See* Christianity: Christianity in Japan; Sakoku; and Shimabara.]

During the Tokugawa period, Nagasaki, the principal port of Hizen, was the only port open to foreign trade, and that only on a limited basis with the Chinese and the Dutch. The Dutch, confined to the man-made island of Deshima in Nagasaki Harbor, served as the shogunate's "window on the West," and provided the Japanese with knowledge about European astronomy, medicine, arts, and so on. Essential in the dissemination of this knowledge were the physicians attached to the Dutch trading establishment on Deshima. Japanese scholars interested in "things foreign" flocked to Nagasaki, and subsequently created the *rangaku* ("Dutch learning") movement. [*See* Deshima *and* Rangaku.]

Hizen was also famous for its porcelain and other arts. The famous Imari and Kakiemon porcelain produced during the Tokugawa period filled the mansions and palaces of Europe, while the more exquisite Nabeshima wares were produced for the exclusive use of that daimyo family. Woodblock print artists and painters who specialized in foreign themes constituted the "Nagasaki school."

John Bowers, *Western Medical Pioneers in Feudal Japan* (1970). C. R. Boxer, *The Christian Century in Japan, 1549–1650* (1967). Englebert Kaempfer, *The History of Japan, Together with a Description of the Kingdom of*

*Siam, 1690–1692,* 3 vols. (1906). Takeshi Nagatake, *Famous Ceramics of Japan,* vol. 4, *Imari* (1982).

RONALD J. DiCENZO

**HLUTTAW,** the central executive organ of the Burmese monarchy. In the Konbaung-dynasty period (1752–1886), the Hluttaw supervised all administrative affairs, including religion, through up to one hundred administrative departments. Directing its work were ministers called *wungyi,* usually but not always four in number, who were appointed by the ruler and served at his pleasure. Typically supervised by the crown prince, the Hluttaw was a large structure within the royal fort, manned round the clock by a staff and at least one *wungyi.* Only the king's private affairs and the guard units of the interior palace were not controlled by the Hluttaw; these were handled by the Byedaik, a privy council outside of Hluttaw control. The Hluttaw is known to have existed in the Pagan period (1044–1287), but little is known of it until the early seventeenth century, when it had probably assumed the above form and function.    WILLIAM J. KOENIG

**HMONG** (also known as Meo or Miao), people of upland northern Southeast Asia and South China, of particular importance in the recent history of Laos and of the international opium trade.

The Hmong can be associated linguistically only with the Yao people, and their origins are similarly obscure. They were early neighbors of the Chinese in the Yellow River valley, and through the succeeding four or five millennia they can be traced through Chinese records to locations farther and farther south, pushed before the expanding Chinese empire. They achieved some degree of political centralization in southeast China in the early centuries of the common era, but their attempts to assert independence were thwarted by imperial China. The historical records of China and Vietnam continue to mention Hmong insurrections almost continually from the ninth century to the twentieth. Defeats thrust them farther southwest, and they appeared in Laos and then in Thailand in the last half of the nineteenth century.

Of an estimated eight million Hmong in Asia, most live in China, with only about fifty thousand each in Laos and Thailand. They have a highly developed kinship and clan organization but have rarely displayed political organization above the village level. Most practice their traditional religion, although Christian missionaries have had some success with them in Southeast Asia and have created a written system for the Hmong language. Most Hmong practice slash-and-burn rice agriculture, moving their villages periodically to work on new land. In Laos they were driven into opium production and also became heavily involved as mercenaries and soldiers on both sides in the Indochina conflict, notably under General Vang Pao. Because of their involvement with the US government, many subsequently emigrated to the United States.

[*See also* Vang Pao.]

"The Meo," in *Minority Groups in Thailand* (1970), pp. 573–688. A. W. McCoy, *The Politics of Heroin in Southeast Asia* (1972).    DAVID K. WYATT

**HO** (Haw), Chinese brigands who pillaged Laos and Vietnam in the 1870s and 1880s. They were mainly Chinese who fled either the chaos of the Taiping Rebellion or the Chinese government's successful efforts to end the rebellion. They took refuge as brigands in the highlands of northwestern Vietnam and adjacent areas of Laos and were organized in bands known by the colors of their banners. The Red Flags, headquartered in eastern Siang Khwang Province, sacked Vientiane and the middle Mekong Valley in 1872; the Black Flags of Dien Bien Phu, led by Deo Van Tri, took Luang Prabang in 1887 after repeatedly threatening Hanoi. The Luang Prabang kings and their Siamese suzerains were unable to restore order, and the French suppressed the last of the brigands only early in the twentieth century.

[*See also* Dupuis, Jean; Un Kham; Garnier, Francis; *and* Black Flags.]

E. S. Laffey, "French Adventurers and Chinese Bandits in Tonkin," *Journal of Southeast Asian Studies* 6 (1975): 38–51. Henry McAleavy, *Black Flags in Vietnam* (1968). Hugh Toye, *Laos: Buffer State or Battleground* (1968).

DAVID K. WYATT

**HOA HAO.** Founded by Huynh Phu So (1919–1947) in 1939, the Vietnamese Hoa Hao Buddhist sect has its roots in the Buu Son Ky Huong ("strange fragrance from the precious mountain") movement of the mid-nineteenth century. Named for Huynh's home village in the southern province of Chau Doc, the Hoa Hao developed ties with the Japanese occupation forces and later with Vietnamese Trotskyites. Although often weakened by factional dispute, the Hoa Hao resisted communist infiltration and later fought government forces during the first year of the Ngo Dinh Diem regime. Although defeated in 1955, the movement remained a powerful anticommunist force in the western Mekong Delta.

[See also Huynh Phu So and Ngo Dinh Diem.]

Bernard Fall, "The Political-Religious Sects of Vietnam," *Pacific Affairs* 28.3 (September 1955): 235–253. Hue-Tam Ho Tai, *Millenarianism and Peasant Politics in Vietnam* (1983).          BRUCE M. LOCKHART

**HOA LU,** capital of Dai Co Viet during the Dinh and Former Le periods (968–1009), located in a narrow river valley near the present town of Gia Vien, about sixty-five kilometers south of Hanoi. Hoa Lu was the birthplace of Dinh Bo Linh, also known as Dinh Tien Hoang ("first emperor"), and the place from which he extended his power over the Red River Delta. The temple of Dinh Tien Hoang is located here.

[See also Dai Co Viet; Dinh Bo Linh; and Le Dynasties.]

Keith W. Taylor, *The Birth of Vietnam* (1983).

JAMES M. COYLE

**HOANG NOA THAM.** See De Tham.

**HO CHI MINH,** founder and leader of the Vietnamese communist movement and president of the Democratic Republic of Vietnam from 1945 until his death in 1969. He was born Nguyen Sinh Cung on 19 May 1890 in Nghe An Province in central Vietnam. His father, Nguyen Sinh Sac, had received a traditional Confucian education and entered the imperial bureaucracy, but he eventually resigned, allegedly to protest growing French domination over his country. As a child, Ho attended the prestigious National Academy in Hue but, possibly in response to his father's political views and growing contempt for traditional education, abandoned schooling before graduation. After a brief period as a schoolteacher, he signed on as a cook's apprentice with a French steamship company.

After spending several years at sea, Ho settled in London during World War I; there he worked in a restaurant and was first exposed to Marxist ideas. Moving to Paris, he adopted the pseudonym Nguyen Ai Quoc (Nguyen the Patriot) and first came to public attention when he presented a petition to the Versailles Peace Conference demanding independence for Vietnam in accordance with the principle of self-determination. He also became active in radical circles and in 1920 became a founding member of the French Communist Party. During the next three years he worked actively among radical exile groups from the colonies who were living in France, participating in an Intercolonial Union formed under Communist sponsorship and publishing an anticolonial journal, *Le Paria (The Pariah)*.

In 1923 Ho was summoned to Moscow, where he studied Marxist doctrine and worked at Comintern headquarters. Already identified as a vigorous spokesman for the anticolonial cause, he served as a delegate with the Peasant International and urged the Communist International to take the lead in promoting revolution in Asia. In late 1924 he was sent to Canton as an interpreter for the Comintern mission to the revolutionary government of Sun Yatsen. His real assignment was to establish a communist movement in French Indochina. Within months Ho recruited radical Vietnamese patriots living in exile in South China into a new revolutionary organization, the Vietnam Revolutionary Youth League. In conformity with prevailing Leninist theory and Ho's own proclivities, the league's program combined social revolution with nationalism and soon became a leading force within patriotic circles in Vietnam.

In the spring of 1927 Ho was forced to leave Canton because of Chiang Kai-shek's crackdown on local Communists. He spent the next three years in Europe and in Siam, where he recruited within the Vietnamese exile community living in the provinces. In early 1930 he returned to South China to resolve a factional squabble within the league and, at a meeting held in Hong Kong, presided over the formation of a formal Communist Party. He remained in Hong Kong as liaison officer for the Comintern's Far Eastern Bureau and was imprisoned by British authorities in 1931. Released in 1933 as a result of pleas by a British civil rights organization, he went to Moscow and spent the next several years in the Soviet Union, reportedly recovering from tuberculosis. There were rumors that he was in Stalin's disfavor because of his nationalist views, but in August 1935 he attended the Seventh Comintern Congress.

In 1938 Ho went to China, where he briefly visited Chinese Communist headquarters in Yan'an and then served as a guerrilla training instructor in central China. In the summer of 1940, with war approaching, he returned to South China and established contact with leading members of the Indochinese Communist Party. The following May, with most of Vietnam under Japanese occupation, he chaired a meeting of the Central Committee just inside the Vietnamese border. It announced the formation of the League for the Independence of Vietnam (Viet Minh for short), a new front organized under Party leadership to seek independence from French rule and Japanese military occupation. During the next few years—interrupted by another stint in a Chinese prison—Ho led the Party in seeking popular support for the Viet Minh front and building up its guerrilla forces for an uprising at the close of the war.

In August 1945, Viet Minh forces launched an insurrection to seize power throughout Vietnam. Hanoi was occupied with little resistance, and in early September a Democratic Republic of Vietnam was created, with Ho Chi Minh—in his first public use of the name—as president. For the next several months Ho attempted to broaden the popular base of the new government while seeking a negotiated settlement with France. Politically astute and conciliatory, he managed to reduce the distrust of rival nationalist leaders and reached agreement on a coalition cabinet at the end of the year. Early in 1946 a National Assembly was elected and confirmed him as president. In the meantime, protracted negotiations with the French representative in Indochina resulted in a preliminary agreement calling for the creation of a Vietnamese "free state" within the French Union. Both achievements, however, were short lived. In the summer of 1946, the tenuous alliance between the Viet Minh and the nationalists broke down, and the latter were driven out of the government. Meanwhile, negotiations with the French foundered when they retreated from the terms of the preliminary agreement. In September, despite the misgivings of Party colleagues, Ho signed a *modus vivendi* in Paris, but on his return to Hanoi, tensions between Vietnamese and French forces escalated, and in December war broke out.

During the next several years, Viet Minh forces retreated to the hills and fought against French forces in the lowlands. By 1954, the French had wearied of the war and sought a negotiated settlement. Once again, militant elements in the Party resisted a compromise, but Ho used his formidable influence to gain the approval of his colleagues, and in July an agreement was reached calling for a truce and a temporary division of Vietnam into a communist north and a noncommunist south.

After 1954, Ho Chi Minh remained president of the Democratic Republic of Vietnam and chairman of the Party but gradually turned over day-to-day responsibilities to trusted lieutenants such as Pham Van Dong, Truong Chinh, and Le Duan. He played a symbolic role as head of state and as a mediator of Party disputes and was active on the international scene, where he promoted Vietnamese national interests within the socialist bloc and attempted to prevent the widening split between Moscow and Beijing. Convinced of the importance of Soviet friendship, he was also sensitive to the brooding presence of China and attempted to maintain cordial relations with the leaders of both communist states. During the 1960s, he appeared to decline in health and his role was reduced to occasional public appearances. He died of an apparent heart attack on 3 September 1969, at the age of seventy-nine.

Ho Chi Minh's importance to modern Vietnam can hardly be exaggerated. He was not only the founder of the Communist Party but also its recognized leader during most of its first half-century of existence. He provided it with ideological guidance, international prestige, a tradition of internal unity, and a sense of realism that on many occasions enabled it to triumph over adversity. Today he remains the symbol of the nation. His memory is enshrined in a mausoleum in Hanoi and in a new name for Saigon—Ho Chi Minh City.

[*See also* Vietnam Revolutionary Youth League; Indochinese Communist Party; Viet Minh; Vietnam, Democratic Republic of; French Indochina War; Pham Van Dong; Truong Chinh; Le Duan; *and* Communism: Communism in Southeast Asia.]

Anonymous, *Our President Ho Chi Minh* (1970) and *Ho Chi Minh: Selected Writings* (1977). Joseph Buttinger, *Vietnam: A Dragon Embattled* (1967). King Chen, *Vietnam and China, 1938–1954* (1969).

WILLIAM J. DUIKER

HO CHI MINH CITY (formerly Saigon), major city in the Socialist Republic of Vietnam. During the period before the Vietnamese expansion into the Mekong Delta, Ho Chi Minh City—then known as Prey Nokor—was an important trading center in the Cambodian empire. As early as 1623, Vietnamese strength and Cambodian weakness enabled Dai Viet to gain control of customs rights for the city. In 1698 the Vietnamese annexed the delta territory and established the provinces of Tran Bien (Bien Hoa) and Phien Tran (Gia Dinh), placing a viceroy in the city in 1699.

At the time of the Tay Son rebellion, the Gia Dinh area was of increasing strategic importance. The citadel of Gia Dinh, on the outskirts of what is now

Ho Chi Minh City, was occupied and reoccupied by the Nguyen and Tay Son forces, the latter finally gaining firm control in 1783. Five years later, Nguyen Anh (Emperor Gia Long; r. 1802–1819) returned with a larger and stronger army and retook Gia Dinh. The city then became the base for his operations against the Tay Son in the region. Once the Tay Son were overthrown and the Nguyen empire established, Gia Dinh continued to play a key administrative and military role, while Cho Lon, the Chinese section, was a commercial center. It also attracted French interest, however, and military operations between 1859 and 1861 resulted in the 1862 Treaty of Saigon, ceding three delta provinces to France.

The French occupied the three southwestern provinces in 1867, and Saigon became the capital of the colony of Cochinchina. As such it remained the center of French power in southern Indochina throughout the colonial period, and the city of Saigon became more European and cosmopolitan in character than Hanoi or Hue. Similarly, as the capital of the Republic of Vietnam, it was perhaps most severely influenced by the American presence. After the fall of the South Vietnamese government in April 1975, Saigon was renamed Ho Chi Minh City.

[See also Cho Lon; Cochinchina; Gia Long; Saigon, Treaty of; Tay Son Rebellion.]

BRUCE M. LOCKHART

## HODGSON, BRIAN HOUGHTON (1800–1894), pioneer Buddhist scholar, linguist, and naturalist who served as the British Resident in Kathmandu from 1833 to 1842. Hodgson's researches and extensive collection of Sanskrit, Newari, and Tibetan Buddhist manuscripts were a major catalyst to the development of Buddhist scholarship in the middle of the nineteenth century. His writings on the history, language, and ethnology of Nepal remain an invaluable source in the study of the Himalayan region.    RICHARD ENGLISH

## HO DYNASTY, Viet ruling house (1400–1407), founded by Ho Quy Ly, maternal relation of the last Tran emperors. After reigning nine months, he abdicated in favor of his son Ho Han Thuong but retained power as *thai thuong hoang* (retired emperor). The Ho were overthrown by the Chinese invasion of 1406.

Ho Quy Ly, also known by his adoptive name of Le Quy Ly, was made a minister in 1371 by his cousin, Emperor Tran Nghe-tong (r. 1370–1373).

As *thuong-hoang* (1373–1394), the diffident Nghe-tong allowed Quy Ly to gain control over both military and civil affairs. Engineering the deposition and execution of emperors Tran Nghien-de (Phe-de, r. 1377–1388) and Thuan-tong (r. 1388–1398), Quy Ly became regent for his three-year-old grandson, Tran An-tong (r. 1398–1400). In 1400 Quy Ly assumed the style of emperor by resuming his family name of Ho, proclaiming a new title for his reign, and changing the name of the country from Dai Viet to Dai Ngu.

After the defeat of the last of the Cham invasions (1390), Quy Ly began to implement an ambitious program of reforms designed to alleviate the economic and social crisis of the late Tran. The army was reorganized and increased and a program of military construction initiated. Paper money was introduced to help relieve a currency shortage. Personal taxes were graduated according to individual landholdings, which in 1397 were limited to no more than ten *mau* for all but princes. Slaveholding was strictly restricted.

Ho Quy Ly's usurpation, his bloody suppression of opposition, and his reforms brought him the enmity of many of the powerful families, few of which supported the Ho when Chinese armies invaded in November 1406. Ho Quy Ly and Ho Han Thuong were captured by the Chinese (16–17 June 1407) and deported to China, bringing the Ho dynasty to an end.

E. Gaspardone, "Le Qui-Ly," in *Dictionary of Ming Biography,* edited by L. Carrington Goodrich (1976). Thomas Hodgkin, *Vietnam: The Revolutionary Path* (1981).

JAMES M. COYLE

## HŌGEN AND HEIJI WARS, two civil disturbances of the late Heian period (794–1185) in Japan. The first conflict arose from strife within the imperial house and the Fujiwara regent's house. In the imperial house, the retired emperor Toba had crossed the former emperor Sutoku by enthroning his foe Go-Shirakawa in 1155. The split in the regent's house ranged former regent Fujiwara no Tadazane and his favorite son Yorinaga against his eldest son Fujiwara no Tadamichi. Upon the death of Toba in 1156, the frustrated Sutoku joined forces with Tadazane and Yorinaga; they employed two malcontent warriors, Minamoto no Tameyoshi and Taira no Tadamasa, to carry out a coup. Go-Shirakawa, however, commanded Taira no Kiyomori and Tameyoshi's son, Minamoto no Yoshitomo, to lead a night attack against Tadamasa and Tameyoshi. As a result of the victory, Sutoku was ban-

ished to Sanuki, Yorinaga was killed, and both Tameyoshi and Tadamasa perished at the hands of their relatives. The Hōgen War marked not only the destruction of Sutoku's faction, but also the militarization of court politics and Kyoto society.

The Heiji War occurred three years later in 1159. Taira no Kiyomori and Fujiwara no Michimori advanced rapidly in the esteem of ex-emperor Go-Shirakawa, while Minamoto no Yoshitomo and another courtier, Fujiwara no Nobuyori, grew jealous. When Kiyomori made a pilgrimage to Kumano Shrine, the two attempted another coup. They killed Michimori, imprisoned both Emperor Nijō and Go-Shirakawa, and had themselves appointed to offices they desired. Kiyomori returned to the capital and defeated Nobuyori in the streets of Kyoto. Nobuyori was executed and Yoshitomo was murdered as he fled eastward. While the Hōgen War marked the rise of the military in Kyoto politics, the Heiji disturbance delivered a serious blow to the Minamoto clan and ensured the rise of Taira no Kiyomori.

[See also Heian Period.]

Edwin O. Reischauer, trans., "The Heiji Monogatari," in Translations from Early Japanese Literature, edited by Edwin O. Reischauer and Joseph Yamagiwa (1951).

WAYNE FARRIS

HOHHOT. See Huhehaote.

HOKKAIDO, the northernmost of the four main islands of the Japanese archipelago. Hokkaido is bounded by the Sea of Japan, the Sea of Okhotsk, and the Pacific Ocean; it is separated from Sakhalin by the La Pérouse (Sōya) Strait (sixty-four kilometers), from Honshu by the Tsugaru Strait (thirty kilometers), and from Kunashiri (one of the Kurile Islands) by the Nemuro Strait (seventeen kilometers). The Nemuro Strait forms a frontier with the USSR. Soviet-occupied Kaigara Atoll in the Habomai Islands lies only 3.7 kilometers from Cape Nosappu, Hokkaido's eastern tip.

With an area of 78,509 kilometers, Hokkaido is the second largest of Japan's four main islands. Japanese sources commonly give Hokkaido's area as 83,519 square kilometers, an area that includes the southern Kuriles (Kunashiri, Etorofu, Shikotan, and the Habomai Islands), occupied since 1945 by the USSR.

At 22 percent of Japan's area, Hokkaido accounts for only 5 percent (5,656,808 in 1982) of Japan's population. The southern and western parts of the island are the most densely populated. A quarter of Hokkaido's residents live in the prefectural capital, Sapporo (with a population of 1,444,981 in 1982).

Hokkaido lies at the northern limit of the temperate zone and has a climate similar to that of northern Europe and southern Canada. The eastern side of the island facing the Sea of Okhotsk has the coldest winters. However, snowfall is heaviest on the side facing the Sea of Japan.

Hokkaido's fauna and flora differ from those of Honshu and share traits with those found in the Soviet Maritime Province and on Sakhalin. Pine, birch, beech, oak, and larch forests cover 76 percent of the island. Arable land is found mostly on the plain drained by the Ishikari River and on the Oshima Peninsula (Hokkaido's southern extremity). Coastal marine life is rich, although heavy exploitation has reduced the numbers of some species of fish, notably herring and salmon.

*History.* Until about 12,000 years ago, Hokkaido was at various times linked to Sakhalin and Honshu by isthmuses, facilitating access to the island by prehistoric migrants. Remains of Paleolithic (circa 30,000 BCE) and Neolithic (early Jōmon, circa 5,000 BCE) cultures have been found on Hokkaido. Relics of the Okhotsk Culture (circa 400–1000 CE) on Hokkaido link the island with a maritime culture that extended around the Okhotsk Sea littoral.

Eighth-century Japanese chronicles relate of expeditions against northern barbarians called variously "Ezo," "Emishi," or "Ebishi"; these may have been ancestors of the Ainu. The origin of the Ainu and the date of their earliest habitation of Hokkaido have not been established, but it is generally thought that Ainu were on Hokkaido by the tenth century CE.

The earliest Japanese contacts with Hokkaido cannot be determined with precision. They probably date from the twelfth century, when merchants crossed the Tsugaru Strait to an island referred to as "Ezo" in order to trade with the "Ezo." With the growth of knowledge of northern geography, the term Ezo came to refer to Hokkaido, Sakhalin, and the Kuriles collectively.

During the fifteenth century the Kakizaki, retainers of the Andō clan of northern Honshu, crossed the Tsugaru Strait and wrested control of the Oshima Peninsula from the Ezo barbarians. In the late sixteenth century the Kakizaki renounced their vassalage to the Andō and in 1600 were enfeoffed by Tokugawa Ieyasu with a new family name, Matsumae.

Ezo was ruled by the lords of Matsumae throughout the Tokugawa period (1600–1868), except during two interims (1799–1821, 1854–1868) when the shogunate assumed direct control in order to strengthen the northern frontier. Matsumae clan influence, which in 1600 had been confined to the Oshima Peninsula, gradually spread throughout the island and, by 1800, onto Sakhalin and the Kuriles. Ainu rebellions in 1669 and 1789 did not remove the aboriginal population from subjection to and dependence upon a system of Japanese trading posts. A fishing industry grew as Ezo marine products found a national market and export via Nagasaki to China. Rice began to be cultivated on the Oshima Peninsula, and modest efforts toward colonization were made under shogunal auspices. Hakodate, on the Oshima Peninsula, was one of two ports opened by Commodore Matthew C. Perry in the Treaty of Kanagawa (1854). Hakodate soon became a regional center for foreign commerce, attracting a number of Russian residents. [*See* Kanagawa Treaty.]

The fall of the Tokugawa shogunate and the creation of an imperial government under the nominal leadership of the Meiji emperor in 1868 was accompanied by a civil war in northern Japan. Diehard shogunal supporters led by Enomoto Takeaki (1836–1908), having escaped from Edo (Tokyo) in several warships, seized Hakodate in 1868. Enomoto's short-lived Ezo government surrendered in 1869 to imperial forces. [*See* Enomoto Takeaki.]

One of the first acts of the Meiji government in northern Japan was to give Ezo a new name: Hokkaido ("northern sea route"). The island was placed under the authority of the Hokkaido Colonization Office (Hokkaidō Kaitakushi). From 1869 until 1882, the Kaitakushi implemented a wide range of programs designed to strengthen Japan's northern frontier against Russian encroachment: road and port construction, colonization by farmer-soldiers, land reclamation, coal mining, and the establishment of light industries. In the introduction of new agricultural technology, a notable role was played by American advisers such as Horace Capron and William S. Clark. Clark's 1877 exhortation ("Boys, be ambitious!") to students at the Sapporo Agricultural College (subsequently Hokkaido University) has become part of Hokkaido folklore. Under Kaitakushi auspices, former warriors (notably from fiefs that had supported the Tokugawa shogunate in 1868 and hence enjoyed little favor with the Meiji government) were resettled in Hokkaido as farmers. In 1871, Sakhalin was placed under the purview of the Hokkaidō Kaitakushi. In 1875, when Japan renounced its claims to sovereignty over Sakhalin to Russia in exchange for the central and northern Ku-

riles (Treaty of Saint Petersburg), the entire Kurile arc became for administrative purposes part of Hokkaido.

Upon the abolition of the Kaitakushi in 1882, Hokkaido was divided into three prefectures (Hakodate, Sapporo, and Nemuro). In 1886, these prefectures were united and placed under the Hokkaido Office (Hokkaidō-chō), which has until the present overseen the island's administration and development.

Being a frontier area, Hokkaido enjoyed less local administrative autonomy than did other prefectures until after World War II. Development plans were centrally formulated and regional offices were appointive rather than elective. Only in 1948 did the new Local Administration Law give Hokkaido an elected governor and the same administrative system as other prefectures.

Hokkaido suffered less than other parts of Japan from American bombing raids in 1944–1945. The island absorbed heavy influxes of refugees from Soviet-occupied southern Sakhalin and the Kuriles in 1945–1947. Moreover, thousands of Japanese who had emigrated to Manchuria in the 1920s and 1930s were resettled in Hokkaido during the early postwar years.

*Current Development.* In 1951, the Hokkaido Development Office (Hokkaidō Kaihatsu-chō) was created as an organ directly under the cabinet and charged with responsibility for guiding the island's economic growth. Compared to the rest of Japan, Hokkaido's postwar economy (4.5 percent of Japan's gross national product in 1982) has a proportionally large agricultural sector and a small manufacturing sector. Hokkaido leads Japan in the production of wheat, hops, soybeans, potatoes, onions, and sugar beets. Livestock raising, dairy production, and beer and wine production are also important industries. The Kitami area leads the world in the production of peppermint. Rice is grown on the Oshima Peninsula but is not a major crop.

Hokkaido fisheries account for 20 percent of the total Japanese catch. Important to the Hokkaido industry are salmon, scallops, cod, herring, sardines, crab, and sea kelp. Some 80 percent of the Hokkaido harvest is taken from within the 320-kilometer Soviet economic zone created in 1977, underlining the importance of Soviet-Japanese relations for the local economy.

The current (1978–1987) Hokkaido Development Plan calls for more government investment in public works and for diversification in the private sector. Major projects include the new Ishikari Port, an automobile production complex at the Tomako-mai Industrial Base, and a plant at Chitose to produce high-density integrated circuits.

Isolation has affected Hokkaido's economy and society. The rest of Japan is occasionally referred to as *naichi* (roughly translatable as "homeland") in local parlance. Communications have improved but have not overcome the sense of isolation. Ferry service to Honshu is cumbersome, and inclement weather can make for turbulent crossings of the Tsugaru Strait. In 1954, a ferry capsized off Hakodate in a typhoon, causing the loss of 1,011 lives.

Hokkaido's traditional isolation will be dramatically reduced with the completion of the fifty-two-kilometer Seikan Tunnel (longest in the world). The tunnel will pass under the Tsugaru Strait, linking Hokkaido and Honshu by rail. Test borings began in 1946, but the decision to build a tunnel was not made until 1970. The target date for completion was 1983, but technical problems have caused delays. Trains are expected to start running in 1987 or 1988.

Hokkaido's proximity to the USSR makes it a strategically sensitive zone. Japan deploys approximately one-third of its Self Defense Forces on the island. Reinforcement of Soviet garrisons on the southern Kuriles in 1978 provoked scenarios of a Soviet invasion of Hokkaido in the popular media. Local opinion is divided on the "northern territories problem" (Japan's proprietary claims to the southern Kuriles, occupied by the USSR in 1945). Irredentism is said to be stronger in Hokkaido than in other parts of Japan. Yet local Soviet-Japanese friendship societies are very active, especially among fishermen.

In the popular Japanese imagination, Hokkaido conjures up images of open spaces, natural beauty, a cold climate (tourists flock to Hokkaido to ski and to avoid summer heat), American-style farms, quaint European architecture (Hakodate's Russian Orthodox churches, Yoiichi's Scottish distillery), the Ainu (some 15,000 of whom live on the island), and a spirit of unpretentious independence among the *dosanko,* or Hokkaido-born.

John A. Harrison, *Japan's Northern Frontier* (1953). F. C. Jones, *Hokkaido* (1958). George A. Lensen, *Report From Hokkaido: The Remains of Russian Culture in Northern Japan* (1954).        JOHN J. STEPHAN

**HO-LING** (*pinyin* romanization, Heling), one of two fifth-century Javanese coastal centers with which the Chinese court interacted. Chinese dynas-

tic chronicles record the visit of the North Indian Buddhist pilgrim Gunavarman to Ho-ling in Central Java on his way to China. There he stayed for several years, patronized by the queen mother, preaching Buddhist theology with great success, and advising the king of Ho-ling on whether to attack his enemies. This Chinese record reports the emergence of Ho-ling from among several competing groups and the assistance of an Indian adviser, which denotes the use of Indic culture as the basis for the establishment of the local ruler's supremacy over other chiefs. Ho-ling sent envoys to China in 430 and 440, but it is not mentioned in sixth-century Chinese records, suggesting that international contact with Central Java was limited until the 640s and 660s when Ho-ling again sent embassies; it was visited around 640 by a Chinese monk who remained to study under a Javanese master.

[*See also* Java.]

W. J. van der Meulen, S.J., "In Search of Ho-ling," *Indonesia* 23 (1977): 87–111.        KENNETH R. HALL

**HOLKARS.** Shepherds by caste, the Holkars derived their family name from Hol Murum, a village near Pune, India. Malharrao, the son of Khanduji, was the founder of the house. He entered the service of the *peshwa* (leader of the Maratha confederacy) in 1721 and became *subahdar* (district governor) of Malwa in 1730. Indore (in Madhya Pradesh) became the capital of the Holkars. A master of guerrilla warfare, Malharrao fought against the *nizam* and the Rajputs. His son Khanderao (1723–1754) died at Kumbher. Khanderao's wife, Ahalya Bai (1725–1795), known for her efficiency and charity, acted as regent for her son Malrao (1745–1767). Tukoji, a distant cousin of Malharrao became *subhedar* (1767–1797). He had four sons: Kashirao (1797–1808), Malharrao (d. 1797), Tukoji (d. 1801), and Yeshwantrao (d. 1811). The latter fought against the *peshwa* and the English, and in 1805 became recognized as legal ruler of Indore. His son Malharrao (d. 1833) became the feudatory of the English by the Treaty of Mandasor (1818); by the terms of this treaty, he retained only Indore. [*See also* Indore; Peshwa; Ahalya Bai; *and* Marathas.]        A. R. KULKARNI

**HO-LO-TAN.** Historians have connected Chinese references to Ho-lo-tan with four undated mid- to late fifth-century inscriptions of King Purnavarman, who ruled the Tarum River basin. Just east of present-day Jakarta, this area was known as Taruma-nagara in the inscriptions. Ho-lo-tan sent seven tribute missions to the Chinese court between 430 and 552. Chinese records of Ho-lo-tan reflect the instability of that age. In the report of a 436 mission the king of Ho-lo-tan, who held the Indic title Vishamvarman, was said to live in fear of his enemies both inside and outside his realm; he thus requested diplomatic assistance and weapons from the Chinese. At that time Ho-lo-tan, once a peaceful and prosperous land, was being attacked from all sides; its people (the king's supporters) were fleeing the country. When the king's son usurped the throne, Vishamvarman was forced into exile. Historians speculate that Purnavarman, the ruler of Tarumanagara, conquered neighboring Ho-lo-tan shortly after 452, the date of Ho-lo-tan's last embassy to China.

[See also Ho-ling.]

W. J. van der Meulen, S.J., "In Search of Ho-ling," *Indonesia* 23 (1977): 87–111. O. W. Wolters, *Early Indonesian Commerce: A Study of the Origins of Srivijaya* (1967).                    KENNETH R. HALL

## HOMBYAKUSHŌ.

Under Tokugawa rule in Japan the social status restrictions created divisions of samurai, peasants, artisans, and merchants; agriculturalists, however, were by no means uniform in privileges and wealth. *Hombyakushō,* literally "principal, basic peasants," were farmers with land and houses registered in their names by the cadastral surveys conducted during the late sixteenth century; they were responsible for providing the land-tax *(nengu)* and labor requirements levied against a village. Landless and dependent peasants worked for the landed and lacked representation in village councils or "shares" *(kabu)* of village land.

The *hombyakushō* system replaced earlier arrangements in which large numbers of agriculturalists labored in semi- or unfree situations under large landowners, a situation that had its origins in the *shōen* of medieval times. [See Shōen.] By recognizing a landholding peasantry it enabled authorities to assign responsibility for tax and labor at the same time that it established a degree of incentive for the village elite. Under this system agricultural productivity rose rapidly in the seventeenth century. As the land filled up in the eighteenth century, growth slowed, but new currents of commercialization related to the urbanization that resulted from the growth of castle towns and central cities like Kyoto, Osaka, and especially Edo brought changes in landholding patterns as well. In many areas new families were established; in others land-holdings increased in size as differentiation within the agricultural village increased. Authorities deplored this, and new families usually found themselves with fewer privileges in terms of access to common land, water resources, and village councils than older families possessed. Yet the essentials of the old order laid out in the cadastral registers remained: villagers with land and influence continued to allocate the tax that was levied against the village, to dominate the village councils, and to possess substantial houses, indicating a rising standard of living, education, and culture.

Albert M. Craig, ed., *Japan: A Comparative View* (1979). Susan B. Hanley and Kozo Yamamura, *Economic and Demographic Change in Preindustrial Japan, 1600–1868* (1977). Thomas C. Smith, *The Agricultural Origins of Modern Japan* (1959).                    MARIUS B. JANSEN

## HOME RULE LEAGUE.

The Home Rule for India League was founded by Annie Besant in Madras in 1916 as an agency to work for Indian self-government. In the same year Bal Gangadhar Tilak started the Indian Home Rule League in Bombay. Initially, cooperation between the two groups made home rule a popular issue, but Besant's withdrawal from politics after 1918, Tilak's death in 1920, and the start of Mohandas Gandhi's Noncooperation movement in 1920 caused the movement to lose its place at the center of Indian nationalist efforts.

[See also Besant, Annie; Tilak, Bal Gangadhar; and Gandhi, Mohandas Karamchand.]

R. C. Majumdar, ed., *The History and Culture of the Indian People: Struggle for Freedom* (1969). Arthur H. Nethercot, *The Last Four Lives of Annie Besant* (1963).
                    JUDITH E. WALSH

## HŌNEN

(1133–1212), also called Genkū and Hōnenbō, was the founder of the Jōdoshū, or Pure Land school, of Japanese Buddhism. Although the Jōdoshū was not formally recognized as an independent school until the early seventeenth century, Hōnen played a critical role in freeing Pure Land teaching from the Tendai matrix in which it had developed. [See Tendai.] Hōnen is also revered as one of the precursors of the popular upsurge of Buddhism in the thirteenth century known as the Kamakura-period revival of Buddhism.

Hōnen was born the son of an official in Mimasaka Province. As a child, honoring the wishes of his dying father, he vowed to dedicate himself to the religious life. At the age of fifteen he entered the Tendai monastery of Enryakuji on Mount Hiei as a novice. Like other Tendai monks he studied the full range of Buddhist sutras, with particular emphasis given the *Lotus Sutra* and esoteric practices. By the time Hōnen entered Enryakuji, Pure Land devotionalism was a strong current among monks there, many of whom were influenced by the *Ojōyōshū (Essentials of Salvation)*, Genshin's treatise on the Pure Land. After his ordination Hōnen withdrew to a life of seclusion, prayer, and meditation at Kurodani, just outside Kyoto. Here Hōnen deepened his conviction that faith in Amida, expressed through the fervent invocation of Amida's sacred name, the practice of the *nembutsu*, offered the best hope of rebirth in the Pure Land for all men and women.

In 1198 Hōnen wrote the *Senchaku hongan nembutsu shū (Collection of Passages on the Original Vow of Amida in Which the Nembutsu Is Chosen as the Paramount Means of Achieving Rebirth)*. This included passages from the Pure Land sutras, with commentaries by Shandao and Hōnen. In it Hōnen argued that in an age of religious decline, *mappō*, the path of personal sanctity and self-effort, *jiriki*, was too hard for lay men and women, even for monks and nuns, to follow. However, the Pure Land path, *jōdo*, relying only on the "other power," *tariki*, of the Buddha Amida and calling only for the devoted invocation of the *nembutsu*, was an easy path that offered the only hope of rebirth in a degenerate age.

Hōnen was a sincere and gentle monk whose simplicity and holiness quickly earned him a reputation as a saintly monk. He attracted many followers and patrons and spread his message of trust in Amida among the courtiers and townspeople of the capital. Although Hōnen was unassertive and conciliatory in expressing respect for other Buddhas, his exclusive devotion to Amida and the *nembutsu* and the popularity he enjoyed among people of all social levels aroused the hostility of Enryakuji monks. In 1207 his opponents prevailed on the court to have him punished. He was exiled to Shikoku. He died shortly after he was permitted to return to the capital in 1211.

Hōnen's Pure Land teaching is perhaps best summed up in the *One Page Testament*, written a few days before he died:

> The method of final salvation that I have propounded is neither a sort of meditation . . . nor is it a repetition of the Buddha's name by those who have studied and understood the deep meaning of it. It is nothing but the mere repetition of the "Namu Amida Butsu" with-

out a doubt of His mercy, whereby one may be reborn into the Land of Perfect Bliss. . . . Those who believe this . . . should behave themselves like simple-minded folk, who know not a single letter, or like ignorant monks and nuns whose faith is implictly simple. Thus without pedantic airs, they should fervently practice the repetition of the name of Amida, and that alone.

> (Coates and Ishizuka, pp. 728–729)

Hōnen thus offered the guarantee of salvation to the poor as well as the powerful, to women as well as men, and to the sinful as well as the righteous. Six leading disciples carried Hōnen's message of the Pure Land throughout the country and laid the foundations of the Pure Land school. Among them the most influential disciple was Shinran (1173–1262), who advocated utter reliance on Amida and founded the True Pure Land school, Jōdo Shinshū.

[*See also* Pure Land *and* Amidism.]

H. H. Coates and Ryugaku Ishizuka, *Hōnen the Buddhist Saint: His Life and Teaching* (1925). Wm. Theodore de Bary et al., comps., *Sources of the Japanese Tradition*, vol. 1 (1958).    MARTIN COLLCUTT

**HONG BANG DYNASTY**, considered to be the first Vietnamese dynasty. The eighteen Hong Bang kings are commonly referred to as the Hung Vuong (Hung kings). Ruling over the kingdom known as Van Lang, the Hong Bang monarchs were traditionally believed to have reigned for over 2,600 years, beginning in 2879 BCE, and they came to have a quasi-mythological status. Recent historians, however, have come to view them as the leaders of a real dynasty that ruled over Van Lang from the seventh century BCE until the establishment of An Duong Vuong's kingdom in the third century BCE.

[*See also* Hung Vuong; Van Lang; *and* An Duong Vuong.]

BRUCE M. LOCKHART

**HONG DUC CODE**, the oldest extant Vietnamese legal code, promulgated during the reign of Emperor Le Thanh Tong (1460–1497). Comprising 721 articles in ten chapters, the code reaffirms a Confucian social hierarchy while giving a more Vietnamese emphasis to women's rights to property, inheritance, and divorce. It also attempts to improve the people's livelihood by reducing land-tenure abuses and providing for more widespread cultivation. The Hong Duc Code remained in effect until the end of the Le dynasty but was superseded by the Gia Long Code in the early nineteenth century. [*See also* Le Thanh Tong *and* Gia Long Code.]

Thomas Hodgkin, *Vietnam: The Revolutionary Path* (1981).
                                    BRUCE M. LOCKHART

HONG KONG. A British-governed territory, Hong Kong (Mandarin Chinese, Xianggang) is situated at the mouth of the Pearl River in Guangdong Province, China. Its total area of 398.25 square miles comprises Hong Kong Island (29 square miles), Kowloon Peninsula and Stonecutters Island (3.75 square miles), and the New Territories stretching from north of the peninsula to the Shenzhen River, with 236 adjacent islands (365.5 square miles).

*Archaeological Background and Early History.* The Hong Kong region is spotted with archaeological remains showing evidence of settlements in primitive times. Recent excavations reveal two main Neolithic cultural traditions that suggest contacts with the northern Chinese Stone Age cultures of Longshan (around 3000 BCE). [*See* Longshan Culture.]

Little is known of the early indigenous inhabitants, yet it is likely that they were members of the ancient Yue tribes of South China and were of Malayan-Oceanic origin. The abundance of shore sites of remains of these early peoples suggest that they subsisted mainly on fishing, gathering, and perhaps some form of agriculture. It is not known whether they had migrated or been assimilated by the latecomers, as little trace of them has been left.

According to ancient Chinese chronicles the Hong Kong region was first brought under the suzerainty of China between 221 and 214 BCE. Archaeological remains of pottery and discovery of coins from this period also suggest the advent of Chinese of the Qin (221–207 BCE) and Han (206 BCE–220 CE) dynasties. The Han tomb at Li Cheng Uk (Li Zheng Wu), Kowloon, gives evidence of the presence of Han Chinese, but no clue of any large settlement. The region must have remained for some time a frontier area spotted with garrisons and their provisioners. Chinese migration on a large scale did not begin until the Song dynasty (960–1279). The oldest existing villages of the Tang clan in the New Territories can be dated to the eleventh century. Other existing families have also come at various times from the Song and Yuan (1279–1368) onward. The two major ethnic groups are Punti (Mandarin, Bendi; "local

people") and Hakka (Mandarin, Kejia; "guest people"), with a majority of the latter having arrived relatively late, in the early Qing dynasty (1644–1911).

*Founding and Extension.* The island of Hong Kong was ceded to Britain in 1842 by the Treaty of Nanjing at the end of the Opium War (1839–1842), the causes of which have been attributed to conflicts between China and Britain over questions of diplomacy, trade, jurisdiction, and the sale of opium. Yet Britain's decision to resort to arms and to demand the cession of land must also be explained in the light of its growing interest and expansion of activities in the East. When Sino-Western trade was confined to Guangzhou under the Cohong system, the idea of securing a place from China had been expressed in Macartney's Embassy (1793), Amherst's Mission (1816), and again in that of Napier (1834). Historical evidence indicates that British merchants were pushing actively in the early 1830s for the acquisition of Hong Kong. Despite the fact that some British had preferred Zhoushan Island and that Lord Palmerston was very dissatisfied with the cession, as Hong Kong was to him "a barren island with hardly a house upon it," the island was retained as Charles Elliot, Henry Pottinger, and others realized its strategic and commercial significance, lying right on the path of the chief trade route to China and with a deep and sheltered harbor. The possession was to serve then as a British diplomatic, commercial, and military post in the East. [*See also* Cohong *and* China Trade.]

Kowloon Peninsula, on the northern side of the Victoria Harbor, had been used by the British troops for camping in the 1850s. When China suffered defeat again by the Anglo-French expeditions in 1858, the resulting Convention of Beijing (1860) ceded the peninsula, including Stonecutters Island, to Britain. The extension of the Hong Kong boundaries to include the New Territories on a ninety-nine-year lease was one of the concessions forced upon China by the foreign powers following its defeat by Japan in 1895. The demand from Britain in 1898 was based on its claim for the defense of Hong Kong against France, Russia, and Germany in their encroachment for "spheres of influence" in China.

*Growth of Hong Kong (1841–1941).* At the time of the British takeover, the island's population numbered about 5,000 farmers and fishermen. After 1841, Chinese laborers, encouraged by prospects of work, began to come to the new settlement and by 1844 the population reached 19,000. Yet Hong Kong's early growth was unspectacular as compared

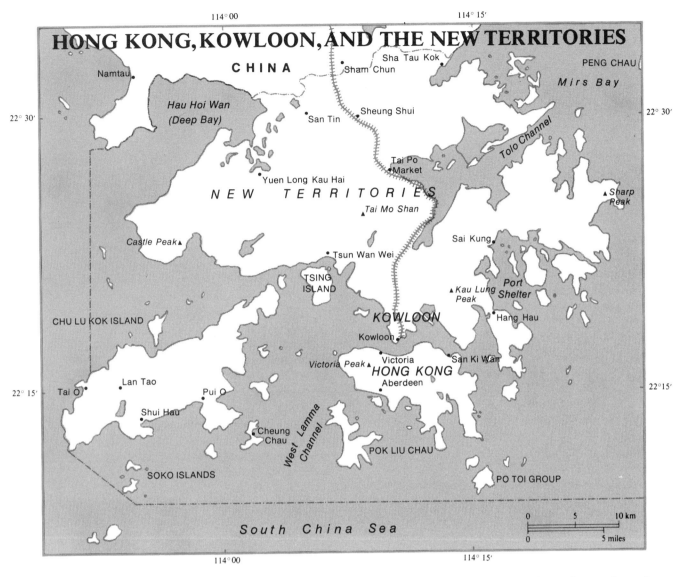

## HONG KONG, KOWLOON, AND THE NEW TERRITORIES

with Shanghai's development, and conditions were not conducive to attracting emigrants of respectable background. Then the Taiping Rebellion (1851–1864) created unsettled conditions on the mainland, resulting in thousands of people of every social class and occupation seeking refuge in the colony. By 1861 the population had risen to about 119,300, of whom 116,335 were Chinese. This pattern was to be repeated and is significant among the factors that made Hong Kong a predominantly Chinese community. The political disturbances at the turn of the century, the 1911 Revolution, and the long period of unrest that followed in China again forced large numbers of people to find shelter in Hong Kong, bringing the population by 1911 to 456,939 and by 1931 to 878,947.

Hong Kong's development began with the expansion of population in the 1850s. Its continued growth, however, was the product of a number of factors operating in the second half of the nineteenth century and after. These included the opening of China to Western trade and influence, followed by the opening of Japan (1854) and Korea (1876); the opening of trade routes in the Pacific Ocean and with Europe (Suez Canal, 1869); the development of England as an industrial and commercial power; and its free trade and laissez-faire policy. In addition, the geographical position of Hong Kong, its harbor, and the security provided by the Hong Kong administration were also important reasons for prosperity. Its entrepôt trade at first was mainly with Britain, India, and China, with opium as a major commodity. Later in the century other goods such as rice, sugar, and textiles became more important, and the areas of trade were extended to Japan, Korea, Southeast Asia, and the Western Pacific. By

1880 the position of Hong Kong as an entrepôt port was firmly established, handling in average about 30 percent of China's external trade. Meanwhile, related commercial enterprises such as shipping, banking, and insurance also prospered. After the turn of the century, although Hong Kong was surpassed by Shanghai as the center of British economic interest in China, its intermediary trade with South China, Southeast Asia, Japan, and the Western Pacific continued to increase.

Other internal developments of Hong Kong during this period included its urbanization, mostly concentrated on the island and the peninsula, which, owing to its hilly land, necessitated reclamation early in 1851. Henceforth, the city continued to expand by more reclamation and cutting into rocks. Little change was made in its administration; the colony had a governor nominated by the crown and nominated Executive and Legislative councils with official majorities. The first unofficial members of the Legislative Council were nominated in 1850, those of the Executive Council, in 1896. The Chinese community was greatly underrepresented as they did not have a representative in the Legislative Council until 1880 and in the Executive Council until 1926.

*Japanese Attack and Occupation (1941–1945).* When war was declared between China and Japan in 1937, Hong Kong received again large influx of refugees (100,000 in 1937, 500,000 in 1938, and 150,000 in 1939). When war broke out in Europe in September 1939, Japan was able to extend its power over the whole of East and Southeast Asia, making Hong Kong's position precarious. Emergency legislation for the mobilization of manpower and material supplies was passed. Hong Kong had only four defensive battalions; reinforcement consisting of two Canadian battalions arrived on 16 November 1941.

The Japanese attack came on 8 December 1941, almost simultaneous with its attack on Pearl Harbor. The invasion came from the mainland and the British troops withdrew to the island on 17 December. After a week's resistance the defenders, including the local Volunteer Corps, were overwhelmed; Hong Kong surrendered on Christmas Day. [*See also* World War II in Asia.]

For three years and eight months Hong Kong suffered under the Japanese military occupation. Trade virtually came to a standstill. All British institutions were abolished. Prisoners of war and British civilians were interned. The food supply was disrupted and public services such as communication and medical and health care were all neglected. Many people escaped to mainland China, while others moved to Macao. The Allied blockade and heavy Japanese losses in the war culminated in an even more serious food shortage in 1944 and 1945. The Japanese then organized mass deportations from Hong Kong. Those who stayed suffered increased oppression, and when Hong Kong was recovered after the Japanese surrender on 14 August 1945, the population of Hong Kong had dwindled from the 1941 figure of 1.6 million to about 600,000.

*The Postwar Years.* The postwar years marked a new era in the history of Hong Kong, an era that witnessed an unprecedented growth of population, rapid industrialization, urban expansion, extension of social services, and modifications in government structure.

Hong Kong made a spectacular recovery after the war. By 1947 population rose to an estimated 1.8 million. The war and disturbances in China caused a mass influx of refugees. Although entry to Hong Kong was restricted by a quota from 1950 onward, both legal and illegal immigrants continued to flow in. This immigration, together with a high rate of natural increase, brought the population to about 3 million by 1960. Natural increase began to drop in the 1960s, but immigration was on the increase, particularly in 1962 and from 1978 to 1980. The influx began to decrease in 1981 as a result of a revision of immigration policy, yet the population had reached 5.2 million by 1982.

Traditional middleman trade made a good recovery in the immediate postwar years, which was disrupted by the United Nations' embargo on trade with China during the Korean War (1950–1953). Confronted with the stagnation of entrepôt trade and the pressure of providing for the greatly increased population, Hong Kong began its industrialization. Despite a great shortage of natural resources, raw materials, machines, and markets, its industrialization has been extremely successful for a number of reasons. The influx of immigrants from China created a labor supply, as well as entrepreneurship, skill, and capital, especially from Shanghai. Capital also came from the boom of intermediary trade in the immediate postwar years and from Southeast Asia in the 1950s. Later, investment came even from developed countries, such as the United States. Other important contributing factors include relative political stability; free trade, laissez-faire policy; low taxation; facilities in banking, insurance, and shipping; and good connections with overseas markets.

Hong Kong's main products include textile, clothing, plastic goods, watches, and electronics. Its chief markets have been Southeast Asian countries until about 1965, and since then, the United States, United Kingdom, and West Germany. The main suppliers are Japan, China, and the United States. Traditional entrepôt trade began to revive from about 1965, with marked increases in 1973 and again since 1979, owing first to the widening of Hong Kong's trading connections and, since the 1970s, to the expansion of China's external trade. Domestic export, however, remained dominant, occupying more than 70 percent of the total export. Industrial and commercial growth together made Hong Kong the world's third largest container port and the leading banking and financial center in Asia in 1982.

Urban renewal in the old city districts, rapid urbanization of New Kowloon, and the development of new towns in the formerly rural areas of the New Territories are all important features of postwar urban growth in Hong Kong. Construction of highrise buildings, multilane highways, tunnels, overpasses, and mass transit underground railways have completely changed the face of Hong Kong.

Rapid growth has created problems in education, housing, and social welfare. As a result, the government has gradually begun to play a larger role in some important aspects of social services. Free primary education was introduced in 1971 and was extended to nine years in 1978. Public housing was begun in 1953, arising from the need to accommodate 50,000 fire victims, but a marked increase and improvement appeared only after 1973. In 1982 more than 2 million people (about 41 percent of the total population) lived in estates for the low-income group. In the area of social welfare, major advances have been made since 1968, particularly in the initiation of a public assistance program and personal social work for the young.

The Young Plan, a government proposal for constitutional reform, was brought up for discussion in 1946. It was dropped in 1952, owing mainly to political change in China and the influx of refugees to Hong Kong. The basic pattern of colonial rule has since then remained unchanged, but modifications have been introduced in its government and administration structure. Major changes include expansion of the Executive and Legislative councils, especially in the increase of unofficial Chinese members and representatives from different professions. The function of the Urban Council has also been expanded and its composition has changed, to consist of an equal number of appointed and elected unofficial members. District Offices were initiated in 1968 to provide a direct dialogue between the government and the people. The 1982 establishment of District Boards, which consist of elected members from the constituents, is yet another step toward providing a better forum for public consultation and participation at the district level.

*Relations with China.* Hong Kong's relationship with China is the most important factor affecting the growth of Hong Kong. In order to feed its population, Hong Kong has always been dependent largely on supply from the mainland. Its fluctuations in population and trade have meanwhile been chiefly the result of events in China. The repercussions of Chinese political movements in Hong Kong are also evident. The Chinese nationalist and anti-imperialist movements in the 1920s were reflected in Hong Kong by a seamen's strike in 1922, followed by a more serious general strike of 1923 to 1926 that crippled the economy and all aspects of life in Hong Kong for almost fifteen months. The Cultural Revolution and antiforeign movements in China caused mounting tension in Hong Kong in 1966, developing into a series of disturbances and demonstrations against the Hong Kong government in 1967. Unrest was rampant until the end of the year, when an accord between China and Hong Kong was reached.

Hong Kong has also made contributions to China. It served as an important center for the introduction of Western knowledge during the Self-Strengthening and reform movements in late Qing China, largely through publication of translations, books, and newspapers, and through the supply of some British-educated men. Its schools in fact turned out people like Wu Tingfang, Wang Chonghui, Sun Yat-sen, and others who helped shape the destiny of modern China. Hong Kong can also claim to be the cradle of the 1911 Revolution; it was a center for the spread of revolutionary ideas and the organization of insurrections against the Manchus. In the area of economics, since the 1860s Hong Kong has been an important distributing center for China's overseas trade, although the volume fluctuates with changing situations in China and abroad. In recent years, with the advance of the "four modernizations program" in China, the role of Hong Kong has widened. It is becoming more and more important as a gateway for capital, material, and technological imports into China.

With the approach of the expiration of the New Territories lease in 1997, agreements have already been negotiated between China and Britain concerning the future status of Hong Kong. The Chinese have agreed that, while it will be an integral part of China, Hong Kong's economy will have a special status. The colony's return to China will certainly mark a new era in its history.

Nigel Cameron, *Hong Kong, the Cultured Pearl* (1978). G. B. Endacott, *A History of Hong Kong* (2d ed., 1973) and *Hong Kong Eclipse* (1978). T. B. Lin, R. Lee, and U. E. Simons, eds., *Hong Kong: Economic, Social and Political Studies in Development* (1979). Lo Hsiang-lin, *Hong Kong and its External Communications before 1842* (1963). William Maecham, *Archaeology in Hong Kong* (1980). Ng Lun Ngai-ha, *Interactions of East and West: Public Education in Early Hong Kong* (1984). Alvin Rabushka, *Hong Kong: A Study in Economic Freedom* (1979).                                    NG LUN NGAI-HA

**HONG REN'GAN** (1822–1864), cousin and early convert of Hong Xiuquan, the leader of the Taiping movement. After studying Christianity and Western science and technology with missionaries in Hong Kong and Shanghai for seven years, he joined the Taipings at Nanjing in 1859, becoming Shield King, generalissimo, minister for foreign affairs, and finally regent to Hong Xiuquan's son.

Hong introduced orthodox Christianity and submitted proposals to democratize Taiping rule, create Western-style economic modernization, and extend social welfare. Blocked in these efforts by the nepotism and corruption of other Taiping leaders, Hong Ren'gan was executed by imperial troops in 1864. Some scholars believe that if the Taipings had been successful and had implemented Hong Ren'gan's proposals, China would have modernized in the same way Meiji Japan did and would have been spared its "century of humiliation" by the West.

[See also Hong Xiuquan and Taiping Rebellion.]

P. RICHARD BOHR

**HONG XIUQUAN** (1814–1864), messianic leader of the Taiping Rebellion (1851–1864) in China. A Hakka, Hong was born on 1 January 1814 in a small village near Guangzhou (Canton), Guangdong Province. His youthful ambition was to restore the reputation of his family, once active in scholar-official life, by succeeding in the civil service examinations. Because he was academically precocious, Hong's relatives supported him for several years of examination training in the village school. There he studied the Confucian curriculum, which taught respect for the family, reverence for the social hierarchy, and loyalty to the dynasty.

Hong did well in the first step of the examination process, but in 1837 he became despondent over his third failure to pass the crucial exam that would have allowed him to compete for bureaucratic office. This precipitated a vision in which Hong was transported to heaven. There he met the Heavenly Father, who complained that Confucian orthodoxy and the religious traditions that reinforced it had made the Chinese abandon monotheism and morality for polytheism and decadence. He commissioned Hong as "Heavenly King" to purify the Chinese and reunite them with their Heavenly Father.

During the next six years, Hong taught school and continued his exam study. After his fourth failure in 1843, however, he broke with Confucianism. In that year, he studied a tract entitled *Good Words to Admonish the Age (Quanshi liangyan)*, which he had first seen just prior to his vision. Written by China's first Protestant minister, Liang Fa (1789–1855), the work contained scriptural extracts and homiletical essays that criticized Chinese religion and culture for lacking both filial devotion to God and moral consciousness. It advocated individual spiritual transformation and depicted an egalitarian Kingdom of Heaven as an earthly possibility. From this tract Hong became convinced that the Heavenly Father in his dream was none other than God, that he himself was the younger brother of Jesus Christ, and that his mission was to usher in the Heavenly Kingdom at some point as yet undetermined.

Hong baptized himself in accordance with Liang's description of the Protestant rite. He also smashed his family's ancestral tablets and religious images as well as the Confucian tablet in his schoolroom. For this iconoclasm, Hong was expelled from his village. In 1844 he visited relatives in the southeastern part of the neighboring province of Guangxi, where he was appalled to witness the terrible suffering of his fellow Hakka from unemployment, hunger, disease, lawlessness, and opium addiction.

In 1845 Hong returned to his native village. During the next two years, he wrote essays and poems that claimed that the Heavenly Father was the same creator-sustainer-judge as the deity revealed not only in the Bible but also in China's pre-Confucian classics. He lamented the emperors' patronage of Daoism and Buddhism, which, he charged, had seduced the Chinese into theological error. Having become alienated from the Heavenly Father, Hong thought, the Chinese people had lost their moral sense. He also accused the emperors of usurping the Heavenly Father's position as China's ruler.

Hong insisted that Confucian ethics were too hierarchical and that the only solution to China's problems was the extension of universal love. This would form the basis of a millennial kingdom where justice and equality would be achieved under theocratic rule of the Heavenly Father and Hong's vice-regency. This he dubbed the Taiping Tianguo ("heavenly kingdom of great peace").

During February and March of 1847, Hong read the Bible and studied Protestantism with an American Southern Baptist missionary in Guangzhou. Inspired to lead a crusade for moral reform, he returned to Guangxi. There he became the leader of the God Worshipers Association, which his convert Feng Yunshan (1822–1852) had organized around Hong's teachings among a number of Hakka villages. He wrote the God Worshipers' prayers (patterned on the Lord's Prayer) to seek forgiveness of "sins" and deliverance from adversity. His new morality was based on the Ten Commandments, which he modified to prohibit the use of tobacco, alcohol, and opium, as well as gambling, lawlessness, feuding over land, and such superstitious practices as witchcraft. These injunctions were reinforced with biblical and Chinese notions of retribution.

Hong's egalitarian ethics found expression in the primitive communism and disaster relief of the God Worshiper's Sacred Treasury. His worship combined Protestant baptism and hymn singing with Chinese-style offerings of food and incense to the Heavenly Father. To demonstrate his followers' break with the orthodox order, Hong led the God Worshipers in defacing temples and smashing religious objects.

In 1850 the emperor ordered the eradication of what had grown to one million God Worshipers. Interpreting this as a sign that the Heavenly Kingdom had begun, Hong declared insurrection on 1 January 1851. He compared the Manchus' "oppression" of the Taipings to the subjugation of the Jews by the Egyptians before the Exodus and claimed that the Heavenly Father was ready to bring them into the new Kingdom and to restore his rightful place as emperor of China. Hong's nationalistic pronouncements, vivid eschatology, and puritanical regulations—coupled with the Hakka shamanism practiced by Hong's lieutenants—inspired the courage and discipline among Taiping troops that helped win early victories against the Qing forces.

By 1853 Hong was comparing himself to the biblical messianic figure of Melchizedek. He developed a rigid theocratic government and designed a new social order based on ancient Chinese utopian ideas and biblical egalitarian concepts. Among his innovations were policies for an equal system of landholding, sexual equality, distributive justice, social welfare, and a simplified language. He also abolished prostitution, concubinage, and footbinding, and advocated a relationship of equality between China and foreign countries.

While other Taiping "kings" actually ran day-to-day affairs, Hong remained chief celebrant and religious thinker. In 1853 he wrote a series of biblical commentaries in order to put the Taiping movement into what he understood to be a more precise Judeo-Christian perspective. After that year Hong lapsed into mental instability. During the fall of Nanjing to imperialist troops in 1864 he committed suicide. As his pre-1853 writings become more widely studied Hong may be recognized as one of modern China's most syncretistic thinkers.

[See also Hakka; Hong Ren'gan; Qing Dynasty; and Taiping Rebellion.]

Eugene Powers Boardman, *Christian Influence upon the Ideology of the Taiping Rebellion, 1851–1864* (1952). J. C. Cheng, *Chinese Sources for the Taiping Rebellion, 1850–1864* (1963). Theodore Hamberg, *The Visions of Hong-Siu-Tshuen, and Origin of the Kwang-si Insurrection* (1854). P. M. Yap, "The Mental Illness of Hung Hsiu-ch'uan, Leader of the Taiping Rebellion," *Far Eastern Quarterly* 13 (1953–1954): 287–304.

P. RICHARD BOHR

**HOOGHLY RIVER.** *See* Hughly River.

**HORSFIELD, THOMAS** (1773–1859), American naturalist and antiquarian. He graduated with a degree in medicine from the University of Pennsylvania in 1798 and after visiting Jakarta in 1800 returned to the island in 1801 to research its natural history. He traveled extensively in Java and received additional government patronage during the British occupation of the island (1811–1816); at this time he extended his interest to Javanese antiquities. From 1812 to 1813 he visited Bangka and in 1818 traveled in central Sumatra. In 1819 he was appointed curator of the East India Company's museum in London, and in 1824 he published his *Zoological Researches in Java and the Neighbouring Islands*.

J. S. Bastin and D. T. Moore, "The Geological Researches of Dr. Thomas Horsfield in Indonesia 1801–1819," *Bulletin of the British Museum* 10.3 (1982): 75–115. T. Horsfield, J. J. Bennett, and R. Brown, *Plantae Javanicae Rariores* (1838–1852). JOHN S. BASTIN

HŌRYŪJI ("temple for the dissemination of the Law"), Buddhist temple situated southwest of the present-day city of Nara in Japan. Constructed about 607, Hōryūji was extensively destroyed by fire in 670 and was reconstructed shortly thereafter. At least some of what are thought to be its original buildings still stand; these are famous as the oldest wooden structures in the world.

Hōryūji is said to have been built under the patronage of Prince Shōtoku (574–622), one of the leading figures in the reform and centralization of the Japanese state in the seventh century by means of extensive cultural borrowing from China. Although representative of the architectural style of temples in China during the Six Dynasties period (220–589), Hōryūji has its own distinctive layout. The most important feature of this layout is the placement of a five-story pagoda (reliquary) and the Golden Hall, which houses the principal icons of the temple, on an east-west axis rather than the north-south axis common in China.

Hōryūji is one of the most important repositories of East Asian Buddhist art, especially sculpture, from the seventh century. It also stands as the principal monument of Japan's advance to higher civilization at this time.

[*See also* Yamato; Shōtoku Taishi; *and* Sculpture: Japanese Sculpture.]

PAUL VARLEY

HOSTAGE CRISIS. On 4 November 1979, Iranian students seized the United States embassy in Tehran and took hostage its diplomatic staff; fifty-two Americans were held until 20 January 1981. This "hostage crisis," provoked by extremist supporters of Ayatollah Khomeini, radicalized the Iranian Revolution and shattered US-Iran relations.

President Jimmy Carter ruled out the use of force and sought a peaceful settlement of the crisis. Owing to Iran's hard line and lack of a clear authority empowered to negotiate, however, negotiations made no progress. The mediation efforts of UN secretary-general Kurt Waldheim failed in February 1980, as did an ill-fated US military rescue mission in April of that year.

Iran's need for arms and money after Iraq's invasion finally moved the crisis toward resolution in late 1980. The election of Iran's parliament provided a body capable of defining a settlement, and, with Algeria as mediator, Tehran and Washington agreed on the release of the hostages in exchange for the return of Iranian assets in America that had been

FIGURE 1. *Hōryūji, Nara.* General view of the temple complex.

"frozen" after the ascendancy of Khomeini. A commission in The Hague was appointed to hear private claims.

In the United States, the crisis was the main focus of attention for both the Carter administration and the public. Carter's failure to free the hostages contributed not only to his defeat by Ronald Reagan in the 1980 presidential elections but also to a political shift toward the right and a revival of patriotic fervor.

Zbigniew Brzezinski, *Power and Principle* (1983). Barry Rubin, *Paved with Good Intentions: The American Experience and Iran* (1980). John Stempel, *Inside the Iranian Revolution* (1981). Cyrus Vance, *Hard Choices* (1983).                    BARRY RUBIN

**HOYSALA DYNASTY**, the most important dynasty of medieval Karnataka, India. At the end of their rule the Hoysalas also had considerable power in the northern part of Tamil Nadu. The first rulers (beginning c. 1006) allied themselves wiith the Gangas. As the Gangas lost control, the Hoysalas gained power and were able to consolidate much of the Kannada-speaking area.

Vinayaditya (r. 1047–1098) established his capital at Dorasamudra (present-day Halebid) and declared himself a feudatory of the Late Chalukyas. Inscriptions report that he waged many campaigns with the Late Chalukyas against adversaries such as the Paramaras of Malava (Malwa), ranging as far north as Dhara in Madhya Pradesh.

Vishnuvardhana (r. 1108–1142) began to enlarge the kingdom. It was during his reign that a style of temple architecture associated with the Hoysalas developed, with well-known examples at Belur, Halebid, and Somanathapura, but others are found throughout the state. A large number of Jain and Hindu (both Shaivite and Vaishnavite) temples were built during Hoysala rule.

The next king of note was Ballala II (r. 1173–1220), who usurped the throne and embarked on an active campaign along the Tungabhadra River. In 1192 he took imperial titles, and with the fall of the Late Chalukyas he took much of northern Karnataka. During his reign the Hoysalas also allied themselves with the Cholas. Someshvara (r. 1235–1260?), grandson of Ballara II, was raised in the Tamil country, and on inheriting the kingdom choose to stay south. Ultimately the kingdom was divided between his two sons, only to be reunited on a much-reduced basis under Ballala III (r. 1292–1343). Toward the end of his reign the growing empire of Vijayanagar and the new Islamic powers led to the collapse of the empire. His son ruled for only a few years, probably dying in about 1346.

[*See also* Chola Dynasty.]

J. D. M. Derrett, *The Hoysalas; A Medieval Indian Royal Family* (1958). R. C. Majumdar, ed., *The History and Culture of the Indian People* (1957), vol. 5, chapter 9, pp. 226–233. B. Sheik Ali, ed., *The Hoysala Dynasty* (1972).                    ROBERT J. DEL BONTÀ

**HSIEN-PEI.** *See* Xianbei.

**HSINHPYUSHIN** (1736–1776), third ruler of the Konbaung dynasty (1763–1776) of Burma. The second son of King Alaunghpaya, Maung Ywa took the throne on 29 November 1763, possibly by poisoning his brother Naungdawgyi.

Under Hsinhpyushin's rule, Konbaung military power and imperial achievement reached their zenith. Throughout his reign, however, he faced considerable opposition, particularly from his next younger brother, the Amyin prince, whose support among officials was so strong that the king feared to execute him despite repeated plots and provocations. Nor was Hsinhpyushin strong enough to discipline his blatantly corrupt and disobedient ministers and other high officials, although they were involved in major revenue embezzlement scandals. The officials also largely frustrated his attempt to conduct a revenue inquest in 1765 to improve control of administration.

Continuing Alaunghpaya's plan for the conquest of the Tai states east of the Salween River, in 1764 Hsinhpyushin launched two major campaigns from north and south in a grand pincer movement on his eastern frontier. This ambitious strategy achieved its final goal three years later with the sack of the Tai capital of Ayudhya.

Disorder occasioned by the reimposition of Burmese authority in the Sino-Burmese border area led to concurrent war with China between 1765 and 1769. After an initial local clash, the Burmese generals Maha Sithu and Maha Thiha Thura outmaneuvered and generally outfought three large Chinese armies. Maha Thiha Thura forced the last Chinese general to negotiate a treaty that would govern future relations, but it was rejected by Hsinhpyushin, who was enraged that his general had let the Chinese go.

The Chinese war had caused a premature Burmese withdrawal from Thailand and permitted the resurgence of Thai power. In 1773 Hsinhpyushin attempted to employ the earlier pincer strategy to subdue the Thai, but he had little success until Maha Thiha Thura assumed command of the southern campaign in 1774. As Maha Thiha Thura's forces prepared for a final descent on Bangkok, Hsinhpyushin's death on 10 June 1776 caused his son Singu to recall the armies to consolidate his own position. This move ultimately ended Burmese dominance of the eastern frontier.

[See also Konbaung Dynasty; Alaunghpaya; Naungdawgyi; and Maha Thiha Thura.]

WILLIAM J. KOENIG

**HSIUNG-NU.** See Xiongnu.

**HSÜAN-TSANG.** See Xuanzang.

**HSÜN-TZU.** See Xunzi.

**HUAINANZI,** a collection of essays written by scholars attached to the court of Liu An (d. 122 BCE), prince of Huainan, which reflects the broad interests and syncretic nature of Chinese thought in the Han period (206 BCE–220 CE). Patterned after the *Lushi chunqiu (Spring and Autumn Annals of Lu),* the *Huainanzi* contains twenty chapters covering such diverse topics as cosmology, astronomy, rulership, military strategy, and a postface that provides a summary of the contents. In addition to serving as a compendium of existing knowledge, the *Huainanzi* offers innovative political alternatives to the Confucian and Legalist doctrines that dominated the Han court. Although it incorporates the vocabulary and ideas of these schools, the *Huainanzi* is decidedly Daoist in its perception of man and government. The *Huainanzi* is the most complete statement of early Han Daoism.

Liu An, the grandson of the Han founder, Gaozu, was enfeoffed as prince of Huainan after his father committed suicide en route to exile. Liu An also committed suicide following the discovery of his plot against the throne. He was famous as a writer and patron of literature. Of his works, only the *Huainanzi* is extant. He presented this text to Emperor Wu between 139 and 127 BCE.

[See also Daoism.]

Roger T. Ames, *The Art of Rulership: A Study in Ancient Chinese Political Thought* (1983). Evan Morgan, *Tao: The Great Luminant* (reprint, 1969). Burton Watson, *Early Chinese Literature* (1962).

M. LAVONNE MARUBBIO

**HUANG CHAO** (d. 884), leader of a great rebellion between 875 and 884 that devastated almost all of China except the modern province of Sichuan and left the Tang dynasty fragmented into regional regimes, thus hastening its collapse.

A prosperous merchant from modern Shandong involved in the illicit salt trade, Huang nevertheless had ambitions of entering officialdom. Failing in this, he took advantage of widespread social unrest caused by famine conditions, oppressive taxation, and the exorbitant cost of salt and tea under a strict government monopoly system that had driven many peasants into banditry. In 875 he raised a bandit force and joined up with another bandit leader in Henan, Wang Xianzhi. When Wang was killed in 878, Huang succeeded him. Marching southward, Huang's force was swelled by a desperate rural populace. He took the great city of Canton (Guangzhou) in 879, ordering the slaughter of about 120,000 of its inhabitants, a majority of the population, including many foreigners. Turning northward, in 880 he captured the eastern capital of Luoyang and the western capital of Chang'an in quick succession, with a terrifying destruction of life and property.

Huang now declared the establishment of the Great Qi dynasty, but it was a complete failure owing to the harshness of his rule and his inability to gain the support of the power brokers of traditional China, the scholar-gentry class. Driven from Chang'an early in 883 by loyalist forces led by the Shato Turk Li Keyong, and having lost all hope of success, Huang committed suicide in mid-884 while attempting to reach his old base in Shandong. Huang Chao has been hailed by Chinese Marxists as a hero leader of the peasant class, although given his social origins, indiscriminate destruction of life, and attempt to establish an old-style dynasty, it seems unlikely that he ever sought to advance peasant interests per se.

[See also Rebellions in China and Tang Dynasty.]

Howard S. Levy, trans., *Biography of Huang Ch'ao* (1955).

HOWARD J. WECHSLER

**HUANG HE.** See Yellow River.

**HUANG TAIJI** (1592–1643), Manchu ruler, Nurhaci's eighth son and successor. Although Huang Taiji is known in some Western sources as Abahai, the name does not exist in any Chinese or Manchu documents. A brilliant warrior, he played an important role in many battles. In 1616 he became one of the Four Senior Beile, the others being Daisan, Amin, and Manggultai. At the time of Nurhaci's death, Huang Taiji controlled the Plain and Bordered Yellow Banners, then the most powerful units of the Manchu Eight Banners. With strength and prestige he outstripped his rivals and succeeded to the throne in 1626. His reign was divided into two periods: Tiancong (1627–1636) and Chongde (1636–1643).

During the first few years of Huang Taiji's reign he ruled the state jointly with the other three Senior Beile. Through patient maneuvers he was able to rule alone beginning in 1632. To weaken the power of other princes he created new offices in the banners and filled them with his own men. Meanwhile, his lenient measures won the cooperation of many Chinese. Huang Taiji repeatedly invaded China proper and China's allies, Korea and the Chahar Mongols. He finally subjugated the Chahar Mongols in 1634 and Korea in 1637, leaving the Ming dynasty as his only enemy. In 1635 he adopted "Manchu" (Manzhou) as the name of his people; a year later he renamed his state "Qing" and proclaimed himself emperor.

Besides the Mongol and the Chinese Eight Banners that he founded respectively in 1635 and 1642, Huang Taiji organized a sinicized bureaucracy after the Ming model. Between 1629 and 1636 he created the Literary Office (wenguan), which later developed into the Three Inner Courts (nei sanyuan), the Six Boards (liubu), and the Censorate (yushitai). He was also responsible for the introduction of the pointed Manchu script that became standard. Huang Taiji was succeeded by Fulin, his ninth son.

[See also Manchus and Qing Dynasty.]

Arthur W. Hummel, ed., *Eminent Chinese of the Ch'ing Period (1644–1912)*, vol. 1 (1943), pp. 1–3.

PEI HUANG

HUANG XING (1874–1916), a leader of the 1911 republican revolution in China. Huang studied in Japan and founded the Society to Revive China (Huaxinghui) among radicals from Hunan Province. In 1905 he joined Sun Yat-sen to found the Revolutionary Alliance (Tongmenghui), in which he was renowned as an organizer and military strategist. Huang planned several unsuccessful uprisings and commanded the revolutionary army after the Wuchang Uprising in 1911. He was minister of war in the provisional government, served as a director of the Guomindang (Nationalist Party), and joined the opposition to President Yuan Shikai in 1913.

[*See also* China, Republic Period; Guomindang; Sun Yat-sen; *and* Xinhai Revolution.]

Chün-tu Hsüeh, *Huang Hsing and the Chinese Revolution* (1961).
MARY BACKUS RANKIN

HUANG ZONGXI (1610–1695), Chinese scholar and official. A native of Yuyao, Zhejiang Province, Huang was the son of a prominent leader of the Donglin Academy and a disciple of the Ming loyalist and martyr, the philosopher Liu Zongzhou. Huang became a leader in the Fushe and served in minor capacities in the Southern Ming court. After 1649 he devoted himself to teaching and scholarship, making major contributions in the fields of historical studies and political theory. He compiled an anthology of Ming-dynasty Confucian writings and commenced work on a similar anthology for the Song and Yuan periods. His own writings on Ming history were utilized by the compilers of the official *History of the Ming (Mingshi)*. His treatise *A Plan for the Prince (Mingyi daifang lu)* went even further than Gu Yanwu's writings in attacking the whole system of Chinese dynastic rule. Huang not only harshly criticized the arbitrary exercise of imperial authority but also questioned the efficacy of individual heroic efforts to rectify abuses of imperial power without a basic change in the system itself. In addition, he proposed institution of an independent school system to provide comprehensive, universal education and to serve as a forum for the expression of public opinion.

Wm. Theodore de Bary, *The Liberal Tradition in China* (1983), pp. 67–90.
JUDITH A. WHITBECK

HUBEI, province in central China; its population in 1982 was 47,804,150 and its area is 180,000 square kilometers. Hubei can be divided geographically into two regions. The eastern region, which makes up two-thirds of the province, forms the northern Yangtze River basin, a low-lying plain surrounded by mountains to the north and southeast. The western third of the province is a rugged, hilly area with cultivated land in the river basins and valleys. Han peoples have settled the plains of Hubei since the first millennium BCE, although it was most intensively settled from the seventh to the eleventh century following the development of a rice-surplus agriculture. With mild winters, hot, humid summers, abundant rainfall, and a long growing season (280–300 days), Hubei still supports a rich and diverse agriculture, producing many crops in addition to rice. In the late nineteenth century, the plain of Hubei was the first area of the Chinese interior to develop modern industry. Today, the largest city of the province, Wuhan, is one of the most important centers of heavy and medium industry in China, as well as a key commercial, rail, and communications center.                                    JOHN A. RAPP

HUE (Phu Xuan), seventh largest city of the Socialist Republic of Vietnam (1973 population, 209,043) and a noted cultural and religious center. Hue is located in central Vietnam, approximately 525 kilometers south of Hanoi and 650 kilometers north of Ho Chi Minh City (Saigon), and is situated on the Song Huang (Perfume River).

Originally named Phu Xuan, Hue served as the permanent capital of the Nguyen lords (1687–1774), of Vietnam (1802–1884), and of the protectorate of Annam (1887–1945). The "citadel" (kinh thanh) of Hue, a square measuring two and one-half kilometers per side and encompassing both an "imperial city" (hoang thanh) and a "forbidden city" (tu cam thanh), was built during the reigns of the Nguyen emperors Gia Long and Minh Mang and was modeled after the capital of the emperors of China at Beijing.

The city suffered extensive damage during a French attack in 1885 and the Tet Offensive of 1968.

[See also Nguyen Lords; Nguyen Dynasty; Minh Mang; and Tet Offensive.]

"Hue, Past and Present," Vietnamese Studies 37 (1973). A. B. Woodside, Vietnam and the Chinese Model (1971).                                JAMES M. COYLE

HUGHLY RIVER, the Bhagirathi branch of the Ganges River in Bengal, India. The Hughly became a busy channel of world commerce at the end of the sixteenth century, when the Portuguese established themselves at what came to be known as Hughly, the chief center of East-West trade in eastern India. The Dutch and the English also came to have their trading headquarters in and around Hughly. Later, the British East India Company moved to Calcutta. The French settled at Chandernagore and the Danes in Serampore, all situated on the western bank of the river between Calcutta and Hughly. By the mid-eighteenth century Calcutta, situated on the east bank of the river, eclipsed all other settlements.

[See also Calcutta; East India Company; Dutch East India Company; and French East India Company.]

Amiya Kumar Banerjee, Hooghly: West Bengal District Gazetteers (1972). A. B. Chatterjee, "The Hooghly River and its West Bank: A Study in Historical Geography," Geographical Review of India 25 (1963).

PRADIP SINHA

HU HANMIN (1879–1936), leading revolutionary writer and theorist of the Guomindang (Kuomintang, KMT, or Nationalist Party). Born near the city of Canton (Guangzhou), Hu was one of Sun Yat-sen's chief subordinates. With Sun and Wang Jingwei he participated in revolutionary plotting that contributed to the overthrow of the Qing dynasty in 1912. For a brief time after that revolution Hu served as military governor of Guangdong Province, but in 1913 he was forced to leave office, and he resumed his revolutionary partnership with Sun Yat-sen. Following Sun's death in 1925, Hu—along with Wang Jingwei and Liao Zhongkai—appeared as a likely successor as leader of the KMT, but that role fell instead to Chiang Kai-shek in 1926. Although Hu served as president of the Legislative Yuan from 1928 until 1931 in the National Government headed by Chiang, he was known during the last decade of his life as Chiang's persistent right-wing critic and rival for power.

[See also Chiang Kai-shek; Guomindang; Sun Yat-sen; and Wang Jingwei.]

LLOYD E. EASTMAN

HUHEHAOTE (Hohhot), the provincial capital of the Inner Mongolia Autonomous Region, is situated on the western Baotou-Huhehaote plain near the Mongolian steppe lands. The city, formerly known as Guisui, was founded in 1581 and subsequently developed by the Ming (1368–1644) and Qing (1644–1911) dynasties as a trading and frontier administrative center.

Since 1949, under Chinese industrial development policies, Huhehaote's population has grown to a total of 747,000. Huhehaote's chief industries include fertilizer and chemical plants, diesel engines, and sugar refining. In addition, Huhehaote and the entire border region have been of great strategic importance in providing defense installations to buffer the Mongolian People's Republic to the north.                                ANITA M. ANDREW

HUK, or Hukbalahap, Philippine peasant movement, guerrilla army, and rebellion. Both *Huk* and *Hukbalahap* refer to three related rural organizations concentrated in central Luzon, north of Manila.

*Huk* comes from *hukbo* (army), which appears in the Tagalog name of the two principal groups. The Hukbo ng Bayan Laban sa Hapon (Hukbalahap), or the People's Anti-Japanese Army, was the region's most popular resistance organization during World War II. The Hukbong Mapagpalaya ng Bayan, or the People's Liberation Army, commonly known as the Huks or Huk rebellion, was strongest between late 1946 and early 1952.

Many who participated in the Huk rebellion had been in the Hukbalahap and in peasant associations during the 1930s and 1940s. These organizations, composed mainly of the families of rice and sugar-cane tenant farmers, sugar mill laborers, and small landowners, had advocated agrarian reforms, generally strongly opposed by landlords, mill owners, and government authorities. The opposition, in turn, caused peasants and their sympathizers to rebel.

Officials and local elites responded with hostility because their domination was threatened by the peasantry's regional organizations. Many large landowners were also determined to alter customary tenancy conditions to their favor without consideration for their tenants' precarious economic situation. Moreover, many who had cooperated with the Japanese regime remained influential afterward and attacked former members of the Hukbalahap. Finally, numerous American and Filipino authorities believed the peasant organizations were communist and stoppable only by force.

The Communist Party of the Philippines (PKP) was sometimes aligned with, and helped lead, the agrarian organizations, the Hukbalahap, and the Huk rebellion. The alliance was intermittent, however, because the objectives of the PKP leadership did not consistently coincide with those of the Huks. The PKP also tried unsuccessfully to carry the rebellion into other regions of the country.

By 1953 the rebellion was clearly diminishing, and by 1956 the movement was reduced to only a few scattered bands of armed men and women. Most participants had grown weary of war, and new government programs convinced many of them that tenancy reforms were possible. Moreover, the government's reorganized military became more effective and considerably less abusive to villagers.

In the 1960s some Huk bands remained in parts of central Luzon, and these constitute the third group to which *Huk* sometimes refers. Villagers' opinions of them varied; some saw them as Robin Hood figures while others considered them robbers. Some Huk bands sold "protection" to the organized prostitution and gambling organizations that thrived outside the United States' Clark Air Force Base in Angeles City, central Luzon.

[*See also* Philippines *and* Taruc, Luis.]

Benedict Kerkvliet, *The Huk Rebellion* (1977). E. Lachica, *Huk* (1971). William J. Pomeroy, *The Forest* (1963). Luis Taruc, *He Who Rides the Tiger* (1967).

BENEDICT J. TRIA KERKVLIET

HULEGU (c. 1217–1265), founder of the Mongol Ilkhanid dynasty of Iran. During his rule, from 1256 to 1265, Hulegu established the boundaries and basic policies of Ilkhanid rule. His successors ruled Iran for approximately one hundred years.

Hulegu was Genghis Khan's grandson and the brother of Mongke Khan, who in 1251 sent him to extend and consolidate Mongol rule in the Middle East. Hulegu conquered Iran, Mesopotamia, and Syria, the last of which, however, he soon lost. In the course of his campaigns he suppressed the Isma'ili sect (known as the Assassins) and from 1256 to 1257 destroyed their strongholds; in 1258 he sacked Baghdad and killed the Abbasid caliph.

Hulegu was Buddhist but also favored Christians, and formed an alliance with the pope and European kings against the Arab Mamluks. He likewise promoted Islamic culture, patronizing the Persian historian Juwaini and the Shi'ite scholar Nasir al-Din Tusi, for whom he built an observatory.

[*See also* Ilkhanid Dynasty.]

*The Cambridge History of Iran*, vol. 5, *The Saljuq and Mongol Periods*, edited by J. A. Boyle (1968), pp. 340–355. René Grousset, *The Empire of the Steppes*, translated by Naomi Walford (1970), pp. 359–367.

BEATRICE FORBES MANZ

HUMAYUN (1508–1556), Indian Mughal emperor. Humayun succeeded his father, Babur, to the throne in 1531, a position that he held until 1540. He became emperor again in 1555, only to die of a fall within a year of his accession. Humayun had inherited troublesome brothers and a shaky empire surrounded by hostile regional powers. The most determined hostile element, however, lay within the empire, toward the east. The Afghans, from whom

Babur had snatched the throne at Panipat, still commanded considerable strength, and an ambitious and competent leader was preparing them for the final trial with the Mughals. In 1540 the Afghan Sher Shah retrieved the imperial throne, which he held for five years; during this period Humayun wandered about in western India and Persia. The second Afghan attempt at empire-building in India lasted a mere fifteen years. Internal Afghan dissension facilitated Humayun's return.

[*See also* Babur; Mughal Empire; *and* Sher Shah.]

Ishwari Prasad, *Life and Times of Humayun* (1955).

HARBANS MUKHIA

# HUME, ALLAN OCTAVIAN

HUME, ALLAN OCTAVIAN (1829–1912), Indian civil servant from 1849 until 1882. Of liberal views, he believed that Indian interests were inadequately represented in government. Devoting his remaining life to promoting the Indian cause both in Britain and in India, he helped fround the Indian National Congress in 1885.

[*See also* Indian Administrative Service *and* Indian National Congress.]

USHA SANYAL

# HUNAN

HUNAN, Chinese province located south of the Yangtze River; the third-largest rice- and tea-growing province in China. Its population was about 60 million in 1980, with a density nearly triple the national average. Hunan lies in the same latitude as Egypt and Florida. Surrounded by mountains on the east, south, and west, it is drained by three river systems flowing from the south through Lake Dongting to the Yangtze River.

From the early eighth century BCE, Hunan was the core territory of the Chu dynasty, which very nearly unified China before succumbing to the Qin in 223 BCE. In terms of political institutions, Chu appears to have originated the *xian* (county) administrative system. In artistic terms, there is much evidence that Han-dynasty normative painting techniques originated in Chu, as did one of the major strands of Chinese poetry, from the *Chuci (Songs of the South)*.

Hunan's academies did not produce a large number of successful imperial scholars during the Qing period (1644–1911), but from the province came the major leaders of the anti-Taiping struggle in the mid-nineteenth century—Zeng Guofan, Zuo Zong-tang, Hu Linyi, and others. Mao Zedong and Liu Shaoqi are among the Hunanese who were instrumental in founding the People's Republic of China. These were not cosmopolitan men but, rather, men of strong political character.

ANGUS W. MCDONALD, JR.

# HUNDRED FLOWERS CAMPAIGN

HUNDRED FLOWERS CAMPAIGN (26 May 1956–8 June 1957), period during which the Chinese Communist Party (CCP) encouraged intellectual and artistic diversity in the People's Republic of China. The name derives from the slogan used to initiate the campaign: "Let a hundred flowers bloom and a hundred schools of thought contend." While the fruits of these Hundred Flowers months were literary and intellectual, their significance is tied to their political results. Political calculations determined the launching and later the reversal of the campaign. Impending changes in economic direction made support by intellectuals desirable; disciplining Party members became a goal; and the effects of de-Stalinization in the Communist bloc were felt by Party and intellectuals alike.

The first public notice given of moderated controls was a speech by Lu Dingyi in which he explained some (never published) remarks by Mao Zedong, including the above slogan. Response was halting, and in February 1957 Mao restated his encouragement, now extending divergent opinions to include criticism of the Party. The goal thus widened from winning over intellectuals to disciplining cadres through criticism by intellectuals. The criticism that followed was most vigorous in what proved to be the campaign's last month, May 1957. At meetings and in print, this reached even top leadership and the Party system itself; demands were made to redress past wrongs, especially the case of Hu Feng, who had criticized some of Zhou Yang's policies as leader of the movement; student unrest was widespread. The intensity of the criticism and its source (chiefly young intellectuals, nurtured by the Party) constituted an unexpected challenge and justified the campaign's opponents within the Party. The reversal in policy came with an editorial in *People's Daily* that said there must be countercriticism (by cadres) as well as criticism. The antirightist drive followed immediately, lasting also a year. Control was reimposed by dismissals and by selective "struggle meetings," focusing on Ding Ling and Feng Xuefeng.

[*See also* China, People's Republic of; Communism: Chinese Communist Party; Lu Dingyi; Ding Ling; *and* Zhou Yang.]

D. W. Fokkema, *Literary Doctrine in China and Soviet Influence, 1956–1960* (1965). Merle Goldman, *Literary Dissent in Communist China* (1967). Roderick MacFarquhar, *The Origins of the Cultural Revolution* (1974). Hualing Nieh, ed., *Literature from the Hundred Flowers* (1981).

SHAN CHOU

**HUNG VUONG.** According to Viet legend, Hung Vuong, the son of Lac Long Quan (Lac Dragon Lord) and the fairy Au Co, became king of the Viet kingdom of Van Lang in 2879 BCE. Tradition holds that he was succeeded by seventeen rulers, each named Hung Vuong, until their Hong Bang dynasty was overthrown by An Duong Vuong.

Archaeological evidence suggests a historical basis for the Van Lang kingdom and points to a date between 1000 and 500 BCE for Hung Vuong's reign. It has also been suggested that Hung Vuong may have been the title adopted by the overlords of Van Lang.

The legend of Hung Vuong is especially significant in that it shows that the Viet kingdom was contemporary with China but separate from it.

[*See also* Lac Long Quan; Au Co; Van Lang; Hong Bang Dynasty; *and* An Duong Vuong.]

Keith W. Taylor, *The Birth of Vietnam* (1983).

JAMES M. COYLE

**HUNS.** By the middle of the fourth century CE, a nomadic pastoral people related to the Huns of the west and the Xiongnu of Chinese records had occupied Transoxiana, driven its Iranian population south or absorbed them, and formed a nation known as the White Huns. To them the Iranians applied the name of an ancient Iranian hostile tribe, the Hiyun (Avestan, Kh$^v$yaona); the Greeks called them the Chionites, and the Indians called them the Hunas.

In about 350 they invaded the eastern Sasanid provinces but were defeated by Shapur II, came to terms with him, and joined him (under their own king Grumbates) in his campaign in Roman Mesopotamia. In 392, the Huns swept from the northern Caucasus into the Iranian provinces as far as Mesopotamia, but were again defeated and driven back. Yet wave after wave of the Hunnic people settled along the Oxus. A fresh horde, the Kidarites, occupied Bactria and Gandhara, inheriting the territory of the now-defunct Kushan dynasty. They and the Chionites were in turn replaced, in the fifth century, by a new group the Iranians called Heptaran

(or Heftalan; Greek, Hephthalites; Arabic, Haytal, pl., Hayatila; Chinese, Yeda), who were soon very much iranized, becoming sedentary and fair in complexion, according to the Byzantine historian Procopius.

As a leading power in Transoxiana and Bactria, the Hephthalites posed serious threats to the Sasanid empire. In 427, Bahram Gur successfully campaigned against them, while Peroz (r. 459–484) received their support in 457 when he dethroned his brother. Turning against them, Peroz was badly defeated and captured by the Hephthalite king, Khushnivar. He was ransomed and released but was soon annihilated when he tried a second time to invade Transoxiana. The disaster made a great impression in the Persian and Byzantine empires and augmented a period of Hephthalite supremacy. Kawad, son of Peroz, paid the Hephthalites a large sum and regained the throne with their help. Finally, the Turks arrived in Central Asia and made an alliance with Khusrau Anushirvan, son of Kawad; together they annihilated the Hephthalites in 557, driving them to the far side of the Oxus. Hephthalite survivors were still active in the military affairs of Herat and Badghis down to the seventh and eighth centuries.

The original language of the eastern Huns has vanished. They employed the Bactrian script and language in their records—even their royal and tribal names are often of Iranian derivation—and imitated the Kushan-Sasanid coinage. They are associated with the cremation of the dead (attested among the Chionites), the straight sword and compound bow, and the strange custom of artificially elongating their skulls upward (a feature often seen on their coins).

[*See also* Chionites; Kushan Dynasty; *and* Sasanid Dynasty.]

Richard N. Frye, *The History of Ancient Iran* (1984), pp. 346ff. Otto J. Maenchen-Helfen, *The World of the Huns* (1973), pp. 52ff. W. M. McGovern, *The Early Empires of Central Asia* (1939).　A. SHAHPUR SHAHBAZI

**HURLEY, PATRICK J.** (1883–1963), American diplomat; ambassador to China (1944–1945). Born in the Oklahoma Territory, Hurley served in the army in World War I and became secretary of war (1929–1933) under President Herbert Hoover. Although prominent in the Republican Party, he served Franklin D. Roosevelt in several special assignments. In 1944, he was sent to China to improve Sino-American relations, which had deteriorated as a result of the tension between the US commander, Joseph W. Stilwell, and Chiang Kai-shek. He stayed on as ambassador and sought unsuccessfully to mediate between Chiang's government and Mao Zedong's Chinese Communist Party. In November 1945, he resigned abruptly and charged that his efforts had been undermined by communist sympathizers in his embassy and in the State Department.

[See also Chiang Kai-shek; Stilwell, Joseph W.; and World War II in China.]

LYMAN P. VAN SLYKE

**HUSAIN, ZAKIR** (1897–1969), Indian educator and politician. Although his family's roots were in the Farrukhabad district of Uttar Pradesh, Zakir Husain was born in Hyderabad (Deccan), where his father had gone to practice law in the courts of the *nizam*. Returning to the North for his education, Husain graduated from Aligarh Muslim University. During the Khilafat and Noncooperation movements he joined other Aligarh "old boys" in rejecting their old school as a government pawn. He was instrumental in the founding of a Muslim "National" University, the Jamia Millia, located in New Delhi. He left India in 1923 to study economics in Berlin, receiving a doctorate there in 1926. On his return to India he involved himself in the politics of the Congress Party, becoming its educational expert. He served in a number of prestigious posts, including vice-chancellor of Aligarh Muslim University (1948), representative to UNESCO (1956), and governor of Bihar (1957). He became the third president of India in 1967, but died while in office.

[See also Khilafat Movement.]

*Asian Recorder* (1969). *Dictionary of National Biography* (1974).
GREGORY C. KOZLOWSKI

**HUSAIN IBN ALI** (626–680), the grandson of Muhammad and the second son of Fatima and Ali ibn Abi Talib. Encouraged to raise the claims of his family against the Umayyads and motivated by a personal vision of an ideal Islam, Husain went into battle and met a tragic end at Karbala in Iraq. The date, 10 Muharram 61 AH, is commemorated as Ashura throughout the Shi'ite world by annual ritual lamentation and pilgrimage to the Shi'ite shrines, especially Karbala. The figure of Husain gave rise to many legends, while the events surrounding his death are the subject of popular drama in Iran and elsewhere.

[See also Ashura.]

Mahmoud Ayoub, *Redemptive Suffering in Islam: A Study of the Devotional Aspects in Twelver Shi'ism* (1978). Roy Mottahedeh, *The Mantle of the Prophet* (1985).
JEANETTE A. WAKIN

**HUSAIN SHAHI DYNASTY,** Bengali dynasty whose name derives from Alauddin Husain Shah, ruler of Bengal from 1494 to 1519. His successors were Nusrat Shah (r. 1519–1532), Firuz Shah (r. 1532–1533), and Mahmud Shah (r. 1533–1538). The Husain Shahis patronized the cultural life of Bengal—most prominently through architecture and literature. Husain Shah made Ekdala his capital and established a progressive administration. He extended his kingdom to the borders of Orissa, occupied northern Bihar, invaded the Ahom kingdom of Assam, and recovered Chittagong from Arakanese occupation. His son, Nusrat Shah, annexed Tirhut and entered into conflict with Babur, but was forced to sue for peace. During this period two famous mosques—Bara Sona Masjid (Great Golden Mosque) and Qadam-i Rasul (Foot Impression of the Prophet)—were constructed at Gaur, and the Hindu epic *Mahabharata* was translated into Bengali. Assassinated by his eunuchs in 1532, Nusrat was succeeded by his son Alauddin Firuz Shah, who in turn was killed by his uncle Ghiyas ud-Din Mahmud Shah. Ghiyas, the last king of the dynasty, was expelled from Bengal by Sher Khan Suri.

[See also Bengal.]

M. R. Tarafdar, *Husain Shahi Bengal 1494–1538* (1965).
FARHAN AHMAD NIZAMI

**HU SHI** (1891–1962), leading liberal scholar and educator in China. While studying in America (1910–1917), Hu came under the influence of John Dewey, whose experimentalistic method had a profound impact on his life. Hu returned to China in 1917 to become a professor of philosophy at Beijing University and subsequently played a crucial role in the new literary and cultural movements. Perhaps his single most important contribution to China's twentieth-century cultural transformation was his advocacy of a plain, vernacular, and "living" language (*baihua*), to replace what he called the "dead" classical language (*wenyan*). As an easier and simpler means of communication, the vernacular language had far-reaching consequences beyond its apparent literary significance. It contributed to increased literacy and hastened the dissolution of the obsolete social and political order.

Hu, an energetic proponent of liberalism, individualism, and women's liberation (what he called "Ibsenism"), was a tireless critic of Confucianism. He was equally critical of Marxism. In his famous 1919 debate with Li Dazhao, "Problems versus Isms," Hu, using the Deweyan evolutionary approach, rejected radical, all-embracing solutions to China's myriad problems. Social ills, he contended, could only be cured by tackling individual, specific problems. Contrary to Hu, Li Dazhao argued that the entire "system," not separate problems, was the issue. Nothing short of a revolution based on the Marxist model could change China's corrupt system. Hu, unwavering in his belief, continued to apply his experimentalist methods to the study of Chinese vernacular novels, cultural history, and philosophy, all of which yielded considerable scholarly results.

Although sympathetic to the Nationalist government, Hu refused to identify with it completely. Nonetheless, in his later years he served as China's ambassador to the United States (1938–1942) and was later made chancellor of Beijing University (1946–1948). Hu left for the United States before the Communist takeover in 1949 and returned to Taiwan in 1958 to assume the presidency of Academia Sinica. He died four years later.

[*See also* May Fourth Movement.]

Howard L. Boorman, ed., *Biographical Dictionary of Republican China* (1967–1971). Chow Tse-tsung, *The May Fourth Movement: Intellectual Revolution in Modern China* (1960). Jerome B. Grieder, *Hu Shih and the Chinese Renaissance: Liberalism in the Chinese Revolution, 1917–1937* (1970).          CHANG-TAI HUNG

## HUSSEIN, SULTAN OF JOHOR AND SINGAPORE (r. 1819–1835), often called Tunku Long. The eldest son of Sultan Mahmud III of Riau and Johor, Hussein failed to succeed his father in 1812 on the latter's death; instead, his younger brother, Abdul Rahman, was proclaimed sultan. In 1819 Hussein was brought to Singapore by Temenggong Abdul Rahman. Both signed a treaty with Sir Thomas Stamford Raffles giving the island to the English. The English recognized Hussein as sultan of Singapore and Johor and gave him a pension. He maintained a residence of Kampong Gelam in Singapore. He shared little in the prosperity of Singapore and had considerable financial difficulties. He died in Melaka, virtually powerless. It was not until 1855 that his son Tunku Ali was recognized as sultan.

[*See also* Johor; Singapore; *and* Abdul Rahman.]

A. H. Hill, ed., *Hikajat Abdullah* (1970). Carl A. Trocki, *Prince of Pirates* (1979).          CARL A. TROCKI

HU WEIYONG (d. 1380), prime minister of the first Ming emperor of China from 1377 until his death in 1380. A native of Anhui Province in eastern China, he had joined the emperor's cause early on and won his trust. After serving in the provincial administration for almost a decade, in 1373 he was brought into the secretariat and in 1377 made prime minister. Two years later he was implicated in a case of treason and was finally beheaded in 1380. There followed a prolonged purge of the bureaucracy in which thousands were executed. The central government was reorganized and the office of prime minister permanently eliminated.

[*See also* Ming Dynasty *and* Zhu Yuanzhang.]

Edward L. Dreyer, *Early Ming Government: A Political History, 1355–1435* (1982).          JAMES GEISS

HU YAOBANG (b. 1915), chairman of the Chinese Communist Party from 1981 to 1987. Hu replaced Hua Guofeng, who in 1976 had succeeded both Zhou Enlai as premier and Mao Zedong as Party chairman. Born into a poor peasant family in Hunan Province, Hu became a protégé of Deng Xiaoping in the early 1940s. He was twice purged with Deng, during the Great Proletarian Cultural Revolution and again in 1976 after the death of Zhou Enlai, before being elevated by Deng to the highest Party post. In January 1987 Hu was forced to resign as chairman in the wake of widespread student demonstrations calling for greater democratic freedom. Prime Minister Zhao Ziyang was named acting Party chairman; Hu, however, retained his seat in the Politburo Standing Committee.

[*See also* Communism: Chinese Communist Party; Deng Xiaoping; *and* Zhao Ziyang.]

EDWARD L. FARMER

HUYNH PHU SO (1919–1947), also referred to as Huynh Giao Chu, founder of the Vietnamese Hoa Hao Buddhist sect in 1939. Gaining a reputation as a healer and prophet, Huynh Phu So declared himself to be a reincarnation of the nineteenth-century Buddha Master of Western Peace. His followers increased in number and were concentrated in his native Chau Doc and neighboring southern provinces. Although the Hoa Hao suffered from French repression, Huynh received protection from the occupying

Japanese. After the war, attempts to work with the Viet Minh failed, and Huynh Phu So was executed by the Communists in May 1947.

[*See also* Hoa Hao.]

Bernard Fall, "The Political-Religious Sects of Viet-Nam," *Pacific Affairs* 28.3 (September 1955): 235–253. Hue-Tam Ho Tai, *Millenarianism and Peasant Politics in Vietnam* (1983). BRUCE M. LOCKHART

**HWARANG** ("flower youths"), bands of elite young unmarried men organized in Silla, one of three competing kingdoms on the Korean peninsula that in 668 finally overcame its rivals and established the first unified dynastic rule in Korea. The purpose of these bands was to prepare young men for military and government service; they provided Silla with the leadership that made the unification possible. Tales of the valor and prowess of *hwarang* heroes such as Sadaham, Kim Yu-sin, and Kwanch'ang are perennial favorites in the Korean tradition.

Members of *hwarang* bands devoted themselves to both spiritual and military cultivation. The *hwarang* ethos derived from a combination of indigenous elements and motifs borrowed from the recently imported Buddhist and Confucian traditions. The influence of the latter two is evident in the famous Five Commandments formulated for the *hwarang* by the Buddhist monk Wŏn'gwang in the early seventh century: (1) serve the king with loyalty; (2) serve one's parents with filial piety; (3) practice fidelity in friendship; (4) never retreat in battle; and (5) refrain from wanton killing. The indigenous elements are reflected in the frequent retreats of the *hwarang* to sacred mountains and river sites for spiritual practices, including ritual songs and dances performed for the nation's tranquillity and prosperity, and in their devotion to spiritual forces or deities associated with such places. *Hwarang* enjoyed great prestige and were even identified with Buddhist bodhisattvas in the popular mind.

[*See also* Silla.]

Woo-keun Han, *The History of Korea*, translated by Kyung-shik Lee (1971). Wanne J. Joe, *Traditional Korea: A Cultural History* (1972). Ki-baik Lee, *A New History of Korea*, translated by Edward W. Wagner (1984).

MICHAEL C. KALTON

**HYANGGA**, term for the twenty-five extant Old Korean poems spanning the seventh to the tenth century. *Hyangga*, like the Japanese *waka* or *uta*, means "native songs." Of the three variant forms, the most polished and popular consisted of two stanzas of four lines plus a conclusion of two lines (eighteen poems). The ninth line usually begins with an interjection. The lyrics of the *hyangga* are transcribed into Chinese logographs chiefly on the basis of phonetic values in a system known as *hyangch'al*, somewhat like the method used in the Japanese *Man'yōshū* (c. 759).

*Hyangga* themes include praise of Silla's elite corps of knights *(hwarang)*, the magical power of poetry, the Confucian concept of statesmanship, and the temporality of man. Eighteen of the poems, however, are Buddhist in inspiration and content and reflect contemporary trends in Korean Buddhism—the cults of Maitreya (the future Buddha), Amitabha (Buddha of Infinite Light), Avalokiteshvara (He Who Observes the Sound of the World), and the emulation of the bodhisattva vows and practices, as in Great Master Kyunyŏ's eleven devotional poems.

Verbal felicity and symbolic resonance grace some *hyangga*. For example, the "Ode to Knight Kip'a" concludes with a correspondence between the knight and the pine that "scorns frost, ignores snow." Like Homer in the *Iliad* (6.146–150), "Requiem" uses the trope of comparing the generations of man with the scattering of leaves. The sixth poem by Kyunyŏ (923–973) likens the enlightened mind to "a moonlit autumn field / Ripe with the gold fruit of knowledge." The decipherment of transcription is still a problem in understanding the meaning of the poems, and new readings of the lyrics are often a debated topic among scholars.

Peter H. Lee, *Poems from Korea: A Historical Anthology* (1974). PETER H. LEE

**HYDARI, AKBAR** (1869–1942), also known as Nawab Hydar Nawaz Jung Bahadur, a title earned in Hyderabad state service, was a member of the extended Tyabji family of Bombay. He began his career in the Indian Finance Service, later moving to Hyderabad, where he served as accountant general and finance secretary (1905–1911), home secretary (1911–1920), finance member (1921–1937), and finally president of the executive council, the equivalent of prime minister (1937–1941). Throughout his life he was active in social reform and educational causes. He proposed the foundation of Osmania University in Hyderabad, India's first vernacular-medium university, in which Urdu was the language of instruction. He was a supporter of close cooperation between the *nizam* and the British and attended the London Round Table Conferences in 1930 to 1931 as a representative of Hyderabad.

K. Krishnaswamy Mudiraj, *Pictorial Hyderabad*, vol. 2 (1934), pp. 23–28.    GAIL MINAULT

HYDERABAD, city in Andhra Pradesh, India, and formerly a state in a region now divided among Andhra Pradesh, Karnataka, and Maharashtra.

*History.* The city of Hyderabad, historically the capital of the largest and richest Indian princely state, ruled by the *nizams,* was founded in 1590 by the ruler of Golconda, Muhammad Quli Qutb Shah, who preferred the site of the present city on the banks of the Musi River to his rocky fortress. Golconda commanded the main trade and military routes across the Deccan plateau and was thus of great strategic importance to any ruler seeking to control southern India. It was also a place of legendary wealth, as evidenced by its diamond market. These facts were not lost on the acquisitive Mughal emperor Aurangzeb, who conquered Golconda in 1687, incorporating the Hyderabad area into the Mughal empire. [*See also* Aurangzeb.]

The most capable Mughal governor of the Deccan was Nizam ul-Mulk Asaf Jah (1671–1748). The *nizam* was so successful that he was recalled to Delhi to help check the decay in the central administration, but he gave up in disgust and returned to the Deccan in 1724. Although he remained loyal to the Mughal emperor thereafter, his realm was for all practical purposes independent. During British rule, Hyderabad had a large degree of autonomy as the most important of the princely states, and only became part of independent India in 1948, following police action by Indian forces. [*See* Nizam al-Mulk.]

At times, Hyderabad's independence was tenuous, as during the struggle for succession following Nizam ul-Mulk's death in 1748, when the contest between French- and British-backed candidates involved the European trading companies in Indian politics as never before, and entrained events that led to British rule over much of India. Again in the mid-nineteenth century, the parlous state of Hyderabad's finances risked direct British intervention. The prime minister, Salar Jang I (r. 1853–1883), salvaged the situation by a reform of the revenue administration, importing Western-educated talent from outside the state. He thus continued a Hyder-

abadi tradition of recruiting administrators from North India at the expense of the then-ruling elite, Hindus and Muslims who had come to Hyderabad with the first *nizam*. Salar Jang succeeded in maintaining the autonomy of the *nizam's* government but created cleavages in the ruling class that plagued Hyderabad politics to the end of Asaf Jahi rule. [*See* Salar Jang I.]

*Language and Culture.* As Hyderabad was the political junction of North and South, so was its culture a composite. Urdu, "the language of the camp," was spoken by North Indian armies in their invasions of the South, and first attained literary distinction, written in Persian script, at the Deccan courts. Muhammad Quli Qutb Shah himself was a poet in Deccani Urdu. Deccani court painting achieved a delicate blend of Hindu form and Muslim taste for surface detail. Hyderabad's cultural symbol, the Char Minar, a great arch with four minarets, dates from the Qutb Shahi period and blends Iranian prototypes with a grandeur of scale characteristic of Hindu and Muslim monuments of the broad, barren Deccan. The composite culture of Hyderabad persisted under the *nizams* with Urdu as the medium of everyday discourse of Hindu and Muslim elites alike. The vernaculars of the rural districts were patronized in the primary education system, while Urdu became the language of government and higher education, especially after the founding of Osmania University in 1917. After its incorporation into independent India and the reorganization of states along linguistic lines, Hyderabad became the capital of the Telugu-speaking state of Andhra Pradesh in 1956. Urdu lost its place as a language of elite cosmopolitanism, but it remains a link with the languages of North India and is thus symbolic of the meeting of North and South that still occurs in Hyderabad.

[*See also* Golconda; Deccan; Mughal Empire; *and* Andhra Pradesh.]

Yusuf Husain Khan, *The First Nizam* (2d ed., 1963). Karen I. Leonard, "Hyderabad: The Mulki–Non-Mulki Conflict," in *People, Princes and Paramount Power: Society and Politics in the Indian Princely States,* edited by Robin Jeffrey (1978), pp. 65-106. Karen I. Leonard, *Social History of an Indian Caste: The Kayasths of Hyderabad* (1978). K. Krishnaswamy Mudiraj, *Pictorial Hyderabad,* 2 vols. (1929–1934). H. K. Sherwani, *Muhammad Quli Qutb Shah: Founder of Haiderabad* (1967).

GAIL MINAULT

# I

IBAN, important ethnic group of northwest Borneo, numbering over 300,000 in Sarawak, or 30 percent of the population. Traditionally shifting cultivators who practiced an animistic religion, the Iban (also called the Sea Dayak) were once interior Borneo's most aggressive headhunters. From the sixteenth through the eighteenth century a major migration brought most Iban from West Borneo (Indonesia) into the Lupar and Rejang river basins; later they spread throughout Sarawak and into Brunei. Some Iban fiercely resisted the control of the Brookes, the Englishmen who governed Sarawak as rajas, for decades. The Brookes suppressed headhunting and employed Iban as soldiers. Many Iban adopted Christianity under their rule. In recent decades some Iban have taken up rubber planting or successfully entered politics, government service, and other professions.

[See also Sarawak; Dayak; Brooke, Sir Charles Vyner; Brooke, Sir James; and Brooke, Sir Charles.]

Robert M. Pringle, *Rajahs and Rebels: The Ibans of Sarawak under Brooke Rule, 1841–1941* (1967). Vinson H. Sutlive, *The Iban of Sarawak* (1978).

CRAIG A. LOCKARD

IBN BATTUTA (1304–1378?), Muslim traveler throughout Asia, born in Tangier, Morocco. Almost all that is known about Ibn Battuta comes from his own narrative of his travels. During his first pilgrimage to Mecca he vowed "never, so far as possible, to cover a second time any road" that he had once traveled, and he certainly journeyed more extensively than any other recorded medieval traveler. Ibn Battuta dictated his travels to Ibn Juzayy, who put the work into literary style. Ibn Battuta often conflated his experiences into a somewhat artificial itinerary. The full text of his work was rediscovered in North Africa in the early nineteenth century.

On his third journey Ibn Battuta spent two or three years in Mecca. His interest began to turn from piety alone to an ethnographic interest in the cultures and peoples he saw. He then traveled overland in North Africa and Syria, exploring Arabia, Mesopotamia, Persia, and Asia Minor. With the assistance of various Muslim sultans and religious authorities, he made a journey by way of Constantinople (in the retinue of the khan of the Golden Horde) and Samarkand to India, where he resided almost eight years at the court of the sultan of Delhi, Muhammad ibn Tughluq, who deputed Ibn Battuta to China as one of his ambassadors in 1342. His was an adventurous journey: he was delayed in Calicut, the Maldive Islands, the Coromandel and Malabar coasts, Bengal, Assam, and Sumatra, landing finally in Zayton (Quanzhou, in Fujian), and then journeying to Beijing. Ibn Battuta's stay in China was relatively short; in 1347 he returned to the West by way of Sumatra and the Malabar coast, arriving in Tangier around 1350. Later he went to Spain and traveled in West Africa.

Ibn Battuta's glowing description of India was treated with skepticism by contemporaneous Arabs but is, on the whole, borne out by comparison with works by Indian historians. His account of his travels in China is not as detailed as much of the rest of his work, perhaps because he viewed his experiences in China as outside the cultural and social history of Islam.

H. A. R. Gibb, trans., *The Travels of Ibn Battuta, A.D. 1325–1354*, 4 vols. (1929; rev. ed., 1958–).

THEODORE NICHOLAS FOSS

IBN SINA, more fully Abu Ali al-Husain ibn Sina; physician, natural philosopher, scientist, and encyclopedist, born near the Central Asian town of Bukhara in 980. After a tumultuous life, Ibn Sina died in the Persian city of Hamadan in 1037. Known to the Latin West as Avicenna, he was particularly famous for his medical and philosophical works.

Most of what we know of Ibn Sina's life derives from an autobiographical account that was completed by one of his most trusted students and friends, Abu Ubaid al-Juzjani. From that biography we know that Ibn Sina had completed most of what an educated medieval Muslim scholar would have learned by the age of sixteen. By then he had become such a famous physician that he was sought after by the Samanid dynast of Bukhara and was allowed to complete his education at the Samanid ruler's private library; he claims to have completed this by the age of eighteen.

His medical masterpiece is *Al-qanun;* in it he recast the Greek medical corpus—especially the writings of Galen and Hippocrates—in an accessible, comprehensive fashion that made it the most desirable pedagogical textbook for over seven hundred years. Al-qanun is composed of five main divisions: book 1 deals with the philosophical foundation of medicine and general medical theories; book 2 deals with pharmacological subjects; book 3, by far the largest part of the text, is an extensive listing of pathological diseases arranged in the order of the body parts; book 4 is devoted to fevers, special diseases such as smallpox, and general problems connected with medical practice; and book 5 is devoted to what was known in medieval Islamic tradition as *aqrabadhin,* the study of the properties of simple and composite drugs.

Ibn Sina's most famous philosophical work is his *Shifa,* which, on the whole, is a reformulation of the Aristotelian philosophical corpus. Like Aristotle, he starts with logic and ends with metaphysics. But unlike Aristotle, he includes extensive treatises on mathematics and astronomy: the first is a version of Euclid's *Elements,* and the second is an edited version of Ptolemy's *Almagest.*

It is not the case, however, that Ibn Sina was content merely to mimic the Greek authors without adding anything of his own. Many original ideas are scattered throughout his works, an extensive reading of which will allow them to be fully appreciated.

[*See also* Astrology and Astronomy, Islamic *and* Medicine.]

A.-M. Goichon, "Ibn Sīnā," in *The Encyclopaedia of Islam* (new ed., 1960–).    GEORGE SALIBA

IBRAHIM, sultan of Johor (1873–1959), became sultan in 1895 on the death of his father, Sultan Abu Bakar. He ruled the state through the turbulent period in which it passed from nominal independence to British colonial rule to Japanese rule (from 1942 to 1945) and finally to independence within the Federation of Malaya. Educated in England, Ibrahim traveled widely after becoming a sultan, making frequent visits to Europe and Britain.

Although a general adviser from Britain was accepted in 1910 and Johor became an "unfederated" state, the Malay administrators of Johor continued to exercise significant control over the state's day-to-day affairs. Ibrahim's administration oversaw the beginnings of modernization in Johor, including the opening of a railroad linking the west to Singapore and to the Malay states to the north and the expansion of rubber planting. In the postwar period he played an important role in opposing the Malayan Union plan.

[*See also* Johor; Abu Bakar; Malayan Union; *and* Unfederated Malay States.]    CARL A. TROCKI

ICHIKAWA DANJŪRŌ. *See* Danjūrō.

ID FITR, literally, "festival of the breaking of the fast," is the annual festival celebrated on the first of Shawwal for three to four days, immediately following the month-long fast of Ramadan. The Id Fitr, although known as the "little" festival in comparison to the "great" festival of sacrifice (Id Qorban), is celebrated with much enthusiasm because it marks the end of hardships connected with the fasting and the exhausting devotions undertaken during the last ten nights of Ramadan. For instance, in Iran the special prayer prescribed for both festivals is performed publicly only on Id Fitr, whereas the Qorban festival is observed privately. The Fitr celebrations begin the sunrise with the payment of *zakat* (alms), the amount of which is fixed in the law books; then the public prayer, followed by a sermon, is held, preferably in the open area known as *idgah* or *musalla.*

[*See also* Id Qorban; Ramadan; *and* Zakat.]

Gustave E. Von Grunebaum, *Muhammadan Festivals* (1951).    ABDELAZIZ SACHEDINA

ID QORBAN, literally "festival of sacrifice," also known as the "great" festival; annually celebrated on the tenth of Dhu al-Hijja, the day when the pilgrims sacrifice at Mina during the *hajj,* the pilgrimage to Mecca. The festival is celebrated with much enthusiasm by the pilgrims, who are directly engaged in a series of devotional acts, of which the culmination is the ritual of sacrifice. The sacrifice of a sheep, a camel, or a cow on this day, however, is not limited to pilgrims; rather, it is recommended that all Muslims reenact this pious act wherever they happen to be.

On the occasion of the Id Qorban, as on the Id Fitr, public prayer is held for the whole community; the service is followed by a sermon explicating the significance of the festival. Books of Islamic jurisprudence are full of recommendations concerning bathing, the donning of new clothes, and the use of perfumes on the *ids*.

[*See also* Id Fitr.]

G. E. Von Grunebaum, *Muhammadan Festivals* (1951).

ABDELAZIZ SACHEDINA

**IDRIS** (1849–1916), sultan of Perak. Son of a *bendahara* (chief minister) and great-grandson of a sultan of Perak, Idris at first supported his cousin, Sultan Abdullah, against James W. W. Birch, a British officer who had been appointed as an "adviser" to Perak, but did not join the Perak rising in November 1875. Idris later served on the State Council and as judge of the Supreme Court. In 1887, although he was not in direct line according to the Perak custom of rotation, Idris succeeded his father-in-law, Yusuf, to the throne. A staunch believer in British "protection," Idris was much respected by the British, but at the 1903 durbar he deprecated the increasing centralization of the Federated Malay States.

[*See also* Perak; Birch, James W. W.; *and* Federated Malay States.]

A. J. STOCKWELL

**IGLESIA FILIPINA INDEPENDIENTE.** *See* Philippine Independent Church.

**IHARA SAIKAKU** (1642–1693), Japanese poet and prose writer. Until his forties Ihara Saikaku was known primarily for his prodigality as a writer of comic linked-verse *(haikai)*. In 1682 his first prose work, a burlesque, *The Life of an Amorous Man (Kōshoku ichidai otoko)*, ushered in the age of the new plebeian hero. This and subsequent works, such as *Five Women Who Loved Love (Kōshoku gonin onna)* and *The Life of an Amorous Woman (Kōshoku ichidai onna)*, established the tone of much of subsequent Tokugawa-era fiction in that they invented heroes for the newly emerging merchant class. Sexual exploits replaced military exploits; the "pleasure quarters" replaced, or rather became, the battlefield. Very much against the official orthodoxy, both men and women become heroes when they sacrificed all for forbidden love. From 1686 to 1688 Saikaku also produced a large number of works that deal with samurai honor and vendetta, but these are not considered among his best; only later would the samurai become fertile ground for heroic treatment. The most important work of his later years was *The Japanese Family Storehouse (Nippon eitaigura, 1688)*, in which he returned to the merchant class with a collection of stories that deal with typically bourgeois values. One finds no sense of overt hostility to the status quo in his works, and yet he constantly surprises with his coolly ironic mode of narration. Saikaku was rediscovered by early Meiji writers and ever since has been extolled, not without reason, as Japan's Daniel Defoe.

[*See also* Tokugawa Period *and* Genroku Culture.]

Donald Keene, *World within Walls* (1976). Ivan Morris, trans., *The Life of an Amorous Woman* (1963). G. Sargent, trans., *The Japanese Family Storehouse* (1959).

RICHARD BOWRING

**IKEDA MITSUMASA** (1609–1682), *tozama* daimyo of the early Tokugawa period famed for his administrative abilities and for his Confucianism. In 1617 Ikeda Mitsumasa was transferred because of his youth from his inherited domain, with an income of 420,000 *koku* (measures of rice), at Himeji in Harima Province (modern Hyōgo Prefecture) to Tottori, with an income of 320,000 *koku*. In 1632 he was moved to Okayama (315,000 *koku*) in Bizen Province (modern Okayama Prefecture), where he established his reputation as one of the three great daimyo administrators of the period. Politically, Mitsumasa institutionalized centralized control over his retainers and over the commoner populace of his domains in accordance with Confucian principles of government delineated with the assistance of his personal adviser, the Confucian Kumazawa Banzan (1619–1691). Vehemently anti-Buddhist, Mitsumasa supported Shinto and utilized shrines for registration of religious affiliation. In education, he established a domainal school in 1641 and "writing schools" for commoners in 1668. Mitsumasa courted the goodwill of the Tokugawa by marrying one of the shogun's adopted daughters, and in 1644 he erected a shrine to Tokugawa Ieyasu modeled on Toshogu at Nikko. He retired in 1672.

[*See also* Tozama Daimyo; Tokugawa Period; *and* Kumazawa Banzan.]

John W. Hall, *Government and Local Power in Japan, 500–1770: A Study Based on Bizen Province* (1966).

RONALD J. DiCENZO

**IKE TAIGA** (1723–1776), Japanese painter, central figure in the transformation and popularization of Chinese-inspired literati painting. A prolific and versatile painter as well as an innovative calligrapher, Ike Taiga helped to achieve a synthesis of Chinese and Japanese traditions that came to be known as Nanga ("southern-school painting") or Bunjinga ("literary men's painting"). His name is often written *Ike no Taiga,* but like many devotees of Chinese culture, he himself preferred *Ike Taiga,* so that his name would conform to the Chinese pattern—a single-character surname followed by a binomial given name.

The son of a farmer, he received his early training in calligraphy at Mampukuji, a Zen temple in Kyoto. He began his professional career as an apprentice in a Kyoto fan shop, where he executed designs after the *Bazhong huapu,* a Chinese painting manual that, together with the *Mustard Seed Garden,* exerted a profound influence on Japanese literati painters.

Taiga gained initial renown in the 1740s through his skill as a finger painter. In 1748 his love of travel led him to Edo, where he was much impressed by the then-fashionable Western-style perspective pictures. His many "true view" *(shinkei)* landscapes reveal the influence of a Western spatial system as well as his keen observation of famous sites.

Unlike Chinese literati painters, Taiga was open to a wide range of themes and styles. He painted traditional Chinese literary subjects, such as Chinese culture heroes, landscapes, bamboo, orchids, and chrysanthemums, as well as themes from Japanese folklore, Buddhist and Daoist subjects, and genre pictures. His painting style reveals a coloristic sensibility and boldness of design that reflect his interest in the Sōtatsu-Kōrin tradition. His exceptional talent and versatility as an artist and calligrapher combined with his charismatic personality made him a legend in his own time.

[*See also* Painting: Japanese Painting.]

Stephen Addiss, *Zenga and Nanga: Paintings by Japanese Monks and Scholars* (1976). James Cahill, *The Scholar Painters of Japan* (1972). Yonezawa Yoshiho and Yoshizawa Chu, *Japanese Painting in the Literati Style* (1974).

CHRISTINE M. E. GUTH

**IKKI.** Most often translated "peasant revolt," although more literally meaning "banding together," *ikki* is a generic term for a variety of protests, petitions, and rebellious actions by Japanese commoners during the Edo period (1600–1868). Such protest predates this period: religiously based compacts (e.g., *ikkō ikki*) and warrior alliances (e.g., *kokujin ikki*) were common bases of political and military action before Tokugawa rule. And such protest did not end with Tokugawa rule: many early Meiji protest actions paralleled *ikki* in motive, structure, and technique. But *ikki* was essentially a protest form determined by the political, social, and economic context of the Edo period.

*Ikki* are generally viewed as defensive efforts by peasants to protect established ways and levels of living, directed mainly against the feudal government and its agents and merchant allies. *Ikki* are therefore often described as a form of class struggle, yet they were hardly ever aimed at reform, much less transformation, of the political status quo: they bore very little connection to the eventual overthrow of the Tokugawa regime; they included a subtype (*murakata sōdō*) that consisted of conflict and litigation within the peasantry; and (especially in the later Edo period) they were frequently aimed at the acquisition of new rights and political positions within the feudal system. They were primarily defensive and restorative, instrumental and concrete in their goals, explicit in their demands, almost always nonviolent toward people, and usually well organized, not moblike.

***Types of Ikki.*** There were many types of *ikki,* including, in roughly increasing order of disruptiveness, the following seven major categories:

1. *chōsan,* the collective flight of peasants to escape misrule
2. *fuon,* minor unrest implying discontent with current policies or conditions
3. *shūso,* the presentation of demands or petitions to officials
4. *osso* or *jikiso,* direct appeal to a higher level of government than that closest to the people
5. *gōso,* collective demonstration and belligerent confrontation with authorities
6. *uchikowashi,* riot with widespread destruction of property and often forcible appropriation of goods and food
7. *hōki,* full-blown rebellion, often involving more than one feudal domain

The less extreme forms of *ikki* were often legal, albeit circumscribed; *osso* and *gōso,* on the other hand, were harshly dealt with as contraventions of the feudal order, whatever their substantive merits.

There were many variations on the above forms; other major types of *ikki* included the *murakata sōdō,* which was intra- or intervillage conflict over communal or political rights or local-level political or economic issues, and, during the last years of the Edo era, the *yonaoshi,* an intense and often millenarian form of intraclass conflict directed at better-off peasants and/or merchants and village officials, stimulated by the chaotic economic and political conditions of the day and aimed at a downward redistribution of wealth and power. Whether the *yonaoshi* were forward or backward looking is a matter of some debate; they do seem to be a transitional form of popular protest amid the downfall of an *ancien régime.*

*Causes and Goals.* In general, *ikki* were caused by three types of factors: economic, resulting from dearth or high food prices; fiscal, resulting from excessive taxation or governmental restrictions on commerce; and administrative, resulting from illegal or rapacious rule. Correspondingly, they aimed most often at acquisition of food and seed, price reductions, tax reductions, trade liberalization, and discipline or removal of unjust officials. Relatively remote regions, the recurrently famine-stricken far north, areas with more commercialized agriculture, and less tightly governed Tokugawa (as opposed to daimyo-ruled) lands seem to have been relatively susceptible to *ikki.* It would be a mistake to relate poverty or feudal exploitation directly to *ikki;* they were more usually provoked by a departure from established practices in welfare and relief, taxation levels, and administration, especially by a failure to allow for short-term dearth or to permit personal gain. Absence of governmental coercive forces on the land, commercial opportunities, the chancy presence of frustrated local leadership or arbitrary officials, and official fiscal deterioration are important explanatory factors, and it was as often the upwardly mobile as the downtrodden who protested. In a society in which wealth, rights, status, and power were so unequally distributed, protest was frequent: more than seventy-five hundred *ikki* were recorded during the period between 1590 and 1877.

*Evolution.* The frequency and nature of *ikki* were not constant during the Edo era. Overall, the trend was toward (1) more *ikki*—from five per year between 1590 and 1640 up to fifty-seven annually between 1830 and 1871; (2) more *ikki* of the more disruptive types such as *gōso* and *uchikowashi;* and (3) more plebeian leadership, with the typical confrontation less often between village elites (representing their constituents) and the government and more often between better-off peasants and others within villages.

The Edo era opened with frequent flight by disgruntled peasants and with large-scale insurrections, often directed against the imposition of Tokugawa rule. As the seventeenth century wore on, both types faded, and orderly petitions *(shūso)* and equally peaceable (albeit illegal) *osso* by village representatives approaching a now well-established regime increased. In the beginning of the eighteenth century, *bakufu* and *han* budgetary problems spurred greater efforts at extraction, both through taxation and official trade monopolies, and peasant resistance grew in intensity (with *gōso* becoming prominent) and scope (as peasants faced increasingly common threats nationwide, cross-domain protest grew). The late eighteenth century saw another wave of fiscal reform, combined with widespread crop failures, and another resultant wave of *ikki,* including unprecedented numbers of *uchikowashi* food riots.

The nineteenth century, including the first years of the Meiji era, was characterized by *gōso, uchikowashi,* and *murakata sōdō,* as the peasantry had become too fragmented to present a united front to the feudal authorities. The 1830s were characterized by another cycle, and the pitch of popular protest reached new heights during the economic and political chaos following the opening of Japan to foreign intercourse in the 1850s. Demands became more universalistic and goals more apocalyptic with the promise and then the achievement of political transformation; the failure of the Meiji regime to meet newly aroused expectations, combined with the imposition of unforeseen reforms, sparked a last wave of traditionalistic *ikki* in the 1870s before the establishment of new extractive, land-tenure, and regulative institutions that pushed commoners' demands into different channels and forms.

*Response and Result.* The most common official response to *ikki* throughout the Edo era was whatever was necessary to pacify the protesters (from studied inaction to concessions to armed repression), followed by punishment (often visited on officials as well as people) and, although governmental duplicity was common, limited but substantive amelioration of the popular condition. Indeed, despite bloody repression of specific *ikki,* there was a limit beyond which the elites could not go without seriously harming their peasant tax base and splitting themselves in policy debate. Many *bakufu* policies became dead letters owing to such resistance, and many demands were fulfilled even though they had been raised illegally.

Peasant gains were real, moreover, because some forms of *ikki* were legal. Although during the Edo era the main focus of proscription became organized protest, simultaneously, provisions for effective articulation of legal demands were augmented. Thus, *ikki* were less an agonized, inchoate cry by the most oppressed than a calculated utilization of all means available to maintain popular standards of justice, thus ameliorating the worst aspects of an authoritarian system.

[*See also* Osso.]

Aoki Michio, *Ikki* (1981). Hugh Borton, *Peasant Uprisings in Japan of the Tokugawa Period* (1938). Stephen Vlastos, *Conflict and Collective Action in Rural Japan* (1984).                    JAMES W. WHITE

**ILAVA**, caste living in India's southwestern coastal state of Kerala. The Ilavas are sometimes held to have migrated from Sri Lanka about the third century BCE, bringing with them the coconut palm, the cultivation of which was once considered their customary occupation. Originally they were considered a low, but not the lowest, caste in Kerala. *Ilava* was their usual name in southern and central Kerala, but similar people farther north were known as *Tiyya*. In the twentieth century the Sri Narayana Dharma Paripalana (SNDP) Yogam, a caste association inspired by the revered religious leader Sri Narayana (c. 1855–1928), challenged the disabilities suffered by the Ilavas as a low caste. After Ilava leaders threatened mass conversion to Christianity in the early 1930s, Travancore (the princely state roughly corresponding to southern Kerala today) granted in 1936 all castes the right to enter temples. The turmoil of these years, however, led many Ilava youths toward the Communist Party, of which Ilavas have often been regarded as chief supporters.

[*See also* Kerala *and* Communism: Communist Parties in South Asia.]

A. Aiyappan, "Ilavas and Culture Change," *Madras Government Museum Bulletin 5* (1943); *Social Revolution in a Kerala Village* (1965). Robin Jeffrey, *"The Social Origins of a Caste Association: The Founding of the S.N.D.P. Yogam, 1875–1905," South Asia* (October 1974): 39–59.                    ROBIN JEFFREY

**ILBERT BILL**, bill proposed to give Indian magistrates in the Indian Civil Service limited jurisdiction over Europeans in criminal cases. (Indian judges in presidency towns already had this jurisdiction.) Written in 1883 by Courtenay Ilbert, law member of the executive council headed by Lord Ripon (George Frederick Robinson), the measure aroused violent and widespread opposition among the resident British community, including members of Ripon's own government. Protest meetings were held; petitions circulated and representatives were sent to London to lobby against the bill. Arguments against the proposal were frequently racial, with leaders of the agitation claiming that Indians were unqualified by race and character to judge Europeans. The government refused to withdraw the bill, but in December Ripon agreed to a compromise. In exchange for the extended jurisdiction the final bill guaranteed Europeans a trial by a jury, at least half of whose members were to be Europeans.

[*See also* Robinson, George Frederick.]

Edwin Alan Hirschmann, *White Mutiny* (1980). Laxman Prasad Mathur, *Lord Ripon's Administration in India* (1972).                    JUDITH E. WALSH

**ILCHINHOE**, pro-Japanese popular movement in Korea during the last years of the Yi dynasty (1392–1910). Begun as a Seoul-based reform organization in 1904 by Song Pyŏng-jun (1858–1925), it inherited a national organizational base by amalgamating with the Chinbohŭi, an association led by Yi Yong-gu, leader of the Tonghak religious movement. After amalgamation, the Ilchinhoe became explicitly pro-Japanese and accepted financial support from the Japanese army; between 1905 and 1910 it worked to bring about annexation with Japan.

The early Tonghak connection ended when Yi Yong-gu was expelled from that church in 1904, yet the Ilchinhoe retained many Tonghak followers. Building a national organization after 1904, Song Pyŏng-jun worked closely with Japanese activist Uchida Ryōhei, leader of the ultranationalist Amur Society (Kokuryūkai). Uchida and Japanese military leaders were quick to see the potential of the Ilchinhoe. At Uchida's behest the Ilchinhoe supported Japanese extremists critical of their government's deliberate pace with regard to annexing Korea. In 1905 the Ilchinhoe petitioned King Kojong directly, enumerating the advantages of protectorate status.
[*See also* Uchida Ryōhei.]

After the establishment of the Japanese Protectorate, the Ilchinhoe gained increased prominence with the elevation of Song Pyŏng-jun to rank of home minister in the Yi Wan-yong cabinet in 1907.
[*See also* Yi Wan-yong.] The Ilchinhoe leaders

aligned themselves with the Japanese military by advocating immediate annexation after the failure of the Korean mission to be recognized by the Hague Peace Conference in 1907; they even went so far as to petition the king to abdicate in favor of Japanese rule. In doing so Ilchinhoe members and offices became targets for reprisals by Korean patriots, and police protection was ordered for Ilchinhoe officials.

Between 1907 and its disbandment in 1910, the Ilchinhoe continued to grow. It attracted opportunists of all sorts, and it was favored by local Korean officials who worried about appearing anti-Japanese. At its height the Ilchinhoe claimed more than 150,000 members, although this number was probably exaggerated. It was disbanded after annexation as part of the general proscription on Korean political organizations.

[*See also* Tonghak *and* Yi Dynasty.]

MICHAEL ROBINSON

**ILI**, area in Xinjiang north of the Tian Shan range; traditional homeland of pastoral nomads. The Ili River, which flows west from Xinjiang into Lake Balkhash, provided the water resources for the Turkic inhabitants of the region. Kazakh herdsmen have constituted and still constitute the vast majority of the population. Qing China conquered Ili in the middle of the eighteenth century but was repeatedly plagued by native discontent and rebellion. In 1871 tsarist Russian troops capitalized on one of the rebellions to occupy the region, but the English and French compelled them to withdraw and to restore Ili to Chinese control. Occasional flare-ups by the Kazakhs have continued to the present.

In 1954 China set up the Ili Kazakh Autonomous District, pledging greater self-determination for the Kazakhs. Yet in 1962 sixty thousand Kazakhs, enraged by the government's policy of encouraging Chinese colonists to move to Ili and by its efforts to compel them to join communes of herdsmen, fled across the border into the USSR. Since the Cultural Revolution of 1966 to 1976, tension has subsided. Large petroleum reserves have been discovered around the town of Karamai, which makes Ili even more vital to Chinese interests. Equally critical, Ili borders on Soviet Central Asia, a vulnerable area in which China needs to achieve peace and stability.

George Moseley, *A Sino-Soviet Cultural Frontier: The Ili Kazakh Autonomous Chou* (1966).

MORRIS ROSSABI

**ILKHANID DYNASTY.** The Ilkhans were a Mongol dynasty that ruled Iran from 1256 to about 1350. They were descendants of Genghis Khan and until 1295 remained dependent on the great khans in Mongolia and China, as their title, "subordinate khans," implies. The period of their rule was economically and politically difficult but rich in cultural achievements.

The Mongols conquered the northeastern Islamic world in the 1220s; in 1251 Genghis Khan's grandson, Great Khan Mongke, gave the vice-regency of the Middle East to his brother Hulegu and sent him to complete its subjugation. In 1256 and 1257 Hulegu destroyed the strongholds of the Isma'ili sect that had plagued the leaders of Sunni Islam; in 1258 his troops took Baghdad and killed the Abbasid caliph.

Hulegu reigned from 1256 to 1265; during his rule he established the boundaries and many of the policies of the Ilkhanid realm. Hulegu's forces tried to attack Syria, but in 1260 the Mamluks defeated them at the battle of Ain Jalut. Despite numerous campaigns, the Ilkhans were never able to gain control over Syria. Their territories thus reached their full extent, bounded by the Euphrates in the west, the Caucasus Mountains to the north, and the Oxus and the Punjab rivers in the east. Having destroyed the powers within the center of the realm, Hulegu left local dynasties intact in its borderlands, demanding tribute and interfering occasionally in their affairs. [*See also* Hulegu.]

The Ilkhans maintained unfriendly relations with their neighbors, including the Mongol states to the north. The Mamluks, who threatened the Ilkhans in the west, soon found a useful ally in the khans of the Golden Horde, who declared war on the Ilkhans in 1262. Their attack failed, but the Caucasian frontier remained contested throughout the Ilkhanid period. In 1270 the Chagatai khans of Central Asia invaded Khurasan; this was the first of many such invasions. Since the Mamluks also threatened the crusader states of the Levant, Hulegu sent envoys to the Western powers suggesting a joint campaign. The European rulers were eager to cooperate, and over the next forty years the Europeans and the Ilkhans repeatedly discussed campaigns but never actually coordinated one.

Hulegu's son Abaqa (r. 1265–1282) continued his father's policies, strengthening the European alliance and again attempting the conquest of Syria. Abaqa's death in 1282 from excessive drinking, a common problem among the Ilkhans, began the first of several succession struggles. He was succeeded by his brother Teguder (Ahmad), the first Muslim Ilkhan, but in 1284 Abaqa's son Arghun seized power. Arghun (r. 1284–1291) suffered from the rebellion of one of his greatest Mongol commanders, and from this time internal discord remained an almost constant problem for the Ilkhans. The next Ilkhan ruler, Abaqa's son Geikhatu (r. 1291–1295), is best remembered for his debauchery and his disastrous experiment with paper currency—known from China—which he introduced briefly in 1294 to alleviate his financial straits. In 1295 Geikhatu's cousin Beidu deposed him, to be overthrown the same year by Arghun's son Ghazan.

Most early Ilkhans were Buddhist or Christian and often favored their Christian and Jewish subjects at the expense of the Muslims. Ghazan (r. 1295–1304), however, converted to Islam and reinstated it as the official religion, a move accompanied by unusual manifestations of religious hostility. At Ghazan's accession the fiscal administration and the economy were in chaos. He reorganized the currency, the tax structure, and the system of military support. These reforms did much to restore prosperity, and by Ghazan's death in 1304 Ilkhanid rule approximated the traditional patterns of Islamic government. [See also Ghazan.]

Ghazan's brother and successor, Oljeitu (r. 1304–1316), attempted to expand Ilkhanid power within the Middle East; he annexed what is now southern Afghanistan but failed to conquer Gilan, on the southern Caspian littoral. At Oljeitu's death the throne passed to his eleven-year-old son, Abu Sa'id (r. 1317–1335). Much of the power within the realm now fell to Mongol commanders; although the Ilkhans were still able to protect their borders, internal order was lost. With the death of Abu Sa'id in 1335 the line of Hulegu became extinct. For a few years khans from other lines held the throne with the help of regional powers, but by the 1350s Ilkhanid rule had ended.

In administering their territories, the Ilkhans depended heavily on Middle Eastern bureaucrats, most of whom spoke Persian. These viziers held great power and wealth and became deeply involved in court politics. There was constant ministerial infighting that often resulted in personal disgrace; almost all Ilkhanid viziers died by execution.

Although the Mongols came into the Middle East as foreigners and destroyed several of its major cultural centers, the khans and their viziers actively promoted Islamic culture and spent unprecedented sums of money on building projects and patronage of the arts and sciences. They opened the Islamic world to outside influence, importing scholars, artists, and scribes from India, China, and Europe. Chinese influence was particularly prevalent and proved highly fruitful in the realm of art; it was at this time that Persian miniature painting first developed, based partly on Chinese models. Historical writing also flourished, and two Ilkhanid viziers, Ata Malik Juwaini and Rashid al-Din, are among the greatest Persian historians. [See also Painting: Iranian and Central Asian Painting.]

The severe economic depression of the Ilkhanid period has often been ascribed to the ravages of the Mongol conquests and the exploitative administration of the early Ilkhans. Scholars have now shown that this decline had begun before the Mongol invasion; while the Mongols accelerated the decline of agriculture and of urban population, they cannot be seen as the only cause of these trends.

Mongol rule brought a major change in political and religious life. Before 1258 local Islamic dynasties had sought legitimation through their relationship to the caliphate. By destroying this institution, the Ilkhans strengthened the concept of individual dynastic legitimacy, thus preparing the ground for the later regional empires of the Middle East. With the end of the caliphate and of Isma'ili power, moderate Twelver Shi'ism gained greater popularity and acceptance.

During the Mongol period Iran was perhaps the greatest cultural and scientific center of the Islamic world, and Persian began its long ascendancy as the language of high culture. Many scholars seek the origins of modern Iran in the Ilkhanid period, when for the first time Iran was controlled nominally by one ruler, separately from most Arab regions of the Islamic world.

[See also Chagatai and Mongol Empire.]

J. A. Boyle, ed., *The Saljuq and Mongol Periods* (1968), vol. 5 of the *Cambridge History of Iran;* and "The Il'khans of Persia and the Princes of Europe," *Central Asiatic Journal* 20 (1976): 25–40. E. G. Browne, *A Literary History of Persia* (1928), vol. 3, pp. 3–158. René Grousset, *The Empire of the Steppes,* translated by Naomi Walford (1970), pp. 347–391.    BEATRICE FORBES MANZ

**ILTUTMISH.** Shams ud-Din Iltutmish (r. 1210–1235), a Mamluk sultan, consolidated Turkish rule in North India. He organized the governing class, the army, the *iqta* land-revenue assignment system, and the currency of the sultanate. A great builder and patron of arts, he enhanced the glory of Delhi and made it his capital. Iltutmish was an intensely religious Muslim and obtained an investiture from the caliph in the year 1229.

Of Ilbari Turkish lineage, Iltutmish was in boyhood sold into slavery at Bukhara. In 1192 Aibak bought him at Delhi. Iltutmish married his master's daughter and had a meteoric career: head of the bodyguard; *amir-i shikar;* amir of Gwalior; and on Aibak's death in 1210, sultan of Delhi. During the Khokar campaign Muizuddin manumitted him. Iltutmish led expeditions into Rajasthan and eastern India but avoided conflict with the Mongols in the northwest. His tomb is near the Qutb Minar.

[*See also* Qutb ud-Din Aibak; Mamluks; Delhi Sultanate; *and* Delhi.]

A. B. M. Habibullah, *The Foundation of Muslim Rule in India* (2d rev. ed., 1961). Khaliq Ahmad Nizami, *Some Aspects of Religion and Politics in India during the Thirteenth Century* (1961).    FARHAN AHMAD NIZAMI

ILUSTRADO, Spanish word, meaning "learned" or "intelligent," that came into popular usage in the Philippines in the late nineteenth century to denote anyone considered well educated according to local standards. The term has been more commonly used in Philippine historical writings to refer to the Filipino educated elite, primarily during the period from 1870 to 1920.

In the late nineteenth century, the expansion of colonial educational institutions led an increasing number of Filipinos to seek higher education both in Manila (at the University of Santo Tomas) and in Europe. There were never any articulated standards for recognition as an *ilustrado* (it was an ascribed status), but in Manila the minimum qualifications appear to have been a university degree (most frequently in law or medicine) and a demonstrated proficiency in the Spanish language.

The significance of this very small sector of the colonial society derives from the leading roles that many *ilustrados* came to play in the major political events of the period. It was this body of Western-educated Filipinos who, among other things, first articulated the concept of a Filipino people and nation. Because most *ilustrados* came from wealthy, often *mestizo* (mixed Filipino, Spanish, and Chinese) families, recent historical writing has tended to view them as a distinct class within the colonial society. *Ilustrados,* however, should be viewed as a subset of the late nineteenth-century Filipino urban and provincial elites, keeping in mind that though wealth and social position greatly facilitated educational attainment, individuals from wealthy families did not monopolize access to higher education. Moreover, it was their exposure to Western education, more than their economic and social positions, that led most *ilustrados* to have a significant influence on the ideas and events of their time.

[*See also* Philippines *and* Philippine Revolution.]

Cesar A. Majul, "Principales, Ilustrados, Intellectuals and the Original Concept of a Filipino National Community," *Asian Studies* 15 (1977): 1–20. Clarita T. Nolasco, "The Creoles in Spanish Philippines," *Far Eastern University Journal* 15 (1970): 1–201. John N. Schumacher, *The Propaganda Movement: 1880–1895* (1973). Peter W. Stanley, *A Nation in the Making: The Philippines and the United States, 1899–1921* (1974).

MICHAEL CULLINANE

ILYAS SHAHI DYNASTY. Shaking Tughluq authority in Bengal, Sultan Shams al-Din Ilyas Shah founded the Ilyas Shahi dynasty in 1342. His son, Sikander Shah (r. 1357–1389), consolidated the dynasty's authority; the less effectual rule of his successors, however, allowed a Hindu minister, Raja Ganesh, to seize power in 1417. Ilyas Shahi rule was restored in 1437 and lasted until 1487. The longest-lived independent Bengal sultanate, the Ilyas Shahis were able administrators particularly noted for their architectural patronage, especially of the enormous Adina Mosque in Pandua, their first capital.

[*See also* Bengal.]

Jadu-Nath Sarkar, ed., *History of Bengal*, vol. 2 (1948).    CATHERINE B. ASHER

IMAM. The basic meaning of the Arabic term *imam* is "leader" or, literally, "the one who stands at the forefront"—for example, in front of the Muslim congregation during public prayers. Theoretically, however, this person either is the highest-ranking spiritual authority in the whole of the Muslim community or serves as a representative and substitute of that person. Thus, in the earliest period following the death of the prophet Muhammad, when practically all Muslims could assemble in one location, such a position was held only by the true "vicar" *(khalifa)* to the office of prophethood itself.

For Sunni Islam the first four "Rightly Guided" caliphs—Abu Bakr, Umar, Uthman, and Ali—are the true imams, and all subsequent leaders share that position with sharply descending rank and importance over the passage of time. It remains a point of doctrine, however, that the establishment of the imamate is permanently obligatory *(wajib)* and that there should be no more than a single imam at one time. By extension of this concept, the founders of the four Sunni law schools—Abu Hanifa, al-Shafi'i, Malik, and Ibn Hanbal—are also considered imams. Many authorities make a clear distinction between the imamate and kingship, the latter being purely worldly and a political expediency.

In Shi'ite Islam a living imam occupies a unique role in the sacred world as the sole, infallible fountain of religious truth and correct guidance. Most Shi'ites accept a highly restricted lineage of imams all descended from Ali ibn Abi Talib, the Prophet's cousin and son-in-law. So special is their function that, for example, pilgrimage to the abode or tomb of an imam assumes the force of a religious obligation.

Among Ithna Ashari (Imani, Twelver) Shi'ites, the living imam is the twelfth in the line of Ali through Husain; this imam disappeared from ordinary contact with his followers in 874. Since 940 he has been in total occultation (ghaiba), but he will return in the future to establish justice and rid the world of evil.

Other Shi'ites (Isma'ilis, Zaidis) accept modifications in the concept of the imamate and hold a different line of imams to have been correct. For example, one branch of the Isma'ilis maintains that the current Agha Khan is the forty-ninth imam in a direct, unbroken line from Ali.

[See also Agha Khan; Caliphate; and Husain ibn Ali.]

Moojan Momen, *Introduction to Shi'i Islam* (1986). Abdulaziz Sachedina, *Islamic Messianism* (1981).

PAUL E. WALKER

IMAM BONDJOL (1772–1864), Indonesian religious leader. Tuanku Imam Bondjol was originally named Mohammad Sjahab and in his youth was called Peto Sjarif, Malin Basa (Mualim Besar), and Tuanku Mudo. The name—or, more precisely, the title—Tuanku Imam Bondjol derives from the fortified village of Bondjol, founded in 1806–1807 in the valley of Alahan Panjang. Imam Bondjol was a student of Tuanku Nan Rintjeh; after his teacher's death Imam Bondjol became the most important leader of the fundamentalist Islamic Padri movement in the Minangkabau in western Sumatra. He also fought the Dutch, who tried to intervene after 1821. He was captured by the Dutch in 1837 after the fall of Bondjol and banished to Cianjur, Ambon (1839), and then to Manado, Sulawesi (1841).

[See also Padri and Minangkabau.]

Christine Dobbin, "Tuanku Imam Bondjol (1772–1864)," *Indonesia* 13 (April 1972): 5–37.

C. VAN DIJK

IMARI. *See* Ceramics: Japanese Ceramics.

IMPERIALISM. From earliest recorded history there have been empires and, therefore, "imperialism." Each empire has imposed its own rules and administration upon other peoples, who thereby find themselves in a dependent relationship to the dominant—or "imperial"—power. Empires are typically characterized by a centrally organized authority in which decisions are made, often arbitrarily, according to priorities of the ruling power and with little if any consultation of those affected by these decisions. An imperial order traditionally describes an asymmetrical power relationship that is usually maintained by political control and military strength but may also be enforced by economic and diplomatic pressure.

Although imperialism is thus a premodern as well as modern phenomenon, the term is commonly applied to the extension of European, American, and Japanese influence and power on a global scale at the end of the nineteenth century and the early years of the twentieth. European powers initiated this expansion, but modern imperialism cannot be seen as merely a manifestation of European history. Imperialism in this latter sense inaugurated a new era of world history, one marked by an unprecedented intensification of contacts between peoples of the world in several dimensions, including political, economic, and cultural ones. It is in this uniquely modern sense that imperialism will be considered.

From the beginning of its use in the late nineteenth century the term *imperialism* has meant many things. It has characterized a historical period, the so-called age of imperialism, from about 1870 to World War I, and has also been used in connection with the extension of "great power" rivalries into the non-European world. For Marxists, *imperialism* denotes the final stage in the development of finance capitalism and capitalist exploitation of less developed parts of the world, but even outside Marxist analysis it has become a term of polemical attack and criticism, connoting a state of mind or an attitude of cultural supremacy and arrogance. Finally, *imperialism* describes a more general process of expansion and ensuing relations between states and peoples.

*Historical Overview.* European influence and penetration of the non-European world in 1870 was relatively modest compared with what it was to become at the turn of the century. This is equally true whether this expansion is measured in terms of areas of formal political domination or on a scale of economic activity. By the twentieth century the scramble for direct territorial control in Africa and, to a lesser extent, in Asia and the Pacific was well under way. The competition for economic influence in China and Latin America was also accelerating as capital flow and commerce increased sharply between centers of surplus and areas that became fields of investment or suppliers of raw materials.

The initial steps in Europe's late nineteenth-century expansion began without much premeditation. A series of disconnected episodes in Africa and Asia touched off a process of extending existing holdings, or of seeking assurance of continued and expanded trade opportunities, or of securing existing investments that had already been established. In Africa, the French government proclaimed a protectorate over the territory controlled by the insolvent *bey* of Tunis in 1881; the following year Great Britain sent an expedition to suppress a nationalist, anti-European uprising in Egypt and to protect the Suez Canal. In western and equatorial Africa, French and British explorers, traders, and soldiers advanced up river systems toward the interior while agents of King Leopold of Belgium obtained control over much of the Congo basin. In eastern and southwestern Africa, Germany entered this sudden land rush. Bismarck's Colonial Congress of Berlin in 1884 and 1885 did little more than regulate the European rivalry for African territory. Within a generation much of Africa had fallen under direct European control, and by the outbreak of war in Europe in 1914 all of the African continent, with the exception of Liberia and Ethiopia, had some form of European administration.

In Asia, French expansion into Tonkin (northern Vietnam) during the 1870s and 1880s initiated a rivalry with Britain in Southeast Asia and southern China. Protectorates over Laos and Burma led to agreement between France and Great Britain to allow a reduced and precariously independent Thai state as a buffer between their colonial territories. Meanwhile, Russia, Japan, Germany, and Italy developed their own appetites for concessions in China. A military victory over China in 1895 gave Japan predominant influence on the Korean peninsula and control of Taiwan. [*See also* Sino-Japanese War *and* Taiwan.] Merchants and soldiers of the Russian empire, having advanced into Central Asia and Siberia, looked upon Manchuria and also Korea as areas of potential expansion. Between 1895 and 1900 the imperial powers pressed the Qing dynasty for territorial and commercial privileges, and European banks granted loans to pay off war debts or to finance railroad construction. Fearing exclusion of its commerce from a China divided into "spheres of influence," the United States in 1899 urged an "open door" policy that was only nominally accepted by the imperial powers.

By the turn of the century China appeared to be on the verge of partition. An antiforeign uprising in China, that of the Yihetuan (Boxers), brought an international military expedition to Beijing in 1900 to relieve the diplomatic legations. The ruling Qing dynasty faced possible collapse under a combined threat of external intervention and domestic upheaval. Yet the imperial powers hesitated to add the burden of administering the population of China to existing responsibilities. [*See also* Yihetuan.] Japan and Russia did go to war over dominance in Manchuria, but this imperial conflict did not lead immediately to direct annexation. A balance among the imperial forces was reached with a series of agreements among France, Britain, Russia, and Japan in 1907: China was to be exploited but not partitioned.

By the beginning of the twentieth century the United States had entered the imperial age with the Spanish-American War, which brought the Philippines, Guam, Puerto Rico, and, indirectly, Cuba into an American domain. The United States invoked the Monroe Doctrine to justify intervention in the Caribbean, Mexico, and the Isthmus of Panama. Despite the Monroe Doctrine's warning to Europe, British, German, French, and Italian capital penetrated Latin America at the turn of the century.

Imperialism reached an apogee with World War I and its settlement. The war began as a strictly European conflict but soon spread to Africa and the Pacific. African and Asian troops and labor were recruited to sustain the European war effort. In the peace settlement of 1919 the victorious imperial states, notably France, Britain, and Japan, received territory as "mandates" under League of Nations supervision. These mandated territories were in fact administered as colonial possessions. They were carved out of former German and Ottoman territories in Africa, the Pacific, and the Levant. Despite growing anti-imperial resistance during the interwar years, the pattern of conquest continued with Mussolini's subjugation of Ethiopia in 1935 and 1936

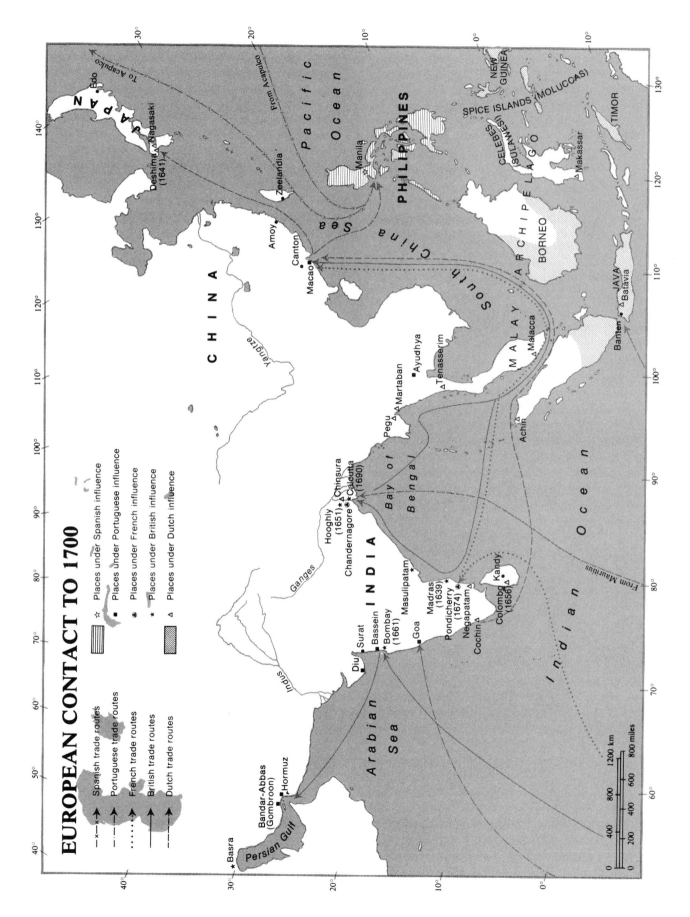

**EUROPEAN CONTACT TO 1700**

Spanish trade routes
Portuguese trade routes
French trade routes
British trade routes
Dutch trade routes

☆ Places under Spanish influence
■ Places under Portuguese influence
◉ Places under French influence
★ Places under British influence
△ Places under Dutch influence

and Japanese expansion into Manchuria and China in 1931 and 1937, respectively.

This powerful thrust of imperial expansion did not go unchallenged. Some opposition and resistance to imperialism had always existed, but the victory of Japan over Russia in 1905 gave an important impulse to anti-imperialist movements. The Japanese victory, although the triumph of one ambitious, imperial state over another, demonstrated that a non-Western society, if industrialized and strengthened by nationalist ideology, could defeat a Western military power. [*See also* Russo-Japanese War.] In the decade before 1914 a series of nationalist uprisings swept through Vietnam, India, and Persia and led to the Young Turk revolt in the Ottoman empire. Imperial expansion and domination were no longer considered inevitable. Moreover, the war heightened demands for self-determination, although such appeals were ignored at the Paris Peace Conference in 1919. The Russian Revolution opened prospects of joining demands for a new social and economic order to the resistance movements in the empires. Between the wars, political and ideological conflict, combined with the economic dislocations of the Great Depression, strained the ability of the imperial states to retain their grip upon subject peoples.

World War II marked the beginning of the end of late nineteenth-century-style imperialism. Of course, the war had many imperial characteristics: Germany's attempts to create a vast continental empire in Europe and Russia, Italy's grasp for supremacy in the Mediterranean basin, and Japan's search for a Greater East Asian Co-Prosperity Sphere, ostensibly directed against Western imperialism but seeking economic domination over much of East Asia and the western Pacific. Great Britain struggled to defend an empire; both Vichy and DeGaulle's Free French invoked the empire to claim France's continued status as a world power, despite military defeat in 1940; the United States fought to protect overseas interests and developed global strategic goals in the course of winning the war; and the Soviet Union's security objectives led to a dependent Eastern Europe in the postwar period.

A major consequence of the war was to reveal the vulnerability of imperialism. Defeat in Europe discredited the authority of French and Dutch rulers of empire. Great Britain had ultimately triumphed but had exhausted its resources in the process. Coherent nationalist movements, linked to demands for a new social and economic order, gained strength and made the price of maintaining empire too high.

Political opposition to imperialism emerged within the European states and eroded the psychological certainty and self-confidence of an earlier age. The retreat from empire in the twenty-eight years after 1945 was as sudden and decisive as the expansion of the late nineteenth century had been. Legacies of this imperial age remained with a persistent and sometimes growing gap between the technological and economic strength of the former imperial powers and the "Third World" of Asia, Africa, and Latin America. Continued economic and cultural ties have thus raised fears of a neocolonial relationship.

*Analysis.* A number of attempts have been made to explain the nature and impact of imperialism. They range from treating the phenomenon as a movement that developed from economic conditions in the industrializing nations to arguments about the political goals and strategic concerns of the imperialist powers.

The early practitioners of imperialism, whether politicians, journalists, missionaries, explorers, merchants, or military officers, provided various justifications for their activities. Arguments for empire included prospects of economic gain, an enhancement of national power, the scientific value of exploration, and the uplifting task of bringing the benefits of a more advanced civilization and culture to "backward" peoples. Often these arguments adopted the language of a competition for glory and power as each nation sought its "place in the sun," fulfilled a "manifest destiny," assumed a "civilizing mission," or acted as a "chosen people," revealing an underlying drive for supremacy.

After the rationales or apologies for empire had been made, analysts sought the underlying causes of imperialism. Among the earliest explanations were those that viewed imperialism as a historically inevitable part of a capitalist economic system. According to J. A. Hobson, V. I. Lenin, R. Hilferding, and others, accumulations of capital surplus brought a search for markets and profitable investment overseas and permitted imports of raw materials necessary for the industrial system. For Hobson, a liberal, this activity benefited certain industrial interests or investors at the expense of higher salaries and purchasing power for the masses. Lenin, writing after Hobson and during World War I, considered imperialism to be both the highest and the final stage of capitalism. For Lenin, capitalism's contradictions, competitiveness, and drive for monopolistic control had led to a self-destructive, imperialist conflict.

Critics of a predominantly economic explanation

of imperialism insist that the costs of empire outweighed any economic gains. They note that overseas investment did not require conquest or direct control, citing in support of this argument the French empire, which offered relatively insignificant markets for either products or investment. Areas of direct dominance in Africa or Asia were often less valuable or profitable than investment in developing areas, a policy favored by Russia or the United States. Moreover, the extraction of raw materials often followed rather than preceded intervention, serving as a benefit but not necessarily as a cause of imperialism.

Arguments for the noneconomic foundations of imperialism initially focused upon the extension of great power rivalries into Asia, Africa, and Latin America. The search for national power and prestige led to French expansion as compensation for military defeat in 1871, to a German drive for world-power status, to British efforts to contain Russian expansion, to an Anglo-French rivalry and scramble for territory in Africa and Asia, to the competition of all imperial powers for spheres of influence in China. In this analysis, imperialism resulted more from strategic or diplomatic calculations based upon an abstract concept of a balance of power than from the manifestation of economic rivalries or pressures. With a nation's strength measured by its ability to project power overseas, heightened nationalist sentiments permitted a mobilization of resources that made imperialism possible.

Other theories have emphasized what may be described as the psychological component of the imperialist impulse. Joseph Schumpeter argued that overseas conquest resulted from the aggressiveness or "atavism" of precapitalist, "feudalistic," and military classes in the industrial states. Others, not necessarily followers of Schumpeter, have concluded that imperialism satisfied and was an expression of a drive for power in which domination was sought for its own sake. This impulse appeared in all imperialist states, whether liberal-democratic, such as Great Britain, France, Italy, or the United States, where the military exercised a minor influence, or authoritarian-imperial, such as Germany, Russia, or Japan, where the role of the military and "precapitalist" classes was more influential.

While differing in approach, the early theorists of empire agreed that a "new" imperialism emerged after 1870. More recently, scholars have questioned the validity of a distinction between the new imperialism and an earlier time of relative indifference toward imperialism in Europe. For Immanuel Wal-

lerstein and his school, capitalist expansion during the era of commercial empires in the sixteenth and seventeenth centuries marked the beginning of a global economic system, a movement that gained in intensity with the emergence of industrial capitalism at the end of the nineteenth century. For neo-Marxists, the persistence of economic imbalances between have and have-not nations has meant the continuation of economic, cultural, and political dependencies even after the decolonization of the twentieth century. From a quite different perspective, two British scholars, Ronald Robinson and John A. Gallagher, have insisted that there was little fundamental difference between the "informal" imperialism of the early nineteenth century and the "formal" empires of conquest and domination after 1870. The advocates of empire would have preferred trade without conquest, but turned to the latter when confronted with conditions overseas that required intervention to protect commerce or to keep strategic areas from falling into the hands of hostile authority. While criticized, the arguments of Gallagher and Robinson have compelled historians to move away from an exclusively Europocentric explanation of imperialism to consider developments in Africa, Asia, and Latin America as part of the process.

Clearly, imperialism has yet to be fully explained by any single, general theory. The result is a series of explanations of varying weights that may be differentially sorted and aggregated to explain individual cases of overseas expansion. Thus imperialism may be described and identified, but its origins, causes, and influence continue to be debated.

[*For further discussion of Western involvement in Asia, see also* East India Company; Fort William; Government of India; Governor-General of India; Plassey, Battle of; Anglo-Burmese Wars; Portuguese; Ethical Colonial Policy; Dutch East India Company; French East India Company; Java, British Occupation of; Java War; Manila Galleon; Spain and the Philippines; Philippines, British Occupation of; Philippine-American War; Qing Dynasty; China Trade; Maritime Customs Service; Treaty Ports; Triple Intervention; Shandong Question; Deshima; Korea, Japanese Government-General of; Shōwa Period; World War I in Asia; *and* World War II in Asia. *For the colonial history of specific areas, see the articles on each country.*]

Winfried Baumgart, *Imperialism: The Idea and Reality of British and French Colonial Expansion, 1880–1914* (1982). Raymond F. Betts, *Europe Overseas: Phases of Imperialism* (1968). B. K. Fieldhouse, *Economics and Empire, 1830–1914* (1973). Tom Kemp, *Theories of Impe-

*rialism* (1967). George Lichtheim, *Imperialism* (1971). William Roger Louis, ed., *Imperialism: The Robinson-Gallagher Controversy* (1976). Wolfgang J. Mommsen, *Theories of Imperialism* (1980). Roger Owen and Robert Sutcliffe, eds., *Studies in the Theory of Imperialism* (1977). H. L. Wesseling, ed., *Expansion and Reaction: Essays on European Expansion and Reaction in Asia and Africa* (1978).                          J. KIM MUNHOLLAND

## IMPERIAL RESCRIPT ON EDUCATION

(Kyōiku Chokugo), pronouncement issued in the name of the Meiji emperor on 30 October 1890, declaring the basis of Japanese education to be the ethical teachings handed down by the imperial ancestors. Following the Meiji Restoration of 1868, which opened Japan to the adoption of Western ideas and technology, translations of American and French textbooks were used in schools, even in courses in ethics. Alarmed by the spread of Western ideas of individualism and utilitarianism, conservative officials drafted the rescript to assert that education had a moral purpose of teaching the people to be loyal to the emperor and obedient to the authority of the state.

The rescript was presented as though it had been written by the emperor himself as a statement of his thoughts for the guidance of his people. To emphasize that it was his personal and direct gift, it did not bear the countersignature of a cabinet minister. Prime Minister Yamagata Aritomo (1838–1922), who engineered the issuing of the rescript in spite of the disapproval of such leading statesmen as Itō Hirobumi (1841–1909), prevailed upon Inoue Kowashi (1844–1895) to prepare a draft. It passed through numerous revisions, as the emperor's Confucian lecturer Motoda Nagazane (Eifu; 1818–1891) urged more explicit expression of Confucian ethical principles. The resulting document, a text of less than one page, defines loyalty and filial piety as the abiding values of the Japanese people. It enjoins the loyal subjects to observe the five relationships of Confucianism, "pursue learning and cultivate the arts, . . ." and, "should emergency arise, offer yourselves courageously to the state; and thus guard and maintain the prosperity of Our imperial throne coeval with heaven and earth. . . . The Way here set forth is indeed the teaching bequeathed by Our imperial ancestors, to be observed alike by their descendants and the subjects, infallible for all ages and true in all places" (official translation).

The rescript was regarded as sacred scripture. It was ceremoniously intoned by the principal of every school in Japan at an annual assembly. Detailed commentaries were issued to explain its application to the writing of textbooks and the design of education. It served to turn in a more authoritarian direction the course of educational policy, which had for two decades undergone frequent changes under the influence of competing Western ideas, both liberal and conservative, and traditional native values. The rescript carried to all subjects the moral guidance given in the Imperial Rescript to Soldiers and Sailors of 1882, a document that had also been planned by Yamagata. There was ambiguity in the constitution of 1889 about the locus of sovereignty, but the Imperial Rescript on Education made it clear that subjects owed absolute loyalty to the emperor. This was an important principle to establish on the eve of convening the first session of the Diet. The rescript was one of a series of measures taken to sanctify the religious and political authority of the emperor, which in turn consolidated the power of the ruling oligarchs. The rescript remained in effect until 1945.

[*See also* Imperial Rescript to Soldiers.]

Carol Gluck, *Japan's Modern Myths: Ideology in the Late Meiji Period* (1985). Donald H. Shively, "Motoda Eifu: Confucian Lecturer to the Meiji Emperor," in *Confucianism in Action*, edited by David S. Nivison and Arthur F. Wright (1959), pp. 301–373.

DONALD H. SHIVELY

## IMPERIAL RESCRIPT TO SOLDIERS.

Issued by the Meiji emperor on 4 July 1882, the rescript (Gunjin Chokuyu) enunciated a code of ethics for all soldiers and sailors that was to govern the ideals and conduct of the modern Japanese armed forces. It is often coupled with the Imperial Rescript on Education (1890) as a major pronouncement underpinning the moral ideology of pre–World War II Japan, an ideology that defined service to the nation in terms of absolute loyalty to the emperor. The 2,500-word rescript asserted that the emperor, as commander in chief, expected servicemen to protect the state and guard the empire. These duties were to be carried out according to five principles: loyalty, propriety, valor, righteousness, and simplicity.

The rescript spelled out how each of these precepts was to be fulfilled. Loyalty, for example, meant an unquestioned obedience to the emperor and the avoidance of political activities. Propriety demanded strict discipline, the acceptance of the authority of superiors, and the considerate treatment of those of inferior rank. Valor required courage to fulfill one's duty and never despising an inferior or fearing an enemy. Righteousness meant honesty and faithfulness in personal relations and in carrying out assigned duties. Simplicity enjoined servicemen to avoid luxury and to cultivate frugality. All five injunctions were to be put into practice in a spirit of sincerity.

In this way, the rescript defined the ethical basis for conduct that would build a disciplined military force. Unlike many previous instructions issued by the military to regulate the conduct of servicemen, this rescript codified military ideals into a sacrosanct doctrine that gave the precepts the status of sacred obligations. It was widely disseminated soon after its promulgation; officers memorized it, and major parts of it frequently were recited by the rank and file. The inculcation of absolute loyalty to the emperor as supreme commander and the stress on spiritual training and values were the features of Japan's modern armed forces that most attracted the attention of foreign observers. Transmitted throughout the population through former servicemen and patriotic organizations, the injunctions of loyalty and duty to the emperor embodied in the rescript became a central feature of the national ideology of prewar Japan.

[See also Imperial Rescript on Education.]

Wm. Theodore de Bary, Donald Keene, and Ryusaku Tsunoda, comps., *Sources of Japanese Tradition* (1958), p. 705.
ROGER F. HACKETT

**IMPEY, ELIJAH** (1732–1809), chief justice of the Supreme Court of Calcutta from 1774 to 1783. From Trinity College, Cambridge, and from Lincoln's Inn (called to the bar in 1756), he represented the East India Company before Parliament in 1772. His appointment in India was created under the Regulating Act of 1773. His fame (or infamy) arises from the trial of Raja Nanda Kumar (Nuncomar) in 1775: the jury having pronounced guilt of forgery, Impey imposed the death sentence and Nuncomar was hanged. Impey was charged with acting in collusion with the governor-general, Warren Hastings; an enquiry was held and he was exonerated. In 1780 Impey stirred up further controversy by becoming president of the company's new Sadr Adalat (High Court). Eventually, at the instigation of enemies, he was recalled to face charges of corruption. He successfully defended himself and the impeachment was dropped.

[See also Nuncomar and Hastings, Warren.]

Sophia J. F. Stephen, *The Story of Nuncomar and the Impeachment of Sir Elijah Impey*, 2 vols. (1885).
ROBERT E. FRYKENBERG

**IMPHAL,** a town in eastern India that is now the capital of the state of Manipur. In 1944 it was the site of a decisive battle in which a British garrison held off advancing Japanese troops (aided by the Indian National Army under the leadership of Subhas Chandra Bose) and thereby halted the Japanese advance through Burma, marking the end of Japan's attempt to invade India. [See also Bose, Subhas Chandra; Indian National Army; and Manipur.]
ROBIN JARED LEWIS

**INDENTURED LABOR.** See Emigration: South Asian Emigration.

**INDEPENDENCE OF MALAYA PARTY** (IMP). The IMP was founded as a multiracial political party in September 1951 by Dato Onn bin Ja'afar, who had resigned from the presidency of the United Malays National Organization because of its unwillingness to offer membership to non-Malays. Ja'afar felt that a postindependence system made up of ethnic parties would aggravate ethnonationalist tensions. Strong opposition from Malays, who feared that the IMP would diminish their political dominance, compelled previously supportive Chinese and Indian leaders to withhold their backing. Thus, the IMP was soundly beaten by the new Malay and Chinese Alliance Party, formed in response to the IMP's concept of multiracial parties, in the February 1952 Kuala Lumpur election. A noble experiment, the IMP never really enjoyed solid support, and it was dissolved in 1953.

[See also Onn bin Ja'afar, Dato; United Malays National Organization; and Alliance Party.]

Gordon P. Means, *Malaysian Politics* (2d ed., 1976).
STANLEY BEDLINGTON

**INDEPENDENCE PARTY AND CLUB,** organizations led by like-minded members of the ruling class of the late Yi dynasty (1392–1910) who championed the cause of an independent Korea. Leaders of the Independence Party sought to detach Korea from its traditional status as a Chinese tributary state and transform it into a fully sovereign, modern nation. The Independence Club, formed in late 1896 and dissolved in late 1898, worked for the same purpose but through a more articulate set of ideas and through an organized mass movement.

The Independence Party (Tongnipdang) was also known in popular parlance as the Enlightenment and Independence Party (Kaehwa Tongnipdang), the Enlightenment Party (Kaehwadang), the Progressive Party (Hyoksindang), and the Pro-Japanese Party (Ch'inildang). The last of these designations refers to the fact that members of the Independence Party often sought and obtained the support and encouragement of Japanese officials and civilians in their anti-Chinese stance.

The most prominent members of the circle were Kim Ok-kyun, Pak Yŏng-hyo, Hong Yong-sik, Sŏ Kwang-bŏm, Sŏ Chae-p'il (later known as Philip Jaisohn), and Yu Kil-chun. Drawing their inspiration from the modernization of Meiji Japan and from their modest knowledge of the achievements of the West, members of the Independence Party dreamed of making Korea over into an "Asian France." (They believed that Japan would be the "Great Britain of the Orient.")

While the Independence Party was not identified with any unified ideology or reform platform, its members, explicitly and through indirect suggestion, embraced with varying degrees of enthusiasm ideas that made them a progressive force. From their memorials, correspondence, and diaries, as well as from contemporary foreigners' observations about them, it becomes clear that although they did not formally reject the official Neo-Confucian orthodoxy, they were dissatisfied with it and wanted to find a formula that would help them preserve the most desirable parts of Korea's heritage while enabling them to bring in what they believed were the helpful gifts of the West for advancing and strengthening Korea politically, militarily, socially, and economically. This groping for a workable fusion of Eastern and Western civilizations remained an elusive search, but the members of the Independence Party did manage to bring into public focus ideas and proposals that were for the most part not only fresh but even revolutionary for the times. Thus, Kim Ok-kyun and Pak Yŏng-hyo both advocated Korea's adoption of Protestant Christianity as one of the keys to overall national advancement, although neither converted to the faith himself. As individuals, members of the Independence Party also espoused many other modern proposals, ranging from the encouragement of Western knowledge through state-sponsored modern schools and newspapers to the introduction of modern industrial and commercial enterprises into the country, the dismantling of the stifling class structure of Korea, the elevation of the status of women, the recognition of the "natural rights" of all Koreans and of popular participation in government, the insistence on the accountability of public officials to the people, the adoption of the rule of

law in the judicial system, and the gradual induction of modern elective bodies at local and national levels. Underlying these proposals was often a Social Darwinian assumption that they would make for a stronger and a more prosperous Korea.

Even before many of the above ideas could be talked about in public, the Independence Party sought to capture political power through a palace revolution. On 24 December 1884 the group (with the exception of Yu Kil-chun) seized control of the palace and the king in a bloody strike and announced the formation of a reform government. Within three days, however, a coalition of conservatives and cautious innovators, who represented the majority force in the bureaucracy, struck back at the coup leaders with the aid of overwhelming Chinese support. The Independence Party was ousted from power. Some of its members, including Hong Yong-sik, were killed in the streets by angry mobs or later executed as rebels by the government. Kim Ok-kyun, Sŏ Kwang-bŏm, Pak Yŏng-hyo, and Sŏ Chae-p'il fled to Japan. For nearly a decade Kim was hunted by agents of the Korean government. He was finally assassinated in Shanghai in 1894 and his dismembered body brought back to Korea for public display. Pak and the two Sŏs went to the United States, where Sŏ Chae-p'il was eventually to gain undergraduate and medical degrees, American citizenship, and an American wife, as well as the anglicized name of Philip Jaisohn. [See also 1884 Coup d'État.]

Despite its failure to gain power, the Independence Party embodied a significant though small step in Korea's hesitant progress toward modernization. It symbolized an irreversible intellectual opening of Korea that paved the way for future innovation. An ironic consequence of the Independence Party's coup was to increase the involvement of both China and Japan in Korean affairs. The Sino-Japanese War of 1894 to 1895 was the culmination of this new trend. [See also Sino-Japanese War.]

The Independence Party's creed of Korea for Koreans and national advancement was, however, picked up by the Independence Club (Tongnip Hyŏphoe) in late 1896. The club was the brainchild of Philip Jaisohn, who had been forgiven and invited back to Korea in early 1896 as an adviser to the Privy Council, itself an advisory body. Jaisohn soon took upon himself the mission of not only strengthening the national consciousness of Koreans but also educating them about the achievements and merits of what he called the Christian civilization of the West. Partly for this reason, he persuaded the government to help him set up a Korean-language newspaper. Weaning Koreans away from China meant to him the exclusive use of the purely native script *han'gŭl*, the study and glorification of Korea's own national heroes, the celebration of Korea's indigenous achievements, and an awareness of the contrasts between the weak and backward-looking civilization of China and the forward-looking and prosperous civilization of the Christian West. A newspaper published jointly in *han'gŭl* and English was begun on 7 April 1896 and remained wedded to these themes in its editorials. It was appropriately called the *Independent (Tongnip sinmun)*.

In July 1896 Jaisohn moved to enlist the throne and high government officials as well as members of the public in the launching of three commemorative projects that he believed would be symbolic reminders of the independence that both China and Japan had recognized and pledged to respect through the Sino-Japanese Treaty of 1895. These three projects were the Independence Gate, the Independence Hall, and the Independence Park. The first was to be built at the site of a gate where envoys from China had been traditionally received by the Korean government according to the rules of the suzerain-vassal relationship between the two countries. The second was to be constructed where a guest house for Chinese dignitaries had stood. Both old structures seemed symbols of Korea's humiliation and needed to be supplanted. An association was formed for this purpose, and it soon came to be known as the Independence Club. Among those prominent in it were Yun Ch'i-ho, an American-educated young Christian official named Yi Sang-jae, Han Hyu-sŏl, An Kyŏng-su, and Namgung Ok, all of whom may best be described as reformist Confucians. The park project was abandoned later owing to lack of funds, but the other two were completed in 1897.

Independence Hall became the site of many public discussions and debates, conducted by the club according to Roberts' Rules of Order, on all manner of questions dealing with the related themes of national independence and social, political, and economic advancement. The Hall thus joined the newspaper in the crusade for public enlightenment. Although the club had its own official monthly organ called *The Great Korean Independence Club Report (Tae Chosŏn tongnip hyŏphoe)*, the *Independent* remained its more eloquent, though unofficial, mouthpiece.

Beginning in late 1897 the club underwent a dramatic transformation structurally and functionally. The club seemed to have struck a responsive chord across the nation. Thousands read its ideas through the *Independent*. Hundreds attended its frequent debates in the Independence Hall. Seeing this popularity, Jaisohn gradually expanded the forum of his editorials to include such sensitive political questions as popular sovereignty, the inalienable rights of the people, the duties and responsibilities of government officials, the need to guard Korea from the pernicious effects of collusion between corrupt Korean officials and self-seeking foreign powers (especially Russia), the necessity of popular participation in government through a national assembly, and the like. The club also began to form branches across the country. Jaisohn's idiom was suffused with arguments influenced by Locke, Rousseau, and Bentham that made both the monarch and the conservative officials nervous. Consequently, he was pressured to return to the United States, which he did in mid-May 1898. Yun Ch'i-ho then took over the leadership of both the club and the newspaper.

Yun and his associates, many of whom were young men fired with Jaisohn's idealism, not only kept the club's activism alive but also gave it a militant edge. Syngman Rhee (Yi Sŭng-man), the future first president of the Republic of Korea, was especially noteworthy among them. Against Yun's advice, the younger members of the club often moved its activism onto the streets, forging an informal alliance with many smaller popular groups representing a cross section of the society and holding frequent mass meetings and demonstrations. In late 1898 this activism led to a confrontation between the club and the government over the question of whether or not the Privy Council ought to be transformed into a modern legislative assembly. The club's proposal showed an eagerness to see the Privy Council function as a kind of one-chamber parliament to which the council of ministers would be accountable for the performance of its functions. The club's arguments for this proposal were drawn from Western democratic theory as well as the populism expressed in the writings of the ancient Confucian philosopher Mencius. At first King Kojong (r. 1864–1907) accepted the proposal. To many conservatives and to the monarch, however, the proposal soon looked like a subversive attempt aimed at eventually turning Korea into a republic. Alarmed at this possibility and irritated by the club's activism, the conservatives persuaded the king to ban the club in early November 1898.

The Independence Club left a lasting imprint on Korea's political development. It made Korean nationalism a deeply felt force in the psychology of the people. Many Koreans continued to draw their inspiration from the club. For the first time, many people thought of themselves as citizens with inherent rights rather than as subjects with nothing but duties toward the state. This too remained part of the club's long-term bequest to the nation.

[*See also* Kim Ok-kyun; Pak Yŏng-hyo; Yu Kil-chun; Yi Sang-jae; Yun Ch'i-ho; Jaisohn, Philip; Rhee, Syngman; Kojong; *and* Yi Dynasty.]

Harold F. Cook, *Korea's 1884 Incident* (1972). C. I. Eugene Kim and Han-Kyo Kim, *Korea and the Politics of Imperialism* (1967). Chong-sik Lee, *The Politics of Korean Nationalism* (1965). James B. Palais, "Political Participation in Traditional Korea, 1876–1910," *Journal of Korean Studies* 1 (1979).          VIPAN CHANDRA

**INDIA.** India as a modern, independent nation dates from 15 August 1947, when it achieved its formal independence from Great Britain, but its culture and civilization are among the oldest and most enduring in the world. In terms of population, India is second only to China, with a population of about 762,507,000 in 1985. With a land area of approximately 3,287,000 square kilometers, it is about one-third the size of the United States. The major religions of India are Hinduism (83.5%), Islam (11%), Christianity (2.6%), Sikhism (2%), and Buddhism (0.7%); the rest (0.2%) are chiefly the religions of the tribal peoples. It is a republic, with a federal structure consisting of twenty-one states and eight union territories, and a parliamentary democratic system of government. The capital is New Delhi, situated in the union territory of Delhi.

The name *India* has been used in the Western world since at least 500 BCE to designate the homeland of Indian civilization; it refers to a great peninsular landmass known as the subcontinent, which juts into the ocean and seas from the Asian mainland. In the classical Sanskrit sources the area is referred to as *Bharat,* but *India* was adopted as the official name in the new constitution in 1950, although in its Hindi version, *Bharat* is used. The name *India* is probably derived from *Hind,* the word the Persians had for the territory on their eastern borders. To the Greeks, India was the end of the inhabited world, a land of marvels filled with strange people with exotic customs and manners, and something of that attitude lingers in the Western imagination. The reality behind the fantasy is that in outlook, worldview, and practices Indian civilization does indeed often differ radically from the other great civilizations. After Europeans realized that Co-

lumbus had not reached India, the term *East Indies* was used to differentiate India from the West Indies. India was also known as Hindustan, following the Persian usage.

After the British conquest the whole of the subcontinent and adjacent territories were governed as the Indian empire. After 1947, when the area gained independence, it comprised two major nations, India and Pakistan, and, since 1971, Bangladesh. In this article, the history of the whole area will be treated as India up to 1947, but after that, attention will be given to the Republic of India. Pakistan and Bangladesh constitute independent entries. The reader should also consult the many articles on particular kingdoms, dynasties, and movements mentioned here as well as those on the various Indian religions, languages, and literatures.

*Historiography.* Before sketching an outline of historical developments in India, it should be noted that very little of what is defined in the West as "history" is found in all the immense body of Indian literature that has come down to us. This has often led Westerners to assume that India has no "history." This is, of course, not true, but refers to the fact that within the Indian literary tradition, so rich in other genres, the writing of history, as understood in the Western, Islamic, and Chinese cultures, did not evolve. Why this is so is not easy to understand, but it is probably rooted in attitudes to time, the place of man in the universe, and his relation to transcendental forces. India has, indeed, historical writings, but they are very different from those of the other great traditions. These texts are known as the Puranas and are concerned with the complex relations of men and gods. They move in a time frame of millions of years and in a spatial dimension that encompasses the whole cosmos, although India is clearly the terrestrial base. For people outside this tradition who came in contact with India as travelers, invaders, or rulers, this mode of historical interpretation was so alien that it seemed fabulous and superstitious.

The earliest historical—in the Western sense—writing about India comes from the Greeks. In the fourth century BCE, Herodotus, "the father of history," gave India considerable attention. Subsequent Greek and Roman historians included India in their survey of world history, and medieval writers continued to use the Greek and Roman accounts.

The second great tradition of historical writing on India comes from Muslim historians and chroniclers, who gave fairly detailed accounts of the military and political activities of the invaders from

Central Asia and the kingdoms they established. Muslim historiography in India concentrated on the successes and failures of individual rulers, not on events as the outcome of social and political forces. This emphasis on history as the narrative story of kings was one legacy of Muslim historiography.

A third tradition of historical writing is largely the product of nineteenth-century British and German scholarship, with its emphasis on "original sources" as the basis for a factual, empirical history. It was on the groundwork of this achievement, despite its limitations and its biases, that much subsequent work, whether by Indian or foreign scholars, has been based. Historical writing on India has probably overemphasized the negative and positive effects of conquests and invasions on Indian society, especially in the modern period. The result has been to portray Indian society as a passive recipient of influences, thus slighting the resiliency and creativity of Indian culture. What is ignored is the enormous vitality of Indian society that permitted it to withstand foreign intrusion and crippling blows. The inner dynamics of India's social structure, the mechanisms that made survival possible, usually referred to as the "caste system," is possibly not a source of weakness but of strength.

The function of religion in the Indian historical experience also has been misunderstood. There was an undoubted tendency among Western historians to see a direct causal connection between what were regarded as social evils (such as caste, poverty, and the treatment of women) and religious doctrines. Max Weber, for example, suggested that India had not experienced the same kind of industrial and economic transformation as had Europe because the teachings of Hinduism made men turn away from striving after economic and social improvement. Hindu society, he insisted, was "not capable of giving birth to economic and technical revolutions from within itself, or even of facilitating the first germination of capitalism in its midst." Careful examination of the relationship of religion and society has to a large degree been lacking in the work of both Indian and foreign writers, and as a result, much of the distinctiveness of the Indian experience has been misunderstood, especially the way in which religious doctrines, intractable physical realities (such as the cycle of the seasons), and social structures reinforce each other.

But of all the legacies from the European, or Western, origins of modern Indian historiography, the most crucial has been the placing of the nation-state at the center of historical experience. For Westerners in the nineteenth century the grand themes of history were the development of the modern state, the formation of constitutional government, the growth of democracy, and, above all, the rise of nationalism. Indian writers tended to accept this emphasis on the existence of a united nation-state as the highest of social and political goals and have sometimes argued that all the movements characteristic of the European political experience—constitutionalism, democracy, nationalism—had in fact existed in India in the past, or else that they were prevented from developing by the oppressive force of British imperialism. This emphasis on the nation-state and nationalism as the focus of history meant that little attention was paid to the possibility that India's political and social development, while quite different from that of Europe, might still be as creative and offer as satisfying a social existence to its people. This concentration on the idea that a united nation-state encompassing the whole of the Indian subcontinent was the only satisfactory goal of history had profound consequences in the twentieth century for the peoples of the region.

One immediate and persistent problem in trying to sketch Indian history is that it is very difficult to find a satisfactory method for periodization, that is, for dividing history into periods that make it possible to grasp movements and developments. A system of periodization that was once widely used was to speak of the Hindu period (from the earliest beginnings up to 1200 CE), the Muslim period (from 1200 to 1700), and finally the British period. There is widespread agreement that the use of religious designations badly distorts reality, as does the use of "British"; all these terms ignore continuities and overstress both religion and foreign conquest. The alternative periodization into ancient, medieval, and modern, drawn from the Western model, avoids some of the false emphasis of the other system, but it, too, distorts historical developments by suggesting parallels with the West that do not exist. For our present purpose it is simplest to avoid either of these divisions and to use instead only dates and descriptive headings.

Terminology also presents special problems in writing about India's past, because we are forced to use terms that are familiar to us from Western history such as *king, kingdom, state, empire,* and *feudalism.* All of these words have meanings that are misleading when applied to India. *Kingdom,* for example, in Western history implies notions of territorial boundaries, sovereignty, and possession of power that are alien to the India experience. In the

Indian context, *king* or *maharaja* probably means an overlord who is acknowledged by lesser rulers, but it does not mean that he controls all sources of power such as the collection of taxes and armies, the characteristic mark of state power in modern Western history.

***The Land: Setting for History.*** The land borders of India are great mountain ranges, consisting of the Himalayas on the north and northeast and their extensions on the northwest, the Hindu Kush and the Sulaiman Range. The Arabian Sea, the Indian Ocean, and the Bay of Bengal are its maritime boundaries. Within this area five geographic regions can be identified that have shaped the course of Indian history by defining regional kingdoms and determining social and economic development. (Geographers usually speak of three divisions, but those given here seem to be in conformity with geopolitical realities.)

The first of these five regions is the mountain zone, stretching in a great arc in the northwest from barren shores on the Arabian Sea to the jungles and hills that separate India from Burma. The mountain areas have not merely been barriers, isolating India from its neighbors; they have been centers of vital cultural and historic movements, differing greatly from each other and from those of the people of the plains. The second division is the vast plain formed by the Indus, Ganges (Ganga), and Brahmaputra rivers. This area has been the center of most of the great empires that have dominated India. To the west is a third division, the great deserts of Rajasthan and southeastern Pakistan. Although geographers do not usually consider this one of the major divisions (they include it within the Indo-Gangetic Plain), it has been the center of quite distinctive historical developments. The fourth region is the peninsular plateau, the Deccan, divided from the Ganges Plain by the Vindhya and other low mountain ranges. At times this area has been incorporated into northern empires, but it has itself been the center of important kingdoms. Beyond the Deccan plateau, there are narrow fertile coastal plains in Orissa, Tamil Nadu, and Kerala, that have had their own distinctive political societies. Although India has few good seaports, a number of them in each of these regions have been centers of coastal as well as overseas trade.

Internal geographic divisions have been determining factors in India's historical experience, as has its location in relation to its neighbors. The Himalayas have posed great difficulties, but not insuperable ones, for communications with China, the home of another ancient Asian civilization. At times, especially in the early centuries of the common era, there have been significant cultural and commercial relations by sea with Southeast Asia. The closest and most continuous relations between India and the outside world, however, were from the northwest. From the most ancient periods there were contacts with the Iranian plateau and later with Central Asia. India was a self-contained and self-sufficient civilization, but never an isolated one.

In analyzing Indian cultural and historical development, some historians have been inclined to give a preponderant place to climate, but the regional differences are so great that causal relations between climate and Indian civilization are not easy to make. The main features of the climate, however, have great bearing on the economy, especially agriculture.

Because of the protective shield of the Himalayas, India is not affected by the cold air currents of Central Asia. Most areas of the country endure very high temperatures for a large part of the year, with readings over 100° F being common. The daily average temperatures are high throughout most of the area, ranging from 79° F (26° C) in the Punjab to 85° F (30° C) in Tamil Nadu. The major climatic feature is the tropical monsoon, which means that rainfall is concentrated in a rainy season of two or three months. Art and literature bear frequent witness to the enormous importance of the monsoon, and there is a constant awareness of how human life is dependent upon the dramatic forces of nature.

***3000–600 BCE: Early Civilizations.*** Human settlements in India have been traced to the sixth millennium BCE in widely scattered areas of the subcontinent, but the earliest settled agriculturalists seem to have appeared in the Baluchistan area, in what is now Pakistan. From these beginnings came the great civilization that developed in the Indus Valley around 2500 BCE. The ruins of two of its major cities, Mohenjo Daro and Harappa, were discovered only in the 1920s, and since then archaeologists have found many more sites in widely separated parts of western India. Its writing has not yet been deciphered but it seems certain that there are direct links between the Indus Valley civilization and later Indian cultures. It was once believed that the civilization was suddenly destroyed by invaders or some great disaster, but current studies suggest that the decay of the urban centers took place over a long period, and by about 1700 BCE the area seems no longer to have had a common civilization.

Around this period, migrants known as Aryans appeared from the northwest. Very little is known with certainty about these peoples, although they have been the subject of intense speculation. They seem to have originated in Central Asia or southern Russia and moved toward western Asia, the Iranian plateau, and India. Two aspects of Indian culture that are of great importance are associated with them. One is the growth and spread of the Indo-European language family in the subcontinent, out of which developed the Indo-Aryan groups of languages. These include classical Sanskrit as well as many of the modern languages of India, such as Hindi, Bengali, and Marathi. The other great influence traceable to the Aryan migratory peoples is the vast body of Vedic literature, so called from the earliest of the texts, the Vedas. These texts, while providing little information about historical events, are an immense storehouse of mythologies, rituals, and religious and philosophic ideas. They have proved the basis for much of the Indian religious traditions.

In the period from 1000 to 500 BCE, new centers of urban life, the first since the decay of the cities of the Indus Valley civilization, appear in the Ganges Plain. The growth of towns, settled agriculture, trade, and the use of iron were all related to the change in the status of tribal or clan rulers. Kingdoms with territorial limits, courts with elaborate rituals, and rudimentary administrative structures are referred to in the literature, as is also the nature of the social structure. There is constant emphasis on the role of the brahmans, with great power accrued to them through their control of ritual practice and religious knowledge, and to the other three groups, or *varnas*, into which society was supposed to be divided: the *kshatriyas* (warriors, landowners), the *vaishyas* (farmers, merchants), and the *shudras* (laborers). These ideas of social organization were later related to the complex social structures known in Western literature as castes. These developments took place mainly in the Gangetic heartland; elsewhere, especially in eastern India and in the South, other social and cultural patterns continued, which through the centuries interacted with the Aryan or the Brahmanic pattern. This was particularly true of the countries in the South, whose languages were not Indo-Aryan but belonged to the Dravidian language family. There was undoubtedly much interaction with other ethnic and linguistic groups, and it was out of this very complex amalgam that Indian culture, and the religion and social structures we know as Hinduism, ultimately evolved.

*600 BCE–300 CE: The First Empires.* The millennium from 600 BCE to 300 CE was a time of intense cultural and social change, but the roots of these activities were firmly embedded in the great historical movements of the previous two millennia. The political history of the subcontinent during this period is characterized by the rise of empires, that is, territorial and ethnic units that expanded their center of power and brought other political and ethnic groups under their domination. Each of the five geographic divisions of India mentioned above had its own separate political history, and in addition, the imperial powers that appear in this time tend to have their centers in the northwest (in what is now northern Pakistan), in the Ganges Plain in North India, or in South India in the Deccan plateau. This period also saw the birth of two great religious movements, Buddhism and Jainism; there is undoubtedly a connection between the rise of new religions and the creation of large political units, but the connections are obscure and speculative. Buddhism spread from its homeland in North India to all of Asia, whereas Jainism remained a small but important sect within India. A third important feature of the period was continued urbanization and increased trade, not only within the subcontinent but with Southeast Asia and the Roman empire as well.

Throughout this period there were repeated contacts in the northwest with the empires of the Iranian plateau, and by about 520 BCE the area west of the Indus became part of the Achaemenid empire. From the point of view of the Western world, the most famous of these contacts came when Alexander the Great conquered the Achaemenid empire and advanced into Gandhara (around Islamabad, the modern capital of Pakistan) in 326 BCE. Alexander's departure from India and his death in 323 prevented the incorporation of Indian territory into his empire, but the principalities established by his generals opened up communication with India, notably with the Maurya dynasty.

In North India, Maghada (in what is now Bihar) had become a powerful kingdom, and about 324 BCE it came under the control of Chandragupta Maurya. His capital was Pataliputra (modern Patna) and from it he controlled large areas of northern India. Under his grandson Ashoka (c. 272–232 BCE) Maurya power was extended over much of India. In modern Indian historiography Ashoka is hailed as the great unifier of India, a man of profound religious tolerance, and the creator of a just society.

Although Ashoka was undoubtedly a ruler of genius, it is probable that his empire was not a centralized bureaucracy but rather a loose federation of rulers who were forced for a time to acknowledge

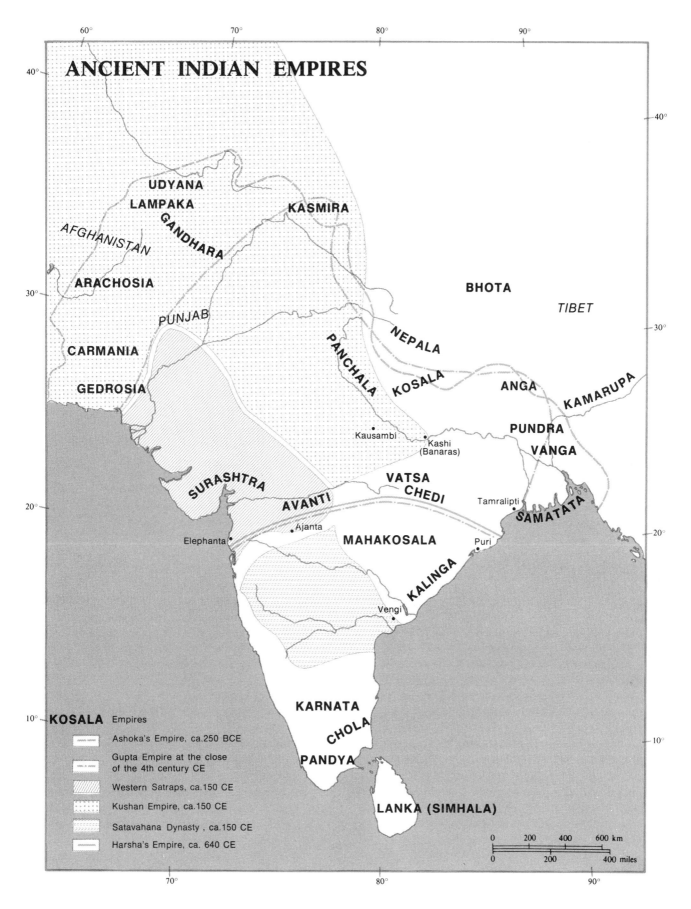

# ANCIENT INDIAN EMPIRES

UDYANA
LAMPAKA
AFGHANISTAN
GANDHARA
KASMIRA
ARACHOSIA
BHOTA
TIBET
PUNJAB
NEPALA
CARMANIA
PANCHALA
KOSALA
ANGA
KAMARUPA
GEDROSIA
PUNDRA
VANGA
Kausambi
Kashi
(Banaras)
SURASHTRA
VATSA
AVANTI
CHEDI
Tamralipti
SAMATATA
Ajanta
Elephanta
MAHAKOSALA
Puri
KALINGA
Vengi

KARNATA
CHOLA
PANDYA

LANKA (SIMHALA)

**KOSALA** Empires

Ashoka's Empire, ca.250 BCE

Gupta Empire at the close
of the 4th century CE

Western Satraps, ca.150 CE

Kushan Empire, ca.150 CE

Satavahana Dynasty , ca.150 CE

Harsha's Empire, ca. 640 CE

| 0 | 200 | 400 | 600 km |
| 0 | 200 | | 400 miles |

the Maurya dominance. The disappearance of the Maurya kingdom around 200 BCE did not mean a period of cultural and economic decay, for there is evidence that, despite what would now be thought of as political disunity, trade flourished and many of the kingdoms that emerged were centers of culture, with rulers who were patrons of religion, art, and literature. Among the best known of these dynasties are the Sungas and the Satavahanas.

In South India (the modern states of Tamil Nadu, Karnataka, Andhra Pradesh, and Kerala) kingdoms were established by the second century BCE that, despite dynastic changes, remained centers of culture, religion, and trade. The Tamil literature of the time shows a rich local religious and social culture that was gradually being influenced by elements from the Aryan traditions of the North. These included the Sanskrit language and the Brahmanical religious rituals and ideas, as well as Buddhism and Jainism.

This movement from the North has sometimes been spoken of as "conquest," but there is no real evidence in these early periods of long-scale military conquests, even by the Mauryas, in the South. The more likely process is one of gradual diffusion of ideas, values, myths, rituals, and the Sanskrit language in the southern regions. The result was the development of very rich cultural traditions in the South, the evidence of which is the beginning of temple building and the creation of an impressive Tamil literary tradition. There were also extensive trading contacts with the outside world. Inscriptions and hoards of coins, as well as literary evidence in Latin literature, attest to the export of Indian luxury goods—textiles, ivory, spices, precious stones, and exotic animals—in exchange for Roman glass, pottery, gold, and silver. Trade from South Indian ports was also conducted with Southeast Asia, and it was at this time that Indian culture began to influence what is now Cambodia, Bali, Java, Thailand, and other areas.

After the decay of Maurya power, the North came under the rule of local dynasties as well as various intruders from the northwest, the most important of whom were the Scythians, known in Indian history as the Sakas, nomadic tribes from Central Asia. One of these tribes established a powerful kingdom that lasted from about 78 to 200 CE.

This dynasty, known as the Kushans, had its capital near modern Peshawar in Pakistan, with Mathura, south of Delhi, the main city in the southern part of the kingdom. Culturally, this period is of importance because the Kushan patronage helped spread Buddhism throughout northern India and Central Asia. It also saw the beginning of new styles of art, especially sculpture, that are associated with Buddhism; Gandhara is noted for its strongly Hellenistic style and influence on Indian art.

In both the North and the South, the period from 250 BCE to 300 CE was one of great social and cultural change. The land area under cultivation expanded, with resulting increases in government revenue, which made support possible for religion, art, and literature. Trade, both by sea from the ports of South India, and overland in the North to Central Asia and Iran, provided for intellectual contacts with other civilizations as well as for the exchange of material goods. Scholarly works in grammar, law, and science codified and defined the tradition. In religion, two schools of Buddhism, Theravada and Mahayana, developed, while the older Brahmanical tradition began to transform itself into what we now think of as Hinduism. The great gods, Shiva and Vishnu, became prominent, with an emphasis on devotional worship. Krishna and another great cult hero, Rama, became objects of worship as incarnations of Vishnu. Worship of female deities was common, especially of the great mother goddess.

*300–1200 CE: Political and Cultural Definition of the Indian Tradition.* The first two centuries of this period in the North were politically dominated by the Gupta dynasty, which lasted from about 320 CE to the beginning of the sixth century. This empire was probably not a centrally administered kingdom, however, but an area where conquered rulers acknowledged Gupta overlordship by paying tribute while maintaining their own local power. Gupta dominance was weakened both by internal struggles and by invasions in the Northwest by the peoples known in European history as the Huns. The Huns did not establish any enduring kingdoms in India but were probably absorbed as local rulers. In the following centuries new dynasties appeared in North India, of which the most important were the Rajputs, a class whose descendants became rulers of many kingdoms throughout the North, but particularly in what is now Rajasthan.

Two questions regarding the political life of this period in North India are of particular interest. One has to do with the actual way in which political power was exercised, the other with ideas of kingship. Some scholars have referred to the political arrangements that developed in North India from the sixth century onward as "feudalism." Rulers tended to assign land on a permanent basis to religious groups as well as to secular groups, who were

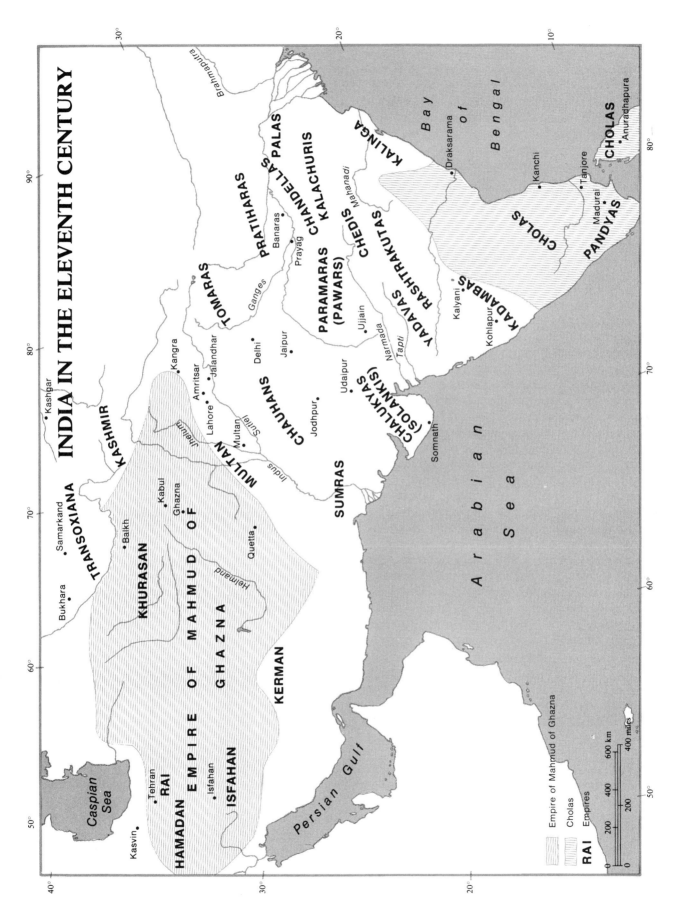

# INDIA IN THE ELEVENTH CENTURY

Caspian Sea

TRANSOXIANA

KASHMIR

KHURASAN

EMPIRE OF MAHMUD OF

GHAZNA

KERMAN

HAMADAN

ISFAHAN

RAI

MULTAN

TOMARAS

PRATIHARAS

PALAS

CHANDELLAS

KALACHURIS

CHEDIS

PARAMARAS
(PAWARS)

CHAHHANS

SUMRAS

CHALUKYAS
(SOLANKIS)

KALINGA

RASHTRAKUTAS

YADAVAS

KADAMBAS

CHOLAS

PANDYAS

CHOLAS

Bay of Bengal

Arabian Sea

Persian Gulf

Kashgar

Samarkand

Bukhara

Balkh

Kabul

Ghazna

Quetta

Tehran

Isfahan

Kasvin

Kangra

Amritsar

Lahore

Jalandhar

Multan

Delhi

Jaipur

Jodhpur

Udaipur

Ujjain

Banaras

Prayag

Somnath

Kalyani

Kohlapur

Draksarama

Kanchi

Tanjore

Madurai

Anuradhapura

Brahmaputra

Ganges

Sutlej

Jhelum

Indus

Helmand

Narmada

Tapti

Mahanadi

Empire of Mahmud of Ghazna

Cholas

Empires

RAI

0    200    400    600 km
0    200    400 miles

in effect the officials of the ruler. This meant that these officials become a hereditary class, with state offices and control of temple lands remaining in the possession of a family. Payment for services to the state came from land assigned by the king, not from his revenues. This arrangement made the officers independent of the ruler, and it gave their families bases of political power. Many of these landowner-officials were brahmans, who combined secular power with religious status. This dispersal of power from the king's court to numerous centers of local power was probably an important factor in ensuring the preservation of religion and culture, despite invasions and dynastic change.

Ideas of kingship in India, as elsewhere, evolved over time and were clearly related to actual social and political conditions, but a few generalizations can be made on the evidence of the Gupta and post-Gupta period in North India. One is that, unlike in many other ancient societies, in India the king was not regarded as a god, even though he might be thought of as being divinely appointed. Many rulers were men of low caste or foreigners who had won power through usurpation, assassination, or military conquest, and the brahmans provided them with an acceptable genealogy. In this way, while mobility was made possible, the norms and values of the society were preserved, with an emphasis on stability and order even while great alternations were being made in political control. In traditional Indian political thought the king was neither a law-giver nor a divine being; his function, or his duty, was to maintain the ideal fabric of society as described in the great legal and religious texts and as expounded by the brahmans. He was, in a sense, a policeman, a guardian of morality, of the accepted norms of society.

In the South, the old dynasties—the Cheras, the Pandyas, and the Cholas—declined, and new ones appeared, of which the chief was the Pallava. As in North India, the kingdoms were not centralized bureaucratic states, and much evidence exists indicating that the southern kingdoms were closer to what have been called "segmentary states" than to the more familiar "unitary states" of European history. In the Chola kingdom, for example, military power was not exclusively controlled by the ruler, as in a unitary state, but was dispersed among many chieftains, who, when it suited their interest, would unite with others to carry out wars, not for territory but for treasure. It was also these chieftains, not the Chola rulers, who were in a position to make land grants to brahmans and others. Villages were related economically and politically, not to the central dynasty, but to local rulers. The Chola dynasty did not possess, then, political and territorial sovereignty in the Western sense but ritual sovereignty that emphasized the greatness inherent in the king. The Chola king conferred part of his greatness upon lesser rulers who, in accepting it, became "little kings."

These complex political systems in both North and South India provided the environment for intense intellectual, religious, and artistic creativity. Examples of its productivity are the poems of Bhartrihari, the plays of Kalidasa, the philosophy of Shankara, the paintings and sculpture at Ajanta and Ellora, and the architecture of the Mukteshwar temple at Bhubaneswar and the Kandariya temple at Khajuraho.

The exuberant creativity that had demonstrated itself in so many expressions of the human spirit appears to have weakened in the eleventh and twelfth centuries. No particular reasons can be assigned for this, but it is no doubt related to many political, social, economic, and religious forces. Moreover, the complexities of their interaction were compounded by a powerful new pressure from outside.

*1200–1700: The Realignment of Politics and Cultures.* This pressure came from the Turks, a Central Asian people who by the tenth century were in control of the Indian borderlands in what is now Afghanistan. The process of decline and decay in Indian civilization has often been attributed to the Turkic invasions, but while this was undoubtedly a factor, it is almost certain that the loss of vitality had preceded the Turkic conquests. Virtually no aspect of Indian civilization disappeared as a result of the coming of the Turkic peoples and Islam; its resilience was such that it was able to withstand not only these invasions but also, at a later date, the coming of the pervasive power of Western imperialism.

It is equally important to recognize the enormous importance of the introduction of a vibrant new religious and social system into the subcontinent, where for nearly three thousand years a civilization had developed and matured. The civilization existing in India and the one brought in by the Turks and other Islamic peoples were both highly evolved and complex systems, complete in themselves. Neither the conquerors nor the conquered were barbarians ready to adopt the civilization of the other.

The coming of the Turkic people in the eleventh and twelfth centuries was not the subcontinent's first experience with followers of Islam: that had begun in 711 when an Arab general from the eastern provinces of the Umayyad empire attacked and conquered Sind, in what is now Pakistan. The Arab conquests in Sind established a permanent Islamic presence there, but they had little influence on the rest of India, since the area was isolated by deserts and, in the North, by powerful Indian rulers. The second intrusion of Muslims into India came not from the Arab world, but from Central Asia. The Turkic chieftains had established themselves by 962 in Ghazna in Afghanistan. In the later tenth and eleventh centuries they moved through the northwestern areas of India and established bases in the Punjab, as far east as Lahore. Then Muhammad, the ruler of Ghur, a principality in Afghanistan, defeated an alliance of Indian rulers in 1192 at Tarain, North India. He established his rule at Delhi, which was the northern outpost of the great Indian king Prithviraj, whose capital was at Ajmer.

Using Delhi as a base, the Turkic commanders expanded their control during the next century into most regions of India. They encountered great resistance from local rulers in their expansion, first into neighboring Rajasthan, then down the Ganges toward Bengal, and finally, in the fourteenth century, to the South, but despite reverses they succeeded in exerting their control everywhere except in the extreme South and East.

*Delhi Sultanate.* The period of Turkic rule from 1192 to 1526 is referred to as the Delhi sultanate to distinguish it from the period after 1526 when the Mughal dynasty was in control. Only very briefly was there centralized control from Delhi; the more usual situation was the existence of independent kingdoms established by commanders of the armies of the sultan of Delhi. Bengal, Gujarat, Malwa, and the Bahmani sultanate in the Deccan all became important kingdoms in their own right. The new rulers had to assure a regular collection of taxes from the peasants and loans of money from the trading classes, and as they did not have enough resources in manpower to change the existing relationships, they generally worked within the existing order. Thus many of the old landed classes remained in effective control at the local level.

For much the same reasons, the new rulers in Delhi did not attempt large-scale forcible conversion of the population to Islam. Many pious religious leaders believed that this forced conversion was the duty of Muslim rulers, but with few exceptions, the Delhi rulers followed the commonsense policy of putting the collection of revenue and the creation of a peaceful society before the ideological demands of religion, which might have led to mass resistance and dislocation. Most of the actual administrative staff of the government were Hindus, as were many of the officers of the army.

While the Muslim rulers of India did not use force on a large scale to bring about conversions, one of the most important results of their conquest was the growth of a very large Muslim population in India. Although most of the population remained Hindu, more than two hundred million of the world's Muslims now (as of 1986) live in the subcontinent. The great concentrations are in the extreme west, in what is now Pakistan, and in the east, in Bangladesh. The reason for this is probably that the populations of these areas traditionally were less deeply rooted in the Hindu social and religious system, and therefore Islam found an easier entrance. Most of the converts were probably from low-caste groups who had not been brought effectively into the Hindu class structure. Other large concentrations are in the great urban areas—Delhi, Agra, Lucknow, Ahmedabad, and Hyderabad. Here many converts appear to have been members of artisan classes, who perhaps found economic and social advantages in the religion of the conquerors. Many of the upper-class Muslims had their origins outside India, as did many of the scholars, artists, and religious leaders.

The Muslims did not form a cohesive community. They were divided by very deep regional, linguistic, sectarian, and class differences, just as was the Hindu population. It is misleading to think of Hindus and Muslims as two self-conscious communities confronting each other in this period. Much nearer the reality is to see groups and classes, sometimes both Muslim, contending within an intricate social and political mosaic.

Hindu rulers by no means disappeared from India during the period of Turkish ascendancy. From 1336 to 1646 large areas of South India were controlled by the great empire of Vijayanagara, which had established its authority over many of the smaller and older Hindu kingdoms of the region. A strong military power, with widespread trading and commercial activities, Vijayanagara provided support for scholars and artists from the traditional Hindu culture. On the east coast, Orissa was the center of strong Hindu kingdoms that were subjected to relatively little Islamic influence. In Rajasthan, although the Rajput chieftains were subject to the Muslim rulers, their courts remained centers of indigenous culture and Hindu spirituality. In the far east, Assam continued to remain virtually outside the control of the dynasties of North India.

*Mughal Empire.* The Mughals (a branch of the Timurid line) constitute the Islamic dynasty that is associated with the most brilliant cultural achievements and the one that longest maintained an extended empire. It is also the one best known in the Western world, for its period of greatness coincided with the beginning of European expansion into Asia in the sixteenth and seventeenth centuries. Numerous European travelers marveled at the wealth and splendor of the Mughal court and the great cities of the empire.

Babur (a direct descendant of Timur, the great conqueror of the fourteenth century, and, through his mother's family, of another great warrior, Genghis Khan) had gained a foothold in North India from a base in Afghanistan in 1526, but it was only in his grandson Akbar's time (1556–1605) that the position of the dynasty was secured. A succession of able rulers through alliances and conquests extended Mughal control over the rest of India, until during the reign of Aurangzeb (1658–1707) virtually all of South Asia, including Afghanistan, was part of the empire. This final expansion was followed by a rapid decline in the power of the Mughal dynasty, and in the first fifty years of the eighteenth century, successor states, usually controlled by commanders and governors of the Mughals, were established in Bengal, Hyderabad, and Oudh. Elsewhere, indigenous regional groups challenged imperial control. These included the Marathas, the Rajputs, the Jats, and the Sikhs; the Afghan chiefs also broke away during this period. Finally, this period saw the emergence of European powers, especially the French and British, as actors in the Indian scene.

The decline of the great Mughal empire has been a subject much discussed by both Western and Indian historians ever since the eighteenth century. Some have explained it in terms of dynastic failure, that is, the weakness and ineptitude of the later rulers. Others have traced the decline to religious tensions generated by Aurangzeb's attempts to strengthen Islam at the expense of Hinduism. Economic historians have seen overexploitation of the peasantry as leading to a breakdown of the revenue system. The expansion of territorial control has also been regarded as a source, on the grounds that the mechanisms of the imperial government were too weak to control such a vast territory. There is almost certainly no one cause of the decline, since all of these factors were present to some extent throughout the whole period of Mughal rule.

The result of the decay of imperial power was not a lapse of the subcontinent into anarchy and chaos, but rather a dispersal of power to new centers—the successor states and the regional groups. Culturally,

the eighteenth century is one of great creative activity, as evidenced by poetry and painting and by building activity in such centers as Lucknow and Jaipur in the North and Madurai and Mysore in the South. The activities of the Europeans were also part of this century of ferment and change, and these provided the focus for the next period, when the subcontinent became much more a part of the world economic and political system than it had been in previous centuries.

*1700–1947: India Becomes Part of the World System.* There are a number of ways of interpreting the history of South Asia from the decline of the Mughal empire to the coming of independence to India and Pakistan in 1947. One is to emphasize the intrusion of the West, with an emphasis on the transforming changes introduced in the form of new ideas, new technology, and new methods of government into an ancient and moribund society. But others, looking at the same historical experience, have seen a record of exploitation and oppression, destruction of much that was of value in the old society, and its replacement by the shoddy and meretricious.

These opposing evaluations overestimate the extent to which Western influence penetrated into the fabric of Indian society. To a very large extent the characteristics of Indian civilization determined the nature of the Western impact, and the Indian relationships with Western economic, political, and cultural forces must be seen in terms of India's own history; one should not be misled by assuming identities, or even important similarities, with the intrusion of Spain in the New World or Britain and France in Africa.

Perhaps the most instructive way to look at the Western relationship with India is to see it as part of the great worldwide movement of change beginning in the sixteenth century that created a world much more closely interlinked than had ever existed before. Military conquest is only one aspect of the intrusion, and not necessarily the most significant. The roots of the linkage of India with this international system were economic and have remained so. After 1600, when the British, French, Dutch, and other European traders came to India, they were in search of goods that were in demand in Europe, such as spices, cotton cloth, silk, opium, and indigo. What India wanted in return was gold and silver, and by the end of the nineteenth century India was part of the world market. This movement from a subcontinental economy to an international one was fairly slow and affected certain parts of the country, such as the areas near the great new seaports of Calcutta, Bombay, and Madras, much more than others.

The trade between India and the rest of the world was not carried on by individual European entrepreneurs but by trading companies, which held monopolies on the trade between India and their home countries. It was not the British government but the British East India Company, an organization of merchants and traders, that began the economic involvement between India and England and that eventually became the Government of India. The company remained in control of the administration of its Indian territories in a formal sense until 1858, but real power had long before been passed to the British government. The East India Company found it advantageous to make agreements with the local rulers and to get concessions from them. Then if a ruler was in difficulty the company would see the opportunity for getting greater concessions, or, when conditions were favorable, with the help of allies in the court or trading community, it would place its own candidate on the throne. Finally, the Indian in a position of power would be replaced by company officials. This was essentially the way in which the East India Company gained power in Bengal between 1757 and 1775. Elsewhere, it gained control through invasion and conquest, as in the territories of the Sikhs in the Punjab and of the Marathas in Central India.

The East India Company was able to defeat the Indian rulers because of superior military equipment and better organization. In addition, it was able to hire Indian soldiers and to discipline them so that they made an efficient army. The active collaboration of elite groups in Indian society was also necessary. It was conquest from within, then, based on Indian means and resources, that made British control possible. It was a slow process, for not until 1850 were the British masters of all of the subcontinent, and even then they were threatened with uprisings and rebellions, as in 1857/1858. From that time on, however, British rule was remarkably secure for almost a century until finally, in 1947, it yielded to political, not military, pressures.

During the nineteenth century all power was concentrated in the hands of a few thousand British officials, without any control through popularly elected assemblies. But this was a despotism with no real parallel elsewhere. The British did not have to answer to an elected government in India as they did to the British Parliament. Furthermore, it was a despotism that ruled within the confines of its own laws and that had created a legal system that provided as fair a measure of protection to the citizens as existed in most countries. The new legal codes and courts were based on English models, which were alien to Indian customs, but they were so quickly accepted and adapted to Indian conditions that in the end they often appear quite different from the originals. The press was remarkably free to criticize the government and its officials. The higher levels of administration had a reputation for honesty and fairness, and as in the case of the legal system, the bureaucracy adjusted itself to Indian needs and demands in such a way that it soon appeared to be Indian, rather than Western. Of all Asian and African countries, with the exception of Japan, India was the first to have a modern bureaucratic structure, and thus it became part of the world political system, even though its rulers were British, not Indian. India had the framework of a nation long before achieving independence.

Economic and political factors combined to provide the setting that made possible the interaction between Indian and Western culture. India had long had access to the Western, but there is little evidence of Western knowledge being appropriated before the nineteenth century. An example is the printing press, which had been introduced into India by the Portuguese in the seventeenth century but which appears not to have excited any interest in Indian society itself. The contrast with the nineteenth century—when the printing press created a virtual revolution in communication through newspapers, pamphlets, and books—is startling. That the fusion of Indian and Western interests took place in the new economic structures and political institutions is best shown in Calcutta, the capital of British India.

Nowhere does one see more plainly than in Calcutta that Western culture was not something imposed on an unwilling and hostile population; instead, a lively, self-confident intelligentsia, involved in the economic and political changes that were taking place, reached out to extract from Western culture the knowledge that would benefit India. The key to attaining this knowledge on which the future depended was the English language, which was prized by Indians then and later, not so much for the richness of its literature as for the fact that it was the way to link their country and themselves with Europe and the West. When Indians turned outward they looked not to China or Japan but to the West and, above all, to the English-speaking West.

The nationalist movement, which began at the end

of the century and culminated in the end of British rule in the subcontinent in 1947, was the direct product of economic, political, and cultural interaction. Indian nationalism was not an ideology imported from the West but was a very distinctive creation of all the complex forces that had gone into the subcontinent's historical experience. Indian nationalist leaders, while demanding freedom and self-rule, accepted many aspects of the culture of the imperial power, claiming constitutional government, freedom of the press, and democracy as their rights as citizens of the modern world.

Another characteristic feature of Indian nationalism is the nature of the leadership of the Indian National Congress, the organization founded in 1885 to give expression to India's political aspirations. Its spokesmen were almost always men who had won distinction in one of the professions and who were respected by the British as well as by their own countrymen. Even in the later period, when attitudes hardened and lines between the British and the nationalist leaders were more firmly drawn, the ultimate validity of the nationalist cause was acknowledged by the British rulers, and there was remarkably little antagonism toward the British or toward the West in general. Indian nationalism also differed from other modern nationalist movements in that it did not call for social revolution or a transformation of society: it was essentially a political movement aimed at transferring power from British to Indian hands. This was true even in the period when Mahatma Gandhi dominated the Indian National Congress in the 1920s and 1930s. Although radical, his social program was not linked to any particular political ideology, and he sought a revolution through personal decision and inner change, not through government control.

Almost from the time of its founding, the goal of the Indian National Congress—that is, a democratic, representative government—was questioned by some Muslim leaders, who argued that this meant rule of Muslims by Hindus, who were the overwhelming majority of the population. To this was added the argument that Muslins and Hindus were not simply religious groups, like Catholics and Protestants in the West, but rather were nations. This belief in the separateness of the Muslims became the central tenet of the Muslim League, an organization founded in 1906. The League found a potent spokesman in the 1920s and 1930s in Mohammad Ali Jinnah, who insisted that both Hindus and Muslims had a national identity rooted in and defined by their religion. This was vigorously rejected by the Indian National Congress, for the Congress ideal was a plural society in which religion was not a defining characteristic of nationality, but a private profession that did not interfere with one's national loyalty. The Muslim League under Jinnah formulated what can best be thought of as an alternative nationalism. On the one side was the nationalism of the Congress, exemplified by Nehru and Gandhi and a host of others, including many Muslims. On the other was the nationalism of the Muslim League, which by the 1940s was beginning to demand a separate homeland for India's Muslims. This struck at the very heart of the Congress's concept of an Indian nation that was coterminous with the India that had been politically unified by the British in the nineteenth century.

By the end of World War II, two great facts had become inescapably clear. One was that the British would not attempt to maintain their rule for very long; the other was that transfer of power and sovereignty to a single national entity seemed to present insuperable problems. In the face of this, the decision was made to partition the subcontinent and to create a separate homeland, Pakistan, for the Muslims. Lord Mountbatten, as governor-general, carried out the final settlement. The leadership of the Indian National Congress, which for so long had opposed the idea, accepted it with bitterness as the only way to achieve independence. Even the Muslim League was not happy in the final division, for not only did it attain less territory than had been hoped for but it was in two pieces, West Pakistan and East Pakistan, separated from each other by the expanse of India. Nor was Pakistan a home for all the Muslims of the subcontinent: sixty million of them remained in India.

***Post-1947: The New India.*** On 15 August 1947, British rule in the subcontinent ended with the transfer of power to the governments of India and Pakistan. There was enormous dislocation and suffering as twelve million people moved from one country to another, but within a few months the countries managed to stabilize their borders. The main problems for both countries were in creating a stable political system, dealing with economic problems, providing a measure of social justice to the poverty-stricken masses, and defining relations with each other and the rest of the world.

Work on a constitution, based upon the existing system instituted in 1935, was begun before 1947 and became effective on 26 January 1950, which is the official independence day of India. It declares India to be a "sovereign democratic Republic" and

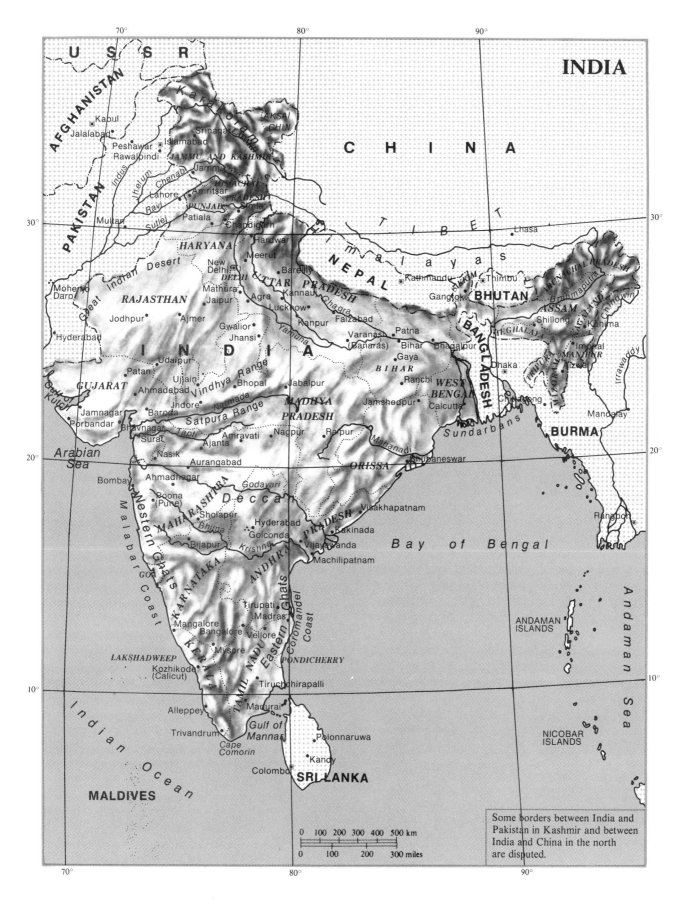

INDIA

70°    80°    90°

U  S  S  R

AFGHANISTAN

•Kabul
Jalalabad•

Peshawar•
Rawalpindi•

PAKISTAN

•Multan

30°

Mohenjo
Daro•

Great Indian Desert

RAJASTHAN

•Jodhpur

Hyderabad•

•Ajmer

I  N  D  I  A

GUJARAT

Jamnagar•
Porbandar•
Bhavnagar•
Surat•

Gulf of Kutch

•Ahmadabad
•Baroda

Satpura Range

Tapti

•Nasik

Arabian
Sea

Bombay•

20°

Ahmadnagar•
•Poona
(Pune)

MAHARASHTRA

Malabar Coast

Western Ghats

GOA

Sholapur•
•Bhima
•Bijapur

Deccan

•Hyderabad
•Golconda
Krishna

KARNATAKA

Mangalore•
•Bangalore

LAKSHADWEEP

Mysore•

•Vellore

KERALA

Kozhikode•
(Calicut)

Alleppey•

10°

Trivandrum•

Indian Ocean

Cape
Comorin

MALDIVES

TAMIL NADU

Tirupati•
•Madras

Eastern Ghats

Coromandel Coast

•PONDICHERRY

Tiruchchirapalli•

Madurai•

Gulf of
Mannar

Colombo•

SRI LANKA

•Polonnaruwa

•Kandy

Srinagar•
KARAKORAM

AKSAI
CHIN

JAMMU AND KASHMIR

Jammu•

Islamabad•

Indus

Jhelum

Chenab

Lahore•  •Amritsar
Ravi

Sutlej

PUNJAB

•Patiala

•Chandigarh

•Simla

HIMACHAL
PRADESH

Hardwar•

HARYANA

Meerut•

New
Delhi•

DELHI

•Bareilly

Mathura•
•Agra

•Jaipur

Gwalior•

•Jhansi

Udaipur•

•Patan
Ujjain•

Indore•

Vindhya Range

•Bhopal

Narmada

MADHYA
PRADESH

Amravati•
•Nagpur

Ajanta•

Aurangabad•

Godavari

Vijayawada•

ANDHRA PRADESH

Machilipatnam•

C  H  I  N  A

T  I  B  E  T

•Lhasa

Himalayas

NEPAL

•Kathmandu

Gangtok•

UTTAR PRADESH

Kannauj•
•Lucknow

•Kanpur

Yamuna

Ghagra

Faizabad•

Varanasi•
(Banaras)

•Patna

BIHAR

•Gaya

Bhagalpur•

SIKKIM

Thimbu•

BHUTAN

ARUNACHAL PRADESH

Brahmaputra

ASSAM

Shillong•

•Kohima

NAGALAND

MEGHALAYA

BANGLADESH

•Dhaka

Chindwin

Imphal•

MANIPUR

TRIPURA

Aizwal•

MIZORAM

30°

•Ranchi

WEST
BENGAL

Jabalpur•

•Raipur

Jamshedpur•

Calcutta•

Mahanadi

Chittagong•

Sundarbans

BURMA

Mandalay•

20°

ORISSA

•Bhubaneswar

Visakhapatnam•

Kakinada•

Bay  of  Bengal

Irrawaddy

Rangoon•

ANDAMAN
ISLANDS

Andaman Sea

10°

NICOBAR
ISLANDS

0  100 200 300 400 500 km

0    100    200    300 miles

Some borders between India and
Pakistan in Kashmir and between
India and China in the north
are disputed.

70°    80°    90°

has a bill of rights providing for equality before the law, freedom of speech, and freedom of religion and forbidding discrimination on the grounds of religion, sex, or caste. There are two houses in the central legislature, one with direct election, the other with members elected by the state legislatures. The president is the ceremonial head of state, with real power residing in the prime minister, who is the leader of the political party with the majority of the seats in the Lok Sabha, the directly elected house.

India was the successor state to the old Government of India and had the advantage of retaining the capital and most of the civil and military services, as well as the industrial centers. Pakistan had to create its governmental structure almost overnight; it had few industries and did not have the advantage of continued leadership from those who had achieved its independence. Jinnah died in 1948, and his successor, Liaqat Ali Khan, was assassinated in 1951. After that, a series of governments tried to maintain parliamentary democracy, but the increasing disorder and factionalism led to a military takeover in 1958 by Ayub Khan.

In India, under Prime Minister Nehru, there was a commitment to parliamentary democracy, a socialist pattern of society, and in foreign affairs, a policy of neutralism and nonalignment, but above all there was a commitment to the preservation of national unity. The first general elections were held in 1952, and although the Indian National Congress at first had no real challenger, a multiparty system developed. Great stress was placed on India as a secular state, that is, one where all religions had equal status. Nehru and his party were convinced that the economic problems of the country would be solved only through government planning, and a series of five-year plans attempted to bring about rapid industrialization and an increase in agricultural productivity. While there have been great difficulties in implementing the plans, nevertheless there has been remarkable progress in modernizing large sectors of the economy.

Nehru remained prime minister until his death in 1964. His successor, Lal Bahadur Shastri, died in 1966, shortly after signing an accord with Pakistan. Shastri was succeeded by Indira Gandhi, Nehru's daughter, who proved to be a formidable politician. The high point of her popularity came after war with Pakistan in 1971, but in 1975 she declared a national emergency, which effectively instituted authoritarian rule and stifled political opposition. In 1977 she was voted out of office by the Janata party under Morarji Desai. She was triumphantly returned

to power in the election of 1980 and remained prime minister until her assassination in 1984, when she was succeeded by her son Rajiv.

Nehru had formulated a foreign policy of neutralism and nonalignment that was intended to keep India from being entangled in great power rivalries while at the same time permitting it to take an active role in world affairs. India asserted its hegemony in the region in an unmistakable fashion in 1961 when it seized Goa, the last enclave of the Portuguese empire in India.

India's relations with its two neighbors, Pakistan and China, however, were of central concern. Animosities caused by the trauma of partition, border disputes, and the quarrel over control of Kashmir led to war between India and Pakistan in 1948 and again in 1965, wars that ended both times in a negotiated cease-fire. India had signed a treaty of friendship with China in 1954, but there were frequent disputes over the boundaries between the two countries. War broke out in October 1962 when the Indian army moved into territory claimed by the Chinese. While the war lasted only one month, it embittered relations, with each side continuing to claim that the other was illegally occupying territory. Then in 1971 tensions increased in the subcontinent when civil war broke out in East Pakistan as its leaders moved to secede from Pakistan. India supported the secessionists, and as the war ended in a victory for them and for India, East Pakistan declared its independence as the new country of Bangladesh.

The emergence of Bangladesh can be seen as a continuation of the process of transfer of power that had begun in 1947 as the political unification that had been created in the nineteenth century by the British broke down. The three national units—India, Pakistan, and Bangladesh—arose from the working of forces within the subcontinent itself. Of the three, India's greatly superior industrial base and its defense forces (the fourth largest in the world) gave it a position of power that none of the other South Asian states could challenge and that often made them regard India with uneasy suspicion.

India's relations with the superpowers, the Soviet Union and the United States, depended in large measure on the effects of their policies on the subcontinent. Thus India perceived the Soviet Union as having been consistent in its support, while the United States was believed to favor Pakistan and China over and against India's interests. The foreign policies of the countries of South Asia are the logical working out of the links that were forged with the world system in the nineteenth century. As the old world order alters, great changes are certain to follow, while new kinds of economic, political, and cultural links are forged. The countries of the area do not have identical interests, despite a long shared history and cultures that have much in common. They often have conflicting concerns, and their future will be molded as they seek internal political stability and justice for their people while working out relationships with each other and with the great powers that will serve their social and political needs.

[*Many of the places, individuals, dynasties, political parties, and religions discussed in this article are the subject of independent entries, several of which contain additional maps detailing specific periods of Indian history.*]

Raymond Allchin and Bridget Allchin, *The Rise of Civilization in India and Pakistan* (1982). A. L. Basham, *The Wonder That Was India* (1954; reprint, 1985). Judith M. Brown, *Modern India: The Origins of an Asian Democracy* (1985). *Cambridge Economic History of India*, vol. 1, edited by Tapan Raychaudhuri and Irfan Habib; vol. 2, edited by Dharma Kumar and Maghnad Desai (1983). Wm. Theodore de Bary et al., eds., *Sources of Indian Tradition* (1958; reprint, 1987). H. H. Dodwell, ed., *Cambridge History of India*, 6 vols. (1922–1953). R. C. Majumdar, ed., *The History and Culture of the Indian People*, 11 vols. (1951–1977). Maureen Patterson, ed., *South Asian Civilization: A Bibliographic Synthesis* (1981). Cyril H. Philips, ed., *Historians of India, Pakistan and Ceylon* (1961). Joseph Schwartzberg, ed., *A Historical Atlas of South Asia* (1978). Vincent Smith, *The Oxford History of India* (rev. ed., 1967). Percival Spear, *India: A Modern History* (1961). Romila Thapar and Percival Spear, *A History of India*, 2 vols. (1966). Stanley Wolpert, *A New History of India* (1982).                  AINSLIE T. EMBREE

INDIA, PARTITION OF. *See* Partition of India.

INDIAN ADMINISTRATIVE SERVICE, the highest administrative and personnel system in India. In British India it was known as the Indian Civil Service (ICS); the Pakistani equivalent after independence was the Civil Service of Pakistan (CSP).

The earliest ICS administrators were recruited without special training, but as British control expanded, both training and a contractual arrangement (through "covenants") between the East India Company and its employees were deemed necessary. By the end of the eighteenth century new members of the Covenanted Civil Service were trained first in Calcutta and then in London. Nomination was the usual means of entry. In 1853 entry to the renamed Indian Civil Service became possible through competitive examination, although as before only British were accepted (despite the provisions of the Charter Act of 1833 to the contrary). The transfer of power from the East India Company to the Crown in 1858 was accompanied by a royal proclamation that reiterated the provisions of the 1833 Act. As the examinations were held only in London, it was difficult for Indians to appear and it was not until 1864 that an Indian entered the service. Beginning in 1923, examinations were held in India as well. By the end of the British period the majority of ICS officers were Indians, although this was evident primarily in the lower ranks.

Starting with the base of the government at the district level, the service provided a "steel frame" for rule. ICS officers served simultaneously as district collectors (of revenue), district magistrates (for law and order), and deputy commissioners (de facto cabinet chiefs). The district experience was preliminary and essential for advancement to positions at the provincial (now state, in India) and central levels, culminating in secretaryships in New Delhi, Islamabad, and Dhaka.

The Indian Administrative Service (IAS) and the CSP have maintained the entry by examination system and the resulting elite status of the group (as also of the equally prestigious foreign services). Reforms have been proposed, and some implemented, that would dilute the often aloof stance of IAS/CSP officers and would, more importantly, place emphasis on developmental work rather than simply revenue and law and order duties.

[*See also* Government of India; East India Company; Pakistan; Bangladesh; *and* Haileybury College.]

Ralph Braibanti, ed., *Asian Administrative Systems Emergent from British Imperial Tradition* (1966). N. C. Roy, *The Civil Service in India* (1958). Philip Woodruff, *The Men Who Ruled India*, 2 vols. (1953, 1954).

CRAIG BAXTER

INDIANIZATION, term commonly employed to designate the process by which a great part of Southeast Asia was influenced by Indian culture in the early centuries of the common era.

With the exception of the Vietnamese, who were under Chinese political domination for most of the first millennium CE, the earliest political entities in mainland Southeast Asia and in the Malay-Indonesian Archipelago were Indian-style kingdoms that adopted Sanskrit as the language of their courts and supported numerous Buddhist monks and brahman priests. Many of these kingdoms are known to us only by Chinese names and through Chinese sources. Such evidence attests, notably, the rise of Funan (in what is now Cambodia) and Linyi (in central and southern Vietnam) about the second century and the presence of various small trading principalities around the Gulf of Siam and in the Malay Peninsula. In the fourth and fifth centuries the beginnings of indianization appear in Indonesia. Archaeological remains and Sanskrit inscriptions recording the affairs of rulers with Indian-style names speak for later centuries.

The significance of the evidence has been much debated. It is now thought unlikely that the impact of Indian civilization was as sudden as Chinese sources suggest. More plausibly, Funan may have witnessed a gradual spread of Indian culture with no abrupt political discontinuity. For centuries, Indian activity in many areas may have been confined to the cosmopolitan trading ports, with little influence on the indigenous peoples of the hinterland.

There is no real evidence of how indianization began. The old military colonization theory has few supporters now. In the 1930s, J. C. van Leur argued that indianization was merely a superficial borrowing largely confined to court ritual. Most historians now avoid such extreme theories, but the ground between them is a field open for speculation.

[See also Funan.]

G. Coedès, *The Indianized States of Southeast Asia*, translated by Susan B. Cowing (1968). K. S. Sandhu, *Early Malaysia* (1973). Paul Wheatley, *The Golden Khersonese* (1961). O. W. Wolters, *History, Culture and Region in Southeast Asian Perspectives* (1982).

IAN W. MABBETT

## INDIAN NATIONAL ARMY.

Organized in 1942 by Mohan Singh in cooperation with the Japanese, the Indian National Army (INA) was reconstituted after a crisis in late 1942. Under the auspices of the Indian Independence League (IIL), and led from mid-1943 by the nationalist leader Subhas Chandra Bose, the INA fought with the Japanese in the Burma Campaign (1944–1945). Its aim was to make contact with nationalist forces within India and to help liberate the country from the British Raj by force of arms. It had a women's regiment named for a heroine of 1857, the *rani* of Jhansi. [See Lakshmi Bai.]

With British defeats in Malaya, Major Fujiwara of Japanese intelligence made further contacts with Indian nationalist groups, and then with Major Mohan Singh, a captured officer, all of whom wanted to work against the British. Fujiwara inspired Mohan Singh to organize Indian prisoners of war who volunteered to fight against their former army. The military organization (INA) was linked to the civilian one (IIL), which was set up in June 1942. By September, an INA division had been assembled, but in December a crisis occurred over the terms of cooperation between the Indians and the Japanese. Mohan Singh was imprisoned, others resigned, and Rash Behari Bose reorganized the IIL and the INA.

In May 1943, Subhas Chandra Bose arrived from Germany and in July took command of the IIL and the INA, both of which he reorganized and expanded. Making a considerable impression on the Japanese general Tōjō, Bose soon formed the provisional government of Azad Hind (Free India), and INA troops joined the Japanese in the battle for Imphal, capital of Manipur state, on the Burma-India frontier. Although there were perhaps 40,000 men in the INA, a much smaller number fought and were defeated with the Japanese. Bose fled and died in a plane crash on Taiwan in August 1945.

After the war, the trials of INA officers in the Red Fort in Delhi (November–December 1945) helped inspire patriotism against the British and undermine their confidence in the Indian armed forces. This was a factor in the decision of the British to leave India.

[See also Bose, Subhas Chandra.]

A. C. Chatterji, *India's Struggle for Freedom* (1947). K. K. Ghosh, *The Indian National Army* (1969). Joyce C. Lebra, *Jungle Alliance: Japan and the Indian National Army* (1971). Hugh Toye, *Subhash Chandra Bose: The Springing Tiger* (1978).    LEONARD A. GORDON

## INDIAN NATIONAL CONGRESS.

Founded in Bombay in 1885, the Indian National Congress led India's nationalist struggle for freedom from British colonial rule. After independence in 1947, the Congress became India's largest, most successful, and most durable political party. The history, organization, and leadership of the Indian National Congress have made it one of the oldest, most unique, and most effective nationalist movements of Asia and Africa.

The origins and development of the preindependence phase of the Congress movement can be divided into three distinct phases: the period of the moderates (1885–1905), the period of the extremists (1905 to the end of World War I), and the Gandhian era (1920–1947). Each phase was marked by a different style of leadership, increasing differentiation of the Congress membership, and the development of more clearly defined political objectives.

The emergence of Indian nationalism and the creation of the Indian National Congress were made possible by the development of the colonial education system and the rise of the new urban, Western-educated English-speaking Indian elite. This elite was drawn predominantly from the old upper-caste Hindu literati trained in the modern professions of law, medicine, education, and journalism at Bombay, Calcutta, and Madras universities. Representing Indian diversity but held together by English language and education, they sought to organize themselves to give expression to their common grievances and aspirations. [*See also* Education: Education in South Asia.]

The new English-speaking elite responded positively to a call by Allan Octavian Hume, an English liberal and former member of the Indian Civil Service (ICS), to organize an association "for the mental, moral, social and political regeneration of the people of India." Hume believed it was essential to create an organized mechanism through which Indian leaders could express their demands and needs to the colonial government. [*See* Hume, Allan Octavian *and* Indian Administrative Service.]

The first meeting of the Indian National Congress in Bombay in 1885 reflected the modest demands of its founders. While praising the positive contributions of British rule, they demanded greater indianization of the civil service at the higher levels, the broadening of the electoral base of the colonial Legislative Council, and greater government assistance in the development of indigenous industry. These demands were to be pressed through the constitutional device of an annual petition of grievance to British authorities.

The liberal nationalism of the Congress's first generation was followed by the development of a more radical, indigenous nationalism of the second generation, which drew its inspiration from Hindu revivalism. This new generation was drawn from the lower middle class of urban India, had less exposure to English education, and was unable to achieve high status and position in the new colonial order. They developed a strong sense of grievance against the British based on religious, economic, social, and political frustrations. In western India, they responded to the militant Hinduism of Bal Gangadhar Tilak, a Maharashtrian brahman. [*See* Tilak, Bal Gangadhar.] In Bengal, Tilak's militancy was paralleled by the development of terrorist and anarchist movements that invoked the patronage of the goddess Kali. Bengali militancy was fueled by the British decision in 1905 to partition the state of Bengal in order to facilitate its effective administration. Bengalis responded by organizing mass demonstrations and boycotts of British goods. Out of these agitations there arose a new militant nationalism that transformed the character of the Indian National Congress. The new militants fought bitter battles with the old moderates for control of the Congress, and the resulting compromises gradually transformed the Congress from a middle-class pressure group into a nationalist movement demanding self-government for India. [*See also* Swadeshi.]

The most significant development in the history of the Congress came after World War I, with the rise of Mohandas Karamchand Gandhi as leader of the nationalist movement. Gandhi had a profound impact on the leadership, organization, appeal, tactics, and goals of the Congress. He restructured the Congress organization into what he termed a parallel government that would win the loyalty of the Indian people. The president of the Congress along with the Working Committee and the party executive committee were to be the prime minister and cabinet of the movement. The All-India Congress Committee (AICC), composed of several hundred state leaders, was to be the Parliament of the movement. The annual conference of party delegates was to provide a broad representational base to determine party programs and select its leaders. [*See* Gandhi, Mohandas Karamchand.]

Gandhi's organizational skills were matched by his broad national appeal. He attracted a wide sector of Indian society, including the rising indigenous industrial elite, which provided him with financing; the lawyers of the smaller district towns; the rural peasantry, whose cause he championed; and Indian traditionalists attracted to his successful political adaptation of traditional Hindu symbols. For a brief period Gandhi even succeeded in gaining the cooperation of a large number of Muslims. [*See also* Khilafat Movement.]

Most important, Gandhi developed a unique form of mass mobilization and political action based on a nonviolent civil disobedience, called *satyagraha*. Civil disobedience placed a primacy on mass political mobilization, organization, and leadership and transformed the Congress from an urban, middle-class phenomenon into a mass movement unique in the Third World. Gandhi's civil disobedience campaigns of 1921–1922, his famous salt *satyagraha* of 1930–1933, and the Quit India movement of 1942 broadened and deepened the mass base, political appeal, and all-India character of the Congress and played a significant role in the achievement of independence in 1947. [See Satyagraha.]

Although just before his assassination in 1948 Gandhi urged that the Congress be disbanded and transformed into a social service organization, his successors refused to accept his advice. They saw the Indian National Congress as an essential instrument for maintaining the unity of India and consolidating India's freedom, development, and security in the wake of partition, war with Pakistan, and economic crisis. Led by Jawaharlal Nehru, the nationalist elite was determined to create a new democratic political order for India based on mass franchise in which the Congress would play a major role. [See Nehru, Jawaharlal.]

For the first twenty years after independence, from 1947 to 1967, the Congress Party became the dominant party of India. It controlled an absolute majority in the newly created national Parliament and ruled almost every state in India's federal system. Under the leadership of Nehru, the Congress consolidated and integrated the republic, framed a new constitution that created a British-style parliamentary system of government, and established a national consensus on key issues of planned development, security, and a nonaligned foreign policy.

Congress dominance during the period between 1947 and 1967 was the result of more than simply the charisma of Nehru and the legacy of the independence movement. The long history, tradition, and style of Congress development resulted in a highly institutionalized political organization capable of the effective management of India's diversity. The nationalist leadership that grew up under Gandhi's tutelage had evolved an especially effective integrative style based on bargaining, mediation, consensus, and compromise. This very approach also evolved a domestic and foreign policy consensus that enabled the Congress to preempt the slightly left-of-center and reformist middle ground of Indian politics. This left-of-center position pushed the political opposition to the right and left extremes, limiting their political appeal. The reconciliation approach developed under Prime Minister Nehru from 1947 to 1964 was continued by his successor Lal Bahadur Shastri, who died in 1966. [See Shastri, Lal Bahadur.]

The rise to power of Indira Gandhi, Nehru's daughter, beginning in 1966, had a profound impact on the later development of the Congress Party and Indian politics. During Mrs. Gandhi's rule from 1966 to 1984, the entire character of the Congress Party and the Indian political system was transformed. Mrs. Gandhi personalized the power of the party and government and centralized it into her own hands. In the process she split the party twice, first in 1969 and again in 1978, and was responsible for the defeat of the Congress in the 1977 election. The defeat followed almost two years of harsh emergency rule during which Mrs. Gandhi sought to alter the basic character of the Indian political system. [See also Gandhi, Indira.]

Restored to power in 1980 following the collapse of the fragmented Janata government, Mrs. Gandhi attempted to structure the party in such a way as to insure the succession of her sons—first Sanjay, and then Rajiv. Sanjay's accidental death in an airplane crash made Mrs. Gandhi's task somewhat more difficult. Yet her success was demonstrated in late 1984 when Rajiv Gandhi was immediately selected as prime minister and leader of the Congress Party when his mother was assassinated. [See Gandhi, Sanjay and Gandhi, Rajiv.]

The Congress Party of Indira Gandhi and her sons was very different from the old Indian National Congress. The organizational structure became a hollow shell, and all real power was concentrated in the hands of Mrs. Gandhi. In fact, the party itself was named the Congress-I—I for Indira. Mrs. Gandhi served as both prime minister and president of the Congress and used existing party structures to control the organization from the top down. Despite the party's constitutional requirement that elections be held every two years, none were held from 1972 to 1984. Meetings of the Working Committee, the AICC, and the annual conference, which under Nehru and Shastri were frequent, now became rare. State Congress chief ministers, state party presidents, and even district level party functionaries were all appointed from New Delhi. Personal loyalty to the prime minister was the only criterion for selection, and the party was deliberately kept fragmented and divided to facilitate central control.

Mrs. Gandhi's leadership style altered the federal character of both party and government. She reversed the earlier tradition of cooperative federalism and restructured the federal base of the Indian polity. The results were the disintegration of the state Congress governments, the rise of mass protest movements, and an authoritarian response when it appeared that the opposition might successfully challenge Congress rule. Emergency rule from 1975 to 1977 brought a series of constitutional amendments that significantly altered the character of the Indian political system. [See also Emergency in India, The.]

Mrs. Gandhi's defeat in the 1977 Indian election brought a temporary halt to the process of centralization and the restoration of a democratic political order. Her return to power in 1980, however, resulted in an accelerated decay in center-state relations, threatened the basis of the federal compact reached by India's Constituent Assembly, and posed severe and dangerous consequences for Indian unity. The inability of personally appointed state leaders to cope with local problems overloaded the central government and resulted in revolt against the center and local defeat for the Congress in many states.

The desire to maintain a monopoly of control aggravated local crises in Assam, the Punjab, Kashmir, and Karnataka. In particular, the crisis in the Punjab escalated out of control and resulted in an Indian Army assault on the Sikh temple in Amritsar. The action alienated the Sikh community and ultimately led to Indira Gandhi's assassination in October 1984 by Sikh members of her own bodyguard.

Her death, and the succession of her son Rajiv Gandhi, marks another major milestone in the century-old history of the Indian National Congress. Despite its questionable descent, the Congress–I continues to consider itself the direct successor of the great Congress tradition. The future of that tradition will depend on the actions Rajiv Gandhi takes to restore it. His massive victory in the December 1984 Indian elections has provided him with a historic opportunity to shape not only the future of the Congress Party but of India itself.

Michael Brecher, *Nehru: A Political Biography* (1959). Judith Brown, *Gandhi's Rise to Power: Indian Politics 1915–1922* (1972). Mohandas Gandhi, *An Autobiography, or the Story of My Experiments with Truth* (1927). Henry C. Hart, ed., *Indira Gandhi's India: A Political System Reappraised* (1976). Stanley A. Kochanek, *The Congress Party of India* (1968). John R. McLane, *Indian Nationalism and the Early Congress* (1977). Anil Seal, *The Emergence of Indian Nationalism: Competition and Collaboration in the Later Nineteenth Century* (1968). Myron Weiner, *Party Building in a New Nation* (1967).

STANLEY A. KOCHANEK

INDIAN OCEAN, third largest of the world's great oceans, after the Pacific and the Atlantic. This ranking is correct even if the Indian Ocean is held to include the waters that stretch to the Antarctic continent. In fact, the exact boundaries of the Indian Ocean have never been agreed upon. While some geographers do consider it to extend through both the Northern and Southern hemispheres, most would limit its expanse to the Northern Hemisphere

or would restrict it to include only the Arabian Sea and the Bay of Bengal. In Western classical sources the Indian Ocean was conceived of in an even more limited sense, namely, as the waters immediately adjacent to the coasts of the Indian subcontinent, which was long the geographical and commercial centerpiece of the region.

The character and climate of the Indian Ocean have facilitated the trade and commerce among the civilizations of West Asia, Africa, India, and Southeast Asia, which have given the ocean its great significance since ancient times. The Indian Ocean is the most pacific of the world's great oceans, and its tropical and semitropical climate presents few of the hazards faced by sailors in waters such as the North Atlantic. The regular monsoon winds have also encouraged travel across the ocean in both directions. *Monsoon,* from the Arabic word *mausim* ("season"), is the name given to the winds that in the Northern Hemisphere blow from the southwest to the northeast in the late spring or early summer and then reverse direction to come from the northeast to the southwest in the late fall. The nature of the monsoon is thought to have been discovered, or at least to have become widely known, in the first century CE, making it possible for navigators to sail directly from southern Arabia to the Indian coast in a month's time and to complete a round-trip journey from Arabia to South or Southeast Asia within a period of six months.

The extent of the trade conducted between West, South, and Southeast Asia in ancient times is evidenced by references to Indian products in texts such as Pliny's *Natural History* or the detailed Greek geographical work *The Periplus of the Erythraean Sea,* usually dated to the first century CE; excavated Roman commercial settlements in southeastern India offer further testimony. Later evidence consists of Chinese references to Persian merchants in southern Chinese ports, reports of West Asian Jewish merchants from southwest Indian trading centers, and precise Arab navigational texts, such as the late fifteenth-century work *Kitab al-Fawa'id,* by Ahmad bin Majid al-Najdi. These and other sources point to a flourishing trade, one that the Portuguese and other European powers sought to interdict and control for themselves, following Vasco da Gama's "discovery" of the sea route to India in 1498.

If movement across the Indian Ocean was predominantly motivated by commercial interests, the trade had important cultural effects as well. One of the earliest and most substantial examples of this phenomenon was the exportation of certain ritual and mythological components of Hinduism from

India to Southeast Asia. Beginning in a significant way in the first century CE in the Funan kingdom of Cambodia, brahman priests were imported by sea to create royal cults in which Hindu deities sanctioned the legitimacy of Southeast Asian dynasties. Mahayana and Theravada Buddhism also followed sea routes from India to Indochina, but Hindu and Buddhist exports later waned in the face of Arab-Muslim trade and settlement. Apart from the Arab conquest of the Sind in the early eighth century CE, the first substantial Muslim settlements in South Asia came as Muslim-Arab traders settled in western Indian ports. [See Mappilas.] While only minimal conversion took place as a result of this activity, the extention of Muslim trade across the Bay of Bengal to Indonesia, Malaysia, and the Philippines established the cultural foundations for the later widespread conversion of populations in those areas.

Vasco da Gama's voyage initiated a new era in the history of the Indian Ocean, leading to the establishment of European colonial states throughout the area. It was the Portuguese, too, who first developed a strategy to control the entire Indian Ocean trade by constructing coastal fortresses from the Red Sea to China. Later, the British realized the hegemony that the Portuguese had only tentatively achieved, and in the nineteenth century British maritime supremacy enabled them to dominate trade and suppress the slave trade throughout the entire Indian Ocean area. With Japanese expansion in the 1930s the British position rapidly declined, and in the postwar period the rise of independent states in the region meant that no one state dominated. By that time the principal economic and strategic interest in the Indian Ocean was focused on its northwestern appanage, the Persian Gulf, whose oil is critical to the economies of all states in the region as well as those in Europe and North America.

[See also Indianization; Portuguese: Portuguese in India; and Gama, Vasco da.]

Alvin J. Cottrell and R. M. Burrell, *The Indian Ocean: Its Political, Economic and Military Importance* (1972). Auguste Toussaint, *History of the Indian Ocean* (1966). Peter J. Webster, "Monsoons," *Scientific American* 245.2 (1981): 108–118.    STEPHEN FREDERIC DALE

**INDIES PARTY** (Indische Partij), early radical political organization in the Dutch East Indies (Indonesia), one of the first to define Indonesian nationalism on countrywide political, rather than narrow social or cultural, grounds.

Founded in 1911 by Eduard Douwes Dekker

(1879–1950), the Indische Partij called for independence of the Indies from Dutch rule. Several prominent Javanese intellectuals, including Tjipto Mangunkusumo and Suwardi Surjaningrat, soon joined him. In 1913 the colonial government refused recognition to the party and exiled these three leaders, destroying the party. Its brief history constitutes an important transitional phase in the introduction of socialism in Indonesia and in the definition of Indonesian nationalism.

[See also Douwes Dekker, Eduard.]

DAVID K. WYATT

**INDIGO**, a blue-black dye produced from the indigo plant. Indigenous to South Asia, indigo was exported to Europe as early as the time of the Roman empire; its name is derived from the Greek word *indikos* ("Indian"). In the nineteenth century indigo was a major export commodity of the East India Company. Conflicts between European planters and Indian peasants disrupted the production of indigo between 1859 and 1860, but it remained an important Indian commodity until 1897, when it declined owing to the competition of German aniline dyes.

[See also Blue Mutiny.]

Jogesh Chandra Bagal, *Peasant Revolution in Bengal* (1953). Blair Kling, *The Blue Mutiny* (1966).

JUDITH E. WALSH

**INDIOS.** Christopher Columbus named the inhabitants of the islands he found on his first landing Indians because he thought he had discovered India. Thereafter the word *indios* was used by the Spaniards for all native inhabitants of the South American mainland and for the natives of the Philippines as well. In the nineteenth-century Philippines, *indios* had a derogatory ring to it, describing those who were unfamiliar with the Spanish language, uneducated, and in general outside the pale of Western civilization. *Filipino*, on the other hand, was used to describe a Spaniard born in the Philippines. Only in the twentieth century was the word *filipino* used to describe native inhabitants of primarily Malay ancestry. [See also Philippines.]

NICHOLAS P. CUSHNER

**INDO-ARYAN LANGUAGES AND LITERATURES.** The Indo-Aryan languages belong to the Indo-Iranian branch of the Indo-European language family and are primarily spoken in India, Nepal, Pakistan, Bangladesh, and Sri Lanka. Before reaching Iran and India, the Indo-Iranians most probably dwelled in Soviet Turkestan. From this region they moved southward, the Iranian branch moving into what is now Iran and the Indo-Aryan branch moving into the Indian subcontinent some time in the early centuries of the second millennium BCE. The precise circumstances surrounding the separation of Iranians from Indo-Aryans and the entry of the latter into the Indian subcontinent are not known.

The testimony of the *Rig Veda*, the earliest Indo-Aryan document, makes it clear that the Indo-Aryans (or Aryans) encountered different indigenous non-Aryan populations in the subcontinent. [*See also* Vedas.] After some initial conflicts, Aryan and non-Aryan cultures and societies gradually converged. The genetic connection between the Indo-Aryan languages and the Indo-European language family is balanced by the impact of the non-Aryan languages of the subcontinent, that is, the Dravidian, Austro-Asiatic, and Tibeto-Burman languages. [*See also* Dravidian Languages and Literatures.] By the time of the late Vedic Brahmana texts, the speakers of Indo-Aryan were already an ethnically mixed people. The development of the caste terminology shows that many non-Aryan elements were incorporated into this later, aryanized Indian society. Non-Aryans and possibly non-Vedic Aryans were raised to the status of brahmans (priests) and *kshatriyas* (warriors). In classical Hinduism the pre-Aryan, proto-Hindu elements seem to have regained their strength in an aryanized form, as the ethnic non-Aryan segment of this culturally aryanized society steadily increased in proportion. By this process of convergence, the Indo-Aryan languages were thoroughly indigenized and came to share many features belonging to non-Aryan languages, finally becoming part of what M. B. Emeneau called "India as a linguistic area."

In general terms, the history of Indo-Aryan can be divided into three broad periods: Old Indo-Aryan, beginning around 1500 BCE; Middle Indo-Aryan, beginning around 500 BCE; and New Indo-Aryan, beginning around 1000 CE. It is difficult to give precise closing estimates for these periods, because most major Indo-Aryan languages continued to be used as literary languages long after they ceased to be spoken vernaculars; Prakrit works, for example, were composed as late as the seventeenth century, and Sanskrit still continues to be used as a literary language. For the same reason, while these three periods generally mark successive phases, they

actually overlap considerably, and therefore the dates given for these periods can only be approximations.

*Old Indo-Aryan Languages.* Aryans are assumed to have entered the Indian subcontinent from the northwest during the first half of the second millennium BCE. The Aryan migration into the subcontinent was not a single massive invasion: Aryan tribes continued to filter into the northwestern part of the subcontinent over a period of many centuries. They brought with them not one unified language but a host of related dialects.

The early phase of Old Indo-Aryan is represented by the language of the Vedic texts. The earliest extant Vedic text is the *Rig Veda*, a collection of religious hymns, the oldest of which probably date to the middle of the second millennium BCE. The archaic language of these hymns is close to Avestan, a language of ancient Persia, but also shows unmistakable Indian features. The language of the *Rig Veda* shows the presence of many dialects. While some of the phonological features of euphony (*sandhi*) can most certainly be attributed to later editors, others, such as the retroflex consonants in the *Rig Veda*, have led to heated debates.

The *Rig Veda* was followed by other Vedic texts. The *Sama Veda* is a collection of similar hymns that were put to music to be sung during Vedic rituals. The *Yajur Veda*, available in multiple recensions, contains prayers and formulas to be recited at the sacrifices. The *Atharva Veda* contains hymns designed for many diverse purposes, ranging from healing the sick and destroying enemies to meditation and magic. The Vedic traditions later produced prose texts called Brahmanas, giving details of sacrificial performances, and Upanishads, devoted to philosophical and mystical speculation. While the language of the *Rig Veda* and other Vedas may be called Early Vedic, the language of the Brahmanas and Upanishads can be called Late Vedic. From Early Vedic to Late Vedic one can clearly observe the movement of the Indo-Aryan speakers from the northwestern corner of the subcontinent to the central and eastern regions, during which the language and the literature show increasing signs of convergence with that of the indigenous populations.

The later phase of Old Indo-Aryan is generally called Sanskrit (*samskrita*, "perfected, polished"). It represents a convergence of several dialects of Old Indo-Aryan. An elite literary form of this language was codified by the grammarian Panini (c. 400 BCE) and his successors Katyayana (c. 300 BCE) and Patanjali (c. 200 BCE). There were also more or less vernacular forms of Sanskrit in existence, as seen in the great epics *Mahabharata* and *Ramayana,* in inscriptions, and also in Buddhist and Jain Hybrid Sanskrit texts. Sanskrit had regional and other scholastic dialects, but it is clear that these gradually lost their importance and that a standardized form of the north-central *(madhyadesha* or *aryavartta)* Sanskrit eventually became the dominant literary language throughout India.

While the composers of Vedic hymns had Vedic dialects as their first languages, Sanskrit gradually ceased to be a first language and became a highly respected second language that had to be learned from grammar books but that was used extensively in literary and scientific works throughout India. The accentual distinctions of Vedic Sanskrit were alive at the time of Panini but were soon lost. Similarly, distinctions of meaning between different past tenses were lost in the classical language. Words that expressed different shades of meaning in the earlier language gradually became synonyms. Thus, in the process of becoming a learned second language the outer shell of Sanskrit was well preserved up to the present day, but its inner structures—semantic and syntactic—as well as its phonetic realization, were to some extent influenced by the first languages of its speakers. An extensive and exclusive literature in the classical language, including the dramas and poetry of Kalidasa (c. 400 CE), was produced during its golden age, from 300 to 900 CE. Sanskrit continued to be the language of every branch of Hindu learning—logic, philosophy, grammar, ritual, medicine, architecture, mathematics, and astronomy. Sanskrit continued this role even through the Islamic period, when its role as the political lingua franca was taken over by Persian. In any case, Sanskrit functioned for about 3,500 years as the language of religion, culture, and learning in India and in foreign lands influenced by Indian religions and culture. To the present day it continues to be the cultural source language for India and has been given the place of an official language in its constitution.

***Middle Indo-Aryan Languages.*** The term *Middle Indo-Aryan* refers to Pali and to many Prakrit and Apabhramsha languages. This is a group of both colloquial and literary languages that through a process of gradual and natural change diverged phonologically and grammatically from the Old Indo-Aryan languages, so that from the middle of the first millennium BCE we can speak of a distinct Middle Indo-Aryan phase in the evolution of Indo-Aryan languages. There are scattered indications of their prior existence in the form of the so-called prakrit-

isms in the Vedic texts. In contrast to the Sanskrit language, which represented the elite variety of Indo-Aryan, the Prakrit languages were felt to be more ordinary; the word *prakrit* literally means "natural."

The Middle Indo-Aryan languages inherit a large part of their vocabulary from the Old Indo-Aryan languages, either with some change *(tadbhava),* or without any change *(tatsama),* while they contain a large local vocabulary *(deshya).* Among them, the Prakrits and Pali were used widely for preaching by "protestant" religious movements such as Buddhism and Jainism from about the fourth century BCE. Their high political importance is seen from their exclusive use in the inscriptions of the emperor Ashoka (third century BCE), and they continued to be used in the early centuries of the common era in inscriptions. There is significant religious and secular literature composed by Hindu and Jain authors in the Prakrits, while Pali is found in the canon of the Theravada Buddhism of Sri Lanka.

The latest phase of the Middle Indo-Aryan languages is seen in the Apabhramsha languages. Apabhramsha literature was produced from about the fifth to about the thirteenth century CE. These can be categorized as follows:

**1.** *Religious languages:* Pali is the language of the Theravada Buddhist canon; Ardhamagadhi, the language of the oldest Jain canonical texts. Apabhramsha was also used for religious literature, and there are Jain varieties of Maharashtri and Shauraseni Prakrits as well.

**2.** *Literary languages.* A large number of Hindu and Jain literary works were composed in Maharashtri (e.g., the *Sattasai,* the *Ravanavaho,* and the *Gaudavaho),* in Paishachi (e.g., the *Brihatkatha),* in Apabhramsha (e.g., the *Paumacariu),* and in other varieties of Middle Indo-Aryan.

**3.** *Dramatic languages.* Varieties of Maharashtri, Shauraseni, and Magadhi occur in Sanskrit dramas as languages to be spoken by certain characters (e.g., the *Mricchakatikam* and the *Shakuntalam).* Some plays are written entirely in Prakrit (e.g., the *Karpuramanjari).*

**4.** *Prakrits described by the grammarians.* Prakrit grammarians beginning with Vararuci (c. 200 BCE) described different Prakrits and varieties of Apabhramsha in their works.

**5.** *Inscriptional Prakrits.* Beginning with the inscriptions of Ashoka (c. 300 BCE), Prakrit inscriptions were produced throughout India and Sri Lanka. These inscriptions reflect regional differences as well as a historical evolution.

**6.** *Buddhist Hybrid and Jain Hybrid Sanskrit.* These varieties of Sanskrit are generally considered to be either a type of Middle Indic Sanskrit or partial sanskritizations of some Prakrit originals.

**7.** *Extra-Indian Prakrits.* Prakrit languages were used for inscriptions and religious texts discovered in regions such as Khotan and Niya in Central Asia.

While Pali, Ardhamagadhi, and early inscriptional Prakrits may be called early Middle Indo-Aryan languages, different varieties of Apabhramsha represent the latest phase of Middle Indo-Aryan and form a link with the New Indo-Aryan languages. Throughout their history, the Middle Indo-Aryan languages coexisted with various phases of Old Indo-Aryan and New Indo-Aryan languages, and as such were subject to mutual influences. Although the Middle Indo-Aryan languages were clearly colloquial at one time, they soon became scholarly literary languages and continued to be used in this way long after they ceased to be spoken by anyone. In this respect, their eventual status was somewhat similar to that of Sanskrit, although Sanskrit always retained its position as an elite language and continued to be used in that role much longer than the Middle Indo-Aryan languages.

*New Indo-Aryan Languages.* Originating from the late Middle Indo-Aryan varieties of Apabhramsha, the New Indo-Aryan languages began to assume their identity by the end of the first and the beginning of the second millennium CE. The phonetic and morphological changes that mark the Middle Indo-Aryan languages are intensified, and with the loss of most inflectional forms the Indo-Aryan languages switch over to the analytical type. They inherit a large part of their vocabulary from the Old Indo-Aryan and Middle Indo-Aryan languages. However, their origin coincides with the influx of Islam into the subcontinent, and they are influenced by the various languages of Muslim invaders and immigrants, that is, they contain a large number of loanwords from Persian and Arabic as well as from several Turkic languages. From the sixteenth century onward the subcontinent came into contact with European colonial powers. Portuguese, Dutch, and French each influenced the linguistic climate there, but ultimately it was English that most strongly affected the New Indo-Aryan languages. With the coming of independence to the subcontinent the languages have assumed different new roles and are following different directions. Hindi, Urdu, Bengali, Nepali, and Sinhalese have emerged as national languages, whereas other languages have either the status of regional, official, or purely local languages.

Depending upon political and cultural demands, these languages are undergoing such processes as de-anglicization, sanskritization, persianization, de-persianization, and so forth.

One can consider these languages from many different points of view. From a genealogical point of view, scholars such as George A. Grierson (1851–1941) proposed a division of the New Indo-Aryan languages into Inner, Outer, and Transitional groups, believing these to be created by two distinct migrations into India. The Outer group included Lahnda (or Western Punjabi) and Sindhi in the northwest, Marathi in the southwest, and Oriya, Bihari, Bengali, and Assamese in the east. The Transitional group included Western Hindi, Punjabi, Gujarati, Bhili, Khandeshi, Rajasthani, and the various Pahari languages. Kashmiri and Shina are Dardic languages, currently believed to be a branch of Indo-Aryan that is strongly influenced by the neighboring Iranian dialects. S. K. Chatterji and others discount the idea of Inner and Outer languages and divide the New Indo-Aryan languages into five regional groups: (1) Northwestern (Sindhi, Lahnda, and Eastern Punjabi), (2) Western (Gujarati and Rajasthani), (3) Central (Western Hindi), (4) Eastern (Eastern Hindi, Bihari, Oriya, Bengali, and Assamese), and (5) Southern (Marathi). On typological grounds, G. A. Zograph divides these languages simply into Western, Eastern, and Transitional types.

In terms of their official status, the New Indo-Aryan languages may be grouped into five sets: (1) official or national languages (Hindi in India, Urdu in Pakistan, Bengali in Bangladesh, Nepali in Nepal, and Sinhalese in Sri Lanka); (2) regional or state languages (Hindi, Bengali, Assamese, Oriya, Marathi, Gujarati, Punjabi, Sindhi, and Kashmiri); (3) literary languages with semiofficial status (Maithili, Bhojpuri, Marwari, Dogri, and Konkani); (4) minor languages (Bhili, etc.); and (5) local subdialects (dialects of Marathi, Hindi, etc.).

Most of the New Indo-Aryan languages had no academic status until very recent times, that place being reserved for Sanskrit, Persian, or English. However, the New Indo-Aryan languages functioned as religious and literary languages for the masses, and thus most of the literature produced in these languages was in the form of religious devotional poetry, ballads, erotic popular poetry, and so forth. Many of these languages—particularly Bengali, Marathi, and Hindi—have extensive literatures. Hindi, for instance, is rich in devotional poetry. The Muslim poet Amir Khusrau (1254–1325 CE) wrote poetry in what he called Hindvi. [*See*

Amir Khusrau.] The poet-saint Kabir (fifteenth century CE) composed many poetic works, of which *Bijak* is most influential. [*See* Kabir.] In the sixteenth century, the famous devotional poets Tulsi Das and Surdas wrote Hindi versions of the Rama and Krishna stories. [*See* Tulsi Das.] From 1700 to 1900, Hindi literature passed through a period of ornate erotic poetry, the most prominent example of which is Bihari's *Satsai.* The modern period of Hindi literature, beginning around 1900, has been characterized by the increasing strength of the literature, particularly in the years following Indian independence in 1947, after which Hindi was raised to the status of a national language.

Similar histories characterize most major New Indo-Aryan literatures. At present these languages are undergoing important adjustments because of their widespread use in education, the news media, television and radio broadcasting, administration, and technical literature. This has affected the New Indo-Aryan languages as well as their literatures. Western genres such as the novel and the short story have been incorporated into New Indo-Aryan literatures. With a large educated readership and an increasing pool of new writers and poets, most New Indo-Aryan languages now have extensive and flourishing literary traditions.

[*See also* Dravidian Languages and Literatures.]

Jules Bloch, *Indo-Aryan from the Vedas to Modern Times,* translated by A. Master (1965). Thomas Burrow, *The Sanskrit Language* (1955; rev. ed., 1973). S. K. Chatterji, *Indo-Aryan and Hindi* (1960). Edward C. Dimock, Jr., ed., *The Literatures of India: An Introduction* (1974). S. M. Katre, *Prakrit Languages and Their Contribution to Indian Culture* (2d ed., 1964). Richard Pischel, *Comparative Grammar of the Prakrit Languages,* translated by Subhadra Jha (1965). Michael C. Shapiro and Harold F. Schiffman, *Language and Society in South Asia* (1981). G. A. Zograph, *Languages of South Asia: A Descriptive Grammar* (1982).                      MADHAV M. DESHPANDE

**INDOCHINA.** Referring to the present-day nations of Vietnam, Kampuchea, and Laos, the term *Indochina* signifies the confluence of Indian and Chinese cultural currents. The colony of French Indochina, originating in the Indochinese Union established in 1887, was divided into the protectorates of Tonkin, Annam, Cambodia, and Laos and the colony of Cochinchina. (The leased territory of Guangzhouan in China was later incorporated as well.) From 1945 to 1954 the future status of Indochina's component states vis-à-vis France was the subject of prolonged negotiations and warfare, resulting in the 1954 Geneva Treaty. While Indochina as a political entity ceased to exist in 1954, the term has remained in use to denote the three countries collectively.

[*See also* Geneva Conference of 1954.]

Ellen Hammer, *The Struggle for Indochina 1940–1955* (1955). Stanley Karnow, *Vietnam: A History* (1983).

BRUCE M. LOCKHART

**INDOCHINA WAR.** The Second Indochina War (1959–1975) began as a struggle for control of South Vietnam, and most of the combat occurred in South Vietnam. Fighting in Laos, Cambodia, and North Vietnam was largely an outgrowth of the struggle for South Vietnam.

At the beginning of 1959, the Republic of Vietnam under Ngo Dinh Diem had almost uncontested military control of South Vietnam. The remnants of the Viet Minh organizations in the south carried out some antigovernment violence, mostly assassinations. However, directives from Hanoi limited this to a low level, considerably less than what the South Vietnamese Communists could have accomplished if cut off from external support and guidance. There was also armed activity by noncommunists, especially the Hoa Hao and Binh Xuyen.

At the Fifteenth Plenum of the Lao Dong Party Central Committee, Communist leaders in Hanoi authorized serious guerrilla warfare by South Vietnamese Communists against Diem's government in Saigon. The decision probably became final at the second session of the Fifteenth Plenum (May 1959) but possibly at the first session (January). Infiltration of men and supplies from North to South Vietnam soon commenced.

Early in 1960, the Communist-led guerrillas, generally called the Viet Cong, began a massive wave of assassinations, raids, and ambushes. The authority of the Saigon government virtually disappeared in many areas.

In December 1960, the National Liberation Front was established as the official leadership of the guerrilla war already in progress. The Lao Dong Party had effective control of this organization, but both its nominal leadership and its rank and file included many noncommunists, especially members of the Cao Dai and Hoa Hao religious sects.

Up to 1963, the armies on both sides were poorly equipped and relatively small. The Viet Cong relied heavily on captured weapons. Saigon got much more support from the United States than the Viet Cong got from North Vietnam, but still nothing like the amount it would receive in later years.

In this preliminary phase, the war was not really a struggle of South against North Vietnamese. Viet Cong troops, officers, and political cadres were almost all South Vietnamese; the infiltrators from North Vietnam during this period were mostly native southerners returning to their homes after a few years in the north. The Army of the Republic of Vietnam, or ARVN (often called the South Vietnamese Army), on the other hand, contained many North Vietnamese. Supreme command over the Viet Cong was exercised by the Lao Dong Party leadership in Hanoi, a mixed group of North and South Vietnamese Communists. (Those born in South Vietnam included Premier Pham Van Dong and Lao Dong Party First Secretary Le Duan.) Diem's government in Saigon was likewise run by a mixed group of North and South Vietnamese. Finally, the Saigon government began to use foreigners (mainly American pilots supposedly engaged in training) in combat on a substantial scale in 1962; the Communist combat forces did not include foreigners.

The fact that the Viet Cong seemed almost purely South Vietnamese, while the government did not, smoothed the guerrillas' path in the countryside. In addition, the Viet Cong were rural in orientation, while most officials of the Saigon government were urban men with little interest in the peasantry. Diem carried out some land redistribution, but for the most part his government supported absentee landlords attempting to collect rent from tenant farmers. The Viet Cong sided with the tenants against the landlords.

In most areas the Viet Cong attained a closer relationship with the peasants than did the Saigon government. The result was a classic case of guerrilla warfare. The Viet Cong mingled with the people, often remaining concealed by day in areas they effectively ruled by night. The ARVN, much less deeply rooted in village society, had more men and more guns but could not find the guerrillas to bring its weight to bear on them. In any case, the ARVN was poorly led, poorly motivated, and not very aggressive in combat.

A conflict pitting the Catholic Ngo Dinh Diem against Buddhist religious leaders placed Diem at odds with much of the urban population in 1963. The United States decided that Diem's performance in both cities and countryside was so ineffective that he could not win the war against the guerrillas. It encouraged officers of the ARVN to overthrow

Diem; he was deposed and shot in November 1963. A period of great instability followed in Saigon.

There was escalation on both sides during 1964. Increasingly powerful guerrilla units clearly appeared to be defeating the ARVN. The Ho Chi Minh Trail, through Laos, was improved to allow more infiltration of men and supplies into South Vietnam from the north, and for the first time the Communist infiltrators entering South Vietnam included substantial numbers of North Vietnamese.

The number of US military personnel in Vietnam increased in 1964 to over 23,000. The United States briefly bombed North Vietnam in August 1964, following the Gulf of Tonkin incidents, two supposed clashes (the first genuine, the second probably imaginary) between US and North Vietnamese vessels off the coast of North Vietnam.

By early 1965 it was plain that the Saigon government could not survive without greatly increased US support. The United States at this point introduced ground combat units to South Vietnam for the first time and began systematic bombing of North Vietnam. US bombing of South Vietnam and Laos, already under way, soon expanded greatly.

Several years of stalemate followed. Expanding US forces with overwhelmingly superior weaponry imposed heavy casualties on the Viet Cong and North Vietnamese forces, but recruitment within South Vietnam and infiltration from the north made good these losses. Moreover, Communist forces in South Vietnam were larger and better armed at the beginning of 1968 than at the beginning of 1965.

During Tet (the Vietnamese new year) of 1968, which came at the end of January, the Communists took advantage of the customary Tet truce to attack the cities of South Vietnam. Their goal was to apply such a shock to the ARVN that it would collapse. The United States was caught partly, and the ARVN almost totally, by surprise.

The plan did not succeed, though it may have come close. The rural guerrillas attacking the cities, fighting in an environment with which few of them were familiar, suffered huge casualties. The Viet Cong never completely recovered from this defeat.

While Tet was a military disaster for the Communists, however, they won a political victory. In the months before the offensive, US spokespersons had been making optimistic statements about Communist weakness. The offensive demonstrated that these statements had been unrealistic; it could not have taken place the way it did if the Communists had been as weak as US representatives had said.

After the offensive, American generals decided

that considerably more US military personnel were needed in Vietnam. The contrast between this apparent pessimism and the optimism of December 1967 undermined the generals' credibility when they claimed, correctly, that Tet had been an American victory. The anticommunist forces also suffered other public relations disasters, such as the killing of a Viet Cong prisoner by an ARVN general in full view of American television cameras.

For the next four years, Communist strength in South Vietnam declined. The Viet Cong, weakened by the Tet Offensive, suffered further losses from the massive air and ground pressures brought against them. Increases in the number and armament of North Vietnamese forces in South Vietnam only partly compensated for this.

The link between the Communists and the South Vietnamese peasantry, while not broken, was greatly weakened. Both the proportion of the Communist forces who were natives of South Vietnam and the proportion who were operating in areas of relatively dense population were declining. The Saigon government finally decided in 1970 to abandon its alliance with absentee landlords and distribute most rented land free of charge to the tenants. Finally, the Phoenix Program caused serious losses among Communist political and administrative personnel.

While the Communist forces weakened, the ARVN grew somewhat stronger. However, the war was growing less popular with the American voting public. The US government, therefore, rather than making a maximum effort to finish off its enemy, treated Communist weakness as an opportunity to withdraw US forces from Vietnam (which reached their peak level, 543,000, in April 1969). ARVN strength did not grow enough to compensate. The net result was that both sides—Communist and anticommunist—were weaker militarily at the beginning of 1972 than they had been at the beginning of 1968.

Fighting in Laos had begun in 1959. The North Vietnamese Army controlled the Ho Chi Minh Trail, a network of supply routes leading through southeastern Laos to South Vietnam. The North Vietnamese also partly controlled the Laotian Communist movement, generally called the Pathet Lao, and supported it with supplies, training, and some troops. The United States supported the Lao government forces and also a far more effective force of Hmong (Meo) tribesmen under General Vang Pao. The US Air Force began bombing Laos in 1964 and expanded the bombing greatly in 1968 and 1969.

The North Vietnamese Army and the Viet Cong had bases and supply routes in the sections of Cambodia bordering on South Vietnam. Up to 1969 they occupied only small areas close to the border. But in 1969 the United States began secret bombing of the Communist base areas in Cambodia, and an anticommunist government under General Lon Nol came to power in Phnom Penh. In 1970 US ground troops assaulted the base areas. The North Vietnamese Army responded by spreading its Cambodian bases over a much wider area to reduce their vulnerability and began supporting the Cambodian Communist movement generally called the Khmer Rouge.

In March 1972 the Communists launched a major offensive in South Vietnam. This was carried out mainly by North Vietnamese troops, which attacked with heavy equipment directly across the demilitarized zone separating North from South Vietnam. They also moved through Laos and Cambodia to hit targets farther south. The ARVN, with massive US air support, managed to stop this offensive, but it had to divert resources away from the struggle against the Viet Cong, who after four years of decline began to regain strength.

A peace agreement was finally signed in Paris in January 1973. It called for the withdrawal of US troops from South Vietnam but not for the withdrawal of North Vietnamese troops. The Saigon government signed this agreement with great reluctance.

The Paris agreement ended US involvement in combat, but it did not stop the fighting among the Vietnamese for even one day. During most of 1973, the ARVN was more aggressive than the Communists in actual combat operations. The Communists were fairly restrained, not wanting to provoke a US return to combat operations in Vietnam, but they were strengthening their forces and preparing for future offensive action.

During 1974, as the collapse of the Nixon administration in the United States reduced the likelihood of a US return to Vietnam, the Communist forces became somewhat bolder. In October they decided to try a major offensive. They took all of Phuoc Long Province without much trouble in early January of 1975. When they took Banmethuot on 12 March, President Thieu decided to abandon his remaining positions in the central highlands. The planning and leadership of the evacuation were atrocious; most of the units involved disintegrated in panic. This triggered an ARVN collapse in other areas, and the Communist forces marched into Saigon on 30 April after comparatively little fighting.

The US Congress halted the bombing of Cambodia in August 1973, but fighting on the ground continued unabated. The Khmer Rouge (who unlike the Pathet Lao were essentially independent of their North Vietnamese patrons) took power on 17 April 1975, shortly before the fall of Saigon.

Combat in Laos had subsided in 1973. The Pathet Lao took power almost peacefully in August 1975.

[*See also* Vietnam; Ngo Dinh Diem; Viet Minh; Hanoi; Hoa Hao; Binh Xuyen; Cao Dai; Pham Van Dong; Le Duan; Tet Offensive; Laos; Pathet Lao; Cambodia; Lon Nol; Khmer Rouge; *and* Paris Peace Conference.]

James P. Harrison, *The Endless War: Vietnam's Struggle for Independence* (1982). Arnold R. Isaacs, *Without Honor: Defeat in Vietnam and Cambodia* (1983). Stanley Karnow, *Vietnam: A History* (1983). Jeffrey Race, *War Comes to Long An* (1972).                EDWIN E. MOISE

**INDOCHINESE COMMUNIST PARTY,** the first formal communist party in French Indochina, founded in 1930. In 1925 the Vietnamese revolutionary Ho Chi Minh had established the Vietnam Revolutionary League, a proto-Marxist organization dedicated to the dual goals of national independence and social revolution. A small core of committed revolutionaries, called the Communist Youth Group, served as the nucleus of the organization and the embryo of a future communist party. To provide an ideological basis for that party, league members were given instruction in Marxist doctrine at a training institute in Canton.

By 1929 radical members had become increasingly critical of the predominantly patriotic and reformist character of the league's program and demanded the creation of a formal communist party. At a national congress held in May, the radicals broke with the league and established a separate Indochinese Communist Party. For the next several months, the two groups competed for Moscow's recognition as the sole legitimate revolutionary organization in Vietnam. The Comintern instructed Ho Chi Minh, then living in Siam, to patch up the quarrel and unite the factions into a new communist party. In February 1930 a new Vietnamese Communist Party was established under his sponsorship in Hong Kong, and a provisional Central Committee was selected. In October, at the first meeting of the committee, a formal program and statutes were accepted, and a new name was adopted—Indochinese Communist Party—on the basis of Moscow's conviction that the Party would be more effective if it operated throughout French Indochina.

The first few years were difficult. In the fall of 1930, Communist participation in the Nghe-Tinh peasant revolt led to severe repression by colonial authorities. The Party's local apparatus was virtually destroyed, and most of its national leaders were imprisoned or executed. For the next three years, the Central Committee ceased to exist, and Party leadership was vested in an External Bureau based in South China and manned by members who had returned from studying in Moscow. The Party's revival was also hindered by prevailing Comintern strategy, which instructed member parties to concentrate their recruitment efforts within the working class.

The situation began to improve in 1935. At its Seventh Congress, held in August, the Comintern adopted a new strategy calling on communist parties to cooperate with all peace-loving and democratic forces in popular fronts against the common danger of world fascism. The new policy had a stimulating effect on the fortunes of the Indochinese Communist Party, resulting in a temporary end of official repression in Indochina and permitting it to broaden its popular base in Vietnam. During the next few years, membership in the Party and its front organizations increased rapidly as Communist activists worked in rural villages and among the urban middle class. After 1938, however, the Popular Front declined, and in September 1939 the Party was once again forced to retreat underground. In November the Central Committee announced preparations for an armed uprising to seize power, but three revolts by local Communist forces in 1940 proved abortive. In May 1941, in the shadow of the Japanese occupation of Indochina, the Party announced the formation of a new united front of all patriotic forces to seek independence at the close of the war. To maximize popular appeal, Communist direction of the new organization was disguised, and the ultimate goal of social revolution was subordinated to the cause of nationalism.

In August 1945, taking advantage of the surrender of Japan, Viet Minh forces launched a general uprising and seized power throughout the country. In September an independent Democratic Republic of Vietnam was established in Hanoi. Most of the key positions in the new government were occupied by Communists, but during the fall, President Ho Chi Minh was able to induce members of rival parties to join in a coalition cabinet. In November, as a gesture to encourage noncommunist participation, the Party announced its own dissolution.

In actuality, the Party simply retreated underground, and when war broke out with France in late

1946, it directed the resistance through its domination of the government and the Viet Minh front. In 1951, the Party reemerged at a national congress held in Tuyen Quang Province. For cosmetic reasons, the name was changed to the Vietnam Workers' Party, but the leadership and strategy remained intact. At the moment of metamorphosis, the Party boasted a national membership of over 500,000.

[See also Ho Chi Minh; Vietnam Revolutionary League; Nghe-Tinh Uprising; Vietnam, Democratic Republic of; and Viet Minh.]

Anonymous, *An Outline History of the Viet Nam Workers' Party* (1970). William J. Duiker, *The Communist Road to Power in Vietnam* (1981). Kim Khanh Huynh, *Vietnamese Communism, 1925–1945* (1982). Douglas Pike, *History of Vietnamese Communism, 1925–1976* (1978). Alexander B. Woodside, *Community and Revolution in Modern Vietnam* (1977).

WILLIAM J. DUIKER

**INDOCHINESE UNION,** coalition of five French possessions under central administration in Southeast Asia. First set up in embryonic form by the French government in 1887 as a means of grouping together French possessions in Vietnam and Cambodia, the Indochinese Union was formally created under the leadership of the dynamic governor-general Paul Doumer ten years later. The union consisted of the three parts of colonial Vietnam (the protectorates of Tonkin and Annam and the colony of Cochinchina) and the protectorates of Cambodia and Laos under a governor-general appointed in Paris. It was replaced by the French Union after World War II.

Joseph Buttinger, *Vietnam: A Dragon Embattled* (1967).
WILLIAM J. DUIKER

**INDO-GREEKS.** *See* Greeks.

**INDONESIA, REPUBLIC OF.** The boundaries of present-day Indonesia, embracing some thirteen thousand islands and a total area of more than five million square kilometers of land and sea, were drawn by Dutch colonial rulers and the exigencies of European imperial expansion in the late nineteenth and early twentieth centuries. On this account there is a certain artificiality in considering the nation's long history separately from that of neighboring and often overlapping linguistic and ethnic areas. Nevertheless, Indonesia lies at the heart of an ancient and very broadly defined world of Malay civilization stretching from Madagascar to the South Pacific, which suggests an essential historical continuity in the region and provides adequate justification for accepting Indonesia as a workable, though by no means rigid, historical unit.

The Solo region of Central Java has yielded evidence of occupation by hominids as early as one million years ago. Material from a nearby archaeological site indicates the existence of the earliest example of *Homo sapiens*, known as Wajak man, who may have lived about forty thousand years ago. Although earlier views depended heavily on theories of waves of migration populating Indonesia's islands from various parts of the Asian mainland, prehistorians today increasingly emphasize continuous human habitation and a picture of closely related cultures becoming gradually differentiated over time, due only in part to migration from other areas.

The archipelago appears to have undergone a transformation between about 2000 BCE and 500 BCE, during which time bronze and iron metallurgy appeared, a sophisticated maritime technology evolved, and wet-rice agriculture began to take hold. These developments may be connected to the remarkable expansion that brought early Indonesians to Melanesia and the coast of East Africa during the same period. In any case, well before the beginning of the common era there were Indonesian peoples and cultures acquainted with the wider world and with both goods and ideas carried by global trade. They themselves had contributed to the material culture of that world and cannot have been merely passive acceptors of outside influences.

Like the Chinese and other Asians, Indonesians were much stimulated by Indian religious thought and interested in a surrounding galaxy of political, social, and artistic ideas. Scholars disagree about precisely how and why the cultural transfer took place, but it was a long, fluid process guided predominantly by Indonesian perceptions and needs. Hinduism and Buddhism, often in local variation, made their mark. Indian scripts were adapted to indigenous languages (which appear to have been unwritten until the late fourth century), and particularly in Java the great Hindu epics known as the *Ramayana* and *Mahabharata* became the foundation for a rich tradition in the arts. Indian legal and social theories had their effect as well, for local rulers adopted Sanskrit titles and claimed extended symbolic and actual powers. Supported and frequently controlled by small elite groups, these rulers became the central figures of *kraton,* or courts, on which

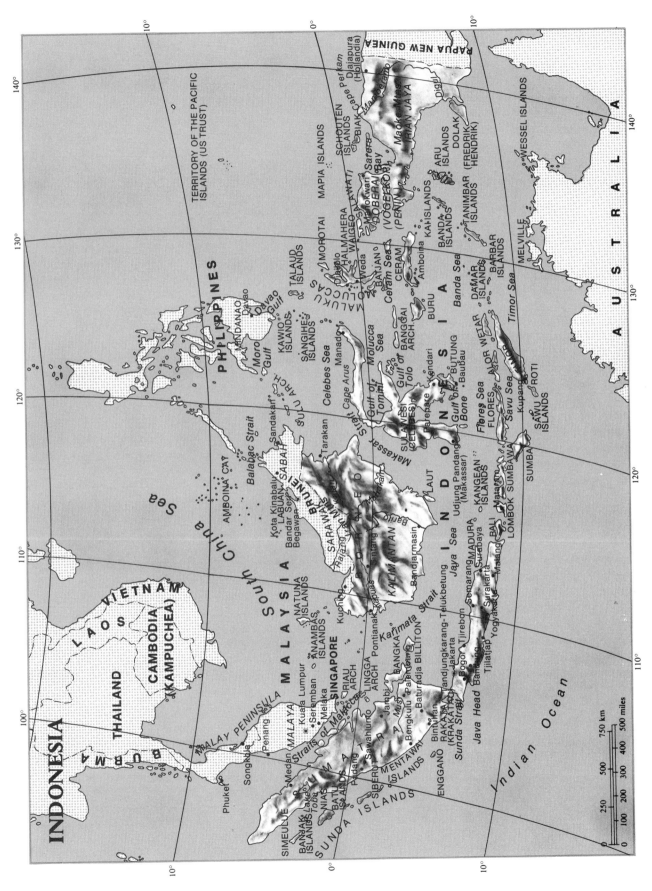

were focused larger politico-economic units than had existed previously. While the effects of all this on the general populace can only be guessed, it seems likely that on the one hand the distance gradually widened between ruling elite and the rest of society, while on the other hand important elements of the new, changing culture were slowly but widely accepted.

Chinese sources and a handful of indigenous epigraphical materials mention a number of small principalities in the archipelago before about 550 CE, and in the following two centuries we can glimpse the emergence of larger, imperial states. Srivijaya in Sumatra and the Sailendra-Mataram realm of Java have often been treated as examples of two distinct patterns of indianized Indonesian civilization, characterized by maritime trading and inland agriculture, respectively. [See Srivijaya; Sailendra; Mataram; and Indianization.] The characteristic glory of the former was said to be a far-flung and profitable trading network, and of the latter the magnificent stone monuments of Central and East Java, such as the Borobudur and Prambanan. In many important respects, however, these states were not dissimilar and clearly belonged to the same general cultural sphere. Both sought to wield economic and military power on the seas, and both sought more universalistic political and administrative forms with which to bind disparate local powers. In these pursuits Srivijaya was at first the most successful, but after the end of the eleventh century Javanese successor states to Mataram showed considerable accomplishment in this direction.

At the end of the thirteenth century the East Javanese kingdom of Majapahit aspired to a kind of neoclassical revival of the style and powers associated with the earlier Hindu-Buddhist states. Under the rule of Hayam Wuruk (r. 1328–1389) and his forceful minister Gajah Mada (d. 1364), Majapahit's commercial and political reach extended as far as the Malay Peninsula to the north and the Maluku islands to the east. [See Majapahit; Hayam Wuruk; and Gajah Mada.] A self-conscious golden age bloomed at the kingdom's center, capturing imaginations far beyond. Majapahit did not unify the archipelago in any modern sense, but it did promote a distinct cultural and commercial pattern. Majapahit's successes, as much as its failures, were responsible for the weakening of the hegemony after the mid-fifteenth century. Trading practices, laws, and much else in the Majapahitan system were admired and imitated by small breakaway states; new economic and political classes brought ferment to

society throughout the archipelago. These forces, interacting with fresh opportunities provided by the expansion of the Islamic world and the arrival of the West, came to characterize a turbulent period of adjustment lasting until well into the eighteenth century.

Much about the islamization of Indonesia remains unclear to scholars. The religion and its cultural aura attracted followers at different times, in different ways, and with different results in various parts of the archipelago. In Aceh, for example, conversions in the late thirteenth century soon produced an intensely Islamic society and state, while conversions among Majapahit's elite in the fourteenth century began a long and complex process of cultural accommodation. [See also Aceh.] An unstable mix of religious proselytization and political adventurism brought both Indonesians and a number of foreigners, including Muslim Chinese, to the fore in the public life of a number of small, highly competitive states. Propagation of the Islamic faith among the general populace did not always take place gradually or without violence. For these reasons some writers have tended to view Islam as a disruptive force, responsible in large part for weakening the archipelago's economy and sweeping away the unifying cultural and political influences of the great Hindu-Buddhist states. [See Islamization of Southeast Asia.]

Yet Islam made its own very substantial contributions of a universalist nature. Muslim missionizing zeal and the concept of the *ummat,* or larger Moslem community, almost certainly encouraged a larger and more closely interlinked trading network in the archipelago than had existed earlier. Although not centralized politically, this development nevertheless was widely recognized as flowing, over a period of several centuries, from a small number of new religious and trading centers, such as Melaka on the Malay Peninsula and Aceh in northern Sumatra. These same centers also were the principal sources of new cultural forms with a unifying effect. Under Islamic influence, for example, the use of a recognizably modern form of Malay (the foundation for the contemporary Indonesian language) became even more widespead than it had been in the early Majapahit period and came for the first time to be written nearly everywhere in essentially the same fashion, an adapted Arabic script. The effects of Islamic literary tradition and ideas about the arts in general varied locally, but on the whole they proved more penetrating and more binding over physical and cultural distance than had their Hindu-Buddhist counterparts.

The arrival of Europeans in the archipelago at the start of the sixteenth century did not signal a new era in Indonesian history and initially at least is best seen in the context of existing patterns of change. The Portuguese, who conquered Melaka in 1511 and during the next eighty years traded, warred, and occasionally missionized in the Malukus, possessed neither the technological superiority nor the numbers to build the commercial monopoly they desired. The Dutch, who followed at the very end of the century and in 1602 founded the Dutch East India Company (VOC), were better equipped and organized. Despite its utterly ruthless application of force, however, the VOC was also more mastered by than master of the trading system of the archipelago. [*See* Dutch East India Company.] Establishing a base on the then-isolated West Java site of present-day Jakarta (1619), the Dutch followed the era's pattern of small-state foundation, discovered that their trading practices and goods were determined mostly by others, and were drawn reluctantly into local political and territorial entanglements. [*See also* Jakarta.] The introduction of coffee to West Java beginning in 1695, in addition to a series of succession disputes in the Central Javanese kingdom of Mataram, led to economic and social changes that by the mid-eighteenth century transformed Dutch functions into those of a colonial power. After 1799 the VOC gave way to a colonial state structure under the direct control of the government of the Netherlands.

In Java during the nineteenth century the Dutch and the indigenous elite gradually reached a classic accommodation, in theory a model for subsequent colonial relationships but in fact unique. After the Java War (1825–1830), the Dutch instituted the profitable but exploitative *kultuurstelsel*, or cultivation system, which combined an earlier forced-delivery approach to cash crops with a newer notion of encouraging production by exacting land rent payments. The Javanese ruling class was co-opted into this system but emerged a politically weakened, dependent, and largely static domestic bureaucracy. The rest of society was left to react to the economic forces thus set in motion. [*See* Java; Java War; *and* Kultuurstelsel.] Elsewhere in the Indonesian realm, where the Dutch had earlier been too weak to establish control, the colonial arm now began to reach. The Minangkabau, Ambonese, Makassarese, Buginese, Balinese, and Acehnese, as well as the peoples of South Sumatra, West and Southeast Kalimantan, and much of the Lesser Sundas, all lost their independence between the 1820s and 1906. In these areas the Dutch found it neither possible nor desirable to attempt to establish a Java-like system of rule; each locale developed its own position within the colonial system, and while the Dutch did not precisely divide in order to rule, authorities nevertheless appreciated and then perpetuated differences within the larger framework.

On the whole, and despite much argument to the contrary, the Dutch period must be judged a destructive one in Indonesian history. In time, however, colonial rule did produce a centralized administrative structure and, willy-nilly, new generations of Indonesians intent on building their own, independent state around it. This vague class, rooted perhaps equally in the traditional elite and in the yeasty mix of colonial urban society, appeared first in Java but soon possessed representatives from throughout the archipelago. Expressing themselves literally and figuratively in the language of the colonizers, the earliest members of this group, such as the young aristocrat Kartini (1879–1904), seemed to waver in their thinking about the colonial relationship. By the late 1920s, however, a new generation had appeared, made up of people who were clear in their belief that independence was inevitable and that they were the proper heirs to a larger, modern Indonesian political and social leadership. Many ideological paths were chosen, including communism and Islam, but in broad outline the goals were remarkably similar. And if a precise conception of "the nation" often seemed lacking, the enormous success of the young, charismatic Sukarno (1901–1970) in giving broad appeal to a romantic, syncretic vision of the Indonesian future suggests that a powerful nationalist sentiment did exist. [*See also* Sukarno.]

During the 1930s the effects of the Great Depression, along with fears of a Pacific war, heightened tensions between the Dutch community and the coalescing Indonesian independence movement; the Japanese arrival in March 1942 therefore occasioned little public sympathy for the old colonial power. Hopes for the New Order, however, quickly proved misplaced. The Japanese had no intention of granting independence, and to make matters worse they proved to be ruthless and clumsy rulers in a region they understood very poorly. Largely because of their own ineptitude and, after mid-1943, their worsening military position, the Japanese came to depend uneasily on members of the prewar independence movement for support. Japan certainly did not create Indonesian nationalist fervor, but it was forced to permit it to grow; even more significant,

Japan's New Order provided a place within the state for many of those elite Indonesians who had spent the Dutch period as anticolonial critics, on the outside looking in. In this important sense, the occupation years continued a social transformation begun much earlier.

Between the Japanese surrender in August 1945 and the appearance of the first Allied troops six weeks later, a rudimentary independent Indonesian state was called into existence—by Sukarno on 17 August—and surprisingly quickly given administrative and emotional substance. That the fledgling nation was also prepared to defend its freedom became clear when British reoccupation units met fierce resistance from both the general populace and the celebrated *pemuda,* or activist youth. The courageous defense of Surabaya against Allied assault on 10 November, still remembered by Indonesians as Heroes' Day, is the most spectacular example of this resistance. Thus began a bitter political and military struggle with the Dutch that was not resolved until 27 December 1949, when the Netherlands formally surrendered sovereignty over its former colony.

This national revolution, which compared with others in the region was both flexible and effective in reaching its immediate goal, nevertheless raised and left unsolved a number of significant internal controversies. These included a fundamental disagreement over the role of religion in national life, contention over the ideology and government best suited to the new nation, deep division between military and civilian forces on many important issues, tensions between Java and the central government on the one hand and the Outer Islands and regional governments on the other, and, finally, differences over the proper path to economic development. Political life during the ensuing years focused upon these controversies, accompanied by fiscal disarray and armed challenges to the authority of Jakarta and the central government, until in 1959 a hybrid political form dubbed Guided Democracy was brought to life. The brainchild of Sukarno, who had been made president in 1945 and remained in that position for more than two decades, Guided Democracy attempted to resolve national conflicts through consensus or *musyawarah,* leaving President Sukarno himself with the responsibility of creating this consensus and balancing increasingly contentious forces, among them the Indonesian Communist Party (PKI) and the military. [*See* Partai Komunis Indonesia.]

The experiment did not succeed. In late 1965 Indonesia was shaken by an upheaval now widely known as the Gestapu. Over a period of about six months as many as 700,000 persons may have been killed in political and religious conflict; tens of thousands were imprisoned. [*See also* Gestapu.] The exact circumstances that precipitated this crisis are a matter of considerable debate, but over a period of several years, the army, which had assumed national leadership under Suharto, gradually consolidated its rule and established what it termed a New Order in concert with student, technocrat, and Muslim support. In 1967 Sukarno was formally removed from the presidency, and in 1971 the first elections since 1955 were held. Suharto's presidency, until then a matter of appointment, was affirmed in this fashion, and the New Order received the public imprimatur it sought. Although alliances and emphases within the political structure have made important shifts in the interim, Suharto and his vision of government remain paramount in Indonesia today. [*See* Suharto.]

The nature and realization of this vision are subjects of continuing controversy and have attracted both defenders and vigorous detractors, who tend to see in the New Order either salvation or ruination. Such determinations, however, are surely premature and are equally dependent on the idea that the New Order's policies represent an abrupt change from those of the period immediately preceding it. While the present government's receptiveness to capitalist development, antipathy toward communism, and emphasis on the growth of a powerful, centralized state represent obvious departures from the policies of Guided Democracy, other New Order hallmarks do not. It was in precisely the late Sukarno period, for example, that the so-called functional groups, or *golongan karya,* so prominent in New Order thinking about political roles of social groups, were first given credence; that Western parliamentary government was denigrated as nothing but "free-fight liberalism"; and that heavy reliance was placed on the consensus-creating powers of the Pancasila national philosophy. [*See also* Pancasila.] Furthermore, from the perspective of social history there is reason to argue that the New Order represents not so much the rise of a new elite as the triumph of a much enlarged middle class, divided during the revolution and confronted with obstacles during the immediate postcolonial era, in a struggle stretching back to the 1930s.

Whatever the case, Indonesia today is a nation with a rapidly growing population of over 160 million, a foreign debt exceeding $25 billion, an annual per capita income of under $500, and a spectrum of social and religious tensions. The alternatives that may realistically be considered in dealing with these issues are likely to be exceptionally limited, and national survival may in the longer view depend less upon political or social forms than unadorned economic substance.

Benedict R. Anderson, *Java in a Time of Revolution* (1972). H. J. Benda, *The Crescent and the Rising Sun* (1958). Harold Crouch, *The Army and Politics in Indonesia* (1978). Clifford Geertz, *Agricultural Involution* (1963). J. D. Legge, *Indonesia* (3d ed., 1980). Ruth T. McVey, *The Rise of Indonesian Communism* (1965). M. C. Ricklefs, *A History of Modern Indonesia* (1981). O. W. Wolters, *Early Indonesian Commerce* (1967).

WILLIAM H. FREDERICK

**INDONESIAN COMMUNIST PARTY.** *See* Partai Komunis Indonesia.

**INDONESIAN NATIONALIST PARTY.** *See* Partai Nasional Indonesia.

**INDONESIAN PEOPLE'S MOVEMENT.** *See* Gerindo.

**INDONESIAN REVOLUTION,** turbulent period of struggle for independence between 1945 and 1950, officially known since 1966 as the War of Independence. The term *revolution,* however, best explains the unleashing of violent forces that took place during the period.

Military defeats in the Pacific persuaded the Japanese to allow preparations for independence in Java from May 1945. Before the Japanese surrender on 15 August, a representative group of leaders had agreed on a constitution for a unitary Indonesian republic, embracing the whole former Netherlands Indies; had denied an Islamic character for the future state; and had accepted the leading role of Sukarno and Mohammad Hatta. The Japanese surrender set off a confrontation between these leaders and young urban activists *(pemuda),* who kidnapped Sukarno and Hatta on 16 August in the hope of forcing a revolutionary proclamation of independence in defiance of the Japanese. Eventually a compromise proclamation was negotiated in the house of Admiral Maeda, a sympathetic Japanese, and read by Sukarno at his house on the morning of 17 August.

In the following five days a preparatory committee, originally selected to meet under Japanese auspices, appointed a president and vice president (Sukarno and Hatta), ministers already highly placed in Japanese-led departments, and governors for provinces throughout the archipelago. But it was only during September and October, as mobilized crowds threatened the Japanese with violence and anarchy, that the officials were able to wrest control from the Japanese in Java and Sumatra. In the process leaders appointed from above were frequently pushed aside by populist radicals. Along the northern coast of Java and in northern Sumatra, in particular, social revolutions swept away the aristocratic elite in favor of Muslim and Marxist politicians. Only the democratization of government under Sutan Sjahrir and the organization of an army command from the locally based junior officers trained by the Japanese succeeded in curbing and localizing these social revolutions in late 1945 and early 1946.

British Indian troops occupied Jakarta for the Allies only on 30 September 1945 and five other cities in Java and Sumatra during October. By this time Indonesians had taken effective authority and thousands of weapons from the demoralized Japanese. Strong resistance to the British occupation of Surabaya (28 October–13 November) made it clear to the British that they could not occupy the whole country by force. Lord Mountbatten therefore encouraged talks between the Dutch and the Indonesian republic. These were facilitated by the republic's timely shift in November 1945 to a parliamentary style of government led by Sjahrir (who was prime minister and foreign minister) and Amir Sjarifuddin (defense minister), the two most prominent noncooperators with the Japanese.

Allied forces encountered less resistance in Borneo and eastern Indonesia and reestablished Dutch authority there by January 1946. Negotiations therefore led toward mutual acceptance of a federal Indonesia in which the republic would represent Java and Sumatra and Dutch-created federal states would represent Borneo and East Indonesia. Even though both sides accepted this formula in the Linggajati Agreement of November 1946, their goals remained far apart. Attempting to force the issue, the Dutch launched an attack on 20 July 1947 to occupy the wealthiest regions of Java and Sumatra. Federal states were quickly established, exploiting ethnic sentiment in these regions. It was a Pyrrhic victory, however, for it involved the United Nations in finding a peaceful solution and necessitated the inclusion in the federal states of many genuine nationalists who would not support the Dutch in a showdown with the republic.

Republican cabinets fell regularly because of the unpopularity of their compromises with the Dutch, even though their successors pursued the same foreign policy. Sjahrir led three successive cabinets but gave way in June 1947 to Amir Sjarifuddin, the most prominent leftist. In January 1948, when Amir in turn fell, Sukarno by-passed the Parliament, dominated by the left, to appoint a presidential cabinet of Muslims and nationalists under Hatta. Now isolated from government, the left accepted the militant communist leadership of Musso, a returnee from Moscow, which led it into the Madiun Rebellion of September 1948. By ruthlessly crushing this rebellion, Sukarno and Hatta increased their stature in the United States and the United Nations and began the unification of the army, which had been divided ideologically as well as regionally.

The Dutch attacked again on 19 December 1948, capturing all remaining republican-held cities and the main civilian leaders. US and federal state pressure obliged the Dutch to restore the republican government to its capital, Yogyakarta, in July 1949 and to accelerate negotiations toward full independence. Meanwhile the army had been the undisputed champion of popular guerrilla resistance and thus believed itself entitled to a central role thereafter.

It was a federal Indonesia to which the Netherlands transferred sovereignty on 1 January 1950. By 17 August 1950 all federal states dissolved themselves into a unitary Republic of Indonesia.

[See also Sukarno; Hatta, Mohammad; Java; Sumatra; Sjahrir, Sutan; Amir Sjarifuddin; Surabaya; Mountbatten, Louis; Musso; and Madiun.]

Benedict R. Anderson, *Java in a Time of Revolution* (1972). George Mc T. Kahin, *Nationalism and Revolution in Indonesia* (1952). Anthony Reid, *The Indonesian National Revolution* (1974).          ANTHONY REID

**INDONESIAN SOCIALIST PARTY.** See Partai Socialis Indonesia.

**INDORE.** Along with Baroda and Gwalior, Indore was one of the three major Maratha princely states in late eighteenth-century India. Its founder, Malhar Rao Holkar (1694–1764), rose as military leader in the Maratha drive northward and eventually became the Maratha governor of Malwa. His most notable successors were his daughter-in-law, Ahalya Bai (r. 1766–1795), who was reputed to be both an able administrator and a model of Hindu piety, and Yeshwant Rao (r. 1798–1811), who concluded a treaty with the British in 1806 that recognized Holkar as independent of the *peshwa* but confined to the area south of the Chambal River. Another war and a second treaty in 1818 further reduced Indore's territory but confirmed its status as a British client. In 1931 Indore had an area of 9,519 square miles, a population of 1,318,237, and an average annual revenue of 13,600,000 rupees. In 1948 it joined the Madhya Bharat union of princely states and in 1956 was incorporated into Madhya Pradesh State of independent India.

[See also Princely States and Madhya Pradesh.]

Edward Thompson, *The Making of the Indian Princes* (1943).          BARBARA N. RAMUSACK

**INDRAPRASTHA,** ancient New Delhi, was the capital of the Pandava brothers, the epic heroes who are said to have founded the city in about 1000 BCE. It is identified with the modern Purana Qila area, still called Indapat. Because of its strategic importance as a major gateway to mainland India, Indraprastha retained its historic identity throughout the ages. It was not, however, until the rise of the Tomaras in the tenth century, and after Prithviraj III of the Chauhan dynasty made it his second capital in the late twelfth century, that Indraprastha (or more correctly, medieval Dhillika, or Kila-i Pithora, and other designations by which the epicenters of the city were known) became the seat of a major political power. Since then the city has remained a dominant political force, serving as a capital of pan-Indian powers.

[See also Delhi and Prithviraj Chauhan.]

SHIVA BAJPAI

**INDRAPURA,** capital of the kingdom of Champa (on the central coast of Vietnam) during the ninth and tenth centuries.

Indrapura was in modern Quang-nam Province and was capital of Champa during what must have been the kingdom's last great days. It became capital in 875, made so by Indravarman II, a new king apparently without royal antecedents. In the century that followed the kingdom prospered, but with the rise of a newly independent kingdom in Vietnam, a new threat to Champa's security grew to the north. War with Vietnam brought the destruction of Indrapura in 982 and its abandonment in favor of Vijaya, much farther to the south, in 1000.

[See also Champa; Cham; and Vijaya.]

G. Coedès, *The Indianized States of Southeast Asia,* translated by Susan B. Cowing (1968).

DAVID K. WYATT

**INDUS RIVER,** one of South Asia's great rivers, flowing from Tibet through Kashmir and Pakistan's Punjab and Sind provinces into the Arabian Sea, a distance of some 1,900 miles. Its basin was the site of the Indus Valley civilization, which flourished from approximately 2500 BCE to 1900 BCE and had its centers at Harappa and Mohenjo-Daro.

[See also Indus Valley Civilization.]

J. Fairley, *The Lion River: The Indus* (1975).

ROBIN JARED LEWIS

**INDUS VALLEY CIVILIZATION.** South Asia's first phase of urbanization has come to be known as the Harappan or Indus civilization (c. 2500–1900 BCE). Centered on the greater Indus Valley of India and Pakistan, this, the largest of the Old World's Bronze Age civilizations, was nowhere suggested in the corpus of ancient historical texts that come to us from India's distant past.

It was archaeologists D. R. Bhandarkar, R. D. Banerji, and Daya Ram Sahni, working under the direction of Sir John Marshall, who explored and then excavated the two great centers of this civilization: Mohenjo-Daro and Harappa. Their work began in 1922 and continued at Mohenjo-Daro until 1931. This was an era of great archaeological discoveries. Howard Carter uncovered Tutankhamen's tomb in 1923. Leonard Woolley excavated the royal cemeteries of Ur in 1926. Li Chi and Hiang Ssu-yung began excavating at Anyang in 1928.

As can be seen on the accompanying map (map 1), the settlements of the Indus civilization are found in the transborder area between modern India and Pakistan. This is the region through which once ran the mighty Sarasvati River of classical Indian texts. The Sarasvati, or Gagra-Hakra as it is known today, is now dry and has been since sometime in the first millennium BCE, but there are many Harappan villages and towns along its banks, as well as along the main branch of the Indus River in Sind, and the rivers of the Punjab as well. These settlements have been taken to indicate that the Harappans were, to a large degree, floodplain farmers. Food grains re-

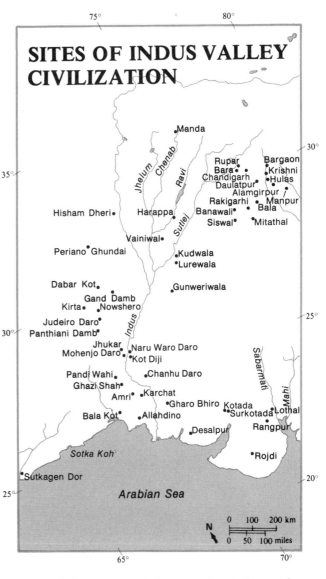

covered from controlled excavation indicate that they grew both barley and wheat, but more of the former than the latter. There is a possibility that rice was cultivated in some regions, especially in the southeast around the site of Lothal. Harappans also grew cotton and made it into cloth.

While we have good evidence for floodplain agriculture, we have no direct evidence for the construction of massive canals that moved river water from its natural course to adjoining environments that would not have been naturally flooded. Most of those who have looked at the problem suggest that the system in use was one that employed the yearly inundation of the rivers in June through September to naturally irrigate cultivated fields.

The Harappans also kept a wide range of domesticated animals, including cattle, sheep, goats, and water buffalo. From the city of Mohenjo-Daro comes our earliest evidence for the domesticated chicken. The openness of the Harappan settlement grid has led to the suggestion that the Harappan subsistence economy also involved a fair amount of pastoral nomadism, probably based on cattle but with sheep and goats as a complement. On the whole, the reconstruction of the subsistence system is remarkably reminiscent of the present, at least in its gross outlines.

There have been substantial excavations in at least seven Harappan settlements: Mohenjo-Daro, Harappa, Kot Diji, Amri, Chanhu-Daro, Lothal, and Sur Kotada. A large number of other sites have been excavated on a smaller scale (e.g., Allahdino, Bala Kot, Rangpur, Rojdi, Rupar). These excavations, and systematic exploration, give us an insight into regional organization, and provide us with an imperfect yet important insight into the nature of Harappan life.

Large settlements such as Mohenjo-Daro (eighty hectares), Harappa (c. sixty hectares), and the recently discovered Ganweriwalla (eighty hectares) in Pakistani Cholistan invariably have a bipartite settlement plan. There is a large low area that has been determined by excavation to be the residential and commercial portion of the city. This is opposed to a higher, smaller district with public architecture, some of which seems to represent places with some kind of ritual function. It is curious to note that so far no Harappan temples have been found. This is not to say that there is a lack of evidence for religious beliefs and practices, but rather that the Harappans did not express this aspect of their way of life in monumental architecture. In this they stand in distinct contrast to the Mesopotamians, the ancient Egyptians, and the ancient Chinese, as well as to the three great New World urban cultures: the Inca, the Maya, and the Aztec.

The bipartite settlement plan is also found at a number of places at the second order of magnitude: towns like Lothal, Sur Kotada, and Kalibangan. But at others the situation is either different (e.g., Chanhu Daro) or ambiguous (e.g., Judeirjo Daro, Nowshero). Small village sites like Allahdino and Amri are generally single entities with an undifferentiated architectural pattern.

Harappans were given to using durable materials for much of their construction. The cities of Mohenjo-Daro and Harappa, as well as the town of Kaligangan, were built almost entirely of baked bricks at a proportion 1:2:4. This is a ratio much in fashion in the West, but Harappan bricks are generally about one-half again as large as Western ones. The use of burned bricks has led to the remarkable preservation of these settlements. Straight streets and the overall grid plan that the Harappans developed for such places can still be seen. All of this taken together gives the visitor a remarkable experience, especially at Mohenjo-Daro, where over ten hectares of remains have been exposed. Original walls tower to a height of twenty feet or more above main streets and side lanes. One can cross a threshold here or peer through a window there. Trash shutes and bathing facilities remain in place. The whole suggests an urban environment that the people have only recently departed, not a city over four thousand years old.

The Harappans were a literate people. Their pictographic script has not yet been deciphered but has been preserved for us in the form of inscriptions on square stamp seals, graffiti on pottery, and other representations. Much work has been done on this body of writing, only some of which is worth serious attention. There is now a sound concordance of the Harappan system of writing (Mahadevan, 1977) that contains valuable tabular matter and an interesting introductory essay. The work by Walter Fairservis (1983) represents one approach to an examination of the iconography of the Indus seals as well as to assigning meaning to those signs that are unambiguously pictographs.

Harappan stamp seals, some with Indus writing, have been found in Mesopotamia and have provided the early excavators of Mohenjo-Daro with evidence that this civilization was truly ancient, dating to the third millennium BCE. There are other ties as well between the sites in the greater Indus Valley and Mesopotamia. Some of these are stylistic but others represent direct Harappan imports to places such as Ur, Kish, Tell Asmar, Tell Agrab, Nippur, and Khafaje. The materials in question include a wide range of Indus beads, especially those of baked and reddened carnelian. Some of these were etched in characteristically Harappan patterns. Other cultural materials of Indian origin found in Mesopotamian sites include metalwork; "games men," ceramics including, but not limited to, an odd kind of "knobbed ware"; kidney-shaped pieces of shell intended as inlay for furniture; and a type of seashell known as *chank* shells. Most of this material is concentrated around the period named for the Akkadian ruler Sargon the Great (c. 2370–2284 BCE or a little later).

Further evidence for trade and commerce between Mesopotamia and ancient India comes to us through a body of Mesopotamian cuneiform texts that were written as records, and accounts of maritime trade between the two lands. These date to the same era as the archaeological finds, although references continue on after the demise of Harappan urbanization. They are informative documents, however, not only in terms of their insights about Mesopotamian civilization and foreign relations of the Harappans, but for the chronology of the Indus civilization as well.

The notion that the date 2300 BCE is central for the chronology of the Indus civilization is also borne out by the masses of radiocarbon dates that are now available. We have learned that this chronometric tool is an invaluable one, but it involves an area of scholarship that must be approached with the same critical eye that a historian uses when examining a body of literature, some parts of which may be at significant odds with the others.

There is a good argument that the inhabitants of the greater Indus Valley were involved in a yet-to-be-understood process leading to urbanization during the first half of the third millennium BCE. This culminated in what can be called the Urban Phase of the Harappan cultural tradition, between about 2500 and 1900 BCE. It was over this span of time that the cities of Mohenjo-Daro and Harappa, along with the other places mentioned here, were occupied, functioning parts of a civilization. We take the following to be the mark of this level of sociocultural integration: (1) marked social classes and craft and career specialization; (2) evidence of a state, and formal leadership with a supporting bureaucracy; and (3) cities, or urban centers.

A long period of cultural "gestation" preceded the emergence of the Harappan Urban Phase. Recent French excavations at Mehrgarh, near Sibi in Pakistan, have revealed a Neolithic, or food-producing, economy on the plains of the Indus Valley as early as 6000–6500 BCE. This work, as well as earlier excavations in Baluchistan at Kili Ghul Mohammad, tells us that the Harappans had direct ancestors in the region for a full four thousand years prior to the emergence of an urban form of social organization. On the other hand, the transition between the Pre-Urban Phase and the Urban Phase seems to have been remarkably short. There appears to have been a critical two- to three-hundred-year period within which the pace of cultural change quickened within this entire region. Such processes have not yet been sufficiently investigated for us to fully describe them, let alone offer a concise explanation for their operation. These entwined tasks are one of the immediate challenges on which archaeologists are currently working.

A similar challenge is presented to scholars who would study the impact of the Indus civilization on later, historical South Asia. We know that beginning about 2000 BCE most of the Indus settlements were abandoned or fell into disrepair. Sir Mortimer Wheeler, one of the most authoritative spokesmen on this topic, once suggested that Mohenjo-Daro had at one point become a "slum" inhabited by "a swarming lower-grade population" (1968, p. 127). Thus the Urban Phase of this cultural tradition gave way to something far more parochial in character. Gone are the urban settlements and so too are the evidences we have for marked social classes and craft and career specialization. Our studies of ancient geography lead us to believe that after about 2000 BCE the state and bureaucracy were increasingly less significant parts of Harappan life.

There is no widely accepted, or even convincing, explanation for the demise of the Harappan Urban Phase, but three things are abundantly clear: (1) The Aryan invasions are an unlikely vehicle of destruction based on the lack of evidence of warfare and the chronological gap between the eclipse of the cities (c. 2000 BCE) and what is taken to be the central point in Indo-European movement into the subcontinent (c. 1500–1000 BCE). (2) The cultural tradition of the Harappan peoples did not perish with the "fall of the cities." There is ample evidence from all of the regions of the civilization for continuity of life into historical eras. In the transborder region of Punjab, Haryana, and Rajasthan, in fact, a large number of sites have been found that take us through what was once thought to be an Indian "Dark Age." (3) The abandonment of many Mature Harappan settlements along the ancient Sarasvati River seems to be coincident in time with the eclipse of the Urban Phase. This can be tied to the drying-up of this river system and would have involved a drop in subsistence productivity. Such a situation may never provide us with the kind of concise historical explanation that archaeologists seek to provide. However, such trauma in what seems to be the center of Harappan agricultural productivity must have played a significant role in second-millennium history within the greater Indus Valley.

There are now clear ties between the Harappan civilization and the true beginnings of South Asian history. This makes more believable something that has been suspected since the discoveries of these ancient cities. There is abundant iconography within the Harappan culture for us to have a clear sense that snakes and other animals, as well as flowers and trees, even plant life in general, played a significant role in the beliefs of these people. We can also perceive an opposition of wild and tame—possibly even domesticated/undomesticated—playing on a broader order/disorder theme running through this material. Themes like this are important parts of medieval, even modern, Hinduism. They appear in Harappan material as motifs on seals and other forms of glyptic art as well as in the painted pottery and figurines. It is from these sources that an extremely important link between the Indus civilization and modern Hinduism can be established.

Work on ancient India's earliest cities has made it abundantly clear that the beginnings of South Asian life as we know it can be traced to this cultural tradition. This is possibly clearest in the seasonal pattern of village-based life, the agricultural regime, and in the role pastoralists play in the subsistence system. This can be further extended into the beginnings of the present-day pattern of settlement and the extraction of a wide range of resources. The major cultivars of South Asia, rice, wheat, sorghum, and the other millets (e.g., *joward, bajra,* and *ragi*), can be traced to Harappan settlements within either the Urban or Post-Urban phases. The same is true for the domesticated animals on which South Asians depend: cattle, water buffaloes, goats, sheep, chickens, and the like. There is further evidence in Harappan contexts for exploitation of the timber resources of the Himalayas, the agate beds of Rajpipla, precious stones from Kashmir, and lapis lazuli from Afghanistan.

Less clearly related to a cultural ecology is the probable origin of the wide range of beliefs that have been integrated into Hinduism, especially at the folk level. It is in these areas of research that a study of the Indus civilization has had its greatest impact on understanding the time depth of this remarkable region of the world.

[*See also* Aryans.]

D. P. Agrawal, *The Archaeology of India* (1982). Bridget Allchin and F. R. Allchin, *The Rise of Civilization in India and Pakistan* (1982). Walter A. Fairservis, *The Roots of Ancient India* (2d ed, 1975) and "The Script of the Indus Valley Civilization," *Scientific American* 248 (1983): 58–66. Iravatham Mahadevan, *The Indus Script: Texts, Concordance and Tables* (1977). Gregory L. Possehl, ed., *Ancient Cities of the Indus* (1979) and *Harappan Civilization: A Contemporary Perspective* (1982). H. D. Sankalia, *Prehistory and Protohistory of India and Pakistan* (2d ed., 1974). Mortimer Wheeler, *The Indus Civilization* (3d ed., 1968).     GREGORY L. POSSEHL

INJU DYNASTY, Iranian family that wielded power in western Iran from 1304 to 1357. *Inju* is a Mongol term referring to royal domains, and the

family began as administrators of such property for the Ilkhan rulers. During the turmoil following the death of the last Ilkhan, Abu Said, in 1335, the Injuids struggled against several rivals to hold onto power in Shiraz and Isfahan. They eventually lost to the Muzaffarids. Some of the great fourteenth-century poet Hafiz's earliest poems praise the enlightened rule of the Injuids in Shiraz, which became the center of Iranian literary culture at that time.

[*See also* Ilkhanid Dynasty; Muzaffarid Dynasty; *and* Hafiz.]

Lawrence Lockhart and Peter Jackson, eds., *Cambridge History of Iran*, vol. 6 (1986), pp. 11–13, 926–934.

RICHARD W. BULLIET

INNER MONGOLIA, the southern half of the grass-covered steppes north of the cultivated regions of China, separated from Outer Mongolia by the Gobi desert. While Outer Mongolia is now the independent Mongolian People's Republic, Inner Mongolia is a province-level unit of the People's Republic of China, with the formal designation Inner Mongolia Autonomous Region. This present-day division of the steppe has been paralleled in the past. Chinese dynasties usually exercised influence over whatever nomads lived in Inner Mongolia, while the lands north of the Gobi were beyond their purview.

Geographically, the grassland is broken by stretches of sandy desert, which becomes the most common form of terrain in the Alashan region in the west. The Edsin Gol in the extreme west is the most important of the many brackish and seasonal rivers that end in salt lakes and marshes. In the extreme north, however, the Khalkha and Orkhon rivers and the Buir and Hulun lakes are connected to the Amur drainage system. The major break in the continuity of the grasslands is in the center of Inner Mongolia, where the Yellow River flows north out of Ningxia, turns east for about 200 miles, and then turns south to form the border between Shanxi and Shaanxi provinces. The grasslands to the south of the bend in the Yellow River—the Ordos region—have always been inhabited by nomadic peoples; the Yellow River in turn has made it possible to support Chinese cities and garrisons in the heart of the steppe.

Inner Mongolia has been inhabited by a succession of nomadic peoples, most importantly the Xiongnu, Wuhuan, Xianbei, Turks, and Mongols. Economically and militarily, these societies were based on their herds of livestock, whose grazing requirements dictated a cyclic pattern of migration.

They often needed grain supplies, which they obtained by trade or raid from their agricultural Chinese neighbors. Their beliefs and social patterns encouraged the nomads to warfare even in the absence of economic motives. Since the boundary between permanent steppe and marginally cultivable agricultural land fluctuated and could never be precisely defined, successive Chinese regimes were forced to take elaborate measures to control the nomads. These measures included (1) building walls, with infantry garrisons and beacon towers, sometimes joined to cover the entire area of the border, as in the Han and Ming; (2) creating military colonies with Chinese settlers; (3) fighting the nomads in their own manner, using armies of Chinese cavalry; and (4) using the diplomatic system of "bridle and saddle" *(jimi)*, under which nomadic chieftains were awarded Chinese titles, seals, and insignia and given lavish gifts in return for nominal amounts of tribute. If well handled, this system could induce a status competition among the chieftains, which Chinese authorities could manipulate.

During the Ming dynasty (1368–1644) most of the population of Mongolia was converted to Tibetan Lamaist Buddhism. A succession of wars under the Kangxi, Yongzheng, and Qianlong emperors of the Qing dynasty brought all of Mongolia, along with Xinjiang and Tibet, under firm Qing control. These events fundamentally changed the situation in Inner Mongolia. The Qing created the modern distinction between Inner and Outer Mongolia by creating a separate bureau for each area in the Mongolian superintendency *(lifanyuan)*, the agency established to manage the affairs of the Central Asian tributary princes. The Inner Mongols were divided into seven leagues *(meng)*, each in turn divided into a number of banners *(qi* or *khoshun,* to be distinguished from the banners of the Eight Banner system). Each banner was given a fixed area, so that traditional nomadic practices withered and died. The largely ceremonial captain-generals *(mengzhang)* of the leagues were chosen from the princes *(jasakh)* of the banners, who were hereditary subject to confirmation by the *lifanyuan.* The banner princes held titles equal to those of the Qing imperial family and were eligible for high military positions. Their subjects suffered from oppressive rule and from Chinese moneylenders and immigrants in the banner lands.

The last three decades of the Qing saw efforts to bring the borderlands under regular provincial administration in order to prevent alienation to foreign powers. Part of Inner Mongolia in consequence was alienated to the three Manchurian provinces. With the fall of the Qing in 1911/1912, Outer Mongolia became independent and the remainder of Inner Mongolia was divided into four new provinces (Ningxia, Suiyuan, Chahaer, and Reheer). Attempts to restrain Chinese immigration into Inner Mongolia were now totally abandoned, and the provincial governments themselves turned into prizes of warlord politics. After the Guomindang reunification of China in 1927, the Inner Mongolian princes began to demand the creation of a single autonomous Mongolian area within the Republic of China. The Guomindang consistently refused this demand, and as a result Prince De, the most important Mongol leader, collaborated with the Japanese during their occupation of North China.

The Chinese Communist victory in 1949 led to the formation of the Inner Mongolia Autonomous Region. As part of the overall nationalities policy of the new regime, the Mongols of the autonomous region were encouraged to publish in their native language and alphabet and to maintain their national customs. Chinese immigration continued, however, and the Han Chinese came to constitute the majority of the population. Throughout China the Great Proletarian Cultural Revolution of the 1960s saw indiscriminate attacks on minority cultures. In Inner Mongolia these took the form of banning the official use of the Mongolian language, placing Han Chinese in all positions of importance, and detaching the eastern and western parts of the region. In the late 1970s these policies were rescinded, and the Inner Mongolia Autonomous Region was restored to its 1950s boundaries.

C. R. Bawden, *The Modern History of Mongolia* (1968). June Dreyer, *China's Forty Millions* (1976). Yingshih Yu, *Trade and Expansion in Han China* (1967).
EDWARD L. DREYER

INOUE ENRYŌ (1858–1919), prominent Meiji-period Japanese Buddhist thinker and educator. The son of a True Pure Land priest from Niigata Prefecture, he began his schooling in the Nagaoka School of Western Studies. From there he entered the seminary of the Higashi Honganji, a large temple belonging to the True Pure Land school (Jōdo Shinshū). He took the name Enryō when he was ordained as a Jōdo Shinshū priest. Inoue was among the first of the Buddhist clergy to secure admission to Tokyo University, where he studied philosophy.

Inoue graduated in 1885. Two years later he established a private academy for the study of Buddhist philosophy, the Tetsugakukan, which later developed into Tōyō University. Here he devoted himself to teaching and writing. Inoue became a vigorous critic of Christianity and a proponent of Buddhism and Japanese nationalism. He argued that Buddhism was better suited to modern society than was Christianity, that Eastern civilization was rooted in Buddhism, and that the revitalization and reform of Buddhism and Eastern philosophy would strengthen Japan as an independent Asian nation.

Inoue devoted his life to the promotion of Buddhism and Eastern thought and to the assertion of Japanese nationalism. He established a National Association of Philosophy in Japan. He argued for the universality of philosophy, stating that it was not something found only in the West but also had deep roots in Japan. He started several journals of Eastern and Western philosophy and was a regular contributor to the influential nationalist journal *Nihonjin (The Japanese)*. Inoue traveled widely throughout Japan, other parts of Asia, Europe, and the United States. He died in Dalian (Dairen) while on a trip to encourage the revival of Buddhism in China and Manchuria.

Through his many lectures, books, and journal articles Inoue was a major contributor to the revival of Buddhism in mid-Meiji, to its alignment with the ideals of the Meiji state, and to its acceptance as a possible counter to the excessive influence of Christianity and Western thought on Japan.

Fumio Masutani and Yoshimochi Undo, "Buddhism," in *Japanese Religion in the Meiji Era*, edited by Kishimoto Hideo and translated by John F. Howes (1956).

MARTIN COLLCUTT

## INOUE KAORU

INOUE KAORU (1836–1915), Japanese government leader of the Meiji period. Inoue was Itō Hirobumi's closest and lifelong friend. Throughout his life, Inoue felt a binding duty to protect or perform unpleasant tasks for Itō, his more prudent and less brave junior colleague from Chōshū. Both men participated in the attack against the British Legation (1862), went to England (1863), and rushed back to try to prevent the clash between the four-power fleet and Chōshū (1864). Inoue nearly paid with his life when Chōshū radicals attacked him during those hostilities.

Inoue spent most of his Meiji administrative career at the heart of the government. His positions included finance vice-minister and minister (1871–1873; 1898), foreign minister (1879–1887), home minister (1893–1894), public works minister (1878–1879), and agriculture and commerce minister (1888–1889). He also went through his public

life bathed in controversy, in part a reflection of his cantankerous personality. He resigned from the Finance Ministry in 1873 over policy differences with Ōkuma Shigenobu, the finance minister. He was sent to Europe from June 1877 to July 1878 to study fiscal and economic matters, but this may have been an "exile" brought on by differences with Ōkubo Toshimichi, the home minister. He helped Itō oust Ōkuma Shigenobu from the government in 1881, and he himself was forced to resign as foreign minister six years later, when he was attacked by others in the government for his overemphasis on introducing European culture and for giving away too much to achieve treaty revision. He was somewhat more successful in Korea and helped to negotiate the Kangwha and Seoul treaties of 1876 and 1885, respectively.

Inoue moved easily in and out of government (his last post was in 1898), and he was active in financial and industrial circles. He had close ties with the Mitsui conglomerate.

[*See also* Itō Hirobumi *and* Meiji Period.]

GEORGE K. AKITA

## INOUE KOWASHI

INOUE KOWASHI (1844–1895), Japanese government leader of the Meiji period. He was born into a high-ranking Kumamoto *han* samurai family and was adopted by the Inoue family. By the age of twenty-seven he had obtained a post in the Justice Ministry (December 1871) and almost immediately thereafter was sent to Europe (May 1872). In 1888 and 1889 he was chief secretary of the Privy Council and then a privy councillor (1890–1892). He also served as education minister for one year, from 1893 to 1894.

Inoue was a gifted thinker and writer whose talents were recognized and fully utilized by prominent Meiji leaders such as Iwakura Tomomi, Itō Hirobumi, and Yamagata Aritomo. His hand is evident in nearly all the crucial documents of the middle Meiji period. The unifying conceptions he brought to his task were the need to create the institutional and ideological bases to serve the nation's ends, an appreciation of both Western and Japanese ideas and values, and moderation and realism. Among his chief contributions are the Gunjin chokuyu (Imperial Rescript to Soldiers and Sailors, 1882), which laid the basis for the indoctrination of conscripts but can also be seen as an admonition against military meddling in politics; and the Kyōiku Chokugo (Imperial Rescript on Education, 1890), which when first promulgated was seen as a moderate statement on the emperor as repository of native traditions and morality, a concept acceptable to opinion molders of all stripes. His greatest contribution was in helping to draft the Meiji Constitution (1889), which, one scholar noted, was "drafted with Inoue listening with one ear to the German specialist Hermann Roesler"; another has judged it to be, "given its premises and aims, a truly impressive testimony to the political insight and genius of the founders of modern Japan."

[See also Imperial Rescript to Soldiers; Imperial Rescript on Education; and Meiji Period.]

GEORGE K. AKITA

INOUE NISSHŌ (1886–1967), ultranationalist activist in Japan. Inoue was born in Gumma Prefecture; his given name was Akira. After attending Takushoku College without graduating, he went to Manchuria, where he was employed by the South Manchurian Railway Company, working concurrently as a spy for the Japanese army. After the outbreak of the Chinese Revolution in 1911 he went to China, where he spent some years as an agent of the Japanese military adviser to Yuan Shikai.

In 1916 Inoue returned to Japan. After an unsuccessful attempt to establish himself in business, he became a priest of the Nichiren sect of Buddhism, remaining active as an ultranationalist. In 1921 he joined the nationalist leader Tōyama Mitsuru in establishing the Tokyo Secret Society for Defending the Country. In 1928 he set up the Gokokudō ("temple for defending the country") in Ibaraki Prefecture, where he propagated to local village youths his ideas on how to save Japan. At that time he became associated with the agrarian nationalist leaders Gondō Seikyō and Tachibana Kōzaburō, as well as with young naval officers serving at the Naval Aviation School in the nearby town of Tsuchiura.

In 1930 Inoue organized his civilian followers into the Ketsumeidan ("blood brotherhood"); the group's intent was to assassinate leading "traitors" among politicians and financial magnates. Each member of the group was assigned a particular victim on the basis of ichinin issatsu ("one man, one killing"). In February and March 1932 two members of the group assassinated former finance minister Inoue Junnosuke and the chief director of the Mitsui company, Dan Takuma. In May, Inoue's followers from the navy took part in the May Fifteenth Incident, in which Prime Minister Inukai Tsuyoshi was assassinated.

Inoue hid for a few weeks at the house of his friend Tōyama Mitsuru, but then gave himself up. He was sentenced to life imprisonment but was released in the general amnesty of 1940. After his release he stayed for some time at the house of Konoe Fumimaro. He was active in various right-wing organizations in the postwar period.

[See also Tōyama Mitsuru and Konoe Fumimaro.]

Thomas R. H. Havens, Farm and Nation in Modern Japan (1974). Masao Maruyama, Thought and Behavior in Modern Japanese Politics (1963). Richard Storry, The Double Patriots (1957).

BEN-AMI SHILLONY

INQUILINO, leaseholder or tenant on the landholdings of Spanish religious orders in the Philippines. The practice of using inquilinos to clear and cultivate large estates began as early as the late sixteenth century. The inquilino paid a fixed rent (terrazgo or canon) in money or kind to the owner. By the nineteenth century, inquilinos, particularly on the friar estates of central and southern Luzon, had emerged as wealthy, predominantly absentee leaseholders who controlled large landholdings that were cultivated by subleasees or sharecroppers, known as kasamas. These latter-day inquilinos played important roles in the commercial and political developments of their time.

MICHAEL CULLINANE

INTANON, chao of Chiang Mai (r. 1871–1897), the last semi-independent ruler of northern Thailand. In the reign of his father-in-law, Kavilorot (1856–1870), the expansion of British teak cutting from Burma north into Chiang Mai upset the traditional internal balance of power and, with the insecurity of American missionary activities there, threatened foreign political intrusion. King Chulalongkorn of Siam responded by appointing Intanon, a weaker candidate, to the throne of Chiang Mai on Kavilorot's death and by steadily curbing the chao's powers of taxation and land control until, by his death in 1897, Intanon had virtually no powers. His successors were little more than symbolic figureheads. [See also Chiang Mai; Kavila; and Chulalongkorn.]

DAVID K. WYATT

INTRAMUROS, the old Spanish city of Manila, on the promontory bordered by the Pasig River and Manila Bay. Previously settled by Filipinos, the site was occupied in 1571 by Spanish forces under Miguel Lopez de Legazpi and was completely surrounded by stone fortifications by 1593. Private residences, government and military buildings, churches and rectories, and warehouses were all constructed within the walls, thus the term *intramuros*. It was not until the eighteenth century that Spaniards began living outside the walls, as the city of Manila expanded to include contiguous districts and municipalities inhabited by Filipinos, Chinese, and *mestizos*. Much of the Intramuros was destroyed during the Pacific War and is currently undergoing restoration.          MICHAEL CULLINANE

**IQBAL, SIR MUHAMMAD** (1877–1938), poet and philosopher whom Pakistanis revere as a founding father of their nation. Born in the Punjabi town of Sialkot to a family of Kashmiri brahman converts to Islam, Iqbal grew up in an atmosphere of piety, hard work, and modest comfort. His formal education was along Western lines: he attended first the Scotch Mission College in Sialkot, then Government College in Lahore (1895–1899). But he was also tutored by the well-known Arabic and Persian scholar Sayyid Mir Hasan and began to write Urdu poetry, taking the famous poet Navab Mirza Khan Dagh as his literary mentor.

From 1899 to 1905 Iqbal taught Arabic, history, and economics at Oriental College in Lahore and continued to make his reputation as an Urdu poet. Then from 1905 to 1908 Iqbal studied abroad, receiving a doctorate in philosophy from Munich and a law degree from Lincoln's Inn. During this period he decided to adopt Persian as his primary poetic language, probably in order to reach a wider Islamic audience. Returning to Lahore, Iqbal earned his living by practicing law from 1908 to 1934, when his health deteriorated. He died after a long illness.

In 1915 Iqbal published his major Persian philosophical poem, *Asrar-i khudi (Secrets of the Self)*; its continuation, *Rumuz-i bekhudi (Mysteries of Selflessness)*, appeared in 1918. These poems initiated a series that included *Payam-i mashriq (The Message of the East*, 1923), a response to Goethe's *West Östlicher Divan*; *Zubur-i 'ajam (Iranian Psalms*, 1927); and *Javid nama* (1932), which has been called "an Oriental *Divine Comedy*." His generally shorter, more lyrical Urdu poems were also published in several collections, notably *Bang-e dara (The Sound of the Bell*, 1924) and *Bal-e Jibril (Gabriel's Wing*, 1936). A collection of his English lectures on Islamic philosophy was published as *The Reconstruction of Religious Thought in Islam* (1930).

At his best Iqbal is one of the great Urdu poets and a great Indo-Persian poet as well. But his wide-spread reputation is based not only on his poetic gifts but also on his philosophy, which is forcefully—and even at times a bit heavy-handedly—expressed in all his works. His philosophy is radically activist, vitalist, and voluntaristic. He rejects all forms of fatalism, passivity, resignation, and materialism; he demands that the human will and spirit transcend all barriers, soaring beyond them into a God-like closeness to God. In Western terms, if poetically he is indebted to Goethe, Dante, and Milton, philosophically he is the heir of Kant, Fichte, Schopenhauer, Bergson, and above all Nietzsche. But Iqbal is by no means intellectually subservient to Western culture; he in fact provides a strong critique of its materialistic self-complacency. Although he addresses himself particularly to Muslims, his real concern is with the restless dynamism and self-transcendent upward struggle of the human spirit.

Always interested in political questions, Iqbal spoke against mere "nationalism," with its attendant risk of "atheistic materialism"; he valued "a man's faith, his culture, his historical traditions" far more highly than "the piece of earth with which the spirit of man happens to be temporarily associated." But he came to believe that partition was the only feasible way to secure the rights of self-development for all the various cultural groups in India, and he was the first influential person to say so publicly (in the 1930s)—thus his status as a founding father of Pakistan.

[*See also* Pakistan.]

Sir Muhammad Iqbal, *The Secrets of the Self*, translated by R. A. Nicholson (1944), and *Gabriel's Wing*, translated by Annemarie Schimmel (1963). Hafeez Malik, ed., *Iqbal: Poet-Philosopher of Pakistan* (1971). Syed Abdul Vahid, *Iqbal: His Art and Thought* (1959).

FRANCES W. PRITCHETT

**IRAN.** Historically, as today, Iran has been bounded on the south by the Persian Gulf and the Gulf of Oman, on the west by the Zagros Mountains, and on the northwest by the Caspian Sea, the Caucasus Mountains, and the mountains of eastern Anatolia. However, its modern political frontiers in the east and northeast are products of the nineteenth-century rivalry between Russia and Great Britain. In earlier periods Iran sometimes extended well into present-day Afghanistan, Pakistan, and the Soviet Central Asian republics.

*Climate and Geography.* The land of Iran is characterized by mountain ranges surrounding interior plains. The sparse rains and snows of winter make

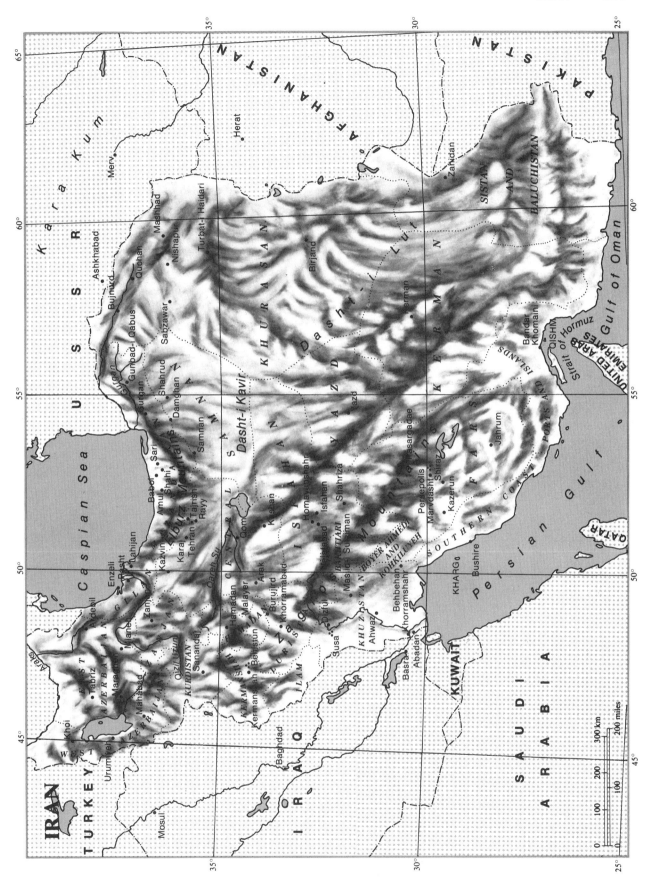

IRAN

1:10,000,000

possible dry farming and pastoralism in mountainous areas, particularly in the west. Elsewhere, this precipitation replenishes a groundwater supply that is tapped by water tunnels called *qanats*. *Qanats* supply water to thousands of Iranian villages. Because of the technical characteristics of this system, villages are found mostly in the piedmont areas of the country.

Central Iran is a relatively flat desert region with large expanses of salt produced by the evaporation of groundwater. It is sparsely inhabited and difficult to cross. The Persian Gulf and Indian Ocean coastal regions are similarly arid and inhospitable. In contrast, the Caspian coast is well watered, with subtropical vegetation. The steep and almost impassable Elburz Mountains, which rise behind a narrow coastal plain, cut off the region from the central plateau. Until the twentieth century, malaria and geographical isolation prevented this coast from becoming a major political or population center.

While mountain barriers and desolate coasts have made Iran difficult to enter from most directions, its frontiers are easily crossed in the east. The mountains that extend eastward from the Elburz are lower and end entirely near the city of Mashhad. Routes from there to Central Asia or the western reaches of the Hindu Kush in Afghanistan have been repeatedly used by invaders and migrating peoples. The southeast offers similar easy passage into the Baluchistan province of Pakistan, but the extreme aridity of this region has made it a less important transit zone.

***Early History.*** Peoples speaking languages of the Indo-Iranian subgroup of the Indo-European language family probably entered Iran from the northeast early in the second millennium BCE. The indigenous inhabitants with whom they intermingled to form the ancestors of the later Iranian population are little known. The Elamites of the province of Fars in the southwest had a written language unrelated to Iranian. Other pre-Iranian languages are unknown.

The ancient Iranians gradually developed an identity separate from the related peoples who moved on to occupy northern India. However, their cultural and religious traditions long remained similar. In Iran a priest named Zoroaster (Avestan, Zarathushtra) reformed the Indo-Iranian polytheistic faith along ethical lines and preached a religion with one god, Ahura Mazda, and an underlying dualistic theology pitting Good against Evil. The Avesta is the religious book of the Zoroastrian religion.

Scholars debate the dates and geography of Zoroaster's life, but his religion was practiced at the time of the earliest historically attested Iranian dynasties, the Medes and the Persians. Media lay in the central Zagros Mountains; Persis (the name is the Greek form of *Fars*) lay in the southwest. The history of the Medes and of the Persian Achaemenid dynasty (named for an ancestor, Achaemenes) is known primarily from Greek historians such as Herodotus, from the great cliffside inscriptions in Old Persian at Behistun, and from the excavation of palaces and tombs at Persepolis and Pasargadae.

Cyrus the Great, who founded the Achaemenid dynasty around 550 BCE, and his successors Darius I and Xerxes invaded the lands of the Greeks. The last Achaemenid ruler, Darius III, suffered defeat at the hands of Alexander the Great in 330 BCE. During the intervening period the Iranian empire established itself as the dominant power in the Middle East and the nemesis of any state lying to the west of it. This confrontation between an Iranian empire and a western adversary has recurred repeatedly in Iranian history. Mesopotamia has sometimes been the domain of the enemy, as in the early Islamic period and during the recent Iran-Iraq war; sometimes this domain has been an area that, despite having a mostly Semitic and non-Iranian population, was an extension of Iranian imperial territory as under the Achaemenids, Sasanids, and Parthians; and it has sometimes been a contested war zone, as in the Safavid period. Achaemenid relations with kindred peoples to the east are poorly known, but pastoral tribes pushing south from Central Asia posed a problem.

The Achaemenid rulers used the title "king of kings" (modern Persian, *shahanshah*). They also distinguished between their provinces in Iran and Aniran ("non-Iran"). Some later dynasties tried using the Achaemenid example to legitimize their rule, most recently the Pahlavis in the twentieth century.

After Alexander's death in 323 BCE his general Seleucus emerged as the controller of his Iranian territories. Like his predecessors, Seleucus and his descendants had difficulty controlling Iran's eastern frontiers. By the year 303 he had lost Alexander's Indian provinces to Chandragupta Maurya. A separate Greek kingdom arose in Bactria in northern Afghanistan. The Seleucids focused their interest on the west and extended their power to the Mediterranean, with capitals at Antioch in Syria and Seleuceia on the Tigris River.

The Arsacids were the leaders of the Parthians, an Iranian people who followed a pastoral way of life southeast of the Caspian Sea. They established a kingdom that expanded in the wake of the Seleucids' increasing concern with the west. The Arsacid or Parthian dynasty ruled from around 250 BCE to 226 CE. It is the least known of the major Iranian dynasties despite being a formidable enemy of the Romans. The Silk Route across Central Asia to China, which first became active during the Parthian period, gave rise to an exchange of cultural influences between the two ends of Asia.

The Sasanids, a family of Zoroastrian priestly origin in Fars, overthrew the Parthians and established Zoroastrianism as the official and exclusive Iranian religion. Christians, Jews, Buddhists, and Manichaeans, a sect begun by the prophet Mani in the third century CE, were sometimes persecuted and sometimes tolerated. The hierarchical Zoroastrian church and its leader the shah confronted on the west a similarly organized Christian church led by the emperors of the late Roman or Byzantine empire established by Constantine in 330. The rival empires fought off and on for three centuries.

Meanwhile, new peoples entered Iranian territory from Central Asia. Some spoke Iranian languages (e.g., Sogdian); others spoke Turkic languages. Buddhism was the dominant religion, although Manichaean and Christian missionaries had spread from Iran deep into Central Asia. The eastern border of the Sasanid empire fluctuated. The numerous small principalities beyond the border are poorly known.

*Islamic Iran.* The prophet Muhammad proclaimed the religion of Islam in a series of revelations (which came to be called the Qur'an) that came to him between 611 and his death in 632. He lived in Mecca in western Arabia, and the earliest Muslims, or believers in Islam, were Arabs. Motivated at least in part by religion, the Arabs embarked on conquests after Muhammad's death. Around 636 they defeated the Sasanids and captured Ctesiphon, the capital. The last Sasanid shah died a fugitive in eastern Iran in 651.

The caliphate was the governing institution established by Muhammad's successors to rule the newly conquered empire. The capital of the caliphate moved from Arabia to Damascus, Syria, in 661 and to Iraq in 750. A new capital was built at Baghdad on the outskirts of the old capitals of Seleucia and Ctesiphon. Arab governors sent by the caliphs ruled Iran. Medieval Islamic historians and geographers seldom wrote about Iran as such; they wrote instead about individual provinces such as Fars and Khurasan. There were many provincial capitals.

Most Iranians converted to Islam over a period of three centuries. The first generations of Iranian Muslims assimilated the culture of Arab conquerors and did not write in their native language. But from about 800 onward more and more Iranians wrote an Iranian language derived from the Middle Persian languages of the Sasanid period. This language is properly referred to as New Persian or Farsi, although it is usually simply called Persian. It is written in the Arabic script and has a substantial admixture of Arabic loanwords. Many Iranians continued to write Arabic, including some of the greatest writers and thinkers in the history of Arabic letters, such as Ibn Sina and al-Ghazali.

The literature written in New Persian frequently embodied an Iranian cultural tradition that survived the loss of national independence and unity. The *Shahnama,* an epic poem that recounts the tales of the mythical pre-Achaemenid rulers of Iran as well as of the historical shahs, was completed by Firdausi around 1000. It drew upon poetic sources that were preserved in both written and oral form from the pre-Islamic period.

As the Abbasid caliphate lost power in the ninth century, several Iranian dynasties of different origins arose in various provinces. The major Iranian dynasties were the Tahirids, the Saffarids, the Samanids, and the Buyids. In Baghdad Iranian influence at the court of the caliph steadily increased, until in 945 a Buyid ruler took control of the city.

The Buyids adhered to the Shi'ite form of Islam, which reveres Muhammad's son-in-law and cousin Ali and his descendants as the divinely appointed leaders of the Islamic community, despite their chronic inability to gain and hold political power. The Buyids retained the Sunni caliphate because the twelfth of the recognized imams, or divinely appointed leaders descended from Ali, had disappeared without a successor a half century earlier. Historians debate the degree to which Iranians adhered to Shi'ism at this time. Written sources indicate that most Iranians were Sunni, but these mostly emanate from the cities. Little is known about small towns and villages.

Prior to the Arab conquests most Iranian cities were small. Iranian aristocrats lived on rural estates and held their wealth in land and treasure. In the ninth and tenth centuries urbanization on an unprecedented scale changed the character of the country. Numerous cities arose with populations at least in the 50,000–100,000 range (e.g., Nishapur, Rayy, Isfahan, Shiraz). They developed into dynamic manufacturing and cultural centers. A recirculation of wealth from the deposed aristocracy and a centralization of tax collection in the governing centers chosen by the Arabs contributed to this urbanization, as did a migration of converts to Islam from rural or outlying areas. The new cities were predominantly Muslim, and Iran became one of the most influential regions of Muslim intellectual activity.

From around 1000 on the independent Iranian dynasties rapidly gave way to new dynasties of Turkic origin. Turkic peoples had been making slow inroads into Iranian territory for several centuries, but until the late tenth century they mostly remained in Central Asia in a tribal and nomadic society oriented primarily toward horse-breeding. The movement of Turkic tribes in large numbers into Iran is poorly chronicled. Many of the Turks were at least nominally Sunni Muslims, but when and how their conversion came about is obscure.

The Ghaznavids were the first Turkic ruling dynasty in Iran, but they were defeated by the Seljuks and pursued their later history in Afghanistan and India. The rulers at this time usually took the title "sultan," the Arabic word meaning "power." The Seljuks established a large empire and brought the rule of the Buyids to an end in 1055. They freed the Abbasid caliph from Shi'ite control, but they allowed him little more political power than the Buyids had. The Seljuks employed some notable Iranian administrators, of whom Nizam al-Mulk was the most famous.

Family feuding contributed to a rapid decline of Seljuk power in the twelfth century. Iran had been suffering for a century from economic difficulties partly brought on by political disorder and nomadic incursions. Urban populations had been falling because of famine, epidemics, and migration to more prosperous areas. These trends accelerated when nomadic depredations reached a peak in the second half of the century and the dynasty of the Khwarazmshahs, established by a lieutenant of one of the Seljuk sultans, proved overly rapacious.

In 1219 Genghis Khan led his Mongol army out of Central Asia and overwhelmed the army of the Khwarazmshah. He conquered eastern Iran and left armies in the west to expand Mongol territory after he withdrew in 1221. The devastations of the Mongols are proverbial, but Iran was already in a deep state of economic and demographic decline before they arrived. The conqueror's grandson Hulegu resumed Mongol expansion westward in a second invasion in the 1250s. He established a separate Mongol state, subordinate to that of the Great Khan in Mongolia, to be ruled by his descendants. This was called the Ilkhan empire, from the title of the ruler.

Several of the Ilkhans took steps to rebuild the Iranian economy. Ghazan Khan converted the dynasty to Islam. Their center of rule was in Azerbaijan, the northwestern province, which had seldom played an important role in earlier Iranian history. Eastern Iran, which had flourished in the earlier Islamic centuries, never fully recovered economically or regained political importance. The population of Azerbaijan adopted the Turkic language of the tribes that settled in the region both before and after the Mongol invasion. The Mongol language left little imprint on Iran because few Mongols settled permanently in Ilkhan territory.

The last Ilkhan, Abu Sa'id, died in 1335. Politically, Iran dissolved into regional dynasties of varying origins. Some claimed power in the name of a descendant of Genghis Khan. Others, such as the Sarbadarids in the northeast, based their rule on religion. Sufism, or Islamic mysticism, began to develop into organized brotherhoods, some of which had political ambitions. Some Sufi brotherhoods were Sunni, others Shi'ite. The distinction was often unclear, since their emphasis was on emotional religious experience rather than legal strictures and definitions.

Timur, known in English as Tamerlane, swept away these petty dynasties in his merciless conquest of Iran in the 1390s. He was a Turkic ruler from Central Asia with an ambition to outdo the incredible conquests of Genghis Khan, one of his ancestors. When he died in 1405 he had subdued every adversary from the Aegean Sea to Delhi and was on his way to attempt the conquest of China.

Timur's descendants could not hold his empire together. Iran again fell apart among rival petty dynasties. The Akkoyunlu state centered in Azerbaijan was one of the most powerful. Its rulers first showed special favor to the hereditary leaders of a Sufi order known as the Safaviyya, but they later grew fearful of their popularity with the Turkic tribes. In 1501 Isma'il, the leader of the order, declared himself shah and established the Safavid empire. He relied militarily on Turkic-speaking tribes who wore the red headdress of the order and were therefore called the Kizilbash ("red head") tribes. Isma'il declared Shi'ite Islam the religion of his new state, even though the Safaviyya had at one time been Sunni like most of the Iranian population.

The Safavid empire fought the Ottomans frequently with mixed success. Their wars fixed the Zagros Mountains as the western border of Iran down to modern times. Safavid power and culture flourished in the early seventeenth century under

Shah Abbas I. Isfahan, the capital, became a magnificent showplace. Shah Abbas established a large Armenian community there. Surviving mosques, silks, carpets, and miniature paintings show this to be one of the most creative and flourishing periods in Iranian history.

Iran converted almost entirely to Shi'ism during the Safavid period. Flanked by hostile Sunni states, Iran assumed a national political identity that embodied Shi'ism virtually as part of its definition. Outstanding Shi'ite philosophers and theologians made the period an important one in Islamic intellectual history.

However, administrative and economic problems, combined with rivalries between Turks and Iranians, undermined the empire. By 1722 it was so weak that an army of marauders from Afghanistan was able to take and plunder Isfahan. An able general, who dispensed with the fiction of Safavid rule and himself took the throne as Nadir Shah, rebuilt an ephemeral empire and conquered as far east as Delhi. But Iran rapidly fell apart again after his death in 1747.

The Zand family based in Shiraz was for a while the most powerful poiitical force in Iran, but in the 1780s a family of leaders of the Qajar tribe eclipsed the Zands and established a new unified Iranian state. The Qajar dynasty, which never approached the Safavids in power, wealth, or culture, ruled throughout the nineteenth century. The Babi and Baha'i religious movements were the most important social developments of the era. Occasional efforts at reform and westernization, prompted partly by the model of changes taking place in the Ottoman empire and partly by fear of Russian and British encroachment, produced no significant increase in power. By the end of the century the country was weak and in debt to foreign creditors. The shahs were perceived as squanderers of the national wealth.

***Iran in the Twentieth Century.*** The largely peaceful Constitutional Revolution of 1906 forced the shah to declare Iran a constitutional monarchy with legislative powers vested in a *majles*, or parliament. The shahs did not fulfill their constitutional promises, however, and Russian and British encroachment became increasingly perilous. In 1924 a military commander named Reza Khan seized control of the country and deposed the Qajars. He became Reza Shah and adopted the family name Pahlavi.

Reza Shah undertook a radical modernization program patterned on that of Ataturk in Turkey. But he made slower progress because Iran was poorer and had been more isolated from European influences than the Ottoman empire had been. At the outbreak of World War II Britain and Russia feared that Reza Shah might favor the Germans. They occupied Iran and forced him to abdicate in favor of his son Mohammed Reza Shah.

Mohammed Reza Shah was not a forceful ruler. In 1953 he was almost overthrown by the popular and nationalistic prime minister Mohammed Mossadegh, but he retained his throne with British and American help. Thereafter he became a more energetic and skillful ruler, and the United States developed close relations with Iran, which it saw as a strategic ally against the Soviet Union. The US encouraged rapid modernization, and oil revenues, which began before World War I but skyrocketed after 1973, made radical changes possible. Iran developed an industrial base, a complex infrastructure, and a large public education system.

In modernizing the country the shah ran roughshod over all opposition. Iran became an absolute monarchy. Most opponents were powerless or too captivated by the country's growing wealth to offer serious resistance, though a revolutionary underground did gain adherents. However, the opposition of certain religious leaders to the shah's reforms proved more dangerous. In Iran, unlike in most other parts of the Islamic world, religious leaders remained at the center of an independent network of institutions, from which they exerted great popular influence and derived financial resources. Moreover, Shi'ism had gone through an intense period of theological and philosophical debate in the nineteenth century, and religious leaders had taken an active part in political affairs.

In 1978 a revolution broke out that forced the shah to flee the country early the following year. The leader of the revolution was the religious leader Ayatollah Ruhollah Khomeini, under whose direction the Islamic Republic was established. In the aftermath of the revolution many countries feared that Iran would become a model for further violent revolution. In 1980 this fear was intensified by the humiliation of the United States through the seizure of its embassy and the holding of hostages. In 1981 Iraq invaded Iran in an effort to overthrow the Islamic Republic. As the war dragged on inconclusively, the fear of revolutionary Iran diminished. But the Islamic Republic seemed well established, and the long history of monarchy in Iran at an end.

[*See also* Abbasid Dynasty; Achaemenid Dynasty;

Afghanistan; Ayatollah; Babi; Baha'i; Buyid Dynasty; Caliphate; Constitutional Revolution; Hostage Crisis; Ilkhanid Dynasty; Imam; Iran-Iraq War; Islam; Khomeini, Ruhollah Musavi; Khurasan; Manichaeism; Pakistan; Parthians; Persian Literature; Qajar Dynasty; Safavid Dynasty; Samanid Dynasty; Sasanid Dynasty; Seleucid Dynasty; Seljuk Dynasty; Shi'a; Sufism; *and* Zoroastrianism.]

A. Bausani, *The Persians* (1971). E. G. Browne, *A Literary History of Persia*, 4 vols. (1902; reprint, 1956). Richard N. Frye, *The Heritage of Persia* (1962) and *The Golden Age of Persia* (1975). Nikki Keddie, *Roots of Revolution* (1981). Roy P. Mottahedeh, *The Mantle of the Prophet* (1985). A. U. Pope, ed., *The Survey of Persian Art*, 6 vols. (1938). Roger Savory, *Iran under the Safavids* (1980). Ehsan Yarshater, ed., *The Cambridge History of Iran*, 7 vols. (1968–).          RICHARD W. BULLIET

**IRAN-IRAQ WAR.** Iraq invaded Iran in September 1980, starting a border, ethnic, and ideological war that produced hundreds of thousands of casualties, many of them civilians. Baghdad hoped that Iran's internal turmoil, international isolation, and army purge would give Iraq an easy victory and a claim to regional leadership. At the same time, Iraqi leaders worried that Ayatollah Khomeini's revolution might undermine Iraq's relatively secular and Sunni-dominated regime.

The war has passed through four phases. First came a seemingly triumphant Iraqi offensive that captured most of Iran's oil-rich Khuzistan province. In mid-1981, however, Iran rallied to push back Iraqi forces. The Iranian army crossed into Iraq in July 1982 and launched a series of failed "final offensives." Then Iraq struck back in a "war of the tankers" beginning in late 1983 with air attacks against ships carrying Iranian trade and oil exports. The military deadlock led each side to try to destroy its enemy's economy in a war of attrition.

By late 1982 Iraq was eager to settle the war, but Ayatollah Khomeini demanded the overthrow of Saddam Hussein's government. Successful Iranian attacks in the southern region around Fao and Basra between 1985 and 1987 raised the prospects of an Iranian victory. This caused many countries to reassess their interests in the war and transformed the conflict from a stalemate into a dangerously unpredictable focus of world tension. On an ideological level, Baghdad counterposed Arab nationalism and anti-Iranian sentiments to Iran's Islamic fundamentalism. Saudi Arabia and Kuwait helped Iraq with huge loans while Syria sided with Iran.

Stephen Grummon, *The Iran-Iraq War* (1982). Shirin Tahir-Kheli, *The Iran-Iraq War: Old Conflicts, New Weapons* (1983). Sepehr Zabih, *Iran since the Revolution* (1983).          BARRY RUBIN

**IRRIGATION.** Neither unique to nor universal in Asia, irrigation typifies Asian agriculture. Monsoons deliver large quantities of rain in a few months; great rivers—the Indus, Ganges, Brahmaputra, Irrawaddy, Mekong, Yangtze, and Huang He—threaten flood; and droughts promise famine. Under a controlled water flow, rice thrives and most crops yield more.

To control water by lifting, diverting, diking, storing, and channeling has thus preoccupied Asia for millennia. Throughout this time, water control has challenged technical ingenuity and social institutions. Hydraulic control requires intense labor and reliable social arrangements to put people to work when and where needed. Social institutions must also resolve conflicts among the various people whose coordinated effort irrigates the land, lest conflict jeopardize the harvest. Physical control over water entails social control over labor and rivalry.

Logically, then, state authorities have played key roles in irrigation development from the beginning, as irrigated agriculture invigorated states. Although the earliest massive state-sponsored irrigation work may be the Peony Dam, built in the late sixth century BCE on the Huai River in China, momentous state sponsorship began in China around 200 BCE, when the density of waterworks defined China's key northern economic area. By this time, irrigation builders had also turned rivers in the Ganges River valley to rice cultivation; the *Arthashastra* indicates that by Maurya times (c. third to second century BCE) rulers assumed responsibility to provide for irrigation in India. State investment in irrigation—commanding land and labor to reap taxes in return—enhanced state material and moral power and also boosted land productivity; it helped to fulfill a ruler's mandate to protect and promote prosperity.

That mandate has inspired state sponsors of irrigation for more than two millennia. After 500 CE the number of such works expanded tremendously, and authoritative personnel, performing labor control and other necessary functions, diversified as irrigation methods were adapted to various Asian physical and cultural milieus. At about the same time, China's key economic area shifted south, into and beyond the Yangtze River basin. Water work shifted accordingly; for example, grain tribute gave priority to the construction of the Grand Canal, built from the sixth to the fourteenth century.

South India and Sri Lanka also saw widespread state-sponsored irrigation in this period. The Grand Anicut, on the Kaveri River in present-day Thanjavur District of Tamil Nadu, became one of the world's largest dams; nearby, another dam built by the Cholas produced what remained for centuries the world's largest reservoir. Sri Lanka carried out the most intricate irrigation construction of all, to divert, dam, store, channel, and distribute mountain water from the central highlands, training it along imperceptibly sloping land for many miles to nourish paddy fields in the semiarid north. This project was the crowning achievement of preindustrial irrigation engineering.

As irrigation moved into new settings, its adaptors carved the Asian landscape into motifs that became as much a part of everyday life as nature itself. Long canals from great navigable rivers characterize the plains of North China and North India. By contrast, on hillsides in central and South China, and in India's river basins as well as on the gently sloping semiarid plains of the Indian peninsula and Sri Lanka, countless dams, channels, and reservoirs store precious water from relatively short rivers. On rain-drenched slopes in Japan, China's Sichuan Province, Southeast Asia, and western India, terraced fields themselves constitute countless tiny reservoirs that regulate water flowing from mountain streams. In the central Yangtze River basin dikes hold back river and lake water and let irrigation in through sluice gates, making farmland from lakes and swamps and creating islands of habitation and cultivation. Almost everywhere, wells water gardens and define patches of green in dry surroundings.

Vast stretches of orderly, intricately built irrigation systems suggest central planning. Yet even huge state projects depended in the long view of Asian history on local initiative by lineages, warrior chiefs, villages, and religious institutions. State sponsorship improved the environment for local construction, but religious institutions as often led the way. Buddhist monasteries in Sri Lanka, Hindu temples in South India, and Sufi mystics in Bengal organized labor and capital to push irrigation into frontiers. Religious institutions are still responsible for irrigation in some parts of Asia today, notably in Bali. Everywhere, villagers themselves provided most of the labor and served most institutional functions in irrigation building, repair, and operation. Vast irrigated landscapes came into being bit by bit, essentially the product of local needs, political power, labor, and technical ingenuity.

After 1200, following more than a millennium of continuous expansion, irrigated agriculture began to encounter technological and social obstacles to further development. In Sri Lanka, a man-made malarial environment forced Sinhalese civilization out of its heartland. In India and China, Inner Asian warriors disrupted states that had supported irrigation, although the Vijayanagar empire and the Yuan dynasty sponsored work in South India and southwest China, respectively. When, the political climate having improved, broad-based irrigation expansion began again in China, nature produced new crises. Frantic dike building on the Yangtze during the seventeenth century constricted drainage routes to such an extent that the river broke through, and floods decimated the population. Another growth cycle began under the Qing (1644–1912), when official dikes on the Yangtze attracted private builders in abundance; but again under stress by the late eighteenth and early nineteenth centuries, the Yangtze, like the Huang He, flooded China and aggravated Qing instability. The Qing state was able to do progressively less to solve irrigation problems.

It was the eighteenth century that brought early modern India its most severe political instability, as wars ripped through centers of irrigated agriculture. The nineteenth century brought peace; a powerful empire under British control; massive new state construction, particularly on the Indus and in the western Gangetic Plain; and widespread private investment, particularly in major river valleys. Evidence suggests that by the end of the nineteenth century the limits of these activities had been reached. Although salinization did not plague the Indus River valley until after 1900, it posed a problem for considerable parts of the Gangetic Plain. In Bengal, drainage blocked by roads and railways produced malaria, waterlogging, and floods. In old irrigated areas where social distress became more and more disruptive, particularly in Bengal, output did not increase to match population after 1900. The colonial system, for all its achievements, left critical problems unattended: small-scale irrigation—the many little reservoirs, dams, diversion, and drainage works that provided for much of India's cultivation—languished and often decayed because economic and political incentives did not attract investors public or private.

In the twentieth century rapidly expanding populations and rising human expectations have had to confront limitations in the number of waterways available for irrigation works. No vast frontiers like the Irrawaddy delta and the lower Punjab, opened up in the last century, remain for irrigation expansion. There is more water to tap for cultivation, much of it underground, but as with dikes on the Yangtze there are limits to healthy depletion of the water table. For millennia irrigated agriculture has expanded by putting more water and more human labor to work on more land to produce more per acre. Now the challenge that faces irrigators is to produce more output per drop of water and per worker.

Two styles of social response to this problem stand out, the first political, the second technological. Since 1950, national governments have followed the example set by Japan in assuming a strong, activist role in agricultural development. In Sri Lanka, a national scheme has revitalized and expanded the classic irrigation base, creating a new frontier for colonization. Similarly, India, China, and Southeast Asian nations have central bureaus to coordinate state irrigation efforts and to channel foreign and domestic capital into water control projects. Water is thus politically charged, nowhere more so than in South Asia, where interstate or international disputes center on every major river system. In China and elsewhere the extent of central, regional, and local control over irrigation development and water also provokes controversy.

More technical breakthroughs have occurred in the last thirty years than in all of the previous millennium. High-yield seed varieties, motorized pumps, lined and redesigned channels, pesticides, and fertilizers promise to make water more productive, with what eventual environmental consequences it is too early to tell. Since the 1960s, when government efforts began to shift toward providing incentives and infrastructure so that farmers might realize the promise of the Green Revolution, technological change has put farmers themselves at center stage in irrigation development.

Human welfare in Asia still depends on reaping the benefits and preventing the destruction water can bring. Irrigation remains as critical today as in ancient times in efforts to increase food supply, agricultural employment, rural incomes, and living standards.

[See also Agriculture and Economic Development.]

Ester Boserup, *Population and Technological Change: A Study of Long-Term Trends* (1981). Ch'ao-ting Chi, *Key Economic Areas in Chinese History As Revealed in the Development of Public Works for Water Control* (1936). E. Walter Coward, ed., *Irrigation and Agricultural Development in Asia: Perspectives from the Social Sciences* (1980). Mark Elvin, *The Pattern of the Chinese Past* (1973). Clifford Geertz, *Agricultural Involution: The Process of Ecological Change in Indonesia* (1963). Dharma Kumar, ed., *The Cambridge Economic History of India*, vol. 2 (1983). Joseph Needham, *Science and Civilisation in China*, vol. 4, part 3 (1971).          DAVID LUDDEN

IRWIN, BARON. *See* Wood, Edward Frederick Lindley.

ISAACS, RUFUS (marquis of Reading; 1860–1935), viceroy of India between 1921 and 1926. After a successful legal career, he assumed office during Mohandas Gandhi's noncooperation campaign of 1920 to 1922. He responded cautiously, but eventually the Ali brothers, Motilal and Jawaharlal Nehru, and Gandhi all were jailed. Lord Reading's most notable attempt at reform, increasing the number of Indians in the Army and Civil Service, was rejected by the British home government and never instituted.

Denis Judd, *Lord Reading* (1982).          JAMES A. JAFFE

ISE, collective designation for a group of Shinto shrines located in the city of Ise, Mie Prefecture, Japan. The Ise complex comprises the Inner Shrine, enshrining the sun goddess Amaterasu Ōmikami, the Outer Shrine, enshrining Toyouke Ōkami, and associated smaller shrines. *Ise* is used to refer to all of them collectively and to the land on which they are situated. From ancient times the area has been deemed a sacred place; it is the seat of the ancestral deities of the imperial house, a favorite pilgrimage destination, and, in modern times under State Shinto, the shrine of the entire Japanese nation.

The Outer Shrine's origins lie in prehistory, while the Inner Shrine is thought to date from the late fifth to the mid-sixth century. Under the *ritsuryō* code no one but members of the imperial family could worship there, and Ise became the center of imperial rites. Of these, the Niiname-sai (a first-fruits festival) and the Daijō-sai (an enthronement ceremony) were the most important in an elaborate ritual calendar, one delineated in the *Engishiki* (927). Both rites take the form of an offering by the emperor of pure food to the deities and consumption by him of a ceremonial meal that the deities are believed to share.

The Inner and Outer shrines are constructed of pure materials in an ancient style of architecture showing influence from Oceania. According to a tradition originating with Emperor Temmu (r. 673–686), the shrines are rebuilt every twenty years, though in fact the custom fell into desuetude in the Middle Ages and was later revived by the Meiji emperor (see figure 1).

Court Shinto ceremonies and the Ise priesthood were formalized during the ninth century. After the introduction of Buddhism (mid-sixth century), however, the cult of the *kami* (the Shinto gods) was pervasively subordinated to Buddhism, a trend not entirely ignored even at Ise. Ise priests took for granted the existence of Buddhas, and numerous Buddhist temples were built at Ise in spite of prohibitions; these numbered about three hundred by the mid-nineteenth century.

It was at Ise that Shinto doctrines were first systematically expounded, by the school known as Watarai, Ise, or Outer Shrine Shinto. This school was founded by the Watarai line of priests of the Outer Shrine. Using the conceptual scaffolding provided by Confucian and Buddhist thought, Watarai Ieyuki (1256–1362) and Watarai Tsunemasa (1263–1339) proclaimed that Toyouke Ōkami (the deity of the Outer Shrine) was the one god of the universe, beneath whom all other *kami* could be ranked and of whom Buddhist divinities were but pale, phenomenal manifestations. This idea was presented in Ieyuki's *Ruijū jingihongen*, and the school used as its sacred scripture the Five Books (*Shintō gobusho*), relating the history and traditions of the Ise Shrines, which were composed in the early or mid-Kamakura period (1185–1333). The doctrinal formulations of this school provided the intellectual basis for such later developments as Yoshida and Suika Shinto. Beginning in the late fourteenth century, priests of the Outer Shrine spread Ise Shinto through the country, laying the groundwork for later popular devotion to Ise.

In spite of a prohibition on commoners worshiping at Ise, the Outer Shrine accepted private donations, and shrine traditions became known in Mino and Owari provinces, where shrine lands were numerous. A thirteenth-century diary reveals that a commoner donated decorative copies of the Buddhist *Heart Sutra* and had the *Ninnokyō* (*Sutra of the Benevolent Kings*) recited at Ise as a form of donation. Shamans (*miko*) from Kumano delivered oracles at Ise, entering a state of spirit possession through sacred dance, as did nuns from Kumano (*Kumano bikuni*), who remained in residence at Ise

FIGURE 1. *Ise Shrine*. Rice warehouse within shrine compound, freshly rebuilt.

until the mid-nineteenth century. Many Buddhist priests, including Ippen, founder of the Ji (Time) school, went to Ise to copy and recite sutras and to perform austerities, believing Ise to be the central shrine of the nation. These examples show that the nominal prohibition of Buddhist observances at Ise was ignored in practice, and that for much of Japanese religious history, Ise, like so many other temples and shrines, has been a place for the worship of both Shinto and Buddhist divinities, most people making no hard and fast distinction between the two religions.

Relations between Inner and Outer shrines were not always harmonious. In 1486 a quarrel between the two was settled only when the provincial governor burned the town where the Outer Shrine was located. A suicide in the wake of this event provoked the notion that the shrines had become polluted and that as a result the imperial regalia had magically taken flight to Kyoto, the seat of the Yoshida priestly line. This idea was an early instance of the belief in boons from Ise falling from the sky in a variety of forms, especially protective talismans, an idea lasting until the beginning of the Meiji period (1868–1912).

Commoner pilgrimage to Ise developed to mass

proportions in the Tokugawa period (1600–1868). Tokugawa pilgrims believed Amaterasu to be a deity of abundance and fertility and went to Ise seeking health and prosperity. The popular conception of the shrines changed in the Meiji period, however, the emphasis shifting to Ise as the ancestral and protective shrine of the imperial house and therefore the place where all imperial subjects should worship. The notion that this-worldly benefits could be gained there declined in favor of the idea that paying tribute at Ise is an expression of patriotic sentiment. This perception of Ise is still alive, as seen in the regular and well-publicized visits of conservative politicians to the shrines as a means of securing the sympathies of those voters who look nostalgically upon the conservative, not to say reactionary, mores of prewar Japan.

[*See also* Shinto *and* Ise Mairi.]

HELEN HARDACRE

ISE MAIRI, pilgrimage to the Ise Shrine in Japan. With the development of currency and transportation routes between the fourteenth and sixteenth century, pilgrimage to temples and shrines began to flourish. Of the various routes, *Ise mairi* attracted the greatest movement of people in the entire Tokugawa period (1600–1868), culminating in mass pilgrimages called *ee ja nai ka*.

Village confraternities organized for pilgrimage were formed by an order of irregular Ise (Shinto) priests called *oshi*. Powerful *oshi* bought and sold rights to confraternities, some controlling as many as four to ten thousand households. By the end of the Tokugawa period, hardly a village in the country (except for the northeast) lacked an Ise confraternity, and some villages had several.

*Oshi* traveled once or twice a year to their confraternities, distributing almanacs, protective talismans, and purifying wands in return for "first fruits"—cash contributions assessed in proportion to the rice tax. On these rounds *oshi* stopped at inns called *Iseya*, conducting lectures on Ise traditions as well as prayers and purification rites. As far as the peasantry was concerned, the principal interest of the pilgrimage itself was to secure boons, such as a good harvest, prosperity, and well-being. When confraternities traveled to Ise, they stayed at their *oshi's* inns, of which there were about eight hundred by the period's end. The *oshi* delivered prayers to the deities on behalf of the members and provided such entertainment as *kagura* (sacred dance) and an escort to plays and other secular amusements available nearby.

A popular belief held that everyone should make the Ise pilgrimage at least once, and confraternities were frequently led by Buddhist priests. Strictly speaking neither a Buddhist nor a Shinto observance, *Ise mairi* was in many areas so much a part of village life that a young person could be regarded as adult only after making the pilgrimage..

The *oshi's* almanacs were influential in spreading knowledge of the sixty-year cycles at which mass "thanks pilgrimages," *okage mairi*, to Ise were expected to occur. Even in ordinary years pilgrims averaged 400,000 annually; there were many more in *okage mairi* years. In 1705 there were 3,469,000 *okage mairi* pilgrims, 2 million in 1771, and between 4 and 5 million in 1830.

The last great *Ise mairi* occurred as part of the *ee ja nai ka*, "anything goes" pilgrimages, to a number of temples and shrines in 1867 and 1868. Rumors of talismans falling from the sky sparked three-day outbreaks of singing and dancing along the pilgrimage routes, with participants often only partially dressed or in transvestite attire. While this mass hysteria was easily manipulated by a variety of political interests, it was too volatile to be controlled. Its inspiration was repeatedly refueled by revelations proclaiming the advent of the Ise deities to deliver the people.

[*See also* Ise.]

HELEN HARDACRE

ISFAHAN (earlier Aspahan/Sepahan, from Old Persian *aspa dana,* "horse-producing region") was a province of Media, lying to the east of the Zagros Mountains and watered by the Zayanda Rud. The region retained its importance down to the Arab conquest in the middle of the sixth century, and its center, the city of Isfahan, became the main city of the province of Jibal. It had also been a major Jewish center since the third century CE, but it was predominantly Muslim by the tenth century.

Various dynasties, especially the Seljuks, used Isfahan as their provincial capital, providing it with architectural monuments such as the Jurjir Mosque (tenth century), the magnificently domed Friday Mosque (eleventh to fourteenth century), and the Darb-i Imam (fourteenth century). Unlike many Persian cities, Isfahan escaped Mongol destruction, but it was sacked and its population massacred by Timur in 1388. Two hundred years later it became a major city of the Safavid empire.

In 1598 Isfahan was chosen as the capital of Iran by Shah Abbas I. Under his rule, the city was embellished with grandiose religious and royal monuments, parks, a wide and attractive avenue with four rows of trees (Chahar Bagh), and ceremonial squares. It gained world fame as a center of art, producing textiles, metalwork, polychrome tiles, mosaic works, and miniature paintings. The city was especially well known for the seventeenth-century Isfahan school of painting, led by Reza Abbasi and characterized by portraiture and naturalistic subjects, and for its large silk and wool floral "Isfahan carpets." On account of its political, artistic, and social importance, Isfahan was nicknamed "Nisf-i Jahan" ("half of the world"), a term still fondly used whenever the city's qualifications are mentioned. By the end of the Safavid period, the city had a population of 600,000, which included many Zoroastrians, Jews, and Christians, and a number of Europeans. Of particular importance were a group of Christian exiles from the Georgian town of Julfa, who founded the village of New Julfa next to the capital. The most celebrated Safavid monuments were clustered around the Maidan-i Shah ("royal

square"), an open area 500 by 155 yards, used for polo and archery as well as for state occasions: the Masjid-i Shah ("royal mosque"), the Masjid-i Shaikh Lutfullah, and the Ali Qapu ("royal gate").

Isfahan was sacked and the Isfahanis were massacred by the Afghan conquerors in 1722, and its revival as a chief Iranian city and center of art came only in the twentieth century, when it was provided with a university, a steel mill, and an airport, as well as with a textile industry. In 1966 its population was 425,000, but it rose to 520,000 in 1972 and had reached over 1,000,000 in the mid-1980s; this unplanned growth has brought social and demographical problems along with it. Always noted for their religious conservatism, the Isfahanis played an important role in the establishment of the Islamic Republic in Iran in the late 1970s.

[*See also* Abbas I; Carpets; Painting: Iranian and Central Asian Painting; *and* Safavid Dynasty.]

Oleg Grabar, "Isfahan as a Mirror of Persian Architecture," in *Highlights of Persian Art*, edited by Richard Ettinghausen and Ehsan Yarshater (1979), pp. 213–241. R. Hillenbrand, "Safavid Architecture," in *Cambridge History of Iran*, vol. 6, *The Timurid and Safavid Periods*, edited by Peter Jackson and Laurence Lockhart (1986), pp. 776–812. Roger Savory, *Iran under the Safavids* (1980), pp. 154–176.          A. SHAHPUR SHAHBAZI

**ISHANAPURA,** capital city and kingdom of Ishanavarman I, early seventh-century ruler of the Khmer state known to the Chinese as Zhenla. The previous two rulers, Bhavavarman and Mahendravarman (Chitrasena), had extended the power of Zhenla up and down the Mekong River. Ishanavarman's first capital was on the Mekong, but he moved it to a city that he then named after himself. The site, on the Stung Sen River northwest of the Great Lake, at Sambor Prei Kuk, had been controlled earlier by kings of Aninditapura. Chinese authors, including Xuanzang and Ma Duanlin, mention the city. Ishanapura is represented by some impressive ruined monuments and is one of the biggest complexes of stone buildings anywhere in Southeast Asia.

Lawrence P. Briggs, *The Ancient Khmer Empire* (1951). G. Coedès, *The Indianized States of Southeast Asia*, translated by Susan B. Cowing (1968).          IAN W. MABBETT

**ISHIDA BAIGAN** (1685–1744), Japanese moral thinker. Ishida Baigan was born the second son of a petty peasant-landlord in present-day Kyoto Prefecture. At the age of eleven he was apprenticed to

FIGURE 1. *The Shah Mosque, Isfahan.* The mosque forms one side of Shah Abbas's royal square, which also includes the Safavid palace and the entrance to the bazaar.

a merchant family in the city of Kyoto. However, this family encountered financial difficulties five years later, and Baigan returned to his home village. After experiencing city life during the culturally rich, extravagant Genroku era (1688–1704), he was forced to work on the family farm under the supervision of a stern father for eight years. In 1707, at the age of twenty-three, he again apprenticed himself to a Kyoto merchant house, but not primarily to become a merchant: the study and propagation of ethical teachings was his main motive. He would remain at this establishment, a textiles shop, for twenty years, until 1727. From 1729, he taught and lectured trimonthly at his own residence, attracting forty to fifty serious disciples. Some of them would spread his ideas (known as "the teaching of the heart") to sixty-nine cities and towns in sixty-five daimyo domains spread over twenty-eight provinces by the beginning of the nineteenth century. Baigan wrote two main works: *Dialogues on City and Country* in 1738 and *On Ordering the Family* in 1744. Both were written in simple, colloquial Japanese.

Baigan's ideas center on the ethics and social role of the merchant class. According to Confucian doctrine, society should esteem peasants for being primary producers and honor warrior-rulers for exemplifying righteousness in disregard of personal profit. By contrast, merchants warranted no respect because they made their living by garnering profit, supposedly without regard to virtue. Since the Tokugawa social system was based on hereditary status, merchants were treated—and thought of themselves—as socially and morally inferior beings. Baigan asserted that merchants were not intrinsically inferior to warriors in morality because they performed an equally important social function: "bringing repose to people's hearts" by supplying and distributing for consumption articles needed in daily life. The merchant's acquiring profit was similar to the warrior's receiving rice stipends—neither act was parasitic or demeaning. Merchants, according to Baigan, earned society's contempt only to the extent that they did business unscrupulously. He sought to instill in them the virtues of honesty, thrift, diligence, charity, and the prompt return of borrowed money or goods, so that they would contribute to the welfare of society and exemplify a virtue equal to that of the warriors.

Baigan's disciples propagated his teachings throughout the nation and at all levels of society. After his death, "learning of the heart" ceased to be a Kyoto-based doctrine appealing mainly to the merchant class; it won adherents among peasants and warriors as well. Baigan, then, helped establish a value system for a mercantile economy in Tokugawa Japan, thus facilitating the implementation of capitalism during the Meiji period.

[*See also* Tokugawa Period *and* Genroku Culture.]

Robert N. Bellah, *Tokugawa Religion* (1957).

BOB TADASHI WAKABAYASHI

**ISKANDAR MUDA** (c. 1581–1636), sultan of Aceh (1607–1636). Iskandar began to advance his interests with the coming of the anti-Portuguese English and Dutch about 1600. About 1615 the English temporarily replaced the Gujaratis as importers of Surat cloth. When new Europeans, including the French and the Danes, increased the demand for pepper, the sultan brought the pepper ports under control and tried to centralize all foreign trade at the capital. He set up a licensing system that kept the Europeans divided and allowed him to reap the benefit of foreign competition. Apart from the harbor dues the king had a large income from personal trading.

Aceh reached the pinnacle of glory under Iskandar Muda. Using resources from trade and taxation he built the kingdom into a strong centralized state, governed by an elaborate bureaucracy. He had a monopoly of firearms, and his armed forces were strong enough to curb the nobility (Orang Kaya) and keep the Europeans at bay. With his powerful fleet Iskandar Muda scoured the Melaka (Malacca) Strait, bearing down several times upon Johor (1613, 1623) and Portuguese Melaka (1614, 1629). Although he failed to destroy his enemies, he succeeded in making Aceh the strongest Malay power in western Indonesia. The Acehnese empire reached Aru in the east and Padang in the west—a stretch of 1,100 miles without much hinterland. It included Pahang, Kedah, and Perak in Malaya and the island of Nias off Sumatra's west coast.

Iskandar Muda has been harshly judged by European observers, who invariably point to the streak of cruelty in his nature. But even they admit that the king had a commanding personality and was a man of judgment. The Malay chronicles look upon Iskandar Muda as the greatest king of Aceh and one who kept a grand court. He is remembered as a lawgiver and a patron of learning who bestowed favor upon such unorthodox Malay authors as Hamzah Fansuri and Syamsuddin of Pasai. In 1629 his grand expedition against Portuguese Melaka ended in a disaster and virtually wiped out his navy. Iskandar Muda died with his foreign aims unaccomplished.

[*See also* Aceh *and* Pepper.]

Teuku Iskandar, "A Document Concerning the Birth of Iskandar Muda," *Archipel* 20 (1980). Anthony Reid, "Trade and the Problem of Royal Power in Aceh: Three Stages: c. 1550–1700," in *Precolonial State Systems in Southeast Asia: The Malay Peninsula, Sumatra, Bali-Lombok, South Celebes* (1975).       ARUN DASGUPTA

**ISLAM,** the religion of the Muslims, founded on the Qur'anic revelations transmitted through the prophet Muhammad (570–632). The Arabic root *slm* conveys the ideas of safety, obedience, submission, commitment, and dedication. The word *islam* signifies the self-surrender that characterizes a Muslim's relationship with God.

*Revelation in Islam.* Islamic tradition records that in 610 Muhammad began to receive revelations from God through the mediation of the angel Gabriel. During Muhammad's lifetime the various revelations were preserved in the memories of his followers, although some few were written down. All the revelations, however, were collected in the Qur'an (i.e., "recitation") within twenty years of the Prophet's death. Muslims assert unequivocally the divine authorship of the Qur'an; Muhammad is but the instrument through which it was revealed.

Islam, as the youngest of the great religious traditions of the West, is best understood in relationship to the two great traditions that preceded it, Judaism and Christianity. The Qur'an, which is understood to be God's actual word and his final revelation, does not abrogate the scriptures of the Christians and the Jews. Instead it is the corrective by which these earlier texts are to be judged, for the Christians and Jews have distorted their books.

The Qur'an text itself is significantly different in form from either the Hebrew Bible or the New Testament. The 114 chapters, or *suras,* are organized in neither thematic nor chronological order. In general, the longer *suras* are first and the shorter *suras* last. All the *suras* but one begin with the invocation "In the Name of God, the Compassionate, the Merciful."

Eschatological concerns with death, judgment, heaven, and hell are Qur'anic themes familiar from previous experiences of prophetic revelation. The Qur'an affirms a radical monotheism; God is com-

pletely transcendent and all-powerful, and he sustains creation at every instant. No image of God is possible, nor does he beget other divinities. There are, however, innumerable spiritual powers in the universe: angels, devils, *jinnis,* and lesser spirits.

God revealed his will in the past to the Jews and Christians, but, the Qur'an attests, they have failed their covenant with God. It is now the duty of the Muslim community to create a society that will embody God's will for his people. The Qur'an, however, is not primarily a practical guide or legal text. It provides the general ideals for individual and community practice, even though sections of the Qur'an text do in fact deal with specific legal matters (e.g., divorce, inheritance, etc.).

Even though the Qur'an recalls many themes from Judaism and Christianity, it places its unique stamp on the familiar. The role of prophet *(nabi),* for example, undergoes reinterpretation in Islam, where he is superseded by the apostle-messenger *(rasul).*

The title *prophet* is accorded to many more individuals in the Qur'an than in the Hebrew Bible or New Testament (e.g., Abraham, Noah, Zachariah, and John the Baptist). On the other hand, the title *rasul,* or messenger, is far more restricted. The majority view among Muslims is that a *rasul* is sent by God with a revelation in book form to a community. His role is both religious and social. In general, therefore, every *rasul* is a prophet, but not every prophet is a *rasul.* The later Muslim tradition adds that, whereas the prophet might fail and be killed, the mission of a *rasul* is guaranteed success by God. Both *nabis* and *rasuls* are free from grave sin; thus God's word is protected from human corruption.

*Hadith (Tradition) and Shari'a (Islamic Law).* Theoretically, the Qur'an is the primary source of guidance in the Islamic community *(umma).* The Qur'an text does not, however, provide solutions for every specific problem that might arise. To determine norms of practice, Muslims turned to the lives of Muhammad and his early companions, preserved in the *sunna,* the living tradition of the community.

Originally the *sunna* varied from place to place, reflecting the pre-Islamic local customs of a particular region. By the ninth century, however, the diversity evident in local traditions was branded a corrupting innovation *(bid'a).* Efforts therefore were made to collect, record in writing, and authenticate traditions ascribed to the Prophet and his early companions. These written compendia of *hadith* (traditions) codified the *sunna* and eliminated any further need for reliance on divergent local sources. The two most important collections of *hadith* are those of al-Bukhari (d. 870) and Muslim (d. 875).

Within the Muslim community the *hadith* are considered by most to be historical fact. It is on this issue that non-Muslim scholars diverge from traditional Islam. While some *hadith* have a core of historical fact, many seem to be later creations. Often they reflect the community's attempts to solve practical and theoretical problems. By linking these later solutions to the Prophet, the composers of new *hadith* ensured them permanent validity. [*See also* Hadith.]

A development parallel to the collection and codification of *hadith* was the articulation of the *shari'a*, Islamic law. In the same way that the codification of *hadith* was an attempt to create uniformity in the *sunna*, the development of religious law is characterized by an ever-increasing effort to eliminate diversity in legal theory and practice. [*See also* Shari'a.]

The earliest Islamic judges (*qadis*) relied on the general ethical principles of the Qur'an, the local practice of the particular region and personal discretion to determine their legal opinions. During the eighth and ninth centuries more and more reliance was placed on written, authoritative *hadith,* thus reducing the need for personal discretion and providing a more universal basis for the development of law.

This process culminated in the work of Shafi'i (d. 820) who insisted that only *hadith* going back to the prophet Muhammad were worthy bases for law. Secondarily analogical and systematic reasoning could be used; however, nothing must be allowed to override the authority of a tradition from the Prophet.

During this same period four principles emerged as the bases (*usul*) of Islamic law: the Qur'an, *hadith* ascribed to the prophet Muhammad, the consensus of the community of legal scholars (*ijma*), and analogical reasoning (*qiyas*). Without doubt, the first two principles predominated, with *hadith* the major influence.

Four schools of law have survived the classical period. They differ in detail, not substance. The Hanafi school (named after Abu Hanifa, d. 767) has numerous adherents in Iraq, Syria, Central Asia, and the Indian subcontinent. Moreover, Hanafi law was the official school of the Ottoman empire. The Maliki school (named after Malik, d. 774) is prominent in North and West Africa as well as in parts of Arabia. The Shafi'i school prevails in parts of Egypt,

Arabia, and East Africa, and especially in Indonesia, Malaysia, and other parts of Southeast Asia. Finally, the Hanbali school (named after Ibn Hanbal, d. 855) is currently best known as the legal school of the Wahhabis in Saudi Arabia.

***The Five Pillars of Islam.*** In addition to the all-encompassing *shari'a* there are five pillars that support the structure of the Islamic community. The first is *shahada,* or the confession of faith: "There is no god but God, and Muhammad is the messenger of God." To embrace radical monotheism and Muhammad as seal of the prophets is to enter fully into the community of truth. The remaining four pillars are involved not with dogma but with praxis: the way one leads the Muslim life.

*Salat,* prayer five times a day, constitutes the second pillar and envelops all human time in the mantle of Islam: daybreak, noon, mid-afternoon, sunset, and evening. *Salat* must be performed in a state of ritual purity. Despite the fact that the prescribed ablutions entail the washing of the hands, mouth, teeth, nostrils, arms, head, ears, and feet, they should not be confused with personal hygiene. The object of these actions is to pass from a state of ritual impurity caused by bodily evacuations, sleep, and sexual contact to a state of ritual purity. [*See also* Salat.]

While some Muslims perform their prayers in the mosque, this is not required. The only prayer service that all are urged to attend is the Friday noon prayer. The occasion is solemnized further by a sermon (*khutba*).

The third pillar of Islam, *zakat* (almsgiving), is a practical sign of Islam's commitment to human equality. Ideally, neither social custom nor economics should create distinctions among the faithful. Islamic law requires that one tender a percentage of one's wealth and yearly production to the *umma* for the care of the needy, orphans, and for the support of clerics, the *ulama*. The amount ranges from 10 percent to much lower percentages, depending on the commodity taxed. [*See also* Zakat.]

Of the five pillars of Islam, the two most dramatically visible to the observer are the month-long fast of Ramadan and the Hajj, the pilgrimage to Mecca. During Ramadan Muslims fast from dawn to sunset, abstaining from all solids and liquids. While the days of Ramadan are spent in arduous fasting, the nights are set aside for family feasting, socializing, and acts of piety. The conclusion of Ramadan is the occasion for the most widely celebrated festival in the Islamic world, the Id al-Fitr, the festival of breaking the fast. The twenty-seventh day

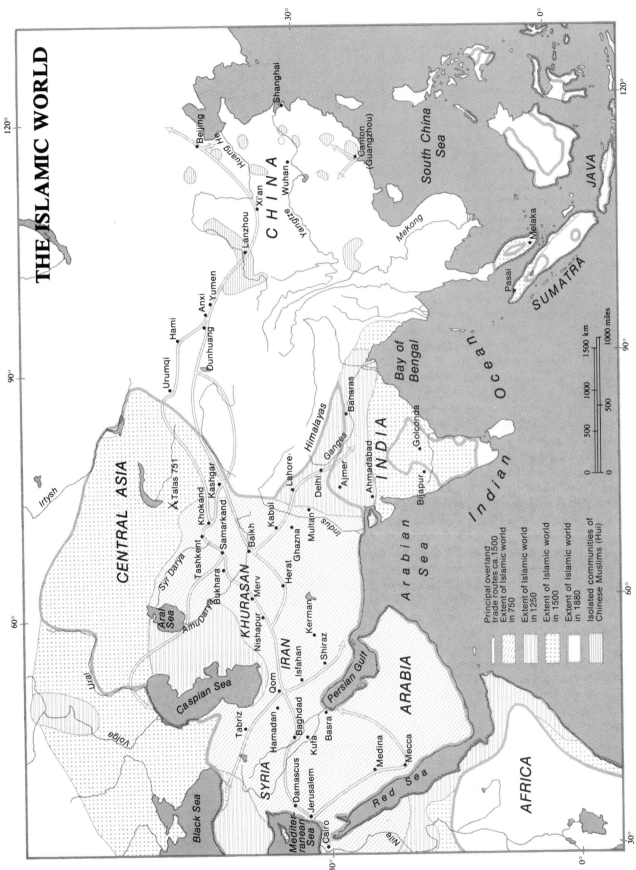

# THE ISLAMIC WORLD

Principal overland trade routes ca.1500
Extent of Islamic world in 750
Extent of Islamic world in 1250
Extent of Islamic world in 1500
Extent of Islamic world in 1880
Isolated communities of Chinese Muslims (Hui)

CENTRAL ASIA

CHINA

Beijing
Shanghai
Wuhan
Canton (Guangzhou)
Xi'an
Lanzhou
Yangtze
Huang He
Yumen
Anxi
Hami
Dunhuang
Urumqi
Mekong

South China Sea

JAVA

SUMATRA
Melaka
Pasai

Bay of Bengal

Indian Ocean

Banaras
Ganges
Himalayas
Lahore
Delhi
Ajmer
Ahmadabad
INDIA
Golconda
Bijapur

Arabian Sea

X Talas 751
Kashgar
Khokand
Tashkent
Samarkand
Syr Darya
Bukhara
Amu Darya
Aral Sea
KHURASAN
Balkh
Kabul
Ghazna
Herat
Merv
Multan
Indus
Nishapur
IRAN
Kerman
Shiraz
Isfahan
Qom
Caspian Sea
Hamadan
Tabriz
Volga
Ural
Baghdad
Kufa
Basra
Persian Gulf
ARABIA
Damascus
Jerusalem
SYRIA
Cairo
Mediterranean Sea
Black Sea
Irtysh
Medina
Mecca
Red Sea
Nile
AFRICA

1000 miles
1500 km    1000    500    0
500    0

of Ramadan, known as the Lailat al-Qadr (Night of Power) commemorates the beginning of God's revelations to Muhammad. [*See also* Ramadan *and* Id Fitr.]

The fifth pillar of Islam, the Hajj, the pilgrimage to Mecca, is unique among sacred journeys because every Muslim man or woman is duty bound to perform the rites of the Hajj once in a lifetime. If the journey is either physically impossible or an undue financial strain on the family, one is excused.

The religious obligation of the Hajj must be fulfilled during the first ten days of the month Dhu al-Hijja; the eighth, ninth, and tenth are the most critical days. The tenth of Dhu al-Hijja is the occasion for the most solemn of Islamic festivals, the Id al-Adha, the festival of sacrifice, also known as the Id Qorban. A blood sacrifice is offered of sheep, goats, cattle, or camels. The flesh of the sacrifice is intended for distribution to the poor. [*See also* Pilgrimage *and* Id Qorban.]

While not officially numbered among the pillars of Islam, the concept of *jihad,* sometimes translated "holy war," is fundamental to the structure of the Islamic community. *Jihad* functions on two levels: first, as a principle of personal renewal, second as a means of defending the community. The primary *jihad* is the battle one fights with one's own evil tendencies. In addition, *jihad* is related closely to the social dualism at the heart of Islam. The world is divided into two realms: the *dar al-Islam* and the *dar al-harb,* the part of the world that has been islamized and the part that remains untouched by the transforming power of the revelation. Consequently, a major impetus within Islam is to extend the range of the *dar al-Islam* and protect it from incursions from the *dar al-harb.* Whenever the *dar al-islam* is threatened, it is incumbent on Muslims to rally to its defense, to engage in *jihad.* [*See also* Jihad.]

**Shi'ism.** The Islamic community is an amalgam of cultures, ethnic groups, and political perspectives. Diversity is evident as well in the fundamentally different approaches to religious authority taken by the two major sectarian groups in Islam, the Sunnis and the Shi'ites.

After the death of the Prophet in 632, a member of his inner circle was chosen to lead the community. True religious authority, however, did not reside in the caliph (*khalifa*), but in the Qur'anic revelations and the remembered words and actions of the Prophet, later collected and codified in the *hadith.* The caliph was intended to be the custodian of the temporal affairs of the community. The power of interpretation in religious matters was exercised by those community members trained in the religious sciences. Those Muslims who espoused this vision of religious and political authority became known as Sunnis, or followers of the well-trodden path of tradition. [*See also* Sunni.]

A minority position affirmed that succession to Muhammad should be hereditary, because God had provided the Prophet and his family with unique powers of religious insight and political charisma. None of Muhammad's male children survived him. The aspirations of the hereditary faction were focused on Ali, Muhammad's first cousin and son-in-law, the husband of the Prophet's daughter Fatima. They became known as Shi'ites, or partisans (of Ali).

The hereditary heir to authority in Shi'ism is called the imam. The usual transmission of the office of imam is from father to son. Disputes as to the rightful successor to the imamate have led to further divisions within the Shi'ite community. By the end of the ninth century, the line of imams was broken by the disappearance of the incumbent. Shi'ite theology explains that the imam did not die but has gone into hiding (the technical term is *occultation*). Eventually the imam will return in physical form to restore the Islamic community to its rightful place as the embodiment of the ideals of the revelation. One group of Shi'ites, members of the Isma'ili sect, are unique in that they possess a living imam. [*See also* Shi'a; Imam; *and* Isma'ili.]

**Philosophical Theology (Kalam).** During the formative period of Islamic philosophical theology (eighth to tenth century), Muslim thinkers addressed questions related primarily to the radical monotheism at the heart of Islam. Perhaps the most critical dilemma was the apparent contradiction in the Qur'an between God's complete transcendence and anthropomorphic descriptions of him. The classical solution treads a middle path and affirms both sides of the paradox. God is totally transcendent, yet he does possess hands, a face, and other attributes, but in a way that we cannot understand.

Related to the question of God's transcendence and perfect unity is the tension in the Qur'an between his omnipotence and human freedom. How could human independence be affirmed without contravening the basic Qur'anic principle that no being is able to infringe upon God's all-pervasive power and control? The granting of such freedom to man is condemned as the cardinal sin of *shirk,* associating something or someone with God.

A group of creative thinkers known as Mu'tazilis, who were strongly influenced by Arabic translations of Greek philosophical texts, staunchly defended man's accountability for his actions and God's justice. To overemphasize God's omnipotence, insisted the Mu'tazilis, would reduce humans to automatons and attribute to God responsibility for all actions, good and evil. [See also Mu'tazili.]

Opponents of the Mu'tazilis accused them of shirk, for by stressing man's freedom they implied that he was an independent agent, able to determine his own fate. The question was not resolved by choosing one or the other extreme position—radical freedom or predestination. The classical synthesis, formulated by al-Ash'arī (d. 935) and his school, does, however, lean more toward predestination. Ash'ari defended God's absolute omnipotence and taught that all human actions are creations of God alone. He rejected secondary causality, for to ascribe independence to laws of nature would be tantamount to shirk. The sun rises and sets, therefore, not because of some internal law of the cosmos, but because God creates the event anew every day.

Ash'ari's solution to the problem of God's involvement in evil was to deny any intrinsic value in human actions. Something is good because God commands it, evil because he forbids it. Lying, for example, is evil only because God decided it would be so. One learns what is good and evil not through human reason, but by careful attention to God's will, made explicit in the Qur'an, hadith, and shari'a. In fact, human reason often leads people astray because it appears irrefutable in its logic. [See also Ash'ari.]

The conflict between reason and revelation was resolved creatively in the work of Abu Hamid al-Ghazali (d. 1111). Ghazali insisted that philosophical methodology was acceptable as long as it did not come into conflict with the truths of revelation. When conflict arose, the conclusions reached by human reason had to be corrected in the light of the irrefutable truth of God's word. Ghazali's magnum opus, the Ihya ulum al-din (The Revivification of the Religious Sciences), remains today one of the most influential works in kalam. [See also Ghazali, al-.]

Ghazali's integration of philosophy and revelation was not universally accepted. Two hundred years after his death Ibn Taimiyya (d. 1328) fiercely attacked Ghazali's view that the goal of all human actions is knowledge of God. This, he insists, is the error philosophers have always made. On the contrary, the true goal of human actions is knowledge of God's will and knowledge of the means to implement it, that is, the shari'a. While Ibn Taimiyya

did not have widespread influence during his own lifetime, his work had substantial impact on the development of various Islamic revival movements; the most notable is the eighteenth-century Wahhabi movement that has shaped present-day Saudi Arabia.

[See also Caliphate; Muhammad; Qur'an; and Sufism.]

The Encyclopaedia of Islam, edited by H. A. R. Gibb et al. (new ed., 1960–). S. D. Goitein, Studies in Islamic History and Institutions (1968). Ignácz Goldziher, Introduction to Islamic Theology and Law, translated by Andras and Ruth Hamori (1981). William Graham, Divine Word and Prophetic Word in Early Islam (1977). Fazlur Rahman, Islam (1979) and Major Themes in the Qur'an (1980). Joseph Schacht, An Introduction to Islamic Law (1964). William Montgomery Watt, The Formative Period of Islamic Thought (1973). PETER J. AWN

## ISLAMIZATION OF SOUTHEAST ASIA.

Islamization affected primarily the peoples of Malaysia, Indonesia, and the Philippines; it is nearly as obscure as the indianization process of several centuries before. The surviving evidence for islamization is small, sometimes contradictory, and often fails to answer important questions. Although several theories explaining islamization have been proposed, the fundamental inadequacy of the extant evidence has never been overcome. For example, we know that Muslims traveled throughout Southeast Asia long before we have evidence of the establishment of local Islamic states or the conversion of local peoples. One problem of all islamization theories is to explain this interval.

The contemporaneous evidence consists primarily of travelers' accounts and inscriptions (mainly gravestones). This material often reflects ignorance or misinformation on the part of foreign observers and, in the case of gravestones, leaves one uncertain whether the deceased was a foreign or indigenous Muslim since in either case an Arabic personal name would have been used. Nevertheless, there is sufficient coherence in the evidence to present a general picture of events. The most significant records are noted below.

The earliest record of the establishment of an Islamic state in Southeast Asia was provided by Marco Polo, who reported that the town of Perlak in North Sumatra, which he visited in 1292, was Islamic. The gravestone of the first Islamic ruler of the nearby town of Samudra, Sultan Malik al-Salih, has survived and is dated AH 696 (1297 CE). Thus, before the end of the thirteenth century the first recorded Islamic states of Southeast Asia had been founded in North Sumatra. When the Moroccan traveler Ibn Battuta (a Muslim himself) visited Samudra in 1345–1346, he found the ruler to be an adherent of the Shafi'i school of law, which consequently came to dominate all islamized areas of Southeast Asia. [See Shafi'i.]

A fragmentary inscription from Trengganu in northeast Malaysia documents the introduction of Islam there. Although it is an Islamic legal code, it employs many Sanskrit terms, suggesting that it was written during an early stage of islamization. Unfortunately the date at the end of the stone is incomplete; the possible readings range from AH 702 to AH 789 (1302 to 1387 CE), with the most probable date falling between 1302 and 1329 CE.

By this time Islam had reached the southern Philippines. A gravestone at Jolo in the Sulu Archipelago marks the death in AH 710 (1310 CE) of a foreign Muslim who had apparently established himself as a local ruler. In 1417 three Muslim rulers of Sulu undertook an embassy to the Chinese court.

One of the most important series of gravestones comes from the Trawulan and Trayala graveyards near the site of the Hindu-Buddhist court of Majapahit in East Java. Because these stones bear decorative motifs associated with the Majapahit dynasty, are close to the court site, and are dated with the Hindu-Javanese Shaka era and Old Javanese numerals rather than the Islamic *anno hijrae* and Arabic numerals, we can conclude that they mark the graves of indigenous Javanese Muslims who were aristocrats, perhaps members of the royal family. The earliest of these stones is dated Shaka 1290 (1368 CE). Thus the first records of Javanese Muslims suggest that the conversion process started at the top of society and the center of the kingdom when Majapahit was at its height, but the evidence is too fragmentary to be definite.

About 1400 the greatest of the Malay trading states was founded at Melaka (Malacca). Traders from many parts of the Islamic world were soon found there. Its first ruler, Parameswara (reigned c. 1390–1413/1414), apparently converted to Islam late in his reign. There appears to have been an abortive Hindu-Buddhist reaction in 1445–1446, after which Islam was firmly established as the religion of the kingdom. Various tombstones and Chinese sources record these events. Melaka's rulers and traders appear to have acted as major supporters of the dissemination of Islam to other areas of the Malay, Indonesian, and Philippine archipelagoes.

Two gravestones from Brunei dated AH 835 and (probably) 905 (1432, 1499 CE) show that Muslims died there, but whether they were indigenous or foreign Muslims is unknown. It was also about this time that Islam began to spread among the Cham of what is now southern Vietnam, themselves speakers of an Indonesian language. After their capital Vijaya (Binh Dinh) fell permanently to the Vietnamese in 1471, many Cham fled southward and adopted Islam; those events, however, are obscure.

Immediately after the Portuguese conquest of Melaka in 1511, Tomé Pires wrote an astute and critical description of the Malay-Indonesian area. Pires had visited Melaka, the north coast of Java, and some parts of Sumatra from 1512 to 1515 and gathered reports about the rest of the Malay-Indonesian area. He reported that Sumatra was islamized from Aceh in the north down the east coast to Palembang, as were the kingdoms of Malaya, Central and East (but not West) Java, Brunei, and some parts of Maluku (Moluccas); the rest of the Malay-Indonesian area was, so far as Pires knew, not yet islamized by his time.

Two Javanese manuscripts that reveal something about early Islamic teachings in the area survive from the sixteenth century (probably from its later years). As both were brought to the Netherlands by the first Dutch expedition of 1595–1597, their date is not in doubt. They probably came from Java's north coast. Both reveal some influence of Malay upon their language; they may be Javanese writings based on teachings in Malay and/or Arabic. Most important, the contents of both are orthodox Islamic mysticism (Sufism). This confirms the early importance of Sufism, at least in some areas.

Based upon such evidence, theories of islamization have been proposed and altered or rejected in the light of new evidence or new theories. Much of this has concerned the origin of the first bringers of Islam, a debate that is probably illusory in its assumption that there was a single source, as L.-Ch. Damais observed in 1968. In the nineteenth century, J. Crawfurd proposed that Arabs and Indian Muslims brought Islam; S. Keyzer pointed to Egypt as the source; G. K. Niemann, J. J. de Hollander, and P. J. Veth proposed Arabs in general; J. Pijnappel suggested the Arabs of Gujarat and Malabar on the west coast of India; and C. Snouck Hurgronje preferred South India as the source. In the twentieth century R. A. Kern emphasized the role of Gujarat, G. E. Marrison pointed to South India, and S. Q. Fatimi to Bengal. Slametmuljana, H. J. de Graaf, and Th. G. Th. Pigeaud also demonstrated that Chinese Muslims played a role. In the second half of the twentieth century the debate focused upon whether the original agents of conversion were traders or mystics (Sufis), with the former being championed particularly by G. W. J. Drewes and the latter by A. H. Johns.

The evidence does not support the idea of a single source for Southeast Asian Islam. While it does show that Sufism was important, trade is also a necessary part of the explanation. The process called islamization probably contained two significantly different aspects: foreign Muslims who brought their religion with them and became Malays, Javanese, or whatever, and local peoples who converted to Islam. It is unlikely that there will ever be adequate evidence to describe, let alone explain, these processes in much detail.

Armando Cortesão, ed. and trans., *The Suma Oriental of Tomé Pires,* 2 vols. (1944). G. W. J. Drewes, ed. and trans., *The Admonitions of Seh Bari* (1969). A. H. Johns, "Sufism as a Category in Indonesian Literature and History," *Journal of Southeast Asian History* 2 (1961): 10–23. M. C. Ricklefs, *A History of Modern Indonesia c. 1300 to the Present* (1981).                M. C. RICKLEFS

ISMA'IL I (Abu al-Muzaffar; 1487–1524), shah of Persia from 1501 to 1524 and founder of the Safavid dynasty. In 1499 Isma'il, then head of the Safavid order, emerged from hiding in Gilan and made his bid for temporal power. His defeat of an Akkoyunlu army at Sharur in 1501 gave Isma'il possession of Azerbaijan, and he was crowned at Tabriz, which became the capital of the new Safavid state.

One of Isma'il's first acts, and one that was to have profound consequences for the subsequent history of Persia, was to proclaim the Ithna Ashari (Twelver) form of Shi'ite Islam to be the official religion of the state. By this act, Isma'il imparted to his kingdom a sense of national identity and differentiated it from the powerful Sunni states on its borders, namely, the Ottoman empire to the west and the Uzbek state to the east. Isma'il spent the next decade in consolidating his power in the rest of Persia. This involved the crushing of residual Akkoyunlu forces and the expulsion of the Uzbeks from the northeastern frontier province of Khurasan. Isma'il also extended Safavid suzerainty to "L'Iran extérieur" by the capture of Baghdad and the occupation of Iraq in 1508.

The subversive activities of Safavid officers and militant Shi'ite propagandists in eastern Anatolia, an area of the Ottoman empire that had a substantial Shi'ite population, provoked the Ottoman sultan Selim to invade Persia in 1514 with two hundred thousand men. The Ottoman artillery and muskets played a major role in the crushing defeat inflicted on Isma'il at the battle of Chaldiran on 23 August 1514. Tabriz was occupied by the Ottomans, and Selim intended to winter there and proceed with the conquest of the rest of Persia the following spring. His plans were frustrated by a mutiny of the Janissaries that forced him to withdraw from Azerbaijan, and the only territory permanently lost by the Safavids as a result of their defeat was northern Iraq.

The effects of the defeat on Isma'il himself, however, were severe and permanent. His pretensions to invincibility and semidivinity shattered, he spent the remaining years of his life in seclusion, giving no direction to affairs of state and never again leading his troops into action in person. As a result, the Uzbeks made significant gains on the northeastern frontier, and Babur, the future emperor of India, captured the key strategic city of Kandahar in 1522. During this period, Isma'il tried without success to engineer an alliance with various European powers against their mutual enemy, the Ottoman empire.

On his accession, Isma'il was faced by a number of intractable problems to which he offered novel but ultimately only partially successful solutions. First, there was the problem of imposing the new state religion, Ithna Ashari Shi'ism, on a country that was still at least nominally Sunni. Second, he had to temper the revolutionary ardor and find an outlet for the martial energies of the militant Sufis of the Safavid order, and to incorporate their organization if possible within the administrative structure of the state. Third, he had to try to reconcile the rivalries between the two principal ethnic groups in the state: the predominantly Turkish military elite who had brought the Safavids to power (whom he had inspired by the recitation of poems of a heterodox nature, of his own composition, in their native Azeri Turkish dialect), and the Persian bureaucrats and members of the religious classes.

On his death in 1524 Isma'il was buried in the family mausoleum at Ardabil. He had four sons (his successor, Tahmasp; Sam; the renegade Alqas; and Bahram) and five daughters.

[*See also* Safavi *and* Safavid Dynasty.]

Roger M. Savory, "Ismā'īl I," in *The Encyclopaedia of Islam* (new ed., 1960–); and *Iran under the Safavids* (1980).                ROGER M. SAVORY

ISMA'ILI, one of several designations (Fatimi, Sevener, Qarmatian, Assassin) for a member of a prominent branch of Shi'ite Islam that separated from other forms of Shi'ism in insisting that the correct imam to follow Ja'far al-Sadiq was his son Isma'il—hence this particular name for the sect.

The Isma'ilis rose to challenge Sunni orthodoxy in the latter half of the ninth century CE and to found a major dynasty, the Fatimids, in North Africa, Egypt, and Arabia in the following century. Remarkable for its clandestine centralized propaganda organization (the *da'wa*) and a sophisticated Neoplatonic theological doctrine, the movement at first flourished in various places throughout the medieval Muslim world but later began to decline; it eventually broke up into a number of branches and offshoots. One of the latter, the Druze, remain important in Levantine affairs of the modern Middle East.

The two main branches died out in Egypt and North Africa but survived in the Yemen and in Iran under different lines of leadership. The eastern, or Nizari, Isma'ilis achieved special notoriety for their use of political terrorism and murder to intimidate opponents; they thus acquired the name *Assassins*. Their imams ruled from Alamut in northern Iran until it was destroyed by the Mongol army of Hulegu in 1256. The sect itself continued in obscurity until the nineteenth century, when its imam once again emerged to prominence under the title *Agha Khan* and its headquarters was moved to Bombay, India. The current Agha Khan is leader of this group.

A numerically smaller branch, the western, or Tayyibi, Isma'ilis, continue to exist in Yemen, with a large following in the Gujarati area of India. One subgroup, the Da'udis, transferred the leadership permanently to Surat and Bombay, where the current head (*da'i mutlaq*) resides.

[*See also* Bohras; Agha Khan; *and* Alamut.]

PAUL E. WALKER

**ITAGAKI TAISUKE** (Inui; 1837–1919), Japanese political leader of the Meiji period and founder of the Jiyūtō (Liberal Party). Itagaki was born into a samurai family in Tosa. A disciple of Yoshida Tōyō, he opposed the Tokugawa shogunate and actively reformed the Tosa military. During the wars leading to the Meiji Restoration he played an important role in suppressing Tokugawa holdouts in Aizu. After the Restoration he spearheaded reforms in Tosa, and in 1871 he joined the government in Tokyo.

Protesting the decision in 1873 not to go to war with Korea, Itagaki resigned his position and returned to Tosa to organize a movement for representative government. In the mid- to late 1870s he helped to found a series of political associations, including the Risshisha and Aikoku Kōtō. In 1881

he founded the Jiyūtō, through which he called for the establishment of a British-type parliamentary system with cabinets responsible to parliament and not the crown. Itagaki's decision to leave Japan for a study tour of the West in 1882 and growing radicalism in the Jiyūtō forced the temporary disbanding of the party in 1884. With the granting of the constitution in 1889, however, it was reorganized and with various permutations in name has remained one of the major parties in Japanese politics. As president of the Jiyūtō in the 1890s Itagaki remained a central figure in the new Japanese Diet. In 1895 he accepted the post of home minister in the second cabinet of Itō Hirobumi, and in 1898 he joined Ōkuma Shigenobu to form the Ōkuma-Itagaki cabinet, which lasted for a brief four months but has often been described as Japan's first "party cabinet." Itagaki used the establishment of the Seiyūkai in 1900 to retire from active politics.

Itagaki's political reputation was largely based on his role as spokesman for the Popular Rights Movement in the 1870s and 1880s. During this period he was influenced by the ideas of John Stuart Mill and Jean-Jacques Rousseau. In opposition to the conservative Meiji oligarchs, Itagaki and the Jiyūtō favored popular sovereignty, human equality, and the right of revolution. When he was stabbed in 1882 by a young rightist who regarded such ideas as treason, Itagaki is recorded to have shouted: "Itagaki may die, but liberty will not die!"

[*See also* Risshisha; Seiyūkai; *and* Meiji Period.]

F. G. NOTEHELFER

**ITHNA ASHARI,** an Arabic term meaning, literally, "twelver," which designates an adherent of the numerically dominant form of Shi'ism in Islam.

From earlier allegiance to a particular line of imams descended from Ali ibn Abi Talib through Ali's son Husain and later through Ja'far al-Sadiq's son Musa al-Kazim, the major doctrines of this sect began to focus on the mysterious disappearance of the shadowy Twelfth Imam in 874, which became a unique religious event and an important turning point. In the initial period (874–940), this imam, whose very existence was doubted by opponents, was said by followers to be in seclusion and therefore reachable only through the mediation of special representatives (*babs*). This period, called the minor occultation, was followed by a permanent occultation of the same imam, who, although hidden, nevertheless remains the living proof of God's grace to the world and is the ultimate source of his truth for mankind. It is this imam in messianic form, in fact, who will be revealed in the final days, when he will lead the righteous to victory over their enemies.

Ithna Ashari Shi'ism tended to avoid conflict with Sunni Islam by accepting what is basically a quietist position with regard to the leadership of the Muslim community. The practice of precautionary dissimulation of religious beliefs *(taqiyya)* was accepted and often even made obligatory. Nevertheless, there developed an elaborate doctrinal literature supporting the sacred history of the imams and the special role of the hidden, twelfth imam. Under these conditions the sect flourished in certain regions of the Muslim world and was recognized finally as the official religion of the state in Iran under the Safavid dynasty (1501–1736). In addition to its dominant position in Iran, Ithna Ashari Shi'ism has a large following in Iraq and important pockets of adherents in other Muslim countries.

[*See also* Shi'a.]

PAUL E. WALKER

**I'TIMAD UD-DAULAH** (d. 1621), *vazir* (chief minister) under the Mughal emperor Jahangir. Originally named Ghiyas Beg, he was a native of Tehran whose utter penury compelled him to seek better prospects in India. The emperor Akbar admitted him into imperial service and he rose to be *mansab* (a military rank) of 1,000 soldiers. On becoming emperor Jahangir gave him the title *i'timad ud-daulah* ("trust of the empire"). His daughter Nur Jahan became empress after he had established himself in service, and his son Asaf Khan held high offices in Jahangir's reign. His magnificent tomb is in Agra.

[*See also* Jahangir *and* Nur Jahan.]

Beni Prasad, *History of Jahangir* (1962).

HARBANS MUKHIA

**ITŌ HIROBUMI** (1841–1909), Japanese government leader of the Meiji period. Itō was the only person of peasant stock among the Meiji leaders. During Itō's youth, however, his father was adopted into a samurai family of modest rank. Itō studied at Yoshida Shōin's private academy (1858), was swept up by the convulsive events that led to the Meiji Restoration, and participated in the attack on the British legation and the assassination in 1862 of Hanawa Jirō, a National Studies (Kokugaku) scholar. After an unauthorized trip to England in 1863, however, he rejected his radical antiforeign views and became a proponent of Western learning.

Itō's talents were recognized by the leaders of the Meiji government, Kido Takayoshi and Ōkubo Toshimichi. He became governor of Hyogo Prefecture before he was thirty years old (1868–1869) and then went to the United States to study fiscal and currency questions (1870). In 1872 he collaborated with Ōkuma Shigenobu to build Japan's first railroad. He succeeded Ōkubo as home minister when the latter was assassinated in 1878, and three years later, in a masterful, bloodless purge, ousted Ōkuma from the government and succeeded him as finance minister. Since he was also *sangi* (state councillor), he became, as had Ōkubo before him, de facto "prime minister." It is a measure of the quality of Meiji leadership and of the political stability they had created that Itō went abroad for a year and a half (1882–1883) to study under leading European constitutional scholars immediately after the purge.

The two decades following Itō's return may be described as the "Itō years," in which he enjoyed a series of political successes and was the principal architect of the new European-style governmental structure. In 1884 the Imperial House Law and the peerage were established, followed in 1885 by the creation of the cabinet system. He became Japan's first prime minister (1885–1888) and again held that post on three separate occasions (1892–1896, 1898, 1900–1901). Itō was the first president of the Privy Council that was founded in 1888 to discuss the Meiji Constitution he had helped to draft. The promulgation of the constitution in 1889 was followed by the establishment in 1890 of the two-house Diet, in which Itō was the first president of the House of Peers. More significantly, Japan was the first Asian state to hold a national election for members of a legislative body.

His domestic achievements were matched by foreign affairs successes. He was prime minister when, with Mutsu Munemitsu, he accomplished what had eluded other Meiji leaders, an agreement with Great Britain (1894) to do away with extraterritoriality in 1899. During the same tenure Japan fought and won its first major war, against China (1894–1895). [*See* Sino-Japanese War.]

Itō displayed to an exceptional degree the qualities characteristic of Meiji leaders: pragmatism, flexibility, moderation, and a preference for compromise and workable, realistic solutions. These traits were evident in two of his final major achievements. He formed the Seiyūkai (1900), a political party composed of members of a former antigovernment party and bureaucrats, a political mix still evident today. He was Japan's first resident-general of the Protectorate of Korea (1905–1909). He favored an even-handed, moderate policy of reform that would respect Korean sensibilities even while Japan's national interests were served. He was assassinated by a Korean in Harbin on 26 October 1909.

[See also Seiyūkai; Meiji Restoration; and Meiji Period.]

GEORGE K. AKITA

ITŌ JAKUCHŪ (1716–1800), Japanese painter. Itō Jakuchū is considered, together with Nagasawa Rosetsu (1755–1799) and Soga Shōhaku (1730–1781), one of the three great eccentric painters of the Edo period (1600–1868).

Born the son of a Kyoto greengrocer, in 1755 he retired from the family business to devote himself to painting. Like many of his contemporaries, he received training in the workshops of the Kanō school and studied Chinese painting of the Yuan (1280–1368) and Ming (1368–1644) dynasties. A highly prolific artist, his works are found in major collections in Japan and the United States.

Jakuchū's most representative paintings include a series of thirty scrolls known as the Colorful Realm of Living Beings. Completed in 1770, this ambitious series depicts a bewildering variety of flora and fauna in luminous colors and in an almost surrealistic manner. Jakuchū also left his mark in the field of monochrome ink painting: his free, wildly exuberant renderings of plants and animals, especially roosters, were much imitated by his followers. Late in life, he developed close ties with Mampukuji, a Zen monastery of the Ōbaku sect. This connection stimulated the corpus of paintings on religious themes he is believed to have executed between the 1770s and 1790. Jakuchū's eclecticism, wit, and interest in local crafts are given expression in the many folkish paintings he made in his last years.

Although he was influenced by the work of Chinese bird-and-flower painters and by the decorative school of Sōtatsu and Kōrin, his scintillating colors, sense of form and design, and subject matter are testimony to his highly individualistic artistic sensibility.

[See also Painting: Japanese Painting.]

Harold Stern, Birds, Beasts, Blossoms, and Bugs (1976).

CHRISTINE M. E. GUTH

ITŌ JINSAI (1627–1705), Japanese Confucian, founder of the Ancient Learning (Kogaku) school of Japanese Confucianism. Itō Jinsai was the son of a Kyoto lumber merchant. From the age of sixteen, he was a follower of the thought of the Chinese Neo-Confucian thinker Zhu Xi (1130–1200), but he revolted against these teachings, spent eight years in self-imposed seclusion, and then, in his thirties, began formulating his own brand of Confucianism. Jinsai remained a private scholar his entire life, refusing all offers of employment from the daimyo. His academy attracted over three thousand students from all parts of Japan. Jinsai and his son, Tōgai, dominated the Tokugawa Confucian intellectual world until the rise of Ogyū Sorai's school in the early to middle eighteenth century.

Jinsai's scholarly concerns were ethics and philology. He found the tradition of Zhu Xi studies distasteful because its teachings were too metaphysically abstract and its moral code too rigorous. For him, the Confucian Way must be "plain and familiar," not abstruse; it must be approbatory of the natural passions of men in society, not repressive of these as sources of evil. Zhu Xi and latter-day Confucians misconstrued the true Way, he maintained, because they based their views on "canonical" texts or parts of such texts mistakenly attributed to Confucius. Jinsai, through strict, philologically empirical research, sought to identify those texts properly attributable to the greatest of all sages, Confucius, and to reject as spurious those that were not. He declared that the true Way was revealed in the Analects and Mencius—when read and interpreted correctly—and that the essence of that Way lay in humanly natural love and affection.

[See also Neo-Confucianism and Ogyū Sorai.]

Yoshikawa Kojirō, Jinsai, Sorai, and Norinaga (1983).

BOB TADASHI WAKABAYASHI

ITŌ MIYOJI (1857–1934), Japanese government leader of the Meiji period. Itō was born in Nagasaki; his father, a commoner, was possibly a clerk-interpreter. Itō studied English and at sixteen became an interpreter for the Hyōgo prefectural government. At nineteen, he impressed Itō Hirobumi with his ability in the English language and was appointed a low-ranking national bureaucrat. He was as close to Itō as anyone other than Inoue Kaoru, and he progressed steadily upward as he followed his mentor. He was with Itō in Europe from 1882 to 1884 to study constitutional systems. His positions included cabinet secretary in the first Itō cabinet (1885); chief secretary of the Privy Council (1888, when Itō was president); and chief cabinet secretary in the second Itō cabinet (1892). He became a privy councillor in 1889 and received an imperial appointment to the House of Peers (1890). He was minister of agriculture and commerce in the third Itō cabinet (1898).

Itō Miyoji is typical of the talented and ambitious men from other than Satsuma, Chōshū, Tosa, and Hizen who were used freely by the Meiji leaders in building the Meiji state. Inoue Kowashi (from Kumamoto), Kaneko Kentarō (from Fukuoka), Mutsu Munemitsu (from Wakayama), and Hara Takashi (from Iwate) are other prominent examples. *Han* boundaries were also ignored when leaders chose able men as sons-in-law, such as Suematsu Kenchō (from Fukuoka, son-in-law of Itō Hirobumi), Funakoshi Mitsunojō (from Hiroshima, son-in-law of Yamagata Aritomo), and Tsuzuki Keiroku (from Ehime, son-in-law of Inoue Kaoru).

Itō excelled as a wordsmith. He assisted in drafting the Meiji constitution, drafted the declaration of war against China (1894), and wrote speeches and documents for Prime Minister Terauchi Masatake (1916–1918).

[*See also* Itō Hirobumi *and* Meiji Period.]

GEORGE K. AKITA

IWAKURA MISSION, Japanese diplomatic and educational mission to the West, inaugurated as part of the reforms of the Meiji Restoration. Lasting from 23 December 1871 to 23 July 1873, the Iwakura Mission (named after its head, Iwakura Tomomi) stands as a symbol of the progressive ideology of post-Restoration Japan. Commissioned by the Meiji emperor, the embassy involved more than one hundred people, the large majority of whom had never before left Japan. Its makeup was especially significant in that it included many leaders of state as well as an entourage of clerks, attendants, and students. The aims of the mission were threefold: first, to serve as representatives of the emperor in spreading good will and to demonstrate Japan's intent to reform and modernize its institutions; second, to exchange views on "unequal treaties" that Japan had negotiated; and third, to examine Western society and culture and discover the extent and nature of its wealth, power, and enlightenment.

The mission circumnavigated the globe, stopping first for an unexpectedly extended seven-month stay in the United States in an unsuccessful attempt to negotiate a new treaty in Washington. The mission crossed the US on the newly completed transcontinental railroad, viewing firsthand the frontier West

as well as the industrial East. After a transatlantic voyage the mission spent four months in Britain, but attempted no further treaty negotiations.

[*See also* Meiji Period and Iwakura Tomomi.]

Sidney Devere Brown and Akiko Hirota, trans., *The Diary of Kido Takayoshi*, vol. 2 (1985). Marius B. Jansen, *Japan and Its World: Two Centuries of Change* (1980). Marlene J. Mayo, "The Western Education of Kume Kunitake, 1877–1878," *Monumenta Nipponica* 28.1 (1973): 3–67.

J. SCOTT MILLER

IWAKURA TOMOMI (1825–1883), one of Japan's most influential statesmen of the nineteenth century and the only court noble to shape significantly the Meiji government in its early years. Iwakura was born into the low-ranking Horikawa family in Kyoto but was adopted into the Iwakura household. He served as a chamberlain to Emperor Kōmei. In 1858 he helped persuade the emperor to withhold approval of the Harris Treaty, advocated by the shogun, and later helped arrange the marriage of Princess Kazu to the shogun Iemochi. He fell into disfavor with both the court and the shogunate and went into retreat from 1863 to 1867, emerging to assist Saigō Takamori and Ōkubo Toshimichi in ousting the shogunate, restoring the emperor to power, and establishing the new Meiji government. He was involved in drafting the Charter Oath and the prefectural system, and in his later years he helped establish the Fifteenth National Bank and the Japan Railway Company.

Iwakura is most famous, however, for serving as leader of an official mission, known as the Iwakura Mission, which went to the United States and Europe in 1871 to observe legal, political, educational, and social conditions. Upon his return in 1873 Iwakura advocated the adoption of a constitution after the Western model, but he was against popular rights. A strong advocate of the emperor's interests throughout his lifetime, Iwakura spent his last years managing the emperor's property.

[*See also* Meiji Restoration; Meiji Period; *and* Iwakura Mission.]

J. SCOTT MILLER

IWASAKI YATARŌ (1838–1885), founder of the Mitsubishi *zaibatsu* and the most successful entrepreneur of the early Meiji period in Japan. Iwasaki's initial exposure to Western learning came in an 1850s reform movement in Tosa. In the late 1860s he took charge of the Kaiseikan, a Tosa agency for industrial promotion. Through currency speculation, manipulation of the Tosa domain's debt, and utilization of his role as an official, he adroitly transformed the Kaiseikan from a domain agency into his own private firm, which took the name Mitsubishi in 1873.

As a steamship company, Mitsubishi grew rapidly in the 1870s through arms transport contracts and government subsidies. These financed successful competitions in 1875 and 1876 against American and British firms. Although Iwasaki then strengthened his monopoly in coastal steamships through a bureau for financing shippers, he soon began purchasing mines and stopped buying ships. With Mitsubishi shipping services deteriorating, in 1882 the government established a second steamship company, the Union Transport Company, also supported by trading firms like Mitsui and regional shipowners. A reckless competition then ensued until the Union Transport and Mitsubishi shipping assets were merged in September 1885 to form the Nippon Yūsen Kaisha (NYK).

Iwasaki spread his risks, often using money saved from salary reductions imposed during competitive shipping struggles to invest in mines. Famous for his "one-man" rule, he in fact aggressively recruited well-educated managers and gave them major responsibility. He was succeeded by his younger brother Yanosuke.

[See also Mitsubishi.]

William D. Wray, *Mitsubishi and the N.Y.K., 1870–1914: Business Strategy in the Japanese Shipping Industry* (1984). Kozo Yamamura, *A Study of Samurai Income and Entrepreneurship* (1974).    WILLIAM D. WRAY

# J

JACINTO, EMILIO (1875–1899), Filipino political activist and important member of the Katipunan, the secret and separatist society that aimed to obtain independence for the Philippines, help the poor and oppressed, and fight religious fanaticism.

Called "the brains of the Katipunan," Jacinto was a law student who, like most of the Katipuneros, came from a middle-class background. Although Jacinto was not one of the founders of the organization, Andres Bonifacio, who founded the Katipunan, quickly recognized his talent and dedication, making him a member of the supreme council. Jacinto's *Kartilya* took the place of Bonifacio's "Decalogue" as the primer of the Katipunan.

Jacinto was well versed in the works of nationalist Jose Rizal as well as the revolutionary books that had inspired Bonifacio. Jacinto's published writings (which appeared in the Katipunan's newspaper, *Kalayaan,* or *Freedom,* edited by him) and unpublished writings in Tagalog vividly expound the major themes that preoccupied Rizal—human dignity, racial equality, austere morality, dedication to the people, and rejection of the hypocrisy of institutionalized religion.

[*See also* Katipunan; Bonifacio, Andres; *and* Rizal, Jose Mercado.]

Teodoro A. Agoncillo, *The Revolt of the Masses* (1956). Epifanio de los Santos, *The Revolutionists* (1973).

JOHN N. SCHUMACHER, S.J.

JA'FARI, the Ithna Ashari (Twelver) Shi'ite school of Islamic law. It was named after Ja'far al-Sadiq (d. 765), the sixth of the Twelver imams, who is believed to be its founder. The period of Ja'far's leadership coincided with a period of intellectual activity in Islam, especially the systematization of the *shari'a* through collection of the *hadith* litera-

ture. The eminent figures Abu Hanifa (d. 768) and Malik (d. 795) were occupied by the attempt to fulfill this need in Sunni Islam. Ja'far al-Sadiq's Fatimid ancestry greatly enhanced his prominence in Medina, and he in effect became the fountainhead not only of the Ja'fari school of law, but of all Shi'ite intellectual as well as traditional sciences. His prestigious and generally acknowledged leadership gave ultimate recognition to the line of the Husainid imams among the Shi'ites, whereas his enlistment as an authentic transmitter of the prophetic traditions in the Sunni "chains of transmission" *(isnads)* gave recognition to the Ja'fari school of law as a valid interpretation of Islamic revelation. The emphasis on *aql* (the intellect) as a major source of Islamic law has become a distinguishing mark of Ja'fari legal theory. Today, the Ja'fari school is regarded by the Sunni scholars of al-Azhar as the "fifth school" in addition to the four Sunni ones.

[*See also* Ithna Ashari; Shari'a; *and* Shi'a.]

Mahmoud Shaltut, *Two Historical Documents* (1963).

ABDELAZIZ SACHEDINA

JAFFNA, historic seaside city (population in 1983, around 125,000), capital of the northern region of Sri Lanka, long an administrative and regional center. The city is itself located within Jaffna Peninsula—the northernmost area of Sri Lanka, linked to the rest of the island by the narrow Elephant Pass isthmus. This area was the heartland of the ancient Tamil kingdoms. Jaffna District (area, 999 square miles; population, around 850,000) is a northern administrative division of Sri Lanka, which includes the peninsula and extends somewhat south of it. The population consists predominantly of Tamils, who originally migrated from South India at least by the first millennium of the common era; Hinduism is their religion and they speak Tamil. The area has an arid climate; its principal occupations are agriculture, dry farming, and, recently, some industry and services.

[*See also* Sri Lanka *and* Tamils in Sri Lanka.]

N. E. Weerasooria, *Ceylon and Her People* (1971).

RALPH BUULTJENS

JAGAT SETH, "banker of the world," a title given by the nawab of Bengal in about 1723 to Fatehchand, a member of the powerful banking family that had come to Bengal from Marwar in Rajasthan. [*See* Marwaris.] The family had enormous wealth and power, receiving taxes in Bengal from the tax-farmers and transmitting them to the nawab and to the emperor in Delhi, as well as making large loans to the nawab and to the foreign merchants trading in Bengal. Jagat Seth was deeply involved in all the transactions that led to the rise of British power in Bengal. He was a major influence in bringing about the downfall of Nawab Siraj ud-Daulah (r. 1756–1757) and in the East India Company's gaining control of Bengal, for he participated in the conspiracy that replaced Siraj ud-Daulah with Mir Ja'far, who was intended to be the company's puppet. After the Battle of Plassey in 1757 Jagat Seth seems to have been responsible for offering Robert Clive, the victorious British commander, a vast fortune from the treasury and for arranging for him to receive a *jagir*, or an assignment of the taxes from a district, worth £30,000 a year. After the East India Company consolidated its control over Bengal the Jagat Seth family lost its role as bankers to the rulers. [*See also* Bengal; East India Company; Clive, Sir Robert; Plassey, Battle of; Siraj ud-Daulah, *and* Mir Ja'far.]

ROBERT E. FRYKENBERG

JAGIR (lit., "holder of a place"), a Persian term, used, however, only in Mughal India. It signified the territory whose land revenue was assigned to a *mansabdar* (officer) as his salary. A *jagir* was usually assigned for three or four years. Theoretically the revenue due from a *jagir* corresponded to the salary of the *jagirdar* (*jagir*-holder); actually, there was considerable discrepancy. Late in the seventeenth century the gap between the supply and demand of *jagirs* widened greatly and created a crisis.

[*See also* Mansabdari System *and* Mughal Empire.]

Satish Chandra, *Parties and Politics at the Mughal Court, 1707–1740* (1959).    HARBANS MUKHIA

JAHANGIR (1569–1627), son and successor of the Mughal emperor Akbar. He was born to a Rajput princess, daughter of the raja of Amber; Akbar named him Muhammad Sultan Salim after the famous saint Shaikh Salim Chishti, whose blessings he had sought for the birth of a son. Eminent tutors such as Abdur Rahim Khan-i Khanan looked after Salim's education. During the last years of Akbar's reign court intrigues forced Salim to rebel against his father but he soon became reconciled with him. On Akbar's death in 1605, with the support of nobles like Nawab Murtaza Khan, Salim ascended the throne as Nuruddin Muhammad Jahangir. He soon remitted certain taxes and duties, allowed regular inheritance of the property of nobles, prohibited the cutting of limbs of criminals, and built many hospitals.

Jahangir married Nur Jahan, widow of Sher Afgan, in 1611. Gradually Nur Jahan became a power in politics, her relatives rose to important positions in the administration, and the Irani faction came to dominate the nobility. Politics at the court led to the revolt by Jahanigir's son Shah Jahan, an attempted coup by the noble Mahabat Khan, and other contumacious activities. Guru Arjun, the revered leader of the Sikhs, was put to death on Jahangir's orders for helping Prince Khusrau when the latter rebelled against the emperor in 1606. Jahangir subjugated Mewar (1614), conquered Ahmadnagar (1616), captured Kangra (1620), and lost Qandahar (1622). He maintained good relations with the Portuguese, the Jesuits, and the English, whose envoys visited his court. Some cases of conflict with the Europeans are also recorded. He did not interfere in religion and abandoned Akbar's experiments in religious leadership. Jahangir was a kind-hearted person with a deep sense of justice. He was also devoted to the arts. Under him painting reached a high-point of development, Persian and Hindi literature flourished, and architecture was patronized. His memoirs throw interesting light on his policies and personality.

[*See also* Mughal Empire; Akbar; Nur Jahan; *and* Shah Jahan.]

Jahangir, *Memoirs of Jahangir*, translated by A. Rogers and edited by H. Beveridge, 2 vols. (1909–1914). Beni Prasad, *History of Jahangir* (3d ed., 1962).

FARHAN AHMAD NIZAMI

JAINISM, an Indian religion dating from at least the sixth century BCE and considered heterodox by Brahmanical Hinduism. The Jain community adheres to a unique, interrelated set of cosmological and soteriological beliefs that, while having changed to a certain extent over time, have always set the Jains apart from other strands of Indian society.

Jain cosmology posits that time endlessly repeats itself, like a cosmic wheel, with six ascending spokes followed by six descending spokes. In the middle two spokes of each ascent and descent are born twenty-four Tirthankaras ("ford-makers") or Jinas ("conquerors"; hence the followers of the Jinas are known as Jains) who come to preach the Jain teachings. In the current descent, the first Jina was Rishabha, who lived millions of years ago. He initiated the Jain teachings and was the first king, creating the order of human society. After a succession of twenty-one Jinas came Neminatha, or Arishtanemi, a cousin of Krishna. Parshva, the twenty-third Jina and son of a noble family of Varanasi, lived in the ninth century BCE, some 250 years before Vardhamana Mahavira, the twenty-fourth and last Jina. The historicity of Parshva is generally accepted by scholars; thus Mahavira was not the founder of Jainism but the reformer of a preexistent ascetic tradition.

Mahavira ("the great hero") was a senior contemporary of the Buddha. He was born into a noble family near Vaishali in present-day Bihar. After thirty years as a householder, he formally renounced the world and wandered for twelve years before attaining enlightenment (*kaivalya, kevala-jnana*). He wandered and preached in the area of what is now Bihar, western Bengal, and eastern Uttar Pradesh for another thirty years before his death and final liberation (*moksha*, nirvana), held by the Jains to have taken place in 527 BCE. Many scholars date the event in 468 or 447 BCE.

The details of the spread of Jainism following Mahavira's *moksha* are still very unclear. The Maurya emperors (fourth to third century BCE) and King Kharavela of Kalinga (second century BCE) gave the Jains some official support. Jainism spread down the eastern coast of India into Andhra, Tamil Nadu, and possibly Sri Lanka in the early centuries BCE. Jains played an important role in the development of Tamil culture. According to a seventh-century CE Digambara tradition, Jains first came to Karnataka around 300 BCE, under the leadership of the sixth preceptor after Mahavira, Bhadrabahu, who led a number of Jains—including the emperor Chandragupta Maurya—to Sravana Belgola near Mysore to escape a famine in the North. In parts of South India, Jain monks preceded brahmans as bearers of Indo-Aryan culture. In Karnataka the Jains were closely allied with several ruling dynasties between the third and fourteenth centuries, including the Gangas, Rastrakutas, and Hoysalas. The flowering of Karnataka Jainism is seen in the writings of authors such as the monk Jinasena and the general Camundaraya, in the development of Kannada literature, and in the magnificent fifty-seven-foot-high standing image of Bahubali (a son of Rishabha) erected at Sravana Belgola in the late tenth century.

To the west, Mathura was a flourishing Jain center from 100 BCE into the early centuries of the common era. Gujarat and Saurashtra soon became the center for Jains in western India. In the middle of the fifth century a council at Valabhi, in Saurashtra, saw the final recension of the Shvetambara canon. Jain monks and laymen were influential in the courts of the Chavada, Chaulukya (especially the polymath monk Hemacandra), and Vaghela dynasties from the eighth to the thirteenth century. Rich Jain merchants and ministers endowed the magnificent mountain temple-cities of Girnar, Shatrunjaya, and Abu, and commissioned illustrated manuscripts.

The history of the Jains has been marked by a number of schisms. The most serious took place in 79 CE, when the Digambaras ("sky-clad") and Shvetambaras ("white-clad") split. The Digambaras insist on total nudity for monks, deny the possibility of women attaining nirvana, deny the authority of the Shvetambara canon, insist that an enlightened Jina requires no bodily sustenance, and disagree with the Shvetambaras on certain aspects of the biographies of the Jinas. Both groups have seen iconoclastic reform movements: the Terapanthis (fifteenth century) and Taranapanthis (sixteenth century) among the Digambaras, and the Sthanakavasis (seventeenth century) and Terapanthis (eighteenth century) among the Shvetambaras. Today, Digambaras are found mostly in Karnataka and parts of Rajasthan and Central India, while the Shvetambaras are concentrated in Gujarat and Rajasthan. Communities of Jain merchants are found in every major urban center in India, although they constitute (as of the 1971 census) only 0.47 percent of the total population.

Jain doctrine characterizes all that exists as being composed of six universals (*dravyas*): life (*jiva*), the defining characteristic of which is consciousness (*cetana*), and five kinds of "non-life" (*ajiva*), namely physical matter (*pudgala*), space (*akasha*), time (*kala*), and the principles of motion (*dharma*) and rest (*adharma*). The *jiva* in its unbounded state possesses the four infinitudes: perception (*darshana*), knowledge (*jnana*), bliss (*sukha*), and ability (*virya*).

But *jivas* are bound by karma, which for the Jains is an invisible material substance, not a process as it is for the Buddhists and Hindus. Karma adheres to the *jiva* and prevents the exercise of the four infinitudes. The religious practice of the Jain renunciant consists in stopping the influx of new karma *(samvara)* and eliminating previously acquired karma *(nirjara)*. At the core of Jain renunciant practice are the "three jewels": right faith *(samyagdarshana)*, right knowledge *(samyagjnana)*, and right conduct *(samyakcaritra)*. Right conduct is encapsulated in the five great vows *(mahavrata)* that the renunciant takes upon initiation: (1) *ahimsa* (non-injury to all living things), (2) *satya* (telling only the truth), (3) *asteya* (not taking what is not given), (4) *brahmacarya* (complete celibacy), and (5) *aparigraha* (renunciation of all possessions). *Ahimsa* has formed the basis of both Jain religious practice and social ethics; as a result, Jain laity are known for their strict vegetarianism and their preference for such occupations as trade and banking, which entail a minimum of violence.

Eberhard Fischer and Jyotindra Jain, *Art and Rituals: 2500 Years of Jainism in India* (1977). Kendall W. Folkert, "The Jainas," in *A Reader's Guide to the Great Religions,* edited by Charles J. Adams (2d ed., 1977), pp. 231–246. Helmuth von Glasenapp, *The Doctrine of Karma in Jain Philosophy* (1942). Hermann Jacobi, trans., *Jaina Sutras,* 2 vols. (1884–1895). Padmanabh S. Jaini, *The Jaina Path of Purification* (1979). Cimanlal J. Shah, *Jainism in North America* (1932). Ram Bhushan Prasad Singh, *Jainism in Early Medieval Karnataka* (1975). R. Williams, *Jaina Yoga* (1963).                    JOHN E. CORT

**JAIPUR.** The Kachwaha clan of Rajputs, who claim descent from Kush, the second son of Rama, the epic king of ancient Ayodhya, was the ruling family of the Indian princely state of Jaipur. According to legend Dhola Rai established the Kachwaha state in 967 CE near its modern location, where it was first known as Dhundar and then Amber. Located midway between Delhi and Ajmer, the Amber state had the distinction or dishonor, according to one's perspective, of being the first Rajput state to initiate close ties with Muslim emperors. In 1562 Raja Bihari Mall offered a daughter in marriage to Akbar, a union that produced the emperor Jahangir. Raja Man Singh, Bihari Mall's adopted son and successor, became probably the most prominent Mughal general under Akbar.

In 1728 Maharaja Jai Singh II began the construction of a new capital, which gave the name of Jaipur to the state. His planned city embodied a synthesis of Rajput and Mughal architectural styles, reflecting the close political and cultural bonds that had existed for over a century and a half. Jaipur entered treaty relations with the British in 1818. Jaipur state was integrated into the state of Rajasthan, a union of former princely states, in 1949. Jaipur city, with a population of about 980,000 (1981), remains the capital of Rajasthan state in independent India. It is a major commercial and tourist center.

[*See also* Princely States; Rajasthan; *and* Rajput.]

Jadurath Sarkar, *A History of Jaipur* (1984). M. L. Sharma, *History of the Jaipur State* (1969).

BARBARA N. RAMUSACK

**JAISALMER.** Rawal Jaisal, a Bhatti Rajput of the Yadu clan, built the first fort at Jaisalmer in 1156 and thus founded the most remote Rajput princely state in India. He chose this location in the Thar Desert reputedly at the invitation of a hermit who pointed out its secular advantages of a freshwater lake near a high ridge that dominated the surrounding barren plain. Over the centuries Jaisalmer developed into a major oasis on caravan routes to Afghanistan and Persia. The state offered a bride to Akbar in 1570 and Maharawal Mulraj entered treaty relations with the British in 1818. The growth of Bombay as a trading center and a network of railways that bypassed Jaisalmer caused a precipitous decline in the trading economy of Jaisalmer. In 1931 the state had an area of 16,062 square miles, a population of 67,652 (which had declined from 115,701 in 1891), and an average annual revenue of 404,000 rupees. In 1948 it joined the Greater Rajasthan Union of independent India.

[*See also* Rajasthan.]

James Tod, *Annals and Antiquities of Rajast'han Or, the Central and Western Rajpoot States of India,* vol. 2 (1832; reprint, 1971).                    BARBARA N. RAMUSACK

**JAI SINGH** (d. 1667), raja belonging to the distinguished Kachchawaha clan of Rajputs. Jai Singh served three Mughal emperors and was awarded the titles *umdat ul-mulk* ("scion of the empire") and *mirza* ("prince"), as well as the highest *mansab* (rank), with 7,000 horses at his command. He fought and won numerous battles in every corner of the empire and was equally known for his diplomacy. His greatest triumph was the treaty he negotiated with the Maratha leader Shivaji in 1665,

FIGURE 1. *City Wall, Jaisalmer.*

though this proved short-lived. The failure of his campaign in Bijapur brought him into disgrace and he died soon after, a broken old man.

[*See also* Rajput *and* Mansabdari System.]

HARBANS MUKHIA

JAISOHN, PHILIP (Sŏ Chae-p'il; 1863–1951), one of the most articulate spokesmen of the independence and enlightenment movements of late-nineteenth-century Korea. In later years Jaisohn intermittently worked for many Korean causes.

A scion of a prominent *yangban* clan of Taegu, Jaisohn received a traditional education in the Confucian classics. Soon his contacts with a small group of Korean progressives, notably Kim Ok-kyun, Pak Yŏng-hyo, Sŏ Kwang-bŏm, Hong Yong-sik, and Yu Kil-chun, made him an eager student of things modern and Western. In 1882 he passed the highest traditional civil service examination (*munkwa*) with distinction but decided to go to Japan with the help of Kim Ok-kyun. During 1883 he studied modern military skills and organization at the Toyama Military Academy in Tokyo. Upon his return to Seoul

he became involved in the Independence Party's attempt in late 1884 to capture power by force. In the short-lived reform government created by the party, he was appointed vice-minister in the Board of War. The break-up of this government at the hands of its Chinese-backed opponents forced Jaisohn to flee first to Japan and then to the United States. [*See also* 1884 Coup d'État.]

During the period from 1885 to 1895 Jaisohn remained in America, acquiring secondary and college education. In 1892 he earned a degree in medicine, became an American citizen, converted to Christianity, married an American (Muriel Josephine Buchanan), anglicized his name, and served as a physician in Washington, D.C., as an assistant to the famed doctor Walter Reed.

Upon the formation of a Japanese-backed reform government after the Sino-Japanese War in 1895, Jaisohn was invited back to Seoul to serve as adviser to the Privy Council. With his own resources, combined with the backing of Yu Kil-chun, a member of the cabinet, Jaisohn also started Korea's first all-*han'gŭl* newspaper, the *Tongnip sinmun (Independent)* and later founded the organization Tongnip

Hyŏphoe (Independence Club). Both organs were designed to help strengthen popular enthusiasm and support for Korea's independence and modernization.

In May 1898, after the Japanese-backed reformers lost influence, Jaisohn was forced to return to America by the antagonistic conservative bureaucracy. From then until 1947 he practiced medicine in Media, Pennsylvania, and at the same time took an active part in cultivating the support of Korean expatriates as well as Americans for the cause of Korean independence. He traveled widely, writing and lecturing and working with members of other Korean organizations and the Provisional Government in exile. In June 1947 he returned to Seoul as senior adviser to the US military government of Korea, and, despite his American citizenship, was frequently but unsuccessfully approached by various Korean political groups to run for the country's presidency. In September 1948, after the formation of the Syngman Rhee presidency, Jaisohn returned to Media, where he remained until his death.

[See also Independence Party and Club.]

Chong-sik Lee, *The Politics of Korean Nationalism* (1965). Channing Liem, *America's Finest Gift to Korea: The Life of Philip Jaisohn* (1952).    VIPAN CHANDRA

**JAJMANI,** a term derived from *yajamana,* the Vedic Sanskrit word for a patron employing a brahman priest to perform a religious sacrifice. By extension, *jajmani* relations are hereditary ties of obligation between a food-producing family and families supplying them with goods and services, usually within a single village or small region. In what has been called the *jajmani* system, the services of specialists are reciprocated with traditionally specified gifts of food, clothing, and sometimes money. *Jajmani* relations typically span generations and link a patron landowning family with single client families of priests, potters, tailors, leatherworkers, washermen, weavers, carpenters, and the like, each practicing traditional caste occupations and also exchanging goods and services among themselves. The equity of such bonds has been much debated. *Jajmani* ties are found in most regions of India but are now weakening as cash transactions gain in importance.

[See also Caste.]

Richard Lannoy, *The Speaking Tree: A Study of Indian Culture and Society* (1971). David G. Mandelbaum, *Society in India* (1970). William H. Wiser, *The Hindu Jajmani System* (1936).    DORANNE JACOBSON

**JAKARTA,** capital and largest city of Indonesia (1980 population, 6.5 million). Jakarta is situated on a swampy plain at the mouth of the Ciliwung River on the northwestern coast of Java. The first town known on this site was Sunda Kelapa, port of the kingdom of Pajajaran in the twelfth century. Conquered in 1527 by the sultanate of Banten and renamed Jayakarta ("victorious"), it was destroyed in 1619 by Jan Pieterszoon Coen, who founded in its place the port of Batavia as regional headquarters of the Dutch East India Company (VOC). Built like a Dutch canal town, Batavia was fortified against hostile neighbors. The VOC encouraged European and Chinese immigration and imported slaves from all over Asia. Some tension existed (and continued) between the ethnic groups, as can be seen by the massacre of Chinese in 1740, after which the Chinese were resettled outside the walls in the "Chinese camp" (now Glodok). As a result of ethnic intermingling, the language of the town became Malay (now Bahasa Indonesia).

In the late eighteenth century Batavia was notoriously unhealthy owing to the spread of waterborne diseases, notably malaria. (Drainage and water supply problems continue to plague the lower town.) Europeans moved to higher land farther south where they built Weltevreden (Gambir) around a large square called Koningsplein (Medan Merdeka). In 1810, after the collapse of the VOC, the colonial administration was moved to Weltevreden, although old Batavia (Kota) remained the business center. Batavia's status as a port was enhanced by the building of a modern harbor at Tanjung Priok (completed in 1886). Chinese settled around markets like Tanah Abang and Senen, while Indonesians lived in kampongs, unplanned urban villages. After the slave trade was abolished in 1812, local immigration provided the labor force. The population grew slowly (from 47,000 in 1815 to 115,000 in 1900), allowing acculturation and giving rise to a unique Indonesian ethnic group, the Orang Betawi.

In 1905 the Batavia municipal government was established with a limited representative council and centrally appointed mayor. Population growth accelerated: by 1930 Batavia had 435,000 people, mostly Javanese immigrants. Settlement spread southward: the European suburb of Menteng was planned in the early twentieth century, and in 1935 the township of Meester Cornelis (Jatinegara) was incorporated into the municipality.

During the Japanese occupation (1943-1945) Batavia's name was changed to Jakarta, a version of Jayakarta. Independence was declared there in

1945. After a period of shared British-Dutch-Indonesian administration, the Dutch seized control of the city again in 1947, and in 1949 Jakarta became the capital of the Republic of Indonesia. As a major center of administration, commerce, industry, education, and culture, it attracted massive immigration, causing severe overcrowding and reducing the Orang Betawi to a small minority. Growth focused on the southwestern area: from Medan Merdeka highways were built to the elite suburb of Kebayoran Baru. In 1961, when the population reached 2.9 million, Jakarta was accorded the status of Special Capital Region, ruled by a powerful centrally appointed governor. Under its most famous governor, Ali Sadikin, Jakarta underwent extensive modernization.

[*See also* Indonesia, Republic of; Pajajaran; Banten; Coen, Jan Pieterszoon; *and* Dutch East India Company.]

Lance Castles, "The Ethnic Profile of Jakarta," *Indonesia* 1 (1967): 153–204. A. Heuken, *Historical Sites of Jakarta* (1982).                    SUSAN ABEYASEKERE

## JALLIANWALA BAGH MASSACRE.

The killing of unarmed protestors by the British army in 1919 at Jallianwala Bagh, a garden courtyard in the city of Amritsar in the Indian state of Punjab, made a significant impact on India's movement for national independence. A rising tide of violent nationalist protest had led General R. E. H. Dyer, the commander of the army in Amritsar, to adopt harsh measures, including one that required all Indians passing the house where a European woman had been assaulted to crawl on their knees. On 13 April 1919 a crowd gathered in the Jallianwala Bagh courtyard to protest, and although there was no provocation and the only exit had been blocked, the troops fired on the crowds, using some 1,650 rounds of ammunition in ten minutes. Approximately four hundred people were killed and twelve hundred were injured.

The Indian National Congress responded with a storm of protest, and the distinguished poet Rabindranath Tagore renounced the knighthood that the British had previously conferred upon him. A commission of inquiry was established by the British government, headed by Lord Hunter, and although the commission chastised Dyer, it was regarded by Mohandas Gandhi and the other Congress leaders, who officially had boycotted the commission hearings, as "a thinly disguised whitewash." Thereafter the name of the massacre became a rallying cry for those in the nationalist movement who sought a more aggressive policy of protest against British rule.

[*See also* Indian National Congress; Amritsar; Gandhi, Mohandas Karamchand; *and* Tagore, Rabindranath.]

MARK JUERGENSMEYER

**JAMAT-I-ISLAMI**, reformist movement founded in 1941 by Maulana Abu'l A'la Maududi in response to the Muslim League's "Pakistan Resolution" of the previous year. Maududi and his followers opposed the idea of Pakistan on the grounds that it would not be a genuine Islamic state but a secular nation controlled by europeanized pseudo-Muslims. The League's Pakistan, they argued, would only serve to encourage Hindu nationalism and anti-Islamic bigotry. The Jamat-i-Islami called on Muslims to practice the faith as defined by Maududi and thus strictly and slowly convert non-Muslims by their example.

After the partition in 1947, Maududi left India reluctantly. Once in Pakistan, he and the Jamat became the government's most persistent and best organized critics. Intolerant of the Ahmadiyya (followers of Mirza Ahmed [1835–1908], who claimed to be a prophet in the line of Muhammad), the Jamat was banned and Maududi was imprisoned after being blamed for the 1953 riots against that sect. The Jamat managed a comeback, however. Although small, it was highly visible, and the sponsorship of an islamicization campaign by Zia al-Haq made certain elements of the Jamat program the official policy of the government.

The Indian branch of the Jamat-i-Islami reconstituted itself in 1948 with Maulana Abul Lais Islahi as its leader. Although little direct contact occurred between the branches, the program of the Indian Jamat-i-Islami continues to stress political quietism and religious purity. It devotes itself to such issues as religious education and relief for Muslim victims of riots, and actually supports the idea of a truly secular (i.e., religiously neutral) state.

[*See also* Maududi, Abu'l A'la; All-India Muslim League; Pakistan; Partition of India; *and* Ahmadiyya.]

A. Ahmad, *Islamic Modernism in India and Pakistan* (1967). W. C. Smith, *Islam in Modern History* (1959).

GREGORY C. KOZLOWSKI

**JAMBI**, or Djambi, city on the Hari River in south-central Sumatra. It was one among a series of upriver ports that emerged in the post-fifth-century era to service the international maritime trade that passed through the Strait of Melaka.

In 683 Jambi, then called Malayu, was conquered and became subject to the authority of the Palembang-based Srivijaya state. In 1024–1025, the South Indian Cholas plundered Srivijaya's ports, and between 1079 and 1082 Jambi replaced Palembang as the central port in the Srivijaya realm. The ruins of a temple complex west of the modern city date from this period. Jambi was raided by the Javanese monarch Kertanagara about 1275 and subsequently became subject to Javanese overlordship. In 1375 it had become part of the Minangkabau kingdom founded by Adityavarman. By the early seventeenth century, when the Dutch and English established factories there, Jambi had become a market center for pepper. The independent Jambi sultanate participated in a series of wars with Johor in the 1660s and 1670s; Jambi's forces sacked the Johor capital in 1673, but Jambi was in turn plundered by Johor's troops in 1679. During the late nineteenth century the Jambi region became a center for Dutch rubber estates.

[See also Srivijaya; Minangkabau; Pepper; and Johor.]

O. W. Wolters, *The Fall of Srivijaya in Malay History* (1970).
                                          KENNETH R. HALL

**JAMI** (1414–1492/1493), Nur al-Din Abu al-Barakat Abd al-Rahman, poet, mystic, and scholar of the fifteenth century, considered by many the last great classical poet of Iran. He was born in Jam (hence his pen name Jami, a town in Khurasan, but spent most of his life in Herat (in present-day Afghanistan), where his family had moved when he was still a boy. Jami received his formal education in the Nizamiyya school of Herat and later in Samarkand, then a prominent center of learning. Apart from a tour of the towns in Khurasan and a pilgrimage to Hejaz, during which he also visited Damascus, he hardly left Herat. He enjoyed the high esteem of princes and kings; the Ottoman sultan corresponded with him and tried to persuade him to go to Anatolia. He belonged to the Naqshbandi order of Sufis. Jami died in Herat at the age of eighty-one and was buried next to his spiritual mentor Sa'd al-Din Kashghari. Among his numerous works are his *Diwan* (in three parts), *Haft awrang, Nafahat al-ons* (an important biographical dictionary of Sufi shaikhs), and *Baharistan* (a collection of sayings and anecdotes in imitation of Sa'di's *Gulistan*).

[See also Persian Literature and Sa'di.]

E. G. Browne, *A Literary History of Persia* (1928), vol. 3, pp. 507–548. C. Huart, "Djāmī," in *The Encyclopaedia of Islam* (new ed., 1960–). J. Rypka, *History of Iranian Literature* (1968), pp. 286–288.

                                      MANOUCHEHR KASHEFF

**JAMMU**, district of the state of Jammu and Kashmir in India, with an estimated population (1981) of about two million. The town of Jammu is the capital of the state during the winter months because the climate is milder; this also lends greater political power to the district. Until recent years the road to Kashmir did not run through Jammu, and its barren hills, without either the beauty or fertility of the Valley of Kashmir, did not attract invaders from India. The result was that throughout the centuries when North India was controlled by Muslim rulers, the people of Jammu, known as Dogras, remained Hindu, and were ruled by independent Rajput chieftains. In the middle of the eighteenth century the powerful Raja Ranjit Deo extended his control from the Ravi River in the east to the Chenab in the west, but after his death around 1780 there was a dispute over succession to the throne; the Sikhs, who had established their power under Ranjit Singh at Lahore, made Jammu a tributary. They made Gulab Singh, a descendant of Raja Ranjit Deo's family, raja of Jammu in 1820. He is said to have been cruel and oppressive, but he extended his power over neighboring hill rajas. He conquered Ladakh, the remote Buddhist territory in the northern mountains, and in 1841 his armies, under the able general Zorawar Singh, invaded Tibet but were driven out. By then the Jammu territories had almost encircled Kashmir, which had been taken over by the Sikhs, and when war broke out between the Sikhs and the British in 1845, Gulab Singh sided with the British. As a reward, after the defeat of the Sikhs the British sold the Kashmir territories to Gulab Singh. He and his successors thus became the rulers of the combined state of Jammu and Kashmir. While the rulers were Hindu, the people of Kashmir were almost 90 percent Muslim, and the Kashmiris believed that they were exploited by the Hindus of Jammu. The ancient animosties produced by differences in religion, language, culture, and by economic grievances, real or fancied, are reflected in the political alignments of the modern state of Jammu and Kashmir.

[See also Kashmir; Singh, Ranjit; and Sikhism.]

                                         AINSLIE T. EMBREE

JANA SANGH, Indian political party founded in 1951 by Syama Prasad Mookerjee. It drew its inspiration from the traditions of nineteenth-century Hindu nationalism and its organizational strength from the Rashtriya Swayamsevak Sangh (RSS), a militant, paramilitary Hindu cultural organization. Despite its open membership and emphasis on the development of *bharatiya*, or Indian culture, the party became identified as a pro-Hindu communal party.

The party developed a strong base in the Hindu heartland of northern India. It participated in coalition governments in five states between 1967 and 1971; in Lok Sabha elections, it polled 9.4 percent of the vote in 1967 and 7.4 percent in 1971. Its support came from urban shopkeepers, white-collar workers, professionals, and some peasants. In 1977 the Jana Sangh merged with the Janata Party, but broke with the Janata in April 1980 to become the Bharatiya Janata Party (BJP).

[*See also* Rashtriya Swayamsevak Sangh.]

Craig Baxter, *Jana Sangh: A Biography of an Indian Political Party* (1969). M. A. Jhangiani, *Jana Sangh and Swatantra* (1967).          STANLEY A. KOCHANEK

JANATA MORCHA ("people's movement"), a movement conceived in Tihar Jail in 1976 when leaders of all opposition parties were imprisoned by Prime Minister Indira Gandhi during the Emergency (1975–1977) in India. Essentially a conglomerate of five constituent political parties, each dominated by a major opposition political figure—the Bharatiya Lok Dal (Charan Singh), Congress-O (Morarji Desai), Congress for Democracy (Jagjivan Ram), Jana Sangh (Atal Behari Vajpayee), and Socialists (George Fernandes)—the Janata came to power in a wave of rural, low caste, and minority protest against Indira Gandhi's Congress-I in March 1977 elections and was voted from power in the December 1979 elections.

During its two and one-half years in office, the Janata government succeeded in restoring freedom of speech, assembly, and the press, as well as the right of habeas corpus and the independence of the courts. Both internal and external emergency decrees were lifted and constitutional amendments and laws passed to diminish the authoritarian constitutional powers used by Mrs. Gandhi during the Emergency period. The Janata Morcha formulated an innovative rural-based labor-intensive economic development strategy based in large part on private voluntary associations and small, cottage industries, but the strategy was never effectively implemented because of divisions within Janata ranks and the dissembling opposition of urban-based politicians.

[*See also* Emergency in India, The; Gandhi, Indira; *and* Desai, Morarji.]

Marcus Franda, "India's Double Emergency Democracy: Transformations, Reactions and Adaptations, and Implications," three-part series in *American Universities Field Staff Reports* 19.17–19 (1975), and *India's Rural Development: An Assessment of Alternatives* (1979).

MARCUS FRANDA

## JAPAN

### HISTORY OF JAPAN

Japan is an archipelago composed of four main islands and numerous smaller islands. Its principal history has been played out in the central islands of Honshu, Kyushu, and Shikoku. Hokkaido, to the north, was fully occupied only in the nineteenth century, and the Kurile island chain, lost to Russian occupation in the closing days of World War II, became known to Japanese only in the eighteenth century. To the south, Okinawa and other Ryūkyū islands came under loose control of the southern Japanese domain of Satsuma in the seventeenth century, and were incorporated under central rule in the 1870s.

*Prehistoric Japan.* A number of groups inhabited the Japanese islands well before the dominance of powerful clans or lineages initiated the process of unification that produced the early Japanese state. Because the modern Japanese state of the nineteenth century based its legitimacy on the shadowy mythology compiled at the dawn of Japanese literacy, the way was not open for free speculation on prehistoric Japan until the Japanese defeat in World War II. Since then the boundaries of prehistoric Japan have been greatly pushed back. Although pottery shards, stone tools, pit-dwellings, and skeletons offer little hope of providing a full record, the scholar's problem has been further complicated by the imprecision of chronological terms. *Jōmon,* for example, is descriptive, describing the first pottery; *Yayoi* is a place name associated with a pottery find. Neither carries the analytical force of *Paleolithic* or *Mesolithic.* Contemporary archaeologists distinguish the following sequence: first, bands roaming rather widely; next, people using Mesolithic tools to ensure survival; then, Jōmon people living a more sedentary tribal life based on food gathering; and finally, Yayoi agricultural societies ruled by shaman chieftains and armed with knowledge of metallurgy.

Throughout much of the early period Japan was connected to the continent, and the islands were formed as sea level rose. The history of early societies in Japan extends for an estimated thirty-three thousand years, becoming "Japanese" with the building of burial mounds (*kofun*) around 250 CE.

The Paleolithic stage (28,000–10,500 BCE) involved the separation of the Japanese islands from the continental shelf, a process that was probably not complete until about 18,000 BCE. Preceramic, Paleolithic sites have been identified since 1949, most of them in the Kantō region. Core and chipped and flake stone tools have been found in numerous sites since then. The principal bridges to the continent were at the northern and southern extremities, and temperature considerations made the southerly route through Korea from North China the logical entry. As long as the southern land bridge existed new arrivals must constantly have appeared.

Stratigraphy, typology, and radiocarbon dating combine to suggest that Japan's earliest pottery originated in northwest Kyushu, where finds have been dated to about 10,000 BCE. These dates antedate those accepted for the earliest Chinese pottery, and establish the antiquity of early societies in Japan. Jōmon cultures are divided into Early (5000–3500 BCE), Middle (3500–2400 BCE), and Late (2400–1000 BCE). Jōmon is usually described as Neolithic; the existence of agriculture in later Jōmon is still unclear, but it is clearly absent in early Jōmon. Consequently some scholars prefer the term *proto-Neolithic*, but most retain the term *Jōmon*. The term *jōmon* itself refers to "rope pattern" designs on pottery. [See Jōmon.]

Yayoi culture, named for an area of Tokyo in which excavations first revealed this post-Jōmon culture, represents the entry of East Asian agricultural techniques and the use of iron. Yayoi corresponds roughly to the early imperial age of China, and may have been affected by some of the population movements that accompanied the developments of Qin and Han times. Wet-rice cultivation made possible dramatic increases in population, and was accompanied by the formation of social classes and the development of early forms of political organization. By late Yayoi the Japanese archipelago was home to ten or fifteen times the population of Jōmon culture. Yayoi culture spread from Kyushu to the north. Pottery containers were used for burial, and pots were now wheel-thrown. Yayoi sites also contain bronze bells and bronze weapons, some probably of continental origin. [See Yayoi.]

The indistinct countours of this shadowy past begin to harden with the creation of the Yamato state on the historic Yamato Plain of central Japan, an area that bore the early capitals of Nara and Kyoto and was serviced by the seaports of the Sakai and Osaka area. Unification took place under the aegis of the Sun line, one of a number of competing lineage or clan structures, probably in existence from the late Yayoi period. Each such lineage claimed linkage with divine entities (*kami*) of natural origin, and the Sun line's claimed ancestry from the sun goddess, combined with a probable advantageous position of access to continental technology and weaponry, served it well in establishing its preeminence. In the seventh and early eighth century the official court scribes who compiled the *Kojiki* (712) and *Chronicles of Japan* (*Nihon shoki*, 720) encased these claims in a cycle of myths that described the divine creation of the Japanese isles, the origins of a beneficent sun goddess (Amaterasu Ōmikami) associated with cultivation of rice in the Land of Reed Plains, who was progenitor of the first ruler (Jimmu) to unify the island empire. These accounts assimilated the evidence of involvement on the Korean peninsula as aspects of Japanese domination and power, and provided the basis for the mythic foundations of empire under Jimmu in 660 BCE, a date derived from the dictates of Chinese numerology. [See Yamato; Kojiki; Nihon Shoki; Amaterasu Ōmikami; *and* Jimmu.]

Yamato political institutions centered around a complex of "clan" (*uji*) lineages, each with its tutelary deity. Some clans were honored by special titles (*kabane*) conferred by the *ōgimi* ("great king"). The highest titles were given as a hereditary right to *uji* leaders who served directly at court or held power bases near the capital. Periods of centralization found powerful rulers extending their influence through the grant of such titles, but early chronicles also speak of geneological falsification by political rivals in periods of weakness.

Occupational groups (*be, tomo*) were attached to the dominant units of court and powerful *uji*. Hereditary heads of these units or corporations, who might or might not possess *kabane*, controlled the activities of the group in performing service or producing goods or products for the court or *uji* to which it was attached. Occupational groups began as servile in status, but in time many specialized in important artisan roles for the production of weapons, and of mirrors for ceremony, and for technological tasks connected with irrigational systems. The early chronicles mention numerous *be* made up of immigrants from the Korean state of Paekche. [See Uji *and* Be.]

By late Yamato times participation in continental

struggles intensified with requests from Paekche for assistance against Koguryŏ and, later, Silla. Paekche sent embassies and hostages to reinforce its requests, and, in the sixth century, Buddhist images, the first recorded evidence of the entry of the continental faith. Japan in turn approached the fifth-century southern Chinese court of (Liu) Song for help against Koguryŏ. Activity on the Korean peninsula was also impelled by a growing desire for material and techological gains; Korea seems to have been a principal source for iron ore as well. [See Koguryŏ and Paekche.]

In the sixth century, however, Yamato influence on the peninsula was in decline; at the same time the continued diffusion of influence from the continent brought efforts to organize a group of literate officials in service to the court, to register and organize at least part of the population, and to register and allocate resources in royal lands (*miyake*) for national purposes. Districts were being organized and officials appointed. By the late sixth century the Soga clan, probably of immigrant origin, had emerged as clear leader at court, committed to the sponsorship of Buddhism and more intense participation in south Korea. Japan was ready for the massive designs of national reconstruction associated with the "great change" toward continental institutions of the seventh century.

***The Chinese Model.*** The Taika ("great change") Reforms of 645 constitute a great divide in Japanese history comparable to the Meiji Restoration of 1868. In the former case Japan turned to China, and in the latter to the West, for institutional models as guide in a planned program of social engineering and modernization appropriate to its time. In each case international relations played a major role in internal renovation. In the seventh century the rise of Tang China was threatening the arrangement on the Korean peninsula to which Japan had become accustomed, while in 1868 the Western imperialist advance on East Asia seemed to carry with it threats to Japanese national sovereignty. In each case an extended period of preparation made possible the changes that followed in quick order. In the nineteenth century the Tokugawa shogunate had begun the experimentation with Western forms and weapons, and in the seventh century an extended influx of Chinese culture and institutions prepared the country for transition.

That preparation had advanced particularly after 587, when the Soga seized power at the Yamato court. This political change ushered in a period sometimes characterized as the Asuka Enlightenment. The strong Chinese character of innovations

that followed may be credited to the success of the Sui dynasty in reuniting China in 589 CE. Tributary relationships were reestablished with the three Korean states of Koguryŏ, Paekche, and Silla. The Soga-dominated Yamato court sent an embassy to the Sui capital. Thereafter there was an increasing flow of missions to China that continued into the ninth century. [See Soga.]

Under Soga dominance the Yamato court supported Buddhism within Japan. Buddhist priests and continental-trained or inspired artisans led in the crafts, building, and scholarship that sparked the culture of the Asuka age. Forty-six Buddhist temples were founded during the period, including the famous Hōryūji, a temple associated with the regent Shōtoku Taishi. Knowledge of Chinese writing was advanced by priests and scholars sent to Japan by the king of Paekche. That process had begun before the Soga coup of 587. It seems clear that increasing numbers of court officials were conscious of the importance and advantage of Chinese script and books well before the Soga rise to power. In 593, however, Suiko, the first female ruler to be invested, ordered court nobles to support Buddhism, while her nephew and regent, Prince Shōtoku, began the activities that brought him his reputation as the principal sponsor of Japanese Buddism. The Ikarugaji (the present Hōryūji) was built near his palace. It became and remains the great repository of Asuka culture, with a wealth of images, some of Korean provenance, that make it the premier temple of Japan. By 614 Korean priests were prominent among the 1,385 clerics at Hōryūji. [See Hōryūji.]

Japanese awareness of the advantages of Chinese institutions became stronger after the 600-member mission to the Sui court of 607. Shōtoku was closely associated with continental interests politically as well as culturally. He prepared an expeditionary force against Silla in 602. The next year he directed the adoption of system of court ranks similar to those of Koguryŭ and Paekche; in 604 he issued his celebrated Seventeen Injunctions (sometimes referred to as a "constitution"), replete with Confucian and Buddhist phraseology and morality; and in 607 and 608 he initiated diplomatic exchange with the Chinese court. Each of these undertakings significantly prefigure the changes that were to follow in 645. [See Shōtoku Taishi.]

At the center of Yamato power the Soga leaders were becoming steadily more arrogant and self-willed. By the time students who had been dispatched to China with the original embassy returned to Japan several years later, the Soga dominance had resulted in deep hatreds that flared in a coup d'état.

The Soga killed Shōtoku's son and his family in 643. Two years later Prince Nakano Ōe and Nakatomi Kamatari, progenitor of the Fujiwara lineage, engineered a coup within the palace, utilizing a welcoming ceremony for Korean envoys to assassinate the Soga leader. He was immediately replaced by Kamatari as the paramount influence at court, who set about initiating the changes collectively known as the Taika Reforms.

These changes had as their purpose the establishment of a system of centralized government headed by an absolute sovereign, who would function in a manner similar to the Chinese emperor. Elements of the Wei, Sui, and Tang institutions were used as examples. Guides and counselors were drawn from the body of students who had been part of the mission to the Sui capital between 607 and 608, and from the large number of refugee scribes and scholars who came to Japan from Korea after the intervention of Chinese armies resulted in the defeats of first Koguryŭ and then Paekche.

Efforts to establish centralized control made it necessary to organize and control the clan (uji) heads. This was done by incorporating them in a new structure of ranks and honors. The Buddhist temples were placed under a new court bureaucracy. Revenue needs led to census surveys and registers. An orderly and uniform allocation of rice fields followed; they were scheduled to be redivided regularly in accordance with population changes. The result of this was an administrative order known to historians as the ritsuryō state, organized on the principal that land and people were to be controlled from the center. Laws for population registers and tax and land allocation made possible a regular collection of produce assessments and labor duty, and the whole was controlled by a sovereign (tennō) who ruled through a Chinese-style bureaucratic structure at the same time that his sacral links to the sun goddess and kami worship were elaborated to guarantee an unchallengeable predominance. [See Taika Reforms and Ritsuryō State.]

The Nara period (710–794) stands as a great age in the development and maturation of Japanese civilization. The court-sponsored poetry anthology, the Man'yōshū, and the early chronicles are the earliest Japanese texts to survive, and provide the beginning point for all consideration of early Japanese culture. [See Man'yōshū.] Administrative codes, modeled on those of China, provide the first solid evidence of political and institutional practice. Also modeled on the Chinese example was the capital, Heijōkyō (modern Nara), which was laid out with broad avenues in a grid pattern emanating from an imperial palace in a north-central location. The classic beauty and severity of early Buddhist art and architecture make Japan the great museum of early East Asian Buddhist style and craftsmanship. [See Nara Period.]

In 794 the capital was moved to modern Kyoto, then called Heiankyō ("capital of peace and tranquillity"). This move provides Japanese historians with a new division, the Heian period (794–1185), which ends with the establishment of warrior rule in Kamakura. In fact, however, it can as well or better be grouped with the Nara age as a period of aristocratic rule, perhaps divided at the year 1000 to allow for the steady deterioration of the ritsuryō order thereafter. Throughout the early part of the age succession disputes continued to mark the political history at the capital. The more important development involves the rise of the Fujiwara family to dominance at court; it controlled the imperial line by providing it with consorts, and the governmental processes by manning new, extrastatutory offices set up to bypass the immobility of the traditional aristocratic ranks. One element of the ritsuryō order, however, and in some ways its most important, survived in ideal: the concept of a "public" population (kōmin), whose produce and tax rightly belonged to the sovereign, as opposed to a system in which "private" interests would control men and their product. By late Heian times private estates (shōen) were threatening this concept, and in the medieval centuries feudal division seemed to extinguish it altogether, but by the sixteenth century the warrior unifiers and their principal vassals were once again speaking of "public matters" and "the realm" (kōgi, tenka) and accepting Confucian rhetoric that renounced privatization of the realm. [See Shōen.].

Heian culture stands as the great achievement of early Japan. Buddhism continued its growth, but became shaped by denominational influences as new schools capable of appealing to larger numbers replaced the esoteric cults of the early period. Priests like Saichō (Dengyō Daishi), Kūkai (Kōbō Daishi), and Ennin (Jikaku Daishi) became the spiritual teachers of the age. Missions to the Tang court of China continued into the ninth century, but they were given up with the conclusion that China had left the Buddhist path and had little further to teach. [See Saichō, Kūkai; and Ennin.] In writing, a Japanese syllabary, drawn from Chinese characters, developed alongside Chinese symbols, and native poetry, especially the thirty-one-syllable waka, became an essential social grace. The native syllabary led to a surge of artistic creativity. Aristocractic women produced much of the great literature of the age, including the *Tale of the Genji* (*Genji monogatari*), while men tended to write in the more "manly" Chinese idiom. The contact with China and Chinese civilization had created a profound consciousness of Japan's as a civilization distinct from that of China. Art, in architecture, statuary, and painting, continued to center on Buddhism. Even here, however, a distinct *Yamato-e*, or "Japanese painting," developed in conscious contrast to the imported idiom. [*See* Genji Monogatari; Painting: Japanese Painting; *and* Heian Period.]

**Warrior Ascendancy.** With the decline of central power the Heiankyō court found itself calling on warrior families for assistance. A provincial class of warriors had been developing in the provinces in the service of local officials and estate managers. In the east there was a loose league headed by the Minamoto, in central Japan they were grouped around the Taira. Both groups claimed a connection with the court, and both grew as ambitious young men found themselves blocked at the capital. Discord between retired emperors and reigning emperors, and internal differences within the Fujiwara, split the Kyoto aristocracy and led it to call in provinical warriors to help settle its disputes. Minamoto and Taira found themselves enlisted on opposite sides in such disputes. In the so-called Hōgen War (1156) victory went to the Minamoto, but in the Heiji War (1159) the Minamoto were defeated and Taira Kiyomori emerged as victor. Kiyomori provided an imperial consort, took the highest of court titles for himself, and ruled with a high hand. Minamoto partisans had meanwhile been biding their time, however, and in a series of battles that became a heroic saga the Minamoto triumphed by 1185. Japan would remain under military rule until the fall of the Tokugawa shogunate in 1867. [*See* Hōgen and Heiji Wars; Taira no Kiyomori; *and* Minamoto.]

Minamoto Yoritomo (1147–1199) received honors and privileges from the court after his victories in 1185, and in 1192 he was appointed *sei-i tai shōgun* ("barbarian-subduing generalissimo"), a title originally conferred during campaigns against the Ainu to the north. Yoritomo chose to keep his headquarters separate from the Kyoto court with its intrigues and jealousies, and established his headquarters at the port of Kamakura in Sagami Bay, not far from present-day Tokyo. At Kamakura he kept institutions, which he modeled on house laws, to a sparse minimum: a Board of Retainers (Samuraidokoro), a Secretariat for General Adminis-

tration (Mandokoro), and a Judicial Board (Monchūjo), which had the responsibility of ruling on disputes over land estates. As a peacekeeping device he received permission from the court to appoint military governors (*shugo*) in all provinces, and military stewards (*jitō*) to watch over private estates. In their simplicity and efficiency these institutions stood in sharp contrast to the complex rank-bound institutions that had come to prevail in Kyoto. [*See also* Mandokoro; Shugo; *and* Jitō.]

Yoritomo did not, however, succeed in his plans to inaugurate a shogunal dynasty. His suspicion of his brothers and cousins had led him to charge the most able of them, particularly his younger brother Yoshitsune, with treason, and his vengeful retribution for real and supposed infidelity destroyed the senior and most able level of possible descendants. Following his demise in 1199, Yoritomo's two choices as successors, both ineffectual, were murdered. Rule then came to be exercised by the Hōjō, a family that had sheltered Yorimoto and provided him with a wife during his long exile to the north.

The great crisis of the Kamakura period was the Mongol invasions dispatched by Kublai Khan to conquer Japan in 1274 and 1281. On both occasions strong Mongol forces managed to get ashore in Kyushu against stout samurai resistance, only to be defeated by the elements as a typhoon struck their ships. Later nationalists credited this to divine intervention in the form of a "divine wind" (*kamikaze*), a name that would recur in future crises. The Kamakura government had no assurance that it would not have to face a third Mongol onslaught, but the costs of preparedness and the government's inability to reward its servants with confiscated lands combined to weaken its standing with its vassals. [*See* Mongol Empire: Mongol Invasions of Japan.]

The Kamakura years were for the most part marked by law and order and, under conditions of peace, productivity and commercial activity advanced strikingly. Guilds of shipping merchants developed to convey freight along Japan's coasts, and provisioners also organized themselves in *za*, or guilds, to carry out their tasks.

The period was one in which culture and literacy, previously confined to small groups at the capital, came to be far more widely diffused throughout the country. In no respect was this more evident than in the transmission and diffusion of Buddhism. The structured esoteric sects of the Nara and Heian periods that had ministered to the needs of the wealthy and powerful now spawned teachings that emphasized the simplicity of faith and the efficacy of chanting and prayer. Popular Buddhism transformed Japanese religious consciousness, whether in prayers to Amida, the Buddha of the Western Paradise, or invocation of the *Lotus Sutra* as taught by the monk Nichiren. [*See* Amidism *and* Nichiren.] The new warrior leaders were themselves usually firm believers in Buddhism. In Kamakura a giant image of Amida Buddha was built, and the Nara temples received shogunal help in their attempts to finance rebuilding and maintenance. [*See* Kamakura Period.]

In the fourteenth century the Kamakura *bakufu* was replaced by a new line of Ashikaga shoguns, who established their headquarters in Kyoto's Muromachi sector, thereby providing the name historians customarily use. In 1333 the emperor Go-Daigo attempted to reassert court primacy in the brief and unsuccessful Kemmu Restoration, and after an extended but futile stand of his supporters in the Yoshino area during which there were rival northern and southern courts (Nambokuchō) the lines were brought together again by the shogun Ashikaga Yoshimitsu in 1392. [*See* Go-Daigo; Kemmu Restoration; Yoshino Line; Nambokuchō; *and* Ashikaga Yoshimitsu.]

In Muromachi times the shoguns were less powerful than the Hōjō had been at the height of Kamakura rule, but the structure of the imperial court survived in even more attenuated form. The provincial military governors (*shugo*) increased in power and combined with *jitō*, who had been assigned to watch over tax receipts, to work toward a much more directly military rule. Ashikaga power rested on leagues of *shugo*, and several among these latter assumed regional autonomy and considerable power. The *bakufu*, however, controlled the central heartland of Japanese civilization and also relations with China. These grew in commercial importance. Guilds, customs stations, and a growing commercialization of the economy brought increasing use of coinage and eagerness for access to currency and goods imported from China.

Piracy accompanied trade. Bands of marauders (*wakō*) based on coastal islands harrassed the coastal areas of Korea and China. In order to control the *wakō*, the Ming dynasty was anxious to secure Japanese compliance; its interests coincided with shogunal desires to increase trade and access to Chinese goods. At the end of the century Ashikaga Yoshimitsu accepted tributary status with China, adopted for himself the title "king of Japan," and took steps to control the marauders. His successors,

however, failed to maintain this policy. [*See* Piracy: Japanese Piracy in Korea *and* Piracy: Japanese Piracy in China.]

In the fifteenth century successional disputes in the Ashikaga line found powerful vassals supporting rival candidates. In the Ōnin War, which ranged between 1467 and 1477, much of Kyoto was destroyed, nobles and monks fled to the provinces, and Japan sank into endemic feudal war. The same process, however, served to spread the culture of the capital to the provinces, and the provision of supplies for the armies served to fuel the economic development that was underway. As powerful regional *shugo* struggled for mastery, new provincial forces took shape behind their backs. Powerful regional despots recognized the significance of their time by referring to the age as one of "warring states" (*sengoku*) reminiscent of that of preimperial China. Gradually neither the impotent court nor the ineffective *bakufu* could exert control; instead many small domains began to take shape, each dominated by retainer bands whose leaders strove for stability and mastery through uneasy alliances loosely cemented by the exchange of hostages. Neither administrative nor landholding arrangements of the *ritsuryō* state could survive this ferment. Japan had become feudal. [*See* Ōnin War *and* Sengoku Period.]

Despite its political disorder, the Muromachi age was a time of rapid economic growth and cultural diffusion. The collapse of the structured world of *shōen* gave free reign to market forces and production for exchange. Regional markets became common and production for distant consumers stimulated the development of transport and commercial organizations. War preparations created large markets for metallurgy and building. What was true in the provinces was even more the case in and around Kyoto, to which the Ashikaga shoguns compelled their major vassals to come and which experienced dramatic growth in commercial activities of many sorts. The *bakufu* in fact supported itself from this commercial sector.

The Ashikaga shoguns, particularly Yoshimitsu and Yoshimasa, lived lives of cultural gratification and eagerly sought the company and products of artists, priests, and poets. Great Zen Buddhist temples sprang up near Kyoto and Kamakura; their priests took the lead in facilitating intercourse with Ming China. Under their aegis trade and culture played as great a part in that contact as religion and diplomacy. Feudal lords in other parts of Japan did their best to attract some of that wealth to their shores as well. [*See* Muromachi Period.]

***Reunification.*** The sixteenth century was a time of upheaval and disorder, but at century's end Japan was substantially unified and pacified. This was the result of three trends. The first was a gradual growth in the size of domains that local figures with retainer armies were carving out. Warfare, alliance, and marriage politics helped pacify the principal geographic divisions. Larger riparian works made it possible for local rulers to extend their control to more efficiently sized economic units; in the process their political potential grew accordingly. Second, the entrance of new foreign technology changed the face of warfare and brought the victory to leaders who had access to firearms. Larger forces of professional soldiery ruled out the extremes of political participation that had been possible in a world of arrows, spears, and mounted samurai. Third, a generation of formidable warlords brought a new ruthlessness and thoroughness to their campaigns. The greatest of these were Oda Nobunaga, Toyotomi Hideyoshi, and Tokugawa Ieyasu.

The gradual coalescense of regional forces into provincial or multiprovince agglomerations can be seen in area after area. In the island of Shikoku, for instance, a warlord called Chōsokabe accumulated followers from each redoubt that was captured, rewarded his principal vassals with kinship standing, and brought the fertile plain at the southern side of that fan-shaped island under single rule. Mountain redoubts gave way to a regional castle at the mouth of the rivers that ran through the alluvial plain. With the valley under control, the daimyo (lord) began to consider crossing the mountains that divided the island and seizing lands along the Inland Sea.

Others elsewhere in Japan had prior access to the weapons brought by the Europeans who came to Japan in the 1540s. Portuguese came first to the island of Tanegashima off the coast of Kyushu. In the decades that followed, the work of Iberian missionaries met with astonishing success. Francis Xavier and the Jesuits he led were representatives of a late-feudal Europe, and they found much in the samurai code they encountered to admire. "It seems to me," Xavier wrote his superiors, "we shall never find among heathens another race to equal the Japanese"; he praised the qualities of honesty, courage and respect for status he saw. Drawn from an aristocratic and feudal background themselves, the Jesuits maintained a highly hierarchic order, and they seemed representatives of a military society. They also profited from the eagerness of Japenese daimyo to avail themselves of the trade—much of it in Chinese goods—and weapons that accompanied the missionaries. At Nagasaki the Jesuits were able to establish a permanent base, owing to the conversion of the daimyo. By 1582 the Jesuits were able to claim 150,000 converts. In part these impressive numbers represented expressions of official favor: not a few daimyo converts responded by ordering the destruction of Buddhist temples and encouraging the conversion of their top retainers. Nevertheless, the number of Japanese who chose exile and death over recantation in subsequent persecutions showed that the missionaries had made major gains. Evidence of European disunity followed to confuse the picture. The union of Spain and Portugal was followed by competition from Franciscans and Dominicans, who preached among the commoners and alarmed the authorities, and the appearance of Dutch and English after 1600 suggested the possibility of Western trade without Western religion. [*See also* Christianity: Christianity in Japan; Xavier, Francis; *and* Nagasaki.]

The first steps toward unification were made under the leadership of Oda Nobunaga (1534–1582). Nobunaga began with four districts in the province of Owari, the present Nagoya Plain, and by the time of his assassination had brought most of central Japan under his control. He marched into Kyoto in 1568, nominally at the request of the hapless shogun Ashikaga Yoshiaki, and quickly established domination over the shogunal court. He took steps to separate the court and shogun from the samurai order to prevent tampering with his control over the feudality, and ultimately he drove the shogun into exile. Nobunaga refused appointment to office under existing structures, and instead spoke of his governance as "the realm," making it clear that he and he alone could define that realm and its interests.

Nobunaga was ruthless in steps he took to eliminate possible sources of division. The Jesuits were recipients of his favor, and he granted them rights to travel and proselytize. The armed monks on Mount Hiei in Kyoto were surrounded and exterminated; his armies were ordered to burn every building and kill every inhabitant. Buddhist political power never recovered.

Nobunaga bound his vassals with regulations and assigned them their lands. He ordered local surveys and cadastral registers, and worked to destroy the autonomous power of the local gentry that had proved troublesome to military despots. In some areas he initiated measures to disarm the populace by calling in all weapons. His determination pacified the countryside, but not his vassals. In 1582 a company of his men marching through Kyoto turned on

Nobunaga; they attacked his headquarters and killed him. [*See* Oda Nobunaga.]

The work of unification was continued by Toyotomi Hideyoshi (1536–1598), an outstanding lieutenant of Nobunaga and a man whose origins were more humble by far than those of his peers. Hideyoshi first crushed the vassals responsible for Nobunaga's murder and then set out to win over his fellow generals. While professing loyalty to Nobunaga's heir and family, he gradually took the lines of power into his own hands. Victories over coalitions of feudal lords in Shikoku (1585), Kyushu (1587), and at Odawara (1590) seemed to offer hope of an end to fighting.

Hideyoshi continued and extended Nobunaga's pattern of social pacification and stratification. All over Japan commoners were ordered to turn in their weapons, and farmer-soldiers had to choose between full-time agriculture or military service. Land surveys brought an accurate and uniform tally of acreage and productivity. The missionaries, whom Hideyoshi had courted for a time until his reduction of Kyushu, were ordered to leave in 1587. Some did, but more remained to work quietly among their converts. [*See* Toyotomi Hideyoshi.]

**Tokugawa: Early Modern Japan.** Hideyoshi planned to have his son Hideyori (1593–1615) inherit his position and lands, and appointed his five great vassals as guardians. Predictably, they soon quarreled; Tokugawa Ieyasu (1542–1616) emerged as the new hegemon after his victory at Sekigahara in 1600. Ieyasu had spent much of his youth as a hostage in the turbulence of Sengoku politics; he shifted to the support of Nobunaga when that seemed expedient, and emerged as Hideyoshi's chief rival after Nobunaga's death. [*See* Tokugawa Ieyasu *and* Sekigahara, Battle of.]

Ieyasu and his immediate successors, the shoguns Hidetada and Iemitsu, utilized and invented infractions of discipline to rearrange the territorial map quite completely. Approximately one-fourth of the productive land of the country was kept in *bakufu* hands: four million *koku* as Tokugawa holdings (the *tenryō*), and three million allocated to vassals of less than daimyo status (i.e., less than 10,000 *koku*-rated domains.) For its own lands the bakufu maintained full responsibility through commissioners (*bugyō*) of finance, temples, and the like, while lower officials like deputies (*daikan*) and inspectors (*metsuke*) completed the administrative system. These offices were reserved to Tokugawa vassals, and hereditary rank was usually appropriate to the post involved. The *bakufu*'s central council of elders (*rōjū*) was staffed by hereditary (*fudai*) daimyo, and a junior council (*wakadoshiyori*) was concerned with matters of house policy. In contrast to the approximately 145 *fudai* daimyo, the hundred-odd "outside" (*tozama*) daimyo who had submitted after Sekigahara, although they included some of the largest domain holders in the land, were rigidly excluded from participation in *bakufu*—and hence national—politics. [*See* Tozama Daimyo.]

*Bakufu* control of daimyo was strict. Injunctions warned them of their duties; their marriages had to be approved; they were expected to contribute to *bakufu* building projects for temples, castles, and the like; they were forbidden to have more than one castle or to repair it without central approval; and they were barred from establishing checkpoints or toll stations. Most important of all, however, was the system of alternate attendance (*sankin kōtai*), which was gradually tightened and regularized. By the 1630s all daimyo had to spend alternate years in residence at the shogun's capital of Edo (modern Tokyo), where they maintained an average of three great estates each, and where they left their immediate family members as hostage during their absence home. In the early years confiscation or reduction of fiefs was frequently based on failure of a daimyo to appear at the appointed time. The theory behind this was that, in peacetime, the daimyo's attendance was a form of service duty comparable to military service in time of war. The vast expenditures required for travel and for maintenance of the estates at Edo, which came to be the single largest drain on daimyo finances, had the effect of enfeebling the military capacity of the daimyo, thus contributing to shogunal security. Feudal lords in their turn collected their vassals in their castle towns for more or less full-time residence. As a result, the military elite became a circulating, urbanized population.

Within their domains, however, the daimyo enjoyed substantial autonomy. Only a few dozen administered domains of province size, but they all maintained councils, magistrates, and bureacracies comparable to those of the Tokugawa house itself. They were expected to support their establishments from their own domains. The *bakufu* required of them service or duty and not taxes. In Edo the daimyo estates were closed areas, special enclaves in which the local dialect, customs and traditions obtained. With the passage of time, however, Edo naturally came to loom ever more important in the eyes, tastes, and expectations of the high feudality. Their subordinates were even more free to mix together, in fencing school, salon, or amusement area. The *sankin kōtai* system played an important role in making the separate sections of Japan into a national unit by the end of Tokugawa rule. [*See* Sankin Kōtai *and* Bakufu.]

The jealous concern with security that reduced daimyo to a traveling and hotel existence also characterized Tokugawa relations with the imperial court. Ieyasu spent most of his time after Sekigahara in the Osaka-Kyoto area making certain that most daimyo would not be able to communicate directly with the court. Injunctions to the court nobles stressed that they should concentrate on cultural affairs, and a high-ranking *bakufu* official was stationed in Kyoto to direct and also to restrict the emperor and nobles.

The problem of foreign relations remained real. In 1600 the Iberian presence had been supplemented by that of Dutch and British traders, and the Japanese saw the possiblity of retaining foreign trade without running the danger of Christian (Catholic) subversion. European rivalries were transmitted to Japan, as Spanish and Portuguese denounced the northerners as pirates while the Dutch and British assured the Japanese of the dangers of missionary-borne imperialism. Ieyasu was eager to build up foreign trade, and at first he was inclinded to tolerate and even to encourage the European presence. He soon became worried that the Hideyori Osaka cause could be linked with that of Catholicism, however, and began the persecution of Christians several years before his attack on Osaka in 1614. [*See* Osaka Campaigns.] In 1637 a troublesome rebellion at Shimabara in Kyushu attracted the support of significant numbers of retainers of formerly Christian daimyo, and this apparently direct association of Catholicism and rebellion led to strong and ultimately ferocious proscription of Christianity. Spanish and Portugese were expelled, and Japanese were forbidden to go abroad or to return on fear of death. Thenceforth trade was limited to Chinese and Dutch traders at Nagasaki, and, via the daimyo and lord of Tsushima, with Korea. In 1609 the daimyo of Satsuma took control of the island of Okinawa, and a modest amount of China trade via Okinawa was also tolerated. But essentially, Japan entered a "seclusion" (*sakoku*) stage, and maintained those regulations until they were challenged by the United States in the visit of Commodore Matthew C. Perry in 1853. [*See* Shimabara *and* Seclusion.]

The overwehelming primacy of the Tokugawa *bakufu* thus gave to late feudal, or early modern, Japan a curious combination of feudal institutions and central authority comparable to that of the early modern states of Europe. Travel controls extended throughout the country. Christian surveillance led to the requirement that all be registered with Buddhist temples and reported as Buddhist adherents. Strict controls prevented daimyo from venturing outside their approved paths and gave *bakufu*-licensed merchant guilds special opportunities for the small volume of foreign trade that was tolerated. The *bakufu* controlled the mining of precious metals and it alone could mint coins. Daimyo realms had substantial autonomy, but the growth of urbanization, travel, and commercial activities drew them ever closer into a system of regional interdependence.

Tokugawa cultural life was rich and varied. The great urban agglomerations produced a commoner class and culture that accepted many of the expectations of the samurai master class but also had an impact on that class. Schooling and literacy spread rapidly. By 1700 most of the samurai were receiving some written education; their bureaucratic posts and cultural role as the heads of society made it imcumbent upon them to combine civil and military values. Ironically, the burgeoning repertoire of the *kabuki* stage, which grew ever more popular despite the misgivings of shogunal moralists, projected samurai values in warrior dreams and disseminated them to the commoners. Plays like the *Battles of Koxinga* and *The Treasury of Loyal Retainers*, with its famous tale of the forty-seven *rōnin* who avenged their lord early in the eighteenth century, became classics for all time. [*See* Tokugawa Period.]

In the eighteenth century, an important intellectual movement known as Kokugaku ("national studies") found scholars trying to see what Japanese culture was like before it was affected by that of China. They wrote glowingly of Japan's divine past and of its present mission. One of the long-run effects of the rise of Kokugaku was a stronger focus on Japanese identity in the face of imported aspects of Chinese civilization. Probably inevitably, this came to focus on the emperor in Kyoto as a symbol of that identity. As successive scholarly generations strengthened and emphasized these trends, many of them railing at the evils of imported Chinese values as they did so, there was a rekindling of interest in the imperial court. So too with the worship of *kami*, in an effort to recreate a Shinto that had become a satellite religion of Buddhism. [*See* Kokugaku.]

The nineteenth century brought reminders that the seclusion edicts of the 1630s might be difficult to enforce and maintain. Napoleonic disturbances extended to Japan, for the Dutch East India Company, its bases in Holland and in Java lost to the French and English, respectively, hired American ships to supply the Nagasaki station. Suspicious about these strange "Dutch" ships, *bakufu* officials interrogated the Dutch merchant factor closely and learned of the American revolution, the French revolution, the invasion of Russia, and the new strength of Europe. "Dutch studies" (*rangaku*) experts were coopted for government service, and books on military matters were added to those on medical matters as important for the national purpose. Translations from Dutch, although not arranged or planned in any systematic way, became steadily more important, and even *bakufu* officials began to see the wisdom of finding out about the outside world in case its ships should come to Japan. [*See* Rangaku.] They did come. Rezanov, a representative of the tsar of Russia, arrived in 1804; the *Morrison*, carrying shipwrecked Japanese sailors (who were refused entry) arrived in 1837, and commodores Biddle and Perry of the United States arrived in 1846 and 1853, respectively. [*See* Rezanov, Nikolai Petrovich *and* Perry, Matthew C.]

The Western powers, fresh from their collaborative effort to punish the Chinese in the Opium War, seemed likely to want as much from Japan. The shogunate was insufficiently funded for rearmament, and its accustomed alliance of vassals proved seriously inadequate, first to counter domestic insurrection, and then to hold off the foreigners. Consequently, the *bakufu* officials reluctantly accepted treaty relations with Perry and Townsend Harris and concluded that the political structure should be modified in order to be able to counter the crisis in foreign relations that was upon Japan. [*See* Harris, Townsend.]

*Meiji Japan.* The reopening of Japan to foreign contact after more than two centuries of seclusion created tensions that brought down Tokugawa rule. The presence of foreigners in the treaty ports reinforced and underlined doubts that had been developing for more than a century. If samurai were unable to expel the barbarians, their position at the top of the social order seemed unwarranted. If the shogun was unable to defend the country, the legitimacy of his position was in doubt. Political economists and Confucian moralists had long wrestled with injustices and irrationalities in the system. Scholars of national learning had pointed to the neglect of the throne and deplored departures from Japan's "national morality." In many parts of the country the rural elite was restive under restrictions castle-town samurai administrators were putting on economic development to favor the urban guilds. Scholars knowledgeable about the West knew that Japan was in a poor position to negotiate or resist Western demands.

Consequently, requests for treaties brought by Commodore Perry and Townsend Harris reactivated politics. The shogunate requested daimyo opinion before responding to Perry. Daimyo consulted their advisers, and soon the problem produced a ripple effect that suggested participation even to lower samurai ranks, where it had explosive effects. Ordinary procedures seemed inadequate in a time of crisis. Issues became related to the positions attributed to the Kōmei emperor in Kyoto, and powerful daimyo proposed linking treaty issues to shogunal succession to ensure the leadership of an able and mature person. Areas shielded from debate throughout the Tokugawa years were thrust into the forefront of political discussion.

A series of Tokugawa missions to the West revealed the inevitable course of future policy. The first brought ratification of the Harris treaty to the United States; future missions to Europe brought detailed knowledge of the sources of Western strength in industrial progress; by the time of the Tokugawa fall a youthful Tokugawa family member and possible successor was a student in France.

In 1866 a *bakufu* attempt to discipline Chōshū radicals, who had seized power within the domain after an earlier setback, misfired and revealed the weakened state of Tokugawa military power. Thereafter events moved rapidly. Tokugawa opponents at court and in Satsuma prepared for possible violence, and Satsuma and Chōshū entered a secret alliance. Tosa leaders proposed to the new shogun, Tokugawa Yoshinobu (Keiki), that he resign his office, confident that he would be first among equals in a collegial directorate that would replace the faltering *bakufu*. Yoshinobu did so in the fall of 1867, but he was outmaneuvered by a court order that he surrender his domains as well. When he attempted to march on the court his units were ambushed and retreated to Osaka. The Boshin civil war followed. The sharpest fighting came not with Tokugawa forces, but from northern daimyo who distrusted the coalition of southern domains whose armies now advanced as "imperial" forces. Tokugawa Yoshinobu surrendered Edo in the spring, and by summer it was renamed Tokyo and designated the new national capital. Fighting by holdouts who had moved to Hokkaido came to an end in late spring of 1869. [*See* Tokugawa Yoshinobu *and* Meiji Restoration.]

At the outset the Meiji Restoration was thus little more than a shift of power within the ruling class. Japan's hazardous position in international affairs required sweeping changes, however, and the new leaders swiftly indicated their intent to utilize the throne to carry out a sweeping program of national renovation. The young Mutsuhito, whose reign name Meiji ("enlightened rule") symbolized this program, issued the Charter Oath in April 1868 that indicated an end to "evil customs" of the past and a search for "wisdom throughout the world" for ways in which all classes could realize their just aspiration. Decisions were to be based on "councils widely convened." Every effort was made to reassure doubters that their opinions would be taken into account, but it was also clear that Japan would restructure its institutions along Western lines in the interest of imperial rule. [See Mutsuhito and Charter Oath.]

Political centralization required reclaiming the 250-odd domains for governmental control and incorporating them into a system of new administrative units. The old divisions were swiftly reduced in number and combined in size to number (initially) seventy-five, and, in time, forty-seven. For the first time the central government's writ ran throughout the country. Many problems lay ahead, but the outlines of the future seemed more clear.

While planning and implementation proceeded in many areas, the core of the leadership, a group of about fifty men including secretaries, left on a twenty-one month trip around the world that brought them back in 1873. This Iwakura Mission was accompanied by an equal number of students and former lords. [See Iwakura Mission.]

Before the mission's departure steps had been discussed to restructure basic aspects of Japanese government and society. In 1873 a new and uniform land tax assessed in money and based upon the value of the land (worked out on the basis of average harvest yields) substituted for the old rice levy. A conscription system was set up to build a new, Western-style armed force. Ambitious plans for a national and uniform education system replaced the mixture of samurai academies, parish schools, and private academies that had proliferated during the last century of Tokugawa rule.

In 1881 the government leaders had the emperor announce plans for a constitution that would be promulgated in 1889, thereby seizing the initiative and keeping preparation of the document out of the hands of the People's Rights (Jiyū Minken) leaders. When the Meiji constitution went into effect the party leaders were co-opted as a parliamentary opposition, and a movement that began as a fundamental challenge to the legitimacy of the governing oligarchy had been tamed and brought into the political system. By then, Japanese had also gained considerable experience in electoral assemblies, for provincial assemblies, however limited their power, had been meeting for more than a decade. [See Jiyū Minken.]

In the course of these developments the Meiji leadership group became more narrow. Men from Tosa and Saga had been substantially eliminated. The initial triumvirate of Saigō Takamori and Ōkubo Toshimichi (of Satsuma) and Kido Takayoshi (of Chōshū) died in 1877 and 1878, Kido of illness, Saigō in his Satsuma Rebellion, and Ōkubo by assassination. The second echelon survived to become the elder statesmen (genrō): Itō Hirobumi and Yamagata Aritomo from Chōshū, Matsukata Masayoshi and Kuroda Kiyotaka from Satsuma, and the court nobles Iwakura Tomomi (d. 1883) and Saionji Kimmochi (d. 1940). Parlimentary and press opponents often referred to this group as the "Sat-Chō clique," but their long tenure and close association together gave Japan remarkably coherent leadership and congruity of direction. [The figures named above are the subject of independent entries.]

The 1880s were a period of institution building in local and national government. In economics Finance Minister Matsukata, who took office in 1881, brought the inflation that had raged during the years of samurai revolts under control through vigorous deflationary policies, selling off government pilot plants and enterprises and curbing government expenditures. The agricultural depression to which historians have attached Matsukata's name produced a number of farmer revolts that were swiftly suppressed by the new armed forces the government had at its disposal; the new order of individual tax obligations, weaker traditional and communal sanctions, and stronger machinery of coercion meant that land alienation and tenantry rose rapidly. Modern centralized police power entered every village, and rationalized administrative boundaries replaced the congeries of hamlets of Tokugawa times with the structured village grid of contemporary Japan.

Itō Hirobumi and others charged with preparations for a constitution journeyed to Europe, where they concluded that the institutions of central European monarchies, particularly those of Prussia, would be the most appropriate models for Japan's new system. In 1884 a cabinet system was introduced to replace the Nara-Heian Council of State

(Dajōkan) that had functioned as the center of government, and Itō became the first prime minister. A new peerage, made up of former court nobles and former daimyo, was established despite considerable protest against introducing archaic class distinction from Europe. By the end of the decade Itō and his colleagues were reviewing the constitution they had prepared (with German advisers) in the presence of the emperor in the new Privy Council. The Meiji constitution was formally promulgated in 1889 as promised.

Foreign policy was by no means forgotten, but the leaders had become convinced that thoroughgoing institutional reforms were prerequisite to the Western powers' approval of treaty reform. Asian adventures, after a brief expedition to punish Taiwanese aborigines for the murder of Okinawan fishermen in 1874 (which established Japan's claim to Okinawa), were put aside. Japan did succeed in "opening" Korea to foreign relations in 1876 and worked out treaty relations with China, but hesitant and maladroitly handled efforts to sponsor modernization in Korea in 1882 and 1884 led to violence and an agreement with China the following year that both sides would stay their hand in the interest of giving first attention to domestic modernization. In Tokyo the government tried to secure the approval of Western powers for partial changes in the unequal treaty system that bound Japan. The Japanese public became increasingly restless with the slow progress these efforts made, and the early political parties were quick to see that charges of weakness in foreign policy were a highly effective political device.

When the Meiji constitution went into effect it proved that its framers, despite their caution, had conceded significant elements of power which could, in time, create a new setting for Japanese politics. The document's caution was shown in its treatment of the throne. To the emperor was ascribed full sovereignty, but he graciously pledged himself to rule with the advice and consent of the Imperial Diet. Basic freedoms were laid down except as modified "according to law." A two-house legislature was established. The House of Peers was elected by ranks within the peerage and augmented by imperial appointments and representatives of the highest taxpayers, while the House of Representatives was elected by a limited franchise (initially slightly more than 500,000 in number) based upon property tax qualifications. Failure to approve a government budget meant that the previous year's budget would continue in force.

The constitution was vague on administrative power because to specify it would have seemed to weaken the emperor's prerogatives. As things worked out the prewar prime minister was essentially a first among equals; his selection was not explained, and in practice the leadership clique made its suggestions to the emperor. Despite this, the lower house, soon dominated by the representatives of the parties formed in the People's Rights Movement, proved a refractory institution that cabinets found difficult to control. At first the *genrō* alternated in office as prime minister, with weight shifting from Chōshū to Satsuma. Efforts to manage the parliamentary support that was now essential saw government leaders try to pressure party men through dissolution of the Diet by imperial proclamations, violence in elections, and coopting party leaders in the hope that political rewards would make them more cooperative. By 1900 Itō, the leading oligarch, had found it necessary to enter the party fray himself by organizing a party (Rikken Seiyūkai) that enlisted many of the original Liberal Party men. In 1918 Yamagata, then the leading *genrō*, reluctantly agreed to the appointment of a party leader, Hara Takashi (Kei), as prime minister, and throughout the 1920s an era of "party cabinets" became the accepted norm. [*See* Seiyūkai; Hara Takashi; *and* Taishō Political Change.]

A major problem in the implementation of parliamentary government was the integration of the armed services in the governing apparatus. The constitution left these under the emperor's command in order to avoid political interference, and in 1900 Yamagata managed to strengthen this by inserting the provision that ministers of war and navy be chosen from active duty generals and admirals. Thus, civilian control of the armed services was explicitly ruled out. Moreover, the adoption of the (Prussian-inspired) General Staff system for both services meant that the chief of the General Staff had independent access to the throne to report and propose, and further weakened the civilian counterpoise to military influence. At the educational level a network of special schools to train officer candidates completed the bifurcation of civilian and military hierarchies.

In 1894 to 1895 and 1904 to 1905 successful wars against China and Russia, respectively, greatly strengthened the confidence and standing of the armed services and their ability to demand and support larger forces. The Sino-Japanese War grew out of a decision that the time had come to challenge China's increasing control of events in Korea. Japan's modern forces proved more unified in spirit and equipment and better led than their Chinese counterparts, and on land and sea the war produced an unbroken series of victories. These were greeted with enthusiasm by a nation tired of Western (and Chinese) condescension, and Japanese of every persuasion hailed the outcome. The Treaty of Shimonoseki (1895) provided a large Chinese indemnity and cession of Taiwan and of the Liaodong Peninsula in southern Manchuria, but Germany, France, and Russia combined in the Triple Intervention to make Japan surrender that continental foothold. The treaty had two additional important provisions: Japan joined the Western powers as a beneficiary of the Unequal Treaties in China, and demanded and received (to the benefit of all the powers) the privilege of establishing manufacturing plants in China. Second, Korea was wrested from the Chinese tributary order and declared "independent," something that in practice made it eligible for domination by Japan. The war thus catapulted Japan from Asian "semicolonial" status to Western imperialist. Treaty reform with the Western powers in 1894 brought to a conclusion a half-century's struggle to regain diplomatic equality. Events were to prove that Japan's sovereignty had been regained at partial cost to China's. [See Sino-Japanese War; Shimonoseki, Treaty of; and Triple Intervention.]

The Triple Intervention, however, reminded Meiji Japanese that they were still a second-class power. The 1898 imperialist pressures on China that followed Japanese disclosure of China's weakness saw Russia moving into the Manchurian foothold Japan had been forced to surrender. In the disturbances accompanying the Chinese Boxer Rebellion of 1900, in which Japan furnished the bulk of the troops for the relief of the Beijing legations, Russia extended its occupation to all of Manchuria, and thereafter intervened in Korea as well. To meet this new threat the Japanese military budget expanded steadily. Diplomatically, alliance with England in 1902 protected Japan from interference by other powers if it set out to settle scores with Russia, as it did in 1904. This time the cost to Japan was far heavier, but its remarkable victories on land and sea established it as one of the great powers in the eyes of even the most skeptical. President Theodore Roosevelt, at the behest of Baron Kaneko Kentarō, helped bring the Russians to the conference table for the Treaty of Portsmouth in 1905. Japan now reclaimed the Liaodong Peninsula in South Manchuria and secured the southern half of the island of Sakhalin. Russian influence was removed from Manchuria and, more

important, Korea, to which the Japanese government sent Itō Hirobumi as resident-general. Itō's efforts to influence and direct change in Korea were only partly successful, and after he was slain in 1909 by a Korean nationalist, An Chung-gŭn, pressures for annexation of the peninsula led to the seizure of Korea as a colony in 1910. [See Russo-Japanese War; Portsmouth, Treaty of; An Chung-gŭn; and Korea, Japanese Government-General of.]

The institutional preparations of the 1880s made possible rapid progress in modern economic manufacturing. War and the preparation for war, and textile exports to Korea and China, speeded this process. By the time the Meiji emperor died in 1912 Japan was well on its way to becoming a modern industrial society. [See Meiji Period.]

*Japan Between the Wars.* The Taishō period (1912–1926) has less distinct contours than does the Meiji, because the failing emperor Yoshihito was succeeded by his son Hirohito as regent several years before succeeding formally to the throne. Hirohito's Shōwa period (1926–) in turn divides into eras of war and peace, and the cataclsymic changes that accompanied and followed the Pacific War constitute a more important dividing point than the emperor's ascension to the throne.

Japan emerged from the Meiji period an imperial power. Although living up to its obligations of the Anglo-Japanese Alliance by occupying German holdings in China and the South Pacific during World War I, it stood aloof from other conflicts and utilized the period to strengthen its position in China while its economy took giant strides during the preoccupation of the Western economies with the war. After the war Japan was a member of the council of the new League of Nations established at Versailles, and contributed a high official to the secretariat of that organization in the person of Nitobe Inazō. Japanese diplomacy in the decade following the war showed Japan to be an internationalist and responsible member of the concert of powers. Japan held to a moderate course in China during the Nationalists' Northern Expedition (1926–1927), but toward the end of the decade concerns for the maintenance of its position in Manchuria produced efforts to prevent the extension of Chinese Guomindang (Kuomintang) rule to that northern area. In Korea, the harshness of early Japanese rule brought on the Independence Movement of 1919 and gave way to the relatively milder policies of "civilian rule," although always under military direction. [See Twenty-one Demands; Northern Expedition; and March First Independence Movement.]

Japan now experienced most of the problems of other industrialized societies. The rapid economic growth of World War I came to an end with the return of Western industrial states to international competition, leading to large-scale labor disputes. Home Ministry bureaucrats who attempted to work out labor regulations in hopes of anticipating social radicalism were usually thwarted by pressure groups whose representatives sat in the lower house of the Diet. Tenant-landlord problems resulting in thousands of disputes found authorities somewhat more responsive and helpful. Government bureaucrats tried to prelude radicalism by a mixture of concessions and repression. The Universal Manhood Suffrage act of 1925 extended the vote to all adult males with the result that an electorate of twelve million provided far greater public participation than even before. Simultaneously, however, a Peace Preservation Act of 1925, strengthened in 1928, set stern penalties for participation in organizations that were contrary to the "national polity" (kokutai) and critical of private property, that is, communist and anarchist leftist movements. [See Peace Preservation Law.]

The interwar period had important precursors of liberalism as well as harbingers of suppression. After the cabinet of Hara Takashi (1918–1921), the first prime minister chosen from the ranks of party leaders, ministries fell under bureaucratic and conservative direction until 1924, when a united party movement to "defend the constitution" produced a political party (Minseitō) cabinet led by Katō Takaaki (Kōmei). Foreign Minister Shidehara Kijūrō, whose China policy during the Nationalists' Northern Expedition avoided confrontation and intervention, directed diplomatic policy in the main-stream of internationalist thinking, a path he tried to follow a second time during the incumbency of Hamaguchi Osachi (1928–1931). Minseitō cabinets made efforts to lessen the obstructive powers of the House of Peers, increase the franchise, introduce social legislation, and reduce both the size and the power of the armed services. The Hara government carried through reductions worked out at the Washington Conference of 1922, and the Hamaguchi cabinet, under the premier's strong leadership, did the same after the London Naval Conference of 1930. Courage was not always rewarded, however, as both Hara and Hamaguchi fell victims to assassins. The period of party cabinets came to an end with the assassination of Prime Minister Inukai in 1932.

It would be wrong to see Japanese politics in the 1920s as a simple confrontation between the military and civilian forces, although the institutional position of the military gave them great advantages when they were united in pursuit of an issue. Opportunistic civilian politicians delivered leadership of the Seiyūkai to General Tanaka Giichi, who followed the Minseitō as prime minister in 1927, and Tanaka proved the victim of his own rhetoric on China policy by twice sending troops to China to block Chiang Kai-shek's unification campaign. Adventurist officers in the Kwantung Army also engineered the assassination of warlord Zhang Zuolin in Manchuria, an act that led to Tanaka's fall from office. Army conspirators did not stop there, however, and soon staff officers of the same army were plotting the takeover of all Manchuria, which came in 1931 despite the efforts of the Shidehara foreign office to limit it. [See Shandong Intervention; Kwantung Army; Manchurian Incident; and Mukden Incident.]

The next decade saw Japanese armies slowly advance south from Manchuria despite the lack of a clear policy or agreement to do so. By 1937, when the "China Incident" plunged Japan into a war it was never able to stop, Japanese armies seemed to have reached agreement with Chinese local forces in the Beijing area. Unfortunately, local initiative and an unexpected firmness in resistance on the part of the Chinese led to all-out war that was opposed by even some of the militarists who had led in planning for Manchuria. [See World War II in China.]

During the early part of the decade the Japanese rural economy was hard hit by the collapse of the silk market in the wake of the world depression. In the air of crisis that followed the assassination of Inukai in 1932, the last genrō, Saionji, decided that it would be necessary to abandon party cabinets for a time and instead called on a retired admiral, Saitō Makoto, to take the helm. Saitō was the first of a number of retired military figures who, it was hoped, would be able to restrain the military and ward off terrorist action by right-wing organizations. Disagreements ran deep within the military, however, for age and rank cliques produced plotting in the hope of forcing a military government that would "purify" what was seen as the corruption of party politics. The most violent of a number of incidents came in 26 February 1936, when an entire army division rose in response to its junior officers, encircled the palace, and assassinated a number of senior government figures. An angry Emperor Hirohito insisted on the suppression of rebels, but the incident left senior army officers (the "Control faction") in a stronger position, as they were perceived as essential to public order. [See February Twenty-sixth Incident.]

Many Japanese were also becoming convinced that liberal democracy had failed in the West, and speculation was widespread that some more controlled form of government should be substituted for the ineffective and contentious structure of the political parties. By the late 1920s the popular and enigmatic Prince Konoe Fumimaro seemed a possible leader and symbol for some such structure, as he was acceptable to all elements of the political spectrum. Konoe was called to head three cabinets from 1937 to 1941, and a new Imperial Rule Assistance Association he headed substituted for the old parties. He proved a disappointment to hopes held of him by right and left alike. He held for an uncompromising stand on China, declaring that Japan would no longer treat with the Nationalist government, thereby condemning the army to a war it could not end. He appointed leading ultranationalists to high cabinet posts, giving them the opportunity to speak for the government. Toward the end of his third cabinet he hoped vainly for an agreement with the United States, and when that proved elusive he resigned to make way for General Tōjō Hideki. [See Konoe Fumimaro and Tōjō Hideki.]

In 1939 the outbreak of World War II in Europe and swift German victories made Japanese militarists eager to seize the Southeast Asian colonies of Britain, France, and Holland in order to guarantee Japanese sources of military and industrial raw materials. Foreign Minister Matsuoka Yōsuke campaigned sucessfully for an alliance with Germany and Italy (1940), which he thought would intimidate the United States. When this was followed by the Japanese move into French Indochina the United States government concluded that Japan was inseparably bound to a worldwide fascist aggressive alliance. United States sanctions cutting off scrap metal and then oil to Japan had the effect of convincing Japanese planners of the need for a war to secure economic independence. The movement of the United States fleet to Hawaiian waters added the need to immobilize that force before moving on Southeast Asia, and led to the Pearl Harbor strike in December 1941. [See Pearl Harbor and World War II in Asia.]

*Postwar Japan.* The reforms carried out under the Allied Occupation of Japan under the direction of General Douglas MacArthur, in a context of war weariness and disillusion, had the effect of transforming Japan. A drastic land reform program, carried out almost without compensation for owners, made owner-farmers out of tenants and provided the basis for a future domestic market. A new constitution, which replaced the Meiji constitution, de-

fined the emperor as "symbol of the state" instead of as source of sovereignty, and included a long bill of rights that makes it one of the most liberal documents in force anywhere. Article 9 pledged the abandonment of war as an "instrument of national policy" and renounced the accumulation of war potential, and gave to the new document its popular name as the "Peace Constitution." The civil code was revised in accordance with sentiments expressed in the democratic constitution, and the powers of the family head, which had been built into the old code, disappeared. Politics under the new constitution found the two political parties of prewar days resurrected and ultimately combined in a new Liberal Democratic Party, which has held power almost uninterruptedly since the war's end. In the early Occupation years the Foreign Office, deprived of any foreign relations to conduct, played an important role as liaison between Japanese government and Occupation headquarters.

Early Occupation programs included vigorous "trust-busting" programs and determination to break up the great prewar combines, but as the Japanese economy stagnated and world politics changed in the light of the American-Soviet confrontation Washington modified these plans and broke up only the largest of the trading complexes (*zaibatsu*). Rules of economic organization changed also with the encouragement of labor union organization, which transformed the immediate postwar industrial order. Education also was democratized and extended in efforts to break the dominance of the prewar hierarchical structure: as economic health returned a dramatic expansion of higher education found Japanese youths attending hundreds of institutions of many kinds.

The Occupation continued until 1952, but in midcourse the reforming enthusiasms of the opening years were modified as United States officials became concerned about radicalism, low productivity, and Japan's place in an East Asia possibly dominated by the emerging Communist Chinese state. Purge decrees originally designed for prewar militarist supporters now served to restrict communist radicalism as well. The resulting resurgence of confidence on the part of Japanese conservatives brought efforts to modify or blunt many of the Occupation measures. The United States' need to work through the Japanese government had in any event made it possible for it to strain reformist impulses through bureaucratic filters; in addition, the parlous state of the economy in post-surrender times greatly increased the authority and importance of fiscal bureaucrats in particular. For most of the postwar period service as minister of finance was virtually prerequisite to consideration for prime minisiter. Japan's directed growth under bureaucratically designed "industrial policy" frequently operated to restrict market access to outside goods until Japanese manufacturers had prepared for high-volume production.

Nevertheless the chief Occupation period reforms reflected Japanese desires as well as American design, and survived to transform the Japanese economy and society. Owner-farmers in agriculture, worker negotiations in labor, great variety in ownership and management, untrammeled civil rights and freedoms, and the democratic machinery of governmental representation removed most of the behind-the-scenes controls that had made it possible for a small number of backstage players to manage events in prewar days. After a Defense Agency (responsible to the prime minister) was established to oversee modest Self Defense Forces in the 1950s, it was denied all the institutional prerogatives that had complicated the prewar scene. The throne, in turn, shorn of the worshipful veneration granted the emperor as descendant of the sun goddess Amaterasu in prewar times, retained no more power than it did in England. [See Occupation of Japan.]

Japan's post-Occupation cabinets kept a low profile in international affairs, accepted American guarantees for Japanese security, and concentrated on steps to improve the economy. The "Japanese miracle" began to take shape in the years of the Korean War, when Japanese factories played an important supporting role for that struggle, and continued and accelerated in the 1960s with Prime Minister Ikeda Hayato's so-called Income Doubling Plan. By the time of the "oil shocks" of the 1970s Japan had achieved the highest growth rates of any major country, had become the second most productive society in the noncommunist world and possibly in the entire world, the world's largest importer of raw materials in almost every category, and the world's largest producer in category after category, including automobiles. An ironic outcome of this was that Japan's real war aims—access to the markets and materials of all countries—had been achieved despite its defeat in the effort to establish regional autarchy in the Pacific War. The Japanese population of 120 million enjoyed a per capita income of more than US $10,000, the world's highest life expectancy, one of the world's most equitable income distributions, and was one of the world's most highly educated. The isolated country Commodore Perry had "opened" in 1853 was now the most in-

ternationally dependent in its need for resources and markets, and had achieved the status it sought by means of peaceful trade.

Hugh Borton, *Japan's Modern Century* (1975). John Whitney Hall, *Japanese History: New Dimensions of Approach and Understanding* (1966) and *Japan from Prehistory to Modern Times* (1970). Thomas R. H. Havens, *Valley of Darkness: The Japanese People and World War Two* (1978). Marius B. Jansen, ed., *Changing Japanese Attitudes toward Modernization* (1965). Donald Keene, *An Anthology of Japanese Literature* (1955). William W. Lockwood, *The Economic Development of Japan: Growth and Structural Change* (1974). Ivan Morris, *The World of the Shining Prince: Court Life in Ancient Japan* (1979). Hugh T. Patrick and Henry Rosofsky, eds., *Asia's New Giant: How the Japanese Economy Works* (1976). Edwin O. Reischauer, *Japan: The Story of a Nation* (1981). George B. Sansom, *A History of Japan*, 3 vols. (1958–1963). Ryusaku Tsunoda, Wm. Theodore de Bary, and Donald Keene, eds., *Sources of Japanese Tradition* (1958). Paul Varley, *Japanese Culture* (1977).

MARIUS B. JANSEN

## GEOGRAPHIC REGIONS OF JAPAN

Japan is an archipelago composed of four main islands and thousands of smaller islands. The four main islands, from north to south, are Hokkaidō, Honshū, Shikoku, and Kyūshū. These four constitute an area of approximately 365,734 square kilometers (143,619 square miles) extending from thirty-one to forty-five degrees north latitude. The archipelago is home to approximately 120 million people.

Japan is most commonly divided into nine distinct regions: Hokkaidō, Tōhoku, Chūbu, Kantō, Kinki, Chūgoku, Shikoku, Kyūshū, and Okinawa. Five of these are divisions of the main island of Honshū; the other four are separate islands or, in the case of Okinawa, an island chain. Each of the nine regions is commonly further subdivided.

Hokkaidō, the northernmost of Japan's main islands, is the second largest in area. It was the last of the main islands to be settled by the Japanese people and was formerly known by the names Ezo, Matsumae, and Oshima. A frontier area during the Tokugawa period, its economy was based on herring and salmon fishing, rather than the rice cultivation that sustained most of the rest of Japan.

Hokkaidō is bounded by the Sea of Okhotsk on the north, the Pacific Ocean on the east, the Sea of Japan on the west, and the Tsugaru Strait, separating Hokkaidō and Honshū, on the south. The majority of its population lives on or near the Ishikari-

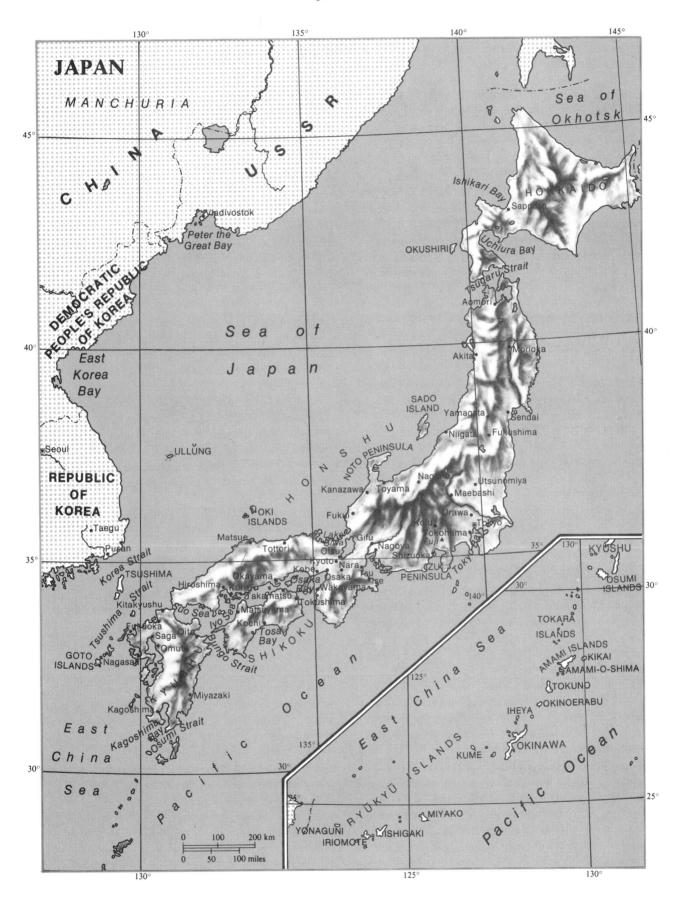

Yufutsu plain, on the southwest of the island. Its major city and prefectural capital is Sapporo, with a population of 1.04 million (1975; 1.4 million, 1983 estimate). Another 4 million residents are scattered among the sixty-seven districts into which the island is divided. [See Hokkaido.]

The island of Honshū, home to over 90 million of the Japanese people, comprises the five regions of Tōhoku, Chūbu, Kantō, Kinki, and Chūgoku. It is bounded on the west by the Sea of Japan and on the east by the Pacific Ocean. Although the island's greatest breadth from east to west is only slightly more than 360 kilometers (220 miles), the two coasts exhibit distinct differences in climate. The eastern coast, as far north as Tokyo Bay, is warmed by the Pacific current known as Kuroshio; the western coast is more subject to the continental climate of northern Asia.

The Tōhoku region has historically been one of the island's more economically depressed areas, and it remains so to this day. It comprises six prefectures at the northernmost regions of the island: Aomori, Akita, Iwate, Miyagi, Yamagata, and Fukushima. Prefectural capitals, respectively, are Aomori City, Akita City, Morioka, Sendai, Yamagata City, and Fukushima City. The economic nexus of the region is Sendai, the largest city in northern Honshū, with a population of over 500,000.

The Chūbu area is located in north-central Honshū, below the Tōhoku region and to the west of the Kantō, Japan's most populous region. Chūbu comprises nine prefectures: Niigata, Toyama, Ishikawa, Fukui, Shizuoka, Yamanashi, Nagano, Aichi, and Gifu. Prefectural capitals, respectively, are Niigata City, Toyama City, Kanazawa, Fukui City, Shizuoka City, Kōfu, Nagano City, Nagoya, and Gifu City. The Chūbu area is often divided into the subgroupings of Hokuriku, comprising Niigata, Toyama, Fukui, and Ishikawa, on the coast of the Sea of Japan; Tōsan, comprising the inland mountainous areas of Nagano, Gifu, and Yamanashi; and the Tōkai, composed of Shizuoka and Aichi on the coast of the Pacific Ocean. The former two regions tend to have more in common with the Tōhoku region to the north, while the last is more similar to the Kinki region to the south.

The Kantō region is the political and economic heart of Japan. It centers on the megalopolis including the nation's capital, Tokyo, and Yokohama-Kawasaki. The present status of the region seems all the more remarkable when one considers that in pre-Tokugawa times it was an underpopulated area, known as Musashino, of less than central impor-

tance. The Kantō comprises six prefectures, Ibaraki, Tochigi, Gumma, Saitama, Kanagawa, and Chiba, as well as metropolitan Tokyo. Prefectural capitals, respectively, are Mito, Utsunomiya, Maebashi, Urawa, Yokohama, and Chiba City. The region lies on the Kantō Plain, the largest expanse of flat land on the Japanese islands.

The Kinki region, also known as the Kamigata and Kansai, centers on the Osaka-Kyoto-Nara area and is Japan's second most populous region and its cultural capital. It is reputedly the first region that the Japanese people settled in significant numbers, and Kyoto was the imperial capital for hundreds of years before Tokyo (or Edo, as it was previously known) was settled. There are presently two large metropolitan areas, Osaka and Kyoto. The region comprises five prefectures: Shiga, Nara, Wakayama, Mie, and Hyōgo. Prefectural capitals, respectively, are Ōtsu, Nara, Wakayama City, Tsu, and Kōbe.

The Chūgoku region, in southernmost Honshū, is composed of the five prefectures of Okayama, Hiroshima, Yamaguchi, Tottori, and Shimane. Prefectural capitals, respectively, are Okayama City, Hiroshima City, Yamaguchi City, Tottori City, and Matsue. The Chūgoku region may be further divided into the two subregions of Sanyō ("sunny side") and Sanin ("shady side"). Okayama and Hiroshima, on the coast of the Inland Sea, compose the Sanyō region, while Tottori and Shimane, on the Sea of Japan, make up the Sanin region. Yamaguchi, at Honshū's extreme southwest, shares a common boundary with both regions.

Shikoku, with an area of 18,256 square kilometers (7,245 square miles), is the smallest of Japan's main islands and also the least heavily populated. Its approximately 4 million people are scattered among the island's four prefectures. Ehime and Kagawa border the Inland Sea, while Tokushima and Kōchi face the Pacific Ocean. The prefectural capitals, respectively, are Matsuyama, Takamatsu, Tokushima City, and Kōchi City.

Kyūshū, the southernmost of Japan's major islands, is home to approximately one-tenth of Japan's population. It can be divided into the Kita-Kyūshū, or northern Kyūshū area, which is primarily industrial, and the more rural and economically depressed area to the south. The island comprises seven prefectures: Fukuoka, Ōita, Miyazaki, Saga, Nagasaki, Kumamoto, and Kagoshima. The prefectural capitals all share their names with those of their prefectures.

The southernmost of Japans's regions is Okinawa, which was known as the Ryūkyū Islands (Chinese,

Liuqiu) during the Tokugawa period. During that time it was a separate kingdom with tributary relationships with both the Kagoshima fiefdom and China. It became a prefecture of Japan in 1881, following negotiations with China. After World War II it was administrated by the United States, until full sovereignty was restored to Japan in 1972. Over one-quarter of the island's 945,000 inhabitants live in the prefectural capital of Naha.

THOMAS R. SCHALOW

JATS, a large group of agriculturalists in North India, variously classified by anthropologists and writers as a caste, a tribe, a race, and an ethnic group. Although it is not easy to define the Jats in terms of characteristics that hold throughout the whole area where they are found, they nevertheless have a sense of self-identity and are recognized by others as forming a cohesive group. They constitute a majority in the eastern districts of the Punjab and are found in considerable numbers in the northwestern districts of Uttar Pradesh, in the areas of Madhya Pradesh around Gwalior, in northern parts of Rajasthan, and in smaller numbers in Sind and Kashmir. They are divided among the three main religions of North India—Hinduism, Islam, and Sikhism—but they tend to retain their primary identity as Jats.

In the nineteenth century there was a great interest in the racial origins of the Jats, with some writers claiming that they were pure Aryans, others that they were descendants of the Huns or Scythians. It is not race, however, but a complex of similarities in social customs and organization that sets them apart from other groups in the same areas. Polygyny, the practice of having more than one wife, was, for example, fairly common among the Jats until the Hindu Marriage Act of 1955 made it illegal. It is also said that prior to the twentieth century female infanticide was practiced. Widow remarriage, which is not permitted in most higher Hindu castes, was also customary. Great emphasis is placed on family and lineage, especially in terms of land ownership, so that historically land was owned not by a single chief, as was the pattern elsewhere in North India, but by individual families. It has been suggested that this made the Jats more egalitarian and more unwilling to acknowledge outside authority. Jat villages were organized into groups known as *khaps*, which exercised social control and provided defense against enemies. Kinship groups (made up of the family and lineage) were an important element in determining *khap* leadership. The *chaudhuri* is an important figure in the Jat community; he is the head of the families whose clan is regarded as having conquered or colonized that particular area in the remote past.

The Jats in the area around Delhi are frequently mentioned in the later Mughal chronicles as troublesome bandits on the roads leading from Delhi to Agra. During the reign of Aurangzeb (1658–1707) a number of uprisings led by Jat chieftains took place in the area around Mathura, and in the eighteenth century they became a strong military power as Mughal authority weakened. Contemporary evidence suggests that the Jat chieftains saw themselves as defenders of Hinduism against the Muslim rulers of Delhi. In the middle of the century Badan Singh, a Jat chieftain, established his rule over the area around Mathura, and built a great fortress at Bharatpur. This became the center of a larger kingdom under his able successor, Suraj Mal, who ruled from 1756 to 1763. The Jat rulers successfully opposed the advance of British power until 1826, when their fort was finally stormed.

The Jats have adapted their sense of solidarity and self-identification to modern electoral politics in order to get their candidates elected to office, and thus they remain a significant force in the political life of North India. The Jat politician Chaudhuri Charan Singh had an important role in creating the Janata party, which defeated Indira Gandhi in 1977. Singh became prime minister briefly in 1979.

[*See also* Caste *and* Suraj Mal.]

E. A. H. Blunt, *The Caste System of Northern India* (1931). M. C. Pradhan, *The Political System of the Jats of Northern India* (1966).    AINSLIE T. EMBREE

JAUNPUR, district seat in the Indian state of Uttar Pradesh, located on the Gomati River. Little is known about Jaunpur before 1321, when Ghiyas ud-Din Tughluq made it a regional headquarters. Jaunpur remained Tughluq until 1394, when, taking advantage of turmoil within the weakened Tughluq state, Malik Sarwar, the governor of Jaunpur, established the independent Sharqi sultanate. Upon the governor's death in 1399, Sharqi territory extended from Bihar to Aligarh; owing to their proximity to Delhi, the Sharqis were frequently at war with the Lodis until the final victory of the Lodis in 1495, ending Sharqi rule.

Under the Sharqi rulers Ibrahim (r. 1401–1440), Mahmud (r. 1440–1457), and Husain (r. 1458–1495), Jaunpur, considered a second Shiraz, was the major Islamic cultural and religious center in North India; moreover, the production of at least one Jain manuscript from Jaunpur at this time suggests an atmosphere of sectarian tolerance. Under the Sharqis, the magnificent Atala and Jami mosques, modeled on the Tughluq Begumpur mosque in Delhi, were erected, as was an impressive fort. With the defeat of Husain Sharqi, Jaunpur's importance waned until Akbar's reign, when the city again regained prominence under Mun'in Khan, the Mughal governor, who constructed an arched bridge, still in use today, over the Gomati. Jaunpur's significance lessened under the later Mughals.

[See also Tughluq Dynasty and Lodi Dynasty.]

J. Burton-Page, "Djawnpur," in *Encyclopaedia of Islam*, (new ed., 1960–). A. Fuhrer and Edmund W. Smith, *The Sharqi Architecture of Jaunpur* (1889). Mian Muhammad Saeed, *The Sharqi Sultanate of Jaunpur* (1972).

CATHERINE B. ASHER

JAVA, island in the Greater Sunda Islands group, Indonesia. Some one thousand kilometers long, it is situated between 105° and 115° east longitude and between 6° and 7° south latitude. According to the 1980 census, Java has a population of nearly 91 million, approximately double the figure recorded in the 1930 census, which reported 27.8 million ethnic Javanese, 8.6 million Sundanese, and 4.3 million Madurese in Indonesia's total indigenous population of 59.1 million. Before this time Java's population is uncertain, but it seems that it had grown from about 3 million (perhaps more) in 1800 to over 25 million in 1900. The area west of approximately 109° east longitude is largely populated by ethnic Sundanese people, with the exceptions of an area around Banten on the north coast, which is Javanese, and the Indonesian capital of Jakarta, which has many different ethnic groups.

Throughout much of its history, Java has been a major cultural, political, and economic force in the Malay-Indonesian area, often exerting influence beyond its own shores. It was the site of Taruma Nagara, one of the earliest historical kingdoms in the Indonesian archipelago. Its king, Purnavarman, left four Sanskrit inscriptions near Jakarta and Bogor in West Java that are dated from about 450 on paleographic grounds. For over a thousand years thereafter, all the recorded states of Java were indianized, that is, they adopted Hindu and Buddhist cultural forms. They were mainly centered on the Javanese-speaking heartland of Central and East Java.

Little is known of the history of the Sundanese area between the fifth and sixteenth century. In the late seventh century it seems to have been dominated by the Sumatran-based empire of Srivijaya, and in 932 an Old Malay inscription from there refers to a king of Sunda. During the eleventh century Sunda may have come under Javanese influence. In the fourteenth century the kingdom of Pajajaran, with its capital near Bogor, was founded, but little is known of its history. Pajajaran's port of Sunda Kalapa (now Jakarta) was taken by Islamic forces about 1527, and the court fell to Banten about 1579, at which point the Sundanese began to embrace Islam. West Java has since been generally regarded as the home of devout Muslims. It was there, for example, that the Darul Islam rebellion originated in 1948.

Eighth-century inscriptions from Central Java indicate the presence of several petty states there; they were apparently brought under the suzerainty of a single monarch by the late ninth century. These states were responsible for the construction of many famous temples, including Borobudur, Mendhut, Prambanan, Candhi Sewu, and Kalasan.

King Balitung's charters, dating from the late ninth and early tenth centuries, are found in both Central and East Java, as are those of his two immediate successors; clearly both areas were claimed by these kings. But King Sindok ruled East Java alone from 928. The reasons for the shift of the court from Central to East Java are unclear; in any case it was to be over six hundred years before major kingdoms again appeared in Central Java. This was not the beginning of indianized civilization in East Java, however, for inscriptions go back to 760 there.

The kingdom governed by King Airlangga (first half of the eleventh century) was located in Janggala in northeast Java, but thereafter until the sixteenth century the central courts were located farther inland along the Brantas River valley. Kadiri (c. 1059–1222) was succeeded by the kingdom of Singosari (1222–1292) and by Majapahit (1294– c. 1527). During this time Javanese influence overseas was felt through military expeditions against south Sumatra and Bali and through political and trading relations. Under King Hayam Wuruk (Rajasanagara, r. 1350–1389), Majapahit experienced one of the golden ages of pre-Islamic Java; his court is described in the panegyric poem *Nagarakertagama*, composed in 1365. Many other major works of Old Javanese literature were composed during the period of East Javanese dominance.

From the fourteenth century onward Islam spread

throughout Java. Evidence suggests that the first Javanese Muslims were people at the Majapahit court, perhaps members of the royal family, but by the early sixteenth century Islamic political strength was centered on the north coast while Majapahit (or its rump) remained Hindu-Buddhist. About 1527 Majapahit fell to Islamic forces led by the kingdom of Demak, which had apparently been founded in the last quarter of the fifteenth century by a foreign (probably Chinese) Muslim. From about 1546 to 1587 hegemony was apparently claimed by the kingdom of Pajang (near present-day Surakarta), the first kingdom to be located in the interior of Central Java for over six centuries; little, however, is known of its history.

By the end of the sixteenth century initiative had passed to the contending princely lines of Mataram (near present-day Yogyakarta) and Surabaya. This contest ended with the defeat of Surabaya in 1625 by Mataram's Sultan Agung (1613–1646). The Mataram dynasty was the longest in Java's history; its members still control the courts of Surakarta and Yogyakarta.

When the Dutch East India Company (VOC) established its headquarters at Batavia in 1619, a new element entered Java's political and economic history. The VOC intervened militarily in Banten in 1682 and soon dominated the state. Its military intervention in the Mataram empire from the 1670s onward led to some eight decades of crisis. A series of rebellions and wars ended in the partition of the kingdom between the courts of Surakarta and Yogyakarta according to the Treaty of Giyanti (1755) and also resulted in the near-exhaustion of the VOC, which was by then well on the road to bankruptcy.

In the early nineteenth century the European governments at Batavia (the Dutch-Napoleonic from 1808 to 1811, the British from 1811 to 1816, and the Dutch thereafter) intervened more aggressively into all aspects of the island's affairs, choosing and deposing monarchs, sacking the court of Yogyakarta in 1812, and attempting to change local social, political, and economic arrangements and to exploit Java's resources for the benefit of the colonial regime. The Java War (1825–1830) ended with the firm establishment of Dutch colonial power throughout Java. The Dutch then introduced the so-called cultivation system (kultuurstelsel), which required that Java's peasantry produce cheap tropical produce that could be sold on the world market through the Netherlands. This system was a great success for the Netherlands. While there is some argument about its overall impact on the Javanese

peasantry, there is no doubt that much compulsion was employed and that many Javanese suffered.

By about 1900 Java's precolonial political, social, and economic arrangements had been thoroughly distorted by the impact of colonial rule and the country's rapid increase in population to over 25 million. The indigenous elite had been demilitarized, tamed, and somewhat demoralized; the peasantry had been exploited and exposed to world economic forces. The stage was thus set for social and political unrest and the emergence of new forms of leadership. After 1901, the Dutch concentrated many of the educational and social developments of their new colonial ethical policy in Java. For all these reasons Java, along with Minangkabau, became one of the two regions that led Indonesia to adopt new cultural and political forms in the twentieth century.

The main anticolonial and nationalist political movements of the period from 1900 to 1942 were all headquartered in Java, although they often had branches in Minangkabau as well. Modernist Islam first flowered in Minangkabau, but Muhammadiyah (founded in Yogyakarta in 1912) became one of its main vehicles, especially after 1925. That the colonial capital Batavia was located in Java, that in 1930 Java and Madura (which were united administratively from 1828) had nearly 70 percent of the total Indonesian population, and that much modern economic development took place in Java contributed to its nationalist dynamism and leadership over other areas. Nevertheless, Dutch colonial authority remained intact and, indeed, deeply entrenched throughout Java until 1942.

During the Japanese occupation of Indonesia (1942–1945), Java's population was mobilized to support Japan's war effort. Japanese encouragement gave nationalist leaders, notably Sukarno, opportunities denied them by the Dutch. Java's leadership in national affairs was thereby further promoted, and it was in Jakarta (Batavia) that Sukarno and Mohammad Hatta proclaimed Indonesia's independence in August 1945.

The Indonesian Revolution of 1945–1950 was primarily fought in Java and Sumatra. The people of Java suffered some of the worst hardships of the revolutionary period; it was there that the Dutch effort to reconquer met some of its toughest resistance. In the years since Indonesia's achievement of independence, the location of the capital city and the concentration of political forces in Java, the large proportion of the national population (62 percent in 1981) found there, its greater levels of urbanization and economic development, and its numerous institutions of higher learning have guaranteed Java's continuing role as a focal point of national affairs.

[See also Indonesia, Republic of; Banten; Jakarta; Indianization; Srivijaya; Pajajaran; Darul Islam; Airlangga; Majapahit; Hayam Wuruk; Nagarakertagama; Islamization of Southeast Asia; Mataram; Agung; Dutch East India Company; Giyanti, Treaty of; Java War; Kultuurstelsel; Madura; Ethical Colonial Policy; Minangkabau; Muhammadiyah; Borobudur; and Prambanan.]

Herbert Feith, The Decline of Constitutional Democracy in Indonesia (1962). F. H. van Naerssen and R. C. de Iongh, The Economic and Administrative History of Early Indonesia (1977). Deliar Noer, The Modernist Muslim Movement in Indonesia, 1900–1942 (1973). Anthony Reid, The Indonesian National Revolution 1945–1950 (1974). M. C. Ricklefs, A History of Modern Indonesia, ca. 1300 to the Present (1981).          M. C. RICKLEFS

## JAVA, BRITISH OCCUPATION OF.

The British conquest of Java was undertaken in order to remove the threat of French influence in Indonesia during the Napoleonic Wars. The conquest was effected during August and September 1811 by naval forces under Rear Admiral Sir Robert Stopford (1768–1847) and land forces from India commanded by General Sir Samuel Auchmuty (1756–1822). The occupation (1811–1816) was sanctioned by the governor-general, Lord Minto (1751–1814), who disobeyed his instructions to withdraw British forces from Java after the conquest because it would have placed unarmed Dutch colonists in jeopardy. An interim administration was established with Thomas Stamford Raffles (1781–1826) as lieutenant-governor and an advisory council consisting of Dutch and British members. The government attempted to create a stable currency by withdrawing the inflated paper money and introduced a new revenue system based on free cultivation and the collection of land rent. A new legal code was promulgated on British principles of justice, and the authority of the Indonesian rulers in the directly administered regions of the island was reduced in favor of British officials. British power was also asserted in Central Java when Yogyakarta was captured in 1812 and a new ruler, Hamengkubuwana III (1769–1814), was placed on the throne.

Because revenues from the land-rent system and from the sales of coffee did not meet the costs of the administration and maintenance of a large British army, the directors of the East India Company in London grew disenchanted with Java, leading to its restitution to the Netherlands under the terms of the Anglo-Dutch Convention of 1814. Raffles was removed from office in March 1816 after being charged with corruption, and his successor, John Fendall (1760–1825), handed over control of the government to the Netherlands Commissioners in August 1816.

[See also Java; Raffles, Sir Thomas Stamford; Law: Law in Southeast Asia; and Hamengkubuwana.]

J. S. Bastin, The Native Policies of Sir Stamford Raffles in Java and Sumatra (1957). Thomas Stamford Raffles, Substance of a Minute . . . on the Introduction of an Improved System of Internal Management and the Establishment of a Land Rental on the Island of Java (1814) and The History of Java (1817).          JOHN S. BASTIN

## JAVANESE WARS OF SUCCESSION.

The three Javanese Wars of Succession mark important stages in the political development of Central Java during the eighteenth century.

The first (1704–1708) followed the succession of Susuhunan (King) Amangkurat III (r. 1703–1708), the son of the previous monarch. His uncle Puger sought the support of the Dutch East India Company (VOC), which recognized him as Susuhunan Pakubuwana I (r. 1704–1719). In 1705 VOC forces marched to Kartasura; Amangkurat III fled to East Java and there eluded his enemies for three years. During this time he was associated with Surapati. After bitter campaigns in East Java in 1706, 1707, and 1708, Amangkurat III surrendered to the VOC, believing that he would be allowed to remain somewhere in Java; instead he was exiled to Ceylon. The succession had now been altered to Pakubuwana I's line, the legitimacy of which seems to have been doubtful.

Upon Pakubuwana I's death his son Amangkurat IV (r. 1719–1726) became susuhunan with VOC support. Two of his brothers, an uncle, and other senior courtiers opposed his succession, but their attack upon the court in 1719 failed. Thus began the Second War of Succession (1719–1723), which coalesced with other rebellions already in progress since 1717. These ended, after heavy losses through disease and battle, in victory for the VOC forces supporting Amangkurat IV.

The third and longest Javanese War of Succession (1746–1757) began with the rebellion of Prince Mangkubumi against his brother Susuhunan Pakubuwana II (r. 1726–1749). Upon the latter's death Mangkubumi took royal titles and thus rejected the succession of his nephew Pakubuwana III (r. 1749–1788). The end result was a military stalemate between VOC forces and the rebels that led to the partition of the kingdom according to the Treaty of Giyanti in 1755.

[See also Java; Pakubuwana; Dutch East India Company; Mangkubumi; and Giyanti, Treaty of.]

M. C. Ricklefs, *A History of Modern Indonesia, c. 1300 to the Present* (1981).    M. C. RICKLEFS

# JAVA WAR

JAVA WAR (1825–1830), uprising against the Dutch and their allies in Surakarta and Yogyakarta led by Prince Dipanagara (1785–1855). The origins of the war lay in the political tensions in the Yogyakarta sultanate; the agrarian and economic difficulties in Central Java, especially the harvest failures of the early 1820s; the increased fiscal burdens on the tax-paying peasants; and land hunger and the oppressive role of the Chinese as tax farmers. Many of these problems were very deep-seated and can be traced back to the eighteenth century.

Dipanagara's leadership transformed what would have been an inchoate agrarian uprising in 1825 into a widespread rebellion involving many disparate groups in Javanese society. Foremost among these were the members of the Javanese religious communities (santri), which looked upon the prince as a spiritual leader who would strengthen the institutional status of Islam in Java and give them a new social prominence. Important support also came from younger members of the Yogyakarta aristocracy and from the peasantry, who regarded Dipanagara as a messianic leader, a "just king" (ratu adil) who would institute a new age of justice and plenty after a period of decay.

The war, which had the character of a series of provincial uprisings loosely coordinated by Dipanagara at the center, took the Dutch by surprise, and for a time it seemed that they would be forced to abandon the whole of Central Java. After Dipanagara's defeat at Gowok just outside Surakarta on 15 October 1826, however, they moved onto the offensive and adopted a policy of food denial against the Javanese forces by building small forts to guard the areas in the plains that had been "pacified" by their troops. Bitter quarrels between Dipanagara's religious and aristocratic supporters (principally between Dipanagara and his chief religious adviser, Kyai Maja) undermined Javanese resistance, and

from 1827 onward important Javanese commanders began to defect to the Dutch.

With Dipanagara's capture at Magelang on 28 March 1830, the war was eventually brought to an end. It cost the lives of about a quarter of a million Javanese and left one-fourth of the cultivated area of Central Java devastated. The Dutch victory heralded the beginning of a new colonial age in which the European government was for the first time paramount in Java.

[See also Java; Dipanagara; Santri; Yogyakarta; and Ratu Adil.]

Peter Carey, *Pangéran Dipanagara and the Making of the Java War (1825–30): The End of an Old Order in Java* (1986).    PETER CAREY

# JAXARTES RIVER

JAXARTES RIVER (Syr Darya), a large Central Asian river rising in the Tian Shan range in the Kirghiz SSR from two branches, the Naryn on the north and the Karadarya on the south. These join in the Ferghana Valley just south of Namangan to form the Jaxartes. The river flows through the Soviet Uzbek and Kazakh republics, both desert areas, to empty into the inland Aral Sea.

In the tenth century the Syr Darya formed the northern border of the territory disputed between the Samanids and the Karakhanids; it is often thought of as having marked a symbolic border between nomadic and pastoral Turan and settled and agricultural Iran. It was here, through their involvement as mercenary troops first for the Karakhanids and then for the Samanids, that Turkish Oghuz (Ghuzz) clans first established themselves from a base at Djand, a city on the east bank of the river at its lower reaches. In the latter part of the tenth century descendants of these Oghuz immigrants joined under the leadership of Seljuk and established an independent dynasty that was to dominate Transoxiana, Khurasan, central Iran, and Iraq for the succeeding 150 years and, through a subsidiary branch, most of Asia Minor in the twelfth and thirteenth centuries.    RHOADS MURPHEY, JR.

# JAYABAYA

JAYABAYA, twelfth-century ruler of Kediri in East Java (r. 1137–1159) to whom are ascribed a series of prophecies (jangka) relating to the historical cycles through which Java would pass until the Javanese year 2000. These foretold alternate eras of prosperity (jaman raharja) and turbulence (jaman musibat; jaman edan) and envisaged the appearance of a messianic "just king" (ratu adil) who would institute a golden age *(jaman emas)* of justice and plenty. These prophecies, which were based on the Indian *kaliyuga* cycles, became particularly popular with the Javanese peasantry during times of crisis and sustained them in the hopes of the coming of a liberator who would rid them of fiscal oppression. During the colonial period, they were an important element in some of the numerous agrarian uprisings against the Dutch in Java.

[*See also* Java *and* Ratu Adil.]

Sartono Kartodirdjo, "Agrarian Radicalism in Java: Its Setting and Development," in *Culture and Politics in Indonesia,* edited by Claire Holt (1972), pp. 71–126.

PETER CAREY

JAYAKAR, MUKUND RAMRAO (1873–1959), Bombay lawyer, politician, and philanthropist. He was a prominent member of a group known as the liberals, which included such other well-known figures as Tej Bahadur Sapru. The group disagreed with many of the policies of Mohandas Gandhi and the Indian National Congress but wanted to maintain unity among Indian nationalists. Jayakar and Sapru acted as mediators to bring about a meeting in 1931 between Gandhi and the governor-general, Lord Irwin, to make an agreement for a more independent constitutional plan for India. He was a member of the Bombay Legislative Council (1923–1926) and the Central Legislature (1926–1930). He represented the liberal group at the Round Table Conferences in London from 1930 to 1932, maintaining contacts with British politicians as well as with the leaders of the Indian National Congress. He was one of the founders of Poona University and was its first vice-chancellor (1948–1956).

[*See also* Gandhi, Mohandas Karamchand *and* Sapru, Tej Bahadur.]

M. R. Jayakar, *The Story of My Life,* 2 vols. (1958–1960).    USHA SANYAL

JAYAVARMAN I, late seventh-century ruler of the Khmer kingdom known as Zhenla. He succeeded his father, Bhavavarman II (not Bhavavarman I, founder of Zhenla's fortunes), who had succeeded Isanavarman I, and he enjoyed a peaceful reign lasting from before 657 to after 690. Inscriptions left by him have been found at Mekong sites from the coast to as far north as Bassac (Vat Phu) in southern Laos, and he was responsible for monuments built at Ba Phnom and Vat Phu. According to Chinese

sources, the period following his reign witnessed the division of Zhenla into separate parts.

[*See also* Zhenla.]

Lawrence P. Briggs, *The Ancient Khmer Empire* (1951). G. Coedès, *The Indianized States of Southeast Asia,* translated by Susan B. Cowing (1968).    IAN W. MABBETT

JAYAVARMAN II, founder of the kingdom of Angkor, in Cambodia. Later rulers of Angkor founded their legitimacy largely on links with him. No inscriptions are extant from his reign, which is known from later records. There have been uncertainty and debate about the chronology of his reign and the nature of his power.

Jayavarman II was a Khmer prince who, at the end of the eighth century and the beginning of the ninth, united the Khmer people, at least nominally, under his own authority. At the time, the Javanese claimed suzerainty over the disunited Khmers, and it was from Java that Jayavarman came to establish himself at a series of successive capitals and to create a unified Khmer kingdom out of the various rival principalities. In 802, at his temporary capital at Mahendraparvata in the Kulen Hills, to the north of Angkor proper, he instituted the *devaraja* ("god-king") cult, which commemorated unity and independence. His last capital was at Hariharalaya, a few miles southeast of Angkor proper, and this site remained the capital under later rulers until the reign of Yasovarman I.

Jayavarman's reign is conventionally dated 802–850, but he may have had a substantial kingdom before 802 and may not have lived to 850. The extent of his territorial power has been debated. He probably did not succeed in creating a genuinely centralized state; great vassal families remained as nodes of local autonomy and potential dissidence. According to C. Jacques, he died in 834 at about eighty-four years of age.

[*See also* Angkor; Cambodia; Hariharalaya *and* Devaraja.]

Lawrence P. Briggs, *The Ancient Khmer Empire* (1951). G. Coedès, *The Indianized States of Southeast Asia,* translated by Susan B. Cowing (1968). O. W. Wolters, "Jayavarman II's Military Power: The Territorial Foundation of the Angkor Empire," *Journal of the Royal Asiatic Society* (1973): 21–30.    IAN W. MABBETT

JAYAVARMAN VII, ruler (r. 1181–c. 1218) of the Cambodian kingdom of Angkor. The chronology of his reign and the attribution to it of various extant structures were long uncertain, but it is now generally accepted that it was he who built the city of Angkor Thom and its central shrine, the Bayon, as well as a large number of other religious monuments and public works, marking his reign as a period of extremely vigorous building activity.

A son of Dharanindravarman II (r. 1150–c. 1160), Jayavarman was able to take the throne only after driving out the Cham invaders who in 1177 overran the country. In 1181 he made himself master of the kingdom and was then able to begin construction of Angkor. He defeated Champa and put on the Cham throne his own nominee, the Cham prince Vidyanandana, who had been a loyal follower but later turned against him. Jayavarman extended the empire of Angkor as far as Say Fong (in modern Laos) and made claims over parts of Burma and the Malay Peninsula. Among many shrines attributed to him are the Ta Prohm and the Preah Khan. His energetic program of public works included the building of 121 rest houses and 102 hospitals, the detailed provisions for which are recorded in inscriptions.

Most rulers of Angkor looked to Shiva for identification, but Jayavarman took as his patron the bodhisattva Avalokiteshvara, the compassionate savior. He saw himself as a bodhisattva, steering his subjects toward Buddhist salvation. One of his inscriptions says of him:

> His feet were a chaplet of lotus on the heads of all the kings; he overcame his enemies in battle; loaded with jewels of virtue he took the Earth to wife, and gave her his glory for a necklace. . . . He suffered from the ills of his subjects more than from his own; for it is the grief of the people that causes the grief of kings, and not their own grief.

After his reign, there were no more grandiose temples commemorated in flowery Sanskrit inscriptions, and it has been suggested that his extravagant demands on his subjects as soldiers and laborers exhausted the energies of the kingdom. (Other explanations of Angkor's decline are, however, at least as plausible.) The image presented by his extravagant works hovers curiously between megalomania and Buddhist compassion.

[See also Angkor; Angkor Thom; and Cham.]

Lawrence P. Briggs, *The Ancient Khmer Empire* (1951). David P. Chandler, *A History of Cambodia* (1983). G. Coedès, *The Indianized States of Southeast Asia*, translated by Susan B. Cowing (1968).    IAN W. MABBETT

## JAYAWARDENE, JUNIUS RICHARD (b. 1906), prime minister (1977–1978) and president (since 1978) of Sri Lanka. Involved in national politics since the early 1940s, Jayawardene became a prominent member of the United National Party at its inception in 1946 and held senior ministerial appointments in every government the party formed. Although his organizational ability was highly valued and he had a personal following, his leadership ambition was thwarted by the stronger position held within the party by Dudley Shelton Senanayake. Jayawardene's inability to develop a firm personal electoral base proved to be a distinct handicap.

Following the death of Senanayake in 1973, Jayawardene took hold of the party reigns, and under his guidance the party emerged as the most dynamic political organization in Sri Lanka. The landslide victory at the 1977 polls, which gave the party the firm control of the legislature, enabled Jayawardene to initiate new policies, most notably an explicit commitment to free-market philosophy in the economy and a pro-Western bias in the foreign policy, in both respects marking the rejection of the party's move toward the center that had occurred in the 1960s. A new constitution was proclaimed in September 1978, introducing a presidential structure, and Jayawardene became Sri Lanka's first executive president. He easily won a new term of office in 1982. Jayawardene has committed the country to an ambitious large-scale development program, and Sri Lanka's economy, which had been stagnating in the pre-1977 period, has shown a remarkable robustness under him. His unquestioned leadership within the party and the fractured political opposition have permitted Jayawardene to dominate national politics in a fashion no other leader has been able to do. Jayawardene has failed, however, to use this unique standing to address the major political problem facing his government: the grievances of the Tamil minority. A rapid deterioration of Sinhalese-Tamil relations has taken place, which has been exemplified in the powerful articulation of the idea of a separate state for the Tamils.

[See also Sri Lanka; United National Party; Tamils in Sri Lanka; and Senanayake, Dudley Shelton.]

VIJAYA SAMARAWEERA

## JESUITS

### AN OVERVIEW

The Society of Jesus, a Roman Catholic religious order founded by Ignatius of Loyola and constituted in 1540, mandated to its members the apostolic purpose "to go . . . to whatsoever provinces they [the popes] may choose to send us—whether they are pleased to send us among the Turks or any other infidels, even those who live in the region called the Indies." While Christianity had been introduced much earlier in various parts of Asia, the Jesuits revived the evangelistic spirit in the age of discovery and colonization. One of the original seven Jesuits, Francis Xavier, reached Goa in 1541 as papal nuncio, then journeyed from India to Melaka (Malacca; 1545 and 1547) and the Moluccas (1546). In 1549 he traveled to Japan, where for more than two years he worked to establish Christian settlements. He returned to Goa in 1552 and from there set sail for China with a Portuguese embassy. He died off the Chinese coast, having established a Jesuit presence throughout Portuguese Asian outposts. [See Xavier, Francis.]

With the Treaty of Tordesillas in 1494, Pope Alexander VI had divided the world into spheres of influence for Spain and for Portugal. The line, drawn before even a general geographic knowledge of the new worlds was available, gave Africa and India to Portugal and the New World to Spain; however, the demarcation was drawn in such a way that the Philippines were included on the side of the New World and Brazil was placed under Portugal's control, the so-called *padroado*. Thus did the Portuguese Province of the Society of Jesus have jurisdiction over almost all of Asia. By the year 1574 some forty-two Jesuits were ready to set sail from Lisbon for the Far East.

In 1573 Alessandro Valignano was appointed "visitor," highest Jesuit authority, of the missions in the East Indies from Goa to Japan. He arrived in Asia in 1574 and spent thirty-three years there. He developed, with the aid of his confreres, a strategy under which the missionaries modified their ethnocentric Western social concepts when there was no compromise of Catholic dogma and adapted to the cultures in which they were laboring. In the hierarchical societies of Asia, the Jesuits decided to focus their evangelistic hopes on the upper strata of society. [See Valignano, Alessandro.]

By the first decade of the sixteenth century Jesuits were working in many parts of Asia. The Italian Roberto De Nobili, in Madurai, India, took on the guise of a *sannyasin*, a Hindu ascetic, and studied Tamil and Sanskrit while teaching the Christian gospel. [See De Nobili, Roberto.]

Matteo Ricci, another Italian, who had entered China in 1583, at first took the outward appearance of a Buddhist monk and later that of a Confucian scholar. Ricci also became proficient in Confucian philosophy and the deportment of a Chinese man of letters. By artful moral persuasion and friendship,

Ricci made his way to the Chinese capital. At his death in 1610 Ricci had left his imprint on the high echelons of court and government. Having made converts from Macao to Beijing, Ricci laid the groundwork for generations of missionaries. From his time to the end of the eighteenth century some nine hundred Jesuits worked in China. [See Ricci, Matteo.]

In Japan, where Christianity showed such promise that some of the daimyo converted to it, the Jesuits became deeply involved in local shogunal politics and with Portuguese commercial interests in Japan. Domestic political shifts, Spanish rivalry emanating from the Philippines, and Franciscan disagreement over missionary method caused serious political and religious problems for the mission. Then in 1600 English traders landed on the Japanese coast. In 1614 Tokugawa Ieyasu ordered that all the Jesuit missionaries be expelled and that the Japanese Christians return to Buddhism. The greatest apostolic success in East Asia was thus thwarted and driven underground, and Japan became a closed country, *sakoku*, until the mid-nineteenth century. [See Seclusion *and* Kirishitan.]

Throughout the seventeenth century, Portugal maintained its nominal *padroado* over all of the Catholic missionary activity in Asia, with the exception of the Philippines, which remained under Spain's jurisdiction. This was done at great cost of manpower and with immense political wrangling. Not only was there pressure from various national and philosophical factions among the Catholic national groups but pressure was being exerted by the Protestant English and Dutch. Trade and national honor were at stake as well as the conversion of souls. [See Spain and the Philippines.]

With Japan closed, the Japanese Province of the Society of Jesus governed from Macao, turning much of its attention to Indochina. To this mission was sent another remarkable man, Alexandre de Rhodes. He labored in Cochinchina and Tonkin for five years until he was driven out. He pleaded to Europe that the hope for the Asian church was the building and maintaining of a native clergy supported by European bishops. Throughout his remaining years in Asia he worked to see this plan implemented and saw some success before his death in 1660. [See Rhodes, Alexandre de.]

In China after 1685, the French Jesuits were given a unique semiautonomous status as the *mission française*. Juridically, China remained as a vice-province under the Province of Japan, even though its missionary activity was moribund. India was divided into two provinces, that of Goa and that of Cochin or Malabar. Debate over missionary method continued to boil over into controversy. National groups within the Jesuit order differed as to apostolic approach to indigenous cultures. Non-Jesuit Catholic orders, the Franciscans and Dominicans, and especially the Missions Etrangères de Paris, were critical of Jesuit missionary methods and criticized the Jesuits for being too accommodating to social practices that smacked of superstition or pagan heresy. In China the debate over the admissibility of certain filial practices, civil observances, and religious terminology and the use of a Chinese-language liturgy by Chinese converts caused deep rifts within the church. This Chinese Rites Controversy went on for centuries. In India, too, a similar struggle was waged over the acceptance of Malabar Rites among Indian Catholics. It was not until the twentieth century that some neutral ground of accommodation was gained.

In China the Jesuits continued to have influence at court as scientists and technicians. They contributed substantially to China's knowledge of the West, and through their frequent reports to Europe they built the Western ideal of the highly regarded benevolent despotism of China in eighteenth-century Europe. By carefully navigating the imperial bureaucratic waters, the few court priests smoothed the way for the missionaries in the field to conduct their business in relative security. The China Jesuits survived the change of dynasties from the native Chinese Ming to the Manchu Qing with little trouble. A few priests even aided the Chinese in the successful completion of the Sino-Russian Treaty of Nerchinsk in 1689, which aimed to settle the border dispute between China and Russia.

In the Philippines, under Spanish control, the Jesuits followed closely the civil and military incursions into new areas. The sheer number of islands and the difficulty in maintaining a continuity of mission made evangelism there difficult.

In the last third of the eighteenth century the Jesuit order was in great turmoil. The nation-states of Europe were beginning to feel a power apart from the ultramontane Catholic church. The Age of Reason was in full flower, and the Society of Jesus appeared as a threat both to state and deism. Slowly but inexorably the Jesuits were banished from country after country, starting with Portugal in 1759 and ending with a general worldwide suppression in 1773 decreed by the pope. (Only in the Russia of Catherine the Great were the Jesuits allowed to exist as an order, and this was more Russian defiance of

Rome than support of the Jesuits.) The Asian missions were cut off from their sources in Portugal, Spain, France, Rome, and the many other lands from which the missionaries had come. The Jesuit principles of mission, which had been more than two hundred years in formation and development, were jettisoned. The church in India lay in virtual ruin. At the Chinese court ex-Jesuits continued to minister to the aging Qianlong emperor, but in the provinces anti-Christian persecution again built momentum. Other entities within the Catholic church sought to take up the mantle of the Jesuit order in parts of Asia with varying degrees of success.

With the defeat of Napoleon in 1814 came the universal restoration of the Jesuit order. The reestablishment of the missions took some time. The Jesuits did not return to China until 1842. They did not go back to Japan, which had showed such promise in the sixteenth century, until 1908. In the late nineteenth century Jesuits from several European countries sought to revive the ancient missions in India, much to the chagrin of the English overlords.

In the twentieth century there has been an attempt to look upon the Catholic church in each Asian country not as an arm of European mission but as an independent, mature part of the whole. Despite the political turmoil in various parts of the Asian continent, Christianity has survived and expanded and the Jesuits continue to work where they are allowed. Much more emphasis has been put by the order upon indigenous control within an Ignatian, Jesuit model of spirituality. In India and Indonesia the Jesuits have been especially successful in attracting local people into their ranks.

[See also Christianity.]

William V. Bangert, S.J., *A History of the Society of Jesus* (1972). C. Wessels, S.J., *Early Jesuit Travellers in Central Asia, 1603–1721* (1924). H. de la Costa, *The Jesuits in the Philippines, 1581–1768* (1967). George H. Dunne, S.J., *Generation of Giants: The Story of the Jesuits in China in the Last Decades of the Ming Dynasty* (1964). Felix Alfred Plattner, *Jesuits Go East* (1950). Johannes Laures, S.J., *The Catholic Church in Japan* (1954). Charles R. Boxer, *The Christian Century in Japan* (1951). Malcolm Hay, *Failure in the Far East* (1957). J. Correia-Afonso, S.J., *Jesuit Letters and Indian History* (1969).

THEODORE NICHOLAS FOSS

## JESUITS IN CHINA

The history of the Jesuits in China (1552 to about 1950) may be divided into two periods separated by an intermediary phase from 1773, when the Society of Jesus was abolished by Pope Clement XIV, to 1814, when it was reestablished by Pope Pius VII. Of the two periods, the premodern one is by far the more glorious, in part because the Roman Catholics had the China Mission field to themselves and in part because Western imperialism, with its many negative aspects, had not yet intruded into missionary activities. The glory of the premodern period derives not solely from the fact that nearly 1,000 (the best source lists 920) Jesuits participated in the China Mission, but more fundamentally from the fact that in the seventeenth and eighteenth centuries the Jesuits' extensive educational system in Europe and their exciting missionary program was stirring the spiritual enthusiasm of some of the brightest young men of that time. The Jesuits excelled in preparing their novices with excellent educations, including training in the most advanced scientific and technological fields of their day. This happy combination of inherent brilliance and extensive learning was particularly appropriate to China, where European missionaries were encountering not a "primitive" culture, but one of the oldest and most sophisticated civilizations in the world.

The founder of the Jesuit China Mission was Francis Xavier (known in Chinese as Fan Jige; 1506–1552). Although he never penetrated the Chinese mainland and died on the offshore island of Shangchuan, his efforts served as an inspiration to later Jesuits. It is important to recognize that the Jesuits in China worked cooperatively and collectively in a way that blurs any attribution of individual achievements. It is with this fact in mind that one designates Matteo Ricci (Li Madou; 1552–1610) as the formulator of the famous missionary approach of Jesuit accommodation. Not only did Ricci have superiors (such as Alessandro Valignano) and confreres (such as Michele Ruggieri) who contributed to the formulation of the accommodation program, but he also had followers who continued to develop and evolve the program. Jesuit accommodation was developed to meet the unique demands of the mission field in China. Although Jesuit missionary policy as a whole stressed the accommodation of Christianity to indigenous elements of a non-Judeo-Christian culture, nowhere had the missionaries encountered such an advanced culture as in China. This forced them to make difficult choices about what to accept and what to reject. If they accepted elements of Chinese culture that contradicted the Christian faith, the accommodation would become theologically invalid. If, on the other hand, they did not accept certain essential elements

in Chinese culture, then the Chinese would reject Christianity out of hand as too alien to Chinese culture.

Since the Jesuits had chosen to concentrate on converting the Chinese literati as the first step toward converting the entire society, elements associated with the literati assumed crucial importance. These elements included the choice of a Chinese name for the Christian God, and the rites performed to honor Confucius and familial ancestors. Was it permissible, these early Jesuits wondered, to use ancient Chinese terms such as Shangdi ("lord-above") or Tian ("heaven") to refer to God, or were these terms too tainted with pagan associations to be accurate? If too tainted, was it then possible to use the Chinese neologism Tianzhu ("lord of heaven"), or was it necessary to develop a Chinese transliteration for the name of God? In regard to the crucial matter of rites, were the rites dedicated to Confucius and to ancestors acts of worship or were they essentially acts of social honor and civil respect? Jesuit accommodation, with its inherent sympathy and respect for Chinese culture, tended to favor the indigenous cultural elements in deciding the above questions, but this produced a negative reaction among some Christians. Although limited to few Jesuits, this criticism included many non-Jesuit missionaries in China as well as Jesuit leaders in Europe. The resulting debate was known as the Rites Controversy and did great damage to the Christian mission in China.

Nevertheless, not all aspects of Jesuit accommodation were so controversial. The Jesuits rejected Buddhism as an accommodative component and instead chose Confucianism. This choice was understandable, given the fact that Confucianism was the official philosophy of the scholar-officials and thus of the group with which the highly educated Jesuits shared the most in common. The Jesuits criticized the coarseness and superstition of many Buddhist monks of that time and praised the Confucian scholar-officials' refinement and emphasis on learning. In addition, the latter presented a highly attractive power base to the Jesuits, who were accustomed in Europe and elsewhere to working close to the apex of the power structure. Nevertheless, the choice of Confucianism and the scholar-officials as the accommodative core in a Chinese-Christian synthesis may be criticized on at least two grounds. First, it was time-bound by the unique set of circumstances that existed at the time of their formulation in the early seventeenth century. Second, the Jesuits appear to have underestimated the scholar-officials' inflexibility and resistance to external influences.

The specific circumstances were part of late Ming-dynasty culture, which was experimental, had a looser sense of Confucian orthodoxy in comparison with other periods in Chinese history and was radical in its willingness to synthesize various teachings into a harmonious unity. The Jesuits tried to utilize the late Ming eclectic spirit, which had attempted to treat the three traditional teachings of Confucianism, Buddhism, and Daoism as essentially one teaching. Such syncretism would have been unthinkable in other periods of Chinese history, when the exponents of these respective teachings competed and clashed with one another for adherents and imperial patronage. The Jesuits attempted to utilize this syncretic spirit by seeking to displace Buddhism in a synthesis with Confucianism. In this viewpoint, whereas Christianity complemented Confucianism, it competed with Buddhism. While Confucianism was more of a moral and social teaching that spoke only implicitly, if at all, of spiritual forces, Buddhism spoke specifically and in great detail on spiritual matters. Confucianism's relative silence on spirits and its emphasis on moral and spiritual cultivation were seen as reconcilable with Christianity's explicit treatment of spiritual forces and one God. Furthermore, elements like the Chinese emphasis on filial respect was very much in accord with the Christian honoring of one's parents.

Although there are many indications that the Jesuit position was valid for the late Ming, it clearly became less tenable after the Manchu invasion of 1644 and the return to a stricter sense of orthodoxy during the Qing dynasty. With the decline of the syncretic spirit, the literati became less willing to accept the synthesis of Confucianism with a foreign religion. In fact, the literati became less willing to accept the blending of Confucianism with any non-Confucian elements, including Buddhism and Daoism. There was a reassertion of the transmission of the *dao* (the Way) from the ancient sages through Confucius to the present. There was little place in such a perspective for a foreign religion. This was the current against which Jesuits of the late seventeenth and eighteenth centuries had to struggle, and it made conversions of eminent literati far more difficult than they previously had been.

Although cultural conditions in China became less fertile for Christianity, the Jesuits continued to find employment in prominent positions at the court, but they lived as an island of Christianity in a sea of Chinese hostility. The continued prominence of the Jesuits in China during the late seventeenth and entire eighteenth centuries was indicative of the quality of the missionaries sent to China and the spiritual discipline of the Society of Jesus. Men like Johann Adam Schall von Bell (Tang Ruowang; 1592–1666) and Ferdinand Verbiest (Nan Huairen; 1623–1688) would have been outstanding in practically any environment, but the cause and collaboration of the Jesuits in China raised them to a unique position in history. Schall and Verbiest were the first Europeans to head the important Bureau of Astronomy, where Jesuits held prominent positions for more than 150 years. Schall and Verbiest were also close to the Manchu emperors of China and initiated a series of daily Jesuit contacts with the throne. If the prospects for the conversion of Chinese literati to Christianity peaked in the late Ming between 1600 and 1644 (the year of the transition of dynasties), the prospects for Jesuit influence on the Manchu rulers of China peaked in the early Qing, between 1644 and 1705.

The promise of Jesuit influence on the Chinese throne and possibly conversion from the top down was a distinct possibility in these years. It was aided by Jesuit brilliance, training, and spiritual discipline but was hindered by the contentiousness that became ever more exacerbated during these years. Not only did Jesuits contend with other Christian missionaries over the Rites Controversy and other issues, but Jesuits also contended with one another. In the process, they presented a sad contradiction to their preaching of peace and harmony. One of the greatest sources of contention among Jesuits themselves was based upon nationalistic differences. More than one-third of all Jesuits (314) during the premodern period of the mission were Portuguese. This was, in part, a reflection of the Portuguese *padroado* (monopoly granted by the papacy over missionary and other activities in Asia) and, in part, a reflection of the Portuguese crown's support of missionary causes. There were also many Italian Jesuits (99), but they had regional rather than national affiliations. Corresponding to the rise of France in the late seventeenth-century political scene in Europe, however, came the increase in the numbers of French Jesuits, of whom there were 130 in the premodern period. The French Jesuits and their masters in Europe were unwilling to honor the Portuguese monopoly, and as a result Portuguese Jesuits such as the favorite of the Chinese throne, Tomé Pereira, contended with increasing arrivals of Jesuits from France. This contention diminished the efficacy of Christianity in the eyes of the Chinese throne.

[*See also* Cattaneo, Lazzaro; Ricci, Matteo; Schall von Bell, Johann Adam; Valignano, Alessandro; Verbiest, Ferdinand; *and* Xu Guangqi.]

George H. Dunne, *Generation of Giants: The Story of the Jesuits in China in the Last Decades of the Ming Dynasty* (1962). Kenneth Scott Latourette, *A History of Christian Missions in China* (1929). David E. Mungello, *Curious Lord: Jesuit Accommodation and the Origins of Sinology* (1985). Antonio Sisto Rosso, *Apostolic Legations to China of the Eighteenth Century* (1948). Arnold H. Rowbotham, *Missionary and Mandarin: The Jesuits at the Court of China* (1942). John D. Young, *Confucianism and Christianity: The First Encounter* (1983).

DAVID E. MUNGELLO

## JESUITS IN INDIA

The Roman Catholic Society of Jesus, known as the Jesuits, is an order of monks devoted to educational and missionary work. Soon after their founding in 1540, the Jesuits, as champions of the Counter-Reformation, distinguished themselves as catechists, humanists, linguists, philosophers, theologians, and confidants of Iberian royalty. Maritime expansion to the East Indies opened up prospects of spiritual and temporal conquest, and Portuguese kings deputed Jesuit clergy to colonial possessions in India and the Orient as ambassadors, chaplains, and proselytizers. Operating in proximity to colonial forts and under the protection of Portuguese forces, the Jesuits concentrated largely on the littoral tracts of the west and southeast coast of India, founding churches and colleges, converting indigenous maritime castes, and acting as chaplains of fort garrisons.

Although they indulged in their usual intellectual activities by setting up printing presses and producing the first printed books in indigenous languages, the Jesuits' intellectual and pastoral pursuits were severely stymied by the weakness of Portuguese colonial power. Jesuit contingents seldom forayed inland except to visit the courts of native kings, thereby duplicating Jesuit strategy in Europe, where influence gained at the court had deep impacts on the effectiveness of Jesuit ministry. Jesuit delegations to the Mughal court and to the courts of Calicut and Travancore failed to convert royalty but nonetheless won for the Jesuits considerable power as guardians and mentors of princes, liaisons between indigenous and colonial powers, and protectors of convert Christian communities. The early Jesuit mission, distinguished by such missionaries as Francis Xavier, Henry Henriquez, Rudolph Acquaviva, and Anthony Stevens, did much to further the expansion of Christianity with the zealotry of the Iberian Inquisition but without deeper cultural roots. [*See also* Xavier, Francis *and* Henriquez, Henry.]

Jesuit missionary methods underwent radical transformation in 1607 with the advent of Roberto de Nobili. The indigenization of missionary methods in adopting the dress and cultural mores of brahman communities and other high castes saw the focus of Jesuit activity shift to the temple center of Madurai. Between 1623 and 1759 Jesuit missions spread inland to Trichinopoly, Salem, Coimbatore, Tanjore, Tinnivelly, Golconda, and Mysore, ministering to a flock of nearly 206,500 converts. In 1774 Pope Clement XIV's Brief of Suppression of the Society of Jesus was promulgated to Portuguese possessions in India, and the *padroado* clergy and the Paris Foreign Mission formally displaced Jesuits from their missions. In April 1838 the "Multa Praeclare" promulgated by Pope Gregory XVI restored the now decadent Indian missions to the Jesuits. The restoration was marred by schism and stormy clashes because Goanese *padroado* clergy contested the reassignment of Jesuits to their former missions.

Between 1891 and 1923 Jesuit churches in India increased from 200 to 632. Jesuit provinces of the new mission concentrated on the nurturing of an Indian clergy and this, coupled with the assignment of Jesuit provinces from the United States and Europe to various parts of India, saw Jesuit activity expand greatly, especially in the field of education. By 1970, 572 Jesuits, or roughly one-third of the Jesuits in India, staffed schools and colleges spread throughout the subcontinent. Jesuit colleges employed 3,745 lay teachers and catered to 112,335 students: 86,812 in 88 schools and 25,523 in 21 colleges. Today, fewer than 300 of the nearly 3,000 Jesuits in India are foreigners. There are 10 Indian Jesuit provinces and 5 Jesuit regions, each having its own college and several high schools, not to mention parishes and mission stations. Jesuits also run a Social Training Center in Bangalore, two theologates, one in Delhi and one in Pune, an Indian Social Institute in Delhi, and a philosophate in Madras.

[*See also* Portuguese: Portuguese in India; De Nobili, Robert; *and* Goa.]

J. Castets, *The Madura Mission* (1924). J. Correia-Afonso, *Jesuit Letters and Indian History* (1955). D. Ferroli, *The Jesuits in Malabar*, vol. 1 (1938). K. Patel and A. Verstraeten, *What They Think* (1972).

PATRICK ROCHE

**JEWS.** The Jewish communities in India, Iran, and China, although now disintegrating, have had a long history, characterized by varying degrees of isolation from Jews elsewhere and integration with the civilizations of their neighbors.

***Persian Jews.*** Dating back to the Babylonian exile, the Jewish Diaspora in Persia developed significantly during the Sasanid period (226–642). After the Muslim conquest, Jews were granted *dhimmi* (protected people) status in exchange for enduring certain political, social, and fiscal disabilities. Jewish sectarian and messianic movements flourished under early Islam. Most Persian Jews were artisans, although under the Abbasids, a wealthy merchant class developed, especially in Ahwaz, Isfahan, and Shiraz, and soon Jews became court bankers to the caliphs, viziers, and in the eleventh century, the Seljuk sultans. Although they prospered under the religious tolerance of the Mongol Ilkhanid dynasty (1258–1336), the Jews, then numbering thirty thousand, suffered a reverse of fortunes under the Shi'ite Safavids (1502–1736) owing to the Shi'ite belief in the "ritual uncleanliness" of nonbelievers. Until the Safavid period, Jewish authorities in Baghdad had controlled the cultural, religious, and educational affairs of the Persian Jews. Now, however, the Persian communities became independent, as Jews of Isfahan assumed the leadership. Shi'ite intolerance lasted throughout the nineteenth century, despite the attempts of European Jewish organizations to intervene with the Qajar Shah Nasir al-Din (1848–1896). The promise of emancipation and equality during the constitutional period of 1905 to 1906 proved abortive; hostilities toward the Jews continued. The establishment of schools in the nineteenth century by the French Alliance Israélite Universelle, followed by American Jewish aid after 1918, alleviated some of the plight of Persian Jews, but the power of the Shi'ite clergy was only broken temporarily under the Pahlavis (1925–1979), whose secularizing and westernizing policies led to the political emancipation of the Jews. The Jewish population increased after 1949, as thousands of Iraqi Jews migrated to Iran, although many of these, as well as the poorer Iranian Jews, eventually emigrated to Israel. The economic situation of those who remained (between seventy and eighty thousand from 1953 to 1979) improved. Their condition took a drastic turn for the worse with the accession of the Khomeini regime in 1979, and a new wave of emigration ensued. Fewer than thirty thousand Jews, including many recent Iraqi immigrants, remained in Iran in 1984.

***Indian Jews.*** In India, the Jewish population is made up of three communities—the Cochin Jews, the Bene Israel, and the Baghdadi, or Iraqi, Jews. The earliest extant documentation of the presence of Jews in Cochin are two copper plates engraved in ancient Tamil, detailing land rights and privileges granted by a Hindu ruler to a Joseph Rabban, the head of a Jewish settlement in Cranganore on the Malabar Coast. Dated by scholars to a period between 970 and 1035, the plates were probably given to Jewish merchants who originally came from Palestine, or possibly Yemen and Aden, at an unknown time and intermarried with the indigenous population. Dark in hue, they were designated as "black" Jews by a "white" Jewish community that seems to have developed in Cochin by the sixteenth century. Consisting of immigrants from Europe (primarily Spain) and the Middle East, this group constructed their own *pardeshi* ("foreign") synagogue in 1568. Three endogamous and ritually separated castelike groups crystallized: "black" Jews, "white" Jews, and *meshuarim* (descendants of manumitted, converted slaves and of the illegitimate offspring of unions between "white" Jews and indigenous mistresses). The protection of the raja of Cochin enabled the Jews to survive the persecution of Portuguese rule (1502–1663), after which they enjoyed an era of religious freedom and commercial prosperity fostered by the Dutch hegemony over Cochin (1663–1795). During the British period that followed, the Jews lost their predominance in the import trade and their position declined. Traditional in their observance of Sephardic rites, the Cochin Jews at their peak numbered about twenty-five hundred. [*See also* Cochin.]

Bene Israel communal traditions maintain that they are descendants of the ten lost tribes of Israel, their ancestors having left Palestine in the second century BCE. Despite scanty evidence, different theories date the arrival of this group to periods ranging from the sixth century BCE to the seventh century CE and these suggest, variously, that they came from Palestine, Yemen, or even Babylon. Spreading into the Konkan villages south of Bombay, the Bene Israel were cut off from the mainstream of Jewish life until the eighteenth century but celebrated some essential holidays, practiced circumcision, followed dietary laws, recited the Shema, and abstained from their oil-pressing occupation on the Sabbath. In the mid-eighteenth century, as many members of the Bene Israel community moved to Bombay seeking employment, they established contact with Jews of Cochin, who, along with Protestant missionaries in the nineteenth century, contributed to a revival of their Judaism. The Bene Israel enjoyed a wave of intense social and communal activity from 1916 to 1927, when they established communal organizations and Anglo-Marathi periodicals. Although a number of Bene Israel became high-ranking government administrators, military officers, and professionals, by the mid-twentieth century most members of the community, numbering more than twenty thousand, could be categorized as lower-middle-class.

Toward the end of the eighteenth century Arabic-speaking Jews from Iraq and other Arab countries arrived in India, establishing themselves in commerce in Bombay and Calcutta. Along with Jews from Persia and Afghanistan, they became known collectively as Iraqi, or Baghdadi, Jews. Many were wealthy merchants dealing in cotton, jute, and tobacco, or pioneering in the textile industry. The Sassoons in particular contributed significantly to the civic development of Bombay. As in Cochin, the Indian environment contributed to caste overtones among Jewish relations in Bombay: the Baghdadis refused to recognize the Bene Israel as proper Jews, owing to the latter's "ritual laxness," hazy origins, and darker complexions. In the 1930s and 1940s, an influx of Central European Jews fleeing Nazi persecution temporarily augmented the Jewish communities in India. Although they had never experienced anti-Semitism from Indians, the Jews of India responded, for a variety of reasons, to the almost simultaneous emergence of India's independence and that of the state of Israel by emigrating. By the mid-1980s, no more than five thousand, mainly Bene Israel, remained in India.

*Chinese Jews.* Although Jewish communities may have existed in China from the Tang (618–907) or even the Han (206 BCE–220 CE) dynasties, the earliest reliable evidence of the presence of Jews dates from the eighth century, suggesting that there may have been communities in Canton (Guangzhou) and Khotan and later, during the Mongol Yuan dynasty (1279–1368), in Hangzhou and Beijing. The only Jewish community to survive, however, was that of Kaifeng, the capital of the Song dynasty (960–1279). Historians disagree over the origin of these Jews (Persia, Yemen, or Palestine) but the group seems to have settled in Kaifeng before 1127, bringing Western cloth, perhaps cotton. Their prayer books were in Judeo-Persian, and they spoke New Persian, the lingua franca of Central Asia. They built their first synagogue in 1163, repairing or rebuilding it repeatedly at least until 1850, soon after which the final synagogue seems to have been destroyed.

From sources including the Jews' own stone inscriptions dated 1489, 1512, 1663, and 1679, tablet inscriptions in the synagogues, their scrolls of law, prayer books, and other writings in Hebrew and Chinese, and from reports of visitors, particularly Jesuit missionaries in the sixteenth and seventeenth centuries, scholars believe the Kaifeng community flourished by the sixteenth century. Many members became military commanders and scholar-officials; some were merchants. Never numbering more than between one thousand and fifteen hundred and divided into seven clans, the Jews maintained their distinct identity, despite intermarriage and the adoption of Chinese surnames, for a number of centuries, owing to the tolerance of the Chinese, who regarded them as a Muslim sect. Some did convert to Islam. After the sixteenth century, their isolation from other Jewish communities seems to have contributed to a decline in their knowledge of Judaism and Hebrew. By the end of World War II racial assimilation was almost complete, although some 200 to 250 traceable descendants of the original Kaifeng Jewish community seem to have survived, with little Jewish identity. In the early 1980s a few individuals still remembered their Jewish ancestry and some of the rituals that grandparents had practiced.

Modern Jewish communities developed in China in the nineteenth and twentieth centuries as Russian Jews settled in Harbin and Tianjin, while European and Sephardic Jews from India, Iraq, and Egypt founded communities in Shanghai and Hong Kong. Refugees from Nazi persecution augmented these communities during World War II, when that of Shanghai increased to about twenty-five thousand Jews, but as in India, most of these communities disintegrated soon after the war. In 1984, approximately thirty Jews lived in all of China.

Walter Joseph Fischel, "Persia," in *Encyclopaedia Judaica,* edited by Cecil Roth and Geoffrey Wigoder, vol. 13 (1971), pp. 302–319; and "Bene Israel," in *Encyclopaedia Judaica Yearbook* (1975–1976), pp. 244–247. Walter Joseph Fischel and Paul Gottlieb, "India," in *Encyclopaedia Judaica,* vol. 8, pp. 1349–1359. Baruch Gilead, "Iran," in *Encyclopaedia Judaica,* vol. 8, pp. 1439–1444. Paul Gottlieb, "Cochin," in *Encyclopaedia Judaica,* vol. 5, pp. 621–628. B. J. Israel, *The Jews of India* (1982). Donald Leslie, *The Survival of the Chinese Jews* (1972). Laurence Loeb, *Outcaste: Jewish Life in Southern Iran* (1977). Ezekiel M. Musleah, *On the Banks of the Ganga: The Sojourn of Jews in Calcutta* (1975). Michael Pollak, *Mandarins, Jews and Missionaries* (1980). S. Soroudi, "Jews in Islamic Iran," *Jerusalem Quarterly* 21 (1981): 99–114. Schifra Strizower, *The Bene Israel of Bombay* (1971). Michael Zand, "Bukhara," in *Encyclopaedia Judaica Yearbook* (1975–1976), pp. 183–192.

JOAN G. ROLAND

JHARKHAND, "land (khand) of the scrubs (jhar)," the name for the forest tracts of middle India; one of the first occurrences of the term is in a thirteenth-century inscription from Orissa. The legend of Jharkhand as the homeland of India's indigenous peoples was adopted by a political party formed by tribals whose objective was to create a Jharkhand state. This was to be carved out of the Chotanagpur-Santal Pargana region of Bihar and contiguous regions of other states.

[See also Adivasis; Santal; Orissa; and Bihar.]

K. S. Singh, "Medieval Tribal Bihar," in History of Bihar, vol. 2, part 1 (1984).          K. S. SINGH

JHELUM RIVER, one of the rivers that gave the Indian state of Punjab its name, "the Land of Five Rivers." The other four rivers are the Sutlej, the Beas, the Ravi, and the Chenab. The rivers are fed from the snow belt of the Himalayas, so they are more important for irrigation than the rivers of peninsular India, which are dependent upon the monsoon. There were small irrigation canals in the regions of the five rivers from ancient times, but more large-scale irrigation works were not developed until the end of the nineteenth century. The greatest development in the Jhelum area took place from 1905 to 1917 in what was known as the Triple Project, when three doabs, or plains between rivers, that had previously been barren were irrigated. The creation of canal colonies, with settlers from elsewhere in the Punjab, led to highly productive farming. Many of the farmers were Sikhs, and after the partition of India in 1947, when the Jhelum region became part of Pakistan, they left their land and fled to India. This led to some dislocation, but the area recovered its productivity and is now one of the most important agricultural regions in Pakistan.

AINSLIE T. EMBREE

JIANG QING (b. 1913), widow of Mao Zedong and a member of the Gang of Four. Born in Shandong Province, Jiang Qing grew up without her father, who must have either deserted her mother or died when she was young. After only five years of primary education, Jiang enrolled in an acting school, where she had an affair with its head, Zhao Taimou, when she was seventeen years old. Jiang followed Zhao to Qingdao when he became a lecturer of a newly established university. When Zhao became involved with another well-known actress, Jiang had an affair with the actress's brother Qiwei,

who worked underground for the Communists under the assumed name of Huang Jing. Through his introduction Jiang joined the Communist Party around 1933. Meanwhile, under the pseudonym of Lan Ping she appeared in several films produced in Shanghai. Jiang's acting career was not very successful and she remained poor. During this time she married the film critic Ma Jiliang, also known as Tang Na, but the marriage soon broke up.

After the Japanese occupation of Shanghai in 1938 Jiang Qing went Yan'an, where she attended the Lu Xun Art Institute and met Mao Zedong, who was a regular speaker there. Despite the objections of his colleagues, Mao married her in 1938 on the condition that she would not involve herself in politics. Mao and Jiang had two daughters.

Jiang Qing was not visible in Chinese politics until the early 1960s, when she became interested in revolutionizing Chinese literature and art. During the Cultural Revolution she rapidly emerged as one of the most powerful, but also the most hated, of political figures. After assuming the role of adviser to the Cultural Revolution Small Group in May 1966, she led the Cultural Revolution in a more radical direction, frequently making inflammatory speeches. She was elected to the Politburo in 1969, remaining in that position until her fall in 1976. Jiang has been reported to be extremely arrogant, vengeful, hysterical, and ruthless, allegedly aspiring to be the official successor to her husband as leader of China in spite of her lack of the necessary qualifications.

[See also Gang of Four and Great Proletarian Cultural Revolution.]

Hong Yung Lee, The Politics of the Chinese Cultural Revolution (1978). Roxane Witke, Comrade Chiang Ch'ing (1977).          HONG YUNG LEE

JIANGSU, Chinese coastal province surrounding the independent municipality of Shanghai. With a population of 60,521,114 (1982 census) in an area of 102,200 square kilometers, Jiangsu is one of the most densely populated areas of China.

Jiangsu formed part of several states in the Spring and Autumn (722–481 BCE) and Warring States (403–221) periods and was incorporated into the Qin empire in 221 BCE. Following the fall of the Latter Han in 220 CE, the area was part of a series of southern states. Reincorporated into the empire under the Sui in 589, Jiangsu grew rapidly in population and productivity, exporting large quantities of grain north via the Grand Canal. By the twelfth century the region had become the economic and political center of China, with the largest cities and the most productive agriculture and trade. The city of Nanjing was an early capital of the Ming dynasty (1368–1644), during which Jiangsu remained a leading commercial and agricultural area, with a huge irrigation and waterworks network and a politically influential upper class. Under the Republic of China, Nanjing was again the capital of China from 1928 to 1938.

Jiangsu today remains a center of agriculture, while industry is also important, especially food processing and cotton and silk textiles but also including other light and heavy industries. In addition to Nanjing, the provincial capital, major rail, transport, and communications centers include Xuzhou, Suzhou, and Wuxi.                    JOHN A. RAPP

**JIANGXI**, province in south-central China that encompasses a population of 33,184,827 (1982 census) in an area of 160,000 square kilometers. Although incorporated into the Chinese empire comparatively early, Jiangxi was not economically important until after the construction of the canal system in the seventh century. From the eighth to the thirteenth century the tea and silver trade increased its prosperity and agricultural population. After coastal ports were opened to foreign shipping in the nineteenth century, Jiangxi declined as a major transport route. A bastion of warlordism in the early twentieth century, the province became a base of the Communist Party in the period of the Jiangxi Soviet (1928–1934). From 1938 to 1945 Jiangxi suffered under the Japanese occupation.

Jiangxi is located in a subtropical region in the drainage basin of a tributary of the Yangtze River; its irrigated agriculture centers on the labor-intensive cultivation of rice, along with winter wheat and other crops. There is comparatively little industry, although coal is mined in the west and other mineral reserves exist in the southeast, including tungsten, tin, and copper. Nanchang, the provincial capital, is a commercial, administrative, and industrial center. Other important cities include Jingdezhen, Fuzhou, Shangzhao, Yingtan, Jiuzhang, and Ji'an.
                    JOHN A. RAPP

**JIAOZHI.** The term *jiaozhi* first appears in the *Liji*, where it describes the sleeping habits of "southern barbarians." From the second century BCE it was used by Chinese as the name of a prefecture (*jun*)

in northern Vietnam. From 111 BCE until the end of Han, it was also applied as the name of a "circuit" (*bu*) that included all of modern Guangdong, Guangxi, and northern Vietnam. It was an administrative toponym in the Hanoi area during the period of Chinese overlordship and was subsequently used by the Chinese as a name for Vietnam.

Jennifer Holmgren, *Chinese Colonisation of Northern Vietnam* (1980). Keith W. Taylor, *The Birth of Vietnam* (1983).                    KEITH W. TAYLOR

**JIAOZHOU**, province established in northern Vietnam during the third century after the removal of direct Chinese dynastic control. It evolved during the subsequent era of the Southern Dynasties (fifth and sixth centuries) as a sometimes formally submissive, sometimes openly rebellious frontier province and had its own cycle of political stability that mirrored in reverse the fortunes of dynasties in southern China. Provincial autonomy led to a brief era of independence in the sixth century. Under the Tang, other provinces were established in northern Vietnam, and Jiaozhou was limited to the region around modern Hanoi.

Jennifer Holmgren, *Chinese Colonisation of Northern Vietnam* (1980). Keith W. Taylor, *The Birth of Vietnam* (1983).                    KEITH W. TAYLOR

**JIAYUGUAN**, known as the "end of the Great Wall"; a Ming-dynasty fortress commanding the western entrance to the Gansu corridor, the narrow passage along the northern edge of the Qilian mountain range followed since ancient times by caravans between China and the Middle East. About two hundred miles east of Yumenguan, site of the famous Jade Gate built during the Han dynasty (206 BCE–220 CE) and rediscovered and described by Aurel Stein in 1906, the Ming fortress was begun in 1372, the location having been chosen for its fresh water supply. The western gate was built in 1495, the eastern in 1506 to 1507. After 1539 the height of the fortress walls was nearly doubled, and from 1539 to 1541 and in 1573, outlying low walls were added. [See also Great Wall.]

                    ARTHUR N. WALDRON

**JIHAD**, military action undertaken primarily for the expansion of the Islamic state but also for its defense. Because it is the only form of war permitted by Islamic religious law—armed conflict between Muslims is forbidden—*jihad* is sometimes misleadingly termed "holy war." *Jihad* is a duty for every able-bodied male Muslim, at least until a sufficient number arises to meet the needs of a particular conflict. The concept of *jihad* is implied in the principle that Islam is a universal religion and therefore a universal polity; all peoples are invited to submit to Muslim rule or face armed conflict, and peace with non-Muslim states is temporary only. Excluded, however, as objects of *jihad* are Christians, Jews, and Zoroastrians who have submitted to the political authority of Islam. Further, *jihad* is incumbent only when it is clear that the military outcome will be favorable; the duty may be suspended, too, when interests dictate acceptance of tribute instead. In Twelver Shi'ite law, *jihad* can take place only with the reappearance of the absent imam.

[*See also* Islam.]

Rudolph Peters, trans., *Jihad in Mediaeval and Modern Islam: The Chapter on Jihad from Averroes' Legal Handbook 'Bidāyat al-Mujtahid' and the Treatise 'Koran and Fighting' by the Late Shaykh al-Azhar, Maḥmūd Shaltūt* (1977).                              JEANETTE A. WAKIN

**JILIN**, province in northeast China; its population in 1982 was 22,560,053. One of China's three Manchurian provinces, Jilin was part of several nomadic dynasties on the border of Chinese cultural influence until early in the twentieth century, when it underwent large-scale Chinese immigration. Its industry was first developed under the Japanese occupation, when its rail and power network was first constructed. Since 1949 Jilin's industry and agriculture have further developed, with the largest concentration of heavy industry in the capital, Changchun. Timber, iron ore, coal, and some copper reserves exist in the mountainous regions in the south and east, which are also the homelands of a significant Korean minority.

Jilin is also the name of a city, formerly the capital of Jilin Province. Established in the seventeenth century, it was primarily a regional market town and lumbering center. In the 1930s the Japanese turned Jilin (Japanese, Kirin) into a petrochemical center for their Manchurian war industry. After 1949 much of the industrial plant that had been removed by the Russians at the close of World War II was rebuilt. Today Jilin contains a large number of chemical and fertilizer plants, as well as major ferroalloy and sugar-refining industries. Its population in 1982 was 1,090,000.                    JOHN A. RAPP

**JIMMU.** According to the pseudohistorical accounts in *Nihon shoki* and the *Kojiki*, Jimmu Tennō was Japan's first emperor. His great-grandmother was Amaterasu, the sun goddess, and his father was the god Ninigi no Mikoto, ruler of the "Central Land of Reed Plains" (i.e., Japan).

At age forty-five, Jimmu proposed an eastward military campaign from his base in southeastern Kyushu in order to "bestow the blessings of imperial rule on remote regions." After proceeding from Toyo (northern Kyushu) through Aki (on the western tip of Honshu) and Kibi (Okayama Prefecture), he reached a point near modern Osaka. However, Jimmu's advance toward his destination in Yamato (Nara Prefecture) was opposed by a local chieftain, and when one of his trusted lieutenants was wounded, Jimmu decided to approach Yamato via Yoshino. Further adventures awaited Jimmu; he fended off a poisonous vapor with a magic sword and was guided to Yamato over treacherous mountains by a giant crow.

Once in Yamato, Jimmu met the resistance of the local gods. At one point, eighty divine bandits awaiting Jimmu in a narrow mountain pass were killed by eighty sword-bearing cooks from Jimmu's party. At last, on the first day of 660 BCE, Emperor Jimmu assumed the imperial dignity in the Palace of Kashiwara in the southern Nara basin. He remained on the throne for seventy-six years, until his death at the age of 127.

Jimmu is a mythological, not a historical, figure. Many of Jimmu's feats were more likely performed by later emperors; for instance, Jimmu's ascension to the throne via Yoshino is reminiscent of the emperor Temmu's experiences during the civil war of 672. The date when Jimmu was supposed to have ascended the throne has been shown to have been invented by the compilers of the *Nihon shoki*, who, believing that great revolutions occurred every 1260 years, counted back 1260 years from Suiko's reign to date the foundation of the empire at 660 BCE. Thus Jimmu Tennō is a fictional character created by early eighth-century apologists who sought to increase the prestige of the imperial house by pushing its origins into the distant past and linking it directly with the Shinto deities.

Still, certain aspects of the Jimmu legend may reflect reality. For example, while it may have come by more peaceful means, most cultural innovation seems to have spread from west to east in Japan. Jimmu's battles in Yamato may have been based on wars fought among local leaders, and Jimmu's character was probably modeled on that of one such magnate.

In the Meiji period, Emperor Jimmu became an object of national worship. The day on which he ascended the throne (11 February) was established as a state holiday and the two-thousandth anniversary of his accession in 1940 was celebrated with great patriotic fervor. The eleventh of February is celebrated as National Foundation Day even today.

[*See also* Kojiki *and* Nihon Shoki.]

W. G. Aston, trans., *Nihongi* (1896). Donald Philippi, trans., *Kojiki* (1969).    WAYNE FARRIS

**JI'NAN**, Chinese city, chief administrative seat in Shandong Province since the Ming dynasty; population, 3,348,615 (1982). The old walled city of Ji'nan was in a beautiful site located in a natural depression near the south bank of the Yellow River, in front of the northwest corner of the Shandong central mountains. Sandstone outcroppings in the depression created the famous springs and renowned Daming (Brilliant) Lake as Ji'nan's special scenic features.

In the twentieth century Ji'nan's role as Shandong's most important city has been rivaled by Qingdao, but Ji'nan has remained more important because of its combination of political, cultural, and transportation functions. Ji'nan became a railroad junction city in 1910, linked with Tianjin, Qingdao and the lower Yangtze Valley. After 1911 increasingly autonomous provincial governments heightened the city's political significance. Foreign influence, first German and then largely Japanese, penetrated along the railway from Qingdao, but never dominated the city. Ji'nan and Shandong were never under the effective control of China's various central governments between 1916 and 1949. After 1949 the city wall was torn down and the city expanded, primarily as a center for transportation and industry, as well as retaining its role as the administrative and educational capital of Shandong.

David D. Buck, *Urban Change in China: Politics and Development in Tsinan, Shantung, 1890–1949* (1978).

DAVID D. BUCK

**JI'NAN INCIDENT**, a military clash in early May 1928 between advancing units of the Chinese Northern Expedition and a Japanese Expeditionary Force especially dispatched by Prime Minister Tanaka Giichi to protect Japanese lives and property in Shandong against violence or confiscation. The National Revolutionary Army troops, under Chiang Kai-shek's orders, broke off the fighting, but the Japanese commander renewed the assault on the Ji'nan city garrison. Japanese troops occupied Qingdao, Ji'nan, and the interconnecting railway for a year, withdrawing only after the new Republic of China's government assumed the previous government's obligations to Japan; the Chinese agreed to pay for improvements made during the Japanese occupation of parts of Shandong from 1915 to 1923. The Ji'nan Incident marked the new belligerent attitude of the Tanaka cabinet toward Chinese nationalism, a shift from the policies associated with Foreign Minister Shidehara, who had joined the Western powers in a joint policy of accommodating moderate Chinese nationalist demands.

[*See also* Northern Expedition *and* Shandong Intervention.]

David D. Buck, *Urban Change in China: Politics and Development in Tsinan, Shantung, 1890–1949* (1978), pp. 157–164.    DAVID D. BUCK

**JIN DYNASTY** (265–420), last native dynasty to rule China prior to the conquest dynasties of foreign origin in the early medieval period. Traditional nomenclature blurs together under the Jin name two governments sharing almost nothing in common other than the bloodline of their imperial family. The Western Jin (265–317) was a traditional, autochthonous regime based in the North China Plain, with its capital at Luoyang for most of its history. The Eastern Jin (318–420), on the other hand, was set up by refugees from the North, who established the first Chinese empire to have its capital south of the Yangtze River, at Jiankang (modern Nanjing).

*Western Jin.* The history of the Western Jin is inextricably interwoven with that of its predecessor, the Wei state (220–265) of the Three Kingdoms. The ruling Cao family failed in its attempts to institutionalize and legitimize its power after its initial military success, and lost control of the government in 249 as the result of a coup led by one of its generals, Sima Yi. Yi's two eldest sons continued the family's military dictatorship within the framework of the Wei ruling house, deposing and murdering Cao "emperors" as necessary, until 265, when Yi's grandson, Sima Yan, formally usurped the throne as founding emperor of the Jin.

Although Yan's reign saw the conquest of the southeastern state of Wu and the concomitant reunification of China in 280, he was responsible for several decisions that proved to have terrible consequences. In the hope of strengthening the Sima family against the kind of coup his own ancestors had carried out against the Cao, he enfeoffed his relatives with actual territories within the state. (This act violated the pattern established by the Han dynasty of giving imperial princes only nominal title over areas actually administered by governors responsible to the emperor himself.) These princes were allowed to maintain personal armed detachments in the interests of a dispersed security apparatus. After the demobilization of the main imperial army following the victory over Wu in 280, however, the released soldiery swelled not only these autonomous corps but also both the ambitions and the fears of their princely masters.

Perhaps even more disastrous was Sima Yan's choice of an empress. Yang Yan presented him with a mentally incompetent heir (Sima Zhong, 259–306), and persuaded him to allow a marriage between the crown prince and Jia Nanfeng (257–300), the ruthless daughter of a powerful family. On her deathbed in 276, Yang Yan extracted from Sima Yan a promise that her first cousin Yang Jin would be made empress, thus setting up a contest for power between two in-law cliques that led to the so-called War of the Eight Princes (300–306).

The progressive destruction of the Yang, Jia, and Sima families as the war went on was of far less significance than the war's effect on the non-Chinese population of North China. For centuries a variety of Central Asian peoples had been filtering into the zone of sedentary agriculture, retaining their own leaders and their social cohesion. Some of this had been encouraged by Chinese emperors happy to have a buffer of horse-riding peoples between their taxpaying peasantry and the predators of the steppe, but with the deterioration of effective central rule in the first millennium of the common era, tribal groups moved more and more at will within the watershed of the Yellow River. Warring parties were quick to appeal to the greed of the leaders of these highly mobile and feared fighting formations. Inevitably, experience of the fragmented condition of the Jin elite led the non-Chinese commanders to the reasonable conclusion that there was no serious obstacle to their acting in their own political interest.

What had begun as a palace intrigue and then swelled into a civil war employing foreign auxiliaries now became an alien conquest of North China. Luoyang fell to non-Chinese forces in 311, and the substitute capital of Chang'an was taken in 316. It is important to note that this was not an invasion by external barbarians, but a breaking out by peoples of alien origins and institutions from a paradoxical status of intimate marginality within the Chinese system. The ensuing century of violent political reorganization, known in Chinese as the period of the "Five Barbarians and Sixteen Kingdoms," is evidence not of the vicious backwardness of the Turkic, Mongol, Tibetan, and other peoples who contested for power but of the inadequacy of traditional Chinese institutions to deal with the actual demography of East Asia in this era. Indeed, it is only under the auspices of these alien tribes and their political descendants that new institutions were forged that gave enough executive power to the imperial throne and its agents to bring about a genuine reintegration of imperial China. Ironically, when that day came, the foreigners on the dragon throne would look back to the Western Jin as a model of political legitimacy.

*Eastern Jin.* Although initially little more than a loose conglomeration of frontier manors weakly subordinated to a family of military adventurers, the southeastern Three Kingdoms state of Wu (222–280) demonstrated that ethnic Chinese were beginning to spread south of the Yangtze River in large numbers for the first time. Far from advancing in a vacuum, they exterminated, absorbed, or drove out the native inhabitants of this extraordinarily different ecosystem as they came, triggering secondary migrations of the Tai and Viet peoples that have not yet ended, as they continue to move into the lands of the prior occupants of Southeast Asia.

As conditions in North China deteriorated at the beginning of the fourth century, the Yangtze frontier began to look more and more attractive to powerful figures in the Western Jin. Military men with vaguely defined authority over the southeast began to dabble in the family politics of the Yangtze Delta, considering it a convenient bolt-hole should the Western Jin collapse entirely. In 307, with a similar plan in mind, the military dictator in Luoyang, Sima Yue, commissioned a minor prince, son of his second cousin, with the grandiose title "General Pacifying the East in Charge of All Military Affairs of Yangzhou [the delta], Granted a Baton [signifying independent authority], Garrisoning Jianye [Jiankang, modern Nanjing]." On 13 October 307 the prince, Sima Rui, rode into that city with a handful of attendants, Sima Yue being unwilling to spare any troops from the fighting in the North China Plain.

Over the next several years, Sima Rui worked out a mutually satisfactory accommodation with the local elite. They supplied and officered militia forces that kept the peace in his name. With the fall of

Luoyang in 311, however, Sima Rui was suddenly catapulted from being an insignificant princeling exiled to a backwater into the position of being the only member of the imperial family left in undisputed control of a territorial base. First a trickle and then a flood of refugees began to appear on the north bank of the Yangtze, hoping to find security in the unknown lands to the south. Almost overnight Sima Rui had the manpower resources both to seal his northern border against non-Chinese incursions and to reduce his southern backers to increasingly helpless bystanders as he put together a new regime. Following the receipt of news of the death of the Western Jin emperor, Sima Rui declared himself the first emperor of the Eastern Jin in April 318.

The next hundred years saw a complex balancing act. The flow of refugees from the North was the source of the dynasty's power, on the one hand, but also the greatest threat to its social stability on the other. One means of handling this problem was to establish the truly dangerous groups on the north bank of the Yangtze, with the job of fending off still more dangerous strangers. In order to avoid the difficulties facing an army of occupation, the government had to divide the southern elite as quickly as possible, isolating and crushing families that would not reconcile themselves to northern domination and co-opting the rest. Another challenge facing the Jiankang government was that of defining "China" in such a geographical context. Was China merely wherever the legitimate emperor happened to be, or was any location other than the North China Plain merely a temporary base from which to mount a campaign to recover the sole legitimate heartland? The northern refugees divided sharply between those who saw the South as a land of opportunity, and those who saw it as the land of exile, a division complicated by the fact that devoting oneself to the recovery of the North tended to be the quickest route to major military command and its accompanying influence.

Given the unending warfare with foreign-led states to the North, it is not surprising that power in the South slipped from the hands of refugee officials into those of refugee soldiers and ultimately into the grasp of native soldiery with no commitment to the traditions of the northern court. One of these generals, Liu Yu, having overawed the Jiankang regime with a series of military victories, attained dictatorial powers by the early 400s, and by declaring himself first emperor of the (Liu) Song dynasty in 420 brought an end to the Eastern Jin.

[See also Three Kingdoms and Southern and Northern Dynasties.]

Étienne Balazs, *Chinese Civilization and Bureaucracy* (1964).                    DENNIS GRAFFLIN

JINGDEZHEN, Chinese city in northeast Jiangxi Province on the southern bank of the Yangtze River; population, 270,000 (1980). Jingdezhen has a long history as the premier porcelain center of China.

Pottery had been made in the clay-rich environs of Jingdezhen as early as the Latter Han dynasty (25–220) and by the third century the town was designated as a supplier to the imperial court. It was only during the Tang dynasty (618–907), however, that porcelain production began on a large scale. Factors such as a sustained imperial patronage, an abundant supply of fine clays and wood for the kilns, and access to water transportation networks all contributed to Jingdezhen's development. Craftsmen in Jingdezhen experimented with a variety of designs, clays, and glazes, reaching an artistic peak in the fifteenth century with the development of the distinctive "blue and white" porcelain of the Ming dynasty (see figure 1).

FIGURE 1. *Flask*. Jingdezhen blue-and-white ware with a dragon and floral decoration. Porcelain with underglaze decoration in cobalt blue, fifteenth century. Height 47 cm., diameter 35.6 cm.

By the sixteenth century the porcelain industry in Jingdezhen greatly expanded as a result of the development of a national market structure. In addition, its wares were exported to Korea, Japan, and Inner Asia; by the eighteenth century Jingdezhen porcelain had even become an important part of European import trade.

Both Jingdezhen and the porcelain industry experienced a decline in the late nineteenth century as the supply of the fine porcelain clay was gradually exhausted. Since 1949 the economy of Jingdezhen has been revitalized by extensive modernization of the porcelain industry, access to new sources of raw materials, and an improved transportation system. As a result, the majority of Jingdezhen's population is now engaged in work related to the porcelain industry.                                    ANITA M. ANDREW

JINGGANG SHAN, mountain range spanning the border between Hunan and Jiangxi provinces in China. These mountains provided refuge for Mao Zedong and his remnant forces of fewer than one thousand men from September 1927, following the abortive Autumn Harvest Uprising, to early 1929, when Mao moved to western Fujian to establish a new base.

In 1928 Mao was joined by Zhu De, who was leading about one thousand men. Together they reorganized and expanded their forces, creating the Fourth Red Army with Zhu as commander and Mao as political representative. Mao's famous "three major disciplines" and "eight rules of conduct," formulated at this time, became the basis for the generally good relationship between the soldiers and the populace that characterized the Red Army henceforth. Although often at odds with Comintern policy and the central leadership of the Chinese Communist Party, the Mao-Zhu strategy of partisan warfare framed at Jinggang Shan became the prototype for successful rural revolution in China.

[See also Mao Zedong and Zhu De.]

Jacques Guillermaz, *A History of the Chinese Communist Party, 1921–1949* (1972). John Rue, *Mao Tsetung in Opposition, 1927–1935* (1966).

PETER J. SEYBOLT

JINMEN (Quemoy), island complex of fourteen islets spread over 69 square miles, situated in the mouth of the Xiamen (Amoy) Bay in southern China. It contains a civilian population of 50,411 (1983), who speak the Amoy dialect. Jinmen became a refugee base in the 1600s for the Ming loyalist Zheng Chenggong (Koxinga). Recently it has been developed for modern agriculture and industry. Although it is within 1.5 miles of territory controlled by the People's Republic of China (PRC), Jinmen is occupied by about 166,000 troops from the Republic of China (ROC), thereby blocking the Amoy harbor. It has threatened to be a flashpoint in the continuing dispute between the Nationalist and Communist regimes.

Within a month after gaining control of Beijing, the Communist armies launched an unsuccessful attack on Jinmen on 25 October 1949. At the beginning of the Korean War (27 June 1950) the US provided military protection to Taiwan against the Chinese Communists. In 1953 the US encouraged the ROC to strengthen the island defenses. The PRC responded with armed attacks, forcing Nationalist civilians and troops from the nearby Ta Chen islands. Through intensive aerial bombing and shelling it sought to interdict the resupplying of the island military bases. The most active military engagements occurred in the summer of 1958. After negotiations in Warsaw between the US and the PRC, China announced on 25 October 1958 that all bombing of Jinmen airfield, wharf, and beach landing areas would stop on even days of the month. The Nationalists could resupply the island on even days without fear of armed attack. On the odd days, the bombing was sometimes intense; on 17 June 1960, for example, 86,000 artillery shells were launched.

US commitment to the defense of Jinmen and Matsu became a campaign issue in the 1960 presidential election between Senator John F. Kennedy and Vice-President Richard Nixon. President Nixon's initiative in 1972 to improve relations with the PRC resulted in cessation of explosive shelling in favor of shells with propaganda leaflets. In recent years there has been an increase in informal contacts and clandestine trade between Taiwan and the Chinese mainland. Although the Nationalists and Communists are no longer openly engaged militarily over these islands, their future remains uncertain.

[See also Matsu.]

Melvin Gortov, "The Taiwan Strait Crisis Revisited: Politics and Foreign Policy in Chinese Motives," *Modern China* 2.1 (January 1976): 49–103. Morton H. Halperin and Tang Tsou, "The 1958 Quemoy Crisis," in *Sino-Soviet Relations and Arms Control*, edited by Morton H. Halperin (1967), pp. 265–303.    RICHARD C. KAGAN

JINNAH, FATIMA (1893–1967), youngest sister of Mohammed Ali Jinnah. After becoming a dentist in 1922, she opened a clinic in Bombay. She moved into her brother's house after the death of his wife and remained his constant companion until his death in 1948. Her main contribution to the Pakistan Movement was giving up her clinic in order to take charge of Jinnah's household, enabling him to devote his time to public life. After Jinnah's death, although she remained politically inactive, she always championed the cause of democracy, women's rights, refugees, and the underprivileged. In 1965 she ran in the presidential election against Ayub Khan as a candidate of the Combined Opposition Parties, but lost. The electors were made up of the electoral college of the Basic Democrats, who were highly amenable to official persuasion.

[See also Jinnah, Mohammed Ali and Pakistan.]

S. RAZI WASTI

JINNAH, MOHAMMAD ALI (1876–1948), the founder of Pakistan, popularly known as Qaid-i-Azam ("the great leader").

Born in Karachi in a Khoja mercantile family, Jinnah had his early education at Karachi and Bombay and then proceeded to Lahore. There he joined the Lincoln's Inn and in 1895 became the youngest Indian barrister to be called to the bar. He returned to Karachi in 1896 and a year later moved to Bombay, where he was able to build a flourishing practice, becoming in due course one of India's foremost lawyers.

Jinnah's first wife died while he was in England. In 1918 he married Ruttenbai, the daughter of Dinshaw Petit, a Bombay Parsi millionaire, despite her parents' tenacious opposition. After a period of estrangement Ruttenbai died in 1929. Jinnah's sister, Fatima, remained his close companion until his death. [See Jinnah, Fatima.]

During his student days in England, Jinnah had come under the spell of nineteenth-century British liberalism. He admired Gladstone and Morley and became associated with Dadabhai Naoroji, the first Indian member of the British Parliament. When he returned to India his faith in liberalism and evolutionary politics was confirmed through his close association with three Indian National Congress stalwarts—G. K. Gokhale, Pherozeshah Mehta, and Surendranath Banerjea. These chief formative influences in his early life, buttressed by his own experience as a lawyer in a predominantly non-Muslim but cosmopolitan metropolis convinced him of the primacy of initiative, enterprise, and hard work, and goaded him to start his political career in 1905 from the Congress platform. He was secretary to its president Naoroji in 1906, and he soon became prominent in national politics. [See Indian National Congress.]

In 1910 Jinnah was elected by Bombay Muslims to the Imperial Council, and his parliamentary career spanned some thirty-seven years. From 1912 onward he began wielding increasing influence in Muslim politics. At his insistence, the Muslim League (founded in 1906) adopted self-government as its ideal. He joined the league in 1913, becoming its president three years later. He brought the Indian National Congress and the Muslim League together and was chiefly responsible for the Congress-League Pact (1916), a joint scheme for postwar reforms, which conceded Muslims the right to separate electorates. For his untiring efforts to effect a communal settlement, the poet and political leader Sarojini Naidu hailed him as "the ambassador of Hindu-Muslim unity." Since he stood for civil liberties, he resigned from the council in 1919, when the Rowlatt Bill was passed into law; and since he stood for "ordered progress," moderation, gradualism, and constitutionalism, he left the Congress in 1920 when it opted for Mohandas Gandhi's direct action and noncooperation platform. Jinnah also resigned from the Home Rule League, whose Bombay branch he headed, when Gandhi, upon his election as president, unilaterally changed its constitution and nomenclature. Jinnah's ascendancy to national leadership thus received a serious setback, obliging him to withdraw from active politics for the next three years. [See also Gandhi, Mohandas Karamchand and Home Rule League.]

In 1924 Jinnah reorganized the Muslim League, of which he had been president since 1919, and devoted the next seven years attempting to bring about unity among the disparate ranks of Muslims and to develop a rational formula to effect a Hindu-Muslim settlement, which he considered the precondition for Indian freedom. He attended several unity conferences, wrote the Delhi Muslim Proposals (1927), pleaded for the incorporation of basic Muslim demands in the Nehru Report (1928), formulated the "Fourteen Points" (1929) as minimum Muslim demands for any constitutional settlement and as a riposte to the Nehru Report, and participated in the Round Table Conference (begun in 1930) in London, called by the British to formulate a new constitution for India.

Despairing alike of the "negative" Congress attitude and of chronic disunity in Muslim ranks, he went into self-exile in London (1931), but returned to India in 1934 at the fervent pleas of his followers. From 1936 onward, despite heavy odds, he breathed new life into the moribund Muslim League, gave it a coherent all-India policy and program, set up a machinery to fight elections in early 1937, and cooperated with the Congress against pro-British parties. The poor showing of the Muslim League in the 1937 elections led to the formation of one-party Congress governments and the exclusion of the Muslim League from power in the Hindu majority provinces. Jinnah responded to the developing Congress policy by reorganizing the league in October 1937 on a more popular basis, changing its creed to "full independence" and going to Muslim masses for grassroots support. He was thus able to exploit both Muslim passion for freedom and heightened disenchantment with the Congress in order to gain support for the league's platform, put pressure on the otherwise reluctant provincial leadership to fall in line, and consolidate his claim as the sole spokesman of Indian Muslims. He was rewarded by overwhelming league victories in by-elections from 1938 onward and the celebration, at his call, of a "deliverance day" by Muslims in December 1939, on the Congress's exit from power. His leadership of Muslims was also recognized by the British when they needed the league's support in the war effort.

In March 1940, at the league's session, Jinnah pronounced the 100 million Indian Muslims a nation in its own right, and on that basis demanded a separate independence for predominantly Muslim regions of northwestern and eastern India. Popularly known as Pakistan, this demand was first ridiculed and then vehemently opposed by the Congress. Nor were the British amenable to the idea of partitioning the subcontinent. But Jinnah organized his movement so adroitly that the Pakistan demand gathered momentum within a few years, became the central issue in all subsequent constitutional proposals, and was overwhelmingly voted for by Muslims in the 1945–1946 general elections. In the long, drawn-out controversy centering on certain provisions of the Cabinet Mission Plan (1946), Jinnah proved himself a strategist of a rare caliber and outmaneuvered the Congress, causing an insoluble deadlock that led directly to the plan of 3 June 1947, under which India was partitioned. Pakistan was established in August 1947.

Because of Jinnah's critical role in its emergence, Pakistan has been termed a "one-man achievement." For the same reason, the Muslim League

nominated him as governor-general, and the Pakistan Constituent Assembly elected him as president. Although aged and weak, he carried the heaviest burden in Pakistan and worked hard to secure its survival in rather treacherous circumstances. He died of overstrain, after a brief illness.

[See also Pakistan and All-India Muslim League.]

Jamil-ud-Din Ahmad, ed., Speeches and Writings of Mr. Jinnah, 2 vols. (1976). Sharif al Mujahid, Quaid-i-Azam Jinnah: Studies in Interpretation (1981). A. H. Dani, ed., World Scholars on Quaid-i-Azam Mohammad Ali Jinnah (1979). H. V. Hodson, "A Political Biography," Pakistan: Past and Present (1977). Sarojini Naidu, ed., Mohomed Ali Jinnah: An Ambassador of Unity (1918). Matlubul Hasan Saiyid, Muhammad Ali Jinnah: A Political Study (1945).                    SHARIF AL MUJAHID

**JINPINGMEI**, Ming-dynasty novel in one hundred chapters, author unknown, first published 1610 or 1611. Long known as a pornographic novel, Jinpingmei is also seen as pivotal in the development of the traditional Chinese novel. The plot is ramified, detailing the lives of Ximen Qing, his six wives (three of whom are named in the title), their household members, and numerous friends and other minor characters. The ending promises Buddhist redemption and reincarnation. In telling this story, Jinpingmei incorporates existing short stories of many kinds (crime, erotic, literary), histories, drama, Buddhist chantefables, and, especially, popular songs; the basic plot, its realism, and the characterizations, however, are the novel's own.

[See also Chinese Literature.]

Clement Egerton, The Golden Lotus (rev. ed., 1972). Patrick D. Hanan, "A Landmark of the Chinese Novel," in The Far East: China and Japan, edited by Douglas Grant and Maclure Millar (1961), pp. 325–335.

SHAN CHOU

**JINRIKISHA** ("man-powered vehicle"), known in the West as rickshaw, a two-wheeled carriage that first appeared in Japan in 1869. The product of three enterprising men, a grocer, an ex-samurai, and a wheelwright, early jinrikisha were little more than large, two-wheeled cargo wagons with a seat, four upright posts, and a canopy. The original designers received government permission in 1870 to operate jinrikisha, setting up shop in the busy market area of Nihonbashi in Tokyo. Meiji entrepreneur Akiba Daisuke modified the jinrikisha, using a newly imported Western carriage as his prototype. He reduced the size, added a boxlike seat and flooring, laquered the exterior, and even added springs. This became the standard for subsequent *jinrikisha* design. Even later, metal wheels, rubber tires, and a lighter frame were added to the design.

*Jinrikisha* were normally powered by one runner. When occasion warranted, however, two or even three runners were used simultaneously to increase speed. Rates of charge varied from city to city and according to the distance the rider wanted to cover. The increasing popularity of *jinrikisha* led to the rapid disappearance of the palanquin *(kago);* by 1871 there were reported to be nearly 25,000 *jinrikisha* in Tokyo alone. Beginning in 1873, *jinrikisha* were exported to Shanghai, Hong Kong, Singapore, India, and other countries. With the advent of streetcars and automobiles *jinrikisha* began to gradually disappear. Today, they are to be seen only as curiosities catering to the tourist industry.

J. SCOTT MILLER

**JINSHIN WAR,** Japanese conflict that takes its name from the *jinshin* year of the sixty-year calendrical cycle, which corresponds to 673. Following the death of Emperor Tenji in 671, a successional dispute arose between Tenji's son Prince Ōtomo and the prince's younger brother Ōamabito. Originally offered the throne by Tenji on his deathbed, Ōamabito had declined, taken the tonsure, and withdrawn to the detached palace at Yoshino, south of Asuka. After Tenji's death in the sixth month of 673, however, Ōamabito led an army to the barrier at Fuwa in Mino Province, thereby cutting off Ōtomo's forces from eastern Japan. A series of military engagements followed, leading to victory for Ōamabito on the twenty-second day of the seventh month. Ōtomo committed suicide. Ōamabito moved the capital from Ōmi, the site of Tenji's palace on the shores of the present Lake Biwa, back to its traditional location in Asuka. He took the throne as Emperor Temmu and reigned until his death in 687. The Jinshin War loomed large in the historical imagination of those of the latter half of the seventh century and was described by Kakinomoto no Hitomaro in his lament for Ōamabito's son Prince Takechi *(Man'yōshū* 2.199).

[*See also* Temmu *and* Man'yōshū.]

IAN HIDEO LEVY

**JINWEN,** or New Text, was the name of a school of Chinese philosophy that represented a religious trend in early Han Confucianism and a religio-political movement in the late nineteenth century. *Jin-wen,* literally "modern script," denoted the official or clerical script *(lishu)* used during the Former Han dynasty (206 BCE–8 CE). The term applied by extension to the officially recognized "modern script" version of the classics that had been transcribed from memory by scholars who survived the collapse of the Qin dynasty (221–207 BCE). The main ideas of the early Han New Text school were contained in the *Gongyang Commentary* to the *Spring and Autumn Annals,* an interpretation of Confucianism that centered on the person of Confucius as a kind of demiurge or uncrowned king who foresaw the end of the Zhou dynasty (1122?–256 BCE) and the beginning of a new era.

Another set of classics written in the "ancient" pre-Han seal script *(chuanshu)* was later found in a wall of the Kong (Confucius) family residence and began to attract the interest of more politically conservative scholars. The subsequent "discovery" of the *guwen,* or "ancient script," *Zuo Commentary* to the *Spring and Autumn* classic lent support to the "Old Text" advocates' portrayal of Confucius as both a teacher who yearned for the restoration of ancient feudal institutions and a judge of the moral character of historical figures. During the brief Xin dynasty (9–23), these Old Text classics were declared orthodox and the *Zuo Commentary* supplanted the New Text *Gongyang Commentary* as the officially sanctioned interpretation of the *Spring and Autumn Annals.* Although the New Text classics reemerged with the establishment of the Latter Han dynasty (25–220), the New Text classics and commentaries steadily lost appeal; after the fall of the dynasty they were neglected.

Over the course of succeeding centuries a few scholars, including the Song Neo-Confucian Zhu Xi (1130–1200), expressed doubts about passages in various Old Text classics. These versions, however, continued to be recognized as authentic and orthodox until Qing-dynasty (1644–1911) "evidential studies" *(kaozheng xue)* scholars systematically proved the Old Text version of the *Book of Documents* a forgery. The way was then opened for reexamination of other classics and the eventual emergence of a philologically tenable New Text position. By the third quarter of the eighteenth century, scholars in Changzhou (notably Zhuang Cunyu and Liu Fenglu) turned their attention to the *Zuo* and *Gongyang* commentaries on the *Spring and Autumn Annals.* Gradually, these scholars became aware of the alternate Old and New Text versions and of the differing political and philosophical premises that informed these Han-dynasty schools.

[*See also* Guwen *and* Kaozheng Xue.]

Chang Hao, *Liang Chi-chao and Intellectual Transition in China, 1890–1907* (1971). Benjamin Elman, *The Unravelling of Neo-Confucianism: The Lower Yangtze Academic Community* (1984). Liang Chi-chao (Liang Qichao), *Intellectual Trends in the Ch'ing Period*, translated by Immanuel Hsu (1959).    JUDITH A. WHITBECK

JITŌ. Generally translated as "military land stewards," the term *jitō* refers to the feudal land-management officials appointed by the Kamakura shogunate, the warrior government of Japan during the thirteenth and early fourteenth centuries. The *jitō* owed their origins to the fact that when Minamoto Yoritomo defeated the Taira in 1180–1185 he acquired but little land with which to reward his followers. The Taira had generally been managers of land, rather than its proprietors, and Yoritomo had no warrant to seize lands that his enemies had only managed. By 1187, however, he had reached an agreement with the imperial court allowing him to assign his followers to take over the posts of land-management officials who had fought for the Taira. His appointees were referred to as *jitō*, as were later shogunal supporters who were assigned to the posts confiscated from warriors who fought against the shogunate in the Shōkyū Incident (1221).

Typically, *jitō* replaced officials known as *geshi* (or *gesu*). The latter were bailiffs who were the ranking resident officials on the estates of absentee noble proprietors. (Where *jitō* were assigned to lands lying outside private estates, they replaced ranking local magistrates.) As successors to these bailiffs, the *jitō* were technically required to continue rendering whatever service to the land's proprietors the bailiffs had rendered before them. Often, however, they did not.

The *jitō* were able to escape rendering accustomed services because, unlike the bailiffs, they were not subject to proprietary discipline. A bailiff who misbehaved could be dismissed by the proprietor he served, but a *jitō* could be dismissed only by the shogun. And while the Kamakura shogunate was generally disposed to uphold the proprietary interests of the old civil and ecclesiastical nobility, it was seldom willing to dismiss even the most intransigent *jitō*. As a result, *jitō* were gradually able to usurp control of much of the land they managed, and by the beginning of the Muromachi period they were well on their way to becoming the proprietary lords of land, rather than mere officials. The process by which they achieved this is among the most important issues in Japan's medieval history.

[*See also* Kamakura Period.]

Jeffrey P. Mass, *Warrior Government in Early Medieval Japan* (1974).    PETER J. ARNESEN

JIUJIANG, Chinese city on the banks of the Yangtze River north of the Lushan mountains in Jiangxi Province. Founded in the Han dynasty, Jiujiang was linked by road with the imperial porcelain works at Jingdezhen during the Ming and Qing periods and served as a river port for the shipment of porcelain, tea, rice, tobacco, cotton, and ramie.

During the Taiping Rebellion (1851–1864) the rebels held Jiujiang for four years before it was recaptured. Zeng Guofan's fleet suffered a major naval defeat at the hands of the Taiping rebels at Jiujiang in 1855. Under the Conventions of Beijing following the Second Opium War, Jiujiang was one of eleven additional treaty ports opened to foreigners. Chiang Kai-shek had his summer residence south of the city, an area famous as a resort.

Yu-wen Jen, *The Taiping Revolutionary Movement* (1973).    SALLY HART

JIYŪ MINKEN (Freedom and People's Rights Movement, or Popular Rights Movement), a nationwide political movement of Meiji-era Japan. The movement's three central objectives—establishing a parliament, reducing land taxes, and accomplishing treaty revision—were all directed against the oligarchy of the Satsuma and Chōshū cliques. The movement began in 1874 when Itagaki Taisuke, Gotō Shōjirō, Etō Shimpei, Soejima Taneomi, and other governmental leaders, angry because the government had repudiated an agreement to "punish Korea," petitioned the emperor for the establishment of a popularly elected parliament. Organization began with Itagaki's Risshisha, a Tosa-based political society, that same year.

In the initial stage, the movement was led by *shizoku* (former samurai) with an elitist mentality and orientation. Before long, however, more local political and learning societies joined forces, primarily over the issue of land taxes. The Aikokusha (Patriotic Society), which had been formed in 1875 with the Risshisha at its core, evolved by 1879 into a more popularly representative organization. The movement demanding the opening of a parliament reached its peak in 1880 and 1881, when the Jiyūtō (Liberal Party) was formed. It is considered to have ended when a struggle against a treaty revision plan proposed by Foreign Minister Inoue Kaoru was ruthlessly suppressed by the Peace Preservation Law of 1887. Its more conclusive end came a year later when the coalition movement of former liberals and progressives (Kaishintō) was broken with Ōkuma Shigenobu's betrayal of its members by joining the cabinet; Gotō Shōjirō did the same in 1889.

It is sometimes said that the Meiji constitution was promulgated in 1889 on the debris of the Jiyū Minken. The movement is considered to be the first of three separate periods of democratic development in modern Japanese history. The second is known as the Taishō democracy, in which the General Manhood Suffrage Law was enacted in 1925 and party cabinets became the rule. The third period is the development inaugurated during the Allied Occupation of Japan after 1945. The Popular Rights Movement, however, had its own limitations. The immediate origins of the movement were found among those who advocated that Japan conquer Korea; they resigned from the Council of State (Dajōkan) when their proposal was rejected. Among them were Itagaki Taisuke and Gotō Shōjirō of Tosa, Etō Shimpei of Saga, and Saigō Takamori of Satsuma. Etō and Saigō led revolts of discontented former samurai against the central government in their own provinces in 1874 and 1877, respectively [See Saga Rebellion.] After Etō and Saigō died, their views were inherited by rightists such as Tōyama Mitsuru of Fukuoka, who in 1881 reorganized his local popular rights society into the Genyōsha (Black Sea Society), predecessor of the Kokuryūsha (Amur, or Black Dragon, Society). He and his organization, although pan-Asianist, would act more like states-rights supporters (kokken shugisha).

As a movement dominated by former samurai, the Jiyū Minken was markedly elitist, at least at the outset. The founders of the Risshisha recognized that there were farmers and merchants with more means than former samurai but considered them so much poorer in intelligence and self-discipline as to be incapable of exercising political leadership. This sort of assessment of the political qualifications of commoners was shared by those in the government. They believed that the Popular Rights Movement was not a truly enlightened national development but agitation among ignorant masses on the part of discontented former samurai and retired officers of the government. There were more perceptive statesmen like Kido Takayoshi, however, who, impressed by what primary education had given the local children of the northeastern region, reflected critically upon bureaucratic despotism. He came to believe that a greater Japan could be built through a balanced development between cities and countryside, in order to increase the common people's potential force. Recent discoveries of constitutional drafts prepared by discussion groups composed of literate commoners show that both government and liberal movement leaders' estimates of popular capabilities were too low.

Another shortcoming of the movement was its limited concern for the freedom and rights of lesser elements in society, such as the new commoner class, the Okinawans, the Ainu, and others. Some of the leading ideologues of the movement, however, notably Ueki Emori and Nakae Chōmin, spoke of the Ainu's position from a universalistic humanitarian point of view. While not within the movement, Tanaka Shōzō of Tochigi Prefecture, a concerned local leader, also defended the Okinawans from a localist and environmentalist point of view. There was also a Popular Rights activist, Iizuka Morizō, who after the collapse of the Chichibu peasant uprising of 1884 went deep into the Ainu country in Hokkaido.

[See also Risshisha; Kokuryūkai; Itagaki Taisuke; Etō Shimpei; Saigō Takamori; Tōyama Mitsuru; Ueki Emori; and Nakae Chōmin.]

Roger W. Bowen, *Rebellion and Democracy in Meiji Japan* (1980). Nobutaka Ike, *The Beginnings of Political Democracy in Japan* (1950). Irokawa Daikichi, *The Culture of Meiji Japan* (1985).        KIMITADA MIWA

**JIZYA,** capitation tax paid by *dhimmis,* or "people of the book," according to Islamic law. "People of the book" were peoples who Muslims believed had received God's word from "messengers" before the prophet Muhammad but who had imperfectly preserved it. This warranted their protection (*dhimma*) within a Muslim state and payment of the *jizya* in compensation. Legists agree that Christians and Jews are *dhimmis* but disagree on other religious communities.

The intermittent enforcement of *jizya* with regard to Hindus, Buddhists, and Zoroastrians marked the legitimate, if subordinate, presence of these groups in Muslim realms in Iran, India, and Central Asia. It also provided a form of patronage on the part of sultans for the *ulama,* Muslim religious authorities.

[See also Dhimmi.]

RICHARD W. BULLIET

**JODHPUR,** city in Rajasthan, India, founded 12 May 1459 by Rao Jodha, a Rathor Rajput, who had a magnificent fort built on the hill overlooking the present city. It remained merely a large village until the reign of Jodha's decendant, Rao Malde (r. 1532–

FIGURE 1. *Jodhpur Fort.*

1562), whose expansionist policies required the employment of many soldiers and administrators. Rao Malde also greatly embellished the defenses of the fortress, which became one of the strongest in North India. During the Mughal period Jodhpur was the capital of the Rathor rajas who served the Mughal emperors. Its population increased significantly in these years, and many buildings were constructed by local Rajputs newly wealthy from participation in Mughal service. In the British period Jodhpur was the capital of the princely state of Jodhpur, also called Marwar.

[*See also* Rajput; Rajasthan; Princely States; *and* Marwar.]

RICHARD DAVIS SARAN

JOGJAKARTA. *See* Yogyakarta.

JOHNSTON, SIR ALEXANDER (1775–1849), puisne justice (1805–1810) and chief justice (1810–1820) of Sri Lanka. Ardent champion of the judiciary, Johnston was a key figure in the conflict that dominated the early history of British rule in Sri Lanka, competition for power and status between the executive and the judiciary. Although his main impetus was personal ambition for power, Johnston was genuinely interested in the rights of the colonial peoples and was responsible for the introduction of the jury system in 1811. Closely involved in Indian affairs in England, Johnston became a familiar witness before the parliamentary hearings on the charter of the East India Company.

[*See also* East India Company.]

*Dictionary of National Biography* 30 (1892): 52–53.

VIJAYA SAMARAWEERA

JOHOR, southernmost state of the Federation of Malaysia, bounded on its west coast by the state of Melaka (Malacca) and on the east by Pahang. Its maritime boundaries are the Strait of Melaka, the Strait of Johor (formerly Tebrau), which separates it from Singapore, and the South China Sea. The name is derived from the Johor River, a large estuary that forms the eastern end of the Johor Strait.

When Melaka fell to the Portuguese in 1512, Sultan Mahmud I fled to Johor and eventually established a capital at Bentan in the Riau Archipelago, an area that until the nineteenth century was generally considered a part of Johor. The Johor kingdom inherited the Melakan dynasty and some of its territories, particularly those to the south in the archipelago and in Sumatra. The territories to the north, particularly Perak, Kedah, and Trengganu, never really came within the orbit of Johor as they had within Melaka's. These states either remained independent or came under Siamese or Acehnese influence. The Johor kingdom, however, attained a measure of prosperity as an entrepôt and, after weathering the challenges of the sixteenth century, found an ally in the Dutch. In 1641 the Johor Malays aided the Dutch in ousting the Portuguese from Melaka.

Traditional Johor was an entrepôt state patterned after Melaka and Srivijaya. It was based on the loyalty of the Orang Laut (sea peoples), control of shipping in the straits, and the maintenence of a capital. The site of the capital was shifted numerous times between 1512 and 1700, generally because of attacks or the installation of a new ruler. Most often the capital was located at a site on the Johor River (e.g., Batu Sawar, Kota Tinggi, and Johor Lama) or else it was in the Riau Archipelago, usually at Bentan.

In 1699 Sultan Mahmud II, the last surviving heir of the Melakan dynasty, was assassinated, and Bendahara Abdul Jalil assumed the throne, beginning a new dynasty. As Leonard Andaya has shown, this act led to a long and costly civil war and the eventual rise to power of Bugis mercenaries, some of whom gained hereditary control over the office of Yang Di Pertuan Muda and effectively dominated the state into the nineteenth century. Under Bugis control Johor/Riau enjoyed considerable prosperity until 1784, when it was destroyed by the Dutch. In 1819 Temenggong Abdul Rahman, a dissaffected Malay chief who had taken territorial control of the southern part of the Malay Peninsula (Johor), signed a treaty with Thomas Stamford Raffles giving the British East India Company control of the island of

TABLE 1. *Sultans of Johor, 1511–1984*

| Sultan | Reign Dates |
|---|---|
| Mahmud Syah I | 1511–1528 |
| Alauddin Riayat Syah II | 1528–1564 |
| Muzaffar Syah | 1564–1570 |
| Abdul Jalil Syah | 1570–1571 |
| Ali Jalla Abdul Jalil Syah II | 1570/71–1597 |
| Alauddin Riayat Syah III | 1597–1615 |
| Abdullah Ma'ayat Syah | 1615–1623 |
| Abdul Jalil Syah III | 1623–1677 |
| Ibrahim Syah | 1677–1685 |
| Mahmud Syah II | 1685–1699 |
| Abdul Jalil Riayat Syah IV | 1699–1718 |
| Abdul Jalil Rahmat Syah | 1718–1722 |
| Sulaiman Badrul Alam Syah | 1722–1760 |
| Abdul Jalil Muazzam Syah | 1760–1761 |
| Ahmad Riayat Syah | 1761 |
| Mahmud Syah III | 1761–1812 |
| Abdul Rahman Muazzam Syah | 1812–1819[1] |
| Hussein Syah | 1835[2] |
| Ali; Temenggong Tun Ibrahim | 1835–1862 |
| Abu Bakar | 1862–1895[3] |
| Ibrahim | 1895–1959 |
| Ismail | 1960–1981 |
| Iskandar | 1981– |

1. Sultan of Lingga to 1830. 2. Sultan of Johor and Singapore.
3. Temmenggong Seri Maharaja, 1862–1868; maharaja, 1868–1885; sultan, 1885–1895.

Source: Haji Buyong Adil, *Sejarah Johor* (1971).

Singapore. Raffles also recognized Tengku Long as Sultan Hussein of Johor. In 1824 the Anglo-Dutch Treaty effectively split the old Johor empire along the line currently separating Malaysia and Singapore from Indonesia.

The modern state of Johor was founded by Temenggong Ibrahim (c. 1835–1862), who after 1844 began to encourage Chinese pepper and gambier planters from Singapore to settle in Johor. During the nineteenth century the Temenggongs maintained cordial relations with the British government of the Straits Settlements and with the Chinese merchants of Singapore. By the 1880s they had succeeded in establishing an effective government over the territory currently known as Johor. In 1885 Abu Bakar was recognized as sultan of the State and Territory of Johor. In 1910 Sultan Ibrahim agreed to accept a British general adviser, and the state became a part of British Malaya as an unfederated state. Johor became independent within the Federation of Malaya in 1957 and joined Malaysia in 1963. The cap-

ital of the state is Johor Bahru, which is situated in the Johor Strait and is linked to Singapore by a causeway.

[*See also* Malaysia; Melaka; Riau; Srivijaya; Orang Laut; Mahmud Syah II; Abdul Jalil Riayat Syah; Bugis, Abdul Rahman; Raffles, Sir Thomas Stamford; East India Company; Hussein, Sultan of Johor and Singapore; Anglo-Dutch Treaty; Ibrahim; Gambier; Temenggong; *and* Abu Bakar.]

Leonard Y. Andaya, *The Kingdom of Johor 1641–1728* (1975). Carl A. Trocki, *Prince of Pirates: The Temenggongs and the Development of Johor and Singapore 1784–1885* (1979). R. O. Winstedt, "A History of Johore, 1365–1895," *Journal of the Malayan Branch of the Royal Asiatic Society* 10.3 (December 1932): 1–167.

CARL A. TROCKI

JOLO, capital of the Sulu Archipelago in the southwestern Philippines, extending for two hundred miles from the Zamboanga Peninsula to northeast Borneo.

In the late eighteenth century, the Sulu sultanate, as the center of a maritime trading zone bounded by Mindanao, Sulawesi, Borneo, and Palawan, was referred to as *el reyno de Jolo*. The Taosug ("people of the current"), the dominant ethnic group in the Sulu Archipelago, are the sole residents of Jolo Island, the historical seat of the Sulu sultanate. Traditionally, the Tau Gimba ("people of the interior") lived in small dispersed settlements and cultivated upland rice, tropical fruits, and vegetables. The Tau Higad ("people of the coast"), who were far more dependent on the sea and marketplace for a livelihood, took a direct interest in pearl and shell fisheries, interinsular trade, and slave raiding. In the first half of the nineteenth century, Jolo, as the capital of the Sulu sultanate, became the focal point of a broad system of trade and the center for marketing of slaves, outfitting of seafaring marauders, and defiance of Spanish incursion. An inexorable process of fragmentation of Taosug trade through a combination of colonial warfare, capitalist development, and Asian enterprise (Chinese and Arab) led to Jolo's decline as a regional entrepôt by the end of the nineteenth century.

Thomas M. Kiefer, *The Tausug Violence and Law in a Philippine Moslem Society* (1972). James Francis Warren, *The Sulu Zone 1768–1898: The Dynamics of External Trade, Slavery and Ethnicity in the Transformation of a Southeast Asian Maritime State* (1981).

JAMES FRANCIS WARREN

JŌMON is the name given to Japan's Neolithic era (10,000–200 BCE). The term literally means "rope pattern" and describes the elaborate, swirling designs that characterize much of the pottery of the age. The Jōmon period also witnessed the development of stone-polishing techniques. Unlike Neolithic man in China and other major cultural centers, however, the inhabitants of Japan subsisted primarily by hunting, fishing, and gathering, not by settled agriculture.

About twenty thousand years ago, the world's fourth (and most recent) Ice Age ended. As the climate warmed, the polar ice caps melted and sea level rose. The land bridge that had provided a walkway for giant woolly mammoths, humans, and other Old Stone Age residents of the Japanese archipelago was submerged for the final time. By the Jōmon period, world temperatures had climbed above current averages, and the sea covered much of what is coastal plain today. Of course, the newly created islands were not completely isolated, as is evidenced by similarities between Jōmon civilization and that of contemporaneous southern Korea.

Archaeologists have estimated the population of the archipelago in the Jōmon era at between 125,000 and 250,000. Population reached its peak by about 5000 BCE and then began to decline. Life expectancy was approximately fifteen years, with death rates highest among the newborn and those over forty. Skeletal remains suggest that Jōmon people were tall, averaging five feet six inches.

The typical Jōmon village was small. Archaeologists usually find between six and ten dwellings per village; each dwelling is large enough to accommodate between four and eight persons. The standard dwelling was a pit with an oven in the center and a makeshift grass roof. While early Jōmon villages were mere camps constructed between hunting expeditions, later settlements give an impression of greater permanence.

Archaeologists have been blessed with a rich inventory of relics from Japan's Neolithic era. Communities usually disposed of shells and bones by piling them up in large heaps that resisted decomposition in Japan's acidic soils. The shell mounds (kaizuka) may be up to two hundred meters in diameter, and are a treasure trove of human and animal remains, tools, weapons, pottery shards, and jewelry. About two thousand shell mounds have been found.

The shell mounds tell scholars a great deal about diet. Over 90 percent of the animal bones uncovered are deer and wild boar. Jōmon people also enjoyed

FIGURE 1. *Jōmon Figure.* Latest Jōmon period (1000–250 BCE), Kamegaoka-type figure. Gray earthenware statuette with some black reduced areas and traces of red pigment on the headdress. Height 25 cm.

seafood such as tuna, mackerel, and oysters and other mollusks. Residents of eastern Japan fished for salmon. Hunting and fishing equipment was made mostly of polished stone and bone. Fishing gear included hooks, harpoons, gigs, and nets. Rafts and log canoes must have served as fishing vessels. Hunters relied on stone and bone clubs, spears, and the bow and arrow. Obsidian was a prized material for arrowheads. In the early Neolithic period individual hunters prowled for game, but soon bands were formed. The dog, the only domesticated animal known to Jōmon Japanese, aided in the chase.

The simple, unglazed pottery that lends its name to the era was hand-built and fired at a relatively low temperature. A revolutionary improvement was made when potters learned how to make flatbottomed containers that stood upright. This advance encouraged the use of the pots for storage as well as cooking. In the middle Jōmon age, in central and eastern Japan, the classic "rope pattern" pots made their appearance. The bold designs suggest verve and an emotional approach to life, in contrast to the

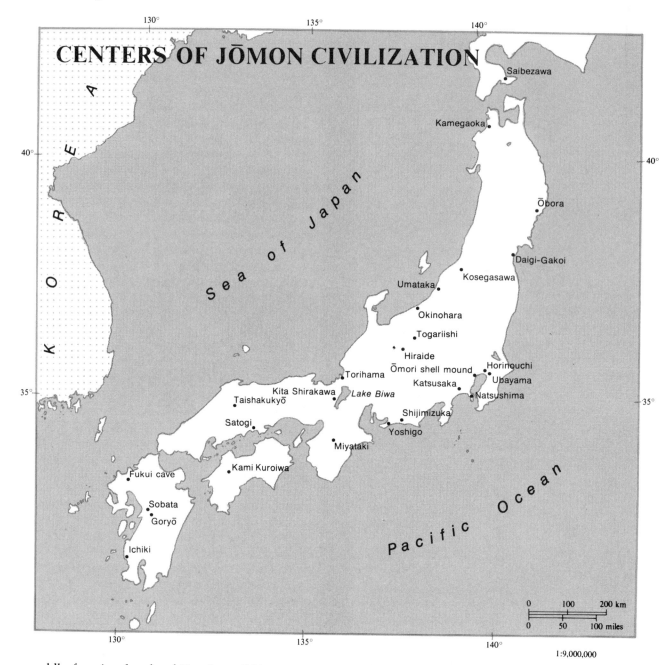

**CENTERS OF JŌMON CIVILIZATION**

Saibezawa

Kamegaoka

Ōbora

Daigi-Gakoi

Sea of Japan

Kosegasawa

Umataka

Okinohara

Togariishi

Hiraide

Ōmori shell mound    Horinouchi

Torihama    Katsusaka    Ubayama

Kita Shirakawa    Lake Biwa    Natsushima

Taishakukyō    Shijimizuka

Satogi    Yoshigo

Miyataki

Kami Kuroiwa

Fukui cave

Sobata    Pacific Ocean

Goryō

Ichiki

K O R E A

0    100    200 km

0    50    100 miles

1:9,000,000

coldly functional style of Yayoi-era (200 BCE–300 CE) pottery.

Neolithic Japanese had a lively social life. Bone and stone earrings, beads, combs, hairpieces, and armbands decorated the bodies of Jōmon persons. Skulls unearthed in shell mounds are often missing a few front teeth. Since most examples are young adults, many archaeologists believe mutilation was part of a rite of passage. Several burial plots have been excavated. Skeletons are usually found with legs and arms flexed; after the early Jōmon era, bodies were sometimes buried in large jars.

The best-known expression of Jōmon spiritual life is the clay figurine of the human form *(dogū)*. Figurines are usually missing a limb, an indication of their use in acts of sympathetic magic. When a person broke an arm or leg, a figurine was made and the injured extremity was snapped off in an attempt to heal the patient.

As the end of the Jōmon age approached, magico-religious practices increased. The expanded use of magic suggests that Jōmon culture may have reached a natural limit. In western Japan, attempts were made to deal with a subsistence crisis by adopting settled agriculture. In the Kantō and northern Japan, however, Jōmon culture continued on through the first stage of the Yayoi age. Hokkaido was a stronghold of Jōmon ways into the Meiji period.

[*See also* Yayoi.]

John Whitney Hall, *Japan: From Prehistory to Modern Times* (1970). J. E. Kidder, *Japan before Buddhism* (1959).    WAYNE FARRIS

**JONES, SIR WILLIAM** (1746–1794), orientalist, founder of the Asiatic Society of Bengal. Unlike most of his contemporaries, Jones went to India with an established reputation as an oriental scholar. He knew Arabic and Persian, had published a grammar of Persian and treatises on Oriental literature, and challenged the French orientalist A. H. Anquetil-Duperron. When he came to India, where he was a judge of the Supreme Court, his linguistic pursuits turned to Sanskrit. His translation of Kalidasa's *Shakuntala*, at first viewed with suspicion in an age of literary hoaxes, demonstrated the importance of Indian literature. His translation of the *Manava Dharmashastra (Laws of Manu)* established the primacy of this text, which to this day overshadows other Hindu lawbooks. Jones also pursued his studies of Arabic lawbooks, begun in England, and commissioned digests of Hindu and Muslim laws for the administration of civil justice in India. He did not live to complete the translation of either digest. Current scholarly opinion no longer credits Jones with the founding of historical Indo-European linguistics, yet his speculations on the origin of languages and civilizations fueled interest in comparative studies. With the Asiatic Society, which he founded in 1784, Jones provided an institutional base for the diffusion of oriental studies, his life-long aim.

[*See also* Anquetil-Duperron, A. H.; Kalidasa; *and* Asiatic Society of Bengal.]

Garland Cannon, *Sir William Jones: A Bibliography of Primary and Secondary Sources* (1979). Garland Cannon, ed., *The Letters of Sir William Jones* (1970). William Jones, *The Works of Sir William Jones* (1799).

ROSANE ROCHER

**JONES ACT,** statute announcing the intention of the US government to "withdraw [its] sovereignty over the Philippine Islands as soon as a stable government can be established therein." It went into effect on 29 August 1916 and functioned as a de facto constitution for the Philippines until 1934.

The Jones Act had been proposed by Representative William Atkinson Jones during the presidency of William Howard Taft. From 1901 legislative power in the Philippines was exercised through a Philippine Commission, which comprised both executive and legislative (upper house) branches of government. Until October 1913 the American commissioners constituted the majority. The Jones Act replaced the commission with an elective senate. It extended the franchise to all literate males who met minimum property requirements. It also incorporated a bill of rights.

American lawmakers saw the act as a conservative step whereby Filipinos, under the tutelage of an American governor-general, would learn the elements of self-rule. Filipino legislators, however, wanted to prepare themselves for self-government in the shortest time possible, and by 1918 they had passed measures to achieve that effect. Francis Burton Harrison, the governor-general at the time, was sympathetic to the Filipino viewpoint, and between 1918 and 1921 Filipinos were able to develop a semiparliamentary form of government. In late 1921, however, Leonard Wood became the chief executive of the islands. Wood interpreted the act in a more conservative manner, and his approach was seen as a backward step by Filipinos. Although Wood's actions received the support of Washington and the supreme courts of both the United States and the Philippines, the hostility they generated made everyone realize that the Jones Act had to be modified. It was superseded by the Tydings-McDuffie Act, which established the Philippine Commonwealth (1936).

[*See also* Philippines; Taft, William Howard; Philippine Commissions; Harrison, Francis Burton; Wood, Leonard; Tydings-McDuffie Act; *and* Philippines, Commonwealth of.]

Francis Burton Harrison, *The Corner-stone of Philippine Independence* (1922). Maximo M. Kalaw, *The Case for the Filipinos* (1916). Michael Paul Onorato, *A Brief Review of American Interest in Philippine Development and other Essays* (1972). Peter W. Stanley, *A Nation in the Making* (1974).    MICHAEL PAUL ONORATO

# JOURNALISM

## JOURNALISM IN CHINA

The roots of Chinese journalism lie in the publication of an official gazette that summarized edicts and official acts of the emperor in the capital on a daily basis during the Ming (1368–1644) and Qing (1644–1911) dynasties. Popular journalism resembling that in the West began with the treaty port press of the nineteenth century. Missionary-run newspapers, like those of John Fryer and Y. J. Allen, carried much material in translation and were important early influences. The reform-minded translator and editor Wang Tao was one of the earliest and most important pioneer figures in Chinese journalism. By the beginning of the twentieth century the treaty port press, with counterparts overseas run by students, was taken to represent "public opinion" and thereby recognized as a force in Chinese politics. At the same time in the interior, highly nationalistic journals like the *Subao* in Hunan became targets of government repression and a cause célèbre.

The new foreign-protected press in the treaty ports and overseas was the vehicle by which Republican revolutionaries like Sun Yat-sen and constitutional monarchical reformers like Liang Qichao and Kang Youwei attacked the Qing dynasty and vied for support amid a highly volatile political climate. After the fall of the dynasty (1911–1912), the new government of President Yuan Shikai recognized the power of the press by trying to control it as much as possible. Government censorship therefore has been a crucial factor in the development of the Chinese press in the twentieth century. During the chaos of the warlord period from 1916 to 1926 the Chinese press thrived as the diversity and outspokenness of the treaty port press spread to the interior. Major journals like Chen Duxiu's magazine *New Youth (Xin qingnian)* had an incendiary influence on the May Fourth Movement of 1919, for example. [*See also* Chen Duxiu *and* May Fourth Movement.]

Two key figures in the development of the press in the 1920s and 1930s were Shao Piaoping and Zou Taofen. Shao was a fearless editor working mostly in Beijing. After 1916 he was arrested four times and finally assassinated in 1926, but not before establishing China's first journalism school and news agency. Editor and publisher Zou Taofen emerged in Shanghai in the early 1930s as the most popular journalist of the period. Indeed, in retrospect the high point of an independent, outspoken Chinese press probably came with Zou and his colleagues in the mid-1930s. Their sense of outrage and their creativity were heightened by the brutally crude efforts of Dai Li's secret police.

Behind the Japanese lines in the rural "liberated" areas during the war years of 1937 to 1945, a new guerrilla press was developing as well as the beginnings, in Yan'an, of what became the Xinhua News Agency, the official press of the People's Republic of China. The Chinese press of today represents a merger of the more tightly controlled Communist Party press in guerrilla areas with the older, more freewheeling dailies like the *Wenhui bao* and *Dagong bao* in Shanghai and Tianjin respectively. Until recently, Party controls and the guerrilla tradition had dominated the latter. Since 1979, however, a reversal of sorts seems to be taking place. Despite the "democracy wall" suppressions of 1979, the press seems to be finding in a modest way its own independent and critical voice vis-à-vis affairs of state. [*See also* Democracy Wall.] Investigative reportage *(baogao wenxue)* in the hands of masters like Liu Binyan has been especially popular. Liu Binyan himself, however, was ultimately perceived as a threat to the stability of the state, and in the crackdown that followed the wave of student demonstrations in December 1986, Liu's Party membership was revoked. Moreover, journalism schools are enjoying a renaissance, partly because of the exponential explosion in the number of publications now rolling off Chinese presses and the need for staff.

The future of Chinese journalism should be interesting, although in all likelihood certain continuities will remain. A major theme will continue to be the close connection between journalism and politics. In Hong Kong and Taiwan as well as the People's Republic, the accomplished journalist is expected to be both a politician and a writer. The pretense of "objectivity" or the attempt to screen politics out of news reporting is unlikely ever to become a major concern of Chinese journalism as it is in the West.                STEPHEN R. MACKINNON

## JOURNALISM IN INDIA

Indian journalism had its beginning on 29 January 1780 with the appearance of the first edition of *The Bengal Gazette or the Calcutta General Advertiser,* edited by William Hickey. The *Gazette* was banned by the officials of the East India Company for libel, but in subsequent years other journals appeared in Calcutta, Madras, and Bombay. These were in English and were mainly gossip meant for the local European community, with some news reprinted from the London newspapers. Censorship by the government was an issue from the beginning, with the editors claiming the same privileges for freedom of the press that existed in England. The argument against this was that conditions in India were so different that a free press would lead to seditious attacks on the government and threaten the continuation of British rule in India.

A famous clash between an editor and the government came in 1823, when the governor-general deported James Silk Buckingham for publishing what was regarded as a seditious libel in his paper, the *Calcutta Journal.* Silk's credo that an editor's duty was to admonish the rulers, "to warn them furiously of their faults and to tell disagreeable truths," has, in general, been characteristic of journalism in India. This attitude became even more difficult for the government with the growth of journalism in Indian languages. The first of such journals was *Dig Darshan,* published in Bengali in 1818 by the Baptist missionaries at Serampore, but in 1821 Rammohan Roy, the great social reformer, started a Bengali paper, *Sambad Kaumudi.* [*See* Roy, Rammohan.] Others appeared in Persian, Hindi, Gujarati, and Tamil during the next twenty years. Many of these papers were short-lived, and most had circulations of less than one thousand, but they reached a wide audience as they were often read aloud to nonliterate listeners.

Despite autocratic foreign rule India enjoyed a remarkable degree of press freedom, owing largely to the initiatives taken by the governors-general in the period from 1825 to 1857. [*See* Governor-General of India.] It was difficult in both theory and practice to deny freedom of speech to English editors of English journals, and Indian editors soon claimed the same rights. The landmark victory for the press was an act passed in 1835, when Sir Charles Metcalfe was governor-general, that repealed most of the existing restrictions on the press. The uprisings in North India in 1857 that challenged British rule in India led, however, to new attempts to control the press, especially the newspapers in Indian languages. What was known as the "Gagging Act" was passed in 1857 to prevent the publication of news sympathetic to the rebels and critical of the government, but it lapsed after peace was restored. Fear of the press remained, however, and in 1878 the government passed the Vernacular Press Act to censor publications in Indian languages. The act was aimed not only at preventing seditious criticism of the government but also at the publication of material that might excite ill feeling between different religious communities. Since the act applied only to publications in Indian languages, Indians claimed that it was based on racial discrimination. The protests were so widespread that it was repealed by Governor-General Ripon in 1881, but the reaction to the act was an important element in the growth of nationalist feeling.

The press, in both English and Indian languages, played a crucial role in the nationalist movement.

On the one hand there were the great English-language newspapers, such as *The Times of India* and *The Statesmen,* which generally supported the government and criticized the activities of the Indian National Congress, but gave coverage to them, while on the other hand there was a very flourishing nationalist press in both English and Indian languages. One of the most famous of these was the *Kesari,* published in Marathi by Bal Gangadhar Tilak, which spread Tilak's fiery nationalist sentiments to a wide audience. [*See* Tilak, Bal Gangadhar.] The fact that the press was free to propagate nationalist ideas and to criticize the government is a crucial factor in explaining the nature of the development of Indian nationalism. Mohandas Gandhi, for example, made use of the press, editing and writing a great deal of the material in such papers as *Young India* in English and *Navajivan* in Gujarati. Other groups, including the Muslim League, spread knowledge of their views through newspapers so that there was a great deal of publicity given to competing points of view.

Journalism in both Indian languages and English continues to flourish in independent India. It is difficult to acquire exact figures, as many newspapers and journals cease publishing and others are started every year, but there were in 1985 about 1,200 daily newspapers and 5,500 weeklies. They are published in at least 16 languages, with the largest numbers in Hindi, for a total of about 3,000. About 500 each are published in English, Marathi, and Bengali, and nearly 700 in Urdu. These figures are somewhat misleading, however, for some of the papers have very small circulations. Hindi journals have the largest total circulations, with about 8 million, followed by English, with about 5 million. The newspaper with the largest circulation is, however, the Bengali daily *Ananda Bazar Patrika,* with a circulation of nearly 500,000, while a paper in Malayalam, the *Malayala Manorama,* published from three different cities in Kerala, has a circulation of nearly 600,000. An important aspect of newspaper circulation in India is that while 75 percent of the population is classified as rural, it is estimated that 75 percent of the readers are found in towns and cities, reflecting both the much higher literacy rate of the urban areas as well as their greater prosperity. Another significant fact about the Indian media is that while the newspapers and journals are privately owned, both radio and television are wholly controlled by the government, which gives the print media a special role in criticizing official actions and policies.

[*See also* East India Company; Emergency in India, The; Indian National Congress; Metcalfe, Sir Charles; *and* Mutiny, Indian.]

Margarita Allan Barns, *Indian Press* (1940). Nadig Krishna Murthy, *Indian Journalism* (1966). D. R. Mankekar, *Press Versus the Government: Before and During Emergency* (1978). *Mass Media in India* (annual). *Press in India: Annual Report of the Registrar of Newspapers for India* (annual).    AINSLIE T. EMBREE

## JOURNALISM IN JAPAN

A Western-style press emerged in Japan in the nineteenth century. There had already existed printed broadsheets, often illustrated, known as *kawaraban,* which reported human interest stories and which had a broad popular appeal, but these lacked the serious treatment of news and issues that would characterize the later press. The Tokugawa shogunate had, from its founding in the seventeenth century, prohibited and punished the publication of news and discussions of public affairs.

After Japan's ports were opened to foreign trade, an English merchant published Japan's first newspaper in any language, the *Nagasaki Shipping List and Advertiser,* at Nagasaki in June 1861, but he soon moved his enterprise to Yokohama, where the *Japan Herald* began publication that same year. By the time of the Meiji Restoration in 1868 a number of other Enlish-language newspapers had appeared in Yokohama. Two Japanese-language papers made their appearance: the *Kaigai shimbun (Overseas News),* published by Joseph Heco, a one-time castaway who had returned from the United States, and the *Bankoku shimbun (International News),* published by an English clergyman who was chaplain to the British mission.

With the Meiji Restoration, Tokyo, as Edo was renamed, became the center for journalism, and leadership in journalism was taken from foreign hands by now-unemployed samurai who had been scholar-bureaucrats in shogunal employ. During the spring and summer months of 1868, while the "imperial" forces were fighting the civil war, these men brought out at least seventeen *shimbunshi,* as the news sheets came to be called.

For a brief five years the new government experimented with a subsidized press in service of the regime, but after 1874 the press lost its official patronage and became and remained privately owned. The present pattern of national, regional, and local newspapers emerged in the first decade of the twentieth century, between the Sino-Japanese and Russo-Japanese wars. The major dailies were by then already large, capital-intensive enterprises that used the latest printing technology to satisfy a rapidly rising reader demand.

Although privately owned, the press was not completely free prior to Japan's defeat in World War II. Press laws restrained editors, and post- rather than prepublication censorship made it ruinously expensive to flout official guidelines. These were inevitably more strongly enforced during periods of political strain and national emergency.

Contemporary Japan has one of the world's highest rates of newspaper circulation. In the early 1980s there were, in addition to five daily English-language newspapers with modest circulation, three major dailies with regional branches that circulated in more than twenty million (morning edition) and twelve million (evening) copies, as well as a multitude of financial, sports, and other dailies. Of these special-interest newspapers, the business and financial papers *Sankei shimbun* and *Nihon keizai shimbun* also had circulations of close to two million each.

Albert A. Altman, *"Shinbunshi:* The Early Meiji Adaptation of the Western-style Newspaper," in *Modern Japan: Aspects of History, Literature and Society,* edited by W. G. Beasley (1975), and "The Press," in *Japan in Transition: From Tokugawa to Meiji,* edited by Marius B. Jansen and G. Rozman (1985).    ALBERT A. ALTMAN

**JUMNA RIVER.** *See* Yamuna River.

**JUNG BAHADUR RANA** (1817–1877), first of Nepal's Rana prime ministers and ruler of the country from 1846 to 1856 and again from 1857 to 1877. As a young and ambitious captain in the royal artillery, Jung Bahadur orchestrated the infamous "Kot Massacre" in September 1846, which brought about the demise of his chief rivals at the royal court in Kathmandu. He subsequently won an arrangement from King Surendra Shah (1847–1881) under which he and his family were invested with hereditary rights in perpetuity to absolute authority in Nepal. Jung Bahadur was the chief architect of the Rana political system, which was based on a highly centralized administration of the Nepalese kingdom controlled by members of the Rana family. He also established the pattern for Nepal's relations with British India, whose support was necessary for the survival of the Rana autocracy. He personally led units of Nepal's army in support of the British during the Revolt of 1857. This action won him titles and honors from the British Raj, as well as the return of territories ceded by the British in the Anglo-Nepali War of 1814–1816, and set the stage for a formal arrangement with the British for the recruitment of Gurkha soldiers.

[See also Rana; Kot Massacre; and Kathmandu.]

B. L. Joshi and L. Rose, *Democratic Innovations in Nepal* (1966).                                        RICHARD ENGLISH

**JUNXIAN SYSTEM,** method of territorial administration in China. The system was instituted in its fully developed form during the Qin dynasty (221–207 BCE) to replace earlier systems of feudal rule. The entire empire was divided into *jun*, "commanderies," under centrally appointed military administration; the *jun* were further divided into *xian*, "districts," under the control of a civil or military official also appointed by the central government. The *junxian* system has remained the model for Chinese territorial administration to the present time. The principal change has been that, except in frontier regions, *jun* military administration has been replaced by *sheng*, "provinces," under civil control. The *xian*, administered by a magistrate appointed from the ranks of the imperial civil service (bureaucrats chosen through the examination system), was the basic unit of imperial rule at the local level until 1911. In the People's Republic of China counties are still called *xian*.

The principal form of rule in Shang and Zhou China was quasi-feudal or feudal. Aristocrats, linked in a hierarchy of personal loyalty often based on real or putative kinship ties, ruled their territories and collected revenues from them, owing only specified obligations to their feudal superiors. By the beginning of the seventh century BCE a new territorial unit called the *xian* was created in the southern state of Chu that was an administrative district governed by an official appointed by and reporting to the central government. This marked the beginning of a transition from feudal to bureaucratic government in ancient China. *Xian* administration quickly spread to the northern states of Jin and Qin, and thence elsewhere in northern China.

With the conquest of all of China by Qin in 221 BCE, the old feudal states (*guo*) were abolished and replaced by *jun* under centralized control. Although *guo* were reinstituted in early Han times, the Han government fairly quickly moved to reassert central administration on the *junxian* model, which thereafter remained the norm.

[See also Qin Dynasty.]

H. G. Creel, "The Beginnings of Bureaucracy in China: The Origin of the *Hsien*," *Journal of Asian Studies* 23 (1964): 155–184. Cho-yun Hsu, *Ancient China in Transition* (1965).                              JOHN S. MAJOR

**JURCHEN,** a people of Tunguz origin based in eastern Manchuria who flourished in the twelfth and thirteenth centuries. Wanyan Aguda, a very able chieftain, established the state of Jin in 1115, and in 1125 and 1127 the Jin conquered the Khitan Liao dynasty (907–1125) and the Northern Song (960–1127). The Jin state occupied North China until 1234, when it was conquered by the Mongols.

The name Jurchen first appeared in Chinese history in 903. The people were identified with the Sushen, the Yilou, and the Mohe tribes by traditional historians. Archaeological excavations in Xituanshan, Jilin, seem to suggest that the Xituanshan culture represents the cultures of the Sushen of the sixth century BCE and the Yilou of the third century CE. Among the remains, the bones of pigs are abundant, a fact indicating an important feature of the Tunguz way of life. It is evident in historical sources that the Mohe, a people active in eastern Manchuria from the sixth to the eleventh century, were closely related to the Jurchen, and were subjugated by the Jurchen in the eleventh century.

During the Liao dynasty the Jurchen settled in eastern Manchuria. Evidence shows that in many areas of Jurchen territory farming was predominant. Archaeological findings related to the Liao-Jin periods in the middle Sungari River region show remnants of iron plows. The people planted rice, millet, and wheat as their staples, and when they took up arms, they sent soldiers to till the newly acquired land.

The people constructed houses and walled towns. The clans lived in clearly defined areas and confined their activities to their own lands. These aspects of Jurchen life—the walled towns, farmland, and domesticated animals including the pigs—indicate that they lived in a semiagricultural society. There were other aspects of Jurchen life, such as hunting, fishing, and stockbreeding, that enabled the people to endure hardship and to improve their fighting skills. These pursuits also offered a chance for recreation.

The Jurchen used cavalry as their main force in war, and had a great number of horses when they rose to power. Because each male adult member of the tribe participated in hunting and fishing, he was automatically a soldier. During wartime, the chieftain of a clan or lineage became *mengan*, head of a thousand men, or *mouke*, head of a hundred men.

In 1116 Wanyan Aguda, slightly changing this system, organized every three hundred households into a *mouke* and ten *mouke* into a *mengan*. Soldiers would bring their own supplies and weapons, and all warriors were mounted. In short, hunting and stockbreeding, especially horse breeding, provided great mobility, one of the major reasons for the Jurchen conquest of Liao and Northern Song; their mobility also led many historians to consider the Jurchen a nomadic people.

The Jurchen clans were partrilineal; each clan consisted of a few lineages, such as twelve lineages for the Wanyan clan, and fourteen lineages each for the Tudan and Wugulun clans. The Wanyan clan had marital relations exclusively with a few neighboring clans. Lineages were the basic units of the Jurchen; every lineage occupied a village or walled town. Differentiation in social classes was not obvious in pre-Jin times. Social stratification became more evident after the people received Khitan and Chinese influences. The Jurchen, in unifying the clans and conquering other peoples, used prisoners of war as a slave class. Slavery existed in another form: early Jurchen law stipulated that in case of capital punishment the family members of a criminal became slaves. If relatives of the criminal wanted to redeem their status, they had to pay a ransom of horses, cattle, and other property to the court. To compensate the plaintiff, the defendant had to give away members of his family as slaves. Corporal punishment was an important element in Jurchen law; those whose crimes were not serious were subject to beating, or had to provide recompense with property. Criminals might lose ears or noses as marks of punishment. The Jurchen adopted the Chinese law code in 1145.

The Jurchen practiced polygamy and levirate. When a man died, his brother could take his wife, or his son or brother's son could take his concubine. The Jurchen imperial family adopted primogeniture with great difficulty, as manifested in disputes for several generations rising from contested succession to the throne.

The original religious system was shamanistic. The shaman had the power to kill by magic and was thought able to predict the sex of an unborn child or cure disease. Like the Khitan, the Juchen worshiped the sun. Buddhism was introduced from Korea, but the Jurchen also believed in Daoism, especially the Quanzhen sect.

During the Jin period, most of the Jurchen settled in North China and adopted the way of life of the Chinese agrarian society. Jurchen rule gave rise to a new social structure in North China. The conquerors and Chinese bureaucrats, landlords, and gentry constituted the upper class. Among the commoners the population under the control of the *mengan* and *mouke* enjoyed more privileges than others. Both the government and landlords owned slaves, whose status was fixed largely by Jurchen conquest wars. The number of slaves undoubtedly exceeded that of the Northern Song. The population of North China reached the figure of 48.5 million in 1195. Jurchen population in 1182 was about 6.15 million, which included 1.34 million slaves, who were actually non-Jurchen. In addition, a little less than one-third of the Jurchen still lived in Manchuria. These figures indicate that in general they were outnumbered by the Chinese at an approximate rate of 1 to 10, with a proportion even more in favor of the Chinese in North China.

There existed many barriers between the conquerors and the conquered. Such barriers naturally led to political and social conflicts. Rebellions of the Chinese and Khitan broke out in the early 1160s, almost causing the destruction of the dynasty. By the end of the Jin dynasty most of the Jurchen were assimilated by the Chinese. They spoke Chinese, adopted Chinese clothes, sinicized their surnames, married with the local population, raised their children according to Chinese norms and educational ideas, and practiced Chinese customs.

During the wars against the Mongols in the last years of the Jin, many Jurchen perished. A few served the Mongol rulers of the new Yuan dynasty (1279–1368), and the process of Jurchen sinicization continued throughout the Yuan period. When the Ming conquered the Yuan one could hardly find a Jurchen in China. In Manchuria, however, many Jurchen tribes were still active. By the end of the Ming (1368–1644) they had reorganized their tribes into the Manchu state. They adopted the Mongolian script to write their language, and for a while they called their state the Later Jin (Hou Jin).

Despite of the long process of the sinicization, there are presently still a few descendants of the Jurchen who remember their origins. In Fujian and Taiwan there is a clan with the surname of Nian whose members believe that they are the descendants of Wanyan Nianhan, a meritorious general in the early Jin; a clan genealogy has been preserved as evidence for their claim.

[*See also* Jurchen Jin Dynasty.]

Kwang-chih Chang, *The Archaeology of Ancient China* (rev. ed., 1977). Chi Li, *Manchuria in History* (1932).

Henry Serruys, *Sino-Jürced Relations during the Yung-lo Periods, 1403–24* (1959). Jing-shen Tao, *The Jurchen in Twelfth-Century China: A Study of Sinicization* (1976).

JING-SHEN TAO

## JURCHEN JIN DYNASTY.

Established by the Jurchen, a Tunguz people in eastern Manchuria, in 1115, the Jin dynasty destroyed the Khitan Liao in 1125 and the Northern Song in 1127. It occupied North China until 1234, when it was conquered by the Mongols.

The Jurchen chieftains served the Liao and Koryŏ as vassals in the eleventh century. In the early twelfth century they encroached upon Korean borderlands and defeated the latter's armed forces. Having established the Jin in 1115, Wanyan Aguda (Taizu; r. 1115–1123) turned against the Liao, routing the latter's army in 1117. An alliance was formed with the Song in 1120 against the Liao. The Song, however, did little to bring about the fall of the Liao, while the Jurchen army took all five Liao capitals. The Jin returned the Yanjing area to the Song in accordance with the treaty of 1123, which also stipulated the payment of annual presents to the Jin. However, owing to Song acceptance of the Jin official Zhang Jue, who defected with the prefecture of Ping, and to the Song refusal to observe the agreement of paying a large amount of taxes collected in the Yanjing region, the Jin launched attacks against the Song in 1125 and 1126. In early 1127 the Jurchen army took Bianjing, capital of the Northern Song, and captured the Song rulers.

Besides able leadership, the military organization seems to have been an important factor in Jurchen successes. The *mengan mouke* system organized all male adults into military units, which also facilitated the occupation of newly acquired land as a sociopolitical system. The Jurchen also recruited a number of non-Jurchen soldiers to fight for them.

As brilliant warriors, the Jurchen were not only excellent horseback riders, but also quick to master Chinese strategies and to borrow Chinese weapons. They developed effective war machines to attack walled towns in a siege, including various kinds of ladders and bridges, catapults, and heavily covered carts carrying sandbags for filling up the moat around the town. Later, the most remarkable weapons they borrowed were firearms. With modifications and improvements, the firearms included bamboo guns, cannons, grenades, and even rockets. All of these were employed on a large scale during the siege of Kaifeng in 1233 to defend the city against the invading Mongols.

The Jurchen did not plan to occupy North China after the destruction of the Northern Song. To exercise indirect rule two puppet regimes with Zhang Pangchang and Liu Yu as heads were set up in succession. Meanwhile, the Southern Song was established with Zhao Gou as the new emperor (Gaozong; r. 1127–1161). The Jin attempted to eliminate Gaozong and sent expeditions against him in 1129 and 1130, driving him to the southeast. Emperor Gaozong managed to make Hangzhou his capital and consolidate the dynasty. The Jurchen abolished the second puppet regime of Qi in 1137, and in the following years made other attempts to reunify China. A treaty was finally concluded between the two states in 1141, stipulating that the Song become a vassal state of the Jin, sending annual tribute of 200,000 taels of silver and 300,000 bolts of silk to the Jin. The boundary line between them was demarcated along the Huai River in the east and the Dasan Pass in Shaanxi in the west.

Taizu's successors Taizong (r. 1123–1135), Xizong (r. 1135–1149), and Hailing (r. 1149–1161) adopted Chinese institutions to form a Chinese-style bureaucracy. Hailing moved the capital in 1153 from Manchuria to Yanjing, where the Secretarial Council (*zhongshu sheng*) and the Court Council (*menxia sheng*) were abolished to centralize power. The Presidential Council (*shangshu sheng*) became the only institution in charge of all state affairs, and directly administered a three-level (*fu, zhou,* and *xian*) local governmental system.

Peace lasted for twenty years. The ambitious Jin ruler Hailing, however, attempted to achieve reunification of the whole of China. He launched attacks against the southern state in 1161. His fleet was destroyed by the Song navy, and his attempt to cross the Yangtze River at Caishi, Anhui, was stopped by the Song forces under the temporary command of a civil official, Yu Yunwen. Before making another effort to cross the Yangtze, Hailing was murdered by the riotous generals.

Following the unsuccessful northern expedition sent by the Song emperor Xiaozong, the two states again made peace in 1165. In the new settlement the Song emperor improved his position by replacing the term "tribute" with "money" (*bi*) for the annual payments, and the amount was reduced to 400,000 units. The vassal-overlord relationship was replaced by one between the younger uncle (Emperor Shizong of Jin) and nephew (Emperor Xiaozong of Song).

Before the assassination of Hailing, Wanyan

Wulu, Hailing's cousin, had already ascended the throne. Alarmed by the degenerating results of sinicization, Wulu (Shizong; r. 1161–1189) made efforts to preserve the Jurchen culture. By this time the Jurchen not only attained high positions in the government and enjoyed many political and economic privileges, but also received different treatment in other aspects. In legal affairs, because of their privileged positions and their connections with powerful officials or noble families, the Jurchen commoners always benefited. Powerful and wealthy Jurchen gradually became major landlords. Not only did the government assign much land to the Jurchen, but a number of landowners were able to acquire large estates through purchase and encroachment of the poor as well. Accompanying the rise of the big estates was tenantry. Powerful families seized land from the poor and employed tenants. They also had a number of slaves to do household and farm work for them.

Deeply involved in the Chinese agrarian society, the Jurchen inevitably suffered from maladjustment. Although as a whole the Jurchen owned more land and enjoyed more privileges than the non-Jurchen peoples, their life in China tended to decline into poverty and loss of martial spirit. Many Jurchen were addicted to alcohol, refusing to work. Some lost their holdings and became paupers. All these problems caused Shizong to inaugurate a program for the revival of Jurchen culture and for the consolidation of the Jurchen regime. Shizong tried to promote the martial spirit by strengthening military training, with an emphasis on hunting. He ordered Jurchen subjects to study the Jurchen language in special schools and created Jurchen *jinshi* degrees for the graduates. He also set up a bureau to translate Chinese classics into Jurchen. Although he sponsored a program to revitalize the Jurchen culture, he identified ancient Chinese customs with those of the primitive Jurchen culture. For example, he ordered the ministers to study and reinstitute ancient and Tang ceremonies as well as Jurchen rituals. In order to consolidate his regime, Shizong introduced measures to limit the holdings of big landlords and to distribute land to the poor. He reformed the taxation system and dispatched agricultural inspectors to promote farming among the Jurchen population.

During the reign of Shizong's successor Zhangzong (r. 1189–1208), the Jin stopped another Song northern expedition from 1206 to 1208. Song annual payments were increased to 600,000 units, and the Jin emperor became the elder uncle of the Song ruler. In the latter half of the twelfth century the Jin

entered into a period of cultural achievement. The most important contributions were made by Chinese scholars. Wang Ruoxu and Zhao Bingwen offered new interpretations of classics, literature, and history. The Jin published more books than had previous alien dynasties. There was a rise of vernacular literature in late Jin times. The Yuan drama, with its origins in the Song, acquired its characteristics during the last years of the Jin and the early Yuan.

The people in the late Jin were inclined to simple and popular religious sects. The most important was the polytheistic and ascetic Quanzhen sect of Daoism, which combined the teachings of Daoism, Confucianism, and Buddhism.

The Mongol invasion resulted in the capture of the capital of the Jin in 1215, and the Jurchen court was forced to move to the southern capital of Kaifeng. The decline of the Jurchen dynasty continued until the Mongols, with the assistance of the Southern Song, conquered it between 1233 and 1234.

[See also Jurchen and Song Dynasty.]

Hok-lam Chan, *The Historiography of the Chin Dynasty: Three Studies* (1970). Herbert Franke, "Treaties between Sung and Chin," in *Études Song in Memoriam Étienne Balazs*, series 1, no. 1, edited by F. Aubin (1970). Morris Rossabi, ed., *China among Equals: The Middle Kingdom and Its Neighbors, 10th–14th Centuries* (1983). Jing-shen Tao, *The Jurchen in Twelfth-Century China: A Study of Sinicization* (1976). Stephen H. West, *Vaudeville and Narrative: Aspects of Chin Theater* (1977).

JING-SHEN TAO

**JUSTICE PARTY,** an early twentieth-century political party in the Madras Presidency, India. Dating from the "Non-Brahman Manifesto" (1916), the Justice Party claimed that the Indian National Congress was dominated by brahmans and that nonbrahman interests could best be furthered by working loyally within the institutions of British rule. Itself dominated by higher nonbrahman castes, the party formed a provincial government after elections in 1920 and introduced several major reforms. Although in decline by the 1930s, the legacy of antibrahmanism remained in the post-Independence period, especially in the "Dravidian" parties of Tamil Nadu.

[See also Indian National Congress and Dravidian Movement.]

C. Baker, *Politics of South India 1920–1937* (1976). R. Hardgrave, Jr., *The Dravidian Movement* (1965). E. Irschick, *Politics and Social Conflict in South India* (1969).

FRANKLIN A. PRESLER

JUTE, a fibrous plant used primarily for the manufacture of cordage and sacking, is thought to have originated on the Indian subcontinent. The British East India Company began to export jute from the Indian subcontinent in the 1790s. In 1854, with the outbreak of the Crimean War, the supply of jute was cut off from southern Russia, and jute cultivation in India was thereby increased. The first steam-driven jute mill in India was opened in 1855, and by 1882 twenty jute mills lined the Hughly River. When India was partitioned in 1947 much of the jute-producing land fell within the borders of East Pakistan, while the processing facilities remained within the Indian state of West Bengal.

Today jute is second to cotton in world fiber consumption. Attempts to cultivate it elsewhere have resulted in plants with fiber inferior to that obtained from plants grown in India. India and Bangladesh together currently produce nearly 90 percent of the world's jute; the total annual yield in each country usually exceeds a million tons. Ten percent of the cultivated land in Bangladesh is planted with jute.

WILLIAM F. FISHER

JUYONGGUAN, less than forty miles from the imperial palace in Beijing, the site of the most frequently visited section of the Ming defensive wall. This portion of the wall guards the most convenient pass through the mountains that separate the capital from the Mongolian steppe beyond. Mentioned in the *Huainanzi* (c. 130 BCE), the pass was fortified by the Northern Qi in 554 and held by the Jin against the Mongols. The exquisite Yuntai, a ceremonial arch decorated with Buddhist images and bearing a celebrated set of inscriptions in Lantsha (the Nepalese script for Sanskrit), Tibetan, Phags-pa Mongolian, Uighur, Xixia, and Chinese, was erected here in 1343–1345. The walls that guard the northern end of the pass, known by most simply as the "Great Wall of China," were built in Ming times.

[*See also* Great Wall.]

ARTHUR N. WALDRON

# K

KABIR (1398?–1448?), North Indian devotional poet, leading figure in the Sant school, best known for iconoclastic verses attacking religious hypocrisy, superstition, and narrow orthodoxy, while urging an immediate personal experience of a supreme being beyond form and attributes. Probably born to a family of Muslim weavers in Varanasi, Kabir shows more Hindu than Islamic influence in his poetry. His most often-used name for God is Rama, and popular tradition says that he was a disciple of the famed Hindu guru Ramananda.

Kabir is believed to have been illiterate. His verses—most in the form of songs or aphoristic couplets—were transmitted widely across the country by oral tradition and set down over the centuries by devotees and admirers. The question of authenticity among the vast corpus of works attributed to him is far from settled. Three broad sets of writings are recognized as most important, although the oldest of these—the Sikh *Adi Granth*—was not compiled until about 1603, perhaps a century and a half after Kabir's death. Originating in the Punjab, the *Granth* includes several hundred compositions attributed to Kabir. In the late seventeenth century the Dadu Panth in Rajasthan collected a set of writings that included many verses attributed to Kabir, among them the *Bijak,* sacred book of the Kabir Panth.

[*See also* Bhakti *and* Indo-Aryan Languages and Literatures.]

Charlotte Vaudeville, *Kabir,* vol. 1 (1974). *The Bijak of Kabir,* translated by Linda Hess and Shukdev Singh (1983).

LINDA HESS

KABO REFORMS, a sweeping modernization of the Korean social and governmental structure undertaken in 1894 under the auspices of the Japanese.

In the summer of 1894, triumphant over the Chinese forces in the first stage of the Sino-Japanese War (1894–1895) and determined to bring Korea under its influence after more than a decade of frustration, Japan took aggressive steps to reform Korea along Japanese lines. The Japanese seized the royal palace in July and the Japanese minister to Korea, Ōtori Keisuke, extracted from King Kojong a promise of cooperation. A new cabinet was formed consisting of progressives. Headed by Kim Hong-jip, an old hand at international negotiation, it also included in key posts such pro-Japanese progressives as Pak Yŏng-hyo and Sŏ Kwang-bŏm, who returned from ten years of exile after the failure of the 1884 coup.

The first measure taken was the renunciation of Korean tributary relations to China and the proclamation of Korea's complete independence. In August the Japanese cabinet chose one of four alternative plans submitted by the foreign minister, Mutsu Munemitsu, and settled on a basic Korean policy: Japan would recognize Korean independence but Japan should directly or indirectly protect and assist her to maintain this independence. The signing of the "Provisional Articles" obliged Korea to accept Japanese advice on internal reforms. Sensing resistance from the traditional Korean elite, the Japanese government in October sent Home Minister Inoue Kaoru, a powerful member of the oligarchy, as minister to Korea to oversee the reform. Arriving with a lengthy blueprint, Inoue presided over the cabinet three times a week to pass a total of 421 resolutions.

The reform measures were epochal in nature and comprehensive in scope. Breaking with the traditional social and political system, they were meant to remodel Korean society and government. The royal family could no longer interfere in state affairs and the role of the king was limited to action in consultation with the cabinet. The six bureaus of the traditional Yi government were replaced by eight ministries under the leadership of the prime minister, and civil and military officials were given equal status. The civil service examination system was abolished and with it the privileged status of the *yangban*, the hereditary elite class. Slavery and discrimination against those engaging in the traditionally despised professions (butchers, tanners) were outlawed. Social mores were challenged—widows could remarry without sanction and men were encouraged to cut off their topknots, to smoke short rather than long pipes, and to wear dark clothes in place of the traditional white clothing.

These reforms met with enormous resistance. Imposed on Korean society from above, the reform challenged central tenets of the traditional way of life, particularly attacking central features of the Confucian worldview and the privileged position of the most powerful class in Korean society, the *yangban*. Predictably, the public reaction was intense and nationwide. The reform was further hampered by a lack of funds. Three million yen that Inoue sought and had been promised by the Japanese government to finance these measures did not materialize. Soon the Korean cabinet was divided between a pro-Japanese group and pro-Western group, the latter of whom resented the high-handedness of the Japanese.

Developments in international affairs were particularly unfavorable to Japan. The Shimonoseki Treaty, which Japan and China signed in April 1895, formalized the end of the Chinese claim to Korea. Immediately afterward, however, the Triple Intervention by Russia, Germany, and France forced Japan to retrocede the Lioadong Peninsula to China and to honor Korean independence. [*See also* Shimonoseki, Treaty of *and* Triple Intervention.]

In May 1895 the Japanese cabinet reversed its Korea policy, gave up the reform effort, and recalled Inoue. King Kojong declared a resumption of power and Queen Min's family returned to power. A new pro-Western cabinet was formed. The Korean government allied itself with Russia, which came to show an increasing interest in Korea. The Japanese resident minister, Miura Gorō, reacted sharply, assisting in an attack on the royal palace in which Queen Min was murdered. Japanese prestige suffered as a result, and the Japanese hold on Korea became quite tenuous while Russian influence grew.

Although Japan had to wait another ten years for complete control of Korea, the Kabo Reforms were the first real step toward it. Moreover, several measures, such as the abolition of the civil service examinations and the class system, repre-

sented the first substantial attempt at a structural modernization of Korean society.

[*See also* Kojong; Min, Queen; *and* Yi Dynasty.]

Hilary Conroy, *The Japanese Seizure of Korea, 1868–1910* (1960). C. I. Eugene Kim and Han-Kyo Kim, *Korea and the Politics of Imperialism* (1967). W. H. Wilkinson, *The Corean Government: Constitutional Changes, July 1894 to October 1895, with an Appendix on Subsequent Enactments to June 30th, 1895* (1897).

JaHyun Kim Haboush

**KABUKI**, a popular Japanese theatrical form originating early in the seventeenth century. Like the puppet theater known today as *bunraku*, *kabuki* enjoyed great popularity throughout the Edo (Tokugawa) period (1600–1868) as entertainment for the urban commoners. In its colorful costumes, lively music and dance, dramatic action and bravura, and appeal to the emotions, it differed markedly from the subtlety and restraint of the earlier *nō* plays, which were considered the appropriate form of drama for the samurai.

The conventional account of the origins of *kabuki* opens with the appearance in Kyoto of Okuni in 1603. An itinerant dancer who claimed association with Izumo Shrine, she and her troupe are said to have performed skits and dances on a makeshift stage in the dry riverbed of the Kamo River, the carnival district at the eastern edge of the capital. In the following years, troupes of prostitutes (*onna kabuki*) appeared in this quarter, drawing audiences of samurai and townspeople with their sensual dances and risqué burlesques. Because their behavior excited quarrels and duels, women were permanently banned from the stage in 1629. *Kabuki* was also performed by troupes of youths (*wakashu kabuki*). Since they too were involved in prostitution, these troupes were banned in 1652. As a consequence of reforms demanded by the authorities, plays of several acts with more plot structure gradually evolved, and the appeal of the performance shifted gradually to the skill in acting technique displayed by mature performers. *Kabuki* continued to be centered on the actor, who demanded of the playwright material to suit his personality and style. The playwright sketched the plot and wrote out only parts of scenes, leaving it to actors to improvise lines that best displayed their voice and delivery. Since old plays and themes were repeatedly reworked and elaborated, few texts survive from before the end of the eighteenth century, and these only in rough manuscript. *Kabuki* drew much of its material from plays written for the puppet theater, which were far superior in dramatic structure. Furthermore, the literary quality of the texts of the puppet plays was higher, as they were composed for reciters to narrate and sing. The most talented dramatists, such as Chikamatsu Monzaemon (1653–1725) and Takeda Izumo II (1691–1756), preferred to write for the puppet theater. The plays *Kanadehon chūshingura (The Treasury of Loyal Retainers,* 1748), *Sugawara denju tenarai kagami (Sugawara and the Secrets of Calligraphy,* 1746), and indeed half of the classical *kabuki* repertoire came from the puppet theater.

The staple of *kabuki* as well as puppet stage was the *jidaimono,* or period pieces, long plays based on heroes and historical events of centuries past that included a liberal admixture of legend and fiction. They were usually five-act plays, but there was a continuing trend toward ever more intricate plots and additional acts. A second type of play, the three-act *sewamono,* or talk-of-the-town piece, appeared after 1700. They dramatized a current scandal or piece of gossip in contemporary commoner society, such as a double love suicide *(shinjū),* an embezzlement, or a murder. A theater program, which lasted from sunrise to sunset, characteristically included a *jidaimono,* a *sewamono,* and occasionally a short dance piece *(shosagoto).* In the nineteenth century, single acts or scenes that had been favorites were elaborated into independent plays. Such works, together with dance pieces often adapted from *nō* plays, such as *Kanjinchō (The Subscription List),* make up most of the famous eighteen plays of the Ichikawa family *(kabuki jūhachiban)* selected by the actor Danjūrō VII (1791–1859).

Among the first celebrated actors to contribute to the formulation of *kabuki* acting styles was Sakata Tōjūrō (1647–1709) of Kyoto and Osaka, who was especially favored for his realistic depiction of the great lover in the pleasure quarter. In Edo, Ichikawa Danjūrō (1660–1704) developed the *aragoto* ("rough stuff") style of exaggerated posturing and bombastic language to play superhuman heroes. But the most significant achievement was the evolution of the difficult techniques of the female imperson-

FIGURE 1. *Kabuki Performance.* Scene from the play *Hama matsukaze.* Shown here (left to right) are Miyawaki Shinji as Konobei and Matsuoka Yutaka as Kofuji.

ator *(onnagata)* on the stages of Kyoto and Osaka by actors such as Yoshizawa Ayame (1673–1729), Mizuki Tatsunosuke (1673–1745), Segawa Kikunojō (1693–1749), and others. The *onnagata* abstracts the essential characteristics of women's movements and speech in a stylized manner. This technique became so well established over the centuries as the conventional image of women's roles that attempts by women in modern times to play these parts have not been considered successful.

Early *kabuki* was performed on borrowed *nō* stages, and then in rudimentary playhouses, but by 1700 *kabuki* theaters were roofed structures with three tiers of boxes and seating for a thousand people. Among the important innovations of the theater in the early eighteenth century was the *hanamichi*, a runway extending from the stage to the back of the hall to be used for dramatic entrances and exits. The revolving stage was invented in Japan in 1758, and numerous trap doors in the stage and *hanamichi* were added. Actors appeared in lavish costumes, wigs, and stylized makeup for the male parts. Dance pieces and some other scenes were accompanied by sung narrative to a *shamisen* accompaniment in a variety of styles, such as Nagauta, Tokiwazu, Kiyomoto, Gidayū, and others. Stage music from clappers, drums, gongs, flutes, fiddles, and other instruments was used to set the mood and play on the emotions.

Critical booklets evaluating actors *(yakusha hyōbanki)*, which began to appear in 1656, turned increasingly from the appraisal of the physical appeal of young actors to criticism of acting ability and the merits of the play. Actors, along with prostitutes, were the main subject of *ukiyo* woodblock prints from the late seventeenth century. After the development of theater posters by Torii Kiyomoto in 1690, prints characteristically depicted actors in dramatic postures drawn from their current roles. Bold portraits of actors' faces by Shunshō, Sharaku, and others appeared in the late eighteenth century.

The visual effect of *kabuki* as performed today in modern theaters has been changed considerably by much larger stages decorated with elaborate stage scenery, drop curtains, spot lights, and stage lighting. The performance, however, is reasonably faithful to the traditional style, for the actors are mostly from acting families and have been taught from an early age the techniques of mime, dance, and elocution for the standard repertoire. The usual format for performances now includes a daily matinee and evening program of about five hours each at which different numbers are presented. Rarely is an entire play performed, but rather a variety of favorite scenes from traditional plays with the addition of plays or scenes composed in modern times *(shin kabuki)*. Although leading actors of Edo times were idolized by theatergoers, government policy classified them as semi-outcastes. Today, however, actors are recipients of official honors as skilled exponents of a traditional art. The establishment of the Kokuritsu Gekijō (National Theatre of Japan) in 1966 has been a stimulus to the preservation of the classical repertoire, the training of young actors, and research on the history of *kabuki*.

[*See also* Bunraku; Nō; Chikamatsu Monzaemon; *and* Danjūrō.]

Earle Ernst, *The Kabuki Theatre* (1974). Samuel L. Leiter, *Kabuki Encyclopedia* (1979). Masakatsu Gunji, *Kabuki,* translated by John Bester (1969). Yasuji Toita, *Kabuki: The Popular Theatre,* translated by Don Kenny (1970).                   DONALD H. SHIVELY

KABUL, capital of the Afghan state since 1776, lies midway between Central Asia and India, a position that has been a key to its historical, commercial, and geographic significance. Babur launched his Mughal empire from here in 1526, and his descendants (1526–1707) retained it as an important provincial center.

Kabul's population rose from 140,000 in 1876 to almost 1,000,000 in 1978. Today it approaches 2,000,000, on account of the flood of internal refugees triggered by the Soviet occupation of Afghanistan that started in December 1979. The ethnic composition of Kabul, inhabited predominantly by Persian-speaking Tajiks in 1876, must have been considerably modified as a result of these changes.

[*See also* Afghanistan.]

*Imperial Gazetteer of Afghanistan, Kabul Province,* 2 vols. (1910).                   ASHRAF GHANI

KACHIN, tribal polity of northernmost Burma and adjacent parts of India and China whose main constituent people call themselves Jinghpaw (Singhpo in Assam).

Because its political-ethnic system is largely defined by a long-term relationship with the Tai-speaking Shan of the adjacent valleys and plains, Kachin cannot have existed before sometime in the twelfth or thirteenth century, when the first Shan principalities, in particular the state of Mongmao, seem to have come into being. This, however, is only inference, as we have no unambiguous reference to these people—in Burmese, Chinese, or European records—until the nineteenth century at the earliest and only the vaguest indications about the Singhpo in the records of the Ahom (subsequent to their founding in the thirteenth century).

E. R. Leach (1954) insists that what he calls *gumsa* (actually, *gumtsa*)—the system of hereditary tract chieftainships in which the chiefs and their lineages own all the land and receive dues (usually a hindquarter of every slain animal) as a consequence of their ritual control over the spirits guarding the territory—is an outcome of a recurrent attempt by Kachin chiefs to assume the prerogatives of Shan princes. According to Leach, *gumlao* (a variant of *gumsa*), in which there is no individual chief of a village or tract and no system of ritualized chiefly dues, is at once a reaction to princely pretensions and a consequence of the tendency for such chieftainships to break down owing to the inability of a lineage-based tribal polity to support the sharp distinction between rulers and subjects. The smaller Shan principalities in the region were often subject to Kachin takeover, and the chiefs involved sometimes attempted to become Shan.

According to LaRaw Maran (1967), however, this admittedly unstable system was not the same thing as the standard Kachin chieftainship, called *gumchying gumsa,* which was found northwest of the Shan-occupied valleys and seems to have been much more stable. It was apparently based upon a long-term relationship with the Ahom, with the more important Shan states, and with both the Burmese kingdom and the Yunnanese marches of China, and it imposed taxes upon such things as the Tibetan pack trade.

The *gumtsa* tended to revert to *gumchying gumsa* through a type of chieftainship called *gumrawng gumtsa* and did not in general alternate with *gumlao.* Furthermore, *gumlao* was not a so-called democratic form of polity. Rather, as its very name indicates (the *gum* prefix signifies anything connected with claims to aristocratic privilege), it was a system in which novel economic opportunities opened up the possibility of wider competition (among members of chiefly clans only) for power and for the ritual privileges of chiefly status, so that this status ceased to have any close connection with exclusive claims to territorial paramountcy. The oscillation between standard chieftaincies and *gumlao* polities seems to be a fairly recent development, caused by the expansion of the China-based caravan trade into Burma and Thailand as well as by expansions owing

to the development, from the eighteenth century onward, of the opium trade in this region of the world (whether or not the Kachin themselves were growing much opium). As a deliberate ideological movement, *gumlao* also seems to owe something to the spread of Shan-Buddhist ethical concepts to the Kachin.

The expansion of both *gumsa* and *gumlao* Kachin into the Shan territories of the upper Irrawady River region brought them into greater conflict with the Burmese kingdom, just as Singhpo, in Assam, increasingly came into conflict with the British in the nineteenth century. Indeed, there is some evidence that when the British marched on Mandalay in 1885, Kachin forces (no doubt along with Shan) were also moving on Mandalay from the north.

Today the Kachin have a constituent state in Burma. Since at least 1962–1963, they have been much involved in insurgency, partly in collaboration with their kin in the Kachin autonomous region of the People's Republic of China.

E. R. Leach, *Political Systems of Highland Burma: A Study of Kachin Social Structure* (1954) and "Imaginary Kachins," *Man* 19.1 (1983): 191–206. LaRaw Maran, "Toward a Basis for Understanding the Minorites in Burma: The Kachin Example," in *Southeast Asian Tribes, Minorities, and Nations,* edited by Peter Bunstadter (1967), pp. 125–146.          F. K. Lehman

KADAZAN, formerly known as Dusun, a group of closely related peoples living in western Sabah, Malaysia. Most Kadazans grow wet rice on the coastal plains or in upland valleys, but some practice shifting cultivation. Long contact and intermarriage with Malayo-Muslim coastal peoples and, more recently, with Chinese and Europeans have greatly modified traditional Kadazan culture. Many have embraced Islam or Christianity, but a proportion still practices the traditional religion. Efforts by coastal Kadazan leaders since the 1950s to promote a stronger sociopolitical unity have been only partly successful. Today many Kadazans are active in politics, government, business, or other professions. In 1970 the Kadazans numbered some 184,512, or 28 percent of Sabah's population.

[*See also* Sabah.]

George Appell, "Ethnographic Profiles of the Dusun-speaking Peoples of Sabah, Malaysia," *Journal of the Malaysian Branch of the Royal Asiatic Society* 41 (1968): 131–147. Margaret Roff, "The Rise and Demise of Kadazan Nationalism," *Journal of Southeast Asian History* 10 (1969): 326–343.          Craig A. Lockard

KAEMPFER, ENGELBERT (1651–1716), German-born physician best known for his *History of Japan* (1727), a work based on information gathered while serving from 1690 to 1692 as physician to the Dutch trading station on the island of Deshima in Nagasaki harbor. Although much of its historical analysis has been revised by subsequent scholarship, Kaempfer's *History* remains an invaluable eyewitness record of Japanese society in the late seventeenth century. Especially noteworthy are the revealing descriptions of the cloistered life of the Dutch of Deshima and the detailed accounts of two Dutch tribute missions to the shogun's court in Edo (Tokyo) in 1691 and 1692.

Kaempfer was born 16 September 1651 in Lemgo in northwestern Germany. He received extensive training in both the sciences and the humanities in German, Dutch, Swedish, Polish, and Prussian schools. He had a great interest in travel and in 1683 left medical studies at the university to become secretary to a Swedish trade mission to Persia. Less than a year later he entered the employ of the Dutch East India Company as a surgeon-major. Following service in the Persian Gulf, India, and Batavia (Jakarta), he arrived in Japan in September 1690 to serve as physician to the Dutch factory. During his two-year stay Kaempfer collected a wealth of information, often surreptiously through informants or by bribing officials, on the geography, language, politics, religion, foreign trade, and natural history of Japan.

In 1693 Kaempfer returned to Europe intending to devote himself to preparing his papers for publication, but his medical practice precluded extensive writing. When he died in 1716 at the age of 65 he had published only a single volume of travel notes. Shortly after his death, the Kaempfer manuscripts were purchased by Hans Sloane, whose library, including the Kaempfer manuscripts, became part of the collection of the British Museum in 1759. The first edition (1727) of Kaempfer's *History* was an English translation of the unpublished German text. Other editions followed in many languages, and the work became world famous.

[*See also* Deshima *and* Rangaku.]

John Bowers, *Western Medical Pioneers in Feudal Japan* (1970). Engelbert Kaempfer, *The History of Japan* (3 vols., 1906).                    RICHARD RUBINGER

KAESŎNG, city near the Yellow Sea coast in central Korea. Kaesŏng was the capital of the Koryŏ kingdom from 918 to 1392.

In the early tenth century Kaesŏng, then known as Songak, served briefly as the capital city of the Silla rebel Kungye. One of Kungye's lieutenants, Wang Kŏn, the future founder of the Koryŏ kingdom, came from this area, where his family had achieved prominence through their success in maritime trade. When Wang Kŏn became king in his own right, he made Songak his capital and changed its name to Kaesŏng. Becoming Koryŏ's official capital in 919, Kaesŏng was also known as Songdo and Kaegyŏng. Its strategic position, surrounded by hills on the banks of the Imjin River, had once made it an important part of Silla's northwest defense chain. According to the geomantic practices that were strictly followed in Korea during that period, Kaesŏng was such a propitious site that in making it his capital, Wang Kŏn was said to have assured the lasting prosperity of his dynasty.

Kaesŏng was sacked several times. First besieged by Khitan forces in the early eleventh century, it was subsequently overrun by these invaders in 1010. In the thirteenth century it was captured by the Mongols, who attacked the city during their invasions of Korea. Kaesŏng was also nearly destroyed by several domestic revolts. For example, in 1126 the aristocrat Yi Cha-gyŏm attacked and burned the palace, and during the later period of military rule (1170–1270) religious and slave revolts wrecked parts of the capital.

Despite the destruction Kaesŏng remained one of the world's most magnificent cities. Divided for administrative purposes into five wards, its population reached a peak in the eleventh century. Traders from China, Japan, and the Arab world and officials from the Mongol empire and beyond came to Kaesŏng to visit. A wall surrounding Kaesŏng, completed in 1029, protected the city and guarded its wide avenues and government buildings. Kaesŏng was also a religious center, with more than seventy Buddhist temples within the city itself, and the economic and cultural center of Koryŏ. Scholars and artisans produced masterpieces of literature and art to grace its homes and buildings. Houses tiled in celadon, extensive libraries, and huge gardens and parks further enhanced the splendor that was Kaesŏng.

EDWARD J. SHULTZ

KAGOSHIMA BOMBARDMENT. After the Richardson (Namamugi) Incident of 1862 in Japan, English representatives demanded that Satsuma *han* pay a steep indemnity and punish the victim's assailants. Satsuma declined, however, and Neale, the British chargé d'affaires, finally ordered his vessels to chastise the recalcitrant domain. When his squadron seized three steamships in Kagoshima harbor a three-hour artillery duel ensued. Satsuma's ten batteries were damaged, and part of the city was burned to the ground by English rockets. The British vessels were also damaged, and sixty seamen were wounded or killed. The ships withdrew to the mouth of the harbor for repairs the next day and then sailed off.

Both sides were reluctant to undergo this exercise again. Earnest negotiations followed in Yokohama, leading to a timely rapprochement between Satsuma and the English. An agreement reached in November 1863 provided that Satsuma would pay an indemnity of £25,000 and punish Richardson's attackers. The English agreed to aid Satsuma in future efforts to purchase warships.

[*See also* Richardson Incident.]

THOMAS M. HUBER

**KAIFENG,** Chinese city in Henan Province; capital of the Northern Song dynasty (960–1126) and, from 1214 to 1234, of the Jurchen Jin dynasty (1115–1234). Kaifeng was the last imperial capital in the Yellow River valley, the ancient center of Chinese civilization. As the Northern Song capital, Kaifeng became one of China's major political, economic, and cultural centers. Its proximity to the Yellow River and location near the head of the Grand Canal gave Song Kaifeng access to both the North China Plain and the new economic centers of the southeast. The city's unplanned and unregulated growth during this period, when its population grew to about one million, contrasted sharply with the orderly layout of the Tang capital, Chang'an, but reflected the dramatic commercial development of the day.

Prior to Song times Kaifeng served as an administrative center with various names. During the Warring States period it was known as Daliang, the capital of Wei. In the Han dynasty it was the seat of Chenliu Commandery. During the Eastern Wei it became Liangzhou and in Northern Zhou and Sui times it was Bianzhou. In the Tang dynasty it gained in importance, becoming the seat of the Henan inspection circuit. It then gained the name Kaifeng-fu, which it held also as capital of Jin, Han, and Zhou during the Five Dynasties period. In the Yuan period it was reduced in status to the capital of Henan Province with the name Bianliang. It remained the provincial capital in Ming and Qing with the name Kaifeng.

PETER K. BOL

**KAIPING,** Chinese city located in Inner Mongolia, site of Kublai Khan's summer capital, the famous Shangdu, or Xanadu. Under the Ming dynasty (1368–1644) Kaiping was an important military outpost, although in 1430 it was moved within the Great Wall, some one hundred miles away.

Edward L. Farmer, *Early Ming Government: The Evolution of Dual Capitals* (1976).    JOHN A. RAPP

**KAKATIYA DYNASTY.** Before the rise of Vijayanagara, the Kakatiyas were the most important dynasty in northern Andhra Pradesh, India. Ruling from the first half of the eleventh century to the 1320s, they were known as prolific builders of temples and large reservoirs. At first feudatories of the Late Chalukyas of Kalyani, they consolidated their power during the Kalachuri interregnum.

At the breakup of the Chola empire the Kakatiyas joined the Hoysalas and the Pandyas in the division of Chola territory. Ultimately rule passed to a daughter, Rudramba, who is mentioned by Marco Polo. After her death the arrival of Muslims from Delhi put an end to Kakatiya rule.

[*See also* Vijayanagara; Chola Dynasty; *and* Pandya Dynasty.]

R. C. Majumdar, ed., *The History and Culture of the Indian People* (1957), vol. 5, pp. 198–203. Ghulam Yazdani, ed., *The Early History of the Deccan* (1960), part 9.    ROBERT J. DEL BONTÀ

**KALA** (U Kala), whose birthdate is unknown, was the author of the *Mahayazawindawgyi*, the earliest of the large, royal chronicles of Burma, thought to have been written in the early eighteenth century CE during the reign of King Taninganwe (1714–1733) of the Restored Toungoo dynasty. Born into a rich family, U Kala had the means as well as the inclination and ability to produce his magnum opus and several smaller chronicles, such as *Yazawin chok* and the *Yazawin lat*, the "abridged" and the "middle" chronicles of kings.

U Kala used poems, biographies, and inscriptions as source material for the *Mahayazawindawgyi*. Later chronicles, such as the *Hmannan (Glass Palace)* and the *Yazawinthit (New Chronicle)*, were modeled on U Kala's work in terms of style, approach, and facts. Moreover, *Mahayazawindawgyi*, which begins with legendary King Mahasammata and ends with King Taninganwe, is probably one of the best primary sources of information on the Toungoo dynasty available.

[*See also* Toungoo Dynasties *and* Glass Palace Chronicle.]

Paul J. Bennett, *Conference under the Tamarind Tree: Three Essays in Burmese History* (1971). Victor B. Lieberman, *Burmese Administrative Cycles: Anarchy and Conquest, c. 1580–1760* (1984).

MICHAEL AUNG-THWIN

**KALACHURI DYNASTIES.** The Kalachuris of Chedi, the region around modern Jabalpur, in Madhya Pradesh, India, are known to historians from the sixth century CE, but became particularly prominent in the late ninth and tenth centuries, when they undertook successful military campaigns against enormously powerful neighbors, among them the Pratiharas and Rashtrakutas. The Kalachuris ruled until the early thirteenth century. Devotees of the Hindu god Shiva, they patronized Shaivite temples and monasteries. Their records are dated in an era commencing in 248/249 CE, commonly called the Kalachuri-Chedi era. Several other Kalachuri dynasties are known, all probably related to this Chedi line. Best known among these were the Kalachuris of Kalyana, one of several families who ruled in the Deccan. In the mid-twelfth century they conquered the prominent Chalukya dynasty, remaining in power until 1184, when power reverted to the Chalukyas.

[*See also* Chalukya Dynasties.]

V. V. Mirashi, *Inscriptions of the Kalachuri-Chedi Era* (1955). Ghulam Yazdani, ed., *The Early History of the Deccan* (1960).    FREDERICK M. ASHER

**KALAHOM**, military ministry and organ of provincial government in premodern Siam. It was originally constituted by King Borommatrailokanat of Ayudhya in the fifteenth century as the military division of the state, with four great generals and their departments balancing the four departments under the Mahatthai. By the end of the seventeenth century the Kalahom took charge of the administration of the southern provinces, combining military and civil functions there, while the Mahatthai did the same for the central and northern provinces. The Kalahom was redefined as the Ministry of Defense under King Chulalongkorn in the 1890s.

[*See also* Borommatrailokanat; Mahatthai; *and* Chulalongkorn.]

H. G. Quaritch Wales, *Ancient Siamese Government and Administration* (1934; reprint, 1965). David K. Wyatt, *Thailand: A Short History* (1984).

DAVID K. WYATT

**KALIBAPI**, an acronym for Kapisanan sa Pagilingkod sa Bagong Pilipinas (Association for Service to the New Philippines), was the sole legal political party during the Japanese occupation of the Philippines. Organized on 8 December 1942, the Kalibapi announced its goals as the reconstruction of the "New Philippines," the restoration of peace and order throughout the islands, and the complete adherence of the Filipinos to the principles of the Greater East Asia Co-Prosperity Sphere. The Kalibapi enlisted the participation and support of practically every important prewar Filipino politician remaining in the country. Its members wrote the constitution and selected the officials of the wartime republic proclaimed 14 October 1943.

[*See also* Philippines.]

David Steinberg, *Philippine Collaboration in World War II* (1967).    GRANT K. GOODMAN

**KALIDASA**, Sanskrit poet and dramatist who flourished probably in the late fourth century CE. Little is known about his life. His works mark the highest development of both drama and court poetry in Sanskrit; they are characterized by great elegance and complexity and are free of the preciosity of other writers of *kavya*, or high poetry. His three dramas, employing both prose and verse, are the early *Malavikagnimitra*; *Vikramorvashi*, his last play; and *Shakuntala*, his masterpiece. His other works are the elegiac *Meghaduta (The Cloud Messenger)*; the epic *Raghuvamsha (The Dynasty of Raghu*, part of which retells the *Ramayana); Kumarasambhava (The Birth of the War God*, describing Shiva's love for Parvati); and the descriptive *Ritusamhara (The Seasons)*. Using subjects drawn mostly from myth and the epics, Kalidasa's poetry celebrates nature and, like Shakespeare's late romances, conjugal love and happy family life.

A. Berriedale Keith, *The Sanskrit Drama* (1964). Barbara Stoler Miller, ed., *Theater of Memory: The Plays of Kalidasa* (1984).    DAVID RUBIN

**KALIMANTAN.** An island of some 290,000 square miles, Kalimantan (formerly Borneo) has a population of approximately ten million people, 75 percent of whom are Indonesian citizens residing in the four Indonesian provinces of North, South, East, and West Kalimantan and the rest either residents of Malaysia's two states on the north side of the island, Sarawak and Sabah, or of the tiny north-coast Sultanate of Brunei, with a population of

200,000 (1982 est.). The island's relatively infertile, hilly interior; its long, winding rivers, many accessible only to small craft; and its broad lowland swamps aproning much of its coastline have contributed to two historically important features of its demography: low population density and striking ethnic diversity.

Dozens of indigenous ethnic groups, the Iban and other Dayak tribes most numerous among them, have long occupied the island's interior. They practiced shifting cultivation and other forms of agriculture, as well as resource collection appropriate to their tropical jungle ecology, and existed in varying degrees of autonomy under traditional leaders. In premodern times they were occasionally, and only marginally, subject to the powers that held sway along the coasts and lower rivers. These were members of regionally expansive ethnic groups, at times Javanese and Bugis but predominantly Malays, whose sultanates ringed the island in the early modern centuries and had river-mouth capitals at Brunei (source of the island's modern name), Pontianak, Bandjarmasin, and lesser sites. From these entrepôts Chinese and other traders carried away sparse but valuable commodities: rattan and bird's nests; jungle gums and resins; gold, diamonds, and pearls; and rice grown by small populations of sedentary farmers subject to the sultans.

Europeans penetrated this trade beginning in the sixteenth century and increasingly so thereafter. During the nineteenth century, through a long and diverse process of negotiated acquisition and conquest, all Borneo was incorporated into Western empires. The larger, southern portion of the island was annexed to Netherlands India, and the northern section was acquired by independent colonizers under the protection of Britain—James Brooke and his family in Sarawak, the British North Borneo Company in Sabah. The sultan of Brunei also accepted British "protection" in 1888.

Various elements of modern colonial economic exploitation were introduced at this time, including plantation agriculture (especially rubber), lumbering, and oil and mineral extraction. As elsewhere in Southeast Asia, these new developments were accompanied by the arrival of new Chinese communities. With the exception of what was then British North Borneo (now Sabah), however, these processes were limited. Of more importance were the imposition of modern colonial administrations and the increasingly effective incorporation of interior peoples into the machinery of state.

Following World War II, Indonesia, independent from 1949, claimed the former Dutch territories in Borneo; these became the Indonesian provinces of Kalimantan. Likewise, Sarawak and Sabah were joined to Malaya, another British possession, and briefly to Singapore as well, to make independent Malaysia in 1963. These areas are now being developed comprehensively—politically, culturally, and economically—as constituent members of neighboring but fundamentally different modern Southeast Asian nation-states. Brunei, which enjoys a disproportionate share of the region's petroleum, remained a British protectorate until 1984 and is now an independent monarchy.

[*See also* Sarawak; Sabah; Brunei; Iban; Dayak; Brooke, Sir James; *and* Indonesia, Republic of.]

Graham Irwin, *Nineteenth-Century Borneo: A Study in Diplomatic Rivalry* (1955). Frank M. Lebar, *Ethnic Groups of Insular Southeast Asia* (1972). Michael Leigh, *The Rising Moon: Political Change in Sarawak* (1974). Robert Pringle, *Rajahs and Rebels: The Ibans of Sarawak under Brooke Rule, 1841–1941* (1970). Tjilik Riwut, *Kalimantan Membangun* (1979). K. G. Tregonning, *A History of Modern Sabah* (1965).    JAMES R. RUSH

**KALINGA,** the ancient name of the coastal lands between the Mahanadi and Godavari rivers. Kalinga was known to Panini (c. fifth century BCE) and was ruled by the Nandas and Mauryas. The emperor Ashoka fought a bloody battle in Kalinga—a battle that proved to be a turning point of his life and career, inspiring him to eschew all war and rule by the principle of *dhammavijaya,* or righteousness. The earliest notable king of Kalinga was Kharavela (second century BCE), a patron of Jainism. Kalinga was eventually split up into a number of small states, and several dynasties ruled over them in sequence. It was an important outlet for external trade with Southeast Asia.

[*See also* Ashoka; Orissa; *and* Maurya Empire.]

R. C. Majumdar, ed., *The Classical Age* (1954) and *The Age of Imperial Unity* (1968).    A. K. NARAIN

**KALMUKS.** Dzungaria, in Xinjiang (Sinkiang) Province, China, is the original homeland of a people known in the West as Kalmuks (Kalmucks, Kalmyks) and in Inner Asia as Oirats, a general term for Derbets, Torghuts, Khoshuts, Baits, Dzakhachins, and Minggats, all closely related linguistically and ethnically. In the 1620s a considerable number of them, mostly the Torghuts, migrated to the lower Volga region of Russia. Until the mid-eighteenth century the Kalmuk khanate enjoyed virtual independence from the Russian empire. In 1771 about three-fourths of the Kalmuks, approximately 169,000, fled Russia and reached Dzungaria after suffering great losses. They became Chinese subjects, while those who had remained were integrated into Great Russia.

Until the turn of this century, the Kalmuks in the Astrakhan and Stavropol provinces and the Don Cossacks region of Russia led a predominantly nomadic way of life. Their principal occupation was horse and cattle breeding and agriculture. In the Civil War period some Kalmuks sided with the Bolsheviks, while others supported the anti-Bolshevik forces. The latter fled Russia in 1920 and settled in France, Yugoslavia, Bulgaria, and Czechoslovakia.

The Kalmuks in Russia gained the status of an autonomous region in 1920, and in 1935 their area became a republic. At the end of 1943 the entire Kalmuk population was deported to Siberia because of its alleged collaboration with the Germans. In 1957 they were allowed to return home and their autonomy was restored.

At present, there are about 1,000 Kalmuks in the USA who immigrated in 1951 and 1952, as well as between 750 and 800 in various European countries and 146,631 in the USSR (122,167 in the Kalmuk Autonomous Republic) as of January 1979. As Tibetan Buddhists and Mongolian-speaking people they occupy a unique position in the West.

[*See also* Dzungaria *and* Oirats.]

Paula G. Rubel, *The Kalmyk Mongols: A Study in Continuity and Change* (1967). René Grousset, *The Empire of the Steppes: A History of Central Asia,* translated by Naomi Walford (1970), pp. 502–542; notes, pp. 628–632.                        ARASH BORMANSHINOV

**KAMAKURA PERIOD** (1185–1333), an era in Japanese history that takes its name from the garrison town of Kamakura on Segami Bay in central Honshu, not far from modern Tokyo. Kamakura was the seat of the warrior government known as the Kamakura *bakufu,* which dominated the political life of Japan during the period. The Kamakura *bakufu* was the first in a series of warrior regimes that governed Japan until the mid-nineteenth century. Thus, the Kamakura period is generally viewed as the formative phase in the development of warrior government in Japan. It is also seen as the early phase of what is frequently described as a medieval society *(chūsei)* in Japan.

*Political History.* The Kamakura period saw a relative decline in the power and influence of the imperial court and religious institutions in Kyoto

and a countervailing growth in the influence of the Kamakura *bakufu* and its provincial vassal warriors. The period also witnessed a loosening of the system of private estates, or *shōen,* that had sustained the court nobility. Related to this were improvements in agriculture and the beginnings of commercial development, market activity, and the use of money. Culturally, the period is characterized by the emergence of an incipient warrior ethic, *dōri,* and the blending of courtly and martial styles; creative new developments in art, literature, and thought; a powerful surge of popular reform in Buddhism; and the active introduction of the culture of Song-dynasty China by Zen monks. In the late thirteenth century the country was threatened by several attempted Mongol invasions. Although frustrated by Japanese defenders and bad weather, these invasions created strains in warrior society that contributed to the eventual destruction of the Kamakura *bakufu* in 1333.

The Kamakura *bakufu* was established by Minamoto Yoritomo (1147–1199). Yoritomo, the son of Minamoto Yoshitomo, (1123–1160), was exiled to Izu in eastern Japan by Taira Kiyomori after the failure of an uprising in which his father took up arms against the Taira. With the destruction of Yoshitomo and other Minamoto leaders and the exile of Yoritomo, Kiyomori consolidated his power over the imperial court. His ambition was to establish an enduring Taira family dynasty and to rule Japan in the name of the emperor through the organs of court government, just as the Fujiwara had done for centuries. As Yoritomo grew to manhood he built up his power in the east through a marriage alliance with the Hōjō clan, gathered Minamoto and other eastern warriors to his cause, and determined to avenge the death of his father by overthrowing the Taira. While Yoritomo directed the campaign from the east, Minamoto Yoshinaka (1154–1184) and Yoritomo's younger brother, the brilliant general Yoshitsune (1159–1189), drove the Taira from Kyoto to their eventual destruction at Dan no Ura in 1185. [*See* Dan no Ura.]

While his generals were pressing the Taira in the west, Yoritomo was consolidating his warrior government in the east. In 1180 he established a warrior council, the *samurai dokoro,* to control his own direct vassals, the *gokenin.* In 1184 he set up two more councils, the *kumonjo* and *monchūjo.* The former was an administrative council headed by Oe Hiromoto (1147–1213), a lower ranking aristocrat-administrator brought from Kyoto especially to advise Yoritomo. The latter, also headed by a Kyoto noble, Miyoshi Yasunobu, handled the investigation of appeals and disputes brought by vassals. These councils, which began on the model of the chancelleries of the court and noble families, provided the administrative structure for warrior rule as victories over the Taira were achieved and political power and the loyalties of warriors flowed increasingly in the direction of Kamakura.

With the Taira defeated, Yoritomo set about destroying other possible rivals to his power and extending his authority into provinces throughout Japan. Immediately following the defeat of the Taira in 1185, Yoritomo appointed his lieutenant Amano Tōkage supervisor of Kyushu vassals. In the same year, using as his justification the need to maintain local order and to secure assistance in arresting his brother Yoshitsune, whom he branded a traitor, Yoritomo secured an edict from the imperial court allowing him to appoint provincial constables, *shugo,* and estate stewards, *jitō.* Yoshitsune sought the protection of the northern Fujiwara. This provided Yoritomo with a pretext to invade northeastern Japan in 1189 and eliminate his brother and Fujiwara warrior power in one initiative. Kasai Yoshishige, who led Yoritomo's victorious forces in the campaign against the Fujiwara, was appointed commander of all vassals in the northeast. Thus, by 1190 Yoritomo had acquired unchallenged military control over the country. In 1192 Yoritomo secured from the court his appointment as *sei-i taishōgun.* This shogunal title provided the capstone and final legitimation for his *bakufu.*

The right to appoint *shugo* and *jitō* was an institutional innovation that gave Yoritomo considerable authority and had far-reaching implications. *Shugo* were appointed province by province. They were powerful vassals designated by Yoritomo to supervise military affairs within their provinces. Their basic duties were threefold. Serving as the liaison between the *bakufu* and provincial society, they organized the military service of the provincial vassals, maintained local order, and arrested rebels. The origins of *jitō* have been traced to the Heian period. From 1185, when Yoritomo's right to appoint his vassals as supervisors of the public domain and of the provincial estates of the court nobility was recognized, their numbers increased and their ties with Kamakura were strengthened. In return for a portion of the tax income of the land, *jitō* policed the estates, oversaw tax collection, and helped maintain local order. Not surprisingly, they often sought to enhance their personal power at the expense of the absentee proprietor of the holding.

In this period the local warrior vassals of the shogun were known as *gokenin,* or "honorary housemen." The honorific *go* indicated a close personal relationship with the shogun. A requirement for *gokenin* status was that the vassal's family have held family domains, *honryō,* for at least three generations and that he be granted a document from the shogun confirming these holdings. Their duties included military service in war and guard duty in Kamakura and Kyoto in peacetime. Orders from the *bakufu* were conveyed to *gokenin* through the *shugo.* The *gokenin* provided the local base of the pyramid of political power and vassal loyalties upon which the authority of Yoritomo and the *bakufu* depended.

The economic base of the Kamakura *bakufu* was control over the eastern provinces, Kantō *bunkoku,* coupled with tax income from direct shogunal domain, Kantō *goryō.* Much of this latter was from holdings in estates confiscated from the defeated Taira and awarded as spoils to Yoritomo. Taken together, these provided the *bakufu* with firm control over the heartland of eastern Japan and a network of landed interests throughout the country.

Yoritomo had dreams of establishing a Minamoto warrior dynasty. Those dreams were frustrated within a few years of his death. He was succeeded by his young and ineffectual sons Yoriie (1182–1204) and Sanetomo (1192–1219), both of whom were appointed shogun but were assassinated in office. With their untimely deaths the Minamoto shogunal line ended. Power within the *bakufu* was steadily assumed by the Hōjō, a leading vassal family of Yoritomo. When Yoritomo had been sent in exile to the Kantō as a child he had been placed under the guardianship of Hōjō Tokimasa (1138–1215). He later married Tokimasa's daughter Masako. After the death of Yoritomo, Masako helped her father and brother, Yoshitoki, assume greater power within the *bakufu.* Tokimasa had a hand in the assasination of Yoriie. With the death of Yoriie and Sanetomo and the elimination of other powerful rivals like the warrior families Hiki and Wada, the Hōjō were able to assume a dominant position in the *bakufu.* It became, in effect, a Hōjō *bakufu* to a degree that it had never been a Minamoto *bakufu.* The Hōjō controlled the *bakufu* until its demise in 1333. They chose to rule, however, not as shoguns but as regents *(shikken)* to shoguns. With the Minamoto line extinct, they brought Fujiwara boys or imperial princes from Kyoto to serve as puppet shoguns. Hōjō rule has been described as conciliar. Certainly vassal interests were voiced in such executive

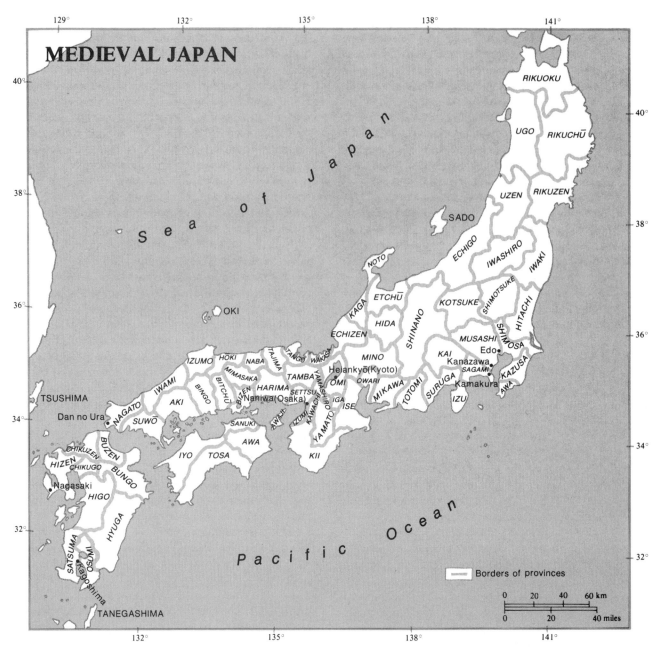

MEDIEVAL JAPAN

warrior councils as the *hyōjōshū*. On the whole, however, the Hōjō dominated these councils and packed them with closely related vassals and loyal officials. Hōjō family control over the *bakufu* became much more pronounced after Tokiyori's destruction of the rival Miura clan in 1247.

Yoritomo's victory did not eliminate the imperial court or deprive it of all its authority. In fact, Yoritomo's authority as shogun and the Hōjō regency were sanctioned by the court. At the same time, while Yoritomo claimed to be an agent of the court, his establishment of a separate regime in Kamakura was regarded by Kyoto as a usurpation of power.

Members of the imperial family and court nobles did not easily relinquish hopes of recovering their former authority. In 1221 the senior cloistered emperor Go-Toba (1180–1239) issued an edict calling for the overthrow of the Kamakura *bakufu* and the arrest of Hōjō Yoshitoki. He refused to send an "imperial" shogun to Kamakura and demanded that several *jitō* appointments be rescinded. Go-Toba anticipated division within the *bakufu* and the loss of support of *gokenin* for the *bakufu*. Some western warriors and monk-soldiers from the powerful monasteries rallied to the court but there was only a feeble challenge to the *bakufu*. Most *gokenin* saw their self-interest in supporting the Hōjō, and the campaign ended with a decisive *bakufu* victory. The Hōjō promptly exiled three cloistered emperors, executed nobles who were alleged to have been ringleaders, and established preeminent power vis-à-vis the court. After the uprising, the Hōjō intervened in the imperial succession and Hōjō Yasutoki and Tokifusa were stationed at Rokuhara in Kyoto to supervise the court and maintain order in the capital. From this time on, the office of Rokuhara *tandai* (Kamakura deputies) was monopolized by the Hōjō family. It became a supervisory authority for western Japan.

The *bakufu* also confiscated three hundred domain-holdings from supporters of the court and warded them to *gokenin* as prizes or appointed *jitō* to oversee them. The *bakufu* extended its authority considerably by the appointment of these new *jitō*. At the same time, the stage was set for increased friction between *jitō* and *shōen* proprietors, and disputes over holdings proliferated. The increasing flood of litigation was handled in *bakufu* courts, which acquired a reputation for providing fair and speedy justice. In addition to settling land disputes the Hōjō gave considerable attention to clarifying the laws and practices, or *dōri*, peculiar to warrior society. Many of these were codified in the *Goseibai shikimoku*, compiled in 1232. This provided a precedent for succeeding warrior legal codes and gave coherence to the warrior order in medieval society.

During the thirteenth century the Mongols were extending their conquests on the continent. Having conquered Song China and the Korean kingdoms, Kublai, the Mongol khan, looked for an opportunity to bring Japan into submission. When diplomatic overtures were rejected by Hōjō Tokimune, a great invasion involving some thirty thousand Mongol warriors and Korean seamen was launched in the tenth month of 1274. Some Mongols landed on the beaches of northern Kyushu, and Japanese warriors had trouble holding the invaders at bay. Fortunately for the Japanese, a storm intervened, wrecking the Mongol armada. A second invasion was dispatched in 1281. Mongol fleets that had attacked the islands of Tsushima and Oki entered Hakata Bay in the sixth month. They were again dispersed by storms. These storms were known as "divine winds," *kamikaze*. Shrines and temples claimed credit for calling them up through their prayers for the protection of the country. The intervention of nature at this critical juncture contributed to a belief, expressed then and later in times of crisis, that Japan was a divinely protected land, *shinkoku*.

Although the invasions failed and the Mongols took no territory, the impact on *bakufu* politics of the Mongol incursions was considerable. Tokimune and his *bakufu* advisers, and especially Kyushu warriors, were obliged to bear the costs of a permanent defense system. Kyushu *gokenin* were forbidden to come to Kamakura or Kyoto to make appeals for spoils. An appeals board was set up in Kyushu. This *chinzei tandai*, as it was known, incorporated military command in Kyushu with judicial functions. At the same time, in the name of strengthening policing powers in Kyushu, the *bakufu* strengthened its exclusive authority in the region and monopolized Kyushu and western shugoships through the appointment of Hōjō administrators. The burdens of defense and lack of war spoils, combined with samurai indebtedness and fragmentation of main and branch families, created severe strains in warrior society. The exclusion of most vassals from the inner circles of power around the regent led to growing disaffection with Hōjō authority, increasingly seen as arbitrary and despotic. When a challenge to that authority was mounted by emperor Go-Daigo in the 1320s the Hōjō were unable to hold the allegiance of some of their most powerful vassals. In 1333 they were overthrown by an alliance of Go-Daigo, members of the court, Buddhist clergy, and such powerful eastern warrior houses as the Ashikaga and Nitta.

***Economy, Society, Culture.*** The growing influence of warriors in society was reflected by their intrusion into the estates, *shōen*, that had hitherto been the exclusive preserve of the court nobility. *Jitō*, who had been granted legal rights within *shōen* by the *bakufu*, sought to extend their influence within the holding. In some instances they withheld taxes from the proprietor and forced concessions, *wayo*, or actual division of the estate, *shitaji chūbun*. *Shugo* with supervisory rights in the provinces also sought to assert their influence over local *shōen*. It has been suggested that the institutional loosening of the *shōen* that was taking place in this period contributed to a freeing of some farmers' energies for market production. More extensive use of double cropping and other small improvements in agricultural technology may also have contributed to the creation of an agricultural surplus. Certainly, local markets held on a regular basis were becoming more common. While rents were still largely paid in rice or other produce, copper cash was being imported from China by the end of the thirteenth century and was in use along the Pacific coast of Honshu and around Kamakura and Kyoto. Money-lending was practiced, and many warriors became so indebted that the *bakufu* felt obliged to issue a debt moratorium edict, a *tokusei,* for Kantō *gokenin* in 1297. While rural life in some areas was becoming more prosperous and diversified, it was also marked by sporadic violence and unrest. In many parts of the country bands of warriors and farmers known as *akutō,* literally, "evil (or powerful) bands," controlled local life and resisted the authority of the Kamakura *bakufu.*

The cultural life of the Kamakura period blended courtly, warrior, and popular elements. It was marked by the continued cultural predominance of the court and by the creation of a distinct warrior cultural style that expressed warrior values of *dōri* or *musha no narai,* the customs of the warriors, while drawing heavily on the learning and culture of the court nobility. Buddhist monks and monasteries, especially Zen monasteries, were active contributors to the culture and, from the Kamakura period, there was popular participation in religion and culture. The age witnessed a popular upsurge of Buddhist devotion, and such popular musical and dancing entertainments as *dengaku, sarugaku,* and *taue uta* flourished in the countryside.

Although the imperial court was being eclipsed politically during the thirteenth century, courtiers maintained their literary and cultural leadership. The composition of Japanese poetry, *waka,* enjoyed renewed vitality and the age saw the compilation of a number of anthologies, of which the most influential was the *Shin kokin waka shū* (1205), containing the poetry of cloistered emperor Go-Toba and his circle. Courtiers also recited, compiled, and read military tales, *gunkimono.* Of these the finest was the *Tale of the Heike (Heike monogatari),* which expressed the pathos of the rise and destruction of the Taira family at the hands of the Minamoto. History and belles lettres were also courtly avocations. The aristocratic monk Jien (1155–1225) offered a Buddhist view of historical change in his *Gukanshō* while arguing in favor of a union of court and *bakufu.* Kamo no Chōmei (1153–1215), a poet and literary associate of Go-Toba, established a hermitage outside the capital and in his *Hōjōki* gave expression to the ideal of the recluse. In addition to its leadership in literary and scholarly activities, the court continued to set styles in art, music, architecture, dress, and manners.

Warrior culture was a blend of martial and literary elements, *bu* and *bun.* Yoritomo and his successors all exhorted their warriors to maintain martial skills and live frugal, outdoor lives. Virtues of loyalty, bravery, family honor, and willingness to give or take one's life for one's honor or one's lord were stressed as the essence of the ideal of the warriors. At the same time, Yoritomo and his successors who headed the *bakufu* were all, to some degree, forced to deal with the court and thus remained subject to its influence. The third Minamoto shogun, Sanetomo, was criticized within the *bakufu* for his excessive devotion to the composition of *waka* and the styles of the imperial court, but there were many warriors who enjoyed such literary pursuits and a few who took brides from Kyoto. The use of lower ranking courtiers as *bakufu* officials and the bringing of Fujiwara infants and imperial princes to Kamakura as shoguns also brought infusions of court culture to Kamakura. With time, the Hōjō regents and their leading retainers became practitioners and sponsors of scholarship and the arts. In painting, portraiture, and sculpture there was in the Kamakura period what Japanese scholars frequently refer to as a "realistic tendency." The vigorous, muscular sculpture of Unkei and Kaikei in particular is said to have been expressive of the directness of the warrior spirit of the age.

***Religious Life.*** Warriors and courtiers patronized Buddhism. Through the newly imported Zen school, especially the Rinzai *gozan* monasteries in Kyoto and Kamakura, they were put in direct contact with the learning and cultural styles of China in poetry, painting, and architecture. Zen, however, was not the only new development in Buddhism in the Kamakura period. One of the most vigorous and creative movements was the articulation and spread of what has been called the "new Buddhism" of the Kamakura age. Looking for surer paths to salvation in an age of spiritual deterioration *(mappō)* and disheartened by the laxity and formalization of traditional monastic Buddhism, reformers broke with older schools such as Tendai to establish new and popular teachings. The most powerful popular current was undoubtedly the Pure Land movement, based on faith in the compassion of the Buddha Amida. Hōnen, who broke with Tendai in advocating the supreme efficacy of the invocation of Amida's name (the *nembutsu),* Shinran, his radical disciple, and the wandering mendicant Ippen all stressed the supreme importance of devotion to Amida and of reliance on the *nembutsu* as a means of triggering Amida's vow to save sentient beings. They found followers at all social levels and throughout the country and originated respectively the Pure Land (Jōdo), True Pure land (Jōdo Shin), and Timely (Ji), schools of Japanese Buddhism. Shinran in particular rejected the monastic ideal and

FIGURE 1. *Great Amida Buddha of Kamakura*. The Great Buddha of the Kōtokuin, a symbol of the Kamakura shogunate. Bronze, completed in 1253. Height 11.38 m.

offered a path to salvation for the lowliest of men and women. The Kamakura period also witnessed a revival of devotion to the *Lotus Sutra*. This was carried furthest by Nichiren, who argued that the teaching of the *Lotus Sutra* offered all that the country needed for spiritual salvation and protection and that other teachings should be suppressed. The vitality and success of the newer schools of Buddhism did not go unnoticed by monks of the older schools. Their initial reaction was to try to have advocates exiled and the teaching proscribed. When that failed to quell the upsurge, the followers of the new teachings were excluded from the older schools and forced to establish their independence. At the same time, the vitality of the popular movement stimulated a surge of reform within the older Buddhist schools. With the revival of the Ritsu, or Vinaya, school there was renewed emphasis on the maintenance of monastic discipline.

While it would, of course, be misleading to distinguish the Kamakura period too sharply from the Heian and Muromachi ages that preceded and followed it, it should be clear from the above discussion that the age had certain clearcut characteristics that allow us to think of it, without exaggeration, as a new phase in the development of Japanese society and culture. Although the Kamakura *bakufu* was eventually overthrown, basic institutions and laws of warrior government had been firmly established and tested during the thirteenth century. The model of an emperor *(tennō)* acting as sovereign with a shogun serving as military hegemon and effective ruler of the country would recur in succeeding centuries. In the process of consolidation of warrior rule, political and economic influence of the imperial court waned. The change was not sudden, but had clearly gone far by the end of the thirteenth century. Go-Daigo's attack on the *bakufu*, culminating in the Kemmu Restoration of 1333 to 1336, was intended to reverse the dilution of imperial authority, but the collapse of the short-lived restoration set the process in motion again. Socially, the advent of warrior power brought changes in the balance of local power in the provinces and in *shōen*, where the power of the court nobility and their agents was undercut or replaced by that of *shugo, jitō*, or *akutō*. The changes in *shōen* management were part of a larger set of economic developments in which market activity and the use of money began to play a more significant role in medieval commerce. The arrival of warriors on the center stage of history was also reflected in art, literature, and architecture. In religion, too, even if the new schools of Buddhism derived much of their doctrine and practice from older Buddhism, they aroused a new and popular fervor as they carried their message to newly emerging groups in society: warriors and farmers in the provinces. In the performing arts, it is in the Kamakura period that we see the beginnings of popular participation. Here, too, the patronage of warriors was evident.

[*See also* Minamoto; Taira no Kiyomori; Bakufu; Shōen; Mongol Empire: Mongol Invasions of Japan; Kemmu Restoration; Heian Period; *and* Muromachi Period.]

Masaharu Anesaki, *Nichiren, the Buddhist Prophet* (1916). Alfred Bloom, *Shinran's Gospel of Pure Grace* (1965). Martin Collcutt, *Five Mountains: The Rinzai Zen Monastic Institution in Medieval Japan* (1982). Heinrich Dumoulin, *A History of Zen Buddhism* (1965). Jeffrey P. Mass, *Warrior Government in Early Medieval Japan* (1974) and *Court and Bakufu in Japan* (1982). Robert Treat Paine and Alexander Soper, *The Art and Architecture of Japan* (3d ed., 1981).    MARTIN COLLCUTT

**KAMA SUTRA,** by Vatsyayana, a text on erotics and social conduct of uncertain date but generally placed in the early Gupta period (i.e., the fifth century CE). Modeled on Kautilya's *Arthashastra,* it proposes *kama* (sexual love) as an alternative to *artha* (economics, statecraft) and *dharma* (spiritual discipline) as a valid end for life. In addition to classifying sexual techniques, it describes the lifestyle of the *nagaraka,* or gentleman-about-town, with aphorisms on standards of elegance and refinement, festivals, courtship, marriage ceremonies, and love potions.

Vatsyayana, *The Kama Sutra: The Classic Hindu Treatise on Love and Social Conduct,* translated by Richard F. Burton (1962).                    DAVID RUBIN

**KAMBUJA,** Sanskrit name for the Khmer or Cambodian people, by which they designated themselves in inscriptions from the Zhenla period (seventh and eighth centuries CE) onward. Literally "born of the race of Kambu," the term refers to the origin myth according to which the Cambodian "solar" dynasty, from which rulers traced their origins, began from the union of the holy sage Kambu Svayambhuva with the nymph Mera, who had been sent by the god Shiva. A semilegendary line of kings leads to the rulers of Sresthapura in what is now Laos. According to a myth of Indian origin, the kingdom of the Kambujas was created, and the name adopted, by the founder Kaundinya, who married an indigenous *nagi* spirit.

[*See also* Cambodia; Khmer; Kampuchea; *and* Zhenla.]

Lawrence P. Briggs, *The Ancient Khmer Empire* (1951). G. Coedès, *The Indianized States of Southeast Asia,* translated by Susan B. Cowing (1968).    IAN W. MABBETT

**KAMBUN,** an abbreviation of the Japanese phrase *kandai no bunshō,* which literally means "writings of the Han dynasty." In early Japan the term was used to refer to any text written in Chinese characters, but later it came to denote as well many styles of Japanese incorporating Chinese word order and *kanji* (Sino-Japanese characters). *Kambun's* function in Japan was analogous to that of Latin in postmedieval Europe: originally the vehicle of transmission for religious, political, philosophical, and literary texts, it gradually became the language of those disciplines, providing a written language for scholarly and offical communication. Many Chinese *kambun* texts, including the Confucian analects and

Buddhist sutras, found their way to Japan. Native Japanese *kambun* differed from traditional Chinese, due to both a misuse of Chinese and the need to express certain concepts in a starkly contrasting Japanese grammar. "Decoding" *kambun* took two forms: the first, predominant until the tenth century, was a literal reading of the document in Chinese. The second, called *kundoku,* involved using rules of inversion to read the document in an order that translated the Chinese into semi-Japanese; these rules became codified around the end of the sixteenth century and included the addition of small Japanese particles, inflections, and markers as reading clues. The combined effect made reading *kambun* much like doing an arithmetic calculation: certain markers took priority over others, producing a summary of the Chinese that sounded like Japanese. Domestically produced *kambun* exist from about the fifth century; early documents include the writings of the sovereign Shōtoki Taishi, the *Nihon shoki,* and *kambun* poetry. Confucian texts were studied in the eighth century, and a strong connection between *kambun* and Confucianism continued, as seen in the Neo-Confucian writings of the Edo (Tokugawa) period. Public notices, at first written in pure Chinese, began to include Japanese vocabulary and particles, resulting in a *kambun*-style documentation from around the Kamakura period called *tokantai. Kambun* continued to be the language of scholarly texts until early into the twentieth century.

[*See also* Nihon Shoki.]

E. Sidney Crawcour, *An Introduction to Kambun* 1962). "Kanbun," in *The Encyclopedia of Japan* (1983). Roy Andrew Miller, *The Japanese Language.* (1967).

J. SCOTT MILLER

**KAMO NO MABUCHI** (1697–1769), Japanese poet and religious thinker, a leading member of the Kokugaku ("national learning") school, a Shinto revivalist movement. Born the son of a Shinto priest in what is now Shizuoka Prefecture, Kamo no Mabuchi began his studies in 1733 under Kada no Azumamarō and by 1746 had distinguished himself enough to be employed by the Tayasu collateral branch of the Tokugawa shogunal family.

Mabuchi had great esteem for the ancient anthology of poems the *Man'yōshū,* compiled in the eighth century. He believed that *Man'yōshū* poems embodied the indigenous, pure spirit of the ancient Japanese before they had come into heavy contact with corrupting alien influences. But unlike other prominent Kokugaku scholars, notably his disciple Motoori Norinaga, Mabuchi considered that ancient Japanese spirit to be one in which heartfelt, earthy emotions spontaneously erupted into verse, with little regard for restrictive poetic conventions or notions of elegant refinement. Moreover, Mabuchi believed that the restoration of antiquity, when men's acts supposedly conformed authentically to such pristine emotional expressionism, would reform society and politics. These views constituted an ahistorical romanticism ungrounded in contemporary social realities.

[*See also* Kokugaku *and* Motoori Norinaga.]

BOB TADASHI WAKABAYASHI

**KAMPAKU**, regent for a reigning Japanese emperor, a post developed in the ninth century as the emperor-centered bureaucratic order began to be modified in the interests of efficiency and the Fujiwara lineage. The title *sesshō* had already been developed to denote a regency for an immature sovereign. In 887 Fujiwara no Mototsune, who had already served as *sesshō*, was the first to be appointed *kampaku*, in effect continuing the leading role he had held earlier. The post became hereditary in the Fujiwara lineage. As the imperial court lost ground in the Kamakura period, titles and functions continued, albeit in attenuated form, and the *kampaku* title became available to the Fujiwara branch families *(gosekke)* that headed the hierarachy of aristocratic nobles. In the late sixteenth century the unifier Toyotomi Hideyoshi used the title *kampaku* and also transferred it to his adopted successor Hidetsugu, who held the title until he was replaced as heir by Hideyori in 1595. The office was abolished at the time of the Meiji Restoration.

MARIUS B. JANSEN

**KAMPUCHEA**, Khmer-language pronunciation of the Sanskrit place-name Kambuja, usually transliterated into English as "Cambodia." The term *Kampuchea* was first used in the ninth century CE, ostensibly to commemorate a North Indian tribe but perhaps also because the word was relatively close to the Cambodian people's name for themselves, the Khmer. Under the French protectorate (1863–1954) Cambodia was known as Cambodge, but in a brief period of independence in 1945, local officials insisted that the term appear in European languages as Kampuchea. A similar rejection of "imperialist" transliteration was made by Pol Pot's Democratic

Kampuchea (1975–1979) and the People's Republic of Kampuchea (from 1979).    DAVID P. CHANDLER

**KAMPUCHEA, DEMOCRATIC,** the regime that governed Cambodia between 1975 and 1979; also the name chosen by the Cambodian coalition government in exile in 1981.

Democratic Kampuchea (DK) came to power following a ruinous civil war and sought to transform Cambodian society along lines that were allegedly Marxist-Leninist in inspiration but that in fact sprang largely from Maoist ideas of revolution, shared by a small group of people in the politburo of the Communist Party of Kampuchea (CPK) under the leadership of Pol Pot. Once in power this group embarked on an extremely radical program, evacuating cities; closing schools, factories, and shops; abolishing currency and postage; and herding most of the population onto hastily organized collective farms. Huge irrigation schemes were undertaken, but many failed because of insufficient expertise. People with skills were often considered "class enemies" and were assassinated in large numbers; hundreds of thousands of others died of malnutrition and overwork.

In 1976 the regime took the name of Democratic Kampuchea and promulgated a constitution, but the CPK admitted its existence only in 1977, under pressure to do so from the Chinese. By that time, war had broken out along the border with Vietnam. The CPK began to purge itself of members suspected of being pro-Vietnamese; several of these had served on the CPK Central Committee. In early 1979 Vietnamese forces, accompanied by several thousand Cambodian sympathizers, invaded Cambodia and swept Democratic Kampuchea from power. However, they failed to kill or capture what remained of the leadership, and these men, including Pol Pot, continued to direct guerrilla forces against the new, pro-Vietnamese regime. Because its alliance with China ensured support from a wide range of anti-Soviet nations, Democratic Kampuchea retained its seat at the United Nations for many years after it had been removed from power.

[*See also* Cambodia; Communism: Communism in Southeast Asia; Kampuchea, People's Republic of; *and* Pol Pot.]

David P. Chandler and Ben Kiernan, eds., *Revolution and its Aftermath in Kampuchea: Eight Essays* (1983). Michael Vickery, *Cambodia 1975–1982* (1984).

DAVID P. CHANDLER

**KAMPUCHEA, PEOPLE'S REPUBLIC OF,** the pro-Vietnamese regime that has governed Cambodia since January 1979, following the Vietnamese defeat of Pol Pot's Democratic Kampuchea. The People's Republic of Kampuchea (PRK) operates under a constitution promulgated in 1981, itself modeled closely on the constitution of Vietnam. As in most communist countries, the National Assembly, elected in 1982, is used primarily to ratify decisions made by Party leaders. The president of the PRK since its foundation has been Heng Samrin; since the end of 1981, Samrin has also served as secretary-general of the Kampuchean Revolutionary People's Party (KPRP), which traces its roots to the early 1950s, when the anti-French struggle in Cambodia was directed to a large extent by the Vietnamese.

Because of the almost universal horror in Cambodia for the Pol Pot era, the PRK, despite its dependence on a foreign power, was able to draw on considerable popular support in its first few years in office. Many of its policies, which contrast sharply with those in effect under Pol Pot, have also been popular. These include the revival of secondary and tertiary education, the repopulation of urban centers, and tolerance for trade. At the same time, its leaders are allowed very little room for political maneuver by the Vietnamese, and it is fair to describe the PRK as a satellite of Vietnam.

[*See also* Cambodia *and* Kampuchea, Democratic.]

Michael Vickery, *Cambodia 1975–1982* (1984).

DAVID P. CHANDLER

**KANAGAWA TREATY,** first American treaty with Japan, signed in 1854. Commodore Matthew C. Perry's expedition to Japan had two objectives; one was to open Japanese ports to American ships trading with China or engaged in whale fishing, the other was to establish trade relations with Japan. Both challenged the Japanese policy of national seclusion (*sakoku*).

The American aims were stated in letters that Perry presented at Uraga in July 1853. Even though the Tokugawa *bakufu* had received advance notice of the expedition, Perry's appearance precipitated a crisis in Edo. There was wide agreement among Japanese that the American squadron represented a threat that Japan lacked the means to counter. Most officials and feudal lords, led by Abe Masahiro, head of the Tokugawa council, concluded that Japan could only hope to minimize concessions, but two powerful minorities disagreed. Tokugawa Nariaki

and his allies insisted that resistance, by force if necessary, was the only way to prevent foreign domination of Japan. Others, notably Ii Naosuke, argued that Japan must enter actively into relations with the West in order to acquire the wealth and military science that would make defense possible.

The majority view prevailed. When Perry returned in February 1854, the *bakufu's* negotiators concentrated their efforts on ensuring that the treaty made no clear provisions for trade. In this they succeeded, helped by Perry's own attitude, which gave priority to the needs of shipping. On other major points they accepted Perry's demands. The Treaty of Kanagawa, signed on 31 March 1854, promised good treatment for shipwrecked seamen, so redressing a longstanding grievance, and opened the ports of Shimoda and Hakodate as ports of supply. From the *bakufu's* viewpoint, both ports were suitably remote from the shogun's capital.

The treaty, soon followed by similar agreements with Britain and Russia, marked the first breach in Japan's seclusion policy. Two major unresolved issues were the question of trade, later taken up by Townsend Harris as American consul, and Japanese disputes over foreign policy, which took many years to resolve.

[*See also* Perry, Matthew C.; Harris, Townsend; Seclusion; *and* Shimoda.]

W. G. Beasley, ed., *Select Documents on Japanese Foreign Policy, 1853–1868* (1955). Payson J. Treat, *Diplomatic Relations between the United States and Japan, 1853–1895*, 2 vols. (1932; reprint, 1963).

W. G. BEASLEY

**KANAUJ.** *See* Kanyakubja.

**KANAZAWA,** the capital of Ishikawa Prefecture, Japan, on the coast of the Sea of Japan. Kanazawa first emerged in the medieval period as a trading settlement. In 1547 it became the headquarters (*jinai-machi*) of the Honganji sect, organizers of the great *Kaga ikkō-ikki*, a religiously based uprising. Some three decades later, in 1583, the daimyo Maeda Toshiie marched into Kanazawa and made it his castle town.

Toshiie and his successors implemented a series of policies that eventually made Kanazawa the largest city in Japan after the three great metropolises of Edo, Osaka, and Kyoto. Chief among these was the requirement that all samurai families who served the Maeda had to live in the city, which immediately gave Kanazawa a base population of nearly 50,000 persons. This touched off a second great migration, this time among merchants, artisans, and laborers, who moved into Kanazawa to supply the needs of the samurai families. According to a 1666 census, a total of 59,101 merchant and artisan families lived in the city, and Kanazawa's total population, including samurai and religious, surpassed 123,000 persons.

As was characteristic of castle towns, Kanazawa was designed and constructed to meet the military needs of the daimyo. To these ends, the Maeda erected an imposing castle, dug moats and canals, and decreed that each of the city's major social classes, as well as Buddhist temples, should be situated in segregated residential areas. In many ways, however, this urban plan remained more of an ideal goal than an achieved reality, for the community's population tended to ignore the residential divisions, especially after the middle of the seventeenth century. Politically, all major policy decisions and laws were decided by the daimyo and a small inner group of advisers and were enforced by several levels of bureaucrats including both samurai and commoners, a division of responsibility common to most castle towns.

Kanazawa prospered during the seventeenth and eighteenth centuries. It constituted a major consumption center and also became the point of manufacture for most of its residents' daily needs. After the daimyo extended patronage to a group of famous craftsmen, Kanazawa became especially renowned for the production of certain fine arts, such as Kutani and Ohi pottery, gold foil design, lacquer ware, and gold and silver inlay.

The city suffered a decline in the decades following the Meiji Restoration (1868) as large numbers of samurai left to take up new occupations in Tokyo and Osaka. By World War I, however, the city had rebounded; it became the capital of Ishikawa Prefecture, the home of a thriving textile industry, and the location of several institutions of higher learning. Today, the city continues to thrive as the leading economic, political, artistic, and educational center of the Hokuriku region, and in 1975 it had a population of 399,949 persons.

James L. McClain, *Kanazawa: A Seventeenth-Century Japanese Castle Town* (1982). Tanaka Yoshio, *Jōkamachi Kanazawa* (1966).          JAMES L. MCCLAIN

KANCHIPURAM (Conjeeveram), city in the Palar valley of Tamil Nadu, South India, capital of the Pallava dynasty (c. 300?–888 CE) and at one time a flourishing center of Buddhism and Jainism. The eighth-century Kailasanatha Temple is one of the most important of the many temples in the city. Kanchipuram was, and still is, an important center for textile weaving.

[*See also* Tamil Nadu.]

*Encyclopaedia of Indian Temple Architecture*, edited by M. W. Meister (1983), vol. 1, parts 1 and 2. T. V. Mahalingam, *Kancipuram in Early South Indian History* (1969).          MEERA ABRAHAM

KANDY, city in the central highlands of Sri Lanka, founded probably in the beginning of the fourteenth century. Its historical importance began in 1472/1473, when it became the capital of a Sinhalese kingdom in the highlands founded by Vikramabahu, a rebel general of the kingdom of Kotte. It retained its independence in its strategic isolation while major political changes were taking place in the western lowlands. In the second half of the sixteenth century, with the Portuguese strengthening their hold on the kingdom of Kotte, Kandy was drawn into power politics.

In the beginning of the seventeenth century Kandy emerged from the Portuguese wars as the only seat of independent Sinhalese political power on the island. Kandy retained this status until the British assaulted and conquered the town in 1815. During the period between 1597 and 1815, when three European powers ruled over the lowlands successively, Kandy rose in prestige as the sole seat of Sinhalese Buddhist political power, under a dynasty that arrogated to itself all of the attributes of Sinhalese royal legitimacy. Kandy was reconstructed as a royal capital, though not on the grand scale of the previous royal capitals, owing to the relative poverty of the kingdom and its inaccessibility.

The town was square in layout with streets running north-south and east-west, and it had two square enclosures. The smaller square contained temples and the king's palace. The Temple of the Tooth, the major Buddhist shrine, was attached to the palace and was the venue of an annual festival known as Esala Perahara. Two monasteries, Asgiriya and Malwatte, were established in Kandy and remain the most influential centers of Buddhism in Sri Lanka.

Under the British, when the island was divided into provinces for administrative purposes, Kandy became the capital of the Central Province. The growth of plantations in the Central Province gave Kandy some commercial importance as the chief urban center in the region. Road and railway links made the city accessible from the coast and increased its contact with other regions of the hill country. Educational institutions grew and after independence the national university was moved to a suburb of Kandy.

[*See also* Kotte *and* Sri Lanka.]

S. ARASARATNAM

KANGAKU (lit., "Han learning"), a Japanese term that refers not only to learning from the Chinese Han dynasty (206 BCE–220 CE) but all Chinese studies of the classics (other than poetry) down to the Qing dynasty (1644–1912); hence, generally, the study of Confucianism. In Japan, *kangaku* refers to the whole of Japanese scholarship on the Confucian tradition, from the pre-Nara through the Tokugawa periods (645–1868).

One can distinguish three periods in the development of *kangaku*: (1) The assimilation of Han and Tang ("Old School") scholarship at the Japanese court (seventh through twelfth century); (2) the gradual introduction of Song ("New") scholarship, that is, Neo-Confucianism, mainly in Zen Buddhist monasteries (thirteenth through sixteenth century); (3) the flourishing of various Neo-Confucian schools organized by commoners during the Tokugawa period (1600–1868).

Confucianism was introduced to Japan by Korean scholars, allegedly toward the end of the third century CE, and became institutionalized when Emperor Tenji (668–671) established a school that during the Nara period (710–794) became a university where Chinese learning developed into two branches: the study of the Chinese classics and that of Chinese history and literature. The latter grew in importance through scholars such as Sugawara no Michizane (845–903). Fujiwara Yorinaga (1120–1156) attempted in vain to reestablish the former to a place of prominence. Toward the end of the Heian period, (794–1185) specialized houses of hereditary scholars were competing with each other: in history, mainly Ōe and Sugawara; in the classics, Kiyohara and Nakahara.

Although the Kiyohara family remained important through the early seventeenth century, renewal in the study of the classics, through the introduction of Neo-Confucianism between 1200 and 1600, took place mainly in the monasteries. Zen monks returning from pilgrimage brought Neo-Confucian works from China. They introduced tenets of Neo-Confucian thought into their Zen teachings to demon-

strate either the general unity of the two doctrines or, point by point, Zen's superiority. They also attacked the anti-Buddhist polemics that Chinese Neo-Confucians had developed. "New" interpretations found their way into the Kiyohara tradition in the late fourteenth century. They did not, however, replace the "Old" readings. A similar development occured in the Ashikaga College, founded by the first Ashikaga shogun (1338–1358) and revived in 1432. The "Old School" disappeared only with the emergence of lay Neo-Confucian scholars in the early Tokugawa period.

The first generation of these scholars consisted of ex-monks who had learned Neo-Confucianism in the monastery (Fujiwara Seika, Hayashi Razan, Yamazaki Ansai). Soon, however, commoners (sometimes ex-samurai like Nakae Tōju or Yamaga Sokō) gathered students or established academies. Very slowly, the rulers followed suit. The *bakufu* funded the Hayashi school and the daimyo built *han* (domain) schools. By 1871, when the *han* were established, most domains had their own schools of Chinese learning. Arai Hakuseki (1657–1725) and Ogyū Sorai (1666–1728), shogunal advisers, were perhaps the most outstanding Japanese scholars of Chinese learning.

All varieties of Chinese (and Korean) studies of the classics developed during the Tokugawa period, including the Wang Yangming school (Ōyōmeigaku in Japanese). In addition, many scholars became critical of Neo-Confucianism and stressed either an eclectic approach (Amenomori Hōshū, Satō Issai) or a return to antiquity (Mencius for Itō Jinsai, the teachings of the sages for Sorai). The ascendancy of Jinsai's and Sorai's schools of Ancient Learning (Kogaku) was checked in 1790, when Matsudaira Sadanobu required all *bakufu* office holders to pass examinations at the newly established Bakufu College (formerly the Hayashi school) on a narrowly defined Neo-Confucian curriculum, constructed by scholars of Ansai's Kimon school. During the last decades of the Tokugawa period the Mito school sought new inspiration in Chinese learning to stave off the growing political crisis that ultimately brought down the *bakufu*.

The great variety of schools of Chinese learning that developed in Tokugawa Japan is usually explained by the fact that, unlike in China, the state did not (except in 1790), through an examination system for officials, have a stake in defining orthodoxy. Some scholars (de Bary), however, see Japanese Neo-Confucianism developing along lines already established in China. The assumption that

Neo-Confucianism was adopted as an official *baku-fu* ideology from the beginning of the period has also been challenged recently (by Herman Ooms).

[*See also* Neo-Confucianism; Sugawara no Michizane; Ogyū Sorai; Itō Jinsai; *and* Matsudaira Sadanobu.]

Wm. Theodore de Bary and Irene Bloom, eds. *Principle and Practicality* (1979). Tetsuo Najita, *Japan* (1974). Herman Ooms, *Charismatic Bureaucrat* (1975) and *Tokugawa Ideology: Early Constructs, 1570–1680* (1985). Joseph M. Spae, *Itō Jinsai* (1948).    HERMAN OOMS

KANGHWA TREATY. Signed on 26 February 1876 in Kanghwa City by Sin Hŏn for Korea and Kuroda Kiyotaka for Japan, the Kanghwa Treaty was the first modern treaty Korea concluded with any country, and thus marked the end of Korea's traditional seclusion policy. It signified the climax of a long process during which Japan, after 1868 on a new course of inner and outer expansion, strove to revise traditional Japanese-Korean relations that had restricted Japanese to the Japan House in Pusan. Early Japanese demands for change were stubbornly resisted, but after King Kojong assumed the full responsibilities of government in 1874 a gradual reconsideration of Korea's position in a rapidly changing East Asian world began.

When in early 1875 Japan renewed its attempt to "normalize" relations, King Kojong and a few close advisers favored the acceptance of the Japanese overtures, while a conservative officialdom opposed any compromise. The Unyō Incident of September 1875, in which the Koreans were provoked into firing on the Japanese naval ship *Unyō*, encouraged Tokyo to take bolder action. It simultaneously sent a mission to Korea with the demand for the conclusion of a peace treaty and dispatched an envoy to China to explore China's attitude toward her vassal. In November 1875 Mori Arinori went to Beijing and held, in January 1876, intensive yet unfruitful discussions with members of the Zongli Yamen (China's Foreign Office) and Li Hongzhang on China's traditional relationship with Korea. Meanwhile, Kuroda Kiyotaka was dispatched to Korea, where on 10 Febuary he presented a draft treaty of thirteen articles. The Koreans, who had not anticipated a new treaty, reacted with surprising speed; on 18 February the Council of State reached the momentous decision to accept the Japanese proposal. Despite vociferous opposition from outside the government, final treaty negotiations were concluded on 26 February and the treaty was exchanged on 27 February 1876. [*See* Kuroda Kiyotaka; Li Hongzhang; *and* Mori Arinori.]

The treaty, of twelve articles, recognized Korea as an independent state enjoying the same sovereign rights as Japan, and provided for the mutual exchange of envoys after fifteen months from the date of the signature of the treaty. The Japanese envoy was to confer with the president of the Department of Rites; the Korean envoy was to be received by the Foreign Office. Article 3 stipulated that the Japanese were to use the Japanese and Chinese languages in their official communications, whereas the Koreans were to use Chinese. All the old agreements existing between Korea and Tsushima were abolished: trade at Pusan was henceforth to be carried out according to the provisions of the treaty, and Korea agreed to open two additional ports for commercial intercourse with Japan in 1877. Article 6 secured assistance and support for ships stranded or wrecked along the Korean or Japanese coasts. Any Japanese mariner was allowed, according to article 7, to conduct surveys of the Korean coast. Article 8 permitted the government of Japan to appoint an officer for each of the open ports of Korea for the protection of Japanese merchants residing there. Freedom both to carry on business without interference from the authorities of either government, and to trade without restrictions or prohibitions, was guaranteed by article 9. Article 10 stipulated extraterritorial jurisdiction, and article 11 arranged for trade regulations, which were to be agreed upon at the capital of Korea or at Kanghwa within six months of the conclusion of the treaty.

Far from having only bilateral significance, this treaty laid the basis for more far-reaching change in the East Asian order than was realized. The Koreans viewed it as the peaceful continuation of Korean-Japanese relations, while for Japan it meant a reversal of the old system on the basis of the "unequal treaties," especially expressed in extraterritorial jurisdiction. Moreover, it denied the Sino-Korean relationship its traditional quality and thus opened for Japan a new era of diplomatic and economic activities on the Korean peninsula.

[*See also* Yi Dynasty.]

Martina Deuchler, *Confucian Gentlemen and Barbarian Envoys: The Opening of Korea, 1875–1885* (1977). C. I. Eugene Kim and Han-Kyo Kim, *Korea and the Politics of Imperialism, 1876–1910* (1967).

MARTINA DEUCHLER

KANGRA, the most densely populated region of India's Himachal Pradesh state, lying in the foothills north of the Punjab plains. In pre-British days the fertile Kangra Valley, watered by the Beas River, was divided among a number of petty Hindu rajas who gave only nominal allegiance to the Mughal rulers of Delhi. Sikh forces under Ranjit Singh marched on Kangra in 1809 and checked the expansion of the Gorkha empire along the western perimeter of the Himalayas. Following the First Sikh War in 1846, the entire area passed into British hands and was thereafter administered as a district of the Punjab. In 1966, however, the government of India merged Kangra with Himachal Pradesh as an administrative concession to the cultural and linguistic affinities linking the district's population with that of the neighboring hills. Critics of the government, on the other hand, saw the merger as a move to split Sikh domination of Punjab state politics. In 1972 Kangra was partitioned into Hamirpur, Una, and Kangra districts.

[*See also* Himachal Pradesh.]

J. P. Parry, *Caste and Kinship in Kangra* (1979).

RICHARD ENGLISH

KANG SHENG (1899–1975), one of the most powerful members of the Chinese Communist Party (CCP) from the late 1930s until his death. Born in Shandong Province to a landlord family, he joined the CCP in Shanghai in 1924 as a labor union organizer. After studying Soviet security and intelligence techniques in Moscow in the early 1930s, he returned in 1937 to begin his long career as the head of the CCP's secret police. He worked mostly behind the scenes, notably in the massive purges of 1943 and 1951 to 1956, and as a member of the Cultural Revolution Group from 1966 to 1969. He helped to rebuild the Party structure from 1969 until his health failed in the early 1970s, and was elected a vice-chairman of the Standing Committee of the Politburo in 1973. Generally, his fortunes rose and fell with that of other radical associates of Mao, such as Jiang Qing, whom he introduced to Party membership in 1937. Kang was criticized posthumously in the Democracy Movement of 1978 to 1981 and by the reform leaders associated with Deng Xiaoping after their defeat of the remaining Maoist ideologues in 1980.

[*See also* Communism: Chinese Communist Party; Great Proletarian Cultural Revolution; *and* Jiang Qing.]

Frederic M. Kaplan, Julian M. Sobin, and Stephen Andors, eds., *Encyclopedia of China Today* (1979). Donald W. Klein and Anne B. Clark, *Biographical Dictionary of Chinese Communism, 1921–1965* (1971).

JOHN A. RAPP

KANG TAI, member of a Chinese mission to the kingdom of Funan in Indochina between 245 and 300. With his colleague Zhu Ying, he is responsible for the earliest extant account of Funan, thought to have been centered on the lower Mekong region. He recorded the local myth of the founding of the royal dynasty and described the inhabitants, whom he said were ugly and black with frizzy hair and no clothes. He claimed to have persuaded the ruler to order the men to wear clothes.

[*See also* Funan.]

Lawrence P. Briggs, *The Ancient Khmer Empire* (1951).

IAN W. MABBETT

KANGXI EMPEROR, reign title assumed by Xuanye (temple name Shengzu; 1654–1722), the third son of the first Manchu emperor of China, Shunzhi. Kangxi's selection as heir was influenced by his prospects of longevity, as he had survived a smallpox outbreak. He reigned from 1661 to 1722.

Shunzhi's will, thought to be largely forged, appointed four regents, Soni, Suksaha, Ebilun, and Oboi, to manage affairs of state during Kangxi's minority. Among these Oboi gained ascendancy. His leadership was marked by factional activity at court, while nationally he made little attempt to reconcile the Chinese people to alien rule.

In 1661 several thousand Chinese gentry in Jiangnan, where Ming loyalism was especially persistent, were punished by Oboi for tax delinquency. Many officials were demoted or dismissed and some were executed, while many students were deprived of the opportunity of advancement through examination. In the same year there occurred the prosecution of those involved in the compilation and production of Zhuang Tinglong's allegedly anti-Manchu history of the Ming dynasty. The case culminated in more than seventy executions.

Oboi's attempt to resettle certain banner lands in an arrangement more favorable to his own banner was unpopular among the Manchu banners and eventually hastened his fall from power. In 1667 the young emperor began to assert his influence but it was not until 1669 that, assisted by Soni's son Songgotu, he was able to arrest Oboi on charges of corruption and factionalism. Oboi died in prison shortly thereafter.

The next decade and a half saw many changes as Kangxi consolidated his power. A major crisis facing the dynasty was the Rebellion of the Three Feudatories (1673–1681). Wu Sangui (1612–1678) had fought for the Manchu cause since 1644 and his power and wealth were extensive. By the middle 1660s he had virtually established control not only over the provinces of Yunnan and Guizhou, to which he had been appointed, but also over Hunan, Sichuan, Shaanxi, and Gansu. Shang Kexi (d. 1676) and Geng Jingzhong (d. 1682), both former Ming generals, also maintained large armies in Guangdong and Fujian, respectively; by 1667 the joint military forces of the three cost more than half the annual state expenditure. [*See also* Three Feudatories Rebellion.]

In 1673 the emperor decided, against the advice of most senior officials, to abolish the feudatories. Wu thereupon rebelled. Claiming to be general in command of all the armies in the country, he proclaimed a new dynasty, which he called Zhou, and ordered the restoration of Ming customs and ceremonies. He took Guizhou and Hunan and was proceeding north when government troops forestalled him. He was joined by Shang and Geng and for some time the Manchu dynasty was imperiled. It was not until eight years later that government forces suppressed the rebels.

Two years later Shi Lang (1621–1696) succeeded in subjugating the island of Taiwan, which since its capture from Dutch colonists in 1662 by Koxinga (Zheng Chenggong; 1624–1662) had been a stronghold of resistance to the Qing. Taiwan then became a prefecture of Fujian Province. [*See also* Zheng Chenggong.]

During the 1680s the Chinese were concerned by the Russian advance through Siberia and along the Amur River and sent military forces to destroy Russian trading posts. In 1689 Songgotu, assisted by Jesuit interpreters, concluded at Nerchinsk the first treaty made on an equal footing between China and a foreign country. Previously China had been prepared to enter into relations with other countries only when the latter acknowledged tributary status. Thereafter trade and diplomatic relations flourished between China and Russia. The cessation of hostilities with Russia enabled China to turn its attention to the defeat of the Olod Mongol leader Galdan (1697), then threatening its northern and northwestern borders. The ensuing peace lasted until

1715, when another war with the Olods broke out, continuing for forty years. In 1720 China occupied Lhasa. [*See also* Galdan.]

While these matters filled the military stage, Kangxi took steps to establish himself as a Confucian type of ruler and to dissipate the anti-Manchu sentiments held by many capable scholars whose cooperation he sought. In 1671 he issued the Sacred Edict, consisting of sixteen political and moral maxims of seven characters each. Members of the gentry had to expound these maxims to the people twice a month at meetings all were expected to attend.

In 1678 there began a search for fine scholars to be tested and employed personally by the emperor. All senior metropolitan and provincial officials were requested to recommend candidates for the *boxue hongcu* examination held in 1679. Of 202 recommended, 152 sat for the examination and 50 passed. Some declined to take it while others feigned illness to avoid giving offense. Of those who passed, 40 came from southern provinces, in contrast to the earlier preponderance of northerners in Qing officialdom. Many of these southerners had suffered under Oboi's persecutions. All the successful candidates became members of the Hanlin Academy and some were employed as the emperor's personal secretaries in the newly established Imperial Study (*nan shufang*). The newly co-opted scholars compiled the official history of the Ming dynasty, with some informal assistance from such Ming loyalist scholars as Huang Zongxi (1610–1695), who had refused to take the examination. The *boxue* examination, by attracting previously unsympathetic Chinese to government service, marked the beginning of a Manchu effort to collaborate in power. However, the execution in 1712 of Dai Mingshi and others for historical writings allegedly injurious to the Qing indicates that sensitivities continued to run high.

Kangxi contributed greatly to the advancement of learning. He ordered the compilation of many works on art and literature, and patronized the fine and applied arts, assembling Chinese and European artists to work in a specially established studio. He himself was intrigued by Western mathematics, science, and mechanical matters, in which he was instructed by Jesuit missionaries.

Kangxi was fond of hunting, which he regarded as a continuation of the Manchu tradition of active life. From 1683 he made annual hunting expeditions to Jehol (Chinese, Rehe), where in 1703 he built summer palaces. He toured the empire extensively, making one eastern tour, four western tours, and six southern tours. The stated purpose of these was the inspection of rivers and their conservancy; in addition they enabled the emperor to establish personal contact with and to check on his provincial bureaucracy.

Kangxi's central government was headed by the Grand Secretariat, into which the Manchu Three Inner Offices restored by Oboi were incorporated in 1670. Its membership was half Manchu and half Chinese. This arrangement, dating from the 1630s when the Manchu capital had been in Shenyang (Mukden), remained the norm in administration throughout the Qing dynasty. By the turn of the century Kangxi had established the palace memorial system, whereby selected officials could send secret information directly to the emperor, that is, without the intermediary of the Office of Transmission. This system was institutionalized by his successors. From 1668 the Imperial Board of Astronomy was directed by Jesuits after the accuracy of their calculations resolved a controversy over the relative merits of Chinese and Western methods. As for state revenues, the principal source was the land and poll taxes, supplemented by salt, tea, commercial, and other duties. In 1712 the emperor decreed that the poll tax should be permanently based on the population of the previous year.

In 1692 Kangxi legalized missionary work in China. The continuing dispute over the compatibility of such Chinese practices as ancestor worship with Christianity came to a head with the arrival in China in 1705 of the papal legate, Maillard de Tournon. In contrast to the Jesuits' policy of flexibility concerning Chinese practices, de Tournon condemned these as superstition. He further insisted on papal authority over missionaries and their converts in China, to be exercised by a papal nuncio resident in Beijing. His demands offended Kangxi, who had de Tournon imprisoned in Macao, where he died in 1710. Meanwhile some of the Jesuits undertook a general survey of China with the emperor's permission and in 1718 produced a map of the empire.

Geography was a new field of scholarly interest in this period as were phonology and philology. Early Qing scholarship was profoundly affected by the intellectual despair engendered by the decline and fall of the Ming dynasty. Such men as Gu Yanwu (1613–1682), Wang Fuzhi (1619–1692), and Yan Yuan (1635–1704) laid the foundations for the school of Evidential Research that reached its height in the Qianlong period by stressing the need for knowledge to have practical application to society. They attacked the idealism of the Wang Yangming school of Neo-Confucianism while others such as Hu Wei (1633–1714) and Yan Ruoju (1636–1704) further undermined the authority of Neo-Confucianism by exposing as later forgeries certain revered texts and documents. Meanwhile Huang Zongxi and Wan Sitong (1638–1702) set new standards of objectivity both in history and in philosophy. [See also Gu Yanwu; Wang Fuzhi; Kaozheng Xue; and Huang Zongxi.]

The question of succession colored the last twenty years of Kangxi's reign. His designated heir, Yinreng, proved dissolute and unstable. Deeply attached to Yinreng as the only one of his twenty sons to have been born to an empress as opposed to a consort, at first Kangxi punished others such as Songgotu on the grounds of bad influence. Bitter factional struggles accompanied the removal (1708), reinstatement (1709), and final removal (1712) of Yinreng from the position of heir apparent. Kangxi was unwilling to designate a replacement and the recriminations clouding the accession of his fourth son as the Yongzheng emperor testify to the intensity of the succession issue.

[See also Qing Dynasty.]

Wm. Theodore de Bary, ed., *The Unfolding of Neo-Confucianism* (1975). Jean-Baptiste du Halde, *The General History of China* (1736). Robert B. Oxnam, *Ruling from Horseback: Manchu Politics in the Oboi Regency, 1661–1669* (1975). Jonathan D. Spence, *Ts'ao-yin and the K'ang-hsi Emperor, Bondservant and Master* (1966) and *Emperor of China: Self-Portrait of K'ang-hsi* (1974). Jonathan D. Spence and John E. Wills, Jr., *From Ming to Ch'ing: Conquest, Region and Continuity in Seventeenth Century China* (1980). Frederic Wakeman, Jr., *The Great Enterprise: The Manchu Reconstruction of Imperial Order in Seventeenth-Century China* (1985).

JOANNA WALEY-COHEN

**KANG YOUWEI** (1858–1927), leading philosopher of the 1898 Reform Movement in China, known especially for his radical reinterpretation of the Confucian classics to show that they included ideas of reform as well as room for westernization. Born into a renowned Cantonese family, Kang was a brilliant student but found traditional learning lacking in substance. He therefore began exploring Chinese translations of Western ideas in the 1880s. By 1895 Kang was in Beijing participating in the metropolitan examination when word of the Japanese terms for its victory over China reached the capital. Kang, along with Liang Qichao, led a group of students in drafting a petition to reject the terms and urging the continuation of hostilities and a series of reforms.

Subsequently, Kang put together his ideas on revitalizing China in several essays. Besides arguing that Confucius was a reformer, Kang called for China to overhaul its political structure. His basic argument was that China's traditional institutions were designed to protect the dynasty from internal enemies but that China's enemies were at that time from without, rendering the institutions of the past useless. Eventually, the Guangxu emperor heard of Kang's ideas and granted an audience on 16 June 1898, even though all of the emperor's councillors had serious misgivings about Kang's radical ideas. Between June and September 1898, Kang and several others advised the emperor on a series of reforms touching almost every topic. These proposed changes were too radical for Empress Dowager Cixi, who organized a coup d'état on 21 September 1898. Kang fled to Japan, where he remained in exile until after the 1911 Revolution.

Kang's years after 1898 were spent organizing societies to protect the emperor, supporting monarchial restorations, encouraging the establishment of Confucianism as a state religion, or feuding with both his own disciple, Liang Qichao, and the revolutionary camp of Sun Yat-sen. His positions attracted little attention as the revolutionary process of twentieth-century China made his ideas anachronistic.

[See also Liang Qichao and Qing Dynasty.]

Luke S. K. Kwong, *A Mosaic of the Hundred Days* (1984). Jung-pang Lo, ed., *K'ang Yu-wei: A Biography and a Symposium* (1967).    ADRIAN A. BENNETT

KANISHKA, the greatest king of the Kushan dynasty, ruler of northern India, most of present-day Afghanistan and Tajikistan, and parts of Central Asia. His absolute dates of rule are unknown; estimates of the beginning of his reign range from 78 to 225 CE. His length of rule, determined from inscriptions dated in the years of his reign, was about 25 years, and he was succeeded by Huvishka.

Kanishka's predecessor was Vima Kadphises, who introduced the gold coinage of the Kushans in place of silver. Kanishka changed the legends on his coins from Greek to Bactrian, an Iranian tongue written in modified Greek characters. His coins portray many deities, Greek, Iranian, and Indian, but Kanishka is known in Pali Buddhist sources as a great patron of Buddhism who built a large stupa

in present-day Peshawar. His name is mentioned in Chinese and Indian sources, an indication of his fame beyond the Kushan empire, and later rulers claimed descent from him. From varying coins bearing his name numismatists have postulated the rule of a second and third Kanishka.

[See also Kushan Dynasty.]

A. L. Basham, ed., *Papers on the Date of Kaniṣka* (1968).    RICHARD N. FRYE

KANNADA. *See* Dravidian Languages and Literatures.

KANŌ SCHOOL, Japanese school of professional artists who practiced a synthesis of Chinese ink painting and native polychrome painting that was regarded as the official painting style throughout the Edo (Tokugawa) period (1600–1868) and whose prosperity was assured by the patronage of successive generations of military governments. Kanō Masanobu (1434–1530) is considered the founder of the Kanō School. He was trained in Chinese ink painting by Zen monks at Shōkokuji temple and later was designated *goyō eshi,* or painter in attendance to the shogun. He was succeeded in this post by his son Motonobu (1476–1559), who was both a gifted painter and an exceptional organizer.

Motonobu is credited with the formulation of the orthodox Kanō style and with the development of a workshop system in which young artists were trained to work as part of a group, each one assigned a task according to seniority. This system was admirably suited to meet the demands of painting on sliding doors *(fusuma),* which became the chief form of interior decoration in castles, palaces, and temples from the sixteenth century on. Such paintings were designed to span one wall or even an entire room. In adapting the ink painting style practiced a generation earlier to meet the demands of large scale mural compositions, Motonobu laid the foundations for generations of later artists.

Together with Motonobu, Eitoku (Motonobu's grandson, 1543–1590) and Tan'yū (1602–1674) are singled out as the most outstanding members of the Kanō school. Early in life, Eitoku developed a reputation as a dynamic ink painter as well as a master of painting on gold foil ground. Although Motonobu had experimented with the use of gold background, it was Eitoku who brought this practice to full fruition. His opulent, monumental compositions and aggressive brushwork found special favor with the military leaders of the Momoyama period (1568–1600).

Tan'yū was the leader of a new branch of the Kanō school established in Edo after that city became the capital in 1615. Like earlier members of the school, his primary employment was as a decorator of palaces and castles. However, he also made sketches after life of a variety of plants, the earliest such works by a Japanese artist. Noted as a connoisseur, his copious sketches and notes on Chinese and Japanese paintings are of great art historical value.

The Kanō studios, in addition to being the training ground for generations of Kanō artists, also provided an introduction to established painting styles and techniques for artists who went on to establish their own schools. Kamō Einō (1631–1697) although himself undistinguished as a painter, wrote the first history of Japanese painting.

[*See also* Tokugawa Period.]

Yoshiaki Shimizu and Carolyn Wheelwright, *Japanese Ink Paintings* (1976). Takeda Tsuneo, *Kanō Eitoku* (1977). Tsugiyoshi Doi, *Momoyama Decorative Painting* (1977).
                                    CHRISTINE M. E. GUTH

**KANPUR** (formerly Cawnpore), a city on the right bank of the Ganges River in the district of the same name in the state of Uttar Pradesh, India. When the area was acquired by the British in 1801, the site of the present city was only a village, but it grew rapidly, and when the first census was taken in 1872, it had 123,000 people; in 1986 it had an estimated population of 1.75 million. During the nineteenth century it had a large military base, and since it was also on the major highways and railroads connecting North India with Calcutta, it became an important industrial center. The city achieved notoriety as one of the main centers of the Indian "Mutiny," the great uprising that took place in 1857 against British rule. The killing of British women and children by a group

FIGURE 1. *The Four Seasons (Detail).* Manner of Kanō Motonobu (1456–1559). One-half of a six-panel folding screen, part of a pair; ink and light color on paper. Size of each screen: 1.55 m. × 3.61 m.

of rebels there received wide publicity, and was one of the incidents the British press used to illustrate the alleged barbarity of the Indians.

AINSLIE T. EMBREE

KANSEI REFORMS. Initiated by Matsudaira Sadanobu (1758–1829), chief senior councillor from 1787 to 1793, the Kansei Reforms (1787–c. 1800), were the second of three reform programs undertaken by the Tokugawa shogunate in Japan, falling between those of the Kyōhō and Tempō eras of the 1720s and 1830s, respectively. The term also applies to similar reforms in daimyo domains. They were necessitated by the cumulative effects of successive natural disasters and famines (causing numerous peasant uprisings and urban riots), bureaucratic corruption under Tanuma Okitsugu, and severe financial distress created by a 50 percent drop in revenues and steep inflation.

A major purge of officials restored administrative efficiency. Ideological uniformity among shogunal retainers was achieved by introducing compulsory examinations based on a narrowly constructed Neo-Confucian curriculum at the new shogunal academy. In the countryside, tax farming was restored, supplies of rice were stored for emergencies, and abuses by tax-collecting merchants were stemmed.

Financial solvency was achieved through monetary reforms. These included the recoining of silver pieces, a qualitative revaluation of the gold currency, and a quantitative reduction of the copper currency. Officially fixed exchange rates strengthened Edo's financial position; the industrial development of its hinterland was promoted. The financial distress of shogunal retainers was alleviated by a complex schedule of debt cancellations. Rice brokers who functioned as bankers were brought under *bakufu* control. By decree, the prices of many consumer goods were lowered, house and land rents in Edo were reduced, and township expenses were curtailed. Sumptuary laws sought to reduce consumption.

Traditionally, the Kansei Reforms have been viewed as a reactionary reversal of Tanuma's expansionist mercantilism following the Kyōhō Reforms. The picture of a cycle of rally–rout–rally during the Kyōhō, Tanuma, and Kansei eras, however, obscures strong continuities in the growing social dislocations of eighteenth-century Japan. The reforms were temporary remedies that strengthened Edo's position and provided formal structures to harmonize merchant interests and government needs without, however, checking long-term developments in the countryside.

[*See also* Kyōhō Reforms; Tempō Reforms; Matsudaira Sadanobu; *and* Tanuma Okitsugu.]

Herman Ooms, *Charismatic Bureaucrat: A Political Biography of Matsudaira Sadanobu, 1758–1829* (1975).

HERMAN OOMS

KANTŌ EARTHQUAKE. A massive earthquake struck the Kantō region of Japan on 1 September 1923, destroying most of the cities of Tokyo and Yokohama and claiming more than 100,000 lives. It was the most destructive natural disaster in Japanese history.

The earthquake had its epicenter in northern Sagami Bay, some forty miles south of Tokyo, and registered 8.2 in intensity on the Richter scale (7.8 on the Japanese scale). The earthquake caused damage in ten prefectures, but was disastrous only in Kanagawa Prefecture and Tokyo City. The cities of Tokyo and Yokohama together (in a ratio of about three to one) accounted for almost 90 percent of the deaths and more than three-fourths of the destruction. In the two cities combined, almost three families in four lost their homes.

In both Tokyo and Yokohama, it was fire rather than the tremor itself that wrought the most destruction. Dozens of fires began simultaneously when the force of the earthquake upset home cooking fires and triggered chemical blazes. In Tokyo the most catastrophic loss of life was caused by a tornado of flames that killed almost 40,000 people who had taken shelter in an open space on the east bank of the Sumida River.

The chaos in the wake of the earthquake encouraged wild rumors blaming Koreans and radicals for starting fires and poisoning wells. Dozens (perhaps hundreds) of Koreans were killed by vigilante groups, while military police were responsible for the deaths of several labor leaders, including the anarchist Ōsugi Sakae. [*See* Ōsugi Sakae.]

Apart from the immediate destruction, the earthquake had numerous long-term effects on Japan. Economically, the immense costs of reconstruction added a major burden to an already strained economy. Politically, the earthquake introduced a note of sober realism into the socialist and labor movements. Culturally, the disaster wiped out much of surviving Edo tradition and ushered in a new era of modernism, hedonism, and pervasive American influence.

Noel Busch, *Two Minutes to Noon—The Story of the Great Tokyo Earthquake and Fire* (1962). Japan Home Office Bureau of Social Affairs, *The Great Earthquake of 1923 in Japan* (1926).          HENRY D. SMITH II

**KAN-T'O-LI.** From about 441 Kan-t'o-li was the chief port on the southeastern coast of Sumatra sending tribute to China. Its actual location is as yet unclear; all that is known about the port is derived from Chinese dynastic sources. These Chinese records indicate that Kan-t'o-li was the overlord of the "favored coast" that became important when the international maritime route began to regularly use the Strait of Melaka. Strategically located on the western edge of the Java Sea and in the middle of the Strait of Melaka and Sunda Strait maritime passage, Kan-t'o-li served as a distribution center for forest products from the Indonesian archipelago. Although initially Kan-t'o-li traded with the West, during the fifth century it came into direct commercial contact with Chinese markets and soon became the principal Southeast Asian port servicing the exchange of eastern and western goods. By the late seventh century the port had been succeeded as the region's dominant entrepôt by Srivijaya.

[*See also* Srivijaya.]

O. W. Wolters, *Early Indonesian Commerce: A Study of the Origins of Srivijaya* (1967).   KENNETH R. HALL

**KANYAKUBJA** (present-day Kanauj), town on the west bank of the Kalinadi near its junction with the Ganges in the Farrakhabad district of Uttar Pradesh, India. Famous in ancient history and legends as a metropolis of the Panchala region, its strategic location in the central doab enabled Kanyakubja to play a historic role in Indian politics and commerce. Its days of glory began in the mid-sixth century CE when, as the Maukhari capital, it replaced Pataliputra as the seat of imperial India, a position it held until the rise of Delhi under the Muslim sultanate in the thirteenth century. In 612 Emperor Harsha united the Maukhari domains, making Kanyakubja his capital. The Chinese pilgrim Xuanzang, who visited the capital in the seventh century, noted its huge size and architectural magnificence. Kanyakubja served as the capital of Yashovarman (r. 715–752), the "lord of all the North." The city was the focal point of the tripartite struggle for the mastery of India among the Palas of Bengal, the Gurjara Pratiharas of Avanti and Rajasthan, and the Rashtrakutas of the South, from the late eighth through the tenth century. The Gurjara Pratiharas made Kanyakubja their capital in about 815, and ruled their empire until Mahmud of Ghazna sacked the city in 1018, destroying its massive fortifications and temples. The city regained its imperial splendor for the last time as the capital of the Gahadvalas, who were conquered by Muhammad Ghuri in 1194.

[*See also* Harsha *and* Maukhari Dynasty.]

R. S. Tripathi, *History of Kanauj to the Moslem Conquest* (1959).          SHIVA BAJPAI

**KAOZHENG XUE** ("evidential studies"), a school of Confucian thought popular in Qing-dynasty China. The term *kaozheng xue* broadly refers to a search for evidence in books, events, and observable phenomena by embracing both a methodology and an epistemology. More narrowly, *kaozheng xue* thinkers sought to determine the literal accuracy and verifiable authenticity of classical and historical texts through close analysis. Because of the emphasis on concentrated study of lexical texts, some scholars have referred to Evidential Studies as "Han learning." It was also termed *puxue,* "unadorned learning," a reference to its simple, precise, and substantive expository style. First emerging in the late Ming dynasty, Evidential Studies had become the dominant mode of Confucian scholarly discourse in the lower Yangtze region by the middle of the Qing dynasty.

According to Benjamin Elman, Evidential Studies developed as a renewed commitment to linguistic analysis in terms of a new epistemological orientation. The older Song-Ming Neo-Confucian mode of thinking used speculative reasoning and intuitive perception, reducing questions to an underlying principle and drawing conclusions by deductive norms. This new epistemological orientation, however, sought to comprehend concrete, verifiable ideas through comprehensive study of complex and multiple phenomena. Challenged partly by Western exact sciences, this new orientation also found impetus in rectifying the political, social, economic, and intellectual deterioration accompanying the fall of the Ming dynasty. Greater interest was directed toward applying scholarship to practical social and political concerns: "statecraft" *(jingshi)* studies and "applied studies" *(shixue)* flourished.

*Kaozheng* methodology placed great emphasis on the scholar's independent judgment unfettered by and unfiltered through established orthodoxy. Although many pioneer Evidential Studies scholars of the late Ming considered themselves adherents of a particular school of Confucian learning, their mode of inquiry and presentation of critical findings already revealed a degree of autonomy from other intellectual concerns. With the first generation of Qing scholars, "masterless" men linked rudimentary methodological theories of internal and collateral evidence to a disciplinary rationale.

The famous Gu Yanwu insisted that "classical studies are what the study of principle [*li*] was called in antiquity." He envisioned Evidential Studies as the means to cut through the accumulated layers of Song and Ming Confucian philosophical reflection imbued (so he believed) with heterodox Buddhist and Daoist ideas. The Five Classics, rather than the Four Books, were used to arrive at a true understanding of the moral, world-ordering principles of the ancient sages—principles applicable to reforming institutions. Gu's methodological contributions to the ancillary studies of phonology, geography, and epigraphy and his notational method of presentation were further developed by later scholars. Once-revered textual versions were proven to be forgeries as the use of the Han-dynasty lexical aids increased.

During the eighteenth century scholarly reputation and influence increasingly were measured by the rigorous and exacting standards of Evidential Studies. Institutions changed to accommodate the emerging norms of academic discourse. Teaching became extremely attractive in the urban academies. A communication network developed as bibliophiles retrieved lost texts, which printers and booksellers made available to the increasingly sophisticated scholarly community. Privately and officially funded research engaged the talents of aspiring young men who sought recognition as they climbed toward government office. For many, reading and exegesis of the classics and histories offered a viable and respectable alternative to government service and a means of contributing to the preservation and purification of indigenous culture.

By the time the *kaozheng* orientation became entrenched in the leading academies of the lower Yangtze region and enshrined in the Imperial Manuscript Library (Siku Quanshu), the fragile unanimity of the *kaozheng* scholarly community had fractured. By the beginning of the twentieth century, Yao Nai, Zhuang Cunyu, and others found the moral principles of the Song Confucians intellectually compelling enough to take issue with the more radical scholars who attacked, questioned, or simply ignored such writing.

The scholar and official Ruan Yuan (1764–1849)

continued to sponsor academies and individual scholarly projects, scholars continued to devote attention to Evidential Studies, and the *kaozheng* intellectual legacy of skepticism, philosophical eclecticism, specialization, and sensitivity to historical context was extended to other fields of activity. However, the deteriorating social and political situation, an increasing interest in contemporary issues, and the diminishing supply of economic resources combined to discourage the evidential scholarship of classical and historical texts. After the Taiping rebels laid waste the lower Yangtze region in the 1850s and 1860s and destroyed many of the great academies, *kaozheng* scholarship never regained its former status.

[*See also* Gong Zizhen; Gu Yanwu; Jinwen; Liang Qichao; Neo-Confucianism; *and* Ruan Yuan.]

Edward Ch'ien, "Chiao Hung and the Revolt against Ch'eng-Chu Orthodoxy," in *The Unfolding of Neo-Confucianism,* edited by Wm. Theodore de Bary (1975), pp. 271–303. Benjamin Elman, *The Unravelling of Neo-Confucianism: The Lower Yangtze Academic Community* (1984). Joanna Handlin, *Action in Late Ming Thought* (1982). Liang Ch'i-ch'ao (Liang Qichao), *Intellectual Trends in the Ch'ing Period,* translated by Immanuel Hsu (1959). Willard Petersen, *Bitter Gourd: Fang Yizhi and the Impetus for Intellectual Change* (1979).

JUDITH A. WHITBECK

KAPILAVASTU, capital of the Shakya republic, the home state of the historical Buddha, Shakyamuni. Its exact location on the present Indo-Nepal border is disputed owing to archaeological discoveries at Piprahwa in India and Tilaurakot in Nepal. At Piprahwa relics of the Buddha have been found.

[*See also* Buddhism: An Overview.]

R. C. Majumdar, ed., *The Age of Imperial Unity* (1968).
A. K. NARAIN

KAPITAN CHINA, title of the recognized head of a Chinese community in a Malay or colonial port or settlement in the Malay world. The *kapitan* was appointed by the Malay ruler or colonial government to be responsible for taxation and often for the maintenance of law and order among the Chinese. In places where more than one speech group formed a considerable portion of the Chinese population, there was sometimes more than one *kapitan*. Often the *kapitan* was also the head of the local secret society or Triad lodge as well as the most important merchant and contractor. During the nineteenth century the British continued the practice of naming a *kapitan* in their Malayan colonies, with the exception of Singapore, but even there prominent Chinese served much the same function as members of the Legislative Council or as revenue farmers.

Emily Sadka, *The Protected Malay States 1874–1895* (1968). Carl A. Trocki, *Prince of Pirates: The Temenggongs and the Development of Johor and Singapore 1784–1885* (1979).    CARL A. TROCKI

**KARACHI.** The largest city and premier seaport of Pakistan, Karachi grew to prominence only after the British annexation of Sind in 1843. From the later nineteenth century the city became the major distribution center for the Indus Valley, the Punjab, and Afghanistan. Its prosperity, which brought continuing rapid population growth, derived from the export of wheat and cotton, and (after 1947) the development of consumer light industry. The Gujaratis, Parsis, and Hindu Sindhis who built up the city's trade were displaced after partition by Muslim émigrés from India, who shaped the city as an Urdu-speaking enclave largely isolated from its Sindhi hinterland. During the first decade of Pakistan's existence (1947–1958) Karachi served as its temporary capital; it is now the provincial capital of Sind.

[*See also* Sind; Gujarat; *and* Pakistan.]

Alexander Baillie, *Kurrachee Past and Present* (1890; reprint, 1975). Herbert Feldman, *Karachi through a Hundred Years* (1970).    THOMAS R. METCALF

**KARAKHANID DYNASTY,** Turkic dynasty that ruled western and eastern Turkestan (Transoxiana and Kashgaria) from the tenth to the beginning of the thirteenth century. It is considered the first Islamic Turkic dynasty (having converted in the middle of the tenth century); in the Karakhanid court appeared the first Islamic Turkic literature, namely, the *Kutadgu bilig (Wisdom of Royal Glory)* of Yusuf Hass Hajib and the *Compendium of the Turkic Dialects* of Mahmud al-Kashgari. Hence, its importance is not only political but cultural.

The dynasty, also called Ilek-khans, Khans, or Al-i Afrasiyab, arose from the Karluk tribe of Turks. The Karakhanids exhibited a system of double kingship that was a feature among certain Altaic tribes. One ruler governed from Balasagun or Karaordu; his counterpart ruled from Kashgar or Talas. Each ruler carried a Turkic name and adopted a Muslim one after conversion, thus creating a great deal of confusion for historians.

The Karakhanids gained political importance in 999 with the capture of Bukhara and the division of the Samanid realm with Mahmud of Ghazna. In 1041 the dynasty split into two distinct khanates; the Hasanids, in the east, ruled from Balasagun, and the Alids, in the west, ruled first from Ozkend and then from Samarkand. During the twelfth century the eastern khanate fell under the hegemony of the Karakitai and essentially disappeared from sight until 1211, when the Mongol Kuchlug overthrew the Karakitai. At that point the eastern branch of the Karakhanids ceased to exist.

The western khanate fell under Seljuk suzerainty in 1074 and remained so until the battle of Qatwan in 1141. There the Karakhitai defeated the Seljuks under Sanjar and took possession of Turkestan north of the Oxus. Although the western branch was able to break away from the Karakhitai in the thirteenth century, it was soon conquered by the Khwarazmshah, who executed the last Karakhanid ruler in 1212 and brought the dynasty to an end.

[*See also* Bukhara; Kashgari, Mahmud al-; Kutadgu Bilig; Mahmud of Ghazna; *and the map accompanying* Seljuk Dynasty.]

C. E. Bosworth, "Ilek-Khāns," in *The Encyclopaedia of Islam* (new ed., 1960–).    JAMES M. KELLY

**KARAKORUM,** capital of the Mongolian empire, now ruined, on the right bank of the upper Orkhon River, 200 miles west-southwest of Ulan Bator in the Mongolian People's Republic. Founded by Genghis Khan in about 1220 as essentially a tent city, Karakorum became a more settled and cosmopolitan capital during the reign of Ogedei (1229–1241), who ordered the construction of walls and a palace begun in 1235, and attracted foreign craftsmen to assist. William of Rubruck, who visited Karakorum in 1254, provides the earliest firsthand European description of the city. Guyug and Mongke both retained Karakorum as their capital, but in 1267 Kublai established his at Dadu (modern Beijing). After the fall of the Mongol Yuan dynasty in China, the Mongol court returned to Karakorum and resisted the attacks of the new Ming dynasty.

Eventually the city was destroyed, although whether it was in 1388, as some argue, is not clear. The leader of the Khalkha Mongols built the great temple of Erdeni Juu near the site in 1585, perhaps hoping to rally the Mongols. Knowledge of the location of Karakorum was lost until the end of the nineteenth century when the Russian scholar N. M. Iadrintsev located ruins, subsequently proved to be those of the Mongol capital by A. M. Pozdneev.

From 1948 to 1949 a joint Soviet-Mongolian expedition investigated the site, finding the remains of Ogedei's palace, a Buddhist shrine, ordinary dwellings, and traces of irrigated agriculture outside the city, as well as tools, money, and ceramics from China and the Islamic world.

J. A. Boyle, *The Successors of Genghis Khan* (1971). L. Olschki, *Marco Polo's Asia* (1960).

ARTHUR N. WALDRON

KARAKOYUNLU (1375–1468), the "Black Sheep," a federation of Turkmen tribes that ruled much of Persia and Mesopotamia in the fifteenth century. They arose in eastern Anatolia north of Lake Van, far from the centralized, orthodox empires of the Ottomans to the west and the Timurids to the east. Apparently at this time, if not before, Azerbaijan became ethnically Turkish. The Karakoyunlu are regarded as a Shi'ite dynasty, in opposition to the Sunni Akkoyunlu.

The Karakoyunlu were originally organized by Bairam Khwaja (d. 1380), chief of the Baharlu clan of the Ghuzz (Oghuz). Both he and his son, Kara Muhammad Turmush, were in the service of the Jalayirid sultans in Tabriz. Kara Yusuf (1389–1420) declared his independence, took over the former Jalayirid possessions in Azerbaijan and Mesopotamia, and made Tabriz his capital. (However, he fled to the protection of the Ottomans and Mamluks from 1400 to 1406 in order to escape Timur's invasion.)

The most important Karakoyunlu ruler was Jahanshah (1438–1467), who extended the empire to its greatest extent, including eastern Anatolia, Azerbaijan, Iraq, Fars, Kerman, and Oman. Jahanshah built the Gok Masjid (Blue Mosque) in Tabriz, a structure renowned throughout the Islamic world for its beauty.

The Karakoyunlu were hostile to the Safavids, who were later to establish a much more powerful Shi'ite dynasty. They also clashed with the Timurids on occasion; Jahanshah defeated Abu Sa'id in 1458 and briefly occupied Herat. Uzun Hasan, the leader of the Akkoyunlu and chief rival of Jahanshah, defeated him in 1466. This effectively terminated the rule of the Karakoyunlu, and their domains were absorbed by the Akkoyunlu.

A rival branch of the Karakoyunlu, originally established by a son of Kara Yusuf, ruled in Baghdad from about 1411 to 1466, when this branch was put to an end by Jahanshah. The Qutb Shahis of Golconda, an Indian dynasty that ruled in the sixteenth and seventeenth centuries, was founded by a descendant of the Karakoyunlu and kept alive their memory.

[*See also* Akkoyunlu; Azerbaijan; *and* Tabriz.]

V. Minorsky, "The Clan of the Qara Qoyunlu Rulers," in *Fuad Köprülü Armağani* (1953), pp. 391–395, reprinted in Minorsky, *The Turks, Iran and the Caucasus in the Middle Ages* (1978). Roger M. Savory, "The Struggle for Supremacy in Persia after the Death of Tīmūr," *Der Islam* 40 (1965): 35–65. LAWRENCE POTTER

KARA KUM (Turkish, "black sand"), a desert in Turkmen SSR, located to the west of the Amu Darya (Oxus) river, stretching to the Caspian Sea, and bounded on the north by the Ustyurt Plateau. It has an area of almost 150,000 square miles and consists largely of sparsely vegetated sandy soil. It is one of two major deserts in Central Asia, along with the Kizil Kum ("red sand"). JAHAN SALEHI

KAREN, heterogenous peoples living in marginal areas of Lower Burma, along the Thai-Burmese border between the thirteenth and twenty-second parallel, and scattered throughout northwestern Thailand. Although Karen identity is tied in part to knowledge of a Karen language, it is largely determined by cultural affinities, with non-Karen individuals "becoming" Karen or vice versa. Census figures are problematic; best estimates conclude that over 90 percent of the perhaps three million Karen live in Burma and the rest in Thailand.

Few clues to early Karen history remain, but Karen tradition places the original homeland along the upper Mekong River. Linguistic evidence, provided by dialect diversity, indicates that Karen preceded Burmese, Thai, and Mon in present-day Burma, appearing over 1,500 years ago. Various subgroups emerged: Sgaw and Pwo, the largest numerically; a number of minor groups, such as the Kayah; and the Pa-O, linguistically close to Pwo but with many Shan cultural traits. Some linguists consider Karen to be a Tibeto-Burman language, but studies indicate that nearly half the lexicon cannot be identified with Tibeto-Burman nor with any other language group, placing this classification in doubt.

Few references to the Karen occur before the late 1700s. By then, Sgaw lived mainly in the upper delta and Pwos farther south. Almost all Sgaws and Pwos grew either swidden or paddy rice. Most Sgaws practiced their traditional religion, but Pwos occasionally were Buddhist. Although they traded with Mon and Burmese, the Karen were only rarely subject to corvée (unpaid labor).

References to Karen in the area of present-day Kayah State in the late 1700s, when Burmese-Thai wars diverted the attention of major powers from here, indicate the formation of several autonomous states. Recognized as autonomous by the British, they constituted the Karenni States in British India following Kayah submission in 1889.

During the Thai-Burmese wars between 1760 and 1824, some Sgaws and Pwos were spies, mahouts, or porters for either Burma or Siam. Most, however, fled the fighting, and thousands settled in Thai areas. Thai kings recognized some Karen centers as border dependencies and retained Karen rulers into the 1900s.

From the 1820s, American Baptist missionaries preached to Karen. Karen desires to escape Burmese overlordship, similarities between Karen traditions and biblical stories, and a Karen belief that Caucasians bearing a book would enhance Karen status prompted about 30 percent of all Karen, mostly Sgaw, to become Christians. Missionaries devised Karen alphabets and trained Karen teachers, pastors, and doctors. The British Indian government welcomed Karen as civil servants, particularly as teachers and soldiers, and a good number entered the upper ranks. Ethnic awareness developed and led to the foundation of the National Karen Association in 1881; national consciousness developed by the early 1900s.

Although many Karen were assimilated into Burmese life, some Karen leaders did not cooperate with Burmese nationalists. In 1949, soon after Burmese independence and after the British government ignored Karen appeals for a separate Karen state, the Karen National Union rebelled, almost taking Rangoon before a truce was called. During the truce, the government mobilized its forces and eventually pushed the rebels to the Thai border, where resistance continues. Rebel popularity among other Karen is uncertain since many nonrebels continue assimilating into Burmese life. In Thailand, Karen have rarely opposed the government, and since the early 1800s they have been incorporated gradually into Thai life.

[See also Karen National Defense Organization and Burma.]

James Hamilton, *Pwo Karen: At the Edge of Mountain and Plain* (1976). Charles Keyes, ed., *Ethnic Adaptation and Identity* (1979). Harry Marshall, *The Karen People of Burma* (1922). San C. Po, *Burma and the Karens* (1928). Ronald D. Renard, *Kariang: History of T'ai-Karen Relations from the Beginnings to 1923* (1980).

RONALD D. RENARD

**KAREN NATIONAL DEFENSE ORGANIZATION.** Formed in mid-1947 as the military arm of the Karen National Union (KNU), the Karen National Defense Organization (KNDO) has been in rebellion against the government of Burma since late January 1949. Initially organized to defend Karen towns and villages from other rebels, the KNU planned its own revolt in 1949 when the government refused to accede to the KNU's demand for a separate and independent Karen state to be formed out of the Tenasserim Division of British Burma. Many Karen units in the Burma army joined the revolt, but while the government forces have never been able to completely suppress the Karen rebellion, the KNDO and related forces have been forced to exist by smuggling across the border with Thailand.

[See also Karen.]

John F. Cady, *A History of Modern Burma* (1958).

ROBERT H. TAYLOR

**KARKOTA DYNASTY,** empire that flourished in Kashmir from about 627 CE until the mid-ninth century. Lalitaditya (c. 724–760), the most powerful Karkota king, extended his territory considerably, possibly as far as Bengal, although his successors maintained only Kashmir. He built some of Kashmir's most important temples, among them the Sun Temple at Martand. The history of this house is recounted in the famous eleventh-century chronicle of Kashmir, the *Rajatarangini* of Kalhana.

[See also Kashmir.]

P. N. K. Bamzai, *A History of Kashmir: Political, Cultural, Social* (1973). M. A. Stein, trans., *Kalhana's Rajatarangini: Chronicle of the Kings of Kashmir* (1979).

FREDERICK M. ASHER

**KARMAL, BABRAK** (b. 1929), president of Afghanistan since 1979. Born near Kabul into a prominent family, Karmal's father was a general in the king's army. Karmal was jailed from 1952 to 1956 because of his political activities at the university. He was one of the founding members of the People's Democratic Party of Afghanistan. When the party split into several factions in 1967, Karmal became the leader of the faction known as Percham ("banner"). He was elected twice to the Afghan parliament.

After the 1978 communist coup, Karmal became the country's vice president. Soon afterward, however, he was purged from the party and sent as ambassador to Czechoslovakia. Subsequently, he was dismissed even from this post. He remained in Eastern Europe and was brought back to Afghanistan by the Soviets after their invasion of Afghanistan in December 1979. He became the country's president at that time but was replaced in 1986 by Najibullah.

[*See also* Percham.]

ZALMAY KHALILZAD

**KARNATAKA**, Indian state with an area of 191,773 square kilometers and a population of 37,043,451 (1981 census). Karnataka is known for its beautiful temples, magnificent waterfalls, deep gold mines, majestic Western Ghats, and rich flora and fauna. Its historical period begins in the time of Ashoka (273–232 BCE), some of whose inscriptions still stand today in some parts of Karnataka. Subsequently several dynasties from the Satavahanas in the first century BCE to the Wadiyars of modern times ruled successively, contributing much to art, architecture, literature, music, religion and philosophy. It was in Karnataka that *bhakti*, a religious reform movement of medieval times, originated. The movement sparked a literary renaissance, a social transformation, and a great philosophic upsurge.

With the breakup of the Vijayanagar empire in the sixteenth century, Karnataka fell into the hands of petty chieftains for nearly two hundred years until it was unified again under Haidar and Tipu. The British conquered it in wars of 1792 and 1799 and split it into four parts, giving one part each to the Bombay and Madras presidencies, the state of Hyderabad, and to the Wadiyars of Mysore. It took more than 150 years (1799–1956) to undo this partition. This period witnessed two significant events: the struggle for freedom and the reunification of Karnataka.

The proximity of northern Karnataka to Pune, the center of extremist activity, intensified the struggle in the twentieth century. Mohandas Gandhi paid tribute to freedom fighter Karnad Sadasiva Rao of Dakshina Kannada. At the same time , the movement for unification of all Kannada-speaking people under one state gained greater momentum. The idea was strengthened by the Indian National Congress resolutions of 1920 and 1921, by the formation of the Karnataka Unification Sangha in 1924, and by the Motilal Nehru Report of 1928. Journalists, lawyers, and litterateurs further promoted the cause. In 1938 both Bombay and Madras legislatures passed a resolution for a new province. The Congress Manifesto of 1946 confirmed its commitment to linguistic division of the country. The Fazl Ali Commission of 1953 to 1955 finally made the linguistic state a reality. A small state of nine districts overnight became a large state of nineteen districts nearly two and one-half times its original size in area and more than three times its previous number in population.

It was not until 1973 that the state's name was changed from Mysore to Karnataka. Bangalore is its capital. A single political party, the Congress Party, continuously ruled over the area from 1947 to January 1983, when the Janata Party formed the government. It has a bicameral legislature with 63 members in the Legislative Council and 225 members in the Legislative Assembly. It sends 27 members to Parliament. Karnataka's literacy rate is 38.41 percent (1981 census) and it has six universities. It has been steadily making progress in social, economic, educational, and industrial fields.

[*See also* Mysore.]

P. B. Desai, *History of Karnataka* (1970). R. R. Diwakar, *Karnataka through the Ages* (1966). S. Gururajachara, *Some Aspects of Economic and Social Life in Karnataka* (1974). R. S. Mugali, *The Heritage of Karnataka* (1946). B. SHEIK ALI

**KARRAMI**, a Sunni sect important in the eastern part of the Muslim world from the ninth to the twelfth century. The theological doctrines of the founder, Abu Abd Allah Muhammad ibn Karram (806–869), known primarily through the writings of his opponents, included a somewhat anthropomorphic interpretation of God's attributes and a moderate and humane position on the questions of indelible faith, God's justice, the imamate, and the fate of unbelievers and heretics. The pronounced ascetic and pietistic strain of Ibn Karram's teachings, which remained a characteristic of his school, combined with strong and active leadership, sometimes attracted a mass following. Under the first Ghaznavid rulers, they were favored over their powerful opponents, the Ash'ari-Shafi'i *ulama* (scholars); the last period of ascendancy occurred under the Ghurids of central Afghanistan.

[*See also* Ghaznavid Dynasty.]

C. E. Bosworth, "The Rise of the Karamiyyah in Khurasan," in *The Muslim World* 1 (1960): 5–14; and *The Ghaznavids, Their Empire in Afghanistan and Eastern Iran, 994–1040* (1963). R. W. Bulliet, *The Patricians of Nishapur, a Study in Medieval Islamic Social History* (1972). JEANETTE A. WAKIN

**KARTASURA**, a Central Javanese court, the ruins of which are located some twelve kilometers west of present-day Surakarta. There King Amangkurat II (r. 1677–1703) established his new court in September 1680 to replace the court that had fallen to Trunajaya in 1677. In June 1742 Kartasura fell to rebels who supported Sunan Kuning during the so-called Chinese War (1740–1743); in December it fell again to Madurese forces, which were obliged by the Dutch East India Company (VOC) to return it to Pakubuwana II (r. 1726–1749). Kartasura was abandoned for the new court of Surakarta in 1745–1746.

[*See also* Trunajaya.]

M. C. Ricklefs, *A History of Modern Indonesia, c. 1300 to the Present* (1981).    M. C. RICKLEFS

**KART DYNASTY.** The Kart (perhaps Kurt) dynasty ruled parts of northwestern Afghanistan and eastern Iran from 1245 to 1381. The Karts played a crucial role in revitalizing the city of Herat, which had been destroyed by the Mongols in 1222. They were noted patrons of writers, artists, and the *ulama* (religious scholars).

The nine Kart rulers, who bore the title *malik*, theoretically governed on behalf of the Ilkhans in western Iran. Relations between them were marked by distrust, however, for the Ilkhans feared that the Kart rulers would try to attain independence. In addition, they regarded the Karts with disdain as a *tajik* (i.e., indigenous) dynasty, rather than one of Turkish origin. The Karts' longevity is attributable in large measure to their adroit diplomacy.

The founder of the line, Shams al-Din Muhammad Kart (1245–1278), was of Ghurid descent. Succession to rule was marked by periods of turbulence, during which the Ilkhans, Chagatai tribesmen to the north, and Sufis at Jam intervened in Herati politics. The Karts achieved their greatest power under Mu'izz al-Din Husain (1332–1370), whose reign coincided with the decline of the Ilkhans and the Chagatai. A Sunni ruler, he fought against the Shi'ite Sarbadarids, defeating them in 1342. Mu'izz al-Din made a formal declaration of his independence in 1349 but was forced by the Chagatai *amir* Qazaghan to retract it two years later.

Mu'izz al-Din was succeeded in Herat by his son, Ghiyas al-Din Pir Ali. Pir Ali also fought with the Sarbadarids, and occupied Nishapur at times in the 1370s. Pir Ali at first resisted Timur's march into Khurasan but was forced to surrender Herat to him in 1381. Herat was then incorporated into the Ti-murid empire, and the last Kart ruler, Pir Ali's son, was put to death in 1389.

[*See also* Ilkhanid Dynasty.]

LAWRENCE POTTER

**KARTINI, RADEN AJENG** (1879–1904), early champion of education for Indonesian women in Dutch Java, where her father was a senior Javanese official. She was exposed to progressive Western ideas through a Dutch-language grammar school education and through her acquaintance and correspondence with several Dutch women and men. Kartini wrote about the indignities of colonialism, education for the Javanese, the emancipation of women, and about her own cultural identity in a series of personal letters to her Dutch mentors that, subsequently published, have become her major legacy. Kartini encouraged the Dutch to take up the issue of women's education seriously and started a modest vocational school for girls before she died at the age of twenty-five.

Raden Adjeng Kartini, *Letters of a Javanese Princess*, translated by Agnes Louise Symmers (1976). Raden Adjeng Kartini, "Educate the Javanese!" translated by Jean Gelman Taylor, *Indonesia* 17 (May 1974): 83–98.

JAMES R. RUSH

**KARTIR**, Zoroastrian priest who left four inscriptions in Middle Persian regarding his rise in influence under the early Sasanids. His name was probably pronounced *kerdir*, and his inscriptions are located at Naqsh-i Rajab; Naqsh-i Rustam, behind the horse of Shapur I; on the Ka'ba-yi Zardusht, also at Naqsh-i Rustam; and Sar Mashhad. His bust is also carved at Naqsh-i Rajab, Naqsh-i Rustam, Sar Mashhad, and Naqsh-i Bahram. He is known only from his inscriptions, all much the same, covering portions of his career.

Kartir claims to have begun his career as a priest under King Shapur I, and under his son and successor Hormazd he was named Ahura Mazda Mobad, a high religious office. Under Bahram I he continued to prosper, while Bahram II gave him the rank of a noble (*wuzurg*) and made him the *mobad* and judge of the entire empire. Furthermore, Hormazd named Kartir head of the fire temple of Anahita at Istakhr, probably the main Sasanid shrine. He died early in the reign of Narseh. Why his name does not appear in literary sources is unknown.

RICHARD N. FRYE

KARVE, DHONDO KESHAV (1858–1962), pioneer of women's education in India and the rights of Hindu widows. A prominent educator in Maharashtra, Karve faced stiff opposition from orthodox society for his support of education and remarriage for widows. In 1898 he founded the Mahilashram (Widows' Home) in Pune (Poona), and later many educational and service institutions, among them the Indian Women's University.

[*See also* Women: Women in South and Southeast Asia.]

G. L. Chandavarkar, *Maharshi Karve* (1958). Dhondo Keshav Karve, *Looking Back* (1936).

FRANK F. CONLON

KASA, classic Korean poetic form that originated in the fifteenth century as song lyrics written to prevailing *kasa* tunes. The *kasa* is characterized by variable length and a lack of stanzaic division; a tendency toward description, exposition, and also lyricism at times; and verbal and syntactical parallelism. Its norm is a group of two four-syllable words—or alternating groups of three and four syllables—that form a unit and are repeated in parallel form.

Often likened to the Chinese *fu,* or rhymed prose, the *kasa* emerged as a new form with "Hymn to the Spring" by Chŏng Kŭ-gin (1402–1481). Masters of the form in subsequent centuries include Chŏng Ch'ŏl (1537–1594), Hŏ Nan-sŏr-hŏn (1563-1585), and Pak Il-lo (1561–1643). Chŏng's works include "The Wanderings" ("Kwandong pyŏlgok," 1580), a description of the eight famous scenes in the Diamond Mountains, two allegorical pieces protesting the exile's loyalty to the king, and "Little Odes to Mount Star" ("Sŏngsan pyŏlgok"), a celebration of the virtues of his friend's retired life. "A Woman's Sorrow" ("Kyuwŏn ka") by Hŏ is a dramatic narrative on the sorrow of unrequited love. Pak Il-lo combined erudition and lyricism, as in "In Praise of Poverty."

The subject matter of the eighteenth-century anonymous *kasa* by women was the daily life of the middle and lower classes. The themes of later examples of definite authorship include records of officials sent to Tokyo and Beijing, praise of institutions, the farmer's works and days, and the sorrow of banishment. Beginning in the late nineteenth century the *kasa* became either didactic (stressing Korea's need for enlightenment), patriotic, or nostalgic. The "Song of Seoul," which details the institutions and glories of the Yi dynasty, was popular among women.

*Kasa* were sung or chanted, and a particular group called the "Twelve Titles," including the "Song of the Fisherman" and "Song of Plum Blossoms," formed a basic repertory. Although it is no longer alive as a poetic form, the *kasa*, like the *sijo*, is still a performing art.

[*See also* Sijo.]

Peter H. Lee, *Anthology of Korean Literature: From Early Times to the Nineteenth-Century*, 1981.

PETER H. LEE

KASHGAR, a city and oasis in the western part of the Tarim Basin in Xinjiang province of China, predominantly Uighur Turkic in population but incorporated into the Chinese Tang empire in the seventh and eighth centuries CE and reclaimed by Qing rule in 1755, with intervals of de facto autonomy and heavy Russian influence between the 1860s and 1950. Buddhism entered China from India via Central Asia through Kashgar during the second century BCE, and the city's prosperity depended in large part on its role as the gateway for the Silk Route from China into Central Asia and areas to the west. The western Turkic empire displaced Chinese rule after the Battle of the Talas River in 751, and Kashgar remained the intellectual and cultural center of the islamicized Karakhanid state until its conquest by the Mongols in 1211. Timur's troops ravaged Kashgar in the late fourteenth century, and it suffered from chronic attacks in subsequent centuries until the reestablishment of Chinese control.

[*See also* Silk Route.]

RHOADS MURPHEY, JR.

KASHGARI, MAHMUD AL-, Turkic scholar and lexicographer, born in Barsgan at the beginning of the eleventh century. Mahmud became a political refugee around 1057 and finally settled in Baghdad, where he wrote the *Compendium of the Turkic Dialects* in 1077. Nothing else is known of his life. The *Compendium* is a Turkic dictionary/encyclopedia describing the Turkiyya language of the Chigil tribe of the Karakhanid confederation. It also contains information on Turkic grammar, dialectology, folklore, history, and epic poetry; and it includes the first Turkic world map.

[*See also* Kutadgu Bilig *and* Turkic Languages.]

Mahmūd al-Kāshgarī, *Compendium of the Turkic Dialects (Dīwān Lugāt at-Turk)*, part 1, edited by Robert Dankoff with James Kelly (1982). JAMES M. KELLY

KASHI. *See* Varanasi.

KASHMIR. The state of Jammu and Kashmir is one of the twenty-two constituent units of the Republic of India. It is divided into three main administrative divisions, of which Kashmir proper is one. Also known as the Kashmir Valley, it is famous the world over for its unique scenic beauty. Surrounded by high mountains of the Pir Panjal range of the Himalayas (12,000 to 18,000 feet above sea level), the valley is a natural geographical region, eighty-four miles long from north to east and twenty-five miles broad, at a height of more than 5,000 feet. Geological evidence in the form of marine fossils has been found to support the legend of the valley having been a lake at one time. According to these legends, this lake was drained of its waters by the ancient sage Kashyapa, who cut a channel *(kash)* in the mountains *(mira)*.

The physical features of Kashmir include, in addition to the mountain ranges, rivers (notably the Jhelum, one of the major rivers of South Asia), mountain streams, freshwater lakes (including the Wular, the largest such lake in Asia), springs, forests, plateaus, and meadows. Its temperate climate, alluvial soil, and abundance of water resources enable the people to raise rich harvests of paddy and other grain and many varieties of vegetables and fruits.

Kashmiri, an Indo-Aryan language with pronounced Central Asian affinities, is spoken by the people of Kashmir. It was traditionally written in a *nagari* script called *sharada,* but this has gradually fallen into disuse, and today only brahman astrologers and priests use it; otherwise, Kashmiri is now written in the Persian script.

The great majority of the people of Kashmir (about 90 percent) are Muslims; the rest are mostly Hindus and Sikhs. Among the Muslims, who first came to Kashmir at the beginning of the fourteenth century as missionaries of Islam, the Sunnis far outnumber the Shi'ites, and there are many more descendants of converts (the Shaikhs) than of Muslim immigrants (Sayyids, Mughals, Pathans, etc.). Ancient Hindu society was characterized by subdivision into castes, which had, however, lost their rigidity under the influence of Buddhism; Kashmir has been, since the early fifteenth century, composed of only the brahmans—a situation without parallel elsewhere in India. Kashmiri brahmans call themselves the Bhatta and are generally known as the Pandits. Both the Prakrit *bhatta* and the Sanskrit *pandita* mean "a learned person." Over the centuries, many Pandit families have settled in various cities of North India to escape from oppression, but they have retained their identity through endogamy and through the preservation of certain customs and practices. The most famous of these *émigré* Pandits has been Jawaharlal Nehru, the first prime minister of India.

Kashmir has produced the first recognizably historical narrative of India, the *Rajatarangini (River of Kings)*. Written in Sanskrit between 1148 and 1150 by a brahman called Kalhana, the saga begins with the legendary past, drawing upon an earlier text, the *Nilamata Purana,* which describes the mythic origins of the holy places of Kashmir and gives an account of ancient customs and practices. It is only when Kalhana comes to Ashoka (272–232 BCE), who appears only as a local king in this narrative, that it can be said to deal with authentic political history. Buddhism was well established in Kashmir by the time the Fourth Buddhist Council was held there in the second century CE.

The first Kashmiri Hindu king of renown was Muktapida Lalitaditya (699–736 CE). He was a great conqueror and extended the boundaries of his kingdom into the Ganges Valley. He built the massive Martand (Sun) temple in southern Kashmir, the ruins of which bear witness to its original magnificence. His successors seem to have remained mostly within the valley. A hundred years after him, another famous king, Avantivarman (856–883), came to the throne. He is said to have been a benevolent ruler who devoted himself to the welfare of his people; his effort to manage the water resources of the valley was one of his major achievements.

During the rule of Suhadeva (1300–1320), an invasion from Qandhar was met not by the king, who fled to safety, but by a Tibetan Buddhist chieftain, Rinchana. Acclaimed as the new ruler by the people, he is said to have wanted to become a Hindu, but the brahmans would not allow it, and so he embraced Islam. He was succeeded by a Muslim retainer of Suhadeva who took the title of Sultan Shams-ud-Din (1338–1341). The early years of Muslim rule were for the most part peaceful. Hindu society in Kashmir had not been characterized by rigid social divisions, and the Muslim Sufi preachers from Persia and Central Asia seem to have found the people receptive to their faith and teachings. The first of these preachers was Bulbul Shah from Turkestan, who came during the time of Suhadeva, but the most famous one was Mir Sayyid Ali of Hamdan (in Persia), who arrived in Kashmir during the last quarter of the fourteenth century. [*See also* Sufism.]

Kashmir underwent a traumatic experience of religious persecution during the rule of Sikandar (1390–1414) who is remembered as Butshikan ("iconoclast"), for he destroyed nearly all the Hindu temples and forced his Hindu subjects to either embrace Islam, leave Kashmir, or be put to the sword. This resulted in large-scale conversions that in the history of India have a parallel only in Bengal. Sikandar had many mosques built, often using materials from the demolished temples. The most famous of these was the original Jama Masjid (Grand Mosque) of Srinagar.

Sikandar's second son, Zain-ud-Abidin (1421–1492), is the most famous and beloved of the Muslim kings of Kashmir, remembered to this day as the Badshah, ("great king"). He anticipated the great Mughal emperor Akbar in many ways—particularly in his respect for non-Islamic religious faiths, concern for the welfare of the people, patronage of scholarship, and interest in architecture. He encouraged his Hindu subjects to return to Kashmir, which many of them did.

Kashmir was incorporated into the Mughal empire by Akbar in 1587. He and his immediate successors built forts and laid many beautiful gardens in Kashmir. In 1739 Kashmir was conquered by Nadir Shah, the king of Kabul. Afghan rule was a period of great misery and persecution for Kashmiris. It ended in 1819 when the Sikh maharaja of Lahore, Ranjit Singh, invaded Kashmir at the request of the Hindus of the valley. Skih rule, however, was not particularly merciful either, and ended in 1846, when the British defeated the Sikh armies. Gulab Singh of Jammu, a Dogra courtier at the Lahore court, bought a portion of the conquered territories, including Jammu and Kashmir, from the victorious British on payment of a million pounds sterling. The state of Jammu and Kashmir thus came into existence and its boundaries were extended by Gulab Singh (1846–1857) and his son Ranbir Singh (1857–1885).

It was during the rule of the next two Dogra maharajas, Pratap Singh (1885–1925) and Hari Singh (1925–1948), that the modernization of Kashmir began. Modern education and medicine were introduced into the valley by Christian missionaries. Administrative reforms included the first settlement survey, which was conducted in the 1890s. Development of roads, waterworks, and hydroelectric projects took place, and to a considerable extent Kashmir lost its relative isolation from the rest of India. Gradually there was a general awakening among the people, and political parties emerged in the early 1930s. The most influential of the political leaders was Sheikh Muhammad Abdullah (1905–1982), who aligned himself and his people with the nationalist movement in the country and was a close associate of Jawaharlal Nehru.

In 1947, with the lapse of British paramountcy over the Indian states, the maharaja tried to enter into "standstill" agreements with India and Pakistan, but the situation was upset by the incursion of Pathan invaders, backed by Pakistani troops, into the state. This resulted in the first Indo-Pakistan war, and a cease-fire line has been maintained in the state ever since. Sheikh Abdullah, popularly known as Sher-i-Kashmir ("the lion of Kashmir"), became the first head of government after the collapse of the maharaja's rule. Radical land reforms, impressive educational and health programs, and the first steps toward industrial development have characterized the policies of various popularly elected governments of the state since 1947.

Kashmir's political history is intertwined with its cultural heritage. The home of Shaivism—one of the most influential religio-philosophical systems of South Asia—Kashmir has been witness to remarkable experiments in cultural synthesis over the centuries. After the early brahman-Buddhist encounter, which produced a distinctive architectural style, the Muslims brought various handicrafts to Kashmir; the Kashmiri shawl and carpet industries were already famous in Europe in the nineteenth century.

Kashmir has produced great Sanskrit scholars, including the famous Abhinavagupta in the early eleventh century, and a number of brahman and Muslim scholars in more recent times, whose contributions to Persian literature have won recognition in Iran. There has also been a rich and steady Kashmiri literary tradition, of which the first distinguished example is the *Vakhya (Poetic Sayings)* of the Shaivite mystic poetess Lalla (late fourteenth century). A cross-fertilization of the Muslim Sufi and mystic traditions also occurred in the fourteenth century. From these early religious and metaphysical beginnings Kashmiri poetry has expanded considerably in scope. The most illustrious and representative poet of the first half of the twentieth century has been Ghulam Ahmad Mahjur (1885–1952). He sang of the beauty of nature, romantic love, religious tolerance, patriotism, and social justice.

[*See also* Srinagar; Shaivism; Mughal Empire; Jammu; *and* Abdullah, Muhammad.]

P. N. K. Bamzai, *A History of Kashmir* (1962). R. C. Kak, *Ancient Monuments of Kashmir* (1936). R. S. Pandit, trans., *Rajatarangini: Saga of the Kings of Kashmir* (1968). G. M. D. Sufi, *Kashmir*, 2 vols. (1949).

T. N. MADAN

KASRAVI, AHMAD (1891–1946), a prominent Iranian intellectual, was born in Tabriz to an extremely religious family and received his primary education in a religious establishment. Turning against the hypocrisy, superficiality, and rigidity that he saw in the curriculum, he left the clerical establishment and joined the constitutionalists in 1911. Mainly for his ardently anti-Shi'ite stand, he was assassinated in 1946 by a member of an extremist religious organization, the Fida'iyan-i Islam, which had formed in 1945 under the leadership of Ayatollah Kashani in Qom. Kasravi is also known as the writer of several works on Iranian political and social history.

[*See also* Constitutional Revolution.]

Ervand Abrahamian, *Iran between Two Revolutions* (1982). Nikki Keddie, *Iran: Roots of Revolution* (1980). Roy P. Mottahedeh, *The Mantle of the Prophet* (1985).

NEGUIN YAVARI

KATAYAMA SEN (1859–1933), Japanese labor union organizer, socialist, and Marxist revolutionary. Born in Okayama Prefecture, Katayama received his early education in the Okayama Normal School and in Tokyo. In 1884 he went to the United States, converted to Christianity, and attended Grinnell College, Andover Theological Seminary, and Yale Divinity School. Returning to Japan in 1896, he founded Kingsley Hall, a Christian settlement house. By 1900 he had become active as a labor organizer and founding member of the Rōdō Kumiai Kiseikai (Society for the Promotion of Trade Unions) and the Tekkō Kumiai (Iron Workers Union). Increasingly interested in socialism he joined the Society for the Study of Socialism and in 1901 helped Abe Isoo and Kōtoku Shūsui to found the short-lived Social Democratic Party. An outspoken pacifist, he traveled to the Sixth Congress of the Second International in Amsterdam during the Russo-Japanese War (1904–1905) and openly shook hands with the Russian delegate Plekhanov.

Back in Japan after the war Katayama engaged in an open debate with Kōtoku, opposing the latter's belief in direct action in favor of gradualism and a parliamentary strategy. In 1914, following Kōtoku's execution, however, he decided to leave Japan for the United States, where he came under the influence of Bolshevik ideas and abandoned his earlier socialist position for Lenin's teachings.

In 1921, in the wake of the Russian Revolution, Katayama emigrated to the Soviet Union and became an active member of the Communist International and a behind-the-scenes supporter of the Japanese communist movement. He died in Moscow in 1933 and is buried in the Kremlin.

[*See also* Communism: Communism in Japan.]

F. G. NOTEHELFER

KATAYAMA TETSU (1887–1978), Japan's only socialist prime minister, serving from May 1947 to February 1948. Katayama was born in Wakayama Prefecture. He attended Tokyo Imperial University, where he was influnced by Abe Isoo and Christianity. Both influences led him to believe in social reform and socialism. Upon graduation he founded a law office and participated in labor disputes. In 1926 Katayama and Abe organized a socialist party, the Shakai Minshūtō, that merged with other groups to become the Shakai Taishūtō in 1932. Katayama was first elected to the House of Representatives in 1930. He was known for his antimilitarist stand and was forced to leave his party after a Diet member was expelled from the Diet for an antimilitarist speech in 1940.

Katayama became prime minister at a time when Japan was undergoing transformation under the Allied Occupation. He worked for new labor legislation and approved of the dissolution of *zaibatsu* (industrial conglomerates) and the creation of the new Ministry of Labor, but he was also obliged to institute wage and price controls and other measures, bringing criticism from elements of his ruling coalition government. As the economy worsened and support diminished, he resigned. After the Socialist Party split in 1951, his role became an advisory one, and he retired from politics after electoral defeat in 1963.

George O. Totten, *The Social Democratic Movement in Prewar Japan* (1966).

MICHIO UMEGAKI

KATHIAWAR, a peninsular region in southwestern Gujarat in India, bounded by the Rann of Kutch, the Arabian Sea, and the Gulf of Cambay. Archaeological evidence at Lothal and elsewhere indicates that the area was part of the Indus Valley civilization and that later it was included in the Maurya empire. It was part of various empires in the following centuries, and in 1024 CE its great Hindu temple complex at Somnath was destroyed in a raid by the Turkic ruler Mahmud of Ghazna. The region was later incorporated into the territories ruled by the

Delhi sultan and his successors, and it became a part of Gujarat, one of the provinces of the Mughal empire. In the eighteenth century numerous petty chieftains asserted their independence, but they were constantly harassed by the Marathas, especially the ruler of Baroda. A number of these chieftains signed a treaty of protection against the Marathas with the British in 1807, and then in 1820, as part of the settlement of western and central India, they came under British control. They were supposed to be treated as independent sovereigns, but there were over 400 who claimed the status of chieftain, most of them holding little more than large estates. A complicated arrangement was worked out whereby 188 chiefs were given a measure of independent jurisdiction under a British Resident, while the rest were grouped under an official of the residency who exercised jurisdiction on their behalf. The government of India, the paramount power, delegated its authority to the government of Bombay, thus creating a multi-layered system of control. Porbandar, one of these small states, achieved special status as the birthplace of Mohandas Gandhi, whose family had been the chief officials of the ruler. The peninsula includes a number of famous Jain temples, and the last wild Indian lions survive in the forests of the Gir hills.

[*See also* Princely States; Gandhi, Mohandas Karamchand; Porbandar; *and* Marathas.]

AINSLIE T. EMBREE

KATHMANDU, a district as well as a bustling city serving as the capital of modern Nepal. It is the country's administrative and commercial center in which are located the palace of the king of Nepal, the Secretariat and other government buildings, foreign embassies, an international airport, and commercial areas. Kathmandu district has an area of 545 square kilometers and a population of 422,237 according to the 1981 census. The city itself is much smaller, however, with an area of 6.4 square kilometers. Historically, Kathmandu was a separate kingdom during the late Malla period (c. 1480–1768). The old town that constitutes the core of Kathmandu is enlivened by its Newar residents, who constitute about 30 percent of the population. Suburban Kathmandu spreads in a three-kilometer radius around the old town and is settled by the non-Newar Nepali-speaking caste groups who arrived in large numbers after the conquest of Kathmandu by the hill state of Gorkha, under Prithvinarayan Shah, in 1768. In the beginning of the twentieth century the town was one mile long and between one-third and one-fourth of a mile in breadth, with a population of about 40,000.

The name *Kathmandu* is said to be derived from the still-extant pavilion made out of the wood of a single tree and called *Kasthamandapa,* reference to which is found beginning in the twelfth century. The town was formerly surrounded by a protective wall, some of the many gates of which still existed in the late nineteenth century. The old town is a melange of residential courtyards, Buddhist *viharas* (monasteries), and Hindu temples, of which 336 are now extant. Its narrow lanes and streets, occasionally opening up into squares, are the site of almost daily festivities of one kind or another. The town has come to acquire the status of a sacred territory for its Newar residents, so that they view it as an ordered space of religious cosmology and perform ritual circumambulation of it on specified occasions in order to gain spiritual merit.

[*See also* Nepal: History of Nepal.]

H. A. Oldfield, *Sketches from Nepal,* 2 vols. (1880; reprint, 1974). Karl Pruscha, ed., *Kathmandu Valley: The Preservation of Physical Environment and Cultural Heritage, A Protective Inventory,* 2 vols. (1975). Mary Slusser, *Nepal Mandala: A Cultural Study of the Kathmandu Valley* (1982). PRAYAG RAJ SHARMA

KATIPUNAN. The Kataastaasan Kagalang-galang na Katipunan ng mga Anak ng Bayan (Highest and Most Respectable Society of the Sons of the People), commonly known as the Katipunan, was a secret separatist society founded in Manila by Andres Bonifacio on 7 July 1892. The Katipunan pursued three objectives. Its political aim was to separate the Philippines from Spain if the latter continued to oppose political and economic reforms, and its civic aim was to develop the principle of mutual help and to defend the poor and oppressed. Its moral objective revolved around the campaign against religious fanaticism and the policy of obscurantism of the friar orders.

The Liga Filipina, an earlier propaganda-reformist society, influenced the structure of the Katipunan, while the masonic movement inspired its initiation and other ceremonies. The society's leaders as well as rank and file came from the lower classes of Philippine society. Like the Liga, the Katipunan had branches in many districts of Manila. It established various councils corresponding to contemporary national, provincial, and municipal governments: a supreme council in Manila, popular councils in the provinces, and municipal councils in the towns. In addition, it published its own newspaper, *Kalayaan (Freedom),* containing the works of Bonifacio and the editor, Emilio Jacinto, which contributed to the society's rapid growth in southern and central Luzon. On the eve of the Philippine Revolution in August 1896, the Katipunan had about thirty thousand members.

After the outbreak of the revolution, however, the Katipunan became very unwieldy, its very existence put at stake. Regionalism and the struggle for political power by leaders of rival factions endangered Bonifacio's supremacy in the society. Some leaders contended that the Katipunan had ceased to be a secret society since the start of hostilities against Spain and that it had outlived its usefulness; thus they argued that it should be replaced by a more organized body. This issue masked the struggle for power between the Magdalo and the Magdiwang, two Katipunan factions in Cavite. Although he traveled to Cavite to attempt a reconciliation, Bonifacio was drawn into the conflict. When the Katipunan held elections at a convention in Tejeros, Bonifacio lost his status as the supreme authority of the Katipunan to Emilio Aguinaldo, a popular Magdalo leader. Considered a better military leader, Aguinaldo was elected president of the newly established revolutionary government. Bonifacio challenged the elections and, together with other leaders of his persuasion, drew the Naik Military Agreement, which aimed to establish a government independent of, and separate from, that established at Tejeros. But he was charged with sedition and with plotting to undermine the legitimacy of the new government. Tried and sentenced to death by a military court, Bonifacio was executed in Cavite on 10 May 1897. With his death, the Katipunan was said to have come to an end. Nonetheless as the struggle for independence continued to rage, Filipinos throughout the country formed themselves into many *katipunanes* (or revolutionary societies) that drew their inspiration from the first Katipunan.

[*See also* Philippine-American War; Philippine Revolution; Friars; Bonifacio, Andres; Jacinto, Emilio; *and* Aguinaldo, Emilio.]

Teodoro A. Agoncillo, *The Revolt of the Masses* (1956) and *The Writings and Trial of Andres Bonifacio* (1963). Gregorio F. Zaide, *History of the Katipunan* (1939).

MILAGROS C. GUERRERO

**KATŌ KIYOMASA** (1562–1611), powerful daimyo (feudal lord) of the late Sengoku period of Japanese history. The son of a blacksmith, Katō Kiyomasa entered the military service of Toyotomi Hideyoshi at a young age and quickly distinguished himself in battle. He received a fief with an assessed productivity of 3,000 *koku* (measures of rice) in central Japan after fighting with special valor in the Battle of Shizugatake in 1583, when Hideyoshi achieved military supremacy in the Hokuriku region. By the end of the Kyushu campaign four years later, Kiyomasa, together with Konishi Yukinaga and Kuroda Nagamasa, had emerged at the top of Hideyoshi's military leadership, and all three were stationed at strategic points in Kyushu, Kiyomasa himself being invested in 1588 with the northern half of Higo Province, assessed at approximately 240,000 *koku.*

Katō commanded a large contingent of troops in the first Korean invasion. He landed at Pusan just two days after Konishi Yukinaga and trailed his fellow commander into Seoul before pushing into Hamgyong Province in the extreme northeast, where he became bogged down in bitter fighting during the winter of 1592–1593. Katō withdrew to Kyushu as part of the general retreat several months later, but he strongly opposed the peace initiatives suggested by Konishi and became one of the most strident voices within Hideyoshi's councils urging a return to the continent. Katō fought with ruthless ferocity during that second failed attempt, earning the nickname "Tiger of Korea," as well as the eternal enmity of the Korean people.

Back in Japan, Katō joined the victorious Tokugawa coalition in the Battle of Sekigahara in 1600, and for this he was rewarded with the southern half of Higo Province, taken from his former ally, the fallen Konishi, who had fought as a member of the ill-fated western alliance. The new acquisition gave Katō a domain with an assessed productivity of approximately 520,000 *koku,* the tenth largest among the daimyo. To rule over this territory, Katō rebuilt his home castle at Kumamoto and initiated a series of reclamation and irrigation projects that eventually raised the actual productivity of the domain to nearly 740,000 *koku.* The Tokugawa house, however, was never completely certain of Katō's loyalties because of his past association with Hideyoshi, and when Kiyomasa's son and heir, Tadahiro, was suspected in 1532 of complicity in a plot against the third Tokugawa shogun, the domain was confiscated and transferred to the Hosokawa family.

[*See also* Hideyoshi's Invasion of Korea; Konishi Yukinaga; Sekigahara, Battle of; *and* Sengoku Period.]

JAMES L. MCCLAIN

KATŌ TAKAAKI (1860–1926), also known as Katō Komei, Japanese diplomat and politician. The son of a lower samurai in Owari domain (Aichi), Katō graduated at the head of his class in English law from Tokyo University in 1881. He entered Mitsubishi's Mail Steamship Company and was sent to England. He embarked upon an official career in 1887, subsequently serving twice as minister to Britain and four times as foreign minister. The pro-English Katō played a major role in concluding the Anglo-Japanese Alliance of 1902. Politically ambitious, he joined Katsura Tarō's new party, the Dōshikai in 1913. When Katsura died later that year, Katō assumed the presidency of the Dōshikai, a position that he retained in the succeeding Kenseikai (established in 1916). In 1914 he became foreign minister in the Dōshikai-backed cabinet of Ōkuma Shigenobu. He was largely responsible for Japan's entry into World War I on the side of the Allies and for imposing the harsh Twenty-one Demands on the Chinese in 1915. He was soon forced to resign by the enraged Ōkuma, whom Katō had deliberately bypassed in both matters.

Despite his tough China policy and elitist sentiments, Katō committed the Kenseikai to English-style democratic reforms following World War I, the most notable of which were responsible party cabinets, universal manhood suffrage, and trade union legislation. In 1924 Katō formed a coalition cabinet with the Seiyūkai and Kakushin Kurabu. The Katō cabinet's most notable achievement was the passage of the Universal Manhood Suffrage Law (1925), although it also sponsored the repressive Peace Preservation Law. Opposition from nonparty elites and the Seiyūkai prevented significant reforms regarding the House of Peers and labor relations. After the Seiyūkai withdrew from the cabinet in August 1925, the ailing Katō reorganized a minority Kenseikai cabinet. He died in office the following January.

[See also Katsura Tarō; Anglo-Japanese Alliance; Twenty-one Demands; and Peace Preservation Law.]

Peter Duus, *Party Rivalry and Political Change in Taishō Japan* (1968). Itō Masanori, *Katō Takaaki*, 2 vols. (1929; reprint, 1970).    SHELDON M. GARON

KATSU KAISHU (1823–1899), officer of the Japanese government during the Tokugawa shogunate *(bakufu)*. Born into a samurai family of modest means, Katsu Kaishu built a career from his knowledge of the West, the study of which he began in 1845. In 1853 he won official recognition with a memorial, submitted in the wake of the Perry mission, on the subject of national defense. This led, in 1855, to an appointment as translator in the *bakufu's* Foreign Studies Institute, quickly followed by an assignment, later that same year, to the *bakufu's* newly formed Nagasaki Naval Academy. There, under instructors from the Netherlands, Katsu learned enough seamanship to qualify for the command of the *Kanrin Maru* on its voyage from Uraga to San Francisco in 1860.

Thereafter, as commander of Tokugawa naval forces from 1862 to 1864, and again from 1866 to 1868, Katsu was one of the *bakufu's* most powerful officials. Attrition among his colleagues at the beginning of 1868 was to leave Katsu in control of what remained of Tokugawa authority, and in this capacity he was able to negotiate the settlement by which Edo was surrendered to the imperial army and Tokugawa remnants were withdrawn to Shizuoka. This was a task for which his previous political activities, involving cordial relations with many either critical of, or hostile to, the government he served, had made him eminently suited. The new (Meiji) government, however, proved a disappointment. It rewarded him with a series of sonorous titles, but this failed to satisfy him, and in 1875, at the age of fifty-two, Katsu resigned to spend his remaining years in reminiscence and recrimination.

HAROLD BOLITHO

KATSURA TARŌ (1847–1913), field marshal, prince, and three-time prime minister of Japan. Katsura was second in importance only to his mentor Yamagata Aritomo as a soldier-politician of the Meiji period (1868–1912). Born into a Chōshū (now Yamaguchi Prefecture) samurai family, he fought with domain forces against the Tokugawa shogunate. After the Meiji Restoration (1868) he studied Western military science in France and in Germany, where he was an attaché from 1875 to 1878.

Katsura's organizational skill enabled him to help reorganize the army along German lines. In 1886, as a major general, he was army vice-minister. During the Sino-Japanese War (1894–1895) he gained fame as a general. After the war, rewarded with a title, he became governor-general of Taiwan (1896) and then army minister in three successive cabinets (1898–1900). In 1901, as Yamagata's protégé, he began the first of three prime-ministerships. The major events of his first cabinet (1901–1906), an alliance with Britain (1902) and a victory over Russia (1904–1905), won Japan new status as an imperial power and eventually won him the title of prince. During his second premiership (1908–1911) Japan annexed Korea. In carrying out his domestic policies, Katsura reluctantly accepted the need to compromise with the majority party, the Seiyūkai, in order to win passage for growing military budgets. In return, he twice supported the Seiyūkai president Saionji Kimmochi as his successor.

Katsura was criticized as a narrow, ruthless, Chōshū-clique general, and this distrust erupted when he formed his third cabinet in December 1912. The preceding Saionji cabinet had collapsed when the army refused to withdraw its demands for two divisions. Now Katsura, who had retired from politics to serve the newly enthroned Taishō emperor at court, was immediately confronted by the vociferous Movement to Protect Constitutional Government, which accused him of manipulating the emperor and using clique politics to expand the army. Neither his use of an imperial pronouncement to silence his foes nor his formation of a new political party (Dōshikai) saved him. He was forced to resign in February 1913 and died eight months later.

[See also Yamagata Aritomo; Meiji Period; and Taishō Political Change.]

ROGER F. HACKETT

**KAUM MUDA—KAUM TUA,** phrase used to describe modern and traditional elements in Malay society during the first three decades of the twentieth century. The term *Kaum Muda* refers to the Arab-educated religious purists, concentrated largely in Singapore and Penang, who sought to rid Islam of what they considered superstitious accretions so that Muslims would be able to compete in the modern world. The term *Kaum Tua* refers to the traditional Malay aristocracy and religious hierarchy. In general the influence of the modernists was limited by their Arab and Jawi Peranakan origins and the restricted importance of their issues to rural Malay society; moreover, the traditionalists could effectively picture them as dangerous radicals.

William R. Roff, "Kaum Muda—Kaum Tua: Innovation and Reaction Amongst the Malays, 1900–1941," in *Papers on Malayan History*, edited by K. G. Tregonning (1962), and *The Origins of Malay Nationalism* (1967).

RAJESWARY AMPALAVANAR

**KAUTILYA,** also known as Kautalya, Chanakya, and Vishnugupta. According to Indian tradition, Kautilya was a counselor to the Maurya emperor Chandragupta, whom he helped to overthrow the Nandas and found the Maurya dynasty. If so, Kautilya lived at the end of the fourth century BCE. The Sanskrit treatise attributed to him, the *Arthashastra*, the text of which did not come to light until the beginning of the twentieth century, aroused much interest in that it significantly increased our knowledge of ancient Indian law, administration, and politics. Although some scholars still defend its traditional date, others assign it to a much later period, as late as the third century CE, or believe it to be a composite text. Kautilya's ruthless views on international relations—every king is a potential world conqueror *(chakravartin);* a neighboring king is necessarily an enemy; a neighbor's neighbor an ally; and so forth—earned him the title of the Indian Machiavelli.

[See also Hindu Law; Maurya Empire; and Chakravartin.]

*The Kauṭilīya Arthaśāstra,* 3 vols., edited and translated by R. P. Kangle (1960–1965).    LUDO ROCHER

**KAVILA,** *chao* of Chiang Mai (r. 1775–1813), founder of the nineteenth-century successor to the ancient kingdom of Lan Na in northern Thailand. In the chaos of the 1760s and 1770s, when Burma occupied old Lan Na and used it as a base for attacking Siam, the governor of Lampang, Phraya Kavila (or Kawila), proved to be an inspiring and effective leader and general. He impressed the Siamese generals who campaigned in the region in the mid-1770s, and one of them, on coming to the throne of Siam in 1782 as King Rama I, subsequently recognized Kavila as his vassal ruler of all the north, while Kavila's younger sister married the king's younger brother. In 1781, with Siamese backing, Kavila moved his capital from Lampang to Chiang Mai, symbolically reviving old Lan Na. The last of his descendants ruled until 1939 under Siamese suzerainty.

[See also Lan Na; Chiang Mai; Phra Phutthayotfa Chulalok; and Intanon.]

K. Wenk, *The Restoration of Thailand under Rama I, 1782–1809* (1968).    DAVID K. WYATT

**KAYA.** See Mimana.

**KAYASTH,** a caste name borne by three separate communities—the Chitragupta Kayasths of northern India, the Prabhu Kayasths of Maharashtra, and the Kayasths of Bengal. Culturally and structurally distinct, with mother tongues of Hindi, Marathi, and Bengali, respectively, all three groups were originally "writing castes," that is, their traditional occupation was of administrative service to the local political rulers. The name *Kayasth* has come to designate the North Indian Chitraguptas, who exemplify the adaptability and social mobility possible in the caste system. Although having a disputed origin, this community became prominent after Muslim rule had become established in the Indian subcontinent. Kayasth men became proficient in the new administrative languages of Persian and Urdu, and many attained important positions in the central Mughal administration and in provincial outposts throughout the empire. Although Chitragupta Kayasths follow high-caste Hindu domestic practices, their customs and fashions also reflect a close association with the Mughal court culture that dominated much of India for centuries. With the advent of British rule, Kayasths became conspicuously successful in the English educational and administrative systems. Kayasth men and women have been prominent in social reform and in literary and political movements in modern India.

Karen Leonard, *The Social History of an Indian Caste: The Kayasths of Hyderabad* (1978).   KAREN LEONARD

KAYSONE PHOMVIHAN, general secretary of the Lao People's Revolutionary Party (LPRP) since its founding in 1955 and the most powerful political leader in Laos. In addition to his leading post in the party hierarchy, Kaysone has served as prime minister of the Lao People's Democratic Republic (LPDR) since its proclamation in December 1975.

Kaysone was born on 13 December 1920 in the village of Na Seng, district of Khanthaboury, province of Savannakhet in southern Laos, of a Lao mother and a Vietnamese father who was secretary to the French colonial resident of Savannakhet Province. He studied at the Faculty of Law of the University of Hanoi and (apparently before completing his degree) left in 1942 to join the student struggle against the French colonial power and their Japanese mentors. In August 1945 he took part in the overthrow of the Japanese rulers in his home province of Savannakhet.

Kaysone joined the Indochinese Communist Party (ICP), probably in 1946, and devoted his total effort in the post–World War II years to the defeat of the French colonial power in Indochina and the establishment of a communist regime in Laos. In 1946 he was assigned to mobilize Lao residents in Vietnam into the anti-French movement. In 1947 he became chairman of the Resistance Committee for

Northeastern Laos. He is credited with establishing in 1949 a Lao armed resistance unit named Latsavong, which has been labeled the embryo of the current Lao People's Liberation Army (LPLA). In 1950 Kaysone was a founding member of the Lao Government of Resistance and served as its minister of national defense. In 1955, along with twenty-four other Lao who had been members of the ICP, he founded the LPRP and was named its general secretary, as well as commander in chief of the LPLA.

In the period of Lao independence following the Geneva agreements of 1954, Kaysone was the primary leader of the Lao communist revolutionary movement, commonly referred to as the Pathet Lao (PL). In 1958 he directed the PL from headquarters in Vientiane, then under the control of the Royal Lao government. Kaysone ran as a candidate in Attopeu Province for the National Assembly in the supplementary elections of May 1958 and was defeated.

Following the Geneva Conference on the Laotian Question (1962), Kaysone remained in Sam Neua when other PL leaders took ministries in the newly formed tripartite government. When the tripartite government fell apart and hostilities broke out once again in 1964, Kaysone moved the PL headquarters to a complex of caves in the mountains of Sam Neua to seek protection from American bombardment. With the advice and assistance of the Vietnamese, Kaysone continued to lead the revolutionary struggle through the cease-fire of 1972 and the establishment of the LPDR in 1975.

[*See also* Laos; Geneva Conference of 1954; Pathet Lao; Geneva Conference on the Laotian Question; Communism: Communism in Southeast Asia; *and* Indochina War.]

JOSEPH J. ZASLOFF

KAZAKHS. A Central Asian people and a constituent nationality of the USSR, the Kazakhs are of Turco-Mongolian stock; they speak Kazakh, a Turkic language of the Kipchak-Nogai subgroup, and are Sunni Muslims (Hanafi legal school). The 1979 census reported 6,556,442 Kazakhs living in the USSR, of whom 5,289,349 were found in the Kazakh SSR (36 percent of the population of the republic). It is estimated that six or seven hundred thousand Kazakhs live in China, some forty thousand in Mongolia, and about four thousand in Afghanistan. The Kazakh SSR, also known as Kazakhstan, the second-largest republic in area in the Soviet Union (2,717,300 sq. km.), is bounded on the north and west by the Russian SFSR, on the south by the Turkmen SSR, the Uzbek SSR, and the Kirghiz SSR, and on the east by China.

Tribes of Turkic pastoral nomads have lived in this area since the eighth century BCE, ruled in turn by the Saksky, the Massagetae, the Alpans, the Usuns and Kungis, the Karluk khanate, the Karakhanids, the Karakhitai, and the Mongols. The Kazakhs, however, were not consolidated as a distinct people until the middle of the fifteenth century, when a group of disparate Turkic and Mongol tribes (including the Kipchak, Argun, Usun, Naiman, and Dulats) gathered in the Dasht-i Kipchak (the Kipchak steppe, the area between the Chu and Sang Su rivers) to graze on unused pasturelands. There, under the guidance of Janibek and Kirai, sons of Barak Khan of the White Horde, the tribal confederation known as the Kazakh khanate was formed.

The term *Kazakh,* the derivation of which is still under dispute, came into use by residents of the area in the late fifteenth or early sixteenth century, possibly at the time of Qasim Khan (r. 1511–1518). The territory under Kazakh control continued to expand until the last quarter of the seventeenth century; Khan Tauke (r. 1680–1718) inherited a khanate roughly identical in size to present-day Kazakhstan. During this period of expansion the Kazakhs became divided into three distinct tribal confederations (hordes): the Great Horde (Ulu Yuz), Middle Horde (Orta Yuz), and Small Horde (Kichi Yuz). At the end of the seventeenth century Kazakh control of the steppe was threatened from the east by the powerful Kalmuk confederation in Dzungaria. In 1723 the Kalmuks made a successful surprise attack. The Kazakhs fled northwest and northeast in their great retreat *(aqtaban shubirindi)* to the Emba, Yaik (Ural), and Ili rivers, the boundaries of the Russian empire.

The expulsion of the Kazakhs from their pasturelands ended the Kazakh khanate and threatened Kazakh economic self-sufficiency. Until the eighteenth century the Kazakhs were nomads who annually drove herds of sheep, goats, horses, or camels over fixed routes of several thousand kilometers. Kazakh customary law *(adat)* gave each tribe or clan the right to assign usage of pastureland to the constituent *auls* (migratory units), and the *aul* elder *(aksakal)* further divided the grazing lands within his community. After the defeat of the Kazakhs by the Kalmuks the khan of each horde sought to secure lands for his people. In the vain hope that his clans would receive access to Bashkir land, Abu al-Khair Khan of the Small Horde swore suzerainty to Empress Anna Ionnovna in 1731. Semeke Khan of the Middle Horde sought access to the land in western

Siberia and swore loyalty to the empress in 1740, but his successor Ablai Khan did not. The Great Horde came under Kalmuk domination and then, with the defeat of the Kalmuks, under the control of the khan of Khokand.

At the end of the eighteenth century the Russians decided to extend their control over the Kazakh territory, and in the 1830s and 1840s, when civil measures such as the celebrated Speransky Reforms of 1822 had failed, they began the military annexation of the steppe and Turkestan regions. Although Soviet history now applauds the "voluntary unification" of the Kazakh and Russian people, in fact the Russians battled localized resistance for one hundred years (1770–1870). The Russians twice brought in considerable force, defeating Batyr Srym in the Small Horde in the 1770s and Kenesari Qasimov in the Middle Horde in the 1840s.

The Kazakh pastoral economy was transformed by direct Russian rule. The Steppe Positions of 1868 and 1891 asserted the crown's ownership of all land and introduced the principles of restricted Kazakh land usage in the steppe. In the last twenty years of tsarist rule 2.5 million Russian and Ukrainian homesteaders arrived in the Kazakh steppe and settled in northern Kazakhstan. In these same years state-supported secular schools and Muslim religious schools were established in the steppe. Russian rule also led to increased contact between the Kazakhs (hitherto weak Muslims) and Tatar and Turkestani missionaries. The graduates of these various schools, the first Kazakh intelligentsia, became political activists in the pre- and post-revolutionary years.

For most Kazakhs the years of colonial rule brought declining economic fortunes. World War I brought isolation and further hardship, and the announcement of a draft of Central Asian laborers led to widespread Kazakh resistance. After the February Revolution in 1917, the Kazakhs established an embryonic government of national autonomy, the Alash Orda, which resisted the Bolshevik takeover until late 1919. In 1920 Kazakhstan became part of Soviet Russia, achieving union republic status in 1936.

The settlement of the Kazakh nomads and the transformation of the Kazakh livestock-breeding economy were the key agenda items of the 1920s, but the Kazakh communists clashed with Stalin when he introduced forced collectivization. Almost seven hundred thousand families died during the collectivization drive, and almost an entire generation of Kazakh intellectuals, communists and noncommunists alike, were wiped out during the purges.

The industrialization of Kazakhstan began during

World War II, but the industrial work force and management is still dominated by ethnic Russians. More than 70 percent of all Kazakhs work in agriculture and livestock breeding on *sovkhozi* (state farms) or *kolkhozi* (collective farms). Although collectivization destroyed the pastoral nomadic economy, most of the Kazakhs continued to live in ethnically homogeneous *kolkhozi* and drove livestock part of the year. However, Khrushchev's Virgin Land Policy (1954) introduced large-scale wheat farming, as well as several million Europeans, into the six northern *oblasts* (regions) of Kazakhstan. It also led to the elimination of traditional Kazakh livestock-breeding practices in all but the desert regions of western Kazakhstan, as the Kazakhs were again pushed further south onto new ethnically heterogeneous *sovkhozi*, where they had to grow fodder to feed their animals.

The traditional Kazakh culture has also been strongly modified by more than sixty-five years of Soviet rule. Religious and customary traditions have been legally restricted, but age-old practices associated with birth, death, and the attainment of manhood remain universally observed. Virtually all Kazakhs are literate, and they have preserved a distinct literary language. As a minority within their own republic, they are engaged in an uphill battle to transmit their language and cultural heritage. The Kazakh intellectuals born and raised under Soviet rule seem determined, however, to preserve their unique historical and cultural legacy, and so the survival of a distinct Kazakh people seems assured for at least the next few generations.

[*See also* Central Asia; Kalmuks; *and* Siberia.]

Shirin Akiner, *Islamic Peoples of the Soviet Union* (1983). Alexandre Bennigsen and Chantal Lemercier-Quelquejay, *Islam in the Soviet Union* (1967). George Demko, *The Russian Colonization of Kazakhstan 1896–1916* (1960). Zev Katz, ed., *Handbook of Major Soviet Nationalities* (1975). Thomas Winner, *The Oral Art and Literature of the Kazakhs of Russian Central Asia* (1955).

MARTHA BRILL OLCOTT

**KECIL, RAJA,** leader of the Minangkabau rebels who captured the regalia of Johor in 1718. He claimed to be the posthumous son of the murdered Sultan Mahmud, but in all probability he was a Minangkabau adventurer who used to his advantage the relative instability of the newly established Bendahara dynasty and the resentment that its efforts to strengthen its control over Johor had aroused. Claiming connections with both the old Melaka dynasty and the Minangkabau court at Pagar Ruyong,

Kecil won over the Orang Laut who manned the Johor fleet and deposed Abdul Jalil. Although he was driven from Johor by Tun Mahmud's nephew and the Bugis, he kept Siak and became the staunchest enemy of the growing Buginese power in the Melaka Straits, opposing them in Kedah and elsewhere.

[*See also* Mahmud Syah II; Abdul Jalil Riayat Syah; Tun Mahmud; *and* Bugis.]

Barbara W. Andaya and Leonard Y. Andaya, *A History of Malaysia* (1982). R. O. Winstedt, *A History of Johor* (1979).                                    DIANNE LEWIS

**KEDAH,** northernmost state of the Federation of Malaysia, is one of the oldest Malay states. Lying at the southern end of the Isthmus of Kra, facing both the Bay of Bengal and the Strait of Melaka, it was ideally placed to become an entrepôt in the developing India–China trade. It traded tin, pepper, and jungle products common to its Malay neighbors, and there was an abundance of rice grown on the fertile and well-watered Kedah Plain. Archaeological evidence points to the presence of an early Buddhist kingdom in Kedah; some scholars even speculate that it may have been the site of the great Malay thalassocracy of Srivijaya, of which Kedah was unquestionably a part by the seventh century. But by the thirteenth century the contingencies of the China trade led to a decline in Malay power, and Kedah was a tributary of the budding Thai empire.

Throughout Kedah's history Malay, then Thai, power rose or fell in succession. By the fifteenth century Kedah had adopted Islam, and it became even more reluctant to submit to its Buddhist neighbor, throwing in its lot with Islamic Melaka instead. In 1511 Melaka fell to the Portuguese, and the Thai dominated Kedah again, despite all its strategies. In 1619, devastated by a particularly savage attack from Aceh, Kedah was forced to turn to Siam for protection. In the eighteenth century, however, both Thai and Malay power were weakened for a variety of reasons, and trade in the Bay of Bengal steadily increased. Kedah flourished at this time: its rice, tin, pepper, and jungle products were in demand.

Civil wars were fought during the first decades of the century, but from the mid-1720s to 1778 Sultan Muhammed Jiwa Abidin Syah promoted Kedah's prosperity and independence. The Bugis from Riau, however, were attempting to forge an empire in the old Malay heartland, and in 1770 they attacked Kedah with help from forces from Perak and Selangor and rebels from Kedah's own *anak raja*. Although its independence survived, Kedah's prosperity did not. By the end of the century Thai power had also revived. In response, Muhammed Jiwa and his successor tried to forge a protective alliance with the British, who now carried on an important part of the trade to China. To this end Kedah ceded Pulau Pinang and Provence Wellesley to the British East India Company in 1786. But the bid to secure a powerful protector and become free forever of the obligation to send the *bunga mas* (Malay, "golden flowers"; the ornamental gifts made of gold and silver given by the vassal states to their rulers) and fulfill other burdensome trappings of tributary status did not succeed. The British failed to fulfill Kedah's expectations, refusing to see the concessions as anything more than a commercial transaction; it was not in their interest to alienate either the Bugis or the Thai for the sake of Kedah.

The situation became worse for Kedah when the Thai objected to Kedah's arrangement with the English. Moreover, a new series of Thai-Burmese wars put great pressure on Kedah, and it was finally overrun by Siam in 1821. The sultan escaped to Penang but received no solace from the British. In 1842, after several abortive attempts had been made to drive out the Thai, he submitted and was reinstated as ruler. Kedah now regained a large amount of domestic independence. Unlike the southern Malay states, Kedah enjoyed a stable and innovative leadership in the second half of the nineteenth century that carried it through the many changes of the period—marked by population increase and agricultural reform—with minimum disruption.

Reunion with the southern Malay states occurred unexpectedly. In 1909, under an agreement between Britain and Thailand, Kedah was transferred to British rule. Kedah could not be fitted into the existing Federated Malay States machinery, for here there was no excuse to replace the existing bureaucracy with British "advisers." Like Johor and the other former Thai states of Perlis, Kelantan, and Trengganu, Kedah continued to enjoy a large measure of domestic autonomy.

From 1942 to 1945 Kedah was occupied by Japanese forces. When the British returned, they proposed a new constitution, called the Malayan Union, to combine the independent protected states with the Federated Malay States and the Straits Settlements. But the independent states, including Kedah, felt that the provisions of the constitution would endanger many of their rights. The scheme was dropped in favor of the establishment of a looser federation in 1948. Kedah was again part of a larger Malay nation, which became independent in 1957.

[*See also* Malaya, Federation of; Malaysia; Srivijaya; Bugis; Riau; East India Company; Bunga Mas; *and* Malayan Union.]

Sharon Ahmat, *Kedah: Tradition and Change in a Malay State* (1984). Barbara W. Andaya and Leonard Y. Andaya, *A History of Malaysia* (1982). R. Bonney, *Kedah, 1771–1821: The Search for Security and Independence* (1971). C. Mary Turnbull, *A Short History of Malaysia, Singapore and Brunei* (1980).        DIANNE LEWIS

**KEDIRI,** large town on the upper reaches of the Brantas River, East Java. As Kediri-Daha, it was an important regional kingdom until 1222.

The kingdom of Kediri-Daha was the result of King Airlangga's decision to divide his East Javanese kingdom in 1049 so that both his recognized successors could rule. With the Brantas River as the dividing line, the western half became Kediri-Daha and the eastern section Janggala, which in time would spawn the Singosari-Majapahit empire. The magico-religious act of dividing the realm through the supernatural powers of the sage Bharada explains the internecine wars, palace coups, and general centrifugal forces that constantly threatened the unity of the East Javanese polity, especially after the fall of Kediri-Daha in 1222. The Kediri period witnessed an unparalleled flowering of the literary arts, as well as an upsurge in commerce throughout the archipelago.

[*See also* Airlangga; Singosari; *and* Majapahit.]

D. G. E. Hall, *A History of South-East Asia* (4th ed., 1968).        M. C. HOADLEY

**KEIŌ GIJUKU,** the oldest Western-style university in Japan. Keiō Gijuku has its roots in the lessons on the Dutch language that Fukuzawa Yukichi, then a samurai of Nakatsu *han* (domain) in Kyushu, started giving at the *han* office in Edo in 1858. By 1865 these lessons had grown into his own private school for modern learning. It came to be called Keiō Gijuku, after the contemporary era (Keiō), the reign of Emperor Kōmei. The curriculum had developed to such an extent by the late 1880s that in 1890 the school was reorganized, becoming the first private Japanese university with faculties of literature, economics, and law. Since 1898 it has maintained an integrated system of education beginning at the elementary school level. In 1906 a graduate school was added, and in 1917 a school of medicine was founded.

From its earliest days under the leadership of Fukuzawa, Keiō has promoted interchange with foreign institutions of education. Since 1956, seminars have been offered in cooperation with Harvard University, a partnership that led in 1978 to the establishment of the Graduate School of Business Administration, patterned after Harvard's. Today, the university is composed of faculties in letters, economics, law, business and commerce, science and technology, and medicine. There are also research institutes, laboratories, and research centers, such as Keiō Economic and Social Observatory and the Pharmaceutical Institute. Undergraduate enrollment in 1981 was 23,341, and graduate enrollment was 1,336.

[See also Fukuzawa Yukichi; Rangaku; and Education: Education in Japan.]

KIMITADA MIWA

KELANTAN, a once-independent sultanate on the east coast of the Malay Peninsula that is now part of Malaysia. It was long a major center of Malay population, cultural efflorescence, and political activity. Since under colonial rule it did not experience the rapid economic development or the massive Chinese and South Asian immigration that some of the western peninsular states did, its population still consists largely of Malay peasants and fisherfolk. Their numbers and allegiances have critically affected recent Malaysian politics.

The bulk of this population has always resided along or near the Kelantan River, at whose delta an identifiable political entity seems to have existed for some centuries. Until the nineteenth century Kelantan's development was shaped by its involvement in the Gulf of Siam trading system, from which it absorbed a variety of economic, political, and cultural influences, especially from Thailand, Cambodia, China, and the maritime Malay world. During the nineteenth century, Siam extended southward into the Malay Peninsula and sought to transform its hitherto tributary relationship with Kelantan and to impose direct political control. But as a result of a civil war fought for control of Kota Bahru, the new capital, and of its growing trade, Kelantan emerged unified and strengthened under Sultan Muhammad II (r. 1838–1886). The instability that followed his death again made Kelantan vulnerable to outside designs; now, however, Siam was frustrated by the extension of British influence northward from Singapore. Through treaties signed in 1902 and 1909 Britain secured control of Kelantan. After the first treaty it was administered by an Englishman serving under the Thai government; after the second it became, as one of the Unfederated Malay States, part of British Malaya. Except for the years 1941–1945 (when, though nominally transferred to Siam, it was under Japanese rule), Kelantan remained under British control until the Federation of Malaya, precursor of the present Malaysian federation into which it was incorporated in 1948, became independent in 1957.

Despite these various changes in Kelantan's international legal status, a powerful and distinctive Kelantanese cultural and political identity has steadily emerged since the nineteenth century, providing a fundamental continuity to the state's modern history. It fuses three principal elements: a strong local and east coast regional sentiment; a concern with Malay culture and values, pan-Malay as well as local; and an intensifying commitment to Islamic religious orthodoxy, social values, and an assertive politics informed by them. Of these, the third has become increasingly central. In the nineteenth century the commitment to Islam was boosted via connections with the Kelantanese community in Mecca and by refugee Islamic religious teachers from nearby Thai-dominated Patani; in the twentieth, by various worldwide currents of Islamic reformism, nationalism, and sociocultural resurgence. Recently, that emergent Kelantanese identity has found forceful expression through the Pan-Malayan Islamic Party, or Parti Islam (PI). A peasant-backed populist opposition party led by Islamic scholars and intellectuals, the PI held state power in Kelantan from 1959 to 1978 and thereby mounted a major challenge to the domination of Malay—and thus national—politics by the United Malays National Organization (UMNO). After a period of eclipse since 1978, the PI, under new leadership, seems again resurgent. Thus, while it is still geographically the most remote of the peninsular Malay states, Kelantan—the bastion of the PI and hence principal arena of conflict between the two main contenders for Malay support—stands at the center of modern Malaysian politics.

[See also Malaysia; Unfederated Malay States; Federated Malay States; Pan-Malayan Islamic Party; and United Malays National Organization.]

Clive S. Kessler, Islam and Politics in a Malay State: Kelantan 1838–1969 (1978). W. R. Roff, ed., Kelantan: Religion, Society and Politics in a Malay State (1974).

CLIVE S. KESSLER

KEMMU RESTORATION (1333–1336), a brief attempt by a Japanese emperor (Go-Daigo, 1288–1339) to restore rule by the imperial court after the overthrow in 1333 of Japan's first warrior (samurai) government, the Kamakura shogunate (1185–

1333). The restoration is named *Kemmu* after the calendrical era of the years 1334 to 1335.

From at least the ninth century on, the ruling power of the Japanese throne had been arrogated by others, for example, by regents of the courtier family of Fujiwara from the late ninth to the late eleventh century and by abdicated emperors *(in)* from the late eleventh to late twelfth century. [*See* Fujiwara Period.] With the founding of the first shogunate at Kamakura in 1185 came Japan's medieval age and a shift of power from Kyoto to Kamakura, from the emperor and court society to the shogun and warrior society. When the Kamakura shogunate weakened in the early fourteenth century, Emperor Go-Daigo became the head of a loyalist movement to overthrow it. Enlisting the aid of warrior chieftains estranged from the Kamakura regime, the loyalists succeeded in destroying the shogunate in 1333. Go-Daigo interpreted the shogunate's destruction as a mandate to "restore" imperial rule. His restoration was a reactionary attempt to turn the clock of history back five hundred years, to a time when, he believed, emperors had still ruled directly. But the real political requirements of the day involved the need to establish new institutions for governing the warrior class and the means to redress the warriors' continuing assumption of control over land. The Restoration government had little sense of warrior needs and in particular failed badly in adjudicating warrior claims to land. In 1336 Ashikaga Takauji (1305–1358) seized power from Go-Daigo and founded in Kyoto a new military regime, the Ashikaga, or Muromachi, shogunate (1336–1573). Go-Daigo meanwhile escaped and went to Yoshino to the south, where he set up a "southern court" that existed concurrently (1336–1392) with the "northern court" in Kyoto backed by the Ashikaga.

[*See also* Go-Daigo; Ashikaga Takauji; Yoshino Line; *and* Nambokuchō.]

PAUL VARLEY

**KEN ANGROK** (c. 1182–1227), founder of the kingdom of Singosari in East Java.

The *Nagarakertagama* and the *Pararaton*, two Javanese chronicles, give different versions of Ken Angrok's life. The former sums up the story in chronograms for the years 1182, 1222, and 1227, detailing his "appearance," victory over the king of Kediri, and death. The *Pararaton* devotes its longest section to a semimythological account of his life. It recounts Ken Angrok's divine origin; his upbringing by the thief Lembong; his wanderings through East Java, during which he supports himself by assault and robbery; and his career in service of the regent of Tumapel, whom he assassinates and replaces. Two further characteristics of the Angrok story are the acquisition of Ken Dedes, his predecessor's wife, and the *kris* (dagger) forged by Empu Gandring and cursed by its maker and first victim to bring about the death of Ken Angrok and his successors.

Both sources agree that shortly after seizing power Ken Angrok launched a successful revolt against the king of Kediri, winning a decisive battle at Ganter in 1221. The following year the kingdom of Singosari was founded at Tumapel, northeast of Malang, where Angrok reigned under the name Rangga Rajasa until 1227.

[*See also* Singosari.]

M. C. HOADLEY

**KENKOKUSETSU** (National Foundation Day), or Kenkoku Kinembi (formerly known as Kigensetsu), is Japan's national holiday. In 1872 the leaders of the new Meiji government designated 11 February to commemorate the founding of Japan by the legendary Emperor Jimmu in 660 BCE. Defeat in World War II destroyed many of the nationalistic symbols and signs associated with prewar Japan, including Kigensetsu. Prior to Japan's recovery of its independence in 1952, Prime Minister Yoshida Shigeru expressed his desire to restore Kenkokusetsu. In 1966 the Diet, against considerable opposition, passed a bill resurrecting 11 February as a national holiday. Apart from the question of the historical accuracy of the date, Kenkokusetsu has been one of the symbolic issues that divided progressives and conservatives in postwar Japan. Progressives continue to oppose this national holiday on grounds that observance of Kenkokusetsu risks restoration of prewar nationalism, while conservatives have defended the national holiday as a normal exercise for an independent nation.

MICHIO UMEGAKI

**KERALA**, state in the Indian Union located on the southwestern coast, bounded in the east by the Western Ghats and in the west by the Arabian Sea. Its capital is Trivandrum and its major language is Malayalam, which is spoken by more than 95 per cent of the population.

The population in 1981 was 25.4 million, of which 59 percent were Hindu, 21 percent Christian, and 20 percent Muslim. Only a few Jewish families now remain at Cochin; their population in 1971 was just over 100, although as recent as 1941 it was around 1,500. [*See also* Cochin *and* Jews.]

Kerala's literacy rate of 69 percent (1981) is the highest in India (the national average is 36 percent). At 65 percent, female literacy (nationally, 25 percent) is particularly noteworthy. Similarly, Kerala is the only state in India in which women outnumber men (ratio in 1981, 1,034:1,000). These figures reflect the legacy of matriliny, which was once followed by large sections of upper-caste Hindus, as well as the more liberal attitude toward women on the part of many of the Christian sects.

Heavy rainfall (an average of 120 inches a year in Cochin, for example) and a tropical climate have made Kerala a producer of valuable crops since ancient times. Although it covers less than 2 percent of India's area, the state produces 60 percent of the country's coconuts. It also accounts for more than 95 percent of the land in India under rubber and pepper cultivation, 55 percent under cardamon cultivation, and 45 percent under ginger cultivation.

The present state, formed on 1 November 1956 as part of the reorganization of the Indian states on the basis of language, is made up of three political units that existed under British rule: the princely states of Travancore and Cochin, each with its own maharaja, and the district of Malabar and a portion of South Kanara, both part of the Madras Presidency, ruled directly by the British. Travancore and Cochin were merged in 1949 to form the united state of Travancore-Cochin. Malabar and the section of South Kanara were added in 1956, at which time the southern, Tamil-speaking areas of Travancore-Cochin were ceded to the state of Madras (now Tamil Nadu). [*See also* Travancore *and* Princely States.]

The early history of Kerala is sketchy. The country of Chera (Kerala) is mentioned in rock edicts 2 and 13 of the Buddhist emperor Ashoka, dating from the third century BCE. From about 100 CE this Chera kingdom appears to have exerted a certain amount of central control. Local chiefs adopted various aspects of the four-*varna* (caste) system, including the Brahmanic ideal of kingship and a consequent claim to be *kshatriyas* (members of the princely *varna*). During the same period, Buddhism and Jainism entered Kerala from the north (relics are still to be seen today), and the coconut was introduced—apparently by people called Ilavas—from Sri Lanka (Ilam). [*See also* Ilava.]

The Kerala calendar—the Malabar Era (ME)—begins in 825 CE. By this time Kerala was well known to the world beyond India. Indeed, referring to exotic products, such as cinnamon, mentioned in the Old Testament, scholars suggest that Kerala's relations with West Asia predate 1500 BCE. In any case, regular and extensive spice trade with West Asia is well-documented from the first century CE: caches of Roman coins have been found in a number of places. This trade was made possible by the discovery that the southwestern monsoon provided a reliable way of sailing across the Indian Ocean. [*See also* Indian Ocean.]

The spice trade no doubt brought the first Christians and Jews to Kerala. In Kerala today the people who call themselves Syrian Christians claim descent from converts of the apostle Thomas, who is said to have arrived in 52 CE. [*See also* Thomas.] Firm documentary evidence of Christian settlement exists from 849. Muslim traders and settlers may have arrived by the end of the seventh century. [*See also* Mappilas.] Both Christians and Muslims made converts among local people, and this accounts for their substantial numbers today. Muslims are concentrated in the area around Kozhikod (Calicut); Christians, in central Kerala, notably around Kottayam.

By the twelvth century the Chera empire had collapsed; in its place emerged dozens of small, warring chiefdoms, each with similar social characteristics, two of which were unique in India. First, large sections of the caste-Hindu population—notably Nairs—were matrilineal, a fact that fascinated visitors from the time of Ibn Battuta in the fourteenth century. Second, caste stratification was far more pronounced than elsewhere and manifested itself in "distance pollution" or "unapproachability." In the extreme example, a Nambudiri brahman considered himself ritually polluted if he caught sight of a Pulaya slave a hundred yards away. Both features survived into the first half of the twentieth century. [*See also* Nairs.]

The era of European intrusion began in 1498 when Vasco da Gama of Portugal landed at Kozhikod. The Portuguese established a trading post at Cochin in 1500 and played a part in the trade and politics of the coast until the Dutch dislodged them from Cochin in 1663. The British ejected the Dutch in 1795. [*See also* Gama, Vasco da *and* Dutch East India Company.]

The participation of the European seafaring powers in the politics of Kerala's petty chiefdoms introduced a new element that some rulers skillfully exploited. Martanda Varma of Travancore (r. 1729–1758) formed alliances with the British East India Company and the rulers of Madura in the Tamil country. He created a centralized state and pushed its borders from its original area around Kanyakumari to the southern outskirts of what is today Cochin. [*See also* East India Company.]

The Mysore kingdom of Haidar Ali Khan and his son, Tipu Sultan, conquered the northern portion of Kerala—what became Malabar district under the British—in 1773. [*See* Haidar Ali Khan *and* Tipu Sultan.] The British seized Malabar from Tipu in 1792. In 1795 the East India Company, in return for having protected them against Tipu, forced Cochin and Travancore into an alliance that required them to pay a subsidy for the company's troops and to accept a British "resident" or adviser at their courts. The political shape of Kerala was thus set for the next 150 years.

In the first twenty years of their dominance, the British suppressed revolts in both Travancore and Cochin (1808–1809) and Malabar (1793–1805). From 1836, "Mappila outbreaks," attacks by Muslims in Malabar on Europeans and Hindus, troubled the British. The last and greatest was in 1921.

The matrilineal family system disintegrated in the late nineteenth and twentieth centuries, unable to cope with population growth, a rigid legal system, monetization, new values, and economic competition from nonmatrilineal groups. In 1925 Travancore passed legislation permitting individuals to obtain their share of their matrilineal joint-family's assets and separate from the family. This led to a rush of partitions in Travancore and to similar legislation during the next thirty years in Cochin and Malabar.

Two events in the 1920s highlighted political change within Kerala and the fact that the region was being pulled into closer connection with the rest of India. The "Mappila" or "Malabar" Revolt, which began in August 1921, cost more than 2,500 lives and has provoked fierce debate. Marxists write of the "Malabar Revolt," depicting it as a peasant insurgency directed against landlords. A non-Marxist school adheres to the idea of a "Mappila" Revolt, an overwhelmingly Muslim rising sparked by the excitement of the Khilafat agitation that swept India in 1920 and 1921. [*See* Khilafat Movement.]

In 1924 the "Vaikam Satyagraha" in Travancore aimed to gain the right for low castes to use roads running close to the temple in the town of Vaikam. Lasting twenty months, the campaign brought Mohandas Gandhi to Travancore for the first time in March 1925. It petered out with a compromise that allowed low castes to use newly built roads that took them around the temple but beyond the pollution distance. The right of low castes to enter temples was granted in Travancore in 1936 and in Cochin only in 1948. [*See also* Satyagraha *and* Gandhi, Mohandas Karamchand.]

The social upheavals of the 1920s drew many youths into politics. They turned first to Gandhi. Malabar became for the British the most troubled district of the Madras Presidency during the national civil disobedience movements of 1930 to 1934. In the jails young civil-disobedience prisoners were often introduced to Marxism by political detainees from North India. Such youths formed a Kerala branch of the Congress Socialist Party in 1934 and transformed this into a branch of the Communist Party of India (CPI) in 1939.

In Travancore, a civil disobedience movement for responsible government collapsed in 1938, and a Communist-led revolt of workers around the town of Alleppey—called the Punnapra-Vayalar Revolt for the two principal villages involved—was put down with perhaps 700 deaths in October 1946. There were abortive attempts at revolt by Communists from 1948 to 1950 during the period of the CPI's so-called Ranadive Line of militant resistance to Indian governments.

In 1957 at the first elections after the creation of Kerala, the Communists and five Communist-supported independents formed a government after winning 65 of the 126 seats in the legislature and 40.8 percent of the vote. This ministry was dismissed by the central government in July 1959 after widespread demonstrations led by the Congress Party, the Catholic church, and the Nair Service Society. In midterm elections in 1960 an anticommunist alliance reduced the Communists and their supporters to 29 seats, although the combined Communist vote rose to 43.8 percent.

Between 1957 and 1982 Kerala had eight elections. The only government to last more than three years was a coalition led by C. Achutha Menon of the Communist Party of India, which was in power from 1970 to 1977.

A recent social development has been the temporary migration of hundreds of thousands of Malayalis to the states of the Persian Gulf to work on projects resulting from the post-1973 oil boom. The large amounts of money that they have returned to Kerala appear, however, to have gone largely into land, houses, and consumer goods, rather than productive investment.

[*See also* Portuguese: Portuguese in India *and* Communism: Communist Parties in South Asia.]

Stephen F. Dale, *Islamic Society on the South Asian Frontier: The Mappilas of Malabar, 1498–1922* (1980).

P. N. Kunjan Pillai Elamkulam, *Studies in Kerala History* (1970). Robin Jeffrey, *The Decline of Nayar Dominance: Society and Politics in Travancore, 1847–1908* (1976). William Logan, *Malabar*, 2 vols. (1887; reprint, 1951). A. Sreedhara Menon, *Social and Cultural History of Kerala* (1979). M. G. S. Narayanan, *Reinterpretations in South Indian History* (1977). T. J. Nossiter, *Communism in Kerala: A Study in Political Adaptation* (1982). K. M. Panikkar, *A History of Kerala, 1498–1801* (1959). George Woodcock, *Kerala: A Portrait of the Malabar Coast*(1967).               ROBIN JEFFREY

**KERMAN**, Iranian province and the city that is the present administrative center of that province. The founding of Kerman city, probably as a military outpost, is attributed to the first Sasanid king, Ardashir I (d. 240 CE). The site, originally called Beh-Ardashir (Arabic, Bardasir; still the name of a district near the city), did not become the provincial capital until the tenth century.

Parts of the province were first conquered by the Arabs during the caliphate of Umar in the seventh century, but this remote region remained a center of dissidence until it was subdued in 718 by Caliph Umar II. Although the bulk of the inhabitants converted to Islam, Zoroastrians were able to maintain a community that survives to this day. The inhabitants of the province, always exposed to sectarian influences, became predominantly Shi'ite with the advent of the Safavids after 1501. In 1406 the Sufi saint Shah Ni'matullah Vali (d. 1431) settled in Mahan (a village thirty miles from Kerman), where his shrine is still a place of pilgrimage. During the nineteenth century a branch of the Shaikhi sect (followers of Shaikh Ahmad Ahsa'i) gained many adherents in the province. The sect's spiritual leader, referred to as Sarkar Agha, traditionally lives in Kerman city.

In the twentieth century the province's mineral wealth, mainly from copper near Sirjan and coal in Zarand, has been of considerable economic importance. Its handicraft tradition has all but disappeared, for the production of Kerman shawls, once considered comparable to the Kashmiri product, no longer exists. Carpet weaving, which reached its commercial heights in the late nineteenth and the first half of the twentieth century, also has declined.

VAHID NOWSHIRVANI

**KERTANAGARA**, last ruler of Singosari (1268–1292), considered the architect of the Singosari-Majapahit empire in East Java. He completed the process of religious unification by practicing the cult of Shiva-Buddha, as well as Tantric rites, to counteract the centrifugal tendencies in Javanese politics resulting from Airlangga's division of the realm two centuries earlier. Kertanagara also carried out an expansionist policy abroad, bringing Sumatra, Malaya, and Borneo into the Singosari sphere of influence, annexing Madura and Bali, and establishing friendly relations with other Southeast Asian states, notably Champa. Whether it was motivated by imperialism or was simply a reaction to the Mongol invaders, Kertanagara's foreign policy clashed with that of Kublai Khan, whose envoys had been insulted and expelled from Singosari in 1289. The Mongol expedition of 1292–1293, which was sent, among other things, to punish Kertanagara, found that its task had been usurped by Jayakatwang, the prince of Kediri, who a few months earlier had captured the capital and thus ended Singosari rule.

[*See also* Singosari.]

D. G. E. Hall, *A History of South-East Asia* (4th ed., 1968).               M. C. HOADLEY

**KESHUB CHANDRA SEN.** *See* Sen, Keshub Chandra.

**KHADI**, or *khaddar*, is the Indian name for the thick homespun cloth that became a symbol and uniform for the Indian movement for independence. The idea of utilizing only homemade cloth for clothing goods was instituted by Mohandas Gandhi in 1916 as an act of *swadeshi*—national self-reliance—and the practice of spinning to make the yarn for *khadi* became a daily pastime for Gandhi and many of his followers.

[*See also* Gandhi, Mohandas Karamchand.]

MARK JUERGENSMEYER

**KHAFI KHAN, MUHAMMAD HASHIM ALI**, author of an important general history of India written in Persian, the *Muntakhab ul-Lubab*, which he began during the latter years of Aurangzeb's reign (1658–1707), but did not publish until 1732. Khafi Khan belonged to a well-known family of Delhi. His father, Khwaja Mir, served Murad Bakhsh, the youngest son of Shah Jahan. Khafi Khan himself held important offices under Aurangzeb, Farrukh Siyar, and other Mughal rulers. His account starts with Babar's conquest of India and ends with events in the year 1731. For the earlier period he draws on Sadiq Khan's *Shahjahan namah*, but from Aurangzeb onward he provides an excellent account full of original information. Although his Shi'ite prejudices against the Turanis have been criticized, his description of the inner conflicts within the nobility and the details of military campaigns and administrative measures are very useful.

[*See also* Mughal Empire *and* Shah Jahan.]

H. M. Elliot and J. Dowson, *History of India,* vol. 7 (1877). S. R. Sharma, *A Bibliography of Mughal India* (1938).                    FARHAN AHMAD NIZAMI

**KHAKSAR MOVEMENT.** Inayatullah Khan Mashraqi (1888–1963), a Cambridge University wrangler (honor recipient in mathematics) and educator, founded the Khaksar Movement in 1932. *Khaksar* literally means "humble," and great emphasis was placed on social service and military discipline. Starting as a secular party, it soon became highly islamicized. Members always wore khaki uniforms and carried, particularly during parade, a *belcha* (spade). In 1936 it was declared that the members were "to acquire strength, and to be ever ready to sacrifice property and life and even children and wife for God and Islam." In 1939 during Shi'ite and Sunni discord they came in conflict with the government of Uttar Pradesh and in 1940 violently clashed with the Punjab government. Casualties occurred, the organization was banned, and its leader was imprisoned. After that, although it still existed in splinter groups, it became politically ineffective. Its main appeal was to the vague romantic idealism of Indian Muslims at that time.

Hira Lal Seth, *The Khaksar Movement under Search Light and the Life Story of its Leader Allama Mashraqi* (1943).                       S. RAZI WASTI

**KHALJI DYNASTY,** one of the five dynasties of the Delhi sultanate. Jalal ud-Din Firuz (r. 1290–1296) founded the dynasty, Ala ud-Din (r. 1296–1316) consolidated and glorified it, and with Qutb ud-Din Mubarak (r. 1316–1320) it perished in the Baradu Revolt. The Khaljis brought about a change in the nature of the polity by converting the Turkish state into an Indo-Muslim state. They admitted non-Turks and Indian Muslims into the governing class and initiated an expansionist policy that brought Rajasthan, Gujarat, and even the Deccan within the orbit of their authority. To suppress a potentially recalcitrant nobility, Ala ud-Din incorporated revenue-free lands into crown land, controlled social interaction among nobles, and enforced prohibition of alcohol consumption. State share of land revenue was assessed at 50 percent based on type of crop and measurement of land under tillage. Ala ud-Din established direct contact with the peasantry by suppressing the rights of intermediaries, and he attempted to regulate the market in grain, cloth, horses, and slaves by fixing prices according to production or maintenance costs. Strict vigilance and severe punishments assured success. Both philanthropic and militaristic motives are ascribed to these measures. Their area of operation is debatable.

The famous Ilkhanid *wazir* Rashid ud-Din Fazlullah came to Ala ud-Din's court as an envoy. The Khaljis were great builders and patrons of the arts and letters (e.g., the works of Amir Khusrau).

[*See also* Delhi Sultanate *and* Amir Khusrau.]

M. Habib and K. A. Nizami, *A Comprehensive History of India,* vol. 5 (1970). K. S. Lal, *History of the Khaljis* (rev. ed., 1980).               FARHAN AHMAD NIZAMI

**KHALQ.** The Khalq political party of Afghanistan was the largest faction that split from the People's Democratic Party in 1967. Noor Mohammed Taraki and Hafizollah Amin, Afghanistan's first and second communist presidents, belonged to this faction. Khalq had more support among Pakhtuns and favored more radical economic reforms than other PDPA groups.

In 1977, Khalq united with the other major communist faction, Percham, to overthrow the regime. After the 1978 coup, Khalq dominated the government and eliminated the Perchamis. The Khalqis carried out major reforms and moved Afghanistan closer to the Soviets. The government ran into increasing domestic opposition, which it sought to suppress forcefully. Khalqi tactics only fueled further opposition, which in turn caused problems within the regime. In September 1979 a power struggle resulted in the elimination of Taraki by Amin, who himself was later killed by the Soviets. Even though Khalqis were retained in the government after the Soviet invasion, the Perchamis were the dominant faction.

[*See also* Amin, Hafizollah; Pakhtun; Percham; *and* Taraki, Noor Mohammed.]

ZALMAY KHALILZAD

**KHAN, ABDUL GHAFFAR** (b. 1890), also known as Badshah Khan, leader of the Pakhtun (Pathan) nationalists in India's North-West Frontier Province. He participated in the Rowlatt agitation and the Hijrat movement and served in 1920 to 1921 as the president of the Frontier Khilafat Committee. He was a founding member in 1929 of the Afghan Jirga and its volunteers, the Khuda'i Khidmatgars, and played a leading role in organizing the civil disobedience campaigns of 1930 and 1931 to 1932. He was instrumental in bringing his party into the Indian National Congress in 1931 and served as a member of the Congress's central leadership from 1931 to 1947. Following independence, he helped to found the Awami League and the National Awami Party of Pakistan. On several occasions he was arrested or forced to live in exile as a result of his advocacy of Pakhtun autonomy within Pakistan.

[*See also* Awami League; Khuda'i Khidmatgar; *and* Pakhtun.]

Abdul Ghaffar Khan, *My Life and Struggle* (1969). D. G. Tendulkar, *Abdul Ghaffar Khan* (1967).

STEPHEN RITTENBERG

## KHAN, AFZAL. *See* Afzal Khan.

## KHAN, SIR SIKANDAR HAYAT (1892–1945),
prominent politician in the Indian province of the Punjab. He entered the provincial legislature in 1924 after careers in the Indian Army and business and rose to be the chief minister of the province from 1937 to his death. In 1937 he reached an agreement with Mohammad Ali Jinnah under which his party, the Unionists, allied with the All-India Muslim League. [*See also* Jinnah, Mohammad Ali.]

STEPHEN RITTENBERG

## KHAN, TIKKA (b. 1915), Pakistani general.
Tikka Khan served in the Indo-Pakistan wars of 1965 and 1971. As the chief martial law administrator and governor of East Pakistan, he directed the crackdown on the Awami League movement in March 1971. Under Zulfiqar Ali Bhutto he served as the Pakistan Army chief of staff. After Bhutto's fall he joined the opposition to Zia-ul Haq's government. [*See also* Awami League.]

STEPHEN RITTENBERG

## KHANDESH, Indian region occupying the Deccan
tableland, bounded by the Narbada and Tapti rivers. This region, associated with events in the *Mahabharata,* is first documented in the second century BCE. Among subsequent dynasties to rule Khandesh

were the Chalukyas, Chauhans, and Khaljis. From 1370 the Faruqi sultans controlled Khandesh; in spite of their comparatively weak position they warded off neighboring kingdoms until 1600, when Khandesh fell to the Mughals. Maratha forces harassed Khandesh from 1670, gaining full authority there by 1760. In the mid-nineteenth century the British controlled Khandesh; today it falls largely within Maharashtra.

H. K. Sherwani, and P. M. Joshi, eds., *History of the Medieval Deccan,* 2 vols. (1973). CATHERINE B. ASHER

## KHAYYAM, OMAR (c. 1020–1120), one of the
most elusive and important figures of Iranian cultural history. A prominent scholar and scientist from Nishapur, Khayyam was connected with the court of the Seljuk Malikshah and was appointed by the vizier Nizam al-Mulk to reform the calendar system. He is credited with the institution and refinement of the solar calendar and with a number of scientific works in Arabic. His *Ruba'iyyat* ("quatrains") enjoy a great status in the body of Persian poetry; over a thousand have been attributed to him, although in recent reliable editions they number between 140 (Hidayat) and 250 (Arberry).

The authorship of this or any poetry at all by Khayyam is engulfed in an enduring controversy; so, too, is his philosophical orientation. The facts as well as the legendary accounts of Khayyam's life, however, point to a highly gifted man well capable of producing the complex but brilliantly lucid quatrains. An inspired, if at times arbitrarily free, translation of the *Ruba'iyyat* by Edward Fitzgerald (1859) introduced Khayyam to the West, creating an almost cultish interest in "Oriental" poetry.

[*See also* Nizam al-Mulk *and* Persian Literature.]

A. Dashti, *In Search of Omar Khayyam,* translated by L. P. Elwell-Sutton (1971). Omar Khayyam, *Rubā'iyāt,* edited by A. J. Arberry (1949). MARIAM PIRNAZAR

## KHAZARS (c. 650–965), a tribal confederation
of predominantly Turkic stock that controlled the Pontic and Caspian steppes and adjoining lands. Their origins and affiliations within the Turkic language group are problematic. The Khazar khanate emerged from the western territories of the empire of the Turk, which had extended its sway to western Eurasia in the last half of the sixth century. The Turk-Khazar confederation was the ally of the Byzantine emperor Heraclius (r. 610–641) in his

wars with Sasanid Iran. This Byzantine alliance was continued when the Arabs replaced Iran as their principal foe. Arab-Khazar warfare began in 652, at about the same time that the Khazars emerged as an independent khanate; it continued until 737, after which an uneasy border was established in the northern Caucasus. Khazar expansion shattered the Bulghar tribal union, of which some elements were driven to Danubian Europe and the Balkans (c. 679) and some to the Middle Volga (eighth to ninth century); these emigrations soon gave rise to the Bulgarian and Volga Bulghar states.

In the late eighth or early ninth century the Khazar royal house, followed by other tribal elements, converted to Judaism (probably of the rabbinical, not the Karaite, type). At the zenith of its power (ninth century) Khazaria encompassed Kiev in the west, the Khwarazmian steppe in the east, Volga Bulgharia in the north, and the northern Caucasus in the south. Its Turkic, Iranian, Finno-Ugric, Slavic, and Paleo-Caucasian population professed Judaism, Islam, Christianity, and various indigenous beliefs. Itil, the capital on the lower Volga, was a major center of international commerce. Structurally, the khanate was closely modeled on that of its progenitor, the empire of the Turk; it was made up of a sacral kingship with a dual monarchy.

Khazar power, already eroding in the late ninth century under pressure from other nomads and internal discord, fell to a joint assault of the Rus of Kiev and the Oghuz (Ghuzz). A greatly reduced Khazaria subsequently faded from the scene. Its disappearance opened the Pontic steppe to new Turkic nomads who would figure in Byzantium's fall.

[See also Ghuzz.]

D. M. Dunlop, *The History of the Jewish Khazars* (1954). Peter B. Golden, *Khazar Studies*, 2 vols. (1980).

PETER B. GOLDEN

KHIEU SAMPHAN (b. 1931), Cambodian Communist official, born and educated in Kompong Cham. He earned a doctorate in economics in Paris in 1958 and later served in various Sihanouk governments, despite his known leftist orientation. In 1967 he went underground with other members of the Communist Party of Kampuchea (CPK). He joined the Party's central committee in 1971, and after the Communist victory over the Khmer Republic in 1975 he became president of Democratic Kampuchea. He served as one of the regime's spokesmen for foreign affairs and managed to es-

cape the purges that wracked the CPK in 1976–1978. In 1981, after the alleged disbanding of the CPK, Khieu Samphan occupied important positions in an anti-Vietnamese coalition government in exile.

[See also Norodom Sihanouk; Communism: Communism in Southeast Asia; Khmer Republic; and Kampuchea, Democratic.]

DAVID P. CHANDLER

KHILAFAT MOVEMENT (1919–1924), the agitation on the part of certain Indian Muslims pressuring the British government to preserve the spiritual and temporal authority of the Ottoman sultan as caliph of Islam. Integral to this was their desire to influence the treaty-making process following World War I in such a way as to restore the 1914 boundaries of the Ottoman empire. The British government was unmoved and treated the Indian Khilafat delegation of 1920, headed by Muhammad Ali, as quixotic pan-Islamists. The Indian Muslim attempt to influence the provisions of the Treaty of Sèvres failed.

The significance of the Khilafat movement, however, lies less in its attempt to influence British imperial policy in the Middle East than in its impact on the Indian nationalist movement. The leaders of the Khilafat movement—the Ali brothers, their spiritual guide Maulana Abdul Bari, the journalist Abul Kalam Azad, and the leading Deoband divine Maulana Mahmud al-Hasan—forged the first political alliance among Western-educated Indian Muslims and *ulama* (religious scholars) behind the issue of the *khilafat* (caliphate). The European attack on the authority of the caliph was construed as an attack on Islam and thus as a threat to the religious freedom of Muslims under British rule. The Khilafat issue crystallized anti-British tendencies among Indian Muslims that had been increasing since the Balkan wars of 1911 to 1912 and the Kanpur Mosque incident of 1913, which had demonstrated the effectiveness of religious issues in political mobilization. The Khilafat leaders were already nationalists; the religious issue provided the means to Muslim political solidarity in the anti-British cause and a method of communication between the leaders and a potential mass following. [See also Deoband.]

The Khilafat movement also joined forces with the Indian National Congress and Mohandas Gandhi in the noncooperation movement of 1919 to 1922. Gandhi espoused the Khilafat cause, as he saw in it the opportunity to rally Muslim support for the Congress. The Ali brothers and their allies, in turn, provided the noncooperation movement with some of its most enthusiastic troops. The combined movement was the first all-India movement against British rule. It saw an unprecedented degree of Hindu-Muslim cooperation and it established Gandhi and his technique of nonviolent protest *(satyagraha)* at the center of the nationalist movement. Mass mobilization using religious symbols was remarkably successful, and the British Indian government was shaken. In late 1921 the government moved to repress the movement. The Ali brothers were arrested for incitement to violence, tried in Karachi, and imprisoned. The noncooperation movement was suspended by Gandhi early in 1922, following a riot in Chauri Chaura in which the local police force was incinerated inside the station by a mob. Gandhi was arrested, tried, and imprisoned soon thereafter. The Turks dealt the final blow by abolishing the Ottoman sultanate in 1922 and the caliphate in 1924.

The aftermath of the Khilafat movement saw a rising incidence of communal violence. The Mapilla rebellion of 1921 increased Hindu-Muslim suspicions, although the Khilafat leadership denounced the Mapillas for resorting to violence. During the period of 1922 to 1924, Hindu-Muslim relations further deteriorated, with riots often fomented by communal organizations—the Hindu Mahasabha, Shuddhi, and Sangathan among Hindus, and Tanzim and Tabligh among Muslims. Thus, the Khilafat movement, a period of Hindu-Muslim amity and cooperation, ironically resulted in an aggravation of communal differences.

[*See also* Ali Brothers; Indian National Congress; Satyagraha; Gandhi, Mohandas Karamchand; Tabligh Movement; *and* Mappilas.]

P. G. Bamford, *Histories of the Non-Cooperation and Khilafat Movements* (1925; reprint, 1974). Mushirul Hasan, *Nationalism and Communal Politics in India* (1979). Gail Minault, *The Khilafat Movement: Religious Symbolism and Political Mobilization in India* (1982). Francis Robinson, *Separatism among Indian Muslims: The Politics of United Provinces' Muslims, 1860–1923* (1975).                          GAIL MINAULT

KHITAN, a people of proto-Mongol stock, masters of northeastern Asia from the tenth to the twelfth century. The Khitan established the Liao dynasty (907–1125) and later the Western Liao (1124–1211) in North China.

The name Khitan appeared very early in Chinese historical sources. According to the *Weishu* (the Northern Wei dynastic history, compiled in the sixth century), the Khitan made their appearance in China in the fourth century. The *Liaoshi* (the Liao dynastic history, written in the fourteenth century) includes the legend that the people originated from a man riding a white horse who met and married a woman riding a blue cow. After they settled in present-day Jehol, their eight sons became the chieftains of the eight Khitan tribes *(bu)*.

During the Tang dynasty (618–907) the Khitan constituted a menace to the northeastern borders of China. In the early Tang a Khitan chieftain was made the governor of Liaozhou. Another chieftain became the governor of Songmo in 649. Later there were two intermarrying clans among the Khitan, each of which had a Chinese surname (Li and Sun). In 696 there was a large-scale Khitan uprising against the Tang and the Khitan leader claimed the title of khan. The uprising was suppressed by Tang forces and the tribal confederation was broken. Taking the opportunity of the mid-eighth century An Lushan Rebellion, the Khitan began to reorganize and again received official titles from the Tang government.

Before and during the Tang period the Khitan had from eight to ten tribes. Chieftains were selected from these tribes as heads of the confederation. There seems to have been no hereditary succession of the chieftainship. In the early tenth century, a Yelü Abauji was selected as the common chieftain of the Khitan tribes. Abauji united the people and established the Khitan state in 907. When his tenure of nine years was over, he refused to select another chieftain as his successor and continued to rule the people. It was said that his attempt to establish a hereditary succession of the chieftainship was made according to the suggestion of his Chinese advisers. With the assistance of the Chinese the Liao dynasty was established.

During the Liao dynasty most Khitan did not become farmers but maintained their pastoral way of life in the northern part of the empire. While the ruling class was under considerable Chinese cultural influence, it also preserved nomadic custom such as the seasonal camping activities called *nabo*. The *nabo* were places where the emperor and his important officials and their families visited and camped in different seasons. As a matter of fact, the emperors did not stay in the five capitals very long but spent most of the time at the *nabo*, where they hunted, fished, and discussed important matters of the state.

State affairs were monopolized by the intermarrying Yelü and Xiao clans. They occupied most of the important offices by implementing the principle of hereditary prerogative to ensure the solidarity of the ruling class. This principle of hereditary selection also provided the dynasty with talented officials by selecting the ablest son or nephew as the successor, although the choices were limited. A number of statesmen and military officers contributed to the establishment of a Liao-centered world order, with a military power that was superior to that of the Northern Song. One of the most brilliant generals was Yelü Xiezheng, who defeated and killed the famous Song general Yang Ye in 986. By the middle of the Liao dynasty a few Chinese families also became prominent and influential and provided the court with administrative experts, military officers, and diplomats.

At the peak of their power it is estimated that the Khitan had a population of only 750,000, whereas the Chinese under their rule numbered about 2.5 million. There were more than 200,000 households under the control of the military, including many non-Chinese and some Chinese households. These households provided the government with 400,000 soldiers and 100,000 mounted warriors. In total, Yelü Deguang (Taizong) probably had an army 500,000 strong, with which he invaded China in 946.

Throughout the Liao period the Khitan were able to maintain many native ceremonies such as the worship of the sun, the rebirth ceremony in which the emperor went through the act of birth, the coronation ceremony held after the rebirth ritual, the annual sacrificial offerings to the mountains, and the Sese ceremony held to procure rain. They also celebrated Chinese festivals such as the Dragon Boat festival and others relating to agriculture. People of all social classes adhered to the Buddhist faith. Buddhist monasteries possessed great wealth and collected taxes from the households under their jurisdiction. The extraordinary growth of Liao Buddhism was reflected in the early Yuan saying that the collapse of the Liao was caused by the people's indulgence in Buddhism.

The existence of a dualistic political and economic structure, the dominant position of the Khitan officials, the maintenance of the pastoral way of life, and the preservation of many native customs are indications of the limited sinicization of the Khitan. In education, the imperial court and the aristocratic families adopted the Chinese way of life, and many Khitan officials and women of the court were able to compose Chinese poems. Unfortunately, none of the books written by Khitan authors is extant. There were several Khitan masters of Chinese painting. One of them, Yelü Bei, Abauji's eldest son and king of Eastern Dan, fled to the Later Tang and adopted the Chinese name Li Zanhua. There were many modifications of the adopted Chinese institutions and customs. There were also a few Chinese who were khitanized and changed their names into Khitan.

After the fall of the Liao, a large group of Khitan under the leadership of Yelü Dashi fled to Turkestan and established the Western Liao (Xi Liao or Karakhitai), which eventually was conquered by the Mongols. A number of Khitan officials and military officers served at the Jurchen court and gained prominent positions. Others were frustrated under Jurchen rule and staged a rebellion in the early 1160s. The most famous Khitan official is found in the period of the Mongol empire in the person of Yelü Chucai (1189–1243). This Confucian scholar-official served at the courts of Genghis Khan and Ogedei, and made significant contributions to the establishment of Mongol rule in China.

[See also Liao Dynasty; Song Dynasty; and Yelü Chucai.]

René Grousset, *The Empire of the Steppes*, translated by Naomi Walford (1970). Morris Rossabi, ed., *China among Equals: The Middle Kingdom and Its Neighbors, 10th–14th Centuries* (1983). Karl A. Wittfogel and Feng Chia-sheng, *History of Chinese Society: Liao (907–1125)* (1949).
                                                    JING-SHEN TAO

KHIVA, KHANATE OF. The Central Asian state of Khiva, in the region of Khwarazm, flourished from the early sixteenth century until 1920. Its indigenous name was always "the country of Khwarazm," and it became known in Russia and western Europe as the khanate of Khiva only in the eighteenth century. The khanate was founded by nomadic Uzbeks who conquered Khwarazm in 1511 under two sultans, Ilbars and Balbars, descendants of Yadigar Khan. These sultans belonged to the branch of the Chinggisids that had descended, through Arabshah ibn Pulad, from Shiban, the fifth son of Jochi; hence in modern scholarly works the dynastic name is often given as Arabshahid or Yadigarid. The dynasty was usually at odds with another branch of the descendants of Shiban established at the same time in Transoxiana following the conquests of Shaibani Khan; the Uzbeks who came to Khwarazm in 1511 had not participated in the campaigns of Shaibani.

The Arabshahids maintained the political traditions of the steppe, dividing the khanate into appanages granted to all male members (sultans) of the ruling clan. The supreme ruler, who bore the title khan, was the oldest member of the clan elected by an assembly of the sultans. During most of the sixteenth century the seat of the khan was in Urgench. Khiva became the seat of a khan for the first time in 1557–1558 (for one year), but only in the reign of Arab Muhammad Khan (1603–1622) did Khiva finally become the capital. During the sixteenth century the khanate included, besides Khwarazm, the oases in the northern rim of Khurasan and the nomadic Turkmen tribes in the Kara Kum desert as well. An appanage of a sultan often included certain regions both in Khwarazm and Khurasan. Until the beginning of the seventeenth century the whole khanate was a loose confederation of nearly independent principalities under one nominal supreme ruler.

Already before the Uzbek conquest, Khwarazm had lost its former cultural importance as a result of the devastations caused by the incursions of Timur in the 1380s. A sizable sedentary population remained mostly in the southern part of the country. Many of the formerly irrigated lands lay fallow, especially in the north, and urban culture declined sharply. The economic weakness of the khanate was reflected in the fact that it did not have its own currency: the coins of Bukhara were used in Khwarazm until the end of the eighteenth century. In these conditions the Uzbeks could retain their nomadic way of life for a long time. They formed a military estate in the khanate, while the old sedentary population, the Sarts, formed the class of taxpayers. The authority of the khans and sultans depended on the military support of the Uzbek tribes; to counterbalance them, the Uzbek rulers often recruited Turkmens. As a result, the importance of the Turkmens in the political life of the khanate was growing, and they started to settle in Khwarazm. The relations between the khanate and the Shaibanid state in Transoxiana were usually hostile. The Arabshahids were mostly in alliance with Safavid Iran against their Uzbek neighbor, and three times—in 1538, 1593, and 1595–1598—the khanate was conquered by the Shaibanids.

By the end of the sixteenth century, after a series of internecine wars in which most members of the Arabshahid clan were killed, the system of appanages apparently ceased to exist. Soon after this, in the early seventeenth century, the khanate lost its possessions in Khurasan to Iran. The reigns of the famous khan-historian Abu al-Ghazi (1643–1663) and his son and successor Anusha constituted a period of relative political stability and economic progress: large-scale irrigation works were undertaken, and the irrigated lands were distributed among the Uzbek tribes; thus they became further sedentarized. But the country was still poor, and the khans had to fill the empty treasury with the booty obtained in marauding raids against neighbors. From this time until the middle of the nineteenth century, the khanate, in the words of a modern historian, played the role of a "brigand state."

The Arabshahid dynasty became extinct at the end of the seventeenth or the beginning of the eighteenth century. (The chronology and genealogy of the khans who ruled during this period are not quite clear.) By that time the power of the Uzbek tribal chiefs had greatly increased, and they began to invite Chinggisid sultans from the Kazakh steppes to be enthroned as khans. The actual authority passed into the hands of Uzbek chieftains with the titles of *ataliq* and *inaq*. Two major Uzbek tribes, Qongrat and Manghit, competed for power in the khanate, and their feuds were aggravated by the secession of the northern part of Khwarazm, Aral (the area of the Amu Darya delta). The Uzbeks of Aral, who were mainly nomadic, became independent from Khiva and began to proclaim their own Chinggisid khans, who also were only figureheads.

Through most of the eighteenth century Khiva was in a state of turmoil. In 1740 the khanate was conquered by Nadir Shah of Iran, but the Iranian domination remained virtually nominal and ended with the death of Nadir Shah in 1747. In the subsequent struggle between the Manghits and the Qongrats the latter had an upper hand. But the prolonged wars between Khiva and Aral and between various Uzbek tribes, in which Turkmens also actively participated, brought Khwarazm to the brink of total anarchy, especially after the Turkmens of the Yomut tribe captured Khiva in 1767. In 1770 Muhammad Amin Inaq, the chief of the Qongrats, defeated the Yomuts and established his authority in the khanate. He became the founder of a new Qongrat dynasty of Khivan rulers. After that, however, it took the Qongrat *inaqs* more than three decades to consolidate their power against the resistance of other tribal chieftains, and Chinggisid puppet khans were still being enthroned.

In 1804 Muhammad Amin's grandson Eltuzer Inaq was proclaimed khan and the Chinggisid puppet khan was removed. His younger brother, Muhammad Rahim Khan (r. 1806–1825), reunited the country after his victory over Aral in 1811, subdued the Karakalpaks to the northeast of the Amu Darya delta, and tried, with some success, to subjugate Turkmen tribes in the south and Kazakhs in the north. The same policy was pursued by his successors. Eltuzer and Muhammad Rahim finally broke the opposition of the Uzbek tribal nobility with the support of the Sarts and the military strength of the Turkmen tribes, whom they either induced to come to Khwarazm peacefully or brought there forcibly, granting them irrigated lands for their military service. They created a relatively centralized state in which the provincial governors had very little delegated authority. During the first half of the nineteenth century the Qongrats greatly expanded the irrigation systems; thus the Uzbeks became completely sedentarized, and new urban centers began to emerge. Under Muhammad Rahim Khan the khanate began to mint its own coins. Despite all this, the khanate was still short of both human and financial resources, and Khivan raids into Transoxiana and Khurasan and against the Kazakhs and the independent Turkmen tribes became a routine annual occurrence. At the same time, however, the Qongrat period was marked by some cultural achievements: it was during this period that Khwarazm became the main center of the development of Turkic literature in Central Asia.

In 1855 the army of Khiva suffered a crushing defeat at the hand of the Teke Turkmens near Sarakhs, in Khurasan, and the khan Muhammad Amin was killed in battle. This triggered a Turkmen rebellion in Khwarazm that lasted intermittently until 1867. The khanate was weakened economically and politically; a great part of the lands irrigated in the first half of the century was devastated and abandoned, and the khanate lost its control of the Turkmen tribes in the south. At the same time it was drifting toward a fatal confrontation with Russia.

The first Russian attempt at conquering Khwarazm was made by Peter the Great, who dispatched a military expedition to Khiva under Prince Bekovich-Cherkasskii in 1717. The expedition ended in failure and almost all its members were killed. During the nineteenth century tensions between Russia and the khanate grew as a result of the Russian expansion in Central Asia, Russian-Khivan rivalry in the Kazakh steppes, and the plundering of Russian trade caravans by the Khivans. A military offensive against Khiva was launched in the spring of 1873 from several directions, under the governor general of Turkestan, A. P. von Kaufman. Khiva was captured on 29 May, and the khan Sayid Muhammad Rahim II surrendered. A peace treaty signed on 12 August 1873 established the status of the khanate as a Russian protectorate; the khan declared himself the "obedient servant" of the Russian emperor; and all territories of the khanate on the right bank of the Amu Darya were annexed to Russia. The subjugation of the khanate had little effect on the internal affairs of the country, in which the Russians interfered only in order to put down several Turkmen rebellions. Attempts at liberal reforms in the khanate made after the Russian revolution of February 1917 failed, mainly because of acute disagreements between the Uzbek and the Turkmen parts of the population. In the spring of 1918 the khanate fell into the hands of the Yomut chief Junaid Khan. In January 1920 Junaid Khan was overthrown by Soviet Russian troops, who had invaded the khanate assisted by Uzbek and Turkmen opposition to Junaid in Khwarazm. On 2 February 1920 the last Qongrat khan, Sayid Abd Allah, abdicated, and on 27 April 1920 the khanate was proclaimed the Khwarazman People's Soviet Republic.

[See also Khwarazm; Shaibanid Dynasty; and Bukhara, Khanate of.]

Wilhelm Barthold, "Kh$^w$ārizm," in The Encyclopaedia of Islam (1st ed., 1924–1937). S. Becker, Russia's Protectorates in Central Asia: Bukhara and Khiva, 1865–1924 (1968). C. E. Bosworth, "Kh$^w$ārazm," in The Encyclopaedia of Islam (new ed., 1960–). M. Holdsworth, Turkestan in the Nineteenth Century: A Brief History of the Khanates of Bukhara, Kokand and Khiva (1959).

YURI BREGEL

**KHMER,** the predominant ethnic group in Cambodia, as well as the Cambodian language, which belongs to the Mon-Khmer family. The geographical origins of the Khmer people are obscure, but it is likely that they have inhabited the Cambodian region for several thousand years. Their language, which is distantly related to Vietnamese, resembles numerous languages spoken by minority groups in Vietnam, Laos, Malaysia, Burma, and Thailand. The Khmer alphabet, adapted from Indian alphabets toward the beginning of the common era, was modified by the Thai for their own use in the thirteenth century.

DAVID P. CHANDLER

**KHMER ISSARAK** (Free Khmer), anti-French political movement in Cambodia that flourished between 1945 and 1954. Founded in Thailand during the closing months of World War II, the Khmer Issarak movement initially enjoyed the patronage of the Thai government and of the Indochinese Communist Party (ICP), based in Vietnam. During the period 1946–1950, *Khmer Issarak* was applied by the French to cover all anti-French guerrilla forces in Cambodia regardless of their political coloration, but noncommunist Issarak were increasingly wooed over to King Norodom Sihanouk's government while the resistance was gradually taken over by pro-Vietnamese Cambodian Communists, who linked the liberation of Cambodia to revolutionary transformation throughout French Indochina.

Although the Issarak movement did not cause many casualties among the French and Sihanoukist forces, it controlled more than two-thirds of rural Cambodia by 1952. When independence was achieved at the end of 1953, the Issarak lost its raison d'être, and thousands of guerrillas laid down their arms and resumed their former occupations. Approximately one thousand of them, however, as well as many highly placed leaders, sought asylum in North Vietnam to escape reprisals by Sihanouk's anticommunist regime. Many of these men returned to Cambodia in the 1970s to take part in the revolution, only to find themselves purged en masse by the leadership of Democratic Kampuchea.

[*See also* Indochinese Communist Party; Norodom Sihanouk; *and* Kampuchea, Democratic.]

DAVID P. CHANDLER

**KHMER REPUBLIC**, pro-American government of Cambodia (1970–1975) that took office following the overthrow of Prince Norodom Sihanouk and was itself replaced by the regime of Democratic Kampuchea. The Khmer Republic survived nearly five years of civil war and three years of American bombing, but by 1974 it controlled little more than the cities of Phnom Penh and Battambang. Hopes that it would be more democratic than Sihanouk's regime were dispelled by the authoritarianism of Lon Nol and by the exigencies of the war. Supporters of the regime were put to death in large numbers by the Cambodian Communists in 1975–1979.

[*See also* Norodom Sihanouk; Kampuchea, Democratic; *and* Lon Nol.]

DAVID P. CHANDLER

**KHMER ROUGE** (Red Khmer), term used by Prince Norodom Sihanouk in the 1960s and later by Western journalists to designate left-wing opponents of Sihanouk's rule. When Sihanouk was overthrown in 1970, the term was applied to op-

ponents of the new regime. After 1975 journalists often called the communist government headed by Pol Pot, known as Democratic Kampuchea, the Khmer Rouge. The term fell out of use when Pol Pot was deposed by yet another communist regime in 1979, although in the early 1980s it was occasionally used to describe hard-line supporters of Pol Pot.

[*See also* Norodom Sihanouk; Pol Pot; *and* Kampuchea, Democratic.]

DAVID P. CHANDLER

**KHOJAS**, a name used in India to designate Muslims who are followers of the Nizari Isma'ili Shi'ite line of imams. The current imam is the Agha Khan (IV). The movement began in an obscure period, when the reigning imam sent missionary emissaries called pirs from Iran to the Multan coast of India to convert Hindus, an activity that probably started in the thirteenth century. Their methods allowed considerable leeway in adapting Hindu practices and mythological symbols to core Islamic doctrine. As a result, surviving Khoja religious literature consists of a long series of liturgical poetic *ginans* in Indian vernacular languages full of unusual mixtures of Hindu and Muslim religious ideas. Later some Khojas, in doubt about their origins and subsequently their religious allegiances, claimed to be Twelver Shi'ites and therefore stated that they owed no obedience to the Agha Khans as imams. A famous case before the British court of Bombay in 1866 affirmed the status of the Agha Khan and the dissidents broke off to form either Twelver Shi'ite Khojas or Sunni Khoja communities. [*See also* Agha Khan.]

PAUL E. WALKER

**KHOKAND, KHANATE OF.** The Central Asian state of Khokand, in existence from about 1710 to 1876, had its center in the Ferghana Valley. The emergence of an independent state in this region, under Uzbek rulers, dates back to the early eighteenth century.

At the end of the seventeenth century Ferghana became independent of the khanate of Bukhara and was ruled by the *khojas* (Sufi shaikhs of the Naqshbandi order) residing in the village of Chadak. About 1710, Shahrukh Biy, chief of the Uzbek Ming tribe, which inhabited the western part of Ferghana, overthrew the *khojas* and founded an independent principality with its capital in the village of Khokand, where he built a citadel; soon afterward it became a city.

During the eighteenth century the relatively isolated Ferghana Valley attracted a great number of immigrants who had left the central parts of the khanate of Bukhara, especially Transoxiana, because of internal feuds there. The influx of population contributed to the rapid economic development of the region, but it also created a great ethnic heterogeneity and a shortage of irrigated land. The Uzbek tribes, most of whom had become completely or partially sedentary by the eighteenth century, were politically dominant, but their power was contested by the more recent nomadic newcomers from the steppe, the Kipchaks, who preserved their separate ethnic identity. The Kirghiz, who inhabited the eastern part of Ferghana, also played an important political role. The old sedentary population consisted mainly of Turkic-speaking Sarts and Iranian-speaking Tajiks. Contradictory interests of these different groups of population were the source of great tensions, which made the history of the khanate in the nineteenth century especially turbulent.

In the third quarter of the eighteenth century Khokand, with the rest of the Ferghana Valley, had to recognize Chinese suzerainty, which, however, remained nominal. Until the end of the eighteenth century the authority of the Ming rulers was limited to western and central parts of Ferghana. The seventh ruler of this dynasty, Alim Biy (r. 1788/1789–1810), expanded his authority over the whole of the Ferghana Valley and assumed the title *khan*. (The exact date of this event is unknown.) He created mercenary troops of Tajik highlanders, to which later were added troops recruited among the sedentary population. With the help of these troops Alim Khan could suppress the hostile tribal chiefs, which he did with great cruelty, and expand the territory of the khanate. In 1808 he conquered Tashkent, one of the most important commercial centers of Central Asia at that time, and subjugated the Kazakh tribes of the Senior Horde, until then subjected to the rulers of Tashkent. Alim Khan's brother and successor, Umar Khan (r. 1810–1822), continued territorial expansion and in 1814 conquered the city of Turkestan with the surrounding steppe regions; the Kazakhs of the Semirechie region also recognized his sovereignty. Thus, the northern borders of the khanate stretched from the lower reaches of the Syr Darya in the west to the Ili in the east. To assure the submission of the Kazakhs, fortresses in the steppe were built (Ak-Masjid, Auliya-Ata, and others). These fortresses had Khokandian garrisons; they attracted settlers from Ferghana, and very soon they became permanent urban and agricultural settlements. In the reign of Umar Khan's son, Muhammad Ali Khan (popularly known as Madali; 1822–1842), the khanate reached its maximum strength. In several military campaigns Muhammad Ali Khan completed the subjugation of the Kirghiz tribes of the Tian Shan and the Pamirs started by Umar Khan, and he conquered the Tajik mountain principalities of Karategin, Darvaz, and Kulab. Khokandian rule in the Kirghiz lands, as in the Kazakh steppes, was secured by the building of fortresses with permanent garrisons, which also attracted settlers from Ferghana.

The reigns of Umar Khan and Muhammad Ali Khan coincided with a period of intensive economic development of the country that was based on large-scale irrigation works undertaken by the khans and a rapidly growing trade with Russia. The cities of the khanate were growing faster than cities elsewhere in Central Asia, and the Ferghana Valley became the major region of cotton growing and silk production. It was also a period of vigorous cultural activity; Umar Khan, who was himself a poet, was an especially enthusiastic patron of literature. Khokand became the second (after Khwarazm) center of the development of Turkic literature in Central Asia (the language of the chancery was Tajik).

The khanate's period of economic and cultural prosperity came to an end in the 1840s. The cruel and corrupt Muhammad Ali Khan aroused general resentment. The *amir* of Bukhara, Nasr Allah, took advantage of the unrest in Khokand, defeated the Khokandian army, and captured the capital; Muhammad Ali was killed (1842). The Bukharans were soon driven out of the country by a popular uprising, but after this invasion the khanate was for two decades plunged into internecine wars, mainly between the Sarts and the Kipchaks (sometimes assisted by the Kirghiz), as well as between different pretenders to the throne. These feuds were accompanied by acts of the utmost cruelty and carnage (such as the massacre of the Kipchaks in 1852); the situation was aggravated by frequent rebellions in the Kazakh and Kirghiz regions and continuous conflicts with Bukhara. Despite this, the khanate had enough strength to survive and to keep its possessions intact until the Russian conquest.

The conflict with Russia began in 1850 with the Russian expansion in the southern part of the Kazakh steppes. In 1864 Russia captured all steppe regions of the khanate, and in June 1864 Tashkent fell; in 1866 the Russians took Khojend, thus reducing the khanate of Khokand to the Ferghana Valley and the mountain regions to the south of it.

In January 1868 the khanate was forced to sign a commercial convention with Russia that marked the end of hostilities, opened the country to the Russian merchants, and reduced it to a de facto Russian protectorate. In 1875 a rebellion against Khudayar Khan broke out under a religious leader who assumed the name of Pulad Khan, and it became anti-Russian in character. It was put down by the Russian army, and on 19 February 1876 the khanate was abolished; it was annexed to the governorate general of Turkestan at the region (oblast) of Ferghana.

[See also Bukhara, Khanate of; and Ferghana.]

W. Barthold and C. E. Bosworth, "Khokand," in *The Encyclopaedia of Islam* (new ed., 1960–). M. Holdsworth, *Turkestan in the Nineteenth Century: A Brief History of the Khanates of Bukhara, Kokand and Khiva* (1959).                                    YURI BREGEL

# KHOMEINI, RUHOLLAH MUSAVI (b. 1902),
more fully Ayatollah al-Uzma Sayyid Ruhollah Musavi Khomeini, Shi'ite scholar and mystic. Imam Khomeini, leader of the Islamic Revolution (1979) that destroyed the Iranian monarchy and guide and founder of the Islamic Republic, is for many Muslims the greatest figure in their modern history.

Khomeini was born on 24 September 1902 in the western Iranian city of Khomein to a certain Sayyid Mustafa, whose father, Sayyid Ahmad, had settled there some fifty years earlier. (Although of Iranian origin, Khomeini's ancestors had spent several generations in India; Sayyid Ahmad was the first to resettle in Iran.) Sayyid Mustafa was killed five months after Khomeini's birth under circumstances that are disputed, and his mother and a paternal aunt had charge of his early upbringing. In 1918 first the aunt and then the mother died, and it was Khomeini's elder brother who determined the following year that he should begin his *madrasa* (Islamic school) education in the nearby city of Arak under Shaikh Abd al-Karim Ha'eri. In 1920, Ha'eri left for Qom to reorganize the religious teaching institution in that city, and Khomeini accompanied him. Thereafter his whole career, down to his exile from Iran in 1964, was closely associated with Qom; it can be said that he completed the process, begun by Ha'eri, of making Qom the spiritual capital of Iran.

In addition to law—the core of the *madrasa* curriculum—Khomeini devoted much attention during his early years in Qom to traditional philosophy and mysticism; it was these subjects—particularly the latter—that formed the subject matter of his earliest writings. It was also as an instructor in philosophy and mysticism that Khomeini made his debut as a teacher, drawing to himself men who remained his associates during the years of revolutionary struggle, notably the ayatollahs Mutahhari and Montazeri. Although Khomeini's first two decades in Qom were largely devoid of political activity, primarily because of the quietist policies of Ha'eri, he participated in the 1923 protest movement led by Agha Nurollah Isfahani, delivered well-attended lectures on ethics that had political implications, and composed poetry that was partly political in content.

On 14 May 1944, about three years after the deposition of Reza Shah, Khomeini issued his first public declaration, calling on the nation, especially the *ulama* (Islamic scholars), to "rise up for God" and revive Islam in Iran, failing which worse calamities than those inflicted by the first Pahlavi ruler would ensue. At about the same time, he published *Kashf al-asrar (The Revelation of Secrets)*, a book that primarily refuted an anti-Shi'ite tract but also criticized the Pahlavi family and adumbrated *vilayat-i faqih* ("the governance of the jurisprudent"), the political theory that later became the constitutional basis of the Islamic Republic.

After an interval of ten years, Ayatollah Burujirdi succeeded Ha'eri in 1946 as head of the religious institution in Qom. Khomeini was among those instrumental in promoting him, evidently in the hope that he would prove more militant than Ha'eri. Despite Khomeini's repeated efforts at influencing him, Burujirdi maintained a determinedly passive stance to the Pahlavi regime, as a result of which Khomeini continued to refrain from attempting decisive political action. He is said, however, to have had some contact with militant religious personalities of the period, such as Ayatollah Kashani and Navvab Safavi. His main concern during the lifetime of Burujirdi was the teaching of Shi'ite jurisprudence, and such was his success that the number of students attending his lectures rose to five hundred by the mid-1950s.

Thus, at the time of Burujirdi's death in 1962, Khomeini was already a prominent figure in Qom, and when the publication of some of his writings on jurisprudence signaled his availability as a "source of imitation" *(marja-i taqlid)* in succession to Burujirdi, many in the religious institution responded. The beginning of Khomeini's political role and his emergence as a national leader who was well known beyond the confines of Qom came when he led a successful campaign in the fall of 1962 for the repeal of laws governing elections to local and provincial councils. His next and more significant clash with the government came early in 1963, when he denounced the shah's "White Revolution" as a fraud designed only to intensify foreign, notably American, exploitation of Iran. On 22 March 1963 paratroopers raided the Faiziyya *madrasa* in Qom, where Khomeini taught and preached, killing several people. Thereafter, his denunciation of the regime became harsher and more frequent, culminating in the historic speech delivered on the anniversary of the martyrdom of Imam Husain, the Prophet's grandson (3 June 1963). Two days later, Khomeini was arrested and taken to Tehran, whereupon a major uprising broke out, the forerunner of the Islamic Revolution sixteen years later.

On 6 April 1964 Khomeini was released and immediately resumed his attacks on the regime, belying a government announcement that he had agreed not to do so. His new campaign came to a climax on 27 October, when he accused the government of treason because of the agreement on the status of forces it had concluded with the United States. On 4 November he was arrested once again and sent into an exile that was to last more than fourteen years.

His first place of exile was Bursa in western Turkey, but in October 1965 he was transferred to the more congenial environment of Najaf, a center of Shi'ite learning and pilgrimage in Iraq. During the years in Najaf, Khomeini issued periodic pronouncements on Iranian affairs that were smuggled into the country and circulated there at great danger; he also received visits from numerous personalities from the oppositional diaspora as well as from inside Iran. He was thus able to remain in touch with his following, despite the best efforts of the Pahlavi regime, and, far from lapsing into obscurity, he was so well remembered by a significant portion of his countrymen that he emerged in 1978 as the natural and undisputed leader of the revolutionary movement.

The events that culminated in the overthrow of the monarchy began with a demonstration in Qom on 9 January 1978 in protest of the appearance of an article defaming Khomeini in the government-controlled press. Thereafter, a series of demonstrations broke out across the country so that by the end of 1978 nearly all of the Iranian people were demanding the installation of an Islamic government under the leadership of Khomeini. His role was crucial throughout: his declarations provided constant encouragement and guidance, and his refusal to settle for anything less than the abolition of monarchy gave the movement a clear and radical goal.

In the hope of diminishing Khomeini's role, the Pahlavi regime persuaded the Iraqi government to expel him from Najaf in October 1978. Khomeini then established a new headquarters in the hamlet of Néauphle-le-Château near Paris, whence communicating with Iran was, if anything, easier than it had been in Najaf. This last stage of Khomeini's exile was relatively brief; on 1 February 1979, two weeks after the shah had fled, Khomeini returned to Tehran to a massive and tumultuous welcome. On 12 February the surrogate government left behind by the shah collapsed, and a provisional government took office under Khomeini's supervision. The abolition of the monarchy and the establishment of the Islamic Republic were formalized through a referendum held on 30 and 31 March.

Soon after the triumph of the revolution, Khomeini went to Qom, but in January 1980 he came to Tehran for medical treatment, and after his release from the hospital he stayed on in the capital, taking up residence in the northern suburb of Jamaran. This transfer of residence to Tehran was necessitated by the successive problems and crises that beset the Islamic Republic: the divisions that existed between the provisional government and the revolutionary council; the crisis surrounding the detention of the American hostages; the conflicts between President Bani Sadr and the Islamic Republican Party, which ended in the removal of Bani Sadr from the presidency; and the war unleashed by Iraq in September 1980. In confronting these various difficulties Khomeini played a skillful role both as arbiter and as decision maker. His functions as "leader" *(rahbar)* have been constitutionally defined by chapter 8 of the Constitution of the Islamic Republic, but as important as his exercise of these specific responsibilities has been his dominating charismatic presence, still perceived by many to embody the values and aspirations of the revolution. Since 1979 Khomeini's appeal as a pan-Islamic revolutionary has spread widely outside Iran; posters bearing his portrait are to be seen on the walls of Muslim townships from Mombasa to Manila.

[*See also* Ayatollah; Bani Sadr, Abu al-Hasan; Qom; *and* Vilayet-i Faqih.]

Ruh Allah Khumayni, *Islam and Revolution*, translated by Hamid Algar (1981).          Hamid Algar

KHOTAN, a town situated at the edge of the Taklamakan desert between the main range of the Kunlun Mountains and the Kara-Kash and Yorung-Kash rivers in the Xinjiang Uighur Autonomous Region of the People's Republic of China. During the Tang period (seventh to tenth century) Khotan was a principality stretching as far east as the kingdom of Kroraina in the Lop Nur area and as far west as the land of the Kashgars in the Pamirs. The Khotanese kingdom was ruled by a dynasty named Vija, or Visa, and its people seem to have spoken Saka-Khotanese.

In the eleventh century Khotan was conquered by the Karakhanids and, later, by the Karakhitai. During the late Middle Ages Khotan passed to the Chagatai. The city benefited from its position on the Silk Route and was renowned for its skilled artisans. In the eighteenth century it was annexed by the Khojas; from 1877 until the Chinese Revolution Khotan was ruled by the Manchus.

Wilhelm Barthold, *Turkestan down to the Mongol Invasion* (2d ed., 1958). L. Hambis, "Khotan," *The Encyclopaedia of Islam* (new ed., 1960–).   ARIEL SALZMANN

KHUANG APHAIWONG (1902–1968), Thai politician and prime minister (1944–1946). Born in Battambang, Khuang was the son of the Siamese governor Chaophraya Aphaiphubet. He was educated in Bangkok until the age of fifteen, when he was sent to France to study engineering. In Paris, Khuang met with Pridi Phanomyong and Luang Phibunsongkhram, two important Thai political leaders, to discuss and plan the 1932 revolution, which established a constitutional government. In 1935 Khuang was appointed minister without portfolio in the cabinet of Prime Minister Phahon Phonphayuhasena. Three years later he became deputy minister of public instruction under Phibun. As a promoter of the 1932 coup, Khuang was appointed a member of the first National Assembly. Subsequently, however, he founded the Democratic Party and ran during every election except the one boycotted in 1952. Khuang was never defeated at the polls.

Known for his good humor and incorruptible character, Khuang was one of Thailand's few civilian prime ministers. He formed four cabinets between 1944 to 1948 but was finally coerced to resign by the 1947 army coup leaders. From then until his death Khuang remained the undisputed opposition leader and symbol of the Democratic Party.

[*See also* Thailand; Pridi Phanomyong; Phibunsongkhram, Luang; *and* Phahon Phonphayuhasena.]

THAK CHALOEMTIARANA

KHUBILAI KHAN. *See* Kublai Khan.

KHUDA'I KHIDMATGAR ("servants of God"), also known as the Red Shirts, were an organization of Pakhtun (Pathan) nationalists in India's North-West Frontier Province. Founded in 1929 as the volunteers of the Afghan Jirga, they were incorporated into the Indian National Congress in 1931 under the leadership of Abdul Ghaffar Khan. They were organized along quasi-military lines but included a pledge of nonviolence in their rules of conduct. They opposed the creation of Pakistan and after independence worked for Pakhtun autonomy until they were declared illegal in June 1948. [*See also* Pakhtun *and* Khan, Abdul Ghaffar.]

STEPHEN RITTENBERG

KHUN BOROM, hero of the Lao legend recounting the origin of civilization. Angry at the barbarity of primitive peoples, the chief of the gods sent a flood to cover the earth, from which only three chiefs escaped by making submission to the gods. They returned to earth as the flood subsided and with a buffalo began rice cultivation around Dien Bien Phu. After the buffalo died, an enormous vine grew from its remains, and from a pumpkin or gourd emerged dark aborigines and the lighter-skinned Lao. When that population proved unruly, the chief of the gods sent his son, Khun Borom ("venerable chief"), to govern them, and his seven sons spread out to rule all the known Tai world.

[*See also* Tai Peoples.]

René de Berval, ed., *Kingdom of Laos* (1959).

DAVID K. WYATT

KHURASAN, or Khorasan, is at present the name of a province in the northeastern part of Iran. In premodern times the region known as Khurasan was usually much larger, often extending from the Oxus River to the fringes of the central Iranian desert and from the Caspian Sea to the mountains of central Afghanistan.

This area has been a center of east Iranian culture with a history stretching back to ancient times, but as a geopolitical unit it dates only from the Sasanid period. Under the Achaemenids and Parthians, the "upper provinces" or satrapies corresponding to Khurasan included Asagartha, Parthava, and Haraiva. The Sasanids organized Khurasan as one of the "four quarters," or major provincial divisions, of their empire and maintained a military and administrative provincial capital in the Merv oasis, which was also the major entrepôt for long-distance trade. The province was subdivided into a dozen districts, many of which were governed by more-or-less autonomous military aristocrats. In conformance with their general policy of urbanization, the Sasanids also founded some new and important cities in Khurasan, notably Nishapur.

The Arab Muslims began to arrive in Khurasan in 650 CE and by 652 had established control over much of the region, usually by negotiated surrenders rather than outright conquest. They also established a military garrison at Merv to guard the frontier and to attempt to extend control over the peripheral areas. Because of the long distance from the center of the empire, their garrisons soon became colonies. Large-scale settlement by Arabs began as early as 665; in 671, some fifty thousand Arab families reportedly settled in the environs of Merv. As a result, there was a high degree of cultural assimilation in Khurasan that synthesized Iranian and Islamic civilization into a new unity. The increasingly Muslim population of the region played a critical role in supporting the Abbasid revolutionary movement (747–750), and Khurasani soldiers and bureaucrats provided a pillar of support for the early Abbasid caliphs. In 813 the Khurasanis supported al-Ma'mun in his struggle with his brother, the caliph al-Amin. Ma'mun, after becoming caliph, entrusted Khurasan to one of his powerful Khurasani generals, Tahir ibn al-Husain, whose descendants inherited the office for fifty years and were the first of several autonomous dynasties to rule Khurasan.

The Islamic civilization of greater Khurasan reached its zenith under the Tahirid (821–873) and Samanid (819–1005) *amirs*. The subsequent Turkish military dynasties, the Ghaznavids (977–1038) and Seljuks (1038–1194), were unpopular, as they tended to overexploit the province, and they gradually shifted their interests to other areas. Despite much political disorder and urban strife, Khurasan still remained an intellectual and cultural center of Islamic civilization down to the time of the Mongol invasions.

Khurasan never fully recovered from the devastation wrought by the Mongols, although a number of ephemeral dynasties such as the Karts (1245–1389), Sarbadarids (1337–1381), and especially the Timurids (1370–1506) and Nadir Shah (d. 1747) tried to revive the province. More often, the area served as a battleground for rival tribes and rulers down to the nineteenth century. Probably the most important and striking feature of recent Khurasani history has been the emergence of Mashhad as a Shi'ite holy city and religious center.

[*See also* Arabs; Mashhad; Merv; Nishapur; Samanid Dynasty; *and* Tahirid Dynasty.]

E. L. Daniel, *The Political and Social History of Khurasan under Abbasid Rule* (1979). Guy Le Strange, *Lands of the Eastern Caliphate* (1905), pp. 382–432.

E. L. DANIEL

# KHUSRAU ANUSHIRVAN

KHUSRAU ANUSHIRVAN (lit., "of immortal soul"; 531–579) succeeded his father, Kawad I, as Sasanid monarch. As crown prince, he had the Mazdakites massacred in Iraq in 528 and persecuted them in the provinces at the start of his reign. He seized their property, gave it to the poor or returned it to its former owners, and settled the status of uprooted women and children. With the support of the nobles and priests he restored royal power after the Mazdakite disorders. His reforms corrected the abuses that had provoked the Mazdakite movement, and he enjoyed a reputation as a just ruler.

Mazdaean dualism and the study of the Avesta and the *Zand* were established under Khusrau's rule. He completed the cadastral survey of Iraq begun by his father and had taxes calculated per unit of cultivated area instead of as a percentage of the crop. He also levied a poll tax on all adult male subjects. The empire was divided into four sections oriented to the points of the compass; these sections were governed by generals (*spahbads*) and were subdivided hierarchically. Nobles were given pay and equipment for military service, or they were given villages; thus a class of military landlords (*dihqans*) was created.

Khusrau's peace with the Byzantines in 532, which allowed him to carry out his reforms, was ended by the invasion of Syria he undertook in 540 to provide plunder, diversion, and employment for his nobles. His demand for Byzantine payments to defend the Caucasus was thus a pretext for the invasion. The captives taken at Antioch were settled at Veh Antiok Khusrau ("Khusrau's better Antioch"), near Ctesiphon. In 541 Khusrau occupied Lazica and built fortifications at Darband; in 544 he invaded Byzantine Mesopotamia. He also built fortifications on the Gorgan plain against the Hephthalites and, in an alliance with the Turks, defeated them there in about 557. The former Hephthalite territory was divided between Khusrau and his Turkish allies at the Oxus River.

By the terms of the fifty-year peace treaty Khusrau made with Justinian in 561, he evacuated Lazica and granted religious toleration to his Christian subjects in return for annual cash payments from the Byzantines. War with the Turks in 569–570 was followed in 571 by an Armenian revolt. Justin II broke the treaty in 572, but his forces were driven out of Mesopotamia in 573 and defeated in Armenia by 576. The Armenian revolt ended in 578 with a general amnesty. Sometime between 575 and 577 Khusrau had also sent a naval expedition to occupy Yemen. Khusrau's reign was not a period only of military activity, however; he is also remembered for his monumental buildings and for the cultural exchanges among Iran, India, and Byzantium that took place during his rule.

[See also Dihqan; Huns; Mazdak; and Sasanid Dynasty.]

Procopius, *History of the Wars*, edited and translated by H. B. Dewing (1961). Ehsan Yarshater, ed., *The Seleucid, Parthian and Sasanian Periods* (1983), vol. 3 of *Cambridge History of Iran.*          MICHAEL G. MORONY

KHUZISTAN. The Iranian province of Khuzistan is bounded on the west by the Zagros Mountains and Iraq, on the south by the Persian Gulf, and on the north by the province of Luristan. Corresponding roughly to biblical Elam, this region, formed by the alluvial fans of the Karkha and Karun rivers, was the breadbasket of the Achaemenid empire. With the fall of the Sasanid dynasty around 640, Khuzistan passed under Muslim rule. Although the area was centrally controlled by the Buyids, Seljuks, and Ilkhanids, actual power in the Safavid period rested in the hands of local lords, such as the Arab Musha'sha princes who were established in the western districts, known since then as Arabistan. The discovery of oil in 1908 at Masjid-i Sulaiman made Khuzistan the key to Iran's future development. The Iran-Iraq War (1980–) has taken a heavy toll, causing the total, or near total, destruction of several major cities, including Khurramshahr, Abadan, and Ahwaz.

[See also Iran-Iraq War.]

Wilhelm Barthold, *An Historical Geography of Iran* (1984), pp. 183–184. Roger Savory, "Khūzistān," *The Encyclopaedia of Islam* (new ed., 1960–).

ARIEL SALZMANN

KHWARAZM, a geographical term referring to the area lying to the west of the Oxus (Amu Darya) immediately below the Aral Sea (Bahr-i Khwarazm). Its principal cities, Kath, Khiva, and Gurganj (modern Urgench), all served at various times as the seat of government for a succession of independent states whose rule often extended beyond the confines of Khwarazm proper.

Khwarazm was an ancient kingdom of great power and wealth, described as such by Herodotus, and in early Persian records at the time of its conquest by Darius. In the Islamic period, the region was important as a center of commercial activity and served as a staging area especially for goods traveling across the Sarmatian steppe (Dasht-i Kipchak) to the cities of the lower Volga, such as Bulghar, Sarai, and Astrakhan. Deprived of one of its principal sources of economic viability by the loss of Gurganj to Genghis Khan in 1221 CE, the state was soon after (with the death of the last independent Khwarazmshah Jalal al-Din Menguberdi in 1231) incorporated into the lands of the Golden Horde.

Throughout the five-hundred-year period following the conquest of the region by the Arab military commander *(amir)* Qutaiba ibn Muslim in 712 up to the time of the Mongol conquest, despite frequent changes in political regime and dynastic rule over the region, Khwarazm remained essentially intact and served as a bulwark and buffer zone that protected central Iran and the rest of the Islamic world against the southward advance of Turkic migration and military conquest that was sweeping across the steppe from the Tian Shan range of western China to the Carpathian mountains of central Europe.

Khwarazm was protected from the penetration of external influences and people by the barrier of the Kara Kum and Kizil Kum desert areas; thus many features (both pre-Islamic and pre-Turkic) of indigenous cultural heritage were preserved intact. Specialists in the field of historical linguistics have determined that the use of the local Iranian dialect persisted until well into the thirteenth century, and linguistic turkicization came only with the settling of large immigrant populations from Transoxiana and points to the east after the Mongol conquest.

[See also Khiva, Khanate of; and Khwarazmshah.]

Wilhelm Barthold, *An Historical Geography of Iran,* edited by C. E. Bosworth (1984).

RHOADS MURPHEY, JR.

KHWARAZMSHAH, a title of sovereignty assumed by various dynasties who served as independent rulers of Khwarazm in both pre-Islamic and Islamic times. After the Arab conquest of Khwarazm in the early eighth century CE, the local dynasty remained nominally in power, but after the establishment of a secure hegemony by the rival Iranian dynasty of the Samanids in neighboring Khurasan (r. 819–1005 CE), any measure of real independence the Khwarazmshahs had previously possessed was effectively nullified.

The title passed to a succession of different rulers who, while titular heads of state, were in fact subservient to other regional powers, notably the Ghaznavids, who rose to prominence at the turn of the eleventh century. After three centuries of indeterminate rule, Khwarazmian independence was brought to a decisive end in 1042 with the imposition of direct rule over the province by the Seljuk Sultan Toghril Beg, who ruled in Nishapur. The title was revived once again in 1098 by a Turkish military governor named Bilge Tegin who ruled under the Islamic name Qutb al-Din Muhammad, and from the time of his son Atsiz (r. 1128–1156) the bearers of the title ruled independently in both name and fact. It was during this last restoration of Khwarazmshah rule by a Turkic dynasty—which boasted a title now stripped of most of its meaning as a claim to sovereignty over the predominantly Iranian peoples of the Ustyurt Plateau—that the title and position achieved its greatest fame and notoriety under the successors of Atsiz. They stood as imperial competitors and military rivals on an equal footing with the Mongol chiefs and their armies, who were attempting to establish unchallenged domination over the Dasht-i Kipchak and surrounding areas in the late twelfth and early thirteenth centuries.

Wilhelm Barthold, *Turkestan down to the Mongol Invasion* (2d ed., 1958).    RHOADS MURPHEY, JR.

**KHWARNA,** the ancient Iranian concept of divine grace, power, or charisma that accompanies the righteous king or hero but that can be lost or withdrawn if he sins. The Avestan form of the word is *khvarena* (Middle Persian, *farn;* New Persian, *farr*). Many times in Iran's pre-Islamic history rebellion against the ruler was justified by the claim that the *khwarna* had left him and descended on another. *Khwarna* is variously called "divine" or "royal"; the land of Iran is also said to possess *khwarna.*

S. Shahbazi, "An Achaemenid Symbol II. Farnah '(God Given) Fortune' Symbolised," *Archaeologische Mitteilungen aus Iran* 13 (1980): 119–147.    RICHARD N. FRYE

**KHYBER PASS,** principal pass linking Central Asia with the Indian subcontinent. The pass runs in a narrow, rugged defile about thirty miles through the Safed Koh Range on the Afghan border with the North-West Frontier Province of Pakistan. Its max-

imum elevation is approximately 3,500 feet. The pass is traversed by motor road, caravan road, and partially by railroad (built 1920–1925) from Jamrud west to Landi Khana on the Afghan border. It is flanked by several fortified posts within Pakistan. The pass was used by numerous early invading peoples from Central Asia, including the Aryans, Scythians, and Huns, and later by Mahmud of Ghazna, Babur, Humayun, and Nadir Shah Afshar. It was penetrated by the British in 1839 and 1878 during the first and second Afghan wars. Loose British political control was extended over its eastern portion by the Treaty of Gandamak (1879), whereby the British paid an annual allowance to local Afridi tribesmen for the maintenance of peace. An Afridi uprising in 1897 led to a new settlement after suppression by the British, but turbulence continued in the area until 1935.

Thomas Hungerford Holdich, *The Gates of India: Being an Historical Narrative* (1910). James William Spain, *The Pathan Borderland* (1963).

JOSEPH E. SCHWARTZBERG

**KIDO TAKAYOSHI** (1833–1877), Japanese political agitator of the late Tokugawa period, subsequently a statesman of the early Meiji period. Born in Chōshū, Kido belonged to the lower stratum of local samurai, the same segment of Chōshū society that produced most of that domain's radical activists (along with most of its conservative activists).

As a youth, Kido was briefly influenced by Yoshida Shōin, but it was his ten years in the political hothouse of Edo, between 1852 and 1862, that nudged him into the anti-*bakufu* position usually termed "loyalist." His already wide acquaintance with malcontents from other domains increased and was extended to courtiers as well when he was transferred in 1862 from Edo to Kyoto, then the center of antigovernment intrigue. The Teradaya Incident, however, from which he was lucky to escape with his life, cut short his stay.

When he returned, under heavy disguise, to Chōshū in 1865, his experience, his wide range of contacts outside the domain, and his formidable manipulative skills quickly won him a responsible official post. Chōshū's resumption of its anti-*bakufu* policy that year was largely at Kido's insistence, and he played a major part in negotiating the Chōshū-Satsuma alliance of 1866, helping also to plan the coup d'état of 1867. By 1868, when the Meiji government was being formed, Kido was already established as one of its most commanding figures. The Charter Oath was in part the product of his draftsmanship, and he led the movement to abolish the domains and replace them with a prefectural system. In 1871 he traveled abroad with the Iwakura Mission, returning a convert to constitutionalism (albeit of a gradual kind), for which he argued at the Osaka Conference of 1875. By this time, however, his health was waning, and his influence in government declined.

[*See also* Meiji Period *and* Charter Oath.]

HAROLD BOLITHO

**KII.** Premodern province (modern Wakayama Prefecture) of central Honshu, Japan, south of the Kyoto-Osaka region. From Heian times (794–1185), Kii was a place of exile for prominent political figures. Religiously, it has three important sites: the Kumano Shrine complex sacred to Shinto, the Negoro Temple, whose warrior-monks were defeated only by Toyotomi Hideyoshi (1536–1598), and the headquarters of the Shingon sect of Buddhism, founded by Kōbō Daishi (773–835) on Mount Kōya.

Politically, Kii played its greatest role during the Tokugawa period (1600–1868), when it constituted the domain of the *shinpan* ("related *han*") Tokugawa daimyo, whose castle town at Wakayama was the center of a fief with an assessed productivity of 550,000 *koku* (measures of rice). The Tokugawa of Wakayama were one of only three *shinpan* daimyo houses (the others being Mito and Nagoya) that were entitled to provide a shogunal heir should the reigning shogun die without legal issue. The most famous of the Kii daimyo was Yoshimune (1684–1751), who as the eighth Tokugawa shogun won fame for his ambitious if conservative political program known as the Kyōhō Reforms and for relaxing the ban on the importation and translation of European books (1720).

Grant Goodman, *The Dutch Impact on Japan, 1640–1853* (1967). Joseph Kitagawa, *Religion in Japanese History* (1966).

RONALD J. DICENZO

**KIJA CHOSŎN** (Chinese, Jizi Chaoxian), a legendary figure who supposedly immigrated to the northwestern part of the Korean peninsula in the twelfth century BCE and founded the Kija Chosŏn kingdom.

According to Chinese records, Kija was a member of the fallen Shang royal family. When the Zhou kingdom succeeded Shang in 1122 BCE, Zhou's King Wu enfeoffed Kija as the duke of Chosŏn. Kija then went to the Korean peninsula, where he became Chosŏn's ruler. This account first appeared in Chinese histories of the third century CE. It seems to have been written to help justify China's presence on the peninsula. Koreans of the twelfth century who were enamored of Chinese traditions wrote this tale into their histories, giving added credence to the legend.

Modern Korean scholars have been less willing to accept the legend as fact. The Kija story clearly shows early Chinese influence on the Korean peninsula and demonstrates Korea's infatuation with Chinese political tradition, but evidence in support of the legend is sparse. If the descendants of the Shang people had expanded onto the Korean peninsula, there would be Shang Chinese artifacts there. Shang is noted for its sophisticated use of bronze, but the bronze culture that entered the peninsula was a derivative of a Siberian bronze culture and shows little evidence of a Shang heritage.

Some contemporary scholars have suggested that the Kija legend explains the rise of a new ruling family or ruling group in Chosŏn. Chosŏn was founded by the mythical king Tan'gun, who ruled the kingdom, according to legend, until Kija came and took over. [*See* Tan'gun.] Kija may well represent a new line, and more specifically the appearance of the Dongyi race that seems to have entered the area prior to 1000 BCE. It has been suggested that the Shang lineage, which was ethnically different from the Zhou, was of Dongyi stock. With the political changes that came with Zhou's rise to power in China, repercussions spread as far as Manchuria and the Korean peninsula, bringing a shift in the ruling structure. At about the same time that Kija allegedly appeared, a bronze culture, even if not identifiable with Shang, developed on the peninsula. Evolving from this bronze culture was one of Korea's earliest recognizable political states. Kija then can be linked with the possible rise of a new ruling group in the Chosŏn kingdom, with the aftermath of political events that occurred in China in the twelfth century BCE, and with the start of the bronze culture in Korea.

The Chosŏn kingdom, or Ancient (Kija) Chosŏn as it is commonly known today, was situated in the Liao and Taedong river valleys and lasted until the second century BCE. Two characteristic bronze artifacts found in this area and identifiable with Ancient Chosŏn are the bronze mandolin-shaped dagger and the many-knobbed coarse-lined mirror.

Neither of these particular varieties have been found in China but they are common in Siberia. Ancient Chosŏn was a megalithic culture, with the stone monuments called dolmen particularly characteristic. Dolmen symbolize the ability of one individual or group to dominate another, and hence are evidence of growing social stratification. Political states began to emerge as the leaders of Ancient Chosŏn, the possessors of bronze weapons and tools, were able to elevate themselves above others. Bronze was not only useful in war but also in agriculture. Agriculture became much more productive than previously, and new plant varieties such as rice even entered the peninsula during this era, bringing significant changes to living patterns.

Traditional Korean historians, believing in the superiority of Chinese political beliefs, accepted the Kija legend and used it to justify Korea's emulation of Chinese norms. To them Kija was a cultural hero who introduced civilization to Korea. Today Kija symbolizes the dynamism and changes that were beginning to affect the Korean peninsula as early as the twelfth century BCE. A new bronze culture, new political and agricultural developments, and new groups migrating into the peninsula all are evident in this early age.
                                        EDWARD J. SHULTZ

## KIM CHONG-P'IL. *See* Kim Jong Pil.

## KIM DAE JUNG

KIM DAE JUNG (Kim Tae-jung; b. 1925), noted South Korean democratic politician. Kim was born on Haŭi-do, a poor island in Muan County in southwestern Korea. His father, a farmer, moved to the local port of Mokp'o in 1936 to run a small inn. The young Kim successfully managed a firm shipping supplies during the Korean War, during which he also escaped North Korean imprisonment. He also published a small daily newspaper. Kim entered politics in 1954, in an unsuccessful bid for a seat in the National Assembly.

In 1960 Kim was elected to the Assembly and during the democratic regime served as official government spokesman. He was reelected in the three subsequent elections of 1963, 1967, and 1971. Because he had risen to prominence spearheading the unsuccessful 1969 parliamentary effort to prevent a third term for President Park Chung Hee (Pak Chŏng-hŭi), he was chosen as the New Democratic Party's presidential candidate against President Park. Despite harassment and government election controls, Kim received 43.6 percent of the vote, shocking the Park government.

Thereafter, government pressures against Kim mounted: he was nearly killed in a government-engineered "accident." In 1972 and 1973 Kim took his cause to the United States; on the way home, during a short stay in Japan, he was kidnapped by Seoul government agents and nearly killed; his rescue and release in Seoul was only obtained under US government pressure. The incident focused international attention on Kim, but he was soon tried, convicted, and imprisoned on obscure charges including "spreading rumors" during the 1967 and 1971 elections.

On 1 March 1976, while still under house arrest, Kim joined nineteen other social leaders in a call for democratic restoration. Kim was given a five-year sentence and remained in jail until December 1978 for this action; on his release he was returned to house arrest, which was not lifted until 8 December 1979, six weeks after the assassination of President Park. Kim then started to campaign for the elections that were expected to be held in 1980, his plans for splitting the opposition with rival Kim Young-sam causing popular disappointment. In mid-May Kim was arrested in the coup of Major General Chun Doo Hwan (Chŏn Tu-hwan), who accused him of fomenting subsequent demonstrations in Kwangju, which Chun bloodily put down. Washington characterized these charges as "far-fetched." Jailed under a death sentence that was reduced to life imprisonment as a result of international pressure, Kim was then allowed to go to the United States for "medical treatment" in December 1982; he was a fellow at Harvard University from 1983 to 1984.

On 8 February 1985 Kim, accompanied by thirty-seven American well-wishers, returned to Seoul, where police violence caused a much-publicized airport scuffle. Kim was not recommitted to jail, however, but placed under house surveillance, from which he was released on 6 March 1985. Although technically still deprived of civil rights by his 1980 sentence, Kim is resuming an influential role in his nation's reviving political life, striving with renewed hope toward his goal of restoring democracy.

[*See also* Korea, Republic of; Park Chung Hee; *and* Chun Doo Hwan.]

                                        GREGORY HENDERSON

## KIM IL SUNG

KIM IL SUNG (Kim Il-sŏng; b. 1912), president of the Democratic People's Republic of Korea and the general secretary of the Workers' Party of Korea. He is also the first member of the Presidium of the Politbureau of the Central Committee and the chairman of its Military Commission. He is the only leader the North Koreans have known since the establishment of the republic in September 1948 and is known as the "supreme leader" and the "sun of the nation." During the nearly four decades of his absolute rule in the northern half of Korea, he has developed a political thought known as *chuch'e,* a concept of self-reliance.

Kim was born Kim Sŏng-ju, the eldest of three sons of Kim Hyŏng-jik and Kang Pan-sŏk in Man'gyŏngdae, near P'yŏngyang. His younger brother Ch'ŏl-ju died early and his youngest brother Yŏng-ju served him in North Korea until the mid-1970s. Kim Il Sung married twice. His first wife, Kim Chŏng-suk, bore him two sons and a daughter. The elder son, Jong Il (Chŏng-il), is now the most powerful political figure after his father, and he will most likely succeed him to the leadership position in North Korea. [*See also* Kim Jong Il.] The other son died in a swimming accident while still young. His first wife died in September 1949 while giving birth to a stillborn baby. Kim was married to his present wife, Kim Sŏng-ae, in 1962, and it is believed that he has four children from his second marriage.

Kim attended Ch'angdŏk Elementary School in P'yŏngyang and moved to Jilin, Manchuria, and attended a Chinese school called Yuwen Middle School. His formal education ended at about tenth grade when he was arrested and jailed for subversive activities related to a local Communist youth organization. He joined various anti-Japanese guerrilla groups in Manchuria, eventually becoming a member of the Northeast Anti-Japanese United Army, a Chinese Communist guerrilla group in the Dongbei (Manchuria) region. Kim fought in this army unit from about 1935, rising in the ranks and becoming one of its unit commanders in 1941, when the Japanese expeditionary forces drove the guerrillas from Manchuria. Kim fled to an army camp near Khabarovsk in the Russian Maritime Province, where his guerrilla forces were regrouped and retrained by the local Soviet armed forces to be used in the event of a Soviet campaign in the Far East.

Kim returned to Korea in September 1945 with the Soviet occupation forces, and he was picked by them to head the Provisional People's Committee in February 1946. In the wild scramble for power among the returned revolutionary groups, Kim and his partisan guerrillas emerged victorious. Kim became chairman of the local Communist Party and was elected premier of the Democratic People's Republic of Korea in September 1948. In his effort to reunify the divided country militarily, he launched an attack on the Republic of Korea in the south in June 1950, starting the Korean War. The Korean War was not only a fratricidal civil war; the United Nations forces there were pitted against the Chinese Volunteer Army as well. In any event Korea remained divided after the conclusion of the war three years later. [*See also* Korean War.]

In the aftermath of the war, Kim successfully used the opportunity to purge his political rivals, and took on the task of reconstruction of North Korea, which had been devastated by the war. He launched three-year, five-year, and seven-year national economic plans to rebuild his country, and in the process he established an unchallengeable position by eliminating all rival factions, replacing them with his partisan guerrillas.

When the Sino-Soviet disputes intensified, Kim became increasingly nationalistic, and began to follow an independent and self-reliant policy. Kim sided with the Chinese during the first half of the 1960s to stave off a Soviet attack on North Korea, and became reconciled with the Soviet Union in the second half of the 1960s, when the Chinese began to attack Kim during the latter part of the Great Proletarian Cultural Revolution in China. Kim subsequently joined and promoted the nonaligned movement in earnest, and began to build up his own personality cult, even trying to project his leadership role in the nonaligned movement. He is referred to not only as the supreme leader but also as a "matchless patriot, national hero, ever-victorious and iron-willed commander, one of the genius leaders of the international Communist movement and workers' movement."

On the domestic front Kim was virtually free to formulate and implement any policy he desired. By proclaiming a new constitution in December 1972, Kim reorganized his government and shifted his power center from the control mechanism of the Party to the operation of the government. While entrusting the daily operations of the Party to his son, Kim became president of the Republic and headed a newly created supercabinet, the Central People's Committee. With the gradual thaw in the relationship between the United States and China, Kim agreed to a direct dialogue with South Korea, advancing his own policy and formula for peaceful reunification of Korea, but the dialogue soon broke off owing to the irreconcilable differences between the two systems. In the mid-1970s, Kim began to train his son to take over the operation of the Party, and by the time of the Sixth Party Congress in October 1980, he had all but anointed his son as heir to the mantle of power in North Korea.

Kim is credited with developing the idea of *chuch'e,* a self-reliant and creative application of

Marxism and Leninism to the specific conditions unique to Korea. Under this principle of self-reliance Kim formulated what is known as the monolithic ideological system. This system encompassed the thought of self-reliance in ideological stance, independence in political work, self-sustenance in economic endeavors, and self-defense in military affairs. The idea is also known as Kim Il Sung Thought.

Kim has written many essays and made many speeches, and his writings are collected in four different editions of his work. The latest collection, known simply as the *Works of Kim Il Sung,* was published in 1979, and it was scheduled to be completed in time for his seventieth birthday in April 1982, but the publication is still continuing. As the absolute ruler of North Korea, Kim will no doubt continue his rule as long as he lives.

[*See also* Korea, Democratic People's Republic of *and* Communism: Communism in Korea.]

Baek Bong, *Kim Il Sung Biographies,* 3 vols. (1970). Kim Il Sung, *Selected Works,* 7 vols. (1971–1979).

DAE SOOK SUH

KIM JONG IL (Kim Chŏng-il; b. 1942), eldest son and chosen successor of North Korean leader Kim Il Sung (Kim Il-sŏng). Kim was born near Khabarovsk in the Soviet Union, where his mother, Kim Chŏng-suk, a partisan fighter, had retreated from her guerrilla base in Manchuria. Kim was also known in his youth as "Yura." He graduated from Namsan School in P'yŏngyang, a special school for the children of prominent revolutionaries and ranking party officials. He later attended Kim Il Sung University and majored in political economy, graduating in 1964. He was believed to have studied in East Germany in an attempt to become a flyer, but upon his return home he worked closely with his father. He worked in the Organization and Guidance Department of the Communist Party and later managed the Ideological and Propaganda Department of the Party, where he was responsible for the production of many revolutionary plays extolling the anti-Japanese record of his father.

Kim gradually made his presence felt within the Party from the Seventh Plenum of the Fifth Central Committee in September 1973, leading the Three-Revolution Team campaigns. During his training period under his father's tutelage in the 1970s, he was often referred to as the "Party Center," and he launched a number of campaigns to take over the daily operations of the Party, including the Three-

Revolution Red Flag Movement. By the time of the Sixth Party Congress in October 1980, his control of the Party operation was complete. He was elected first secretary of the Central Committee, a ranking member of the Presidium of the Politbureau, a member of the Military Commission, and member of the Central Committee of the Party. When he was elected member of the Seventh Supreme People's Assembly in February 1982, it had become obvious that he was heir apparent to succeed his father as the supreme leader of North Korea. Affectionately referred to as the "dear leader," Kim Jong Il is the most powerful figure behind his father in North Korea.

[*See also* Korea, Democratic People's Republic of *and* Kim Il Sung.]

Ch'oe In Su, *Kim Jong Il: The People's Leader* (1983). Inoue Shuhachi, *Modern Korea and Kim Jong Il* (1984).

DAE SOOK SUH

KIM JONG PIL (Kim Chong-p'il; b. 1926), South Korean coup leader, prime minister, and politician. Kim was born in Puyo, South Ch'ungch'ong Province, into a large family linked with leftist activity. He was reportedly involved in leftist student movements against the US military government while at Seoul Teachers College in 1946. He married the niece of Park Chung Hee (Pak Chŏng-hŭi); her father was shot as a communist during the fall riots of 1946 in Taegu. Kim entered the constabulary in 1948 with the famous eighth class, specializing thereafter in North Korean intelligence.

Beginning in February 1960 Lieutenant Colonel Kim was as deeply involved in plans for a military coup to purify and reconsecrate the government as was Park. A coup planned for May 1960 was forestalled by the April student revolution, but the resolve continued. [*See* April Nineteenth Student Revolution.] On 16 September 1960 Kim was prominent among the sixteen young officers who broke into the office of the chief of staff and demanded his resignation. Tried for breach of military discipline, Kim and a close friend were retired, although later, after the coup, they were reinstated and allowed to retire as brigadier generals. They used retirement to widen the coup group.

Viewing the democratic era as "chaotic," the group struck on 16 May 1961, and easily toppled the surprised government. Kim rapidly became a leader within the new ruling junta and, within days, established and directed the South Korean Central

Intelligence Agency, the new government's chief internal control mechanism. At the core of policy planning, Kim consistently led the hardline group arguing for the prolongation of junta rule. His influence on the new constitution was prominent and, from March 1962 on, he headed recruitment activities for a new political party to support the revolution's aims.

Before it was unveiled on 18 January 1963 this new Democratic Republican Party (DRP) was constructed on centralist principles drawn from the precedents set by the Guomindang (Kuomintang, or Nationalist Party; the ruling party of the Republic of China on Taiwan). Kim led the movement to recruit Park Chung Hee as the party's presidential candidate. He engineered Park's acceptance, which led to his narrow victory in October 1963 and the DRP's stronger one in November. Despite two enforced exiles, Kim maintained control over the DRP and Korea's internal political life with noted agility, leading the government to victories in 1967 and 1971. From 1971 to 1975 he was prime minister. He was also largely responsible for restoration of relations with Japan, visiting Prime Minister Ikeda on 26 October 1961 and 21 February 1962, and signing the Kim-Ōhira memo of 12 November 1962, the basis for the normalization that was ultimately achieved in 1965.

Mounting rivalries with Lee Hurak (Yi Hu-rak) and Park's increasing withdrawal marred the 1970s, but only with Park's assassination in October 1979 did Kim fall from power. On 17 May 1980 Chun Doo Hwan (Chŏn Tu-hwan) had Kim arrested to distance the new regime from the architects of Park's repression. Charged with amassing wealth by abusing power, Kim and two others were stripped of about US $13,000,000 in assets. Only on 6 March 1985 was Kim released from a political ban. He has remained politically inactive since that time.

[See also May Sixteenth Coup d'État; Park Chung Hee; and Korea, Republic of.]

Se-jin Kim, *The Politics of Military Revolution* (1971).

GREGORY HENDERSON

KIM KU (1876–1949), head of Korea's Provisional Government in Exile and noted anti-Japanese nationalist. Kim Ku was born in the rural central Korean province of Hwanghae, the only son of an impoverished farmer. After Korea's liberation in 1945, Kim returned from China to play an active political role in South Korea's formative years until he was assassinated.

Despite his commoner status, Kim began studying the Chinese Confucian classics in 1884. From 1892 he was active in the antiforeign religious Tonghak movement, the revolt of which in 1894 led to the Sino-Japanese War. [See also Tonghak and Sino-Japanese War.] In 1896 he killed a Japanese officer and was imprisoned, escaping in 1898. Following the Russo-Japanese War (1904–1905), when Japan established a protectorate over Korea, Kim was a leader in the Sinminhoe (New People's Association) for defense of the country's independence. He was apprehended in 1909 for complicity in the attempted assassination of the Japanese resident-general; he was imprisoned from 1911 until his parole in 1914. He was active in nationalist organizations until the independence uprising of 1 March 1919. [See also Korea, Japanese Government-General of and March First Independence Movement.]

Fleeing to Shanghai, China, with other nationalist leaders, Kim headed the police bureau of the Provisional Government in Exile. In 1926 he became its prime minister, and later its president. He led in the formation of the Korea Independence Party (established in 1930) and the Korean Nationalist Party (in 1936). Although he sought to promote unity among Korean nationalists, he was in the noncommunist or right-wing camp.

As Japanese control of Korea tightened, Kim turned to terrorist tactics. He masterminded a grenade attack on the Japanese emperor's state procession in Tokyo in January 1932, the bombing of Japanese dignitaries at a picnic in Shanghai three months later, and a second unsuccessful attempt to assassinate the Japanese emperor.

Kim's anti-Japanese activities brought him to the attention of the Chinese leader Chiang Kai-shek, with whom he established a friendly and cooperative relationship. Beginning in 1931, he received Chinese financing for intelligence work; in cooperation with Chiang, he arranged for military training and organized Koreans to fight with the Chinese. The Korean nationalist units were designated the Kwang-bok-kun (Liberation Army) in 1942.

A political enemy attempted to assassinate Kim at a political unity meeting in 1938. He recovered and resumed his leadership of the Provisional Government, which took on new life during World War II.

On 27 November 1945, Kim returned to American-occupied southern Korea, although—like other Provisional Government figures—he was required to come as a private individual. He nevertheless set up offices in the Doksu Palace in Seoul. He led the struggle against trusteeship in December 1945, calling a general strike in defiance of the United States Military Government.

For a time Kim worked with Syngman Rhee (Yi Sŭng-man) to promote national unity and oppose the Communists. He parted company with Rhee by supporting the proposal for UN-observed elections throughout Korea and published a manifesto, *My Appeal,* in favor of it. On the other hand, he opposed the separate election of 10 May 1948 in the southern zone. With Kim Kyu-sik, he met Kim Il Sung (Kim Il-sŏng) and Kim Tu-bong of North Korea in April 1948 at the "Conference of the Four Kims," as a final effort at national unity, but failed to achieve any agreement.

After the establishment of the Republic of Korea in August 1948, Kim Ku headed his own Korean Independence Party, which he organized after his break with Rhee, but a young Korean Army lieutenant shot and killed him on 26 June 1949. In 1962, after Rhee was deposed, the military government of General Park Chung Hee (Pak Chŏng-hŭi) awarded him a posthumous decoration in recognition of his nationalist merit. A statue of Kim stands on a hill overlooking Seoul.

Kim was handicapped by his lack of formal education in a country that expects its leaders to be scholars, and he has been faulted for lack of breadth and subtlety of understanding. He is admired, however, for his courage and his firm lifelong devotion to Korea's cause. He completed an autobiography in 1929, which was republished in Seoul in 1947. Married in 1904, he had two sons and a daughter. His wife died in 1924.

Chong-sik Lee, *Korea and the Politics of Nationalism* (1963).                    DONALD S. MACDONALD

**KIM KYU-SIK** (1881–1950), Korean nationalist leader, Christian layman, and scholar. Kim Kyu-sik was born near Pusan in southern Korea. At the age of six he was taken into the household of the American missionary educator Horace Underwood. Sent to Roanoke College in the United States, Kim graduated in 1903, and was Underwood's secretary for the following decade. He was a leader in founding the Saemunan Presbyterian Church, of which he became an elder in 1912.

In 1911, the year after the Japanese annexation of Korea, Kim took refuge from Japanese persecution by moving to Shanghai, China. He went into business as a trader between North China and Mon-

golia, becoming Ulan Bator branch manager for the Anderson Company. Continuing to be active among Koreans in China, Kim was sent by the New Korea Youth Association as representative to the Versailles Peace Conference in 1918. Although he was not admitted to the conference, he submitted petitions on behalf of Korea and established a press office in Paris.

Following the independence uprising of 1 March 1919, Kim was named foreign minister of the Provisional Government in Exile at Shanghai. He worked with Syngman Rhee's Korean Commission (an unofficial embassy) in Washington. In 1921, reassigned as education minister, Kim returned to Shanghai, but he resigned his post later that year in the course of factional disputes. He resumed his trading activities, traversed the Gobi desert, and witnessed the revolutionary struggles in Samarkand.

In 1922 Kim attended the East Asian Workers' Conference in Moscow with the left-wing Korean leader Yŏ Un-hyŏng (Lyuh Woon Hyung). In 1932 he rejoined the Provisional Government, now at Nanjing, and with Kim Wŏn-bong, another prominent left-wing leader, he organized a United Fighting Front against Japan. Later, in 1941, Kim entered the legislative assembly of the Provisional Government as representative of the Masses Revolutionary Party (Minjung Hyongmyongdang), rejoined the cabinet, and became its propaganda chief. In 1944 he was named vice president of the Provisional Government.

Following Korea's liberation in 1945, Kim returned to Seoul with other Provisional Government leaders. He was the only prominent noncommunist leader to support the trusteeship plan announced at the Moscow meeting of Foreign Ministers in December 1945. He became vice-chairman of the Democratic Representative Assembly under the American military government in early 1946, and later that year he was asked by the military government to lead a coalition committee with Yŏ Un-hyŏng for reconciliation of left-wing and right-wing positions.

After elections in October 1946 for an interim legislative assembly in South Korea, Kim was elected its chairman; but he subsequently resigned in protest against the assembly's powerlessness under the US Military Government and the hostility between left- and right-wing legislators. Kim and Yŏ organized a National Independence Federation as a middle way between left and right extremes, but Yŏ's assassination in July 1947 deprived the Federation of much of its strength. Kim was joined by Kim Ku in opposition to Syngman Rhee's campaign for a separate independent state in the southern half of Korea; in April 1948 both men participated in a "Conference of the Four Kims" with North Korean leaders Kim Il Sung (Kim Il-sŏng) and Kim Tu-bong as a last-ditch effort to prevent division of the country. Thereafter, Kim, aging and in delicate health, played a diminishing political role as moderate elder states-man. He was captured by the North Koreans in their invasion of June 1950 and died of asthma in North Korea on 10 December 1950.

A scholar of English literature as well as a political and religious leader, Kim lectured and taught in both Korea and China. In 1923 he was awarded an hon-orary doctorate by Roanoke College. In 1940 he published *Introduction to Drama of the Elizabethan Era*, and in 1945, *Practical English*. He was married in 1906, widowed in 1917, and remarried in 1919; he had three sons (the first of whom died in infancy), and a daughter.

Chong-sik Lee, *The Politics of Korean Nationalism* (1963).          DONALD S. MACDONALD

**KIM OK-KYUN** (1851–1894), Korean revolu-tionary and member of the reform-minded Progres-sive Party (Kaehwadang, also known as the Inde-pendence Party), which staged an unsuccessful coup in 1884. Born into the powerful Andong Kim family, which dominated political power for the first six de-cades of the nineteenth century, Kim passed the civil service examination in 1872, ranking first among the successful candidates. Serving in the advisory branch of the government, he gained the trust of King Kojong (r. 1864–1907), whose power was eclipsed for the most part by either his father, the Taewŏn'gun, or his consort's clan, the Min family.

In the late nineteenth century Yi-dynasty Korea was challenged by the necessity of transforming a traditional Confucian monarchy in a China-cen-tered world into a modern nation. Japan and China vied with each other for influence over Korea. From the signing of the 1876 Kanghwa Treaty, Japan at-tempted to expand its power to its continental neigh-bor, while China was unwilling to relinquish the traditional tributary relations with Korea. [*See also* Kanghwa Treaty.] In Kim's view, those who were in power were either too conservative or too self-serving and did not grasp the magnitude or the ur-gency of the task of reformation and modernization. In his search for a way to accomplish this goal, Kim formed friendships with like-minded young intellec-tuals including Hong Yŏng-sik, Pak Yŏng-hyo, Sŏ

Chae-p'il (Philip Jaisohn), and Sŏ Kwang-bŏm. Re-ferred to as progressives, they at first studied the writings of the Practical Learning *(sirhak)* Confu-cian scholars but soon turned to Japan as a model.

The conviction that Korea should follow the ex-ample set by Meiji Japan was strengthened by Kim's first trip to Japan in 1882. Not only was he im-pressed by the progress Japan had made, but he also met Fukuzawa Yukichi, the foremost Meiji intellec-tual. Deeply impressed by Fukuzawa, who espoused enlightenment, character building, national inde-pendence and power, Kim came to regard him as his mentor. [*See also* Fukuzawa Yukichi.] During Kim's absence an anti-Japanese mutiny by Korean soldiers in July 1882 resulted in the arrival of three thousand Chinese troops. Kim regarded complete Korean independence from China as the first step in modernization and found the presence in Korea of Chinese troops particularly disturbing. Although this event was a setback for Japan, it was allowed to station six hundred soldiers in Korea and received additional concessions including an indemnity for damages. Korea was required to send to Japan an official mission of apology, headed by another pro-gressive, Pak Yŏng-hyo; Kim joined this mission as well.

On this second trip, which lasted from September 1882 to March 1883, Kim renewed his relationship with Fukuzawa and earned the support of the pol-itician Gotō Shōjirō and Inoue Kakugorō, an activist disciple of Fukuzawa. Kim also published an essay in Fukuzawa's newspaper, *Jiji shimpo*, which he sent to the Korean throne. The only exposition of his reform ideas, it called for improvements in sanita-tion, agriculture, and roads as essential aspects of modernizing Korea. On his return to Korea, Kim, accompanied by Inoue Kakugorō, tried to raise funds from the Western powers to finance these projects. When this effort failed he made a third trip to Japan, with King Kojong's blessing, hoping to obtain a loan of three million *yen* in exchange for mining, fishing, or timber rights. By this time Kim was treated as a celebrity in Japan as the leading Korean progressive, but he was unable to convince Japanese government leaders of the worth of his request. His attempt to negotiate a three-million-dollar loan from the American Trading Company through a representative in Japan also failed.

When Kim returned to Korea after almost a year, in May 1884, he felt the situation required drastic measures. Chinese troops remained on Korean soil, the Min family and its supporters were interested only in maintaining the status quo, and the Western powers were indifferent. Kim and other Progressive Party members planned a coup and received a promise of support from the Japanese minister, Takezoe Shinichirō. On the evening of 4 December 1884 the plotters killed about a dozen people in power and seized the royal palace with the assistance of Japanese troops. On the next day they announced a new cabinet in which Kim headed the Ministry of Finance. The reform program included the abolition of tributary relations with China, the abolition of the class structure, the employment of talents according to strict meritocracy, and a reorganization of government. On 6 December Chinese troops attacked the palace and captured the king. Hong Yŏng-sik died, and Kim Ok-kyun, Pak Yŏng-hyo, Sŏ Kwang-bŏm, Sŏ Chae-p'il, and a few others fled to Japan. Takezoe, who apparently helped the Korean revolutionaries without the explicit approval of his home government, was subsequently censured.

Kim spent the next ten years in exile in Japan, moving from place to place to elude assassins sent by the Korean government. In the early years of his exile, he wrote the *Kapsin illok (Journal of 1884),* an apologia for the coup addressed to the Japanese public, in which he blamed the Japanese government for the failure. Much of the information about the incident derives from this source. Kim was assassinated in Shanghai in early 1894 by a Korean government agent. His murder elicited an outcry in Japan and provided a rallying point in the mobilization of public support for the Sino-Japanese War.

[*See also* 1884 Coup d'État; Independence Party and Club; Yi Dynasty; Kojong; *and* Taewŏn'gun.]

Harold F. Cook, *Korea's 1884 Incident: Its Background and Kim Ok-Kyun's Elusive Dream* (1972).

JAHYUN KIM HABOUSH

KIM TAE-JUNG. *See* Kim Dae Jung.

KIM VAN KIEU. *See* Nguyen Du.

KIM YU-SIN (595–673), the most famous general of the Korean kingdom of Silla. A twelfth-generation descendant of King Suro (r. 42–199), the founder of the ancient kingdom of Kaya, he was both a noble and a warrior. When his ancestors surrendered to Silla in the sixth century, they moved to Kyŏngju, where he was born and raised. In his youth Kim showed promise and, like many other children of the Silla nobility, he became a *hwarang* to learn leadership skills and refine his character. [*See* Hwa-

rang.] Well versed in military technique, he demonstrated keen insight and ability; these traits, coupled with his high lineage, were sufficient to assure Kim elite status. His childhood friend, Kim Ch'un-ch'u, the future King Muyŏl (r. 654–661), married his sister, linking Kim Yu-sin even closer to the royal cause. This marriage symbolized more than the union of two families. It was a merger of an established lineage with aristocrats from outside the traditional power structure, bringing enhanced authority and stability to Silla leadership.

Kim Yu-sin first emerged as a powerful military leader in the 640s and vowed with Kim Ch'un-ch'u ·to unite the peninsula. The unification process was long and it was not until 660 that large-scale warfare erupted. In that year Kim Yu-sin, leading an army of as many as fifty thousand men, attacked Paekche from the east in concert with the Chinese commander Su Dingfang, who led a force from the west. This double-pronged attack routed Paekche.

The war of unification was far from over, as Koguryŏ offered even fiercer resistance in the north. Kim Yu-sin again joined Su and the Chinese troops. On one occasion he guided a shipment of supplies through Koguryŏ lines to relieve a beleaguered Chinese detachment. En route Kim was attacked from behind and lost many men. Within a day, however, he launched a counteroffensive and defeated the enemy. Such bold action was characteristic of Kim and helped assure Silla's ultimate control of the peninsula when Koguryŏ collapsed in 668. Even with Koguryŏ's surrender, however, the Chinese were reluctant to give up their foothold. Kim Yu-sin and other Silla generals turned against China and frustrated its authority; by 676 they had forced China's withdrawal from the peninsula.

Because of his extreme valor, Kim became one of the most decorated individuals in the Silla kingdom and was granted extensive landholdings. Kim's political contributions were significant. Through his efforts unification was achieved. Even more laudable, however, was his constant support of the Silla throne, never challenging its sovereignty even though he commanded immense military power. Through his resolute loyalty, he enabled the Silla nobility to expand its authority internally while incorporating the conquered elites of Paekche and Koguryŏ into the Silla social order. His fame spread throughout East Asia. Even the emperor of Tang China, so an ancient Korean text claims, had heard that "one of the great men of the universe was born in Silla and called Yu-sin."

[*See also* Silla.]

EDWARD J. SHULTZ

**KINGKITSARAT**, first king of Lan Sang–Luang Prabang (r. circa 1707–1726). A son of Surinyavongsa, the only son of the last king of Lan Sang, Kingkitsarat was deprived of his rightful succession to the throne by palace coups. He and his brothers gained the aid of their mother's relatives in Yunnan and in 1706 captured Luang Prabang. His rival, King Sai Ong Hue of Vientiane, appealed to Siam for assistance. The king of Ayudhya sent an army that imposed a partition of old Lan Sang between Vientiane and Luang Prabang in 1707. The kingdom of Luang Prabang thus established was to endure until the end of the French protectorate in 1953.

[*See also* Lan Sang; Luang Prabang; Surinyavongsa; *and* Vientiane.]

DAVID K. WYATT

**KINH DUONG VUONG**, legendary figure associated with the beginnings of the earliest Vietnamese dynasty, the Hong Bang. A descendant of the mythical Chinese ruler Shen Nong, Kinh Duong Vuong ruled over a kingdom known as Xich Quy Quoc ("country of red devils"). Taking as his wife Than Long Nu ("lady dragon spirit"), he fathered Lac Long Quan. The latter, with his wife Au Co, produced the race of kings known as Hung Vuong. According to Vietnamese historical tradition, the Hung kings ruled the kingdom of Van Lang from the seventh to the third century BCE.

[*See also* Lac Long Quan; Au Co; Hung Vuong; *and* Van Lang.]

Keith W. Taylor, *The Birth of Vietnam* (1983).

BRUCE M. LOCKHART

**KINWUN MINGYI** (1822–1908), given name U Gaung, minister and ambassador of King Mindon of Burma.

Born Maung Chin, the son of minor rural gentry in Upper Burma, northwest of Mandalay, Kinwun Mingyi spent most of his youth in Buddhist monasteries and was ordained a monk in 1841. He then joined a monastery in the capital, Amarapura, before leaving the monkhood in 1849 to join the personal retinue of the Mindon prince as a financial secretary. He moved quickly to a post in the Hluttaw, the central institution of Burmese administration, after Mindon became king in 1852. In 1866, after toiling his way through the ranks, Mingyi became the *kinwun* (superintendent of toll stations) and took on responsibilities for foreign affairs. He was sent on two missions to Europe, in 1872 and 1874. He was among those who managed the succession of King Thibaw in 1878, only to find the new king unmanageable. Kinwun Mingyi survived subsequent purges and the British conquest in 1885, and served the British as an adviser. He is remembered as a writer and bibliophile.

[*See also* Mindon *and* Thibaw.]

Paul J. Bennett, *Conference under the Tamarind Tree: Three Essays in Burmese History* (1971).

DAVID K. WYATT

**KIPCHAKS**, a loosely organized, nomadic, Turkic tribal confederation (deriving from the Kimek-Kipchak union) that dominated the steppes from the Danube to Kazakhstan from the eleventh to the early thirteenth century. The western grouping was also called Cuman ("pallid ones"; Russian, Polovtsy), and elements of the eastern grouping were known as Kangli. Their movements contributed to the Ghuzz (Oghuz) and Pecheneg migrations.

The Kipchaks were involved in the domestic affairs of Rus, the Khwarazmshahi state (through marital and military ties), and Georgia (where they helped to drive out the Seljuks). They assisted in the creation of the second Bulghar empire and became a major source of *ghulams* (military slaves) for the Islamic world. These *ghulams* later formed the Mamluk state in Syria and Egypt (1250–1517) and constituted the "slave kings" of the Delhi sultanate (1206–1290). Thus, Iltutmish (1211–1236) claimed descent from the royal clan of the Olberli, a Kipchak tribe of the Volga region.

The lack of central authority not only blunted their attacks on sedentary societies, but left them ill-prepared to face the Mongols of Genghis Khan. They were conquered in 1237. In time, the Kipchaks turkicized the Tatars of the Golden and White Hordes, giving rise to the Kipchak Turkic peoples of the Soviet Union. Kipchak families were also prominent in the service of the Yuan dynasty in China, and sizable numbers of them settled in Hungary in flight from the Mongols.

[*See also* Ghuzz; Mongols; *and* Pechenegs.]

Peter B. Golden, "The *Polovci Dikii*," *Harvard Ukrainian Studies* 3/4 (1979–1980). O. Pritsak, "The Polovcians and Rus," *Archivum Eurasiae Medii Aevi* 2 (1982).

PETER B. GOLDEN

**KIPLING, JOSEPH RUDYARD** (1865–1936), popular writer whose poems, novels, and short stories shaped the British view of India for many generations. Born in Bombay, Kipling spent the first five and a half years of his life there before being sent to England for his schooling. He returned to India in 1882 as a fledgling reporter for the *Civil and Military Gazette* of Lahore, later moving to its sister publication, the Allahabad-based *Pioneer*. For seven years Kipling roamed the country, consorting with "princes and politicals," beggars and bounders; he soon published his first short Indian pieces—*Departmental Ditties* (1886) and *Plain Tales from the Hills* (1888). He returned to London in 1889 to take up his literary career, later achieving international fame and receiving the Nobel Prize for literature in 1907.

Kipling has always been a controversial figure. In some of his Indian works he glorified the rulers at the expense of the ruled, and this is the Kipling that most readers are familiar with today: the belligerent imperialist, "the bard of Empire" whose voice is often cruel, arrogant, and contemptuous of Indians. But there is another Kipling, the one who wrote *Kim* (1901) and *The Jungle Books* (1894–1895), and his voice could be both subtle and compassionate. Kipling's writing can be said to draw its power from the constant tension between the imperial prophet and the creative artist.

*Kim* is Kipling's masterpiece: here the author has at last ceased to propagandize, and the India that emerges from the pages of this deeply lyrical book is a land of vitality and variety. Here an Indian worldview, personified by the Tibetan lama who befriends Kim, is granted equal validity with Western ones, and Kipling seems to be striving for a synthesis of East and West made up of the best that each culture has to offer. Kim's questions ("Who is Kim?" and "What is Kim?") are really addressed to Kipling himself: the boy's search for an identity mirrors his creator's own quest for self-definition amid the confusions of an Indian upbringing and an English heritage.

Charles Carrington, *Rudyard Kipling: His Life and Works* (1955). John Gross, ed., *Rudyard Kipling: The Man, His Work and His World* (1972). Angus Wilson, *The Strange Ride of Rudyard Kipling* (1977).

ROBIN JARED LEWIS

**KIRATA**, legendary aboriginal inhabitants of the Himalayas. Early references to the "golden skinned" Kirata in Sanskrit literature portray them as fearsome, skin-clad cannibalistic hunters skilled in magical arts. In later Hindu epics they are described as having their own kings who allied themselves with Hindu rulers but despised brahmans. In a well-known episode from the *Mahabharata,* the god Shiva assumes the guise of a Kirata to do battle with the hero Arjuna. The Kirata have been associated with the Kiranti of Nepal, who are thought to have occupied the Kathmandu Valley until driven eastward by the Licchavis in the early centuries of the common era.

S. K. Chatterji, "Kirata-Jana-Kṛti," *Royal Asiatic Society of Bengal, Letters* 16.2 (1950): 143–235. K. Rönnow, "Kirāta: A Study on Some Ancient Indian Tribes," *Le Monde Oriental* 30 (1936): 90–169.

RICHARD ENGLISH

**KIRGHIZIA**, region in the USSR inhabited by the Kirghiz. Two groups of Kirghiz are known in Asian history: the Yenisei Kirghiz of southern Siberia and the Tianshan Kirghiz, who inhabit the territory of the present-day Kirghiz Soviet Socialist Republic.

*Yenisei Kirghiz.* The political center of the Yenisei Kirghiz (possibly a fortified town mentioned in Chinese and Islamic sources as Kemijketh or Mitijketh) lay near the confluence of the Yenisei and Abakan rivers, at present-day Abakan, the capital of the Khakas Autonomous Region of the Russian SFSR. This area, populated by Paleosiberian (chiefly Samoyed) peoples, eventually came under the control of a Turkic-speaking group known in Chinese sources as the Gegun (possibly a transcription of the ethnonym *Kyrghyz,* first mentioned in 201 BCE), who moved in from the Altai mountain range. The term *Kyrghyz* appears in the Orkhon Turkic inscriptions, which report wars between the *khaghan* of the Orkhon Turks and that of the Kirghiz (late seventh to early eighth century). There were also, however, family ties and trade between the two polities. Relations with China became lively after the Kirghiz had destroyed the Uighur state in 840 and substituted their own; they then became the major power in Inner Asia. In 924, however, the Khitan (founders of the Liao dynasty in China) broke the primacy of the Kirghiz state and limited its extension.

Chinese sources from the Tang period mention Kirghiz embassies and include descriptions of the Kirghiz and of their country. Both the old term *Gegun* and a new one, *Khakas,* are used for the Kirghiz, and lexical examples are given that show both Turkic and Samoyed words. These sources suggest a range of economics and occupations, including a nomadic pastoral economy, a sedentary agricultural one oriented toward crafts and trade, and an economy based on hunting (including the fur trade) and fishing. The Kirghiz people are described as fair-haired, with blue eyes and a ruddy complexion. These reports may stem from the composite nature of the Kirghiz polity, in which only the ruling stratum was Turkic, while the rest were Paleosiberian agriculturists and hunters, hence the dichotomy in name (*Gegun* is a Kirghiz term; *Khakas*, a Samoyed one), language, way of life, and physical appearance: the fair complexion of the aborigines was more likely to strike foreign observers. The Yenisei Kirghiz had a writing system based on a slightly archaic form of the Orkhon alphabet; this system is preserved chiefly on epigraphic funerary monuments.

By the time Temujin was proclaimed Genghis Khan in 1206, the Kirghiz polity was no longer a unified state led by a *khaghan* but an aristocratic oligarchy, still sufficiently powerful to warrant becoming an early target of the new conquests (1207, definitively in 1218). Mentions of food relief for the Kirghiz hit by famine and of displacement of some Kirghiz to Manchuria can be gleaned from Yuan annals.

When reports about the Yenisei Kirghiz reappear in the seventeenth century, they describe a similar society of a Kirghiz aristocratic confederation dominating non-Kirghiz elements, referred to as Kyshtyms. These records are mostly in Russian (the earliest from 1604) and reflect the advancing Russian conquest of Siberia. The Yenisei confederation of the Altysar, Yeser, and Altyr tribal groups was then tributary to the Altan khans of Mongolia, and subsequently to the Dzungars, but the Russians were rapidly gaining ascendancy.

In comparison with earlier eras, this was a period of decline for the Yenisei Kirghiz. The former literacy had disappeared, with nothing to replace it except for a limited knowledge of the Mongol script and language, used for contacts with the external world (correspondence with Moscow, for example). Agriculture and the crafts lost much of their former vigor, and the fur trade came to exist virtually only to meet the demands of Dzungar and Russian suzerains. Worst of all, the Kirghiz suffered increasing losses in population due to the actions of the Dzungars and Russians. The culmination of this process of decline came in 1703, when the Dzungars, after having devastated the area, drove away the cream of the aristocratic clans of the Kirghiz; the Russians seized the Kirghiz territory immediately afterward (1704–1706), destroying the remaining Kirghiz. These events are conventionally given as marking the end of the existence of the Yenisei Kirghiz. There is evidence, however, that parts of the population did survive and are among the components of the modern Khakass and Tuvin nationalities.

*Tianshan Kirghiz.* Genetic relationship between the Yenisei and Tianshan Kirghiz is still a matter of debate, but it does appear that both groups originated in the general area of the Altai mountain range, with the former group moving east, and the latter, a millennium later (in the course of the fourteenth and fifteenth centuries), west. Certain aspects of the westward movements of the Kirghiz appear to have been connected with similar movements of Western Mongols (known at different times as Oirats, Kalmuks, or Dzungars), and this may have contributed to considerable intermingling and thus to the Mongoloid racial type of the Kirghiz. The two groups were ultimately separated by the islamization of the Tianshan Kirghiz and the conversion to Buddhism of the Mongols. The Dzungars subsequently also affected the Tianshan Kirghiz, to the point of forcing them to abandon the Tianshan mountains and seek refuge in the Pamir and Kunlun ranges; they returned only after the collapse of the Dzungar empire in the second half of the eighteenth century.

Unlike the Yenisei Kirghiz, the Tianshan Kirghiz never succeeded in forming a unified state. They remained a group of mutually contending tribal groups until the Russian conquests in the 1850s and 1870s imposed upon them first a colonial rule and then a Soviet system.

The Tianshan Kirghiz were until their recent sedentarization (1932–1934) almost exclusively mountain nomads, living in yurts and raising horses, sheep, cattle, camels, and yaks. Most were illiterate, but they had a vast body of oral literature (the epos *Manas,* for example).

[See also Kalmuks; Khitan; Oirats; Orkhon Inscriptions; *and* Uighurs.]

Wilhelm Barthold and G. Hazai, "Kirgiz," in *The Encyclopaedia of Islam* (new ed., 1960–). René Grousset, *The Empire of the Steppes,* translated by Naomi Walford (1970).                        SVAT SOUCEK

**KIRIN.** *See* Jilin.

**KIRISHITAN**, the Japanese term for Christianity and Christians used from the mid-sixteenth to the late nineteenth century. *Kirishitan* is the Japanese pronunciation of the Portuguese word *Christaõ.* Christianity was introduced to Japan in 1549 by the Jesuit missionary Francis Xavier, who was followed by a large number of Jesuits, as well as Franciscans and Dominicans. [*See* Xavier, Francis.] Initially spurred by interest in trade with the Portuguese as well as spiritual goals, many Japanese responded enthusiastically to the missionaries, who claimed as many as 150,000 converts by 1582. The mission had the early encouragement of Oda Nobunaga, who saw Christianity as a counter to the powerful Buddhist monasteries. It also had the support of the convert *Kirishitan* daimyo (lords) of Kyushu, who donated land for schools and churches—and even the port of Nagasaki—to the Jesuits and whose domains became strongholds of Kirishitan converts. By the mid-1580s the Jesuits had schools, novitiates, seminaries, churches, and a college, these located in Kyushu, in Nobunaga's capital of Azuchi, and in Kyōto; through these institutions they trained a cadre of native catechists. There was as well a rapidly growing community of faithful in central and western Japan.

Jesuit evangelical success came into conflict with the emerging national hegemony of Toyotomi Hideyoshi after his conquest of Kyushu in 1587. Alarmed at the extent of Kirishitan spiritual and material success in Kyushu and at the threat the new faith posed both to native beliefs and his own supremacy, on 24 July 1587 he decreed: "Since Japan is the land of the gods, it is outrageous that the base doctrines of the Kirishitan are propagated [here]." He ordered the Jesuits expelled. The expulsion order was not enforced, but it signaled the start of an anti-Christian reaction that gained force over the next half-century. Hideyoshi's fears were exacerbated by the arrival of Spanish mendicant friars, who began challenging the Jesuits in 1592. The Franciscans and Dominicans were less accomodating to Japanese custom, and the boasts of a Spanish mariner from the *San Felipe,* cast upon Tosa in 1596, that the friars were but the vanguard for the *conquistadores* confirmed Hideyoshi's fears. He ordered crucifixion for six Franciscans, seventeen of their Japanese converts, and three Japanese Jesuit lay brothers *(irmaō),* who were marched from Kyoto to Nagasaki for public ridicule before their execution on 5 February 1597, the first, but not the last, martyrdom in Japan.

The arrival of English and Dutch Protestant merchants in Japan in the first decade of the seventeenth century made clear to Hideyoshi's successor Tokugawa Ieyasu that trade with Europeans without Kirishitan evangelism was possible. Even so, for a decade after founding the *bakufu* in 1603, Ieyasu permitted the Franciscans to evangelize in eastern Japan because of his interest in relations with Spain. In 1612, however, he prohibited Christianity in his own domains. In 1614, after both the English and

the Dutch had established trading factories in Hirado, and after a mission from James I of England, Ieyasu ordered the expulsion of all missionaries from the land, and he exiled several prominent Kirishitan converts from Japan to Manila or Macao. This order, unlike Hideyoshi's, was enforced, and from 1614 on the experience of the Kirishitan was one of ever-increasing persecution and restriction.

In 1622 the second Tokugawa shogun, Hidetada, unable to stanch the inflow of missionaries, ordered the execution of fifty-five Christians (the "great Nagasaki martyrdom") and in 1624 ordered the Spanish out of Japan altogether. Proscriptions against the Kirishitan were repeated and strengthened through the 1620s and 1630s, while other restrictions were placed on Japanese foreign intercourse to prevent contact with the foreign creed. [*See* Seclusion.] The great Shimabara Rebellion of 1637–1638, although it was at root a peasant revolt against political and economic repression, was viewed by the *bakufu* as a Kirishitan rebellion, as most of the participants were converts. The great difficulty the *bakufu* found in suppressing the revolt prompted the expulsion of the Portuguese traders in the summer of 1639, thus cutting off for the Japanese all contact with the Kirishitan menace. After 1639 the only remaining Kirishitan in Japan were forced to go underground; these were the *kakure,* or "hidden," Kirishitan of southern and western Kyushu, some few cells of which managed to survive until the ban on Christianity was lifted in 1873, their faith and ritual by then an amalgam of Catholic and native Japanese practices.

The *bakufu* implemented various measures to ensure that the Kirishitan meanace was stamped out permanently, most important among them the mandate that all Japanese be formally affiliated with a Buddhist temple and that the responsible officer of every administrative unit (hamlet or urban ward) annually inspect all residents of the unit to certify their Buddhist affiliation. At first enforced only in shogunal domains, as large pockets of Christianity came to light in the 1650s and 1660s the *bakufu* made the system mandatory nationwide. The resultant "sect affiliation records" *(shūmon aratame chō)* are an invaluable source of data for the study of Japanese demographic history. The *bakufu* also prohibited the importation of Western-language books, or any books that mentioned the Christian God. This ban was slightly relaxed in 1720, to permit circulation of "useful" books (i.e., those on medicine, mathematics, astronomy, and the like), but this relaxation was accompanied by strict censorship in Nagasaki to ensure that no Kirishitan propaganda entered. The ban on Kirishitan belief and activity remained in force until 1873, when the Meiji government lifted it in response to pressures from the Western powers.

[See also Christianity: Christianity in Japan and Tokugawa Period.]

C. R. Boxer, *The Christian Century in Japan, 1549–1650* (1951). Otis Carey, *A History of Christianity in Japan* (2 vols., 1909). Michael Cooper, *Rodrigues the Interpreter* (1974). George Elison, *Deus Destroyed: The Image of Christianity in Early Modern Japan* (1973).

RONALD P. TOBY

**KIRKPATRICK MISSION.** Colonel William Kirkpatrick's mission was the first attempt made by the English government of Bengal to establish contacts with Nepal in the late eighteenth century. The mission achieved nothing substantial except perhaps gaining its first peep at this *terra incognita* through Kirkpatrick's firsthand travel accounts. Kirkpatrick's entire stay in Nepal lasted barely seven weeks, from 15 February to 4 April 1793. The mission had been dispatched in response to Nepal's request for help from the English against China. Meanwhile, Nepal concluded a peace with the latter and therefore agreed only reluctantly to receive the mission.

William Kirkpatrick, *An Account of the Kingdom of Nepaul, Being the Substance of Observations Made during a Mission to That Country in the Year 1793* (1811; reprint, 1969). L. R. Stiller, *The Rise of the House of Gorkha* (1972).    PRAYAG RAJ SHARMA

**KISAN SABHA.** Centered on the eastern United Provinces in India, the Kisan Sabha (Farmers' Assembly) was a movement dedicated to the improvement of economic conditions for India's rural poor. The movement arose under local rural leadership around the year 1920, as booming agricultural prices, a rise in the value of land, high profits for the landed, and war recruitment combined to pose an intolerable economic burden on the landless and the poor. Coalescing briefly with the Congress-led Noncooperation Movement, the Kisan Sabha was revived in the 1930s during the Depression.

[See also Indian National Congress.]

USHA SANYAL

**KISHI NOBUSUKE** (b. 1896), prime minister of Japan from 1957 to 1960, bureaucrat, and Liberal Democratic Party leader. Kishi was prime minister during the 1960 crisis over the security treaty with the United States, a near-revolutionary turbulence that seemed to bring into question Japan's postwar political system.

Kishi was born in Yamaguchi Prefecture in southwestern Honshu into a distinguished family that is linked to many notable figures of Meiji Restoration and later history. Satō Eisaku, prime minister in the 1960s, is Kishi's younger brother.

Kishi distinguished himself at Tokyo Imperial University. He rejected his academic mentor's invitation to become his successor and instead entered the Ministry of Agriculture and Commerce in 1917. As a reform-minded bureaucrat, he quickly distinguished himself among his peers and his seniors as an outstanding manager and planner. These qualities found opportunity for employment in the puppet state of Manchukuo, where Kishi served from 1936 to 1939 in a variety of posts charged with industrial development. Kishi returned to Japan as vice-minister of the Ministry of Commerce and Industry just before World War II, and he was in charge of economic mobilization in the Tōjō cabinet from 1941 to 1944. During those years the Ministry of Commerce and Industry became the Ministry of Munitions; after the war it became the Ministry of International Trade and Industry (MITI). Kishi's preparedness for postwar economic planning and reconstruction was exceptional.

After Japan's surrender Kishi was a war-crimes suspect because of his prewar position, but he was not tried. Upon his release he entered conservative politics, counting close allies among bureaucrats, business leaders, and politicians critical of Yoshida Shigeru's willingness to rely upon American help. As prime minister after 1957 he encountered bitter opposition to his proposed renewal of the American tie, and his high-handed Diet tactics, combined with his public image and prewar record, persuaded many Japanese that under his leadership their democracy hung in the balance. Kishi resigned shortly after Diet approval of the security pact, but he continued to play an important behind-the-scenes role in conservative politics.

Junnosuke Masumi and Robert Scalapino, *Parties and Politics in Contemporary Japan* (1961). George R. Packard, *Protest in Tokyo: The Security Treaty Crisis of 1960* (1966).    MICHIO UMEGAKI

**KITA IKKI** (1883–1937; given name, Terujirō), radical right-wing writer and activist in Japan. Kita was born on Sadō Island to a prosperous rural family. In his youth, he was attracted to socialism and in 1906 he published *Kokutairon oyobi junsei shakaishugi (The National Polity and Pure Socialism)*, in which he argued that socialism suited Japan's national principles. The book was banned ten days after its publication.

When the Chinese revolution broke out in 1911, Kita went to China as an observer for the Kokuryūkai (Amur River Society). After the murder of his friend the revolutionary leader Song Jiaoren in 1913, he returned to Japan to write *Shina kakumei gaishi (A Private History of the Chinese Revolution, 1921)*, in which he ascribed the revolution's failure to a lack of Japanese support.

In 1916 Kita went to China and in 1919, while still in Shanghai, he wrote *Nihon kaizō hōan taikō (Outline Plan for the Reorganization of Japan)*. In this book Kita advocated nationalization of excessive wealth, establishment of a welfare state, and the liberation of Asia from Western imperialism by a "revolutionary Japanese empire." In order to achieve these goals, he called for a coup d'état that would allow the "people's emperor" to suspend the constitution and assume direct powers. Although the book was first banned, a censored version was published in 1923. Uncensored, handwritten copies were circulated clandestinely, however, by his followers.

In 1919 Kita returned to Japan as a sinophile, a devoted adherent of Nichiren Buddhism, and a virulent nationalist. With Ōkawa Shūmei, he soon became active in various right-wing organizations. Through his friend Nishida Mitsugi, Kita started an enduring association with a group of young officers. For some years he was financed by the Mitsui concern, which by means of these contributions sought to avert attacks on its leaders.

Kita's followers among the young officers perpetrated the February Twenty-sixth Incident of 1936. When the incident broke out, Kita encouraged the rebels to hold fast until their demands were met. After the rebellion was suppressed, he and Nishida were arrested. Both men were sentenced to death and executed in 1937. Kita is sometimes referred to as the father of Japanese fascism because of his advocacy of curbs on private wealth and state direction of large enterprises.

[*See also* February Twenty-sixth Incident.]

Masao Maruyama, *Thought and Behavior in Modern Japanese Politics* (1963). Ben-Ami Shillony, *Revolt in Japan* (1973). George M. Wilson, *Radical Nationalist in Japan* (1969).          BEN-AMI SHILLONY

**KITCHENER, HORATIO HERBERT** (Lord Kitchener; 1850–1916), commander in chief of the Indian Army from 1902 to 1909. In 1904, under central commands, he reorganized the army administration. In 1905 the British cabinet largely accepted Kitchener's proposal that the commander in chief, rather than the Viceroy's Council, be the final authority over military administration in India, a move that led to the resignation of the viceroy, Lord Curzon.

[*See also* Curzon, George Nathaniel.]

USHA SANYAL

**KIZILBASH** (Turkish, "red head"), the name given to Turkish tribal groups who supported the Safavids beginning in the fifteenth century CE, referring to the distinctive red headgear they wore. It is sometimes used to refer to both the Safavid religious ideology and the Safavids in general.

The Kizilbash originally consisted largely of converts to the Safavid cause from seven major Turkish *uymaqs* (loosely, "tribes") but soon expanded to include most of the large *uymaqs* of the period. While in the early period one could become a Kizilbash simply by converting to the cause of the Safavids, in a short time (at least by Shah Isma'il's reign at the beginning of the sixteenth century) membership in the Kizilbash was restricted to members of certain *uymaqs*.

The Kizilbash came to be a "closed class group with specific military functions" and were distinguished from all other members of the Safavid state. The terms *Turk* and *Tajik* were loosely employed to refer to the members of the Kizilbash and the predominantly Persian-speaking elite, respectively. The former, under the early Safavids, comprised the military and governmental elite of the state, but many Tajiks acquired major government positions in time, and the distinctions of the roles are not altogether clear. The term fell out of use with the end of the Safavid dynasty and became used almost exclusively for the heterodox Shi'ite religious beliefs espoused by the Safavids.

The designation *Kizilbash* is still used in Afghanistan to refer to an urban middle class of Turkish origin believed to have immigrated originally during the reign of Nadir Shah. The largest community of Kizilbash in Afghanistan is in Kabul, but their population is undetermined.

[*See also* Isma'il I *and* Safavid Dynasty.]

Roger M. Savory, *Iran under the Safavids* (1980).

JAHAN SALEHI

KIZIL KUM (Turkish, "red sand"), a desert in Central Asia between the Amu Darya (Oxus) and the Syr Darya (Jaxartes) rivers. The Kizil Kum extends to the south almost to Bukhara, and to the north to a series of hills by the Aral Sea. It lies to the east, across the Amu Darya, of the Kara Kum ("black sand") desert, the other major Central Asian desert.                                    JAHAN SALEHI

KLACWA. *See* Kyaswa.

KLOBUKOWSKI, ANTONI-WLADISLAS, governor-general of French Indochina between 1908 and 1911. Born in 1855, Klobukowski entered government service in 1873 and occupied several posts in the colonial administration in Indochina during the 1880s, including the resident-generalship of Tonkin. After several diplomatic posts elsewhere, he replaced Paul Beau as governor-general of Indochina in September 1908. With popular unrest on the rise, Klobukowski took a tough line, arresting rebels and closing the University of Hanoi. But his efforts to end abuses in the French-run alcohol and salt monopolies aroused opposition in colonial circles, and in 1911 he was recalled from office. Klobukowski died in 1934.

Joseph Buttinger, *Vietnam: A Dragon Embattled* (1967).                              WILLIAM J. DUIKER

KNOX, ROBERT (1641–1720), author of *An Historical Relation of Ceylon*, a widely read work based on his experiences in that country. A sailor by profession, Knox was captured, along with his father, the captain of the *Ann*, and several others when their vessel put in to Kottiyar Bay near Trincomalee, Sri Lanka, for repairs. Knox spent twenty years (1660–1680) in the Kandyan kingdom. His experiences during this long enforced stay and his sensitive understanding of the people among whom he lived formed the basis of *An Historical Relation of Ceylon*, which he published in 1681 after his escape to England. The book is one of the classic accounts of the island's people. In addition to being a celebrated sourcebook on the Kandyan kingdom, the work also made a certain impact on the development of English prose through its influence on the work of Daniel Defoe.

[*See also* Trincomalee.]

E. F. C. Ludowyk, ed., *Robert Knox in the Kandyan Kingdom* (1948).                        K. M. DE SILVA

KŌBŌ DAISHI. *See* Kūkai.

KODAW HMAING, THAKIN, also known as U Lun (1875–1964), Burmese novelist, playwright, editor, politician, and leader in nationalist literary and political circles for more than fifty years. As editor of the first Burmese national newspaper, *Thuriya,* in 1911, he bridged the gap between traditional poetry and court writing and the twentieth-century modernist movement. He never learned English and remained devoted to such premodern interests as alchemy. Active in the university students' strike of 1920, he was patron of the left-wing section of the Dobama Asiayon in the 1930s. During the Japanese occupation (1942–1945) of Burma he served as privy councillor and after independence urged reconciliation between the underground communists and the government. In 1954 he was awarded the Stalin Peace Prize.

[*See also* Dobama Asiayon.]

John F. Cady, *A History of Modern Burma* (1958).

ROBERT H. TAYLOR

KOGURYŎ, Korean kingdom, first mentioned in Chinese records of the end of the first century BCE, that survived until the end of the seventh century. With Silla and Paekche, Koguryŏ was one of the Three Kingdoms of Korean history. It is via the shortened form *Koryŏ,* used to designate a later Korean state, that our word *Korea* derives.

According to later legend incorporated into the Sino-Korean chronicle *Samguk sagi* in 1145, Koguryŏ was established by a prince of divine parentage who fled south to the Yalu River from the Manchurian Puyŏ confederacy in 37 BCE. [*See also* Puyŏ.] Chinese histories such as the *Hanshu* (first century) and *Sanguozhi* (third century), however, paint a very different picture. They suggest that the administrators of the Former Han conquests in Korea and Manchuria may have regarded the five original Koguryŏ tribes as useful clients who would defend the imperial frontiers on the upper Yalu against other potentially hostile groups, and that this situation existed at least as early as 75 BCE. The Koguryŏ "king" in this period may simply have been the chieftain of the leading tribe, the Sonno-bu, used as an intermediary by the Chinese in their dealings with the rest.

The age of "proto-Koguryŏ" as a Chinese client statelet came to an abrupt end in 12 CE, when the

Chinese usurper Wang Mang made an unsuccessful attempt to use the tribes in his campaign against the northern nomads. The tribes rebelled, and the arrest and execution of their king by the Chinese did nothing to ease the situation; the five tribes continued to act together against the empire and Koguryŏ began its long career as China's principal enemy in the northeast. Possibly the severance of ties with the Han frontier administration led to a decline in the prestige of the Sonno-bu; by the end of the first century CE the Sonno-bu kings had been replaced by a ruling house drawn from another of the five tribes, the Kyeru-bu. Under Kyeru-bu leadership the Koguryŏ warrior aristocracy extended its control over various groups of sedentary agriculturalists in northern Korea, such as the Ŏkcho. In the *Sanguozhi* the Chinese note: "In this realm [i.e., Koguryŏ] there are some ten thousand or more who eat in idleness and do no work in the fields, being supplied by the lower orders, who bring them rice, salt, and fish from remote regions."

Clearly, although there was a certain amount of Chinese cultural influence even at this early period of Koguryŏ history, the religion and way of life of the people retained strong connections with the world of the nomads further north. Koguryŏ's religion, for example, seems to have been a type of animism that involved star worship and, among other things, the worship of a god called the Spirit of the Underground Passage, who descended from heaven to his shrine east of the capital in the tenth month and later reascended. At some unknown stage in the history of Koguryŏ this spirit was identified with the ancestor of the royal line. Another feature of Koguryŏ life that showed similarities to practice in other parts of Inner Asia was the custom of uxorilocal marriage, which scandalized the Chinese historians, as did the apparent freedom with which the two sexes could intermingle: "The people love song and dance, and in the towns and villages of their kingdom, men and women gather together every evening and into the night to sing and amuse themselves together."

In 245 the Wei dynasty then ruling northern China made a determined effort to end the prolonged irritation of Koguryŏ raids into Liaodong. Hwando, the capital of Koguryŏ north of the Yalu, was captured and sacked by the Chinese, and the Kyeru-bu king Wigung was hunted into the far north but never captured. The Chinese campaigns destroyed, at least for the time being, the tributary basis of the Koguryŏ state, and Koguryŏ subsequently disappeared from the Chinese records for almost seventy years.

The middle Koguryŏ kingdom emerged from obscurity early in the fourth century, when the civil wars of the Eight Princes and the rebellion of various groups settled in North China had led to the collapse of imperial rule north of the Huai River. The successive Chinese dynasties that strove to retain a semblance of empire south of the Yangtze River were clearly in no position to intervene in Korea, and the Chinese colonies in the Korean peninsula were completely isolated. Ŭlbul (Mich'on, r. 300–331), a descendant of King Wigung, seized the opportunity, and soon after the middle of the century Koguryŏ had taken over most of northern Korea. Farther north, Koguryŏ was able to expand into the Liaodong Peninsula in spite of continued harassment by other nomad groups, one of which sacked Hwando for the second time in 343. By the end of the reign of King Kwanggaet'o in 413 Koguryŏ's territory extended from the Sungari River in Manchuria to the Han River in southern Korea, while the chieftains of Silla in southeastern Korea had accepted Koguryŏ's suzerainty in exchange for protection against raids from the Japanese Yamato state. Only the southwestern Korean state of Paekche, founded by refuges from Puyŏ about a century earlier, continued to resist Koguryŏ domination and prevented the unification of the peninsula. [*See also* Kwanggaet'o.]

Nevertheless, the reigns of Kwanggaet'o and his successor Changsu (413–491) constituted the golden age of Koguryŏ. Numbers of Chinese gentry, fleeing the chaos in northern China, had settled in the kingdom, and several were used as administrators by the rulers, perhaps in a deliberate attempt to bolster royal power at the expense of the old tribal nobility. The heightened status of the king appears in the doctrine of the divine origin of the royal house as proclaimed in a lengthy inscription set up by King Changsu outside his capital in honor of his predecessor. Surrounding this still extant inscription are the stone chambers covered by great earth mounds that are the tombs of the Koguryŏ nobles. The frescoes covering the inner walls of these tombs reveal something of the customs of the period, showing the owners of the tombs hunting, riding on armored horses, or watching displays of dancing and wrestling. Although Buddhism had been introduced into Koguryŏ from China in 372, there is little trace of its influence in these frescoes, which are in many ways the most impressive surviving examples of Korean tomb art.

In 427 the Koguryŏ capital was moved south to P'yŏngyang, the old capital of the Chinese colonies in Korea, and efforts were concentrated upon bringing the kingdom of Paekche to heel. Although forces

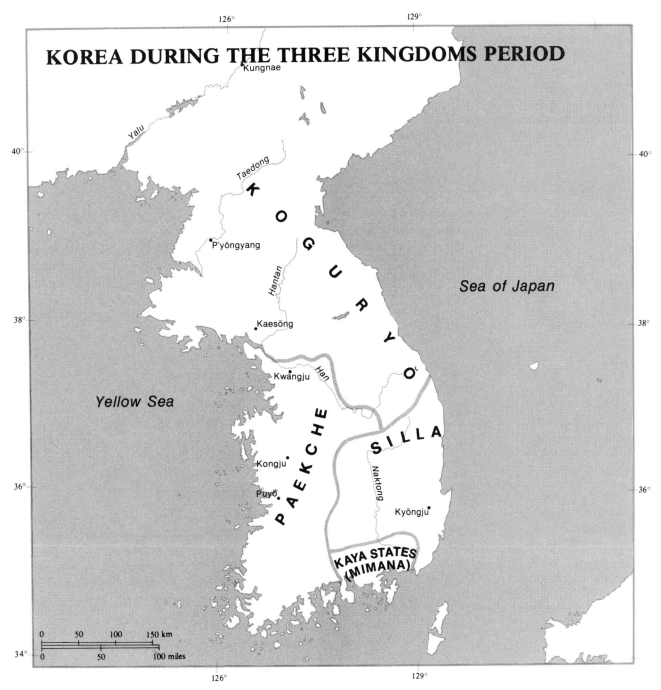

# KOREA DURING THE THREE KINGDOMS PERIOD

Kungnae

Yalu

Taedong

KOGURYŎ

P'yŏngyang

Hantan

*Sea of Japan*

Kaesŏng

Han

Kwangju

*Yellow Sea*

PAEKCHE

Kongju

SILLA

Puyŏ

Naktong

Kyŏngju

KAYA STATES (MIMANA)

0   50   100   150 km
0        50        100 miles

of Koguryŏ crossed the Han River in 475 and occupied the Paekche capital of Hansŏng, however, Paekche simply moved its capital farther south and continued to resist. In addition, since by this time Silla had thrown off Koguryŏ's suzerainty, the opportunity for a unified Korea under Koguryŏ's rule had already passed.

In the first half of the sixth century Koguryŏ's power declined and the court seems to have been distracted by factional strife. In 551 Paekche was able to retake the territory lost to Koguryŏ in 475, only to lose it almost immediately to Silla. In spite

of its political weakness, this phase of Koguryŏ's history was also one of great cultural activity, especially that associated with Buddhism. Mahayana Buddhism, particularly of the Madhyamika school, was now predominant in Koguryŏ, and it was from that kingdom that the religion was now introduced to Silla. In 594 the Koguryŏ monk Hyeja went to Japan to become the tutor in Buddhism to Crown Prince Shōtoku. In 600 the Koguryŏ literatus Yi Mun-jin compiled an account of the early days of the kingdom, the *Yugi sinjip*, which is thought to have formed the basis of the record of Koguryŏ contained in the twelfth century *Samguk sagi*. Unfortunately the *Yugi sinjip* does not appear to have covered the history of Koguryŏ after the fourth century and our knowledge of the subsequent period is still very scanty and based mainly upon references in the Chinese dynastic histories.

From the early fifth century until the end of the sixth century Koguryŏ's relations with the various dynasties that ruled northern or southern China had been entirely peaceful, but this situation rapidly deteriorated after the Sui dynasty reunited China in 589. It soon became evident that the Sui intended to recover all the imperial territory lost at the beginning of the fourth century, including both Liaodong and the Korean commanderies. To some extent this threat is reflected in the patriotic legends of Koguryŏ found in the *Samguk sagi* and evidently derived from the *Yugi sinjip*, with their emphasis on successful resistance to Chinese invasion. The Koguryŏ court also attempted to secure itself by an alliance with the Eastern Turks, but this merely served as a direct provocation to the Sui, who between 612 and 614 carried out several massive invasions of Koguryŏ. These attacks succeeded in inflicting great devastation but met with determined resistance. Although Koguryŏ was brought to its knees, it was the Sui dynasty that cracked and collapsed into civil war within eighteen months of its final, inconclusive invasion of Korea.

Once the Tang dynasty (618–907) had succeeded the Sui, campaigns against Koguryŏ were resumed, largely in response to the insistent appeals for help from the kingdom of Silla, which itself felt threatened by the new alliance between Koguryŏ and Paekche. Nevertheless, in the intervals of peace there was still a good deal of cultural contact between Koguryŏ and China, and Koguryŏ princes studied in the Chinese capital. Other emigrants from Koguryŏ sought the safety of Japan, where they introduced various innovations in music and in dance drama.

The final Chinese onslaught came just after the middle of the seventh century. The pretext for this particular series of invasions was the assassination of the king of Koguryŏ in 642 by a noble named Yŏn'gae Somun, who appointed a puppet king but effectively ruled as military dictator until his death in 666. Even with Silla's help the Chinese invaders made little progress, and it was not until after the conquest of Paekche by the Chinese in 663 and the death of Yŏn'gae Somun that the final collapse of Koguryŏ took place, largely as a result of bickering between the dead dictator's heirs.

After the fall of P'yŏngyang on 22 October 668, large numbers of upper-class families of Koguryŏ were deported to China, and the Chinese attempted to restore their own direct rule in the peninsula. The troops who would have been needed to implement this policy were required on other frontiers, however, and southern Koguryŏ as far as the Taedong River was quickly absorbed by the kingdom of Silla. Silla was never able to control the northern area, which was subject to prolonged political instability. In 677 the Chinese tried to repair the harm they had done by bringing back the last ruler of Koguryŏ, King Pojang, to organize some sort of kingdom in Liaodong, but it proved impossible to revive the Koguryŏ state structure; moreover Chinese suspicion rapidly brought about the deposition of King Pojang.

Until the end of the seventh century successive Chinese regimes tried from time to time to stabilize this frontier by restoring members of the Koguryŏ royal family, but the only real improvement in the situation took place entirely independently of Chinese initiatives, as a result of a revolt of the Malgal tribes around 699. This group, which had formerly played a subordinate role in the old Koguryŏ kingdom, was eventually able to take advantage of the confusion in southern Manchuria to establish the kingdom of Parhae, which survived for more than two hundred years and ruled from the Sungari to the Taedong.

[*See also* Paekche; Silla; *and* Parhae.]

K. H. J. Gardiner, *The Early History of Korea* (1969). W. E. Henthorn, *A History of Korea* (1971).

KENNETH H. J. GARDINER

**KOH-I NUR DIAMOND**, famous diamond included in the crown jewels of Britain. The Koh-i Nur ("mountain of light") diamond was first acquired by emperor Shah Jahan as a gift. Nadir Shah took it when he sacked Delhi and it eventually passed to Ranjit Singh in 1813 when he took prisoner Shah Shuja, who had fled Kabul. When the British annexed the Punjab they insisted that the diamond be given to Queen Victoria. It now adorns the crown of England. [*See also* Shah Jahan.]

LYNN ZASTOUPIL

**KOIRALA, BISHWESHWOR PRASAD** (1915–1982), prime minister of Nepal during its brief period of parliamentary democracy and long-time leader of the country's political opposition. In 1947

Koirala founded the Nepali National Congress (NNC) Party along with other members of the Nepali intelligentsia living in India, including his half-brother M. P. Koirala, D. R. Regmi, and K. I. Singh. Advocating principles of democratic reform, economic development, and Nepali nationalism, the NNC spearheaded the revolutionary movement that overthrew the century-old Rana oligarchy in 1951. In 1959 the NNC won an overwhelming majority in the country's first popular elections. As president of the party, Koirala was appointed prime minister by King Mahendra. However, growing opposition to the new government led by Communist factions and representatives of entrenched Rana interests prompted Mahendra to dissolve Parliament in 1960, less than nineteen months after it had been convened. All political parties were subsequently outlawed and Koirala, along with other NNC leaders, was jailed without trial until 1968, when he was permitted to go into exile in India. Returning to Nepal in 1976, he was arrested on charges of treason and sedition but was acquitted a year later and released to undergo medical treatment in the United States. Koirala figured prominently in Nepal's 1980 national referendum on the restoration of political parties, advocating a policy of reconciliation between the crown and Nepal's democratic interests.

[*See also* Rana; Singh, K. I.; *and* Nepal: History of Nepal.]

B. L. Joshi and L. Rose, *Democratic Innovations in Nepal* (1966). L. Rose, *Nepal: Strategy for Survival* (1971). RICHARD ENGLISH

**KOJIKI** *(Record of Ancient Matters),* a history of the Japanese ruling house commissioned during the reign of the emperor Temmu (r. 672–686) and completed in 712. The *Kojiki* is composed of four parts: a preface that explains why the book was written and three volumes *(maki)* that describe the creation of Japan, its heroic age, and the reigns of the emperors until the empress Suiko (r. 592–628). The contents of the *Kojiki* are similar to those of Japan's first Chinese-style court history, the *Nihon shoki,* but it is written in a mixed style, using Chinese characters both for their meaning and their sound value in Japanese.

According to the preface, Emperor Temmu became concerned about the state of court records sometime after his victory in the civil war of 672. Imperial genealogies *(teiki)* and old tales *(kuji),* which had first been collected about 600, were full of errors. Since status at court was based upon lin-

eage and the titles *(kabane)* conferred by previous rulers, a precise history was an absolute necessity. As the first step in this task, a twenty-eight-year-old courtier named Hieda no Are was asked to memorize the genealogies and stories.

In 712, the courtier Ono Yasumaro wrote down what Hieda no Are had memorized. This new history, the *Kojiki,* was soon eclipsed, however, by the *Nihon shoki* and was accorded less importance throughout the early and medieval eras.

In the Tokugawa period (1600–1867) the status of the *Kojiki* began to rise, primarily as a result of the efforts of Motoori Norinaga. A leader of the Kokugaku ("national learning") movement, Motoori saw in the *Kojiki* a purely Japanese classic, unsullied by such outside influences as Chinese or Buddhist culture. For him it described several "uniquely Japanese" traits, such as *mono no aware* ("pathos"), and he used the work to support his contention that Japan's superiority in East Asia was founded on its imperial line, divine and unbroken. During the chauvinistic 1930s the *Kojiki* was revered with fundamentalist fervor.

Since World War II, scholars have come to look upon the *Kojiki* as a linguistic and ethnological treasure. Anthropologists have found elements of Central and Southeast Asian folklore in many myths. Far from proving the uniqueness of Japanese culture, the *Kojiki* suggests the debt Japan owes to the rest of Asia.

[*See also* Nihon Shoki *and* Motoori Norinaga.]

Basil Chamberlain, trans., *The Kojiki* (1932). Donald Philippi, trans. *The Kojiki* (1969). WAYNE FARRIS

**KOJONG,** posthumous name of Yi Myŏng-bok (1852–1919; r. 1864–1907), the second son of Yi Ha-ŭng (1821–1889), chosen in 1864 as the twenty-sixth Yi king in Korea, succeeding Ch'ŏlchong (r. 1849–1864), who died without an heir. His father was given the title Taewŏn'gun ("grand prince"), and the oldest living dowager, a member of the Cho family of P'ungyang, began her regency (until 1866) for the twelve-year-old king.

During the decade from 1864 to 1873, when power was largely in the hands of the Taewŏn'gun, Kojong received a thorough Confucian education and was married in May 1866 to a fifteen-year-old girl who belonged to his mother's lineage, the Yŏhŭng Min. She became known as Queen Min (1851–1895). During his father's "regency" Kojong certainly was not a mere puppet, and after 1869 he seems to have exerted some independent authority. He had an especially strong sense of justice, was lenient in administering punishment, and showed repeated concern about relief measures. Kojong contributed to his father's downfall in December 1873; later, encouraged by conservative Confucian literati, he abandoned a great number of his father's policies. Eventually he himself became the target of Confucian criticism, and his position became further complicated by the growing influence of the Min, who began in the mid-1870s to occupy posts in the higher echelons of the government.

Despite these various pressures Kojong surrounded himself with men of proven ability in government. The culmination of his pragmatic foreign policy was the conclusion of Korea's first modern treaty, the Kanghwa Treaty, with Japan on 26 February 1876. Well aware of the changing circumstances in East Asia, Kojong was determined to lead Korea out of its international isolation. He concluded treaties with Western powers and launched a self-strengthening program. After the 1882 Uprising, however, Korea became the arena for the growing Sino-Japanese struggle over the peninsula, and the modernization process was increasingly dominated by the Min. Kojong's ability to maintain his own course became more and more limited, and particularly after 1884, with China's intensified interference in Korean affairs, he was degraded to a mere figurehead.

In 1895 Queen Min was murdered by the Japanese, who after defeating China in 1894 faced expanding Russian influence in Seoul and accused the queen of a pro-Russian, anti-Japanese attitude. Kojong himself took refuge in the Russian legation in February 1896 and remained there for one year. A last attempt to assert Korean independence was the proclamation in 1897 of the Empire of the Great Han *(taehan cheguk)* and the elevation of Kojong to emperor. This did not save Korea, however, and Kojong, decried as a weakling, became thoroughly disillusioned. He was finally forced by the Japanese-backed cabinet to abdicate in the summer of 1907. He was succeeded by his son, posthumously known as Sunjong (r. 1907–1910). During the remaining years of his life Kojong lived in retirement. He died suddenly on 22 January 1919 amid rumors that he had killed himself or had been poisoned. His funeral, scheduled for 3 March, served as the backdrop for the March First Independence Movement.

[*See also* Kanghwa Treaty; 1882 Uprising; 1884 Coup d'État; March First Independence Movement; Taewŏn'gun; Min, Queen; *and* Yi Dynasty.]

Martina Deuchler, *Confucian Gentlemen and Barbarian Envoys: The Opening of Korea, 1875–1885* (1977). C. I. Eugene Kim and Han-Kyo Kim, *Korea and the Politics of Imperialism, 1876–1910* (1967). James B. Palais, *Politics and Policy in Traditional Korea* (1975).

MARTINA DEUCHLER

**KOKINSHŪ.** The first anthology of poetry in Japanese *(waka)* to be commissioned by the imperial family, the *Kokinshū (Collection of Ancient and Modern Poetry)* was compiled from circa 885 to circa 914 by a group of talented court poets directly appointed by Emperor Daigo (885–930): Ki no Tsurayuki (868?–945?), Ki no Tomonori (d. circa 905), Ōshikōchi Mitsune (fl. 898–922), and Mibu no Tadamine (d. circa 920). Its 1,111 *waka*, predominantly in the thirty-one-syllable *tanka* form, are arranged by category in twenty sections. The first ten sections contain poetry composed on formal occasions. The subjects include the seasons, parting, and travel. The second ten sections are devoted to informal poetry, with over half the corpus made up of love poetry and the rest being made up of miscellaneous poems and traditional songs and verse. The structure of the *Kokinshū* influenced all future imperial *waka* anthologies—there were twenty more, the last compiled in 1439. All are equally divided between formal and informal poetry, and all but two contain twenty sections.

Tsurayuki and his colleagues compiled the *Kokinshū* by selecting *waka* from three periods: (1) "the past" (c. 750–810), when poetry was still composed in the style of the *Man'yōshū*, the first *waka* anthology (c. 760); (2) "recent times" (c. 850–887), characterized by the work of the "six celebrated poets" (the *rokkasen*: Henjō, 816–890?; Ariwara Narihira, 825–880; Fun'ya Yasuhide, fl. c. 858–883; the monk Kisen, fl. ca. 810–824; Ono no Komachi fl. 833–857; and Ōtomo Kuronushi, fl. 885); and (3) "the present" (887–930), Tsurayuki's own time. Few *waka* survive from the early ninth century, when the most popular literary pastime for the court was composing poetry in Chinese.

The *Kokinshū* marks a radical change in the style of Japanese poetry. The compilers and other poets of "the present"—the early tenth century—influenced by the rational, intellectual style fashionable in Chinese literary circles during the late Six Dynasties period (502–589), produced witty, subjective, individualistic *waka* that differed dramatically from the poetry of the *Man'yōshū*. This new style was of course well represented in the *Kokinshū*. The "six celebrated poets," though criticized on minor points by Tsurayuki in his Japanese preface to the *Kokinshū*, were the first to develop the elegant, rational style that so influenced the compilers' poetics. The *"Kokinshū* style" became the stylistic foundation for classical Japanese *waka*.

Tsurayuki's preface is an important document in its own right. One of the earliest examples of Japanese prose and the first work of criticism in the language, the preface stresses the importance of balancing diction (*kotoba*) and tone (*kokoro*).

[*See also* Man'yōshū.]

Robert H. Brower and Earl Miner, *Japanese Court Poetry* (1961). Jin'ichi Konishi, *A History of Japanese Literature*, vol. 9, *The Early Middle Ages* (1986). Laurel Rasplica Rodd, trans., *The Kokinshū* (1984).

AILEEN GATTEN

**KOKUGAKU** ("national learning"), considered by many to be the most important and influential intellectual movement in Tokugawa Japan, arose in the late seventeenth century. Kokugaku comprised many and varied fields of investigation: classical language and literature; court hierarchy, protocol, and ceremonial; ancient history, society, and folklore; and, finally, Shinto. Despite this diversity, all Kokugaku scholars shared an interest in and veneration for Japan's ancient past. They strove to clarify what Japanese speech, attitudes, beliefs, institutions, and modes of conduct had been like before the coming of Buddhism and Confucianism permanently altered these unalloyed national characteristics.

Kokugaku scholarship contains three distinguishing features: an exaltation of emotive literature as genuinely expressive of human nature, in opposition to a didactic literature expressive of contrived and oppressive Buddhist or Confucian moral norms; a rigorously empirical philological method that rejected latter-day interpretations in order to arrive at the original meaning of ancient Japanese texts; and the presumption of Japan's world preeminence based on an unquestioned belief in the literal truth and absolute value of the accounts given in the ancient texts, especially the *Kojiki* (compiled 712), accounts that Confucian rationalists dismissed as mythical.

We can trace the development of Kokugaku by outlining the major ideas of five of the school's leading figures: Keichū (1640–1701), Kada no Azumamaro (1669–1736), Kamo no Mabuchi (1697–1769), Motoori Norinaga (1730–1801), and Hirata Atsutane (1776–1843).

Keichū, a disenchanted Buddhist priest, found personal solace in the study and recitation of Japanese poetry (*waka*). His contributions to Kokugaku were the establishment of literature as an autonomous realm independent from morality and the introduction of objective, philological methods of literary criticism. Buddhists and Confucians claimed that works of literature should be interpreted as conveying philosophical truths or moral lessons, such as the ephemerality of worldly affairs or the evil of lust, but Keichū held that literature was nondidactic. Moreover, the study and composition of *waka* had been the monopoly of aristocratic families, each of which jealously guarded its teachings as "family secrets." Keichū helped popularize *waka* composition by breaking the aristocrats' hold over literary canons of taste and by relaxing the highly restrictive literary conventions of the court that stifled free expression of emotions.

Keichū's literary studies were primarily a matter of personal satisfaction; he had little concern for sociopolitical affairs. By contrast Kada no Azumamaro, son of a Shinto priest, provided the Kokugaku tradition with a social dimension by linking poetics with Shinto, while viewing Shinto in distinctly nationalistic terms. He contributed the idea that textual research was the key to discovering the "Way of the gods" (*shintō*). His thought is marked by a strong ethnic consciousness and antipathy to alien moral teachings. Kada reputedly petitioned the *bakufu* to establish a state school for Kokugaku in 1728, but this petition was probably forged by his disciples and was never submitted.

Kada's perception that Japan's indigenous Way was revealed in ancient works of literature found culmination in the thought of Kamo no Mabuchi and Motoori Norinaga, though these men differed about what constituted this Way and which ancient texts revealed it. Mabuchi, a Shinto priest, identified the guileless and "masculine" expression distinctive of the poetry of the *Man'yōshū* anthology as conveying the pristine "nobility and uprightness" of the ancient Japanese. By contrast, Norinaga, a merchant turned physician, preferred the elegant and "feminine" qualities of tenth- to thirteenth-century *waka* as a poetic ideal, but sought Japan's ancient Way in the *Kojiki*, a prose chronicle outlining Japan's mythic national origins and the descent of her ruling house from the sun goddess Amaterasu. For Norinaga, this indigenous Way consisted of unquestioning submission to existing political authority—whether good or evil—as ordained by divine will. Japanese moral excellence lay in adhering strictly to this Way:

the Chinese overthrew some twenty dynasties during their history, Norinaga reasoned, while the Japanese submitted reverently to one divine ruling house.

Hirata Atsutane, son of a lower-class samurai, rejected Norinaga's philological rigor and aesthetic, literary concerns, but he carried on and intensified Norinaga's protonationalism. In addition, Hirata drew on Buddhist, Confucian, and Christian moral doctrines to provide an element of religiosity—the promise of paradise after death—calculated to meet human emotional needs. He reasoned that unless commoners felt sure of being rewarded for virtue and punished for vice, they would not follow the Way of the gods and uphold the existing sociopolitical order. He taught that there were two spatially contiguous worlds—the "apparent" and the "hidden." Mortal men lived in the apparent world, which was ruled over by the emperor and was visible from the hidden world; after death their spirits went to the hidden world, which was ruled over by the god Ōkuninushi and was invisible from the apparent world. Ōkuninushi conferred rewards and meted out punishments in his realm based on whether people did good or evil in the apparent world. The criteria for such judgment would be loyalty to ruler, filial piety to parents, and diligence in the family calling. Such teachings, designed to popularize Kokugaku among the masses, bore fruit. By 1841, when the *bakufu* ordered Hirata into domiciliary confinement and forced him to cease publishing, he had over 550 students; after his death his students numbered over 1300, many of whom assumed posts in the new Meiji government. [*See* Meiji Restoration.]

It is tempting to view Kokugaku as an ideology motivating the overthrow of the *bakufu* and the restoration of direct imperial government in 1868. Broadly speaking, such a view is correct. But it is important to note that the thinkers examined here would have disavowed any connection between their ideas and an anti-*bakufu* insurgency. Norinaga and Atsutane in particular sought to enhance *bakufu* rule by arguing that Japan's gods had decreed its establishment and that Japan's indigenous moral code required absolute submission to it. They held that shogunal rule had been sanctioned by the emperor, a descendent of Amaterasu; to obey the shogun was to comply with imperial command. In the 1850s and 1860s, however, the *bakufu* committed acts violating the emperor's personal will: opening Japan to foreign trade, to residence by foreigners, and to international diplomatic intercourse. This discredited the *bakufu* in the eyes of many Japanese imbued with the Kokugaku ideal of absolute obedience to the emperor and justified for them the creation of a government that would be more responsible to him.

[*See also* Kamo no Mabuchi *and* Motoori Norinaga.]

Shigeru Matsumoto, *Motoori Norinaga* (1970).

BOB TADASHI WAKABAYASHI

KOKURYŪKAI (Amur River Society; sometimes given in English as Black Dragon Society), an ultranationalistic Japanese organization that was established in 1901 in Fukuoka by Uchida Ryōhei. An offshoot of Tōyama Mitsuru's Genyōsha, the organization was devoted to combating Russian expansion (whence its name, from that of a river in Manchuria) and to promoting a greater Japanese empire. Its agents engaged in clandestine activities in Korea, China, and Russia, often with the tacit support of the Japanese army. The organization also functioned as a pressure group in Japan to prod the government into adopting a more forceful foreign policy.

The Kokuryūkai called for the elimination of Western imperialism in Asia and assisted movements of national liberation in China and the Philippines. It also sponsored rallies at home against the "weak-kneed' foreign policy of the government and its concessions to Western powers. In 1905 it was one of the sponsors of the violent demonstration at Hibiya Park in Tokyo against the Portsmouth Peace Treaty, which ended the Russo-Japanese War. [*See* Hibiya Incident.]

The Kokuryūkai condemned liberalism, socialism, and communism, and its members helped break industrial strikes in northern Kyushu. Its platform called for "renovation" in government, foreign affairs, defense, and education, and it advocated a synthesis of Eastern and Western culture. The society received support from secret army funds and some sectors of the business world.

Although never a mass organization, the Kokuryūkai exercised considerable influence through its connections with high-ranking officials, intimidation of opponents, and public campaigns. It was dissolved in 1940, when it merged into the Taisei Yokusankai (Imperial Rule Assistance Association).

[*See also* Uchida Ryōhei.]

Delmer M. Brown, *Nationalism in Japan* (1955). Marius B. Jansen, *The Japanese and Sun Yat-sen* (1954). Richard Storry, *The Double Patriots* (1957).

BEN-AMI SHILLONY

KŌMEI (1831–1866), emperor of Japan (r. 1846–1866). Kōmei Tennō's reign was extremely troubled, with Japan endangered by both internal unrest and foreign attack. Within six months of his accession, in a dramatic departure from the normal conventions governing court-*bakufu* relations, the fifteen-year-old emperor—undoubtedly influenced by others—urged the *bakufu* to pay more attention to national security. Thereafter the court rapidly increased its authority in national affairs, for the most part involving the young emperor in these concerns. As he matured, he was to become increasingly involved, largely through his concern that foreigners, repulsive in appearance and indecorous in behaviour, might defile the imperial land. To avoid this disgrace he refused to ratify international treaties, urged the expulsion of foreigners, and called publicly on the gods for protection from foreigners. He was also prepared to encourage opposition to the *bakufu*, but when he was obliged to look at the alternatives Kōmei began to change his mind. It was precisely at this juncture that he died, suddenly (and some say conveniently) at the age of thirty-five.

[*See also* Tokugawa Period.]

HAROLD BOLITHO

KONBAUNG DYNASTY (1752–1885), last major dynasty in Burma. Konbaung history roughly divides into three periods: early martial and administrative vigor from the 1750s to the 1780s, military and administrative decline to the early 1820s, and forcible dismemberment and ultimate extinction in the Anglo-Burmese Wars of 1824, 1852, and 1885.

In the early 1750s, Alaunghpaya, a local official in the Shweibo area of northern Burma, founded the dynasty amid the chaos of the demise of the Restored Toungoo dynasty at the hands of southern rebels. He rallied the local populace, co-opted or destroyed his local rivals, and cleared southern forces from northern and central Burma by 1754. In 1757 he conquered the south and permanently unified the Irrawaddy Valley under Burmese rule. Rebuilding the administrative and military systems, he set out to restore his kingdom to its former imperial dimensions but died on retreat from a failed campaign against the Thai kingdom of Ayudhya.

Alaunghpaya bequeathed a strong administrative and military base as well as revived imperial ambitions to his son Naungdawgyi, whose turbulent reign from 1760 to 1763 was mainly occupied with subduing two major rebellions. His next younger brother, Hsinhpyushin (r. 1763–1776), may have shortened Naungdawgyi's reign with poison. Under Hsinhpyushin's rule, the Konbaung state reached the zenith of its military power and imperial achievement. From 1764 onward Konbaung armies campaigned in the Tai states east of the Salween River, capping their successes with the sack of the Thai capital of Ayudhya in 1767. From 1765 to 1769 Hsinhpyushin's forces also defeated four Chinese invasions and forced China into a treaty governing relations. But in sharp contrast to his military success, Hsinhpyushin faced strong internal political opposition throughout his reign and was unable to deal with blatant corruption among the high officials.

The period of decline was prefaced by the pacific reign of Hsinhpyushin's immature and dissolute son, Singu (r. 1776–1782), who offended the gentry and officials. Singu was deposed by his cousin Maung Maung in 1782, but both were executed a week later by Bodawhpaya, fourth son of Alaunghpaya. Bodawhpaya (r. 1782–1819) fought a long and draining war with Thailand from 1784 to 1811, conquered Arakan in 1784, and taxed and levied the populace heavily for wars and massive public works projects. A severe famine from about 1805 to 1812 further strained the country. Overexploitation by the ruler, agricultural scarcity, and widespread maladministration by officials caused a substantial popular flight from crown service, which significantly reduced military capability and disorganized the economy and society. In his declining years, Bodawhpaya occupied himself with religion and the succession problem, enabling the country to recover somewhat.

After Bodawhpaya, Konbaung history is heavily shaped by relations with Britain and the progressive dismemberment of Burma. In the early reign of Bagyidaw (r. 1819–1837), the Burmese military threat to the British-Indian border led to the First Anglo-Burmese War (1824–1826). Burmese defeat brought the loss of Arakan, Assam, and Tennasserim, a large monetary indemnity, and acceptance of a British residency. The war also ushered in a quarter century of misrule and disorder under Bagyidaw and his successors Tharrawaddy (r. 1837–1846) and Pagan Min (r. 1846–1853).

Bagyidaw lapsed into periodic insanity after 1831. After years of intense factional struggle at court, his half-brother Tharrawaddy deposed him in 1837. Tharrawaddy also became insane and was deposed by his son Pagan Min in 1846. With much of Burma in near-anarchy as the result of cumulative misrule, British authorities used a local incident in Rangoon to draw an unwilling Pagan into war in 1852. The quick Burmese defeat and the alienation from Pagan of gentry and officials enabled a half-brother, the Mindon prince, to depose Pagan in early 1853. Britain unilaterally annexed Lower Burma as the fruit of victory.

The long reign of Mindon (r. 1853–1878), a pious and sincere ruler, was characterized by attempts to modernize and strengthen the truncated kingdom while stoutly maintaining its diplomatic independence. Mindon's reforms, only partly successful, included salaries for officials, a uniform house tax, coined money, and a reorganized provincial administration. He also encouraged economic development and trade with Lower Burma. Mindon refused to recognize formally the British annexation of Lower Burma but rejected the use of military force and allowed the army to deteriorate. He dabbled at relations with other European powers, especially France, and sent several missions to France, Italy, and Britain.

On Mindon's death in 1878, however, the progressive trend came to an abrupt halt and the earlier pattern of factional strife and misrule reappeared. Because Mindon had not designated a crown prince after the first crown prince was assassinated in 1866, a court faction led by the chief queen and the leading reformist minister, the Kinwun Mingyi, placed the twenty-year-old Thibaw prince on the throne. With no political following, the weak and inexperienced Thibaw (r. 1878–1885) was dominated by his wife and mother-in-law, and his administration quickly collapsed amid growing banditry and disorder.

In 1885 an incident involving a fine on the Bombay-Burmah Trading Company became the British excuse for the Third Anglo-Burmese War, whose real cause was British fear of French influence. A quick war late in the year ended the dynasty, Thibaw was exiled to Madras, and Burma became a province of British India.

[See also Alaunghpaya; Ayudhya; Naungdawgyi; Hsinhpyushin; Singu; Bodawhpaya; Anglo-Burmese Wars; Tharrawaddy; Pagan Min; Mindon; Kinwun Mingyi; Thibaw; and Bombay-Burmah Trading Corporation.]

John F. Cady, *A History of Modern Burma* (1958). Walter Desai, *History of the British Residency in Burma, 1826–1840* (1939). D. G. E. Hall, *A History of Southeast Asia* (4th ed., 1968).      WILLIAM J. KOENIG


**KONFRONTASI.** *See* Confrontation.


**KONG LE** (b. circa 1934), Laotian military leader. The son of a Phutai tribesman from southern Laos, Kong Le was born in Muong Phalane in central Savannakhet Province. His military career began in 1948 or 1949 when, after one year of formal schooling at the lycée in Savannakhet, he was recruited by the French to fight the Viet Minh. He rose through the ranks to become a captain in the Territorial Army by 1952. In 1954 he commanded a detachment of thirty men in Luang Prabang.

In October 1957 Kong Le was assigned to attend a Rangers School for the Royal Lao Army, organized by the United States in the Philippines. He returned to Laos in January 1958 to take up command of the Second Paratroop Battalion.

In August 1960 Kong Le directed a coup d'état against the conservative government of Prince Somsanith and called upon Prince Souvannaphouma to lead the government. Following the attack, led by General Phoumi Nosavan in December 1960, Kong Le fled with his troops to the Plain of Jars, where he commanded the neutralist military forces of the government led by Souvannaphouma.

In February 1963 the assassination of Kong Le's chief of staff, Colonel Ketsana Vongsouvan, on the Plain of Jars provoked a breach between Kong Le and a rival officer in the neutralist forces, Colonel Deuane Sunnarath, who joined his forces with the Pathet Lao. Kong Le's fortunes as a neutralist military commander collapsed in the mid-1960s and he went into exile in France.

Kong Le has been engaged in exile politics since the communist takeover in 1975. He was reported to have been in China in the early 1980s, lending his name to the Chinese effort to train anti-Lao government insurgents, although he had returned to France in 1983. His name was also associated with the Lao People's National Liberation Front, a paper resistance organization opposed to communist rule in Laos.

[See also Viet Minh and Laos.]

JOSEPH J. ZASLOFF


**KONGZI.** *See* Confucius.


**KONISHI YUKINAGA** (d. 1600), powerful daimyo (feudal lord) of the late Sengoku period of Japanese history. Born into an important merchant family at Sakai who had been active in the China trade from the late fifteenth century, Konishi Yukinaga entered the military service of the Ukita daimyo family of Bizen during his youth. Later he shifted loyalties to Toyotomi Hideyoshi, who assigned Yukinaga to duty with naval forces in the Inland Sea before discovering his great talents as a field general. Yukinaga soon emerged as one of a trio of top Hideyoshi generals (together with Katō Kiyomasa and Kuroda Nagamasa) and helped lead Hideyoshi's forces into Kyushu in 1587, for which he was rewarded with the southern half of Higo Province, with an assessed productivity of approximately 240,000 *koku* (measures of rice).

In 1592 Yukinaga commanded the largest contingent of Japanese forces in the invasion of Korea. After successfully landing at Pusan, he marched into Seoul on 12 June 1592, after covering nearly three hundred miles in twenty days. Yukinaga then pushed north at the head of some eighteen thousand men, capturing P'yŏngyang in July. By fall, however, Chinese forces had entered the battle at the request of the Korean king; Korean guerrilla action against the Japanese had stiffened considerably; and Admiral Yi's famous turtle boats had begun to disrupt seriously the flow of Japanese supplies. After bitter fighting in the spring of the following year Konishi negotiated an armistice that permitted the bulk of Japanese forces to retreat to Japan, leaving only a rear guard at Pusan.

Four years later, Yukinaga was back in Korea at the head of Hideyoshi's second invasion effort, an action that Yukinaga had opposed. Fighting was even more ferocious and costly to the Japanese this time, just as Yukinaga had feared, and when Hideyoshi died in September 1598, Yukinaga quickly opened peace talks and withdrew Japanese troops from the continent. Yukinaga returned to Higo and then died after fighting on the losing side at the Battle of Sekigahara (1600), where he was an important member of Ishida Mitsunari's western alliance.

Konishi Yukinaga is also remembered as Japan's most powerful Christian daimyo; it was a faith he had inherited from his father. Yukinaga, known also by his Christian name, Don Augustino, built a leper's hospital and orphanage at Osaka, and the missionaries treated his death as that of a martyr.

[*See also* Katō Kiyomasa; Hideyoshi's Invasion of Korea; *and* Sengoku Period.]

JAMES L. MCCLAIN

**KONOE FUMIMARO** (1891–1945), three-time prime minister of Japan who was in power on the eve of the Pacific War. The son of Konoe Atsumaro,

Prince Konoe traced his ancestry back to the Fujiwara regents of the Heian era (794–1185). He assumed his seat in the House of Peers in 1916, becoming its president in 1936. In 1919 he attended the Paris Peace Conference. While progressive in his support of party cabinets, he denounced Britain and the United States for maintaining Western domination in Asia and the rest of the world.

Widely praised for his youthful dynamism, Konoe formed his first cabinet (June 1937–January 1939) with support from the military, business, party politicians, bureaucrats, and even key socialists. Following the outbreak of hostilities with China (July 1937), the Konoe cabinet widened the scope of fighting by pursuing a policy of annihilating the Nationalist government. On the home front, Konoe pushed thorough the National General Mobilization Law and other legislation that increased state power over the Diet and private interests. In his last two cabinets (July 1940–October 1941), Konoe sponsored the New Order Movement and the Imperial Rule Assistance Association, which absorbed the nation's parties, unions, and other associations. His government also approved the occupation of Indochina and concluded the Tripartite Pact with Germany and Italy. As relations with the United States deteriorated during 1941, Konoe unsuccessfully sought a last-minute meeting with President Roosevelt to prevent war. He then resigned to avoid responsibility for the impending Pacific War.

As a senior statesman, Konoe lobbied for a speedy end to the war after mid-1944. In a memorial to the emperor, he warned that protracted war would result in a revolution led by "communists" in the army. After the Japanese defeat, Konoe worked on revising the Meiji Constitution. He committed suicide after Occupation authorities indicted him as a war criminal. In his memoirs Konoe portrayed himself as a foe of authoritarianism and militarism. Others, however, noted that Konoe and his cabinets boldly advanced authoritarian domestic policies while committing Japan to the China war and southern expansion.

[*See also* World War II in Asia.]

Gordon M. Berger, "Japan's Young Prince: Konoe Fumimaro's Early Political Career, 1916–1931," *Monumenta Nipponica* 29 (1974): 451–475, and *Parties Out of Power in Japan, 1931–1941* (1977). Yoshitake Oka, *Konoe Fumimaro: A Political Biography* (1983).

SHELDON M. GARON

**KORAN.** *See* Qur'an.

KOREA. Although not always unified politically, the Korean peninsula is home to a people with a single cultural identity. Korea has been a conduit for intellectual and technological advances from China to Japan, but within Korea these ideas took on new shape, so that Korea occupies a unique niche in the East Asian cultural world.

*Early Korean History.* The earliest evidence of human habitation on the Korean peninsula comes from sites that date from the late Paleolithic era, or about thirty thousand years ago. Paleolithic man lived in caves and rough dwellings on level ground; these early inhabitants of Korea were hunters and gathers. The record of man becomes clearer in the Neolithic era, between 4000 and 3000 BCE. The use of polished stone tools and pottery distinguished Neolithic man from his more primitive forebears; archaeological evidence supports a theory of successive waves of pottery cultures, possibly linked to separate migrations from Central Asia.

The advent of the use of bronze implements in Korea around the ninth and eighth centuries BCE dramatically altered life on the peninsula. The Bronze Age people soon dominated more primitive groups. Rice agriculture began at this time, most probably introduced from China. Social and political organization became more complex as evidenced by larger-sized communities, megalithic burial practices requiring mass labor, and the rise of walled-town communities. Thus, the Bronze Age, which lasted until roughly the fourth century BCE. witnessed the rise of primitive yet powerful tribal communities.

With the introduction of iron to Korea came increased influence from China. The rise of the ancient tribal states in northern Korea, bridging the Yalu River, invited Chinese incursions. Ultimately, the Chinese Han dynasty (206 BCE–220 CE) mounted a successful invasion of Korea and established colonies there. Of the four original Han commanderies, Lelang (108 BCE–313 CE) survived and even outlasted its parent dynasty.

Lelang occupied the Taedong River basin in northwestern Korea and had to defend its territory forcefully from the start against the hostile Korean tribal federations. The Lelang governors, their officials, and numerous colonists brought with them Chinese culture and technology. The impact of Lelang culture, including its political institutions, Chinese writing, burial customs, and technology, was profound. The presence of the colony also accelerated the process, already begun, of tribal amalgamation into larger federations leading eventually to the establishment of small monarchical states. [See Commanderies in Korea, Chinese.]

The so-called confederated kingdoms in Korea emerged in the first century of the common era. The Puyŏ kingdom occupied the Sungari River basin in Manchuria and its ruler was using the designation "king" *(wang)* by 49 CE. Placed between China and another rising confederated state that straddled the upper Yalu basin, Koguryŏ, the Puyŏ people were sought by the Chinese as allies. Ultimately, Puyŏ fell to Koguryŏ, a kingdom that traced its rise to the fourth century BCE. By 159 CE Koguryŏ was in vigorous competiton with Puyŏ and with the tribal peoples occupying the central east coast of the peninsula, the Okcho and Eastern Ye. [See Puyŏ.]

To the south of the Han River, the Three Han states (Samhan) emerged, invigorated by migrations of refugees from the conflicts in north and central Korea. Late to develop because of their relative remoteness, the Three Han states absorbed the earlier Chin state as advanced culture and technology flowed south. Eventually they came to dominate the south: Mahan in the area of modern Kyŏnggi, Ch'ungch'ong, and Chŏlla provinces; Chinhan to the east of the Naktong River; and Pyŏnhan in the area of modern Kyŏngsang Province to the west of the Naktong.

The confederated states had more advanced agriculture and political institutions than did the states to the north. Agriculture was the economic base, but it is clear that animal husbandry, fishing, and hunting also remained important. Chinese records indicate a social structure that delineated commoner and "low households" as well as slaves. At this time kingly authority, supported by an aristocratic elite, emerged. The elite of the confederated kingdoms was concentrated in walled towns that dominated the surrounding countryside. Early kings were chosen by an elective process. Ultimately, kingships became hereditary, but in most of the confederated kingdoms it seems that the aristocracy maintained considerable power, related no doubt to this early collegial pattern of rule. [See Three Hans.]

By the third century CE the confederated states had begun, through the process of conquest and amalgamation, to consolidate, finally forming three powerful, well-developed, and sophisticated entities known as the Three Kingdoms. This period marked the establishment of large integrated political structures on the peninsula and a dramatic Korean participation in the international dynamics that marked the East Asian scene between 300 and 700 CE. Each of the Three Kingdoms—Koguryŏ in the north,

Paekche in central and southwestern Korea, and Silla in the southeast—developed distinctive cultures with common overtones derived from their earlier peninsular antecedents.

**The Three Kingdoms and Unified Silla.** The most powerful of the Three Kingdoms was Koguryŏ. Although mythology dates its formation to the first century before the common era, the first mention of Koguryŏ appears in Chinese records of the second century CE. In the fourth century Koguryŏ expanded as Chinese influence weakened on the peninsula. It eventually seized control of the territory of Lelang and expanded into northern Manchuria as far west as the Liaodong Peninsula and south into the Han River basin. At its height in the 400s, Koguryŏ controlled a vast state that straddled the Yalu River and threatened the neighboring states to the south.

Koguryŏ's decline began in the 550s, when Paekche to the south reasserted its claim to the Han River basin. From this time forward Koguryŏ was under threat from rising Chinese forces in the north as well as their traditional rivals in the south. The reunification of North China under the Sui in 581 marked a significant challenge to Koguryŏ. Although it defended itself brilliantly against three separate Sui invasions between 612 and 614, Koguryŏ, exhausted, eventually succumbed to a combined force from Tang China in league with Silla to the south in 668. [See Koguryŏ.]

Between 300 and 650 the kingdom of Paekche occupied the southwest portion of the peninsula. Paekche grew from an amalgamation of the Mahan tribal federation with remnants of the Puyŏ people who fled Chinese incursions in the north after 285. The weakest of the Three Kingdoms militarily, Paekche was forced to contract beginning in the fifth century. Koguryŏ incursions forced Paekche to move its capital south and to seek an alliance with Silla, only to be betrayed by their Silla allies later. Ultimately Paekche fell in 660 under the weight of a combined Tang-Silla invasion that was mounted to destroy the power of Koguryŏ. The remains of the Paekche aristocracy were eventually integrated into the Silla state after the Silla unification in the late seventh century. [See Paekche.]

The Silla kingdom was last to develop, but it ultimately grew to become the force that first unified the peninsula under a single state after 668. Silla originated among the Chinhan tribes in the southeast. Its early rise to power was helped by an alliance with Koguryŏ in its struggle with Paekche over control of the Han River basin. By the mid-sixth century Silla asserted its control over the central area of the peninsula as well as the tribes of the east coast and the people of Kaya (Mimana) in the south.

After the fall of Paekche and Koguryŏ, Silla moved to consolidate its control over the peninsula. In this later period of its history (668–918), the state is referred to as Unified Silla. Forced to counter Chinese attempts to maintain control in the north, Silla ultimately settled for suzerainty over most of the peninsula excluding territory north of the Taedong River that was occupied by Parhae, which had risen to replace Koguryŏ at the end of the seventh century. [See Parhae.]

The height of Silla power and civilization came in the period between 668 and 780. The capital, Kyŏngju, contained more than seven hundred thousand people and was the center of the vast estates of the Silla ruling class. Buddhism flourished under the patronage of Silla elites, and Silla monks traveled to India and China, participating in the lively intellectual life of the faith. The Silla government also encouraged classical Chinese studies by establishing a Confucian Academy and experimenting with a civil service examination system based on the Tang model. Silla scholars studied in China, and some, like Ch'oe Chi-wŏn, were even admitted into the Tang bureaucracy. [See Ch'oe Ch'i-wŏn.]

Silla's decline after 780 was caused by endemic strife over the kingship and growing regional autonomy on the part of the great landed families in the provinces. By the late 900s Silla authority could no longer be enforced outside its capital district. During their last forty years, Silla monarchs continued to be enthroned, but the peninsula outside the capital was under control of regional powers. Thus, in the last years of Silla new powers emerged, each claiming to be revivals of Paekche and Koguryŏ; the renewed tripartite division of Korea at this time lent the name Later Three Kingdoms to this period. [See Silla and Later Three Kingdoms. A map of Korea during the Three Kingdoms period accompanies the article Koguryŏ.]

**The Koryŏ Dynasty.** Founded in 918 by Wang Kŏn, Koryŏ unified the Later Three Kingdoms in 936. Koryŏ extended the territory of Silla to the approximate area occupied by modern Korea. Wang Kŏn founded Koryŏ by expanding his power base, which was centered on his maritime merchant beginnings in alliance with landed interests of local Silla strongmen in the area around Kaesŏng. Later he absorbed Silla nobles into the Koryŏ ruling strata.

Only after three generations of Koryŏ rule was the dynasty consolidated, as royal authority gradually eliminated independent power bases and created a centralized civilian bureaucracy loyal to the throne. The institution of civil service exams and separate exams for the Buddhist clergy gave former Silla aristocratic elements the advantage in gaining bureaucratic positions and power owing to their experience and education.

Although Buddhism remained an important political force in Koryŏ, Confucianism was increasingly upheld as the new dynasty's political ideology. Dynastic administration came firmly into the hands of the Confucian bureaucracy over time. Although Koryŏ extensively borrowed Chinese institutions, the operation and elaboration of the increasingly complex central bureaucracy was adapted to Korean aristocratic imperatives.

Having long chafed under the increasing civilian monopoly of power, military elements rose in 1170 in a decisive coup. The generals fought among themselves, however, and only after twenty years of strife was order restored, under the leadership of Ch'oe Ch'ung-hŏn. Ch'oe allied with civilian bureaucrats, eliminated rival generals, and created a system of dictatorial rule dominated by his family. The period of military dictators ended with the assassination of the fourth Ch'oe ruler in 1258 after a long and unsuccessful resistance against Mongol invaders. Although the military dictators carried on a long resistance, even moving the court offshore to Kanghwa Island, the Mongols ultimately prevailed. The humiliating subjugation to Mongol power required enormous yearly tribute payments, a Mongol overlord in residence at the Koryŏ capital, and, at one point, the exaction of troops, laborers, ships, and provisions for two ill-fated invasions of Japan, in 1274 and 1281. The Koryŏ kings were required to marry Mongol princesses, and the Koryŏ crown prince was forced to live in the Mongol capital. [See Ch'oe Ch'ung-hŏn and Mongol Empire: Mongol Invasions of Korea.]

Although the Koryŏ dynasty suffered from repeated invasions and endured the humiliation of Mongol subjugation, it maintained a strong presence in East Asia for four and a half centuries. It provided a transition between the Buddhist, aristocratic state of Silla and the Confucian Yi dynasty that followed. Indeed, its very name, Koryŏ, provided the root of the modern English name Korea.

Koryŏ also left an important artistic and technological legacy. Koryŏ celadon, porcelain characterized by a unique blue-green glaze, was prized throughout East Asia; although the technology is extinct in modern times, the refinement and sophis-

tication of Koryŏ ceramics remain a unique testament to this period. Movable metal type was another contribution of Koryo craftsmen to world civilization. Long interested in printing, Koryŏ technicians had already accomplished the herculean task of setting the entire Buddhist canon on woodblocks (these blocks are extant today, stored at Haein temple in South Korea). The passion for proselytizing the Buddhist canon lead to the creation of movable metal type in 1234 (fully two centuries before Gutenburg in Europe); such type was used thereafter in the printing of Buddhist texts. [See Koryŏ Tripitaka and Koryŏ.]

*The Yi Dynasty.* Under the official name of Chosŏn the Yi royal family ruled Korea from 1392 to 1910. The dynasty created a system of government in its first century that laid the base for a period of extraordinary stability. The founder, Yi Sŏng-gye, allied his military lieutenants with emerging Neo-Confucian reformers. Between them they embarked on a broad reform program to redistribute land, reduce the power of the Buddhist church, and strengthen the hold of Neo-Confucian principles in society. Indeed, Neo-Confucianism became state orthodoxy, and over the next few centuries Confucian values and norms spread downward as commoners emulated the Confucian literati elite; law, family practices, and ancestor ritual were all reshaped by the Confucian social engineers. [See Yi Sŏng-gye and Neo-Confucianism in Korea.]

The dynastic foundation was solidified under the third Yi monarch, Taejong (r. 1400–1418), and his son Sejong (r. 1418–1450). Generally acknowledged to be the most brilliant Yi monarch, Sejong was himself responsible for stimulating an enormous burst of cultural creativity, important advancements in statecraft, and legal reforms. In the field of linguistics Sejong personally directed the successful project that created the Korean alphabet, known as *han'gŭl.*

The function and structure of government were elaborated in a National Code promulgated in 1471. Although theoretically the source of all power, the Yi monarchs were restrained by an elaborate system of checks and balances. For example, the three censorial organs (samsa)—the Office of the Inspector-General, Office of Censor-General, and the Office of Special Advisers—were each delegated surveillance duties over the monarch and officialdom. The size and scope of government increased as new offices were added and the reach of administration was extended. In terms of local administration, the country was divided into eight provinces, and each province was further subdivided into counties. All governors and county magistrates were centrally appointed.

The first two centuries of growth, peace, and stability for the dynasty ended with the invasions of the Japanese military leader Toyotomi Hideyoshi in 1592. Although the forces of China's Ming dynasty that arrived to head off Hideyoshi decisively checked the Japanese advance, the depredations of the Japanese and Ming armies laid waste to Korea. Famine induced by the interruption of agriculture added to the already extensive loss of life. It took the dynasty fully half a century to recover, and the invasions left an indelible scar on the minds of Koreans. [See Hideyoshi's Invasion of Korea.] Further compounding the Yi dynasty's problems was the fall of the Ming and rise of Manchu power in China. Loyalty to the Ming incurred Manchu wrath, and two Manchu invasions in 1627 and 1636 forced the Koreans to repudiate the Ming in favor of submission to the Manchu emperor.

Recovery came after 1650 and spread to reforms in the political system as the government moved to regain control over the population and resources. The late-seventeenth-century Uniform Land Tax Law was perhaps the crowning achievement of this period. The new tax law commuted the sundry tribute and in-kind taxes in favor of a uniform tax in rice based on land assessment. The new law spurred commercialization of the economy as did government abandonment of artisan and commercial licensing and monopolies.

After the successful reigns of Yŏngjo (r. 1724–1776) and Chŏngjo (r. 1776–1800), years of relative balance in court-bureaucracy politics, the throne was passed between a succession of minors, each dominated by royal in-law families. With weak royal authority and with competition among lineages attempting to dominate the throne, government efficiency was again sapped by factional strife.

In 1864 a minor, Kojong (r. 1864–1907), ascended the throne, and until his majority in 1874 administration fell under the control of his father, who became known as the Taewŏn'gun ("grand prince"). The Taewŏn'gun attempted reforms to revitalize kingly authority, national defense, and government revenues. His isolationist foreign policy was popular at court, as he took credit for beating back tentative French and US naval incursions entreating commercial relations in the 1860s. His other reforms, however, provoked a strong reaction from elites who were determined to maintain tax privileges and other perquisites of power. Thus, the Taewŏn'gun's program ultimately failed to reassert monarchical power. [See Taewŏn'gun.]

Kojong assumed power in 1874 and was immediately thrust into a foreign policy crisis. Although after 1868 the Koreans had repeatedly rebuffed Japanese requests for recognition of the Meiji government and the establishment of commercial relations, Kojong was eventually forced by a mounting military threat to come to terms with his country's island neighbors. The Kanghwa Treaty of 1876 forcibly "opened" Korea to commercial intercourse. It also spurred Kojong to experiment tentatively with gathering information and foreign technology in the cause of reform. After 1882, at China's urging, Korea signed treaties with the major Western powers to balance the rising influence of Japan. The treaties were unpopular among conservatives, who carried out a campaign to reject the West and all associated with it. [See Kanghwa Treaty and Kojong.]

In 1882 the increasingly divided Korean government was rocked by a mutiny within its own army. The mutiny provoked Chinese interference and a resurgence of conservative antiforeign elements. In reaction to this development, a group of progressives staged a coup d'état with Japanese support in 1884 and attempted to legislate from the top down a sweeping program of reforms and institutional change. This effort, known as the Kapsin Coup, was crushed by Chinese troops. The bloody coup set the cause of reform back a decade and set the stage for the ultimate confrontation between Japan and China over whose political and economic interests in Korea would prevail. [See 1882 Uprising and 1884 Coup d'État.]

Increasing mismanagement in government and the penetration of foreign market forces destabilized the Korean countryside. Peasant anger and frustration at government corruption and increased foreign presence erupted in the massive Tonghak Rebellion in 1894, which engulfed major portions of central and southwest Korea. The rebellion provided China and Japan with an opportunity to send troops, and the Japanese victory in the ensuing Sino-Japanese War of 1894 to 1895 removed Chinese influence from Korea. Russian influence provided the weakened Korean court a brief respite, but after 1895 Japanese power and determination to dominate affairs in Korea steadily increased. [See Tonghak and Sino-Japanese War.]

The chain of events that led ultimately to the fall of the Yi dynasty began with the Russo-Japanese war in 1904. After defeating the Russians, the Japanese proclaimed Korea a protectorate, assumed control of Korea's foreign relations, and inserted Japanese advisers at all levels of the Yi government. Between 1905 and 1909 Itō Hirobumi, the first resident-general in Korea, laid the legal and institutional basis for the ultimate annexation of Korea as a formal Japanese colony.

The protectorate provoked a wide-scale Korean resistance. Intellectuals redoubled their efforts to transform Korean society along modern lines, and patriotic guerrilla bands *(ŭibyŏng)* carried out an armed resistance that was only quelled in 1911. Nevertheless, with international recognition ensured, with firm control of the Korean government, and with overwhelming military force, the Japanese ended the 518-year rule of the Yi dynasty in 1910. [*See* Yi Dynasty.]

*The Colonial Period.* Between the formal assumption of Japanese rule in 1910 and liberation in 1945, Korean society underwent a fundamental transformation. Colonial rule marked the final collapse of the traditional Korean political system, the Yi dynasty, and its aristocratic social underpinnings. Centralized Japanese administration brought sweeping changes in Korean society. A mass education system, a new legal system, modern communications, rationalized taxation, and severe police controls decisively changed Korean daily life. Japanese economic policy accelerated concentration of landholding already underway and the associated spread of tenancy. In the 1930s empirewide industrial policy expanded operations in the Korean colony and in the puppet state of Manchuria; this, in turn, required a massive movement of Korean labor from farms to factories. Finally, Korean intellectual and political life revolved around different approaches to the problem of liberation, and fierce debates emerged over the acceptance of Japanese rule. Although thirty-five years of colonial rule united Koreans in their hatred of the Japanese, the failure of either the domestic or exiled nationalist movement to shake off Japanese rule created a divided and rancorous political climate in the years after liberation from colonial subjugation.

The Korean colony was unusual in several important ways. Its proximity to the Japanese metropole was unique. This allowed the Japanese to bind, strategically and economically, their new colony to the mother country. Railroads became the primary links for markets as well as for military movement. Territorial contiguity also allowed the settlement of large numbers of Japanese. By 1945, seven hundred thousand Japanese were residents of the colony. Thus, Japan became one of the few major world powers to colonize its neighbor, an advantage it enjoyed over the Western powers with their far-flung overseas empires. [*See* Imperialism.]

The colonial state was also the agent of Japanese economic plans for Korea. Semiofficial companies such as the South Manchurian Railway Company were created to build and maintain railroads, and the huge Oriental Development Company financed industrial and agricultural projects. In the 1930s close government cooperation was the hallmark of industrial development in Korea as Japanese entrepreneurs sought to exploit Korean resources and cheap labor. Permits and favorable loans from the central bank helped the government-general guide economic development toward the goals of the Japanese empire.

The Japanese land survey conducted between 1910 and 1918 illustrates the dramatic impact of colonial rule. The Japanese rationalized traditional land relationships to lay a new basis for taxation scaled to productivity. The new land tax in 1918 became the primary source of colonial government revenue that steadily increased as rice production improved. The net result for the Korean peasantry was disaster. Landlords, Korean and Japanese, were favored with taxes that never increased. The system accelerated concentration of landholding already underway. During the colonial period Korean agriculture became increasingly devoted to the production of rice and other staples for the Japanese market. The depression of 1930 to 1931 and concomitant fall of rice prices on the Japanese market, combined with a sudden Japanese move to restrict Korean rice imports, had a disastrous effect on the Korean economy. Mortgage foreclosures and tenancy, already increasing, accelerated between 1930 and 1935. At this time tenancy rates in areas of high land ownership concentration approached 80 percent. In addition, the 1930s witnessed the widespread emigration of Koreans to Manchuria and Japan in search of work.

The colonial state also invested heavily in communications. At liberation, Korea had, perhaps, the finest rail network of all liberated colonies, considerably denser than in China or Southeast Asia. The motives for his heavy investment were strategic and economic. After 1910, the Japanese moved quickly to connect their outer perimeter of interest, Manchuria, with safe harbors on the southern Korean coast. Heavy Japanese investment in communications, rail, road, telegraph, and telephone profoundly affected Korean life. Mobility replaced centuries of isolation, and railroad crossroads and terminuses transformed small villages into bustling urban centers. The railroads moved migrant laborers and intellectuals alike and served to broaden Korean consciousness of a wider world.

Korean reaction to Japanese colonial rule was predictable. Japanese rule galvanized Korean patriotism, and, after 1910, the Korean nationalist movement expanded from its elite intellectual origins to become a mass phenomenon. Between 1910 and 1919, the period of so-called military rule, the Japanese severely restricted political and intellectual organization. By 1919 the pressures pent up by the repression exploded in the famous March First Demonstrations of 1919. One million people in the streets crying for the right of self-determination shocked and embarrassed the Japanese, and the resulting crisis forced a fundamental policy change. [See March First Independence Movement.]

The new administration of Governor-General Saitō Makoto revamped colonial administrative practices. Under the banner of "cultural rule," Saitō provided more cultural autonomy for Koreans, redressed grievances in legal discrimination, and, in general, softened the tone of colonial rule. The goals, however, remained the same. Changing the military policy to a civilian system did not mean the Japanese were abandoning control; rather, colonial rule was strengthened while they attempted to co-opt dissent.

Koreans responded to the cultural policy with a burst of organization. The newly permitted vernacular press expanded and contacts with the reinvigorated exile movement flourished. Between 1920 and 1926 several mass movements were mounted within the legal limits of political activity.

The Korean communist movement originated in the early 1920s as well, but police repression finally drove the movement underground. For the balance of the colonial period, the Korean communist movement remained alive, expressed in a guerrilla movement in the colony. However, growing leftist influence in regional branches and Japanese restrictions precipitated a leadership crisis that doomed the organization in 1931.

In 1927 a united front organization, the New Korea Society (Sin'ganhoe), was formed to bridge the growing schism between moderate, bourgeois nationalists and the radical and communist camps. Tolerated by the Japanese because of its original moderate leadership, the Sin'ganhoe successfully created the beginnings of an effective mass movement in the colony. However, growing leftist influence in regional branches and Japanese restrictions precipitated a leadership crisis that doomed the organization in 1931.

By 1937 the Japanese found it necessary to speed up the process of assimilation in order to further

their military ambitions. The last decade of colonial rule saw the creation of a plethora of mass organizations to support the war against China and, later, against the Allied powers in the Pacific. Youth groups, women's groups, writer's federations, and military units were created to mobilize active Korean support for the empire. By 1942 the Japanese abandoned their program to recruit Korean labor and military volunteers and began to conscript Koreans for both kinds of service. The ultimate expression of Japanese commitment to fictive assimilation was the infamous Name Order of 1940 that required Koreans to adopt Japanese names in place of their own.

Rapid industrialization in Korea and mobilization for the Japanese war effort after 1937 uprooted Korean society. The Korean peasantry, already burdened by heavy tenancy and increasingly impoverished by debt, became a pool of labor for industry in North Korea, Manchuria, and Japan. By one estimate, fully 11 percent of the Korean population was abroad in 1945. Economic development was uneven and predicated on Japanese empirewide planning. Although labor shortages during the war gave many Koreans experience in colonial administration, banks, and economic planning, overall there remained only a small Korean managerial class in 1945. A minority of landlords and Korean entrepreneurs flourished in the last years of the colony, yet the majority suffered under the increasingly harsh mobilization.

The sudden end of colonial rule released the constraints of political repression, but gave rise to new conflicts in Korea. Leaders of the government in exile, conservatives, moderates, socialists, and communists alike returned to struggle for command of the long-dreamed-of national independence. Exiled leaders were joined by intellectuals released from prison and the moderate nationalists who had remained active in the 1940s. Uprooted peasants returned from factories and mines in Manchuria and Japan. Korean military and labor conscripts returned from Southeast Asia and China. They all returned to a homeland transformed by a generation of Japanese rule. Partially urbanized, partially industrialized, Korea was left a dual legacy of skewed economic development and overheated politicization. Economic development, however warped and inequitable, had socially mobilized the Korean population; a generation of Japanese rule had galvanized Korean national consciousness. While the sudden removal of the Japanese achieved national independence, however, the problems created by the colonial experience left a troubled legacy for the

Korean people in the postwar period. [*See* Korea, Japanese Government-General of.]

***Liberation and Joint Occupation.*** The sudden Japanese defeat in August 1945 liberated Korea from colonial rule. Koreans began pouring back into the homeland and the atmosphere was dense with political and class strife. The excitement and expectations of liberation were crushed, however, as the US and USSR assumed control in Korea in a hastily arranged joint occupation in September 1945.

The decision to occupy Korea went back to Allied discussions in 1943 and 1944 regarding trusteeship in former colonial territories after the projected victory in the war. The rapid collapse of Japanese power within weeks of the Russian entrance into the Pacific War provoked a rushed round of negotiations with the ultimate decision to divide Korea at the thirty-eighth parallel, with Russians occupying the north and the US in the south.

US policy had initially intended a true internationalist presence; by 1947, however, US-Soviet rivalry had pushed the US into a stance of containment and US-Soviet negotiations stalled. Thus, the US was willing to use UN-sponsored elections in 1948 in an attempt to legitimate a single Korean government, and in the absence of Soviet cooperation in the North, a single US-supported regime in the South. The Republic of Korea came into being in this manner in the fall of 1948.

Syngman Rhee (Yi Sŭng-man) and his conservative supporters dominated the new government. Although ruling under the authority of a fairly liberal constitution, Rhee used extensive police power and extralegal methods to root out political rivals and suppress leftist elements still active in the South. Between 1948 and the outbreak of the Korean War in June 1950 Rhee's government had to struggle with a depressed economy, rural demands for land reform, peasant insurrection, and a bloody guerrilla struggle with Communist sympathizers.

In the North, Soviet occupiers worked initially with the people's committees led by moderate Cho Man-sik. By 1946 they had replaced this coalition with an Interim Peoples' Committee led by the young guerrilla leader Kim Il Sung (Kim Il-sŏng). Kim's energy and political organizational skills complimented his reputation as a nationalist guerrilla fighter. Under his direction a de facto separate North Korean government emerged in 1946. The Interim Peoples' Committee pushed land reform, established a mass party (the Korean Workers Party), and organized an army in 1946. Kim's efforts to build a military force was augmented by the return of many Koreans with experience in the Chinese civil war.

Soviet domination of the North peaked in the period 1947 to 1948. The Soviets attempted to arrange economic relations in a quasi-colonial manner with North Korea providing strategic raw materials for Soviet manufactured goods. They also worked to limit Chinese influence among the North Koreans. Ultimately, distracted as they were by more pressing problems in Eastern Europe, the Soviets withdrew, ending their intense involvement in North Korea.

***The Korean War.*** The outbreak of fighting between the North and South in June 1950 transformed what had been in effect a low-grade civil conflict since 1946 into a hot war. Both regimes had claimed themselves the only legitimate government of all Koreans since 1948. Indeed, since 1948, the South had been forced to contend with a bloody internal guerrilla struggle. In 1950 a series of events precipitated an open invasion of the South by North Korean forces. The impending successful repression of the guerrilla movement in the South, the return of thousands of Korean troops from the recently concluded Chinese civil war, and Soviet material aid all seemingly convinced Kim Il Sung to invade the South and solve the problem of division once and for all.

The initial fighting drove the South Korean forces and their US allies south. By August the North Koreans had occupied the entire peninsula except for the southeastern corner, the famous Pusan Perimeter. The US counterattacked in September with a massive amphibious landing behind enemy lines at In'chŏn and came close to destroying the North Korean Army. At this point US policy shifted from containment and restoration of the status quo to "rollback." US forces drove north of the 38th parallel in the fall of 1950 and by October were on the Chinese border.

Eventually the war stalemated in a bloody struggle of attrition at roughly the original 38th parallel division. For the next three years the North endured US bombing missions that destroyed their cities and industry. The South, having been overrun several times by the opposing armies, was also devastated. With the South Koreans refusing to sign, an armistice agreement was reached in the spring of 1953. Although subsequent attempts for a formal peace were attempted in 1954 at Geneva, they came to nought. The present peace remains based on only a cease-fire agreement and is maintained by a continued confrontation of masses of soldiers and armor along the demilitarized zone.

The Korean War was an appalling tragedy for the Korean people. It froze the political division of the nation and turned the expectations of 1945 into a

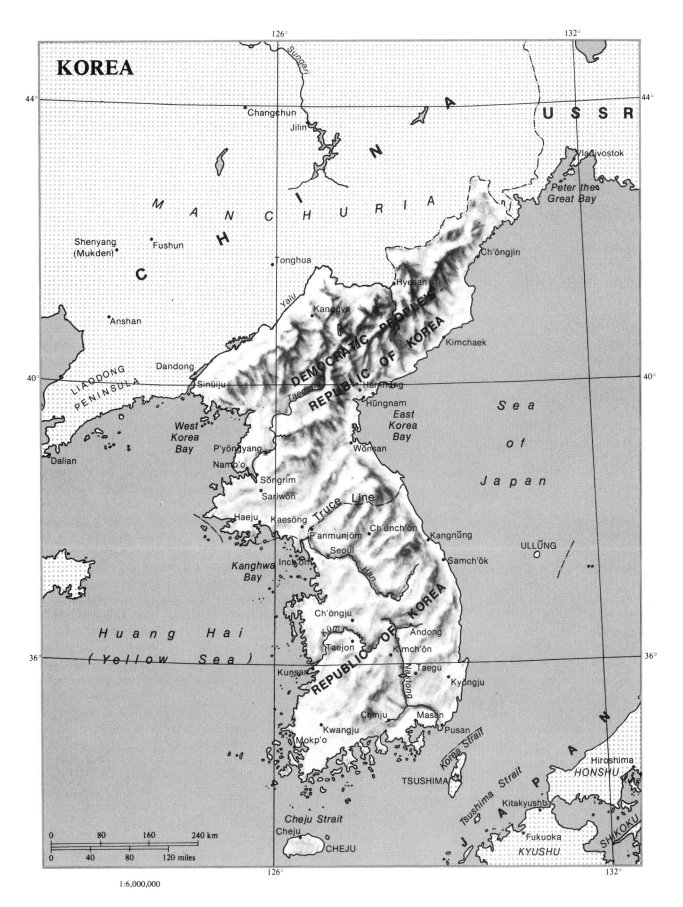

KOREA

1:6,000,000

nightmare of holocaust. The tragedy was further compounded by the fact that the civil war solved none of the outstanding social and political tensions that had been engendered by Japanese colonial rule and the subsequent division of the country. [See Korean War.]

*Modern Korean Society.* In spite of the tragic division, both North and South Korea have rebuilt and pursued aggressive economic development policies that have reshaped Korean society since the mid-1950s. Indeed, the rapidity of change has been breathtaking. It has transformed Korea, North and South, from transitional semi-industrialized societies in the 1950s into middle-class industrial powers.

Less is known of the development of the Democratic People's Republic of Korea since the Korean War because of its isolationist foreign policy and total control of information. A single-party political system ruled by a highly centralized bureaucracy under the total control of its leader, Kim Il Sung, North Korea remains in many ways an enigma to the outside world. Nevertheless, the general shape of its society and economy is known. The North Koreans, using the industrial endowment left by the Japanese, were able to rapidly rebuild with Russian assistance after the Korean War. They are not dependent on foreign energy sources and have created an impressive industrial economy. The stress on economic and political self-sufficiency embodied in the principle of self-reliance *(chuch'e),* however, has hurt their economic growth in the last decade as they outstripped their technological and capital resources. In recent years, the North Koreans have made tentative overtures to the outside world, hoping to find new sources of technology and capital.

After the Korean War, South Korea faced enormous obstacles in rebuilding its society. Almost two-thirds of the population resided in the South, and most industry was located in the North. With its dense population and almost no industrial capacity, South Korean planners had to begin from scratch, investing in power plants, agriculture, and basic industries. US economic assistance was very important in the 1950s as South Korea struggled to feed its population.

Politically, South Korea has attempted, with little success, to build an open democratic system of government. In the 1950s the military threat from the North and internal economic stagnation inhibited normal democratic politics by providing a strong imperative for authoritarian rule. The dissonance between authoritarian controls and the theoretical commitment to democracy has produced serious tensions in South Korean society over the last thirty years. In spite of these problems the people remain committed to democracy; as South Korea modernizes, considerable pressure for government to live up to the letter of constitutional principles has forced the present leaders toward a program of gradual liberalization in the political arena.

Economically, South Korea is committed to private ownership and capitalism. Since 1960 a government-business relationship has emerged to coordinate a successful program of sustained economic growth based on borrowed foreign capital and investment in exporting industries. The per capita income of South Korea was roughly US $100 in the late 1950s; today it approaches $2,000. This rapid accumulation of wealth is the result of careful and flexible government planning, creative use of borrowed capital, and the energy of the private sector. Although often called a "miracle," there were compelling concrete reasons for South Korean success. It was based on the outstanding human resources of Korean society, a disciplined, well-educated work force, and close cooperation between political leaders and private entrepreneurs. Moreover, the industrialization of Korea is rooted in the colonial period; it began more than fifty years ago. Simply put, once the economy was rebuilt after the Korean War and stable political leadership was entrenched, the Koreans were able to concentrate their energies and talents toward a purposeful program of development.

Although wealth has been rapidly accumulated, and many have found mobility upward into the new urban middle class, income distribution remains skewed. The wages of workers have not kept pace with economic growth; indeed, the government restricts free labor organization and strikes. Moreover, there is a growing perception that only certain sectors of society are benefiting from the push for growth. Even the beneficiaries of the boom, the new urban middle class, have become increasingly frustrated by the slow pace of political liberalization. For its part, the government is now faced with issues of equity as Korea shifts from a posture of "growth at all costs" toward a new attention to social spending, economic liberalization (a reduction of government controls and fostering of free market forces), and the evolution of a more open political system. In addition, the constant problem of reunification of the two Koreas is always close to the surface.

[See also Korea, Democratic People's Republic of *and* Korea, Republic of.]

Carl Berger, *The Korean Knot: A Military-Political History* (1964). Frederick M. Bunge, ed., *South Korea, a Country Study* (3d ed., 1982). Tae-Hung Ha, *Guide to Korean Culture* (1968). Sungjoo Han, *The Failure of Democracy in South Korea* (1974). Gregory Henderson, *Korea: The Politics of the Vortex* (1968). Chong-sik Lee, *The Politics of Korean Nationalism* (1963). Shannon McCune, *Korea's Heritage, A Regional and Social Geography* (1956). Ramon H. Myers and Mark R. Peattie, eds., *The Japanese Colonial Empire, 1895–1945* (1984). Dae-sook, Suh, *The Korean Communist Movement, 1918–1945* (1970).                    MICHAEL ROBINSON

**KOREA, CLASS STRUCTURE IN.** The southeastern state of Silla, which united the Korean peninsula in 668, was based on a mass of cultivators ruled by aristocratic clans whose members were graded by "bone ranks" *(kolp'um)* assigned according to descent from both parents. The bone ranks determined the level of national office to which one could rise. In the Koryŏ dynasty, which succeeded Silla in 918, the early ruling group consisted of merit subjects who aided the founding of the kingdom, local magnates who had defected from Silla, and aristocrats from the nonroyal Silla bone ranks. An examination for which only notables could sit was established, a systematic bureaucracy was adapted from Tang Chinese models, and a system of appanages *(chŏnsikwa)*—land whose taxes went to officials—was instituted. The ruling elite that developed was known as *yangban* ("two orders," i.e., civil and military officials), and included both those risen through the examinations and aristocrats whose power was based on hereditary status, intermarriage with the royal house, and untaxed estates cultivated by slaves. Beginning in the twelfth century the growing size of the aristocrats' estates, with their population of slaves exempt from corvée and military service, seriously hindered state finances and led to the downfall of the dynasty.

The succeeding Chosŏn Yi dynasty, established in 1392, curbed the power of the Koryŏ aristocracy by reducing the size of estates and of the slave population. The *yangban* were transformed into a group whose status was maintained primarily through office holding and success in the examinations, although the possession of land and slaves was also necessary to provide leisure to attain literacy in the Chinese of the bureaucracy and examinations. Relatives of existing high officials were granted easy access to office and preferential advancement through the ranks of the bureacracy, while local clerks *(hyangni)*, technicians, and the sons of *yang-* *ban* by concubines or remarried women were barred from the highest ranks of the bureaucracy and eventually came to occupy the new status of *chungin* ("middle people").

Chosŏn society included two other status groups inherited from Koryŏ: the commoners *(sangmin)*, who bore the brunt of state taxation, corvée labor, and military service; and the "base people" *(ch'ŏnmin)*, who either were slaves or engaged in polluting occupations. The commoners were not formally denied access to the examinations or offices, but unlike the middle people (who were so denied) they generally lacked the means and connections necessary to rise to high position. The base people were ineligible for the examinations or office holding, but, being exempt from corvée and military service, were sometimes able to amass considerable wealth. Status group membership was largely hereditary. Strictly speaking, families were supposed to lose *yangban* status after four generations without office. Many descendents of *yangban*, however, retired to the country and were able to maintain *yangban* status there by preserving landed estates, publishing genealogies that attested to their background, preserving Confucian family ceremonies, and cultivating Chinese letters.

Beginning in the sixteenth century the commercialization of the economy led to an increase in free tenancy and wage labor and the rise of a class of capitalist commoner farmers. Although these farmers never seriously challanged the hegemony of the *yangban* in the capital, they were often able to obtain influence in the countryside and even rise to *yangban* status by purchase, or by bribing local status registration clerks. Slave labor gradually declined until it all but disappeared by the early nineteenth century. This four-status system was abolished in the Kabo Reforms of 1894, but old status traditions continued in the countryside well into the twentieth century. [*See also* Kabo Reforms.]

At the time of the Japanese annexation in 1910 some seventy Koreans received Japanese peerages, but throughout the colonial period considerations of wealth and education were the most important determinants of status and power. Many of the old elite had both wealth and education and continued in prominence under the new regime, but those of commoner background often became successful in the lower ranks of the colonial bureaucracy or as entrepreneurs. During the 1920s and 1930s those people of base background waged a vigorous campaign against discrimination through their organization, the Hyŏngp'yŏngsa. The Japanese in Korea had superior access to modern higher education, bureaucratic office, and capital; this led to ethnic stratification in which a good deal of farmland and most wholesaling and modern industry was in Japanese hands. The majority of Korean peasants became landless tenants or laborers.

Following liberation from Japan in 1945, North and South Korea developed in different directions. In the north, land reform was followed by collectivization of farms and businesses so that classes based on ownership of property no longer exist there. One's social position depends upon occupation and Communist Party membership. In the South, postwar land reform eliminated the landlord class and much of the remaining power of the *yangban* as well, although some landless tenants still remain. Commoner villagers began to refuse traditional services previously rendered to *yangban*, and an ethic of equality has been instituted. The rapid industrialization of the 1960s and 1970s led to massive migration to urban areas, and the appearance of squatter settlements around major cities led to fears of the development of an unassimilable urban proletariat. Most migrants, however, have been employed as factory workers or in small self-run businesses, and the distribution of land and income in South Korea is today remarkably equitable for a developing country.

[*See also* Yangban.]

Herbert Barringer, "Social Differentiation, Stratification and Mobility in Korea," in *Korea, A Decade of Development*, edited by Yunshik Chang (1981). Andrew Grad, *Modern Korea* (1944). William E. Henthorn, *A History of Korea* (1971). James Palais, *Politics and Policy in Yi Dynasty Korea* (1980). Herbert Passin, "The Paekchŏng of Korea," *Monumenta Japonica* 12.3 (1956): 195–240.                    CLARK SORENSEN

**KOREA, COLONIAL PERIOD OF.** *See* Korea *and* Korea, Japanese Government-General of.

**KOREA, DEMOCRATIC PEOPLE'S REPUBLIC OF.** In the aftermath of unfruitful negotiations between the Soviet Union and the United States to establish a unified Korean government, the Democratic People's Republic of Korea (DPRK) was established in North Korea in September 1948, with P'yŏngyang as its capital. The two major powers had occupied Korea at the end of World War II and had agreed in December 1945 to establish a Korean provisional government that was to operate under the trusteeship of four world powers (the United States, the Soviet Union, Britain, and China) for a five-year period, but the onset of the Cold War made it impossible for them to arrive at a formula for a unified government. The DPRK's constitution, adopted by the Supreme People's Assembly (SPA) in April, proclaims it to be the sole legal government in Korea, but its authority has been limited to the northern half of the peninsula except for a brief period during the Korean War when its army, the Korean People's Army, occupied most of the peninsula.

The basic framework of the government was laid out under Soviet occupation (1945–1948). Thus, in October 1945 the Soviet command in P'yŏngyang created the Five-Province Administrative Bureau as an executive body for its occupation zone. The Soviet command evidently hoped the Bureau would represent a united front of the communist and noncommunist forces in North Korea, but as the noncommunist elements in North and South Korea opposed the trusteeship, they were eliminated from the political arena.

Communist authorities under the Soviet command evidently determined in December 1945 to push through a program to "democratize" North Korea. Kim Il Sung (Kim Il-sŏng), the Soviet-supported leader, announced in December 1945 that by uniting with "all democratic parties and social organizations," the Communist Party would transform North Korea into a "strong democratic base" by rapidly "democratizing" political, economic, and cultural life there. At the same time he declared that the Party should strengthen the united front with the democratic forces of South Korea, thereby setting the stage for a unified People's Democratic Republic.

In February 1946 the Five-Province Bureau was succeeded by the North Korean Provisional People's Committee, which promulgated, between March and October 1946, laws on land reform, labor practice, equality of the sexes, and nationalization of industries, transportation, and banks. Individual handicrafts and commerce temporarily were to be preserved as private enterprise. The land reform law eliminated the traditional power elite in the villages.

In February 1947 the Provisional People's Committee shed its "provisional" title and on 8 September 1948 the SPA proclaimed the DPRK as an independent sovereign state. The next day the SPA formed a government under Kim Il Sung, who had been the chairman of the People's Committee. In September 1948 he assumed the new title of premier and held that title until 1972, when he was elevated to the newly created office of president. North Korea claimed authority over the entire peninsula as had South Korea in August 1948. The Soviet forces were withdrawn at the end of 1948.

The Korean War (June 1950–July 1953) severely tested the strength of the political support behind the DPRK. While the DPRK's army was highly successful during the initial months of the war, General Douglas A. MacArthur's landing at Inch'ŏn in September abruptly changed the entire course of the war. A large part of North Korea was taken by US and South Korean forces before the Chinese "volunteers" intervened in October, enabling the DPRK eventually to restore its authority over its domain. The war lasted until 27 July 1953, when a cease-fire agreement was signed at P'anmunjŏm. The war involved China and the Soviet Union on the North Korean side, and thirteen member nations of the United Nations contributed armed men and medical units to South Korea. The war also reduced the entire peninsula to rubble; casualties on both sides were enormous. The chances for peaceful unification had been remote even before 1950, but the war dashed even the remotest of hopes. [See also Korean War.]

The Communist leadership discovered during the winter of 1950, when its troops were being decimated by US and South Korean forces, that the political and military structure they had built was fragile. Two-thirds of Party members had to be subjected to various forms of discipline and punishment for infraction of rules. A number of high-level Party and military officers had to be removed from their posts for "acts of cowardice," disobeying orders, inefficiency, and similar charges. A large number of people also aided the enemy or even joined "reactionary" paramilitary units serving the enemy during the period of retreat. A greater number of people simply abandoned the Communists and fled to the South when the UN forces were retreating in the face of Chinese intervention.

An intensive reconstruction effort was launched in both the economic and the political arena at the end of the war. The long-range recovery and development plan was announced by the Central Committee of the Korean Workers' Party (KWP) in August 1953. The plan consisted of three basic stages: a brief, preparatory stage involving "sweeping up the rubble"; a Three-Year Plan (1954–1956) to regain pre–Korean War production levels; and finally, a Five-Year Plan (1957–1961) to lay the basis for making North Korea a socialist and industrial so-

ciety. These plans were pushed through with the fervor of war. While the DPRK received some aid from China, the Soviet Union, and other Communist-bloc countries, it had to rely mostly on internal mobilization. The growth rate of North Korea's industries during these years was substantial: the average annual growth rate was estimated to be 41.7 percent during the period of the Three-Year Plan and 36.6 percent during the period of the First Five-Year Plan.

In 1961 Kim launched the First Seven-Year Plan with the objectives of raising the living standards of the people and expanding the existing industrial base by promoting a major technological revolution. While the initial stage of the Seven-Year Plan seemed to have progressed satisfactorily, economic development began to falter in 1965 and 1966. The deterioration of the relationship between China and the Soviet Union adversely affected the DPRK. The North Korean decision to side with the Chinese in 1962 incurred the displeasure of the Soviet Union, which made no new aid commitment after 1961, although it did honor commitments made in late 1960 for aid through 1964. The stoppage of military aid from the Soviet Union between 1962 and 1964 also necessitated North Korea's utilizing more resources for military buildup after late 1962, which further slowed economic development. As a result, in October 1966 the Seven-Year Plan was extended for three years. The Seven-Year Plan projected an average annual increase in total industrial output of 18 percent, but the actual result was 12.8 percent.

North Korean farms also went through a radical change as the regime decided on agricultural collectivization. The process took place in three stages, each with a successively greater degree of collective ownership and control. By August 1958 the entire farm population had been absorbed into the movement, grouped into some 13,300 cooperatives. In October of the same year cooperatives were reorganized into larger units, having the same boundaries as the ri, the lowest administrative subdivision, numbering 3,700. The cooperative became at once a basic social unit and a basic form of state power for the rural area in that it was designed to integrate rural industry, agriculture, trade, culture and education, and military affairs into a single entity.

Equally radical changes were instituted in the political arena during the postwar years. Even though Kim Il Sung's predominant position in the political system had never been challenged since 1946, he had shared power with men of diverse backgrounds. There were men from the Soviet Union, the returnees from northwest China, and the veterans of underground activities in Korea. Kim, on the other hand, was a veteran of anti-Japanese guerrilla warfare in Manchuria who apparently spent the period from 1941 to 1945 in the eastern maritime region of the Soviet Union. By 1958 practically everyone outside of Kim's inner group had been purged. Since April 1955 the leader had also launched an intensive campaign to remold the Party, stressing ideological fortification, dedication to nationalism, and loyalty to the leader. Exaltation of the leader knew no bounds. After 1968 the cult extended to his family as well.

The Six-Year Plan (1971–1976) was to accelerate the development of the power and mining industries and to reduce the need for imported raw materials and other products. It also called for the expansion of the metallurgical and chemical industries and the extensive introduction of automation and semi-automation. Although the government found it necessary to designate 1977 as a year of adjustment —thus in fact extending the Six-Year Plan by one year—the regime claimed that the Six-Year Plan's targets were overfulfilled and that industrial production had risen at an annual rate of 16.3 percent, or 2.3 percent above the target rate. The training of technical personnel had been emphasized, and their number was reported to have increased from 497,000 in 1970 to 1 million in 1976.

The DPRK, however, encountered a severe problem in foreign trade. In the early 1970s North Korea, undoubtedly spurred by the current of détente, had attempted to break away from the established pattern of heavy reliance on Communist-bloc trade and to venture into the noncommunist world by purchasing a great quantity of machinery and entire plants from Western countries and Japan, but the sudden shift in world economy caused by the oil crisis of 1973 led the DPRK to default on the payments due. The problems were serious enough to cause the government to reshuffle top-level government personnel and lower the targeted industrial growth rate for the Second Seven-Year Plan (1978–1984) to 12.1 percent. As of the end of 1981, the DPRK reportedly owes foreign countries approximately US $3 billion. Its exports in 1980 came to $1.4 billion.

In December 1972 the leadership adopted a completely revised constitution to replace the one that had been in force since 1948 and created a number of new governmental offices and institutions. The basic aim of the leaders in adopting the new constitution was to adapt it to the changes that had taken place since 1948. The myth of the SPA's leg-

islative supremacy was discarded, the supreme authority of the leader was legitimized, and the enormous power of the inner circles of the ruling elite institutionalized. These goals were attained through the creation of a presidency, the establishment of a Central People's Committee (CPC), and the emasculation of the SPA and its Presidium. The president, elected by the SPA for four years, is the supreme commander of the armed forces and the chairman of the National Defense Commission. He heads, "directly guides," and recommends membership of the CPC; convenes and presides over meetings of the Administrative Council (cabinet) when necessary; promulgates the laws and ordinances; and issues edicts. The CPC, a fifteen-member body, is "the highest leadership organ of the state." It draws up the policies of the state; "directs" the work of the cabinet, local people's assemblies and committees, and judicial and procuratorial organs; and guides the work of national defense and state political security. The CPC also serves as a vital link between the state and the party as most of its members are concurrently members of the Presidium of the Politburo of the KWP.

The Sixth Congress of the KWP, held in October 1980, officially confirmed the status of President Kim Il Sung's son, Kim Jong Il (Kim Chong-il; b. 1941), as the successor to the supreme leader, solving the mystery behind the building of the cult of his "revolutionary family." The president had chosen his younger brother Yong-Ju as a potential successor and elected him a member of the Political Committee (Politburo since 1980) of the KWP at the Fifth Party Congress held in November 1970, but he somehow fell into disfavor, and was not even reelected a member of the 248-member Central Committee of the KWP at the Sixth Congress. Kim Jong Il, on the other hand, was installed at the Sixth Congress in the fourth position in the presidium of the Politburo, the second position in the Secretariat, and the third position in the Military Commission. In May 1984 North Korean newspapers began to accord the younger leader virtually equal status with his father in their front pages. Barring unforeseen events, Kim Jong Il will assume positions in the state apparatus as well.

[See also Korea; Communism: Communism in Korea; Kim Il Sung; and Kim Jong Il.]

Frederica M. Bunge, North Korea, A Country Study (3d ed., 1981). Ryu Hun, Study of North Korea (1966). Glenn D. Paige, The Korean People's Democratic Republic (1966). Robert A. Scalapino, ed., North Korea Today (1963).

CHONG-SIK LEE

KOREA, HAN-CHINESE COLONIES IN. *See* Commanderies in Korea, Chinese.

KOREA, JAPANESE GOVERNMENT-GENERAL OF. The Japanese colonial administration was established in Korea following the conclusion of an annexation treaty between the two neighboring states on 22 August 1910. It lasted thirty-five years until the end of World War II in 1945, when defeated Japan was shorn of all colonial possessions.

In the wake of the Russo-Japanese War (1904–1905), Japan occupied Korea militarily and imposed her protectorate in a treaty signed 17 November 1905. For the next five years, the Japanese Residency-General (Tōkanfu) controlled Korea's foreign affairs and a progressively wider range of domestic affairs as well. Emboldened by the acquiescence of the major Western powers, disturbed by widespread Korean resistance, and above all, in pursuit of the goals of national aggrandizement, the Japanese government annexed Korea in 1910, ending the five centuries of rule by the Yi dynasty (1392–1910) on the Korean peninsula.

The Government-General (Sōtokufu) of Korea (or Chōsen, as the Japanese called it) was a centralized bureaucratic structure headed by the governor-general (*sōtoku*), who was by law a general officer in the military service. In fact, all the governors-general but one, Admiral Saitō Makoto, were army generals. Accountable only to the Japanese emperor via the prime minister, the governor-general enjoyed a broad range of executive, legislative, and judicial powers together with emergency military command authorities that made him a virtual dictator. While the central offices were located in Keijō (as the Japanese called Seoul), the local administration consisted of thirteen provinces, further divided into counties, subcounties, townships and villages in a hierarchical chain controlled from the center. Of the eight men who occupied the top post in Korea (two of them on two separate occasions each), three had been war minister in Tokyo concurrently or immediately prior to assignment in Korea, while three others served as the prime minister either prior or subsequent to the Korean tour. In other words, Korea was considered by the Tokyo government an important colonial and military outpost.

The thirty-five year history of Japanese rule may be subdivided into three periods: (1) 1910 to 1919, (2) 1919 to 1936, and (3) 1936 to 1945. In the first period the Japanese created an institutional foundation for a modern, efficient, but brutal colonial administration. One of the most controversial among many "modern reforms" that was introduced early in Japanese rule was a cadastral survey ostensibly designed to establish a more reliable system of farm registry for administrative as well as tax purposes; it had the effect of disallowing misinformed or uninformed farmers continued ownership or cultivation of their farms. Of equal importance was the introduction of a modern public school system that was designed to prepare young Koreans to accept the colonial rule as they learned useful vocational skills. A significant number of dispossessed or disgruntled Koreans chose to or had to leave the homeland, most of them crossing the border to the Jiandao region in southeastern Manchuria. The ruthless suppression within Korea of any anti-Japanese resistance, real or suspected, created a climate of terror. Called a period of "military rule" *(budan seiji)*, these initial years were marked by a drastic reduction of all classes of Koreans to the status of the powerless and voiceless victims of an alien militarist regime complete with a sizable gendarmerie and garrison forces in addition to the regular civilian police.

What began as a peaceful demonstration by Koreans for their national independence on 1 March 1919, the day of the funeral of the former king, Kojong (r. 1864–1907), ushered in the second period. The March First Movement was originally planned by a handful of religious leaders and student activists in Seoul, but it quickly mushroomed into a series of massive demonstrations throughout Korea. Caught by surprise, the Japanese authorities responded with indiscriminate use of brute force that produced hundreds of thousands of casualties and extensive destruction of property. The Tokyo government was alarmed and embarrassed by these events, particularly because of their adverse impact on domestic and world opinion. Tokyo therefore broke with established precedent by appointing a navy admiral, Saitō Makoto, as governor-general, and it promised moderation of its policies in Korea. Saitō proclaimed a "cultural rule" *(bunka seiji)* that allowed a limited range of freedoms of press and association. At the same time, new steps for economic development and agricultural improvement were announced. Many critics of the Japanese policies maintain, however, that the policy shift was more apparent than real. [*See also* March First Independence Movement.]

The March First Movement also marked a turning point in anti-Japanese activities waged by the Korean nationalists in Manchuria, Siberia, China, and

America. In an attempt to create a nucleus to bind together diverse groups in distant localities, a Korean Provisional Government was proclaimed in Shanghai in April 1919. Although its effectiveness was greatly undermined by internecine feuds arising from personal or ideological discord, the exile "government" managed to survive and serve as one of the tangible symbols of Korean nationhood. Another notable development in the post-1919 period was the growth of leftist political groups that presented a major challenge to conservative nationalists.

The quickening tempo of the Japanese military ventures against China and then against the Allied powers in World War II and concomitant changes within Japan itself were reflected in the administration of Japan's Korean colony in the final period. Korea was increasingly viewed as a forward military and industrial base for Japanese military operations on the Asian mainland. Marked advances were made in transportation, telecommunication, mining, energy production, and manufacturing. Korea's industrialization, especially the growth of chemical and heavy industries, was designed for the purpose of sustaining Japan's war-making capacity. Also mobilized for the war were the human resources of the Korean colony. Beginning in 1938 a growing number of Koreans were recruited for the Japanese military, and by 1943 a full-fledged conscription system was sending tens of thousands of Korean young men to the war. At the same time, Korean laborers, including women, were forcibly sent to all parts of the expanding Japanese domain, many of them to be stranded after the war.

As the mobilization of Korea's material and manpower resources grew in intensity, so did the Japanese efforts to regiment and "japanize" the Koreans. If the policy of assimilation was not entirely new in the late 1930s, the scope and magnitude of various measures initiated at this time were certainly unprecedented. Governor-General Minami Jirō (in office 1936–1942) imposed Japanese State Shinto, built around an overzealous version of the cult of emperor worship, upon the Koreans, including protesting Christians. He virtually outlawed the use of the Korean language in schools and public places, and any manifestation of interest in studying Korea's history and cultural traditions was often treated as evidence of anti-Japanese and subversive intent. Koreans who valued their family lineage and traditions were particularly outraged when persistent efforts were made to "persuade" them to adopt Japanese-style surnames and even given names, although

many submitted out of fear. When the Japanese empire collapsed, the Koreans regained their names and their native language. Many other legacies of the colonial rule, however, including the virtually total absence of experience in national self-rule, proved to be greatly more difficult to rectify.

Any attempt to review and assess the record of the Japanese Government-General of Korea runs the risk of partisan bias. On the one hand, a wide range of modern changes did take place in Korea under the Japanese aegis, not only in terms of physical or material conditions of life but also in sociocultural aspects. Every conceivable aspect of traditional Korean life and society felt the impact of modern challenges and had to be modified, supplanted, or discarded. For better or worse, the Japanese were the primary transmitters of modern stimuli, and the process of modernization became sustained and systemic while Japan ruled Korea.

On the other hand, it is undeniable that Japanese rule was imposed and maintained by force and that the majority of Koreans felt victimized, oppressed, and humiliated. Despite the close geographical, historical, and ethnic ties between the two nations, or perhaps because of these ties, the two peoples proved incapable of the integration the Japanese sought to impose. When the Japanese colonial rulers tried to assimilate or japanize Koreans, their words and actions appeared unconscionably hypocritical. The Japanese rulers proclaimed equality (isshi dōjin) as their basic principle but practiced discrimination in matters large and small. Until the end of the colonial period, Koreans had no vote, they were kept out of decision-making roles in the colonial administration, they were discriminated against in both the public and private sectors, and they were denied equal business and educational opportunities. The wartime rations of food and other necessities favored Japanese settlers in Korea, who usually lived in self-imposed segregation from the surrounding Koreans, and their air of superiority and arrogance stirred resentment and resistance among Koreans. Koreans who opposed Japan were hunted down, in and outside of Korea, and met cruel and harsh punishments. The bitter memories of the Koreans have died hard, and education in both South and North Korea after World War II has perpetuated a collective hostility to Japanese colonialism. In North Korea, a former anti-Japanese guerrilla group successfully established its political legitimacy partly on the strength of its past campaigns against the imperialist rulers, while the 1984 state visit of South Korean President Chun Doo Hwan to Japan elicited a highly publicized expression of "regret" for the past "unfortunate" history by the Japanese emperor.

Viewed from another perspective, the Japanese rule of Korea was the first instance of imperial conquest by an Asian nation of another Asian nation in the modern period. In retrospect, it was neither inevitable nor successful. It may also be noted that the Japanese administration of Korea was considerably harsher and created longer-lasting animosity among the colonized people than in the somewhat similar case of the Japanese Government-General of Taiwan (1895–1945).

[*See also* Yi Dynasty *and* Korea. *For the extent of Japan's holdings in northeast Asia during the early twentieth century, see the map accompanying* Meiji Period.]

Andrew J. Grajdanzev, *Modern Korea* (1944). Gregory Henderson, *Korea: The Politics of the Vortex* (1968). Han-Kyo Kim, "Japanese Colonialism in Korea," in *Japan Examined: Perspectives on Modern Japanese History*, edited by Harry Wray and Hilary Conroy (1983), pp. 222–228. Chong-sik Lee, *The Politics of Korean Nationalism* (1965). Andrew C. Nahm, ed., *Korea under Japanese Colonial Rule: Studies of the Policy and Techniques of Japanese Colonialism* (1973).    HAN-KYO KIM

**KOREA, OCCUPATION OF.** *See* Korean War.

**KOREA, REPUBLIC OF.** Established in August 1948, with its capital in Seoul, the Republic of Korea (ROK) emerged in the aftermath of unfruitful negotiations between the Soviet Union and the United States to establish a unified Korean government. The two major powers had occupied Korea at the end of World War II and had agreed in December 1945 to establish a Korean provisional government under the trusteeship of four world powers for a five-year period, but the onset of the Cold War made it impossible for them to implement the agreement. In January 1948 the United Nations General Assembly dispatched the Temporary Commission on Korea to supervise a general election throughout Korea, but the Soviet command did not permit its entrance to North Korea. Elections were held in the US-occupied South Korea in May 1948 for the National Assembly, which adopted a constitution that proclaimed the ROK to be the sole legal government in Korea. Its authority, however, has been limited to the southern half of the peninsula.

The establishment of the ROK came after three years of US occupation characterized by uncertainty and confusion. Although the United States had proposed the division of Korea at the 38th parallel in August 1945, its leaders began to question the strategic value of South Korea by 1947, and no major effort was made to prepare for a viable political and economic system. Syngman Rhee (Yi Sŭng-man), an American-educated nationalist leader, was elected president in 1948, but he inherited a faltering economy that was cut off from the northern part of the country, which had much of the country's natural resources and had provided 70 percent of South Korea's electric power.

Between June 1950 and July 1953, the entire country was thrown into havoc as the war raged over the entire peninsula and reduced it to rubble. Even though the war ended with a truce at P'anmunjŏm, tension between North and South Korea remained high, and the United States continued to station troops in South Korea. The US forces had been withdrawn in 1949, but they were dispatched again in June 1950 soon after the North Korean invasion. [*See also* Korean War.]

Domestic politics between 1948 and 1960 revolved around the opposition's struggle to unseat President Rhee. The constitutional provisions concerning the presidency became the focal point in the drawn-out struggle. Rhee and his supporters forced through constitutional amendments on three occasions to prolong his rule (even resorting to martial law in 1951) while the opposition mustered public support against it. By the late 1950s, however, Rhee became a captive of the political structure that had supported him. In the March 1960 general election, Rhee was reelected by default because his principal opponent died just before the election while getting medical treatment in the United States, but his party's attempt to elect Yi Ki-bung as vice president through fraudulent means touched off massive student demonstrations, and Rhee resigned on 26 April. [*See* Rhee, Syngman *and* April Nineteenth Student Revolution.]

South Korean society changed greatly during Rhee's rule. Educational opportunities were greatly expanded. The land reform law, enacted in June 1949, turned nearly one million sharecroppers, or approximately 40 percent of the total farm households, into small landowners. At the same time, the war gave rise to a large officer corps that developed into an increasingly significant social group.

The government began the task of rehabilitation as soon as the battle zone stabilized near the 38th parallel in 1952. The scarcity of material and the need to maintain a large army caused a high rate of inflation, but by 1958 prices had stabilized. The government also intensified its effort to increase industrial production, placing emphasis on power generation and textile and cement production. The average rise in the gross national product was 5.5 percent from 1954 through 1958. Industrial production led the advance, growing by nearly 14 percent per year. Various members of the United Nations, particularly the United States, provided substantial financial assistance. The economy, however, began to stagnate in 1959.

A transitional government headed by Chang Myŏn (John M. Chang) maintained order after Rhee's resignation and prepared for a new general election of the National Assembly in July 1960. That body revised the constitution on 15 June, instituting a parliamentary form of government with a bicameral legislature. In the July election the Democratic Party won 175 of the 233 seats in the lower house of the National Assembly. A junta headed by Major General Park Chung Hee (Pak Chŏng-hŭi), however, carried out a coup d'état on 16 May 1961, ending the brief democratic interlude. The junta ruled until December 1963, when Park was installed as president under a new constitution drafted by the junta and approved by a national referendum. [*See* Chang Myŏn *and* May Sixteenth Coup d'État.]

Although the Park government exercised considerable control over all aspects of the society through the Korean Central Intelligence Agency (KCIA), opposition parties and the press exercised much freedom, and the presidential and National Assembly elections of 1967 and 1971 were closely contested. There were numerous student demonstrations against the government, particularly in 1965, when it concluded a diplomatic treaty with Japan, Korea's former colonial ruler, and agreed to send forty-five thousand combat troops to Vietnam. But the government managed to control the situation without producing any casualties among demonstrators.

In December 1971 Park proclaimed a national emergency and rammed through the National Assembly a bill granting him complete power to control, regulate, and mobilize the people, the economy, and the press. In October 1972 he proclaimed martial law and submitted to a national referendum a new draft constitution that came to be designated the *yusin* (revitalization) constitution. This 1972 constitution allowed Park to succeed himself indefinitely, to appoint one-third of the National Assembly members, and to exercise emergency powers at will. The president was to be chosen by the more than two thousand locally elected deputies of the

supposedly nonpartisan National Conference for Unification, who were to cast their votes without debate. Park was reelected in December 1972 under the new constitution and subsequently issued numerous emergency decrees to suppress all forms of dissent. Park argued that national security demanded a strong leadership particularly because of uncertainties in US commitment to South Korea's defense. President Nixon had enunciated the Guam Doctrine in 1969, had withdrawn one of the two remaining US divisions from South Korea in 1970, and had made further preparations for troop withdrawal even though tension remained high on the Korean peninsula. Under the pressure of the détente policy of the United States, the ROK government established contacts with the Democratic People's Republic of Korea (DPRK) leadership in the north, and their representatives held series of meetings in 1972 and 1973, but no substantive agreements were reached and the tension remained unabated.

President Park encouraged South Korea's trade with Japan, and the volume of trade rose from US $148 million in 1964 to $2,964 million in 1973, but relations between South Korea and Japan were severely strained between 1973 and 1975 in the aftermath of South Korean agents' abduction of Kim Dae Jung (Kim Tae-jung) from a Tokyo hotel in August 1973. Kim was President Park's opponent in the 1971 presidential elections. The abduction incident and Park's oppressive measures also gave rise to increasingly vociferous opposition from students, intellectuals, and politicians. [*See* Kim Dae Jung.] In August 1974 Park narrowly avoided an assassination attempt by a Korean resident in Japan, but stray bullets killed the president's wife.

Park's strongest defense against his critics had been the high rate of economic growth under his leadership. South Korea's economy had expanded rapidly under his rule, particularly after he "normalized" South Korea's relations with Japan in 1965. The manufacturing sector grew rapidly during the first two five-year economic development plans, which lasted from 1962 to 1966 and 1967 to 1971, and registered 15 percent and 21 percent annual growth rates, respectively. Domestic savings rates grew, and exports rapidly expanded. Commodity exports grew by 44 percent annually between 1962 and 1966, and by 35 percent between 1967 and 1971. The third Economic Development Plan (1972–1976) aimed at the expansion of heavy and chemical industries. The GNP grew by more than 11 percent and exports by more than 50 percent per year. South Korea weathered the worldwide oil crisis of 1973 and 1974 through expansion of construction projects in the Middle East, where South Korean firms earned US $15 billion between 1974 and 1978. The economic growth continued during the first two years of the fourth Economic Development Plan (1977–1981).

In 1979, however, President Park confronted serious problems. The economy suffered from stagnation and a high rate of inflation. Economic problems accompanied by political suppression caused social unrest, and the opposition camp became more vociferous. President Park was also subjected to strong pressure from US president Carter, who announced in March 1977 a plan to withdraw all US ground combat troops over a five-year period and continued to press for the improvement of the human rights climate in South Korea. (President Carter subsequently postponed the plan indefinitely.) In October 1979 students in Pusan and Masan poured into the streets and clashed with police, and the government declared martial law there. On 26 October President Park was shot to death by Kim Jaegyu, the director of the KCIA, who had been responsible for controlling the dissidents. [See Park Chung Hee.]

A brief interlude of political freedom followed the assassination, when opposition leaders and former followers of President Park debated on the content of a new constitution. Choi Kyu-ha (Ch'oe Kyu-ha), the acting president, delayed the constitutional revision, however, thereby precipitating massive student demonstrations in May 1980.

In the meantime, Major General Chun Doo Hwan (Chŏn Tu-hwan), head of the Defense Security Command, took control of the army in December 1979 by arresting the Army chief of staff. He also assumed the directorship of the KCIA in April 1980. On 17 May he issued a martial law decree prohibiting all political gatherings indoors or outdoors and arrested principal politicians. When students in Kwangju, a city of six hundred thousand people 170 miles southwest of Seoul, defied the new decree on the following day and held demonstrations, the Martial Law Command dispatched a special paratrooper force to suppress them. The ten-day confrontation that followed between the army and the citizens of that city left 170 persons killed, including 22 soldiers and 4 policemen, according to official sources. Other sources reported 2,000 dead. General Chun retired from the army and was elected president on 27 August under the 1972 constitution. The junta then carried out a massive purge of political and intellectual elites and revised many principal

laws through an appointed body known as the National Security Legislative Council. In October the junta pushed through a new constitution by a national referendum, and in March 1981 an electoral college similar to the one under the 1972 constitution reelected Chun president for a seven-year term. In June a new National Assembly was elected. The Defense Security Command, however, continued to exercise strong control over the country's politics and press.

President Chun called for the construction of a new society based on justice and fairness, but his administration was marred by numerous large-scale scandals between 1981 and 1983. By mid-1981 inflation was brought under control, and the economy began to resume the pace of growth. President Chun was strongly endorsed by President Reagan of the United States and Premier Nakasone of Japan, but he faced stiff opposition from student activists, who defied the government ban to hold series of demonstrations in the fall of 1984. [See Chun Doo Hwan.]

By 1985 the rapid growth of the Korean economy was producing many changes in the Republic of Korea. Exports led the economy, and large conglomerates dominated foreign and internal commerce. President Chun had conducted successful trade and political negotiations with Japan, becoming the first Korean head of state to be received by the Japanese sovereign, and there were indications that negotiations with the Democratic People's Republic of Korea to the north might be renewed.

[See also Korea and Korea, Democratic People's Republic of.]

Sungjoo Han, *The Failure of Democracy in South Korea* (1974). Gregory Henderson, *Korea: The Politics of the Vortex* (1968). Kim Se-jun, *The Politics of Military Revolution in Korea* (1971). Paul W. Kuznets, *Economic Growth and Structure in the Republic of Korea* (1977). W. D. Reeve, *The Republic of Korea: A Political and Economic Study* (1963). Edward R. Wright, *Korean Politics in Transition* (1975).                    CHONG-SIK LEE

# KOREAN STATE EXAMINATION SYSTEM.
With the founding of the Yi dynasty (1392–1910), Confucianism became the dominant ideology in Korea and for the first time state examinations became the central path to government careers. Civil service examinations had been instituted in 958 by the Koryŏ dynasty (918–1392), but the aristocracy enjoyed wide access to office without participating in the examinations.

The fully elaborated system included three kinds of examinations: the civil service examinations that led to public office; examinations for technical specialists in foreign languages, medicine, astronomy, and law; and military examinations. The general features of these examinations were much like those in China, although they functioned somewhat differently in Korea's more highly stratified society. By law even commoners had access to the civil service examinations, but in fact only members of the elite class, the *yangban,* competed successfully. Indeed, even the "illegitimate" sons of *yangban* fathers and their secondary wives were excluded. Many members of the *chungin,* or "middle people," class came from such a background, and it was mainly *chungin* who took the technical examinations and became specialists in the various government agencies. The military examinations were far less prestigious than the civil service exams, and were in fact open to all, but the highest positions in the military structure were regarded as civil positions and hence could not be attained through the military examination route.

The civil service exams dominated *yangban* life as the major avenue of social standing and economic well-being. The system consisted of a preliminary stage, the *sokwa* or *sama,* and a final stage, the *taekwa* or *munkwa.* The preliminary stage resulted in a licentiate degree, but did not qualify one for any significant official appointment. There were two kinds of licentiate: those who specialized in the classics were *saengwŏn* (Chinese, *shengyuan*), the term for all those who passed the preliminary examinations in China; those who specialized in the literary exams became *chinsa* (Chinese, *jinshi*), the term reserved in China for those who passed the final level of the civil service examinations. Both degrees qualified one to sit for the final course of examinations, but many were satisfied to stop with the licentiate degree, for it already carried great prestige, substantiated one's scholarship, and confirmed the family's social standing.

The examinations originally were to be held every three years, but this schedule was later augmented by a number of special examinations held at irregular intervals to celebrate special occasions in the national life. Both the *sokwa* and *taekwa* examinations involved preliminary examinations at the provincial level and second exams in Seoul; the *taekwa* also involved a third stage, the Palace Examination, which was held in the presence of the king for the final ranking of the exam passers. The *sokwa* selected 1,080 candidates initially and awarded 200 with final success, while the *taekwa* selected 223 and narrowed that down to a final 33. The system was finally abandoned in the modernizing Kabo Reforms of 1894.

[*See also* Korea, Class Structure in; Neo-Confucianism in Korea; *and* Kabo Reforms.]

Woo-Keun Han, *The History of Korea,* translated by Kyong-shik Lee (1970). Wanne J. Joe, *Traditional Korea: A Cultural History* (1972). Ki-baik Lee, *A New History of Korea,* translated by Edward W. Wagner (1984). James B. Palais, *Politics and Policy in Traditional Korea* (1975).

MICHAEL C. KALTON

**KOREAN WAR.** The decade from 1943 to 1953 was the crucible of the period of national division that still troubles Korea. Nothing about the politics of contemporary Korea can be understood without comprehending the events of this decade. It was the breeding ground of the two Koreas, of war, and of a reordering of international politics in northeast Asia. The important dates of this period include 1945, when American and Soviet forces moved into Korea to accept the Japanese surrender; 1948, when each sponsored the emergence of the Republic of Korea (ROK) in the South and the Democratic People's Republic of Korea (DPRK) in the North, and June 1950, when the Korean War began.

Koreans term the American and Soviet occupations "liberation." Their use of such a term is indicative of the bitterness of the period of Japanese colonial rule (1910–1945). The colonial experience was intense and bitter. It brought development and underdevelopment, agrarian growth and deepened tenancy, industrialization and extraordinary dislocation, political mobilization and deactivation, a new role for a strong state, new sets of Korean political leaders, communism and nationalism, armed resistance and treacherous collaboration; it left deep fissures and conflicts that have gnawed at the Korean national identity ever since. Although 1945 was indeed a watershed, the colonial period deeply influenced the American and Soviet occupations and the two Korean states that emerged in 1948.

*American Policy.* In much of the literature on the 1940s, American policy appears to be unformed and tentative, the Americans making few preparations for the responsibilities they assumed in Korea. Diplomatic documents declassified in recent years, however, have suggested more forethought than might have been expected, although the nature of American planning before the Japanese surrender remains controversial. This planning shows that the United States took the initiative in great-power deliberations on Korea during World War II, suggesting a multilateral trusteeship for postwar Korea to the British in March 1943 and to the Soviets at the end of the year.

At about the same time, planners in the State Department drastically altered traditional US policy toward Korea by defining the security of the peninsula as important to the security of the postwar Pacific, and viewing Soviet domination of all of Korea as a threat to postwar security. It was this early planning that reflected a newfound US interest in Korea, and that lay behind the American decision to send troops to Korea in 1945.

When twenty-five thousand American soldiers occupied southern Korea in early September 1945, new problems arose. They found themselves facing a strong Korean impulse for independence and for thorough reform of colonial legacies; by and large Koreans wished to solve their problems alone and resented any inference that they were not ready for self-government. The American military command, along with emissaries dispatched from Washington, tended to interpret this resistance to US desires as radical and pro-Soviet. When Korean resistance leaders set up an interim People's Republic and so-called people's committees throughout Korea in September 1945, the United States interpreted a fundamentally indigenous movement as part of a Soviet master plan to dominate all of Korea. Radical activity, such as the ousting of landlords and attacks on Koreans in the colonial police, was usually a matter of settling scores left over from the colonial period, or of quite legitimate demands by Koreans to run their own affairs. This activity immediately became subsumed within Soviet-American rivalry, so that the Cold War arrived early in Korea—in the last months of 1945.

When the Korean War erupted American policy changed. Had the United States simply sought to contain the Communist thrust into the South, it would have restored the 38th parallel when it crushed the North Korean army. Instead, American forces under General Douglas MacArthur marched into North Korea and sought to destroy the northern regime and unify the peninsula under the rule of Syngman Rhee (Yi Sŭng-man).

For a generation, scholars tended to blame the debacle of the march north on MacArthur, alleging that he violated strict orders not to move precipitately to the Yalu River border and not to provoke Chinese intervention. Again, declassified documentation now shows that the crossing of the 38th parallel reflected a change from containment to a new policy called rollback: as policy planners described it, the United States for the first time had the chance to displace and transform some Communist-held territory. This American thrust, however, brought Chinese forces in on the northern side in October and November 1950; these "volunteers" and a reinvigorated North Korean army pushed US and South Korean forces out of the North within a month, and caused a crisis in American domestic politics as backers of Truman fought with backers of MacArthur over the administration's unwillingness to carry the war to mainland China. Although the war lasted another two years, until the summer of 1953, the outcome of early 1951 was definitive: a stalemate, and an American commitment to containment that accepted the de facto reality of two Koreas and explains why forty thousand US troops remain in South Korea today.

*Soviet Policy.* From the time of the tsars Korea has been a concern of Russian security; the Russo-Japanese War of 1905 was fought in part over the disposition of the Korean peninsula. It has often been thought that the Russians saw Korea as a gateway to the Pacific, and especially to warm-water ports. Furthermore Korea had one of Asia's oldest communist movements. Thus, it would seem that postwar Korea was a great concern to the Soviet Union; many have therefore thought that its policy was a simple matter of sovietizing northern Korea, setting up a puppet state, and then directing it to unify Korea by force in 1950.

We can infer changes in Soviet policy toward North Korea by examining turning points in 1946 and 1949. During World War II Stalin was mostly silent in discussions with Roosevelt about Korea, tending either to humor him and his pet trusteeship projects (which Stalin no doubt thought were naive), or to say that the Koreans would want independence. From 1941 to 1945 Kim Il Sung (Kim Il-sŏng) and other guerrillas were given sanctuary in Sino-Russian border towns near Khabarovsk, given training at a small school, and dispatched as agents into Japanese-held territory. Yet they were not given military equipment, and the Soviet Union maintained formal neutrality with Japan until August 1945. Although the US State Department suspected that as many as thirty thousand Koreans were being trained as Soviet guerrilla agents, postwar North Korean documents captured by MacArthur show that there could not have been more than a few hundred of such agents. When the Soviets occupied Korea north of the 38th parallel in August 1945, they brought these Koreans (often termed Soviet-

Koreans, even though most of them were not Soviet citizens) with them. Kim Il Sung did not appear in North Korea until October 1945, however, and what he did in the two months after the Japanese surrender is not known.

In retrospect Soviet policy seems more tentative and reactive than American policy in the South; Soviet power at that time in the Far East was flexible, and resulted in the withdrawal of Soviet forces from Manchuria in early 1946. A Soviet Union utterly devastated by the war seemed much more concerned with Eastern Europe.

In 1946 this position changed. In February an Interim People's Committee led by Kim Il Sung became the first central government in North Korea; in March a revolutionary land reform ensued, dispossessing landlords without compensation; in August a powerful political party (called the North Korean Worker's Party) came to dominate politics; and in the fall the first rudiments of a Northern army appeared. Powerful central agencies nationalized major industries (they had of course mostly been owned by the Japanese) and began a two-year economic program on the Soviet model of central targets and the priority of heavy industry. Nationalist and Christian leaders were ousted from all but pro forma participation in politics, and Cho Man-sik was held under house arrest. Kim Il Sung and his allies dominated the press, eliminating newspapers that contained opposition sentiments.

It was in the period from 1947 to 1948 that Soviet domination of North Korea was at its height. The Soviets in particular sought to involve the North in a quasi-colonial relationship in which Korean raw materials such as tungsten and gold were exchanged for Soviet manufactures. It is interesting to note that they appear to have sought to keep Chinese Communist influence out of Korea: Kim Il Sung and other guerrillas had fought alongside the Chinese and had often joined the Chinese Communist Party in the 1930s, but in the late 1940s Chinese ideology (meaning Maoism) had to be infiltrated into Korean newspapers and books.

At the end of 1948 the Soviets withdrew their occupation forces from North Korea, signaling changes that were to come in 1949. This decision contrasted strongly with Soviet policies in Eastern Europe. In contrast, no Soviet troops were stationed in Korea again. At the same time, tens of thousands of Korean soldiers who fought in the Chinese civil war filtered back to Korea. This little known but terribly important episode signaled the beginning of the end of Soviet dominance; all through 1949 tough, crack troops with a Chinese, not a Soviet,

experience and orientation returned to be integrated with the Korean People's Army (KPA).

The Soviets kept advisers in the Korean government and military and continued to trade and to ship weaponry to North Korea. Perhaps they hoped to dominate both North Korea and China and establish a monolithic transnational communist unit in northeast Asia. Without military forces, however, and facing strong leaders like Mao Zedong and Kim Il Sung, they could not do so. The year 1949 therefore was a watershed in Soviet policy, when North Korea got some maneuvering room and when the Soviets sought to distance themselves from the perceived volatility of Kim and his allies.

***The Emergence of Two Koreas.*** The greatest mistake one can make in evaluating post–World War II Korea is to assume that Koreans were so malleable that they could be molded and manipulated by the Americans and the Soviets. Much of the focus has been on great-power actions, however, and Korea is seen as an empty "black box," within which Koreans got things done to them. Had there been no Soviet or American occupation, the effects of the colonial period would nonetheless have assured deep divisions within Korean society. The great powers did not invent communism and capitalism; Koreans had begun discovering both in the 1920s if not earlier. The US and the USSR could not automatically control the situation in Korea; Koreans proved recalcitrant even to violent pressures. We may see this pattern in the emergence of separate regimes.

The great powers would choose 1948 as the year when separate regimes emerged—but that is only because the Americans and the Soviets take credit for the establishment of the ROK and the DPRK. Actually, both regimes were in place, unofficially, by the end of 1946. They each had bureaucratic, police, military, and political power. They each had preempted, or at least shaped, the Korea policies of the powers.

In the South, the actual planning for a separate regime began in the last months of 1945. Syngman Rhee, a seventy-year-old patriot who had lived in the United States since 1911 (when he earned a doctoral degree at Princeton), returned in October with the backing of General MacArthur and elements in military and intelligence circles in the United States. A crusty and conservative man of the older generation, he was also a master politician. Within weeks he had won control of conservative and traditionalist factions, many of them from the landed class; he also had found friends among Americans worried about the spread of radicalism, who needed little convincing that Rhee and his allies would be a bulwark against the spread of communism.

In short order the leaders of the American occupation and Rhee began to make plans for a separate administration of southern Korea, for a southern military (which began training in January 1946), for the reestablishment of a national police force, and for a "koreanization" of the governmental bureaucracy left by the Japanese (which was substantially completed by the end of 1946). The Americans staffed the military, the police, and the bureaucracy mostly with Koreans who had experience in the colonial regime; they thought they had no other choice, but in so doing the regime took on a reactionary cast that severely weakened it in its competition with the North.

American power was so great that it was able to influence the formal rules of the game of South Korean politics, and thus the 1948 constitution was a relatively liberal document, guaranteeing basic freedoms of speech and press, a vociferous legislature, and periodic elections. It had certain critical loopholes as well, allowing Rhee to proclaim emergencies or use draconian national security laws to deal with his opposition.

The North Korean regime also emerged de facto in 1946, and also looked forward to a military expedition. Within a year of the liberation the North had a powerful political party, a budding army, and the mixed blessing of a single leader named Kim Il Sung. Although Kim had rivals, we can date his emergence—and his particular style of leadership—from mid-1946. By then he had placed close, loyal allies at the heart of power. His prime assets were his background, his skills at organization, and his ideology.

Kim's ideology tended to be revolutionary-nationalist rather than communist, also from the beginning in 1946. He talked about Korea, not about the socialist international. He spoke of unification, not national division. He discussed nationalism, not Marxism. He distributed land to the tillers instead of collectivizing it (at least until the Korean War began). One can also see in the late 1940s the beginnings of the *chuch'e* ideology (a doctrine stressing self-reliance and independence) so ubiquitous in North Korea today.

Kim's great political weapon was his control of the party and the army. He systematically filtered his allies through the commanding heights of each; when the Korean People's Army was founded in February 1948 it was said to have grown out of Kim's guerrilla army and to have inherited its "revolutionary tradition." When masses of Koreans who fought with the Chinese Communists came back to Korea in 1949, and thereby threatened Kim's power, he had himself declared *suryŏng,* or "supreme leader," a designation that had only been used for Stalin until that time and that continues to be his sobriquet.

*Military Engagement.* For Americans, the outbreak of war in a distant, little-known country was a sudden shock. They assumed that the war started on 25 June 1950, with its antecedents relatively unimportant. They viewed the war as an unprovoked, aggressive attack across an international boundary, directed by the Soviets, an interpretation that remains dominant in American literature on the subject.

In the Korean view, however, the war started in 1945, not 1950; the events of 1950 to 1953 differed only in degree from what had preceded them. Apart from government propaganda, they emphasize the civil aspects of the war. South Korea remains fixated on the question of who started the war, since it has been the winner of that argument for forty years. The war was primarily a civil war, however, fought over the same issues that had existed between North and South since 1945. Furthermore, except for propaganda purposes no Koreans saw the 38th parallel as any more than a temporary boundary fixed by foreigners.

Before the war extensive armed conflict had gripped the border between North and South and the mountainous interior of the South. After sporadic and scattered peasant rebellion between 1945 and 1947, guerrilla warfare began in 1948—first on Cheju Island, then spreading to the mainland after the Communist-aided Yŏsu-Sunch'ŏn Rebellion in October 1948. The Chŏlla provinces in the southwest, parts of the Kyŏngsang provinces in the southeast, the mountainous rib in the middle of the peninsula, and the remote upper east coast were all affected by guerrilla warfare. From 1948 to 1950, generally speaking, the guerrillas tended to be strong in the spring and summer and weak in the fall and winter, the result of severe weather and blockades of mountainous areas by American-advised counterinsurgency forces. Sometimes as many as one thousand guerrillas and counterguerrillas would be killed in a single week; several tens of thousands had died by June 1950.

It would appear that a major suppression campaign in the fall and winter of 1949 to 1950 decimated the remaining guerrillas in the South, which may have suggested the virtues of a conventional warfare strategy to the North. The northern timing was also affected by the return of Koreans who had fought in China. Declassified documentation makes clear that in 1949 the southern forces caused many provocations and battles along the 38th parallel, as did the northerners; but in 1949 the North was not ready to fight.

Although sufficient documentation does not exist to prove the point, it appears now that the Soviets did not order Kim to attack the South; if they did have a role in the events of June 1950, it more likely was an attempt to suck American power into a bloody and useless war, and to pit China against the United States and thereby assure China's orientation toward the socialist bloc. In any case, when Kim's regime was nearly extinguished in the fall of 1950, the Soviets did very little to save it. China picked up the pieces, and the North Koreans have never forgotten it. From this moment on, it was clear that North Korea treasured its relationship with China, whereas it dealt with the Soviet Union because it had to do so, not because it wanted to do so.

Although there remain many murky aspects to the Korean War, it is likely that the frontal attack in June 1950 was mainly Kim's decision, and that the key enabling factor was the availability of as many as one hundred thousand troops with battle experience in China. When the Rhee regime, with American military advisers, largely eliminated the guerrilla threat in the winter of 1949 to 1950, the civil war moved into a conventional phase. Had the Americans stayed out, the northern regime would have won easily. With battle-hardened veterans from the Chinese civil war, the Korean People's Army was a formidable force in the early stages of the war.

The KPA swept down and captured Seoul in three days. As it marched on Taejŏn it encountered American forces for the first time, and devastated them. The battle of Taejŏn was a great victory for the North, as the KPA sent Americans reeling with envelopment tactics that began with what seemed to be large frontal assaults, and continued with large numbers of Koreans bypassing American forces on either side and then surrounding them. Contrary to previous literature on the Korean War, it now appears that during this phase of the war large numbers of southern guerrillas and irregulars helped the KPA, which became a great problem for American and South Korean forces.

The northerners swept through the populous Chŏlla provinces in two or three days, as southern resistance collapsed in this region where the southern left had been strong. Two great columns then marched on Pusan from the southwest and the northeast. MacArthur threw every available resource into holding the Pusan perimeter, which ran roughly from P'ohang on the east coast to just north of Taegu along the Naktong River and down to Masan on the southern coast. Most of August 1950 was consumed with defending these positions, the North Koreans seeking to mass enough soldiers to punch through. Daily situation reports make clear that the tide started to turn only when the Americans developed a preponderance of numbers; the perimeter still barely held back the onslaught in mid-September.

On 15 September the Americans again landed at Inch'ŏn, five years nearly to the day after they had first arrived. This time a massive amphibious landing devastated North Korean forces defending this important port city; after a week of very tough and bloody fighting, Seoul was recaptured by American forces. American commanders then sought to close a trap, marching down from Seoul and north from the Pusan perimeter. The trap closed on tens of thousands of footsoldiers, but all important KPA officers got away, as did large numbers of soldiers who began guerrilla warfare. After Inch'ŏn, some ten thousand guerrillas remained in the Chŏllas, and about forty thousand in the region of the 38th parallel between Ch'unch'ŏn and Wŏnsan.

President Truman approved a document authorizing the march north in late September. By 1 October South Korean units were already crossing the parallel; they marched almost unimpeded up the east coast. The American march on P'yŏngyang was slower going, because the North Koreans needed time to evacuate the capital. The high leadership escaped to a mountain fastness near Kanggye, apparently determined to fight a protracted guerrilla war against the American and South Korean forces. In what most historians have taken to be a major blunder, MacArthur split his commands and columns as they marched toward the Yalu River, making communication between the Tenth Army in the east and the Eighth Army in the west very difficult.

In the fourth week of October, the combined forces reached the Yalu River border with China near Manp'ojin. Suddenly fresh Chinese troops and Koreans who had been held across the border in Manchuria entered the war, cutting up South Korean units particularly badly and causing a collapse along the entire front. American forces fell back quickly and regrouped. Just as suddenly, the Chinese forces disappeared.

In late November, MacArthur again pushed to

the Yalu, launching what he called a "reconnaissance in force" that was, in reality, a major offensive to reach the Chinese border. At this point as many as two hundred thousand Chinese "volunteers" entered the fray, clearing the North of American and South Korean forces in about ten days. MacArthur's forces also faced heavy attacks from guerrillas in the midpeninsula region, necessitating a major amphibious evacuation through the northern port of Hamhŭng. By 1 January 1951 Seoul was again threatened as the Chinese and the reinvigorated North Koreans launched a major New Year's offensive. Seoul fell again on 4 January and for a while it seemed as if American forces would have to evacuate the peninsula.

The failure to predict the Chinese entry into the war remains one of the great controversies of the period. MacArthur and his allies claimed that although they knew there were hundreds of thousands of Chinese soldiers just across the border, they could not predict the intention on the part of the Chinese to use them. In this they are largely correct; intelligence agencies in Washington, including the Central Intelligence Agency, were not much better and tended to predict that the Chinese would not come in. It is also the case, however, that MacArthur may not really have worried much about Chinese intervention, both because he underestimated their fighting skills and thought American forces would devastate them, and because he wanted to extend the war to China. He advocated the use of atomic weapons against the Chinese, and the invasion of South China by Nationalist armies on Taiwan.

It is likely, however, that future historians who did not live through the Truman-MacArthur controversy will be kinder toward MacArthur. Much of the existing literature is a victor's literature, written by people who tend to be anti-MacArthur. Declassified documentation shows that almost all high officials backed the march into the North, hardly anyone predicted the Chinese involvement, and almost no one understood the close, historical connections between the Chinese and the North Korean leadership. Furthermore, those who emerged from the war with unblemished reputations, such as Truman and General Matthew Ridgway, now seem less virtuous.

We now know that Truman was ready to use atomic weapons against the Chinese if major reinforcements entered the war in the spring of 1950; that in the fall of 1951 Truman authorized Operation Hudson Harbor, which involved the simulation of atomic attacks on North Korea, sending lone B-29s to drop dummy A-bombs; and that Ridgway asked for approval to use chemical weapons on the Chinese, only to be told by MacArthur that they were against the laws of warfare. In light of this information, MacArthur may not look bad in the hindsight of historians not caught up in the controversies of the 1950s.

From the spring of 1951 to July 1953, a vicious, bloody positional war ensued, with enormous losses particularly on the northern side; bombing campaigns eliminated most northern cities, and in 1953 even the irrigation system was attacked through heavy bombing runs on large dams. Still, when the armistice finally was signed in 1953 not much territory had changed hands since mid-1951. Many historians tend to think that the twin events of Stalin's death in March 1953 and the new Eisenhower administration's threat to use atomic weapons made the final negotiations possible. The South Korean leadership resisted the armistice, with Syngman Rhee releasing prisoners of war to disrupt armistice negotiations; the ROK never signed the armistice. The great powers and the belligerents attempted to negotiate a peace treaty at Geneva in 1954, but that came to nought and the peace continues to be held only by the armistice agreement and the continuing confrontation of masses of soldiers and armor along the demilitarized zone.

When the war ended, it ended a decade of extraordinary ferment and change. Both Koreas had watched as a virtual holocaust ravaged their country and turned the vibrant expectations of 1945 into a nightmare. The point to remember, perhaps, is that it was a civil war and, as a British diplomat once said, "every country has a right to have its War of the Roses." The true tragedy was not the war itself, for a civil conflict purely among Koreans might have resolved the extraordinary tensions generated by colonialism and national division. The tragedy was that the war changed nothing: only the situation prior to the war was restored. The tensions and the problems remain unsolved.

[See also United Nations Commission for the Unification and Rehabilitation of Korea; Korea, Democratic People's Republic of; Korea, Republic of; Kim Il Sung; Rhee, Syngman; and MacArthur, Douglas A.]

Soon-sung Cho, *Korea in World Politics, 1940–1950* (1967). Bruce Cumings, *The Origins of the Korean War: Liberation and the Emergence of Separate Regimes, 1945–1947* (1981). Bruce Cumings, ed., *Child of Conflict: The Korean-American Relationship, 1943–1953* (1983). Gregory Henderson, *Korea: The Politics of the Vortex*

(1968). George McCune, *Korea Today* (1950). E. Grant Meade, *American Military Government in Korea* (1951). Glenn Paige, *The Korean Decision* (1968). Robert Scalapino and Chong-sik Lee, *Communism in Korea*, 2 vols. (1972). Dae-sook Suh, *The Korean Communist Movement, 1918–1948* (1967).                BRUCE CUMINGS

KORYŎ, the medieval kingdom that ruled over a territory very similar to that of modern Korea for more than four and a half centuries, from 918 to 1392. It is from the name *Koryŏ* that the English *Korea* originates. Koryŏ marks the transition from the Buddhist Silla (57 BCE–935 CE) to the Confucian Chosŏn (Yi; 1392–1910).

Founded in 918 by Wang Kŏn of the state of T'aebong (901–918), Koryŏ unified the Later Three Kingdoms in 936. Wang Kŏn (T'aejo; r. 918–943) was a son of a local chief with an obscure maritime family background from a remote border area (present Kaesŏng) and built his power base on the maritime interests, but he actively sought alliances with many local strongmen of the Silla aristocratic, landed interests, eventually forming an alignment with the beleaguered Silla court, then under attack from Later Paekche (892–936). This alignment drew the nobility of Silla closer to his camp and facilitated its voluntary submission to him in 1935. Wang Kŏn's policy also resulted in a massive absorption of Silla nobles into the Koryŏ ruling strata, creating a power group whose background and interests were basically incompatible with those of maritime upstarts like himself. The conflicting interests of the two principal power groups eventually found expression in a succession struggle that followed the founder's death in 943. The outcome of this struggle saw the successive ascendancy of kings Chŏngjong (r. 945–949) and Kwangjong (r. 949–975), two princely brothers around whom the Silla aristocratic interests rallied, signaling the resurgence of the former nobility as the dominant group in the new dynasty.

The succession struggle also revealed a potential threat to the throne by Wang Kŏn's independent generals. Dynastic consolidation occurred only after King Kwangjong strengthened royal authority through a series of drastic measures aimed at eliminating the independent power bases of generals and creating a centralized civilian bureaucracy loyal to the throne. His actions, particularly his successful introduction of the Chinese (Confucian) civil service examinations for the central bureaucracy and his institution of a separate, competitive ecclesiastical

FIGURE 1. *Wine Pot.* Korean ceramics of the Koryŏ period (918–1392) are famous for their celadon glaze. Height 25.4 cm.

examination system for the Buddhist clergy, moreover had the effect of facilitating the resurgence of the aristocracy of Silla, since the former nobles were as yet the most educated and best qualified group to take the examinations. These examinations, once successfully institutionalized, tended to solidify state control over the two ideologies vital to dynastic governance and also to differentiate the respective social function of the two creeds. Although Buddhism continued to enjoy strong royal patronage under Koryŏ, it was Confucianism that was upheld as the new dynasty's political ideology because of increasing reliance on Confucian literati for the management of government. Throughout Koryŏ, Buddhism therefore flourished more as the spiritual custodian of the kingdom, while the dynastic administration of temporal affairs was, except for a few notable cases, left in the hands of the Confucian bureaucracy. [*See also* Korean State Examination System.]

The process of confucianization of the Koryŏ government, once set in, was accelerated by subsequent government reorganizations that were undertaken before the military coup of 1170. The government

so built featured a structure and nomenclature co-
piously borrowed from those of (mostly Song dynasty) China. In the operation of its government,
however, Koryŏ departed considerably from the
Chinese model. The foremost among the forces compelling such a departure were apparently the nobility, who were the principal bearers of the indigenous
sociopolitical tradition that Koryŏ inherited from
Silla. The new ruling elites, while emancipated from
the strict Silla *kolp'um* ("bone-rank") class restrictions and transformed into the novel Confucian literati under Koryŏ, still formed a tightly knit social
group practicing intermarriage among themselves
and with members of the new royal family. Protected by an array of special privileges, this elite
group gradually evolved into a kind of oligarchy
virtually monopolizing government power. All other
groups had to be content with lesser social functions
assigned to them, thus fixing everyone's station in
society.

*Military Rule.* An abrupt change that shattered
the oligarchical grip over government power came
when a military coup led by the commanding general of the Royal Guard Regiment and his trusted
lieutenants succeeded in 1170; nearly all the oligarchs and their close associates were killed. In a
bold move the coup leaders scrapped the Koryŏ system of civil supremacy by appointing themselves to
the positions of power and eradicating the socioeconomic discriminations to which they had been
subjected under the civilian dominance. Thus, they
ushered in a new era of military supremacy only to
be faced with serious problems arising from abortive
civilian countercoups and widespread uprisings of
the social underdogs, as well as incessant infighting
among generals, problems that they were ill-prepared to handle. They lacked the experience, training, or vision necessary to run a government as complex and sophisticated as the one built by their
former civilian masters. It was a quarter of a century
before they could put together a semblance of government and restore order. The leadership for this
finally came in 1196, from Ch'oe Ch'ung-hŏn
(1149–1219), a scion of a military family, who with
his brother purged all rival generals and assumed
power. He and his son Choe U, who succeeded him,
energetically pursued policies to reintroduce to the
service of the military-dominated government able
civilian literati trained in Confucian statecraft, thus
establishing an effective administrative structure under the control of the Ch'oe house. [*See also* Ch'oe
Ch'ung-hŏn.]

Under the rule of the Ch'oe house, the dynasty
and its administrative machinery remained intact
but were subject to the dictates of the Ch'oe leaders.
Important government decisions, including personnel appointments, were made by the Ch'oe dictator,
assisted by his literati retainers and then transmitted
to the dynastic bureaucracy for implementation; the
Koryŏ king was relegated to the position of a mere
figurehead. To back up their rule, the Ch'oe dictators built an elite troop of bodyguards that displaced
the old royal guard regiments and a new private
army in place of the dynastic central army, both of
which were under their personal command. They
also acquired a vast manorial estate and a huge work
force of tenants and slaves attached to it. Some historians see the makings of an incipient feudalism in
Korea in the pattern of Ch'oe rule, particularly in
the management of its household administration.
Whether or not this is so, the period inaugurated an
era of institutional development remarkably independent of the Chinese model. The upheavals of the
period also produced an unprecedented degree of
social mobility through the rise of the military masters and their lowborn retainers, and by extensive
intermarriage between military and civilian families.

*Foreign Invasions and Mongol Conquest.* The
demise of the Ch'oe house came when the fourth
Ch'oe dictator, Ch'oe Ŭi, was assassinated in 1258
after nearly thirty years of unsuccessful resistance
against the invincible Mongol invaders. Even before
the Mongol incursions Koryŏ had suffered from a
number of foreign invasions. None left as lasting an
imprint on Koryŏ, however, as that of the Mongols.
The first foreign threat appeared when the Khitan
(Liao) destroyed Parhae (Chinese, Bohai) in 926 and
invaded Koryŏ in 993, 1010, and 1018. Koryŏ's firm
resolve to defend its territory, coupled with skillful
diplomacy, however, held these invaders in check,
producing intermittent tributary relations to the
Khitan and corresponding suspension of contact
with the Song, the Khitan's principal adversary in
China. When the Jurchen (Jin) rose in Manchuria
in the twelfth century, Koryŏ again fended off the
new threat by accepting settlements similar to the
ones worked out with the Khitan earlier.

In the following century the Mongols appeared
on the scene; Koryŏ first joined hands with them to
eliminate their common enemy, the Khitan (1219),
but the alliance did not last long because Koryŏ
resisted Mongol demands for exorbitant tribute.
When formal relations ruptured in 1224, the Mongol invasion followed in 1231, and Koryŏ was
forced to surrender. The Ch'oe dictator, refusing to
accept a permanent capitulation, fled to Kanghwa

Island near the mouth of the Han River and took with him the entire ruling structure including the royal court. Protected by a narrow channel separating the island from the peninsula, they braced themselves for a long drawn-out resistance against the sea-fearing Mongols, thus provoking further incursions. The Mongols launched six more major invasions that destroyed everything in their path, but they could not bring the military dictator in the island fortress to his knees. The Ch'oe dictators, relying on coastal transport for provisions collected in the peninsula, withstood the onslaughts for nearly three decades, until war-weary civilian officials in collusion with a trusted slave-lieutenant of the Ch'oe house assassinated the last dictator and sued for peace. Before peace could be restored, however, the civilian advocates of peace, with the aid of the Mongol troops, had to crush the resistance of military diehards opposed to capitulation (1273). [See also Mongol Empire: Mongol Invasions of Korea.]

Koryŏ's final submission transformed the dreaded Mongol domination into harsh reality. Once back in its old capital, the Koryŏ court was compelled to squeeze out of the ruins of the war-torn country the provisions, ships, and soldiers that the new Mongol (Yuan) overlord demanded for its ill-fated invasions of Japan in 1274 and 1281. Even after the failure of those invasions the Mongols maintained their expeditionary headquarters, now as an instrument of control, and exacted cessions of northern frontier territories and Cheju Island, in addition to exorbitant annual tribute. Koryŏ's submission also produced an imperial grant for the new Koryŏ king to marry a Mongol princess—a practice that all subsequent Koryŏ kings were obliged to follow, thus making Koryŏ a "son-in-law" country of the Mongol emperor. The Mongol court thereafter made all Koryŏ crown princes reside in the Mongol capital until they ascended the Koryŏ throne.

This practice further facilitated the deracination of the Koryŏ monarch. Koryŏ seemed no more than an appendage to the Mongol empire as the Koryŏ kings during this period became more Mongol than they were Korean, and some preferred to stay in the Mongol capital, ruling their kingdom through messengers or by proxy. In time Mongol influence also inevitably permeated through the Koryŏ establishment, particularly since knowledge of Mongolian language and customs became a virtual precondition for success in official careers. Still, the period was not without positive contributions for Koryŏ. For one thing, Chinese culture once again began to flow into Korea, transmitting among other things Neo-Confucian studies, which spread among the Koryŏ literati, furnishing an innovative ideology for late Koryŏ reformers to follow in reinvigorating their government.

The Koryŏ leader who launched a bold assault to rid the Koryŏ government of the Mongol interference and who produced a significant, albeit limited, result was King Kongmin (r. 1351–1374). At a time when Mongol power was weakened by internal rebellions, he destroyed the agencies of Mongol control by dismantling their expeditionary headquarters in Koryŏ and recovering the northeastern territory still under the direct Mongol administration. However, when he tried to scale down the large landholdings of the Koryŏ ruling elites that had developed under the aegis of the Mongol court, his attempt backfired, costing not only the royal will for reform but also the life of the reformer-king himself. Nevertheless, King Kongmin's crusade, so far as it had succeeded, laid the groundwork for the subsequent resurgence of a reform movement, this time spearheaded by the Neo-Confucian literati of late Koryŏ who had secured their initial foothold in the Koryŏ goverment as a result of the king's pioneering efforts.

**Neo-Confucianism and the Rise of the Yi Dynasty.** The Neo-Confucian demand for sweeping reform arose in late Koryŏ when the military buildup to meet the rampant Japanese pirate raids then ravaging the coast became a paramount issue in goverment circles. The demand took on an added urgency as forays of Chinese rebels challenging Mongol rule increasingly spilled over deep inside Koryŏ territory, drawing the reluctant Koryŏ government into the fluid hegemonic war being waged in China between the newly risen Chinese Ming and the enfeebled Mongol Yuan. After some vacillation, the Koryŏ government decided to dispatch its army to attack the Ming forces in southwestern Manchuria to stop the persistent Ming maneuvering designed to bring about Koryŏ's submission, and it named two of its best generals to lead the expedition. One of the two, General Yi Sŏng-gye, had open doubts, however, about the wisdom of the decision. When he reached the Yalu River amid heavy monsoon rains, his poorly equipped forces were seriously depleted by desertion and disease. Convinced of the futility of carrying on any further with the apparently doomed expedition, he staged a mutiny, marched his troops back to the Koryŏ capital and took control of the government by overthrowing those in power and replacing the reigning monarch with his brother (1388). Yi then threw his support behind the Neo-Confucian reformers and carried out sweeping reforms, in the process dealing a crushing blow to the Koryŏ establishment, particularly its ruling elite and their allies in the Buddhist monasteries.

Yi, a battle-tested general with a family power base in the formerly Mongol-controlled northeastern frontier area, was, like most reformers, a relative newcomer to Koryŏ government circles, sharing little vested interest with the entrenched aristocratic families who were the principal targets of the reform. When the reformers completed their work, culminating in the reallocation of all landholdings, ostensibly to rejuvenate the financial health of the government but really to break the backbone of the old economic order, they had undermined the very foundation of the dynasty.

The demise of Koryŏ waited only for the fabrication of political justification for the enthronement of Yi Sŏng-gye. The conspirators behind Yi's enthronement found the last obstacle to their plot the Neo-Confucian literati, whose faith in the principles of dynastic legitimacy and loyalty made them the last preservers of the dying dynasty. Although this obstacle was mercilessly removed by political assassinations and banishments, the founders of the Chosŏn (Yi) dynasty could not bury these principles with their stubborn defenders, thus sowing the seed of ideological dissension that plagued the dynasty for centuries to come. Led by the Neo-Confucian literati, life and society under the Chosŏn were to undergo a radical transformation, in which many age-old customs and ideas such as endogamy, equal inheritance for sons and daughters, and aristocratic patronage of Buddhism were forsaken. In their places were substituted novel practices of Chinese origin insisted on by orthodox Neo-Confucian doctrinaires.

[See also Neo-Confucianism in Korea; Yi Sŏng-gye; and Yi Dynasty.]

William E. Henthorn, Korea: The Mongol Invasions (1963). H. W. Kang, "Institutional Borrowing: The Case of the Chinese Civil Service Examination System," Journal of Asian Studies 34.1 (November 1974): 109–125; and "The First Succession Struggle of Koryŏ in 945: A Reinterpretation," Journal of Asian Studies 36.3 (May 1977): 411–428. Ki-baik Lee, A New History of Korea, translated by Edward W. Wagner with Edward J. Shultz (1984), chaps. 5–8. James B. Palais, "Land Tenure in Korea: Tenth to Twelfth Centuries," Journal of Korean Studies 4 (1982–1983): 73–205. Michael C. Rogers, "The Regularization of Koryŏ-Chin Relations (1116–1131)," Central Asiatic Journal 6.1 (1961): 51–84. Edward J. Shultz, "Military Revolt in Koryŏ: The 1170 Coup d'etat," Korean Studies 3 (1979): 19–48.

HUGH W. KANG

**KORYŎ TRIPITAKA**, Buddhist canon of the Korean kingdom of Koryŏ (918–1392), one of the major testaments to the flourishing Buddhist culture of medieval Korea. This collection consists of 81,258 individual woodblocks, each approximately two feet three inches long, ten inches wide, and one inch thick, from which rubbings were taken to produce printed editions of the canon.

Two separate carvings of the Tripitaka were undertaken during the Koryŏ dynasty: the first, begun in 1011 and completed some years thereafter, was destroyed by the Mongols in 1231; the second, made between 1236 and 1251, is still extant. Its xylographs are stored at Haein Monastery, as they have been since 1398. The editor in chief of the second carving was the scholar-monk Sugi (fl. mid-thirteenth century), who followed exacting editorial standards in the canon's production. Sugi's *Koryŏ-kuk shinjo taejang kyojŏng pyŏllok (Supplementary Record of Collation Notes to the New Carving of the Tripitaka of the Koryŏ Kingdom)* gives a precise account of variant readings found in the earlier Chinese and Korean editions of the Tripitaka that he used in collating his new edition. As such it is a major source of information for East Asian Buddhist textual criticism. Modern critical editions of the Chinese Buddhist canon, including the definitive Taishō Tripitaka, take the Koryŏ Tripitaka as their *textus receptus*.

[See also Buddhism: Buddhism in Korea.]

Kai-hyon Ahn, "Publication of Buddhist Scriptures in the Koryŏ Period," in Buddhist Culture in Korea, edited by Shin-yong Chun (1974). Lewis R. Lancaster and Sung-bae Park, eds., The Korean Buddhist Canon: A Descriptive Catalogue (1979), introduction. Nak-choon Paik, "Tripiṭaka Koreana," Transactions of the Royal Asiatic Society, Korean Branch 32 (1951): 62–73.

ROBERT E. BUSWELL, JR.

**KOSALA**, ancient Indian regional kingdom, with Sravasti, Saketa, and Ayodhya as its chief cities, that included most of the districts in the mideastern parts of modern Uttar Pradesh. During the sixth and fifth centuries BCE Kosala was one of the four major states that contended for supremacy over the North Indian heartland. King Prasenjit and the merchant leader Anathapindika were patrons of Shakyamuni Buddha, who spent most of his rainy seasons at Sravasti. Ayodhya, which was the capital of Rama, the celebrated hero-king in the *Ramayana*, continues to thrive as one of the most sacred cities of India. Archaeology has confirmed the antiquity of both the cities.

After the distintegration of the Maurya empire Ayodhya became the center of the region and became a local state with its own coinage. It later flourished as a metropolis in the Gupta period. Vasubandhu, a famous Buddhist philosopher, hailed from the city.

[*See also* Buddhism: An Overview.]

R. C. Majumdar, ed., *The Age of Imperial Unity* (1968).                                          A. K. NARAIN

**KOTELAWALA, SIR JOHN LIONEL** (b. 1897), prime minister of Sri Lanka 1953–1956, best known for his outspoken anticommunist talks at the 1955 Bandung Conference. Son of a policeman who married into great wealth, Kotelawala was a sportsman, planter, and Ceylon light infantry officer who was regularly elected to the State Council and Parliament by overwhelming majorities. As prime minister his intemperate lifestyle alienated many Buddhists and was an important factor in the victory of the Buddhist-oriented Sri Lanka Freedom Party (SLFP) in 1956.

[*See also* Bandung Conference *and* Sri Lanka Freedom Party.]

John Lionel Kotelawala, *An Asian Prime Minister's Story* (1956).                              PATRICK PEEBLES

**KOT MASSACRE,** the event that catapulted Jung Bahadur Rana (1816–1877) and his family into the preeminent rule of Nepal. Taking advantage of divisiveness in the royal family and rivalries at court, Jung Bahadur orchestrated the murder of twenty-nine prominent noblemen, including the entire Council of State, on the night of 14 September 1846, thus positioning himself to be appointed prime minister. The event takes its name from the site of the massacre, the Kot ("armory") near the royal palace in Kathmandu's Hanuman Dhoka Square.

[*See also* Jung Bahadur Rana.]

B. L. Joshi and L. Rose, *Democratic Innovations in Nepal* (1966).                           RICHARD ENGLISH

**KŌTOKU SHŪSUI** (Denjirō; 1871–1911), Japanese socialist and anarchist thinker of the Meiji period. Kōtoku was born in the small town of Nakamura in Kōchi Prefecture. Educated in local schools, and subsequently by Nakae Chōmin in Osaka and Tokyo, he developed an early interest in the Popular Rights (Jiyū Minken) Movement. A young journalist of considerable literary talent, his early career was made in writing for various magazines and newspapers.

By the late 1890s Kōtoku had become interested in socialism. In 1897 he joined the Society for the Study of Social Problems (Shakai Mondai Kenkyūkai), and in 1901 he helped found the Social Democratic Party. The same year he published his first major book, *Nijū seiki no kaibutsu teikoku shugi (Imperialism: The Specter of the Twentieth Century)*. This work was followed in 1903 by *Shakai shugi shinzui (The Quintessence of Socialism)*, the most important Japanese work on socialism written before the Russo-Japanese War of 1904–1905. A pacifist, he denounced the war against Russia in his *Heimin shimbun*. Jailed for these efforts, he left Japan for San Francisco in 1905, where he came into contact with Russian émigrés and members of the Industrial Workers of the World (IWW).

Under these influences Kōtoku shifted his position from socialism to anarchism and a belief in "direct action" and the general strike. In 1906 he split the Japanese socialist movement over these issues, and in 1910 his radical young followers plotted to assassinate the Meiji emperor. Although only peripherally involved, Kōtoku was thought of as the ideological leader of the group. Found guilty, he was executed along with eleven others in 1911.

[*See also* Jiyū Minken.]

F. G. NOTEHELFER

**KOTTE,** the principal Sri Lankan Sinhalese kingdom from the mid-fourteenth to the late sixteenth century. Throughout its history it was under severe external pressure, initially from the Tamil kingdom of the north, which Kotte successfully resisted and eventually repelled, and later from the Portuguese, to whom it ultimately succumbed by the end of the sixteenth century. Of the Kotte kings, Parakramabahu VI (1411–1467) was the last and most powerful Sinhalese monarch to rule the entire island.

The Kotte kingdom took its name from its capital, which was located in the interior a few miles south of Colombo. The city of Kotte remained the capital until 1565, when the port city of Colombo became the capital under Portuguese protection. Until very recently Kotte was a suburb of Colombo, but has regained some of its former importance now as the administrative capital of the island and the site of the new Parliamentary complex.

[*See also* Sri Lanka *and* Colombo.]

K. M. de Silva, *A History of Sri Lanka* (1981).

K. M. DE SILVA

KOXINGA. *See* Zheng Chenggong.

KŌYASAN (Mount Kōya) is the name popularly given to the Japanese monastery of Kongōbuji ("temple of the diamond peak"), established by Kūkai, the founder of Shingon Buddhism, in the year 816. Kōyasan is in Wakayama Prefecture and can be reached easily by train from Osaka.

After his return from China in 806 Kūkai headed several monasteries and established a reputation as a great religious leader at the imperial court in Heian. In 816 he petitioned the emperor to be allowed to establish a monastic center in the mountains to the southeast of the capital: "High peaks surround Kōya in all four directions. I should like to clear the wilderness in order to build a monastery there for the practice of meditation, for the benefit of the nation, and for those who desire to discipline themselves."

Throughout the middle ages Kōyasan remained the spiritual training center of Shingon Buddhism, while Tōji, or Kyōōgokokuji, in the capital served as the administrative center of the Shingon school. The construction of Kōyasan was completed by Kūkai's successors. His fame and the solicitations of wandering mendicants, *kōya hijiri,* brought generous donations from courtiers and commoners. Monastic buildings spread over the mountain top. A tradition quickly developed that Kūkai had not died but had entered a deep meditative trance (Sanskrit, *samadhi*) on Kōyasan. He is still believed to play the role of savior for those who are suffering and is expected to return to earth once again with the coming of the future Buddha, Maitreya. Pilgrims came from all over Japan to the site of his mausoleum, the Okuno-in, and many had the ashes of their deceased relatives buried there.

Kōyasan was granted land for "seven leagues" around the mountain, as well as estates, or *shōen,* scattered throughout Japan. Thus, the monastery quickly became one of the great landholders of medieval Japan. Like Enryakuji and other powerful Buddhist monasteries, Kōyasan had its own monastic army. There were factional disputes within the community and clashes with soldiers from the warrior class or the forces of other monasteries. In 1581 Kōyasan was attacked by the warrior Oda Nobunaga, whose power it had challenged. The monastery yielded to his successor, Toyotomi Hideyoshi. When Kōyasan no longer represented a threat to warrior power, Hideyoshi and the Tokugawa shoguns allowed it to recover some of its former glory. Kōyasan is still a thriving Buddhist community and major site of pilgrimage.

[*See also* Kūkai *and* Shingon.]

Yoshito S. Hakeda, *Kūkai: Major Works, Translated, With an Account of His Life and a Study of His Thought* (1972). Asakawa Kanichi, "The Life of a Monastic *shō* in Medieval Japan," in *Land and Society in Medieval Japan,* edited by The Japan Society for the Promotion of Science (1965).

MARTIN COLLCUTT

KRA ISTHMUS, the narrowest section of the Malay Peninsula, in southern Thailand between Kraburi in the west and Chumphon on the Gulf of Siam. The isthmus is approximately fifteen miles wide, with a maximum elevation of 250 feet, and may have been one of several important transpeninsula trade routes in ancient times. At various times since the late nineteenth century proposals to cut a canal across the isthmus have been made, but because of the expense and the potential damage to Singapore's maritime position, none has succeeded.

J. L. Christian, "The Kra Canal Fable," *Amerasia* 1 (1938): 559–563. A. J. Loftus, *Notes of a Journey Across the Isthmus of Kra* (1883). H. G. Quaritch-Wales, *Towards Angkor* (1937).

DAVID K. WYATT

KRATON, stockaded or walled compound containing the audience pavilions, enclosed courtyards, and living quarters of an Indonesian (especially Javanese) ruler *(ratu)* and his close followers. Usually constructed on a north-south alignment, the Javanese *kratons* were viewed as equivalent to cosmic *mandalas* (sacred circles) from which the power and energy *(shakti)* of a ruler flowed out into the surrounding countryside. Sometimes the royal compounds covered sizable areas and contained extensive populations. They were also bordered to the north and south by broad open squares *(alun-alun)* planted with twin boxed *waringin* (banyan) trees as symbols of the ruler's authority. Around the *kratons* were clustered the residences *(dalem)* of the royal princes and officials.

Thomas Stamford Raffles, *The History of Java* (1817).

PETER CAREY

KRISHNA (Sanskrit, "black"), one of the two principal deities of Hindu Vaishnavism and the eighth incarnation *(avatara)* of the god Vishnu.

The cult and mythology of Krishna developed

over a period of more than two thousand years; the early beginnings of his cult are unknown. Krishna seems to have been a tribal hero of the Yadava tribe of northwest India, who became identified in various ways with the minor Vedic deities Vasudeva, Narayana, and Vishnu. The worship of Krishna-Vasudeva dates to at least the second century BCE, with an inscription on a Besnagar column decreed by the Greek ambassador Heliodoros, a convert.

Within the text of the Indian epic *Mahabharata,* the figure of Krishna as crafty chief of the Yadavas, superhuman hero, charioteer of Arjuna, teacher of the *Bhagavadgita,* and incarnation of the supreme god Vishnu echoes his evolution to a status as a pan-Indian deity during this critical period of the formation of classical Hinduism. In the *Harivamsha,* the Puranas, and later medieval literature, the full life story of Krishna is developed with emphasis upon the child-god: he is portrayed among the cowherds, in his dance *(rasalila)* with the thousand *gopis* (cowherdesses), and especially in his relationship with Radha, an important source of theological and devotional inspiration for medieval and modern *bhakti* (devotional) movements.

[*See also* Bhakti *and* Vaishnavism.]

Jan Gonda, *Aspects of Early Vishnuism* (1954). Bimanbehari Majumdar, *Krsna in History and Legend* (1969).                    RANDOLPH M. THORNTON

## KRISHNA MENON, VENGALIL KRISHNAN

**KRISHNA MENON, VENGALIL KRISHNAN** (1896–1974), Indian diplomat and defence minister. He was born in Calicut into a well-established professional family. As a student he joined the Home Rule and scouting movements, and later was deeply influenced by socialist thought. In 1924 he went to England and became a vigorous spokesman for Indian nationalism. After Independence he became high commissioner in London (1947–1952), member of the delegation to the United Nations (1952–1961), and member of Parliament (1952–1967, 1972–1974). Menon often aroused controversy and strong feelings, but was consistently supported by Prime Minister Jawaharlal Nehru, a close intellectual friend. Appointed defence minister in 1957, he was forced out of office after India's losses in the 1962 war with China.

[*See also* Home Rule League *and* Nehru, Jawaharlal.]

T. J. S. George, *Krishna Menon: A Biography* (1964).
FRANKLIN A. PRESLER

**KSHATRIYA,** second in rank of the four *varnas,* or traditional social divisions delineated in ancient Hindu texts. The four traditional *varnas* (which common use treats as caste) are *brahman, kshatriya, vaishya,* and *shudra.* According to the *Rig Veda,* the *kshatriyas* arose from the arms of primordial man and were supposed to manage society through armed might.

Groups categorized as *kshatriya* have been economically and politically powerful as rulers, warriors, landlords, and farmers. In northern India, such prominent groups include Rajputs, Thakurs, and Jats; Marathas and Coorgs of southern India are also sometimes accorded *kshatriya* status.

The *kshatriya* model of behavior is based upon control of land and emphasizes the just exercise of physical power, honors glorious displays of valor, and usually allows consumption of meat and alcohol (in contrast to the more ascetic and nonviolent *brahman* ideals). Throughout history, many originally lower-ranking subcastes, or *jatis,* have prospered and aspired, often successfully, to membership in the prestigious *kshatriya* category.

[*See also* Brahman; Vaishya; Shudra; Untouchability; *and* Caste.]

Pauline Kolenda, *Caste in Contemporary India: Beyond Organic Solidarity* (1978). David G. Mandelbaum, *Society in India* (1970).          DORANNE JACOBSON

**KUALA LUMPUR,** Malaysia's largest city and federal capital. Kuala Lumpur began as a Chinese tin-mining settlement in the 1850s. From 1868 to 1885 Yap Ah Loy served as *kapitan China,* in effect, "mayor" of the mostly Chinese town. Yap's policies rescued Kuala Lumpur from the ruins of the Selangor Civil War and regenerated the area's tin industry. By the mid-1870s the town was booming, attracting many settlers.

In 1880 the new British rulers moved the Selangor state capital from Klang to the more central and flourishing Kuala Lumpur, and by 1884 it contained 4,000 inhabitants. Already separate neighborhoods for the Chinese, Indian, and varied Malayo-Muslim settlers had developed. In 1891, when Kuala Lumpur became capital of the Federated Malay States, its population had grown to 19,000 (73 percent Chinese). Rubber soon joined tin as a new source of wealth. By 1901 the British had abolished the office of *kapitan* but still tended to deal with the various ethnic communities through their wealthy elite. An appointed multiethnic Sanitary Board appeared in 1890. Kuala Lumpur also became a major educational center, eventually including several universities. To accommodate the growing Malayo-Muslim population, the first Malay land reserve (now Kampong Bahru) was created in 1899. By the 1930s a Malay community was coalescing out of mixed ethnic origins, a process that accelerated after World War II.

Kuala Lumpur became a municipality in 1948 and gained an elected council in 1952. In 1961, however, the council was replaced by an appointed federal commissioner. Population growth increased dramatically in the postwar years, a reflection of Kuala Lumpur's new status as federal capital, rapid commercial development, and an increasing challenge to Singapore's traditional political, economic, and sociocultural primacy in Malaya. In the early 1950s construction began on Petaling Jaya, a major satellite town six miles away that became a combination industrial center and middle-class suburb. By 1970 Kuala Lumpur's population had reached 452,000 (55 percent Chinese, 25 percent Malay, 19 percent Indian); Petaling Jaya contained another 93,000 people. In 1974 Kuala Lumpur was declared a federal territory, no longer administered as part of the state of Selangor.

[See also Malaysia.]

J. M. Gullick, "Kuala Lumpur, 1880–1895," *Journal of the Malayan Branch of the Royal Asiatic Society* 28 (1955), and *The Story of Early Kuala Lumpur* (1956). T. G. McGee, *The Southeast Asian City* (1967). Manjit Singh Sidhu, *Kuala Lumpur and its Population* (1978).

CRAIG A. LOCKARD

KUBLAI KHAN (1215–1294), Great Khan of the Mongol empire from 1260 to 1294 and the founder of the Yuan dynasty in China. Kublai's grandfather Genghis Khan, his uncle Ogedei, and his brother Mongke had conquered an enormous territory that eventually included North China, Central Asia, Korea, Persia, Russia, sections of the Middle East, and, briefly, even parts of Poland and Hungary. Kublai's significance stems from his efforts to govern, rather than to plunder, this vast newly conquered domain. He was the first of the Mongol khans who attempted to administer these lands, not simply to impose military control.

Kublai was born on 23 September 1215 to Tolui, Genghis Khan's son, and Sorghaghtani Beki, a Nestorian Christian noblewoman from the Kereit tribe. Because Tolui often accompanied his father on military campaigns, he spent little time with his son. He and his wife endured long separations, and she had the principal responsibility for rearing their four sons. Tolui was passed over as successor to his father—his brother Ogedei became the *khaghan*, or "khan of khans"—and died in 1231/1232, a few years after his unsuccessful candidacy. His wife was determined to avenge this slight and to wrest control of the khanate from Ogedei's descendants.

Sorghaghtani Beki's contemporaries throughout the known world considered her to be the most remarkable woman of her age. The Persian historian Rashid al-Din wrote that she was "extremely intelligent and able and towered above all the women in the world." A Hebrew physician named Bar Hebraeus said, "If I were to see among the race of women another woman like this, I should say that the race of women was far superior to that of men." She had lofty ambitions for her sons and groomed them for important positions. All four of them were destined to be prominent figures in the Mongol domains. Mongke, the eldest, was to be the Great Khan of the Mongol lands from 1251 until his death in 1269; Kublai succeeded his older brother and ruled China from 1260 until 1294; Hulegu destroyed the Abbasid dynasty, which had governed much of the Middle East and Persia since 749, and established his own dynasty in Persia; and Arigh Boke, as the youngest son, would rule the Mongol homeland.

Sorghaghtani covertly forged alliances with Mongol nobles in the interests of her sons. Although she herself was a fervent Nestorian, she assisted and supported the Muslims, Daoists, and Buddhists. Receiving a domain in North China from her brother-in-law Ogedei, she won over her Chinese subjects by promoting agriculture rather than by converting the economy to pastoral nomadism. By such astute policies, she ingratiated herself with the Mongol nobility. With the help of Batu, the ruler of the Golden Horde in Russia, she was able to have her son Mongke enthroned as Great Khan in 1251. She lived just long enough to enjoy her victory, but not to reap personal profits from her efforts. In the first month of 1252 she succumbed, but not without having dramatically influenced her sons.

Kublai, in particular, was affected by his mother's attitudes and policies. Like his mother, he recognized that the newly conquered territories ought to be granted much local autonomy and ought not to be pillaged. He wanted to rule Xingzhou, the land in North China he received from Ogedei in 1236. Governance of this domain, he knew, required Chinese assistance. His Mongol retinue did not have the requisite administrative skills. He recruited a corps of Chinese advisers and officials who established an orderly and equitable system of taxation and fostered the native agrarian economy. Xingzhou prospered as a result, and Kublai gained the confidence of his Chinese subjects and coaxed those who had fled when the Mongols overran North China to return to their homes. His policy of religious toleration also helped him gain the allegiance of the Chinese within his domains. Eventually he could and did call upon Confucians, Buddhists, Muslims, and Christians for advice, assistance, and actual execution of policy. His territories were, as a consequence, well administered, and he was soon ready to undertake new and greater responsibilities.

Impressed by Kublai's success in Xingzhou and by his ability to attract a loyal group of advisers, his brother Mongke entrusted him with additional assignments. In 1253 Kublai organized an expedition that extended Mongol control into the province of Yunnan, previously the domain of the independent kingdom of Dali. Following the advice of his Confucian adviser Yao Shu (1201–1278), he pacified Dali with little bloodshed. Three years later, Kublai, adopting the recommendations of his Daoist-Buddhist adviser Liu Bingzhong (1216–1274), constructed a summer residence in Kaiping, 36 miles west of the modern town of Dolon Nor in Inner Mongolia. In 1263 he renamed it Shangdu ("upper capital") and established it as his secondary capital. Except for the hunting preserve or park, Shangdu resembled a typical Chinese capital city in its layout, Kublai's signal to his Chinese subjects that he was becoming increasingly sinicized. Marco Polo, who visited Shangdu in 1275, was evidently impressed by the marble palace, the Buddhist temples, and the residences of Kublai's family and officials, around which were beautiful streams, parks, and pavilions. Shangdu (Xanadu) was indeed a "stately pleasure dome," to use Samuel Taylor Coleridge's description in his poem "Kubla Khan." In 1258 Mongke assigned Kublai to resolve a dispute between the Buddhists and the Daoists that threatened the religious harmony and stability of North China. Kublai found the Daoists' claims unwarranted and their actions disruptive. Thus, he sided with the Buddhists and imposed limitations on the Daoists, quelling the religious disturbances for over two decades. Finally, in 1259, Mongke ordered Kublai to lead one army in a three-pronged assault on the Southern Song. Mongke, who commanded one of the armies, died in Sichuan during this campaign, leading to a struggle for power between his two younger brothers.

Both Kublai and his brother Arigh Boke claimed the throne, and their Mongol supporters enthroned each of them. In May of 1260 an assemblage of Mongol nobles met in Shangdu to proclaim Kublai the Great Khan while Arigh Boke was elected *khaghan* in the Mongol capital of Karakorum in June. Many conservative Mongols who wanted to preserve the traditional values and practices of a pastoral nomadic society were upset by Kublai's sinicization. They perceived that Kublai's fondness for the Chinese way of life would alienate him from his Mongol culture. Arigh Boke, based in the traditional Mongol homeland, represented the interests of the upholders of the "old ways." Using the resources of North China, Kublai finally defeated his younger brother in 1264, by denying him the supplies he needed.

The nomadic Mongols continued to challenge Kublai throughout his reign. In 1268 his cousin Khaidu wrested control of much of Central Asia from Kublai's forces. He continued to harass China's northwestern border until his death in 1301, and he garnered much of his support from Mongol traditionalists. The Nestorian Christian Nayan led a rebellion against Kublai in Manchuria in 1287. With a force of 200,000 troops, Kublai personally crushed this rebellion and executed Nayan. In sum, Kublai was not the undisputed leader of the Mongols; legitimacy eluded him.

To quell the criticisms of Mongol conservatives, Kublai needed to follow his grandfather's and uncle's policies of expanding the empire. Military successes enhanced his legitimacy in the eyes of the Mongols. He first sought to pacify the Southern Song dynasty, an objective that had eluded both his uncle Ogedei and his brother Mongke. With the help of two Muslim engineers who brought artillery with them, his troops successfully laid siege to the Song stronghold of Xiangyang in 1273. They then occupied the Song capital of Lin'an in 1276, and in 1279 the last Song emperor drowned in a naval engagement off the southeastern coast of China. After several campaigns from 1277 to 1287, Kublai compelled Burma and Champa (modern South Vietnam) to accept the sovereignty of the Mongols. He was not as successful in two other naval expeditions. His campaigns against Japan, in 1274 and 1281, ended disastrously. A typhoon, which the Japanese dubbed a "divine wind" (*kamikaze*), destroyed much of the Mongol fleet on the second expedition. An expedition against Java in 1292 also was forced to withdraw without gaining the submission of the natives. Despite these last defeats, Kublai's expansionist policy converted many previously hostile

Mongol traditionalists to his side. [*See also* Mongol Empire: Mongol Invasions of Japan *and* Mongol Empire: Mongol Invasions of Southeast Asia.]

Meanwhile, Kublai also focused on governing China. With the assistance of his Chinese advisers, he developed an administration that resembled those established by earlier Chinese dynasties. He reimposed Confucian rituals and reactivated old government agencies; he provided tax exemptions to Chinese Confucian scholars; in 1271 he adopted the Chinese title Yuan for his new dynasty; and, perhaps his most important signal to his Chinese subjects, in 1267 he shifted his capital from Karakorum in the Mongol heartland to Dadu (Khanbaliq; modern Beijing) in China. Yet he was not totally sinicized, nor was he eager to rely solely upon the Chinese for assistance in ruling. He did not reinstitute the civil service examinations as a means of recruiting officials because he wanted to employ non-Chinese in his administration. He also imposed a four-class system, with the Mongols and their Central Asian allies at the top and the Chinese at the bottom. Finally, certain military positions were reserved for Mongols. In short, Kublai wanted to win over the Chinese but still distrusted them.

Kublai did, nonetheless, attempt to promote the Chinese economy. He created a special government agency to help the peasants produce more food. In the 1280s he extended the Grand Canal to Dadu in order to transport grain from South China to the capital. Unlike many Chinese emperors and officials, he was not scornful of commerce. To foster trade, he issued paper money, encouraged the creation of merchant associations (*ortaq*), and organized postal stations that offered shelter, food, and drink to travelers. European and Asian merchants, including the Polos from Venice, arrived at Kublai's court, and goods from Riazan, Melaka, and Herat were transported to Dadu. Kublai also recruited Chinese, Tibetan, and Persian craftsmen to assist in his construction projects.

Kublai served as a patron of Chinese culture. He offered a government position to Zhao Mengfu (1254–1322), one of the greatest calligraphers and painters in Chinese history. He ordered Phags-pa, a Tibetan Buddhist lama, to devise a written script that could be used for all the languages in the Mongol domains. He did not discriminate against the religions in his realm and, in fact, exempted them from taxation. His coterie of advisers included Confucian scholars, Muslim financial administrators, Daoist magicians and soothsayers, Tibetan Buddhist lamas, and Christian traders. In 1291 he enacted a new law code that was, in theory, more lenient than previous Chinese ones. Chinese drama, medicine, and astronomy, which were enriched by foreign influences, all advanced during his reign.

The military campaigns, the building projects, and the patronage of culture were costly. Kublai decided to recruit foreigners to raise the needed revenue. The rebellion by Li Tan in 1262 had caused Kublai to become cautious about relying exclusively on Chinese officials. He thus employed non-Chinese to manage the financial administration of China. These men, in particular the Muslim Ahmad and the Uighur Sengge, alienated the Chinese with their continuous demands for revenue and higher taxes. The resentment against these men led to the assassination of Ahmad in 1282 and the execution, on the grounds of corruption, of Sengge in 1291.

Kublai also faced other failures in the last decade of his reign. Inflation, the result of a large increase in government issuance of paper money, developed at a rapid pace. Conflicts between the Buddhists and the Daoists reemerged. Kublai briefly supported an anti-Muslim campaign. The expeditions against Japan in 1281 and Java in 1292 were costly disasters. Kublai's personal life seemed to be collapsing. His favorite wife, Chabui, died in 1281, and his son and designated successor, Zhenjin, died in 1286. Unable to face these personal and governmental difficulties, he became increasingly self-destructive. He drank and ate in gargantuan quantities. In his last years he was fat and often drunk. He died in 1294, a sad and disillusioned old man.

Kublai's ambition to create a well-governed and unified empire composed of numerous nationalities, ethnic groups, and religions was unrealized. Yet his significance lies in the fact that he was the first of the Mongol conquerors truly to make the transition from conqueror to ruler.

[*See also* Genghis Khan; Hulegu; Ogedei; Mongol Empire: An Overview, *and* Yuan Dynasty.]

John Andrew Boyle, trans., *The Successors of Genghis Khan* (1971). Hok-lam Chan and Wm. Theodore de Bary, eds., *Yüan Thought: Chinese Thought and Religion under the Mongols* (1982). Wai-kam Ho and Sherman E. Lee, *Chinese Art under the Mongols: The Yuan Dynasty (1279–1368)* (1968). John Langlois, ed., *China under Mongol Rule* (1981). A. C. Moule and Paul Pelliot, trans., *Marco Polo*, 2 vols. (1938). Paul Pelliot, *Notes on Marco Polo*, 2 vols. (1959–1963). Morris Rossabi, "Khubilai Khan and the Women in His Family," in *Sino-Mongolica: Festschrift für Herbert Franke,* edited by W. Bauer (1979), and *Khubilai Khan: A Biography* (1985).

MORRIS ROSSABI

KUCHING, largest city in East Malaysia. Kuching was established as a Malay village in the 1820s. Raja James Brooke made the riverine port his capital in 1841, and under his rule the city flourished as an entrepôt for the products of a growing hinterland, exporting rubber, pepper, gambier, sago, gold, and antimony. Malayo-Muslim migrants and Chinese settlers arrived, and the population grew to 8,000 in 1876 (70 percent Malay) and 34,500 by 1939 (55 percent Chinese). In 1970 the municipality recorded 63,535 people (69 percent Chinese, 26 percent Malay), but population in the metropolitan area probably numbered 100,000.

The Brookes governed Kuching through the elites of the various ethnic communities, although a municipal board appeared in 1922. By 1956 this board had been reorganized into an elected municipal council with a Chinese majority. Kuching enjoyed the best educational facilities, many opened by Christian missions, and has both supplied much of the political leadership and generated most of the political movements for Sarawak. In recent years Sibu has challenged it for economic leadership, but Kuching remains the political, cultural, and intellectual hub of the state.

[See also Malaysia and Brooke, Sir James.]

Craig Lockard, *From Kampong to City: A Social History of Kuching, Malaysia, 1820–1970* (1984). Elizabeth Pollard, *Kuching Past and Present* (1972).

CRAIG A. LOCKARD

KUGE, term used in late Heian and medieval Japan to mean "aristocrat." *Kuge* originally referred to the government, but with the rise of the warrior in the late twelfth century, it came to describe the Kyoto aristocracy.

The origins of Japan's aristocracy lie in the seventh century, when the Chinese system of bureaucratic organization and remuneration was adapted to fit Japan's native tradition of hereditary rulers (the *uji*). Only members of powerful *uji*, such as the Fujiwara or Otomo, were allowed access to the upper reaches of government, which were in theory open to all.

During the eighth and ninth centuries aristocratic competition for wealth and power resulted in frequent coups and assassinations. By the middle of the ninth century the northern branch of the Fujiwara had a near monopoly on government posts. For almost two centuries thereafter they received the lion's share of provincial taxes. They also began to organize large landholdings (called *shōen*), which

became immune from taxation by the eleventh century. [See Shōen.]

The heyday of Fujiwara rule and aristocratic culture was the age of Michinaga (966–1027). Court diaries and literature such as *The Tale of Genji (Genji monogatari)* reveal a great deal about life at court. Aristocrats lived on magnificent estates and wore fine silk brocades. Yet despite the opulence of their surroundings, they bathed rarely, ate only twice a day, and suffered from a lack of protein. Favorite pastimes included poetry and calligraphy contests. The status of women was relatively high. The Heian aristocrat valued rank above all, and fine gradations often made for great social differences.

Aristocrats lost their monopoly on political power in the twelfth century. Despite the formation of the warrior government in Kamakura, however, aristocrats remained powerful, particularly in western Japan. They often served as scribes for the illiterate warriors. In the fourteenth century the status of aristocrats suffered a severe jolt as the Ashikaga family created a second warrior government. Many courtiers were reduced to begging in the streets of Kyoto. When the Tokugawa shogunate was formed in 1603, special laws were written for the old aristocracy and many were endowed with stipends. Descendants of the Heian aristocracy were included among the Meiji nobility.

[See also Uji; Fujiwara Lineage; and Heian Period.]

John W. Hall, *Japan from Prehistory to Modern Times* (1973). Ivan Morris, *The World of the Shining Prince* (1964). Edward Seidensticker, trans., *The Tale of Genji* (1977).

WAYNE FARRIS

KUJŌ, a family prominent in Japanese politics during the late Heian and Kamakura periods (eighth to the fourteenth century). In the eighth century the Fujiwara, the most powerful aristocratic family in Japan, split into four branches. By monopolizing the posts of regent (*sesshō*) and prime minister (*kampaku*), the northern branch dominated the court for almost three centuries.

Late in the Heian epoch, a scion of the northern branch, Tadamichi, became prime minister. Each of his two sons founded a new branch family named after his Kyoto residence. The offspring of the eldest son Motozane were called Konoe ("imperial guard"), while those of the second son Kanezane took the name Kujō ("ninth avenue"). In the twelfth century the Kujō divided further, into the Ichijō ("first avenue") and Nijō ("second avenue") branches.

The Kujō made their political fortunes by maintaining a strong alliance with the Kamakura government. Both Kanezane, who worked with Minamoto no Yoritomo, and his grandson Michiie succeeded to high positions at court. This alliance helped the Kujō retain their large portfolio of estates (shōen). Two Kujō scions became the fourth and fifth Kamakura shoguns (early to middle thirteenth century). The family persisted throughout the medieval and Tokugawa eras. The thirtieth head of the Kujō, Michitaka, was a member of the Meiji nobility; his daughter married the Taishō emperor.

[See also Fujiwara Lineage.]

George B. Sanasom, *A History of Japan to 1334* (1958).
                                                    WAYNE FARRIS

KŪKAI (774–835), posthumously known as Kōbō Daishi, revered as the founder of the Japanese esoteric school of Shingon Buddhism. *Kūkai* means "sea of emptiness"; *Kōbō* means "spread the Buddha's teaching"; *Daishi* ("great teacher") is an honorific title granted only to the most eminent Buddhist monks. Kūkai was also a creative religious thinker, a scholar of Chinese and Sanskrit, an educator who established the first school open to commoners in Japan, a wandering pilgrim and ascetic, a builder of roads, ponds, and bridges, the founder of the monastic center on Mount Kōya, a great calligrapher, and, in legend, the inventor of the Japanese *kana* syllabary. He is admired in Japan as a culture hero and universal genius. In legend he is believed not to have died but to have passed into a state of eternal meditation (Sanskrit, *samadhi*) in which he acts as a savior for all suffering people in the long interlude between the departure of the Buddha Shakyamuni and the advent of the future Buddha, Maitreya.

Kūkai was born into the Saeki family, provincial nobility from Sanuki Province on the island of Shikoku. As a child he was sent to the capital to begin the study of Confucianism, Daoism, and the Chinese classics considered essential to the training of a young nobleman and government official at the college for nobles. Kūkai, however, was drawn more by Buddhism than Confucianism. At the age of nineteen he decided to enter the Buddhist life. He received ordination at Tōdaiji and then devoted himself to a reclusive life of wandering, contemplation, and study of the Buddhist sutras.

In 804 he went to China as a member of an embassy dispatched by Emperor Kammu. Kūkai sought in China a teaching that would both clarify his understanding of the difficult esoteric *Mahāvairocana Sutra* and unify the varied, and seemingly conflicting, interpretations of Buddhism he had encountered in a decade of solitary religious quest. In Chang'an Kūkai studied with several monks before becoming the disciple of the Chinese esoteric master Huiguo (746–805). Huiguo took a particular liking to the earnest young Japanese monk and initiated him into all the secrets of the Tantric tradition. Kūkai, for his part, copied and collected new esoteric texts and mandalas and acquired the ritual implements essential to the proper conduct of Tantric ceremonies.

After his return to Japan in 806 Kūkai was appointed abbot of the monastery of Takaosanji (Jingoji) in the suburbs of the Heian capital and permitted to spread his Shingon ("true word") teachings. He won imperial favor and was invited to perform ceremonies for the protection of the imperial court and the nation. In 816 he was granted permission to build a monastery in the forests of Mount Kōya in Kii to be devoted to study and meditation. This developed into Kongōbuji ("the temple of the diamond peak"), or Kōyasan, as it is commonly known, one of the great Buddhist monastic complexes in Japan. In 823 Kūkai was also presented with the partially completed Tōji ("eastern temple") in the capital itself. Named Kyōōgokokuji ("temple of the dharma kings, protectors of the nation"), this became the principal Shingon training monastery, administrative center for the rapidly growing Shingon school, and repository of Shingon art. Kūkai's Shingon teachings and rituals appealed strongly to members of the imperial court and soon permeated Tendai Buddhism. Kūkai's writings not only reformulated esoteric Buddhist teaching, they added depth to Japanese Buddhist thought in general and showed respect for Daoism and Confucianism as well as Buddhism. The Shingon school founded by Kūkai has remained a major force in Japanese Buddhism.

[See also Shingon *and* Kōyasan.]

Yoshito S. Hakeda, *Kukai: Major Works, Translated, with an Account of His Life and a Study of His Thought* (1972). Joseph M. Kitagawa, "Master and Saviour," in *Studies in Esoteric Buddhism and Tantrism* (1965), pp. 1–26.
                                                    MARTIN COLLCUTT

KUKA SECT, a Sikh revivalist movement founded by Baba Ram Singh (d. 1885), a carpenter from a village in Ludhiana district who began preaching his strict version of the Sikh faith in 1857. The highly emotional nature of the group is indicated by its name, which refers to the adherents' practice of setting up a shout (*kuk*) while engaging in military drill.

The sect is also known as the Namdhari, from its emphasis on the constant repetition of God's name *(nam)*. Prophecies circulated that Baba Ram was a reincarnation of Guru Gobind Singh and that he would drive the British out of Hindustan. Baba Ram's own opposition to the British was limited to opening correspondence with a Russian governor in Central Asia. His followers, however, led a series of violent riots against Muslim butchers in Amritsar and other cities between 1868 and 1872. This led to the executions of some eighty Kukas and the exiling of Baba Ram to Burma. His descendants still lead the sect, which numbers some 400,000 members.

[*See also* Sikhism.]

F. S. Bajwa, *The Kuka Movement* (1965). Kushwant Singh, *A History of the Sikhs* (1966), vol. 2.

GREGORY C. KOZLOWSKI

KUKRIT PRAMOJ (b. 1911), Thai politician. He is the son of Prince Khamrob, the director general of the police department, and the younger brother of Seni Pramoj. Kukrit read politics and economics at Oxford and began his career in the Ministry of Finance but soon left for private business. Kukrit was first elected to Parliament in 1946 but resigned his seat in protest of legislated salary increases for members of Parliament.

Kukrit is modern Thailand's most colorful personality. He is well-known as a prolific author, educator, dancer, artist, journalist, orator, movie actor, banker, hotelier, and politician. As owner and the most prominent columnist of the newspaper *Sayam Rat,* Kukrit filled the role of society's gadfly during long periods of military rule. After the student uprisings of 14 October 1973, which ousted the regime of Thanom Kittikachorn, Kukrit emerged as a key political figure. He formed the Social Action Party and in 1975 led a coalition government that negotiated US troop withdrawal from Thailand, recognized the Beijing regime, and opted for improved relations with Vietnam and Kampuchea. Kukrit was replaced by his brother Seni following the April 1976 elections. As head of the Social Action Party, Kukrit is still very active in Thai politics.

[*See also* Thailand; Seni Pramoj; *and* Thanom Kittikachorn.]

John Girling, *Thailand* (1981).

THAK CHALOEMTIARANA

KULINISM was the term used by nineteenth-century social reformers in India to describe the practice of polygamy among the high-caste group of brahmans in Bengal known as "Kulins." Because of their high status in Bengal society, Kulins were much sought after by brahmans of lower rank as husbands for their daughters, and the custom had developed whereby Kulins married numerous times in return for high dowries. Highly publicized cases were reported of old men marrying as many as one hundred wives. When the husbands died, the wives, who might be young women, could not remarry under Hindu law, nor was there any legal provision for their support. The social reformers regarded the custom as especially degrading to upper-caste women and to Hindu society in general, since it was frequently cited by Western critics as an example of the degeneracy of Hinduism. Under pressure from reformers, the High Court ruled that in such marriages the women had to be supported, which, along with other movements for rights of women, such as laws regarding the age of marriage and inheritance, effectively ended the custom.

[*See also* Caste; Vidyasagar, Isvarchandra; *and* Women: Women in South and Southeast Asia.]

AINSLIE T. EMBREE

KULTUURSTELSEL, also known as the Cultivation System. In 1830 Johannes van den Bosch proposed a scheme whereby Java would produce exportable agrarian commodities inexpensively enough that they could be priced competitively on world markets. The plan compelled Javanese peasants to grow and harvest crops that with some preparation or processing could be consigned to the Netherlands Trading Company (NHM) for export and sale in the Netherlands. Each village was to set aside one-fifth of its land for planting a crop designated by the government and to devote one-fifth of its labor—sixty-six days per year per peasant—to tending and processing it. The government would purchase the crop at a fixed price that, according to the plan, would be sufficient to pay the land rent (tax) owed by the village. Of the various crops tried, sugar and indigo proved most successful and, along with coffee, which had long been profitably grown in Java, accounted for most of the profits van den Bosch's system produced for the treasury of the Netherlands.

To get the Javanese village to undertake this commitment, the government restored the Javanese elite *(priyayi)* to positions of prominence and had them assert their traditional rights to deliveries of produce and labor. For this they, as well as the European administrators, were awarded a percentage of the value of the government crops produced in their districts. The peasants were supposed to regard the extra burdens imposed by the system as part of their traditional obligation to their chiefs.

The government's constant need for more money and the greed of European and Javanese administrators led to excesses that resulted in suffering and dislocation for peasants in some parts of Java. These abuses, as well as its antiliberal economic aspects, have led to the characterization of the system as totally exploitative. Nonetheless, some elements of Javanese society benefited under the plan, and it opened Java to production for world markets.

[See also Java.]

Clive Day, *The Policy and Administration of the Dutch in Java* (1904). Robert Van Niel, "The Measurement of Change under the Cultivation System in Java, 1837–1851," *Indonesia* 14 (1972): 89–109.

ROBERT VAN NIEL

KUMARAJIVA (d. about 415), early transmitter of Buddhism to China. A native to Kucha in Central Asia, Kumarajiva began the study of Buddhist teachings at the early age of seven. By the time he was twenty he had studied widely under masters in Kashmir and Khotan and had established a reputation as a brilliant expositor of both Hinayana and Mahayana teachings.

Hearing of Kumarajiva's fame, Fu Jian, sovereign of the Former Qin kingdom in China, sent the general Lü Guang to pacify Kucha and escort Kumarajiva back to the capital at Chang'an. Before Lü Guang could return to China the Former Qin was overthrown. Kumarajiva was consequently forced to settle in Liangzhou, where he remained for nearly twenty years. It is believed that during this period he became well versed in the Chinese language. In 403 Liangzhou was annexed by the Later Qin kingdom and Kumarajiva was finally able to enter Chang'an. The Later Qin ruler, Yaoxing, honored him as state preceptor and provided him with all material and personnel necessary to devote himself full time to the translating and expounding of Buddhist scriptures.

In the last decade of his life, Kumarajiva translated approximately thirty-five works totaling 297 scrolls. His translations of such fundamental Mahayana Buddhist scriptures as the *Lotus Sutra* and the *Vimalakirti Sutra* gained enormous popularity

in China and have been revered as the standard versions throughout East Asia. As an exponent of Mahayana Buddhism, Kumarajiva emphasized the teachings of the Prajna Sutras and the Madhyamika school. He translated three treatises attributed to the Indian patriarch Nagarjuna and one by Nagarjuna's disciple Aryadeva, and lectured extensively on their contents. Eminent disciples such as Sengrui, Sengzhao, Daosheng, and Huiguan spread Kumarajiva's teachings throughout North and South China, where they had a major impact on the development of a genuine understanding of the Buddhist tradition on the part of the Chinese.

[See also Buddhism: Buddhism in China; Six Dynasties; Southern and Northern Dynasties; and Nagarjuna.]

Dale Todaro, "Kumārajīva," in *The Encyclopedia of Religion*, edited by Mircea Eliade (1987), vol. 8, pp. 398–400.

DAN STEVENSON

KUMAZAWA BANZAN (1619–1691), Japanese Confucian scholar and reformer. Kumazawa Banzan was the son of a masterless samurai. In 1634, he obtained a post with an annual stipend of three hundred *koku* (measures of rice) in Okayama domain under the daimyo Ikeda Mitsumasa, but he resigned after five years. In 1642, he studied under Nakae Tōju. In 1645, at the age of twenty-seven, he returned to Mitsumasa's service as a high-ranking domain official with a stipend of three hundred *koku*. But in 1658 he was forced to resign again owing to fierce opposition in the domain and the displeasure of the *bakufu*. Thereafter he moved, or was relocated under orders from the *bakufu*, several times. He died an exile in 1691.

Banzan declared, "I follow neither Zhu Xi nor Wang Yangming [Chinese Neo-Confucian thinkers]—only the ancient sages." His philosophical point of departure was that the sages had created policies best suited to their time and circumstances. Japanese rulers should not hamstring themselves by adhering to ancient Chinese institutions. Instead, they too should formulate policies appropriate to contemporary conditions. However, his specific reform proposals—returning the samurai to the soil, relaxing the system of alternate attendance in Edo, giving warriors rather than daimyo the authority to tax peasants, and halting the opening up of new rice fields—were in fact ill-suited to his times. Daimyo policies of the early Tokugawa period aimed to consolidate and strengthen domain power over both samurai and peasants. Herein lay the biggest cause of his fall from favor in Okayama; his supposed ideological heterodoxy was of little importance.

BOB TADASHI WAKABAYASHI

KU NA, king of Lan Na (r. 1355–1385), brought order to Lan Na (northern Thailand) after a period of warfare. Born about 1324, Ku Na was the eldest son of King Pha Yu (r. 1337–1355) and peacefully succeeded him. Ku Na was exceptionally able and energetic, and he was well educated in the Indic arts and sciences. He promoted the introduction of a new Sinhalese sect of Buddhism in his land, which over the next two centuries was to be a major unifying and intellectual force in Lan Na. His son, Saen Muang Ma, succeeded him in 1385.

[See also Lan Na.]

N. A. Jayawickrama, trans., *The Sheaf of Garlands of the Epochs of the Conqueror* (1968). David K. Wyatt, *Thailand: A Short History* (1984).    DAVID K. WYATT

KUNMING, Chinese city, capital and largest city of Yunnan Province; its population in 1982 was 1.43 million. Traditionally a small provincial administrative town, Kunming began its industrialization after the construction of a railway to Haiphong by the French in 1910. From 1939 to 1945, when the wartime Nationalist government retreated to southwest China, Kunming grew into an industrial, commercial, and transport center. Although it lost much of its industry at the end of the war, after 1949 Kunming was again built up as an industrial center. Today it is a leading producer of copper, lead, and zinc, and also possesses machine tool, electrical equipment, truck, chemical, fertilizer, and cement factories, fueled by hydroelectric and thermal power plants.    JOHN A. RAPP

KUOMINTANG. *See* Guomindang.

KUO MO-JO. *See* Guo Moruo.

KURDISH, the collective, and somewhat loose, term for a number of related Indo-European languages and dialects of the Northwest Iranian branch, spoken by the Kurds. Kurds themselves like to consider all these as Kurdi (Kurdish), even though some of them are distinct languages, each with various dialects of their own.

In the central regions of Kurdistan, a language, which some linguists would like to call "Kurdish proper"—or Kurdi, as the Kurds would call it—with an array of dialects, is spoken. It is divided into two major branches: the northwestern branch called Kurmanji, after one of its major dialects (others being Hakkari, Sinjari, Bahdinani, and Buhtan), and the southeastern Surani branch. The northwestern branch is spoken in the area between Mount Ararat and Lake Urmia in the east and Diyarbakir and Afrin (in the Kurd Dagh region of northwestern Syria) in the west, in some northern sections of Iraqi Kurdistan, and in the Kurdish regions of the Soviet Caucasus. The southeastern dialects are spoken in the south-central regions of Kurdistan, from Bijar (Garrus) to Arbil, southward to Sanandaj, and in other major Kurdish cities such as Kirkuk, Mahabad, Sulaimaniyya, Naqqada, Saqqiz, Khanaqin, and Qala Diza. The major dialects of the southeastern branch are Sanandaji, Mukri, Sulaimani, Warmawa, Pizhdar, and Khushnaw. Kurdi is fortunate in having a large body of literature, written and oral, spanning more than ten centuries. It has traditionally been held in esteem by all Kurds. In this century the rise in prominence of such Surani-speaking cities as Sulaimaniyya, Sanandaj, Kirkuk, and Mahabad has given the Sulaimani branch of Kurdi an unprecedented possibility to become the lingua franca of all Kurds.

The Awraman or Hewraman dialect spoken in the area between Sanandaj and Sulaimaniya, in the Pawa-Mariwan region, may be considered a distinct dialect of Kurdi, separate from either Surani or Kurmanji. It is more likely a language in its own right, akin to Kurdi.

In the northwestern areas of greater Kurdistan, that is, the northern half of eastern Anatolia, Zaza is the principal language, displacing Kurmanji. It is spoken from near Erzurum to Darsim and Kharput. At the early stages of its development, Zaza seems to have been heavily influenced by Gilaki. It may not be safe to assume that it is an offshoot of that language, but Zaza grammar and vocabulary have many southwestern Iranian features found in Gilaki or Persian. [See also Gilaki.]

In the southwestern parts of Kurdistan, from Hamadan and Kermanshah to Ilam and Qasr-i Shirin, Gurani and Lakki predominate. The Kurdish enclaves in Baluchistan speak a Gurani dialect. Many linguists have shown a tendency not to classify Gurani and Lakki as Kurdish, but rather as intermediate languages between Kurmanji and Luri, a southwestern Iranian language. The more prominent dialects of Gurani and Lakki are Pairawandi, Kulyai, Kalhur, Zangana, Nankili, and Kermanshahi.

Even though the Kurds would like it to be, Kurdish—even its Kurmanji and Surani branches—is not the modern form of the language spoken by the ancient Medes. It is more likely that Kurmanji and Surani are offshoots of a dialect related to Median proper. Tati, spoken by a diminishing number of urban-based ethnic groups in western Persia, might rightfully be considered the direct descendant of ancient Median.

Kurdish has been adapted to writing in the past, and the Arabo-Persian alphabet was generally used for this purpose. In modern times, depending on which country the Kurds live in, various alphabets are used: in Turkey, a modified Roman script; in Iraq, Syria, and sometimes in Iran, a modified form of Arabo-Persian; and in the Soviet Union, Armenian and Cyrillic alphabets. Writing in Kurdish is discouraged in Syria and Iran and outlawed in Turkey. The rich Kurdish literature has thus been an essentially oral one, with some notable exceptions in the epic cycle of *Mam u Zin* and the religious material of the Ahl-i Haq sect. There is no general consensus as to exactly how many Kurdish speakers there are, but the total figure of between sixteen and eighteen million seems plausible.

[*See also* Kurdistan.]

J. Blau, *Kurdish Kurmandji Modern Texts* (1968). E. R. McCarus, *A Kurdish Grammar* (1958) and "Kurdish Language Studies," *Middle East Journal* (1960). D. N. MacKenzie, *Kurdish Dialect Studies* (1961–1962) and *The Dialect of Awraman* (1966). E. B. Soane, *Kurdish Grammar* (1913).            MEHRDAD IZADY

**KURDISTAN**, the home of the Kurds, located in the highlands of eastern Anatolia and the northwestern section of the Zagros Mountains. In its present fragmented state, Kurdistan stretches over five international borders, from Iran and Iraq to Turkey, Syria, and the Soviet Union. The country is predominantly mountainous but is interrupted frequently by fertile and well-watered valleys, some of which are, like the plains of Mahi Dasht, of unusual fertility and expanse. Many of the major rivers of the Middle East have their source in Kurdistan, such as the Tigris, Euphrates, Araks, Kura, Kizil Irmak, Safid Rud, and Karkheh. The heartland of Kurdistan is the area bordered on the southeast by two tributaries of the Tigris, the Little and the Great Zab, and on the northwest by Lake Urmia. This area has been known successively as Gutium, Kardush, and Ardalan.

*History.* The origins of the Kurds are still somewhat uncertain. Variations of the word *Kurd* appear regularly in the ancient sources. Of the invaders from the mountainous region of "Gutium," Naram-Sin (2291–2255 BCE), king of Agade (Akkadia), said, "in the mist of the mountains they grew up, they became virile, they acquired stature . . . ." The Gutis set up a dynasty in Sumeria (c. 2250–2120 BCE). Akkadian sources mention a mountain kingdom of Gutium to the east and north of Assyria as one of the regions annexed by the Kassite rulers of Akkadia around 1400 BCE. Assyrian sources of the late second millennium also mention Gutium, the country of the "Gutils" to the east and north of Assyria. Babylonian tablets of the sixth century BCE enumerate the "Kardakas" among the Babylonian royal guards. The "Carduchis," "Cardaces," or "Kurtioi" are credited by Greek and Roman writers with playing a considerable role in the latter history of the Persian Achaemenid empire. In post-Achaemenid times, the form *Gordyene* was more commonly employed by historians; it remained the dominant form until the beginning of the Islamic age, when the term *Kurdistan* was finally established for the country.

The Islamic conquests of the seventh century CE opened a much clearer chapter in the history of the Kurds. Kurds set up various dynasties, both within Kurdistan and beyond, and some of these acquired great distinction: the Shaddadids of Arran and eastern Armenia (c. 951–1174); the Rawwadids of Azerbaijan (early tenth century to 1071); the Marwanids of central and eastern Anatolia (983–1085); and the Ayyubids of Egypt, Syria, northern Mesopotamia, and the Yemen (1169 to the end of the fifteenth century), of whom Saladin, famous for his defeat of the Crusaders, is the most celebrated. The illustrious Safavids of Persia (1501–1722), although a Turkic-speaking dynasty, were quite probably of Kurdish origin as well. The Zands of Persia (1750–1794) were the last Kurds to found a ruling dynasty before the eclipse of Kurdish fortunes in modern times. [*See* Zand Dynasty.]

From 1514 to the middle of the sixteenth century the western parts of Kurdistan passed into Ottoman hands, while the smaller eastern portion stayed under the jurisdiction of various dynasties of Persia. This situation continued until the end of World War I, when the Ottoman portion was divided into Syrian, Iraqi, and Turkish sections. The Kurdish regions of the Caucasus had already passed into Russian hands by the early nineteenth century.

The twentieth century has brought Kurdistan a degree of fragmentation never before experienced by the Kurds. With the advent of modern states and well-guarded national boundaries in the Middle

East, the movement of Kurds and the exchange of ideas and culture among the five fragments of Kurdistan has become exceedingly difficult. This situation has been worsened by the reserved or hostile relations among the countries under whose jurisdiction the Kurds live. Faced with this fragmentation and the outright denial of their national rights the Kurds have become a very politicized and embattled people, usually at odds with the governments under which they live. Kurdish history in the twentieth century has been marked by frustration: deportations, wars, popular uprisings, and the formation and liquidation of many Kurdish political parties and declarations of independence. More than once have the Kurds been caught in political and physical crossfire because of their tenuous existence on the border regions of these states. A major force in the Middle East for millennia, the Kurds, despite their fragmentation, remain a vital nation steadfastly resisting assimilation and elimination.

***Ethnology and Ethnography.*** The Kurds are now predominantly of Mediterranean racial stock, resembling southern Europeans in general coloring and physiology. The linguistic, cultural, and racial "aryanization" of the aboriginal Caucasoid Kurds seems to have begun by the beginning of the second millennium BCE with the continuous immigration and settlement of Indo-European tribes such as the Kassites, Mitannis, Armenians, Medes, Sakas (Scythians), and Persians. This process probably was completed by the middle of the first millennium BCE at the latest, by which time the Kurds had formed the basis of their contemporary ethnic identity.

The Islamic era brought with it yet another wave of immigrations and settlements in Kurdistan: first the Arabs and later the much more numerous Turkic and Mongol tribes; in Kurdistan today there are a few Arabic but many more Turkic and Mongol place and tribal names. Except for the Christian and Jewish populations, and a few Turkmen enclaves in Iraqi Kurdistan, the settlers generally have been assimilated into the Kurdish nation.

The Kurds themselves have proved to be at least as mobile as these immigrants. The early migrations of the Kurds are, however, quite difficult to trace; as early as the time of Strabo, the word *Kurd*, or *kurtioi* as he wrote it, was a very general term loosely applied to all those mountain pastoralists living a way of life similar to that of the Kurds. This general usage of the term continued until about the fifteenth century CE, when all of the semisedentary and tribal peoples of the Zagros range, from the Strait of Hor-

muz to central Anatolia, were still referred to as Kurds. The valor and energy of the Kurdish mountaineers often marked them for military service in the Babylonion, Persian, Greek, Arabian, Turkish, and even Russian armies (the Kurdish regiment played a crucial role in the Battle of Minsk in World War II); large segments of the Kurdish population were sometimes transferred to the far borders of one or another empire to man garrisons against outside intrusions. Thus, Kurdish communities can be found in places as far apart as Ferghana, on the Chinese border; the shores of the Aegean Sea; and the shores of the Indian Ocean.

The more general migrations of the Kurds and their colonization of new territories are less enigmatic but as poorly documented. Many of their movements resulted in the assimilation of the Kurds into the indigenous population. Such was the fate of many populous Kurdish tribes, such as the Shaqaqi, who settled in Azerbaijan, Arran, and Shirvan in the last millennium. The Kurdish immigration into Armenia, on the other hand, has resulted in the gradual colonization of the region by the Kurds. The Kurdish settlement in Armenia proper must have begun before the advent of Islam. By the tenth century CE they were already living in the environs of Lake Van, the heartland of historic Armenia. The annihilation of the Armenians, the last indigenous people of eastern Anatolia, at the end of World War I left the area predominantly Kurdish. This act has effectively converted the Armenian Plateau into a de facto component of contemporary Kurdistan.

***Religion.*** It is safe to assume that the Kurds' adoption of an Indo-European, Iranian language and culture in the course of the first millennium BCE entailed the worship of Aryan deities as well. Zoroastrianism seems to have made inroads in Kurdistan by the end of the Sasanid era (224–640) and the introduction of Christianity and Islam only added to the religious diversity of Kurdistan. At present, the Kurdish-speaking Kurds are nominally Sunni Muslims of the Shafi'i rite, but the bonds of the Kurds to different Sufi orders (*tariqas*), such as the Naqshbandi, Qadiri, and Bektashi, some holding heterodox views, brings the Kurds' "orthodoxy" into question.

The Gurani speakers of southeastern Kurdistan are overwhelmingly of the Ahi-i Haq sect, commonly identified as an extremist sect. In fact, the Kurds were termed *ghulat* ("extremists") by medieval Muslim observers such as Nizam al-Mulk. The Zaza speakers of Anatolia adhere to the more conventional Alawite branch of the Shi'a. A large number of Kurdish Muslims, particularly in the major

Kurdish cities, do, however, adhere to the conventionally recognized Islamic denominations.

The Yazidis, predominantly of the Sanjar region of Iraq and Syria, but also living in eastern Anatolia and the Soviet Caucasus, practice a religion, admittedly non-Islamic, that exhibits many Zoroastrian or even early Aryan cult features. Kurdistan is also home to adherents of Judaism and of many established Christian sects, but their numbers, never large, are presently shrinking.

[See also Kurdish and Iran.]

F. D. Andrews, *Lost People of the Middle East* (1985). H. Arfa, *The Kurds: A Historical and Political Study* (1966). W. Behn, *The Kurds in Iran: A Selected and Annotated Bibliography* (1977). G. Chaliand, ed., *People Without a Country* (1980). J. Creagh, *Armenians, Kurds and Turks* (1980). J. B. Fraser, *Travels in Koordistan* (1840). E. Ghareeb, *The Kurdish Question in Iraq* (1981). M. Kahn, *Children of Jinn* (1980).    MEHRDAD IZADY

**KURILE ISLANDS,** an archipelago of thirty-six islands (area: 15,600 square kilometers) extending northward 1,200 kilometers from Hokkaido, the northernmost of the four main islands of the Japanese archipelago, to the Kamchatka Peninsula, USSR, and dividing the Sea of Okhotsk from the Pacific Ocean. Volcanic eruptions, earthquakes, tidal waves, and sudden storms and fogs create an unstable natural environment. Marine life abounds.

For centuries, the Kuriles have been a stepping stone and meeting ground for diverse peoples and cultures. Prehistoric migrants moved along the arc to and from Siberia and North America. The Ainu had inhabited the Kuriles for several hundred years when Russians and Japanese converged in the seventeenth century from the north and south, respectively.

During the eighteenth century, Russians explored the entire arc and settled its central and northern parts. Sporadic attempts were made to collect tribute from the Ainu in the southern Kuriles.

A Russo-Japanese frontier problem developed toward the end of the eighteenth century. Russian activity in the southern Kuriles prompted the Tokugawa shogunate to dispatch a surveying mission (1786) and to deploy garrisons on the islands of Kunashiri and Etorofu (1798). Problems raised by Russian raids on Etorofu in 1807 were peacefully settled in 1813, but without any demarcation of a frontier.

Russian occupation of Sakhalin, the Amur region, and the maritime regions, together with the Crimean War (1854–1856), again brought the Kuriles to the fore in Russo-Japanese negotiations. The Treaty of Shimoda (7 February 1855) defined the Kurile frontier as running between Etorofu and Uruppu, thus recognizing Japan's sovereignty over the southern Kuriles. Mounting Russo-Japanese friction over Sakhalin (which the Treaty of Shimoda had declared a Russo-Japanese condominium) was resolved by the Treaty of Saint Petersburg (7 May 1875), wherein Japan abandoned all claims to Sakhalin in exchange for acquiring the central and northern Kuriles.

Under Japanese rule (1875–1945), the Kuriles were administered as part of Hokkaido. Kunashiri and Etorofu attracted most of the permanent settlers (18,000 in 1939), who engaged in fishing and agriculture. By the 1930s, some 30,000 Japanese seasonal workers flocked to northern Kurile fishing fleets and canneries.

Japan began fortifying the Kuriles in 1940. Etorofu's Hitokappu Bay served as an assembly point for the task force that struck Pearl Harbor, Hawaii, on 7 December.

Soviet seizure of the Kuriles constituted part of a campaign against Japanese forces on the continent that opened on 9 August 1945. An amphibious force from Kamchatka landed on Shumushu on 18 August and secured the island on 25 August after bitter fighting. The southern Kuriles (including Shikotan and the Habomai Islands off Hokkaido) were occupied without resistance by the Soviet Pacific fleet between 29 August and 3 September.

The Kuriles were formally declared to be Soviet territory on 20 September 1945 and since 1947 have been administered as part of the Sakhalin district. All former residents of Japan were repatriated between 1945 and 1947. The permanent Soviet population (about 18,000 in 1979) is swollen in summer months by seasonal workers. The arc contains several naval and air bases. Since 1978, military forces have been strengthened on Etorofu and Kunashiri.

Tokyo claims that the "northern territories" (Kunashiri, Etorofu, Shikotan, and the Habomai Islands) are "inalienable" Japanese lands and calls for their retrocession. Opposition parties (including the Communists) and (since 1964) the People's Republic of China call for the return of the entire Kurile arc to Japan. Although President Franklin Roosevelt endorsed transfer of the Kuriles to the USSR at the Yalta Conference (1945), Washington since 1956 has officially supported Tokyo's claims to the southern Kuriles. Moscow denies that a territorial issue exists and refuses to make it a subject of negotiation.

The Kurile impasse has prevented the conclusion of a Soviet-Japanese peace treaty.

John J. Stephan, *The Kuril Islands: Russo-Japanese Frontier in the Pacific* (1974).    JOHN J. STEPHAN

**KURODA KIYOTAKA** (1840–1900), Japanese government leader of the Meiji period. Kuroda was born in Satsuma (Kagoshima). He studied Western gunnery and helped to defend Kagoshima against the British bombardment of 1863. [See Kagoshima Bombardment.] He worked to bring about the Satsuma-Chōshū coalition and then distinguished himself in the battles against *bakufu* forces during the early Meiji period. He went to the United States in 1871 and returned to Japan via Europe. As head of the government's Hokkaido Colonization Office, he sought to sell off its holdings. This precipitated the crisis of 1881. One result was the imperial rescript promising the establishment of a Diet in 1890. In 1886 and 1887 he traveled around the world. He was appointed prime minister (1888–1889) and held other prominent posts. He was *sangi* (state councillor; 1874), agriculture and commerce minister (1887–1888), communications minister (1892–1895), and privy council president (1895–1900).

Kuroda's birthplace, his early career, and the support of Saigō Takamori and Ōkubo Toshimichi would seem to indicate a stronger role for him and Satsuma in the Meiji government after Ōkubo's assassination. Although he was duly appointed to high posts, he was never able to win a place for Satsuma as Chōshū's equal. The reason may have been his instability stemming from alcoholism. The disability apparently started early, for Kido Takayoshi records in his diary (8 January 1875) that Kuroda was "drunk again." His appointments, despite his disability, indicate that the Meiji leaders were sensitive to the requirement of maintaining a balance between Satsuma and Chōshū in the government.

[*See also* Meiji Period.]

GEORGE K. AKITA

**KURUKSHETRA** (lit., "field of the Kurus"), now the name of a town in Haryana, 100 miles north of Delhi, originally denoted the settlement area of the ancient Kuru people as against their forested belt, known as Kurujangala ("jungle of the Kurus"). It is famous in the traditional history of India as the place where the great Bharata War was fought between the Kauravas and the Pandavas, the central theme of the epic *Mahabharata*. It was here in the battleground that the god Krishna delivered the *Bhagavad Gita* and exhorted Arjuna to fight for the sake of *dharma* (duty). In this way, Kurukshetra became a *dharmakshetra* ("field of *dharma*") and thus continues to be famous as a sacred place for Hindus.

[*See also* Mahabharata *and* Bhagavad Gita.]

R. C. Majumdar, ed., *The Age of Imperial Unity* (1968).    A. K. NARAIN

**KURUNEGALA,** a rock fortress located in northwestern Sri Lanka, for a brief period in the late thirteenth century the capital of the Dambadeniya rulers. Its present importance dates to the nineteenth century, when, following the creation of the North-Western Province (1845) it became the province's administrative capital. Kurunegala was one of two main trouble spots during a minor rebellion against the British in 1848. Today, it is the center of a rich rice-producing area and one of the principal centers of coconut production.

[*See also* Dambadeniya.]

K. M. de Silva, *A History of Sri Lanka* (1981).

K. M. DE SILVA

**KUSHAN DYNASTY.** The Kushans were one of the clans of the Yuezhi, a Tokharian-speaking tribe that lived originally in Gansu, China. Around 170 BCE the Yuezhi were defeated by the Xiongnu and moved to the west. By 128 BCE they were already established north of the Oxus River; by 100, or a little later, they had conquered Bactria and Sogdiana. They divided their kingdom into five *yabgus* (chiefdoms), one of which was the Kushan; its earliest known chief was Heraus. Sometime early in the first century CE Kujula Kadphises subjugated the other four *yabgus* and created one unified state.

Although their coins and inscriptions identified them as Kushan, the Chinese insisted upon calling them Yuezhi, and the Indian and Western sources called them Tusara/Tukhara and Tokharoi/Tochari, respectively. Kujula ruled for most of the first century and died an octogenarian. He extended the Kushan territories south of the Hindu Kush and into India. The widely circulated coinage of his reign bore such borrowed devices as a bust of Augustus, a Macedonian soldier, Zeus, Herakles, and a cross-legged seated figure that was perhaps an attempt to represent the Buddha. Kujula's successor, Vima Kadphises, further expanded and consolidated the Kushan power and issued gold and copper coins of standardized type and metrology. On the obverse of the coins of his realm he is shown emerging from the clouds; the flames rising from his shoulders indicate divine features. On the reverse Shiva stands beside a bull; the coins' legend announces the king's affiliation to the god.

The golden age of Kushan history begins with Kanishka. Estimates of the date of his accession range from 78 to 225 CE. Whatever the date, it has consistently been used as the beginning of the era, lasting a little over one hundred years, of the early kings named Kanishka, Vashishka, Huvishka, and Vasudeva. The possibility that a second or third Kanishka or a second Vasudeva existed (or even a second Huvishka) cannot be ruled out. Archaeological discoveries and numismatic and other evidence indicate that the Kushan empire was in its heyday during the reigns of Kanishka and Huvishka; under them the Kushan presence extended from Chorasmia (Khwarazm) in Central Asia to Bihar in India.

Kanishka represented one of the four great powers of the world of his time. In an inscription a king named Kanishka appropriates the royal titles used in India, Parthia, China, and Rome: *maharaja* ("great king"), *rajatiraja* ("king of kings"), *devaputra* ("son of god"), and *kaisara* ("Caesar"). The Fourth Buddhist Council, probably held in Kashmir, was convened by Kanishka; thus, Buddhist tradition remembers him as a royal patron second in importance only to Ashoka. In addition, the rise of the Mahayana and the Hinayana Sarvastivada schools took place in large part during Kanishka's reign.

Under Kanishka coins struck with images of Shakyamuni Buddha and possibly Maitreya Buddha were issued. But he and the later king Huvishka were liberal in their religious policy, and on the coins of their reigns were depicted deities belonging to other pantheons, such as the Shaiva, the Greco-Roman, and the Iranian/Central Asian; some of them are shown in more than one form. The list of deities includes Oesho (Shiva), Skando Komaro, Bizago, Mahasena, Helios, Selene, Herakles, Serapis, Athsho, Nana, Arooaspo, Manaobago, Mao, Miiro/Meiro, Oanindo, Oado, Orlagno, Farro, and so on.

Vasudeva, the last of the early kings, issued coins of only one type, that is, with Shiva. From the number and quality of the coins of his reign, as well as from other evidence, it appears that the beginning of the decline of Kushan power had begun by the end of his tenure, although the Kushans continued for another hundred years or so after him. But the empire was fragmented into enclaves ruled by various scions of the dynasty, and it finally fell to the Sasanid and Gupta empires in the middle of the fourth century.

The Kushan polity regarded the king as *devaputra*. The divine legitimation of his authority is conveyed by several images struck on Kushan coinage: a nimbus around the head of a king, a human figure emerging from a bank of clouds, flames rising from the king's shoulders. *Devakulas* ("houses of god"), housing statues of deceased kings, were erected; their maintenance and repair were considered acts of religious merit. The Kushan political organization, however, was not rigidly centralized; elements of limited decentralization are noticeable in the role of *kshatrapas* and *mahakshatrapas*, who were in charge of the territorial administration of the provinces. But the *mahadandanayaka* and the *dandanayaka*, offices of a military hierarchy in which positions were often held by scions of the ruling family, were appointed as checks on the power of these provincial officials.

The strength and glory of the Kushan state in history lay in its economic basis. Not only did the Kushans control the fertile Oxus, Indus, and Ganges-Yamuna river systems, but they also took full advantage of their proximity with China and Central Asia in regulating the silk trade to Rome. Their favorable balance of trade with the outside world is apparent in the large number of gold coins they issued as well as in the hoards of Roman coins found in India. Evidence of religious gifts made by artisans and merchants indicates that Kushan commerce and urban life thrived, with the guilds enjoying a significant role in the control of banking and distributive power.

Although originally Tokharian-speaking, the Kushans wisely adopted the languages, scripts, and cultures of the areas they ruled, modifying the Greek script to suit their needs, issuing documents in a variety of Iranian and Indic languages, and patronizing the religious cults and beliefs prevailing in their empire. Their role in the development of the Gandhara and Mathura schools of art is in itself a significant chapter of ancient Indian art history. Poets and philosophers received royal patronage, and some of the finest examples of Sanskrit literature belong to this period. It is fair to state that the groundwork of the classical age of South Asian history was laid by the Kushans.

[*See also* Sasanid Dynasty; Gupta Empire; Kanishka; *the map accompanying* Parthians; *and map 1 accompanying* India.]

A. L. Basham, ed., *Papers on the Date of Kaniska* (1968). *Central Asia in the Kushan Period,* 2 vols., edited by B. G. Gafurov and others (1974–1975). B. Chattopadhyaya, *Kushāna State and Indian Society* (1975). B. N. Mukherjee, *The Kushan Genealogy* (1967). A. K. Narain, *The Indo-Greeks* (1962; reprint, 1980). B. N. Puri, *India under the Kushānas* (1965). John Rosenfield, *The Dynastic Arts of the Kushans* (1968). D. Sclumberger, "Surkh Kotal," *Antiquity* (1959): 81–86.

A. K. NARAIN

## KUSUNOKI MASASHIGE

KUSUNOKI MASASHIGE (d. 1336), a warrior (samurai) chieftain of medieval Japan whose origins are obscure but who was later apotheosized as the supreme exemplar of imperial loyalism in Japanese history. Kusunoki Masashige rose to prominence in the service of Emperor Go-Daigo (1288–1339), who in the early 1330s supported a movement to overthrow the Kamakura shogunate (1185–1336), Japan's first warrior government. Although only a petty chieftain of a province near Kyoto, the emperor's seat, Kusunoki gained fame as a wily and elusive guerrilla who held the armies of the shogunate at bay until Go-Daigo's loyalist movement could succeed. When the Kamakura shogunate was overthrown in 1333, Go-Daigo sought to restore direct rule by the emperor and end the tradition of warrior government begun a century and a half earlier. But Go-Daigo's restoration regime was an abysmal failure, and in 1336 it lost power to the Ashikaga, or Muromachi, shogunate (1336–1573). Kusunoki, ever loyal to the emperor, died at the Battle of Minatogawa (near modern Kobe) in 1336 in a futile attempt to prevent Ashikaga Takauji (1305–1358), founder of the new shogunate, from capturing Kyoto. Kusunoki's exploits were dramatized in a famous war tale of the age (the *Taiheiki*), and he became idolized for his selfless loyalty to the throne. *Kamikaze* ("divine wind") pilots in World War II often invoked his memory in dedicating their suicide missions.

[*See also* Go-Daigo *and* Kemmu Restoration.]

PAUL VARLEY

## KUTADGU BILIG

KUTADGU BILIG (*The Wisdom of Royal Glory*), the earliest Islamic Turkic (Karakhanid) literary work in poetic form. The *Kutadgu bilig* was written in the Turkic dialect of Kashgar in 1069 by Yusuf Khass Hajib of Balasagun; it is modeled on the "mirror for princes" genre. It comprises 6,645 distichs, is based on the dialogue form, and revolves around four personages, each with an allegorical Turkic name. Kun Togdi ("rising sun") represents justice; Ay Toldi ("full moon"), fortune; Ogdulmish ("highly praised"), wisdom; and Odgurmish ("wide awake"), contentment.

The *Kutadgu bilig* combines Islamic elements and Turkic pagan elements within the framework of an allegorical symbolism unique in Islamic literature. The work, along with Mahmud al-Kashgari's *Compendium of the Turkic Dialects,* served to establish the Turkic tradition within the Islamic cultural sphere alongside the Iranian and Arabic ones.

[*See also* Kashgari, Mahmud al- *and* Turkic Languages.]

Khass Hajib Yusuf, *Wisdom of Royal Glory (Kutadgu Bilig), A Turko-Islamic Mirror for Princes,* translated by Robert Dankoff (1983).

JAMES M. KELLY

## KWANGGAET'O

KWANGGAET'O (r. 391–413), powerful monarch of the Korean kingdom of Koguryŏ. In the two reigns prior to his rule, Koguryŏ experienced considerable state development as Buddhism became officially recognized, a Confucian academy was started, and a strong central power structure was erected. Building on this internal growth, King Kwanggaet'o turned Koguryŏ's energy toward rapid territorial expansion. The king's reign name *Kwanggaet'o* means "broad expander of the domain." A commemorative stele found just across the Yalu River in Manchuria claims that in his twenty-three-year reign King Kwanggaet'o extended Koguryŏ's control over much of Manchuria, subjugating fortresses and people who stood in his path. He assured Koguryŏ's domination of the Liaodong area and made the Sungari River its northern boundary. He successfully stymied Paekche's advances from the south and sent troops to help Silla defeat a combined Kaya-Wa Japanese attack in the Naktong River basin. When his land routes were blocked, he put to the sea, proving himself not only an able general but also a master of naval warfare. By the end of his reign he could claim the conquest of some 64 fortresses and 1,400 villages.

Internally King Kwanggaet'o fostered a strong state. His capital remained at Kungnae-sŏng (modern Tonggou) in the middle of the Yalu River valley, but he recognized the importance of P'yŏngyang, which would become the capital of the kingdom in the subsequent reign. Toward the end of his rule he built nine temples in that area, demonstrating his devotion to the Buddhist faith as well as a commitment to P'yŏngyang's strategic value.

If controversy surrounds King Kwanggaet'o today, it focuses on the memorial stele mentioned above. It was discovered by Japanese personnel in the late nineteenth century, and some contend they altered the text to prove that Japan had conquered parts of the Korean peninsula in the fourth century in order to justify Japan's return to Korea in the twentieth century. There is no conclusive evidence to support this conjecture. Nevertheless, the inscription does indicate that King Kwanggaet'o successfully fought the Wa in southern Korea and became one of Koguryŏ's most successful conquerors.

[*See also* Koguryŏ.]

Hatada Takashi, "An Interpretation of the King Kwanggaet'o Inscription," *Korean Studies* 3 (1979): 1–18.                                    EDWARD J. SHULTZ

**KWANTUNG ARMY.** The Japanese Kwantung garrison took its name from the Kwantung (Guandong) Leased Territory on strategic Liaodong Peninsula in southernmost Manchuria. This territory was received from Russia by the terms of the 1905 Portsmouth Treaty ending the Russo-Japanese War. Apart from the leasehold, the Japanese assumed defense of railroad concessions, particularly the South Manchuria Railway, also acquired as spoils. In 1919 the Japanese government separated military and political responsibilities in Manchuria, reorganizing the Army Bureau at Port Arthur (Lüshun) as Kwantung Army (Kantōgun) Headquarters.

Centrally appointed, the Kwantung Army commander reported not to civilian authority but directly to the war minister and general staff in Tokyo. Operating under Supreme Command Prerogative, he avoided home interference in practice. For a decade after World War I, Kwantung Army officers meddled in Chinese factional politics, culminating in Colonel Kōmoto Daisaku's unapproved assassination of Manchurian warlord Zhang Zuolin in June 1928. Three years later the freewheeling Kwantung Army staff arbitrarily provoked the Manchurian Incident at Mukden, exploiting Nationalist China's nonresistance policy. Within five months, the Kwantung Army overran Manchuria. Puppet state Manchukuo, established in 1932, signed a mutual defense treaty with Japan; the Kwantung Army commander served concurrently as ambassador.

Numbering scarcely 10,000 men in 1931, the Kwantung Army reached twelve and one-half divisions, twenty-three garrison units, and twenty-seven air groups by 1940. Along the 3,000-mile international border, frays punctuated the 1930s as the Russians added strength in Siberia and introduced troops into Outer Mongolia (1936). The Kwantung Army's most serious boundary clashes occurred on the Amur River in 1937 and at Nomonhan in the west in 1939. After Germany invaded European Russia in June 1941, the Japanese military and government seriously considered fighting the USSR. In the summer of 1941 a mobilization euphemistically called Kwantung Army Special Maneuvers was conducted, doubling Kwantung Army manpower to 700,000 and greatly improving logistics. Although no Japanese assault materialized, Kwantung Army strength peaked in the period 1942 to 1943, after the Pacific War began.

As Japan began losing the war, the Kwantung Army was bled of men and matériel for deployment elsewhere. When Soviet forces attacked on 9 August 1945, it took only six days until Tokyo announced capitulation. The Russians claimed they inflicted 84,000 casualties and captured about 600,000 soldiers. The era of Japanese attempts at northeast Asian hegemony had come to a close.

[*See also* Mukden Incident; Nomonhan, Battle of; *and* World War II in China.]

Alvin D. Coox, *Nomonhan: Japan against Russia, 1939* (1985).                                    ALVIN D. COOX

**KY, PETRUS.** *See* Truong Vinh Ky.

**KYAI,** or *kiyayi,* Javanese title used as an honorific address for distinguished and respectable gentlemen, especially men learned in a branch of religious knowledge. In present-day Java the term is usually associated with Islamic scholars *(ulama)* and students of religion *(santri).* Previously, however, it was used more widely to designate men who were worthy of respect for their advanced years or position. Venerable *pusaka* (heirloom) krises, lances, *wayangs,* and gamelans are also given individual names with the title *kyai* to indicate their holiness and power, particularly in court circles. The word is sometimes shortened to *ki,* which also stands for a diminutive of *kaki* ("grandfather").

Clifford Geertz, *The Religion of Java* (1960). Th. G. Th. Pigeaud, *Literature of Java,* vol. 1 (1967).

PETER CAREY

KYANZITTHA, one of the most effective kings (r. 1084–1113) of Burma's Pagan dynasty. Kyanzittha (who appears as Kalancacsa in Old Burmese incriptions) apparently rose to the throne on the basis of his military abilities, rather than his genealogical ties to the royal family. He was noted for continuing and completing the work of political expansion and unification begun by his predecessors Anawrahta and Sawlu.

Kyanzittha successfully synthesized Burman military rule, Mon cultural sophistication, Theravada Buddhism and other religious beliefs, and Pyu cultural foundations to create what was to become the classical Burmese tradition. Although he inherited many accomplishments begun by his predecessors, he did strengthen the military and gave the kind of legitimacy to Burman rule that was desperately needed by the conditions of his reign (in part created by the success of his predecessors). He patronized Mon scholars, artisans, and some of their courtly ways to raise the aesthetic qualities of Pagan art and architecture; purified and reinvigorated Theravada Buddhism while tolerating other religious beliefs; and recognized the society's debt to its predecessors, the Pyu, by tracing part of his genealogy to them. Kyanzittha remains today an exemplar of political leadership.

[See also Pagan.]

G. H. Luce, "The Career of Htilaing Min (Kyanzittha), the Uniter of Burma, A.D. 1084–1113," *Journal of the Royal Asiatic Society* (1966): 53–68, and *Old Burma—Early Pagan* (1969).    MICHAEL AUNG-THWIN

KYASWA, king of the Burmese kingdom of Pagan (r. 1235–1249). The son of King Nadaungmya (Natonmya), he succeeded to the throne without apparent incident at a time in Pagan history when a great deal of money was being lavished upon the Buddhist monastic order (sangha). Kyaswa's reign began to feel the effects of giving tax-exempt land and a flow of labor to the church.

Between 1236 and 1237 he attempted to confiscate what he called illegally held glebe land "upstream and downstream," and he held ecclesiastical courts to determine the purity of the *sangha* and perhaps to register them. Despite loading the investigative bodies with relatives, he apparently failed in both attempts.

Kyaswa was also known for his use of moral aphorisms to appeal to his subjects. Carved on stone, the edicts, in which he compared himself implicitly to the great king Ashoka (who had followed a similar strategy), were dispersed throughout the kingdom. Like most kings and modern rulers of Burma, he lived in a culture that compelled him to build a work of merit that was worthy of a king, endow it with good land to ensure its survival indefinitely, and assign to it tax and crown-service labor that would produce the revenue to maintain it and the members of the order that invariably went with it. His Mahabodhi, a copy of the temple at Bodh Gaya, and his Myinpyagu, another large temple, are the best known of Kyaswa's works of merit still standing today.

[See also Pagan.]

Michael Aung-Thwin, *The Origins of the Classical Burmese State: An Institutional History of the Kingdom of Pagan* (1985).    MICHAEL AUNG-THWIN

KYAUKSE, area of Upper Burma, encompassing approximately 530 square miles and located about 80 miles east of Pagan, that may have been the first home of the Burmans in Burma. Probably the most fertile area of Upper Burma, Kyaukse (which means "stone weir" in Burmese) is irrigated by at least four perennial streams. By the eleventh century (and possibly sooner) it was the granary of the Pagan kingdom. Because it was so extensively irrigated, Kyaukse was able to produce three crops a year. Along with two other similarly endowed areas—Minbu and Taungbyon, south and north of Pagan—Kyaukse contained virtually all the wealth of the Burmese kingdoms.

As a crown property, Kyaukse was settled by people who served the crown in return for rights to the produce. It was referred to as a *khayaing* (Old Burmese, *kharuin*, "core, hub, nucleus") because it was considered a center of the kingdom's wealth. It had eleven fortified villages that functioned as the seats of royal authority; from these, members of the royalty who had been appointed as Kyaukse's governors and as other types of overseers performed their duties. Today Kyaukse retains the economic importance it has had throughout Burmese history.

[See also Pagan.]

G. E. Harvey, *A History of Burma from the Earliest Times* (1925; reprint, 1967). G. H. Luce, "Old Kyaukse and the Coming of the Burmans," *Journal of the Burma Research Society* 42.1 (1959): 75–112.

MICHAEL AUNG-THWIN

KYAW NYEIN (b. 1915), Burmese politician who served as deputy prime minister in 1948 and 1956–1958, as minister for Home Affairs in 1947–1948, and in other cabinet positions during the 1950s. He began his political career in student nationalist politics during the 1930s and during the wartime Japanese occupation of Burma served in various capacities under Ba Maw. In 1946 he was elected secretary-general of the Anti-Fascist People's Freedom League (AFPFL) over a Communist candidate and held this post until 1956. A keen political rival of the Communists, he ordered the arrest of their leaders in March 1948, at the start of the civil war. Following the split of the AFPFL in 1958, he led the Stable faction with U Ba Swe but lost the election of 1960.

[See also Anti-Fascist People's Freedom League and Ba Swe.]

Frank N. Trager, *Burma: From Kingdom to Republic* (1966).                ROBERT H. TAYLOR

**KYAWSWA**, king of the Burmese kingdom of Pagan (1288–1297). He attempted to resurrect the Pagan kingdom, which had been attacked by an external enemy, possibly the Mongols, by winning the succession struggles that followed when Narathihapade was eliminated by his son, Thihathu. Some scholars have argued that although he received the allegiance of most of the royal family and others in relevant positions and seemed to have control over the Pagan court, Kyawswa had begun to lose his power to the so-called Three Shan Brothers, who had rights over the rich Kyaukse area. On the other hand, evidence that he was fully in control is as compelling. For example, he went through the elaborate ritual of coronation in 1289, he continued to dedicate land to newly built monasteries and temples as did his ministers and governors (who, in addition, publicly recognized his suzerainty), and he died a natural rather than a violent death, passing his authority to his legitimate successor, Sawnit.

[See also Pagan.]

Michael Aung-Thwin, *The Origins of the Classical Burmese State: An Institutional History of the Kingdom of Pagan* (1985). Paul J. Bennett, *Conference under the Tamarind Tree: Three Essays in Burmese History* (1971).

MICHAEL AUNG-THWIN

**KYŌGEN**, a classical Japanese theatric form. *Kyōgen* developed in the fourteenth century along with *nō* drama. There are two categories of *kyōgen*: *ai kyōgen*, the interlude between acts in a *nō* play in which a *kyōgen* actor in the role of a local man summarizes the plot of the play thus far and relates the history of the principal character, and independent *kyōgen* skits, usually performed between complete *nō* plays to provide comic relief. The term *kyōgen* usually refers to the latter category. *Kyōgen* literally means "wild words," a Buddhist term for literary or dramatic speech that, though frivolous, might lead to enlightenment. The term was first applied to entertainment of secular content performed between long religious ceremonies; *kyōgen* drama probably evolved from such entertainments. *Kyōgen* and *nō* developed together: Zeami, the playwright and critic who is credited with creating *nō*, mentions both *ai* and independent *kyōgen*. Through the seventeenth century, *kyōgen* actors were held in low esteem, even by fellow actors and musicians. Their art was all but ignored by chroniclers in the fourteenth and fifteenth centuries, and no attempt was made to summarize or record *kyōgen* plays until the early seventeenth century. Over two hundred *kyōgen* plays survive today; all are anonymous. Unlike *nō*, *kyōgen* is generally performed without masks. The earliest form of *kyōgen* play is a festive medley of auspicious song and dance, and one of this type is often the first *kyōgen* presented in a program. There is little humor or satire in this kind of *kyōgen*. The later and better-known examples of *kyōgen* focus on comic situations, or even parody famous *nō* plays. There is little singing or dancing. Many of the plays have two stock characters, a dim-witted lord and his clever servant Tarō Kaja; others involve gods, monks, animals, and demons; and all give a vivid picture of Japanese life in the fourteenth and fifteenth centuries.

[See also Nō.]

André Beaujard, *Le Théâtre Comique des Japonais* (1937). Donald Keene, *Nō: The Classical Theatre of Japan* (1966, rev. ed. 1973). Arthur Waley, trans., *The Nō Plays of Japan* (1957).                AILEEN GATTEN

**KYŌHŌ REFORMS**, the first comprehensive attack by the Tokugawa *bakufu* of Japan on the problems of its maturity. Initiated by Tokugawa Yoshimune, who became shogun in 1716, and named for the era in which they took place, the reforms first of all addressed government finances, reducing expenditure and maximizing income through land reclamation, increased taxation, and daimyo contributions. To make government more effective, a number of corrupt local officials were purged, and high office was thrown open to a broader spectrum of the bureaucracy. The shogun also involved himself in government through the institution of a suggestion box. In the economy at large, efforts were made to curb inflation through price control and currency revaluation. The government also embraced mercantilism, limiting the export of precious metals and trying to replace imported items with Japanese products. The *bakufu's* legal system was rationalized, and stricter measures were taken on gambling and prostitution. By controlling interest rates and refusing to allow creditors to take debtors to court, the government also took steps to protect samurai from the consequences of indebtedness.

On the whole these reforms were unsuccessful. This was in part owing to the Kyōhō famine, which made many measures unenforceable, but more a result of the mistaken assumptions concerning society and human behavior on which they were based. The failure was apparent long before Yoshimune's death in 1751. Peasant resistance forced the taxation policy to be jettisoned, with the result that *bakufu* income declined steadily after 1744. Currency reform, while it had certainly curbed inflation, also invited a general economic depression from which only renewed currency debasement offered escape. All attempts at price control failed, as did efforts to rescue the samurai from debt. The appointment of capable administrators, too, barely survived Yoshimune: within a decade some of his own appointees were to be purged in their turn. Legal reform and greater access to Western books proved the most lasting effects of these policies.

[*See also* Tokugawa Yoshimune; Kansei Reforms; *and* Tempō Reforms.]

HAROLD BOLITHO

KYŎNGJU, Korean city in North Kyŏngsang Province, 34 miles from Taegu, the provincial capital. Kyŏngju was capital of the kingdom of Silla (57 BCE–935 CE) and its environs have furnished rich archaeological evidence for early Korean civilization. The temple of Pulguk (Pulguksa) and the grotto shrine of Sŏkkuram combine with an excellent museum to make the city a principal tourist site. The city is surrounded by huge mounded tombs, some as high as seventy feet, in which royalty or nobility were interred. The most important has yielded a gold crown that is one of Korea's most important historical artifacts. The introduction of Buddhism, however, ended the era of tombs, as was later to be the case in Japan as well.

MARIUS B. JANSEN

KYOTO, the imperial capital of Japan from 794 until 1868. Throughout its premodern history, Kyoto was a city of diverse character. It served as the national center of learning and high culture, the headquarters of major religious institutions, a hub of production and commerce, and the seat of the Ashikaga shogunate. Indeed, Kyoto remained Japan's sole significant city until the late sixteenth century and was one of three leading metropolitan centers (with Edo and Osaka) until the late nineteenth century. Kyoto lost much of its political centrality following the establishment in 1603 of the Toku-

FIGURE 1. *Shakyamuni Buddha.* Sŏkkuram, Kyŏngju, mid-eighth century.

gawa shogunate (which made its capital Edo, present day Tokyo) and was fully eclipsed as a seat of national government when the imperial household assumed residence in Tokyo after 1869. The city has nonetheless prospered in the modern era as a center of education and religion, scientific research and health services, the chemical and electronics industries, traditional crafts, and tourism.

Kyoto lies in a valley, surrounded on three sides by the Tamba Mountains. The Kamo and Katsura rivers flow through the city, joining the Yodo River to the south and thus connecting the landlocked metropolis to Osaka Bay. Long associated with important aristocratic families, the area was chosen as a capital site in 794 following the abandonment of Nara (originally called Heijōkyō) and a brief, abortive attempt to establish the imperial administration in Nagaoka. Like its predecessors, the new capital (originally called Heiankyō, or "capital of peace and tranquillity") was laid out, in emulation of the contemporary Chinese capital Chang'an, in a grid pattern with a north-south axis. It covered roughly 6,000 acres, measuring approximately 3.2 miles from north to south and 2.8 miles from east to west. The city expanded in the premodern era both to the north and to the east, across the Kamo River, while retaining its essential symmetry. The development of the western area of the city has been a modern phenomenon. Kyoto now covers 236 square miles.

The ancient city was dominated by a vast imperial compound. Located in the north-central sector of the city, the Palace itself and the great buildings of state conveyed the majesty and power of monarchical rule—a national and highly centralized system of administration that was aristocratic in organization and bureaucratic in function. Dramatic official buildings had masonry foundations, white plaster walls, wood columns painted in vermilion, green tile roofs, and gold fixtures. Although the city had no outer rampart, both the imperial compound and the individual enclaves within it stood behind gates and walls affording entry only to the elite. Such arrangements prevailed throughout the premodern period; government buildings visible or accessible to common citizens, public gardens and monuments, and even ceremonies of state with a public character are all modern arrivals in the Japanese city.

While population estimates sometimes range to improbably high figures, it seems likely that Kyoto had approximately 100,000 people in the eleventh century, 200,000 in the late sixteenth century, and 350,000 in the eighteenth century. The current population is roughly 1,475,000. Growth was not steady during the premodern period, and declines to below 100,000 people may have occurred during periods of war.

At the heart of Kyoto's premodern population was an aristocracy of 10,000 or more that attracted large constellations of servants, retainers, and skilled craftspeople, including architects, engineers, carpenters, textile workers of every description, potters, metal and lacquer workers, painters, makers of ink and paper, and so forth. This accomplished community of artisans, originally attached to government offices or noble families, formed the nucleus of medieval guilds, which, in turn, produced the independent professional craftspeople of the early modern period. Kyoto's dominance in the traditional crafts, particularly fine textiles, has been continuous.

The variety and excellence of Kyoto's artisans derived fundamentally from the taste, affluence, and ambition of an aristocracy absorbed by beauty. The aristocratic community in the capital emerged as eminent patrons and practitioners of the arts, peerless builders, and—most importantly—literate gentlepeople who produced masterpieces of poetry and prose that remained the foundation of Japan's high culture and gave to its aristocratic interpreters and exponents a lasting cultural authority. The most distinguished literary works of the classical period include the poetic anthology *Kokin wakashū* (completed in the late tenth century), the *Genji monogatari (Tale of Genji)* by Murasaki Shikibu, and the *Pillow Book* of Sei Shōnagon (both completed in the early eleventh century). [*See* Genji Monogatari.] Artistic energy was at its height during the ascendancy of the Fujiwara family, whose heads served as regents to successive emperors and in this way exercised a critical political and cultural influence from the mid-ninth to the mid-eleventh century. The Buddhist temple Byōdōin, located in Uji, survives as a monument to Fujiwara taste. [*See* Fujiwara Lineage.]

Also important to Kyoto's premodern character and population was the Buddhist clergy. Despite early attempts to contain Buddhist influence in the city (by forbidding the Nara sects to transfer their headquarters to the new capital, for example), Kyoto soon surpassed its predecessor in religious influence. Located within and closely adjacent to the city were major monasteries of the classical period that received aristocratic patronage (including Enryakuji on Mount Hiei and Tōji), as well as major temples of the medieval and early modern periods that flourished with more popular support (including the Jōdo temple of Chion'in, the Jōdo Shinshū

FIGURE 1. *Phoenix Hall, Byōdōin, Kyoto.* Hall dedicated to Amida Buddha, built by Fujiwara Yorimichi in 1053.

temples of Nishi and Higashi Honganji, the Nichiren temple of Honkokuji, and many Zen monasteries, such as Nanzenji and Daitokuji). Monks, priests, and students from across Japan studied at Kyoto's temples, which became centers of secular as well as religious education, the intellectual training ground of the nation. [*See* Enryakuji.]

The essential features of Japanese government in the classical Heian period (794–1185)—that is, the imperial institution itself and the large bureaucracy of aristocratic office holders—survived throughout the premodern period. The monarchy, of course, continues to this day. Yet both emperor and aristocracy were consigned to increasingly symbolic roles in the medieval (1185–1467) and early modern (1467–1868) eras. The nobility remained a consequential class of landed proprietors in the middle ages. Practical governing power over the nation, however, came to be exercised by military leaders

of the Kamakura (1185–1333) and Ashikaga (1336–1573) shogunates. [*See* Kamakura Period *and* Muromachi Period.] Both regimes took power after civil wars that occasioned the widespread devastation of Kyoto and that demonstrated the inability of the aristocracy to maintain order without martial deputies to whom they effectively relinquished control. The great imperial compound, symbol of monarchical rule, was never rebuilt after the classical period.

The political dominance that Kyoto shared with the new shogunal capital of Kamakura was recovered when the Ashikaga shoguns chose to make the imperial city their own headquarters. The renewed primacy of the city was reflected in several splendid shogunal residences (including the "gold" and "silver" pavilions, Kinkakuji and Ginkakuji), spacious Zen monasteries supported by the military class (including Shōkokuji), and a rich cultural life that flourished under Ashikaga patronage (ranging, for example, over the fields of monochrome landscape painting, dry rock gardening, *nō* drama, and Chinese poetry).

Prolonged civil war raged in Japan from 1467 until 1590, as warriors throughout the provinces wrested control over land from both traditional noble proprietors and members of the ruling military community. Much of Kyoto's elite was impoverished, and the city was periodically ravaged by battle, rebellion, and natural disaster. Residential "islands" surrounded by moats and walls and protected by stout gates and fortifications took over the urban landscape. Yet the period also saw two salutary developments of lasting import: the emergence of governing organizations of townspeople who administered their neighborhoods in the power vacuum created by shogunal debility, and significant commercial growth (particularly in arms and textiles) as an already strong community of artisans, moneylenders, and merchants became linked to regional and eventually national markets stimulated by the demands of war.

The pacification and political reunification of Japan began with Oda Nobunaga, a provincial daimyo who overthrew the Ashikaga shogunate in 1573 and governed Kyoto through his own deputy. Toyotomi Hideyoshi, Nobunaga's successor, initiated the reconstruction of the city and built new monuments on a lavish scale (including an outer rampart, additional streets, the castle of Jurakutei, and an immense Buddhist icon housed in the temple of Hōkōji). Often using Kyoto as his own political base, Hideyoshi eliminated traditional proprietary privileges in the city (including aristocrats' claims to taxes and rents, as well as guild monopolies) and subordinated all urban institutions to the jurisdiction of his deputy *(shoshidai)*, a practice continued by Hideyoshi's successors, the Tokugawa shoguns. [*See* Oda Nobunaga *and* Toyotomi Hideyoshi.]

The Tokugawa, governing from Edo between 1603 and 1868, maintained a residence in Kyoto but rarely visited the city themselves. [*See* Nijō Castle.] Kyoto continued to develop commercially, yet yielded economic primacy to Osaka and Edo by 1700. The courtly tradition in art and literature was maintained, and popular forms of drama (including *kabuki* and *bunraku*), painting and graphic arts, poetry, and fiction thrived in a city that emerged as a major book publisher. Kyoto became, as well, the national center of pilgrimage and tourism, activities that were served by the bourgeoning number of commercial maps, guide books, and shopping directories.

Kyoto was once more at the center of national politics in the mid-nineteenth century when imperial loyalists mounted a rebellion against shogunal rule in the name of the emperor. [*See* Meiji Restoration.] In 1869, however, the Meiji emperor moved to Tokyo, which became, by the end of the century, the capital of a constitutional monarchy.

Modern Kyoto is the seat of Kyoto Prefecture; it is a prosperous industrial city, the site of major museums and universities, and a tourist mecca. Kyoto was not bombed during World War II, and many of its historical treasures remain. The Imperial Palace, reconstructed in the late nineteenth century, has been the site of modern enthronement ceremonies.

John W. Hall, "Kyoto as Historical Background," in *Medieval Japan: Essays in Institutional History,* edited by John W. Hall and Jeffrey P. Mass (1974), pp. 3–38. Hayashiya Tatsusaburō with George Elison, "Kyoto in the Muromachi Age," in *Japan in the Muromachi Age,* edited by John W. Hall and Toyodo Takeshi (1977), pp. 15–36. Donald Keene, *World Within Walls* (1976). William H. McCollough and Helen Craig McCollough, trans., *A Tale of Flowering Fortunes,* 2 vols. (1980). Ivan Morris, trans., *The Pillow Book of Sei Shōnagon* (1967). R. A. B. Ponsonby-Fane, *Kyoto: The Old Capital of Japan* (reprint, 1956). Edward Seidensticker, trans., *The Tale of Genji* (1976). Wakita Haruko with Susan B. Hanley, "Dimensions of Development: Cities in Fifteenth- and Sixteenth-Century Japan," in *Japan Before Tokugawa,* edited by John W. Hall, et al. (1981), pp. 295–326.

MARY ELIZABETH BERRY

**KYUSHU.** *See* Japan: Geographic Regions of Japan.

# L

LABUAN, small island off the west coast of Sabah, about forty miles north of Brunei. Because Labuan possessed a good harbor, adequate water, a strategic location, and coal reserves, British agents pressured the sultan of Brunei to cede the sparsely populated island as a crown colony in 1846. In 1888 Britain transferred the colony's administration to the North Borneo Chartered Company, but in 1907 Labuan was placed under the jurisdiction of the Straits Settlements. In 1946 Labuan became part of the new British colony of North Borneo (Sabah). The island was an economic liability to the British for much of its history, but many Chinese and Malays settled there. Labuan's economic status has improved considerably since the formation of Malaysia; in 1970 the island's population totaled 17,189.

Maxwell Hall, *Labuan Story: Memoirs of a Small Island* (1958). K. G. Tregonning, *A History of Modern Sabah: North Borneo, Borneo, 1881–1963* (1965).

CRAIG A. LOCKARD

LAC LONG QUAN ("dragon lord Lac"), in Viet legend a descendant of the proto-Chinese agricultural deity Shen Nong. Lac Long Quan left his home in the sea and brought civilization to the inhabitants of the Red River delta. When a northern invader appeared in the delta, Lac Long Quan kidnapped the invader's wife, the fairy Au Co, and took her to Tan Vien Mountain. Au Co then bore Lac Long Quan a hundred sons, fifty of whom returned with their father to the sea and fifty of whom remained in the uplands. Lac Long Quan and Au Co are considered by the Viet people to be their legendary progenitors. The Viet sometimes refer to themselves as the children of the dragon and the fairy.

[*See also* Au Co *and* Tan Vien Mountain.]

Keith W. Taylor, *The Birth of Vietnam* (1983).

JAMES M. COYLE

LAC VIET, the people of the Red River civilization. The term *Lac Viet* is particularly associated with the Dong Son culture, but it may be applied as far back as the Neolithic Phung Nguyen culture (c. 1800 BCE). The Lac Viet practiced wet-rice cultivation, developed their own bronze technology, and traded with neighboring peoples. Lac society was based on the small family and the village commune. Both kinship and inheritance are thought to have been bilateral. At the regional level there was a loose hierarchy of Lac lords, culminating in the king, called the Hung Vuong. Viet tradition holds that the Hung Vuong ruled over a confederation of fifteen Lac tribes.

Lac society survived the political vicissitudes of Chinese suzerainty until it was destroyed after the suppression of the Trung Sisters Rebellion in 43 CE.

[*See also* Dong Son; Hung Vuong; *and* Trung Sisters Rebellion.]

Thomas Hodgkin, *Vietnam: The Revolutionary Path* (1981). Keith W. Taylor, *The Birth of Vietnam* (1983).

JAMES M. COYLE

LADAKH. The region of Ladakh embraces the Ladakh and Karakoram ranges of the western Himalayas and the valley of the upper Indus River. The area is arid, averaging three inches of rainfall a year, and is one of the highest inhabited areas of the world. Historically, trade has always played an important role in the economy. Pastoralism, largely of yak and sheep, is also an important part of the economy, while agriculture is limited to irrigated plots of barley, buckwheat, sour grass, and root crops.

Information about the area prior to the tenth century is limited. The earliest population of Ladakh was probably composed of the Dardis, and a small Dardi-speaking population still exists between Hanu and Morol. In the first or second century lower Ladakh was included within the Kushan empire. Other inscriptions dating to that period supply evidence of cultural intercourse with India, apparently through Kashmir. The Korean pilgrim Hyech'o (Chinese, Huichao), who traveled from India back to China in 727, reported that Ladakh was part of the Tibetan empire and that Buddhism was flourishing in the area at that time. Buddhism first entered Ladakh from India through Kashmir. The influence of Tibetan Buddhism dates to the eleventh century. Ladakh remained a political part of the Tibetan empire until at least the middle of the ninth century, and cultural ties between the two countries continued beyond that time. The origin of the Ladakhi kingdom is connected with the decline of the Tibetan monarchy in the ninth century.

The imperialistic tendencies of some of the Kashmiri sultans after the conversion of Kashmir to Islam brought a new element of instability to the western Himalayas, and Ladakh was invaded through Kashmir several times in the fifteenth and sixteenth centuries. In the next century, however, the Ladakhi kingdom reached a brief pinnacle of power with the conquest of Gu-ge in 1633. Ladakh's ensuing conflict with Tibet (1679–1684) was resolved only after the intervention of the Mughal governor of Kashmir. The resolution of this conflict reduced Ladakh's power and deprived the kingdom of half its former territory. Ladakh never recovered its role of political importance in the region. As part of the conditions for Mughal support, the king converted to Islam and a mosque was established at Leh. From 1834 to 1842 the area was invaded and conquered by the Dogra army of Raja Gulab Singh, who annexed it to the region of Jammu. Thereafter the area ceased to have a separate political identity or a separate history. Ladakh was invaded by Pakistani forces in 1948 and the area is still contested by both India and Pakistan. In the early 1960s Chinese forces penetrated and gained control of the remote area known as Aksai Chin in the northeast.

[*See also* Aksai Chin *and* Kashmir.]

A. H. Francke, *A History of Ladakh* (1977). Luciano Petech, *The Kingdom of Ladakh: c. 950–1842* (1977). D. L. Snellgrove and Tadeusz Skorupski, *The Cultural Heritage of Ladakh* (1977).　　WILLIAM F. FISHER

## LA GRANDIÈRE, PIERRE-PAUL-MARIE DE
(1807–1876), governor of Cochinchina (1863–1868). During his term as governor, de la Grandière worked to consolidate and expand France's territorial gains. Acting independently of Paris, he risked war with Siam to negotiate a treaty of protectorate with Cambodia's King Norodom. He then went on to occupy the three southern provinces still in Vietnamese hands—Vinh Long, Chau Doc, and Ha Tien—after accusing Phan Thanh Gian of supporting anti-French activities there. The provinces were not officially ceded until 1874. De la Grandière also sponsored the important Lagrée-Garnier Mekong Exploration Mission of 1866–1868.

[*See also* Genouilly, Charles Rigault de *and* Norodom.]

Joseph Buttinger, *The Smaller Dragon: A Political History of Vietnam* (1958). John Cady, *The Roots of French Imperialism in Eastern Asia* (1954).

BRUCE M. LOCKHART

LAHORE, the capital of the Punjab and the second-largest city of Pakistan. An ancient city, Lahore is often mentioned in history. The origin of the city of Lahore and its early history are shrouded in mystery. Hindu tradition claims that it was named after the *Ramayana*'s legendary hero Rama's son Loh or Lava. Xuanzang, the Chinese pilgrim, mentions it. It was probably founded at the end of the first or the beginning of the second century. The first authentic reference to Lahore is found in al-Biruni's *Tarikhul Hind*, compiled about 1030 to 1033. The Ghaznavid and Ghori sultans (1098–1206) made it the capital of their empires and adorned it with numerous buildings. Lahore has seen many empires rise and fall, and many invaders and travelers passed through it. The Mughals (1526–1765) enriched its architectural heritage with splendid buildings. Qutb ud-Din Aibak, Jahangir, Nur Jahan, and Asaf Khan are buried in the city. The tomb of Muhammad Iqbal, poet-philosopher and thinker of Pakistan, is in front of Badshahi Mosque. Many famous Muslim saints lived and preached here and devotees from all over Pakistan and many other parts of the world come every year to pay homage.

The mosque of Wazir Khan and the Lahore Fort, built by Akbar and beautified by Shah Jahan, display magnificent examples of encaustic tile work. Other examples of exquisite architectural beauty and grace are Aurengzeb's Badshahi Mosque, a lofty structure of red sandstone ornamented with marble tracing (see figure 1); Jahangir's tomb, also constructed of red sandstone with marble ornamentation; and the Shalamar and Jinnah gardens.

The Sikhs ruled Lahore from 1765 to 1849. Ranjit Singh made it his capital. The British (1849–1947) beautified Lahore with buildings that harmoniously combine Mughal, Victorian, and Gothic styles of architecture. Under British rule Lahore was a major cultural center of North India, especially notable for its role in Urdu literature and Hindu religious reform movements such as the Arya Samaj. Lahore was also a hub of political activity during the freedom movement. Famous Hindu, Sikh, Muslim, and Christian leaders, representing the Indian National Congress, the Muslim League, and other minor political parties, used Lahore as their base for propagating their ideas. Newspapers, journals, and periodicals in Urdu, Hindi, English, and Punjabi were published.

In March 1940 the Muslim League passed a resolution at its Lahore session demanding a separate Muslim state. Suddenly Lahore became politically important for the Congress and the League. After independence in 1947 it became the capital of the Punjab, then of West Pakistan (1955–1969).

Since 1947 Lahore has grown enormously. Its population has increased to many times its former size. There are two universities and many colleges and schools; students have played an important role in its cultural and political activities. Student demonstrations against Ayub Khan, Yahya Khan and Zulfiqar Ali Bhutto led to the downfall of their governments.

Lahore is famous for its eating places, shopping centers, cinema houses, film studios, and theaters, and its families of musicians, singers, and wrestlers.

Many well-known writers, poets, thinkers, and literary figures have lived and worked in this city, enriching its cultural traditions.

Muhammad Baqir, *Lahore: Past and Present* (1952). Syed Muhammad Latif, *Lahore: Its History, Architectural Remains and Antiquities* (1956–1957).    S. RAZI WASTI

LAJPAT RAI, LALA (1865–1928), Indian nationalist leader. He was born in Dhudki, Ferozepore District to an Aggarwal Baniya family, and attended the Government College in Lahore. Lajpat joined the Arya Samaj in December 1882 and the Indian National Congress in 1888. On 9 May 1907 he was deported to Burma for his radical politics and released on 18 November 1907. Lajpat spoke before the Punjab Hindu Conference in October 1909 and left for England in April 1914. He visited the United States in 1914 and Japan in 1915, returning to India in February 1920. In 1925 he presided over two meetings held in Calcutta, a session of the Indian National Congress and one of the Hindu Mahasabha.

[*See also* Arya Samaj *and* Indian National Congress.]

Lala Lajpat Rai, *Autobiographical Writings,* edited by V. C. Joshi (1965), and *Speeches and Writings,* 2 vols. (1966).    KENNETH W. JONES

FIGURE 1. *Badhshahi Mosque, Lahore.* Built by Emperor Aurangzeb (r. 1659–1707).

LAKSAMANA, Sanskrit word meaning "admiral" or "lord of the fleet." In a traditional Malay court the *laksamana* was in charge of the fleet and the coast and was one of Malaya's four principal ministers. Because the wealth of the region was primarily derived from sea-borne trade, the *laksamana* was of great importance. The office tended to be held in one or two of the main families; the first, and most famous, *laksamana* of the Melaka sultanate was Hang Tuah. The *laksamana* family played a major part in restoring power and prosperity to seventeenth-century Johor.

[See also Bendahara; Melaka; *and* Johor.]

C. C. Brown, "Sejarah Melayu or Malay Annals," *Journal of the Malay Branch of the Royal Asiatic Society* 25.2–3 (October 1952). Kernial Singh Sandhu and Paul Wheatley, eds., *Melaka—The Transformation of a Malay Capital c. 1400–1980* (1983).     DIANNE LEWIS

LAKSHMI BAI (1824?–1858), *rani* of Jhansi (in present-day Uttar Pradesh), widow of Gangadhar Rao, the last ruler of Jhansi. Gangadhar Rao died issueless and his state was annexed to British territory by Lord Dalhousie in 1854 through application of the Doctrine of Lapse. The *rani* was provided with a pension but, despite her appeals, was denied the throne. At this time she was approximately thirty years of age and by all accounts was highly capable.

On 5 June 1857 the Jhansi sepoys revolted and killed numerous English residents. Although considerable contrary evidence existed, British officials accused the *rani* of conspiring in the mutiny and massacre. She subsequently led her troops—including a force of women—into battle against British attackers in bloody encounters at Jhansi, Kalpi, and Gwalior. Riding horseback and dressed in male attire, she died in battle on 17 June 1858. Her heroism was remembered throughout India's struggle for independence and is still celebrated in stories and songs.

[See also Mutiny, Indian.]

Michael Edwardes, *Red Year: The Indian Rebellion of 1857* (1973). Joyce Lebra-Chapman, *The Rani of Jhansi: A Study in Female Heroism in India* (1986).

DORANNE JACOBSON

LAMAISM, the Western term for the Buddhism of Tibet. The term was given currency by L. A. Waddell, whose 1895 work *The Buddhism of Tibet, or Lamaism* was the first encyclopedic study of Tibetan Buddhism. Tibetan Buddhists object to the term when it is used (as it was by Waddell) to imply that Tibetan Buddhism is a deviant form of Buddhism. But if one means by it that Tibetan Buddhism is a unique form of Buddhism that focuses on putting the Buddhist teachings into practice by following the precept of one's personal teacher, or lama, then it is not deemed objectionable. *Lama* means "unexcelled," and is the Tibetan translation of the Sanskrit *guru.*

Learned Tibetans are proud of having received the final form of Indian Buddhism, transmitted from the monastic centers at Nalanda and Vikramashila after 700 CE, including what they call the Three Vehicles—Hinayana, Mahayana, and Tantrayana, considered to be, respectively, the monastic, messianic, and apocalyptic forms of Buddhism. The vast literature of the Buddhist Tantras is fully preserved only in Tibet; relatively few such texts remain in India, Nepal, China, and Japan. This extensive Tantric lore enabled the Buddhist missionaries who came to Tibet to develop powerful rituals and contemplations to "tame," as they put it, the uncivilized, shamanistic Tibetans and bring them into the Buddhist fold. The same knowledge was later used by the Tibetans to "tame" the Mongols and then the Manchus. This achievement has been misread by non-Tibetan scholars to mean that Buddhism compromised with or was assimilated by shamanism, a judgment that has led them to the mistaken perception that Lamaism is degenerate, born of a "pact with the devil," as Waddell so colorfully put it.

Atisha (982–1054), an Indian abbot who was the most important of the later missionaries to Tibet, was once asked by his Tibetan disciples, "Which is more important: the scriptures and treatises or the precept of the guru (lama)?" He responded, "The precept of the guru: even though you know all the texts by heart, without the guru's precept, at the time of practice you and the Dharma [the Buddhist teachings] go separate ways." Thus, the guru or lama system had already become established in Indian Buddhism. [See also Atisha.] The guru in Hinayana Buddhism was to be thought of as the representative of the Buddha, the original abbot of the community. The guru in Mahayana Buddhism was thought of as the spiritual friend, vessel of the Buddhas' blessings and inspiration. The Buddhism of the Tantras, however, started from the ritual and contemplative visualization of the guru as the Buddha himself, or even as the quintessence of all Buddhas.

The more intense the pressure on the practitioner to achieve immediate realization, the less remote is the presence of the fruitional exemplar, hence the importance of the lama in Tibetan Buddhism. A further reason why the term *Lamaism* is not at all inappropriate has to do with the unique history of Tibet, in that only there did Buddhist monasticism develop to the point where it expanded beyond the traditional role of alternative social reality, taking upon itself the responsibility of managing the secular society as well as the institutions of education and spiritual training.

[*See also* Buddhism; Tantra; *and* Tibet.]

Tenzin Gyatso (Dalai Lama), *The Buddhism of Tibet* (1974). Hugh E. Richardson and David L. Snellgrove, *Cultural History of Tibet* (1968). R. A. Stein, *Tibetan Civilization* (1972).          ROBERT A. F. THURMAN

FIGURE 1. *Wat Phra That Haripunjaya, Lamphun.* Probably constructed in 1108, the *wat* includes a *chedi* that is sixty meters high and twenty meters wide at the base.

**LAMBERT, GEORGE ROBERT,** British naval officer who played an important role in the Second Anglo-Burmese War (1851–1852). Born in 1795, Lambert entered the navy in 1809. Lord Dalhousie (James Andrew Broun Ramsay), the governor-general of India, gave Lambert the opprobrious title of "combustible commodore" for his apparently unrestrained activities at the start of the Second Anglo-Burmese War. His exaggerated response to the Burmese seizure of two British ships in Rangoon harbor resulted in the commitment of colonial authorities to an ill-considered but irreversible course of war and acquisition. Research suggests that Lambert was a cautious, moderate individual who was strongly influenced by anti-Burmese propaganda spread by Rangoon's English merchants and American Baptist missionaries, both of whom had a long-standing desire for British intervention in Burma. Dalhousie and the English politician Richard Cobden threatened a parliamentary investigation of Lambert's actions, but the resultant government blue book left Lambert virtually unscathed.

[*See also* Anglo-Burmese Wars *and* Ramsay, James Andrew Broun.]

Oliver B. Pollak, "The Origins of the Second Anglo-Burmese War (1852–53)," *Modern Asian Studies* 12 (1978): 483–502.          OLIVER B. POLLAK

**LAMPHUN,** long-established city in northern Thailand. Perhaps originally settled by Mon people, Lamphun became the capital of the kingdom of Haripunjaya in the eighth century CE. According to legend, Buddhist monks there sent to Lopburi for a

ruler and received Princess Camadevi, daughter of the king of Lopburi. Her dynasty continued for some centuries (intermittently after the tenth century under the suzerainty of Cambodian Angkor) until Mangrai, founder of Lan Na, conquered it in 1281. Thereafter it remained an important provincial city, only twenty-five kilometers from Chiang Mai.

[*See also* Dvaravati; Mon; Lopburi; Angkor; Mangrai; *and* Lan Na.]

David K. Wyatt, *Thailand: A Short History* (1984).
DAVID K. WYATT

**LAM SON UPRISING,** a rebellion begun in 1406 against the Ming occupation of Vietnam (then called Dai Viet), following Ho Quy Ly's usurpation of power from the Tran. It was led by Le Loi (c. 1385–1433), a village chief in the Lam Son area of Thanh Hoa Province. In February 1418 he proclaimed himself Binh Dinh Vuong ("pacifying king") and began a series of scattered attacks against the Chinese garrisons. Although the Lam Son movement had some victories during the next four years, it also experienced defeat and hardship, in particular a shortage of rations. By the end of 1422 the rebels' situation was so bad that Le Loi agreed to negotiate a truce, which he signed in March 1423.

When he again took the offensive in 1424, however, Le Loi adopted a strategy advocated by his lieutenant Nguyen Trai. Instead of launching sporadic, local attacks, Le Loy organized a guerrilla movement with broad-based popular support. By initially focusing his attacks on Nghe An, he controlled all of southern Dai Viet (extending approximately to the sixteenth parallel), except for the major cities, by the fall of 1425. In 1426 he began an offensive against Chinese troops led by Wang Tong that was centered on the capital at Dong-do in the Red River delta. Although the Chinese defied his appeals for surrender, Le Loi was able to strengthen his forces and augment his supply of arms and rations while consolidating his administration.

In late 1427 Le Loi's defeat of new reinforcements under Liu Sheng and Mu Cheng finally incited Wang Tong to surrender. The Ming troops returned to China in early 1428, having been spared and even provisioned by Le Loi. He then founded the Le dynasty, ruling as Le Thai To (1428–1433), and inaugurated an era of peaceful Sino-Vietnamese relations that lasted until the dynasty's end.

[See also Le Loi; Le Dynasties; and Nguyen Trai.]

BRUCE M. LOCKHART

## LAND TENURE AND REFORM

### LAND REFORM IN MODERN CHINA

From early modern times until about 1955 almost all the land in China was operated as individual farms. Most land was also held by individual owners, although the owner was not necessarily the same person as the operator. Other ownership patterns were closely related to individual ownership, including ownership by clans, temples, and other institutions that functioned much like private landowners, and land held under rules of customary tenure, which in effect meant that two parties each owned certain specified rights to the land.

Patterns based on individual ownership and operation had existed off and on for more than two thousand years, but they had alternated or coexisted with very different patterns for much of this period. The "well-field" system, under which each of eight families supported itself on one piece of land and worked with the others on one piece for their lord, was a classical ideal. Much land was distributed under state ownership in the "equal field" system of the Northern Dynasties and the early Tang. Serfdom and slavery were widespread in many eras down to the Yuan. From the Ming onward, however, the principal alternative to freehold farming was family-farm tenancy.

When the Qing dynasty was strong, taxes on the owners of land formed one of the main sources of its revenue. During the nineteenth century, however, its ability to collect land taxes declined. After the fall of the Qing in 1911, land taxes went almost entirely to provincial authorities; this remained the rule in most areas until the rise of the Chinese Communist Party (CCP). The severity of taxation varied arbitrarily from one area to another.

In the first half of the twentieth century the level of tenancy was lowest in the area around the Yellow River. Tenancy increased as one moved southward, reaching very high levels in some areas of the far South; it was also high in the northeast. Considerable debate exists as to the average level of land concentration, but the estimate found in many CCP sources—that the landlords and rich peasants, who constituted less than 10 percent of the population, owned 70 to 80 percent of the land—is definitely mistaken. This estimate was formulated very early in the CCP's research on rural conditions and was not revised when later CCP surveys showed it to have been exaggerated.

The question of whether land concentration was increasing or decreasing in the decades up to 1949 must also be treated with caution. In some areas, warlords and other powerful people were taking advantage of unstable conditions to accumulate very large landholdings. In others, the decline of law and order broke up large landholdings, as absentee owners became unable to control their tenants. Patterns of social mobility that created the appearance of a progressive increase in the concentration of landholdings even in areas where no such trend actually existed confuse the issue further.

Sun Yat-sen proposed the slogan "Land to the Tillers," but he died before being faced with the problem of how this should be interpreted in practice. After the split between the Guomindang (Kuomintang, KMT, or Nationalist Party) and the CCP in 1927, the Guomindang lost interest in land reform and did not attempt serious land redistribution during its tenure on the mainland. However, the Guomindang did redistribute much landlord land to the peasants on Taiwan in the 1950s.

The first systematic effort at land redistribution was made by the Communist Party in various guerrilla base areas, mostly in central and southern China, starting shortly after the split of 1927. By 1933 it had formulated exact definitions for demarcating the classes in the countryside. These were based on whether a family's income came from its own labor or from exploitation of the labor of others through tenancy, usury, and the hiring of agricultural laborers. The main categories were the following:

1. *Landlords* had incomes coming essentially from the labor of other people. A family with at

least one member performing major agricultural labor at least 120 days per year was not generally to be classified as a landlord family, even if its income was quite large.

2. *Rich peasants* did major agricultural labor but also got a significant amount of income by exploiting the labor of others.

3. *Middle peasants* were essentially self-sufficient farmers, but they might exploit the labor of others to a small extent (often by hiring labor at times of peak labor demand). Originally, families were classified as middle peasants only if less than 15 percent of family income could be traced to labor done by nonmembers; the limit was raised to 25 percent early in 1948.

4. *Poor peasants* were either tenants or smallholders without adequate land and capital.

5. *Agricultural laborers* were hired workers with no land of their own. CCP policies generally grouped them together with the poor peasants.

There were also minor categories such as peddlars and individuals physically unable to labor. Those who fell into these categories were granted exemptions from the normal principle that those whose incomes came from renting out land should be considered landlords.

The CCP Land Law of 1931, applied in the Jiangxi Soviet, was extremely radical. Landlords were to be stripped of all their land, and rich peasants reduced to extreme poverty. The Land Law was ambiguous about whether land could be taken from middle peasants whose landholdings were greater than the per capita average for the areas in which they lived. Implementation of this law was fairly effective, although there was significant evasion and misapplication.

During the period of Chinese resistance against Japan (1937–1945) the CCP formally abandoned land reform. However, graduated taxes and CCP rent-reduction policies weakened the economic position of the landlords to a point where many of them had to sell significant amounts of land in a depressed market. Between 1945 and 1947 the CCP gradually resumed radical land distribution. These policies were implemented mostly in areas of North China where the amount of land in landlord hands had never been very large. In its efforts to provide enough for worthy poor peasants and agricultural laborers, the CCP by 1947 was taking land not only from landlords and rich peasants, but also from middle peasants who owned more than the average amount of land, and even from some middle and poor peasants who owned less than the local average

but whose parents or grandparents could be shown to have been landlords or rich peasants. Meanwhile, local cadres were told that adequate benefits must be brought to the poor, but were not told exactly how to do this. Directives from the CCP leadership that might have explained exactly whose land was subject to confiscation were often vague and self-contradictory. The Outline Land Law (10 October 1947) resolved some of the uncertainties but left ambiguous the question of whether well-to-do middle peasants could have some of their land taken away. Only in the first half of 1948—with the issuance of supplementary directives forbidding the confiscation of middle-peasant land, the broad distribution of a revised version of the 1933 regulations for class demarcation, and the acceptance of the idea that in some areas the amount distributed to the poor simply was not going to be very large—did the land-reform cadres receive a clear and consistent definition of what they were supposed to do.

In the summer of 1948 the CCP decided that it was unwise to carry out land reform immediately after a given area came under Communist control. Building an effective organizational structure and getting the peasants psychologically prepared would take time. In the interim, only preliminary programs such as rent reduction were to be carried out. The decision did not mean that the CCP was calling a prolonged halt to land reform; at any given time there were always some areas that had been under CCP control just long enough to be ready, under the new criteria, to initiate land reform.

Over the next two years land policy was moderated still further as the CCP became more concerned about the way radical policies, especially attacks on middle and rich peasants, sometimes disrupted agricultural production. The Party was also moving southward into areas where the percentage of the land that was owned by landlords was much larger than in the North, and where the need to take land from people other than landlords therefore seemed less pressing.

A new Agrarian Reform Law was issued in June 1950 to regulate land reform in the tremendous area that had come under CCP control in 1949 and would be ready to begin land reform in late 1950 or 1951. The law confirmed the previous policy of protecting middle peasants from confiscation but added that even rich peasants might be allowed to retain landholdings exceeding the local average. Land that rich peasants worked by family labor or hired labor was not to be taken; even land that they rented out was in some cases to be left untouched.

Land reform was carried out in most of central and southern China between mid-1950 and mid-1952. By the spring of 1953 all ethnically Han areas of the countryside had been covered by the program. Only some national minority areas were allowed to postpone it.

Party land reform was partly an economic program. The CCP wanted to eliminate what it considered to be an essentially parasitic class, the landlords, and place land and capital in the hands of the peasants who actually worked the land. This was certain to elevate income levels among the poor peasants, and the CCP hoped that it would also elevate agricultural production. Beyond this, the land reform had a very important political component. The CCP won tremendous peasant gratitude by its redistribution of wealth. It encouraged peasants to participate in the process of redistribution and not simply to wait passively for the CCP to give them the land. Those peasants who joined most actively and competently generally became the new political leaders of the village, and many of them joined the CCP. The former village leadership, made up mostly of landlords and rich peasants, was overthrown and the landlords lost their economic leverage in the redistribution of wealth. They were also held up to systematic public humiliation. Many were brought before "struggle meetings" at which they had to confess their sins and endure taunts and denunciations by their former tenants. Some were imprisoned or executed. The overall effect was to destroy the old power structure in the villages and substitute one affiliated with the Communist Party.

No reliable figures are available for the number of people executed in the course of land reform. In the areas where the proportion of landlords killed was highest (those that underwent land reform around 1947), the killings were often informal lynchings. Even for areas that underwent land reform under the more formal and less bloody policies introduced in 1950, adequate statistics have not been published. Western scholars generally define land-reform executions rather broadly, and give estimates ranging from around 1 million to 3 million or higher.

The results of these policies were uneven. Economic inequalities were narrowed in most Chinese villages, but only in some areas that had undergone land reform under the very radical policies of 1947 were they eliminated or almost eliminated. In the typical village that underwent land reform between 1950 and 1952, there remained rich peasants and well-to-do middle peasants who owned considerably more than the former poor peasants. The degree of inequality of landholdings tended to increase in the years immediately following land reform; some poor families found themselves in economic difficulty and had to sell part or all of their newly acquired land.

When the CCP gained control of China, it was able to restore effective central control of land taxes for the first time since the late Qing. A tax was placed on households owning agricultural land, graduated rather steeply according to the amount and quality of the land held by each household. The tax was not supposed to fluctuate from year to year, except for remissions in case of disaster. Each year, owners were taxed according to the government's estimate of what their land would have produced in a normal year. This insulated the government from the effects of crop fluctuations, and promoted production by allowing an owner who worked hard and got an unusually large crop to keep all of the extra production.

The pattern of relatively but not completely equal ownership of freehold farms created by land reform was eliminated in the mid-1950s by collectivization. Only in the early 1980s has private land ownership begun to be reintroduced under the new economic policies of Deng Xiaoping.

[See also Agriculture, Collectivization of; Agricultural Producers' Cooperatives; and Responsibility System.]

Joseph Esherick, "Number Games: A Note on Land Distribution in Prerevolutionary China," Modern China 7 (1981): 387–411. William Hinton, Fanshen (1968). Edwin E. Moise, Land Reform in China and North Vietnam (1983). Vivienne Shue, Peasant China in Transition (1980).
EDWIN E. MOISE

## LAND TENURE, REVENUE, AND REFORM IN SOUTH ASIA

Knowledge of the systems of land tenure in South Asia prior to the Muslim period is scant. Early documents inconsistently assert in some places that land was owned by the ruler and in others, by the cultivating peasant. Certainly there were many claimants to the produce of each village. The ruler claimed a share, traditionally a quarter of the produce of rainfed lands and a third of the produce of irrigated lands. The actual share depended upon the power of the ruler and upon how much he wanted to be a "good king" (but even greedy kings made no demands when the crops failed).

Other claimants were the members of the powerful castes in the villages, the cultivating peasantry, and the village artisans, specialists, and other laborers. The dominant castes were sometimes themselves cultivators, sometimes more like petty lords. Dominant caste members and their council governed village affairs. Under what terms other cultivators held land we do not know, other than that they contributed produce to the dominant castes as well as to the ruler and other villagers. Artisans (carpenters, blacksmiths, potters, and so on) and village servants (watchmen, barbers, washermen, temple personnel, etc.) shared in the harvest "according to custom"—a minimal subsistence share in the worst years, somewhat more in better years. Shares of priests depended largely upon the position of brahmans in the local caste hierarchy. Laborers, many of whom were Untouchables, shared in the harvest, but always at a minimal subsistence level. Many laborers were permanent servants of higher caste families and are best thought of as serfs attached to specific families rather than to the land.

Until the late nineteenth century vacant lands remained to which people could move. The availability of these lands had two consequences. First, neither rulers nor locally dominant castes could impose an unduly harsh burden upon those beneath them, as the latter were free to flee and find other land to clear. Second, assuring that land was cultivated and its produce shared, not resolving claims to ownership of specific plots, was of greater concern to the authorities. There was thus not so much a system of land tenure as a hierarchy assuring that land was farmed and its produce shared among all of the villagers.

The Muslim invasions did not alter the basic pattern. Monetization of the economy increased and, in areas close to the centers of power (towns and cities), the ruler's share was increasingly commuted to specie, which peasants could acquire by selling to the towns, royal administrators, and armies.

There is evidence from this period of sales of land, but it is less clear what rights or powers were sold, or how often an effective custom allowed a seller who had departed and later returned to reclaim his rights. People jointly holding (or dominating) an area gave other members of the group a preemptive right to purchase. During periods when central administrations were weak, revenue farmers bought and sold rights to collect the land revenue, but how far down the hierarchy the power to sell obtained is not known. No absolutely clear line separated "ruler" from "lord" from "owner." Only under British rule do we find complete, detailed records.

Early British records give the impression that "lords" or "rulers" did occasionally engage in purchase and sale, but that such transactions were probably pointless in the absence of other sources of power and influence with which to make the purchased rights effective. However, transfers at this level did not change the systems of sharing within villages. Because there was vacant land and because the peasantry lacked power or influence, they had no reason to buy or sell, nor did anyone have reason to buy from them.

Some holdings, later known as "privileged tenures," paid little or no revenue: those of Muslim trusts and Hindu temples; *inams,* a term covering a multiplicity of grants of land from superior to inferior; and *jagirs,* a grant of the land revenue by rulers to those who supplied troops or who had been loyal retainers. There was no end to the complexity and variety of tenures, all of which reflected the structure of power and influence.

British rule broke sharply with the past. Basic to the pattern of thought of Western commercial society are the ideas of property and markets. At first the British felt that the issue was whether the ruler owned the land—with the happy prospect that, if he did, then the East India Company, as successor to emperors and rajas, was justified in collecting all the produce "in excess of the costs of production" (i.e., the competitive rent). The issue, however, became moot before there was agreement on the answer. British worry over who owned the land was more important in principle than it was in practice. Considering the low yields, the company's need for revenue, and the large number of claimants, including many interlopers willing to agree to pay a high revenue in order to get land, the difference between a land revenue tax and a competitive rent was virtually zero. The revenues first assessed by the British usually proved too high, and throughout British rule the share demanded by the government declined.

In the south and west the amount of land revenue was usually settled with individual families. These became known as *raiyatwari* settlements. In the north, as British rule spread westward from Bengal, the view was taken that, regardless of who owned land, a class of improving landlords should be created. The revenue assessment was made with powerful local people, with groups of families claiming joint tenure and sharing by agnatic descent, or with "brotherhoods" sharing "by custom." These became known as *zamindari* settlements, some of which, mostly in the northeast, were permanent settlements: the revenue was fixed in perpetuity in the expectation that the produce would increase and the class of improving landlords would become rich and therefore loyal. As their rule extended, the British learned that their concepts of property did not fit the Indian systems and so they began to fix the revenue in "regular" settlements for thirty or forty years, following which there were reassessments.

Among the effects of British policy were two contrary tendencies. As the British became increasingly aware of the complex nature of Indian interests in the produce of the land, they began to try to protect tenants from the exploitative powers of landlords, who enjoyed not only property rights granted by law but also effective political power in the countryside. These efforts were largely confined to zamindari areas. They were nowhere entirely effective and in many places had little effect at all. Meanwhile, Indians began to realize the opportunities that their new titles provided in an increasingly commercial society and began to accept British ideas about property. Shares in kind became rents in cash and zamindars began to see themselves less as lords, whose prerogatives were certainly being restricted by British law, and more as landlords.

British rule did not, however, substitute the British system for the earlier Indian systems. First, the multiplicity of complex claims to the produce of the land continued. Villagers of all sorts still received shares in the produce of village land (even, for a few, as late as the 1960s). More importantly, title to the land continued to be the record of the assessment of the revenue, as limited by the recorded rights of others. In fact, in raiyatwari as well as in zamindari areas, all tenures were implicitly subordinate, "at the grace of the ruler" and his settlement officer.

Most importantly, subordinate legal rights beneath the zamindars grew in the course of British rule. Some proprietors who lost title because of failure to pay the revenue or because of foreclosure on a mortage sometimes became "exproprietary tenants" with a permanent but alienable right to the same holding. A multiplicity of subordinate tenures were created at the expense of the superior holder. Most common were "occupancy tenancies," hereditary but inalienable rights to the land, subject to a rent fixed by an official. At its most complex, at the end of British rule, there could be un underproprietor, an exproprietary tenant, an occupancy tenant, and a hereditary tenant below the zamindar. The land might actually be farmed by a sharecropping tenant-at-will who might even employ a permanent servant.

In raiyatwari areas, where in principle the raiyat was the farmer, holders of raiyatwari settlements might lease land to tenants who engaged servants or laborers to do the farming. There were also large inam holdings in the raiyatwari areas, a result of many decisions and compromises arrived at by different officers at different times and places. Thus, there were raiyats who were not cultivators, inamdars who could be likened to zamindars, occupancy tenants under zamindars, and tenants under these. Three tiers of interest in the land were common, perhaps even typical.

After achieving independence in 1946–1947, the countries of South Asia engaged in three sorts of land reform: (1) efforts to give tenants security of tenure, (2) laws designed to transfer title to tenants, and (3) limits upon the size of holdings.

Laws granting rights to tenants were little more effective in the independent nations than similar laws had been under British rule. The locally powerful were able to evict tenants or alter the land records. Tenants were deterred from demanding their rights by the threat of violence or the cost of litigation. Laws transferring title to tenants were somewhat more effective. In Kashmir and Uttar Pradesh landlords with large acreages lost much of their land, but elsewhere evasion left many large holdings undisturbed. In East Pakistan (Bangladesh) many titles were easily transferred because Hindu landlords had fled to India.

The policy of transferring title, more and more widely adopted, merged with the policy of limiting the size of holdings. Tenants became the owners of most of the excess land. However, throughout South Asia landowners evaded the ceilings: large holdings were divided among sons (who would, however, have inherited and divided anyway); families formed spurious cooperative societies that could hold large acreages; and, in an unknown number of cases, spurious names were entered in the land records, allowing the original holders to continue to keep control over the land. In no country was there significant transfer of land to landless laborers or village servants.

Land reforms certainly did affect the economic and social structures of landholding in South Asia, and they did alter the relative economic and political positions of castes and other groups. However, the issues of how effective the reforms were, whether they contributed to or retarded economic development, and what their effects on rural society were are matters of dispute. In India those with large acreages lost appreciable amounts of land, so that those owning five to thirty acres came to dominate the countryside. In the other countries the shift from large to middle-sized holdings was not so great, and was least in Pakistan. Increasing commercialization of agriculture, especially in areas where the Green Revolution technologies were widely adopted, undermined the traditional village systems that had provided minimal security of income and status for all villagers. A two-class system of those with access to a hectare or more and those without land or holding only petty plots began to replace the multilayered village hierarchies.

[See also East India Company; Partition of India; and Law: Judicial and Legal Systems of India.]

B. H. Baden-Powell, *The Land Systems of British India*, 3 vols. (1892). *The Cambridge Economic History*, vol. 1, edited by Tappan Raychaudhuri and Irfan Habib (1982), vol. 2, edited by Dharma Kumar and Meghnad Desai (1983). Robert E. Frykenberg, ed., *Land Tenure and Peasant in South Asia* (1977). Ronald J. Herring, *Land to the Tiller: The Political Economy of Agrarian Reform in South Asia* (1983). W. H. Moreland, *The Agrarian System of Moslem India* (1929). Walter C. Neale, *Economic Change in Rural India: Land Tenure and Reform in Uttar Pradesh, 1800–1955* (1962). Daniel Thorner, *The Agrarian Prospect in India* (1956).

## LAND TENURE, REVENUE, AND REFORM IN SOUTHEAST ASIA

Southeast Asia differs from the other chief agricultural regions of Asia in having had, historically, a high ratio of land to labor, meaning that farmholdings were relatively large by Asian standards and that land was in ample supply in the region until the twentieth century.

There is only one major exception to this generalization. In the Red River delta of northern Vietnam pressure on land was already severe by about the fourteenth century. There, land tenure problems became all the more acute because of the tendency of the elite to amass landholdings and remove them from the tax rolls, and nearly every dynasty since the Ho in the fourteenth century attempted land reforms. It is probably no accident that it was only in Vietnam that highly formal patterns of land ownership developed, while elsewhere in the region land was held by tillers on a sort of usufructuary basis, with farmers holding and using land on the understanding that they would render taxes and labor services to the government and the elite. Landholdings could range to an average of ten acres per household in Burma and Thailand, and the local technology of wet-rice agriculture rendered such holdings more than ample to feed a household.

Southeast Asian populations grew at a phenomenal rate in the nineteenth century—perhaps as much as 2 percent per year—but short-term pressure on the land was muted by the opening up of major new rice-producing areas, notably the Mekong Delta of Vietnam, the lower Chaophraya Delta of Thailand, and the Irrawaddy Delta of Burma. Many rice farms were mortgaged on the assumption that rapid increases in rice prices would continue indefinitely, and many farm families were forced from their lands when prices fell, particularly during the world depression of the 1930s. Rural economic conditions have deteriorated for many ever since, and every Southeast Asian government has had to face major tenancy and land tenure problems since the 1950s.

James C. Scott, *The Moral Economy of the Peasant* (1976).                    DAVID K. WYATT

**LANGKASUKA**, ancient state on the Malay Peninsula, centered on the Patani River basin. It is known mainly from Chinese sources from the second century onward and must have based its power on control of transpeninsular trade. It is associated with extensive, unexcavated ruins in the Yarang district of Patani Province, Thailand, where Brahmanic sculptures from the eighth to tenth century have been found. Muslim Patani continued its functions from the sixteenth century onward.

[See also Patani and Tambralinga.]

G. Coedès, *The Indianized States of Southeast Asia*, translated by Susan B. Cowing (1968). Paul Wheatley, *The Golden Khersonese* (1961).       DAVID K. WYATT

**LANGUAGE FAMILIES.** There are two principal ways of cataloging information about languages as they are situated on a continent: the genetic and the typological. The genetic approach is based on the model of a tree and the branches that issue from it at different intervals. The last twig on each branch is ultimately related to all the other twigs, through the nodes that connect it with all other branches. The typological approach views languages from the other end: a hypothetical protolanguage is assumed to have existed in the remote past and can be reconstructed by means of the methods of comparative linguistics. This protolanguage (the trunk) had daughter languages (the branches), which, in turn, had further branches. The progression continues up to the point where a number of languages (living, or attested through surviving documents) can be considered as being related by virtue of having ultimately descended from one and the same protolanguage.

Some languages are genetically isolated. This means that there is simply no other language with which they can be compared for the purpose of reconstructing a protolanguage. Such languages are assumed to be the sole survivors of their own protolanguage and are therefore called *isolates*.

The notion of *phylum* is diametrically opposed to that of the isolate. A phylum is a unit (of languages presumed to be related) larger than the language family: it may consist of two or more such families and, in addition, of any number of isolates. The larger the phylum, the less rigorous the method by which it has been established is likely to be. This accounts for the use of such other terms as *super-family, stock,* and *superstock* in the sense of phylum or multiples of a phylum. Examples of phyla that have been proposed for Asia (as defined in this en-cyclopedia) are Sino-Tibetan, Austro-Tai, Austro-asiatic, Austronesian, and Indo-Pacific.

The results of comparative linguistics are never final and often controversial. The state of our understanding of the genetic composition of a given continent is therefore always in flux, and must be borne in mind when categorizing the languages of that continent. (See table 1.)

It is generally assumed that the diversity of languages was even greater in the past than it is now. A few vestiges of now extinct languages survive as inscriptions, such as those of Harappa and Mohen-jo-Daro (third millennium BCE), found in the Punjab and in the Indus Valley. The genetic affiliation of the languages in these documents has not been determined. Documents have also been found in To-charian, an extinct Indo-European language spoken

TABLE 1. *Language Families of Asia*

| Family or Isolate | Sample Language; Area[1] | Phylum or Further Affiliation Suggested | No. of Branches[2] | No. of Languages[2] | No. of Speakers[2] |
|---|---|---|---|---|---|
| Ainu | Ainu; Hokkaido | none | 1 | 1 | 10,000 |
| Japanese | Japanese; Japan, Ryūkyū Is. | Korean, Altaic | 2 | 2 | 100,000,000 |
| Korean | Korean; ROK, DPRK | Japanese, Altaic | 1 | 1 | 34,000,000 |
| Sinitic (Chinese) | Mandarin; PRC, Taiwan | Sino-Tibetan | 2 | 8 | 600,000,000 |
| Miao-Yao | Miao; PRC, Vietnam, Laos | Sino-Tibetan, Kadai, Mon-Khmer, Tai and Kam-Sui | 2 | 4 | 3,000,000 |
| Kadai | Li; Hainan (PRC) | Tai and Kam-Sui, Austro-Tai | 2 | 4 | 1,000,000 |
| Mon-Khmer | Vietnamese; Vietnam | Austroasiatic | 7 | 90 | 35,000,000 |
| Palaung-Wa | Palaung; Thailand, Burma | Mon-Khmer | 2 | 10 | 1,000,000 |
| Tai and Kam-Sui | Thai; Thailand | Miao-Yao, Kadai, Sino-Tibetan | 4 | 30 | 50,000,000 |
| Malaccan | Jakun; Malaysia | Austroasiatic | 1 | 17 | 37,000 |
| Indonesian | Indonesian; Malaysia to Philippines | Austronesian | 4 | 200 | 150,000,000 |
| Nicobarese | Nicobarese; Nicobar Is. | Austroasiatic | 1 | 12 | 12,000 |
| Andamanese | Andamanese; Andaman Is. | ?Indo-Pacific | 1 | 3 | 1,000 |
| Karen | Bwe; Burma | Tibeto-Burman, Sino-Tibetan | 1 | 8 | 2,000,000 |
| Tibeto-Burman | Burmese; Burma, Thailand | Sino-Tibetan | 5 | 200 | 25,000,000 |
| Khasi | Khasi; Assam (East India) | Mon-Khmer, Austroasiatic | 1 | 1 | 390,000 |
| Munda | Santali; India | Austroasiatic | 2 | 11 | 6,000,000 |
| Nahali | Nahali; Madhya Pradesh | Mon-Khmer; isolate? | 1 | 1 | 1,000 |
| Dravidian | Tamil; India | none | 3 | 21 | 140,000,000 |
| Burushaski | Burushaski; North India, Pakistan | none | 1 | 1 | 27,000 |
| Indo-European | Iran to Sri Lanka, USSR | Semitic, Uralic | 3 | 60 | 450,000,000 |
| Altaic | USSR, Mongolia, PRC | Japanese, Korean, Uralic | 3 | | 3,000,000 |

1. Rough geographical identification, not always complete, is of the locus of the family or isolate. Some families (such as Mon-Khmer, Indonesian, and Indo-European) are deployed over huge territories; this fact is not indicated in the column.
2. Figures are for Asia only.

in Central Asia until about the seventh century CE. Other extinct languages include Sumerian (an isolate), Assyrian-Babylonian, Hittite, and Elamite.

Linguistic diversity can also be plotted on the map. We can ask what typological features are particular to a certain area, regardless of the genetic appurtenance of a given language. Thus, the languages of Southeast Asia typically have short, one-syllable roots and tone (a musical-pitch contour associated with each monosyllabic unit of meaning), but few suffixes. In Chinese $da^4$ $niao^3$ $fei^1$, where the superscript numbers indicate tone, literally means "big bird flies" or "big bird flew." By contrast, a large number of languages, stretching from western Asia as far as Japan, have longer roots, a rich array of grammatical devices (suffixes), but no tone; for example, the Japanese phrase ōkii-na tori ga tob-u, "big bird flies" (or ton-da, "flew"), where -na, ga, -u, and -da are all part of the grammatical elements of the language. Each language and, by extension, each language family (in a grosser way) has its own, particular grammatical profile.

This great typological diversity among the languages of Asia suggests questions about where, when, and how it arose. The answers to these questions are shrouded in mystery: it is not known when, how, and precisely where (or how many times) human language arose and it is not known to what the great diversity of languages (on the globe or in Asia alone) can be ascribed. We do know that lively contact among groups of persons engenders linguistic change (and hence variety), whereas linguistic isolation breeds conservatism. It can therefore be assumed that large-scale prehistorical migrations as well as social and demographic upheavals such as slavery or the decimation of populations through plagues provide the scenario that accounts for the great diversity of language families and language types today. We also know that the language families of the Western Hemisphere originally came from Asia. This suggests that the diversity of languages in Asia may have been even greater in prehistoric times than it is now.

Some language families (Indonesian, Altaic) extend beyond the confines of Asia. The bulk of the Indo-European languages are spoken in Europe. Omitted from the table are the Caucasian phylum (with three branches, some thirty five languages, and about five million speakers) and mention of some Semitic languages in the southwest of Asia.

The effect of cultural history on language is paramount. However, the histories of writing systems, of the nature and varieties of ritual language, and of special codes for expressing politeness found in many Asian languages are to a large extent independent of the genetic (family) appurtenance of a given language.

[See also Altaic Languages; Turkic Languages; Mongolian; Chinese Language; Sino-Tibetan Languages; Austroasiatic Languages; Austronesian Languages; Philippine Languages; Indo-Aryan Languages and Literatures; and Dravidian Languages and Literatures.]

Paul K. Benedict and James A. Matisoff, Sino-Tibetan, A Conspectus (1972). Johannes Friedrich, Extinct Languages (1957). Merritt Ruhlen, A Guide to the Languages of the World (1976). Thomas A. Sebeok, ed., Current Trends in Linguistics, vol. 2, Linguistics in East Asia and Southeast Asia, (1967) and vol. 5, Linguistics in South Asia (1969). C. F. Voegelin and F. M. Voegelin, Classification and Index of the World's Languages (1977).

ROBERT AUSTERLITZ

**LANKA SAMA SAMAJA PARTY** (LSSP), the largest Marxist political organization in Sri Lanka. The dominant theme of the history of the party since its formation in 1935 has been personality conflicts and ideological splits. The first major split in 1939, which removed the Stalinist minority, produced the party's Trotskyist identity, and through the successive conflicts and splits the leadership has rested firmly with the pragmatists. The party and its ancillary youth and trade union movements have focused primarily on the urban southwest and have had little impact upon the rural population. While the party's top leaders have enjoyed personal popularity, the key to its electoral successes has been electoral agreements with the Sri Lanka Freedom Party, with which it twice entered into coalition agreements, in 1964–1965 and between 1970 and 1975. The latter association ended bitterly and proved costly, for the party suffered a complete debacle at the 1977 polls.

[See also Sri Lanka Freedom Party and Communism: Communist Parties in South Asia.]

G. J. Lerski, Origins of Trotskyism in Ceylon (1968). V. Samaraweera, "Sri Lankan Marxists in Electoral Politics, 1947–77," Journal of Commonwealth and Comparative Politics 18 (1980): 308–324.

VIJAYA SAMARAWEERA

**LAN NA**, old Tai kingdom centered on Chiang Mai in northern Thailand. By the thirteenth century, Tai peoples had dominated the north-central part of the Indochinese peninsula (comprising present-day north Thailand, northeast Burma, southern

Yunnan in China, and northwestern Laos) for several hundred years. A number of petty principalities had flourished in the region—among them, Chiang Hung in Yunnan, Keng Tung in Burma, Yonok at Chiang Saen, and Lamphun. By conquering and unifying most of this region, King Mangrai (r. 1259–1317) created a new and more powerful kingdom, Lan Na and, from 1296, a new capital at Chiang

TABLE 1. *Rulers of Lan Na*

| RULER | DATES OF RULE |
| --- | --- |
| Mangrai | 1259–1317 |
| Chai Songkhram | 1317–1318 |
| Saen Phu | 1318–1319 |
| Khrua | 1319–1322 |
| Nam Thuam | 1322–1324 |
| Saen Phu (second reign) | 1324–1328 |
| Kham Fu | 1328–1337 |
| Pha Yu | 1337–1355 |
| Ku Na | 1355–1385 |
| Saen Muang Ma | 1385–1401 |
| Sam Fang Kaen | 1401–1441 |
| Tilokaracha | 1441–1487 |
| Yot Chiang Rai | 1487–1495 |
| Muang Kaeo | 1495–1526 |
| Ket Chettharat | 1526–1538 |
| Chai (Sai Kham) | 1538–1543 |
| Ket Chettharat (second reign) | 1543–1545 |
| Queen Chiraprapha | 1545–1546 |
| Setthathirat (of Lan Sang) | 1546–1551 |
| Queen Ku | 1551 |
| Mekuti | 1551–1564[1] |
| Queen Wisutthithewi (under Burma) | 1564–1578 |
| Tharawaddy Prince (of Burma) | 1578–1607 |
| *Two sons of Tharawaddy Prince* | 1607–1613 |
| Thadogyaw (of Burma) | 1613–1615 |
| Si Song Muang | 1615–1631 |
| Phraya Thipphanet | 1631–1659 |
| *Ruler of Phrae* | 1659–1672 |
| *Burmese Crown Prince* | 1672–1675 |
| *Burmese ruler* | 1675–1707 |
| Nara (Burmese officer) | 1707–1727 |
| Thep Sing | 1727 |
| Ong Kham (from Lan Sang) | 1727–1759 |
| Chan | 1759–1761 |
| Khi Hut | 1761–1762 |
| Abhayagamani (Burmese) | 1762–1768 |
| Mayagamani (Burmese) | 1768–1771 |

1. Mekuti and Queen Ku may be one and the same figure.

Mai. It was a difficult region to rule, for Mangrai as well as his successors. The rugged mountainous topography left the Tai population scattered among innumerable small, upland valleys, and neither Chiang Mai nor any other regional center could muster sufficient resources of manpower or wealth to securely dominate other centers. Only the most able and charismatic leaders could temporarily unite such a landscape, and none succeeded in erecting durable, strong institutions of administration. The kingdom's name, Lan Na—the "million rice-fields"—connotes bucolic decentralization; thus the real identity of Lan Na is less a tradition of political unity than it is one of shared struggle (against nature and outsiders) and common Buddhist and literary tradition. Lan Na's core region encompasses what is now northern Thailand.

In Lan Na's history, political stability and instability alternate until the reign of Tilokaracha (1441–1487), when power and prosperity peaked. This was followed by two long centuries (1558–1774) of more or less constant Burmese occupation, traces of which remain in the region's architecture, cuisine, and language. The revolt of the north and the intrusion of a revived Siam in the 1770s led to a new polity in the north under Kavila but not to a revival of Lan Na as such, which is most gloriously associated in the memory of the northern Thai (Tai Yuan) people with the period from Mangrai to Tilok.

[*See also* Chiang Mai; Mangrai; Ku Na; Tilokaracha; Setthathirat; *and the maps accompanying* Sukhothai *and* Ayudhya.]

David K. Wyatt, *Thailand: A Short History* (1984).

DAVID K. WYATT

**LAN SANG** (Lan Xang), classical kingdom of Laos from the fourteenth century to 1700 that saw the definition of Lao culture and identity. At its greatest extent it covered virtually all of present-day Laos and about half of northeastern Thailand.

Several Lao kingdoms of the Mekong Valley took the name Lan Sang Hom Khao ("kingdom of the million elephants and the white parasol [of sovereignty]"), but the first was centered on Luang Prabang in northern Laos in the late thirteenth century. Although its name was grand, many neighboring Lao principalities (including Siang Khwang and a polity in the Vientiane region) were as powerful—or weak. It was Fa Ngum, a scion of the royal house of Luang Prabang, who in the mid-fourteenth century led a small army up the Mekong River valley to conquer rival states and his grandfather's Luang Prabang, then founded a united Lao kingdom of Lan Sang in 1353. The unity he established, however, was fragile, and the central authority of the kings in Luang Prabang depended heavily on the personal allegiance and assistance of local rulers and dignitaries, for whom Lan Sang was simply a useful fiction. Indeed, in 1373 those dignitaries deposed Fa Ngum and installed his son Un Huan as King Sam Saen Thai (the "king who ruled 300,000 Tai," i.e., Lao, according to a census he carried out in 1376). Sam Saen Thai was an effective and long-lived ruler, surely because of the support he had from the provincial dignitaries, but on his death in 1416 the kingdom's inherent instability became apparent: it had eight kings in twenty-two years.

Lan Sang finally took shape as an effective state from 1442 to 1571, a period in which successive kings in Luang Prabang began to appoint their sons and relatives to govern important provinces and cohesiveness was forged in warfare against Vietnam (1478–1479). King Visun (r. 1501–1520) worked to define a distinctive Lao identity, including its own Buddhism and state religious symbols (especially the Prabang Buddha image, brought to Luang Prabang in his reign) and monuments. His son, Phothisarat (r. 1520–1547), resided most of the time in Vientiane, closer to the center of the Lao population, which was steadily moving down the Mekong River valley and across the Khorat Plateau of what is now Thailand. King Setthathirat the Great (r. 1547–1571) moved the capital to Vientiane and built upon his predecessors' efforts to enter forcefully into the diplomatic life of mainland Southeast Asia to establish Lan Sang as a major power, even becoming concurrently king of Lan Na for a period. Burmese military expansion in the last half of the sixteenth century, however, cut short the Lao kings' state-building efforts, and Vientiane fell to the Burmese in 1570, as Ayudhya had in 1569 and Chiang Mai in 1564.

After three decades of instability Laos was brought back together by King Surinyavongsa (r. 1637–c. 1694), whose reign is remembered as the last golden age of Laos, in which peace reigned and the arts and Buddhism flourished. Foreign visitors to Laos in the 1640s described a powerful, prosperous, and stable state. Its power, however, was based little more solidly than that of Sam Saen Thai or Setthathirat, for the kingdom simply disintegrated on Surinyavongsa's death, about 1694. Although several kingdoms thereafter revived the

TABLE 1. *Kings of Lan Sang*

| | KING | REIGN DATES |
|---|---|---|
| 1. | Fa Ngum | 1353–1373 |
| 2. | Sam Saen Thai (Un Hüan) | 1373–1416 |
| 3. | Lan Khamdaeng | 1416–1428 |
| 4. | Phommathat | uncertain |
| 5. | Yukon | uncertain |
| 6. | Siang Sa | uncertain |
| 7. | Pak Huai Luang | uncertain |
| 8. | Mun Ban | uncertain |
| 9. | Müang Khai | uncertain |
| 10. | Thao Khamkoet | uncertain |
| | Interregnum | three years |
| 11. | Sainyachakkaphat Phaenphaeo | 1442–1479 |
| 12. | Suvannabanlang | 1479–1486 |
| 13. | La Saen Thai | 1486–1496 |
| 14. | Somphu | 1496–1501 |
| 15. | Visunlarat | 1501–1520 |
| 16. | Phothisarat I | 1520–1547 |
| 17. | Setthathirat | 1547–1571 |
| 18. | No Kaeo Kuman (*or* No Müang) | 1571–1572? |
| 19. | Phanya Saensurinthalüsai (Chan) | 1572?–1575? |
| 20. | Voravongsa | 1575–1579 |
| 21. | Saensurinthalüsai | 1580–1582 |
| 22. | Phaya Nakhon (Noi) | 1582–1583 |
| | Interregnum | 1583–1591 |
| 23. | No Müang | 1591–1598? |
| 24. | Thammikkarat | 1598?–1621 |
| 25. | (Crown Prince, unnamed) | 1622 |
| 26. | Phothisarat II | 1623–1627 |
| 27. | Mom Kaeo | uncertain |
| 28. | Ton Kham | uncertain |
| 29. | Sivisai | uncertain |
| 30. | Surinyavongsa | 1637–1694 |
| 31. | Phanya Müang Chan (usurper) | 1694–1700? |

name of Lan Sang, none governed more than a small portion of Surinyavongsa's domains. Lan Sang was succeeded, from about the year 1700, by the kingdoms of Luang Prabang, Vientiane, and Champassak.

What made Lan Sang such an enduring symbol for the Lao? It carried associations of cultural kinship among Lao that bridged local isolation and divisions, and it enabled Lao to maintain their self-respect vis-à-vis their Vietnamese and Siamese neighbors. During the reigns of a few great kings, Laos was a major state in the region.

[*See also* Laos; Lao; Champassak; Luang Prabang; Vientiane; Siang Khwang; Fa Ngum; Setthathirat; Surinyavongsa; That Luang; That Phanom; *and the map accompanying* Ayudhya.]

Maha Sila Viravong, *History of Laos* (1964). David K. Wyatt, *Thailand: A Short History* (1984).

DAVID K. WYATT

**LANSING-ISHII AGREEMENT.** Arrived at in 1917 by Robert Lansing, the United States' secretary of state, and Ishii Kikujirō, Japanese ambassador to the United States, the Lansing-Ishii Agreement was a statement of the positions that the two governments would take on the problem of China. The agreement was an attempt to relax tensions growing out of the collision of Japanese and American policies on China.

When the conversations leading to the agreement began in the summer of 1917 the US and Japan were allies against Germany in World War I. Japan had declared war on Germany in August 1914, succeeded in eliminating Germany as a rival in China within a few months, and then moved rapidly to expand its influence in China. Early in 1915 Japan presented its famous Twenty-one Demands to China, the provisions of which would have had the effect of greatly increasing Japanese influence there. [*See* Twenty-one Demands.] Japan hoped that the European powers, preoccupied with their war in Europe, would be unable or unwilling to defend either China or their rights and interests there.

The United States, still not in the war, however, took a strong stand against the Japanese demands. In response to this Japan dropped the more extreme of its demands, but secured Chinese agreement on the others through use of an ultimatum in May 1915. The US Department of State then set forth the doctrine of nonrecognition, which held that the US would not recognize any treaty or agreement entered into by China and Japan that would impair US treaty rights in China or violate either Chinese political or territorial integrity or the Open Door policy. The nonrecognition doctrine was revived sixteen years later, when it was applied to Japanese actions in Manchuria.

It was against this background that the United States and Japan set out in the summer of 1917 to try to reach an accommodation on their policies toward China. The result was the Lansing-Ishii Agreement of 2 November 1917. The main points of the agreement were that the US recognized that Japan had special interests in China based on the principle of territorial propinquity and that, further,

the US was confident that the Japanese government would live up to its assurances that it would not discriminate against the trade of other nations or disregard their commercial rights under treaties with China; both governments denied that they would infringe in any way on the independence or territorial integrity of China and declared that they would always adhere to the Open Door principle; both powers also pledged to oppose actions taken by any other government against China's independence and integrity and the Open Door.

The Lansing-Ishii Agreement remained in effect until 1922. At that time, as a result of the Washington Conference treaties, the two governments announced that the agreement had been superseded by a set of multilateral treaties worked out for the protection of China.

[*See also* World War I in China.]

A. Whitney Griswold, *The Far Eastern Policy of the United States* (1938). Tatsuji Takeuchi, *War and Diplomacy in the Japanese Empire* (1935). JOHN M. MAKI

**LAN XANG.** *See* Lan Sang.

**LANZHOU,** Chinese city, capital of Gansu Province, and since ancient times an important garrison and trading center. In the mid-1980s the population of this industrial city exceeded 1.5 million. The Yellow River flows through the city, which is also the major railroad junction of northwestern China. In Ming times the site of a pontoon bridge across the river, the city acquired industry only in the late nineteenth century, when Zuo Zongtang used it as a base in his campaigns against Muslim rebels. Soviet influence, strong until the late 1950s, is evident in the design of the modern city, which is a center of oil refining, chemical manufacture, machinery industries, and nonferrous metallurgy, as well as of uranium enrichment and atomic research.

ARTHUR N. WALDRON

**LAO,** major subgrouping of the Tai people, forming the dominant population of Laos and northeastern Thailand. Historically, people dwelling in the kingdoms of Lan Sang and Lan Na called themselves Lao and are contradistinguished from the Shan and Lu of Burma and southwestern China and the Siamese of central Thailand; their ethnic and linguistic affinities are close. The term *Lao* is politically charged in contemporary Laos, where it might best be used with ethnic and linguistic connotations to refer to the lowland-dwelling Lao speakers and where *Laotian* is used to denote non-Lao speakers. The Lao of northeastern Thailand are now referred to as Isan ("northeasterners"), while the Lao of Chiang Mai and the north are known as the Tai Yuan. [*See also* Tai Peoples.]    DAVID K. WYATT

LAO ISSARA (Free Lao), rebel movement started by Laotian members of the Free Thai, which had been fostered by the Allies in Thailand during World War II. When Japan capitulated in August 1945, the US aid and encouragement the Free Lao members had received convinced them that the French would be prevented from returning to Laos. Although Laos's independence, which had been granted by the Japanese, would be preserved, the absence of the French would leave the country subject to takeover by its ancient enemy Vietnam, now seizing its own independence. Prince Souphanouvong, however, long resident in Vietnam, already had enlisted Ho Chi Minh's support for Laotian independence, and in September he appeared in Laos with a Vietnamese military force, thus accentuating the dilemma.

Prince Phetsarath, who was then prime minister, was at Vientiane, the administrative capital, and in touch with the Lao Issara. Under pressure from the Vietnamese in Laos and aided by the Chinese entering Laos by Allied arrangement, he prevented the French from resuming control and reaffirmed independence. He urged King Sisavangvong to declare the union of Laos, including southern Laos, which was not part of his royal domains, and to ignore the French. But the king, who was based in Luang Prabang, was isolated by the rains from Vientiane and its anti-French pressures. He had already announced the continuance of the French protectorate and had welcomed a French mission, as had Prince Boun Oum, the dominant personality of the south; both men feared Vietnam more than they resented France. On 15 September Phetsarath himself, in defiance of the king, declared the union of Laos. After further disagreements, including Phetsarath's support of the Lao Issara, the king dismissed Phetsarath on 10 October. A rebel Lao Issara government was formed on 12 October and the king was forced to abdicate on 4 November. Under Phanya Khammao Vilay, formerly governor of Vientiane Province, the rebel government controlled little of southern Laos or of the countryside elsewhere, which was largely occupied by French-led guerrillas or by the Viet-namese. When the rains subsided, a government delegation went to Luang Prabang and eventually persuaded Sisavangvong to resume the throne as king of a united Laos and to legitimize the Lao Issara, which he did on 24 April 1946.

The French, however, were now returning to Laos in force and rejecting any compromise; they had already defeated a strong Lao Issara-Vietnamese force at Thakhek on 21 March. As the French advanced, Phetsarath and the Lao Issara fled to Thailand, where they were helped by the anticolonial government of Pridi Phanomyong. The Thai welcome, however, cooled when a military government took control of Laos in December 1947 and ordered Lao Issara troops out of the country. Prince Souphanouvong, increasingly involved in guerrilla activity against the French, fell out with his colleagues over the Vietnamese issue, and in May 1949 he was expelled from the Lao Issara.

Meanwhile, most of the movement's leaders had been satisfied by constitutional developments in Laos in 1947, which the king had asked of the returning French, and by effective independence in 1949. They dissolved their organization in October 1949 and returned home from Thailand under an amnesty in November. The new constitution had no role for Phetsarath, who remained unreconciled in Thailand until 1957.

[*See also* Laos; Phetsarath; Souphanouvong; Sisavangvong; *and* Boun Oum.]

John B. Murdoch, *Lao Issara: The Memoirs of Oun Sananikone* (1975). 3349 (pseudonym; largely the work of Phetsarath), *Iron Man of Laos,* translated by John B. Murdoch (1978).    HUGH TOYE

LAOS, landlocked state of mainland Southeast Asia located between Vietnam and Thailand, bordering also on Cambodia (Kampuchea) in the south and Burma and China in the northwest. It has an area of 91,000 square miles and an estimated population of 3.5 million; its capital is Vientiane.

There are many ways of defining Laos as a unit in history, for there are several different units, depending on perspective. Geographically, there is the north, radiating from Luang Prabang, consisting of many narrow river valleys separated by mountains; the central highlands, centered on Siang Khwang; the Vientiane Plain and the area dependent upon it; and the Mekong Valley, stretching south from Paksane to the Cambodian border. In ethnographic terms, there are lowland Laos, inhabited by Lao-speaking, Buddhist, wet-rice agriculturist Lao, and

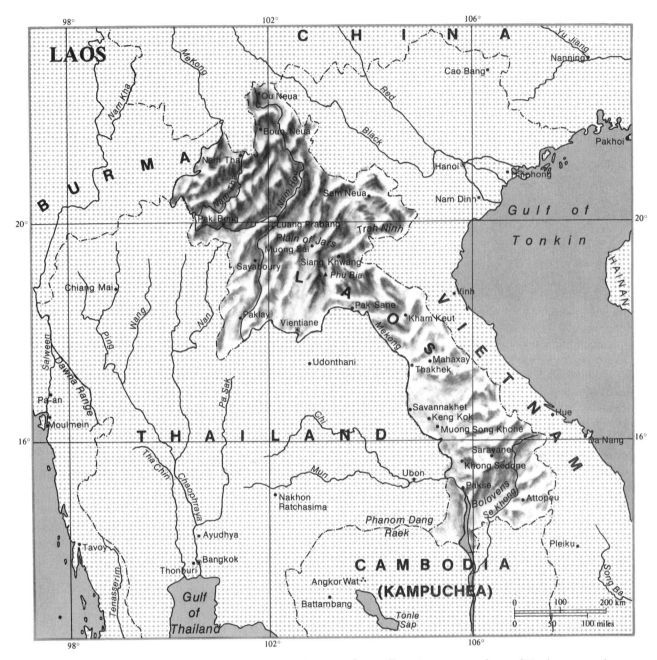

upland Laos, inhabited by non-Lao speakers who number almost half the population. Historically, there is a Laos with modern borders and a very different, historical Laos that at its height of power extended far across the Khorat Plateau of neighboring Thailand. (Today nearly ten times as many Lao live in Thailand as in Laos.) Each of these has in some sense its own history, and thus it is difficult to speak of a single history of Laos.

Laos was inhabited five or more millennia ago by people who probably spoke Austroasiatic languages and whose culture probably resembled that of the Ban Chiang and Dong Son civilizations. In the mid-

first millennium CE, speakers of Tai languages began moving into Laos from the northeast, and until the mid-thirteenth century these people, even those who lived as far north as Luang Prabang, were exposed to Buddhism and participated in the life of the Cambodian kingdom of Angkor. By 1300 major Lao Buddhist and political centers included Luang Prabang; Siang Khwang, a city in the Vientiane area; and That Phanom. In the 1350s, a scion of the ruling house of Luang Prabang militarily united the Lao principalities into the kingdom of Lan Sang. The unity of Lan Sang, however, was fragile and depended on personal relations between the Lan Sang kings and provincial dignitaries and potentates. Only the rare king of Lan Sang—Fa Ngum (r. 1353–1373), Phothisarat I (r. 1520–1547), Setthathirat (r. 1547–1571), and Surinyavongsa (r. 1637–1694) —could make the state an effective power over all the Lao.

The fragility of Lao unity was demonstrated during the period of division, which began about 1700 and continued, it could be argued, until recently. Laos fell apart into three (or even four) smaller kingdoms—Luang Prabang, Vientiane, and Champassak, with Siang Khwang also maintaining some degree of autonomy. All were caught in the major warfare between Siam and Burma that wracked the region in the last half of the eighteenth century and left it, weak and divided, prey to Burmese aggression and Siamese expansion. Siamese military campaigns reduced all four kingdoms to vassals of Siam in the 1770s and began the losses of territory and population to Siam that accelerated in the nineteenth century. King Anuvong of Vientiane (r. 1804–1827) daringly challenged Siam by organizing a massive rebellion in 1827 that succeeded only in extinguishing the kingdom of Vientiane and facilitating direct Siamese control over the middle Mekong Valley. In its aftermath, when Siam became embroiled in warfare with Vietnam, much of the population of central and eastern Laos was transferred west across the Mekong River to what is now northeast Thailand. Laos was too weak to withstand Chinese brigands in the 1870s and 1880s, and Siam as suzerain power was too weak to withstand French imperial expansion westward from Vietnam in the 1880s. The Franco-Siamese Crisis—also known as the Paknam Incident—of 1893 was resolved with Siam's cession to France of Laos east of the Mekong.

But colonial Laos was little more unified than Lan Sang or the three kingdoms had been, and its existence was further complicated by Laos's integration into French Indochina. The French more or less directly ruled the territory from the Vientiane Plain to Cambodia, but they maintained the kingdom of Luang Prabang as a protectorate. France did very little to encourage the formation of an all-Laos elite and trained virtually no professional class. Under the circumstances, the sacrifices so many Lao made in the struggle for Lao independence in the post–World War II period are all the more surprising. On many important issues, however, Lao remained divided. Some saw the only hope of ending French rule to be collaboration with the Vietnamese nationalist movement, which became predominantly communist; others judged their best hope to be to play upon the French need of Lao cooperation to gain concessions for Laos. Fundamentally different tactics grew into profound divisions that persist to the present. Unification under the kings of Luang Prabang satisfied neither radicals nor southerners. Collaboration with Vietnamese communism alienated many patriots who feared Vietnamese imperialism; collaboration with first France and then the United States angered other patriots. The Lao (or Laotian) civil war between what might be termed the moderate accommodationists (neutralists) led by Prince Souvannaphouma and the communist Pathet Lao led by Prince Souphanouvong sputtered from the late 1940s until 1975, when the Pathet Lao won and proclaimed the Lao People's Democratic Republic on 2 December.

[See also Champassak; Geneva Conference on the Laotian Question; Lan Sang; Lao; Lao Issara; Luang Prabang; Paknam Incident; Pathet Lao; Phetsarath; Phoumi Nosavan; Savangvatthana; Siang Khwang; Sisavangvong; Souphanouvong; Souvannaphouma; Vientiane; and Vientiane Agreements.]

Nina S. Adams and A. W. McCoy, eds., *Laos: War and Revolution* (1970). A. J. Dommen, *Conflict in Laos: The Politics of Neutralization* (1971). Hugh Toye, *Laos: Buffer State or Battleground?* (1968). David K. Wyatt, *Thailand: A Short History* (1984).    DAVID K. WYATT

LAOZI, an epithet translatable as "old boy," denoting the supposed author of the Daoist classic *Daode jing*, or *The Way and Its Power*. If we assume that such a person existed, and that certain other traditions concerning him are true, his real name was Li Er (or less plausibly Li Dan), he lived in the Chinese state of Chu during the Warring States period (403–221 BCE), and he was a remote ancestor of the ruling house of the Tang dynasty (618–906 CE). In his many incarnations, Laozi became the subject of a rich religious literature, and his spirit was commonly worshiped.

The authenticity of the transmitted text of the *Daode jing* has recently been confirmed by the archaeological discovery of two manuscript copies that appear to have been written before 180 BCE and differ little from the traditional version except in the order of chapters. The *Daode jing* is characterized by an intuition and an attitude. What is intuitively grasped is a unity underlying the plurality of the phenomenal world, an identity underlying its diversity, and the eternal underlying its flux and impermanence. But the *dao*, or Way, that which is intuitively grasped, cannot properly be named because it transcends all boundaries of meaning and all possible names. It is neither in a state of being or nonbeing because these and all other opposites are reconciled in it. The *de*, or "virtue," of the Way, in the sense of immanent power, is given practical effect by the sage who obtains it (*de*, "to get," cognate with *de*, "virtue"). Intuitive identification with the Way and the acquisition of its power requires quietistic or meditative practices that are only suggested in the text.

The attitude expressed in the *Daode jing* is one of humility. The Way is likened to the "valley spirit" and the "female," and is readily symbolized by water, which is yielding—that is, fluid—and spontaneously seeks out low places. Humility in action is *wuwei*, "not-action," having the sense of spontaneous or natural action after the fashion of the *dao* itself.

The *Daode jing* appears at times to have been addressed to a ruler. It is perhaps for this reason, and because of the importance given to the concept of "power," that it was adopted by, among others, the creators of the syncretic Daoist-Legalist Huang-Lao school of statecraft of the early Han dynasty (206 BCE–220 CE).

[*See also* Daoism.]

Judith Magee Boltz, "Lao-tzu," in *The Encyclopedia of Religion,* edited by Mircea Eliade (1987), vol. 8, pp. 454–459. D. C. Lau, trans., *Tao Te Ching* (1963). Arthur Waley, trans., *The Way and Its Power* (1934). Holmes Welch, *Taoism: The Parting of the Way* (1957).

ROMEYN TAYLOR

## LATER THREE KINGDOMS

**LATER THREE KINGDOMS,** the last stage of the kingdom of Silla (57 BCE–935 CE), a period during which its rulers were opposed by two warlord states that controlled most of the Korean peninsula. During this period of fewer than forty years the old Silla aristocracy was eliminated and new leaders came to the fore.

The decline of Silla began with the murder of King Hyegong in 780, after which the Silla royal line changed frequently, although remaining restricted to the *chin'gol* bone-rank in the aristocratic hierarchy. The constant upheavals undermined the government's authority in the provinces, where local leaders—such as Chang Po-go, early in the ninth century—gained virtual autonomy. By the reign of Queen Chinsŏng (r. 887–897) taxes were no longer reaching Kyŏngju, the Silla capital, and successive years of drought and famine filled the countryside with starving people who turned to banditry in desperation, while Queen Chinsŏng and her male favorites raised money by the sale of offices.

Two figures rose to prominence early in the long civil war. One was Kyŏn Hwŏn, a farmer's son who had formerly served as a guard on the coast and had collected his own band of followers. Kyŏn Hwŏn took over a large part of southwestern Korea and, in 900, when he captured the important city of Wŏnsan, he proclaimed himself king of Later Paekche. Kyŏn Hwŏn was a man of Silla who had no connection with old Paekche; his announcement of a Paekche restoration was no more than a ruse to legitimate his rule and conciliate the population of the southwest.

Kyŏn's main rival was Kung Ye, said to have been the illegitimate son of a Silla king. Kung Ye had been abandoned at birth but rescued and reared by a servant girl. For a time he had been a Buddhist priest under the name Sŏngjong, but in Queen Chinsŏng's reign he became a bandit. After beginning his career in the service of other rebel leaders, Kung Ye built up his own base at Ch'ŏrwŏn, in central Korea. In 901 he took the title king, calling his kingdom first Majin then (from 911) T'aebong. Intensely hostile to Silla, Kung Ye announced that he would avenge the long-vanished kingdom of Koguryŏ, which had been destroyed by Silla in alliance with the Chinese; he also claimed to be Maitreya, the coming Buddha, with the ability to see into people's hearts. The tyranny and growing violence of his rule led to Kung Ye's overthrow in 918, whereupon his lieutenant Wang Kŏn was installed as king, and the name of the kingdom changed to Koryŏ.

Wang Kŏn was the son of a petty magistrate in western Korea; some scholars believe he came of merchant stock. As soon as he could he moved the capital much closer to the western coast, back to his hometown, modern Kaesŏng. In the struggle between Wang Kŏn and Kyŏn Hwŏn that followed, Silla, now no more than the city of Kyŏngju, was merely a pawn. Nevertheless, all three rivals were careful to maintain contacts with China, and it would seem that Kyŏn Hwŏn attempted to emulate Chang Po-go and monopolize the trade between China and Korea. Wang Kŏn fought back, establishing a bridgehead in southern Paekche and defeating Kyŏn Hwŏn in a series of naval battles. Kyŏn Hwŏn, however, remained powerful on land, and in 927 he sacked Kyŏngju; the aristocracy of the old capital were massacred or enslaved, and the last Silla king, Kyŏngsun (r. 927–935), was completely dependent on Wang Kŏn for protection. In 935 Kyŏngsun abdicated in Wang Kŏn's favor, bringing the kingdom of Silla to an end. Earlier in the same year Kyŏn Hwŏn, now an old man, had been overthrown by one of his many sons; after three months as a prisoner in a Buddhist temple he fled to Koryŏ.

With his former rival now a pensioner at his court, Wang Kŏn invaded Later Paekche in the autumn of 936, defeating Kyŏn Hwŏn's son Sin'gŏm at the battle of Ilsŏngun. The conquest of Paekche that followed brought the Later Three Kingdoms period to a close, and united the greater part of the peninsula under the rule of Koryŏ.

[See also Silla; Koryŏ; and Chang Po-go.]

KENNETH H. J. GARDINER

LATTRE DE TASSIGNY, JEAN DE (1889–1952), French commander in chief and high commissioner in Indochina (1950–1951). A temperamental and strong-willed leader, General de Lattre saw the First Indochina War as an essentially Vietnamese conflict, with France aiding Bao Dai's State of Vietnam against the Viet Minh. Despite several military victories in 1951 and the establishment of the "de Lattre line" of fortifications, he is not credited with any major contribution to the French military cause. He was, however, a staunch advocate of a Vietnamese army led by Vietnamese officers. In January 1952, shortly after a largely unsuccessful visit to Washington to request American aid, de Lattre died of cancer.

[See also French Indochina War.]

Joseph Buttinger, Vietnam: A Dragon Embattled (1967).                              BRUCE M. LOCKHART

LAUREL, JOSE P. (1891–1959), leading Filipino legal scholar and politician, president of the Japanese-authorized wartime Republic of the Philippines (1943–1945), and losing candidate for president in 1949. Laurel, who had degrees from the University of the Philippines and Yale University, served variously in the Philippine government as secretary of the interior, associate justice of the Supreme Court, acting secretary of justice, and senator.

Laurel's pre–Pacific War opportunities for true political prominence had seemed stymied by the dominant power of Manuel L. Quezon. When Quezon was in the United States and Laurel was prevailed upon by the Japanese to serve as president, "patriotism and ambition, ideological belief and

pragmatic possibilities, heroism and cowardice all merged in his decision," according to historian David Steinberg (1967). Tried for collaboration after the war, Laurel claimed that he had acted under duress to save the Filipinos from an even worse fate at the hands of the Japanese. The issue was never legally resolved because on 28 January 1948 President Manuel Roxas granted amnesty to all those accused of collaboration. Nevertheless, Laurel's tremendous winning vote in the 1951 senatorial election put the issue to rest politically.

In 1953 Laurel was one of the principal architects of the rise to the presidency of Ramon Magsaysay. Magsaysay, in turn, selected Laurel to head a Philippine economic mission to the United States to seek revisions in the Philippine-American trade arrangements. On 15 December 1954 the multifaceted Laurel-Langley Trade Agreement was signed. The pact guaranteed the Philippines true parity on a reciprocal basis, ended American control of the Philippine peso, assured more equitable tariff quotas, and established a period of twenty years in which special Philippine privileges in the American market would be phased out.

[See also Philippines; Quezon, Manuel Luis; and Laurel-Langley Trade Agreement.]

Theodore Friend, Between Two Empires (1965). David Steinberg, Philippine Collaboration in World War II (1967).                              GRANT K. GOODMAN

LAUREL-LANGLEY TRADE AGREEMENT, 1955 revision of trade relations between the Philippines and the United States, informally named after the chief negotiators for the two sides. It replaced the 1946 Bell Trade Act and was in effect until 1974.

Major provisions of the agreement were as follows: the gradually declining tariff preferences established in the Bell Trade Act were accelerated for US exports to the Philippines and decelerated for Philippine exports to the United States; limits on Philippine exports, other than sugar and cordage, were eliminated; quotas could be imposed on imports that harmed domestic producers; the value of the peso was no longer tied to the dollar; the Philippines agreed to remove its tax on the sale of foreign exchange; the citizens of the two countries were granted the same rights in all business activities; and the Bell Trade Act's grant to US investors of parity with Filipinos in developing Philippine natural resources and operating public utilities was made formally reciprocal by granting Filipinos similar rights in the United States.

[*See also* Bell Trade Act *and* Laurel, Jose P.]

*US Department of State Bulletin* 19 (Sept. 1955): 463–477.                                    STEPHEN R. SHALOM

# LAW

## LAW IN CHINA

One of the world's great legal traditions, with a history of more than two millennia, Chinese law helped to shape the distinctive cultural homogeneity and political unity that have long characterized the Chinese people. Classical Chinese law also served as the model for the formal law of premodern Korea, Japan, and Vietnam.

***Classical Chinese Law.*** Classical Chinese law encompasses the codes and procedures promulgated and enforced by successive Chinese imperial dynasties, together with the shared legal values and customs that complemented the formal law. China's dynastic history began with the unification of all Chinese territory in 221 BCE under the king of the state of Qin, who became the first emperor. During the centuries preceding unification, Qin and other feudal states in the North China Plain placed increasing reliance on written law to establish and maintain political power and social control. Qin laws reflected the statist precepts of the Legalist school of political philosophy, which had gained dominance over the more humanistic Confucian school during the fourth and third centuries BCE. The history of Chinese law and government has been largely shaped by these two conflicting approaches to human nature, social order, and the art of political governance.

Many Chinese historians have attributed the early collapse of the Qin dynasty only fifteen years after its establishment to excessive reliance upon positive law rules, coercively enforced by formal state mechanisms. Subsequent dynasties, the Han, Jin, Sui, Tang, Song, Yuan, Ming, and Qing, which spanned the 2,100 years from 206 BCE to 1911, learned from the mistakes of the Qin. All placed primary reliance upon a pervasive moral code, inculcated through education and example and through the operation of family, clan, and village organizations.

Unlike most Western legal traditions and systems, the exercise of political power and the enactment and implementation of legal rules in Chinese society were not subject to influence by other centers of political or economic power. In contrast with the West, political power in old China was not subject to the constraint of transcendent values and rules bestowed by a divine creator. Nor did Chinese law evolve over time through conflict and compromise between a secular human society and the dominant state political power and authority.

For more than two thousand years, China's emperors relied upon a combination of essentially Confucian moral norms and legalist bureaucratic methods to govern a very large agrarian society. The Confucian moral code was centered upon the notion of continuous self-cultivation and the performance of one's proper social role in a hierarchically structured society. Aggressive pursuit of selfish interests was highly disfavored in traditional Chinese society. Thus, yielding to others was a highly stressed value. Conflicts were to be resolved through compromise, with both sides accepting a mediated solution arranged by respected family elders or community leaders. Litigation in a magistrate's court was avoided if possible, as it was fraught with the risk of loss of reputation, property, and possibly one's life.

Although Confucian moral norms and local mediation were the workhorses of China's traditional legal system, China's imperial rulers also developed a comprehensive set of published rules that emphasized penal regulations almost exclusively. These rules were imposed on the populace by the state. While the imperial criminal codes set forth a rather systematic structure of interlocking rules that reinforced the Confucian standards of Chinese society, the emperor could by fiat change any law at any time.

Despite the persisting primacy of Confucian morality as the core of society and basis of government, written codes of law and formal legal procedures became increasingly comprehensive in scope and more widely utilized over time. The essence of the substantive law of twenty centuries of imperial codes, however, largely reflected Confucian moral norms, what has been called the gradual "confucianization" of Chinese law.

Although the emperor possessed enormous authority in traditional Chinese political legal theory, classical Chinese law exhibited a high degree of regularity and predictability, deriving from general adherence to a number of key legal principles, rules, and procedures. This model has been termed "rule by law" in contrast to the modern notion of "rule of law," which connotes an autonomous legal system, independent of political authority. There are, nonetheless, certain features in this rational bureaucratic model of classical Chinese law that satisfy very modern standards of legality. Thus, prior notice of the criminality of an act was deemed essential to the finding of the criminal intent necessary to punish someone who had violated a law. The same overriding concern with the subjective state of mind of the actor gave rise to the principle of voluntary surrender, which bestowed complete exemption or reduction of punishment on an offender who surrendered to the authorities prior to the issue of an arrest warrant.

Other rules of classical Chinese legal procedure include an automatic new trial if the convicted criminal refused to make written acknowledgment that the judgment was valid as to both law and facts. Furthermore, magistrates were forbidden to accept anonymous accusations, even though they might be true in fact. One can plausibly argue that these provisions show imperial concern with bureaucratic regularity, but not necessarily a recognition of independent constraints on state power. Nevertheless, these rules indicate considerable procedural sophistication.

Classical Chinese legal procedure was, in many respects, in advance of Western legal systems at the time. Thus, as early as the seventh century the Tang-dynasty legal code made mandatory at least three automatic reviews of a sentence of death before the sentence could be carried out. By the time of the Qing dynasty (1644–1911) further levels of review had been added. In addition, family members could appeal conviction directly to the emperor, subject to risk of punishment should the appeal be ruled frivolous.

Other distinctive features of classical Chinese law include the absence of an independent legal profession. Private lawyers were prohibited, subject to severe criminal penalties. They were considered social parasites and fomentors of disputes. Thus, administration of justice was monopolized by the magistrate, who happened also to be chief prosecutor. Accuracy of the investigation and fairness of the judgment was sought through the imposition of absolute liability on magistrates who made mistakes of law or fact, regardless of how well-intentioned and free of fraud or malice they may have been. It was small wonder that magistrates went to great lengths to avoid accepting formal complaints.

A hallmark of classical Chinese law has been a preference for mediation over litigation. The Confucian values that promoted social harmony and encouraged individuals to compromise disputes no doubt joined with magisterial preference to keep formal lawsuits to a small percentage. Nonetheless, there was far more litigation in imperial China than is commonly appreciated. One reason for the persistence of such litigation was the lack of genuine finality in traditional Chinese legal procedure. A case could always be reopened if one party claimed that he was a victim of injustice.

Classical Chinese law reached its maturity during the Tang dynasty (618–907). Drawing on the laws and procedures of the preceding Sui dynasty (589–618), in 624 the Tang rulers promulgated the *Tang Code with Commentaries (Tanglü shuyi)*. Consisting of 502 articles, the Tang Code helped the Tang emperors establish a rule of unprecedented wealth and power.

The Tang Code established a model for later Chinese dynasties; as noted, it was also copied in Korea, Japan, and Vietnam. In all these countries, its influence lasted for more than a thousand years. The Tang Code was divided into two parts, with an initial general part containing 57 articles followed by 445 articles defining specific offenses. The general provisions set forth basic principles of statutory construction and judicial procedure, as well as standards for sentencing and carrying out criminal punishment.

Prior to the twentieth century China possessed no officially promulgated contract law or commercial law. This is not to say, however, that no contracts or commerce existed. In the absence of written code provisions, property rights and commercial relations were guided by customary rules, enforced primarily by guilds or by village elders.

*The Twentieth Century.* The classical legal system—Confucian values underlying a legalist bureaucratic structure—served China reasonably well until the invasion of Western values and power. This invasion, coupled with a population explosion, brought the imperial era to an end in 1911. While a number of young Chinese reformers sought to restore glory and prosperity to China through the importation of liberal values and their attendant legal and political institutions, the more radical promises of the Communist Party prevailed in China's violent civil struggle of the early twentieth century.

The founders of the Chinese Communist Party placed their faith in Marxist materialism, rejecting both the old static Confucian ideal and bourgeois idealism, with its belief in natural law and constitutionalism. Law, like all other elements of the so-called social superstructure, was viewed simply as a tool with which the ruling class sustained its dictatorship over the oppressed classes. Laws and legal institutions were also seen as functional weapons to be employed to achieve intermediate goals on the path from "feudal" society through socialist transition to the ultimate goal of communist society: the withering away of the state.

Operating with such elemental Marxist assumptions about the nature and role of law, it is not surprising that when the Chinese Communist Party seized political power from the Nationalists on 1 October 1949, one of its first acts was to abolish the comprehensive Six Codes that had been laboriously developed over more than thirty years, from a beginning in 1903 under the Qing emperor to their adoption under Chiang Kai-shek in the mid-1930s. The codes comprised the constitution, civil code, code of civil procedure, criminal code, code of criminal procedure, and administrative laws. The discarded rules were not replaced by comprehensive new laws, because Mao Zedong and the Party did not want to straitjacket the revolutionary forces. The political and social priority at the time was to suppress and eliminate enemy classes, feudal habits, and reactionary ways of thought.

In short order, not only was the Nationalist code discarded, but so were most of the lawyers, judges, and law professors trained under the Nationalists. The Nationalist system was replaced by kangaroo courts run by the aroused peasants who enforced "revolutionary justice" over "evil" landlords. When a limited number of courts were reestablished in the early and mid-1950s, they were staffed largely by politically reliable Party members who possessed no formal legal training.

A promising movement toward greater legal formality and predictability, comprehensive codification, and open trials in the mid-1950s was blocked by Mao in 1957, when he pushed through an "antirightist" campaign that purged scores of leading law professors and Party officials who advocated codification and the establishment of a more rational and stable "socialist legality." After the dismal failure of Mao's Great Leap Forward in 1958, advocates of political and economic pragmatism and gradualism in the Party's leadership forced Mao to accept some policy compromises and to promulgate various separate statutes in the early 1960s.

The hopes of those advocating an ambitious program to promulgate codes, train lawyers, and strengthen courts were completely dashed, however, when Mao unleashed the Great Proletarian Cultural Revolution in 1966. Primarily intended by Mao to discredit Party moderates who opposed his leftist commitment to "continuing revolution" and "pol-

itics over economics," the Cultural Revolution quickly got out of hand, eventually paralyzing the Party, disrupting the economy, and decimating institutions of higher education, including virtually all law schools. Law was one of the principal targets of the radical Cultural Revolution faction, which successfully exhorted mobs of youthful Red Guards to "smash the police, procuracy, and the courts."

Law in China today is designed to promote policy aims designated by the leaders of the Chinese Communist Party. Since the reemergence of Deng Xiaoping as China's paramount leader in 1978, the overriding purpose of all policies and all institutional reforms has been to assure the achievement of the "Four Modernizations"—industry, agriculture, science and technology, and national defense. Deng and his supporters, who now command the key positions in every sector of the government, economy, and society, have set in motion a long-range reorientation of laws, personnel training and selection, and policy enforcement procedures, all calculated to enhance stable and rapid economic growth.

Prevailing Party policy stresses the importance of law and the necessity for rapid expansion of the ranks of well-trained legal specialists. In 1978 an eight-year plan for development of law, legal institutions, and legal education was adopted. The program called for the opening of at least one law faculty in each of China's twenty-nine internal divisions, the speedy reestablishment of the legal profession, the expansion of courts, and the progressive drafting and promulgation of criminal and civil codes as well as scores of other important laws and regulations.

Three motivations seem to have triggered China's law reform movement and to provide a continuing impetus for a lasting commitment to build a regular and predictable legal process. These motivations are a popular demand for legal protection against arbitrary behavior by Party or government officials or by other citizens; the need for clear guidelines for domestic economic activity; and a perceived need for a systematic network of civil, economic, and commercial law rules and procedures to attract and protect foreign capital and technology.

Deeply ingrained values, thought patterns, and habits cannot be changed overnight. Promulgation of hundreds of laws and training of thousands of lawyers will not instantly instill faith in legal procedures, no matter how committed leaders may be to replacing personal relations and government dictation with the predictability and fairness of public law and procedures. As noted, China does not have a tradition of placing strong reliance upon legal rules and procedures. Human behavior has been guided not by law so much as by broad moral concepts—Confucian norms of proper behavior—which have been only partly superseded by the new communist morality. Prevailing norms have encouraged unity and harmony and have discouraged the pursuit of personal interests in conflict with the claims of others. The Chinese have favored mediation over litigation and have rejected a "winner take all" victory over one's adversaries.

These deeply entrenched patterns and values will certainly continue to influence the form and function of Chinese law. At the same time, however, the pressures of dynamic development at home and the competition of foreign models promise to bring about substantial and irreversible change in the practice as well as the form of law in China.

[*See also* Confucianism; Legalism; Qin Dynasty; *and* Tang Dynasty.]

Derk Bodde and Clarence Morris, *Law in Imperial China* (1967). Hungdah Chiu and Shao-chuan Leng, *Criminal Justice in Post-Mao China: Analysis and Documents* (1985). Ch'ü T'ung-tsu, *Law and Society in Traditional China* (1961). Jerome A. Cohen, Randle Edwards, and Fu-mei Chang Chen, eds., *Essays on China's Legal Tradition* (1980). Jerome A. Cohen, *The Criminal Process in the People's Republic of China, 1949–1963* (1968). A. F. P. Hulsewe, *Remnants of Han Law*, vol. 1 (1955). Sybille Van der Sprenkel, *Legal Institutions in Manchu China: A Sociological Analysis* (1962).

R. RANDLE EDWARDS

## JUDICIAL AND LEGAL SYSTEMS OF INDIA

India has been the home of four major legal traditions: Hindu, Muslim, British, and that of modern, independent India. Although each of the latter three legal systems was established in India as the result of dramatic political change, none has ever totally supplanted its predecessors. Important elements of the earlier traditions remained in each new system, and all of the earlier traditions are present in contemporary Indian law.

**Dharmashastra.** The autochthonous legal tradition of India is Hindu. The Sanskrit word perhaps closest in meaning to the English term *law* is *dharma,* which refers generally to right or proper conduct, and thus covers such English concepts as law, morality, duty, and obligation. A vast body of Sanskrit texts dealing with these and other normative topics, generally known as the *Dharmashastras,* developed between 600 BCE and 500 CE. In these

texts, obligations and penalties were differentiated according to caste and station in life.

Hindu law knew no hierarchy of legal agencies. There were innumerable overlapping jurisdictions; many groups enjoyed a degree of autonomy in administering law among themselves. Each caste had its own tribunals, sometimes advised by brahmans, and markets, villages, and guilds had councils to decide disputes. These bodies decided cases according to caste or local custom as well as, or instead of, rules derived from the *dharmashastra.*

The *dharmashastra* not only established different rules for different kinds of persons, but it incorporated and certified many bodies of rules not found within its pages. Every aggregation of people—castes, bodies of traders, guilds of artisans, families, sects, villages—was entitled to formulate and apply its own customs and conventions. Custom was not necessarily ancient and it was not unchangeable. It might be minted for the occasion. The power of groups to change custom and to create new obligatory usage was generally recognized. Where matters concerning such groups came before the royal courts, they were to be decided in accordance with the usage of the group.

Royal courts existed in capitals and in some larger towns, where the king or his delegate decided cases on the advice of brahman *shastris,* scholars of the *dharmashastra.* Hindu rulers enjoyed in theory, and sometimes exercised, a general power of supervision over all the lesser tribunals. In theory, only the royal courts could execute fines or corporal punishments, but presumably the various lesser tribunals could pronounce them and invoke the king's power of enforcement. But while some adjudications might have been enforced by governmental power, most depended on expulsion and boycott as the ultimate sanctions. Theoretically, at least, these decisions could be appealed to the king, but available evidence suggests that this occurred infrequently.

In spite of the general prestige of the *dharmashastra* and its brahman exponents, and in spite of the plenary power of the royal courts, neither *dharmashastra* nor the king's law displaced the many bodies of local law; *dharmashastra* itself incorporated the widest tolerance of local law. The fact that *dharmashastra* was the only body of law that was written, studied, and systematically cultivated—in addition to the prestige of its brahman expositors and the patronage of royal authority—caused widespread striving on the part of many groups to broaden it to govern more groups on more legal topics. But this was by absorption and acceptance, not by imposition. At the same time that custom was gradually aligned in some respects with the standards set by the *dharmashastra,* the textual law was itself continuously reinterpreted to accommodate a variety of usages. The relation between the "highest" and most authoritative parts of the legal system to the "lower" components was more like the relation between leading American universities and smaller colleges, or between *haute couture* and discount store fashions, than it was to the type of hierarchical relationship that is associated with a modern legal system. No central power could pronounce binding law or unify the system.

*Islamic Influence.* This diverse, decentralized system became even more complex with the conquest of much of India by Muslim invaders, beginning in the twelfth century. Muslim rulers had royal courts in cities and administrative centers that exercised general criminal (and sometimes commercial) jurisdiction and also decided civil and family matters among the Muslim population. These courts operated according to Muslim law—at least in theory, for the application of *shari'a* (Islamic law) was qualified by custom and royal decrees, by corruption and lack of professionalism, and by arrangements allowing considerable discretion to the courts of first instance. While a hierarchy of courts and a right of appeal existed, it seems that the activity of these higher courts fell short of any sustained and systematic supervision of the lower courts. Hindus were generally allowed their own tribunals in civil matters. Where such matters came before royal courts, the Hindu law was applied. The government's courts did not extend very deeply into the countryside; there was no attempt to control the administration of law in the villages. Presumably, the Hindu tribunals proceeded as before Muslim rule, except that whatever ties had bound these tribunals to governmental authority were weakened; there was no appeal to the royal courts. [*See also* Durbar.]

*British Rule.* A third legal tradition arrived with the British in the seventeenth century. The East India Company's charter gave it the power to discipline its own servants, and a 1618 treaty with the Mughal emperor recognized this power for the company's factory at Surat. As new British settlements were established, new company courts were created in them. These courts were not the same in all locations, however. In 1726 the courts in the presidency towns were made royal courts of uniform structure, deriving their power directly from the king and not from the company, with appeal to the Privy Council in London. Their jurisdiction was confined to cases involving residents of the presidency towns or company factories. But uniformity proved elusive and jurisdictional restrictions proved difficult to maintain in the face of the appeal of these courts to Indian litigants. [*See* East India Company.]

A new plan, put forth in Bengal in 1772 and later adopted in Bombay and Madras, established in each presidency a hierarchy of courts empowered to hear civil cases between all residents—both Indian and European—of the presidency. In suits regarding inheritance, succession, marriage, caste, and religious endowments, the courts were to apply the *dharmashastra* to the Hindus and the *shari'a* to Muslims. The British judges were assisted by brahman advisors in ascertaining and applying Hindu law, and *moulvis* for Islamic law. Presidency-wide hierarchies of criminal courts were established in the 1790s. Thus, by the end of the eighteenth century British courts had completely supplanted those of the Indian rulers throughout the territory of the presidencies. This process continued through the nineteenth century, with new British courts being created as the territory of British India increased.

The law applied by the British courts was derived from many sources. Hindu and Muslim law continued to be applied in the "personal law" areas of inheritance, caste, marriage, and religion. However, the British were not content to depend solely upon Indian advisers for knowledge of Hindu and Muslim law; they also translated many basic works on the *dharmashastra* and *shari'a*. The British judges relied increasingly on such texts, as well as on precedent from their own courts. Outside these areas, the British judges were empowered to decide according to "justice, equity, and good conscience," a rubric under which most cases were decided according to principles and rules of English law. [*See also* Jones, Sir William.]

The anglicization of the law in India increased after 1858, when the British Crown replaced the administration of the East India Company. During the next quarter century a series of codes, based more or less on English law and applicable throughout British India, were enacted. There was virtually complete codification of all fields of commercial, criminal, and procedural law. Separate "personal laws" were still applied to Hindus and Muslims, but the connection between these laws and the original traditions of the *dharmashastra* and the *shari'a* became transformed. After 1862 the courts no longer employed Indian law advisers but instead decided cases on the basis of precedent and the available texts. The traditional methods of refining the doctrines of the *dharmashastra* through the writing of commentaries, and the flexible application by the *shastris* were displaced by the British system of formal rule application and accumulation of precedent. The living process of Hindu law was abandoned; in its place appeared a body of rules known as "Hindu law."

As the law applied in British Indian courts became increasingly anglicized, the traditional legal institutions were also largely displaced. The British courts quickly attracted large numbers of cases. Some indigenous judicial institutions, particularly caste councils, remained active, but in the course of the late nineteenth and early twentieth centuries, most of these bodies became moribund. The British viewed the flood of cases into their courts and the concomitant decline of traditional judicial institutions with some concern, as they thought that indigenous forms of judicial administration would be cheaper, more suited to Indian cases, and less prone than British courts to manipulation and abuse by litigants. Nevertheless, all efforts to divert Indian cases from the courts into other forums failed.

A large and influential legal profession developed as the business and importance of the courts increased. The first judges and lawyers were English, but as the nineteenth century progressed the bar became predominatly Indian, and increasing numbers of Indians were appointed to the judiciary. Lawyers became prominent in public life, and particularly in the movement for Indian independence from Britain.

*Postindependence.* After independence in 1947, the legal system changed again. The Constitution of India, which came into effect in 1950, created a unified, hierarchical judiciary, headed by a Supreme Court. In effect, the constitution preserved most of the court system created by the British, but made the Supreme Court rather than the Privy Council the highest court of appeal. Each state (with a few exceptions, where two states share one court) has a single judicial hierarchy with a High Court at its apex. There are no lower central courts, although specialized tribunals do exist to handle cases in such areas as income tax or labor matters. English is still the language used in most courts.

The caste and local tribunals have largely disappeared. Attempts to resurrect "traditional" justice, in the form of informal village courts *(nyaya panchayats)* to handle minor disputes, have not been successful. When they were created in the 1950s, these *panchayats* attracted large numbers of cases, but most of them have undergone a drop in case filings, to the point of being moribund. It seems that these *nyaya* ("new") *panchayats* offer neither the community justice of the old *panchayats* nor the independence and finality of the courts, and thus have not been attractive to potential litigants. [*See also* Panchayat.]

The adoption of the constitution introduced several entirely new elements into the Indian legal system. One was the basic idea of constitutionalism. In a striking departure from the British idea of parliamentary supremacy, the Indian courts are empowered to strike down legislation and administrative acts that violate provisions of the constitution. This power of judicial review has not been completely accepted by Indian politicians. There has been a dialectical process of Supreme Court assertions of the review power, legislative enactments and constitutional amendments to limit that power, and further Supreme Court decisions preserving the power despite the actions of Parliament.

The battles over the power of judicial review have largely been fought over issues involving the Fundamental Rights, which are guaranteed citizens by Part III of the constitution, roughly analogous to the American Bill of Rights. The constitution provides that citizens may request writs enforcing these Fundamental Rights directly from the Supreme Court or from the high court of their state, without first bringing the matter before a lower court. This ready access to the higher judiciary has ensured that Fundamental Rights issues are frequently raised, and has led to the development of an elaborate constitutional jurisprudence.

In modern India, law is seen as a means for changing society. The Republic of India is a secular and (since 1976) socialist state. The constitution calls for state action to bring about a more equal and just society. Parliament has enacted many laws aimed at achieving that goal. Thus, Article 17 of the constitution abolishes "untouchability," and laws have been enacted that impose penalties for restricting the civil rights of the former Untouchables. Other constitutional provisions empower the state to depart from formal equality to promote the interests of the former Untouchables, members of tribal groups, and other "backward" classes. Pursuant to these provisions, government has erected programs of "compensatory discrimination" involving reservation of such benefits as jobs and places in professional schools for members of these groups. Other laws have been enacted to bring about equal treatment of women, the abolition of dowry, and the emancipation of bonded laborers. The constitution establishes as a Directive Principle of State the policy that the personal law systems applied separately to Hindus and Muslims will be replaced by a uniform civil code. Parliament passed a series of acts in 1955/1956 known collectively as the Hindu Code, which effects a wholesale and drastic reform of Hindu Law. Where earlier legislation introduced specific modifications into the framework of shastric law, the code entirely supplants the *dharmashastra* as the source of Hindu law. Muslim law has been less affected, though the ultimate goal of its replacement remains official policy.

Overall, Indian legal development since the arrival of the British displays increasing rationalization and professionalization—a trend accentuated in independent India. The law is universal in coverage, technically complex, administered by a sizable group of trained professionals, and applied through a unified hierarchy of agencies. Unlike the pre-British systems, it is designed to enforce local conformity to national standards. Yet the price of complexity and hierarchic unity is to make law remote from popular understanding. The system of legal ideas and institutions is now so complex as to supply ample occasion for slippage and opportunity for manipulation, so that uniformity in doctrine and unity in formal structure coexist with diverse practices that diverge from the prescriptions of the formal law.

[*See also* Hindu Law *and* Shari'a.]

M. B. Ahmad, *The Administration of Justice in Medieval India* (1941). J. D. M. Derrett, *Religion, Law and the State in India* (1968) and *Essays in Classical and Modern Hindu Law,* 4 vols. (1978). R. Dhavan, *The Supreme Court of India* (1977). Marc Galanter, *Competing Equalities* (1984). M. P. Jain, *An Outline of Indian Legal History* (1966). P. V. Kane, *History of Dharmaśāstra,* 5 vols. (1930–1962). R. Lingat, *The Classical Law of India* (1973).    MARC GALANTER and ROBERT M. HAYDEN

## LAW IN SOUTHEAST ASIA

From the point of view of legal history and comparative law, Southeast Asia is one of the most complex areas in the world. There are two reasons for this. First, a great number and variety of laws have held sway in the area. Second, complex relations developed within and between the various legal systems of the area. A plurality of laws is the norm rather than the exception.

***Premodern Laws.*** There are six text traditions dating from the eighth to the nineteenth century.

*The Burmese Dhammathat.* The Burmese Dhammathat consists of a number of named texts, known mostly in nineteenth-century copies. They are written in a set form: each has an introduction that explains the source of law (derived from Manu, or Manosara), followed by an exposition of rules, the formal model for which is the Indian Dharmashastras. The earlier Dhammathats tend to enumerate the eighteen titles in *Manu* 8.4–7 and rely heavily on Sanskrit technical terminology. An increasing burmanization, however, is also evident, and such major texts as *Wagaru* and *Dhammavilasa* show considerable departures from the Indian model in their content, form, and use of Indian-derived legal terminology.

*The Thai-Lao Thammasat.* The main text of the Thai-Lao Thammasat is the *Law of the Three Great Seals,* which was rewritten during the reign of Rama I and published in 1805. The purpose of the revision was to restore the laws to their original purity for the better administration of justice. Nonetheless, the concept of law (derived from Manu) as being absolute in nature remained that of the Indian model. Significant change, however, was introduced in form, content, and technique. The form, for example, did not follow *Manu* 8.4–7; instead, the eighteen titles were elaborated into subchapters dealing with specific causes of wrongful action. The content, also, is Thai rather than Indian and takes account of the peculiar implications of Thai social structure. On the technical side, the most important innovation was the incorporation of the temporal decrees (*rajasattham*) of the ruler into the text itself. In theory these were derivative (*sakha-attha*) categories, but in practice they took on the character of being fundamental (*mula-attha*) through incorporation.

*The Java-Bali Texts.* The sources of the Java-Bali texts are in epigraphy dating from the fourteenth century; later manuscripts are known in copies dating from the eighteenth century. Although the texts initially relied on Indian forms, they later assumed an indigenous Java-Bali form. Their content is local, but some of the classifications they use are clearly derived from India. To suit circumstances in Java and Bali, Sanskrit technical terminology is redefined considerably. Because there is no set form for writing the rules, the arrangement is haphazard, with the same or related subjects appearing in widely separated places in the texts; this is in sharp contrast to the Burmese and Thai material. There are substantial difficulties in dating and in the relation of any one text to another. These problems have been compounded by Europeans, who commissioned and/or "revised" texts for administrative purposes.

*The Khmer Epigraphy.* Although there is no Khmer text of law as such, there are rich epigraphic sources dating from the eighth to the fourteenth century. From the evidence they provide it is clear that the Dharmashastras were well known in the Khmer empire. There is also evidence for the existence of a number of judicial bodies and some information about procedure and about the content of substantive law (especially regarding land and other forms of property such as bondsmen and bondswomen). No proper survey from the legal history point of view has been done.

*Texts of Muslim Southeast Asia.* Texts from Islamic areas in Southeast Asia (south Thailand, the Malay Peninsula, Sumatra, Java, and islands of the southern Philippines) are written in Malay or related languages and are known mainly in eighteenth- or nineteenth-century copies. Although there are considerable difficulties in determining the origin and date of these texts, it appears that the text tradition began in the early sixteenth century. While elements of *fikh* (Islamic principles of jurisprudence) appear in some texts, the manuscripts cannot be strictly considered classically Islamic because their content is overwhelmingly indigenous and they are not written in Arabic. Nonetheless, the texts clearly assume a Muslim population, demand some minor adherence to particular parts of *fikh* (mostly in family law and contracts), and derive from rulers (sultans) whose legitimacy is founded on a Muslim polity. Although they primarily deal with matters of interest to an agricultural population (i.e., land matters), the texts also contain important sections on commerce, in which Islamic rules are important. Perhaps most significant, the authority of law is described in wholly religious terms, for example, as ultimately deriving from revelation. Authority is vested in the ruler and exercised by him (through the text provision) by virtue of his position as *ber-khalifha*, the "shadow of God on earth."

*Vietnamese Texts.* The surviving legal material dating from Vietnam's premodern period is especially rich and complex. The Hoang (Hong) Duc Code, originally from the fifteenth century, is known in eighteenth-century rescensions. Considerable administrative and historical material also dates from the eighteenth century. In addition, the Hoang Viet ("imperial Vietnamese") text, sometimes called the Gia Long text, dates from 1812. The Hoang Duc and Gia Long codes are derived from the (Chinese) Tang and Qing codes, respectively, in terms of their form and, to a large extent, their content. This correspondence has led some scholars to say that the texts are Chinese (indeed, the French translation of the Hoang Viet is often read as the only full translation of Qing imperial law), but such a conclusion is not fully justified. While their form (books and

titles) exactly reproduces that of the Chinese original, their administrative regulations introduce specifically Vietnamese features that effectively adapt and/or reorder the formal imperial provisions.

*Summary.* The premodern laws of Southeast Asia are derived, in varying senses, from the great traditions of India, Islam, and China, but none of these surviving materials fully fits any of these categories. On the contrary, Southeast Asian law is the product of a highly original culture. Its main characteristic is a striking process of intellectualism directed toward the immediately practical in the important areas of sovereignty/authority and economic (i.e., agricultural and commercial) order. [*See also* Hindu Law; Hong Duc Code; *and* Gia Long Code.]

**Colonial Laws.** There are six European legal traditions dating from the sixteenth century in Southeast Asia.

*Spanish Laws (the Philippines).* Spain's formal rule of the Philippines began early in the sixteenth century, and in the Royal Decree of 1530 the laws of Spain were extended to the Philippines. In 1680 laws for all colonial territories were specifically drafted for the overseas territories and included in the *Recopilacion de leyes de los Reinos de las Indias,* which had various succeeding editions. It was replaced in 1805 by the *Novissima Recopilacion,* which was in turn replaced by the reformed civil and commercial codes of 1870 to 1889. In addition, a judicial administration (Audencia) based on the Spanish administrative system was organized under regulations dating from 1590 onward. Thus, the substantive law applied was the law of Spain in the various codifications produced from the seventeenth century. Perhaps its most striking characteristic is the formal incorporation of Christian precepts, as defined by Spanish Catholicism, into the law texts. Contemporary Philippine law essentially retains the civil system, although significant changes were introduced during the American occupation, particularly where religion was concerned.

*Dutch Law (Indonesia).* The Netherlands East Indies have a complex legal history. From the point of view of comparative law, the area's most outstanding feature is a formal system of legal pluralism arrived at on a racial-cultural basis. Separate population groups each had their own law. Europeans or persons assimilated to that status followed Dutch civil law, "foreign Orientals" observed Qing law (though it was eventually done away with in the early twentieth century), and native Indonesians were subject to the *adat* laws. There were about nineteen *adat* law groups (*adatrechts-kring*), whose laws were administered in Native Courts (*land-*

*raads*) based on extensive compilations of the rules of particular cultural groups written by officers of the civil service. This formal plurality led to the emergence of a complex body of rules to deal with conflicts between laws of the different law groups. This was called *intergentiel recht,* or interracial (private) law. Islam, however, had no separate existence within this system; its application, in any case, was dependent on whether it was recognized or received under any particular *adat* law group. Although the plural system was formally done away with on Indonesia's independence, Islamic law still has only a limited competence and the *adats* continue to be administered as part of the national law. [*See* Adat.]

*English Law (Burma, Malaysia).* From the very beginning of the nineteenth century English law was instituted in Burma (which until 1937 was part of British India), the Straits Settlements (Penang, Melaka, Singapore), the Federated and Unfederated Malay States (now peninsular Malaysia), and North Borneo (now Sabah) and Sarawak. The considerable variations in the content of English law applicable in each territory and through time are outweighed by the inheritance of common features. First, all territories had in common the principle that English law was the law of general application. As a result, the larger part of substantive English law (e.g., contract, tort, property, trusts, criminal law) applied, though considerable revision, reformulations, and amendments did take place. Second, the English element included the technical processes of precedent (i.e., the formation of a general principle over time by way of individual decisions on particular points) and statutory interpretation. Authority from the metropolitan jurisdiction was freely cited. Third, while it applied generally, English law was always subject to the exception that its application was limited if it damaged, undermined, or was in conflict with the "manners, customs, and religions" of the subject populations. This exception proved very important and gave rise to personal law (i.e., particular and special rules that applied to persons defined on the basis of race or religion), in which Southeast Asia is particularly rich. For example, Burma has Anglo-Islamic law, Anglo-Hindu law, Burmese Buddhist law, and Chinese Confucian law; peninsular Malaysia and Singapore have Chinese law, Hindu law, Islamic law, and Malay *adat* (*adat perpateh, adat Melayu*); and Sarawak and Sabah have Chinese law, Muslim law, and about nine named versions of *adat* laws.

*French Law (Indochina).* France's territories in Indochina consisted of Cochinchina, Annam, Tonkin, Cambodia, and Laos. From the point of view of French law, the countries were divided into the *pays de souveraineté française* (i.e., Cochinchina and Laos, in which the sovereignty of French law was absolute, though changes were instituted occasionally to accommodate local circumstances) and the *pays de protectorat* (i.e., Cambodia, Annam, and Tonkin). The *pays de protectorat* maintained their indigenous systems of laws but introduced numerous alterations in procedure (i.e., courts of justice on French lines were established) and content. Thus, indigenous principles that did not fit in with Western ideas of justice and civilization, such as slavery and torture, were abolished. Such varying jurisdictions, as well as the different laws available (i.e., French civil law in either its metropolitan or revised versions, Annamite, or Tonkin law), gave rise to internal legal conflicts. There were conflicts between metropolitan law and Indochinese law applicable to French citizens in Indochina, conflicts within various legislative regimes within the Union Indochinoise, and conflicts about the different degrees of competence exercised by the various tribunals, whether indigenous or French, in the execution of judgments. The complexity of conflicts was never fully resolved.

The special position of the Chinese should also be noted. They were initially classified as *asiatiques assimilés,* which made them subject to indigenous law of the territory in which they resided, but later acquired the status of "foreign nationals [of China]" by the Treaty of Nanjing (1930) and became entitled to the benefit of the laws of China. Practically speaking, the provisions of the treaty appear to have had little, if any, effect.

*American Law (the Philippines).* The American presence in the Philippines lasted not quite fifty years, but its impact on Philippine law was decisive. The US administration introduced the notion of secularism in private law and also brought in far-reaching and fundamental technical changes, including very important modifications in contracts, civil wrongs, constitutional law, and trusts. So far as administration is concerned, there has been a partial implementation of the precedent system. In other areas, however (especially in family law), the Spanish legacy remains fully intact. From the technical point of view, the most important aspect of law in the Philippines is the relationship between common law and civil law.

*Europeanization of Thai Law.* Thailand was the only country in Southeast Asia to escape direct imperial rule, but between 1856 and the 1920s it was subject to treaties of extraterritoriality imposed by the European powers. These were not done away with until the reform of the Siamese legal system, which began at the end of the nineteenth century with the gradual introduction of codes (civil, procedural, criminal) on European lines. These were drafted with European (mainly Franco-Belgian) advice. Some indigenous features were retained, however.

*Summary.* Southeast Asia's colonial legacy forms the basis of its modern laws. The most striking characteristic is a plurality of source of law (premodern and colonial) combined with European bureaucratic structures for legal administration. So far as content of law is concerned there has been a considerable hydridization, that is, "personal laws" that are based on Asian principles have been given European law forms.

[*See also* Audencia *and* Islamization of Southeast Asia.]

M. B. Hooker, *A Concise Legal History of South-East Asia* (1978).     M. B. HOOKER

**LAW, EDWARD** (Lord Ellenborough; 1790–1871), president of the Board of Control of the East India Company from 1828 to 1830. Ellenborough encouraged British exploration of the Indus River for purposes of trade and strategic defense. Appointed governor-general of India in 1841, he followed an aggressive military policy: he withdrew British forces from Afghanistan, annexing Sind and virtually subjugating Gwalior. Recalled in 1844 for not consulting his council or obtaining sanction for his actions from London, he was nevertheless rewarded with an earldom. [*See also* Sind *and* Governor-General of India.]     USHA SANYAL

**LAWRENCE, JOHN LAIRD MAIR** (Baron Lawrence; 1811–1879), administrator in the Indian Civil Service, younger brother of Sir Henry Lawrence. John Lawrence began his Indian career in 1830; a civil servant assigned to various Delhi Territory districts until 1845, he spent the next phase of his career largely in the Punjab in senior administrative and political capacities. Earning high recognition (including a baronetcy) for directing vital supplies and troops from the Punjab to Delhi in 1857 during the Indian Revolt, he was viceroy of India from 1863 to 1869.     USHA SANYAL

**LAWRENCE, SIR HENRY MONTGOMERY** (1806–1857), soldier-administrator in the Bengal Army. He joined the army in 1822; a gunner in the First Anglo-Burma War (1824–1826), he later distinguished himself as a revenue surveyor in the Northwest Provinces. Directly involved in the British forward movement in Afghanistan and the Punjab, Lawrence and his team of administrators ruled the Punjab through the so-called Lawrence system of benevolent personal "despotism." Appointed chief commissioner of Oudh in March 1857, he died defending Lucknow three months later during the Indian uprising of 1857. [*See also* Mutiny, Indian.]     USHA SANYAL

**LAXMI DEVI,** junior queen of Nepalese ruler Rajendra Shah (r. 1816–1847). Her intrigues against the crown prince brought about the three-way division of royal authority known as *tin sarkar* ("three governments"), which eventually paved the way for the Rana family's rise to power. Laxmi Devi's attempts to avenge the death of a favored member of her king's Council of State touched off the Kot Massacre in September 1846, and, in its bloody aftermath, she was obliged to elevate Jung Bahadur Rana and his descendants to the office of prime minister.

[*See also* Kot Massacre; Rana; *and* Jung Bahadur Rana.]

B. L. Joshi and L. Rose, *Democratic Innovations in Nepal* (1966).     RICHARD ENGLISH

**LE DAI HANH.** *See* Le Hoan.

**LEDI SAYADAW** (1846–1923), internationally recognized Burmese Buddhist monk. A member of the monkhood since early youth, his monastic name was Hyin Nyana and he was taught by the second San Caun Sayadaw, one of the leading monks during the reign of King Mindon. He became a forest monk at the Ledi Forest near Monywa, where he attracted many pupils and where he wrote many of his 102 books on Buddhism. A leading preacher of the Thudhamma (a Burmese Buddhist sect) during the nationalist period, the Ledi Sayadaw was given the first A.M.P. title by the colonial government in 1911 and a doctor of literature degree from Rangoon University in 1918. In many of his writings he attempted to reconcile extremist Buddhists and bring about a consensus of the center.     JOHN P. FERGUSON

**LE DUAN** (1908–1986), secretary-general of the Vietnamese Communist Party from 1956 to his death. Born the son of a carpenter in Quang Tri Province, he became a member of the Indochinese

Communist Party in 1930. Rising to the Central Committee in 1939, he was arrested the following year and spent the war years in prison. After World War II he directed the Party's resistance activities against the French in South Vietnam. Going north in 1956, he was named secretary-general of the Party and confirmed in that post in 1960. After the death of Ho Chi Minh in 1969, he was the most influential figure in the Party.

[*See also* Vietnam *and* Indochinese Communist Party.]

Douglas Pike, *History of Vietnamese Communism, 1925–1976* (1978). Tran Van Dinh, ed., *This Nation and Socialism Are One: Selected Writings of Le Duan* (1979).

WILLIAM J. DUIKER

**LE DUC THO,** leading member of the Vietnamese Communist Party and, for his efforts as the chief North Vietnamese negotiator at the Paris peace talks, corecipient (with Henry Kissinger) of the Nobel Peace Prize for 1973. Born about 1910 in Nam Ha Province near Hanoi, he joined the Party in the early 1930s and spent several years in prison. Elected to the Central Committee in 1945, he eventually became Le Duan's deputy in South Vietnam. After 1954 he returned to Hanoi and was elected to the Politburo. During the war he served on the Central Party Military Commission and the Secretariat. From 1975 to 1986 he was given increasing prominence and was thought to be in charge of Party affairs. On 17 December 1986, in the midst of the sixth national Vietnamese Communist Party Congress, Le Duc Tho was one of four prominent leaders who resigned from the Politburo; this was the largest reorganization in the history of the Vietnamese Communist Party.

[*See also* Le Duan.]

Henry Kissinger, *White House Years* (1979). Douglas Pike, *History of Vietnamese Communism, 1925–1976* (1978).    WILLIAM J. DUIKER

**LE DYNASTIES,** name given to three Viet ruling houses: the Former Le (980–1009), the Later Le (1428–1527), and the Restored Le (1533–1788).

The Former Le dynasty was founded by Le Hoan (941–1005), also known as Le Dai Hanh, an important general of the Dinh period. The assassination of Dinh Tien Hoang in November 979 left a six-year-old child as ruler. With a Chinese invasion imminent, Le Hoan was acclaimed emperor by his troops, an act condoned by the boy-king's mother.

The Former Le's most significant achievement was its preservation of Viet independence and unity. The Chinese invasion of 981 was repulsed, after which Le Dai Hanh carefully cultivated relations with the Song. Two campaigns against Champa (982, 1000) secured the southern frontier and forced the Cham to move their capital to the south.

Le Dai Hanh was the first Viet ruler to strike his own currency and to perform the ceremonial plowing of the first furrow in the spring. While this rite was Confucian, Confucian scholars (Vietnamese, *nho;* Chinese, *ru*) were less important at the Viet court than Buddhist monks, who provided the majority of functionaries.

The death of Le Dai Hanh ushered in a succession struggle, won by the sickly Le Long Dinh, whose brutal and inefficient "lying-down reign" *(ngoatrieu)* lasted four years. The Former Le then ended the way it had begun, supplanted by the family of a general, Ly Cong Uan.

The Later Le dynasty was established by Le Loi, a clan chieftain from Thanh Hoa, in opposition to the Chinese occupation of 1407–1427. After a ten-year struggle, Le Loi and his forces freed Dai Viet from Ming domination. The structure of government that emerged in the early years of Le rule reflected the experience of the war of liberation. Le Loi had surrounded himself with a staff of proved advisers *(dai than)*, many of whom were his kinsmen, and gave them great authority in public affairs. With Le Loi's death (1433), these men and their descendants ran the government on behalf of Le Thai Tong (r. 1433–1442) and Le Nhan Tong (1442–1460). The coup of Prince Nghi Dan, elder half-brother of Nhan Tong (28 October–1 November 1459), led to the countercoup of 21–24 June 1460, in which the *dai than* placed yet another young prince, Tu Thanh, on the throne. The imperial counselors, however, underestimated the political intelligence of Le Thanh Tong (r. 1460–1497) and found themselves merged into the bureaucratic government established by this dynamic ruler in 1471.

During the reign of Thanh Thong the power of Champa was broken and new areas were opened for settlement and cultivation, Viet law was codified, and the supremacy at court of Confucian doctrines over those of Buddhism and Daoism was firmly established. Thanh Thong's policies were continued by his successors Hien Tong (1497–1504) and Tuc Tong (1504–1505), but with the reigns of the "devil king" *(guy vuong)* Uy Muc (1505–1509) and the cousin who deposed him (Tuong Duc, r. 1510–

TABLE 1. *Rulers of the Le Dynasties*

| RULER | DATES OF RULE |
|---|---|
| FORMER LE (980–1009) | |
| Le Dai Hanh (Le Hoan) | 980–1005 |
| Le Trung Tong (Le Long Viet) | 1005* |
| Le Long Dinh (Ngoa Trieu) | 1005–1009 |
| LATER LE (1428–1527) | |
| Le Thai To (Le Loi) | 1428–1433 |
| Le Thai Tong | 1433–1442 |
| Le Nhan Tong | 1442–1459* |
| Nghi Dan | 1459–1460* |
| Le Thanh Tong | 1460–1497 |
| Le Hien Tong | 1497–1504 |
| Le Tuc Tong | 1504–1505 |
| Le Uy Muc | 1505–1510* |
| Le Tuong Duc | 1510–1516* |
| Le Chieu Tong | 1516–1522* |
| Le Cung Hoang | 1522–1527* |
| RESTORED LE (1533–1788) | |
| Le Trang Tong | 1533–1548 |
| Le Trung Tong | 1548–1556 |
| Le Anh Tong | 1556–1573* |
| Le The Tong | 1573–1599 |
| Le Kinh Tong | 1600–1619 |
| Le Than Tong | 1619–1643* |
| Le Chan Tong | 1643–1649 |
| Le Than Tong (second reign) | 1649–1663 |
| Le Huyen Tong | 1663–1671 |
| Le Gia Tong | 1672–1675 |
| Le Hy Tong | 1675–1705* |
| Le Du Tong | 1706–1729* |
| Le De Duy Phuong | 1729–1732* |
| Le Thuan Tong | 1732–1735 |
| Le Y Tong | 1735–1740* |
| Le Hien Tong | 1740–1786 |
| Le Chieu Thong (Le Man De) | 1786–1788* |

*Killed, deposed, or forcibly retired.

1516), disorder increased throughout the state. Tuong Duc died in the course of the rebellion of Tran Cao, and power once again passed into the hands of the military. Chieu Tong (1516–1522) and Cung Hoang (1522–1527) were deposed by General Mac Dang Dung, who proclaimed the Mac dynasty on 12 July 1527.

The Restored Le dynasty was the creation of the Nguyen clan, ancient supporters and relatives of the Le, and their marital relations the Trinh, who rose in opposition to the Mac. Nguyen Kim fled to Laos in 1527, where he was granted a fief at Sam Neua by King Phothisarat of Lan Sang. There, in 1533, Kim persuaded a great-great-grandson of Thanh Tong to assume the style of emperor.

The Le returned to Dai Viet in 1545 and by 1592 had replaced the Mac in the capital. But none of the sixteen Restored Le emperors ever exercised any real power. They presided over a ceremonial court *(trieu)*, while affairs of state were decided at the residence *(phu)* of the *chua* (lord), a hereditary office established and occupied by the Trinh.

With the death of Nguyen Kim in 1545, control of the Le restoration passed to the Trinh. In 1558 Trinh Kiem appointed Nguyen Hoang, son of Kim, as governor of Thuan Hoa and Quang Nam, the southernmost regions of Dai Viet. This geographical separation was the reflection of the political struggle between the two families, each claiming to be acting on behalf of the Le, which dominated the next two centuries until the Nguyen, Trinh, and Restored Le were swept away by the Tay Son Rebellion.

[*See also* Vietnam; Le Loi; *and* Le Thanh Thong.]

Emile Gaspardone, "Mac Dang Dung," in *Dictionary of Ming Biography*, edited by L. Carrington Goodrich (1976). Thomas Hodgkin, *Vietnam: The Revolutionary Path* (1981).                    JAMES M. COYLE

**LEE KUAN YEW** (b. 1923), prime minister of Singapore since 1959. Born in Singapore, he was educated at Raffles Institution and Raffles College and achieved a double first at Cambridge. After practicing law, he was a founder and secretary-general of the People's Action Party (PAP) in 1954. The party's leadership was divided between noncommunist intellectuals such as Lee and procommunists with mostly a trade union background. The moderates retained control in 1956 and 1957 only through the arrests of some "extremists."

Lee became prime minister when PAP won the 1959 elections, but a procommunist group, the Barisan Sosialis, broke away and threatened the party's majority. Lee reacted by supporting the proposal of the Malayan prime minister, Tunku Abdul Rahman, to form Malaysia, winning a 1962 referendum on this issue and defeating the Barisan in a 1963 election. Weakened by arrests, the Barisan withered away; since then only one opposition (noncommunist) member has been elected to the Singapore Parliament. Singapore became part of Malaysia in 1963 but had to leave it in 1965 because of political and economic differences.

Since 1959 Singapore's policies have been largely

set by Lee: a welfare state run on private enterprise lines, encouragement of foreign investment, control through grass-roots organizations, emphasis on discipline and opposition to drugs, creation of armed forces through conscription, emphasis on English in education, and measures to restrict population but promote parentage by elites. No successor is apparent, although several technocrats are being groomed.

[*See also* People's Action Party; Barisan Sosialis; *and* Singapore.]

T. J. S. George, *Lee Kuan Yew's Singapore* (1973). Alex Josey, *Lee Kuan Yew* (1968).          R. S. Milne

**LEGALISM** (Chinese, *fajia*), one of the major schools of Chinese thought that arose during the Warring States period (403–222 BCE); closely associated with the unification of China under the Qin dynasty in 221 BCE. Legalism represented a radical break from other schools of Chinese thought in that there was no discussion of the moral nature of man and the universe, antiquity was rejected as a model for emulation, and no place was accorded to religious goals and practices. Instead, the dominant concerns centered upon the power and authority of the state and the ruler. From the Legalist point of view the conditions of the Warring States period represented deep changes in the nature of the political state in China. The Zhou feudal order was moribund, and a radically different way of structuring the political state was necessary. The complex and interwoven system of interrelationships between the ranks of the feudal order, *li* (ritual or propriety), was no longer the cement of society. While the Confucians wanted to reinstate the system, the Legalists wanted to substitute law as the means to strengthen the state's ability to govern.

Several prominent names are associated with the school. Its actual beginnings, however, are subject to some debate. Guan Zhong (d. 645 BCE), prime minister of Qi and purported author of the *Guanzi*, is regarded by some as the founder of Legalism. This claim is based upon his discussions of the nature and importance of law. Others argue his authorship of the *Guanzi* is too doubtful and the work itself too eclectic to be considered the first major Legalist document. The major names associated with the school are Shang Yang (d. 338 BCE), Shen Buhai (d. 337 BCE), Shen Dao (350–275 BCE), and Han Feizi (280?–233 BCE). Li Si (280?–208 BCE), the prime minister to Qin Shihuangdi (First Emperor of Qin), was also a Legalist, but he was more a practical administrator than a formulator of Legalist doctrine. Several different strains of Legalist thought can be identified. Shang Yang, for example, is said to have been concerned primarily with law *(fa)*; Shen Buhai saw a critical role for methods or techniques *(shu)*; and Shen Dao focused on power *(shi)*. These various elements were brought together and synthesized by Han Feizi.

Law had already been discussed by Guan Zhong, but its application was much broadened by Shang Yang and Han Feizi. Law was seen as a singular authority and standard for society. No longer were there to be individually held standards or decisions subject to special moral relations. The law was uniform and knowledge of the law was to be universal. A severe system of rewards and punishments left little grounds for flexibility. To Shang Yang there was even less room for rewards. Order was simply maintained by the people's knowledge of the severity of the punishments. To Han Feizi both heavy rewards and punishments were necessary.

*Shu* were the methods and techniques that were necessary to maintain the power and authority of the state and the ruler. Shen Buhai saw *shu* primarily in terms of the methods or techniques needed by the ruler to govern. Han Feizi saw *shu* as filling certain areas not adequately covered by the law. The law was in a sense public: ruler, officials, and subjects alike stood in equal relation to its statutes. Methods, however, were the possession of the ruler to be exercised on behalf of his own authority in relation to his subjects, but also to his own officials. It took on a clandestine quality for Han Feizi and assured the authority of the ruler in a way the law could not.

Power primarily referred to the position and status of the ruler. What was important was not the person who was ruler, but the position itself. It was recognized that not all rulers would have the ability to govern well and that the system should be able to function independent of a particular ruler. To this end, there was an increase in the position of the ruler to an unprecedented apex of power. The activities of government moved around this apex while the ruler remained still and aloof, riding the circumstances yet unaffected by them. This has occasioned the reference to the Daoist idea of *wuwei* (nonaction) found in Legalist writings: the ruler in his august power rules without acting.

The actions, however, were severe and uncompromising, and law, methods, and power all contributed to this end. The principle of "actualities and names" *(xingming)* provided the basis for exacting rigid conformity to Legalist principles. Either the individual was or was not in conformity with the duties of his position. Rewards and punishments were the result of the judgment. This demand for rigid control and authority ultimately found its explanation in the Legalists' interpretation of human nature. They argued that human nature was evil and therefore such measures were thoroughly justified to maintain order and stability in society.

Throughout Chinese history a negative judgment has been passed upon the Legalist school as a result of its association with the ruthlessness and brutality of the meteoric rise and fall of the Qin dynasty. The Legalist school did not survive the downfall of the Qin, yet there are potentially at least certain long-lasting effects of the school. According to Derk Bodde and Clarence Morris, Legalism placed an imprint upon Chinese law in the penal emphasis in imperial law codes, the assumption of guilt until proven innocent, the legal use of torture, and the effect of group rather than individual responsibility. In general, the Legalists focused upon modernity rather than antiquity and on practical results rather than moralizing. They also inculcated an egalitarian spirit by insisting that all were subject to the same law. The effect was not to enhance the role of the individual but to cement the authority of the state.

[See also Qin Dynasty; Han Feizi; Li Si; and Shen Buhai.]

Derk Bodde, *China's First Unifier: A Study of the Ch'in Dynasty As Seen in the Life of Li Ssu 280?–208 B.C.* (1967). Derk Bodde and Clarence Morris, *Law in Imperial China* (1967). Wing-tsit Chan, *A Source Book in Chinese Philosophy* (1963). J. J. L. Duyvendak, *The Book of Lord Shang* (1928). K. C. Hsiao, *A History of Chinese Political Thought* (1979). Yang K'uan, *Shang Yang's Reforms and State Control in China*, edited and translated by Li Yuning (1977).

RODNEY L. TAYLOR

## LEGAZPI, MIGUEL LOPEZ DE (1511–1572),

Spanish conquistador and first governor-general (*adelantado*) of the Philippines. Legazpi (then chief clerk of the Cabildo of Mexico City) was chosen by Viceroy Luis de Velasco of Mexico to colonize the Philippines. On 27 April 1565 Legazpi's four-ship expedition arrived in Cebu, where the first permanent Spanish settlement in the Philippines was established. In 1569, after the Portuguese threatened his Cebu settlement, Legazpi transferred his headquarters to Panay. From there he sent Martin de Goyti and grandson Juan de Salcedo to Manila in May 1571, and on 24 June 1572 he declared Manila a royal Spanish city and capital of the colony.

The establishment of Spanish rule in the Philippines was accompanied by very little actual bloodshed. Effectively supported by soldiers and missionaries (Augustinians), Legazpi sought to gain the good will of the *indios,* who were at times hostile or frightened, by "good treatment and the display of kindness." The low level of social and political organization—the natives were loosely organized into small communities called *barangays*—no doubt facilitated the colonization immensely.

Legazpi died of apoplexy on 20 August 1572, but not before establishing the power of Spain in the Philippines. Legazpi's expedition also succeeded in charting a return route from the Philippines to Mexico. Spanish galleons would use this route for over two hundred years for the Manila-Acapulco trade.

[See also Philippines; Manila; Barangay; and Manila Galleon.]

Andrew Sharp, *The Adventurous Armada: The Story of Legazpi's Expedition* (1961).

BERNARDITA REYES CHURCHILL

## LEGGE, JAMES (1815–1897), the first translator

of the Chinese classics into English. Born in Scotland, Legge pursued theological studies and joined the London Missionary Society. Posted to Melaka as a missionary and principal of the Anglo-Chinese College, Legge moved the college to Hong Kong in 1844 and changed the curriculum to train Chinese clergy. In 1876 he accepted the newly established chair of Chinese language and literature at Oxford. Legge's translations of the Confucian classics—the Four Books in 1861 and the Five Classics between 1862 and 1885, with help from Wang Tao—provided the West with the first systematic presentation of the intellectual basis of traditional China.

Alexander Wylie, *Memorials of Protestant Missionaries* (1867).

ADRIAN A. BENNETT

## LE HOAN (941-1005), also known as Le Dai

Hanh, Vietnamese king and founder of the Former Le dynasty. When Dinh Bo Linh was assassinated in 979, Le Hoan, then commander in chief of the army, seized the throne. He led the resistance to the Chinese invasion of 980–981 and invaded Champa in 982.

Le Hoan eventually established peaceful contact with China and fostered the growth of Buddhist monastic influence at the Vietnamese court. Ruling from Hoa Lu, he took the title Dai Hanh ("great deeds") emperor. His many sons ruled different parts of the realm as personal fiefs and, after his death in 1005, discredited their family by fighting over the throne.

[*See also* Le Dynasties.]

KEITH W. TAYLOR

**LE LAI** (d. 1419), Vietnamese officer under Le Loi (1385–1443) in the Lam Son uprising (1418–1428) against the (Chinese) Ming dynasty. Le Lai took an oath of loyalty to Le Loi when the rebellion began and was among those trapped by the Chinese on Chi-linh Mountain in 1419. When Le Loi asked for a volunteer to wear his armor and act as a decoy, Le Lai dressed as his commanding general, went onto the battlefield, and was soon killed by the Ming troops, allowing Le Loi to make his escape.

[*See also* Lam Son Uprising *and* Le Loi.]

BRUCE M. LOCKHART

**LELANG.** *See* Commanderies in Korea, Chinese.

**LE LOI** (c. 1385–1433), also known as Le Thai To and Binh Dinh Vuong, founder of the Later Le dynasty of Dai Viet.

Descendant of a prominent landholding family of Lam Son in Thanh Hoa Province, Le Loi inherited the clan leadership upon the death of his older brother. He supported the movement of the Later Tran pretender Quy Khoang against the Chinese occupation, but with the collapse of Tran resistance (1414) he submitted to the Ming, becoming chief of the district in which his family's holdings were located.

On 7 February 1418, having spent the intervening years attracting followers, Le Loi proclaimed himself Binh Dinh Vuong ("pacifying king") and began a campaign to drive out the Chinese. During this protracted struggle Le Loi narrowly escaped capture, was frequently defeated, and several times agreed to truces with the occupying army, which was engaged in suppressing other anti-Chinese uprisings as well. His persistence, however, wore down the Chinese. The death of the expansionist Ming Yongle emperor (1424) and the rising tide of rebellion in Dai Viet turned the struggle against the Chinese. Having defeated the flower of the occupying army (Tot Dong, September 1426), invested the capital, and routed the main relief force from China (Chi Lang, 10 October 1427), Le Loi offered the local Chinese commander an opportunity to withdraw, which was accepted on 10 December 1427.

Le Loi then cast aside Tran Cao, the pretender behind whom he had legitimized his assumption of power, and set about rebuilding his devastated country. This process had begun even before the defeat of the Ming: civil-service examinations were begun in 1426 and refugees ordered back to their villages in 1427. Le Loi began to set up a strong administration at both the central and provincial levels, promulgated a law code, reestablished the Viet coinage, and organized a tax system.

Le Loi's administrative system relied heavily upon his personal relationships with the imperial counselors (*dai than*). His early death left these notables with great power and delayed the consolidation of Le rule for nearly forty years.

[*See also* Lam Son Uprising; Le Dynasties; *and* Dai Viet.]

Emile Gaspardone, "Le Loi," in *Dictionary of Ming Biography*, edited by L. Carrington Goodrich (1976), pp. 793–797.

JAMES M. COYLE

**LEPCHA,** the earliest known inhabitants of Sikkim. The language and tradition of these Mongoloid peoples link them with the Tibeto-Burman populations of eastern Nepal, but in the wake of their conquest by Tibetan Khams in the 1600s they were converted to Tantric Buddhism. A number of Buddhist texts translated into the Lepcha language have been preserved in what is thought to be an indigenous script. Largely displaced by Nepali settlers in the late 1900s, Lepchas are now concentrated on the Jongu reserve in central Sikkim, where their land rights are protected by the government.

[*See also* Sikkim.]

H. Siiger, *The Lepchas* (1967).

RICHARD ENGLISH

**LE THAI TO.** *See* Le Loi.

**LE THANH THONG** (1442–1497), fifth ruler of the Later Le dynasty of Dai Viet.

The fourth son of Le Thai Thong (r. 1433–1442), Prince Tu Thanh was placed on the throne during the ministerial countercoup of 21–24 June 1460. (An elder half-brother, Khac Xuong, had refused the potentially fatal honor.) By the end of 1463 the young emperor had skillfully outmaneuvered those who had enthroned him and was ruling in fact as well as in name.

A staunch believer in the relevance of Confucian doctrine to Viet kingship, Thanh Thong sought to consolidate his authority by creative application of the Chinese administrative model. The first step in this process was the revitalization and expansion of the examination system, which was begun in 1463, and the enhancement of the prestige of its graduates. This new class of officials found employment in the expanded and revised administration created by the emperor in 1471, which, not incidentally, increased the power of the throne. Support of Daoism and especially Buddhism, which had been so important to earlier Viet dynasties, was limited by imperial decree.

Other achievements of the reign were the promulgation of the famous Hong Duc law code (1483), which formed the basis of Viet law until 1815, and the final defeat of Champa (1471), which removed the major obstacle to the southward expansion of Dai Viet.

Le Thanh Thong's ability and energy, reinforced by that of his officials, allowed Dai Viet to enjoy a long period of relative peace and prosperity. By the second decade of the sixteenth century disorder had returned, but the memory of Thanh Thong's reign, which gradually took on the character of a golden age, sustained the prestige of the Le dynasty even into the nineteenth century.

[See also Vietnam; Le Dynasties; Hong Duc Code; and Champa.]

Thomas Hodgkin, *Vietnam: The Revolutionary Path* (1981). JAMES M. COYLE

**LETWETHONDARA**, one of the most famous poets of the Konbaung dynasty of Burma, was born in 1723 near Shwebo in Upper Burma. He served King Alaunghpaya and his sons in various positions and was awarded five distinguished titles, including Letwethondara. He composed his classic poem "At the Foot of Meza Hill" when exiled by King Hsinhpyushin to a penal settlement in northern Burma. Since then his name has become identified with this poem, a favorite theme of Burmese drama to this day. In addition to his other literary works, Letwethondara wrote treatises on law, military tactics, and military history. He died at Mingun, near Mandalay, toward the end of the century.

[See also Alaunghpaya.]

MYO MYINT

**LE VAN DUYET** (1763–1832), viceroy of Vietnam's Gia Dinh Province under emperors Gia Long (r. 1802–1820) and Minh Mang (r. 1820–1840). A loyal Nguyen follower who had helped defeat the Tay Son, Le Van Duyet was opposed to Minh Mang's enthronement but did not contest his legitimacy. He concentrated his energies on suppressing local revolts rather than on carrying out the emperor's anti-Christian laws, and in 1827 he pleaded the missionaries' cause at the court. After his death and the subsequent revolt of his adopted son, Le Van Khoi, his title and honors were revoked. Emperor Tu Duc reinstated them in 1868.

[See also Gia Long; Le Van Khoi Rebellion; and Minh Mang.]

Nguyen Phut Tan, *Modern History of Vietnam (1802–1954)* (1964). BRUCE M. LOCKHART

**LE VAN KHOI REBELLION.** Le Van Khoi (d. 1834) was the adopted son of Vietnamese marshal Le Van Duyet, who was posthumously dishonored by his enemies. Gia Dinh Province, where he had been viceroy, was incorporated into the central administrative system. These measures caused Le Van Khoi to revolt against Minh Mang (r. 1820–1840) in July 1833, and the rebels soon controlled the six Mekong Delta provinces. The court moved to suppress the rebellion, whose support came primarily from Christian communities loyal to Le Van Duyet's memory. Le Van Khoi called for Siamese help but died in late 1834, and the citadel of Gia Dinh was retaken by August 1835.

[See also Le Van Duyet and Minh Mang.]

Nguyen Phut Tan, *Modern History of Vietnam (1802–1954)* (1964). BRUCE M. LOCKHART

**LHASA** ("place of deity") has been the capital of Tibet since the reign of King Songzen Gampo (r. about 620–649), who first brought Buddhism to Tibet. He built the great temple, the Jo-khang, to house the treasured image of Shakyamuni Buddha that his bride, Wencheng, brought from her father, the Tang emperor Taizong. Lhasa city formed itself in concentric rings of streets around this great structure. Songzen also built a palace on Red Hill overlooking the city, on which site the monumental Potala was built in the seventeenth century. The Tibetan parliament, the Kashag, and other government offices were nearby the Jo-khang in the center of the city. There were many shops and traders' stalls, mostly catering to the streams of pilgrims who were constantly visiting the sacred sites. Prostration and circumambulation were major activities. There was a small circular walk around the central shrines, and a larger one that encompassed the Potala as well as the city. Most accounts of the city are left by members of the British mission, some of whom describe accurately the layout of the city while registering shock about the odd combination of cheerful people and unsanitary conditions. In the later part of the twentieth century the Chinese created a second, Chinese city of barracks built of stones taken from demolished monasteries. The old Tibetan town of thirty or forty thousand people has been left more or less as it was, although most of the more elegant houses and monastic buildings were destroyed during the Cultural Revolution.

[See also Tibet.]

F. Spencer Chapman, *Lhasa: The Holy City* (1938). H. Harrer, *Seven Years in Tibet* (1953). P. P. Karan, *The Changing Face of Tibet* (1976).

ROBERT A. F. THURMAN

**LIANG DYNASTY.** *See* Six Dynasties.

**LIANG QICHAO** (1873–1927), one of China's most skilled publicists of reform ideas in the crucial era between the 1890s and 1920s. Liang belonged to a transitional generation that had been educated in the traditional educational system but that refused to follow the conventional career opportunities. Instead, he opted for the medium of the recently developed Chinese press, where he played a leading role in expanding the political and intellectual horizons of China.

With China's defeat in 1895 by the Japanese, Liang began to edit reform periodicals and to publish essays dealing especially with educational reform. During this period he also established societies for studying China's problems and promoted the ideas of Kang Youwei. Although Liang did not play a prominent role in the reform movement of 1898, he had developed a reputation as a leading thinker behind the reform proposals and was forced to flee to Japan with the coup d'état of September 1898. While in Japan he continued to publish ideas that helped promote the political revolution of 1911 and 1912. Among these ideas were the promotion of new institutions, including a constitution and a parliament, as well as such concepts as individualism and a public-spirited citizenship.

Liang returned to China in October 1912 and formed a political party that supported constitutional reform and competed with Sun Yat-sen's revolutionary party. Liang supported liberal-democratic government and opposed Yuan Shikai's monarchial attempt in 1916 and an imperial restoration effort in 1917. But his principal impact remained as a publicist popularizing new ideas on literature, law, finance, politics, and current events, providing in part the basis for the intellectual revolution of the May Fourth era. By the 1920s Liang lost his enthusiasm for the West and returned to his Confucian roots, emphasizing Confucianism's altruism as a response to the wholesale westernization being promoted in China. The new generation had produced new leaders who overtook Liang, however, although all acknowledged their indebtedness to his essays and periodicals.

[See also Kang Youwei.]

Hao Chang, *Liang Ch'i-ch'ao and Intellectual Transition in China, 1890–1907* (1971). Philip C. Huang, *Liang Ch'i-ch'ao and Modern Chinese Liberalism* (1972).

ADRIAN A. BENNETT

**LIANG SHUMING** (b. 1893), preeminent neo-traditional thinker and rural reconstructionist in China. Criticizing his contemporaries for either slavishly imitating Western models or erroneously embracing Marxist theories, Liang contended that a rejuvenated Chinese culture would be the future culture of the world. China's hope, Liang argued in the 1920s, lay in its ability to revitalize its traditional spiritual and moral values based on the Confucian ideal of harmonizing the "inner" and the "outer" realms. Liang also believed that China's reconstruction should begin at the grass-roots level. He founded the Shandong Rural Reconstruction Institute in 1931 in an attempt to ameliorate rural conditions. The project ended when the Sino-Japanese War erupted in 1937.

Guy S. Alitto, *The Last Confucian: Liang Shu-ming and the Chinese Dilemma of Modernity* (1979). Howard L. Boorman, ed., *Biographical Dictionary of Republican China* (1967–1971). CHANG-TAI HUNG

**LIAO DYNASTY.** In 907 the Yelü clan of the Khitan established the Liao dynasty, which became the most powerful state in East Asia in the eleventh century. It was destroyed by the Jurchen in 1125.

Long after the fall of the state of the Khitan in the twelfth century, the name of the state continued to exist and attracted the attention of the people of

Western Asia and Europe. The term *Khitai*, with variations such as *Cathay*, was used by Central Asians to describe China after the Tang period (618–907), because following the collapse of the Tang only the Liao established sufficient power to maintain relations with some Central Asian states. In the twelfth century a group of the Khitan under the leadership of Yelü Dashi fled to the west and established the Western Liao (Karakhitai, 1124–1211).

With the conquest of China by the Mongols the term *Khitai* was used to designate China, which became a part of the Mongol empire. Although in the thirteenth century a few Europeans already realized that Cathay was indeed China, it was only in the seventeenth century that this fact became universally understood. Even in modern times the term Cathay is sometimes used by Westerners, and in Russia, Greece, and the Middle East, variations of the term are also still used.

The significance of the Liao dynasty is that it established a pattern of the "conquest dynasties" in East Asia, with Sino-Khitan institutions to rule the mixed population. It existed longer than the Northern Song dynasty (960–1127) and occupied a large area in northeast Asia, including present-day Inner Mongolia, southeastern Manchuria, and parts of Shanxi and Hebei provinces.

The founder of the Liao dynasty was Yelü Abauji (Taizu; r. 907–926), who became the emperor of the Khitan in 907 and established political and military institutions for the new state. He recognized Confucianism as the basic political ideology of the state and built Confucian temples, but he also emphasized Khitan language and culture. In foreign policy he interfered in the politics of Five Dynasties China and advanced southward in the northern Hebei region. Although he could not take Yuzhou (Beijing), he destroyed the Korean kingdom of Parhae (Chinese, Bohai) in 926.

*Early Political and Dynastic Difficulties.* Abauji was succeeded by his designated heir Deguang (Taizong; r. 927–947), his second son. His firstborn, Bei, was made the king of the Eastern Dan. The first problem during Deguang's reign was the lack of centralization in the government. Empress Dowager Xiao, Deguang's very able mother, made attempts to centralize power by forcing the officials to obey orders from the central government. Those who dared to oppose the policies of the court were executed.

A second problem was that of the imperial succession. After the sudden death of Deguang in 947, Bei's eldest son was supported by the generals and became the third ruler of the Liao. Lihu, Deguang's younger brother, also aspired to the throne, and raised an army against the new emperor Shizong (r. 947–950). Through the mediation of a few ministers, Lihu gave up and recognized Shizong. Palace feuds, however, did not cease; both Shizong and Muzong (r. 951–968) were murdered. It was only during the reign of Emperor Shengzong (983–1030) that the power of the generals and aristocrats was finally curbed.

A third problem was also related to the powerful aristocrats, who did not always agree with the early rulers on foreign policy. Both Abauji and Deguang were ambitious in their foreign policies. Deguang especially attempted to establish a dynasty in China and adopted the Chinese name Liao for his dynasty. His mother, the empress dowager, however, was against her son's plans. She believed that the foreigners and the Chinese simply could not be ruled under an alien dynasty. It was possible that those who plotted against Shizong were the aristocrats who shared her view and were in favor of a nonintervention policy toward China. Shizong ignored their intentions and planned to invade China, but he was murdered before the dispatch of the expeditionary army. His successor, Muzong, seems to have been overshadowed by the aristocrats; he did nothing to prevent the Later Zhou from invading the Liao state and recovering the Guannan area.

*Liao Administration.* Because of the strong influence of the aristocrats and the fact that Liao territory in North China was not larger than its non-Chinese territory, a dualistic political and economic system gradually developed in the early years of the dynasty. The empire was divided into two parts. The tribal division in the north had at its center the Khitan people, who still had large herds of livestock and led a nomadic life. The northern division of the government was accordingly a mobile organization with the emperor and his important officials moving from one place to another in different seasons. The government of the northern region had the *shumiyuan*, or Bureau of Military Affairs, as the highest political institution. Next was the Office of the Prime Ministers. These institutions administered the general affairs of the state as well as the various tribes of the Khitan in the north. In addition, there were a few offices in charge of the affairs of the imperial household and the families of the aristocrats.

The government of the southern region was responsible for the administration of the Chinese agriculturalists, who were the majority there. It was from this peasant population that the bulk of the taxes were collected. The government consisted of the southern Bureau of Military Affairs and the southern Office of the Prime Ministers. These offices were patterned after those of the Tang but were less important than their northern counterparts.

The Khitan relied upon their tribesmen to consolidate their state. The ruling stratum was constituted mainly of members of the Yelü and Xiao clans, clans that provided the government with most high-ranking officials and military officers. The rulers also utilized Chinese bureaucrats to help administer the state. In order to broaden the basis of the ruling class, Chinese officials were recruited through the civil service examination system. Although only a small number of officials were enlisted through the examinations, quite a few important officials held the *jinshi* degree.

Khitan rulers and aristocrats possessed large estates. The rulers granted counties and even prefectures to imperial relatives and ranking officials who had absolute jurisdiction in their estates. These privileged aristocrats did not pay taxes to the government. This nomadic form of feudalism was to recur in the early years of the Mongol empire. While the government relied upon the Chinese farmers for income, most Khitan commoners tended their herds for a living. Slaves worked for the government as well as for the aristocratic families and landlords. The Buddhist monasteries also owned a great number of slaves.

The Khitan acquired the Yan-Yun region, including modern Beijing, in 936 from the Later Jin ruler Shi Jintang, who became the subject and "son" of Yelü Deguang. After Shi's death, his successor refused to recognize Khitan suzerainty. Thereupon Yelü Deguang invaded the Later Jin, destroyed the Chinese state in 947, and declared the establishment of the Great Liao.

***Relations with Neighboring States.*** The Song and the Liao established diplomatic relations in 974. Emperor Taizong of the Song destroyed the Northern Han in 979 and then invaded the Liao. This attempt to recover the Yan-Yun region, however, was unsuccessful. A second attempt, made in 986, also failed. A friendly relationship was restored in 1005 with the conclusion of the Treaty of Shanyuan, which stipulated that the Song send annual presents to the Liao in the amount of 100,000 taels of silver and 200,000 bolts of silk. Taking advantage of the Song defeat by Xixia in 1040, the Liao sent envoys to the Song court in 1042, demanding the return of the Guannan territory that had been taken from the Liao by the Later Zhou. Another treaty was concluded in the same year, which increased Song annual payments from 300,000 units to 500,000 units.

Part of the annual payments were given to the Khitan for them to persuade the Tanguts of Xixia to restore peaceful relations with the Song. Xixia refusal of Liao mediation resulted in two Khitan military campaigns against the Tanguts, in 1044 and 1049, but the Khitan were repeatedly defeated. Eventually the Xixia again became a vassal state of the Liao, and the Liao often played the role of mediator between the Song and the Xixia. With the making of the treaty of 1042 during the reign of Emperor Xingzong (r. 1031–1055), the power of the Liao reached its apex. A Liao-centered world order was formed, with Koryŏ, Xixia, and a number of Central Asian states participating in it.

During the long reign of Emperor Daozong (r. 1055–1100), the dynasty began to decline. A tragic incident occurred in the imperial palace in 1075 owing to the intrigues of court officials. This incident brought about the deaths of the empress and the crown prince. Daozong was succeeded by his grandson (posthumous title Tienzuo), who became the last emperor of the Liao. The Liao was conquered by the Jurchen Jin in 1125.

[*See also* Khitan *and* Song Dynasty.]

René Grousset, *The Empire of the Steppes,* translated by Naomi Walford (1970). Morris Rossabi, ed., *China among Equals: The Middle Kingdom and Its Neighbors, 10th–14th Centuries* (1983). Karl A. Wittfogel, "Public Office in the Liao and the Chinese Examination System," *Harvard Journal of Asiatic Studies* 10 (1947): 13–40. Karl A. Wittfogel and Feng Chia-sheng, *History of Chinese Society: Liao (907–1125)* (1949).          JING-SHEN TAO

**LIAO MOSHA** (b. 1907), Chinese Communist Party official. Born in 1907 in Hunan, Liao joined the Chinese Communist Party when he was working as a journalist in Shanghai during the 1930s. After 1949 he served as the director of the Educational Department and later of the United Front Work Department of Beijing Municipality. Immediately following Mao's Great Leap Forward (1959–1961), Liao joined Wu Han and Deng Tuo to contribute essays to the column "Notes of the Three-Family Village." During the initial stage of the Cultural Revolution he was purged as revisionist. Liao was rehabilitated in 1979 and became a national member of the Political Consultative Conference.

[*See also* Chinese People's Political Consultative

Conference; Deng Tuo; Great Leap Forward; Great Proletarian Cultural Revolution; *and* Wu Han.]

HONG YUNG LEE

**LIAONING**, northeast Chinese province in southern Manchuria with a population of 35,721,693 (1982 census) in an area of 230,000 square kilometers. Its capital is Shenyang (Mukden). It was an important base for the nomadic conquerors of China from the tenth to seventeenth century; large-scale industrialization and Chinese immigration began only at the turn of the twentieth century, following the construction of railways by the Russians and Japanese. As part of the puppet state of Manchukuo from 1932 to 1945, Liaoning's industry was further developed, although much of it was removed by the Soviets at the end of World War II. Since 1949 Liaoning's industry has been rebuilt to the point where it is the most heavily industrialized and urbanized province of China. Its comparatively mild climate also allows for a fairly diversified agriculture. Liaoning also contains rich deposits of iron, coal, and nonferrous metal ores.    JOHN A. RAPP

**LIAQAT ALI KHAN** (1895–1951), chief lieutenant in the All-India Muslim League and the first prime minister of Pakistan. A member of a wealthy, landed family, he was educated at Aligarh and Oxford, and trained as a lawyer before entering politics. He joined the Muslim League in 1923 and sided with Muhammad Ali Jinnah when the party temporarily split four years later. As the general-secretary of the league from 1936 to independence, he played an influential role in shaping the party's program. Like Jinnah, his political views changed from seeking safeguards for Muslims within a united India to advocating partition and the creation of Pakistan. Liaqat served in the legislature of the United Provinces from 1926 to 1940 and in the Indian Legislative Assembly from 1940 to 1947, where he was the deputy leader of the league's parliamentary party. In 1946 he was appointed the finance minister in the interim government of India created under the Cabinet Mission Plan. With independence, he became the prime minister of Pakistan and, following Jinnah's death in 1948, the leader of the country. In that capacity he was instrumental in organizing Pakistan's new government and defining its policies. He continued to serve as prime minister until his assassination in 1951.

[*See also* All-India Muslim League; Jinnah, Mohammad Ali; Pakistan; *and* Partition of India.]

M. Rafique Afzal, *Speeches and Statements of Quaid-i-Millat Liaquat Ali Khan* (1967). S. M. Ikram, *Modern Muslim India and the Birth of Pakistan* (1965).

STEPHEN RITTENBERG

**LI BAI** (Li Bo; c. 701–762), premier Chinese poet (with Du Fu) writing in the *shi* style; best known for his bold, flamboyant poems celebrating swordsmanship, sheer mountains, love of wine, and the moon. In his youth Li wandered throughout the empire, from Sichuan and Gansu in the west through central China to Shandong and modern Nanjing in the east. Although he served briefly (from 742 to 744) as a poet at the court of Emperor Xuanzong, Li was exiled to the far southwest for his participation in an abortive rebellion (757); he never held the government office traditional for his class. The few known facts of Li's life have been embellished by themes from his poems to create a romantic personality in turn long inseparable from the poems. About one thousand poems (many of which may not be authentic) and several dozen prose pieces survive.

[*See also* Chinese Literature *and* Du Fu.]

Shigeyoshi Obata, *The Works of Li Po, the Chinese Poet* (1922). Arthur Waley, *The Poetry and Career of Li Po* (1950).    SHAN CHOU

**LICCHAVI DYNASTY.** The Licchavis were powerful members of the Vrijji confederacy at Vaishali during the time of the Buddha (c. sixth century BCE). Politically, they seem to have remained a prestigious group until the early Gupta rule (fourth century CE) in India. Nepal's Licchavis are believed to be an offshoot of those in Vaishali. The first documented Licchavi king to rule Nepal was Manadeva (c. 464–505 CE) and its last known ruler was Jayadeva II (c. 733 CE). Although the Licchavis in India observed a republican oligarchical system, their government in Nepal was monarchical. The Licchavis are highly regarded for laying the foundations of Nepal's classical traditions in art, architecture, culture, and economy.

[*See also* Nepal: History of Nepal.]

Hitnarayan Jha, *The Licchavis* (1970). D. R. Regmi, *Ancient Nepal* (3d ed., 1969).    PRAYAG RAJ SHARMA

LI DAZHAO (1888–1927), Chinese Marxist thinker who played a seminal role in introducing Marxist ideology into China and in organizing the northern branch of the Chinese Communist Party.

Li studied in Japan from 1913 to 1916, then returned to China to work with the relatively conservative Progressive Party (Jinbudang). In 1918 he gained national prominence when he was appointed chief librarian of Beijing University and joined the editorial board of the radical journal *New Youth*. Li employed the young Mao Zedong as a clerk in the library; when Li organized the first Marxist study group in China in late 1918 as a result of the influence of the Bolshevik Revolution, Mao was invited to join the discussions. Still, when members of the Comintern approached Li about organizing a communist party in China, he referred them to his friend Chen Duxiu. After Chen Duxiu began the party in Shanghai in 1920, Li undertook to organize the northern branch of the party and was important in Communist Party affairs until 1927. When the Chinese nationalists turned on their former communist allies in April 1927, Li took refuge in the Soviet Embassy compound. He was arrested there by the troops of the warlord Zhang Zuolin and hanged on 28 April 1927. Li's Marxist thinking, which had a great influence on Mao Zedong, had a populist emphasis on the central role of China's impoverished peasantry and the struggle against imperialism.

[*See also* Communism: Chinese Communist Party; Marxism and Socialism: Marxism in China; China, Republic Period; May Fourth Movement; Chen Duxiu; *and* Mao Zedong.]

Maurice Meisner, *Li Ta-chao and the Origins of Chinese Marxism* (1967).                    LEE FEIGON

LIEZI, a collection of anecdotes and essays, ranks with the *Laozi* and the *Zhuangzi* as a masterpiece of early Chinese Daoist literature. The *Liezi* was traditionally attributed to Lie Yukou (c. 450–375 BCE), but is now generally regarded as a work of the third or fourth century CE because of the integration of older material with tales reflecting Buddhist influence. With the exception of the chapter devoted to the hedonist Yang Zhu, the *Liezi* reflects traditional Daoist attitudes toward life and death, reality and illusion, and nonaction and spontaneity.

[*See also* Daoism.]

A. C. Graham, *The Book of Lieh Tzu* (1960). Burton Watson, *Early Chinese Literature* (1962).

M. LAVONNE MARUBBIO

LIGA FILIPINA. The Liga Filipina, organized by the Filipino leader Jose Rizal in Manila on 7 July 1892, crystallized Rizal's basic nationalist ideology. Its purpose was to promote the moral and intellectual education of Filipinos and so achieve the progress that would join them into a nation, even while still under Spanish rule. But some of Rizal's aims—his advocation of mutual aid and progressive reforms, for example—though not subversive individually, clearly challenged Spanish sovereignty when considered in conjunction. Moreover, not all the members of the Liga fully understood Rizal's intent.

This ambiguity showed itself with Rizal's arrest. Andres Bonifacio then used the reorganized Liga's popular councils to create a secret revolutionary organization, the Katipunan. The gradualists within the Liga, alarmed at Bonifacio, soon dissolved the organization into the Cuerpo de Compromisarios, which was pledged to reach a compromise. But when the Katipunan went to arms, membership in the defunct Liga was regarded by the Spaniards as de facto proof of subversive intent, and the *compromisarios* were executed for the revolution they had not made.

[*See also* Rizal, Jose Mercado; Bonifacio, Andres; Katipunan; *and* Propaganda Movement.]

Cesar A. Majul, *A Critique of Rizal's Concept of a Filipino Nation* (1959). John N. Schumacher, *The Propaganda Movement* (1973).

JOHN N. SCHUMACHER, S.J.

LIGHT, FRANCIS (1740–1794), founder of the British settlement on Penang Island, Malaysia. Light entered the Royal Navy in 1759 as a midshipman, was discharged in 1763, and sailed to India in 1765. As captain of a ship out of Madras, he traded with Aceh, Salang, and Kedah. His influence with the Malay ruler of Kedah led to his appointment by the British East India Company in 1786 as superintendent of the new settlement on Penang (Prince of Wales Island).

[*See also* Penang.]

H. P. Clodd, *Malaya's First British Pioneer: The Life of Francis Light* (1948).           JOHN S. BASTIN

LI HONGZHANG (1823–1901), China's best known, most influential statesman of the late nineteenth century. Beginning as a protégé of Zeng Guofan, Li rose to prominence in the 1860s as organizer and commander of the Anhui (Huai) Army, a key force in quelling the Taiping and Nian rebellions. From 1870 he built a many-sided regional power base centered on Tianjin, where he served for a quarter century as governor-general of Zhili Province and commissioner for the northern ports. During these years his leading role in China's Self-Strengthening modernization program was particularly important. The China Merchants Steam Navigation Company, inaugurated by Li in 1872, led to pioneering coal-mine, railway, telegraphic, and manufacturing ventures, as well as educational projects including sending Chinese students abroad.

Li's expertise in "foreign matters," combined with his contacts and loyalty to the throne, increasingly made him China's voice in the era's numerous diplomatic crises. Instrumental in resolving the Margary Incident with Britain in 1876, he was his country's most important negotiator again in terminating the Sino-French War of 1884 to 1885. From the mid-1880s Li sought particularly to secure China's northern frontier, which meant competing with Japan for paramount influence in Korea. This effort came to a sad conclusion in the Sino-Japanese War of 1894 to 1895. The destruction of China's Beiyang Fleet, built by Li as a prize national defense project at Tianjin, not only ended Chinese aspirations to naval prowess but cast doubt on the whole Self-Strengthening program in which Li had played such a key role.

Kenneth E. Folsom, *Friends, Guests, and Colleagues: The "Mu-fu" System in the Late Ch'ing Period* (1968). Immanuel C. Y. Hsu, "Late Ch'ing Foreign Relations, 1866–1905," in *The Cambridge History of China*, vol. 11, *Late Ch'ing, 1800–1911, Part 2*, edited by John K. Fairbank and Kwang-Ching Liu (1980), pp. 70–141. Kwang-Ching Liu, "The Confucian as Patriot and Pragmatist: Li Hung-chang's Formative Years, 1823–1866," *Harvard Journal of Asiatic Studies* 30 (1970): 14–22. Stanley Spector, *Li Hung-chang and the Huai Army: A Study in Nineteenth-Century Chinese Regionalism* (1964).                    IRWIN T. HYATT, JR.

**LIJIA SYSTEM.** A "community" system of levying and collecting land taxes and labor services in China, the *lijia* was an integral part of the "sub-bureaucratic" rural organization of the Ming dynasty (1368–1644).

Ming Taizu (r. 1368–1398), the founding emperor of the dynasty, developed the *lijia* system as part of his grand plan for an elaborate organizational structure in rural China. The official government apparatus did not extend below the county (*xian*) level of administration. Taizu sought to bridge the distance between bureaucracy and rural society. He therefore turned to individuals in the local villages to act as proxy agents for the central government. This system of rural administration grew out of the "Yellow Registers" population registration system of 1381, which levied land taxes and labor services on the basis of surveys assessing the property and number of persons in each household.

The Ming *lijia* system imposed an added supervisory responsibility on the village unit. Communities (*li*) were organized into units of 110 households (*hu*). Each *li* was then subdivided into ten sections (*jia*) of ten households. The heads of the ten wealthiest families were then designated as "community chiefs" and each served a one-year term of office, assuming responsibility both for the collection of local taxes and all material and service levies. The chief also served as the intermediary between the community and the local government. In a similar manner, one section was required to serve as a "section chief."

The *lijia* system was designed to provide a balance of power in rural society. The success of such an organization depended on "unofficial" personnel in the villages and ultimately afforded them a considerable degree of self-governance. The *lijia* system continued to be utilized throughout the Ming dynasty, although the organization was considerably weakened after the death of Taizu. The Qing dynasty (1644–1911) modified the *lijia* system in such a way as to superimpose the mutual surveillance, responsibility, and militia functions of the *baojia* ("watch group") system on the rural administrative structure established by the *lijia*.

[*See also* Baojia System.]

Edward L. Dreyer, *Early Ming China: A Political History, 1355–1435* (1982). Ray Huang, *Taxation and Government Finance in Sixteenth-Century Ming China* (1974). Charles O. Hucker, *The Ming Dynasty: Its Origins and Evolving Institutions* (1978). John R. Watt, *The District Magistrate in Late Imperial China* (1972).                    ANITA M. ANDREW

**LI LISAN** (1897–1967), important early leader of the Chinese Communist Party. Li joined the Party in 1921 in Paris, where he had gone to study. After his return to China, he became an important labor organizer. In 1928 he was made the effective head of the Party. The policy he pursued, which came to be known pejoratively as the "Li Lisan line," consisted principally of armed uprisings against urban areas. The policy failed to mobilize the Chinese masses and led to repeated losses for the Party. In 1931, Li was called to Moscow for corrective study, remaining there until 1945. After the establishment of the People's Republic of China in 1949 he held a series of minor offices.   LEE FEIGON

LIM BOON KENG (1869–1957), major political and cultural leader of the Chinese community in Singapore from the 1890s to 1940s. Born in Singapore, Lim graduated from Raffles Institution and Edinburgh University (in medicine). Along with Song Ong Siang (1871–1941), Lim led a westernized reform group within the Baba Chinese elite that worked to reconcile the ambiguities of multiple Baba loyalties: to Britain, China, and Singapore. Lim helped establish the influential Straits Chinese British Association, which attempted to modernize Straits Chinese culture. He promoted the use of modern Mandarin and the establishment of girls' schools, published English and Malay newspapers, and served on various government councils. Later Lim became president of Amoy University. Returning to Singapore, he served as spokesman for the Singapore Chinese during the Japanese occupation of the country.

[See also Singapore.]

Ong Siang Song, *One Hundred Years' History of the Chinese in Singapore* (1923). C. M. Turnbull, *A History of Singapore, 1819–1975* (1977).   CRAIG A. LOCKARD

LIMBU, a Tibeto-Burman-speaking people inhabiting the easternmost hills of Nepal. Like the Rai, with whom they claim ancestral kinship, the Limbu trace descent from the legendary Kiranti, who are thought to have ruled Nepal before the common era. Despite the Buddhist influence of neighboring Sikkim and the Hinduism of the Nepalese majority among whom they are settled, the Limbu are predominantly animists and employ spirit mediums to propitiate a variety of spirits and deities. They have, however, been integrated into the country's caste hierarchy. The Limbu combine subsistence agriculture with service in the Gurkha regiments of British and Indian armies.

L. Caplan, *Land and Social Change in East Nepal* (1970).   RICHARD ENGLISH

LIN BIAO (1907–1971), one of the most important military leaders of the Chinese Communist Party (CCP); active from the period of the first urban uprisings in the late 1920s until his death after an alleged coup attempt in 1971.

Lin Biao, whose original name was Lin Youyong, was born on 5 December 1907 in Huanggang County, Hubei Province. His father was a small landlord and petty capitalist whose bankruptcy eventually forced the younger Lin to leave home at the age of ten. At fourteen Lin moved to Wuchang, the provincial capital, where he attended middle school and joined patriotic student societies. In 1925 he went to Shanghai as a delegate to the anti-imperialist National Student Association. Soon thereafter he joined the Communist Youth League. In October he was admitted to the Whampoa Military Academy in Canton. In 1926, along with many of the graduating cadets, Lin joined the Communist Party. The next year he joined a forward unit of the Northern Expedition. He was also involved as a junior officer under Zhu De in the failed Nanchang Uprising of 1 August 1927, a date now celebrated in China as the anniversary of the founding of the People's Liberation Army (PLA). After small remnants led by Zhu escaped to southern Hunan, Lin was made commander of one of five columns. His column captured the town of Dayu in 1927 and reached Mao's headquarters at Jinggang Shan in 1928. After the merger of Zhu De's forces with those of Mao Zedong, Lin rose quickly from battalion to regimental commander, gaining his first real guerrilla experience in Jiangxi in 1929 and winning victories in southwest Fujian Province later that year.

From January 1930, after receiving a letter from Mao that criticized the "pessimism" of certain military commanders, probably including Lin himself, Lin seems to have become one of the most ardent exponents of Mao's line of rural guerrilla warfare. Beginning in the early 1930s his troops seemed to have been used more in the guerrilla-style warfare favored by Mao, supporting the frontal attacks and defense of strong points of other CCP forces guided by Soviet advisors. After the reorganization of the Zhu-Mao troops, Zhu De assumed command of the First Army Corps and placed Lin in command of the Fourth Army. These forces were stationed in the newly proclaimed Jiangxi Soviet. From 1930 until 1933 Lin helped to defeat the first four of Chiang Kai-shek's "Annihilation Campaigns," also called Communist-Extermination Campaigns. In January 1932 he commanded the First Army Corps in a thrust into Fujian Province. In 1934, with the start of the Fifth Annihilation Campaign, Lin led a diversionary attack that allowed the main body of the Red Army to escape westward on the start of the famous Long March, throughout which Lin's troops were heavily involved. In 1935 Lin and part of his army reached Shaanxi Province along with Mao and other CCP leaders. [*See also* Communist-Extermination Campaigns.]

In January 1935 Lin's army captured Zunyi in northeast Guizhou and organized the Zunyi Conference, at which Mao became the undisputed leader of the Chinese Communist movement. A year later the Politburo authorized Lin and Peng Dehuai to lead troops in an attack across the Yellow River against the forces of the governor of Shanxi. In July of the same year Lin became the president and political commissar of the Red Army academy.

With the outbreak of war with Japan in July 1937, Lin took over command of the 115th Division of the newly organized Eighth Route Army. In September 1937, after another forced crossing of the Yellow River, Lin led his division to a major victory over the Japanese at Pingxing Pass in northeast Shanxi. After this battle Lin's forces engaged the Japanese at three points in western Shanxi, where Lin was seriously wounded and forced to return to Yan'an. In 1938 he traveled to Moscow, reportedly for medical treatment but also as the CCP representative. While in Russia he wrote an article on the war in China that reflected the line of the Hitler-Stalin alliance.

In 1942, after returning to Yan'an, Lin became vice-president of the Central Party School and Mao's ally in the Party rectification campaign. From October 1942 to mid-1943 he served in the CCP-KMT (Kuomintang, or Nationalist Party) liaison office with Zhou Enlai in Chongqing. Returning to Yan'an, he resumed the presidency of the army academy and directed the training of garrison troops in the Shaanxi-Gansu-Ningxia (Shaanganning) Border Region. [*See also* Shaanganning.]

Lin was elected to the Seventh CCP Central Committee in 1945 and commanded the Communist occupation of key Manchurian cities a year later. After initial losses against KMT armies, Lin's forces retreated to the countryside, where they promoted land reform and engaged in mobile warfare. Lin led the counteroffensives that captured all of Manchuria by the end of 1948 and much of North China by early 1949, including Beijing and Tianjin. In mid-1949 Lin participated in the abortive peace talks between the CCP and KMT, following which he commanded one of the armies that conquered the rest of the mainland by the end of the year. In the final battle of the civil war he led the conquest of Hainan Island in January 1950.

After the founding of the People's Republic of China (PRC) in 1949, Lin held the posts of chief of the central-south administrative bureau and commander of the central-south military region. Although he also held important national posts in the early 1950s, he was largely absent from public life, reportedly because of tuberculosis. By 1955 he had been elevated to the Politburo and named one of the ten marshals of the PLA. He made his first public appearance in five years at the Eighth Party Congress in 1956, where he was listed seventh among the seventeen members elected to the Politburo.

Although largely out of public view in the next two years, by the spring of 1958 Lin began to appear more regularly. In May of that year he was elected vice-chairman of the Central Committee and member of the Standing Committee of the Politburo. In April 1959 he was named a vice-premier and vice-chairman of the National Defense Council. After the purge of Peng Dehuai in 1959, Lin Biao became minister of defense and de facto head of the CCP Military Affairs Committee. From 1959 until his fall Lin was involved in strengthening political control and ideological indoctrination of the PLA. By the early and mid-1960s Lin had begun the cult of Mao Zedong in the army through mobilization campaigns that were later extended to the civilian population in the Great Proletarian Cultural Revolution. In September 1965 Lin ended an official silence of several months to lead the defense of Mao and his policies publicly, beginning with the major speech, "Long Live the Victory of the People's War," in which he linked the Maoist strategy of surrounding the cities from the countryside with the struggles of third world countries against the "cities" of American and Western imperialism. In 1966, after the fall of Liu Shaoqi, Lin became vice-chairman of the Party and heir-apparent to Mao, a position actually accorded to him by name in the 1969 Party constitution.

After the chaos and destruction of the Cultural Revolution had reached an extreme in 1967, Mao called on Lin Biao and the army to restore order. As a result, the army gained considerable political influence, although there was much resentment within the military over Lin's politicization of the PLA and over high-level tolerance of attacks on the army by radicals early in the Cultural Revolution. Thus, when Mao began to fear Lin Biao's increasing influence around 1969 and started to move against Lin's allies, the army failed to line up solidly behind Lin.

At the 1970 Lushan Plenum, where Mao criticized

Lin's "theory of genius" as an excessive and un-Marxist adulation of individual leaders, the split between the two became obvious to Party insiders. Mao later claimed that at this plenum, against his express wishes, Lin and his allies tried to reestablish the post of state chairman, a post abolished after the fall of Liu Shaoqi. Secret coup documents leaked after Lin's fall reveal that after the plenum, Lin supposedly feared Mao's intentions and began consolidating his power in the military. When Mao undercut Lin's plans by transferring or removing key Lin supporters in the army and by moving the Lin-controlled 38th Army out of the Beijing Military Region, Lin stepped up his desperate maneuvers. According to the documents, he allowed his son, Lin Liguo, a high air force official, to launch an attempt to assassinate Mao, the "571 Project." A recent study by Yao Ming-le, however, cites evidence, supposedly from an unnamed high CCP official, that Lin Liguo's plans were only one amateurish part of a wider conspiracy, and that in fact Lin Biao was assassinated by the forces of Mao's bodyguard Wang Dongxing at the instigation of Mao and Zhou Enlai before he could put his plans into action. Nevertheless, the leaked documents and the later official account claim that it was the failure of the 571 Project and the revelation of Lin Liguo's plans to Party leaders (purportedly by Lin Biao's daughter to Zhou Enlai), that led Lin Biao and his wife Ye Qun, along with Lin Liguo and key associates, to attempt to flee to the Soviet Union. The conspirators' plane was allegedly shot down as it crossed into Mongolia on the night of 12 September 1971. All passengers were reported killed, and their partially burned bodies were buried at the spot.

Shortly after the fall of Lin and the arrest or transfer of his remaining followers, indirect criticism of Lin as an ultraleftist began to appear in the press. In the "Criticize Lin Biao and Confucius" campaign of 1973 to 1975, however, Lin was denounced by name as a rightist. After the death of Mao and the arrest and denunciation of the Gang of Four led by Mao's wife Jiang Qing, Lin was again denounced as an ultraleftist and as a leader of the "Lin Biao-Jiang Qing counterrevolutionary cliques." Beginning in 1973 a dissident group denounced Lin as the founder of the "Lin Biao system" of "feudal fascism"—a system of "emperor worship" that encouraged blind obedience to individual leaders. Since 1978 this has continued to be the official line, in spite of indications that accomplishments of disgraced leaders including Lin may no longer be totally expunged from official Party history.

[See also Communism: Chinese Communist Party; Chinese People's Liberation Army; China, People's Republic of; Great Proletarian Cultural Revolution; and Mao Zedong.]

Martin Ebon, *Lin Biao: The Life and Writings of China's New Ruler* (1970). John Gittings, *The Role of the Chinese Army* (1967). Ellis Joffe, *Party and Army: Professionalism and Political Control in the Chinese Officer Corps, 1949–1964* (1965). Michael Y. M. Kau, *The Lin Biao Affair: Power Politics and Military Coup* (1975). Donald Klein and Anne Clark, *Biographical Dictionary of Chinese Communism 1921–1965* (1971). Thomas W. Robinson, *A Politico-Military Biography of Lin Biao, Part 1, 1907–1949* (1971). William Whitson, *The Chinese High Command: A History of Communist Military Politics, 1927–1971* (1973). Yao Ming-le, *The Conspiracy and Death of Lin Biao* (1983).    JOHN A. RAPP

**LINGAYATS**, also known as Virashaivas, Shaivite sect founded during the twelfth century in the Kannada-speaking area of the Deccan in South India. The name (literally, "linga-bearer") is derived from the practice of wearing a small *lingam*, a phallic symbol representative of the Hindu god Shiva, on cords around the neck. This linga, which is never to be removed from the devotee's body, is central to all rituals and must be worshiped daily.

The traditional founder of the cult is Basava, but this claim is not beyond dispute as some scholars assert that he actually nurtured an already-existing belief. It is certain, however, that as minister to the Calukya king Bijjala Kalacuri (r. 1156–1167 CE), Basava fostered the growth of the movement, even to the point of being criticized by his enemies for the excessive court patronage of the Lingayats. His biography and teachings are found in one of the sacred Lingayat texts, the *Basava Purana*.

Although their philosophical doctrines of "qualified monism" and *bhakti* ("devotion") could easily be identified as elements of mainstream Hinduism, the Lingayats are distinctly heterodox in their social observances. Basava denied the authority of the Vedas and rejected the Brahmanical claim of inherent superiority, as well as all caste distinctions. The Lingayat prohibition of child marriages, the allowance of widow remarriage (positions that anticipated nineteenth-century Hindu reform movements), and the burial of the dead (as opposed to the traditional practice of cremation) might indicate an Islamic influence on the early doctrines of the sect. However, many of these practices, especially the denial of caste distinctions and burial of the dead, were either abandoned or modified in later times, with the important exception that the sect remains decidedly anti-Brahmanical.

[*See also* Shaivism *and* Bhakti.]

Surendranath Dasgupta, *A History of Indian Philosophy*, Vol. 5 (1922; reprint, 1975). J. A. Dubois, *Hindu Manners, Customs and Ceremonies*, translated by H. K. Beauchamp (1906). S. C. Nandimath, *A Handbook of Vīraśaivism* (1942). André Padoux, "Śaivism: Vīraśaivas," in *Encyclopedia of Religion*, edited by Mircea Eliade (1987), vol. 13, pp. 12–13. L. Rice, *Mysore and Coorg from the Inscriptions* (1909).    STUART W. SMITHERS

**LINGGA,** largest island of the southern part of the Riau-Lingga Archipelago, is located just south of the equator and just west of 105° east longitude. With the neighboring island of Singkep, Lingga forms the southern end of the Strait of Melaka (Malacca). Today a part of the Republic of Indonesia, the island was formerly part of the Johor empire and was generally ruled from either Riau or Johor. In the late eighteenth century Lingga became the seat of the Johor/Riau sultan (particularly Sultan Abdul Rahman) while the Bugis Yang Di-Pertuan Muda generally controlled the traditional capital of Riau on Bentan. Lingga achieved minor prominence in the nineteenth century as a center of gambier and pepper cultivation and because of some tin mining.

[*See also* Riau; Melaka; Indonesia, Republic of; Johor; *and* Abdul Rahman.]

Raja Ali Haji, *Tuḥfat al-Nafis (The Precious Gift)*, edited and translated by Virginia Matheson and Barbara Watson Andaya (1981).    CARL A. TROCKI

**LINSCHOTEN, JAN HUYGHEN VAN** (1563–1611), Dutch traveler and writer. A native of Haarlem, he gained firsthand experience in the centers of Portuguese trade in Lisbon and Goa as the secretary (from 1583 to 1589) to Goa's archbishop. After nine years in the Portuguese service he returned in 1592 to the Netherlands. There he published two books, *Reysgeschrift van de Navigatien der Portugaloysers in Orienten* (1595) and *Itinerario naer Oost ofte Portugaels Indien* (1596), providing critical maps and detailed descriptions of Portuguese discoveries, Asian trade, and navigation of the Indian Ocean. These works aroused considerable public interest and were, after the Bible, perhaps the most widely read books in Western society during the early seventeenth century. Using his sailing directions, the first Dutch fleet set forth in 1595. An English translation of the *Itinerario (Itinerary to the East, or Portuguese Indies)* appeared in 1598 and was a direct impulse for the formation of the British East India Company in 1600. Linschoten's books not only contained the practical information that was needed for the initial Dutch and English voyages; they also demonstrated that Portuguese power in the East was vulnerable and that Portuguese relations with Asian populations were so bad that there was ample opportunity to enter into competition. He pointed to Java as an excellent center for establishing trade, since the Portuguese rarely went there.

[*See also* Dutch East India Company; East India Company; *and* Portuguese: Portuguese in India.]

Jan Huyghen van Linschoten, *The Voyage of J. H. Linschoten to the East Indies*, 2 vols., edited by A. C. Burrell and P. A. Tiele (1885).    KENNETH R. HALL

**LIN YUTANG** (1895–1976), Chinese author, scholar, and journalist. Lin received his early education at Shanghai's St. John's University. After earning a doctorate from Leipzig University in Germany, he returned to China in 1923 to teach English at Beijing University. Lin did not achieve fame until he launched a successful magazine, *Lunyu (Analects)*, in 1932. The magazine, specializing in satire and humor contrary to traditional didacticism, championed the idea that literature should serve as a channel of self-expression. He continued to advocate the use of simple prose and a humorous style. Lin spent most of his life in America and was known to Western readers through a score of popular books, notably *My Country and My People* (1935).

Howard L. Boorman, ed., *Biographical Dictionary of Republican China* (1967–1971). Adet Lin and Anor Lin, *Our Family* (1939).    CHANG-TAI HUNG

**LIN ZEXU** (1785–1850), a noted official and one of China's most famous modern patriots. From 1820 he served in a variety of judicial, educational, and financial positions, which brought him provincial governorships and a reputation for honesty and fairness. Known also for strong opposition to opium, Lin was appointed by the Daoguang emperor to suppress the drug traffic at its Guangzhou (Canton) center. As an imperial commissioner in 1839 he moved vigorously and effectively against the trade's Chinese participants. His firm actions against their British suppliers, particularly his destruction of some twenty thousand chests of confiscated opium, were no doubt equally salutary. The result at the time of this interference with British trade, however, was the Opium War, a disaster for China and Lin personally. In September 1840 he was dismissed and sentenced to exile in Xinjiang (Chinese Turkestan). By the time of his death, however, Lin had regained enough imperial favor to be appointed to four more brief governorships.

[See also Opium and China Trade.]

Chang Hsin-pao, *Commissioner Lin and the Opium War* (1964). Arthur Waley, *The Opium War through Chinese Eyes* (1958).          IRWIN T. HYATT, JR.

LI PO. *See* Li Bai.

LI SI (c. 280–208 BCE), Chinese official in the service of the state of Qin who rose to the rank of prime minister of the Qin dynasty in 214 BCE. A student of Xunzi, Li Si, like his fellow student and rival Han Feizi, later rejected Confucianism in favor of a strict Legalist doctrine. As prime minister, he was associated with the notorious "burning of books and burial of scholars" of 213 BCE and with the building of the Great Wall. In the confusion following the death of the emperor Qin Shihuangdi in 210 BCE, he was accused of treason; he was executed two years later.

[See also Legalism; Han Feizi; Qin Dynasty; Qin Shihuangdi; and Xunzi.]

Derk Bodde, *China's First Unifier* (1938).

JOHN S. MAJOR

# LITERACY

## LITERACY IN CHINA

The fact that elite culture has been so thoroughly literate throughout most of Chinese history has until recent times hindered exploration of the significance and development of literacy as a theme in Chinese history. It now appears that not only were there always several levels of literacy in China, but indeed changes in the nature and scope of literacy in China account for a number of important changes in Chinese political, social, and intellectual life. Among those who could read or write in China, degrees of knowledge of the written word varied. At one extreme was the examination graduate who could command a vocabulary of several thousand characters, many quite abstract, and readily recall most of the texts of the classics that formed the basis for political and literary discourse. At the other extreme

might have been a villager who knew the several hundred or perhaps a thousand characters, mostly of quite concrete reference, that were necessary for marketing and primitive accounting. There were, no doubt, many illiterates in China—probably more than at a comparable period in the West—but to a striking degree the politics and economy particularly of late imperial China were predicated on some level of popular literacy. The literacy of the common man in China was fostered in lineage and community schools, which could be established and maintained with a relatively small endowment.

The development of printing in the thirteenth century and the widespread dissemination of printed materials that began in the fifteenth and sixteenth centuries changed the character of cultural life in China in a variety of ways. At the popular level, the availability of printed matter has been seen as playing a role in the changing character of religion in early modern China, and certainly lay behind the development of vernacular fiction as a literary genre. On the elite level, printing was probably a force behind the development of textualism and traditions of empirical scholarship, which dominated intellectual life in the Ming and Qing dynasties. A desire to close the gap between elite and popular literacy has motivated reforms in the twentieth century both in the syntax and grammar of the Chinese language and in the form of Chinese characters.

Thomas F. Carter, *The Invention of Printing in China and Its Spread Westward*, revised by L. Carrington Goodrich (1955). Evelyn S. Rawski, *Education and Popular Literacy in Ch'ing China* (1979).          R. KENT GUY

## LITERACY IN SOUTHEAST ASIA

Historically, the spread of mass literacy in Southeast Asia has been facilitated by the fact that Southeast Asian languages—with the important exception of Vietnamese, which was written in Chinese-style characters until modern times—were written in Indian- and sometimes Arabic-style alphabets and by the importance that the religions of the region (Buddhism, Islam, and Philippine Christianity) placed on basic education. That most Southeast Asian farm families were much more prosperous than their Indian and Chinese counterparts also made it possible for families to spare boys from farm labors to learn basic reading and writing at the village Buddhist monastery or Islamic *pondok* school.

Nineteenth-century observers characteristically commented that Southeast Asian male literacy rates ranged from 50 to 90 percent. Except in the American Philippines and independent Siam, however, mass literacy suffered under colonial rule in the late nineteenth and early twentieth century when indigenous religious institutions lost much of their vigor. Postwar independent regimes all devoted considerable resources to developing compulsory primary education for males and females alike, and contemporary literacy rates in Southeast Asia, though threatened by the enormous burden placed on state education by rapid population growth, are among the highest in the less-developed countries of the world. Those in Thailand, Singapore, Brunei, and Malaysia, for example, may favorably be compared with mass literacy rates in the industrialized countries of Europe and North America.

DAVID K. WYATT

**LITERATI PURGES.** There were four "literati purges" *(sahwa)* during the second century of Korea's Neo-Confucian Yi dynasty (1392–1910). These bloody political clashes occurred in 1497, 1504, 1519, and 1545. The literati *(salim,* literally, "forest of literati") who suffered these purges represented a highly moralistic type of Neo-Confucianism, oriented to self-cultivation, that had developed in the countryside among those who shunned government careers. As men of the *salim* mentality began to filter into government their orientation brought them into conflict with the more pragmatic statecraft of Neo-Confucians in the establishment.

The first two purges occurred under the reign of Lord Yŏnsan (r. 1495–1506), a depraved and insane ruler whom historians have never accorded the title of king. Under his tolerant predecessor, King Sŏngjong (r. 1470–1494), *salim* remonstrance had gotten out of hand; the three bureaus that enjoyed this prerogative often acted in concert to oppose policies or appointments, vilified opponents as amoral and vicious, and resorted to power tactics such as mass resignations to get their way. These tactics caused an institutional crisis as the function of remonstrance threatened to overshadow the executive power of the throne and policymakers.

Yŏnsan reacted to such pressure with hostility. In 1498, when he discovered that a scholar preparing the dynastic history had written critically of his grandfather's usurpation of the throne, he struck. This first literati purge saw the execution or exile of some thirty men, a symbolic warning that there should be no challenge or questioning of established authority. As Yŏnsan slipped further into extravagance, sensuality, and paranoia, however, remonstrance continued. In 1504 the official world was plunged into a bloodbath. Anyone remotely connected with past criticism was executed or exiled; the two-year reign of terror finally ended in 1506 with a coup organized by high officials.

A strong reaction characterized the early reign of Yŏnson's successor, King Chungjong (r. 1507–1544). In 1515 a brilliant and charismatic young official, Cho Kwang-jo (1482–1519), emerged at the head of a powerful and idealistic reform movement that swept the political world with its promise of a new era. The young reformers pushed too far and too fast, however, alienating many and finally including the king, who had been Cho's staunch supporter. In 1519, just when Cho seemed at the height of his power, he and his group were suddenly purged, and the *salim* type of Neo-Confucian was again under a cloud.

Chungjong had two sons by different queens; toward the end of his reign, as the princes' maternal uncles maneuvered for the succession, the official world was split into rival factions. The *salim* figures just beginning to reenter government were swept up in the factionalism. Their candidate succeeded to the throne but died almost immediately and the swing of power to the rival faction brought about the final literati purge in 1545.

Within twenty years, however, the *salim* were back and had themselves become the establishment: the purges had succeeded in fusing them into a self-conscious school that regarded itself as maintaining the orthodox essence of the Neo-Confucian heritage. This "*salim* mentality" became a distinctive and lasting feature of Korean Neo-Confucianism.

[*See also* Neo-Confucianism in Korea *and* Yi Dynasty.]

Woo-Keun Han, *The History of Korea,* translated by Kyong-shik Lee (1970). Wanne J. Joe, *Traditional Korea: A Cultural History* (1972). Ki-baik Lee, *A New History of Korea,* translated by Edward W. Wagner (1984). Edward W. Wagner, *The Literati Purges: Political Conflict in Early Yi Korea* (1974).    MICHAEL C. KALTON

**LIU BANG** (247–195 BCE), petty official under the Qin dynasty (221–207), led one of many revolts against the dynasty that broke out in 208 BCE. By 206 his forces had captured the Qin capital of Xianyang, and he proclaimed himself prince of Han. He defeated his main rival, Xiang Yu, in 202. As emperor of the Han dynasty from that date, he spent the remainder of his reign consolidating his power over all of China. He won popular support for the new dynasty by abrogating the Legalist code of Qin and reducing taxes, and he won support from the ruling class through a partial restoration of feudalism. He is generally known by his posthumous title, Han Gaozu.

[*See also* Qin Dynasty *and* Han Dynasty.]

Michele Pirazzoli-t'Serstevens, *The Han Dynasty.* (1982).    JOHN S. MAJOR

**LIU BEI** (162–223), impoverished member of the Han imperial clan who became enmeshed in dynastic intrigue following the Yellow Turbans Rebellion of 184. At first an ally of the general Cao Cao, he later became his bitter rival. Allied with Sun Quan against Cao Cao and enlisting the services of the great hero and general Zhuge Liang, in 211 he attempted to gain control of the empire from his refuge in Sichuan. With the collapse of the Han Dynasty in 220, Liu Bei proclaimed himself emperor of Shu. His Shu Han dynasty, one of the Three Kingdoms (along with Wu and Wei) of the post-Han era, endured until 263.

[*See also* Han Dynasty; Yellow Turbans; *and* Three Kingdoms.]

Rafe de Crespigny, *The Last of the Han* (1969). Achilles Fang, *The Chronicle of the Three Kingdoms (220–265)* (1952).    JOHN S. MAJOR

**LIU SHAOQI** (1898–1969), early leader of the Chinese Communist Party (CCP) and president of the People's Republic of China from 1959 to 1968. Liu was purged during the Cultural Revolution.

Liu Shaoqi was born in Ningxiang County, Hunan, located midway between the provincial capital, Changsha, and the birthplace of Mao Zedong. The youngest son of a rich peasant, Liu attended local primary schools followed by several brief essays at higher education (including an eight-month stay in Moscow) before joining the Chinese Communist Party and devoting the rest of his life to its cause. Liu began as a labor organizer in his native Hunan during the period of the first United Front between the CCP and the Guomindang (Kuomintang, or Nationalist Party) and continued on a clandestine basis after the Communists were driven underground upon the sudden rupture of that relationship in 1927.

During the ensuing period of the First Civil War (1927–1936) and the War of National Resistance (1936–1945), Liu became the leading organizer of Communist underground bases in "white" areas oc-

cupied by Guomindang or Japanese forces, contributing to an invisible growth of Communist power that was to manifest itself decisively in the post–World War II confrontation with the Nationalist regime. A participant in the Long March and an early supporter of Mao Zedong, Liu played a major role in the Zhengfeng rectification movement (1942–1944). During this time he consolidated his leadership, making seminal contributions to Party organization theory and cadre ethics in his essays "On Inner Party Struggle" and "How to Be a Good Communist."

In the post-Liberation era, Liu Shaoqi emerged as the leading custodian of the CCP's organizational integrity and the most influential supporter of Mao's unique approach to political development, two commitments that were to prove increasingly incompatible. As Liu's prestige rose, ultimately taking him to the presidency of the PRC (1959) and Party vice-chairmanship, Mao's leadership simultaneously faltered on his Hundred Flowers (1957) and Great Leap Forward (1958–1960) initiatives. Mao's temporary reversal fostered within the populace an apparently spontaneous shift of allegiance from Mao to Liu. Mao reacted sharply against this in the Great Proletarian Cultural Revolution (1966–1976), allowing his erstwhile heir apparent to be branded "China's Khrushchev," the mastermind of a "bourgeois reactionary line" designed to subvert further progress toward the communist utopia. As such, Liu and his fellow "capitalist roaders" became targets of a mass criticism campaign of unprecedented scope and intensity, culminating in October 1968 in their purge. In Liu's case, the rigors of the experience seem to have aggravated various physical ailments that, left unattended, resulted in his death in November 1969.

Liu's reputation was to outlive his physical demise. The post-1976 reversal of verdicts on Mao Zedong's contributions to communism during his terminal decade eventually resulted in the posthumous vindication of Liu Shaoqi at a memorial ceremony held on 17 May 1980. Although in deference to ideological continuity "mistakes" were still vaguely referred to, the investigation report absolved Liu of most specific accusations, and his *Selected Works* have since been published amid considerable fanfare. Surviving members of his family, led by his widow, Wang Guangmei, and five children, have also been rehabilitated.

The purpose of Liu's rehabilitation was to exonerate those thousands who were stigmatized by association with his "line," led by Deng Xiaoping,

Peng Zhen, and Chen Yun, and to legitimize the policies either for which he was responsible or that were imputed to him in the course of the criticism campaign. In its search for legitimation amid the crumbling iconography of "Maoism," the reform regime of Deng Xiaoping needed martyrs and saints. In fulfilling this new function, Liu Shaoqi symbolized an eclectic mix: a basically Leninist approach to Party organization, stressing internal norms and procedures over substantive ideological concerns; an approach to cadre morality that grafts Marxist theory to Confucian humanism; and a pragmatic approach to development that merges elements of market and plan, monopoly, and bureaucratic pluralism into a functional division of labor.

[*See also* Communism: Chinese Communist Party; China, People's Republic of; Deng Xiaoping; Great Proletarian Cultural Revolution; *and* Mao Zedong.]

Lowell Dittmer, *Liu Shao-ch'i and the Chinese Cultural Revolution* (1974), and "Death and Transfiguration," *Journal of Asian Studies* 40.3 (May 1981): 455–479. Liu Shao-ch'i (Liu Shaoqi), *Collected Works*, 3 vols. (1969).

LOWELL DITTMER

**LIU SONG DYNASTY.** *See* Six Dynasties.


**LI XIANNIAN** (b. 1907), a top economic planner and political leader of China since the 1950s. A native of Huang'an, Hubei Province, Li worked as a carpenter in his youth; joined the Party in 1927; took part in the Communist-led peasant uprisings, the Long March, and the Civil War; and was a military commander and Party leader in central China from 1949 to 1952. Li was appointed a vice-premier and minister of finance in 1954 and has since been one of China's most important economic planners. His career was not adversely affected by the Cultural Revolution; he has been a Politburo member since 1956 and was a Party vice-chairman from 1977 to 1982. Currently he is president of the Republic (China's head of state) and a Politburo Standing Committee member. He is married to Lin Jiamei.

PARRIS CHANG


**LI YUANHONG** (1864–1928), military commander and president of the Chinese republican government in Beijing. Li helped build a modern army in Hubei Province at the end of the Qing dynasty. During the Wuchang Uprising in 1911 revolution-aries forced him to be military governor and briefly to command the revolutionary army. He became national vice president under Yuan Shikai and, later, president (1916–1917, 1922–1923). As president, Li quarreled with militarists and tried to maneuver between factions but never acquired the authority to control policy effectively.

[*See also* China, Republic Period; Yuan Shikai; *and* Xinhai Revolution.]

Howard L. Boorman, ed., *Biographical Dictionary of Republican China* (1968). Andrew J. Nathan, *Peking Politics, 1918–1923: Factionalism and the Failure of Constitutionalism* (1976).    MARY BACKUS RANKIN


**LI ZHI** (1527–1602), Chinese scholar. The great iconoclast of the late Ming, Li Zhi represented the most radical pole within the Taizhou branch of Wang Yangming's School of Mind. Li hailed from a merchant family in Quanzhou, Fujian Province. Although he passed the provincial-level civil service examinations and held several government posts during the period between 1555 and 1581, Li grew alienated from the philosophical orthodoxy of Zhu Xi and the corruption he saw in the traditional bureaucracy. In 1585 he withdrew to a Buddhist temple to devote himself to study and writing.

At the core of Li Zhi's philosophy was a belief in the unity of the Three Teachings (Confucianism, Daoism, and Buddhism). His quest for individualism advocated full expression of personal desires, criticism of traditional morality, and the advancement of "heterodox" ideas. Li was arrested in 1602 and while awaiting trial committed suicide as a final act of nonconformity.

Wm. Theodore de Bary, "Individualism and Humanitarianism in Late Ming Thought," in *Self and Society in Ming Thought*, edited by Wm. Theodore de Bary (1970), pp. 145–248. L. Carrington Goodrich and Chaoying Fang, eds., *Dictionary of Ming Biography, 1368–1644* (1976), pp. 99–102. Ray Huang, *1587: A Year of No Significance* (1981), pp. 189–221.    ANITA M. ANDREW


**LI ZICHENG** (c. 1605–1645), Chinese bandit and leader of a mammoth peasant rebellion that toppled the Ming dynasty in 1644, on the eve of the Manchu conquest.

Son of a prosperous Shaanxi peasant, Li held a position as a post-station messenger before serving in the military. During the 1620s, a time of severe economic depression when the Ming government was dominated by corrupt and greedy eunuchs, Li joined an uncle and other relatives who had taken to banditry. At that time, banditry was spreading rapidly among the impoverished peasants of Shaanxi and Shanxi provinces. The Ming government, with its main forces committed to the struggle against the Manchus in the northeast, could do little to contain the growing domestic strife.

Twice narrowly escaping capture by government troops in the early 1630s, Li joined forces with other bandit gangs and led raids as far south as Anhui. In 1636, after his uncle's capture and death, Li adopted the title Dashing King and led his own forces into Sichuan, where they were eventually turned back. In 1639 Li's fortunes rose again when, after a bad drought in Henan, he found thousands of new recruits, including at least two well-educated scholars who agreed to serve as his advisers. On their suggestion, Li now embarked on a campaign of promoting tax relief and other policies designed to win over more peasants. His notoriety increased in 1641, when he captured the capital of Henan, killed a Ming prince, and distributed property to the poor and hungry. Riding on the crest of what was then the largest peasant rebellion in Chinese history, Li controlled most of north and northwest China by the spring of 1644 and had begun to establish the trappings of government.

On 25 April 1644 Beijing fell in a panic to Li's peasant army of nearly 400,000, and the last Ming emperor hanged himself in despair. Li had already proclaimed a new dynasty, the Shun, but his forces were quickly defeated at Shanhaiguan by superior Manchu troops aided by a Ming loyalist general. Thus, in June Li was forced to abandon his prize and to retreat to the west and south. Within a year he lost all he had won and was killed in Hubei, possibly at the hands of peasants.

Although Li's massive rebellion dethroned the Ming rulers, Li failed to build an effective administration. Moreover, his cruelty as a leader disillusioned many followers and alienated the scholar-officials who in the end preferred to support the alien Manchus.

[See also Ming Dynasty and Rebellions in China.]

James P. Harrison, *The Communists and Chinese Peasant Rebellions, A Study in the Rewriting of Chinese History* (1971). James B. Parsons, *The Peasant Rebellions of the Late Ming Dynasty* (1970).    ROLAND L. HIGGINS

## LI ZONGREN

**LI ZONGREN** (1891–1969), military leader of the Guangxi clique in Guomindang (Kuomintang, KMT, or Nationalist Party) politics. After partici- pating in the Northern Expedition, Li and the Guangxi generals emerged as rivals to Chiang Kai-shek, only to be defeated in 1929. The Guangxi leaders retained their provincial base but thereafter limited their attacks on Chiang to verbal assaults. After the outbreak of the war with Japan in 1937, Li left Guangxi to assume military command at Xuzhou and was credited with China's brief victory at Taierzhuang. As the KMT position collapsed in the civil war, Li mounted a challenge to Chiang's dictatorship. He was elected vice president in 1948 over Chiang's objections and became acting president in the last weeks of the KMT regime. Li moved to the United States until returning to China in 1965.

[See also Chiang Kai-shek; Guangxi Clique; and Guomindang.]

Diana Lary, *Region and Nation: The Kwangsi Clique in Chinese Politics, 1925–1937* (1975). T. K. Tong and Li Tsung-jen (Li Zongren), eds., *The Memoirs of Li Tsung-jen* (1979).    PARKS M. COBLE, JR.

## LOCUST REBELLION

**LOCUST REBELLION.** One of numerous popular rebellions against Vietnam's Nguyen dynasty, the Locust Rebellion broke out in the northern province of Son Tay in 1854. The movement's leader was Le Duy Cu, claimant to the throne of the Le dynasty, which still enjoyed considerable support in certain areas of the country. Although the rebellion was quickly suppressed, it did attract the support of Cao Ba Quat, a well-known scholar who was dissatisfied with life under the Nguyen. The movement is referred to as the Locust Rebellion because Son Tay and Bac Ninh provinces were being plagued by these insects in 1854.

[See also Cao Ba Quat.]

Nguyen Van Thai and Nguyen Van Mung, *A Short History of Vietnam* (1958).    BRUCE M. LOCKHART

## LODI DYNASTY

**LODI DYNASTY,** an Afghan dynasty of the Delhi sultanate, established in 1451. Afghan migrations to India began during the early Turkish period. By the time of Muhammad bin Tughluq the Afghans constituted an important segment of the nobility. An Afghan merchant, Malik Bahram, joined the service of a governor of Multan and served him so devotedly that he entrusted his son Malik Kala with the administration of Daurala. Malik Kala's son Bahlul founded the Lodi dynasty in 1451 and ruled until 1489. He was followed by Sikandar (1489–

1517) and Ibrahim (1517–1526). Ibrahim met his end at the hands of Babur at the Battle of Panipat (1526), following which the Lodi dynasty yielded its place to the Mughal empire.

The Lodis had come to power at a time when the Delhi sultanate had shrunk in dimensions and the contumacious activities of chieftains in the Punjab and the growing ambitions of the Sharqis in the east had created formidable problems. The Lodis sought to introduce principles characteristic of Afghan tribalism into Indian polity. In matters of succession, suitability rather than the principle of heredity guided their action. The army of the Delhi sultanate under them changed its character from "the king's army" to "tribal militia." Some of the privileges and prerogatives of the sultan came to be commonly used by the nobles, and the king came to be looked upon as *primus inter pares*. The three Lodi rulers, however, demonstrated different attitudes in dealing with the nobility—Bahlul's despotism was tempered by Afghan traditions of tribal equality; Sikandar made the nobles recognize the superior status of the monarch; and Ibrahim's overbearing attitude alienated them.

[*See also* Delhi Sultanate; Panipat, Battles of; *and* Mughal Empire.]

S. A. Halim, *History of the Lodi Sultans* (1961). I. H. Siddiqi, *Some Aspects of Afghan Despotism in India* (1969).                      KHALIQ AHMAD NIZAMI

LOESS, a yellow, fine-grained soil deposited in great depths by wind or glaciers. Extensive loess deposits in North China account for some of the special characteristics of that region. Winds scouring the deserts of Central Asia have built up the uncompacted, easily worked soils that cover the Chinese provinces of Shaanxi, Shanxi, Hebei, and Henan. Because of its friability loess is well suited to agriculture. When cut by water it erodes easily leaving vertical cliffs. Cave houses cut into loessial cliffs are a common feature of North China. It is erosion of loess that gives the Yellow River its characteristic color and the heavy sediment that over the ages has formed the North China Plain and extended the shoreline of the Yellow Sea and Gulf of Bohai.

EDWARD L. FARMER

LOMBOK, an island of 4,990 square kilometers, east of Bali. The Sasak people of Lombok were imperfectly islamized by the Javanese in the sixteenth century. Throughout the seventeenth century control was contested between Islamic Makassar and Bima, dominant in the east, and the Hindu Balinese kingdom of Karangasem in the west. By 1740 the Balinese had extended their rule throughout the island, though the east remained more orthodox in its Islam and more capable of periodic rebellion. After a series of wars between rival Balinese factions,

FIGURE 1. *Lodi Tomb, Delhi.*

a united kingdom of Lombok emerged in 1838 with its capital at Mataram. An east Sasak rebellion in 1891 provided a long-awaited opportunity for Dutch intervention in what was by then the wealthiest remaining independent state in Indonesia. The first Dutch expedition in July 1894 was forced to withdraw to the port of Ampenan with heavy casualties. After obtaining reinforcements the Dutch were able to destroy Mataram. Resistance ended with the ritual suicide *(puputan)* of the defeated Lombok court in November 1894.

[*See also* Islamization of Southeast Asia *and* Mataram.]                                ANTHONY REID

LONG MARCH. The Long March is the great epic event in the Chinese Communists' rise to power. It has been glorified in song and story in China as a triumph of human will over immense obstacles, both human and material. According to Edgar Snow's *Red Star Over China*, the most famous English-language account of the march, there were a total of 368 days en route, with an average of almost a skirmish a day. For the major portion of the march, there were only 44 rest days over a distance of about 5,000 miles, or an average of one halt per 114 miles marched. The average distance covered daily was 24 miles, much of it over incredibly difficult terrain, including eighteen mountain ranges and twenty-four rivers. The army passed through twelve provinces, breaking through the barriers of ten provincial warlords and defeating or avoiding government troops. As Snow commented, "However one might feel about the Reds, it was impossible to deny recognition of their Long March as one of the great exploits of military history."

Of the original one hundred thousand men and several dozen women who broke through the government blockade of the Jiangxi Soviet in mid-October 1934, perhaps only five thousand reached northern Shaanxi, where the march ended a year later. Mao's First Front Army numbered about ten thousand in late 1935 but half of it was composed of local Shaanxi recruits. The total number of troops under Communist command at the beginning of 1937 was probably about forty thousand, including those who had already established a base in the northwest, pockets of guerrilla forces scattered throughout China, and the Second and Fourth Front Armies under the command of He Long and Zhang Guotao respectively. The latter arrived in the northern Shaanxi base about a year after Mao, having lost over three-fourths of their troops to bat-

tle casualties, disease, exhaustion, and desertion. The cost of the march had been frightful, but the leadership core of the Communist movement had survived and gained the respite that enabled the Communists to rebuild their forces and expand their territory rapidly once the war with Japan began in 1937.

One of the most important aspects of the Long March was the rise of Mao Zedong to preeminence in the Communist Party. At the last meeting of the Central Committee of the Party before the Long March (the Fifth Plenum), Mao had been demoted. He had lost his position on the Political Bureau, the guiding organ of the Party, and was not included in the new Party Affairs Department or the Party Secretariat. Those offices were dominated by the so-called "returned students," a group of young Moscow-trained Communists who had long been at odds with Mao over his handling of affairs in the Jiangxi Soviet.

Mao's retaliation came during the Long March at Zunyi, a town in Guizhou where the First Front Army halted for a few days in January 1935. The First Front had taken a terrible beating in the early months of the march. Outnumbered by the Nationalists by five or six to one, they had lost seventy percent of their troops, only thirty thousand remained. Qin Bangxian, leader of the Party as general secretary, was severely criticized by Mao and others, resulting in a reshuffling of Party leadership. Zhang Wentian became general secretary, and Mao became chairman of the Central Committee Military Affairs Committee, the most powerful office for the duration of the Long March. He was also reinstated to the Political Bureau and elected to its Standing Committee, and was made a secretary of the General Secretariat. Although nominally he would not head the Party for several more years, after the Zunyi meeting his name was always listed first in Party proclamations.

Mao's second great political struggle during the Long March was with Zhang Guotao, commander of the Fourth Front Army, which had been operating in northern Sichuan while the First Front was struggling north from Guizhou after the Zunyi meeting. When the two armies met their leaders disagreed on strategy and tactics, especially concerning the final destination of the march. After several stormy, inconclusive meetings they compromised by dividing their combined army into two columns with units of the First and Fourth in each. Mao's eastern column, led by Peng Dehuai, Lin Biao, and Ye Jianying, headed north for Shaanxi. Zhang's western column, led by the commander in chief of the Red Army, Zhu De, and the chief of staff, Liu Bocheng, tried to secure a base in Sichuan. In early September 1935 the reinforced western column numbered perhaps sixty thousand, about six times the size of Mao's force. Zhang established a de facto rival central committee in Sichuan. During the next year, however, pressure from Nationalist troops and a series of ill-conceived military maneuvers reduced the western column to less than ten thousand men, including three thousand survivors of He Long's Second Front Army, which had joined Zhang's troops in Sichuan. It was a chastened but still defiant Zhang Guotao who met Mao in northern Shaanxi a year after the latter had arrived. Zhang assumed several positions of responsibility there, but within a few months Mao had rallied the support to drive him from the base area and out of the Party.

The Long March, then, was not, as it is sometimes depicted, a victorious struggle of a unified Communist Party certain of its direction and its future. It was marked by devastating defeats and divisive political battles. The northern Shaanxi base provided temporary refuge, but the Nationalist government of Chiang Kai-shek was still bent on annihilation and was marshaling a huge army for a final campaign.

Curiously, however, it was not a demoralized Communist remnant that outside observers like Edgar Snow found in northern Shaanxi in 1936; on the contrary, they appeared to be very optimistic. Perhaps euphoria resulting from the mere fact of survival against enormous odds is sufficient explanation for their self-confidence, but there were several indications of a change in fortune to reinforce it. In December 1935 students in Beijing, Shanghai, and other cities had provoked a strong, nationwide patriotic response to their mass demonstration to pursuade Chiang Kai-shek to cease his anti-Communist military campaigns and turn his attention to combatting the imperialist designs of Japan. That response was reflected strongly among the troops from northern China who had been designated by Chiang to lead the attack against the Communists. Unhappy about fighting other Chinese instead of the Japanese who occupied their homeland, they kidnapped Chiang in December 1936 and forced a united front with the Communists. [See also Xi'an Incident and United Front.]

The resulting cessation of civil war enabled the Communists to concentrate on establishing base areas throughout northern and eastern China during the war with Japan from 1937 to 1945. The Long March indeed proved to be a turning point for the Communists, who would rule China in a little more than a decade.

[See also Shaanganning; He Long; Lin Biao; Mao Zedong; Peng Dehuai; Ye Jianying; Zhang Guotao; and Zhu De.]

Otto Braun, *A Comintern Agent in China* (1982). James P. Harrison, *The Long March to Power: A History of the Chinese Communist Party, 1921–1972* (1972). Warren Kuo, *Analytical History of the Chinese Communist Party* (1966–). Agnes Smedley, *The Great Road: The Life and Times of Chu Teh* (1956) and *The Long March: Eyewitness Accounts* (1963). Edgar Snow, *Red Star over China* (1938). Helen Foster Snow, *Inside Red China* (1939). Dick Wilson, *The Long March, 1935* (1971).

PETER J. SEYBOLT

**LONGMEN**, site, near present-day Luoyang, of numerous Buddhist cave temples. After the Northern Wei (386–534) moved its capital south to Luoyang in 494, the closer proximity to the influence of Chinese pictorial expression and the existence of deposits of fine gray limestone permitted sculptures of greater refinement of expression than had been known. The new style reached its culmination in the cave known as Binyangdong completed in 523. The site was the object of imperial patronage in the Tang dynasty (618–907), when the emperor Gaozong ordered the carving of the colossal figure of the Buddha Vairocana in 672.

[See also Northern Wei Dynasty.]

Michael Sullivan, *The Arts of China* (1977). Denis Twitchett, ed., *Sui and T'ang China, 589–906, Part 1,* vol. 3 of *The Cambridge History of China* (1979).

JOHN PHILIP NESS

**LONGSHAN CULTURE**, late Neolithic culture of north-central China; it flourished from approximately 2500 to 1800 BCE. Longshan marks the final stage of Neolithic culture in China before the advent of the Bronze Age. The culture, characterized by rice cultivation, polished stone implements, and fine, burnished, wheel-thrown black pottery, is named for a type-site at Longshan, Shandong Province.

The Longshan culture superseded the Yangshao "red pottery" culture throughout North China, as well as the Qingliangang culture in Shandong and northern Jiangsu. The transition was marked by a "Longshanoid" phase, lasting roughly from 3200 to 2500 BCE. The characteristic Longshanoid cul-

FIGURE 1. *Liangzhu Pottery*. This tripod of the third millennium BCE is an example of the typical black pottery found at sites associated with the Longshan culture.

tures—Miaodigou II, Chujialing, and Huating—show substantial regional variation, but all have distinctive features in common. Rice cultivation apparently brought with it an increase in population size, density, and wealth; there was an increased range of domesticated animals; production of pottery, bone, stone, and other artifacts became more specialized and industrialized; and burial patterns and ceremonial implements indicate the development of a social hierarchy and a more complex ritual life.

The fully developed Longshan culture that followed the Longshanoid phase shows a continuation and intensification of earlier trends. Two main regional variants are recognized, one in the central plains and one in the eastern coastal area. The former is characterized by a predominance of gray pottery; the eastern variant is the "classical" Longshan culture, with an abundance of fine, black "eggshell" pottery (see figure 1). The culture of the central plains was followed by the Erlitou culture, marking the earliest phase of the Chinese Bronze Age (around 2000 BCE), while the classical Longshan culture of the Shandong Peninsula and neighboring regions along the coast endured well into the second millennium BCE.

[*See also* Yangshao Culture *and* Bronze Age in China.]

Kwang-chih Chang, *The Archaeology of Ancient China* (3d ed., 1977). David Keightley, ed., *The Origins of Chinese Civilization* (1983).     JOHN S. MAJOR

LON NOL (b. 1913), Cambodian political figure and president of the Khmer Republic (1971–1975). The grandson of a Cambodian provincial governor, he was educated in Cambodia and Saigon and enrolled in the Cambodian colonial civil service in 1935. In ten years time he had risen to the rank of deputy provincial governor. During the late 1940s he was active in conservative political circles and came to the favorable attention of King Norodom Sihanouk. When independence was obtained from France in 1953, Lon Nol embarked on a military career, benefiting from some experience fighting alongside the French against communist insurgents in the early 1950s. He was frequently minister of defense in Sihanouk cabinets and was named prime minister in 1966 and again in 1969. In 1970 he took part in the coup that overthrew Prince Sihanouk and ushered in the pro-American Khmer Republic. Lon Nol's inept leadership and the fervor of communist-led troops opposing him combined to produce a series of disastrous defeats, culminating in the capture of Phnom Penh by communist forces in 1975, soon after Lon Nol had been sent into exile in Hawaii.

[*See also* Cambodia; Khmer Republic; Norodom Sihanouk; *and* Kampuchea, Democratic.]

William Shawcross, *Sideshow* (1979). Michael Vickery, *Cambodia 1975–1982* (1983).     DAVID P. CHANDLER

LOPBURI, ancient city and principality in central Thailand. The site of Lopburi, on the northeastern fringe of Thailand's Central Plain, is of great antiquity, yielding Neolithic remains, and its importance through time must derive from its position as a stage on the overland route between the Chaophraya River basin and central Laos. Early Lopburi, with its Mon population, was an important center of the Dvaravati civilization between the sixth and ninth century, and legends attribute to it the founding of Haripunjaya (Lamphun). In the early eleventh century, having maintained close connections both with the north and with Tambralinga on the Malay Peninsula, the whole of this region was brought within the Angkorian empire under Suryavarman I, and it remained under Khmer control almost continuously through the thirteenth century. Toward the end of that century, however, it was independent, as attested by embassies it sent to China seeking recognition in 1289–1299; during this period it was not included within the expanding kingdom of Sukhothai.

It would appear that the new Thai kingdom of Ayudhya, founded in 1351, resulted from an alliance between Thai Suphanburi, in the west, and Mon/Khmer Lopburi, and it is surely Lopburi that is the source of Ayudhya's statecraft and administrative institutions. Lopburi was a major center in Ayudhya's first century but faded thereafter. It briefly regained prominence as the summer capital of King Narai in the seventeenth century and as a military center for Phibunsongkhram during World War II. Its extensive monumental ruins have made it a popular tourist center today.

[See also Dvaravati; Mon; Lamphun; Tambralinga; Suryavarman I; Angkor; Sukhothai; Ramkhamhaeng; Ayudhya; Ramathibodi I; Narai; and Phibunsongkhram, Luang.]

G. Coedès, *The Indianized States of Southeast Asia,* translated by Susan B. Cowing (1968). David K. Wyatt, *Thailand: A Short History* (1984).    DAVID K. WYATT

**LOP NUR** (Lob Nor) is an uninhabited area of sparse grassland and semidesert adjacent to marshes and salt lakes located at the eastern end of the Tarim Basin in Xinjiang Province, China. Since 1964 it has been the primary test site for the Chinese nuclear weapons program. In the early 1970s, the Soviet Union reportedly probed American reaction to a preemptive strike on the Chinese nuclear installations there and received a strong negative response.

JOHN A. RAPP

**LO THAI,** king of the kingdom of Sukhothai in Thailand (r. 1298–1346 or 1347), better remembered for his religious and cultural achievements than for his political or military activities. Lo Thai was the son of the great king Ramkhamhaeng, but from the beginning of his reign he could not retain his father's vast empire; as early as 1320 he ruled only over the territories immediately surrounding Sukhothai in the upper Chaophraya Valley. During his reign the classic Sukhothai bronze sculptures were cast, and he was a vigorous promoter of orthodox Sinhalese Buddhism in the Tai-speaking world. He died suddenly in 1346 or 1347, eventually succeeded by his son Mahathammaracha I (Luthai).

[See also Sukhothai; Ramkhamhaeng; and Mahathammaracha I.]

A. B. Griswold and Prasert na Nagara, "King Lödaiya of Sukhodaya and His Contemporaries," *Journal of the*

FIGURE 1. *Phra Prang Sam Yot, Lopburi.* Constructed in Lopburi style with laterite and sandstone decorated with stucco, Phra Prang Sam Yot is the architectural landmark of Lopburi. Originally built as a Hindu shrine, it was converted to a Buddhist temple during the reign of King Narai of Ayudhya (r. 1656–1688).

*Siam Society* 60.1 (1972): 21–152. David K. Wyatt, *Thailand: A Short History* (1984).    DAVID K. WYATT

**LOVEK** (Lawaek), capital of Cambodia from 1527 to 1594. During this period, the heyday of Cambodian power between the fall of Angkor in the fifteenth century and the present day, Cambodian kings opened the country up to Western traders and led several military campaigns against the Thai kingdom of Ayudhya. The most prominent of these kings was Ang Chan (r. 1516–1567); the most successful campaign occurred in 1556. Beginning in the 1570s, Cambodian attacks on the Thai alternated with Thai attacks on Cambodia. Thai armies laid siege to Lovek in 1587 and again in 1594. According to a Cambodian legend, Thai soldiers scattered silver coins into the hedges surrounding the capital. To get the money, Cambodians cut down the foliage and were overrun. Another legend relates that in 1594, after sacking Lovek, the Thai carried off two sacred statues, Preah Ko ("sacred cow") and Preah Keo ("sacred jewel"). Preah Ko contained documents explaining the secrets of Cambodian culture; by possessing these, the legend asserts, the Thai were able to dominate Cambodia for the next three hundred years. In the actual siege, the Cambodian king pleaded unsuccessfully for military help from the Portuguese in Melaka and from the Spaniards in the Philippines, then fled to Laos before the Thai armies sacked his capital and carried off its population. Hardly any archaeological evidence of the city's years of greatness survives; a new capital was built at Oudong, south of Lovek, in the early seventeenth century.

For the next two hundred and fifty years, Cambodia was unable to recover its sixteenth-century momentum, and its territory was contested by Thai, Vietnamese, and local factions. Because of these "dark ages," Lovek has retained an honored place in Cambodian chronicle histories, as well as in oral tradition.

[*See also* Cambodia; Angkor; Ayudhya; Ang Chan; *and* Thailand.]

David P. Chandler, *A History of Cambodia* (1983).
DAVID P. CHANDLER

**LOW, SIR HUGH** (1824–1905), English colonial administrator, naturalist, and traveler. During a botanical tour of Borneo Low came under the patronage of James Brooke, and between 1848 and 1877 he held various posts (including acting governor) in Labuan, published *Sarawak, Its Inhabitants and Productions* (1848), and became the first European to climb Mount Kinabalu (1851). Later he became Resident of Perak (1877–1889); there his command of Malay and tact in handling the State Council and ending debt-slavery established the "advisory system," which became the model followed by subsequent British residents in the Malay Peninsula.

[*See also* Brooke, Sir James; Labuan; *and* Perak.]

Emily Sadka, *The Protected Malay States, 1874–1895* (1968).    A. J. STOCKWELL

**LOWER BURMA.** Although the deltaic regions of southern Burma had long been distinguished politically, ethnically, and geographically from the dry zone to the north, the notion of Lower Burma as a distinct unit became prevalent only in the era of British colonial involvement in Burma. As the British usually defined it, Lower Burma extended from the southern fringes of the dry zone as far north as the Thayetmyo district to the southernmost areas of Tenasserim. Lower Burma included the districts that made up the deltas of the Irrawaddy and Sittang rivers and the Salween River valley. At times, for statistical purposes, the districts of the Arakan coast were also included in Lower Burma. In the British era and since independence, *Lower Burma* most commonly refers to the Irrawaddy Delta region.

[*See also* Burma.]

MICHAEL ADAS

**LUANG PRABANG,** city and kingdom of northern Laos; royal capital of French colonial Laos. Now insignificant and isolated, it once was the hub of the Lao world.

Lao people first entered the Luang Prabang region about the seventh century. By the thirteenth century they had become Buddhists and had become involved in the life of the Khmer kingdom of Angkor, some of whose artifacts may be found in Luang Prabang. From 1353 to 1569 it served as the royal seat and administrative capital of the kingdom of Lan Sang, but by the sixteenth century it was increasingly losing place to Vientiane, which was becoming the center of a much larger Lao population and was more convenient of access.

On the dissolution of Lan Sang about 1700, one contender for the throne of Lan Sang—Prince Kingkitsarat, grandnephew of the last king of Lan Sang—fled to Luang Prabang and in 1707 established a new Lan Sang kingdom there to rival the Lan Sang kingdom of Vientiane. In the two centuries that followed, the kings of Luang Prabang cultivated political and kinship relations with the ruling families of principalities across the north of Laos but were never sufficiently strong to be able to challenge Vientiane successfully. First to protect themselves against Vientiane and then for the sake of survival, kings from Surinyavongsa (r. 1771–1791) onward made themselves vassals to the kings of Siam. But their Siamese suzerain was too weak—or too preoccupied with Western threats to its survival—to be able to protect Luang Prabang effectively either against the He invasions from China and Vietnam in the 1870s and 1880s or against French expansionism. Following the Paknam Incident of 1893, Siam ceded its rights in Laos to France.

In the French colonial period, Luang Prabang at least nominally ruled only northern Laos, as a protectorate of France. During World War II and the period of rising nationalism just after the war, the French conceded ever-increasing powers to the kings of Luang Prabang in order to gain their cooperation, and most Lao nationalists came to rally around the kings as representing all the Lao, though not without some resistance from Prince Boun Oum of the house of Champassak in the south. With the proclamation of the Lao People's Democratic Republic in 1975, King Savangvatthana abdicated but chose to remain in Laos with his people. He is thought to have died while undergoing "reeducation" in 1979.

Because both the French colonial and the national independent governments chose to run their administration and center their bureaucracy in Vientiane, Luang Prabang was not a site of military and political contention and never underwent much urbanization. Among historical Southeast Asian cities, it is rare for being unspoiled, bucolic, and astonishingly beautiful.

[*See also* Laos; Fa Ngum; Lan Sang; Khun Borom; Kingkitsarat; Boun Oum; Savangvatthana; Sisavangvong; Surinyavongsa; *and* Un Kham.]

Maha Sila Viravong, *History of Laos* (1964). David K. Wyatt, *Thailand: A Short History* (1984).

DAVID K. WYATT

**LUANG PRADIT MANUTHAM.** *See* Pridi Phanomyong.

**LÜ BUWEI** (d. 235 BCE), one of the major advisers to the king of Qin, the eventual first unifier of China, Qin Shihuangdi. Lü, the marquis of Wenxin, was by background a rich merchant. He entered into the service of the Qin royal court and when the future Qin Shihuangdi ascended the throne at the age of thirteen, Lü acted as prime minister for nearly a decade, a role that made him the virtual ruler of Qin. His own downfall came in 237 BCE over a palace intrigue that eventually prompted his suicide in the year 235. He was responsible for appointing Li Si (280–208) as adviser; it was Li who eventually succeeded Lü Buwei.

[*See also* Li Si; Qin Dynasty; *and* Qin Shihuangdi.]

Derk Bodde, *China's First Unifier: A Study of the Ch'in Dynasty As Seen in the Life of Li Ssu (280?–208 B.C.)* (1967).

RODNEY L. TAYLOR

**LUCKNOW**, a city of 1.1 million people (1981) and the capital of the Indian state of Uttar Pradesh, situated 300 miles southeast of Delhi. It was already a flourishing town and grain market in the sixteenth century, when in 1590 Emperor Akbar named it the seat of the governor of Awadh. Muslims of Indian, Arab, Iranian, and Pathan descent constituted the core of Lucknow's ruling families, the first being closely linked to the Mughal court in Delhi. Emperor Aurangzeb endowed the famous Sunni theological school at Farangi Mahal, which survives as a font of religious and moral authority for the community. With the decline of the Mughal empire in the eighteenth century, Awadh emerged as the leading suc-

TABLE 1.    *Kings of Lan Sang–Luang Prabang*

| KING | REIGN DATES |
| --- | --- |
| 1. Kingkitsarat | 1707–1722 |
| 2. Ong Nok (or Khamon Noi) | 1722–1731 |
| 3. Inthasom | 1731–1756 |
| 4. Inthavongsa | 1756–1757* |
| 5. Sotikakuman | 1757–1771* |
| 6. Surinyavongsa | 1771–1791 |
| 7. Anurutthakuman | 1791–1816 |
| 8. Manghaturat | 1816–1837 |
| 9. Suksoem | 1837–1850 |
| 10. Chantharathep | 1850–1870 |
| 11. Un Kham | 1870–1887 |
| 12. Kham Suk (or Sakkarin) | 1887–1904 |
| 13. Sisavangvong | 1904–1959 |
| 14. Savangvatthana | 1959–1975* |

*Abdicated.

cessor state ruled by a dynasty of Shi'ite nawabs of Iranian descent. [*See* Farangi Mahal.]

Asaf ud-Daulah, nawab of Awadh, transferred his court from Faizabad to Lucknow in 1775 and for the next eighty years Lucknow was the largest and most prosperous precolonial city in the subcontinent. Successive rulers embellished the city fabric with complexes of palaces and gardens, bazaars, mosques, and *imambaras* (Shi'ite religious shrines), with noblemen and merchants following suit on a smaller scale. Under their generous patronage there developed in Lucknow a distinctive cultural style: its exquisitely refined manners, speech, and cuisine; its Urdu poets, musicians, entertainers, and courtesans; its perfumes, cosmetics, finely embroidered clothing, and other luxury goods; and its scores of bankers, jewelers, craftsmen, and artisans became legendary.

In 1856, however, while Lucknow was in full flower, the long-standing political dominance of the British culminated in the annexation of Awadh to the British empire and the banishment of Nawab Wajid Ali Shah. Lucknow offered an intense and

FIGURE 1. *Imambara, Lucknow.*

heroic resistance during the mutiny and rebellion of 1857, but the city was recaptured and pillaged, its citizens savagely chastised, and the cultural epoch was brought to an abrupt close.

A strong British authority was installed in the royal quarter, while the newly created municipal committee reordered civic affairs. A new and spacious cantonment and civil lines were laid out, while roads cut through the old neighborhoods and railway lines connected the city to the hinterland. The *taluqdars,* rural chieftains who traded in their political power for fixed rents from lands they had controlled in Awadh, were now welcomed as the loyal elite to build their city mansions. In 1877, with the abolition of Awadh as a separate political entity, Lucknow's major administrative functions were shifted to Allahabad. In 1920, however, Lucknow became the provincial capital of the United Provinces.

Under British rule Lucknow grew into an important railway junction, a command headquarters for the military establishment, a center for medicine and education, and preeminently an administrative center for the governance of the enlarged province. Only occasionally did the city become the stage for nationalist activity, such as the Lucknow Pact of 1916, but fresh impetus was given to the old, muted Shi'ite–Sunni rivalry that vents itself even today. The partition of 1947 saw the departure of several notable Muslim families and the influx of Punjabi and Sindhi entrepreneurial families. Small-scale modern industry is now growing in Lucknow and relief from urban blight and unemployment may be in sight for its people.

[*See also* Awadh *and* Uttar Pradesh.]

H. R. Nevill, *District Gazetteers of the United Provinces of Agra and Oudh,* vol. 37, *Lucknow* (1904). Veena Talwar Oldenburg, *The Making of Colonial Lucknow, 1856–1877* (1984).          VEENA TALWAR OLDENBURG

**LU DINGYI** (b. 1901), director of the propaganda department of Chinese Communist Youth League (from 1926 until the 1930s), of the Communist army (1930s), and of the Chinese Communist Party (1949–1966), and thus the ultimate enunciator of correctness in arts, education, and publishing (including the *People's Daily*). Lu issued major directives in each Party reform of literature, including that against "extreme leftism" (1951); those of the Hundred Flowers Campaign (1956–1957) and its correction, the antirightist drive (1957); and during the festival on contemporary Beijing opera (1964), the precursor to the Cultural Revolution. In the evolving alliances of 1965 Lu was identified with Peng Zhen, a member of Liu Shaoqi's faction, and was dismissed, arrested, and publicly "tried" in 1966; he was rehabilitated in 1979.

[See also Hundred Flowers Campaign.]

"Comrade Lu Dingyi's Discussion of Education Policy and Other Problems when Visiting Jiaotong University in Shanghai," *Chinese Education* 13 (1981): 34–41. Jürgen Domes, *The Internal Politics of China, 1949–1972*, translated by Rüdiger Machetzki (1973).    SHAN CHOU

**LU JIUYUAN.** See Lu Xiangshan.

**LUMBINI,** a site in Nepal that is recognized as the birthplace of the Buddha. To consecrate the site, the emperor Ashoka built a stone pillar there (c. 249 BCE); this was visited and noted by the Chinese pilgrims Faxian in the fourth century and Xuanzang in the seventh. There is also a shrine with a sculpture of the Buddha's mother, Mayadevi, a group of brick stupas, and a sacred tank. Forgotten for many centuries, Lumbini finally received the attention of Indian archaeologists after General Kharga Singh discovered the Ashokan pillar in 1896. With the assistance of an internationally funded program, Lumbini is being developed into a pilgrimage center.

[See also Ashoka.]

Devala Mitra, *Archaeological Excavations at Tilaurakot and Kodan and Explorations in the Nepalese Tarai* (1972). P. C. Mukherji, *A Report on a Tour of Exploration of the Antiquities in the Tarai (Nepal)* (1901; reprint, 1969).    PRAYAG RAJ SHARMA

**LUNYU,** the Confucian *Analects,* a work that is hard to overestimate for the role it has played in the history of Confucianism and in the cultures of China, Korea, and Japan. The *Lunyu* is regarded as the most reliable and complete record of the teachings and personality of Confucius. The earliest reference to the *Analects* is in the *Liji (Book of Rites),* signifying its presence as a text in pre-Han times. The *Hanshu,* the Han dynastic history, lists three versions of the work: *Lulun,* the *Analects* of the state of Lu; *Qilun,* the *Analects* of the state of Qi; and the *Gulun,* the Old Text version purportedly secreted away along with other classics in the walls of the home of Confucius. Zheng Xuan (127–200 CE) based his version upon the *Lulun* but added material from both other texts. He Yan (190–249

CE), building upon editors such as Zheng Xuan, produced the version of the text still accepted today.

How close to Confucius's own day was the composition of the *Analects?* Its sources were sayings and conversations preserved by disciples. These appear to have been passed from the first generation of disciples to their own disciples before it was compiled. The "authenticity" of the work as recording what Confucius actually taught is to be measured in terms of the accuracy of the records of the disciples, a question largely unanswerable.

The *Analects* was established as a canonical work with the Five Classics under Emperor Han Wudi (140–87 BCE), a part of the official establishment of Confucianism as state orthodoxy. During the Tang dynasty it was included among the Twelve Classics, and in the Song dynasty Zhu Xi (1130–1200) made it a vital part of the new textual tradition of Neo-Confucianism by placing it in the collection known as the Four Books. As a canonical work it has functioned in both public and private capacities, reflecting the sense of Confucian orthodoxy as something that appealed to the aspiring bureaucrat in the context of the civil service examination system and that in turn could be seen as a source of private reflection and learning within the personal Confucian religious life.

[See also Confucius and Confucianism.]

D. C. Lau, trans., *Confucius: The Analects* (1979). James Legge, trans., *The Four Books* (1930). Rodney L. Taylor, "Confucianism: Scripture and the Sage," in *The Holy Book in Comparative Perspective,* edited by F. M. Denny and R. L. Taylor (1985). Arthur Waley, trans., *The Analects of Confucius* (1938).    RODNEY L. TAYLOR

**LUOYANG,** today a small city in northwest Henan Province, China, boasts a history dating back to China's Neolithic era (6000–5000 BCE). A number of ancient imperial capitals have been located in the environs of the present-day city. These include the presumed first capital of the Shang (c. 1523–1027 BCE) and the seats of the Eastern Zhou (771–256 BCE), Eastern Han (25–220), Wei (220–265), Jin (265–420), Northern Wei (386–535), and Sui (581–618) dynasties. Luoyang also served as a secondary capital during the Tang dynasty (618–907).

It was during the Sui dynasty (581–618) that Luoyang first developed as a major commercial center, a process that continued under the Tang. In the Tang period, Nestorian Christianity was introduced at Luoyang by Central Asians and the city was renowned for its imperial library, Buddhist frescoes, and poets. The city declined in significance in the tenth century. From the thirteenth century until 1949 Luoyang served as the provincial capital of Henan. The city was chosen for development as a new industrial city under China's first Five-Year Plan (1953–1957). According to the 1982 census, Luoyang's population was 978,000; its industry includes heavy machinery, glass, ball bearings, tractors, chemicals, cotton textiles, and cement.

ANITA M. ANDREW

**LUTYENS, SIR EDWIN** (1869–1944), famed as the designer of the British imperial capital of New Delhi (built 1912–1931). Lutyens began his career designing romantic English country houses. He subsequently adopted Palladian classicism, with its order, balance, and evocation of past empire, as the style most expressive of the ideals of imperialism. In Delhi he created an axial town plan that joined the symmetries of *beaux arts* design with segregation by rank and income. The centerpiece of the scheme was the viceroy's house, which, though classical in conception and proportions and immense in scale, nevertheless assimilated Indian elements, such as the overhanging cornice, into an integrated synthesis.

[*See also* Delhi.]

Robert Irving, *Indian Summer: Lutyens, Baker, and Imperial Delhi* (1981). Christopher Hussey, *The Life of Sir Edwin Lutyens* (1950).     THOMAS R. METCALF

**LU XIANGSHAN** (1139–1193), also known as Lu Jiuyuan, a Song-dynasty thinker who contributed to the revival of Confucianism in China. A degree holder and minor official, Lu was more famous as a teacher than as a writer. In his lectures Lu emphasized the importance of mind (*xin*) and its identity with principle (*li*). Consequently, Lu has been associated with the intuitive side of Neo-Confucian thought, a side that opposed the views of Lu's contemporary Zhu Xi (1130–1200) and reached fullest expression four centuries later in the thought of Wang Yangming.

[*See also* Neo-Confucianism; Zhu Xi; *and* Wang Yangming.]

Wing-tsit Chan, *A Source Book in Chinese Philosophy* (1963). Wm. Theodore de Bary, Wing-tsit Chan, and Burton Watson, comps., *Sources of Chinese Tradition* (1960).

EDWARD L. FARMER

**LU XUN** (1881–1936), pseudonym of Zhou Shuren, preeminent modern Chinese writer. At his best, with insight and intelligent anger Lu Xun exposed China's condition and the dilemma of intellectuals caught in the demands of life in a backward country in modern times.

Lu Xun's life divides into approximately ten-year segments. In Japan from 1902 to 1909, he turned from medical studies to literature. His translations and journals, ventures with his brother Zhou Zuoren, barely sold, however, and on returning to China, these activities ceased. For nearly a decade he taught biology and then, in Beijing, did administrative work and traditional scholarship. In 1918 Lu Xun published "Diary of a Madman." Eight years of writing and teaching of Chinese literature followed, a period that saw the publication in 1921 of one of his most highly regarded works, *The True Story of Ah Q*. In 1927 Lu Xun moved to Shanghai; by 1929 he was supporting the Communist Party; a year later he helped found its League of Left-Wing Writers. When the Party ordered the league dissolved (1936), Lu Xun formed a splinter group. Reconciliation was achieved two weeks before his death.

Lu Xun's literary output was small compared to his influence—two dozen short stories (collected in *Nahan*, 1923, and *Panghuang*, 1926) and one slim volume each of prose poems, poetry, and retold classical tales. Moreover, in his hands, the satiric essay (*zawen*) attained a perfect, merciless form. Translations, letters, diaries, traditional scholarship, and writings on woodblock engravings make up the larger remainder of his collected works.

In subject, Lu Xun established the major themes of China and the "Chinese character" conceived of as spiritually infirm. In style, he evolved a prose that was terse, abusive, and vivid at a time when wordiness characterized the vernacular movement. The legacy of Lu Xun remains a formidable one, the more difficult to assess because not unflawed. For Communist critics, his elevation beyond criticism has further slowed down evaluation. Lu Xun's followers, however, fell swiftly: by 1957, Feng Xuefeng, Hu Feng, and Xiao Jun had all been purged.

[*See also* Chinese Literature *and* May Fourth Movement.]

Merle Goldman, ed., *Modern Chinese Literature in the May Fourth Era* (1977), pp. 89–102, 161–233. Tsi-an Hsia, *The Gate of Darkness: Studies on the Leftist Literary Movement in China* (1968), pp. 101–162. Leo Oufan Lee, ed., *Lu Hsun and His Legacy* (1985). Lu Xun, *Selected Works of Lu Xun*, 4 vols. (1981).

SHAN CHOU

LY BON (d. 1547; also known as Ly Bi), Vietnamese ruler who led a rebellion against the overlordship of the Chinese Liang dynasty in 541, proclaiming himself Nam De ("southern emperor"). He traced his ancestry to Chinese who had immigrated to Vietnam during the Han dynasty; his family was noted for its military service on the upland frontier. His rebellion was preceded by disappointment at the Liang court and assignment to the Cham frontier. In 545–546, an expedition led by Chen Baxian, eventual founder of the Chen dynasty, defeated Ly Bon in a campaign of four major battles, forcing him to seek refuge in the mountains, where he was betrayed and killed by his tribal allies.

[*See also* Cham.]

Keith W. Taylor, *The Birth of Vietnam* (1983).

KEITH W. TAYLOR

LY CONG UAN (974–1028), Vietnamese king who founded the Ly dynasty, which reigned until 1225. He was educated by Buddhist monks and served as the palace guard commander at the Hoa Lu court. He was made king by general acclamation in 1009 and moved the capital to Thang Long (Hanoi) in 1010. Noted for his erudition and piety as well as for his martial skills, and advised by the famous monk Van Hanh, Ly Cong Van fostered Buddhism as an aspect of royal authority. He was posthumously entitled Ly Thai To.

[*See also* Ly Dynasty.]

KEITH W. TAYLOR

LY DYNASTY, Viet ruling house (1010–1225), founded by Ly Cong Uan, an important official of the Former Le dynasty. Under Ly rule the dynastic institution was first established in Dai Viet and Viet independence of China was reaffirmed.

The early Ly rulers consolidated their authority and strengthened the state through a combination of symbolic acts and practical policies. The capital was moved from Hoa Lu to Thang Long (Hanoi) in 1010, an imperial genealogy was introduced (1026), and the name of the country was changed to Dai Viet (1054). These actions distinguished the Ly house from both the former Viet rulers and the social class from which the Ly originated.

The Ly established a strong, centralized administration based on, but not imitative of, that of China. Officials were selected from the imperial clan and leading families. A temple of literature (*van mieu*) was founded in 1070, and after 1075 some officials were chosen by triennial examinations. The court established taxes (1013), promulgated a penal code (1042), promoted agriculture and trade, and took a leading role in the construction of public works such as roads and dikes.

Ly rule was reinforced by military power. A palace guard of professional soldiers could be augmented, in times of war, by levies on local garrisons, which were controlled by a system of local registration. This system enabled the Ly to overcome internal threats and wage successful campaigns against Champa (1069, 1103) and China (1075–1077).

The Ly period marks the apogee of Buddhist influence at the Viet court. The Ly rulers were avid proponents of the Thien (Dhyana) sect, endowing hundreds of pagodas, sending missions abroad in search of texts, and engaging in Buddhist ceremonies within the confines of the court.

In 1225 the Ly were supplanted by the Tran, who had infiltrated the imperial clan through marriage, but Ly institutions and Ly policies continued for centuries to influence Viet social and political life.

[*See also* Ly Cong Uan; Former Ly Dynasty; Dai Viet; *and* Tran Dynasty.]

Thomas Hodgkin, *Vietnam: The Revolutionary Path* (1981). O. W. Wolters, "Le Van Huu's Treatment of Ly Thanh Ton's Reign (1127–1137)," in *Southeast Asian History and Historiography: Essays Presented to D. G. E. Hall* (1976), pp. 203–226. JAMES M. COYLE

LY NAM DE. *See* Ly Bon.

LY PHAT MA (1000–1054), Vietnamese king. Born in Hoa Lu, he was the eldest son of Ly Cong Uan, whom he succeeded as king in 1028. He established the Ly dynasty on an institutional and intellectual foundation that would endure for nearly two centuries. A devout Buddhist, he patronized the monkhood and built many temples; the famous One-Pillar Pagoda of Hanoi was originally built during his reign. He promulgated the first Vietnamese law book. Many of Vietnam's national spirit cults are associated with or date from his reign. He was posthumously entitled Ly Thai Tong.

KEITH W. TAYLOR

LY PHAT TU was a junior kinsman of Ly Bon. After Ly Bon's death in 547 Ly Phat Tu eventually assumed clan leadership and gained control of the

Vietnamese lands; legends about his defeat of Trieu Quang Phuc, a local Vietnamese hero, echo a concept of talismanic political authority found in pre-Han Vietnamese mythology. His personal name means "son of Buddha," and during his rule an Indian monk, Vinitaruci, arrived from China and founded a new Thien (Chinese, Chan) Buddhist sect. In 602, Ly Phat Tu openly resisted the Sui dynasty. Chinese forces penetrated Vietnam via Yunnan and took him by surprise; he was captured and deported to the Sui capital.

[*See also* Ly Bon.]

Keith W. Taylor, *The Birth of Vietnam* (1983).

KEITH W. TAYLOR

**LY THAI TO.** *See* Ly Cong Uan.

**LY THAI TONG.** *See* Ly Phat Ma.

**LY THUONG KIET** (1019–1105), Vietnamese military ruler. Born in Thang Long (Hanoi), he was a eunuch from childhood. He rose to be commander-in-chief of Vietnamese military forces, gaining fame for capturing the Cham king in 1069. He led Vietnamese forces in the 1075–1077 war with Song China, first leading a preemptive strike that destroyed the Song fleet and briefly captured Nanning, then stopping the subsequent Song invasion at the Cau River; he is credited with writing a famous poem affirming Vietnam's right to be independent of China that dates from this war. Most of his career was spent in Vietnam's southern provinces facing Champa.

KEITH W. TAYLOR

# M

MACAO, Portuguese island colony located on the southern coast of China, lying between the Xi Jiang (West River) and Zhu Jiang (Pearl River) estuaries, approximately one hundred kilometers south of Canton (Guangzhou). The Portuguese name for Macao was derived from the Cantonese names Ngaomen ("gateway to the bay," Aomen in Mandarin) and Ama-ngao ("bay of Ama"). Ama is a goddess of sailors and navigators and is probably a manifestation of the Buddhist bodhisattva of mercy, known in Chinese as Guanyin. A temple dedicated to her at the entrance of the inner harbor to Macao is the oldest building in Macao and probably was standing when the Portuguese first saw Macao around 1555. The first Portuguese settlers arrived in 1557 and named the settlement "Povoação do Nome de Deos na China" ("settlement of the name of God in China"). The settlement was located on a peninsula joined by a narrow isthmus to mainland China. Later, two nearby islands, Taipa and Coloane, were settled.

Originally, trade was the primary livelihood of the colony. When the lucrative trade with Japan ended in 1635, Sino-European trade thrived until the end of the eighteenth century, but the silting up of the harbor and the founding of Hong Kong in the nineteenth century combined to end this trade. During the seventeenth and eighteenth centuries Macao was also important as a base for missionary operations in China and became a refuge during times of persecution as well as a center of the Rites Controversy conflict. Late in the seventeenth century Rome divided the China Mission into the three dioceses of Beijing, Nanjing, and Macao (which included Guangdong and Guangxi provinces). Macao has a history of semiautonomy, rather than independence, from the Chinese mainland government. Negotiations were concluded in 1987 to return Macao to China in December 1999 under the same "one country—two [economic and legal] systems" formula as will be applied to Hong Kong's return to China in 1997. The population of Macao today is estimated at 400,000, of whom 97 percent are Chinese. The colony's chief economic mainstays are tourism and gambling.

[*See also* Jesuits: Jesuits in China.]

C. R. Boxer, *Fidalgoes in the Far East, 1550–1750: Fact and Fancy in the History of Macao* (1948). *Seventeenth Century Macao in Contemporary Documents and Illustrations*, edited by C. R. Boxer (1984). Chang T'ientse, *Sino-Portuguese Trade from 1514 to 1644, a Synthesis of Portuguese and Chinese Sources* (1934).

DAVID E. MUNGELLO

MACAPAGAL, DIOSDADO P. (b. 1910), fifth president of the Philippines (1961–1965).

Macapagal was born in abject poverty on 28 September 1910 in Lubao, Pampanga. As a young boy, he worked in the rice fields during the day and caught frogs in the evening for food. In spite of his modest beginnings, Macapagal was an exceptionally bright student. He went on to the university, where he earned two doctorates, one in law and the other in economics.

Macapagal began his career as a professor at the University of Santo Thomas in Manila. His first government post was with the Department of Foreign Affairs, where he held numerous positions in the law division; there he wrote the Foreign Service Act, which came to be known as the Macapagal Act.

Macapagal was first elected to office in 1949 as a congressman from the province of Pampanga. After serving two terms, he was elected vice-president in 1957. In 1961 he won a four-year term as president. President Macapagal enunciated the doctrine of Asian solutions to Asian problems, which he incorporated into an effort to form a confederation of Malaya, Indonesia, and the Philippines called Maphilindo. Macapagal's goal was to shift Philippine foreign policy from a westward to an eastward orientation. Maphilindo was an attempt to achieve that goal.

Macapagal was unsuccessful in his economic reforms, most notably in failing to solve the rice shortage. He lost his bid for a second term as president to Ferdinand Marcos in 1965.

Diosdado Macapagal, *The Philippines Turns East* (1966).

DAVID R. CLAUSSENIUS

**MACARTHUR, DOUGLAS A.** (1880–1964), American military leader who played a prominent role in Asian affairs before, during, and after World War II. MacArthur was born on an army post in Little Rock, Arkansas, on 26 January 1880. His father, Arthur MacArthur II, was a career army officer who rose to the rank of lieutenant-general. The younger MacArthur was extremely close to his mother, who worked actively to advance his career.

MacArthur's assignment after his graduation from West Point in 1903 was to the Philippines, his first contact with Asia. His tours of duty in the Philippines and Japan from 1903 to 1906 convinced him of the importance of Asia to the United States. He first achieved wide public notice during World War I through his flamboyant personal style, his conspicuous gallantry under fire, and his qualities of leadership. His service in France won him the reputation of being the most brilliant young officer in the US Army.

After three years (1919–1922) as superintendent of the US Military Academy at West Point, MacArthur served a three-year tour of duty in the Philippines. After his return he became in 1927 the president of the US committee for the Olympic games at Antwerp and thereafter went to the Philippines for another two-year tour of duty, returning to become chief of staff of the army. In this position he was responsible for the breaking up of the Depression-era "bonus army," which had marched on Washington in 1932 to demand the payment of a bonus for service in World War I. His action resulted in a storm of criticism and was one of the low points of his career.

MacArthur's term as chief of staff ended in 1935, and he was then appointed, as a US major general, to be military adviser to the Philippines, then preparing for independence. Later he was concurrently made commander of US Army forces in the Far East. He was responsible for the defense of the Philippines

when war broke out on 8 December 1941. The Filipino-American forces under his command were unable to resist the Japanese effectively, but their tenacious defense of Bataan stirred American emotions. MacArthur was ordered by President Franklin Roosevelt to proceed to Australia to take command of a new Southwest Pacific theater of war. He made a difficult escape with his wife, young son, and a small group of officers.

In late 1942 his forces began a counterattack in New Guinea that led northward through the southwest Pacific to the eventual counterinvasion of the Philippines in the fall of 1944. This long campaign was the highpoint of MacArthur's military career.

When the war came to an end MacArthur was appointed Supreme Commander for the Allied Powers (SCAP), in charge of directing the Occupation of Japan. Under his command many changes were initiated that the Japanese people welcomed and adopted as their own.

In late June 1950 the Korean War broke out. The US government recommended that the United Nations assume responsibility for dealing with this breach of the peace and the UN acted to do so. Because the nearest sizable body of armed forces was in Japan under his command, MacArthur was named commander of what became the UN forces in Korea. In the opening weeks of the war the UN forces were almost driven from the peninsula, but in a brilliant tactical maneuver MacArthur's forces landed at Inch'ŏn, far behind the North Korean front line, and succeeded in reversing the military situation. As his armies impetuously moved north to the Manchurian border, the People's Republic of China intervened militarily.

This development and the resulting military setback for the UN forces led MacArthur to demand that he be permitted to attack military bases on Chinese territory. His demand gained considerable political support in the US and led to a confrontation, MacArthur standing alone against the Joint Chiefs of Staff, his immediate superiors, and President Truman, his commander in chief. The result was that in April 1951 President Truman relieved him of his command of both the UN forces in Korea and of the Occupation of Japan.

MacArthur returned to a hero's welcome that led eventually to an abortive move to make him the Republican nominee for president in 1952. Despite an initially enthusiastic public reception, MacArthur soon fell into the relative obscurity of retirement. He died in Washington, D.C., of acute liver and kidney failure on 5 April 1964 and was buried in the MacArthur Memorial in Norfolk, Virginia, his mother's home city.

[*See also* World War II in Asia; Occupation of Japan; *and* Korean War.]

Trumbull Higgins, *Korea and the Fall of MacArthur* (1960). D. Clayton James, *The Years of MacArthur*, 2 vols. (1970–1975). William Manchester, *American Caesar* (1978).                                    JOHN M. MAKI

## MACAULAY, THOMAS BABINGTON (Lord Macaulay; 1800–1859), law member, Government of India (1834–1838); renowned essayist and writer. After emerging from private schools and Trinity College, Cambridge (fellow, 1824), he entered the British House of Commons (1830). As member on the Board of Control (1832; secretary, 1833), his speech helped win passage of the 1833 Charter Renewal Act. Like the governor-general (Lord Bentinck) and his brother-in-law (the chief secretary to the Government, Sir Charles Trevelyan, with whom he lived in India), he blended evangelical and utilitarian ideals. On the Law Commission, he was largely responsible for the Code of Criminal Procedure and the Penal Code. His famous *Minute on Education*, reflecting the views of Bentinck and Trevelyan, is largely misunderstood. Instead of indicating a despotic imposition of English education (and Western learning) upon hapless subjects, this essay was, as research now shows, a response to pressures of an elite urban gentry in India. Classic essays on Sir Robert Clive and Warren Hastings won him further acclaim. He helped to open entry to the Indian Civil Service by competitive examination.

[*See also* Indian Administrative Service *and* Bentinck, William Cavendish.]

John Clive, *Macaulay: The Shaping of the Historian* (1973). C. D. Dharkar, ed., *Lord Macaulay's Legislative Minutes* (1946).              ROBERT E. FRYKENBERG

## MAC DANG DUNG (d. 1541), first emperor of Vietnam's Mac dynasty (r. 1527–1529). Called to suppress revolts against the weakening Le dynasty, Mac Dang Dung was able to defeat the rebels while consolidating his own power. In 1527 he forced the abdication of the reigning Le monarch and proclaimed himself emperor, ruling for two years before abdicating in favor of his son, Mac Dang Doanh (r. 1530–1540), but continuing to direct policy. The Mac were continually plagued by resistance from Le supporters. These loyalists applied to the Ming dynasty for aid, but Mac Dang Dung was able to prevent Chinese intervention by ceding portions of Vietnamese territory in 1540. [*See also* Mac Dynasty.]
                                    BRUCE M. LOCKHART

## MAC DYNASTY, rulers of the heartland of Dai Viet (1527–1592), regarded as usurpers by many contemporaries and by most subsequent Viet historians.

Mac power was established by Mac Dang Dung, a descendant of the illustrious Tran-period official Mac Dinh Chi. Dang Dung entered the Le court as a military official in the 1500s, survived the factional struggles of the 1510s, and gradually became powerful enough to restore order to Dai Viet, depose the last two Le rulers, and proclaim himself emperor (1527). In 1530 he abdicated in favor of his eldest son Dang Doanh (r. 1530–1540) but continued to direct policy as "senior emperor" (*thai thuong hoang*) until his death in 1541.

The Mac coup was bitterly resented by Le officials, many of whom retired and refused to serve the Mac or took up arms against them. Out of their localized uprisings developed a movement to restore the Le dynasty, which gained control of Nghe An and Thanh Hoa provinces in the 1540s.

Most of the Viet, including most of the literati, acquiesced in Mac rule, probably because the Mac were able to restore a measure of peace and prosperity to the country. Mac Dang Dung and his successors were firmly committed to the principles of government espoused by the preceding dynasty. Civil service examinations were renewed, Le legal and administrative codes were reissued, and the historical records of the Le were compiled. A threatened Ming intervention was averted by territorial and diplomatic concessions, and the Mac received Chinese recognition in 1540.

The Mac dynasty was brought down by a combination of internal weakness and external attack. Factional struggles began during the reign of Mac Phuc Hai (1540–1546) and became severe during the minorities of Mac Phuc Nguyen (r. 1546–1561) and Mac Mau Hop (r. 1561–1592). The losers in these struggles frequently joined the expanding Le restoration movement, which by 1560 had reduced Mac control to the capital and the delta lowlands. Mac forces made frequent attacks on restorationist bases in Thanh Hoa and Nghe An, notably between 1570 and 1581, but after 1583 Mac strategy became purely defensive.

The Le restoration forces overran the delta and captured Thang Long in 1592. Mau Hop and his son

TABLE 1.  *Rulers of the Mac Dynasty*

| RULER | REIGN DATES |
|---|---|
| 1. Mac Dang Dung | 1527–1530 |
| 2. Mac Dang Doanh | 1530–1540 |
| 3. Mac Phuc Hai | 1540–1546 |
| 4. Mac Phuc Nguyen | 1546–1561 |
| 5. Mac Mau Hop | 1561–1592 |
| 6. Mac Toan | 1592–1593 |
| 7. Mac Kinh Chi* | 1592–1593 |
| 8. Mac Kinh Cung* | 1592–1625 |
| 9. Mac Kinh Khoan* | 1623–1638 |
| 10. Mac Kinh Vu* | 1638–1677 |

*Mac "pretenders."

Mac Toan were put to death, and the remaining Mac partisans gradually withdrew from the delta into the surrounding highlands. There, in Thai Nguyen and Cao Bang provinces, collateral descendants of the main Mac line adopted reign titles and with Chinese support resisted Le/Trinh pressure until being driven out of Cao Bang in 1677.

[*See also* Mac Dang Dung; Le Dynasties; Nguyen Kim; Trinh Lords; *and* Trinh Kiem.]

Thomas Hodgkin, *Vietnam: The Revolutionary Path* (1981). J. Whitmore, "Mac Dang Dung," in *Dictionary of Ming Biography,* edited by L. Carrington Goodrich (1976).                                JAMES M. COYLE

MADHYA PRADESH, with an area of 443,459 square kilometers, is the largest of the thirty-one states and territories forming the Indian Union. It is the sixth largest in terms of population, which was 52,138,467 in 1981. The low density of population is due to the state's terrain, extensive forests, and poor communications. Madhya Pradesh is situated in central India. Its hilly backbone, which includes the Vindhya and Satpura ranges, forms a watershed for the Narmada and Mahanadi rivers, and for tributaries of the Ganges, Godavari, Jamuna and Tapti river systems. The state's boundaries, which it shares with seven other states, are irregular for linguistic or historical reasons. The main language of the state is Hindi.

As for political institutions, Madhya Pradesh has a single chamber legislature, or Vidhan Sabha, of 320 members. Its chief minister and cabinet are drawn from the majority party, while the government of India appoints the governor. The state is divided into forty-five administrative districts, grouped into eleven divisions. The upper ranks of administration are staffed by the centrally recruited Indian Administrative and Police Services; a state-recruited civil service staffs the middle and lower ranks. The capital city is Bhopal and the High Court is located in Jabalpur.

In 1956 various territories united to form the state of Madhya Pradesh. These territories were (1) Mahakoshal, named after Dakshin Kosala, the fourth-century kingdom in the locality; (2) Madhya Bharat, or Central India, a union of princely states consisting of Gwalior, Indore, and their satellites, formed in 1948; (3) Vindhya Pradesh, after the Vindhya Range, comprised of princely states in the regions of Bundelkhand, Baghelkhand, and Chota Nagpur; and (4) the former Muslim state of Bhopal. In 1955 the States Reorganisation Commission recommended the union of these four territories, and Madhya Pradesh came into being on 1 November 1956.

Madhya Pradesh has faced serious social and economic problems since its inception. Its *per capita* income, which is less than the national figure, was static between 1971 and 1981. More than half the population lives below the poverty line; 80 percent live in the countryside. Poor and largely illiterate tribals and "scheduled" castes form one third of the population. The state's economy is mainly agricultural, much of it at the subsistence level. Poor communications inhibit development; forty of the forty-five districts are industrially backward.

The government is attempting to resolve these problems. Basing its strategy on the state's abundant forest, mineral, and water resources, it has initiated many projects and encouraged private investment. Consequently, the latter is increasing slowly and some progress is noticeable in the public sector—in irrigation and power generation and in the field of social welfare. The government is also promoting cultural activities and encouraging tourism around historical sites at Khajuraho, Sanchi, Mandu and elsewhere. Backwardness and development thus form contrasting aspects of life in contemporary Madhya Pradesh.

[*See also* Bhopal; Indore; Sanchi; *and* Princely States.]

D. Moraes, *Answered by Flutes: Reflections from Madhya Pradesh* (1983). *Times of India Directory and Year Book, 1983* (1983). W. Wilcox, "Madhya Pradesh," in *State Politics in India,* edited by M. Weiner (1968).

DAVID BAKER

MADIUN, town and residency in East Java. Part of the kingdom of Mataram during the sixteenth through the eighteenth century, it came under Dutch sovereignty in 1830. In 1948 tension between West Javanese troops of the Siliwangi Division, associated with the Mohammad Hatta government, and local left-wing troops led to clashes culminating in the Madiun Affair, in which local Communist Party (PKI) supporters took over the town and announced the formation of a new national-front government. The revolt was joined by PKI leaders and was accompanied by clashes between *santri* (those who adhere more or less to Islamic principles) and *abangan* (those only nominally affiliated with Islam) in rural areas. It was crushed by government troops by November 1948.

[*See also* Partai Komunis Indonesia.]

David Charles Anderson, "The Military Aspects of the Madiun Affair," *Indonesia* 21 (1976): 1–63.

ROBERT B. CRIBB

**MADRAS**, India's fourth-largest city, with a population of 3,276,622 in 1981, was the first of the great Indo-British port cities to be founded by the British East India Company. From a modest start in 1639 as a small trading outpost called Fort Saint George, Madras grew in size and importance as British colonial political and economic power extended itself throughout South India during the eighteenth and nineteenth centuries. For over one hundred fifty years, until after India's independence in 1947, Madras functioned as the administrative and commercial capital of the vast Madras Presidency.

Geographically, the choice of Madras for a seaport defied common sense. Its straight, sandy, surf-beaten beach offered no natural refuge for ships. Not until 1911 was an artificial harbor built that was able to withstand the violent monsoon storms. Other natural deficiencies of the site limited Madras's growth relative to that of Calcutta and Bombay. It was not linked to the interior of the peninsula by land or water routes of any importance. With the exception of textiles, its hinterland produced few surplus agricultural or manufactured goods to augment its trade. Maintaining an adequate fresh water supply has been a recurring problem in the city. The lack of abundant local sources of energy delayed its industrial development. Beginning in the late nineteenth century, however, these geographical shortcomings were partly surmounted by the construction of a southern railroad network with its headquarters in Madras.

Commerce and politics, not geography, have thus been the deciding factors in the history at Madras.

English traders were drawn to the area by the flourishing local textile industry and by political concessions made to the East India Company by local rulers. Overseas trade remained its primary function until the late eighteenth century, when textile production declined in the wake of the devastating Carnatic Wars. The aggressive marketing of British cloth in India further impaired the local textile industry and the prosperity of the port, until a demand for agricultural exports brought renewed activity after 1850.

As British power emerged victorious from the complex political struggles of eighteenth-century South India, politics replaced commerce as the chief activity of Madras. The seat of the colonial government of British South India, Madras's influence radiated throughout the region. Its bureaucracy, courts, colleges, and schools attracted migrants to the city and introduced British cultural and political values into South Indian society.

In the late nineteenth century, Madras became one of the active centers of Indian nationalist sentiment. A parallel movement of Tamil cultural nationalism had its early roots in the city as well, reflecting Madras's role as the capital of the Dravidian-speaking region of India. Now the capital of the state of Tamil Nadu, created from the Tamil-speaking part of the old Madras Presidency, Madras remains the ranking metropolis of southern India. It has the most active port of the region, continues as its financial and commercial hub, supports a growing number of modern industries, and with its vigorous colleges, press, film industry, and institutions for the arts is the cultural center for much of South India today.

[*See also* Tamil Nadu; East India Company; *and* Dravidian Movement.]

Susan J. Lewandowski, "Urban Growth and Municipal Development in the Colonial City of Madras, 1860–1900," *Journal of Asian Studies* 34 (1975): 341–360. Susan M. Neild, "Colonial Urbanism: The Development of Madras City in the Eighteenth and Nineteenth Centuries," *Modern Asian Studies* 13 (1979):217–246. N. S. Ramaswami, *The Founding of Madras* (1977). C. S. Srinivasachari, *History of the City of Madras* (1939).

SUSAN NEILD BASU

**MADRASA**, Arabic term denoting an Islamic religious college. Originating in eastern Iran in the tenth century, the *madrasa* began to spread to most parts of the Islamic world in the late eleventh century. Sometimes part of a mosque complex, and often designed as a group of student cells and recitation rooms around a square or rectangular courtyard, the *madrasa* usually had Islamic law at the center of its curriculum. Government-supported modern educational systems supplanted *madrasas* supported by pious endowments in most countries in the nineteenth and twentieth centuries. [*See also* Education: Education in Iran and Central Asia.]

RICHARD W. BULLIET

**MA DUANLIN**, a Chinese scholar who lived during the period of transition between the end of the Song (960–1279) and the beginning of the Yuan dynasty (1279–1368), completed the *Wenxian tongkao (Ethnography of the Peoples outside China)* in 1224. This encyclopedia was based on the highly respected eighth-century Tang encyclopedia *Tongdian* of Du You (735–812), but it added a great deal of additional and updated material collected by Ma Duanlin. His is the most detailed Chinese account of early Southeast Asia and may even contain information that the author himself collected on travels in the Vietnamese, Cham, and Khmer realms. His encyclopedia frequently includes information that was omitted from the *Songshi (History of the Song)*. In his view the Chinese court's contact with Southeast Asian countries was largely for the purpose of commerce and did not have direct political consequences.

KENNETH R. HALL

**MADURA**, island in Indonesia off the northeast coast of Java, opposite Surabaya. It has an area of 2,113 square miles and a population of about 2.5 million.

The history of Madura is inextricably linked with that of Central and East Java. From at least the thirteenth century, Central Javanese kingdoms controlled the island, and Javanese princes were given appanages there. In the course of extending their control over the north coast of Java in the seventeenth century, the Dutch came to dominate Madura; and in 1885 they established a single residency to administer it. It was integrated into the Indonesian Republic in 1949.

[*See also* Indonesia, Republic of *and* Java.]

M. C. Ricklefs, *A History of Modern Indonesia* (1981).

DAVID K. WYATT

**MADURAI.** Noted by the geographer Ptolemy and featured in the Tamil epic *Silappadikaram*, Madurai is the oldest enduring and stable South Indian urban habitat. Together with its extensive hinterland, the city has survived into the twentieth century as a major regional nexus of political, cultural, religious, and economic life.

This urban complex has endured numerous historical transformations, including recent ones linked to modern bureaucratic and educational institutions, while remaining the quintessential seat of Tamil political and social culture. This may be attributed, in part, to its location in what may be India's only cultural cul-de-sac. Located approximately 120 miles north of the tip of India, Madurai is the last in a series of urban complexes that, historically, have been situated along the inland, and largely semiarid, spine of southern India. This location, at the southward narrowing tip of India, has meant that there have been no major regional urban centers south, east, or west of Madurai. As a result, Madurai has remained largely uncontested as an attractive place for the development of synthetic ideologies that linked urban and rural communities, Dravidian and Aryan cultures, clan and caste social organization, and a variety of major linguistic communities. The center of Madurai's traditional sociopolitical culture is the renowned fourteen-acre Pandya temple of the goddess Minakshi, to which pilgrims come from all over India and the world.

[*See also* Tamil Nadu.]

J. Nelson, *The Madura Country* (1860).

CAROL APPADURAI BRECKENRIDGE

**MAEDA**, an important *tozama* daimyo family of the Tokugawa period (1600–1868) of Japanese history. The feudal domain of the Maeda, with an assessed productivity of more than one million *koku* (measures of rice) and comprising much of Kaga, Noto (both in modern Ishikawa Prefecture), and Etchū (modern Toyama Prefecture) provinces, was the largest in Japan.

Rising from obscure origins in central Honshu, Maeda Toshiie (1538–1599) established the family's position through ties to Oda Nobunaga, Toyotomi Hideyoshi, and Tokugawa Ieyasu. His son Toshinaga (1562–1614) fought with Ieyasu at the Battle of Sekigahara (1600), built Kanazawa Castle, and developed the castle town (*jōkamachi*) surrounding it. Toshitsune (1593–1658) participated in the Osaka Campaign (1615) and established branch domains (*shihan*) at Daishōji and Toyama.

The Maeda, especially the fourth daimyo, Tsunanori (1643–1724), won fame as able administrators who consolidated control over their retainers, employed such famous Confucian scholar-advisers as Kinoshita Jun'an (1621–1698), and established poorhouses (1670). They also patronized *nō* theater, the tea ceremony, and Kutani porcelains, and they maintained Kenrokuen, one of the three most famous examples of Tokugawa-period gardens.

As *tozama* daimyo, they were viewed with suspicion by the shogunate and thus were excluded from national politics. Nevertheless, they remained loyal to the Tokugawa until 1868.

[*See also* Tokugawa Period *and* Tozama Daimyo.]

James McClain, *Kanazawa: A Seventeenth-Century Japanese Castle Town* (1982).　RONALD J. DICENZO

MAGADHA. The kingdom of Magadha was one of sixteen ancient North Indian states—both monarchies and republics—traditionally mentioned in Buddhist sources. Its core area was located in what is now Bihar, and was the site of many events in the Buddha's life. Strategically situated along the middle Ganges, it became the heartland of a number of kingdoms from the sixth century BCE to the eighth century CE.

The lists of dynasties and rulers of Magadha may be found in Buddhist as well as in Brahmanical and Jain sources, but they vary considerably from one text to another. By all accounts, however, the first famous king of Magadha was Bimbisara (c. 546–c. 494 BCE), a contemporary and supporter of the Buddha. His capital was at Rajagriha (modern-day Rajgir). He consolidated his kingdom by matrimonial alliances with nearby Kosala and Vaishali and by annexing the territory of the Angas (in present-day Bengal). He ushered in a period of efficient administration, lucrative trade up and down the Ganges, and general prosperity. [*See* Bimbisara.]

Bimbisara was deposed and put to death by his son Ajatashatru (c. 498–c. 462 BCE), who is also well known in Buddhist literature, and who further expanded the kingdom by conquering territories to the west and to the north. As a result, Magadha clearly became the most powerful kingdom in northern India. Its ascendancy and absorption of several small republican states, moreover, marked a final victory in this area for the monarchical system.

Initially hostile to the Buddha, Ajatashatru eventually came to give important support and royal patronage to the early Buddhist community at a crucial time in its development. But he too was murdered by his own son, the second victim in what some scholars have referred to as the parricidal tradition of this particular dynasty.

The number and names of the subsequent kings in this line—also victims of parricide—vary considerably from one source to the next. The last of them, however, was deposed in 414 BCE in a popular uprising led by Shishunaga, who founded a new dynasty. His son, Kalashoka, whose identity is a matter of much scholarly debate, reigned from about 396 to about 368 BCE and is said to have moved the capital to Pataliputra (modern-day Patna) on the Ganges. [*See* Pataliputra.] The Shishunagas, however, were a short-lived dynasty, and soon gave place to the even shorter-lived line of the Nandas (ruled c. 346–c. 324 BCE), the last of whom was overthrown by Chandragupta (c. 324–c. 300 BCE), the founder of the Maurya empire.

With Chandragupta, the glories of Magadha became pronounced. His capital at Pataliputra was visited by ambassadors from abroad (such as the Greek envoy Megasthenes) and was famous as one of the great cities of the ancient world. His empire extended as far as Afghanistan to the west and the Deccan to the south, and, under his son Bindusara (c. 300–c. 272 BCE) and grandson Ashoka (c. 272–c. 232 BCE), it extended over virtually the entire Indian subcontinent. [*See* Chandragupta Maurya *and* Ashoka.]

With Ashoka's death, however, the decline of the Maurya empire began; the empire eventually broke up in approximately 187 BCE. Nevertheless, after several centuries the land of Magadha again became the home of another great empire—that of the Guptas, whose founder, Chandragupta I, acceded to the throne about 320 CE and brought unity and a classical age of culture to North India that lasted until the mid-sixth century.

Thereafter the glory of Magadha faded, though a lesser Gupta dynasty continued to rule in a much reduced Magadhan kingdom until about 800.

[*See also* Buddhism: An Overview; Maurya Empire; *and* Gupta Empire.]

B. C. Law, *The Magadhas in Ancient India* (1946). Radhakumud Mukerji, "Rise of Magadhan Imperialism," in *History and Culture of the Indian People*, vol. 2, *The Age of Imperial Unity* (1951).　JOHN S. STRONG

MAGARS, a distinct ethnic Mongoloid group of Nepal, who speak a dialect of their own of Tibeto-Burman extraction and practice animism. They inhabit mainly the warmer central hills between the Tanhun and Palpa districts of Nepal and subsist primarily through agriculture. Magars today are considered the most hinduized of Nepal's ethnic groups. Many Thakuri high castes seem to have a Magar ancestral background, according to a widely prevailing belief in Nepal. They have made themselves known to the world as Gurkha soldiers in the British, Indian and Nepali army. Socially, they are given a lower caste status by the Hindus.

[*See also* Gurkhas.]

John T. Hitchcock, *The Magars of Banyan Hill* (1966). Francis Tuker, *Gorkha: The Story of the Gorkhas of Nepal* (1957).                    PRAYAG RAJ SHARMA

MAGATAMA are comma-shaped, polished beads used in necklaces of the Yayoi (200 BCE–300 CE) and Tumuli (300–700) periods in Japan. The beads were modeled on the boar-tusk jewelry of the Jōmon age (10,000–200 BCE). In the Yayoi era, the beads' shape was standardized and new materials, notably glass, stone, and jade, were employed. The number of jade beads increased markedly around 500 CE, when local chieftains used the necklaces to symbolize their rank. The political and religious significance of *magatama* is verified by ancient myths: the "gems of Yasaka" were given to the sun goddess, Amaterasu, by her fun-loving brother Susano-o no Mikoto. *Magatama* are one of the three treasures of the imperial family, along with the mirror and the sword.

[*See also* Yayoi.]

George Sansom, *Japan, A Short Cultural History* (1958).                    WAYNE FARRIS

MAGELLAN, FERDINAND (Portuguese, Fernão de Magalhães), Portuguese mariner and navigator. He was born in Sabrosa, Oporto, Portugal in 1480, of noble lineage. Magellan persuaded Charles I of Spain to mount an expedition to reach the Spice Islands by sailing westward and set sail on 20 September 1519 with 265 men and five ships. Having reached the Pacific through what is now the Strait of Magellan, the fleet eventually attained the Marianas and, on 16 March 1521, the Philippines. Magellan died there on 27 April 1521 in the Battle of Mactan while trying to impose Spanish sovereignty on the chieftain Lapulapu. One ship and eighteen men, having circumnavigated the globe, reached Spain on 6 September 1522 with a rich cargo from the Spice Islands.

F. H. H. Guillemard, *The Life of Ferdinand Magellan and the First Circumnavigation of the Globe* (1890; reprint, 1971). Antonio Pigafetta, *Magellan's Voyage, A Narrative Account of the First Circumnavigation*, 2 vols., translated and edited by R. A. Skelton (1969).

BERNARDITA REYES CHURCHILL

MAGSAYSAY, RAMON (1907–1957), president of the Philippines (1953–1957) who ended the Huk insurgency and attempted economic and social reform.

Magsaysay was born to a poor family on 31 August 1907 in Zambeles province. He worked his way through the University of the Philippines and Jose Rizal College, graduating in 1933. He joined a transportation company and rose from a mechanic to a branch manager by the outbreak of World War II in 1941. He fought in the defense against the Japanese invasion, then returned to his home province to join the anti-Japanese guerrilla movement, becoming a successful local commander. On the return of US forces, he was named military governor of Zambeles. With the restoration of civil rule, he won a congressional seat as a member of the Liberal Party and served two terms (1946–1950). President Elpidio Quirino appointed him secretary of defense in 1950, and with much American aid and advice he worked to combat the antigovernment Huk insurgency. By reforming the army to consciousness of its civic responsibilities and by offering land to insurgents who surrendered, he quelled the Huk threat within three years.

Charging the government with corruption and obstruction, Magsaysay resigned in 1953, joined the Nacionalista Party, and contested the presidency in the 1953 elections. He won a four-year term from December 1953. His success at eliminating the Huks was capped with the surrender of their leader, Luis Taruc, in May 1954. Magsaysay continued, however, to work for major reforms, most notably in land distribution and political institutions. He won enormous personal popularity but could not overcome the bitter resistance of entrenched political factions and economic interests, who saw reform as a threat to their domination. He was in the process of building a new coalition of younger, reform-minded politicians when he suddenly died in an airplane crash as he was returning from Cebu to Manila on 17 March 1957. He was succeeded by Vice President Carlos Garcia.

Magsaysay is remembered as a staunchly pro-American, anticommunist reformist whose popularity was based on a popular feeling that he was sincerely working for the interests of ordinary Filipinos.

[See also Huk; Nacionalista Party; Taruc, Luis; Garcia, Carlos P.; and Philippines.]

Carlos P. Romulo and Marvin M. Gray, *The Magsaysay Story* (1956). Alvin H. Scaff, *The Philippine Answer to Communism* (1955). Frances L. Starner, *Magsaysáy and the Philippine Peasantry: The Agrarian Impact on Philippine Politics, 1953–1956* (1961).

DAVID K. WYATT

MAHABALIPURAM (Mamallapuram), a southeast Indian seaport lying some fifty miles south of Madras, is renowned for the monolithic temple complex that dominates its shore. The so-called Seven Pagodas, or *rathas,* were commissioned by the Pallava ruler and founder of Mahabalipuram, Narasimhavarman (c. 625–645 CE), and are recognized as a major turning point in the development of South Indian art and architecture. In addition to the *rathas,* which are hewn from massive boulders, the site also contains several relief sculptures in stone, the *pièce de résistance* being a depiction of the descent of the

Ganges River from heaven. Mahabalipuram flourished as a naval and maritime trading port during both the Pallava and Chola dynasties.

[See also Architecture: South Asian Architecture.]

G. Jouveau-Durbreuil, *Pallava Antiquities,* 2 vols. (1916–1918).
STUART W. SMITHERS

MAHABANDULA (c. 1780–1825), Burmese general and minister. U Yit served first as a minor court factotum, then was titled and appointed governor of Alon by Bodawhpaya (1782–1819). Bagyidaw (1819–1837) appointed him a minister *(wun-gyi)* in 1819 with the honorific title Mahabandula. From that time, he served aggressively as the Burmese commander on the frontier with the British East India Company and played an important role in the events leading to the First Anglo-Burmese War (1824–1826). He was hurriedly recalled from the frontier to deal with the British landing at Rangoon in May 1824, but his death by enemy fire on 1 April 1825 ended serious Burmese military resistance and led to the opening of negotiations in October.

[See also Anglo-Burmese Wars.]

WILLIAM J. KOENIG

FIGURE 1. *View of the Temple Complex, Mahabalipuram.*

MAHABHARATA, the great Sanskrit epic of war, composed between 400 BCE and 400 CE. Outside its kernel story of internecine war, the *Mahabharata* is difficult to summarize. The work has its stylistic and mythological roots in the *Rig Veda* and its narrative sources are probably oral tales of a tribal war fought in the Punjab early in the first millennium BCE. As the tradition was taken over by professional storytellers and intellectuals, many sorts of legend, myth, and speculative thought, such as the *Bhagavad Gita,* were added. In its present form it is a rich encyclopedia of ancient India culture consisting of over one hundred thousand verses divided into eighteen books. Evident within its multiple layers are historical changes as well as conceptual conflicts between competing sets of social values—warrior ethics versus priestly morality, Vedic sacrifical cults versus sectarian devotional religion, and so forth.

The epic's main action revolves around a feud of succession involving descendants of the legendary king Bharata—the five sons of Pandu and their cousins, Dhritarashtra's hundred sons. The feud itself is based on a series of genealogical complications involving divine interventions. Dhritarashtra is born blind and his younger brother Pandu succeeds to the throne of Kurukshetra, an ancient kingdom in the western part of the Ganges River valley. But Pandu suffers a curse, renounces the throne, and retires to the forest with his family. Dhritarashtra assumes the regency for his eldest nephew, Yudhishthira, but his own eldest son, Duryodhana, covets the throne and in various episodes attempts to assassinate his cousins or otherwise frustrate their rights. After thirteen years of exile imposed on them for Yudhishthira's total defeat in a crooked ritual dice game, the Pandavas return to reclaim their kingdom. Duryodhana's refusal makes war inevitable. The eighteen-day-long battle and concomitant philosophizing by various teachers and battle leaders takes up the bulk of the epic. The brutality of warfare is diffused by the symbolization of the characters as universal forces of order (*dharma*) and chaos; the battle ends with the triumph of order over chaos, of the Pandavas over the Kauravas. Like the *Ramayana*, the *Mahabharata* has deeply influenced the religious and cultural life of the whole Indian subcontinent and much of the rest of South and Southeast Asia.

[*See also* Ramayana; Bhagavad Gita; *and* Vedas.]

Alf Hiltebeitel, *The Ritual of Battle: Krishna in the Mahabharata* (1976). *The Mahabharata*, translated by P. C. Roy (1927–1932). *The Mahābhārata*, books 1–5, vols. 1–3, edited and translated by J. A. B. van Buitenen (1973–1978). A Barend van Nooten, *The Mahabharata, Twanye's World Author's Series* (1971).

BARBARA STOLER MILLER

## MAHADAMMAYAZADIPATHI

**MAHADAMMAYAZADIPATHI** (also known as Mahadhammarajadhipati), last king of the Toungoo dynasty of Ava in Burma (r. 1733–1752).

Mahadammayazadipathi is generally regarded as a weak and ineffective king, but at the age of eighteen he inherited from his father a kingdom almost doomed by institutional decline. Fierce factionalism at court, serious slippage of the state's labor resources, growing regionalism especially on the part of the Mon of the coast, and foreign dangers made his survival for two decades a minor miracle. The combination of Mon rebellion and Manipuri raids paralyzed the court, and the capital and dynasty fell to the Mon in April 1752.

[*See also* Ava; Burma; Mon; *and* Pegu.]

G. E. Harvey, *A History of Burma from the Earliest Times* (1925; reprint, 1967). Victor B. Lieberman, *Burmese Administrative Cycles: Anarchy and Conquest, c. 1580–1760* (1984).       DAVID K. WYATT

**MA HAIDE.** *See* Hatem, George.

**MAHA-MEGHAVAHANA DYNASTY.** During the first century BCE in India, much of Orissa was ruled by kings of the Maha-Meghavahana line of the Chedi clan. Commonly called the Chedi dynasty, it is known almost exclusively from King Kharavela, who probably ruled during the second half of the first century BCE. His career, outlined in a lengthy inscription at Khandagiri, near Bhubaneshwar, included military forays into western India and the South, but he probably did not maintain territory beyond Orissa. Kharavela was a Jain but claimed tolerance of all religions, and provided funds for the excavation of rock-cut shrines at Khandagiri.

[*See also* Orissa.]

K. C. Panigrahi, *History of Orissa: Hindu Period* (1981). N. K. Sahu, ed., *Utkal University History of Orissa*, vol. I (1964).       FREDERICK M. ASHER

**MAHARASHTRA,** Indian state with an area of 307,762 square kilometers and a 1981 population of 62.8 million. It is a part of the geological division of India called the Deccan. Its antiquity goes back to the third century BCE. A fourth-century Sri Lankan Pali chronicle mentions it as Maharatta, a Prakrit form of Maharashtra; in the seventh century the Chinese pilgrim Xuanzang refers to it as Moheluocha, and the Aihole (Bijapur) inscription of the Badami Chalukya king Pulkeshin II specifically refers to it. Its origin is attributed to its early inhabitants, Rattas or Rashtrikas, and to its language, Maharashtri-Prakrit, from which the Marathi language of its people is evolved and in which its major work *Jnaneshwari* (thirteenth century) was composed. It was ruled by Hindu rulers such as the Satavahanas (second century BCE to second century CE), Vakatakas (third to sixth century CE), Badami Chalukyas (sixth to eighth century), Rashtrakutas (eighth to tenth century), Kalyani Chalukyas (ninth to twelfth century), and Yadavas (twelfth to thirteenth century), who were followed by Muslim rulers of the Deccan sultanates (fourteenth to seventeenth century).

Maharashtra's cultural unity was earlier brought about through the Marathi language and literature and the *bhakti* movement of the Varakari Sampradaya. The cultural and religious heritage of saints Jnaneshwar, Namdev, Eknath, Tukaram, and Ramdas is still cherished. This cultural unity paved the way for political unity under the Maratha leader Shivaji in the mid-seventeenth century. [*See also* Shivaji.] The expansion of Maratha power in the eighteenth century carried the culture of Maharashtra to occupied regions in North and South India. Under the British, central Maharashtra became a part of the Bombay Presidency, whereas the other two Marathi areas, Marathwada and Vidarbha, remained under Hyderabad State and Central Provinces, respectively. Maharashtra as a full-fledged cultural and political entity, including Desh, Konkan, Marathwada, and Vidarbha, came into existence only on 1 May 1960.

Maharashtra is triangular in shape and is bounded by the Arabian Sea to the west, Madhya Pradesh and Gujarat states to the north, Andhra Pradesh, Karnataka, Goa, and a part of Madhya Pradesh to the east. It represents 10 percent of the area and 9 percent of the population of India. It has thirty districts distributed over seven divisions with Bombay as its capital. It has twenty-nine cities with a population greater than 100,000; 35 percent of the state's population is urban. It is foremost in the production of oilseeds, cotton, and sugarcane, and in the textile industry. Its Chanda teak forests are the best in India. Economically it is the most advanced state, owing to Bombay's location within its borders, yet its other regions are still underdeveloped. The scanty rainfall, ruggedness of the country, and low soil fertility have caused its people to struggle hard for a bare existence. The majority of the people are Hindus; the Maratha community predominates. In the past the long west coast (720 kilometers) attracted Middle Eastern and European traders, who influenced its society and culture. In modern times Lokhitwadi, Jotiba Phule, Mahadev Govind Ranade, Agarkar, Shahu Chhatrapati, and Dr. B. R. Ambedkar launched social reform movements, while Pherozeshah Mehta, Dadabhai Naoroji, Gopal Krishna Gokhale, and Bal Gangadhar Tilak worked for the political awakening and independence of India.

[*See also* Marathas *and* Bombay.]

Iravati Karve, *Maharashtra: Land and Its People* (1968).    A. R. KULKARNI

MAHASENA (247–301), Sri Lankan ruler of the Anuradhapura kingdom. He is credited with commissioning the construction of sixteen tanks (reservoirs or artificial lakes) and four canals in the Anuradhapura area, one tank in the Puttalam district, and the Alahara canal, the source of water for the Minneriya tank in Polonnaruva. These projects involved the state in a massive investment of labor resources on an unprecedented scale, and reflect a notable advance in irrigation technology.

Mahasena was one of the earliest adherents of Mahayana Buddhism in Sri Lanka and led a spirited attack on the Mahavihara, the center of Theravada orthodoxy. He founded the Jetavana Monastery, which supported the Abhayagiri Monastery in its campaigns against the *bhikkhus*, or monks, of the Mahavihara.

[*See also* Anuradhapura *and* Sri Lanka.]

K. M. DE SILVA

MAHATHAMMARACHA, king of Ayudhya (r. 1569–1590), ruled Siam under Burmese suzerainty. Descended from Sukhothai and Ayudhya monarchs through his father and mother, respectively, Mahathammaracha led the plot that enthroned Chakkraphat in 1548 and was rewarded with the new king's eldest daughter and the vice-royalty of Phitsanulok. Apparently jealous of the king, he was less than aggressive in military defense and was captured several times by the Burmese, who made him king. As a vassal of the Burmese monarchs, he worked to rebuild his devastated state but left military action to his sons, Naresuan and Ekathotsarot, who succeeded him on his death in 1590.

[*See also* Ayudhya; Chakkraphat; Naresuan; *and* Ekathotsarot.]

W. A. R. Wood, *A History of Siam* (1926). David K. Wyatt, *Thailand: A Short History* (1984).

DAVID K. WYATT

MAHATHAMMARACHA I (Luthai), king of Sukhothai (r. 1347–1368 or 1374), early king in Thailand who struggled to maintain his historic kingdom. As crown prince in the reign of his father, Lo Thai, Luthai took an active interest in Buddhism and is credited with writing in 1345 the classic work of Thai cosmology, the *Traiphum (Three Worlds)*, evidencing vast scholarship. When his father died suddenly, Luthai had to defeat a usurper, Ngua Nam Thom, to claim the throne. Against an expanding Ayudhya, he strove to ensure his kingdom's survival through diplomacy and seems to have concluded a nonagression treaty with King Ramathibodi I of Ayudhya. The circumstances of his death are not known.

[*See also* Lo Thai; Sukhothai; Mahathammaracha II; *and* Ramathibodi I.]

A. B. Griswold and Prasert na Nagara, "The Epigraphy of Mahadharmaraja I of Sukhodaya," *Journal of the Siam Society* 61 (1973). Frank E. Reynolds and Mani Reynolds, *Three Worlds According to King Ruang* (1982).

DAVID K. WYATT

**MAHATHAMMARACHA II**, king of Sukhothai (r. 1368 or 1374–1398) who came under the suzerainty of Ayudhya (Siam). The son of Mahathammaracha I (Luthai), he came to the throne about 1370 and soon was attacked by Borommaracha I of Ayudhya, who forced him to submit as a vassal. On Borommaracha's death in 1390 Mahathammaracha reasserted Sukhothai's independence. King Ramaracha (r. 1395–1409) of Ayudhya, however, imposed Ayudhya's authority in 1397, even to making Ayudhya law current in Sukhothai. Mahathammaracha II died soon thereafter, succeeded by his son, Sai Luthai (Mahathammaracha III).

[*See also* Sukhothai; Mahathammaracha II; Borommaracha I; Ayudhya; *and* Mahathammaracha III.]

A. B. Griswold and Prasert na Nagara, "A Declaration of Independence and its Consequences," *Journal of the Siam Society* 56.2 (1968): 207–250. David K. Wyatt, *Thailand: A Short History* (1984).    DAVID K. WYATT

**MAHATHAMMARACHA III** (Sai Luthai), king of Sukhothai (r. 1398–1419), struggled to maintain Sukhothai's independence against Ayudhya (Siam). Sai Luthai succeeded his father, Mahathammaracha II, as king in 1398 and in 1400 declared his independence of Ayudhya's suzerainty. He seized Nakhon Sawan and also intervened in a succession dispute in Lan Na (1401). By 1412, King Intharacha (r. 1409–1424) had reestablished Ayudhya's suzerainty, and Sai Luthai had to meekly host Intharacha's visit to Sukhothai in 1417. He died two years later.

[*See also* Sukhothai; Ayudhya; Mahathammaracha II; *and* Mahathammaracha IV.]

A. B. Griswold and Prasert na Nagara, "A Declaration of Independence and its Consequences," *Journal of the Siam Society* 56.2 (1968): 207–250. David K. Wyatt, *Thailand: A Short History* (1984).    DAVID K. WYATT

**MAHATHAMMARACHA IV** (r. 1419–1438), the last king of Sukhothai in Thailand. Mahathammaracha III (Sai Luthai) had finished his reign as a vassal of Ayudhya, and on his death the king of Ayudhya awarded the throne of Sukhothai to Sai Luthai's son, Prince Ban Muang, who reigned as Mahathammaracha IV. He moved his capital south to Phitsanulok about 1430, casting then the great Buddha Jinaraja image. On his death in 1438, King Borommaracha II of Ayudhya abolished Sukhothai, incorporating its territories into his own, and sent his son Ramesuan—the future King Borommatrailokanat—to serve as viceroy at Phitsanulok.

[*See also* Sukhothai; Mahathammaracha III; Ayudhya; *and* Borommatrailokanat.]

A. B. Griswold and Prasert na Nagara, "A Declaration of Independence and its Consequences," *Journal of the Siam Society* 56.2 (1968): 207–250. David K. Wyatt, *Thailand: A Short History* (1984).    DAVID K. WYATT

**MAHA THIHA THURA** (d. 1782), honorific title of U Tha Gyi, a Burmese general and minister. U Tha Gyi was an early and trusted lieutenant of King Alaunghpaya (1752–1760). Appointed governor of Toungoo in 1762, he served as a minister (*wungyi*) from 1764 to 1777 with the honorific title of Maha Thiha Thura. He was the primary architect of the Burmese victory in the Sino-Burmese War of 1765–1769. He was recalled from a successful campaign in Thailand in 1776 to support the accession of his son-in-law Singu (1776–1782). In 1777 Singu deposed him and executed his daughter. Restored to rank and position by Bodawhpaya (1782–1819), Maha Thiha Thura was executed for plotting a coup with Bodawhpaya's younger brother, the Sitha prince, on 23 February 1782.    WILLIAM J. KOENIG

**MAHATTHAI**, for six hundred years the most important organ of Thailand's government. In the fifteenth century King Borommatrailokanat of Ayudhya made this ministry oversee all civil government, giving it primary responsibilities for provincial administration and making the ministries of the capital, palace, lands, and treasury subordinate to it. From the seventeenth century onward its minister often was regarded as the kingdom's prime minister, though control of the southern provinces passed to the Kalahom. Under Prince Damrong Rajanubhab as minister (1892–1915) it became modern Thailand's Ministry of Interior, in charge of provincial administration.

[*See also* Borommatrailokanat; Kalahom; Bunnag Family; Bodindecha Sing Singhaseni; *and* Damrong Rajanubhab.]

Tej Bunnag, *The Provincial Administration of Siam, 1892–1915* (1977). H. G. Quaritch Wales, *Ancient Siamese Government and Administration* (1934; reprint, 1965). David K. Wyatt, *Thailand: A Short History* (1984).

DAVID K. WYATT

**MAHAVAMSA**, chronicle of ancient Sri Lanka in Pali verse, attributed to a *bhikkhu* (monk) named Mahanama about the sixth century CE. Although permeated by miracle and invention, it contains a surprisingly full and accurate chronological and political framework for the study of the island's early history. Despite its gaps and flaws it is a remarkable achievement in historical writing. Future generations treated this as the definitive study of the island's history and regarded it as their duty to bring it up to date. Thus its continuation, called the *Chulavamsa*, surveys the period to the reign of Vijayabahu I (r. 1055–1100), and its second part ends with Parakramabahu I (r. 1153–1186). It was subsequently extended by different authors to the mid-eighteenth century.

[*See also* Dutthagamani; Elara; *and* Sri Lanka.]

K. M. DE SILVA

**MAHAVIRA.** *See* Jainism.

**MAHAYANA BUDDHISM.** *See* Buddhism: An Overview.

**MAHDI** (Arabic, "the guided one"), title of messianic imam in Shi'ism, used in the general Islamic tradition for the awaited descendant of Muhammad who will restore Islamic purity. The title seems to have gained importance through its usage in the prophetic communications *(hadith)*, where it is used for certain individuals in the past and for a messianic figure in the future. The basic emphasis of Islam lies in the historical responsibility of its followers, namely, the establishment of the ideal religiopolitical community, the *umma*, with a worldwide membership of all those who believe in God and his revelation through Muhammad. The seeds of this responsibility, which carries within itself the revolutionary challenge of Islam toward any social order that hampers its realization, were sown by Muhammad himself. In the persistent aspiration for a more just society these seeds have borne fruit in rebellion throughout Islamic history.

In the years following Muhammad's death, a group of Muslims emerged who, dissatisfied with the state of affairs under the caliphate, looked back to the early period of Islam as ideal epoch, unadulterated by the corrupt and worldly rulers of expanding Islamic empire. It was owing to this feeling that many began to look forward to the rule of a descendant of Muhammad, the Mahdi, who would bring an end to corruption and wickedness. The growth of such a hope among the group that has been wronged and oppressed was the inevitable outcome of the consistent stress Islam lays on the realization of the just society, under the divine revelation. The idea of Mahdi was especially important in Twelver Shi'ism, where the firm belief in the return of the twelfth imam as messianic leader became the cornerstone of the creed.

Although the title *mahdi* was used for the first time for Ali and Husain among the Shi'ite imams as a designation of a righteous Islamic ruler, its usage in the messianic sense seems to have been first applied by Mukhtar ibn Abi Ubaid al-Thaqafi, a man with Shi'ite sympathies, to Muhammad ibn al-Hanafiyya, a son of Ali by a woman other than Fatima, in the context of a two-year rebellion against Umayyad authority. Ibn al-Hanafiyya died without achieving anything significant, but the aftermath of the movement was far reaching. It was at this time that the two central beliefs about the Mahdi—his concealment *(ghaiba)* and his return *(raj'a)* at the appropriate time—were introduced.

The decades prior to the end of Umayyad rule in 750 were marked by several Shi'ite revolutions and uprisings headed by leaders claiming to be the Mahdi and demanding a new social order. Although the Abbasid revolution was based on Shi'ite messianic expectations, its leaders abandoned their messianic role after being established as caliphs, and they adopted Sunnism. Even after this disappointment, Shi'ite hopes continued to run high and, consequently, almost all imams from that time on were believed to be the Mahdi, and as such not to have died, and their return was expected. This was especially true of the followers of the first twelve imams. The twelfth imam was, however, by no means the last of those who were proclaimed as Mahdi, and the title has continued to be bestowed to the present day.

[*See also* Caliphate; Imam; Ithna Ashari; Shi'a; *and* Sunni.]

S. A. A. Rizvi, *Muslim Revivalist Movements in Northern India in the Sixteenth and Seventeenth Centuries* (1965). A. A. Sachedina, *Islamic Messianism* (1980).

ABDELAZIZ SACHEDINA

MAHENDRA (1921–1972), ninth Shah king of Nepal who oversaw the modernization of the country's economic and administrative systems. In 1955, Mahendra succeeded to the throne at age thirty-four upon the death of his father, Tribhuvan, and quickly initiated a number of steps toward Nepal's planned economic development. Among these were land reforms, the creation of a National Planning Commission, and a Development Ministry to coordinate foreign aid funds contributed chiefly by the US and India. Under Mahendra's rule Nepal became a member of the United Nations (1955) and the non-aligned movement (1962). Mahendra fulfilled his father's reformist ambitions in 1959 by introducing Nepal's first constitution, which established a bicameral parliament and elections by adult suffrage. Nevertheless, Mahendra was openly skeptical of the viability of a Western-style democracy for Nepal and distrustful of the politicians who came to prominence in the 1950s. In December 1960, prompted by growing antigovernment demonstrations by the Communists and responding to Rana protests over the way in which the majority Congress Party government was proceeding with land reforms, Mahendra dissolved Parliament, suspended constitutional rights, jailed the leaders of the Nepali Congress, and outlawed all political parties. In place of the parliamentary system, Mahendra established in 1961 a "partyless *panchayat* democracy" based on a pyramidal system of elected councils at the village, district, zonal, and national levels, with the king and his personally appointed Council of Ministers at the apex. Mahendra died in January 1972 and was succeeded by Crown Prince Birendra.

[*See also* Tribhuvan, Bir Bikram; Birendra; *and* Nepal: History of Nepal.]

B. L. Joshi and L. Rose, *Democratic Innovations in Nepal* (1966). L. Rose, *Nepal: Strategy for Survival* (1971).                    RICHARD ENGLISH

MAHENDRAVARMAN. *See* Chitrasena.

MAHINDA (third century BCE), one of the great figures in the history of Buddhism in Sri Lanka. In the Sri Lankan historical tradition he is identified as the individual who introduced Buddhism to the island. The *Mahavamsa* devotes considerable space to his arrival in the island as an emissary of the Maurya emperor Ashoka, and to his conversion of Devanampiya Tissa to Buddhism. The work also describes Mahinda as a *bhikkhu* (monk), and one of Ashoka's sons; Indian sources treat him as one of the emperor's brothers. Mahinda may be regarded as the founder of the Buddhist order in Sri Lanka and the inspiration behind the establishment of the Thuparama *dagoba,* the first identifiable place of Buddhist worship in the island. His arrival in the island is dated to the 15th year of Ashoka's reign (c. 255 BCE), and the 236th year after the death of the Buddha.

[*See also* Buddhism: An Overview; Sri Lanka; *and* Devanampiya Tissa.]

James Brow, *Vedda Villages of Anuradhapura: The Historical Anthropology of a Community in Sri Lanka* (1978). W. Rahula, *History of Buddhism in Ceylon: The Anuradhapura Period* (1956).    K. M. DE SILVA

MAHMUD OF GHAZNA (971–1030), the most important ruler of the Ghaznavid dynasty and, according to the contemporary political scientist Nizam al-Mulk, the first Islamic "sultan." He succeeded in 998 to the command of all the territories his father Sebuktigin had administered from Ghazna in central Afghanistan on the Samanids' behalf. After he took Khurasan from the Buyids in 999, his authority was recognized by the caliph al-Qadir; thus, his line was established as independent.

Of greater historical significance, however, were Mahmud's continuous campaigns to the Punjab and parts of Sind, campaigns that opened a new era of Muslim expansion into the Indian subcontinent. These conquests, along with his taxation policies in Khurasan, have made Mahmud a controversial figure. Undisputed, however, is his success at building the largest empire of its day, extending from central Iran through Afghanistan and into northern India.

Mahmud supported Sunni causes, patronized poetry and learning, and built magnificent palaces, apparently motivated, however, more by convention than conviction. Nonetheless, he has achieved nearly legendary status in literary and folk traditions.

[*See also* Ghaznavid Dynasty *and* Sebuktigin, Abu Mansur. *For the extent of Mahmud's empire, see map 2 accompanying* India.]

C. E. Bosworth, *The Ghaznavids* (1963). M. Nazim, *The Life and Times of Sultan Mahmud of Ghazna* (1931).
                    RUSSELL G. KEMPINERS, JR.

MAHMUD RIAYAT SYAH III (1759–1812), sultan of Johor (r. 1761–1812). His election was forced upon the Malays, who preferred a mature candidate, by the Bugis faction, which dominated Johor until it was driven out by Dutch forces in 1784. Mahmud found that in exchange for Dutch support he had to yield to the occupation, and consequent stultification, of Riau. He temporarily overcame the Dutch with the help of Illanun pirates in 1787 but was then forced to flee Riau to avoid Dutch retribution. Refused help by the English, he attempted to unite all Malay and Bugis against the Europeans but without success. The Napoleonic wars caused the Dutch to leave Riau in 1795, and the Bugis and Malays returned, along with their quarrel. On Mahmud's death in 1812 the throne again became a bone of contention, as, perhaps intentionally, he had not clearly specified which of his two sons was his heir and had given one to each faction to raise. The Bugis again forced the success of their candidate, but the confusion was sufficient to give the English opportunity to obtain Singapore.

[See also Johor; Bugis; and Singapore.]

Carl A. Trocki, *Prince of Pirates* (1979). R. O. Winstedt, *A History of Johor* (1979).    DIANNE LEWIS

**MAHMUD SYAH II**, sultan of Johor (r. 1685–1699), was unstable and sadistic, and his irresponsible behavior did much to destroy in a short period the carefully nurtured prosperity that had come to Johor in the late seventeenth century with the decline of Aceh and Melaka. His behavior led to his murder, apparently with the collusion of the Orang Kaya—a radical course of action in a Malay court, which held no crime more heinous than murder. He left no heirs and was the last Johor sultan who could claim direct descent from the Melaka sultans.

[See also Johor and Abdul Jalil Riayat Syah.]

Leonard Y. Andaya, *The Kingdom of Johor* (1975). R. O. Winstedt, *A History of Johor* (1979).    DIANNE LEWIS

**MA HUAN** (1414–1451), Chinese Muslim interpreter who accompanied the eunuch admiral Zheng He on three of his seven maritime missions to Southeast Asia in the early fifteenth century. He wrote about his experiences on these voyages in the *Yingyai shenglan (Description of the Coasts of the Ocean)*, which he originally compiled in 1416 and later expanded; it was published in 1451. This text, together with the *Xiyang fanguo zhi (Record of the Western Barbarians)* of Gongzhen (1434), who accompanied the expedition of 1431–1433 as a secretary, and the *Xingcha shenglan (Description of*

*the Starry Raft)* by the Confucian scholar Feixin (1436), provides valuable firsthand descriptions of Zheng He's efforts to solicit foreign trade in the South China Sea, the Indian Ocean, and beyond, under the third Ming dynasty emperor. Among these Ma Huan's account is considered by scholars to have the highest standard of factual accuracy. His account is especially valuable as a source of information on the small states in the Strait of Melaka region. He describes the founding of Melaka in 1403 and records its early fifteenth-century history.

[See also Zheng He.]

J. V. G. Mills, *Ying-yai Sheng-lan of Ma Huan (1433)* (1970).    KENNETH R. HALL

**MAINE, SIR HENRY** (1822–1888), legal member of the Legislative Council of India from 1862 to 1869, later serving on the India Council in England. His fame rests on his historical study of law in India and Europe and on his thesis that society progresses as its law becomes based on contract rather than status.

[See also Law: Judicial and Legal Systems of India.]

George Feaver, *From Status to Contract: A Biography of Sir Henry Maine* (1969).    LYNN ZASTOUPIL

**MAITLAND, SIR THOMAS** (1759–1824), commander in chief and second governor of Ceylon (1805–1811) during conflicts between civil and military officials. He reformed the European civil service into three classes and required British civil servants to learn Sinhalese and Tamil. Through closer supervision of the civil service, he tried to prevent oppression by indigenous officials.

Walter Frewen Lord, *Sir Thomas Maitland: The Mastery of the Mediterranean* (1897).    PATRICK PEEBLES

**MAJAPAHIT**, Javanese empire in power during the fourteenth and fifteenth centuries; its capital was Trawulan, near Modjokerto, East Java. The kingdom of Majapahit was heir to the Singosari kingdom, which had been centered on Tumapel, northeast of Malang; thus Javanese history classifies the period from the thirteenth to the fifteenth century as the Singosari-Majapahit era. The continuity of this era was interrupted only once by a short revolt staged by the regional kingdom of Kediri in 1292–1293. The rebels were foiled, however, by Prince

Vijaya, who submitted to them initially but then made a secret alliance with the Mongols in return for assistance in unseating the Kediri prince. As soon as his goal was accomplished, Vijaya turned on his former allies and ultimately forced them to return to China. He then moved the capital to Trawulan and there ascended to the throne of the successor kingdom, Majapahit, with the title Kertarajasa Jayavardhana.

Kertarajasa was succeeded in 1319 by his son Jayanagara, who ruled until 1328. Both reigns were punctuated by revolts; the *Pararaton (Book of Kings)* records nine conflicts from 1293 to 1320. Several of these conflicts, such as those of Rangga Lowe in 1295 and Sora in 1292–1300, are celebrated in Old Javanese literature; others were the result of old comrades falling out after defeating the forces of Kediri or Kublai Khan. The most successful of these revolts was led by Kuti, who in 1319 seized the capital. The king, accompanied by a bodyguard, fled the capital under the protection of a young officer named Gajah Mada. Through a daring ruse, Gajah Mada later slipped back into the occupied capital, raised an insurrection, and restored the king to power. As a reward for his deeds he was made minister, thus beginning his rise to unprecedented influence and power.

When Jayanagara died heirless in 1328, one of the daughters of his predecessor was chosen regent for her underaged son, Hayam Wuruk, who ascended the throne in 1350 as Rajasanagara. Only after Gajah Mada's death in 1364 could Hayam Wuruk actively govern the realm. How he did so is related by the *Nagarakertagama*, a chronicle written at his court in 1365; that he did well as a ruler is apparent from his reign's stability and longevity. The reign of his successor Wikramawardhana (r. 1389–1429), however, was a period of decline, complete with civil war, conflicts with Chinese envoys, a famine in 1426, and the gradual loss of the kingdom's internal strength. Until recently most scholars believed that the succeeding half-dozen reigns named in the *Pararaton* continued the process of disintegration. New information, however (provided by the Waringin Pitu inscription of 1447, among others), suggests that an orderly succession of rulers reigned at the old Majapahit capital, including Queen Suhita (1429–1447), King Wijayaparakramawardhana (1447–1451), King Rajasawardhana (1451–1453), King Girisawardhana (1456–1466), King Singdhawikramawardhana (1466–1478), and King Girindrawardhana Ranawijaya (c. 1486). The reason for the final demise of the kingdom is even more uncertain. Although Javanese tradition asserts that Majapahit was conquered in 1478 by a confederation of Islamic states, inscriptional evidence suggests that a Hindu king was reigning at the Majapahit capital in 1486.

In terms of material wealth or trade goods, Majapahit was not a rich kingdom. Its wealth lay instead in agricultural resources, namely, fertile soil and abundant water supplies, as well as in sufficient manpower and an effective administrative organization. Many of the ceremonies described by the *Nagarakertagama* exhibit Hindu or Buddhist overlays, yet in the final analysis they were chthonic rites aimed at improving the soil's fertility. These symbolic acts were supplemented by practical measures to increase agricultural productivity, such as construction and maintenance of dams, dikes, drainage canals, terraced and unterraced rice fields, and so on; these were specifically urged by the ruling circles before representatives of the landed gentry on occasion of the annual court festival.

Given the major role of agriculture to the realm, it was exceedingly important that the producers live in peace with one another and not claim one another's lands. Hence registers, land grants, royal charters, and domain rights were overseen from time to time in an attempt to prevent disputes from arising. If they did arise, however, the Majapahit administration had a well-developed judicial procedure designed to deal with such cases. Perhaps the greatest tribute to the system is that many traces of its governmental and judicial institutions are recognizable in those of later, Islamic Javanese kingdoms.

[*See also* Singosari; Pararaton; Kublai Khan; Gajah Mada; Hayam Wuruk; *and* Nagarakertagama.]

D. G. E. Hall, *A History of South-East Asia* (rev. ed., 1964).

M. C. HOADLEY

**MAJLISI, MUHAMMAD BAQIR** (1627–1699), Iranian religious scholar, strongly exotericist in outlook, who exerted considerable influence on the Safavid state and left behind an important corpus of writings still studied in Iran. Gaining fame as a prodigy of erudition, he swiftly advanced to the position of *mullabashi* ("chief mulla," i.e., head of the religious hierarchy), from which he was able to set the Safavid state on a disastrous course of confrontation with the Sunni Afghans. His main scholarly accomplishment was a vast collection of Shi'ite traditions, *Bihar al-anwar (Oceans of Lights)*. Noteworthy, too, are the shorter handbooks of religious practice he wrote, in Persian, for a broader audience.

S. H. Nasr, "The School of Isfahan," in *A History of Muslim Philosophy*, edited by M. M. Sharif (1966), vol. 2, pp. 930–931. HAMID ALGAR

**MAKASSAR**, a city, language, and ethnic group in southwest Sulawesi. First mentioned as an "island" on the route to the Malukus (Moluccas) by the Javanese chronicle *Nagarakertagama* (1365), Makassar became better known as the capital, state, and language of the dual kingdom of Goa and Tallo as it rose to dominate south Sulawesi in the late sixteenth century.

Malay traders began visiting the port of Makassar in the 1540s and helped it dominate rival ports on the trade route to the Maluku—Bantaeng, Bira, and Selayar. The economic foundation for Makassar's greatness was laid by Karaeng Matoaya, ruler of Tallo (1593–1637) and prime minister of Makassar, who expanded local rice production to supply the Maluku in exchange for cloves and nutmeg. As the Dutch East India Company (VOC) asserted a monopoly over spices from Maluku, other Europeans based themselves in Makassar, where they could buy from Malay and Makassarese traders prepared to defy Dutch claims. The British (1613) and the Danes (1618) established factories, and Golconda, Aceh, and Spanish Manila sent their agents. Makassar became the major Portuguese base in Southeast Asia after the loss of Melaka in 1641, when three thousand Portuguese and four churches were reported in the city.

Matoaya was also responsible for Makassar's acceptance of Islam (1605) and the subsequent wars (1608–1611) in which the Bugis states accepted Islam and Makassar hegemony. Makassar's power also extended to Sumbawa (1617), Buton, and eastern Borneo. As a result of the humiliating Treaty of Bungaya (1667) and a series of defeats by an alliance of Dutch and Bugis (1666–1669), Sultan Hasanuddin (1653–1669) became the last ruler of a strong strong Makassar empire; his successors ruled only Goa. The large urban population was dispersed. The Dutch renamed the northerly Makassarese fort of Ujung Pandang Fort Rotterdam and fortified it strongly. A much smaller city of Dutch, Eurasians, Chinese, Malays, and Bugis grew around the fort to work in the declining Dutch trade to the Malukus and handle local exports, consisting mostly of Bugis slaves.

In the nineteenth century Makassar regained its role as the leading entrepôt of eastern Indonesia. Its population grew from about 5,000 (half of them slaves) in the eighteenth century to 40,191 in 1915, 84,855 in 1930, 384,159 in 1961, and 708,465 in 1980. In 1971 the city's name was changed to Ujung Pandang (by which it had been known locally since early Dutch times). Makassar remains the name of a language and ethnic group embracing about 1.6 million people.

[*See also* Maluku; Goa, Kingdom of; Sulawesi; Dutch East India Company; *and* Bugis.]

Leonard Y. Andaya, *The Heritage of Arung Palakka* (1981). Anthony Reid, "A Great Seventeenth-Century Indonesian Family: Matoaya and Pattingalloang of Makassar," *Masyarakat Indonesia* 8.1 (1981).

ANTHONY REID

**MAKRAN** is the coastal strip of hills, about one hundred miles wide, on the Arabian Sea in southeastern Iran and southwestern Pakistan. While the area is barren and inhospitable, it has been an important link between the Middle East and India since prehistoric times. Alexander and his army retreated from India through the Makran, and Arab traders had settled there before the rise of Islam, and used its harbors as bases for trade with Asia. After the Arab conquest of Sind, Makran achieved considerable prosperity, but it became less important after the Turkic peoples established their power in Afghanistan and linkages with India shifted to the passes through the northwest hills.

AINSLIE T. EMBREE

**MALABARI, BEHRAMJI MERWANJI** (1853–1912), Parsi owner of the Bombay-based newspaper *Indian Spectator*, brought social reform questions to national attention through his writings in 1884 on infant marriage and enforced widowhood. His vigorous campaign for government intervention on these issues directly contributed to the enactment, in 1891, of the Age of Consent Act.

[*See also* Age of Consent Act.]

USHA SANYAL

**MALACCA.** *See* Melaka.

**MALAMATI**, a tendency in Islamic Sufism characterized by rejection of public rituals and dress, absorption in God while engaged in affairs of this world, working for a living rather than relying on God to provide it, concealing one's progress in the spiritual path, and avoiding all display of piety. The adherents receive their name (Arabic, "he who incurs censure") from these last two, and are thus sometimes wrongly confused with certain Sufis who purposely disregarded all social norms. The principle Malamati representatives are identified primarily with Khurasan and include Sahl al-Tustari (d. 896) and especially Abu Yazid al-Bistami (d. 874), who is credited with formulation of the doctrine. Among later orders, the Naqshbandiyya are particularly associated with this school of thought. [See also Sufism.]

J. Spencer Trimingham, The Sufi Orders in Islam (1971).                         JEANETTE A. WAKIN

# MALAVIYA, MADAN MOHAN (1861–1946),
founder of Banaras Hindu University and spokesman for the Hindu Mahasabha. In 1905 Malaviya gave up his law practice to work for the establishment of Banaras Hindu University, an institution that was created in 1916 and modeled after Annie Besant's Central Hindu College. Malaviya was vice-chancellor of the university until 1938. A dedicated nationalist, Malaviya was president of the Indian National Congress in 1909 and 1918. He was twice president of and the most respected spokesman for the Hindu Mahasabha, a communal organization founded in 1914 to protect Hindu interests against Muslim separatist demands. [See also Hindu Mahasabha.]

Sitaram Chaturvedi, Madan Mohan Malaviya (1972). R. C. Majumdar, ed., The History and Culture of the Indian People: Struggle for Freedom (1969).

JUDITH E. WALSH

# MALAYA, BRITISH MILITARY ADMINISTRATION OF. Known as the BMA, the British Military Administration was established in Malaya on 15 August 1945 and remained in force until the creation of the Malayan Union on 1 April 1946. The objectives of the BMA were to reestablish British rule following the Japanese occupation of Malaya, to restore law and order, and to maintain essential services in the immediate postwar months, as well as to prepare for the transition to civilian colonial government. The administration faced two major problems: corruption and inefficiency were rife among its officials, and the Malayan Communist

Party launched a major wave of strikes and demonstrations against the colonial authorities. [See also Malayan Union and Malayan Communist Party.]

F. S. V. Donnison, British Military Administration in the Far East 1943–46 (1956). Martin Rudner, "The Organization of the British Military Administration in Malaya, 1946–1948," Journal of Southeast Asian History 9 (1968): 95–106.         RAJESWARY AMPALAVANAR

# MALAYA, FEDERATION OF, formed in 1948
with the establishment of a central government consisting of a British high commissioner, an executive council, and an initially nonelected legislative council. A corresponding structure was set up at a state level. The federation was in effect a centralized system, but each state's ruler retained the power to rule on the Muslim religion and Malay customs, and the Malays' special position was safeguarded. This made it much more acceptable to the Malays than the abortive Malayan Union scheme (1946). The plan was a stepping stone to independence, chiefly because it allowed the election of more than half the legislature (1955). [See also Malayan Union and Malaysia.]                         R. S. MILNE

# MALAYALAM. See Dravidian Languages and Literatures.

# MALAYAN CHINESE ASSOCIATION, or
MCA, founded in 1949, originally as a welfare organization by Tan Cheng Lock, a respected Straits Chinese. The Emergency had just begun (1948), and the MCA provided a rallying point for opposition to the rebels and raised funds for those affected by resettlement.

In 1952 local leaders of the MCA (now a political party) formed an ad hoc alliance with local leaders of the United Malays National Organization (UMNO) to fight the Kuala Lumpur elections against the Independence of Malaya Party. They were successful and on a national level formed the Alliance Party (1953), later joined by the Malayan Indian Congress.

The role of MCA leaders is difficult because the party is a subordinate member of the ruling coalition. UMNO is the dominant partner and always provides the prime minister, and in the present National Front, as opposed to the previous Alliance, the MCA is not even the sole representative of the

Chinese in the coalition. The MCA is torn between its dependence on UMNO and the demands of those within the party who want it to take a stronger stand for the Chinese. Obviously, it cannot make as strident claims as its chief competitor for Chinese votes, the opposition Democratic Action Party (DAP). The DAP regularly wins more Chinese votes than the MCA, which has to rely on Malay votes cast for it as UMNO's partner. Nevertheless, the MCA does win concessions from UMNO, for example on the implementation of the New Economic Policy and the allocation of university places to Chinese.

[*See also* Tan Cheng Lock; Emergency in Malaysia, The; United Malays National Organization; Independence of Malaya Party; *and* Alliance Party.]

Diane K. Mauzy, *Barisan Nasional* (1983). Gordon P. Means, *Malaysian Politics* (2d ed., 1976).    R. S. Milne

# MALAYAN COMMUNIST PARTY (MCP).

The birth of communism in Malaya came about through an external impetus from the Chinese mainland. In 1923 Comintern organizers under the auspices of the Chinese Communist Party (CCP) first appeared and by 1926 had set up a communist labor group. Several CCP cadres arrived in 1927 to help establish the regional Nanyang Communist Party; a further reorganization in 1930 founded the Malayan Communist Party proper under direct control of the Comintern's Far Eastern Bureau in Shanghai. Economic recession, the Sino-Japanese War, and a burgeoning Chinese nationalism in the mid-1930s enabled the MCP to attract support among Chinese youths and workers and to foment widespread strikes.

During the Japanese occupation the MCP cooperated with the British through its guerrilla arm, the Malayan People's Anti-Japanese Army. Coincidentally, however, the Party made secret preparations to fight the British for national liberation after the war. Between 1945 and 1948 the MCP prepared for guerrilla war and conducted overt labor agitation; in March 1948 the Party embarked on a strategy of armed struggle and by June had gone underground to fight. The guerrilla war lasted until 1960 but failed miserably for two basic reasons: the MCP failed to attract either Malays or substantial numbers of Chinese, and the British first promised and then granted national independence.

Today the MCP is impotent and presents little threat to the government. Its remnants operate in south Thailand, recruiting sparsely from Thai Chinese and Malays. In 1970 the Party split into three bitterly contending factions: the Central Committee, the Marxist-Leninists, and the Revolutionary Faction. In late 1983 the last two groups combined to form the Malaysian Communist Party, still in opposition to the Central Committee.

[*See also* Communism: Communism in Southeast Asia; Malaysia; *and* Malayan People's Anti-Japanese Army.]

Gene Z. Hanrahan, *The Communist Struggle in Malaya* (1954). Anthony Short, *The Communist Insurrection in Malaya 1948–1960* (1975).    Stanley Bedlington

# MALAYAN INDIAN CONGRESS (MIC), Ma-

laysian political association founded in August 1946. Its early political ideology was democratic socialist, but by the early 1950s it had slowly acquired acceptance of free-market capitalism. In 1946–1947 the MIC was affiliated to the radical All-Malaya Council of Joint Action in opposition to the Federation Agreement, but with the collapse of this coalition the party became more prone to internal divisions and suspicions. In the late 1940s it had a strong orientation toward India, but this weakened in the early 1950s as the MIC deepened its involvement in independence politics.

The MIC's ideology and fortunes have always been strongly influenced by the personality of its presidents. John Thivy (1946–1947) and Budh Singh (1947–1950) were both socialists with a strong interest in India; K. L. Devaser (1951–1955) was also a socialist but clearly oriented toward Malaya, and V. T. Sambanthan (1955–1973) brought the MIC into alliance with the United Malays National Organization and the Malayan Chinese Association and into the government of an independent Malaya. Under Sambanthan, the MIC was dominated by Tamil and rural interests and strongly sympathetic to noncommunalism.

The MIC's next president, V. Manickavasagam (1973–1979), was responsible for a major restructuring of the organization, partly in response to the political and economic changes brought about by the New Economic Policy. Under Samy Vellu, who became president in 1979, the MIC became a more militant champion of community interests. Nonetheless, the relatively small size of Malaysia's Indian community has prevented the MIC from assuming more than a modest role in government and restricted Indian politicians to posts within the ministries of labor, transport, and housing.

[*See also* United Malays National Organization; Malayan Chinese Association; Manickavasagam, V.; *and* Malaysia.]

Rajeswary Ampalavanar, *The Indian Minority and Political Change in Malaya, 1945–1957* (1981). S. Arasaratnam, *Indians in Malaysia and Singapore* (1979).

RAJESWARY AMPALAVANAR

## MALAYAN PEOPLE'S ANTI-JAPANESE ARMY (MPAJA).

The MPAJA was the main instrument of War Communism, the second stage of the Malayan Communist Party's (MCP) development. Arrangements to cooperate with the British to fight the Japanese—after the party had received instructions from China in 1940—were cemented in Singapore after the Japanese invasion. Following some brief training by the British and after the British defeat, several small groups of Chinese Communists moved north into Malaya from Singapore to contact MCP groups there and form the nucleus of anti-Japanese resistance.

In January 1942 the first group of the British-trained guerrillas formally established a regiment of the MPAJA in Selangor. Other groups were formed in states throughout the peninsula, and by the end of the war they were reported to number seven thousand guerrillas supported by three hundred thousand civilian helpers. Not all were Communists.

The MPAJA achieved little of military consequence apart from tying down Japanese troops that might have been deployed elsewhere. The Japanese surrender meant that the MPAJA never had to commit its forces to sustained operations. It also expended some of its energy fighting Guomingdang (Kuomintang) guerrillas. Although the MPAJA reestablished contact and received much weaponry and equipment from the British in 1943, it was simultaneously preparing to fight for national liberation once the war was over. When the Japanese surrendered, only part of the MPAJA emerged from the jungle, surrendered its arms, and stood down. From 1945 onward secret MPAJA units, estimated at about four thousand guerrillas, with hidden arms caches, were formed to stay behind. When the MCP went underground in June 1948 to conduct the guerrilla war, these clandestine former MPAJA units were already in place as the spearhead of the Communists' armed struggle.

[*See also* Malayan Communist Party.]

J. H. Brimmell, *Communism in Southeast Asia* (1959). Spencer F. Chapman, *The Jungle Is Neutral* (1951). Gene Z. Hanrahan, *The Communist Struggle in Malaya* (1954).

STANLEY BEDLINGTON

## MALAYAN UNION,

a scheme of government introduced by the British in 1946 but soon abandoned because of strong Malay opposition. The scheme, prepared during World War II, excluded Singapore. The British wanted to streamline the prewar system, which included the Straits Settlements, federated states, and unfederated states. Power was to be centralized, and, in the former two, rulers would be virtually stripped of all power. The British also wanted to make it easier for Chinese and Indians to acquire citizenship (and thus the right to vote in a future democratic regime) and to have access to civil service posts that were closed to them. They may also have wished to recognize Chinese anti-Japanese efforts during the war. At the war's end, however, racial tensions were high, and the Malays were easily mobilized to resist the proposals. Apart from the citizenship issue, the Malays fiercely resented the downgrading of their rulers. Their anger was exacerbated by the coercive methods used by the British to obtain the rulers' assent to the scheme. It was not, however, the rulers who organized opposition but the new United Malays National Organization (UMNO), led by Dato Onn bin Ja'afar. Following the Malay protests the plan was scrapped and replaced by the Federation of Malaya (1948). A major consequence was general recognition that UMNO was the main organization speaking for the Malays, indicating that it was the spearhead of the future independence movement.

[*See also* United Malays National Organization; Onn bin Ja'afar, Dato; *and* Malaya, Federation of.]

James de V. Allen, *The Malayan Union* (1967). M. R. Stenson, "The Malayan Union and the Historians," *Journal of Southeast Asian History* 10 (1969): 344–354.

R. S. MILNE

## MALAY NATIONALIST PARTY (MNP),

founded in October 1945, inherited the legacies of the prewar Kesatuan Melayu Muda and wartime PETA, received support from Communists, and stood for the common Malay and union with Indonesia. Between 1945 and 1948 its presidents were Mokhtaruddin Lasso, Burhanuddin, and Ishak bin Hajji Mohammad; estimates of membership during this period of popularity range from fifty thousand to over one hundred thousand. Along with non-Malays, it vainly opposed the federation proposal that was negotiated between the British, the sultans, and leaders of the United Malays National Organization and inaugurated in 1948.

Although the MNP was not outlawed on the declaration of Emergency (June 1948), several of its leaders (including Ishak and Boestamam) were detained. Its support waned and withdrew to Singapore, where it was proscribed in 1950. Malay radicalism reemerged during the mid-1950s with the formation of the Pan-Malayan Islamic Party, which was derived from the religious wing of the largely secular MNP and from Boestamam's Partai Rakyat Malaya.

[See also PETA; United Malays National Organization; Malaya, Federation of; Emergency in Malaysia, The; and Pan-Malayan Islamic Party.]

Ahmad Boestamam, *Carving the Path to the Summit* (1979). A. J. Stockwell, *British Policy and Malay Politics During the Malayan Union Experiment, 1942–1948* (1979).                    A. J. STOCKWELL

## MALAYO-POLYNESIAN LANGUAGES. *See* Austronesian Languages.

## MALAYS.
The term *Malay (Melayu)* is not restricted to one particular ethnic, linguistic, or cultural group. As defined by the Malaysian constitution, a Malay must "speak the Malay language, profess Islam, and habitually follow Malay custom." In modern Malaysia there are political, educational, and economic advantages available to those who comply with the constitutional definition of Malay. Certain groups and individuals within Malaysia who were not born Malays (e.g., the Mirek of Sarawak and individuals of Chinese and Indian descent) can be legally defined as Malay by conforming to these constitutional requirements.

The concept of who is Malay has not always been so readily defined and appears to have changed over time. The most important literary work in the Malay language, the *Sejarah Melayu (Malay Annals),* is the earliest indigenous source for information about "Malayness." Compiled about 1612 but based on earlier records, it explains that *Melayu* was the name of a river in South Sumatra that flowed near the hill of Si Guntang near Palembang. Si Guntang was the site of the first appearance of three princes of supernatural descent in the Malay world. They were progenitors of the Malay royal lines of Palembang (then Singapore, Melaka, and Johor), Minangkabau, and Tanjung Pura.

Several passages in *Sejarah Melayu* indicate that members of the Melaka court who claimed to be descended from ancestors from the Melayu (Palembang) area were entitled to positions of status and special prestige. *Malay* indicated descent from a select Sumatran-born few and was a term of exclusiveness. This descent-based definition of Malay lost much of its significance with time, but the concept that Malay culture stemmed from the culture of Melaka was maintained.

The cultural dominance of Melaka traditions is reflected in the status accorded to the court of Melaka and its seventeenth-century successor, Johor. Both centers were regarded as representative of what was truly Malay, and they set the standard for Malay culture. Malays were differentiated from non-Malays by their observance of a set pattern of etiquette and behavior believed to have been formulated at the court of Melaka.

During the fourteenth and fifteenth centuries Islam was accepted as the dominant religion at the Melaka court. Gradually, adherence to Islam became another feature that distinguished Malays from non-Malays. By the end of the eighteenth century, William Marsden, a British colonial official living in Sumatra, wrote: "In common speech the term *Malay,* like that of *Moor* in the continent of India, was almost synonymous with Mohametan."

In the nineteenth century the colonial administration in Malaya felt it necessary to differentiate between those people who would be administered by the British and those who were subject to a Malay sultan. Under the 1874 Treaty of Pangkor, a Malay (a subject of a sultan) was defined as one who followed Malay custom (*adat*), spoke the Malay language, and professed Islam. This definition of Malay was reaffirmed in the Malaysian constitution. The official inclusion of Islam as a defining characteristic placed a burden of choice on some peoples, particularly some inland groups in the southern areas of the Malay Peninsula. They had been in the process of gradually adopting Malay customs and language, and in cultural terms they were Malay. But because they were unwilling to convert to Islam, they were legally classified as non-Malay and categorized as Orang Asli (aborigines).

[See also Malaysia; Melaka; Johor; Adat; *and* Orang Asli.]

S. Husin Ali, *The Malays: Their Problems and Future* (1981). G. Benjamin, "In the Long Term: Three Themes in Malayan Cultural Ecology," in *Cultural Values and Tropical Ecology in Southeast Asia,* edited by K. Hutterer and T. Rambo (1985). S. Siddique, "Some Aspects of Malay-Muslim Ethnicity in Peninsular Malaysia," *Journal of Contemporary Southeast Asia* 3.1 (June 1981): 76–87. R. O. Winstedt, *The Malays: A Cultural History,* revised and updated by Than Seong Chee (1981).

VIRGINIA MATHESON

MALAYSIA. Linking the Southeast Asian mainland with the archipelago, Malaysia is characterized by sociocultural heterogeneity and geographical division reflecting a classic "plural society." West Malaysia's eleven states (known traditionally as Malaya) occupy the southern portion of the Malay Peninsula. Larger in territory, East Malaysia includes two states, Sarawak and Sabah, covering the northern third of Borneo. Some 84 percent of the 1980 population of 13.5 million live in the more developed and urbanized Malaya. Ethnic Malays account for 47 percent of Malaysia's population (52 percent in Malaya), followed by Chinese (34 percent), Indians (9 percent), and predominantly non-Muslim Borneo groups (8 percent). Both Malaya and the Borneo states possess broad coastal plains with interior mountain ranges; forest covers some 70 percent of the land. Traditionally most people lived along the coast or the many important rivers.

Malaysia's general history can only be understood in a regional framework, as part of the western archipelago realm. The Straits of Melaka bisect this realm and have long served as a crossroads for peoples and cultures as well as terminus for the ancient China-India trade. Influences from China, India, the Middle East, and later Europe followed the maritime trade to Malaya. Prehistory remains insufficiently studied, but discoveries in Sarawak suggest early human habitation. A few Paleolithic sites have been unearthed in Malaya; Neolithic culture was apparently well established by 1500 to 2500 BCE. Small Malayan kingdoms appeared in the second or third century CE. By this time Indian religious, cultural, and political ideas were beginning to filter into the peninsula. Hinduism and Buddhism became blended with local animism, especially for the royal courts. Already Sumatra and Malaya had developed international reputations as sources of gold and tin (the latter still important), and the inhabitants were renowned seafarers. Between the seventh and the thirteenth century many of the small, often prosperous peninsular maritime trading states may have come under the loose control of Srivijaya, the great Sumatran-based empire. [See also Srivijaya.]

In 1400 a new state was established on Malaya's southwest coast by Sumatran exiles. Soon Melaka became the archipelago's major trading entrepôt, gaining suzerainty over much of coastal Malaya and eastern Sumatra. Islam had already spread into the region in the fourteenth century; Melaka became the main center for the propagation of Islam as well as the terminus for the great Indian Ocean maritime trading network. At its height in the late fifteenth century, Melaka hosted fifteen thousand merchants from many countries. The king became a sultan, and the people of the Melaka area began calling themselves Malays (a probable elite reference to earlier Srivijayan origins). Henceforth the term *Malay* applied to those who spoke a version of the Malay language and practiced Islam; behavior and identity, rather than descent, became criteria for "Malaydom," so that previously Hindu-Buddhist and animist peoples of various origins could identify themselves (and even merge with) the prestigious Malays. Over time a loose cultural designation became a coherent ethnic group spread throughout Malaya, eastern Sumatra, western Borneo, and the smaller islands in between, a region that can be termed the Malay world. However, Islam came to overlay the earlier beliefs, so that before reform movements commenced in the late nineteenth century, few Malays were Muslims in any pure sense; much of Hindu ritual remained important for the elite, and spirits were richly incorporated into Islamic folk beliefs. [See also Melaka and Malays.]

In 1511 the Portuguese captured Melaka, but Islam continued to spread among coastal societies. Sultanates were created throughout the Malay world; usually they were situated at the mouth of a major river and sought to control trade to and from the peoples of the interior, often animist peoples such as the Dayak of Sarawak and Orang Asli of Malaya. Melaka languished under Portuguese control and was captured by the Dutch in 1641. But other, newer and dynamic sultanates such as Johor-Riau, Kedah, and Brunei (on Borneo's northwest coast) took over some of the trading functions, flourishing for several centuries. [See also Johor; Riau; Kedah; and Brunei.] Despite continual movement of archipelago peoples into the area (several Malayan ruling families boast immigrant origins), Malaya and northern Borneo remained sparsely populated into the early nineteenth century. Many present-day Malays are descendants of immigrants from elsewhere in the wider archipelago who arrived during the past two hundred years. Indeed, there was a tendency for immigrants from Java, Sulawesi, and Sumatra to merge with the existing Malay community over time, a process that steadily accelerated with the rise of Malay nationalism and vernacular education in the 1930s. Siam came to control some of the northern Malay sultanates, and southernmost Thailand is still heavily Malay Muslim in population. The Malay sultanates included various, often feuding chiefdoms; occasionally inter- or intrasultanate wars erupted. To Western observers the sul-

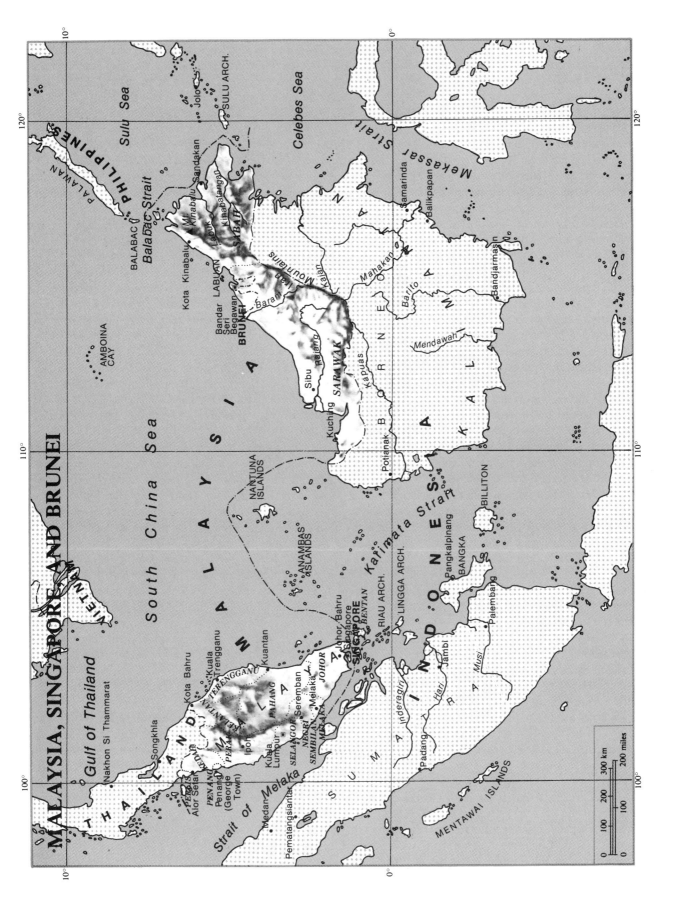

MALAYSIA, SINGAPORE, AND BRUNEI

tanate system seemed politically unstable, but it reflected a chronic situation in which states constituted hierarchical but fluctuating spheres of influence ruling over mobile populations.

Except in Melaka there was little Western influence in Malaya and northern Borneo until the late eighteenth century, when Britain became interested in the area. In 1786 the British annexed Penang, off Malaya's northwest coast; the island soon became a major trading entrepôt with a largely Chinese population. Britain acquired Singapore at the tip of the peninsula in 1819; a fine harbor and strategic location at the southern end of the straits made Singapore the center for Britain's economic and political thrust in the peninsula. The British welcomed Chinese immigrants to the sparsely populated island; soon the predominantly Chinese port became the region's primate city and major base for Chinese economic activity in Southeast Asia. Britain obtained Melaka from the Dutch in 1820 and hence governed the three major west-coast ports, which they termed the Straits Settlements.

By the early nineteenth century Chinese began settling in large numbers in the west-coast sultanates, where they cooperated with local Malay rulers to mine tin. The Chinese organized themselves into tightly knit communities and, allied with competing Malay chiefs, fought wars with each other for control of minerals. Chinese settlers also established towns like Kuala Lumpur and Ipoh, which would soon grow into major cities. British investors became interested in the potential mineral wealth but worried about the political unrest. By the 1870s local British officials began intervening, establishing political influence (sometimes employing force or the threat of force) through a system of British residents (advisers); by 1914 they had achieved formal or informal colonial control over nine sultanates (four acquired from Siam). The various states kept their separate identities but were increasingly integrated to form British Malaya. Meanwhile, an English family, the Brookes, had gained control of Sarawak in 1841, ruling as a family dynasty until 1941. [See also Brooke, Sir Charles Vyner; Brooke, Sir James; and Brooke, Sir Charles.] A British chartered company ruled Sabah (North Borneo) from 1881 to 1941, while Brunei became a British protectorate in 1902.

British rule affected Malaya and the Borneo territories in many ways. The Brookes and the chartered company faced prolonged resistance before militarily consolidating their control, while occasional local revolts punctuated British Malayan rule

as well. On the whole, however, British administration brought peace and security. The Malay sultans retained their traditional status as symbolic rulers at the apex of an aristocratic social system, although they lost some of their political authority. The British believed that the Malay peasants needed to be protected from cultural and economic change, with traditional class divisions maintained. Hence most economic development would be left to Chinese and Indian immigrants, as long as these served long-term British interests. Only the Malay elite enjoyed the benefits of modern education and a place in the new colonial or (in Sarawak) quasi-colonial system as civil servants. But many Malayan and Bornean villages were affected by British taxes and forced to shift from subsistence to cash-crop farming (chiefly rubber), becoming subject to fluctuations in world commodity prices. Nevertheless much economic growth occurred, as British policies promoted transportation development and the planting of gambier, pepper, tobacco, oil palm, and especially rubber, which along with tin became the major export. Malaya and British North Borneo developed classic extractive, plantation-oriented economies geared to meeting the resource and market needs of the industrializing West.

Between 1800 and 1941 several million Chinese entered Malaya, Sarawak, and British North Borneo to work as laborers, miners, planters, and merchants. Tamils from South India were imported as a proletarian group in Malayan rubber estates. Whereas in 1800 Malays accounted for 90 percent of Malaya's population, by 1911 they constituted only half. A plural society was developing, with most Malays in villages, Chinese in towns, and Indians on plantations. The elites of the various communities participated in and benefited from the system, while the British skillfully used "divide and rule" tactics to maintain their control. Through enterprise, cooperation, and organization, many Chinese became part of a prosperous urban-based middle class in control of retail trade. On the whole the various groups lived in their own neighborhoods, followed different occupations, spoke their own languages, practiced their own religions, operated their own schools, and later formed their own political organizations. By the 1930s some mostly ethnically oriented currents stirred in Malaya, Singapore, and Sarawak. Chinese organizations were oriented toward political trends in China, while Malay groups sought either Islamic revitalization and reform or debated the future of Malays in a plural society.

The Japanese occupation (1941–1945) generated tremendous changes in Malaya and the Borneo territories, disrupting the economies and exasperating communal tensions since Chinese and Malays reacted differently to Japanese control. Procommunist, predominantly Chinese guerrillas waged resistance in Malaya. With the end of the war, Sarawak and North Borneo became British crown colonies. The British also introduced some local self-government in Malaya, permitting political parties to coalesce. But from 1948 to 1956 the Malayan Communist Party revolted against the British, a violent but ultimately unsuccessful struggle that had support only from a section of the Chinese community. [*See also* Malayan Communist Party.] By 1957 conservative, pro-British leaders had negotiated independence, led by a Malay aristocrat, Tunku Abdul Rahman. A pattern of multiethnic alliance (later known as the National Front) between mostly ethnically based, generally conservative, elite-led parties would henceforth dominate Malaysian politics. The arrangement has tended to favor the Malays politically, since the major Malay nationalist party, the United Malay Nationalist Organization, or UMNO, leads the alliance and holds most federal offices. But Chinese were granted liberal citizenship rights and maintain strong economic power. Malaya was a federation of eleven states (nine sultanates), symbolically headed by a king elected periodically from among the sultans. Kuala Lumpur became the federal capital.

In 1963 the British agreed to terminate colonial rule over Singapore, Sarawak, and Sabah (North Borneo) by including these historically and ethnically distinct states with Malaya in a new expanded federation known as Malaysia. However, the new, hurriedly formed nation faced many political problems: several years of Indonesian military opposition (known as Confrontation); sporadic communist insurgency in Sarawak; considerable East Malaysian disenchantment over Malayan domination and development policies; and expulsion of Singapore in 1965. [*See also* Confrontation.] Communal tensions in Malaya generated riots and a nationwide state of emergency in 1969–1970. Many non-Malays resisted government attempts to build national unity and identity, such as increasing emphasis on Malay language in education and public life. Government policies aimed at redistributing more wealth to Malays, as well as a growing Islamic revival, particularly worried Chinese. Rural development policies have improved life for many, though some non-Malays and Malays have benefited little.

Nonetheless, Malaysia can boast of many achievements: a quasi-democratic political system (regular elections, moderate political diversity, some civil-liberties restrictions); a highly urbanized society by Asian standards; a prosperous, although somewhat neocolonial, export economy (the major world producer of tin and rubber); some economic diversification (oil, timber, manufacturing); a dynamic mixed economy (free enterprise and an expanding state sector); a growing multiethnic urban middle class; little desperate poverty (although serious regional disparities in development exist); the second highest per capita income in Southeast Asia; high literacy rates and an impressive educational system; and general political stability despite geographical and communal divisions. Malaysia's future prospects probably depend on the ability of political and economic leaders to maintain strong diversified economic growth, alleviate the causes of rural poverty, and promote communal tolerance so that all Malaysians feel they have a continued place in one of Asia's more promising nations.

Barbara Watson Andaya and Leonard Y. Andaya, *A History of Malaysia* (1982). J. M. Gullick, *Malaysia: Economic Expansion and National Unity* (1981). Teck-Ghee Lim, *Peasants and Their Agricultural Economy in Colonial Malaya, 1874–1941* (1977). R. S. Milne and Diane Mauzy, *Politics and Government in Malaysia* (1978). Victor Purcell, *The Chinese in Malaya* (1967). Margaret Roff, *The Politics of Belonging: Political Change in Sabah and Sarawak* (1974). William Roff, *The Origins of Malay Nationalism* (1967). C. M. Turnbull, *A History of Singapore, 1819–1975* (1977).                     CRAIG A. LOCKARD

MALCOLM, SIR JOHN (1769–1833), important administrator for the East India Company, rising to succeed Mountstuart Elphinstone as governor of Bombay from 1827 to 1830. Malcolm was instrumental in convincing Peshwa Baji Rao II to abdicate, setting the stage for direct British control of much of West-Central India. Malcolm was trained under the duke of Wellington, when the latter served in India during the wars with the Marathas, and remained convinced of the policy of firm government by the British in India. Malcolm also wrote some notable histories, including *Sketch of the Sikhs* and *Central India*.                     LYNN ZASTOUPIL

MALDIVES, a state made up of about two thousand islands in an archipelago in the Indian Ocean, five hundred miles west of Sri Lanka. Little is known of the ancient history of the islands, but they were probably settled by about 500 BCE by people from South India and Sri Lanka. There is archaeological evidence of Buddhist influence, but Islam has been the religion of the people since the twelfth century, when a ruler of one of the islands was converted to Islam. While Arab traders and missionaries brought the islands into cultural contact with the Islamic world, the lack of resources in the islands and their distance from main trading routes assured their political isolation for many centuries. The language, known as Divehi, is related to Sinhala, the Dravidian language of Sri Lanka, and is written in the Arabic script with many Arabic and Persian loan words.

The written records of Maldivian political history begin with the advent of Islam, but details about the social life are sparse. One account of the customs of the people has been provided by the famous Arab traveler Ibn Battuta, who lived in the Maldives from 1343 to 1344. Traditionally, the islands were ruled by a succession of hereditary sultans. In theory, the sultans ruled with the advice of the *qazis,* the interpreters of Islamic law, but in practice authority seems to have been centered in the sultan and his council of nobles. The archipelago was divided into provinces, with a dual administration headed by a revenue collector and a judicial officer. These were further subdivided into island administrations. Male, the main island, was the center of political power.

Maldivian economy was almost wholly dependent upon fishing, with a minimum of subsistence agriculture. Trade was carried on with Kerala, a state on the southwest coast of India, and in the fifteenth century one of the rulers of Cannanore (a section of Kerala) claimed sovereignty over the islands. His control, however, was probably quite nominal. The islands were subjected to frequent raids from pirates, but a new phase of contact began with the arrival of the Portuguese in the Indian Ocean at the end of the fifteenth century. They controlled Male from 1528 to 1573, when they were driven out. The next Europeans to arrive were the Dutch, after they had established their power in Ceylon in the middle of the seventeenth century. The British replaced the Dutch in 1796, but in the first half of the nineteenth century they showed little interest in the Maldives. After 1860, however, Indian traders from Bombay who had settled in Male became involved in local politics and, as British subjects, asked for the protection of the British government. This led to a declaration, in 1877, that the Maldives were a protectorate of the British crown; while the sultan retained his authority within the islands, all foreign relations rested in the hands of the government of Ceylon.

The Maldives became independent of the British in 1965. In 1968 the office of sultan was abolished and an elected president installed as head of the state. A republican constitution was created and communication with the outside world was improved. As one of the twenty poorest countries in the world (with a per capita income of $160 in 1978), assistance was received from the United Nations Development Program for social and economic programs. Tourism was encouraged through the establishment of resorts on a number of islands exclusively for foreigners.

H. C. P. Bell, *The Maldive Islands: An Account of the Physical Features, Climate, History, Inhabitants, Production and Trade* (1883). Clarence Maloney, *People of the Maldive Islands* (1980). Urmila Phadnis and Ela Dutt Luithui, *Maldives: Winds of Change in an Atoll State* (1985).

AINSLIE T. EMBREE

**MALIK, ADAM** (1917–1984), Indonesian journalist and politician. He was active in the nationalist Partindo and Gerindo and in 1937 established the Indonesian news agency Antara. With Tan Malaka he founded the Partai Murba, which he represented in Parliament (1956–1960). As trade minister under Sukarno, he opposed the growth of the Indonesian Communist Party (PKI) and proposed the establishment of a single-state party in which the PKI would be submerged. He became one of the leading civilian politicians associated with Suharto's New Order, as foreign minister (1966–1977) and vice president (1978–1983). In later years he was occasionally critical of the New Order's record on human rights.

[*See also* Gerindo; Tan Malaka; Partai Komunis Indonesia; Sukarno; *and* Suharto.]

Adam Malik, *In the Service of the Republic* (1980).

ROBERT B. CRIBB

**MALIKI,** one of the four orthodox schools of law in Islam, named after Malik ibn Anas, who died in the Arabian city of Medina in 795. A celebrated legal scholar, Malik is known above all as the author of *Kitab al-muwatta,* the earliest surviving work on law in Islam; its contents in general reflect the outlook of that early legal tradition associated with the Hejaz. While the Maliki school owed its formative inspiration to the teaching of Malik, the elaboration of its doctrine into a unified, distinctive code of law was in the main the work of his leading disciples, in particular al-Sulami (d. 852), al-Tanukhi, known also as Sahnun (d. 854), and Isma'il ibn Ishaq (d. 895). In addition to the Qur'an, Malikis based their legal rulings on the consensus *(ijma)* or customary law of Medina, and when these failed to provide an adequate basis for law they had recourse to personal judgment *(ijtihad/ra'y)*. Malikis did make use of the *hadith* (the traditions of the Prophet) as a basis for law, but these never constituted the highest court of appeal for them. If Malikis and Hanafis were largely in agreement on the role of reason in the juridical process, they sometimes differed substantively in the realm of positive law, a fact explained largely by their different geographical roots.

Apart from isolated cases, and for reasons that are not entirely clear, Maliki law never won acceptance in the eastern lands of Islam. It has been and remains the dominant school of North Africa.

[*See also* Hadith; Hanafi; *and* Qur'an.]

Noel J. Coulson, *A History of Islamic Law* (1964), pp. 43–48 and index. Joseph Schacht, *Origins of Muhammadan Jurisprudence* (1950).          MERLIN SWARTZ

MALKOM KHAN (1832/1833–1908), prominent Iranian reformer of the nineteenth century. Born in Julfa of Armenian parents, Malkom Khan spent most of his youth getting an education in Paris; he returned to Iran in 1851 to serve in the newly established Dar al-Fonun (the polytechnic school). In 1856 Malkom Khan, highly favored by the prime minister Mirza Agha Khan Nuri, was chosen to accompany the Iranian delegation sent to Paris to discuss the Herat issue with Britain. There, in 1857, he was allegedly initiated into a masonic lodge. Upon his return to Iran, he formed the pseudomasonic Faramushkhana ("house of oblivion") in Tehran in 1858 to facilitate gatherings of enlightened Iranians and the propagation of reformist thought. In the meantime, he published the *Kitabcha-yi ghaibi ya daftar-i tanzimat* and the *Daftar-i qanun*, which dealt largely with legal, political, and administrative reform based on the Western model. Owing to the controversial nature of his activities, he was exiled in 1861 and the Faramushkhana was officially dissolved. He was later pardoned and again exiled to London in 1890 after a lottery scandal, and there he began the publication of his newspaper *Qanun (Law)* in 1891, calling for reform and modernization in his mother country; he collaborated with other reformists of the time such as Sayyid Jamal al-Din al-Afghani and Mirza Agha Khan Kirmani. He participated only marginally in support of the Tobacco Protest of 1906.

[*See also* Qajar Dynasty; Afghani, Jamal al-Din al-; *and* Dar al-Fonun.]

Hamid Algar, *Religion and State in Iran, 1785–1906* (1969) and *Mirza Malkum Khan* (1973). Shaul Bakhash, *Iran: Monarchy, Bureaucracy and Reform under the Qajars: 1858–1896* (1978).          NEGUIN YAVARI

MALLA, an honorific title adopted by royalty in the Indian subcontinent, derived from the Sanskrit word meaning "wrestler" or "very strong man." A Malla tribe or confederation is described as existing in northern India at the time of the Buddha, and a Khasa dynasty in western Nepal also used the Malla title from the twelfth through the fourteenth centuries. The most extensive use of the term *Malla* is to be found in the Kathmandu Valley, where modern historians refer to the period extending from 1200 to 1769 as the Malla Period. The suffix *malla* was commonly added to the names of the kings who ruled during this period, gradually supplanting the honorific *deva* suffix used by the early Mallas and their predecessors. These Malla kings were generous sponsors of public works, and their legacy includes a large proportion of the most significant art and architecture to be found in Nepal today.

[*See also* Kathmandu.]

BRUCE McCOY OWENS

MALOLOS REPUBLIC, short-lived constitutional government following the success of the Philippine revolutionary movement against Spain.

In September 1898, as relations worsened between the Philippine revolutionary army and US troops occupying Manila, Emilio Aguinaldo transferred the capital of his government from Cavite to Malolos, Bulacan, forty-five kilometers northwest of Manila. Preparations were immediately begun for the inauguration of the Revolutionary Congress, which had its first meeting on 15 September in the Barasoain basilica. The congress was dominated by *ilustrados* and sought to restrict the influence of the Katipunan and the power of Aguinaldo. Pedro A. Paterno and Benito Legardo took the lead in persuading its members to override the wishes of Aguinaldo and Apolinario Mabini and establish a committee to draft a constitution.

The Malolos Constitution was written by Felipe G. Calderon and provided for a three-branched republican and parliamentary government. The Assembly of Representatives was to be elected by a restricted suffrage and possessed the greatest share of political authority. Mabini consequently opposed the constitution, insisting that current dangers required emergency powers for the president. A compromise was reached, and Aguinaldo proclaimed the constitution the fundamental law on 21 January 1899.

Two days later the Republic of the Philippines was formally inaugurated. The first Christian republic in Asia, it fell victim to the determination of the United States to assert its sovereignty over the Philippine archipelago. Less than two months after the Philippine-American War began, Aguinaldo was forced to evacuate Malolos to escape the approaching US forces under General Arthur MacArthur. The capital was subsequently moved to San Isidro and later to Cabanatuan, to Tarlac, and, finally, to Bayambang. At Bayambang in November 1899, Aguinaldo announced the shift to guerrilla-style warfare and took refuge in the highlands of northern Luzon. On 23 March 1901 Aguinaldo was captured at Palanan, marking the end of the First Philippine Republic.

[*See also* Philippine Revolution; Aguinaldo, Emilio; Ilustrado; Katipunan; *and* Calderon, Felipe.]

Teodoro Agoncillo, *Malolos: The Crisis of the Republic* (1960). Teodoro M. Kalaw, *The Constitution of the Philippine Republic* (1914). Gregorio F. Zaide, *The Philippine Revolution* (1954).    RICHARD E. WELCH, JR.


MALUKU (also known as Moluccas or Spice Islands), islands of eastern Indonesia between Sulawesi (Celebes), New Guinea, Timor, and the Philippines that served as a magnet for sixteenth- and seventeenth-century European navigators and explorers. Historically, the most important islands of the region were Ternate, Tidore, and Halmahera in the north and Ambon (Amboina), Ceram, and the Banda Islands in the center.

The northern islands were virtually the world's only source of cloves, while the central islands produced nutmeg and mace. Substantial quantities of these spices began reaching the Mediterranean world and western Europe in the fifteenth century, due in part to the entrepôt functions performed by the new sultanate of Melaka (Malacca) after 1400; a major impetus to Portuguese and Spanish expansion was the desire to go directly to the source of these valuable commodities. The Portuguese, after taking Melaka in 1511, entered into an alliance with the sultan of Ternate in 1512, and for much of the next century contended with Spain for control of spice exports from the Malukus. The Dutch and English followed them in the early seventeenth century, with the Dutch East India Company establish-

ing its preeminence after the Amboina Massacre (1623). To establish and maintain a monopoly on rare-spice production, the Dutch confined clove production to a few carefully controlled areas, restricted production to keep prices high, and enforced bans on private trading. Because their direct control came so early and was so intensive, the Malukus' experience of colonialism was perhaps the most intensive in Indonesia, and a substantial Christian population grew there, notably on Ambon. During the Indonesian Revolution a Republic of East Indonesia was established in the Malukus with Dutch encouragement; the Malukus became an autonomous part of the independent United States of Indonesia in 1949. With the unification of the Indonesian Republic in 1950, resistance to indonesianization developed and has never been fully quelled.

[*See also* Indonesia, Republic of; Amboina Massacre; Coen, Jan Pieterszoon; Dutch East India Company; Goa, Kingdom of; Makassar; *and* Spice Trade.]

E. S. de Klerck, *History of the Netherlands East Indies* (1938). M. C. Ricklefs, *A History of Modern Indonesia* (1981). B. H. M. Vlekke, *Nusantara: A History of the East Indian Archipelago* (1959).    DAVID K. WYATT


MALWA. West of the region in India known as Bundelkhand and extending to the eastern border of Rajasthan is the Malwa Plateau, today mostly in Madhya Pradesh. It is named for the Malava kingdom, first encountered there in the fourth century BCE and mentioned by Greek sources. The principal city of eastern Malwa was Vidisha, while that of western Malwa was Ujjaini, also called Avanti. In the late tenth century CE Malwa rose to prominence under the Paramaras, who maintained authority until 1305, when Malwa was conquered by Ala ud-Din Khalji. Under the Khaljis, Mandu became Malwa's premier city. Malwa was absorbed by the Mughals under Akbar and became one of their *subas,* or provinces of the empire.

[*See also* Ujjain *and* Khalji Dynasty.]

Kailash Chand Jain, *Malwa Through the Ages* (1972). D. C. Sircar, *Studies in the Geography of Ancient and Medieval India* (1971).    FREDERICK M. ASHER


MAMLUKS, term used for the early Turkish sultans of northern India who ruled from 1210 to 1290. The term *mamluk* denotes a Turkish officer who was a slave; thus these rulers were also known as comprising the "slave dynasty" of Delhi. The ten main rulers of this dynasty are as follows: Qutb ud-

Din Aibak (r. 1206–1210), Aram Shah (r. 1210), Iltutmish (r. 1210–1235), Ruknuddin Firuz (r. 1235), Raziyya (r. 1236–1240), Muizuddin Bahram (r. 1240–1242), Nasiruddin Mahmud (r. 1246–1266), Balban (r. 1266–1287), Kaiqubad (r. 1287–1290), and Kaimurs (r. 1290). The historian Minhaj (c. thirteenth century) names these ruling houses after individual sultans, thus, Qutbi, Shamsi, and Balbani. With the exception of Aibak, all of these sultans were Ilbari Turks, hence they have also been called the Ilbarites. The state under the Mamluks was ethnically restricted: power rested with the Turks alone and slave officers dominated the governing class. The Mamluks initiated the growth of an urban aristocratic culture and patronized the growth of Indo-Islamic architecture and the Persian language.

[*See also* Delhi; Delhi Sultanate; Qutb ud-Din Aibak; Iltutmish; *and* Raziyya.]

M. Habib and K. A. Nizami, eds., *A Comprehensive History of India* (1970), vol. 5. K. A. Nizami, *Some Aspects of Religion and Politics in India during the Thirteenth Century* (1961).    FARHAN AHMAD NIZAMI

**MANCHUKUO.** *See* Manchuria.

**MANCHU LANGUAGE.** Manchu is a member of the Tunguz branch of the Altaic language family. It is closely related to Jurchen (now extinct) and Xibo, a language currently spoken by approximately twenty thousand people in Xinjiang (Chinese Turkestan). Manchu has been written in an adopted form of the Mongolian alphabet since the end of the sixteenth century. The official language of the ruling Manchu imperial house during the Qing dynasty, it was the vehicle of a large translation literature (mostly from Chinese) as well as the language of an immense body of annals, edicts, and memorials, much of which is preserved in Beijing and Taipei. Only a few native speakers of Manchu remain in several villages in Heilongjiang Province in northeastern China.

[*See also* Altaic Languages *and* Manchus.]

Jerry Norman, *A Concise Manchu-English Lexicon* (1978).    JERRY NORMAN

**MANCHURIA.** The area known as Manchuria comprises the three Chinese provinces of Heilongjiang, Jilin, and Liaoning, today usually called Dongbei ("the northeast"). Originally inhabited by tribal peoples, the area is rich in natural resources that have led to dramatic economic growth in the twentieth century, while its location at the convergence of the Japanese, Chinese, and Russian realms has made it a center of conflict since the nineteenth. With a population of about 100 million, Manchuria today is China's single most important heavy industrial region.

The victory of the Manchus over the Ming in 1644 united the destinies of China and Manchuria, although the ethnically distinct Manchus initially forbade Chinese immigration into their homeland. Russian probes in the seventeenth century were turned back, but the major Russian thrust toward the Pacific in the nineteenth century (Vladivostok was founded in 1860 and the Trans-Siberian Railroad was begun in 1891) could not be resisted. Russian gains worried the Japanese, who obtained control of the Liaodong Peninsula after their victory in the Sino-Japanese War of 1894 to 1895, only to be forced out by Russian-organized diplomatic pressure. Meanwhile, the Chinese under Li Hongzhang sought to use Russia to offset Japan. Russia was permitted to construct the Chinese Eastern Railroad, which by cutting across Manchuria facilitated communications between Vladivostok and the Trans-Siberian, as well as the South Manchurian Railroad, which connected the ports of the Liaodong Peninsula with the industrial cities to the north. Russian troops moved into Manchuria at the time of the Boxer Rebellion.

Victory in the Russo-Japanese War of 1904 to 1905 gave Japan much of the Russian position in south Manchuria. Nearly all Japanese considered a strong position there essential to their island's security, but were willing to accept Chinese sovereignty. The ultimately futile Japanese attempt to reconcile their need for a special position in Manchuria with their cooperative relationship to the Western powers, who favored the "Open Door," is a basic theme of the diplomacy leading to World War II in the Pacific. In 1931 the Japanese Kwantung Army moved unilaterally to occupy Manchuria, an action that was followed by the establishment of the client state Manchukuo (1932–1945).

Soviet troops poured into Manchuria late in the summer of 1945 and seemed prepared either to incorporate the region into the USSR or to install a pliant Chinese Communist regime. Having permitted Chinese Communist forces to move into the area, however, they largely withdrew. In the ensuing Chinese civil war (1945–1949), Nationalist forces advancing from China proper along a narrow railway line proved unable, despite initial successes, to defeat the already-entrenched Communists: the battles fought in Manchuria must be considered among the most decisive of the conflict.

A continuing Soviet military presence in Manchuria was provided by treaty in 1950, and the territory served as a logistical base during the Korean War. Not until after Stalin's death was the Soviet military position completely abandoned. The continued importance of Manchuria was underlined in 1955 when the purge was announced of the chairman of the regional administration, Politburo member Gao Gang: one charge was that he had treated Manchuria as his "independent kingdom." Conflict with the USSR erupted along the border in 1969, and powerful Soviet forces continue to face Manchuria on the east and west.

Industrial development in Manchuria began during Japanese rule and has continued since then. Today Manchuria is the center of heavy industry in China, with extensive coal mines (Fushun), oil fields (Daqing), and steel mills (Anshan). Dalian is an important port, while Shenyang (Mukden), in addition to being a major industrial city, is one of the most important military centers of the People's Republic.

[See also Gao Gang; Kwantung Army; Manchus; Russo-Japanese War; and Sino-Japanese War.]

Kang Chao, The Economic Development of Manchuria: The Rise of a Frontier Economy (1982). Michael H. Hunt, Frontier Defense and the Open Door: Manchuria in Chinese-American Relations, 1895–1911 (1973). Robert H. G. Lee, The Manchurian Frontier in Ch'ing History (1970). George Alexander Lensen, The Damned Inheritance: The Soviet Union and the Manchurian Crises 1924–35 (1974).          ARTHUR N. WALDRON

MANCHURIAN INCIDENT, the conquest and pacification of Manchuria from September 1931 to January 1933 by the army Japan had fielded in the region (Kwantung Army). The origins of the campaign lay in the intensifying struggle in the late 1920s between Japan and China for a predominant position in Manchuria. While Manchuria outside the Kwantung (Guandong) Leased Territory was still considered to be under the nominal control of China, Chinese authority had been eroded by political factionalism within the region, as well as by a growing and vigorous Japanese presence in southern Manchuria. The latter consisted of four principal elements that sought to expand Japanese interests and jurisdiction: the Japanese immigrant community, which had increased in numbers and militancy; the South Manchuria Railway Company, which operated not only the major north-south rail line through southern Manchuria but also many of the

commercial and industrial enterprises there; the Foreign Ministry, which maintained a network of consular posts and consular police throughout the region; and Japan's field command in Manchuria, the Kwantung Army. The army's headquarters were at Port Arthur in the Leased Territory, but its elements (essentially a division, plus some miscellaneous artillery and garrison units) were stationed in several key cities along the South Manchuria Railway, in fulfillment of its mission to protect Japanese lives and property outside the leased territory, including the railway and its "attached lands."

Of all the Japanese elements in Manchuria, it was the staff of the Kwantung Army that was most determined to consolidate control over southern Manchuria by permanently separating it from any control by the Chinese central government in Nanjing. The Chinese government was equally determined to regain actual, as well as nominal, sovereignty in Manchuria, which it wished to incorporate as an integral part of China. In the late 1920s a great tide of Chinese nationalism, the reunification drive by Chiang Kai-shek and the Guomindang (Kuomintang) had begun to approach the borders of Manchuria. In 1930 Zhang Xueliang, the principal warlord in Manchuria, had acknowledged the authority of the government of Nationalist China. Thus, by 1931, the stage was set for a confrontation between China and Japan. On the Japanese side, the Kwantung Army staff, which considered the territory and resources of Manchuria to be a vital strategic importance to Japan, were stridently determined to bring about a violent, rather than a negotiated, resolution of the issue.

Led by two aggressive and energetic colonels, Ishiwara Kanji and Itagaki Seishirō, the Kwantung Army staff, without the direction or authorization of central headquarters in Japan, but with the knowledge of certain middle-echelon officers on the General Staff, laid careful plans over a two-year period for the conquest of Manchuria, in the face of Chinese forces that were greatly superior in numbers and equipment. These plans culminated in the sudden attack by elements of the Kwantung Army on the main Chinese garrison at Mukden on the night of 18–19 September 1931, supposedly in retribution for a Chinese attempt to destroy the tracks of the South Manchuria Railway near Mukden. Actually, the sabotage had been secretly perpetrated by Kwantung Army officers. [See Mukden Incident.]

The initial attack set in motion a runaway campaign for the conquest of southern Manchuria and the annihilation of Chinese regional armies, of which Zhang Xueliang's was the largest. In Tokyo, the civilian government, concerned about the aggressive image of Japan on the world scene, and the General Staff, fearful of possible Soviet intervention in Manchuria, attempted without great success to limit the initiatives of the Kwantung Army. By December 1931 Japanese forces had overrun most of southern Manchuria, had taken control of the provincial capitals of all three Manchurian provinces, and had penetrated northern Manchuria as far north as the Nonni River. Frustrated only in its attempt to annex Manchuria as an outright Japanese colony, the Kwantung Army staff, during the autumn of 1931, negotiated with suitably eminent and pliable Manchurian political figures for the establishment of an "autonomous" client state, Manchukuo.

On its part, the Chiang Kai-shek regime decided it was not yet prepared to confront the Japanese while it still faced internal opposition in China, not the smallest of which was that offered by the Chinese Communists. It did little, therefore, to aid the beleaguered Chinese forces in Manchuria, although it tacitly permitted Zhang Xueliang to move the bulk of his army southwest out of Manchuria, a withdrawal that was completed by January 1932.

In December 1931 the installation in Tokyo of a civilian government more sympathetic to the maintenance of Japanese interests by force, along with personnel shifts in the high command leading to more active support of the operations of the Kwantung Army, opened the way to the subjugation of all of Manchuria. In this final phase of conquest, increasingly massive reinforcements from Japan strengthened the "mopping up" operations against the remaining Chinese resistance, which the Japanese invariably termed "banditry." By January 1933, in any event, these aggressive drives into eastern, northern, and western Manchuria by the Kwantung Army essentially completed its conquest of the region.

The reckless conquest of Manchuria had serious consequences for Japan. It exposed dangerous ambiguities within the Japanese political order and instabilities within the military command structure, and it propelled Japan along a perilous new path of confrontation with China, the Soviet Union, and the United States.

[See also Kwantung Army and Zhang Xueliang. For the extent of Japan's conquest of Manchuria, see the map accompanying Meiji Period.]

Sadako Ogata, Defiance in Manchuria: The Making of Japanese Foreign Policy, 1931–32 (1964). Mark R. Peattie, Ishiwara Kanji and Japan's Confrontation with the West (1975).                          MARK R. PEATTIE

MANCHUS, the name (the origins of which are obscure) applied in 1635 by Huang Taiji (Abahai) to his followers, most of whom were Jurchen, people of Tunguz stock and speakers of a language belonging to the Uralo-Altaic group. The Jurchen Jin dynasty had ruled much of northern China from 1115 to 1234, but following the Mongol conquest the Jurchen were driven into Manchuria, where, living disunited in tribal groups, they developed a number of different ways of life. During the Ming period those in southern Manchuria and the Liao River area took up farming, while those along the Amur and Ussuri rivers in the north lived by hunting and fishing. The tribes in the west Manchurian plain, near Mongolia, followed a nomadic life.

In the mid-sixteenth century a new Manchu state arose as Nurhaci, of the Aisin-Gioro clan of the Jianzhou Jurchen, gradually united the scattered tribes by a skillful combination of warfare, marriage diplomacy, and collaboration with the Ming rulers in China. In 1601 he reorganized the tribal military system into a more bureaucratically controlled banner system: first four, and then in 1615, eight. By 1644 the Manchus were strong enough to take control of China, then in disorder. The period of rule over China weakened the Manchu ethnic and national identity, however, and particularly after the anti-Manchu 1911 Revolution (in which many were slaughtered) assimilation was rapid.

Although the last Qing emperor was re-enthroned as ruler of the short-lived Japanese client state of Manchukuo (1932–1945) and Manchu ways artificially revived, today the Manchu people are largely indistinguishable from Han Chinese. Certain surnames are generally recognized as being of Manchu origin, however, and in the last few years many have reclaimed Manchu nationality. Recent figures put the number of Manchus and related groups in the People's Republic of China at 2,711,000. The Xibo, who number about 44,000 and live in Xinjiang Province, are the descendants of Qing border guards, and appear to be the last remaining group of Manchu speakers.

[See also Huang Taiji; Jurchen; Nurhaci; and Qing Dynasty.]

Gertraude Roth Li, "The Manchu-Chinese Relationship, 1618–1636," in From Ming to Ch'ing, edited by J. D. Spence and J. E. Wills, Jr. (1979), pp. 1–38.
                          ARTHUR N. WALDRON

MANDALAY. Located in the dry central plains of Burma, Mandalay was founded by King Mindon in 1857 and was the last capital of the last dynasty in

Burma. The walled, square inner city, approximately four miles around, was designed to represent Tavatimsa, which to the Burmese was the most important of the Buddhist heavens. Its battlements, towers, gates, "floor plan," and a variety of other features symbolized the best-known characteristics of Tavatimsa. Outside the Shwe Myo Taw, or Royal Golden City, were Mandalay's suburbs, where a large portion of the kingdom's population lived. Inside the city were the king and many members of the court, such as the queens, princes, and princesses, as well as the important ministers; the elite guards who defended the throne and capital; the treasury and regalia; the royal library and the records of the kingdom; the Lion Throne, over which rose the tallest man-made (secular) structure in the land, representing Mount Meru; the halls for audiences, ancestors, and minor thrones, including the crystal palace where the nineteenth-century chronicles were written; and the water clock tower, which announced the status of the universe to everyone.

Like most Burmese capitals, Mandalay was a representation of sacred space, sacred time, and sacred energy. In 1885 much was burned and looted, a large portion of its records destroyed, and most of its treasures stolen. Its king was deposed and exiled, and its raison d'être ended. It was the symbolic as well as actual end of the Burmese monarchy after a history of about a thousand years.

[See also Burma and Mindon.]

Michael Aung-Thwin, "Sacred Space, Sacred Time, and Sacred Energy: Dimensions of the Exemplary Center in Burmese History," in The City as a Sacred Center: Essays on Six Asian Contexts, edited by Bardwell L. Smith and Holly Baker Reynolds (1987). Scott O'Connor, Mandalay and Other Cites of Burma (1907).

MICHAEL AUNG-THWIN


MANDOKORO, political office of the Heian, Kamakura, and Muromachi periods in Japan. Although mentioned in records of the Nara era, the origins of the office lay in the middle Heian epoch. As the system of household administration specified in the Taihō Codes declined, great noble families such as the Fujiwara created substitutes and called them mandokoro. The office managed property and recorded family membership and was staffed by dozens of bureaucrats. Headed by a director (bettō), the mandokoro consisted of a four-tier chain of command and issued orders called kudashibumi. Soon temples, shrines, provincial headquarters, and even shōen also added administrative offices with the same name and similar duties.

In 1190, after his victory in the war against the Taira and appointment as head of the palace guards, Minamoto no Yoritomo established his own mandokoro in Kamakura. Its duties consisted of municipal administration and the adjudication of lawsuits. The organization of Yoritomo's mandokoro was copied from Heian precursors; the bureaucrats who ran the office were even imported from Kyoto. In the early thirteenth century the directorship was normally held as a joint appointment by the Hōjō regent, and the Kamakura office began to decline in importance. In the late Kamakura era a clan known as the Nikaido was promoted to head the office.

The Muromachi shogunate copied Kamakura's mandokoro, even using the Nikaido as supervisors. They did not establish a directorship, however, nor did the Muromachi mandokoro issue kudashibumi. The new office managed economic affairs, overseeing pawnshops, sake brewers, and loans. Eventually the Nikaido were replaced by the Ise family as chief officers of the Muromachi mandokoro. The Ise silently built their own power base in the shogunate from this position.

George Sansom, A History of Japan to 1334 (1958).

WAYNE FARRIS


MANDU. The hill fort of Mandu in Madhya Pradesh, India, was utilized from the sixth century on, but little is known of its history until Dilawar Khan Ghori broke with the Tughluqs and subsequently established Mandu as his capital. In 1405 Ghori's son Hoshang Shah ascended the throne and enlarged the domain. A vital patron of architecture, he erected a mosque and his own white marble tomb, which claimed the admiration of the Mughals two centuries later. By 1436 the Khaljis took Mandu as their capital and further expanded its borders. Under Khalji patronage palaces such as the Jahaz Mahal were constructed, tombs and mosques were built, and manuscripts such as the Ni'mat nama were painted. After 1526 Mandu, considerably weakened, lost its independence and fell under the control of various rulers.

[See also Tughluq Dynasty and Khalji Dynasty.]

R. Skelton, "The Nimat Nama: A Landmark in Malwa Painting," Marg 12 (1959):44–50. G. Yazdani, Mandu: City of Joy (1929).

CATHERINE B. ASHER

**MANGELUN CONVENTION** (1894), also known as the Anglo-Chinese Convention, established the frontier between Burma and China. Chinese knowledge of the area was based on centuries of mule trade in the area. Britain pacified and surveyed the region.

Points of contention included unsuccessful Chinese requests to establish a customs house at the Burmese border town of Bhamo. The British were concerned about maintaining roads, controlling smuggling, and passage for troops. The convention is credited with halting China's advance to the Irrawaddy River and that of France to the Mekong.

Dorothy Woodman, *The Making of Burma* (1962).

OLIVER B. POLLAK

**MANGKUBUMI** (Hamengkubuwana I, r. 1749–1792) was the founder (1755–1756) of the court of Yogyakarta and the greatest monarch of Java's Mataram dynasty in the eighteenth century. Sultan Mangkubumi rebelled in 1746 and was proclaimed king by his followers in 1749. In 1755 he agreed with the Dutch East India Company (VOC)—which supported King Pakubuwana III (r. 1749–1788) of Surakarta but could not defeat Mangkubumi—to partition the kingdom between Pakubuwana III and himself. Thereafter he proved himself to be a firm and able monarch who made Yogyakarta the greatest military power of Central Java in the last half of the eighteenth century.

[*See also* Yogyakarta.]

M. C. Ricklefs, *Jogjakarta under Sultan Mangkubumi, 1749–1792* (1974).    M. C. RICKLEFS

**MANGKUNAGARAN**, minor court established by the Surakarta prince Raden Mas Said (later Adipati Aria Mangkunagara) in 1757 after fighting against the combined forces of the Dutch East India Company (VOC) and his erstwhile ally Mangkubumi (Sultan Hamengkubuwana I of Yogyakarta, r. 1749–1792). During the end of Mangkunagara's reign and that of his successor Mangkunagara II (1796–1835), the fortunes of the Mangkunagaran court became ever more closely allied with that of the Dutch government, especially after the reorganization of the Mangkunagaran forces along European lines by Herman Daendels. The cultural style of the court synthesized European and Javanese elements (particularly in military affairs), and the energetic entrepreneurial policies of Mangkunagara II

and Mangkunagara IV (r. 1853–1881) laid the foundations of a thriving Mangkunagaran estate sector.

The fourth Mangkunagara also achieved renown as a litterateur (Javanese, *pujangga*) and philosopher of distinction. In 1896 the Mangkunagaran became fully independent from the senior Surakarta court (Kasunanan) but lost most of its lands and income after Indonesian independence in 1945 because of its equivocal attitude to the nationalists.

[*See also* Mangkubumi.]

M. C. Ricklefs, *Jogjakarta under Sultan Mangkubumi, 1749–1792* (1974).    PETER CAREY

**MANGRAI**, founder and king of Lan Na (r. 1259–1317), the kingdom centered on Chiang Mai in northern Thailand. Born in 1239, Mangrai was the son of the ruler of the old Yonok kingdom at Chiang Saen; his mother was the daughter of the ruler of Chiang Hung in Yunnan. Almost immediately after succeeding his father in 1259, he began an extended program of conquests and moved his capital southward to Chiang Rai in 1262 and Fang in the 1270s. Jealous of the power and prosperity of Haripunjaya (Lamphun), he planned its conquest for more than ten years, all the while skillfully using diplomacy to placate his enemies and encourage allies, the latter including Phayao and the Shan of Pagan and later the Mon ruler of Pegu.

After taking Haripunjaya (1281), Mangrai determined to move his capital farther south and staked out the site of Chiang Mai ("new city") in 1292, finally constructing it in 1296. Through much of the next twenty years he was occupied in warfare with Mongol China, defending his maternal relatives in Chiang Hung and demonstrating to the Tai his fitness to lead and rule them. The Chinese finally wearied and established regular diplomatic relations with Mangrai's kingdom of Lan Na from 1312. At his death in 1317, Lan Na dominated the interior Tai uplands, but its power still was fragile and largely the creation of a single extraordinary king. His most important legacy was his vision of a single kingdom transcending local petty Tai rivalries. For centuries afterward, his name was associated with a gentle, humane code of laws that, modified, continued in force through the nineteenth century.

[*See also* Lan Na; Lamphun; *and* Phayao.]

A. B. Griswold and Prasert na Nagara, "The Judgments of King Man Ray," *Journal of the Siam Society* 65.1 (1977): 137–160. David K. Wyatt, *Thailand: A Short History* (1984).    DAVID K. WYATT

MANI, founder of the dualistic, gnostic religion known as Manichaeism, was born near Ctesiphon in Mesopotamia probably in April 216 CE. His father belonged to a southern Mesopotamian gnostic, baptist sect, probably the Elkhasaites. His parents were Iranians, and his mother was possibly related to the ruling Arsacid dynasty. At twelve Mani received his first revelation from a spiritual double of himself, causing him to break with his father's sect. His second important revelation came on 19 April 240; thereafter he began his missionary work for his new religion. In 241 he went by ship to Sind; then he returned to Iran and Mesopotamia, where he lived at the court of Shapur I, to whom he dedicated his first book, the *Shabuhragan*. After the death of Shapur, Mani continued his preaching, but under Bahram I (c. 275) he was ordered to appear at court in Gundeshapur (Belapat). He was thrown in prison, and in the spring of 276 he died in chains. According to some stories his skin was stuffed with straw and hung on the gate of the city.

[*See also* Manichaeism *and* Shapur I.]

Geo Widengren, *Mani and Manichaeism* (1965).

RICHARD N. FRYE

# MANICHAEISM,

MANICHAEISM, a religion based on gnostic doctrines and Zoroastrian dualism, founded in the third century CE by Mani. The faith spread throughout the Persian Sasanid empire and beyond in Mani's lifetime, in the west to Europe and North Africa, where the young Augustine practiced it before his conversion to Christianity, and in the east to Turkestan and China. It survived despite persecution by Zoroastrians and Christians, and as a heresy within Christianity it existed until recent times among the Bogomils of southeastern Europe.

Mani was born in northern Mesopotamia on 14 April 216, shortly before the Sasanid overthrow of the Parthians. His mother Maryam was of the noble Parthian Kamsaragan family; according to the tenth-century *Fihrist* of the Muslim Arab writer Ibn al-Nadim, his father, Patteg, a Persian of Hamadan, was a member of the Mughtasila ("those who bathe themselves," *maktak* in Sasanid inscriptions), apparently the gnostic sect of the Mandaeans. Mani was raised in the sect and adopted its calendar of fasts and, apparently, much of its philosophy in his later teachings. At the age of twelve Mani was first instructed by his spiritual "twin" (Pahlavi, *narjamig*, equated by western Manichaeans with the Christian Holy Spirit and by eastern Manichaeans with the Buddha Maitreya), but his full revelation came at twenty-four: he became the apostle of a new religion that was to incorporate and supersede the revelations of all past prophets.

Mani traveled throughout Iran as Manikhayya (Aramaic, "the one alive"; hence, Greek, Manichaios), healing, preaching, and composing hymns. He invented a script based on the Palmyrene character of his native Aramaic that represented with clarity and precision the various Iranian languages into which books and hymns were translated from the Aramaic. In the west, Manichaean books are found in Coptic, Greek, and Latin; and in the east in Chinese. Mani was renowned as an artist; one of his paintings, the *Ardahang*, retained its legendary fame in later Persian Islamic poetry. Although favored, it seems, by Shapur I, for whom he composed his only work in Pahlavi, the *Shabuhragan*, Mani was opposed by the ambitious and ruthless Zoroastrian high priest Kartir. He was summoned to court at Gundeshapur (Beth Lapat) by Bahram I in 274 or 277, hostilely interrogated by the king, perhaps in the presence of Kartir, imprisoned, and executed. In Parthian texts, the death of the Apostle of Light is called by the Buddhist term *parinirvana*—release from the wheel of being and suffering.

Mani's church was persecuted by the Sasanids, and many of the faithful fled northeast across the border on the Oxus, where the community grew to rival, and in the sixth century to claim independence from, the older center of the faith in Sasanid Babylon. The community had been founded, like Manichaean settlements elsewhere, by missionaries, in this case the third-century disciple Mar Ammo, who was accompanied by a Parthian prince and allowed to enter the eastern clime by its guardian spirit, the goddess Ard (Avestan, Ashi; the *yazatas* of prosperity in Zoroastrianism). In this legend is seen the Manichaean tendency to clothe history in local sacred garb; translations of religious terms, as in the case of the Twin, were similarly adapted to regional tradition, although the integrity of the doctrine itself was maintained. Parthian was the main language of the eastern Manichaean church; texts were also written in Pahlavi and the Iranian language of the local Sogdians. Translations were done in the Turkish of the Uighurs, whose king accepted Manichaeism in 762; it was the state religion until the Kirghiz conquest in 840. The Manichaeans lived in the main peacefully with their Christian, Buddhist, and Zoroastrian neighbors, but the damaged condition of most manuscripts attests to Muslim and other harassment, and the community, with its center in later times around Kocho, near modern Turfan, was eradicated in the Mongol invasions of the thirteenth century.

The Manichaean community was divided into two categories of believers, the Hearers (Pahlavi, *niyoshagan*) and the Elect (*dendaran*, literally "holders of the religion"; Zoroastrian Pahlavi, *den*). The Hearers were allowed to marry and to procreate; they provided for the needs of the Elect, who wore white, fasted regularly, observed strict rules of celibacy and vegetarianism, heard the weekly confessions of the Hearers, instructed them, and conducted religious services; the principal feast of the year was the Bema ("platform") festival in commemoration of the departure of Mani, spiritually enthroned among the faithful, from the world. The hierarchy of the Elect consisted of a leader (at Babylon in the west, and after the sixth century, also at Samarkand in Sogdiana), 12 apostles, 72 bishops, and 360 priests.

In the east, ritual life centered around organized monasteries; in the west, private houses and other facilities were used. Many liturgical hymns have been preserved—stirring poetry depicting the terror of the soul in the darkness of this world, its poignant cries for help, its escape from the concentric bonds of captivity of the evil demons, and its triumphant reunification with the Light. The theme of the soul as an alien, light element imprisoned in darkness, from which it is released by the revelation of wisdom concerning its true origins and by its abstinence from the worldly lusts that imprison it, is familiar from such gnostic texts as the Syriac *Hymn of the Pearl* in the *Gospel of Thomas;* the hymn's protagonist, the Soul, is a Parthian prince.

Mani developed an elaborate cosmological scheme peopled by a plethora of divinities invented by him or drawn from Zoroastrianism, Christianity, and Buddhism. In the beginning, the Paradise of Light extended to the north, west, and east, or above, while the Hell of Darkness yawned southward and below. Paradise was ruled by the Father of Greatness (called Zurvan, "time," in Pahlavi texts but not in Parthian ones; this indicates that in Persia the terminology was adapted to Zurvanism), his consort the Great Spirit, and the five Light Elements. There are five corresponding Dark Elements in Hell.

The Devil (Ahremen; Ahriman in Zoroastrianism) came to the boundary of the two worlds by chance and, desiring the Light, invaded it. The Father of Greatness withdrew from the battle that ensued, evoking successive emanations of himself, of the same nature but of various functions (like the divinities of Mazdak), to fight the intruder or to deflect his attention by being captured. One of these is the First Man, Ohrmizd (Ohrmazd in Zoroastrianism; born of Zurvan in the Zurvanist myth), who is seized by the darkness. He calls out for help and is rescued, becoming the prototype for every soul of light caught in this world. In the wars that follow the Living Spirit shapes the world from the corpses of vanquished demons. The redemption of the remaining light trapped in darkness is begun, but is frustrated by the demonic creation of Adam and Eve through Matter (Pahlavi, Az, the female demon of concupiscence in Zoroastrianism). The god Jesus the Splendor enlightens Adam, who renounces procreation, but Eve is seduced by a demon and thereby perpetuates the human species, to whom the Great Nous (Wahman; Avestan, Vohu Manah, "good mind," by whose agency revelation came to Zoroaster) periodically sends prophets, of whom Mani is the greatest.

Mani taught that each soul passes through successive incarnations until it attains release: the Elect ascend directly to the New Paradise, an antechamber of the Paradise of Light; evil men go to Hell. At the end of days, Jesus will return, the cosmos will collapse, matter will be imprisoned, and the freed souls will behold the Father of Greatness in the Paradise of Light. Mani thus inverted the Zoroastrian dualistic world view: the two primordial forces of good and evil are locked in struggle, but the Father of Greatness himself has withdrawn. The world, rather than being in essence a good creation, the ultimate reward, from which evil is to be cast out by the combined efforts of Ahura Mazda—ever present to his beloved creation, man—and ourselves, is for Mani an abortion in which we are lost, far from the alien god. Wisdom is a means of precipitate flight, rather than an instrument of ultimate harmony. The doctrine of reincarnation is adopted from Buddhism. But the figure of Jesus is neither gnostic nor docetic: although the savior is God and not man in Mani's system, his sufferings are not a mere pretense designed to deceive the Archons—our cosmic jailers—but the true agony of light held captive by the dark.

Zoroastrians condemned Mani as a *zandik,* a misinterpreter of the Avesta; a chapter of the ninth-century polemical work *Shkand-gumanig wizar (Doubt-dispelling Explanation)* is devoted to a refutation of his form of dualism. Mani is known from both Sogdian and Arabic sources to have written an epistle to the Armenians, and it seems that his religion was newly diffused through the Byzantine lands in the guise of various heretical Christian sects, the Thondrakites, Cathars, Albigensians, and later the Bogomils, by Armenians who migrated to the Balkans in the ninth century.

[*See also* Ahura Mazda; Mani; Sasanid Dynasty; *and* Zoroastrianism.]

J. P. Asmussen, *X^uāstvānīft, Studies in Manichaeism* (1965) and *Manichaean Literature* (1975). Mary Boyce, *The Manichaean Hymn Cycles in Parthian* (1954) and *A Reader in Manichaean Middle Persian and Parthian* (1975). F. C. Burkitt, *The Religion of the Manichees* (1925). W. B. Henning, "Mani's Last Journey," *Bulletin of the School of Oriental and African Studies* 10 (1942): 941–953, and "The Manichaean Fasts," *Journal of the Royal Asiatic Society* (1945): 146–164. Steven Runciman, *The Medieval Manichee* (1961). Geo Widengren, *Mani and Manichaeism* (1965). JAMES R. RUSSELL

**MANICKAVASAGAM, V.**, president of the Malayan Indian Congress (MIC) from 1973 to 1979, carried out a major reorganization of the party, attracting more urban intellectuals and non-Tamils to the MIC. He also served in several cabinets, heading various ministries. Under his leadership the MIC became a more effective voice for the Indian community in Malaysia, but the relatively small size of the Indian population has limited the MIC to a modest role in government, restricting Manickavasagam and his successors mainly to the ministries of labor, transport, and finance.

[*See also* Malaysia *and* Malayan Indian Congress.]

Rajeswary Ampalavanar, *The Indian Minority and Political Change in Malaya, 1945–1957* (1981). S. Arasaratnam, *Indians in Malaysia and Singapore* (1979).

RAJESWARY AMPALAVANAR

**MANILA**, capital and chief city of the Philippines since the sixteenth century.

By the time the Spanish colonizer Miguel Lopez de Legazpi reached Manila in 1571 it was already a small commercial port with connections to the Asian trading system; its raja was a Muslim, with marriage ties to the sultanate of Brunei and trading connections in Melaka. It was, however, simply one port among many, whether on Manila Bay or among the islands as a whole, that survived on the peddling trade characteristic of the times. Having conquered the city, Lopez de Legazpi chose to make it Spain's headquarters for the conquest and christianization of the archipelago. Manila rapidly became a Spanish colonial city like many in Spanish America, and it was administered through the viceroy in Mexico. There were headquartered the Spanish military, bureaucracy, and missionary orders.

During its first two centuries, Manila—and, indeed, the Philippines—depended economically on Asian traders, especially Chinese, who flocked to Manila to trade luxury goods for Mexican silver dollars. It also depended on the Manila galleon, which sailed to Acapulco annually and made enormous profits that sustained the Spanish administration. The galleon trade also indirectly affected the social composition of Manila and its outlying ports by attracting an entrepreneurial Chinese minority.

It was only after the British conquest and occupation of Manila (1762–1764), and especially following the end of the galleon trade (1811–1815), that Manila established its character as a major port for the movement of bulk commodities, for it was only then that the colonial government seriously began to develop the agricultural economy of the Philippines. Nineteenth-century Manila functioned as the hub of inter-island commerce, receiving shipments of sugar, tobacco, hemp, and other commodities from throughout the archipelago for export and managing imports and the wholesale and retail trade. Provincial families, many mestizo in their origins, with economic interests to look after, now took up residence in the capital, and increasingly they formed an educated, economically powerful, and politically conscious group that the Spaniards found ever more difficult to control. Manila was now both the most cosmopolitan and the most Filipino—not simply Tagalog or Spanish or mestizo—of Philippine cities. The energies of the metropolitan elite made possible the Philippine Revolution (1896–1898) as well as the transition to an independent government during the American colonial regime (1898–1946).

Manila was heavily damaged both in the Japanese conquest of December 1941 and the American reconquest in early 1945. The combination of wartime damage and rapid postwar growth has left little physical evidence of an old Manila, which is perhaps best represented by a few churches and Malacanang Palace, once the seat of Spanish governors and now of the Philippine president.

[*See also* Philippines; Manila Galleon; Indios; Intramuros; Manila Bay, Battle of; Mestizo; Parian; Philippine-American War; Philippine Revolution; Propaganda Movement; *and* Spain and the Philippines.]

Teodoro Agoncillo and O. M. Alfonso, *History of the Filipino People* (1967). J. L. Phelan, *The Hispanization of the Philippines* (1959). E. Wickberg, *The Chinese in Philippine Life, 1850–1898* (1965). D. C. Worcester, *The Philippines Past and Present* (1914).    DAVID K. WYATT

# MANILA BAY, BATTLE OF

**MANILA BAY, BATTLE OF** (1898), naval victory by a US squadron under the command of Commodore George Dewey that destroyed the Spanish Pacific fleet of Admiral Patricio Montojo and paved the way for the cession of the Philippine archipelago to the United States.

Dewey's squadron of six modern warships entered Manila Bay under cover of darkness and engaged the outgunned Spanish men-of-war at dawn on 1 May. The American ships attacked in column formation in a series of lateral passes, and by noon every Spanish ship was sunk or in flames. Following the battle, US Army troops were transported to Manila, and the city formally surrendered on 14 August.

[*See also* Philippine Revolution *and* Philippine-American War.]

Ronald Spector, *Admiral of the New Empire: The Life and Career of George Dewey* (1974). David F. Trask, *The War With Spain in 1898* (1981).

RICHARD E. WELCH, JR.

# MANILA GALLEON

**MANILA GALLEON.** Its conquest of Peru in the 1530s provided Spain with immense quantities of silver that it used to secure the luxuries of the East directly, thereby eliminating Spanish dependence on Portuguese intermediaries. In 1565 a navigational route from Manila to Mexico and back was discovered. The first Manila galleon carried Chinese silks, satins, porcelain, and Southeast Asian spices to Acapulco in 1573, returning to Manila with Spanish silver from the New World. For the next 250 years Manila was the hub of a commercial circuit in which Asian products were exchanged for New World silver.

Since the government of China would not allow Spain to establish a permanent settlement on the China coast (the Portuguese had already secured a trading alliance with Canton and had been granted a trade base on Macao), Spain was forced to find a suitable harbor elsewhere. When Spain seized Manila in 1570, it was already a prosperous port with a well-established commercial community of Chinese and Southeast Asian merchants. These Manila-based traders had become wealthy as marketers of eastern Indonesian archipelago products that were secured via the Sula Sea, but they also traded regularly with Vietnam, Japan, and Siam. Under Spanish rule Manila was not only a Spanish but also a Chinese city. Since the Spaniards themselves could not trade in China, they instead depended on the Chinese community to supply Manila with Chinese products.

The voyage to Manila from Acapulco was a relatively easy eight to ten weeks with the wind, but the way back, which required a more northern route and went against the Pacific Ocean wind currents, took between four and six months. The ship left Manila in late June or early July. Sometimes up to 75 percent of the Asian and European crew died from disease or malnutrition before the galleon reached Acapulco; a 30 to 40 percent loss of crew was usual, and in 1657 the galleon arrived in Acapulco with all its crew dead. To improve the odds of survival on the voyage from the East, the California coast was settled to provision galleons before they made their way south to Acapulco. Although the voyage was risky, it produced high profits. While the Atlantic Ocean trade normally returned a 15 percent profit, it was not unusual to receive 30 to 50 percent interest on one's investment in the galleon trade. During the last decade of the sixteenth century, bullion exports from the New World, two-thirds of which came from Peru, usually ran between three and five million pesos. In 1597, an exceptional year, the bullion sent from Acapulco to Manila reached twelve million pesos. Between 1570 and 1780 an estimated four thousand to five thousand tons of silver were exported to Manila.

At Acapulco, goods were loaded on muleback for transshipment to Mexico City. Peruvian merchants also arrived in large numbers, bringing smuggled Peruvian silver to exchange for Chinese goods. The illegal Peruvian trade in Acapulco and along the coast of Nicaragua became a source of concern for the Spanish crown, which tried to limit it. So much silver was shipped to Manila and so many Asian products were returned that Spanish merchants in Seville, who held a royal monopoly over the New World import and export trade, forced the Madrid government to impose limits on the value and volume of the annual Manila galleon. The galleon trade was officially regulated to guarantee sufficient profit in order to subsidize Manila's Spanish population and government while also protecting the interests of Iberian merchants. Despite royal prohibitions, the volume of the galleon trade always far exceeded the official limits.

Space in the Manila galleon was divided into shares of a fixed size that were controlled by the Spanish community of Manila, which was constituted as a powerful commercial guild (*consulado*). Few of these Spaniards, however, were merchants themselves, but instead sold their cargo space to Chinese merchants or depended on Chinese trade partners who secured cargoes and traded on their behalf. The Spanish church was also a major participant in the trade, often supplying most of the capital to purchase Chinese goods and outfit the galleon and frequently subsidizing the Manila Spanish community between the galleon's annual visits. Spanish residents of Manila were so dependent on the galleon trade that if a galleon was lost or captured the community faced financial ruin.

The ease by which the community normally secured wealth by investing in the galleon trade discouraged it from developing the Luzon interior. The only direct Spanish contact with the Manila hinterland was maintained by Spanish friars, and restrictions on the volume of the galleon trade inhibited Spain's interest in cultivating trading relationships with other Asian states. Only after the British occupied Manila in 1762—and subsequently plundered it—was Manila's Spanish community finally forced to enter the Luzon interior to develop an export crop economy.

[*See also* Manila *and* Spain and the Philippines.]

Emma Blair and James A. Robertson, eds., *The Philippine Islands, 1493–1898*, 55 vols. (1903–1909). Alonso Felix, Jr., *The Chinese in the Philippines*, 2 vols. (1966). John L. Phelan, *The Hispanization of the Philippines: Spanish Aims and Filipino Responses, 1565–1700* (1959).

KENNETH R. HALL

MANIPUR, Indian state of over a million people, situated on the Burmese border. The state is sharply divided, both geographically and ethnically: in the rugged hills, which comprise approximately 90 percent of the area of the state, live twenty-nine different tribal groups constituting one-third of the total population. The remaining two-thirds are concentrated in the Manipur Valley and are predominately Meitei.

Historically, *Meitei* simply designated one of the seven Kuki-Chin speaking clans in the valley, but as the Meitei became politically powerful their name also assumed preeminence. Centered in Imphal, the Meitei dynasties evolved a complex ranking system based on genealogy and expressed in types of service

given the throne. In the eighteenth century Bengali influence led to cultural changes, particularly the adoption of Vaishnavism by the elite. British conquest in 1891 accelerated social transformation and increased the distance between the elite and the masses. Efforts to revive the traditional Meitei culture, such as the following of customary religious rituals and the attempt to replace Bengali script with Manipuri script, have had strong political overtones. These cultural movements aim, with some success, at challenging an alliance among the ruling elite, the national government, and Vaishnavite brahmans.

Resistance in the hills has been far more violent. In 1917 the Kuki tribes rebelled against the British practice of forced labor. Similar grievances and a sense of cultural dislocation were factors in the birth of the Zeliangrong movement, a unification of several Naga groups. Led by a religious charismatic named Jadonang, who was hung by the British in 1931, the movement continued under the leadership of his female first cousin, Gaidinliu, who allied herself with the Congress Party. This movement, with its religious overtones, remains influential in the area.

[*See also* Adivasis *and* Naga.]

T. Hodson, *Naga Tribes of Manipur* (1911). J. Roy, *A History of Manipur* (1958). K. Singh, ed., *Tribal Movements in India* (1982). CHARLES LINDHOLM

MANOPAKORN NITITHADA (1884–1948), Thailand's first prime minister (1932–1933). The son of a cobbler, Phraya (Thai, "governor, minister") Manopakorn (Thongkon Hutasing) was born in Bangkok, attended the Ministry of Justice Law School, and completed further studies in England. He held the posts of Privy Council member, finance minister, and professor of law before becoming prime minister in 1932. He was recommended to the post by Pridi Phanomyong, who hoped that Mano, then an admired judge of the Court of Appeals, would give immediate respectability to Thailand's new constitutional government (established by the 1932 revolution, which overthrew the monarchy). On 1 April 1933, however, Mano suspended parliamentary meetings, claiming that members were too busy feuding and advocating communistic ideas; he was particularly alarmed by Pridi's proposed Economic Development Program. Nineteen days later Mano was unseated by a coup led by Phraya Phahon Phonphayuhasena and fled to Penang, where he lived in exile until his death.

[*See also* Thailand; Pridi Phanomyong; Phahon Phonphayuhasena; *and* People's Party of Thailand.]

Kenneth P. Landon, *Siam in Transition* (1939).

THAK CHALOEMTIARANA

## MANSABDARI SYSTEM.

The Mughal emperor Akbar based his administrative and military organization on this system, by which each state official was given a military rank (Persian, *mansab*), irrespective of his duties, that determined his status and salary. In case of military duty the *mansabdar* ("*mansab*-holder") actually commanded the number of soldiers his rank indicated. As the number of *mansabdars* increased, there began to appear a distinction between the personal rank of the official and the number of soldiers he commanded. This was indicated by *zat* (personal rank) and *sawar* rank (indicating horsemen under command). The gap between the two increased with time. *Mansabdars* were initially paid in cash but later in revenue assignments called *jagirs*. Regular transfer of *mansabdars* throughout the empire was an effective check on consolidation of local power. The growing number of *mansabdars* created pressures on state revenues and contributed considerably to the breakdown of Mughal administration in the eighteenth century.

[*See also* Akbar *and* Mughal Empire.]

Abdul Aziz, *The Mansabdari System and the Mughal Army* (1972). Satish Chandra, *Parties and Politics at the Mughal Court, 1707–1740* (1959).    HARBANS MUKHIA

## MAN SINGH

(1550–1614). In 1562 the Indian Mughal emperor Akbar initiated a policy of conciliating the long-term adversaries of the empire, the Rajputs. The first and chief beneficiary of this policy was the house of the Kachchawaha clan of Rajputs, whose kingdom was at Amber (Jaipur). Man Singh belonged to this house. Akbar cemented the newly forged alliance through matrimony. Man Singh's paternal aunt became Akbar's queen and gave birth to Salim (Jahangir), who in turn married Man Singh's sister. Man Singh himself rose to the highest *mansab*, or rank in the imperial service, outside of imperial princes; he became Akbar's chief general, conquering territories and suppressing rebellions all over the empire.

[*See also* Rajput *and* Akbar.]

R. N. Prasad, *Raja Man Singh of Amber* (1966).

HARBANS MUKHIA

## MANSUR SYAH,

sixth sultan of Melaka (r. 1459–1477). During his reign Melaka came to dominate most of the important tin-, gold-, and pepper-producing areas of the Malay Peninsula, East Sumatra, and the intervening islands. Mansur successfully opposed Thai influence in the peninsula by mounting an expedition against Pahang. His chief minister (*bendahara*), Tun Perak, probably inspired these expansionist policies and personally led many of the expeditions.

[*See also* Melaka.]

C. C. Brown, "Sejarah Melayu or Malay Annals," *Journal of the Malay Branch of the Royal Asiatic Society* 25.2–3 (October 1952). Kernial Singh Sandhu and Paul Wheatley, *Melaka: The Transformation of a Malay Capital c. 1400–1980* (1983).    DIANNE LEWIS

## MANUCCI, NICCOLAO

(1638–1717), Italian traveler. At age fourteen, moved by "a passionate desire to see the world," he left Venice to undertake a journey to India. There he spent over a half century, traveling extensively. In the War of Succession (1657–1658) he attached himself to Dara Shikoh and remained loyal to him to the end. His four-volume *Storia do Mogor* (1653–1708) is a valuable source of information on a wide range of themes for seventeenth-century India.

[*See also* Dara Shikoh *and* Mughal Empire.]

Niccolao Manucci, *Storia do Mogor*, translated by W. Irvine (1907–1908).    HARBANS MUKHIA

## MAN'YŌSHŪ,

Japan's first anthology of poetry and one of the world's greatest collections of archaic lyrical verse. As the fount of Japanese literary expression, the *Man'yōshū* occupies a position comparable to that of the works of Homer for Western literature or the *Book of Songs* (*Shiji*) for Chinese literature. The title, literally "the collection of ten thousand leaves," suggests this was considered the "anthology of all anthologies" from seventh- and eighth-century Japan. Most of the works in the *Man'yōshū* were composed between the 640s and the 750s. The last dated poem was composed in 759, but the anthology is thought to include some later works, possibly some from the ninth century.

The *Man'yōshū* includes some 4,516 poems, collected in twenty *maki*, or "scrolls". There are included some four hundred named poets, but approximately half of the poems in the anthology are anonymous. There is a great variety of poets, "from emperors to beggars," and the collection includes a few works in Chinese as well as "poems of the frontier guardsmen" and "poems of the Eastland" in provincial dialect.

The three classical thematic categories in the *Man'yōshū* are the "poems on various themes" (*zōka*), which include celebrations of imperial excursions; the "personal exchanges" (*sōmon*), largely the poetry of erotic longing; and the "laments" (*banka*, literally "coffin-pulling poems"), the poetry of bereavement. The two major forms are the *chōka*, "long poem," and the *tanka*, "short poem"; both consist of alternating *ku*, or phrases, of five and seven syllables. The writing system is characterized by a mix of Chinese characters used both phonetically and semantically and is strikingly similar to the writing system used in recording *hyangga*, native Korean verse.

The first important poet encountered in the *Man'yōshū* is Princess Nukada, who flourished at Emperor Tenji's Ōmi Court in the 660s. Her "Spring and Autumn Poem" (1.16) is an aesthetic judgment of nature that shows the influence of Chinese parallelism. The greatest poet of the anthology, and one of the two or three greatest figures in classical Japanese poetry, is Kakinomoto no Hitomaro, most of whose work was composed in the 690s. Hitomaro completed a shift that was changing Japanese poetry from a ritual to a lyrical verbal art; his *chōka* are marked by unprecedented scale and rhetorical complexity. Especially renowned are his laments for the imperial family (2.167, 199, etc.), the poems on the death of his wife (2.207–212), and the *chōka* often considered his masterpiece, "Poem upon seeing a dead man lying among the rocks on the island of Samine in Sanuki" (2.220).

Another major poet is Yamanoue Okura, who was a member of Ōtomo Tabito's poetry circle at the Dazaifu in the Nara period. Tabito's circle wrote in Chinese as well as Japanese, and Okura's work, especially his "Dialogue of the Destitute" (5.892), shows the influence of Confucianism and Buddhism. It is the only major discursive, philosophical poetry in the *waka* tradition. Another poet of the Nara period included is Yamabe no Akahito, whose work is characterized by a less religious, more imagistic treatment of the landscape, as seen in his "Poem on viewing Mount Fuji" (2.317) and its celebrated *tanka* envoi (3.318).

The last great poet of the Nara period was Ōtomo Yakamochi. The most prolific of *Man'yōshū* poets, Yakamochi composed in a style that anticipates the more subjective exploitation of nature found in poetry of the Heian period. Yakamochi is traditionally considered the compiler of the *Man'yōshū*, although it is now thought that the work of editing continued for some time after the Nara period.

Ian Hideo Levy, *The Ten Thousand Leaves: A Translation of the Man'yōshū, Japan's Premier Anthology of Classical Poetry* (vol. 1, 1981).    IAN HIDEO LEVY

MAO DUN (1896–1981), pseudonym, meaning "contradiction," of Shen Yanbing, Chinese novelist and literary figure. Mao Dun was a founding member of the Literary Association (1920) and editor of its influential magazine, *Short Story* (1921–1923); he joined the Communist Party in 1921, was a founding member of the League of Left-Wing Writers (1930), and sided with Lu Xun in the League's 1936 split. Fame came with his first novel, *Disillusion* (1927), part of a trilogy about a youth in the Northern Expedition. In the next twenty years there followed short stories, essays, much newspaper work, and half a dozen chiefly topical novels, of which *Midnight* is best known. Under the People's Republic Mao Dun was, until the Cultural Revolution, head of the Writers' Union and minister of culture. His memoirs were published between 1979 and 1981.

Merle Goldman, ed., *Modern Chinese Literature in the May Fourth Era* (1977), pp. 233–280. Mao Tun (Mao Dun), *Midnight,* translated by Hsü Meng-hsiung and A. C. Barnes (1957).    SHAN CHOU

MAO ZEDONG (1893–1976), preeminent leader of the People's Republic of China and first secretary of the Chinese Communist Party (CCP) from 1943 until his death. A keen strategist, capable poet, and able politician, Mao sought to remake China into a modern and industrial power using unorthodox means.

Mao Zedong was born in Hunan Province in the rocky upland village of Shaoshan, Xiangtan County, where 75 percent of the residents were surnamed Mao. His father, Mao Shunshen, was a hard and grasping man who managed to raise himself to moderate wealth. Mao had two brothers, Mao Zemin (1895–1943) and Mao Zetan (1905–1935), and a sister, Mao Zehong (d. 1930). Mao's mother died in the autumn of 1919; his father died within a few months, in January 1920.

Mao began attending the village school in Shaoshan when he was eight years old. After only five years of schooling, however, his father had him return to the farm to work in the fields by day and manage the account books at night. In 1909 Mao, who hated farming, fled the family farm for the next county. There his maternal uncle had obtained his entrance into the Tongshan Higher Primary School. Mao was six years older than the other students, and his ragged clothes and country manners were a source of great embarrassment to him. By early 1911, versed in the traditional classics and alert to the crisis of his country, the seventeen-year-old Mao was ready for larger things. He took a steamer to Changsha, where he was admitted to middle school and began reading newspapers. He rapidly became one of the most avid readers in his age group and later stated that his entire education had been through newspapers.

During the summer and early autumn of 1911 political fever grew in Changsha, fueled in part by a rice shortage in the city and in part by news of the unsuccessful uprising in Canton (Guangzhou) led by another Hunanese, Huang Xing. [See also Huang Xing.] When news came of the Wuchang Uprising of 11 October, Mao and a friend were quick to join the army. He spent six months as a common soldier, reading voraciously. During this period he first encountered socialism in several pamphlets by Jiang Kanghu (1883–c. 1945). Demobilized, the nineteen-year-old Mao applied to various schools before withdrawing to spend six months reading on his own in the provincial library. Eventually, in the spring of 1913, Mao resolved to become a teacher.

During the next five years Mao attended the First Provincial Normal School, where he acquired a great portion of his education and served a part of his apprenticeship as a politician. He learned to write classical Chinese poetry and became a disciple of Yang Changji, a nationally known advocate of combining Western science with Chinese culture. Mao's first significant published article, "A Study of Physical Culture" (1917), stressed patriotism: "If our bodies are not strong, we will be afraid as soon as we see enemy soldiers. How then can we reach our goals and make ourselves respected?" Patriotism was Mao's driving motive for many years, gradually becoming mixed with a quest for personal power. As a student he and his friends founded a night school for workers, based on the idea that an ignorant nation was a weak nation. Upon graduation in 1918, they founded the Xinmin Xuehui (New Citizens Study Society) in an effort to continue the intellectual excitement of school as they scattered around the world. In the fall of 1918 Mao followed Yang Changji to Beijing, where his teacher helped him to obtain a minor library job working for the Marxist thinker Li Dazhao. He returned to Changsha shortly after the outbreak of the May Fourth Movement in 1919 and established the *Xiang River Review* as the local voice of that movement. He quickly earned a reputation as an effective spokesman against warlordism and imperialism. After publishing four issues, the journal was closed down and Mao became editor of Yale-in-China's *Xin Hunan (New Hunan)*. When this journal was also suppressed by the local warlord, Mao continued to write for a newspaper until the failure of a student strike in December 1919 forced him to flee the province. [See also Li Dazhao and May Fourth Movement.]

Mao returned to Changsha in the summer of 1920. He won a job as principal of the primary school associated with his alma mater, and with it the material basis to marry Yang Kaihui, Yang Changji's second daughter, the following winter. He became a leader in several local organizations and began demonstrating his ability to participate fully in emotional meetings, while at the end giving a dispassionate, reliable verbal summary of the proceedings.

In his autobiography, related to Edgar Snow in 1936, Mao declared that by the summer of 1920 he "had become in theory and to some extent in action a Marxist." In August he founded a Marxist study group. However, patriotism in Changsha was still as likely to be associated with anarchism as with Marxism. The Culture Bookstore, founded by Mao and his friends (in a building owned by Yale-in-China) in the autumn of 1920, stocked anarchist books more heavily than Marxist tracts. Anarchism also heavily peppered Mao's involvement with a short-lived, highly emotional movement to establish an independent nation of Hunan in the same year.

Mao followed news from the developing communist movements in Beijing and Shanghai closely, and in January 1921 he announced to his colleagues that he had become a communist. In July 1921 Mao, now twenty-seven, led the Hunanese delegation to the First Congress of the Chinese Communist Party in Shanghai; he returned as secretary of the Hunan Branch of the CCP.

In Changsha in 1920 and 1921 anarchists led a burgeoning labor movement in which Mao was not involved until late 1921. In January 1922 Mao sent a representative of the Hunan party to the coal mines at Anyuan to begin organizing. Within nine months Anyuan miners had become one of the most successful unions in all China, and Mao had sent other members of the Party to organize railroad workers, carpenters, barbers, lead miners, and many others. The labor movement took on a life of its own, over-reached itself, and was cut short by a warlord crack-down in early 1923.

Mao did not attend the Second Congress of the CCP in June 1922, but at the Third Party Congress, a year later, he was elected to the Central Commit-tee. Living now in Shanghai, he threw himself into the task of advancing the alliance between the Com-munist Party and the Nationalist Party (Guomin-dang) of Sun Yat-sen. Representatives of the Com-intern had ordered the Chinese Communists to make this alliance with the national bourgeoisie, but the coalition was fraught with conflict from the begin-ning. [See also Comintern.] After nearly eighteen months as a high official of the CCP and a member of the Shanghai Bureau of the Guomindang, facing attacks from both the right and the left, Mao became ill. He and his wife returned to Shaoshan in February 1925 to recuperate.

The international communist movement already had founded a Peasant International (Krestintern) in October 1923. But Chen Duxiu, secretary of the Party's Central Committee, considered the peas-antry an unreliable element, prone to "feudal" hab-its. In the poor upland area around Shaoshan, sev-eral of Mao's acquaintances from Changsha were establishing night schools for peasants; Yang Kaihui began teaching in one of them. In May and June 1925 the group organized antiforeign National Shame societies, and by July had begun helping peas-ants organize to prevent landlords from selling grain outside the locality. In late August soldiers from the provincial army arrived to quell the threat to prop-erty. Mao fled to Canton.

By October 1925 Mao had become acting head of the Nationalist Party's propaganda department. Never bashful, he now claimed to be more expert on the countryside than anyone of his political rank. The need for increased work among the peasants was the theme of his address to the Second Congress of the Guomindang. He was again elected to be the alternate member of the Guomindang Central Ex-ecutive Committee and in December 1925 became a member of the Peasant Movement Committee. When Chiang Kai-shek took advantage of the Zhongshan Incident of March 1926 to reduce the role of Communists in the Canton government, Mao was removed from his most important posts. At almost exactly the same time he became head of the two-year-old Peasant Moving Training Institute, charged with teaching students to mobilize the rural masses for national revolution.

When classes ended in the fall, the Northern Ex-pedition was already under way. Mao traveled to Shanghai, made a brief tour of rural areas in Zhe-jiang and Jiangsu, and in December gave the keynote address to the First Hunan Peasant's Association Congress in Changsha. He spent January 1927 in-vestigating the situation in five rural counties near Changsha. The resulting "Report on an Investiga-tion of the Peasant Movement in Hunan" (March 1927) has been called "unique within the Chinese Communist movement" because it looks to the peas-ants as the major revolutionary force. It is also a graphic example of how Mao related to the peas-antry en masse; he wrote not from his roots as a peasant's son, but from his role as an agent of rev-olution. The report is also a pro-Comintern docu-ment in the hotly charged debate between the Com-intern and Chen Duxiu, the CCP chairman who rejected the importance of the peasantry in the rev-olution. [See also Chen Duxiu.]

The Communist–Nationalist alliance collapsed completely in June 1927, leaving the CCP in disar-ray, its members hunted criminals. Many of the Par-ty's leaders took part in the Nanchang Uprising of 1 August, now celebrated as the date of the estab-lishment of the Red Army. Other leaders, including Mao, attended an "emergency conference" on 7 Au-gust. Chen Duxiu was deposed as leader of the Party and a series of rural uprisings were planned for Hu-bei, Jiangxi, and Hunan.

The goal of these Autumn Harvest Uprisings was to surround and capture the major cities of the Yangtze region. Mao was sent to Hunan to lead the rising there. But the peasant movement of which he had written glowingly six months earlier had faded. The masses did not rise, and the ragtag, inexperi-enced forces of this uprising were defeated within ten days. Narrowly escaping capture, Mao gathered the remnants—about one thousand men—and re-treated to a traditional bandit lair on Jinggang Shan, 130 miles southeast of Changsha. [See also Jinggang Shan.]

Mao used his redoubtable powers of friendship and persuasion to ally with two traditional bandit leaders. He organized peasant uprisings against landlords, and for a year fought defensive wars both against warlord soldiers and against the leadership of the Communist Party Center, which strongly urged unrealistic policies to make his little army the central force in a nationwide, spontaneous uprising. In May 1928 he was joined by Zhu De's force of ten thousand poorly equipped men. Zhu became commander of the Fourth Red Army, while Mao became political commissar.

In November the Zhu–Mao Fourth Red Army was again reinforced by the arrival of a ragged band of one thousand soldiers under Peng Dehuai, who had rebelled against the Guomindang. Zhu and Mao evolved the famous sloga, "The enemy advances, we retreat; the enemy camps, we harass; the enemy tires, we attack; the enemy retreats, we pursue." But by the winter of 1928 to 1929 the Fourth Red Army was beset by fierce attacks from warlord armies allied with Chiang Kai-shek. On 14 January 1929 Mao and Zhu left Jinggang Shan, crossed Jiangxi Province, and—after a terrible battle in which they lost half their forces—established the Chinese Soviet Republic in a new base near Ruijin.

Mao Zedong, now thirty-seven years old, gradually began to build the strongest center of Communist power in China, based firmly on his experience of what was effective in raising the enthusiasm of the peasants. He undertook a series of social surveys to provide background to land reform and agrarian revolution, further developing his strong sense of the deep ethical ideals of the common people. He formulated independent theories regarding organization, leadership, political training, military discipline, territorial bases, and other matters in essays such as "On the Rectification of Incorrect Ideas in the Party" (December 1929) and "A Single Spark Can Start a Prairie Fire" (January 1930).

The Central Committee in Shanghai, dominated by Li Lisan and living underground in the wreckage of the failures of 1927, preferred to emphasize the urban proletariat's role in the struggle rather than rural revolution. Mao strongly opposed Li's strategic orders in February 1929 to disperse and fight a pure guerrilla war. He only reluctantly obeyed orders in mid-1930 to assault the major cities of central China with his newly expanded forces. Peng Dehuai occupied Changsha for ten days in the summer of 1930, but Mao and Zhu De were driven back from Nanchang. By the end of autumn the Communist forces had been forced to retire into the marches once again. In Hunan the vengeful warlord government executed both Yang Kaihui, Mao's former wife living in retirement, and his sister Mao Zehong.

Busy with matters in other parts of the country, Chiang Kai-shek had not considered the Communists to be a principal threat to his power until these attacks. Now his police intensified the search for Communists in the cities. In the South China countryside his armies undertook five successive Encirclement Campaigns to annihilate the Communists. Even when confronted with the Japanese conquest of the Northeast (Manchuria) beginning in September 1931, Chiang continued to allocate most of his military resources to fighting the Communists. [See also Communist-Extermination Campaigns.]

Numerically inferior, the Communists survived for three years by combining carefully calculated withdrawals and slashing surprise attacks. However, between 1931 and 1934, the leadership was sharply divided between Moscow-supported elements who wanted the revolution to return to the cities quickly, and those (led by Mao) who were intent on adapting Communist theory to local conditions, patiently cultivating rural revolution. This division was at the root of the Communist leadership's inability to decide whether to support an anti-Chiang rebellion in Fujian Province in November 1933, and led to Mao's replacement as political commissar by Zhou Enlai in the same year.

Always a competent political infighter, the embattled Mao secured reelection as chairman of the Central Soviet government when the Second All-China Congress of Soviets met at Ruijin in January 1934. This position would have allowed him to continue his economic work had the Jiangxi Soviet remained viable. But as Chiang Kai-shek's circle of blockhouses, connected by modern motor roads, drew ever tighter around the base area later that year, the question of survival became uppermost. The Central Soviet government at Ruijin dissolved in October and set out on the Long March.

The Long March is an epic of human endurance that lasted 370 days and covered 6,000 rugged miles, with fighting almost every day. The Communists broke out of the encirclement thinking they were marching westward, possibly to establish a new soviet area with He Long in northwestern Hunan. Their attempt to cross the Xiang River in northern Guangxi, however, cost nearly two-thirds of the 100,000 troops who had begun the march. At Mao's urging, the Hunan plan was abandoned and the First Front Red Army moved further westward into Guizhou. [See also Long March.]

In January 1935 the badly battered force took the city of Zunyi in northern Guizhou Province and convened a conference of all major leaders. Mao seized the opportunity to voice severe criticisms of the military line being pushed by the Soviet-backed Party leadership. He argued forcefully that they had fought in too conventional a manner instead of resorting to the guerrilla tactics for which Mao was later to become famous. Zhou Enlai, previously an ally of the Moscow-oriented Party Center, offered a self-criticism and proposed that Mao take over military leadership. Henceforth, Zhou became one of Mao's most trusted subordinates. A goal for the march was decided upon: to go north to fight the Japanese. Mao was not to receive formal leadership over the Party until 1943, but the Zunyi Conference had set the stage for his becoming the undisputed leader of the new China. From the leading core of the march participants, Mao built a cohesive military and Party leadership that survived largely intact for thirty years.

In Yan'an from 1936 to 1947, Mao Zedong led his movement in wars against foreign and domestic enemies. Generals such as Zhu De, Peng Dehuai, Lin Biao, Chen Yi, He Long, Liu Bozheng, and others did the front-line fighting. Zhou Enlai took care of the daily problems of relations with the Nationalists. Mao set himself to a serious study of Marxism-Leninism and wrote prolifically. He articulated a coherent set of ideas for remaking China, and he secured for himself unquestioned supremacy within the Chinese Communist Party.

Mao came to be the supreme dictator of a unorthodox type of revolutionary war, utilizing the crisis of the Japanese invasion and the weakness of Chiang Kai-shek's Nationalist government. Mao's pragmatic military doctrine grew naturally from his experience in Jinggang Shan and Jiangxi, and from his knowledge of traditional Chinese strategic thinking. Tactically, this meant guerrilla mobile warfare, avoiding positional battle unless certain of victory. Strategically, it meant occupying uncontested areas and building an infrastructure for use in the future, while at the same time pursuing a united front with the Nationalists.

Mao began urging a second united front with the Nationalists even before the Long March had ended. In "On Tactics Against Japanese Imperialism," given at a metteing of the Political Bureau in December 1935, Mao outlined his fundamental strategy: "The task of the Party is to form a revolutionary united front by combining the activities of the Red Army with all the activities of the workers, the peasants, the students, the petty bourgeoisie and the national bourgeoisie throughout the country." The task of the Japanese imperialists is "to turn China into a colony while our task is to turn China into a free and independent country with full territorial integrity." Exactly a year later two dissident generals kidnapped Chiang Kai-shek in the Xi'an Incident, and both the Nationalist and Communist sides became more willing to join in a united front against Japan. [See also Xi'an Incident and United Front.]

In the wake of the massive and almost totally victorious Japanese offensives during 1937 and 1938, small groups of Communist soldiers and ad-

ministrators fanned out across the North China Plain and central China, creating pockets of civil-military power in the interstices of the Japanese occupation, filling gaps left where local leaders loyal to Chiang Kai-shek had fled. Beginning in early 1939 Japanese strategy turned to holding operations with occasional forays in force. In response to this relaxation, both the Communists and the Nationalists became more concerned with consolidating their power in the areas they controlled. Chiang Kai-shek imposed a blockade on the Shaanganning Border Area, of which Yan'an was the capital. He brought the Second United Front to an end in January 1941 with a serious attack on the Communist New Fourth Army in southern Anhui Province. [See also New Fourth Army Incident.] From the beginning, Mao looked optimistically for ultimate victory both over the immediate enemy—Japan—and the long-term domestic foe, the Nationalist Party of Chiang Kai-shek. He never lost sight of the practical objective of destroying the enemy's armed forces, but he viewed the political mobilization of the Chinese population as a matter of foremost importance. Military victory was to be a product of rational transformation of social relations within the base area society and a precondition for radical transformation in the nation as a whole.

Mao was in a position to shape the consciousness of wartime China through words as well as deeds. Many people outside the Communist base areas learned about Mao and his ideas from the American journalist Edgar Snow, whose *Red Star over China* (1937) was widely circulated in Chinese translation. Snow portrayed a tall, pale figure with boundless energy, an omnivorous reader who was careless of personal appearance but meticulous about the details of duty. Snow's words about a plain, patriotic, and highly moral figure with "considerable genius" in planning were reinforced by reports from other journalists and by clandestine circulation of Mao's essays. Written in a clear, easy to understand style, such works as *Problems of Strategy in China's Revolutionary War* (1936) and *The Tasks of the Chinese Communist Party in the Period of Resistance to Japan* (1937) contrasted favorably with the turgid prose emanating from the Nationalist side.

As a teacher of revolutionary practice Mao sought to build a strong moral link between Party leadership and the masses. According to Mao, those in the Party must humbly learn from the people while at the same time acting as their teachers. He urged leaders to take the masses' inchoate ideas, systematize them through study, and explain to the masses in their new form so that the masses would embrace them as their own. This "mass line" did not preclude strong moral leadership by the Leninist party. In works such as *On Practice* (1937) and *In Memory of Norman Bethune* (1939), Mao set forth the virtues of hard struggle, self-reliance, selfless behavior, implacable hostility to the enemy, and iron discipline.

The "mass line" also included economic transformation. Communist principles and earlier experience in South China indicated that income redistribution would help mobilize the masses for the patriotic goals. Wartime shortages dictated emphasis on cooperation in production. In Marxist jargon, major benefits could come about from changes in human relations of production, even though there might be only minor changes in the objective forces of production. A decade later, after 1949, the Yan'an program was taken as a model for social revolution in China as a whole.

The CCP needed a leader who could stand in the public mind at the same level as Chiang Kai-shek. In scores of meetings and conferences during the rectification movement of 1942 to 1944, Mao and his followers hammered home the basic Maoist idea of combining theory and practice, instilling new discipline and purpose into the rapidly growing organization and ending the possibility that Moscow-based theoreticians such as Wang Ming (Chen Shaoyu) could challenge Mao's primacy. [*See also* Wang Ming.] Mao's idea of a real theoretician was one who had done as much investigation and organization as he had reading. Few could doubt he had done that. In 1943 he was elected chairman of the Central Committee and the Politburo, and he remained leader of the Party thereafter.

When the Chinese Communist Party held its Seventh National Congress in Yan'an in the spring of 1945, there were nineteen Communist base areas scattered over northern and central China with a combined population of more than 90 million. Party membership was estimated at 1.2 million, with another 900,000 in the armed forces. The newly elected Central Committee and Political Bureau were overwhelmingly composed of experienced men who had proven their ability and loyalty to Chairman Mao. The new Party constitution stated in its preamble that the central guide for all future work was "the thought of Mao Zedong." In a talk entitled "On Coalition Government," Mao summarized his political thought and stated conditions under which the CCP would cooperate with the Nationalists in the postwar period.

Under American guarantees Mao flew to Chongqing in late August 1945 to discuss with Chiang Kai-shek the nature of the postwar government. Even while they met, their armies were racing to accept surrender of Japanese and puppet troops in North China and Manchuria, and to take over their equipment. Chiang's firepower was vastly superior to Mao's, his army several times larger. His grand strategy was to take and hold the cities and rail lines. Mao's strategy during the first year of the ensuing civil war was to build peasant armies, using the countryside to surround the cities. To avoid positional warfare until ready, he even allowed Yan'an to be captured in March 1947. Despite his superior strength, however, Chiang was unable to stem inflation in the economy or corruption and defeatism within his army.

The "mass line" depended on agrarian reform to convince the peasants that revolution was in their interests. During the war against Japan agrarian reform had been restricted to limiting rent and interest, but with the breakup of cooperation with the Nationalists, a more radical policy of "land to the tiller" was adopted in many areas. Mao declared that throughout the civil war period, "the peasants stood with our Party and our army against the attacks of Chiang Kai-shek's troops wherever the land reform problem was solved radically and thoroughly." He appears to have been among the moderates in the Party, however, pressing for protection of the property of "middle peasants" and "small landlords" who did not egregiously exploit the labor of others, for their productive capabilities were critical to the well-being of the economy as a whole. It was this policy that was adopted in the early years after Liberation.

By the end of 1947 the tide had begun to turn. The People's Liberation Army (PLA) in Manchuria and North China shifted to conventional warfare and dealt the Nationalists a series of crushing defeats. During 1948 and the first half of 1949 the Red Armies rolled up the forces of their enemies of twenty-five years, and on 1 October 1949, twenty-eight years after participating in the birth of the Communist Party in China, Mao Zedong stood on the Gate of Heavenly Peace in Beijing to declare at the formation of the People's Republic of China (PRC) that "China has stood up."

Mao was fifty-five years old when he came to supreme national power. He had never been outside of China and he had spent more than twenty years working in the countryside. Now he and his close lieutenants, Liu Shaoqi, Zhou Enlai, Zhu De, and

Chen Yun, were faced with attempting to build a powerful modern economy, a city-based industrial economy upon which a new China, free of foreign domination, could be constructed. The country was prostrate after decades of civil war and foreign occupation. Chiang Kai-shek had fled to Taiwan with US $300 million from the national treasury and five hundred thousand soldiers. Mao recognized the magnitude of the tasks that lay before him. He warned the Party against overconfidence and arrogance. "To win nationwide victory is only the first step in a long march of 10,000 *li*. Even if this step is worthy of pride, it is comparatively tiny; what will be more worthy of pride is yet to come."

Economic assistance from abroad was sorely needed. Attempts to open a dialogue with the United States through Zhou Enlai failed utterly. In December 1949 Mao flew to Moscow for nine weeks of negotiating with Stalin for military support in case of attack and annual Soviet industrial credits of $60 million a year for five years. One of the results was widespread adoption of Soviet-style institutions in government and industry.

Even more important was domestic reconstruction, social and economic. Mao set about the task with revolutionary vigor. In April 1950 he promulgated a new marriage law aimed at abolishing feudal oppression. Two months later a new Land Reform Law was announced. The property of landlords was to be confiscated and distributed among the poor, and the rural gentry was to be destroyed as a class. The intention was to be moderate so as not to reduce food production, but popular enthusiasms were not to be curbed. Some two million people lost their lives during the transformation of China's ancient agrarian system; a permanent underclass of former landlords was created. A new sense of hope was born among the peasants, however, and Mao Zedong achieved a near mythic status: later, even his disastrous errors could not shake the staunch support he enjoyed among China's vast rural majority. [*See also* Land Tenure and Reform: Land Reform in Modern China.]

In August 1950 Mao anticipated demobilization of a substantial part of the People's Liberation Army, but the surprise outbreak of the Korean War taxed China's military and economic resources and exacerbated his inclination toward social discipline through coercion and repression. As the war raged, he launched a thought reform campaign to transform intellectuals through mass criticism and individual self-criticism, the "Three Antis" movement to root out corrupt and inefficient cadres, and the

"Five Antis" movement to direct mass criticism toward merchants and industrialists. Always a strong believer in the power of the human will, Mao sought to encourage "correct" thinking, as well as to solidify his own positions, by encouraging "the cult of Chairman Mao" through publication of new versions of modern history and of the texts that would become the *Selected Works of Mao Zedong*.

The death of Stalin in March 1953 and the end of the Korean War in July gave Mao greater freedom and encouraged moderation and flexibility. The First National People's Congress in September 1954 elected him chairman of the People's Republic of China and of the Council of National Defense. The Soviet Union granted increased financial and technical assistance to China, and in October Nikita Khrushchev visited Beijing. Khrushchev's de-Stalinization speech of 1956, and the subsequent Soviet invasion of Hungary in October, however, wrenched the international communist movement. Convinced that the Chinese people had become good socialists, Mao launched the Hundred Flowers Campaign in early 1957 to encourage intellectuals to speak freely. [*See also* Hundred Flowers Campaign.]

The strong criticism of both Party and government proved to Mao the validity of his 1937 essay *On Contradiction*: human society develops through a continuous series of creating and resolving contradictions. The contradictions within society could be resolved only by a permanent revolution—education and discussion to resolve "nonantagonistic" contradictions among the people, and continued use of force to resolve "antagonistic" contradictions between "ourselves and our enemies." The first to feel the iron fist in the new Anti-Rightist Campaign were those who had spoken out to criticize.

Seeking to force the historical pace and to turn from material incentives toward massive mobilization of burgeoning human resources, Mao launched a collectivization campaign in 1957 to reorganize the countryside into communes. In 1958 he followed up with the Great Leap Forward to modernize China's agriculture and industry at breakneck speed. While there are many disputes about the significance of the Great Leap Forward, and its coincidence with poor weather conditions and weak local management, there can be no question that its failure—and the three years of near starvation that resulted—tarnished Mao's towering reputation. [*See also* Agriculture, Collectivization of *and* Great Leap Forward.]

At the same time, Mao sought to force the historical pace internationally. He disagreed with Khrushchev's hopes for détente with the United States, a disagreement that led to Soviet withdrawal of technicians and aid just as the other problems of the Great Leap were beginning to crest. Mao resigned as chief of state in April 1959, but defeated Peng Dehuai's attempt to dislodge him from his other posts that summer. [See also Peng Dehuai.]

For the next several years, Mao was, in his own words, "in the second rank." His published writings of the period, witty and keenly logical, were largely concerned with a critique of the Soviet Union's flagging revolutionary zeal, a critique that led to the Sino-Soviet split in 1963. Approaching seventy years of age, he was also deeply concerned with his own country's flagging revolutionary zeal and slow pace of economic development. In 1964 he launched a Socialist Education Movement, focusing on the vast numbers of people born since 1950. The Party leadership was in the process of becoming a bourgeois "new class," he believed. Chinese socialism could only be rescued by the young learning from heroic model socialists and from the People's Liberation Army (PLA).

In 1966 Mao launched the Great Proletarian Cultural Revolution, mobilizing masses of young Red Guards to "storm the heights." Under the general leadership of Mao's wife of twenty-five years, Jiang Qing, the stated aim of the Cultural Revolution was to root out old customs, habits, and ways of thought using the "thoughts of Chairman Mao." The Party itself was a prime target. Deng Xiaoping, Peng Zhen, Liu Shaoqi, and other senior leaders were subjected to public vilification and sent to dwell in vile "cow sheds." Hundreds of thousands of intellectuals, Party cadres, and economic leaders were similarly mistreated. [See also Red Guards; Deng Xiaoping; Peng Zhen; and Liu Shaoqi.]

The Great Proletarian Cultural Revolution put great emphasis on revolutionary voluntarism, an idea more associated with the anarchist ideas of the Culture Bookstore of Mao's youth than with the ideas of Karl Marx. The result, in a country where for centuries people had been taught that there is but one truth, was severe disruption of all segments of industry, communication, and government. Red Guard groups began fighting among themselves. Only the PLA, under Lin Biao, offered a coherent structure upon which the country could be rebuilt. Lin became Mao's chosen successor, and the process of rebuilding slowly began from 1967 to 1969. However, a hidden power struggle developed as Lin attempted to shoulder aside Zhou Enlai in 1970.

Zhou was guilty of attempting to deradicalize the Cultural Revolution and to go beyond military power in rebuilding political institutions. He was even prepared, with Mao's backing, to invite President Richard Nixon to visit Beijing. Henry Kissinger visited in July 1971 to prepare the way for Nixon's visit the following February. In September 1971, according to the official version, Lin Biao attempted to assassinate Mao Zedong. When the plot failed, Lin tried to escape to the Soviet Union, but his plane crashed in Mongolia, killing all aboard. [See also Chinese People's Liberation Army and Lin Biao.]

The winding down of the Cultural Revolution accelerated after Lin Biao's death as the authority and apparatus of the Party was put back into place. Mao expressed his regrets for the harsh treatment suffered by officials, who were being rehabilitated in large numbers.

Zhou Enlai died in January 1976. Zhu De died six months later. Only the infirm Mao was left among the founders of the Chinese Communist Party. He had made his last official appearance at the Party's Tenth Congress in 1973. When he died on 9 September 1976 at the age of eighty-two, the leaders of China's political and military bureaucracies lost little time severing the remaining links with the radicals. The "Gang of Four," leaders of the Cultural Revolution, including Jiang Qing, were arrested in October. [See also Great Proletarian Cultural Revolution; Gang of Four; Jiang Qing; Zhou Enlai; and Zhu De.]

Mao's hopes for rebuilding China on the basis of voluntarism, ideological unity, and mass mobilization were thus quickly put to rest. The Communist Party of the Soviet Union had Lenin to fall back on when Stalin was criticized twenty-three years earlier. In deflating the cult of Mao in China, the new leaders, including Deng Xiaoping, have praised Mao's role in the struggle for liberation while criticizing the excesses of his later years. Those attacked during the Cultural Revolution have been restored to a place of honor in part to fill the void created by reducing the stature of Mao. Mao's emphasis on egalitarianism and voluntarism has been replaced by a stress on pragmatism and material incentives.

[See also China, People's Republic of; Communism: Chinese Communist Party; and Marxism and Socialism: Marxism in China.]

Jerome Ch'en, Mao and the Chinese Revolution (1965). Foreign Languages Press, Selected Works of Mao Tsetung, 5 vols. (1967–1977) and Resolution on CPC History

(1949–1981) (1981). Angus W. McDonald, Jr., *Urban Origins of Rural Revolution: Elites and the Masses in Hunan Province, China, 1911–1927* (1978). Maurice Meisner, *Mao's China: A History of the People's Republic* (1977). Stuart Schram, *Mao Tse-tung* (1967). John Bryan Starr, *Continuing the Revolution: The Political Thought of Mao* (1979). Brantly Womack, *The Foundations of Mao Zedong's Political Thought, 1917–1925* (1982).

ANGUS W. McDONALD, JR.

**MAPPILAS.** *Mappila* is the name generally used to identify the Muslims who reside along the Malabar coast of southwestern India. The word *Mappila* is of uncertain origin and is not used by these people to refer to themselves; they prefer to be known simply as Muslims. The Hindus of Malabar originally employed the term as a label for the three foreign mercantile communities of Jews, Christians, and Muslims who permanently settled in the area, but during the European colonial period the term came to be applied exclusively to Muslims.

The Mappilas comprise what may be the oldest Islamic community in the South Asian subcontinent, one that was founded by Arab-speaking Muslim traders perhaps as early as the end of the seventh century CE. These Muslims initially settled in port towns such as Calicut, where some of them intermarried with and/or converted local Hindus. By 1500 CE the Mappilas were estimated to make up 20 percent of the population of the northern Malabar coast. In postindependence India they represent more than 11 percent of the population of the entire coast, which is now incorporated into the modern Kerala State. The contemporary Mapilla community is made up of both merchants and agriculturalists. The majority of the population speaks Malayalam, although some still know the hybrid Arabi-Malayalam dialect, a mixture of Arabic, Malayalam, Tamil, and Sanskrit that uses a modified Arabic script. The community is especially well-known for its long resistance to European commercial imperialism and for its turbulent history during the colonial period, culminating in the Mappila Rebellion of 1921–1922, one of the most serious outbreaks of violence in British Indian history.

[*See also* Kerala.]

Duarte Barbosa, *The Book of Duarte Barbosa*, translated and edited by Mansel Longworth Dames (1918–1921). Stephen Frederic Dale, *Islamic Society on the South Asian Frontier: The Mappilas of Malabar, 1498–1922* (1980). Roland E. Miller, *The Mappila Muslims of Kerala* (1976).

STEPHEN FREDERIC DALE

**MARATHAS.** The origin of the Marathas, the Marathi-speaking community of the Indian state of Maharashtra, cannot be determined with certainty. Whether the term *Maratha* is derived from the word *Maharashtra* or whether the country assumes the name of its dwellers is difficult to say.

Non-Aryan cultural traits among Marathas of all grades are apparent. Several Maratha clans are totemic, and Khandoba (sword father) and Bhavani (mother goddess), the two chief deities of the Marathas, are aboriginal in character. The cult of Khandoba is ancient and non-Brahmanic. Bhavani, the family deity of Shivaji, is one of the *matas* (mother goddesses) of the Dravidians. R. E. Enthoven of the Ethnographical Survey of Bombay Presidency asserts that the Marathas are neither a caste nor a sect; they were originally a tribe that developed caste divisions. He classifies them under three broad groups: (a) Marathas proper, who claim descent from the *kshatriyas* (Rajputs); (b) Maratha Kunbis, the class of cultivators; and (c) Maratha occupational castes. The differentiation between the Marathas proper and Kunbis is based on economic and social status, and now the two terms are considered synonymous. Maratha is a caste name, but in its wider aspect it indicates all Marathi-speaking people of Maharashtra.

References to Marathas and their country are found in the accounts of al-Biruni (1030), Friar Jordanus (c. 1328), and Ibn Batuta (1340). But it is not until the seventeenth century, under Shivaji, that the Marathas came into political prominence. Historians attribute different factors to this rise of Maratha power. To Grant Duff, an early nineteenth-century British historian, it was owing to fortuitous circumstances—"like a conflagration in the forests of the Sahyadri mountains." Mahadev Govind Ranade attributes it to the genuine efforts of the Marathas and Rajwade to increase their strength in the Nizam Shahi, under the patronage of the sultan, in order to check the growing power of immigrant (*pardeshi*) and native (*deccani*) Muslims. Several Maratha chiefs serving under the Nizam Shahi or Adil Shahi—the Bhonsales, the Jadhavs, the Nimbalkars, the Mores, the Ghorpades, the Manes, the Ghatges, the Dafleys, the Sawants, the Shirkes, the Mahadiks, and the Mohites—received training in arms and administration.

Maloji Bhonsale (c. 1552–1606), the *patil* (headman), joined Nizam Shahi with a small band of cavalry. His son Shahaji (1599–1664) served Nizam Shahi, the Mughal empire, and Adil Shahi and came to prominence as a leading Maratha. He bequeathed his *jagir* (a grant of public revenues) of Pune, Supa, which was practically independent, to his son Shivaji (1630–1680), who founded the Maharashtra Raj. Shivaji united the Maratha chiefs from Maval, Konkan, and Desh regions for a higher purpose—the promotion of Maharashtra *dharma*—and carved out a small kingdom by defeating the alien powers. He stabilized the state by establishing an effective civil and military administration and making it economically viable. He was the first Maratha *chhatrapati* (chief) to start a *raj shaka* (royal era) and to issue *shivarai hon* (gold coins) on the occasion of his coronation (1674).

Shivaji's son Sambhaji (1657–1689), in power for a short period of nine years, was confronted with domestic feuds as well as challenges from the Siddis, the Portuguese, and the Mughals. His coldblooded murder (1689) by the Mughals inspired a wave of patriotism in the Maratha country, and under the leadership of his brother Rajaram (1670–1700), the Marathas waged a war of independence against the imperial army of Aurangzeb, who struggled in vain to wipe out Maratha power until his death (1707). Tarabai, Rajaram's widow, declared her son Shivaji II (1700) as *chhatrapati*. But when Sambhaji's son Shahu was released (1707) from Mughal captivity he gained support from the leading Maratha nobility, and a civil war broke out in the Maratha country. Tarabai set up a separate *gadi* (throne) at Panhala (Kolhapur), but palace revolution in 1714 removed both Shivaji II and Tarabai and declared Sambhaji (1698–1760), second son of Rajaram, as *chhatrapati* of Kolhapur, which Shahu finally recognized in the Treaty of Warna (1731).

Under Shahu, the Bhat family of Shrivardhan (Raigad) came to prominence. For example, the Chitpavan brahman Balaji Vishwanath Bhat (1713–1720), who had helped Shahu strengthen his position, became his *peshwa* (prime minister) and brought the *sanads* of Swaraj, Chauth, and Sardeshmukhi from the Mughals. In turn, his son Peshwa Bajirao I (1720–1740) pursued an aggressive policy that expanded Maratha power by implanting the Maratha *sardars* in the north, an area that later developed into the Maratha confederacy. Gujarat, Malwa, and Bundelkhand came under Maratha control, and a new band of Maratha *sardars* like Shinde, Holkar, Gaikwad, and Pawar came to prominence. The peshwaship now became hereditary: Bajirao's son Balaji (1740–1761) succeeded his father and carried the Maratha flag to Attock (Punjab). Shahu died in 1749, and his adopted son Ramraja, who was believed to be incompetent, re-

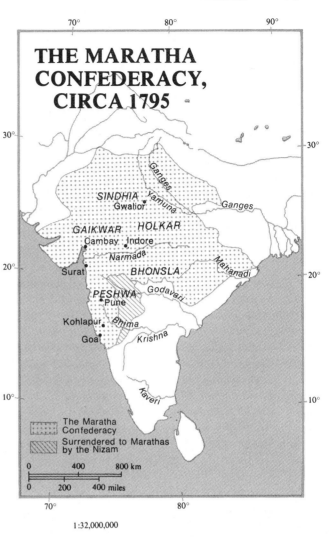

THE MARATHA CONFEDERACY, CIRCA 1795

1:32,000,000

mained a titular *cchatrapati*. Thus the *peshwas* became the de facto rulers of the Maratha country, and Pune became the center of its politics.

The defeat of the Marathas by the Afghan ruler Abdali at Panipat (1761) proved to be a setback, but it did not destroy Maratha power. Balaji's son Madhavrao I (1761–1772), successful in war and administration, restored Maratha's prestige. His premature death was a great blow to Maratha power. Domestic feuds led to the murder of the next *peshwa*, Narayanrao (1773), whose posthumous child, Madhavrao II (1773-1795), managed affairs with the help of a council called Barbhai, of which Nana Phadnis and Mahadji Shinde were prominent members. Power was thus shifted from the *peshwa* to the *karbharis* (managers).

At this time the British, who were the neighbors of the Marathas, gradually stepped into Maratha politics. Although the British were at first (1781) unsuccessful in establishing hegemony, the last *peshwa*, Bajirao II (1795–1818), surrendered control of Maratha to them in 1818. Mountstuart Elphinstone, who was responsible for liquidating Maratha power, then created a Maratha state at Satara. In an attempt to win the sympathy of Marathas, he installed Pratap Singh (1793–1847), a descendant of Shahu, on the throne as raja. Pratap Singh was deposed in 1839, and his brother Shahaji was made raja. The British annexed the state in 1849. Thus, the hegemony of the Marathas, who had dominated the political scene in Indian history for more than two centuries, came to an end.

[See also Maharashtra; Indo-Aryan Languages and Literatures; Shivaji; Deccan Sultanates; Portuguese: Portuguese in India; Mughal Empire; Aurangzeb; Peshwa; and Elphinstone, Mountstuart.]

Grant Duff, A History of the Mahrattas, vol. 2, edited by S. M. Edwardes (1921). R. C. Mujumdar and V. G. Dighe, eds., The Maratha Supremacy, vol. 8 of The History and Culture of the Indian People (1977).

A. R. KULKARNI

## MARCH FIRST INDEPENDENCE MOVEMENT,

a nonviolent protest organized by Korean religious bodies in 1919 after it was clear that despite the Wilsonian rhetoric of self-determination the Versailles settlement at the conclusion of World War I would contain no promise of independence for Korea. The timing of the demonstration was provided by the death of the former King Kojong (r. 1864–1907), who died in January amid rumors that he had been poisoned for his refusal to sign a statement assuring his countrymen that he favored permanent unity with Japan. The funeral ceremonies were set for 3 March, and Seoul was crowded with mourners in white attire.

Korean representatives of major religious communities had been planning an appeal to the world's conscience since the fall of 1918. Nationwide planning was carried out with great secrecy and full cooperation of Buddhist, Ch'ŏndogyo, and Christian leaders. The latter community, principally Presbyterian and Methodist, had led the country in modern education and had a vigorous tradition of self-government. As a Western tradition it was also a natural channel for transmission of Wilsonian ideals.

The signers of the declaration of independence met in Seoul, read their declaration, and awaited arrest. Their declaration made reference to the new and promising role of the United States in East Asia and to the importance of Wilson's Fourteen Points for new nations. Its peroration announced that

"Now is the great opportunity to reform the world and recover our ruined nation. If the entire nation rises in unity we may recover our lost national rights. . . . Rise!"

The startled Japanese colonial authorities responded with brutal suppression. Although the movement was nonviolent, Japanese police records falsified this to cover their own violence. According to Japanese authorities, 553 Koreans were killed and 1,409 were wounded. Postindependence Korean statistics multiply these figures by factors of 13 and 32 (i. e., 7,189 killed and 45,088 wounded); 2 Japanese civilians and 6 gendarmes were killed. As late as the 1980s Japanese textbook references to "riots" fanned these animosities to flame once more.

This violence drew protests around the world and also in Japan, where it provided fuel for the antimilitarist and internationalist enthusiams of the years after World War I. Policies and officials became less repressive, hesitant steps toward Korean local self-government were announced, and the rhetoric and to some degree the fact of colonial control were moderated. A student resistance movement in Kwangju in 1919 and militarist currents of Japan in the 1930s, however, brought new and more systematic suppression of Korean national aspirations.

[See also Korea and Korea, Japanese Government-General of.]

Frank A. Baldwin, "Participatory Anti-Imperialism: The 1919 Independence Movement," Journal of Korean Studies 1 (1979): 123–162. Chong-sik Lee, The Politics of Korean Nationalism (1965). A. C. Nahm, "Missionaries and the March First Movement," in Korea under Japanese Colonial Rule, edited by A. C. Nahm (1973).

MARIUS B. JANSEN

## MARCH INCIDENT,

an attempted coup d'état by right-wing Japanese army officers and civilian nationalists in March 1931. While the driving force behind the plot came from a number of middle-rank officers who were members of the ultranationalist Cherry Blossom Society, a number of senior officers were also involved. Plans centered on the overthrow of the civilian government and the establishment of a totalitarian military regime to be headed by General Ugaki Kazushige, the minister of the army. They called for the mobilization of a mob of ten thousand vagrants, who were to surround the Diet and throw it into confusion, while suicide bomb squads were to attack the residence of the acting prime minister and the headquarters of the principal political parties.

General Ugaki, while not deeply involved in the conspiracy, seems to have played an equivocal role in it, refusing to assist the specific plans of the conspirators, yet maintaining contact with them. Ugaki's ultimate decision not to participate, however, was foremost among the reasons for the collapse of the plot, the details of which were not made public until the end of World War II. The conspirators went unpunished and even uncensured, although several were assigned to the Kwantung Army in Manchuria, where they contributed to the plans of that force to conquer the region in the autumn of 1931. The March Incident, the first of a number of attempts by the Japanese military to intervene forcefully in Japanese politics, demonstrated the growing lack of discipline within the Japanese army and the ominous tensions within Japan generally in the early 1930s.

[See also Manchurian Incident.]

Richard Storry, *The Double Patriots: A Study of Japanese Nationalism* (1957).         MARK R. PEATTIE

MARCOS, FERDINAND E. (b. 1917), president of the Philippines from 1965 to 1986. He was born in Sarrat, Ilocos Norte, and married Imelda Romualdez, daughter of a prominent family of Leyte, in 1954. A graduate of the University of the Philippines Law School and a highly decorated intelligence officer for the US Army during World War II, he served as a Liberal Party congressman in the House of Representatives (1949–1959) and in the Senate (1959–1965). Marcos switched his allegiance to the rival Nacionalista Party and defeated President Diosdado Macapagal in the presidential election of 1965. Marcos initiated major programs for school construction and agricultural development, and in 1969 he was reelected, becoming the first Philippine president to serve a second term.

Discontent grew during the second Marcos administration as a result of unfulfilled campaign promises, inflation, student demonstrations, and mounting crime and corruption. In August 1971 the still-unresolved bombing of the Liberal Party's rally in Manila killed or wounded several opposition leaders. Public order worsened after disastrous flooding in Central Luzon. After a series of mysterious bombings around Manila, Marcos proclaimed martial law throughout the country on 23 September 1972 to prevent "a violent overthrow, insurrection, and rebellion" and to create a "new society" for the Philippines. He dissolved Congress, suspended a constitutional convention that had been convened to implement basic reforms, curtailed civil liberties, and arrested many prominent Filipinos.

In January 1973, Marcos announced the ratification of a new "constitutional authoritarian" form of government. Although a popularly elected national assembly with limited powers was convened in 1978, Marcos continued to rule as a virtual dictator. Imelda Romualdez Marcos became an important political force for her husband, sponsoring several major showcase projects for the arts, trade, and travel. In 1975 she became the first governor of Metro Manila, and in 1978 she was appointed minister of human settlements.

Marcos formally lifted martial law in 1981; however, as economic performance deteriorated and violence increased, he relied increasingly on the military, the constabulary, and his decree powers to govern. Two armed challenges to the Marcos government appeared; one, during the 1970s, was a Muslim secessionist movement led by the Moro National Liberation Front; the other was a spreading Communist insurgency carried out by the New People's Army. In August 1983 former senator Benigno Aquino, Jr., a moderate political rival who had been imprisoned by Marcos for seven and one-half years and was then allowed to go to the United States for a heart operation, returned from exile. Seconds after his arrival at Manila International Airport, Aquino was assassinated, sparking a massive popular insurgency against Marcos. Marcos appointed an investigative commission, which found that several close Marcos allies in the military were responsible for Aquino's murder. A Marcos-controlled trial resulted in the acquittal of all defendants. A new trial began after President Corazon Aquino came to office.

Given the reports of Marcos's failing health, the uncertainties over presidential succession, the increasingly deteriorating economic situation, the new political role of the reform movement within the military, the growing strength of a radical insurgency, and the alienation of the middle class and the business community, two decades of Marcos rule were about to close.

Marcos's first major political defeat, hastening his undoing, occurred when the opposition won a third of the seats in the 1984 National Assembly elections. In response to increasing domestic and American pressure for reform, Marcos announced presidential elections in November 1985. In calling for these elections he hoped to renew his mandate for another six years and reestablish a legitimate succession by electing a vice-president; the office of the vice presidency had been abolished with the enactment of the 1973 constitution. But Marcos had underestimated the strength of the opposition in general and of Corazon Aquino in particular.

Amid charges of widespread election fraud, Aquino claimed victory and called on Marcos to resign. Cardinal Sin and the Catholic church played a pivotal role in ousting Marcos by using the pulpit to deliver support for the victory claimed by Cory Aquino.

A rapid succession of events, beginning with the walkout of thirty computer operators from election headquarters to protest the tampering of election results of 9 February 1986, signaled Marcos's weakening grasp on political forces. Marcos's postelection move to arrest members of the reform movement, including Defense Minister Juan Enrile and General Fidel Ramos, provoked a successful preemptive revolt. When Enrile and Ramos announced their defection from Marcos, Cardinal Sin appealed over Radio Veritas for the people to go to Camp Aguinaldo in Manila to protect Enrile and Ramos, whom he called "defenders of our democracy." For the next four days, the "people power" revolution thwarted Marcos forces, which, when faced with the choice of killing fellow Filipinos in order to reach Enrile and Ramos, chose not to move.

On 25 February 1986, both Aquino and Marcos, in separate ceremonies, took the oath of office for president. After some futile last-minute bargaining with Enrile, Marcos accepted the United States' offer to evacuate him and his family from Malacanang Palace. On the evening of the same day he was sworn into office, Marcos was flown to Hawaii by a US helicopter.

Since seeking refuge in Honolulu, Marcos has maintained contact with and encouraged the opposition in the Philippines. He is widely suspected of financing several coup attempts against the Aquino government, including a plan, foiled by the United States, to return to the Philippines. Marcos faces extensive litigation as the Philippine government attempts to recover an estimated five to ten billion dollars he amassed while in office.

[See also Philippines; Nacionalista Party; Macapagal, Diosdado P.; Moro National Liberation Front; New People's Army; Aquino, Benigno; Aquino, Corazon Cojuangco; and Catholicism in the Philippines.]

John Bresnan, *Crisis in the Philippines: The Marcos Era and Beyond* (1986). Gary Hawes, *The Philippine State and the Marcos Regime: The Politics of Export* (1987).

Robert Shaplen, "A Reporter at Large: From Marcos to Aquino," *The New Yorker*, 25 August 1986 (pp. 33–73) and 1 September 1986 (pp. 36–64).

DAVID A. ROSENBERG

**MARHAEN,** term coined by Sukarno in 1930 referring to individuals who own only sufficient means of production to support themselves at subsistence level. It includes impoverished peasant smallholders, fishermen, street vendors, and the like who, Sukarno argued, made up the bulk of the Indonesian population. While a strict definition of *marhaen* excludes proletarians, who sell only their labor, the term was generally used to refer to all impoverished Indonesians and by extension to the entire Indonesian people, who Sukarno claimed were oppressed by capitalism and imperialism. This concept enabled Sukarno to incorporate Marxist analysis into his nationalist critique of colonialism without promoting class conflict within Indonesian society.

[*See also* Sukarno.]

Bernhard Dahm, *Sukarno and the Struggle for Indonesian Independence* (1969). Soekarno, *Marhaen and Proletarian* (1960).     ROBERT B. CRIBB

**MARING.** *See* Sneevliet, Hendricus J. F. M.

**MARITIME CUSTOMS SERVICE,** Chinese governmental body of the late nineteenth and early twentieth centuries. Although regarded by many as imperialistic, the Customs Service, led in its heyday by Robert Hart, nevertheless facilitated foreign trade, gave the imperial court its principal new revenues, introduced the principle of central fiscal control, and fostered China's various modernization efforts.

The foreign inspectorate in the Chinese customs system was created in Shanghai on 12 July 1854 (after the Chinese customs official fled during the Small Sword Society uprising); this practice was later extended to other treaty ports. As head of the Zongli Yamen (Foreign Office), Prince Gong appointed Horatio N. Lay inspector general of customs in 1861; Robert Hart replaced him in 1863. The Service was known in Chinese as the Haiguan, or Maritime Customs, in order to distinguish it from the traditionally established collectorate (Changguan), known to the Westerners as the Native Customs. The traditional Chinese superintendents of maritime customs continued to exercise their functions of banking and remitting duties, but their position gradually lost prominence.

The Imperial Maritime Customs Service, an organization under the authority of the Zongli Yamen, consisted of several offices, such as the inspectorate general's office in Beijing, the statistical and printing office in Shanghai, the office of the nonresident secretary in London, and the offices of the commissioners of customs in various open ports. Under the able leadership of Hart, the Customs became China's first modern civil service, and its staff consisted of some 700 foreign employees (representing 22 countries) and 3,500 Chinese by 1895.

In addition to applying the customs tariff and collecting a growing revenue for the central government, the Customs provided other useful services: the coastwise lights, charts for navigation, and the services of pilotage and berthing of ships; the modern procedure of customs handling and appraisal of goods; and the publication of essential trade statistics and reports. Its revenue collections were used for many modernization projects: to buy gunboats and equip modern-style troops, to finance the new language schools, to send diplomats and maintain legations abroad, and to create a modern postal service. Because the Customs was staffed by many foreigners and its revenues were used in the twentieth century as security for China's foreign loans and indemnities, however, Chinese patriots condemn it as imperialistic. There were three foreign inspectors general after Hart: Sir Francis Aglen (1911–1928), Sir Frederick Maze (1929–1943), and Lester Knox Little (1943–1950).

[See also Hart, Robert and Zongli Yamen.]

John K. Fairbank, K. F. Bruner, and E. M. Matheson, eds., The I. G. in Peking: Letters of Robert Hart, Chinese Maritime Customs, 1868–1907, 2 vols. (1975). Stanley F. Wright, Hart and the Chinese Customs (1950).

YEN-P'ING HAO

**MARRIAGE.** See Family and Marriage.

**MARSHALL, GEORGE C.** (1880–1959), American diplomat who led a doomed peace mission to China from December 1945 to January 1947. General Marshall was a World War II hero and postwar statesman who had limited Asian experience. His task was to prevent the outbreak of civil war between the Communists led by Mao Zedong and the Nationalists led by Chiang Kai-shek, as well as to foster the creation of a coalition government. At first, because of his prestige and sincerity, a ceasefire was arranged. By the summer of 1946, however, the agreements had broken down, mostly because Chiang Kai-shek wanted to get on with the war as soon as possible. By the end of the year Marshall gave up and returned to Washington to become secretary of state. Since then, the Marshall mission has received much criticism for its naiveté and failure. Although on the surface US support for Chiang continued after the mission, in reality Marshall's failure represented a turning point after which Washington's material aid and enthusiasm for the Nationalists dwindled.

STEPHEN R. MACKINNON

**MARTIN, WILLIAM ALEXANDER PARSONS** (1827–1916), American Presbyterian missionary who won prominence as a secular educator in late nineteenth-century China. Originally from Indiana, Martin went to Ningbo, where in the 1850s he developed a taste for literary work in Chinese. His translation of an international law text brought him official notice and led to teaching at the Tongwenguan (Interpreters College) in Beijing. In 1869 Martin became the institution's president, and for the next three decades he directed its pioneering effort to train aspiring Chinese civil servants in Western science as well as in languages. Broadminded and flexible, W. A. P. Martin was a key figure in Sino-foreign cooperation and in the modernizing "uplift" movement among Protestant missionaries.

Ralph Covell, W. A. P. Martin: Pioneer of Progress in China (1978). W. A. P. Martin, A Cycle of Cathay, or China North and South with Personal Reminiscences (1900).

IRWIN T. HYATT, JR.

**MARWAR.** The name Marwar derives from the Sanskrit Marudesha, or "Land of Death," the ancient name for the arid region lying between the Indus River in the west and the Aravalli Mountains in the east. In the medieval period the name came to refer only to that part of Rajasthan contained within the boundaries of the old Jodhpur princely state. After the invasions of western Rajasthan that the Khiljis carried out from 1305 to 1315, the Rathor Rajputs were able to extend their rule over the other Rajputs of this region, and by the death of Rao Jodha in 1489 they controlled virtually all of Marwar. During the reign of Rao Malde (1532–1562) the influence of Marwar in Rajasthani affairs reached its peak. It was probably at this time that Marwari became the major literary language of Rajasthan.

[*See also* Marwaris; Rajput; *and* Rajasthan.]

RICHARD DAVIS SARAN

MARWARIS. The arid, famine-prone, and militarily contested areas of Marwar, Ajmer, Jodhpur, Sirohi, and Bikaner in central Rajasthan, India, have for centuries seen the emigration of many of their people, poor and rich. Those who have gone into business as moneylenders, bankers, traders, and later as industrialists—often Jains—are called Marwaris. They have spread throughout India to cities and remote villages to carry on business. Sometimes thought usurious, they were, for example, officially cited for rapaciousness in reports on the Deccan agrarian riots of the early 1870s. Under British rule many Marwaris moved to Calcutta to take advantage of its new opportunities; often from this center some families entered into dominating positions in Indian commerce and industry, among them the Birlas, Dalmias, Jains, Jaipurias, Goenkas. Their business organization is often based on family and clan, such as Oswal, Mahesri, Agarwal, Porwal, Srimal, and Srisrimal. Marwaris often retain kin ties to their areas of origin and remit money and support institutions there.

[*See also* Birla Family.]

D. R. Gadgil, et al., *Notes on the Rise of Business Communities in India, Preliminary Memorandum* (1951). T. A. Timberg, *The Marwaris, from Traders to Industrialists* (1978).

HOWARD SPODEK

# MARXISM AND SOCIALISM

## MARXISM IN CHINA

Marxist theory first became known to Chinese intellectuals in the first decade of the twentieth century, largely as a by-product of their interest in anarchism and other Western socialist doctrines. Although there was some intellectual interest in Marxism at the time among several associates of Sun Yat-sen, there were no Chinese Marxists until the May Fourth era began in 1919.

The reasons Marxism struck few responsive chords among the emerging revolutionary intelligentsia in the early years of the century seem fairly obvious. In its orthodox, pre-Leninist form, Marxism rested on the central proposition that socialism presupposed capitalism, that modern large-scale in-

dustry and a mature industrial proletariat were the essential prerequisites for a socialist revolution. Consequently, it was a doctrine that addressed itself to the workers and intellectuals of the advanced industrialized countries of the West. It had little relevance or appeal to nationalist intellectuals in largely agrarian China. The disheartening political message orthodox Marxism conveyed to those Chinese intellectuals who were attracted to socialist ideals was that there was little to do but to wait passively on the political sidelines until modern capitalist productive forces had completed their necessary historical work.

*Initial Acceptance.* It was not until 1919—under the triple impact of the Russian Revolution, the arrival of the Leninist version of Marxism, and the May Fourth Movement—that significant numbers of Chinese intellectuals saw Marxism as relevant to their situation and began to embrace the doctrine. The anti-imperialist passions generated by the May Fourth Movement politicized a portion of a Chinese intelligentsia that was increasingly disillusioned with the West and Western liberalism. Leninism, in turn, offered a place for economically backward lands in an international revolutionary process, a place for peasants in the making of modern revolutions, and a central place for intellectuals in the organization and leadership of a revolutionary party. Further, the concrete example of the Bolshevik Revolution served to identify Marxism with political success in a backward country as well as to convey the messianic expectation of the imminence of a worldwide revolutionary transformation. The coincidence of these three factors, where internal and external events were so inextricably intertwined, produced China's first Marxists in the years between 1919 and 1921, as well as the Chinese Communist Party, formally established in the summer of 1921.

Marxism had emotional and psychological as well as political and intellectual appeals in China. The imported doctrine found its original Chinese roots among nationalist intellectuals who were also cultural iconoclasts. They had rejected (and often condemned in totalistic fashion) traditional Chinese values in favor of modern Western democratic and scientific ideas, but they harbored burning nationalist resentments against the Western powers that had impinged upon China and had for so long humiliated their country and its people. Marxism partially filled the emotional void created by the tension between nationalism and iconoclasm, for Marxism (particularly in its Leninist form) was a Western doctrine that condemned the capitalist and imperialist West, thereby both satisfying the intelligentsia's nationalist impulses and reaffirming their westernizing intellectual inheritance. At the same time, Marxism precluded a retreat to a "feudal" Chinese tradition that had been rejected as useless and morally evil. To become a Marxist was thus a way for a Chinese intellectual to reject both the capitalist West and a precapitalist Chinese culture. Under a Marxist banner, China, along with Russia, could be seen at the forefront of modern nations in an international process of socialist revolution.

*Early Interpretations.* Of the early converts to Marxism, the most prominent were Chen Duxiu and Li Dazhao, leaders of the westernizing New Culture Movement of 1915 to 1919 and the cofounders of the Chinese Communist Party. However, the two arrived at strikingly different interpretations of Marxism in the 1920s, illustrating the enormous diversity in Chinese treatments of the newly imported doctrine. Chen, the leader of the Party in its first phase (1921–1927), received Marxism as an international revolutionary message and tended to interpret the theory in a more or less orthodox Western Marxist-Leninist fashion. He viewed the cities as the main revolutionary arena, with the rural areas following their lead. The urban working class would be the bearer of the socialist future, and the peasantry was granted only an auxiliary role in the revolutionary process. With a firm faith in the objective historical laws set forth in Marxian texts, Chen believed that the level of economic development ultimately would determine China's social development and the corresponding political stages of the Chinese revolution.

Li Dazhao, in contrast, placed his socialist hopes not in the workings of objective laws but rather in his faith in the power of human will and consciousness to shape historical reality in accordance with socialist ideals. He looked to the countryside rather than the cities for the sources of China's regeneration and identified the peasantry rather than the proletariat as the truly revolutionary class. And his strongly nationalist proclivities led him to view China as an organic "proletarian" nation in the world capitalist order, a nation destined to play a special role in the forthcoming international revolutionary transformation. The powerful voluntarist, populist, and nationalist impulses that governed Li's domestication of Marxism foreshadowed the version of Marxism-Leninism that was to become dominant in China—the doctrine that eventually came to be known to the outside world as "Maoism."

*Maoism.* Announcing itself as a distinctive ideological current early in 1927 in Mao Zedong's then-heretical "Hunan Report," Maoism celebrated the spontaneous revolutionary activities of the peasantry as a "raging tidal wave" destined to sweep away everything before it—and also attributed to the peasants themselves those elements of revolutionary creativity and standards of political judgment more orthodox Leninists necessarily reserve for a Communist party. The conditions that permitted the dominance of Mao and his agrarian-oriented ideas were prepared by the Guomindang (Kuomintang, or Nationalist Party) counterrevolution of 1927, which destroyed Communist political power in the cities, severed the link between the Chinese Communist Party and the urban working class, and confined the revolution to China's rural hinterlands. It was in the most backward rural areas of an economically backward land that Maoism grew and flourished. While Marxism, and especially Marxist historical theory, influenced a wide variety of Chinese intellectuals, including some anticommunists such as Hu Hanmin, it was in its Maoist form that Marxism found its most significant political expression in China.

As a Chinese variant of Marxism-Leninism, Maoism was theoretically elaborated during the Yan'an era (1935–1945) of the Communist Revolution. The "thought of Mao" was formally canonized as the official ideology of the Chinese Communist Party in 1945, four years before the establishment of the People's Republic, and it was to remain the dominant version of Chinese Marxism for another three decades. Mao's "sinification of Marxism" implied (even if it did not theoretically acknowledge) wholesale departures from many basic premises of Marxism and Leninism in favor of ideas conventionally condemned by Marxists as "utopian" and "populist." It included a voluntaristic belief that the consciousness and moral qualities of people were decisive in determining the course of history. Maoism rejected the Marxist proposition that capitalism was a necessary and progressive stage in historical development, and instead tended to champion the socialist advantages of backwardness. It was a doctrine that inverted the Marxist conception of the relationship between town and countryside in modern history, perceiving the true sources of social progress and revolutionary creativity residing in the rural areas rather than the modern cities. It rejected the Marxist faith in the modern industrial proletariat as the agent of socialism, looking instead to the revolutionary potential and innate "socialist wisdom" of the rural masses. These departures from Marxist orthodoxies were prerequisites for the unorthodox strategy of "people's war" that brought the Chinese Communists to power in 1949, whereby the radical potentials of the countryside were mobilized to "surround and overwhelm" the conservative cities.

*Mao Zedong Thought.* Many of the distinctive features of Maoism during the Yan'an era remained (or reemerged) to characterize postrevolutionary Maoism, now canonized as an official state ideology known as Mao Zedong Thought. Yet between official theory and actual practice there developed ever wider chasms. Maoist ideology continued to celebrate the virtues of rural life even while the resources of the Maoist state were devoted largely to industrializing the cities. The Maoist regime laid the foundations for China's modern industrial revolution, but Maoist ideology continued to convey a populist-type hostility to the necessary features of modern industrialism—a distrust of occupational specialization, of a specialized division of labor, of experts and expertise, and of large-scale organization. As industrialization inexorably began to transform the character of Chinese social life and consciousness, Maoist theory insisted ever more ardently that human consciousness and radical social change were more the preconditions than the products of modern economic development.

Over the postrevolutionary era, Maoism acquired an increasingly utopian character, reflected in part in the doctrine of "permanent" or "continuous" revolution that demanded a rapid passage through the bourgeois and socialist phases of development to the achievement of a communist society. Through a "continuous" process of increasingly radical social and ideological transformations, the utopian goals prophesized in Marxist theory were to be striven for (and realized in at least embryonic form) in the here and now, in the very process of constructing their Marxian-defined economic prerequisites, prevailing conditions of material scarcity notwithstanding. Accompanying the theory of "permanent revolution" was the doctrine of the continuance of class struggle under socialism; the entire era of "the transition from socialism to communism" would generate ceaseless social contradictions and would be propelled by persisting class struggles. And the notion of the advantages of backwardness received ever more radical expression in Mao's celebration of the alleged "poor and blank" character of the Chinese people (and thus their special revolutionary potential) and his startling thesis that "the more backward the economy, the easier the transition to socialism."

Yet however far Mao Zedong departed from the premises and logic of Marxism and Leninism, postrevolutionary Maoism was distinguished by a retention of a vital vision of a future socialist utopia, and by an unusual willingness to confront the dilemma of reconciling the means of modern economic development with ultimate Marxian ends. One can question the success and the results of the effort, but it would be difficult to ignore the historical uniqueness of the attempt that was made to reconcile the means and ends of revolution.

In the end, Maoism sowed the seeds of its own demise. If Maoism celebrated the alleged socialist advantages of backwardness, it also was a doctrine committed to the modernization of a backward China. It was under a Maoist ideological banner that China was fashioned into a modern nation-state and transformed by an industrial revolution. In its political methods and ideology, however, Maoism continued to reflect the backward environment in which it was born and the very backwardness it strove to overcome. Insofar as the Maoist regime was successful in its effort to modernize China, many Maoist beliefs seemed increasingly anachronistic in a changing China populated by new generations ever further removed from the backward rural conditions that had molded the revolution and the mentalities of many of its leaders. Thus, Mao's successors were soon to discard most of what was distinctively Maoist in the ideology they continue to present under the label "Marxism-Leninism–Mao Zedong Thought."

*The Post-Mao Period.* In the post-Mao period Chinese Marxist thought has been marked by a rejection of the radical, utopian, and egalitarian features of the Maoist ideological heritage in favor of a return to more orthodox Marxist and Leninist beliefs. Among Chinese Marxist intellectuals there has been a revival of interest in the Western Marxist tradition. While the emphasis has been on study and reconsideration of the original writings of Marx and Engels, this has been accompanied by growing interest in the whole body of Western Marxist thought, not excluding a good many theorists (such as Kautsky, Lukacs, Gramsci, and the writers of the Frankfurt School) hitherto excluded from the official Marxist-Leninist pantheon. In the post-Mao years Chinese Marxist scholars have pursued inquiries into such previously forbidden or neglected areas as the writings of the young Marx, Marxist humanism, the concept of alienation, Western Marxist aesthetics, the theory of the Asiatic mode of production, and a vast variety of topics in both Chinese and world history. In contrast to the Maoist era, when there was much Marxian ideological fervor but little study of Marx, the post-Maoist era has produced what is undoubtedly the most intensive and impressive period of serious Marxist scholarship in the history of the People's Republic.

Official state Marxism in the post-Mao era has been characterized by a generally economically deterministic version of the doctrine. An orthodox-type Marxian belief in the operation of objective economic and social laws, often treated as analogous to the laws on nature, has replaced the Maoist emphasis on human will and consciousness as the crucial factors in history. The Maoist theory of permanent revolution has been abandoned in favor of the conventional Marxist view that social relations and consciousness are ultimately determined by the level of productive forces. The Maoist insistence on class struggle as the motive force of historical progress has given way to an evolutionary conception of socialism developing from lower to higher stages in a relatively stable and gradual fashion, with each succeeding stage essentially determined by the level of economic development. In place of the Maoist notion of the advantages of backwardness has come the orthodox Marxist view that capitalism is a progressive historical epoch and the necessary prerequisite for socialism. While Mao had come to view the social and ideological products of capitalism as the main barrier to the achievement of socialism, his successors identify the main enemy as the lingering influences of Chinese feudalism—and imply that "Chinese-style socialism" will incorporate many of the features historically associated with capitalism for many decades to come.

In the post-Maoist version of Chinese Marxism, the principal contradiction in Chinese society is no longer between the "bourgeoisie" and the "proletariat" but rather between advanced (and presumably socialist) relations of production, on the one hand, and backward productive forces, on the other. The prescribed solution is modern economic development in the most rapid and efficient possible fashion, with all social and other considerations subordinated to the single-minded pursuit of the Four Modernizations. In this sense, official post-Maoist Chinese Marxism is essentially an ideology of modernization, which, like its Soviet counterpart, rests on the comforting assumption that the development of modern productive forces will more or less automatically guarantee the eventual arrival of communism, still proclaimed to be the desired social end. In the meantime, and also similar to Soviet Marxism, socialist and communist goals are postponed to an indefinite time in the future while their pre-

sumably necessary economic foundations are being laid.

The striking changes in Chinese Marxist thought over the post-Mao years call into question the widely held thesis that Marxism has undergone successive phases of "disintegration" or "decomposition" in its journey eastward—to Russia and especially China—from its homeland in Western Europe. Whatever the utility of this view for understanding Chinese Marxism in its Maoist phase, it clearly is an untenable characterization of recent Chinese Marxist thought. Post-Maoist Marxist literature, far from showing signs of "decomposition," is above all marked by a revival and reinvigoration of many original and orthodox Marxist conceptions and ideas. Indeed, the authors of this literature, both official ideologists and members of the intelligentsia, seek to establish firm (albeit politically selective) links to the Western Marxist theoretical and intellectual tradition. While the ultimate outcome of the post-Mao period of ideological flux is not easily predictable, it is now clear that the history of Marxism in China did not come to an end with the canonization of Maoism but rather has resumed processes of intellectual and ideological change that are proceeding in new and unanticipated directions.

[*See also* Communism: Chinese Communist Party; Chen Boda; Chen Duxiu; Li Dazhao; Mao Zedong; *and* May Fourth Movement.]

Arif Dirlik, *Revolution and History: The Origins of Marxist Historiography in China, 1919–1937* (1978). William Joseph, *The Critique of Ultra-Leftism in China, 1958–1981* (1984). Maurice Meisner, *Li Ta-Chao and the Origins of Chinese Marxism* (1967) and *Marxism, Maoism and Utopianism* (1982). Stuart Schram, *Mao Tsetung* (1967). Benjamin Schwartz, *Chinese Communism and the Rise of Mao* (1951) and *Communism and China: Ideology in Flux* (1968). John B. Starr, *Continuing the Revolution: The Political Thought of Mao* (1979). Frederic Wakeman, *History and Will: Philosophical Perspectives of Mao Tse-Tung's Thought* (1973).

MAURICE J. MEISNER

## MARXISM AND SOCIALISM IN SOUTHEAST ASIA

In Southeast Asia, Marxism, a more disciplined ideology than socialism, derives in part from the pre–World War I social democratic tradition in Europe and more particularly from the Russian Revolution; socialism traces its origin to many schools of thought, including English Fabianism and post–World War I European social democracy, as well as indigenous Asian philosophies and even religions.

Both ideologies figure prominently in the evolution of nationalist movements in Southeast Asia. In Indonesia, for instance, Dutch radicals working in Java before World War I founded the Social Democratic Association, the earliest Marxist group in East Asia and a precursor of the Indonesian Communist Party (PKI); Marxists, nationalists, and socialists, though often rivals for leadership of the independence movement, also collaborated toward the common goal. In Burma, rudimentary Marxist ideas permeated the nationalist Thakin movement at the University of Rangoon in the late 1930s. Marxist and socialist ideas brought home by Filipinos studying in the United States were present in the Philippine nationalist movement in the same era. Even in independent Siam, where there was no need for a national liberation movement, socialist ideas were introduced tentatively by students returning from the Sorbonne.

Socialism could not, of course, be put into practice until the colonies gained their independence after World War II. In some new nations it then became complementary to nationalism; socialism was to economic independence from imperialism what national liberation was to political independence. Much lip service was accordingly paid to socialism. Indonesia and Burma, for instance, were especially persistent in their claim of building a socialist economy. Even Cambodia's Prince Sihanouk proclaimed Khmer socialism in royal Cambodia. The depth of the socialist experience, however, has been shallow and the performance dismal.

By the 1980s a catalog of socialist and Marxist achievement in Southeast Asia would read like this: Socialism is still the official ideology of Burma, since Ne Win proclaimed the Burmese Way to Socialism (BWTS) in 1963, shortly after toppling the faltering parliamentary regime; the accomplishments are not impressive, but the ideology persists. In Singapore, Lee Kuan Yew came to power in 1959 on a broadly socialist platform, but all that remains of his socialism are the impressive social services of the People's Action Party regime. In the former Indochina states, all of them Communist—Vietnam, Laos, and Cambodia—Marxism is, of course, the underlying ideology and will remain so as long as the heirs of Ho Chi Minh hold power in Hanoi. Elsewhere throughout Southeast Asia, Marxist and socialist ideas are confined to small dissident or resistance movements, most of them illegal and several of them in insurrection for a quarter of a century.

[*See also* Communism: Communism in Southeast Asia.]

Stuart R. Schram and Helen Carrère d'Encausse, eds., *Marxism and Asia: An Introduction and Readings* (1969). Frank N. Trager, *Marxism in Southeast Asia: A Study of Four Countries* (1959). CHARLES B. McLANE

**MASHHAD** (Arabic, literally "a place where a martyr died"), term for the gravesites of the Twelver Shi'ite imams, who were believed to have suffered a martyr's death. The Qur'an attests that the martyr is granted special heavenly privileges (3:163), and the concept of the sufferings of the imams as reflected in their sad vicissitudes played an important role in the development of the sanctity of their shrines. Since all imams received a martyr's death, their tombs became the places for annual visitation of the Shi'ites, who firmly believed that their love and devotion for the martyred imams, expressed through their visits to their shrines, would win them forgiveness for their own sins, and that their loyalty to the imams would enable the faithful to share in the final victory of the messianic imam, the Mahdi. Pious Shi'ites looked upon the shrines as places where they could share in the imam's sanctity.

Among all the imams, however, it was Husain ibn Ali, the third Shi'ite imam, who enjoyed the status of "Chief of the Martyrs." His tomb was probably the first *mashhad* in Shi'ite piety and was regarded as sacred immediately after his martyrdom in 680 CE. The concept of *mashhad* with its pious implications was well developed by the ninth century, when the strong emphasis on the visitation (*ziyara*) to Karbala led the Abbasid caliph Mutawakkil to destroy the tomb in 850/851 and prohibit under threat of heavy penalties the visiting of the *mashhad*.

The tombs of other imams were also regarded as *mashhads*. The Mashhad Ali at Najaf, a town six miles west of Kufa, became a place of veneration in the early Abbasid period. The *mashhad* at Kazimain, a town near Baghdad, enshrines the tombs of Musa al-Kazim and Muhammad al-Jawad, the seventh and ninth imams of the Twelvers. In Samarra, a town to the north of Baghdad, are buried Ali al-Hadi and Hasan al-Askari, the tenth and eleventh imams; the eighth imam, Ali al-Rida, is buried in Sanabad, in the district of Tus, now known as the celebrated town of Mashhad (Iran). But of all the *mashhads* Karbala has preserved its unique place in Shi'ite piety, and the visitation to it has come to be placed on a level equal to, if not higher than, the pilgrimage to Mecca (*hajj*). The shrines of all the imams were richly endowed, and lavish gifts were given by different Muslim rulers, especially the

Shi'ite dynasties. The shrines became the center of life in the towns that grew around the precincts. They are also important centers of Shi'ite learning, and as such they gave impetus to the founding of important *madrasas* (schools) around them.

[*See also* Ali al-Rida; Husain ibn Ali; Madrasa; *and* Mahdi.]

Mahmud Ayoub, *Redemptive Suffering in Islam* (1978). D. M. Donaldson, *The Shī'ite Religion* (1933).

ABDELAZIZ SACHEDINA

## MASJUMI.

The Masjumi, or Madjelis Sjuro Muslimin Indonesia, was founded in 1943 as a federation of Indonesian nonpolitical Islamic organizations. In November 1945 it was transformed into a political party. At first the Masjumi was a party uniting the Indonesian Islamic organizations, but in 1947 the Partai Sarekat Islam Indonesia (PSII) left it, as did the Nahdatul Ulama in 1952. The departure of these two traditionalist groups turned the Masjumi into a party for modernist Indonesian Muslims and earned it considerable support outside Java. Among its principal leaders were Natsir, Sukiman, Roem, and Sjafruddin Prawiranegara. In the 1955 general election Masjumi received 20.9 percent of the vote. The party was banned in 1960 after it refused to condemn those of its leaders who had joined the Pemerintah Revolusioner Republik Indonesia (PRRI)/Permesta rebellion.

[*See also* Sarekat Islam; Nahdatul Ulama; Sjafruddin Prawiranegara; *and* Pemerintah Revolusioner Republik Indonesia/Perdjuangan Semesta.]

C. VAN DIJK

## MATARAM,

region in south-central Java that was the site of major kingdoms in at least two periods of Javanese history. The first was in the eighth and ninth centuries, when power was disputed between the Shaivite rulers *(rakryan)* of Mataram, of which the first known king was Pu Sanjaya (732–c. 760), and the Buddhist dynasty of the Sailendra ("lords of the mountain"). It was during this period that most of the great Shaivite and Buddhist monuments and temple complexes *(candhi)* in Central Java, such as Prambanan, Borobudur, and Mendhut, were built.

During the reign of Shaivite Pu Sindhok (929–947), the royal capital was transferred to the Brantas River Valley in East Java for reasons that are still unclear. Six centuries later, probably in the 1570s, a certain Kyai Gedhe (later Ki Ageng) Pamanahan (died c. 1584), a vassal of the ruler of Pajang, occupied the Mataram area and founded a new dynasty that lasted until the partition of Central Java at the Giyanti peace settlement of 1755.

Pamanahan's son, Panembahan Senapati Ingalaga (reigned c. 1584–1601), is thought (from the evidence of later Javanese chronicles) to have been the founder of Mataram's imperial expansion. He defeated Pajang about 1587 to 1588, then expanded his power northward to the Pasisir and eastward down the Sala and Madiun river basins, coming into direct conflict with the powerful port city of Surabaya. He also built a new *kraton* at Kutha Gedhe and was buried there in the impressive royal graveyard. His successor, Panembahan Seda-ing-Krapyak (c. 1601–1613), continued Mataram's struggle against Surabaya and established the first contact with the Dutch East India Company (VOC), allowing the Dutch to establish a trading post at Japara.

But it was the next ruler of Mataram, Sultan Agung (r. 1613–1646), who brought the new state to the height of its greatness through a series of successful military campaigns against the remaining north-coast principalities, Madura (1624) and Surabaya (1625). He also built a fine new court complex at Karta (1614–1622), three miles to the south of Kutha Gedhe. His military successes, however, brought him into conflict with the VOC, which had just established a new trading entrepôt at Batavia (1619). In 1628 and 1629, Agung twice tried to capture the VOC fortress there, but the Dutch were able to repulse him, mainly because of their naval superiority. This was the last time until the Java War (1825–1830) that Dutch authority on Java was seriously threatened. For the rest of his reign, Agung was busy facing down challenges to his authority in Central and East Java, most notably by campaigns against Giri (1636) and Blambangan in the Eastern Salient (1636–1640). He also requested and received authorization from Mecca to style himself as sultan (1639–1641). After his death in 1646, the empire that he had established began to split apart under the rule of his inept son, Sunan Amangkurat I (r. 1646–1677), who effectively lost control of the north coast and was evicted from his new *kraton* at Plered by the forces of Madurese rebel Raden Trunajaya (d. 1680). Had it not been for the intervention of the VOC, which eventually defeated Trunajaya in 1678–1679 and guaranteed the succession of Amangkurat's son, Sunan Amangkurat II (r. 1677–1703), it is likely that Mataram would have collapsed completely.

The ensuing period, known as the Kartasura era (1680–1745) from the name of Amangkurat II's new court complex in Pajang, was extremely turbulent. Internecine rivalries wracked the court, and the VOC became ever more influential, politically and economically, in the Javanese hinterland.

[*See also* Sailendra; Giyanti, Treaty of; Kraton; Dutch East India Company; Java War; Agung; *and* Amangkurat I.]

M. C. Ricklefs, *Modern Javanese Historical Tradition: A Study of an Original Kartasura Chronicle and Related Materials* (1978) and *A History of Modern Indonesia* (1981).                                   PETER CAREY

**MATHURA.** Recent archaeological excavations show that Mathura, located on the west bank of the Yamuna River some ninety miles south of Delhi, India, has been a thriving mercantile city since the fourth century BCE. Beginning in the Saka period there is evidence of the religious complexity of Mathura, for it played host to religious institutions established by Jains and Buddhists while also producing a wealth of Brahmanical sculpture. Greek geographers, relying on documents of the fourth and third centuries BCE, made reference to a cult of Herakles there—undoubtedly a reference to the god Krishna—and Krishna's popularity since that time has contributed to Mathura's status as one of India's great places of pilgrimage *(tirtha)*. A time-honored formula stipulates that there are seven major *tirthas* in the subcontinent, and Mathura is usually included among them.

Mathura serves as the hub of the Braj region, where Krishna is said to have spent his youth. According to traditional accounts, it was to rescue Mathura's throne from its usurpation by the wicked king Kamsa that Krishna descended to earth. But just as the focus of Krishna's story has shifted in the course of time from this confrontation to his idyllic childhood in the surrounding Braj countryside, so has another *tirtha* come to serve as the primary focus for pilgrimage to Braj since medieval times. This is Vrindavan, located some six miles upriver from Mathura, a site clairvoyantly "discovered" by the Bengali saint Chaitanya (1486–1533) as he journeyed through Krishna's homeland. [*See* Chaitanya.] He identified it as the place where Krishna first danced his amorous *rasa lila* (musical drama) with the cowherding maidens of the region. At intervals after leaving Braj, Chaitanya deputed a set of trusted devotees to establish theological and ritual institutions in Vrindavan, and they were soon joined by representatives of a number of other sects, making

Vrindavan a theologically cosmopolitan locale despite its rural setting. Every year, particularly in the rainy season, Vrindavan is thronged with pilgrims from near and far, who witness *rasa lilas* enacting episodes in the life of Krishna. These *rasa lilas* are well known throughout North India and beyond.

[*See also* Krishna; Chaitanya; *and* Vaishnavism.]

Frederic Salmon Growse, *Mathura: A District Memoir* (3d. ed., 1883). John Stratton Hawley, *At Play with Krishna: Pilgrimage Dramas from Brindavan* (1981).

JOHN STRATTON HAWLEY

**MAT SALLEH REBELLION.** Mat (Mohammed) Salleh was the most important leader to resist the spreading power of the British North Borneo Chartered Company in nineteenth-century Sabah. British sources mostly characterize him as a treacherous rebel waging a reactionary battle against company-sponsored law and order; a revisionist interpretation portrays him as a traditional Malayo-Muslim leader of popular resistance, perhaps even a nationalist hero, against a company rule imposed by force. A part-Sulu, part-Bajau chief from northwestern Sabah, Mat Salleh clashed repeatedly, beginning in 1894, with company representatives over their attempts to collect taxes. In 1897 his forces raided the British settlement at Gaya Island. Conflict erupted again, and Mat Salleh was killed at Tambunan in 1900. Ironically, his activities resulted ultimately in an increased company presence on the west coast.

[*See also* Sabah.]

Ian D. Black, *A Gambling Style of Government: The Establishment of Chartered Company Rule in Sabah, 1878–1915* (1983). W. K. C. Wookey, "The Mat Salleh Rebellion," *Sarawak Museum Journal* 7 (1956): 405–450.                                   CRAIG A. LOCKARD

**MATSU** (Mazu), a complex of nineteen islets with an area of 11.3 square miles located in the Taiwan Straits, commanding the mouth of the Min River and opposite the Chinese port of Fuzhou in Fujian. Matsu has a population of 15,000 (1974 census). Like Jinmen, Matsu is occupied by troops from the Republic of China, but it is not as prominent a target for Communist gunners. [*See also* Jinmen.]

RICHARD C. KAGAN

**MATSUDAIRA SADANOBU** (1758–1829), initiator of the Kansei Reforms (1787–c. 1800), the second of three reform initiatives in Tokugawa-era Japan. Born in Edo, Sadanobu was the third son of

Munetake, the founder of the junior Tokugawa collateral house of Tayasu, and grandson of Yoshimune, the eighth Tokugawa shogun. Through adoption Sadanobu became the daimyo of Shirakawa (1783–1819), senior councillor *(rojū shuseki)* of the *bakufu* (1787–1793), and, from 1788 to 1793, shogunal regent *(hosa)*.

Sadanobu became *bakufu* leader in 1787 with a reputation as an able administrator for having successfully led his domain through four years of crop failures. The *bakufu* then faced a grave financial, political, and moral crisis that was the combined result of successive natural disasters, famines, destructive riots, and bureaucratic corruption under its previous leader, Tanuma Okitsugu. Sadanobu purged Tanuma's clique and instituted bureaucratic reforms. He increased Edo's economic independence from Osaka, alleviated the indebtedness of shogunal retainers, established *bakufu* control over moneylenders, built reserves against emergencies, and reestablished financial solvency. He also resisted the first foreign attempt to open the country when Adam Laxman tried to establish trade relations between Japan and Russia in 1792, and he reasserted *bakufu* authority against proimperial sentiment among courtiers and some daimyo.

Also a literateur and ardent Confucian, Sadanobu established a shogunal academy for the compulsory education, in a narrow curriculum, of shogunal retainers seeking office. The measure drew considerable protest, as did his stringent sumptuary laws. After his early dismissal from his *bakufu* posts in 1793, Sadanobu continued his daimyo rule and produced a number of miscellaneous literary works.

[See also Kansei Reforms.]

Herman Ooms, *Charismatic Bureaucrat: A Political Biography of Matsudaira Sadanobu, 1758–1829* (1975).

HERMAN OOMS

MATSUKATA MASAYOSHI (1835–1924), Japanese government leader of the Meiji period. Matsukata was born in Satsuma (Kagoshima) to an impecunious samurai family. He did not play a significant role in Kagoshima's defense against British bombardment (1863) or fight in battles against the *bakufu* (shogunal government). He was, however, favored by Ōkubo Toshimichi, one of the principal architects of the Meiji state and himself a native of Satsuma; this circumstance explains his rise in the early Meiji government. Like most Meiji leaders he traveled in the West (in 1878, to France, England, Germany, and Holland).

From the beginning of his career in 1871 Matsukata was chiefly associated with what became the Finance Ministry. He was finance minister for some fifteen years in all, his first term beginning in 1881. Although he was also home minister (1880), privy councillor (1903–1917), lord keeper of the privy seal (1917–1922), and twice prime minister (1891–1892, 1896–1898), it was on Meiji Japan's fiscal structure that he left his imprint. His premier achievement was not the Matsukata deflationary policy that bears his name; that policy was in place before he became finance minister. Rather, his lasting contribution to the Meiji state was the creation of a stable paper currency backed by silver and then by gold. This policy helped to solve the Meiji government's fundamental fiscal problem, that of earning the people's confidence. Matsukata, however, could not duplicate his success as a fiscal manager in the political arena. Even as prime minister in 1891 he depended on the support of other *genrō*. His lack of political skill and influence contributed to Satsuma's being politically overshadowed by Chōshū after Ōkubo's death. Even so he had outlasted all the *genrō* from Satsuma and Chōshū when he died in 1924.

[See also Meiji Period.]

GEORGE K. AKITA

MATSUO BASHŌ (1644–1694), Japanese poet of the early Edo (Tokugawa) period. Matsuo Bashō is best known for his *haiku* (a verse form consisting of seventeen syllables) but equally famed for evocative travel records *(kikō)*, which combine prose with *haiku*. Without question the preeminent master of the *haiku* form, Bashō also ranks among the most gifted poets in Japanese literary history. His principal achievement was to raise the genre of *haikai* (informal linked verse, which includes *haiku*) to a fine art.

Bashō was born in 1644 in Ueno, Iga Province (present-day Mie Prefecture), to a low-ranking samurai family. While still a boy he became an attendant of Tōdō Yoshitada, a young relative of the lord of the province, and served him until Yoshitada's death in 1666. His master's premature death seems to have been the chief impetus behind Bashō's decision to abandon the life of the military aristocracy for that of a professional *haikai* poet. He had shown an early aptitude for poetry composition, publishing his first two *haiku* in a Kyoto anthology in 1664. In 1672, after drifting between Ueno and Kyoto, Bashō moved to Edo (modern Tokyo). Within a few years he had made a name for himself in the shogun's capital and had attracted a respectable number of students. In 1680 they built him a cottage in a quiet part of Edo and planted a banana tree *(bashō)* in its garden. The poet took his pen name from this tree.

Bashō produced some of his finest poetry during the course of several journeys undertaken between 1684 and 1694. A journey in 1689 through the northern part of Honshu provided Bashō with material for the best of his travel accounts, *The Narrow Road to the Deep North (Oku no hosomichi)*. Bashō died in Osaka in the autumn of 1694 while travelling. His deathbed poem exemplifies the spare, haunting style of his mature work:

Taken ill while traveling:
Dreams wander aimless
Through sere fields.

[*See also* Haikai.]

Donald Keene, *World within Walls* (1976). Makoto Ueda, *Matsuo Bashō* (1970; reprint, 1982). Nobuyuki Yuasa, trans., *The Narrow Road to the Deep North and Other Travel Sketches* (1966).    AILEEN GATTEN

## MATSUOKA YŌSUKE (1880–1946), Japanese

diplomat and statesman. Originally from Yamaguchi Prefecture, from the age of thirteen until he was twenty-two he lived in the western United States, in the midst of racism against Asians. There Matsuoka learned a lesson that would critically affect his stance toward Americans: if you are unjustifiably hit by a bullying American hit him back immediately; otherwise you will never have a chance to raise your head before him. This view was only to intensify as he grew older.

As a career diplomat after 1904, Matsuoka served mostly in China and developed a special interest in the northeastern provinces of that country. After the Manchurian Incident of 1931 to 1933 he represented Japan at the League of Nations in Geneva. When the League rejected Japan's position in 1933, Matsuoka led the delegation in walking out of the meeting. He believed his political life had finished, but to his surprise he was received in Japan as a national hero for having served notice on the "bullies" of the West. For a time he campaigned throughout Japan for the dissolution of political parties and for the creation of a nonparty government, envisioning a state not unlike the totalitarian states of Mussolini and Hitler, but he then retired from the political scene to become president of the South Manchurian Company.

In 1940 Matsuoka became foreign minister in the second cabinet of Konoe Fumimaro. It was he who coined the term "Greater East Asia Co-Prosperity Sphere," naming the institutional objective of Japan's ambitions in Asia. As a step toward consolidating a Eurasian continental power bloc as a means for obtaining a bargaining position relative to the United States, he concluded the Axis Alliance in September 1940 and, as a stopgap, the Soviet-Japanese Neutrality Pact in April 1941. When Hitler started war against the USSR, however, Matsuoka's colossal scheme for peace collapsed: the Axis alliance blocked any chance of restoring amiable relations between Japan and the United States, and in spite of all his wishes Japan declared war against the United States in December 1941. After the war, Matsuoka was brought to trial at the International Military Tribunal in Tokyo, but he died from chronic tuberculosis in June 1946.

KIMITADA MIWA

## MAUDUDI, ABU'L A'LA (1903–1979), jour-

nalist, political activist, and Muslim revivalist thinker. Educated by his father along traditional lines, Maududi began his career as a journalist, founding his own review, *Tarjuman ul-Qur'an*, in 1935. An opponent of both Indian and Pakistani nationalism, he founded a political party/revivalist organization, Jamat-i Islami, in 1941. Forced to migrate to Pakistan, he quickly established himself as a severe critic of the country's political leadership. The government banned his party and imprisoned him several times, once under a sentence of death that was later revoked. Toward the end of Maududi's life, General Mohammad Zia-ul Haq embraced some of his ideas and incorporated them in his islamization program.

Maududi's writings stressed the evils created by imperialism and international capitalism. He argued that the universal acceptance of Islam would eliminate poverty, injustice, and the oppression of the masses. His admirers consider him the most systematic thinker of modern Islam, while his critics dismiss him as an impractical romantic. Nonetheless he has an international reputation in the Muslim world, and revivalists have a particular respect for his thought.

[*See also* Zia-ul Haq, Mohammad.]

A. A. Maududi, *The Islamic Law and Constitution* (1960). W. C. Smith, *Islam in Modern History* (1957).

GREGORY C. KOZLOWSKI

## MAUKHARI DYNASTY.

The Maukhari dynasty (c. 540–606 CE) ruled the Ganges Plain from its capital, Kanyakubja (Kanauj), which thereafter replaced Pataliputra as the center of imperial India. Participating in the counter-offensive against the Hunas (Huns), which coincided with the collapse of the Gupta empire, the Maukharis subjugated the Later Guptas of Magadha and Malava in Rajasthan, and strengthened their position against the Hunas of the northwest by matrimonial alliance with the Pushyabhutis of Sthanvishvara. The Maukharis campaigned as far as Andhra in the southeast and the Punjab Hills in the northwest in order to consolidate their rule over Uttar Pradesh and large areas of surrounding states. The dynasty was destroyed by the allied forces of the rulers of eastern India and Malava in 606, leading to the union of the Maukhari domains with those of Harsha in 612.

[See also Kanauj; Magadha; and Harsha.]

E. Pires, *The Maukharis* (2d ed., 1982). B. P. Sinha, *The Decline of the Kingdom of Magadha* (1954).

SHIVA BAJPAI

## MAUNG NU. See Nu, U.

## MAURITIUS.

A small island in the southwestern Indian Ocean, Mauritius was controlled by the Dutch during the seventeenth century, by the French in the eighteenth, and by the British from 1814 until independence in 1968. Sugar plantations using African slave labor were established by French settlers who, with the mixed-race creoles, formed a social elite that gave a lasting French character to the island's culture. During the nineteenth century, following the abolition of slavery, the British introduced indentured Indians as a plantation labor force. Sugar remains the overwhelming source of income, and Indians now constitute two-thirds of the population of Mauritius.

[See also Emigration: South Asian Emigration; Dutch East India Company; East India Company; French East India Company; and Indian Ocean.]

Burton Benedict, *Mauritius* (1965). Hugh Tinker, *A New System of Slavery* (1974). THOMAS R. METCALF

## MAURYA EMPIRE.

In power from about 324 to about 187 BCE, the Maurya empire owes its name to the house of the Mauryas, under whose rule the Indian subcontinent saw, for the first time in history, a considerable degree of political unity.

The dynasty was established by Chandragupta Maurya (c. 324–c. 300 BCE), who overthrew the last of the Nanda kings through the connivance of his minister Chanakya. The latter, also known as Vishnugupta or Kautilya, was a political genius and the reputed author of a famous treatise on government, the *Arthashastra*. [See also Kautilya.]

Chandragupta conquered much of North India in a series of military exploits. Legend has it that in his youth he actually met Alexander the Great, but his real confrontation with the Greeks in Northwest India came in about 305 BCE, when he defeated the forces of Seleucus Nicator, the Macedonian satrap of Babylonia, and actually pushed the empire's frontier further west into what is now Afghanistan. A peace treaty was concluded with the Seleucids and the new border held for over one hundred years. [See also Alexander III and Seleucus I.]

Chandragupta was succeeded by his son, Bindusara (c. 300–c. 272 BCE), who was known to the Greeks as Amitrochades (from the Sanskrit epithet Amitraghata, "killer of enemies"). Actually, he maintained good relations with the Seleucids; a probably apocryphal anecdote has it that he wrote to the successor of Seleucus, Antiochus I, asking to buy some figs, some wine, and a sophist. Antiochus replied that he was sending the figs and wine, but that Greeks were not in the habit of selling sophists. Bindusara is also credited with quelling a number of internal uprisings and expanding the empire in the South through conquests in the Deccan.

The Maurya dynasty reached its apogee, however, with the reign of Bindusara's son, Ashoka (c. 272–c. 232 BCE), one of the most remarkable rulers India has ever had. He is still renowned today for the enlightened policies he set forth in his rock edicts—the *dharma* with which he sought to unite the empire ideologically—and, in the Buddhist tradition, he came to be seen as a model monarch whose support of the community of monks inspired Buddhist rulers all over Asia.

After Ashoka, however, the dynasty saw a succession of sovereigns who are generally lumped together as the "last Mauryas." Their rule was marked by decline and even their names are not altogether certain. The Tibetan historian Taranatha lists only three successors to Ashoka; Buddhist sources such as the *Ashokavadana*, however, give the names of six rulers, while the Hindu Puranas have a quite different list of ten monarchs, all for a period of less than fifty years. In fact, some of these "last Mauryas" may have reigned simultaneously in different parts of the empire, which proved to have overextended itself. Weakened by its own administrative weight, by foreign invasions in the Northwest, and by the rise of autonomous states in the South, the Maurya empire finally collapsed in about 187 BCE, giving way in its Ganges homeland to the new Shunga dynasty founded by Pushyamitra (c. 187–c. 75 BCE).

The origins of the Maurya family are unclear. According to the Pali Buddhist tradition, Chandragupta belonged to a *kshatriya* clan, the Moriyas, who lived in Pipphalivana in Nepal, and who had come late to the Buddha's funeral but were nonetheless given some of the embers of his cremation fire as their share of relics. Other sources, however, suggest a family of less noble origins; classical historians, who knew Chandragupta as Sandrocottus, portray him as a brigand and upstart of low caste.

The Maurya capital was at Pataliputra (present-day Patna), the chief city of the old kingdom of Magadha. [*See also* Pataliputra.] Megasthenes, the Greek ambassador whom Seleucus sent to Pataliputra, fortunately left a detailed account of life in that city. His information is not always to be trusted, but when taken together with the *Arthashastra*, a fair picture of the organization and culture of the Maurya empire emerges.

Megasthenes was much impressed by the large capital city and its immense, luxurious imperial palace. Though in constant fear of assassination, the emperor personally and publicly administered justice; all the details of social and economic life were systematically regulated and watched over by a highly developed bureaucracy and an elaborate network of spies. The economy, in all its important aspects, was controlled by the state, and mines, forests, large farms, munitions, and spinning industries were state owned and managed.

Megasthenes claimed that the people were divided into seven endogamous groups—"philosophers," peasants, herdsmen, traders, soldiers, government officials, and councillors—though the accuracy of this statement and its relationship to caste are a matter of some dispute. The army was composed of the four traditional Indian divisions: forces mounted on elephants, on chariots, cavalry, and infantry, and tended to be large (Chandragupta's forces reputedly numbered 600,000 men). Fortification was a science in itself.

Finally, in terms of religious life, the empire may perhaps best be characterized as pluralistic. Brahmanism, Buddhism, Jainism, the Ajivikas, and wandering mendicants of other types all seem to have coexisted side by side. Although Chandragupta appears to have had some affinity for the Jains, Bindusara is said to have supported brahmans, and Ashoka's connections with Buddhism are well known. The general religious policy of the Mauryas was to encourage tolerance. Ashoka, in fact, in one of his edicts specifically calls for sectarians to respect one another and to refrain from denigrating other faiths.

In modern times the Maurya empire is remembered as one of the golden ages of Indian history—a time when the country was united and independent. It therefore comes as no surprise that today, the national flag of India should have as its chief emblem an old symbol of the Maurya era: the lion capital from one of King Ashoka's pillars.

[*See also* Chandragupta Maurya; Ashoka; *and* Megasthenes.]

V. R. Ramachandra Dikshitar, *The Mauryan Polity* (1932). B. G. Gokhale, *Aśoka Maurya* (1966). John W. McCrindle, ed. and trans., *Ancient India as Described by Megasthenes and Arrian* (1926). K. A. Nilakantha Sastri, *Age of the Nandas and Mauryas* (1967). Romila Thapar, *Aśoka and the Decline of the Mauryas* (1961).

JOHN S. STRONG

MAY FOURTH MOVEMENT, originally a protest against Japanese territorial ambitions in China; more broadly, a political and literary student movement that presaged the rise of the Chinese Communist Party.

On 4 May 1919 more than three thousand students from thirteen Beijing universities assembled at the Gate of Heavenly Peace to protest the Versailles Peace Conference's decision to uphold Japan's claim to parts of China's Shandong province. Emotions were taut as the students heard speeches reviling certain Beijing government officials who had, since the infamous "Twenty-one Demands" of 1915, shown themselves willing to sell the nation for Japanese money. [*See also* Versailles Treaty of 1918 *and* Twenty-one Demands.] As the demonstration moved in noisy parade toward the foreign legation quarter, some of the students decided to lodge an even more forceful protest; they stormed through cordons of police and armed bodyguards, beat the ambassador to Japan senseless, and set fire to the house of the minister of communications. Fighting continued until the police were reinforced and several dozen students arrested. The Beijing government launched a series of repressive measures against the students and arrested some of their professors. These actions in turn set off an unprecedented paroxysm of modern nationalism throughout the nation. In the weeks that followed, students, merchants, and labor organizations in other cities carried out strikes and demonstrations in support of the Beijing students and their cause.

In the end, the Chinese representatives in Paris refused to sign the treaty, the students and professors were released from jail, and certain government ministers resigned. Some historians date the true birth of modern China from these events, which altogether lasted but six weeks. The "May Fourth Movement" was in its narrowest sense a patriotic outburst of a new generation of urban intellectuals, in league with other segments of the recently expanded urban populace, against the foreign imperialist powers and the Beijing warlord government.

In the twentieth century, however, the Chinese often have made the date of a particular incident serve as a symbol of an extended series of events as well as a related complex of attitudes, emotions, and ideas, which then are loosely referred to as a "movement." "May Fourth" is by far most important of these symbolic dates, and universally regarded as the most significant historically because it gave birth to the Chinese Communist Party, Chinese Marxism-Leninism, a new totalistic kind of antitraditionalism, and a pointedly anti-imperialistic mass nationalism. It also introduced a hitherto un-Chinese emphasis upon the redemptive power of youth and on the young as a vehicle for national salvation.

**The New Culture Movement and Chen Duxiu.**
May Fourth is also the vaguest and most complex of these movements, because its leadership, participants and antiestablishment posture overlap with that of the longer and more sweeping "New Culture Movement," an antitraditional intellectual and social ferment during the decade between 1916 and 1926. The May Fourth demonstrations were a symbolic pivot of this broader movement, which in turn was but one stage in the ongoing process of China's cultural transformation to adjust to the modern world.

The New Culture Movement was first associated with Chen Duxiu (1879–1942) and his magazine *New Youth,* which he founded in 1915 in Shanghai. In its pages, Chen issued a clarion call to young China to destroy all of old China, its institutions, habits, ethics, and thought as well as all its authorities and patriarchies. His call for cultural revolution was not in itself completely unprecedented, but in the decade previous to 1916 tens of thousands of foreign-trained intellectuals had returned to China's cities, where a totally new class, the modern student

of Western-style schools, had sprung up. Within a year *New Youth* had become the most influential periodical in the nation and Chen had become the leader of a sizable group of kindred spirits all over China.

Chen advocated a wholesale adoption of rationalistic Western culture and civilization, which he epitomized by the terms *science* and *democracy.* Quite unmoved by appeals to Chinese cultural identity and national pride, he and his coterie obstreperously flaunted the foreignness of their cultural revolution by using the transliterations of English words (*saiensi, demokelaxi*) instead of the Chinese terms. In the New Culture Movement there is something of the implacable rationalism of the French Enlightenment. Its war cry "Overthrow Confucius and sons" was in the same spirit as Voltaire's "Écrasez l'infâme." This intellectual outburst dealt a shattering blow to Confucianism and ushered in a new iconoclastic attitude toward all of the Chinese past.

The intellectuals related their frustrated nationalism and their Western-oriented antitraditional cultural iconoclasm on two levels. First, they identified the political establishment, which they held responsible for China's appalling failure as a modern nation, with Chinese tradition and Confucianism. Second, they assumed, as had previous generations, that in order to achieve the wealth and power of the Western nations, China had to borrow culturally from them. In the seven decades previous to 1919 China had gradually increased the scope and depth of these borrowings to include more and more of Western culture. In the 1860s and 1870s it had begun with military hardware and related technologies. In the 1870s and 1880s this was expanded to include economic institutions and organizations. In the twenty years following that, China imported Western science and scholarship, as well as education and government, and began to send its young abroad for study. Finally, in 1912, even the monarchy was abandoned for a Western-style democratic republic, together with its political processes and organizations. Yet throughout the entire period, China seemed to become poorer, weaker, and increasingly abused internationally. The conclusion that the young intellectuals drew was that the only thing Western left to borrow—and the only thing Chinese left to jettison—was culture itself, the whole way of life and its underlying spirit.

A crucially important figure in the May Fourth Movement was the chancellor of Beijing University, Cai Yuanpei (1876–1940), whose tenure (1916–

1926) both coincided with and made possible the May Fourth Movement. Cai's devotion to absolute academic freedom, his liberal attitude toward experimentation, and his encouragement of the talented young made the university the center of the movement as well as the intellectual hub of the nation. In 1917 Cai appointed Chen Duxiu the university's dean of arts and letters, which brought him together with a host of like-minded men returned from study abroad. Cai was equally devoted to diversity, appointing men from a wide spectrum of intellectual and political viewpoints. Another of his appointments, university librarian Li Dazhao (1889–1927), more conservative culturally than most, was yet a cofounder of the Chinese Communist Party. Significantly for later history it was Li, not Chen, who was Mao Zedong's mentor during his brief sojourn at Beijing University in 1918–1919. [See also Chen Duxiu; Cai Yuanpei; and Li Dazhao.]

**Individualism, Iconoclasm, and Other Isms.** One of the dominant concepts of the May Fourth Movement was the liberation of the individual, a value that ran directly counter to the very keystone institution of Chinese society, the family. The new urban educated youth began to ignore, and sometimes aggressively violate, the ancient principles of family organization. Sons and daughters ignored marriages arranged by their parents and openly defied traditional customs and codes. Fu Sinian (1896–1950), the student marshal of the May Fourth demonstration and later a famous scholar, titled a 1919 article on the Chinese family system "The Source of All Evil." Thus, the basic unit of Chinese society and the entire hierarchic network of social relations and obligations that had shaped it for millennia were under unprecedented and systematic attack.

The sacred authorities of the past became fair game to the new intellectuals. Confucius and the ancient sages went from being demigods to villains. Inspired by Western critical scholarship, a new generation of historians, such as Gu Jiegang (1895–1980) and Qian Xuantong (1887–1939), set out to prove that the sage-king founding fathers of China were myths and that the Confucian classics were mere assemblages of later interpolations. Wu Zhihui (1864–1953), a major intellectual of the period, advocated putting all the ancient writings "into the toilet for thirty years."

The modern press burgeoned during the May Fourth era as foreign-trained intelligentsia and their students founded hundreds of new magazines devoted to introducing Western thought and culture. These publications also provided a forum in which,

for the first time in China, national, social, and intellectual problems were discussed. The general tone and inspiration of most can be surmised by their names: *New Tide, New Woman, New Society, New China, New Man, New Learning, Youth and Society, Young China, Young World,* and so on. Older, established publishers began to follow their lead, and replaced their editors with younger, aggressively modern-minded men. Their editors and contributors infused hundreds of Western-derived "isms" into the Chinese scene, all of which were widely discussed and debated: feminism, Ibsenism, utilitarianism, anarchism, naturalism, relativism, Bergsonism, and so on. The issues and controversies in their pages were, in a way, a telescoped recapitulation of those of the nineteenth- and early twentieth-century West. Translations from Western languages became a major industry. In the decade after 1915, tens of thousands of translations of Western writings—everything from Nietzsche and Freud to William James and Charles Seignobos—were published. Much of Western fiction also was rendered into Chinese, so that by the 1920s Shakespeare, Tolstoy, and Dumas were as well known as traditional Chinese literary greats.

**Hu Shi and the Colloquial Literature Movement.** One of those cultural innovations associated with May Fourth that had the most immediate and profound effect was the general abandonment of China's classical written language (*wenyan*, which had not been a spoken tongue for thousands of years if ever) for a language closer to modern colloquial Chinese (*baihua*). The New Culture figure most closely associated with this idea was Beijing University professor Hu Shi (1891–1962), a student of John Dewey and enthusiastic disciple of American pragmatism and liberalism. While still a student in New York, Hu published articles calling for all serious literature to be written in *baihua* to produce a "living literature" instead of the dead, sterile, stylized writing of the past. Chen Duxiu immediately and vociferously supported him and began publishing *New Youth* in *baihua*. Despite strenuous opposition from some of China's older literary authorities, it was an idea whose time had come. In 1920 the Ministry of Education decreed that *baihua* would be the language taught in public schools. By the 1930s, almost all writing was in some form of *baihua*. Thus, the previous three thousand years of Chinese writings of all sorts was rendered largely inaccessible to later generations. By the same time, Chinese writers almost universally had adopted the Western literary forms of novel, short story, play, and poetry, and the native Chinese forms began to disappear. [*See also* Hu Shi.]

The earliest and most famous *baihua* writer was Lu Xun (pen name of Zhou Shuren; 1881–1936), also a professor at Beijing University for a time. His bitterly satirical stories of rural life struck Chinese traditional culture and society blows more telling, perhaps, than all the polemics of Chen, Hu, and their colleagues. His novelette *The True Story of Ah Q* (1921) is the only modern Chinese piece of fiction to have won universal international acclaim. After 1949 the Communist authorities enshrined him as the creator of the *baihua* literary revolution and the foremost cultural revolutionary of the May Fourth period. The 1920s saw a profusion of literary coteries, all of which based themselves upon various European literary theories. As in Chinese thought in general, the 1920s saw a steady leftward drift in the literary scene, and by the early 1930s Marxist theories of "revolutionary" literature dominated. [*See also* Lu Xun.]

***Split in the Movement.*** By the 1920s the intelligentsia, which had just a few years before thought of the "West" as a monolithic entity comprehensively symbolized by "science and democracy," now began to perceive its inner tensions and complex alternatives. Out of this came a permanent split within the ranks of the May Fourth intelligentsia. In the summer of 1919 Li Dazhao organized the Society for the Study of Marxism in Beijing. Simultaneously in Shanghai, Chen Duxiu organized the nucleus of a Chinese Communist Party, which in July of the next year held its first congress. The May Fourth Movement was after this composed of two broad groups, a left wing oriented toward political action and social revolution, and a liberal wing that maintained a scholarly aloofness toward politics and devoted itself to gradual cultural reform.

The impact of the May Fourth Movement, however profound, was limited to a relatively small group of urban intellectuals. All these tides from the West left the vastness of rural China unaffected. Only decades later did nativized forms of these influences begin to transform the rural Chinese and their traditional way of life.

Howard Boorman, ed., *Biographical Dictionary of Republican China*, 4 vols. (1967–1971). Chou Tse-tsung, *The May Fourth Movement: Intellectual Revolution in Modern China* (1960). Charlotte Furth, ed., *The Limits of Change: Essays on Conservative Alternatives in Republican China* (1976). Jerome Greider, *Chinese Intellectuals and the State in Modern China* (1981). Joseph R. Levenson, *Confucian China and its Modern Fate*, 3 vols. (1958–1965). Benjamin I. Schwartz, ed., *Reflections on the May Fourth Movement: A Symposium* (1972).

GUY R. ALITTO

**MA YINCHU** (1882–1980), highly respected Chinese economist and demographer. Born in Zhejiang Province, Ma studied economics in the United States, receiving his B.A. from Yale in 1907 and Ph.D. from Columbia in 1910, and taught at Beijing National University and other Chinese universities. He was a member of the legislative Yuan under the Guomindang government, but criticized its economic policy during and after the Anti-Japanese War.

Ma cooperated with the Communists after 1949, serving as president of Beijing University and in many other positions. He came under heavy political attack and was ousted from the university in the late 1950s because he criticized the programs of Mao Zedong's Great Leap Forward and the official government population policy. He was rehabilitated in 1974 and appointed honorary president of Beijing University in 1978. Ma's publications include *The Economic Reform of China* and *My Economic Theory, Philosophy, and Political Stand*.

PARRIS CHANG

**MAY SEVENTH CADRE SCHOOLS.** Deriving its name from Mao Zedong's instructions of 7 May 1966 that the military should not only prepare for fighting, but also run schools, factories, and agriculture, the first such school was set up to reeducate the cadres who made ideological mistakes during the Cultural Revolution in China. In the schools that sprang up all over China after 1969, the errant cadres received ideological education while laboring. The ostensive purpose was to help the cadres to raise their ideological awareness, but the schools in many cases actually functioned as forced labor camps: the participants were subjected to a tightly controlled rigid schedule, built their own schools, and grew their own food. After Mao's death the horrors of the schools were reported and they were eventually abolished.

[*See also* Great Proletarian Cultural Revolution.]

HONG YUNG LEE

**MAY SIXTEENTH CIRCULAR.** Issued by the Chinese Communist Party on 16 May 1966, the document held that the Party propaganda apparatus had largely misrepresented Mao's theory of class struggle in the debate over Wu Han in the preceding six months. By unequivocally stating that the main target of the Cultural Revolution was "bourgeois academic authorities" as well as some unidentified Party leaders who were allegedly acting as representatives of the bourgeois class, the document raised the possibility that the Party itself would be the target of the Cultural Revolution. Later the target was more clearly defined by the official adoption of the term "the power holders taking the capitalist road within the Party." The circular also set up the Cultural Revolution Small Group, staffed mostly with radical intellectuals under the leadership of Jiang Qing, who took control of the Party propaganda machine.

[See also Great Proletarian Cultural Revolution and Wu Han.]

HONG YUNG LEE

MAY SIXTEENTH COUP D'ÉTAT. On 16 May 1961 the short-lived democratic government of the Republic of Korea, which had replaced the dictatorship of Syngman Rhee (Yi Sŭng-man) less than a year earlier, was overthrown by a group of military leaders headed by General Park Chung Hee (Pak Chŏng-hŭi), who proceeded to rule South Korea until his assassination in 1979.

A so-called democratic republic had been hurriedly launched in South Korea in August 1948 with a hastily drafted constitution that provided for a presidential system of government. This government, headed by Syngman Rhee, was put to a severe test when the Korean War erupted in June 1950. The survival of the Republic of Korea was assured by the American military intervention under the auspices of the United Nations, but the war that raged for three years had far-reaching impact on the body politic of South Korea.

In the name of national survival, the republican governmental superstructure was radically altered to make President Rhee an autocratic ruler. Under urgent pressures of war, the South Korean military became the fourth-largest standing army in the world by the end of the Korean War. Internally, the military emerged as the most powerful and effective organization in the country, in both the absolute and the relative sense. South Korea had become an immense garrison.

Meanwhile, the Second Republic of Korea was inaugurated with a responsible cabinet system when the massive student uprising of April 1960 toppled the Rhee government, which had become oppressive and corrupt. [See also April Nineteenth Student Revolution.] The Second Republic was headed by Premier John M. Chang (Chang Myŏn), a genteel Catholic layman who evidently believed in democracy. His cabinet was unable, however, to govern the country, in turmoil with staggering economic problems, including an unemployment rate above 20 percent of the work force, and unending student demonstrations (some two thousand) within about nine months following the so-called Student Revolution.

Various military groups reportedly planned coups in Korea, stimulated by the successes of Abdel Nasser of Egypt (1956), Ne Win of Burma (1958), and Ayub Khan of Pakistan (1958). Rumors were rampant in Korea that various factions of the Korean military were about to execute antigovernment moves. The most oft-mentioned group was one with ties to the National Youth Corps (Chokch'ong). The Chang government apparently intended to head off these groups by retiring some ringleaders from active military service, but the cabinet was preoccupied with daily crises of bare survival. A coup organized and headed by Major General Park Chung Hee, supported by a large number of lieutenant colonels including Kim Jong Pil (Kim Chong-p'il), General Park's nephew by marriage, struck the heart of the republic, Seoul, in the predawn hours of 16 May 1961. The force actually taking part in the coup was made up of a few thousand officers and men, and the only military force actually dispatched to the Han River bridge to stop them was a "company" of about fifty military policemen. Only a few of these military policemen were wounded, as the coup force quietly overpowered the halfhearted resistance.

Unlike Rhee and Chang, both of whom were American-educated and Western-oriented, Park and many of his devoted followers were products of a Japanese military education. Their model of development tended to be prewar Japan, although they paid lip service to close ties with the United States. After two years and seven months of the rule by the military junta, the Third Republic of Korea was inaugurated on 17 December 1963 with general-turned-civilian Park as the elected president. President Park, however, faced a "legitimacy crisis" in the eyes of many Koreans, particularly intellectuals and precoup political leaders. The Park regime concentrated its energy on rapid economic development, the normalization of relations with Japan, and apparently the perpetuation of Park's political power during his life. The preoccupation with economic development, coupled with pro-Japanese policies—particularly after the Normalization Treaty of 15 November 1965—brought South Korea into the Japanese economic orbit through Japanese loans, technology transfers, and relationships between the Korean managerial elite under Park and conservative ruling groups in Japan.

Park was assassinated on 26 October 1979 by his own hand-picked director of the Central Intelligence Agency. Months of uneasy transition were followed by another military coup on 12 December 1979, this time led by General Chun Doo Hwan (Chŏn Tu-hwan), who was subsequently "elected" president of the Fifth Republic. The coup of 16 May thus marked a turning point in South Korea's political upheavals and inaugurated prolonged rule, briefly interrupted, by the military and elite groups it coopted.

[See also Chang Myŏn; Park Chung Hee; Kim Jong Pil; and Korea, Republic of.]

Se-jin Kim, The Politics of Military Revolution in Korea (1971). John P. Lovell et al., "Recruitment Patterns in the Republic of Korea Military Establishment," Journal of Comparative Administration 1 (February 1970): 428–454. John K. C. Oh, Korea: Democracy on Trial (1968).

JOHN KIEH-CHIANG OH

MAY THIRTIETH INCIDENT, nationwide eruption of anti-imperialist sentiment in China that helped catapult the Guomindang (Kuomintang, or Nationalist Party) to revolutionary victory by 1927. In early 1925 an industrial depression and poor working conditions provoked bitter labor unrest. During one of a series of strikes in Shanghai, guards at a Japanese-owned factory shot and killed one of the strikers. Two weeks later, on 30 May, British-led police shot into a crowd of workers and students who were protesting the earlier killing, resulting in twelve more Chinese deaths. Nationalistic sentiment was already at fever pitch, and these events led to a paroxysm of xenophobia among all social classes throughout the nation. On 23 June, in a related demonstration in Canton (Guangzhou), British and French troops killed another fifty-two Chinese protestors, which in turn led to a general strike and boycott against the British in Hong Kong that lasted fifteen months. These events greatly stirred Chinese political passions, resulting in the rapid growth of both the Guomindang and the Chinese Communist Party and in the popular acceptance of revolutionary change.                     LLOYD E. EASTMAN

MAZANDARAN. The Iranian province of Mazandaran is situated along the southern littoral of the Caspian Sea, bordered on the west by the province of Gilan, on the east by the province of Astarabad or Gourgan, and on the south by the Elburz Mountains. According to the philologist Nöldeke, the region's name is derived from the Pahlavi compound Mazan-dar, "the gates of Mazan," and was thus distinguished from its eastern districts, known as Tapuristan (Pahlavi, "land of the Tapurs"), the basis of the Arabic Tabaristan. The Iranian name reappears in geographies of the Seljuk period. Sari, Amol, and Chalus are the major cities. Mazandaran's extremely mountainous terrain—Mount Demavand rises to 9,900 feet—explains in part the ability of local feudal lords to retain political power in many areas, from the time of the Arab invasion until the Timurid era. It was only under the Safavid shah Abbas that Mazandaran was fully incorporated into the Persian empire (1596).

[See also Gilan and Tabaristan.]

Wilhelm Barthold, An Historical Geography of Iran (1984), pp. 230–243. R. Vasmer, "Māzandarān," The Encyclopaedia of Islam (old ed., 1924–1938).

ARIEL SALZMANN

MAZDAK, Zoroastrian heresiarch who flourished during the reign of the Sasanid king Kawad (488–531) of Iran and was killed by the latter's son Khusrau I, who for his deed received from grateful Iranians the epithet Anushirvan, "of immortal soul." Mazdak was the son of a Persian, Bamdad; his teachings go back to the Zoroastrian sect of the Zardushtagan. He preached that there arose from the primal elements two cosmic managers of good and evil; the former ordered the world through a pyramidal scheme of spiritual powers similar to the hierarchy of the Sasanid state. Good and evil have become intermingled by chance or accident; in consequence, fate governs the world, and all men are equal beneath it. Property, wives, and power therefore ought to be held in common by all.

These communistic doctrines found support among the Iranian masses, who were impoverished by ceaseless imperial wars, priest-ridden, and oppressed by the wealthy, dynastic nobility; Mazdak's program struck at the heart of the Sasanid social order, with its elaborate system of inheritance and next-of-kin marriage designed to concentrate property in the hands of a few and to prevent any social mobility. Kawad, who had regained his throne after a coup d'état by the nobility only with the aid of Hephthalite armies, thought to save his own throne and undermine the power of the nobles by patronizing Mazdak. But when the latter attacked the privileges of the crown itself, the crown prince Khusrau was allowed to have the Mazdakite leadership massacred by surprise; as king, Khusrau instituted reforms with sensitivity to noble interests.

The third century of Islam, with its economic and social unrest, saw a revival of Mazdakite ideas, often allied to Islamic and Buddhist doctrines, among the Abu Muslimiyya and other revolutionary sects in Khurasan. For all its outward resemblance to Zoroastrianism, the doctrine of Mazdak replaces cosmic purpose with impersonal chance, and its gods are materialistic processes rather than moral attributes of divinity. The social aspects of Mazdakism appear to be logical corollaries of its atheistic philosophy, and the subject has accordingly been most carefully studied by scholars in socialist countries.

[See also Khusrau Anushirvan and Zoroastrianism.]

Ehsan Yarshater, "Mazdakism," in The Cambridge History of Iran, vol. 3, The Seleucid, Parthian and Sasanian Periods (1983), pp. 991–1024.

JAMES R. RUSSELL

MCMAHON LINE, a de facto, although disputed and undemarcated, boundary between the Indian Union territory of Arunachal Pradesh (North-East Frontier Agency until 1971) and the Tibet Autonomous Region of China. The McMahon Line runs mainly along high crests of the Greater Himalayas from Bhutan northeastward past the gorge of the Brahmaputra River, then veers southeast to the border of Burma. (China accepted a short extension of the line east and south along the Sino-Burma border in 1960.) A fairly precise drawing of the line was made possible as a result of British surveys conducted in 1912–1913.

The line was proposed by the British, who were represented by Sir Henry McMahon, at a tripartite conference of British, Chinese, and Tibetan diplomats held at Simla in 1913–1914 to determine the limits and future status of Tibet. It was agreed to by Tibet, which hoped to bolster its claims to independence from China, but it was rejected by China. A dispute as to its alignment along the questionably delimited westernmost sector of the line led to repeated skirmishes and, late in 1962, to large-scale military action. Chinese troops broke through India's defenses and reached the plains of Assam; but, with winter approaching, the Chinese unilaterally withdrew to their previous positions. China has not subsequently pressed its claims by military means.

Alastair Lamb, The McMahon Line: A Study in the Relations between India, China, and Tibet, 1904–1914, 2 vols. (1966). Neville G. A. Maxwell, India's China War (1970).                           JOSEPH E. SCHWARTZBERG

MEDAN, modern and largest city in Sumatra. Medan's status as a significant center dates to 1870, when Jacob Nienhuys made it the base of his fast-growing tobacco enterprise, the Deli-Maatschappij. This planters' town was linked by railway to the older Deli River port capital of Labuan in 1886 and to the seaport of Belawan in 1888. The resident of the east coast of Sumatra moved his capital from Bengkalis to Medan in 1887, and the sultan of Deli moved to his opulent Maimun Palace in the city. The Dutch (in 1938) and the republic (in 1945) declared Medan the capital of all Sumatra. Since 1950 the city has administered only North Sumatra, which is the largest Indonesian province outside Java.

The fastest-growing Indonesian city, Medan has expanded from a population of 26,990 (1911) to 76,584 (1930), 479,098 (1961), and 1,378,955 (1980). It is now the country's fourth most populated city and has long had the highest proportion of Chinese inhabitants (35 percent in 1930) as well as a mixed Indonesian population that has contributed disproportionally to the modern Indonesian language, literature, and press.

[See also Sumatra.]

ANTHONY REID

MEDES (Old Persian, Mada), an ancient northwestern Iranian people. In the ninth century BCE, the Medes lived in the Zagros Mountains and in regions as far to the east as Raga (Rayy, south of present-day Tehran); in 834 BCE the Assyrian king Shalmaneser III invaded the land of Mada, but Urartu seized the territory five years later. These two powers to the west and north greatly influenced the early culture of the Medes and of their southern cousins, the Persians.

In 715, Dayaukku (Deioces) joined Urartu in a rebellion against Assyria; his successor Ukhshatar (Cyaxares I) consolidated the Median kingdom.

Urartu and Assyria were weakened in the eighth century by invasions of the nomadic Cimmerians from the north, who became allies of Media; the old kingdoms were further shaken by the Scythian invasions of the seventh century, and in 612 Huvakhshathra (Cyaxares II) sacked the Assyrian capital Nineveh and conquered Anatolia as far west as the Halys River. He was succeeded by Astyages, who ruled the first Iranian empire from his capital at Ecbatana (modern Hamadan). His daughter Mandane married Cambyses, son of the Achaemenid Persian king Cyrus I. Their son, Cyrus II, defeated Astyages in 550 and incorporated Media into the kingdom of the Achaemenids.

The Medes practiced at first a polytheistic religion like that of the other pre-Zoroastrian Iranians; the faith of Zoroaster reached them via the trade route that ran from Bactria to Raga, the only western Iranian site mentioned in the Avesta; it was adopted by the priestly tribe of Media known as the Magi. This term later came to be a general designation of the Zoroastrian priesthood (Old Persian, *magu; magupati*, "chief magus"; Pahlavi, *mobad*). A temple site with a fire altar, carefully infilled in ancient times, has been excavated at the Median site of Tepe Nush-i Jan; the archaeologist D. Stronach regards it as a Zoroastrian sanctuary, but Mary Boyce argues against this interpretation.

No Median literary monuments are known, and there are few remnants of Median material culture. Most information on the Medes is gleaned from onomastics, from the historical inscriptions of the Assyrians and the Persians, and from Greek historians, especially Herodotus in Book One of *The Histories*.

[*See also* Achaemenid Dynasty.]

W. Culican, *The Medes and Persians* (1965).

JAMES R. RUSSELL

**MEDICINE.** Three primary traditions of humoral medicine were separately elaborated in Chinese, Indian, and Greek centers of learning, these becoming special branches of learning between the fifth century BCE and the fifth century CE. Ideas and products passed between these centers, yet the medical traditions maintained their distinctive character and continue today in modified but recognizable forms.

The works of Galen (130–200 CE) and other Greek physicians were translated into Arabic during the Middle Ages, and this Greco-Arabic tradition spread with the diffusion of Islam to other parts of Asia. The learned tradition is still cultivated in South Asia, though it has disappeared in its homeland. Western scholars often call it "Arabic medicine," but in South Asia it is called "Greek medicine" (*Yunani tibb*), while advocates of cultural revivalism in the Middle East prefer the religious designation "Islamic medicine." The last is most appropriate for traditions that combine magic and religious curing with humoral medicine. These syncretic traditions vary regionally, as well as between rural and urban areas and different social classes, but they provide a major source of health care throughout the range of Islamic societies from North Africa to Indonesia and the Philippine Islands.

Texts attributed to Hippocrates (460–377 BCE) mention drugs from India, and medieval Muslim scholars knew a great deal about both Chinese and Indian medicine. For example, in the ninth century the historian al-Tabari was familiar with the classic Indian texts, and elements of Chinese sphygmology were assimilated to Galen's theories by the Persian physician Ibn Sina, or Avicenna (980 to 1037 CE), whose *Al-qanun fi al-tibb (Canon of Medicine)* is the text of greatest authority among learned practitioners in modern India, Pakistan, Sri Lanka, and Bangladesh. Over the centuries the knowledge of other forms of humoral medicine did not alter the fundamental character of Greco-Arabic science, which was based on the four elements (earth, air, fire, and water), with health conceived as a balanced relationship *(mizaj)* of four humors *(akhlat)*: black bile, yellow bile, blood, and phlegm. Assimilation with other health care traditions had far greater consequences for regional popular culture and folk practices and, over the past century, for the displacement of learned humoral practice by cosmopolitan medicine in most Islamic countries.

The earliest and most influential text for Chinese medicine was the *Huangdi neijing (The Yellow Emperor's Manual of Corporeal Medicine)*, composed during the second and first centuries BCE. About three-quarters of this work is concerned with theories related to acupuncture, the practice of inserting needles into the body at specific therapeutic points, and with moxibustion, the burning of tender from mugwort leaves on or just above the same points that are used in acupuncture. Based on an analogy with hydropic systems of rivers and their tributaries, canals, and reservoirs, the text held that health is sustained by the flow of pneuma (*qi*) in the body as it accommodates to internal and environmental circumstances. The application of needles or heat at points along the channels help maintain the flow or to correct disruptions in it. The points of intervention were largely determined by reading the patient's pulse, and they were said to correspond to the 365 degrees of celestial circles, the days of the year, and so on. This system of correspondences was elaborated in conceptions of the five elements—earth, metal, water, fire, and wood—and in conceptions of yin and yang, which were characterized by such properties as femaleness and maleness, quiescence and movement, and so on.

The Chinese, Greco-Arabic, and Indian traditions were all grounded in systems of correspondence that aligned the organization of society, the universe, and the human body and other forms of life into an all-embracing order of things combining such qualities as heat/coldness, moistness/dryness, lightness/darkness, subtlety/materiality. These systems also aligned the seasons of the year, the directions of the compass, and the cycle of birth, growth, and death. Because they provided a comprehensive way of conceiving patterns that ran through all of nature, they served as classificatory and mnemonic devices to observe health problems and to reflect upon, store, and recover empirical knowledge, but they were also subject to stultifying theoretical elaboration, self-deception, and dogmatism.

Another major early text for Chinese medicine was the *Shanghan lun (Treatise on Fevers)*, composed by Zhang Zhongjing (142–210 CE). It represents a different tradition of Chinese humoralism than that of the *Huangdi neijing*, one oriented to drug therapy and much less concerned with theoretical schemata. Similarly, different schools of learning existed in the other humoral traditions, and this pluralism was enhanced by ritual curing and empirical practices such as bonesetting and midwifery.

The Indian tradition of medical science is known as Ayurveda ("knowledge of longevity"). Its earliest and greatest text is the *Caraka Samhita,* a manual or encyclopedia compiled by the physician Caraka in the first century CE, in which medicine is divided into eight branches: general principles, pathology, diagnostics, physiology and anatomy, prognosis, therapeutics, pharmaceutics, and ways to assure therapeutic success. A somewhat later manual, the *Sushruta Samhita,* is famous for its treatment of surgery.

Ayurveda was based on a theory of five elements *(bhuta)*—earth, water, fire, air, and ether—and three humors *(dosha)*—wind, bile, and phlegm. As in the Chinese and Greco-Arabic traditions, the equilibrium of humors maintained health, and their dis-

equilibrium caused illness. An individual's age, sex, and temperament regulated the humoral equilibrium in relation to the season, food consumption, and other activities. Physical manipulations were used, but therapy depended mainly upon modifying the patient's diet and surroundings and on the use of numerous medications. Some medicines required elaborate preparation, and some used herbs gathered from distant mountains, as well as gold, precious stones, or parts of animals.

The medical systems of all Asian countries are dominated in the present century by cosmopolitan medicine. Although colleges, research centers, and other modern professional institutions have been created to cultivate Asian medicine in some countries, the main concern of ministries of health and of international agencies is always, and necessarily, the development and regulation of cosmopolitan medical institutions. In legal consideration, economic power, social status, and technological competence, the institutions stand out. Governmental planners usually treat these institutions as if they were the only significant sources of health care. Yet humoral medicine and ritual curing coexist everywhere with cosmopolitan medicine, and for the vast majority of people they are embedded in everyday life to provide the culturally dominant mode of health care. Even in Japan and in centers of modernity like Hong Kong, Jakarta, and Bombay, traditional humoral medicine and ritual curing are strongly represented. They persist because they are grounded in long-standing traditions that govern personal hygiene, food preparation, and other domestic activities. And they persist because the systems of correspondences essential to humoral thinking continue to provide the basic metaphors for experiencing the body and for understanding one's life in the ongoing Hindu-Buddhist, Islamic, and East Asian civilizations.

Michael W. Dols, *Medieval Islamic Medicine* (1984). Jean Filliozat, *The Classical Doctrine of Indian Medicine* (1964). Charles Leslie, *Asian Medical Systems: A Comparative Study* (1976). Lu Gwei-Djen and Joseph Needham, *Celestial Lancets: A History and Rationale of Acupuncture and Moxa* (1980). Manfred Ullmann, *Islamic Medicine* (1978). Paul U. Unschuld, *Medicine in China*, 3 vols. (1985–1986). Francis Zimmermann, *The Jungle and the Aroma of Meats* (1986).    CHARLES LESLIE

**MEGASTHENES** (c. 350–290 BCE), a native of Ionia sent to India as an ambassador to the court of Chandragupta Maurya by Seleucus Nicator, the

Macedonian satrap of Babylonia. His embassy (c. 305 BCE) followed the settlement of a war between Seleucus and Chandragupta, during which the latter managed to expand the frontiers of his empire west of the Indus.

Megasthenes is most famous for his book *Indika*, an account of the geography, government, customs, social structure, superstitions, and history of North India, based on his travels and his life at the Maurya capital of Pataliputra. Megasthenes' lack of critical acumen has often been noted, but his work became one of the chief sources of knowledge about India in the ancient Western world. It was much used by later historians such as Strabo (first century BCE) and Arrian (second century CE), and remains an important contemporary record of Maurya civilization.

[*See also* Maurya Empire; Chandragupta Maurya; *and* Seleucus I.]

John W. McCrindle, ed. and trans., *Ancient India as Described by Megasthenes and Arrian* (1926).

JOHN S. STRONG

**MEGHALAYA.** Sandwiched between Bangladesh and Assam, the Indian hill state of Meghalaya actually combines two former British hill districts, the Garo Hills and the Khasi-Jaintia Hills. A steep and relatively barren region, Meghalaya is known as the location of perhaps the wettest place on earth—Cherrapunjee. It is also the home of two unique tribal peoples who make up 80 percent of the one million inhabitants of the region. These are the Garo and the Khasi, both characterized by matrilineal, matrilocal social organizations. The Mon-Khmer-speaking Khasi traditionally had a more hierarchical political system than that of their Garo neighbors, and the Khasi chiefs (*syiems*) continue to be powerful as cultural arbitrators and political leaders. The Bodo-speaking Garo, on the other hand, were loosely ruled by elders.

This region was the first to feel the influence of Christian missionaries (1842), and the division between Christian and non-Christian has had important political ramifications. Fear of assimilation into India, however, has led to alliances and reassertions of cultural identity by Christian and non-Christian alike. Under the All Party Hill Leaders Conference (APHLC) the people of the region united in a peaceful struggle for statehood—a struggle that met with success in 1972. The comparative tranquility of Meghalaya during this transitional period was due perhaps to the willingness of the matrilineal tribesmen to accept outsiders into their midst. Since statehood, however, this willingness has been sorely tested by migrants who dominate local trade and business. The resulting violent demonstrations against outsiders have marred Meghalaya's pacific reputation among the "seven sister" states of India's Northeast.

[*See also* Adivasis.]

H. Bareh, *Meghalaya* (1974). J. Bose, *Glimpses of Tribal Life in North-East India* (1980). K. Singh, ed., *Tribal Movements in India* (1982).

CHARLES LINDHOLM

**MEIJI EMPEROR.** *See* Mutsuhito.

**MEIJI PERIOD.** [*This article treats the entire period of Meiji rule. For a more detailed discussion of the political events that led to the imperial restoration of 1868, see* Meiji Restoration.]

The Meiji Restoration was the pivotal event in modern Japanese history; it is the starting point for any discussion of major developments that followed in the Meiji period (1868–1912) and beyond. The Restoration nearly did not happen. The groups behind the coup d'état that made the Restoration possible entangled themselves in a comedy of errors. On 3 January 1868, however, a coup succeeded, and the leaders declared the restoration of imperial rule (*ōsei fukko*). The splendiferous reign name, *Meiji* ("enlightened rule"), only later (3 October 1868) came to dignify both the coup and the period that followed. The subsequent achievements stand in stark contrast to the thin reed upon which the coup leaders stood that first month of 1868.

For the simile of a pivot to have meaning, we must look backward to the Tokugawa institutions, structures, and developments that shaped the contours of post-Restoration Japan. One of the most critical of these was the vertically structured Tokugawa polity. From Edo, the shogun's government and bureaucracy administered the shogunate's domain and the major cities, and controlled the functions and policies with countrywide implications, such as *sankin kōtai* (alternate attendance of lords in the capital), foreign trade, defense, and minting. Then came some 260 domains, governed by the daimyo and their bureaucracies, in effect small "countries" whose autonomy remained intact so long as it did no violence to the shogunate's countrywide responsibilities and concerns. In the domains' villages, towns, and cities were hundreds of self-governing bodies of commoners. If the relationship of shogunate to domain was that the shogunate controlled while the domains administered, that relationship also obtained between the domain government and the self-governing bodies. The number of samurai in the countryside was miniscule. Most lived in castle towns. Here, too, the chōnin ("city people," that is, the commoners) were given a large measure of autonomy. These tens of thousands of self-contained islands of stability go a long way in explaining Japan's ability to make the transition from the Tokugawa order to the Meiji: the Meiji leaders' efforts were not deflected to coping with the concerns of the great bulk of the Japanese.

The Tokugawa may have been a rigidly status-bound society, but by late in the period it was remarkably free in economic terms. The capitalist economy that is the hallmark of the Meiji period finds its antecedent in the Tokugawa, when one "representative" tenant farmer could turn a tidy profit by raising twenty-five thousand daikon (white radishes). Merchants from Osaka, driven by anticipation of financial gain, would annually flock hundreds of miles to the region described in Kawabata Yasunari's Snow Country for the chijimi cloth fair. It was, again, the autonomy enjoyed by the commoners that enabled them to thrive in an economy propelled increasingly by market forces and becoming more "national" by the mid-nineteenth century.

A five-hundred-year coal supply was one of only two natural resources significant to modernization available to Japan at the beginning of the Meiji period. The other was its people—industrious, creative, and educated. The Meiji leaders could call upon a body of samurai and commoners whose literacy was comparable to that of advanced, contemporaneous European countries. More important than literacy, perhaps, was the widespread diffusion of the "modern" notion that change for the better was not only possible but desirable. It lessened their burden considerably that the Meiji leaders did not have to drag the majority of the Japanese people unwillingly into the new era.

The new leaders, who in the decades before the Restoration had used words such as "plot" in their letters, now had to build responsibly. All the acts that followed the coup were based on the realistic decision that Japan must not antagonize the Western powers. This first principle in Japanese foreign policy guided the conduct of Japanese leadership to the 1930s. Having made this decision, the leadership

then concentrated on domestic reforms, and the Tokugawa polity was the first problem they confronted. A polity divided into some 260 semiautonomous, mutually jealous and suspicious entities was poor material with which to build a modern nation. A unified nation had to be created, and the leaders proceeded slowly and cautiously, a procedure and tempo they followed throughout the Meiji period.

They built on a decision taken in April 1868 by Katsu Kaishū, a bakufu official, and Saigō Takamori, from Satsuma, that Edo would be handed over peaceably to the anti-bakufu coalition. The agreement enabled the new leaders to control immediately the administrative center for the former bakufu domain, nearly a quarter of Japan's total area.

Although the bakufu domain was under its control, the government coalition had had to fight its way north. The Boshin War, especially the Echigo (ended 10 September 1868) and Aizu (ended 8 October 1868) campaigns in northwestern Japan, were bloody and closely contested. These campaigns gave the Sat-Chō (Satsuma-Chōshū) coalition momentum, since it had won every significant military battle. Each victory enhanced its claim to being kangun, or forces in the imperial service. The Sat-Chō commanders were also gaining experience in leading and coordinating disparate domain forces. The contributions of men and material by other domains meant also that the vertical Tokugawa polity was slowly breaking down. Therefore, when the coalition finally turned to the problem of the Tokugawa polity, the notion that the Sat-Chō leaders were in command was not novel, and it had the support, sometimes lukewarm, of more than a handful of domains.

The Meiji leaders knew what had to be done, but they did not have a master plan. Events were moving too quickly from the fortuitous success of the coup to the country's pacification. They could lean on precedents neither from their own history nor from that of China, the traditional source of political models. The nation-building experiences of the West, so far as they were known, seemed inapplicable to their situation. Their task must have loomed awesomely. This, and the lack of a military force, may account for their caution. The leaders had perforce become prudent and careful in the most revolutionary phase of their lives, for the most circumspect among them, like Itō Hirobumi and Yamagata Aritomo, had participated in terroristic or illegal political actions in the bakumatsu period.

A two-pronged approach was taken, the first part of which involved using the emperor as the focus of transdomainal loyalty and the symbol of the new government's legitimacy. This was the easier part. Mutsuhito was a lad of sixteen. He was led before his "subjects," first on a trip to Osaka (1868) and then, accompanied by thousands, to Edo (November 1868–January 1869). These were the first of the one hundred two trips made during his reign, including six grand tours to all parts of the country. Some eighty years later, his grandson Hirohito, too, was to serve the political purposes of alien rulers by being paraded before his subjects.

The second aspect of this approach involved incremental steps taken judiciously and always through consultation with court nobles, daimyo, and samurai from important domains. The goal was the elimination of the domains. The daimyo had to be dislodged or persuaded to return their territories and their people to the court (the government in Tokyo). The government had neither the power nor the inclination to force the issue, so the first move was made by the four domains that had toppled the *bakufu*. In March 1869 the samurai leaders of the four domains persuaded their daimyo to return their territories and people to the court *(hanseki hōkan)*. Some other daimyo followed suit. In July 1869 the government, having taken the precaution of appointing many key daimyo to important government positions, ordered the remaining daimyo to comply. Here again, the transition was eased by appointing all daimyo as governors of their domains. But the daimyo now served as officials of the Tokyo government. It was not until two years later that the government was confident enough to move firmly against the daimyo-governors. Its strength had been bolstered by the formation of the Imperial Guard, composed of ten thousand fighting men from Satsuma, Chōshū, and Tosa (April 1871). In August 1871 the daimyo-governors were told that they were no longer governors and that their domains would become prefectures. Samurai, with their own staffs, were appointed in place of the daimyo-governors. The samurai were practiced administrators, having served as such in domain and Tokugawa administrations or in the new government. The use of ex-Tokugawa retainers and supporters reflected the willingness of the new government to use "men of ability" wherever they might be found.

The destruction of the Tokugawa polity and the creation of a centralized, national government was so important that Yamagata Aritomo later called it the "Second Restoration." The confidence that the success of the Second Restoration engendered can be measured by the Iwakura Mission, led by most of the Meiji leaders, which left Japan for more than one and one-half years (1871–1873) as an experiment in learning firsthand of the West. [*See* Iwakura Mission.] It is also measurable by the government's willingness to move apace on socioeconomic renovations affecting two of Japan's most important constituencies, the samurai and the farmers. In their effects on the samurai, these renovations would stanch a drain on the treasury; in their effects on the farmers, they would also help to fill its coffers.

The government first moved against the samurai. It divided the class into two groups: the lower part was made commoners by fiat; the upper part, other than daimyo, remained *shizoku,* or samurai clans. The government assumed responsibility for their stipends, once the domains' function. This may have enhanced the sense of one government over all, but it was an intolerable burden for a government embarking on other costly tasks of modernizing Japan. The leaders moved with care to eliminate this burden. It first offered the *shizoku* an option to exchange stipends (in rice) for cash and levied a graduated income tax on them (1873). In late 1875 all stipends were converted into cash, but the government still faced annual payments. The following year the government ordered the compulsory commutation of all stipends into interest-bearing bonds (5 to 7 percent) capitalized at between five and fourteen years of income, depending on the size of the stipend. The government was able to immediately reduce its outlay for *shizoku* support by about 30 percent, and it no longer faced the prospects of continuous payment.

The number of *shizoku* involved, some 311,000, was not trifling. Yet this remarkable socioeconomic revolution, initiated by a part of their number to eliminate the pride of status and hereditary income of all, was accomplished with relatively little bloodshed. If the *shizoku* had had a proprietary interest in the land, as did the gentry in China, the reaction would have been different. Samurai also had become inured to lowering expectations, since they alone among all classes during the Tokugawa had been suffering a consistent drop in income. That many among the lower ranks were already working with their hands during the Tokugawa period softened their demotion to commoner ranks. The tradition of domain loyalty militated against the rise of concerted transdomainal opposition, as did tensions between higher and lower samurai ranks. In addition, there were those like Abei Iwane, who petitioned the governor of Fukushima Prefecture (7 January 1874) to surrender his 16 *koku* (measure of rice) stipend. His grounds were that keeping it contravened the government's policy of enlightenment (modernization), and was shameful in light of the commoners' struggle to adjust to the new conditions. The governor calculated that among the *shizoku* in the domain 10 to 20 percent shared Abei's enthusiasm. Significantly, the governor recorded nothing of rebelliousness, and this in a stronghold of anti-Sat-Chō sentiment. The enthusiastic minority, driven by idealism, fueled by excitment for the new age, and dispersed throughout the land, may have pulled along many of the uncommitted or doubtful.

The land-tax reform is the third major achievement of the first Meiji decade. By eradicating the cumbersome and inequitable Tokugawa tax system of payment in produce, it laid the basis for a modern capitalist economy that was more efficient in channeling human and material resources for modernization's tasks. To fix the tax base, the government determined the monetary value of 84.44 million parcels of agricultural lands of various kinds and issued 109.33 million certificates of land ownership. This was completed within three and one-half years, from July 1873 to the end of 1876.

The government imposed two conditions on the tax reform to reduce opposition from those who would be most affected. The total tax revenue was to be no larger than that collected under the Tokugawa, and tax burdens were to be uniform throughout Japan. Uniformity meant that tax burdens in some areas rose sharply, but overall the tax burden on most farmers may have decreased slightly; real income rose gradually but surely from 1873 to 1899. A deflationary period in the 1880s, in which the government corrected for the high expenditures of the reform and disorder of the early decade, has drawn much attention, but over the entire Meiji period agricultural output rose nearly 2 percent annually. Efficiency, uniformity, and predictability increased both the effectiveness of market forces and the integration of regional markets.

There were uprisings, some serious, among the cultivators, but nearly all were local and easily pacified. The growth of tenancy and the increasingly desperate plight of tenants compelled to regularly pay taxes in bad times are costs of the reform that are often cited. Recent studies, however, show that tenancy did not rise dramatically and that the lot of the tenant was not generally as bad as has been suggested.

The salient characteristic of Japan's mid-nineteenth century transitional period is the demise of the samurai, in terms of lives lost and pride and status demolished. The danger of samurai uprisings preoccupied the government during its first decade. The middle 1870s saw unrest in the southwest, which had been a center of Meiji support, and where also, perhaps, expectations for the new order had been highest. The government's failure to take military measures to avenge supposed affronts from Korea sparked a demand for representative institutions from part of the governing coalition, inaugurating the movement for "freedom and people's rights" *(jiyū minken undō)* that led to political parties, as well as to samurai insurrections that culminated with the great Satsuma Rebellion of 1877. [*See* Jiyū Minken.] Yamagata Aritomo's letters to Itō Hirobumi in this decade hardly mention farmers' uprisings; he complained of former samurai's espousal of "people's rights," but he was more concerned by their capacity for armed attack than by their sloganeering. Major enlightenment figures like the educator-publicist Fukuzawa Yukichi (1835–1901), whose treatises circulated in hundred of thousands of copies, deprecated the political agitation of the former samurai.

The three premier leaders of the first decade passed from the scene within a year of one another. Saigō Takamori committed *hara kiri* after the Satsuma Rebellion (1877), Kido Takayoshi died of illness (1877), and Ōkubo Toshimichi, probably the greatest of Meiji leaders, was assassinated (1878). Their places were taken by Ōkuma Shigenobu, Itō, and Yamagata. Ōkuma and his supporters were purged from the government in October 1881 in moves orchestrated by Itō. Such was the nature of political change in Meiji Japan that Ōkuma would return as prime minister (1898 and 1914) and some of his followers would have illustrious careers in and out of government.

Ōkuma's ouster left Itō and Yamagata as the two most important political leaders. As they moved front and center, their brush strokes in letters to others changed from the tiny scrawls of the first Meiji decade to large and bold strokes. None of the Satsuma leaders filled the vacuum created by Ōkubo's untimely death. Only Matsukata Masayoshi made the transition to Chōshū leadership, but he was patronized by the Chōshū *genrō* ("elders") even when he was prime minister (1891 and 1896). Sat-Chō unity, so crucial in the first decade, had given way to Chōshū dominance. Consultation did not cease, but by the 1900s Hara Kei's diary notations showed that Matsukata was consulted only occasionally.

Ōkubo had been the principal actor in laying the foundations of Japan's modern state. The changes were aimed at specific groups: daimyo, samurai, and farmers. The other major reforms were based on the premise that Japan had to tap the resources of all its people. These renovations bear Itō and Yamagata's marks. Significantly, both came from humble backgrounds. Itō's social status was that of a farmer, and Yamagata's that of a *chūgen*, the lowest rank among the samurai.

Reform in education during the Meiji period owed much to the Tokugawa heritage. The Meiji leaders very early carried forward this inheritance by urging the establishment of elementary schools (1869). Within three years, universal compulsory education was decreed. Some farmers violently opposed the loss of their youthful labor to schools, as well as the taxes levied to support the schools, but a national system soon took root. There was little opposition when in 1908 the government added an additional two compulsory years to the original four. By the end of the Meiji, Japan had the world's highest school attendance rate. A literacy rate of 98 percent had also been achieved.

There was general agreement that education should serve state purposes. The means toward this end, however, were subject to considerable and heated debate. In 1890 authorities concluded the debate through a decree, the Imperial Rescript on Education, which declared "loyalty and filial piety . . . [to be] the glory of the fundamental character of Our Empire, and . . . the source of Our education." Reading of the document assumed an almost sacral importance in school ceremonies, and its issuance led to a controversy about the compatability of Christianity, which grew rapidly in the 1880s, with patriotism. Together with the earlier Rescript to Soldiers and Sailors (1882), the statement was designed to provide an ideological and moral foundation for the new Japanese citizen-subject. Nevertheless, both documents were phrased in generalities capable of varied interpretation, and neither service nor educational personnel were as uniform in their response as some writers have suggested. Many teachers, like Red Shirt in Natsume Sōseki's *Botchan*, prided themselves in being at the forefront of Western learning. The textbooks, though uniform throughout Japan from 1903, did not preach a message of narrow nationalism through all their four revisions in the first four decades of the twentieth century. Until the 1930s, there was considerable stress on Japan's international role. The usual portrayal of tight, centralized control over

education also breaks down in consideration of the autonomy exercised by the localities, where education accounted for nearly half of town and village budgets in the last five years of the Meiji. [*See Imperial Rescript on Education.*]

The institution of universal conscription (1873) and the creation of mechanisms for local self-government (1898–1899) may be considered in tandem. Yamagata, the guiding force behind them both, had intended them to be so considered. He reasoned that if the nation were to demand military service of its youth, then it should permit their fathers, and later those who had served, the right of self-governance. The Tokugawa heritage of the idea of self-governance has been stressed. There was also Tokugawa precedent for commoners serving militarily alongside samurai. In Tokugawa cities, samurai intendants used commoners for police duties. Both anti-*bakufu* domains and the *bakufu* used commoners as regular troops (e.g., Chōshū's *kiheitai*), irregulars (e.g., Tosa's *kaientai*), or as vigilantes (e.g., the *bakufu's shinsengumi*). Itō and Yamagata had led military units of commoners in the *bakumatsu* period. The conscription system nonetheless was revolutionary in making commoner participation in the nation's armed forces regular and universal. Initially the innovation was not popular. Samurai were outraged at the destruction of a monopoly they had enjoyed for centuries. Farmers preferred shouldering hoes to guns. Elements from both groups rebelled. All were put down.

The conscription system should not be perceived as the beginning of a militaristic, expansionist Japan. Rather it should be seen in relation to the Meiji leaders' decision that war with the West was unthinkable. The army was to provide for domestic stability and security. The leading Western powers to whom Japanese leaders looked for inspiration all had citizen armies. The army was a vehicle for social mobility as well, and this further helped to promote social stability. The basic training provided to lowly recruits and the technological education provided officers created new opportunities for many.

The generalization that the Meiji transformation was tightly controlled from the center does not withstand an accounting of Meiji economic development. In the first twelve years, it is true, industrialization was encouraged through government owned and managed pilot plants. On 5 November 1880, however, as part of Matsukata's deflationary policy, most government-owned plants were offered for sale. The outstanding feature of Meiji economic development, which built on Tokugawa antecedents of growing domestic manufacture, interregional trade, and population mobility, is that it followed Adam Smith's "natural pattern" of progress from agriculture and handicrafts to light and then heavy industry. Moreover, the stimulus for Japan's modern economic growth was the capitalistic domestic market. Foreign and colonial markets, at their maximum (1927–1936), accounted for but a 20 percent share of Japan's gross national product. Significantly, the Japanese were becoming an economic challenge to the West. Western cotton-spinning machines were not fully introduced into Japan until the late 1870s. But by 1897 exports of cotton yarn surpassed imports, despite protective tariffs imposed by the West. By the first decade of the twentieth century Japanese cotton goods had driven American merchandise from the Korean and Manchurian markets. By the 1920s they had captured the Asian market from China to India.

The capstone of the Meiji transformation was the establishment of constitutional government. Yamagata saw it as such and called it the "Third Restoration." Perhaps this was the most revolutionary innovation. Others can be seen as built on Tokugawa institutions and trends, but the concepts of legally enshrined individual rights and limitations on governmental powers were alien. Further, the idea of parties and factions went against the grain; majority rule sanctioned by law was a thoroughly novel conception, and public oratory and competition for votes would have been unthinkable in Tokugawa Japan. So the Meiji leaders proceeded slowly. The landmarks are clear: the consultative assemblies of governors in Tokyo (1875); the creation of prefectural assemblies (1878); the imperial promise (1881) to promulgate the constitution in 1889; the creation of the peerage and cabinet systems (1885); the establishment of the local government system; and the gradual elevation of the emperor to a position "above the clouds," to prepare him for his role as a constitutional monarch (the last grand imperial circuit was in 1885).

The Meiji constitution, the establishment of the Diet (1890), and their unceasing travels to the West show the Meiji leaders' recognition that Western strength was based as much on political institutions as on technology and arms. This may have been a crucial reason for the success of their reforms.

The sharing of political power on a national scale, minimal at first, was achieved without revolution by the masses, and this was a source of considerable pride. There was widespread interest in and demand for constituent assemblies, however, and the government was determined to control the timetable for their creation. There were legal restrictions on the political opposition, and opposition leaders were jailed and fined, but the path to constitutional government was not strewn with the bodies of the opposition. Once the constitution was established, the Meiji leaders never reverted to the *status quo ante* —this in the face of the growing strength of the political opposition, which increased with every passing election, until a working two-party system was in place (by 1924). This is an achievement still unmatched by any non-Western country.

In a memorandum submitted in 1880, Yamagata could not conceal his pride in the government's domestic achievements: "It is true that the Meiji Restoration's achievements are outstanding . . . [but these gains] are nothing compared to the question of Japan's relationship with other countries, which in turn is tied to Japan's rise and fall." This is a clear statement on the Meiji leaders' priorities. They were prudent in their dealings with the Western powers and were willing to go to great lengths to accommodate themselves to these powers. Japan was involved in three major wars during the lifetime of the Meiji leaders: the Sino-Japanese War of 1894 to 1895, which brought Japan international equality and an alliance with England (1902); the Russo-Japanese War of 1904 to 1905, which consolidated the path to empire; and World War I, which offered Japan the opportunity to consolidate its position in China. The *genrō*, however, were hesitant in 1914, and this contrasted with the confidence of the younger leaders, including civilians such as Foreign Minister Katō Kōmei, who directed negotiation of the Twenty-one Demands (presented to China in 1915 in order to extend Japanese rights on the mainland). Hara Kei commented in the Taishō period (1912–1926) that as long as Yamagata lived, Japan would never fight America, however much younger army officers talked about it. When Yamagata died (1922), Tokutomi Sohō wrote that if Yamagata could have written his own epitaph, it would read: "After me, the deluge." Both men were right. [See Sino-Japanese War; Anglo-Japanese Alliance; Russo-Japanese War; *and* Twenty-one Demands.]

In the last years of the Meiji period there were signs everywhere that Japan's leaders had helped to change irrevocably the face of the nation. The first graduates of the state and private universities were filling the upper reaches of the bureaucracy and the industrial and commercial enterprises. Political parties were becoming part of the larger establishment, and former bureaucrats were assuming leadership

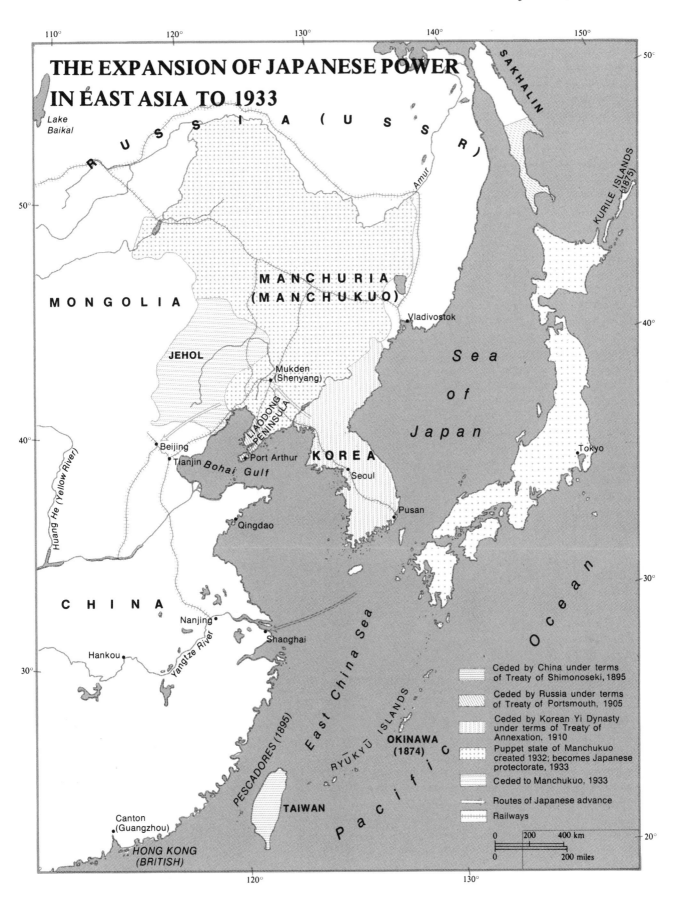

# THE EXPANSION OF JAPANESE POWER
# IN EAST ASIA TO 1933

*Lake Baikal*

R U S S I A ( U S S R )

SAKHALIN

MONGOLIA

M A N C H U R I A
(M A N C H U K U O)

JEHOL

*Amur*

Vladivostok

KURILE ISLANDS (1875)

Mukden
(Shenyang)

LIAODONG PENINSULA

Beijing

Tianjin *Bohai Gulf*

Port Arthur

KOREA

Seoul

S e a
o f
J a p a n

Tokyo

Pusan

*Huang He (Yellow River)*

Qingdao

C H I N A

Nanjing

*Yangtze River*

Hankou

Shanghai

*East China Sea*

RYŪKYŪ ISLANDS

OKINAWA
(1874)

P a c i f i c
O c e a n

PESCADORES (1895)

Canton
(Guangzhou)

TAIWAN

HONG KONG
(BRITISH)

Ceded by China under terms
of Treaty of Shimonoseki, 1895

Ceded by Russia under terms
of Treaty of Portsmouth, 1905

Ceded by Korean Yi Dynasty
under terms of Treaty of
Annexation, 1910

Puppet state of Manchukuo
created 1932; becomes Japanese
protectorate, 1933

Ceded to Manchukuo, 1933

Routes of Japanese advance

Railways

0    200    400 km

0         200 miles

roles in them. Service ministers were consorting openly with party heads. Newspapers whose earliest function had been to educate the masses, with government encouragement, were now part of the capitalistic economic structure: they were inciting mobs against the government and were seeing circulation figures rise, riot by riot. Urbanization kept pace with industrialization, which was moving into the intermediate stage of chemical fertilizers, heavy machinery, and cement and wood pulp manufacture. Government leaders were beginning to show concern over growing labor unrest and "dangerous" socialistic thought. On the whole, however, the Meiji leaders had built well in the face of the smallest margins for error, the paucity of natural resources, the existence of unequal treaties and tariffs, and the threatening context of a world where "all great nations in the fullness of their strength have desired to set their mark upon barbarian lands" (von Treistschke). They did so without resorting to an iron fist or subjecting Japan to direct or indirect foreign control.

The distance Japan had traveled in four decades is measurable by the honors bestowed on the surviving leaders. Yamagata, who had started life as a lowly *chūgen* and who in 1864 had been fired on by a fleet including French ships, in 1889 met with France's president. Itō, who was not permitted to use the officers' toilet on his first trip abroad (1863) and had to squat on a plank projecting from the ship, could smile in satisfaction at his honorary degree from Yale (1901).

In his diary, Kawasaki's mayor noted on 30 July 1912 that His Imperial Majesty had passed away at 12:43 A.M. and at 1:00 A.M. it was announced that Crown Prince Yoshihito was emperor. The other notation for the same day concerned itself with the mayor's visit, along with fifteen other "lobbyists" of the town, to the Tokyo office of the Fuji Gas and Cotton Spinning Company to urge the construction of a branch factory in Kawasaki. The Meiji period had ended, but everywhere in Japan life went on.

[*The figures mentioned in this article are the subject of independent entries. See also* Mutsuhito *and* Charter Oath.]

George Akita, *Foundations of Constitutional Government in Modern Japan, 1868–1900* (1967). William G. Beasley, *The Meiji Restoration* (1972). Hilary F. Conroy, *The Japanese Seizure of Korea, 1868–1910: A Study of Realism and Idealism in International Relations* (1960). Albert M. Craig, *Chōshū in the Meiji Restoration* (1961). Marius B. Jansen, *Sakamoto Ryōma and the Meiji Restoration* (1961). William W. Lockwood, *The Economic Development of Japan: Growth and Structural Change, 1868–1938* (1954). James I. Nakamura, *Agricultural Production and the Economic Development of Japan, 1873–1922* (1966). Herbert Passin, *Society and Education in Japan* (1965). Thomas C. Smith, *Political Change and Industrial Development in Japan: Government Enterprise, 1868–1880* (1965). Harry Wray and Hilary F. Conroy, *Japan Examined: Perspectives on Modern Japanese History* (1983).
GEORGE K. AKITA

**MEIJI RESTORATION.** The Meiji Restoration of 1868 marked the shift of power from the Tokugawa shogun to the court of the boy emperor Mutsuhito, who adopted the reign title of Meiji, "enlightened rule." The events of 1868 represented little more than a shift of power within the old ruling class, but the larger process of which the restoration was a harbinger would end the ascendancy of the warrior class and replace the decentralized structure of late feudalism with a centralized modern state, one committed to building the national power that would enable Japan to compete in the international order. The Meiji Restoration, or "Renewal," as it might better be translated, thus stands as a turning point of Japanese history and a major event for East Asian and indeed world history.

*Political Background.* As political history the events of 1868 capped a process that had begun with the crisis created by the arrival of Commodore Matthew C. Perry in 1853, but they were powerfully affected by discontents and currents of change that had a far longer history. Tokugawa institutions, urbanization, and economic change had unified Japan more than the fractured political divisions would suggest, but the formal structure of decision making had remained unaltered since the seventeenth century. Tokugawa vassals who served on central councils continued to enjoy a monopoly on national offices, while lords of the largest domains and even heads of cadet houses were excluded from participation. The regime did its best to suppress knowledge of the Western approach to Asia, but word of China's disastrous Opium War was spread through *rangaku*, or "Dutch (i.e., Western) learning," and Chinese books that entered through Nagasaki. Currents of Kokugaku ("national learning") had produced an ethnic nationalism and had awakened respect and concern for the imperial court that would make it a rallying point for the disaffected and thus doom Tokugawa efforts to maintain the court's insulation from national politics. [*See also* Perry, Mattew C.; Rangaku; *and* Kokugaku.]

Consequently, when the shogunate, presented

with Perry's request for diplomatic and trade relations, tried to build a consensus for a decision it knew it would have to make by inviting the recommendations of feudal lords and the imperial court, its action had the effect of politicizing first the feudal lords, then the court, and then lower-ranking members of the samurai order. In effect, the inability of the "barbarian-subduing generalissimo" *(sei-i tai shōgun)* to control his barbarians first weakened and then destroyed his mandate to rule.

The treaty worked out by Perry in 1854 provided for the coming of a consul. Townsend Harris, in turn, worked out a commercial treaty in 1858 by making persuasive use of the disasters that China had met in its efforts to ward off the West. [*See* Harris, Townsend.] Tokugawa officials expected clear sailing in securing the pro forma approval of the imperial court to this treaty, but to their astonishment approval of the treaty became entangled with the issue of shogunal succession. The head of the cadet house of Mito, Tokugawa Nariaki, had anticipated Togugawa efforts in Kyoto with arguments that the national crisis required a mature and able successor (his son, Hitotsubashi Keiki), rather than a minor from another cadet house who would, in normal times, have been the choice.

Tokugawa traditionalists rejected this interference with a brusque show of force. A new administration headed by Ii Naosuke signed Harris's treaty on its own, settled the succession issue in favor of the future shogun Tokugawa Iemochi, and then moved to punish lords, nobles, and their agents who had presumed to lobby for a different course of action. A number of great lords were forced into retirement, and at lower levels over one hundred men were sentenced, eight to execution, six of them to be beheaded like ordinary criminals. Among these was the scholar-teacher Yoshida Shōin of Chōshū, posthumously exalted as a paragon of patriotism. Violence brought counterviolence. In March 1860 Ii Naosuke, the *bakufu*'s first minister, was assassinated by plotters whose manifesto charged him with indifference to the emperor's will.

The politics of the 1860s were played out in the presence of the foreign powers whose representatives and merchants were admitted to the ports opened by the Harris treaty. Foreign trade worsened an inflation that was already in progress. Further, the presence of Westerners provoked anti-Western terrorism, which in turn brought threats of Western retaliation. Hapless Tokugawa administrators found themselves under domestic pressure to grant the foreigners less and under foreign pressure to restrain antiforeignism. Responsibility for foreign affairs brought many bureaucratic careers to an early end.

Politics were also played out in a setting of terrorism. The assassination of the shogun's first minister began a period of violence that transformed Japanese politics. The activists were imperial loyalists who styled themselves *shishi*, "men of high purpose." They were usually of modest rank, status, and income, less inhibited by formal duty than their superiors, and more able to communicate with their fellows from other domains. Frustration with lives of limited opportunity combined with ethnic and loyalist zeal to produce a conviction that "higher duty" to an imperial loyalty should outweigh normal dictates of status subordination. This led them to remonstrate with their superiors, at times to strike them down, and at others to flee their lords' jurisdictions to enter the exciting world of national politics. In such a setting the slogan "Sonnō, jōi," ("Revere the emperor; expel the barbarian") became their battle cry. Since their cause won out and their associates became the leaders of the Meiji state, these activists became heroes of modern Japanese patriotism.

***Role of the Outer Domains.*** While two-sworded and reckless men could unsettle matters, changes of substance required the efforts of major domains. In the southwest the leaders of the Satsuma, Chōshū, and Tosa domains were major actors on the national scene. So, until a civil war destroyed its strength, was the Tokugawa cadet house of Mito. The southwestern fiefs had disproportionately large numbers of samurai. They were integrated territorial units with a proud history of regional consciousness, resources that made it possible to build military strength, and a centuries-old resentment of Tokugawa rule. They were in many respects more old-fashioned and "feudal," less commercialized and market oriented, than the Tokugawa heartland of Japan.

In the years after 1860 Chōshū, Satsuma, and Tosa competed in proposing political changes that would increase the participation of the imperial court and the great domains in national politics. This pronounced goal of reconciliation between court and camp, or emperor and shogun, known as *kōbu-gattai,* led to extensive shogunal concessions in 1862 that relaxed requirements for local lords' attendance at Edo and created new posts for Hitotsubashi Keiki (who had been denied the shogunal succession in 1858) and another Tokugawa collateral. The young shogun, Tokugawa Iemochi, visited the sovereign at Kyoto and adopted a pose of ritual humility. He was to die, still a youth, at Osaka on his third visit to the imperial capital in 1866. The succession then went to Hitotsubashi Keiki (Tokugawa Yoshinobu), who never once visited the shogunal capital of Edo during his brief tenure as shogun. Thus, Kyoto became a rival national center and capital.

Meanwhile, Chōshū and Satsuma discovered for themselves that talk of expelling the West could never be translated into fact. Chōshū tried shelling foreign ships off its shores in 1863, and Satsuma samurai murdered an Englishman who fell afoul of a Satsuma daimyo procession. Both domains were shelled by Western ships, and both responded by importing Western guns and sending students to the West to study Western technology. Units equipped with rifles would prove superior to traditionally armed units in the fighting that lay ahead. [*See* Shimonoseki Bombardment *and* Richardson Incident.]

It required several years before an effective regional alliance was worked out against the Tokugawa, however, because the domains distrusted each other as much as they distrusted the *bakufu*. In 1863 Satsuma units helped Tokugawa units expel Chōshū from Kyoto, and after a counterdrive against the imperial palace by Chōshū radicals was thwarted, Satsuma joined the *bakufu* in an expedition to chastise Chōshū as an "enemy of the court." A new and more conservative Chōshū administration quickly subdued its radicals and submitted to *bakufu* demands. It seemed the Tokugawa would prevail. Monetary, military, and administrative measures modernized the *bakufu* and built up its strength in its home domains, until Satsuma leaders began to fear they might be next to feel the edge of Tokugawa power.

Suddenly the tide turned. Chōshū radicals rebelled against their superiors and resumed power after a short civil war. When the *bakufu* announced a new expedition against Chōshū, Satsuma refused to participate. A badly managed Tokugawa expedition was mauled by Chōshū units that were fighting with their backs to the wall. The death of the young shogun Iemochi gave the *bakufu* an excuse for halting military action and was soon followed by the death of the emperor Kōmei as well.

All this violence was played out against a background of terrorism and Western demands for additional ports and concessions. A galloping inflation and widespread uneasiness combined with poor crop yields to produce demonstrations, rebellions, and millenarian "renewal" movements among ordinary Japanese.

Two Tosa *shishi*, Sakamoto Ryōma and Nakaoka Shintarō, helped Satsuma and Chōshū leaders to form an anti-Tokugawa alliance. Iwakura Tomomi, a prominent Kyoto noble, provided channels to the court hierarchy and the boy emperor Mutsuhito. Soon two schemes for ending the Tokugawa power monopoly were in motion. The Tosa daimyo prepared a proposal that the new shogun resign his offices and remain as first among equals in a new, conciliar setting. The shogun, Tokugawa Yoshinobu, accepted this advice and proffered his resignation to the throne in November 1867. He was outmaneuvered, however, by the leaders of Satsuma and Chōshū. They had secured court authorization for direct action and were not prepared to accept a compromise settlement. In meetings from which the shogun was excluded they secured orders for him to surrender his lands as well as his offices. When he hesitated, and then advanced on Kyoto to remonstrate with the court, his units were ambushed at Toba and Fushimi and he himself declared in contempt as an "enemy of the court." Restoration of imperial rule having been announced, the restoration war began as units of Satsuma, Chōshū and Tosa armies, now termed the "imperial army," advanced to the east and north. The war, named Boshin (for the era title), ended with surrender of Tokugawa naval holdouts in Hokkaido in June of 1869.

Tokugawa resistance was half-hearted. The last shogun was in doubt as to his policy and never close to *bakufu* hard-liners. Most of the opposition the "imperial" armies met was based on suspicion that the southwestern domains planned to set up a new shogunate. The restoration coup was thus the product of a fierce competition for leadership in the cause of reconstruction and modernization. There was nearly universal agreement that government needed to be reconstructed, and the issue was who should undertake the job.

During the first stages of the fighting, in April of 1868, the new government issued a five-article imperial oath to reassure the daimyo that all would have a place in the new order that was to come. The Charter Oath, as it has become known, was phrased with skillful generality. It promised that councils would be convened to carry out affairs of state on the basis of "common opinion," it spoke of full opportunity for commoners as well as for officials, it stressed the abolition of "evil customs of the past," and spoke of a search "throughout the world" for knowledge, in order to "strengthen the foundations of imperial rule." This document served to ease the transition from old order to new. Designed to re-assure feudal lords that their privileges were secure, it became a harbinger of reforms that would be based on general opinion and in line with modern practices as observed throughout the world. By the last quarter of the twentieth century the emperor Hirohito was citing it as authorization and prece-dent for the democratic reforms carried out after World War II. By then, however, debates among historians as to the motive force, social content, and historial significance of the Meiji Restoration had assumed an intensity reminiscent of the passions that ran in mid-nineteenth-century Japan.

[See also Tokugawa Period; Meiji Period; Charter Oath; and Mutsuhito.]

W. G. Beasley, *The Meiji Restoration* (1972). W. G. Beasley, ed., *Select Documents on Japanese Foreign Policy, 1853–1868* (1955). Albert N. Craig, *Chōshū in the Meiji Restoration* (1961). Thomas M. Huber, *The Revolutionary Origins of Modern Japan* (1981). Marius B. Jansen, *Sakamoto Ryōma and the Meiji Restoration* (1961). Marius B. Jansen and G. Rozman, eds., *Japan in Transition from Tokugawa to Meiji* (1986).

MARIUS B. JANSEN

MEIREKI FIRE. The great Edo fire of 1657, the third year of the Meireki period, was the greatest disaster in Japanese history until modern times. The fire broke out on 2 March after a period of pro-longed drought, in the temple of Hommyōji in the Hongō district of Edo. Legend relates that the fire began from sparks cast off by the ceremonial burn-ing of the kimono *(furisode)* of a young girl who had recently died; the resulting disaster is hence of-ten known as the "Furisode Fire."

Driven by a strong northwest wind, fire ravaged Edo for more than forty hours, by which time two-thirds of the city lay in ruin, including the great donjon of Edo Castle. Traditional reports of more than 100,000 lives lost are doubtless exaggerated, but the toll was certainly in the tens of thousands. Relief and reconstruction in the wake of the fire imposed severe financial strains on the shogunate, which took extensive preventive measures, including the relocation of temples and daimyo mansions, the construction of firebreaks, and the reorganization of the fire-fighting system.    HENRY D. SMITH II

MEKONG EXPEDITION, French exploration of the Mekong River (1866–1868). On establishing control over southern Vietnam and Cambodia in the early 1860s, putting them astride the lower Mekong, the French dreamed of using the Mekong as a water avenue into the fabled wealth of China's interior. Promoted by Francis Garnier and commanded by Lieutenant Doudart de Lagrée, an expedition to ex-plore the Mekong left Saigon on 5 June 1866. Pass-ing Champassak, Vientiane, and Luang Prabang, it ascended the river to Jiang Hong in Yunnan, crossed overland to the Yangtze River, descended it to Shanghai, and returned to Saigon in June 1868. The journey proved the river unnavigable for commerce, but it also whetted French interest in Laos, which France seized in 1893.

[See also Garnier, Francis.]

M. Osborne, *River Road to China* (1975).

DAVID K. WYATT

MELAKA (Malacca), located on the west coast of the Malay Peninsula, was the center of intra-Asian trade at the end of the fifteenth century. A century earlier it had been merely a fishing village, but it changed when it was chosen as headquarters by Pa-rameswara, a Palembang prince who may have had connections with the old ruling family of Srivijaya. Situated at the narrowest point of the straits between Sumatra and the peninsula, Melaka was the ideal meeting place for seaborne trade from both East and South Asia.

The city's meteoric rise owed as much to political as geographic factors. Parameswara made his ven-ture just as China's new Ming dynasty, seeking to resume the tributary trade, needed a dependable port in the southern ocean that would be its ally and thus keep the trade route free of piracy. From 1400 to 1430, Melaka exchanged many tributary missions with China, and the Chinese protection it received allowed it to survive challenges from Siam and other competitors.

The inspired and courageous leadership of its first three rulers also played an important part in Me-laka's rise. Recognizing the need to woo the trade—the greatest asset of any aspiring political entity in the Malay world—Melaka's leaders provided safe and convenient facilities. They installed a regular governing body and a good judicial system, codified port regulations, and formed a functional bureau-cratic organization that guaranteed the safety of merchants and valuable cargoes. When the Chinese emperors began to lose interest in the overseas trade, Melaka's leaders worked to attract the important trade of Muslim North India by controlling many of the nearby pepper-producing areas; in 1436 Melaka's third ruler adopted Islam. By the 1560s the Melaka sultanate controlled Pahang, Siak, Kampar, Trengganu, and Johor and had achieved a *modus vivendi* with Siam.

By the end of the century Melaka was a thriving cosmopolitan port, a market of exceptional wealth where spices, pepper, Indian cotton cloth, cinnamon, Chinese silks, porcelains and other goods, precious metals, glassware, and woolen cloths from the West were available. Its trade revenues supported a sultanate that was to set the pattern for Malay courts for centuries. To the Portuguese, who visited it in 1508, Melaka seemed, according to Tomé Pires, "a land that cannot depreciate, on account of its position, but must always grow."

In an attempt to monopolize the city's trade, the Portuguese captured Melaka in 1511. Their military victory was due as much to the internal dissension among the Malays as to Portugal's technological advantages. Melaka's trade, however, was not so easily captured; the Portuguese adopted an alternative route via West Sumatra and the Sunda Straits, and many Indian merchants diverted to the new port of Aceh in North Sumatra. Sultan Mahmud of Melaka fled to Bentan and later Johor, where the sultanate regrouped about him. Johor and Aceh launched repeated attacks on Melaka, now a European-style stone fortress and the Portuguese headquarters in Southeast Asia. Melaka lost its dominance of Asian trade, though the Portuguese retained the port till it was taken in a grueling siege by the Dutch East India Company (VOC) in 1641.

Melaka was of more strategic than commercial importance to the Dutch and thus was not the center of Dutch operations in the archipelago. Although they had hoped to inherit the sultanate's privileges and profit from its monopoly of pepper and tin production in the Malay states, the Dutch realized after a few decades that this could not easily be achieved and largely abandoned their attempt. Melaka's trade was restricted in accordance with the VOC's "buy cheap, sell dear" policies and in order to prevent it from competing with Batavia. Melaka was not a profitable post for the VOC during most of its tenure.

In the eighteenth century the growth of European, and especially English, trade to China revived Melaka's position a little, but the port now had to compete with a number of Malay trade centers. Dutch monopolistic policies drove the English to establish their own port at Penang in 1786 and at Singapore in 1819, causing further ill effects for Melaka. Moreover, silt made the port increasingly un-

suitable for major shipping. In 1795 it fell to the English, who planned to transfer its remaining residents and trade to Penang. Although they did destroy all the old fortifications, the English abandoned these plans, largely because of arguments by Thomas Stamford Raffles, among others, that Melaka retained such an important place in the conciousness of the Malays that its possession by a hostile power was dangerous to English interests. The Dutch returned briefly from 1818 to 1825, after which Melaka became one of the English Straits Settlements. It remained under English rule, except for the brief interregnum of the Japanese invasion, until it became part of independent Malaya in 1957.

[*See also* Palembang; Srivijaya; Dutch East India Company; *and* Malaya.]

C. C. Brown, "Sejarah Melayu or Malay Annals," *Journal of the Malayan Branch of the Royal Asiatic Society* 2–3 (October 1952). M. A. P. Meilink-Roelofsz, *Asian Trade and European Influence* (1962). Tomé Pires, *Suma Oriental,* 2 vols. (1944). Kernial Singh and Paul Wheatley, eds., *Melaka: The Transformation of a Malay Capital* (1980). O. W. Wolters, *The Fall of Sri Vijaya in Malay History* (1970).                                    DIANNE LEWIS

**MENANDER,** identified with Milinda of the Buddhist work *Milindapanho,* ruled (c. 155–130 BCE) over larger parts of modern Afghanistan and Pakistan. The greatest of the Indo-Greeks, he led an expedition to the Ganges Valley, possibly reaching Pataliputra, but had to retreat on account of internal dissensions. He issued a plentiful coinage and an inscription perhaps dated in his reign. One of his copper coin types shows a *dharmachakra,* which may confirm his Buddhist leanings. According to Buddhist tradition he abdicated his throne in favor of his son and retired from the world; according to Plutarch he died in a camp, but there were rival claims for his ashes, and monuments were built on them in various cities.

[*See also* Greeks.]

A. K. Narain, *The Indo-Greeks* (1957).

A. K. NARAIN

**MENCIUS** (371–289 BCE), latinized form of the name Mengzi ("Master Meng"), a major Confucian of the Warring States period (403–222 BCE) in China, and for later Confucians second only to Confucius in importance. A native of Zou in present-day Shandong, he studied under a disciple of Zi Si, the grandson of Confucius. His career is in certain respects similar to that of Confucius. Mencius traveled from state to state for about forty years offering advice to the rulers to bring an end to the civil strife of the period; this advice was largely ignored. He attacked other schools of thought of his own day, particularly the Mohists and the Daoists, and sought a return to the ways of the sages of antiquity, Yao and Shun, as well as that of the founders of the Zhou dynasty, King Wen and the Duke of Zhou. Mencius saw the classics, regarded as the records of the sages, as the main body of education and the means to rectify the conditions of the day.

Mencius's political advice consisted of calling for a virtuous ruler, a true king, and a humane government. Such a ruler would be motivated not by profit (li) and utility (yong), but righteousness (yi) alone. Righteousness was defined in terms of the inherent moral nature of any political decision as it affected the good of the people, not the privilege of the ruler. There was in fact a moral imperative for the true king: such a person could not bear to see the suffering of others. The true king ruled with the mandate of Heaven (tianming), a religious sanction to political authority. If these conditions were not fulfilled and the king was a tyrant, then the people had the right to revolt.

For Mencius the good of the people could best be served by returning to the ideal political and economic structure of the early Zhou, essentially a feudal order. Distinctions between ranks were to be maintained with the belief that harmony would result from the respect and fulfillment of such distinctions, the Confucian concept of zhengming, rectification of names. In economic terms Mencius recommended a return to the so-called "well-field" system, a structure that provided both private and shared farming responsibilities. Although traditional institutions were encouraged, there is a shift in attention for Mencius from the privileges of the ruling class to the rights of the ruled.

This attention to the individual is based on Mencius's belief in the perfectability of each person. Expanding upon the ideas of Confucius, Mencius concludes that human nature (xing) is inherently good. It is part of man's nature that upon seeing a child about to fall into a well, he would rescue the child. An individual is born with "four beginnings" of goodness: humaneness (ren), righteousness (yi), propriety (li), and wisdom (zhi). These beginnings must be fully developed through education in order for one to become a moral person. In some they are not developed and evilness results from violation of the inherent nature.

Not considered a major interpreter of Confucius for a number of centuries, Mencius began to emerge from obscurity during the Tang-dynasty Confucian revival, but his work only became canonized during the rise of Neo-Confucianism in the Song, when Zhu Xi (1130–1200) included it in the Four Books. Since that time his interpretation of Confucianism substantiated Neo-Confucian political, philosophical, and religious ideals throughout East Asia, whether in the setting of the civil service examination or in personal self-cultivation.

[See also Confucius; Confucianism; Neo-Confucianism; Warring States Period; and Xunzi.]

K. C. Hsiao, A History of Chinese Political Thought (1979). D. C. Lau, trans., Mencius (1970). I. A. Richards, Mencius on the Mind (1932). Vincent Shih, "Metaphysical Tendencies in Mencius," Philosophy East and West 12 (January 1963): 319–341. A. F. Verwilghen, Mencius: The Man and His Ideas (1967). Arthur Waley, Three Ways of Thought in Ancient China (1939).

RODNEY L. TAYLOR

**MEO.** See Hmong.

**MERV**, an oasis and town on the lower reaches of the Murghab River in the present-day Turkmen SSR. Archaeological evidence is still sparse, but irrigated agriculture was well developed there by 1200 BCE, judging from references in early Indian texts, and the area was incorporated into the Persian state by the time of Darius I. The town appears to be more recent and was probably first founded by the Seleucid Antiochus I (280–261 BCE).

The Arab conquest swept over the area in 651 CE, and the town was rebuilt as the new capital of Khurasan, later becoming the center of the Abbasid movement in the eighth century. Under the Abbasid caliphs Merv was one of the great centers of Islamic learning, famous especially for its libraries. Agriculture remained productive, and sericulture and weaving were prominent. Agriculture depended almost entirely on irrigation provided by a dam on the Murghab that long antedated the town. Urban growth depended largely on Merv's location on the main caravan route through Central Asia to China, and the city became one of the great emporia of Asia, serving caravans and selling its own products. The Seljuks occupied the oasis in the eleventh century, and under their effective rule Merv achieved its greatest growth until the destructive Mongol conquest of the area in 1221. The Mongols razed the town and the dam, and Merv never recovered, owing in part to the disruption caused by continuing conquest and raiding, but also to the deflection and progressively reduced trade volume of the main caravan routes, especially after the opening of sea routes westward from East Asia. In 1884 the area was incorporated in the Russian empire, and by the late 1880s two new dams had been built on the Murghab.

[*See also* Khurasan *and* Turkmenistan.]

Wilhelm Barthold, *Turkestan down to the Mongol Invasion* (2d ed., 1958).    RHOADS MURPHEY, JR.

**MESTIZO,** term used in Spanish America to denote people with mixed Indian and Spanish ancestry. In the Philippines, where there are large numbers of Chinese and relatively few Spaniards, the word *mestizo* applied to people of mixed Chinese and Malay ancestry, and differentiations were made between Chinese mestizo, Spanish mestizo, and later, American mestizo. In Spanish America the term *mestizo* carried with it the image of the shiftless, lazy, and troublesome, probably because mestizos were often of illegitimate birth. In the Philippines, on the other hand, mestizos had more social prestige, and the word did not have the stigma that it had in Latin America.    NICHOLAS P. CUSHNER

**METALWORK.** Iran and Central Asia have rich mineral deposits of both precious and base metals, which their inhabitants have long fashioned into utensils, arms, coins, and art objects. Most examples of early Iranian metalwork come from tombs, treasures, or hoards, often excavated clandestinely; thus we have a skewed picture of the material culture. Luxury objects in gold and silver are overrepresented, and the context and provenance of these objects are often unknown; they can be dated only by comparison to other media or by internal stylistic chronologies. Many identifications and attributions are controversial.

For example, the Zawiya treasure, a trough with bronze strips containing gold, silver, and ivory objects, was discovered by a shepherd boy on a mountainside in northwestern Iran in 1947. These objects combine Urartian and Scythian styles and have been attributed to a local dynasty of the ninth to the seventh century BCE. The fortress where the treasure was discovered might have been destroyed by Scythian raiders, whose own royal tombs have yielded significant numbers of gold objects in the "animal style."

Both the Achaemenid and Sasanid empires had elaborate civilizations requiring rich cultic vessels. The Achaemenid royal treasure included superbly sculpted gold rhytons (drinking vessels) in animal shapes and fluted silver vases with ibex handles. The more than one hundred bowls or plates of precious metal confirm the renowned wealth of the Sasanid court. Many show a king hunting or killing game, but the meaning of other scenes is less clear. So is their exact dating, for these silver plates continued to be produced after the Arab conquest, probably in inaccessible areas such as the mountains south of the Caspian Sea, where the population was not converted to Islam until the tenth century.

Islam discourages the use of silver and gold for the manufacture of luxury objects, and in the Islamic world these metals were used mainly for minting coins. As they are clearly dated, coins are important sources for establishing the historical record. Sasanid coins have portraits of emperors with distinctive crowns; they are one of the best sources of iconography. Islamic coins are decorated with inscriptions; they document the development of epigraphic style.

FIGURE 1. *Incense Burner.* Fashioned in the shape of a lion, this bronze incense burner from Khurasan, dated 1181–1182, is an example of Iranian metalwork of the Seljuk period. Height 85 cm., length 80 cm.

Most metalware from Islamic Iran is made of baser alloys, either bronze or brass (the two are frequently confused). Unlike pre-Islamic examples, most served domestic or religious functions; the major types are lamps, perfume bottles, mirrors, inkwells and penboxes, caskets, ewers, and cups. Even these objects do not represent the society as a whole, for the excavations at Nishapur in northeastern Iran revealed a whole "underworld" of medieval Iranian metalwork—smaller, less exotic pieces not considered of commercial value and overlooked by clandestine diggers.

These quotidian objects stand in direct contrast to the most famous pieces of Islamic metalwork, such as the Bobrinsky Kettle, now in the Hermitage. The tiny (six inches high) bucket is cast in bronze, incised, and inlaid with silver and copper, with niello decorating the inlay. Its inscriptions indicate that it was made for a merchant in Herat in 1163. Although modeled on a bath bucket, the quality of its decoration—scenes of combat, revelry, and gaming and elaborate inscriptions—testifies to the sophistication of the school of metalwork that flourished in northeastern Iran in the eleventh and twelfth centuries. Later dynasties continued this tradition of luxury wares.

[See also Money: Money in the Ancient Near East and Money: Money in the Islamic World.]

James W. Allan, *Nishapur: Metalwork of the Early Islamic Period* (1982). Eva Baer, *Metalwork in Medieval Islamic Art* (1983). Prudence O. Harper, *Silver Vessels of the Sasanian Period* (1981). Assadullah Souren Melikian-Chirvani, *Islamic Metalwork from the Iranian World 8th–18th Centuries* (1982). Edith Porada, *The Art of Ancient Iran* (1965).                    SHEILA S. BLAIR

**METCALFE, SIR CHARLES** (1785–1846), a prominent administrator for the East India Company, serving on the governor-general's council and as lieutenant governor of the Northwest Provinces. Metcalfe introduced the village settlement for revenue purposes, arguing that it was the truly indigenous system of India. As acting governor-general after William Bentinck's resignation, Metcalfe lifted restrictions on the press, a controversial move that prompted his superiors to refuse to make him Bentinck's permanent successor. Metcalfe later served as governor of both Jamaica and Canada.

[See also Bentinck, William Cavendish and Law: Judicial and Legal Systems of India.]

D. N. Panigrahi, *Charles Metcalfe in India* (1968).

LYNN ZASTOUPIL

**MEWAR.** The name *Mewar* is derived from the ancient term *Medapata,* referring to the southern part of the Indian state of Rajasthan. From early times it was the homeland of the Guhila Rajputs, who ruled from their capital at Chitor. The Guhilas were severely defeated by the Khiljis in 1303, when Chitor was taken after a bloody siege. However, they recovered rapidly in the next few decades under the leadership of the Sisodiya branch of the Guhila family, and by the end of the fourteenth century Mewar was once again the center of a powerful Rajput kingdom. During the reigns of Rana Kumbha (1433–1463) and Rana Sanga (1509–1528) the power of Mewar was at its peak. These rulers fought on equal terms with the sultans of Gujarat and Malwa and dominated the other Rajput kingdoms of Rajasthan and central India throughout much of their reigns. In 1527 Rana Sanga, then at the height of his influence, was defeated at Khanua (near Agra) by the Mughal emperor Babur. Mewar suffered through a subsequent period of invasion and warfare that ended only with the Mughal–Sisodiya alliance arrived at in 1614.

[See also Chitor and Rajput.]

RICHARD DAVIS SARAN

**MIAO.** See Hmong.

**MIKI TAKEO** (b. 1907), prime minister of Japan from 1974 to 1976. Miki was born in Tokushima Prefecture on the island of Shikoku. A graduate of Meiji University, he also studied several years in the United States at the University of California at Berkeley. He entered national politics in 1937 with his election to the House of Representatives and served continuously thereafter. After World War II he became involved in the activities of a small centrist party, Kokumin Kyōdōtō, and served in the cabinet of Katayama Tetsu as minister of communications. The merger of the Liberal and Democratic parties in 1955 placed him outside the mainstream, but his skill as leader of a small faction brought him increasing prominence. He served as director general of the Economic Planning Agency, as minister of international trade and industry, and as minister of foreign affairs in the cabinets of Satō Eisaku.

After the fall of Tanaka Kakuei in 1974, Miki was elected head of the Liberal Democratic Party in a move against traditional politics. There were few notable achievements in his term of office, excepting the policy creating a ceiling for defense spending of 1 percent of the gross national product. When the conservatives did poorly in the 1976 elections, Miki was forced out of office.    MICHIO UMEGAKI

**MILINDA.** *See* Menander.

**MILL, JAMES** (1773–1836), utilitarian reformer who held important positions in the Examiner's Office of the East India Company from 1819 to 1836. His famous book, *A History of British India,* appeared in 1818 and became a textbook at Haileybury college; the work is noted for its scathing attack on the British orientalists' idea that Hinduism was once a refined and sublime religion. Mill's tenure in the Examiner's Office was marked by a concern for reform of India. He focused on stimulating revenue and educational reforms through the government of India, hoping to instill Western ideas of science and self-reliance into Indian society.

[*See also* Haileybury College *and* Utilitarianism in India.]

Eric Stokes, *The English Utilitarians and India* (1959).
LYNN ZASTOUPIL

**MILL, JOHN STUART** (1806–1873) British economist and philosopher. He followed his father, James Mill, into the Examiner's Office of the East India Company in the years 1823 to 1858. Mill continued his father's reformist policies, focusing on improving education, the civil service in India, and administration in the Indian dependencies. He held out hopes for educating India into representative institutions under the aegis of British government and insisted on allowing educated Indians to hold the highest civil service positions in India. He refused a post on the new India Board, instituted when the company was abolished after the Revolt of 1857, fearing that English politics would replace the company's rational administration.

[*See also* Mill, James *and* East India Company.]

Eric Stokes, *The English Utilitarians and India* (1959).
LYNN ZASTOUPIL

**MIMANA,** the Japanese term for one of the states of ancient Korea created by the Kaya confederation. The state is also known as Imna, Kaya, or Karak. Located on the southern tip of Korea, the state was supposedly created in 42 CE, was dominated by "Wa" people during the late fourth century, and was absorbed by the Korean kingdom of Silla in 562. The subject of Mimana's historicity is sur-

rounded by controversy that boiled up as recently as the Japanese textbook controversy in 1982.

According to the eighth-century Japanese text *Nihon shoki,* an Empress Jingū conquered the region in the fourth century. Administration was handled by a Japanese representative who relied on village headmen to supply fish, agricultural products, and iron ore as tribute. In the fifth and early sixth century Japan ceded territories to its ally Paekche in compensation for lands conquered by the northern kingdom of Koguryŏ, but in 562 Silla occupied Mimana. Silla and the Nara court remained bitter enemies over the Mimana issue throughout the eighth century.

The text in question, however, was compiled to establish the legitimacy of the Japanese imperial house, and Japanese scholars did not begin to attach decisive importance to it until the "national studies" (Kokugaku) movement of mid-Tokugawa times. Its assertions of Japanese invasions of and control over part of Korea were particularly congenial to nationalist scholars during the Meiji Restoration, as Japan began to dominate Korea, and they became accepted scholarship in modern Japan and Japanese-occupied Korea.

After World War II, Korean and Japanese historians began to question the historicity of Mimana as a Japanese colony and emphasized instead the immense cultural contribution made by Korea to early Japan. Egami Namio suggested that it was Japan that had been under Korean influence and not vice versa, and that "horse riders" from the mainland had entered Japan from Korea and dominated its elite and, in all probability, provided its sovereign. Excavations of the ancient tomb at Takamatsuzuka near Nara in 1972 revealed murals and artifacts strikingly similar to those found in Korea and China. Opinions among specialists remain sharply divided about Mimana-Kaya, although no historians question the importance of Korean civilization for that of early Japan.

[*See also* Yayoi.]

J. Russell Kirkland, "The 'Horseriders' in Korea: A Critical Evaluation of a Historical Theory," *Korean Studies* 5 (1981): 109–128. Gari Ledyard, "Galloping Along with the Horseriders: Looking for the Founders of Japan," *Journal of Japanese Studies* (1975): 217–254. Chong-sik Lee, "History and Politics in Japanese-Korean Relations: The Textbook Controversy and Beyond," *Journal of Northeast Asian Studies* (1983): 69–93. Suematsu Yasukazu, "Japan's Relations with the Asian Continent and the Korean Peninsula before 950 A.D." *Cahiers d'Histoire Mondiale* 4 (1958).    WAYNE FARRIS

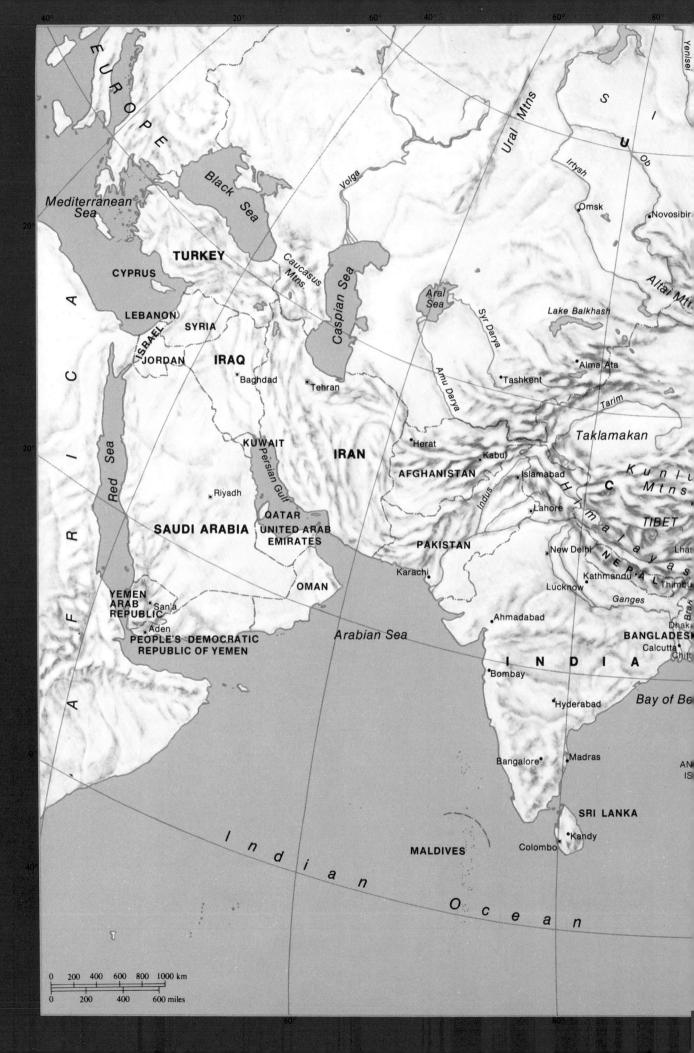